Museum
Registration
Methods
6th Edition

AMERICAN ALLIANCE OF MUSEUMS

The American Alliance of Museums (AAM) has been bringing museums together since 1906, helping to develop standards and best practices, gathering and sharing knowledge, and providing advocacy on issues of concern to the entire museum community. Representing more than thirty-five thousand individual museum professionals and volunteers, institutions, and corporate partners serving the museum field, the Alliance stands for the broad scope of the museum community.

The AAM's mission is to champion museums and nurture excellence in partnership with its members and allies.

Books published by AAM further the Alliance's mission to make standards and best practices for the broad museum community widely available.

MRM6

Museum Registration Methods
6th Edition

EDITED BY JOHN E. SIMMONS AND TONI M. KISER

ROWMAN & LITTLEFIELD
Lanham • Boulder • New York • London

Published by Rowman & Littlefield
An imprint of The Rowman & Littlefield Publishing Group, Inc.
4501 Forbes Boulevard, Suite 200, Lanham, Maryland 20706
www.rowman.com

6 Tinworth Street, London SE11 5AL

British Library Cataloguing in Publication Information Available

Library of Congress Cataloging-in-Publication Data

Library of Congress Control Number: 2020904516
ISBN: 978-1-5381-1310-3
ISBN: 978-1-5381-1311-0
ISBN: 978-1-5381-1312-7

Contents

PART 1   THE PROFESSION

PART 2   COLLECTION MANAGEMENT POLICIES

PART 3   THE BASICS

FIGURES

TABLES

Sample Collection Forms

ACKNOWLEDGMENTS

The production of this book has been a community effort, with so much owed to so many that we cannot acknowledge everyone who helped by name. However, a very special thank-you goes to all of the contributing authors of this edition and their predecessors, with particular thanks to the editors of the previous two editions, Rebecca Buck and Jean Gilmore.

John is forever grateful to Julianne Snider for her support, advice, technical expertise, help with figures, and general wise counsel during the course of this project.

Toni would like to thank Scott Kiser for his understanding of such an important project and the help provided during many editing and writing sessions.

We thank our editor at Rowman & Littlefield, Charles Harmon, for the opportunity to take on this project and for his continual interest and support.

Letter from the Chair of the Collections Stewardship Professional Network of the American Alliance of Museums and the President of the Association of Registrars and Collections Specialists

In 1958, Dorothy Dudley and Irma Bezold Wilkinson published the first edition of *Museum Registration Methods*, a groundbreaking work on best practices in the care and management of museum collections. Since then, the American Alliance of Museums (AAM) has kept *Museum Registration Methods* in print through five editions, each representing a major leap forward in the evolution of the collections profession.

Much has changed in collection practices since the first edition of *Museum Registration Methods* appeared more than sixty years ago. Best practices, functions, roles, and responsibilities have continually adapted to meet the needs and expectations of museums, audiences, and other key stakeholders, and new job titles have been introduced to reflect changes in the profession. While the role of the registrar remains an integral and critical museum function, there may be staff members with different titles or specializations who are responsible for registration and collections management.

Since the publication of the fifth edition of *Museum Registration Methods* a decade ago, the profession has adapted and grown significantly. There are new areas of specialization and additional responsibilities, including the care of digital objects, increased emphasis on provenance research, and changes in the legal landscape, along with recognition of the importance of achieving equality and diversity in the profession. The AAM Collection Stewardship Professional Network in collaboration with the Association of Registrars and Collections Specialists (ARCS) continue to promote and advocate for the interests of the profession and champion the highest standards of professionalism.

Museum Registration Methods has long been the most comprehensive definitive resource for collections professionals, and this sixth edition continues to build on that body of knowledge to offer timely professional guidance on digital collections, provenance research, repatriation, loans, exhibitions, shipping, collections storage and care, databases, and much more.

We are indebted to Toni Kiser, John Simmons, and the contributing authors to this volume for their tireless work and dedication to updating and expanding *Museum Registration Methods* for the next generation of museum professionals, and to all who have contributed their time and expertise to this endeavor in the past, particularly Rebecca A. Buck and Jean Allman Gilmore, whose significant contributions in the fourth and fifth editions have made an indelible imprint on collections work.

The profession continues to thrive and flourish through a belief in shared expertise, experience, and knowledge. This sixth edition of *Museum Registration Methods* is a testament to that collaborative spirit as we continue to strive for the ideal in our work.

DANIELLE HALL BENNETT
PRESIDENT
ASSOCIATION OF REGISTRARS AND
  COLLECTIONS SPECIALISTS

SEBASTIÁN E. ENCINA
CHAIR, COLLECTIONS STEWARDSHIP
  PROFESSIONAL NETWORK
AMERICAN ALLIANCE OF MUSEUMS

PREFACE

JOHN E. SIMMONS AND TONI M. KISER

IN A RECENT best-selling novel, the protagonist finds "an elegantly embossed card" in an exhibit case indicating that an object has been removed and loaned to another institution. The narrator explains that the card is called a *loan log* or a *title card* and is used by museum curators "in exchange for" an object that is on temporary loan (as if there were some other kind). The narrator then explains that two of these cards are printed for each object that is loaned—one card is exhibited to thank the lender (mistakenly called a "donor" in the novel) and the other held "as collateral" for the object on loan.[1] Alas, but this is how misunderstood our profession is by the public at large—not only are there no such things as elegantly embossed cards used as collateral for loaned objects, the novel credits the curator, and not the registrar or collections manager, with conducting the loan process. Collections work is now, and has always been, largely invisible.[2] Despite its invisibility, registration and collections care are the heart of the museum and are constantly evolving to meet new challenges.

A quantitative measure of the changes in the profession since the publication of the first edition of *Museum Registration Methods* (*MRM*) in 1958 can be made by comparing the size of the first edition with the fifth edition. The first edition was a modest 225 pages, weighed less than 1½ pounds, and included contributions from 15 professionals. By 2010, the fifth edition of the book (*MRM5*) had grown to 516 pages with contributions by 68 authors, and weighed in at 4 pounds.

While preparing this edition we have noted several significant differences compared to *MRM5* that reflect recent changes in the profession. For one, the job titles *registrar* and *collections manager* are now virtually synonymous (see CHAPTER 1A, "A Very Brief History of the Profession"). This edition includes a new chapter on the management of extremely large collections—specifically, those of the National Park Service (see CHAPTER 1D, "Caring for the Nation's Treasures—the National Park Service Museum Program") but also retains chapters intended to help very small museums (e.g., chapter 4B, "Manual Systems"). What was "The Registrar's Bookshelf" in previous editions now contains far more references to material available on the internet—so much that it has been renamed "Resources for Registrars and Collections Managers" in this edition and includes links to the American Institute of Conservation wiki,[3] the Canadian Conservation Institute publications,[4] Connecting to Collections,[5] and the National Park Service Museum Management Program,[6] among others. However, it is important for those of us in the profession to keep in mind that not everything has been scanned and posted on the web; there is still a significant body of information useful to registrars and collections managers that is available only in print form (particularly older information).

Unfortunately, along with the increase in useful information on registration and collections care, there has been an increase in bogus information. It is easy to find this stuff, such as the recent viral video of someone vigorously scrubbing the surface of a painting with a brush and an unknown solvent and scores of recommendations for inappropriate and damaging methods for cleaning and housing objects; it is not recommended to clean paintings by rubbing them with a raw potato, to de-acidify documents by submerging them in warm water with antacid tablets, to mark objects with nail polish, or to wrap things in tissue paper and store them in old egg cartons, yet this sort of bad advice persists on the internet and in television shows. Critical thinking and discernment are increasingly necessary skills for registrars and collections managers.

Another significant change is the nature of the materials being added to collections. In the decade since *MRM5* was published, there has been a steady growth in born-digital artworks and documents. Born-digital objects pose serious preservation problems for museums because at present there are no reliable means to preserve digital information for the long term. The best we can do is embark on expensive programs of continual file conversion as software and hardware change, although we know from past experience that file conversion ultimately results in data deterioration and loss.

The role of provenance research in museums is increasingly important for documenting and preserving objects, particularly with the increase in looting of cultural patrimony occurring worldwide, from Latin America to Africa and particularly in recent zones of conflict in Afghanistan, Iraq, Syria, and other locations in the Middle East. A recent exhibit at the Museum of Islamic Art in Doha (Qatar) called "Syria Matters" highlighted the destruction of cultural heritage with 120 exquisite objects from the collections of museums around the world. That such an exhibit could be assembled is the result of the work of dozens of nameless registrars and collections managers who labor behind the scenes to document and preserve objects of significance to humanity. That this exhibit needed to be assembled is a sad testimony to the threats to cultural heritage worldwide.

The challenges we face in the future are many and complex. Museum collections continue to grow as objects are added, while the objects already in the collections are aging and deteriorating; at the same time, there are fewer collections care staff members relative to the size of collections in museums and far less funding for collections care is available than in the past. It may seem to be an uncertain future, but registrars and collections managers are enormously creative and resilient and what we do is fundamentally important to museums and other collecting institutions. When we look back at the history of registration and collections care and consider how much the profession has evolved and adapted over the last six decades, the future of museum registration and collections care looks bright indeed. •

NOTES

1. D. Brown, *Origin* (New York: Doubleday, 2017), 278.

2. K. F. Latham, "The invisibility of collections care work." *Collections* 3, no. 1 (2007): 103–112.

3. Available at: http://www.conservation-wiki.com/wiki/Main_Page.

4. Available at: https://www.canada.ca/en/conservation-institute.html.

5. Available at: https://www.connectingtocollections.org/.

6. Available at: https://www.nps.gov/museum/.

PART I | THE PROFESSION

1A | A VERY BRIEF HISTORY OF THE PROFESSION

JOHN E. SIMMONS

THE ORIGIN OF the institutions we now recognize as museums can be found in the cabinets of curiosities of the late Renaissance, but modern museums did not emerge and proliferate until the nineteenth century as collecting institutions diversified into the art, history, science, and other specializations we have today.[1] The objects in the cabinets of curiosities were organized and cared for, but we know very little about what was done or by whom, although there are a few tantalizing clues. An illustration of the cabinet of Ferdinando Cospi (1606–1686) from Bologna is one example. The image appeared in a five-volume catalog of Cospi's collection that was written by Lorenzo Legati (d. 1675) and published in 1677. The woodcut shows the collection's caretaker and guide, a dwarf named Sebastiano Biavati, standing in the collection and holding an Egyptian sculpture (FIGURE 1A.1).[2]

In a woodcut showing the collection of Levinus Vincent (1658–1727) in Amsterdam there is a young boy in the lower right corner, apparently helping visitors to the cabinet find the objects they wish to see.[3] The catalogs of the cabinets of curiosities were important documents, the products of diligent research—the way the objects were ordered and described can tell us much about how the objects in the collections were understood.[4] Often the owner of the cabinet hired a specialist scholar to write the catalog, as did John Tradescant the Younger (1608–1662) in London. Tradescant contracted a lawyer and antiquarian named Elias Ashmole (1617–1692) to help catalog his collection, known as the *Musaeum Tradescantianum*.[5] Through a series of legal maneuvers, Ashmole later managed to wrest control of the collection from the widow Hester Pooks Tradescant (d. 1678) after her

FIGURE 1A.1 SEBASTIANO BIAVATI IN THE COLLECTION OF FERNANDO COSPI, 1677. HTTPS://COMMONS .WIKIMEDIA.ORG/WIKI/FILE:FERDINANDO_COSPI_COLLECTION.JPG.

husband's death and donated it to Oxford University where it was renamed the Ashmolean Museum.[6]

The first comprehensive works to address the acquisition, organization, and care of collections appeared early in museum history. In 1565, Samuel von Quiccheberg (1529–1567), published *Inscriptiones; vel, tituli theatric amplissimi* (*Inscriptions, or, Titles of the Most Ample Theater*), which is now recognized as the first museological treatise on the care and organization of collections.[7] More than 150 years later, the next significant contribution to the topic was published in German in 1727 by an object dealer in Hamburg named Caspar Neickel,[8] but there was still no recognized museum profession at that time. Museums typically employed a curator along with a few anonymous assistants who had minimal on-the-job training. This situation did not begin to change until the late 1800s when the collections care profession slowly began to emerge.[9]

THE REGISTRAR

Rebecca Buck has traced the first use of the title *registrar* in a museum to 1881 when Stephen C. Brown (d. 1919) was hired at the Smithsonian Institution to head the Office of the Registrar.[10] The word *registrar* has been in use since at least 1571 to refer someone who keeps written records (as did Elias Ashmole for the Tradescant collection), so the word was a logical title for that role in museums.[11] Around 1905 the Metropolitan Museum of Art in New York started using the title of registrar, followed by the Museum of Fine Arts in Boston in 1906.[12] By this time museum curators were beginning to publish their ideas about the organization of objects and to recognize that specialized knowledge would be required for collections and their associated information to be preserved to serve as rational tools of inquiry in the future.

By early in the twentieth century there were three basic ways to train for museum work: (i) learning on the job; (ii) short-term training offered by one of the new museum associations; and (iii) a few opportunities to undertake museum training in a university setting.[13] By this time, collection catalogs had long since evolved from simple inventories into descriptive texts and had been standard features of collections

for more than two hundred years. With the increasing sophistication of collection catalogs, documentation standards and object provenance became more exacting and specialized. Two important factors in the development of the registration profession at this time were (i) the increase in university-based training programs and (ii) advent of professional museum associations. The oldest of the latter, the Museums Association, was founded in the United Kingdom in 1889. The American Association of Museums (now the American Alliance of Museums [AAM]) was founded in 1906, followed by many similar organizations around the world.[14]

Many of the fundamentals of museum registration were derived from the library profession, particularly the work of Melvil Dewey (who developed the Dewey Decimal System while working in Amherst, Massachusetts, beginning in 1874); Henry Watson Kent of the Metropolitan Museum in New York; and one of the most significant museum leaders of the era in the United States, John Cotton Dana of the Newark Museum.[15] In her research on the history of registration, Buck turned up one of the earliest descriptions of a museum registrar's job, published in 1907:

> The duties of this officer have been systematized and co-ordinated to those of the Director and other members of the Museum staff. All objects of art offered either by way of gift or purchase, are received by him and duly receipted for. If not accepted, they are returned to the owner by him. After the Trustees have accepted an object, it is immediately numbered, accessioned, sent to the photographer's studio to be photographed, returned to the Registrar's Office, and there awaits placement in the room for recent accessions. A list for the monthly Bulletin, classifying and describing the different objects, is then prepared and temporary labels are attached to those so accepted.
>
> The business of the Museum in receiving and dealing with all objects of art received by it has been thoroughly systematized.[16]

The Museum of Fine Arts in Boston described the registrar's position in 1907:

It shall be the duty of the Registrar of the Museum to receive and deliver objects of art at the Museum, to attend to Custom House business and to loans and deposits with or by the Museum; to attend to the immediate accessioning of objects, and to render assistance to those in charge of departments in their further registry; also to verify the registers of the Museum under the Director and when desired by him; to record any restrictions attached to objects and to aid the Director in maintaining these restrictions; to attend to the photographing of the objects; to aid the Director and those in charge of departments in arranging for the storage, installation, cleaning and repair of objects, and to direct any persons assigned to this work not already responsible to others; and to render such other assistance in the work of the Museum as the Director may determine.[17]

THE COLLECTIONS MANAGER

In his book on the history of museum studies, Jesús Lorente identified three components that were fundamental to establishing the museum profession: (i) specialized publications; (ii) professional associations; and (iii) formal training courses,[18] all of which blossomed in the twentieth century and enabled the collections care profession to progress from people with on-the-job-learning and informal apprenticeships to a core of university-trained professionals who could access a range of technical literature and who had official channels for communication with colleagues through museum associations.

The title *collections manager* came into use in the mid-1970s in natural history museums in the United States.[19] Although some natural history museums had registrars,[20] the position was not common. Historically, most hands-on collection work and registration was done by curators or by curatorial assistants working under their direction. As both collections and collections-based research increased in size and complexity, it became obvious that specialists were needed to take over the documentation and care of the collections because the job descrip-

tions of most natural history curators were increasingly focused on research and administration.[21] A 1990 survey of collection care positions in the United States and Canada demonstrated that the tasks of collections managers included the registration and care responsibilities traditionally assigned to registrars in other museums but with a greater emphasis on hands-on collections care and use of electronic registration systems.[22] Although there were some attempts to distinguish between a registrar and a collections manager (e.g., a registrar was primarily involved with recordkeeping and a collections manager with hands-on collection work), the responsibilities of the two positions quickly converged and the job titles have become synonyms (see CHAPTER 1B, "The Straw that Stirs the Drink—The Role of the Registrar in the Museum World").

MUSEUM REGISTRATION METHODS— DUDLEY AND WILKINSON

One of the most important developments in registration as a profession was the publication of *Museum Registration Methods*. The idea for the book was hatched in 1952 at a registrar's session at the annual meeting of the AAM in Minneapolis, Minnesota. The leaders who stepped up to take on the task were Dorothy Dudley and Irma Bezold Wilkinson.

Dorothy Dudley (1903–1979) graduated from Wheaton College in Massachusetts and undertook a twelve-monthlong apprenticeship program at the Newark Museum in 1925 at a monthly salary of just fifty dollars.[23] She became the museum's registrar in 1932 and, in 1936, moved on to the Museum of Modern Art in New York, where she spent the remainder of her career. In New York, Dudley met Irma Bezold Wilkinson (1906–1997), who had graduated from the University of Wisconsin in 1929 and went to work for the Metropolitan Museum of Art in 1930. Wilkinson served as the museum's registrar from 1949 to 1963 (she was also an authority on Middle Eastern and Islamic Art).

To get their project started, Dudley and Wilkinson sent a questionnaire to more than two hundred museums around the country to solicit input from their colleagues, and they reviewed the then scant literature on registration and collections care. They took a draft of their book to the 1954 AAM meeting in Santa Barbara, California, where it was presented and formally approved. Dudley and Wilkinson wrote in the introduction to their book that:

> The results of our survey indicated that the responsibilities of the registrar in many museums include not only the making and keeping of records, but also work related to the entry, exit, safekeeping, and cataloguing of museum objects; while in some museums registration is the responsibility of curators who supply the registrar with the information needed for his records. In all museums, however, the basic procedures for registration were similar, whether handled by a curator or a registrar.
>
> We have included in this manual the procedures of a registration department where the registrar's duties include, in addition to the recording of objects, their physical handling as they move in and out of a museum and arrangements for their packing, shipping, storage, and insurance. We have also included articles on cataloguing for registrars who make catalogue records under the direction of, or in consultation with curators. In planning the illustrations we did not attempt to set up an ideal system of registration forms, but rather to give a representative selection of those currently in use.[24]

At the time they prepared the first edition of *Museum Registration Methods*, Dudley and Wilkinson were both experienced registrars (Dudley was fifty-five years of age, and Wilkinson was fifty-two), which is undoubtedly a big part of why the book was so successful; the first edition reflects their combined decades of professional training and experience, as well as their consultations with others in the profession. In the introduction to the first edition, they explained that they wrote the book because so many people were asking them for advice, but they emphasized that "cooperative labor and support produced this manual."[25] With this simple statement, Dudley and Wilkinson set a tone for the profession that en-

dures today—registrars and collections managers are an amazingly collaborative, supportive, and friendly community.

Within ten years, the first edition of *Museum Registration Methods* was out of print and the profession was changing. Among other developments, the AAM had organized a task force to address loans in museums that produced a white paper on safe lending policies,[26] and there had been significant changes in US tariff legislation. There were new import and export requirements, insurance of collections was becoming more complicated, the design of packing crates was changing, and a few museums were beginning to experiment with computers in collection registration. This prompted Dudley and Wilkinson to produce a second edition, this time published jointly by the AAM and the Smithsonian Institution, that appeared in 1968, and then a third edition in 1979. The third edition mostly followed the format of the first two editions, but with updated information and new chapters addressing registrars in natural history museums and historic houses and the growing use of computers. The third edition also included the sad news that Dorothy Dudley had died while the book was in galley proof.

.

THE NEW MUSEUM REGISTRATION METHODS—BUCK AND GILMORE

The biggest format shift came with the fourth edition, which had two new editors—Rebecca A. Buck and Jean Allman Gilmore—and was appropriately titled *The New Museum Registration Methods*. Buck and Gilmore had interviewed Wilkinson in 1994[27] and reported that "Irma Wilkinson did not like nonsense; she told us that everyone in the profession should first understand the importance of the object and that their professionalism would flow from that understanding."[28]

The development of the profession can be seen by comparing the contents of the first five editions of *Museum Registration Methods* (see TABLE IA.I and FIGURE IA.2). One of the most significant changes was the expansion of the registrar's duties. In the first three editions, the storage and care of objects were described as "generally the province of curators and

Table 1A.1 Evolution of Museum Registration Methods

Edition	First	Second	Third	Fourth	Fifth
Date	1958	1968	1979	1998	2010
Editors	Dorothy H. Dudley and Irma Bezold	Dorothy H. Dudley and Irma Wilkinson	Dorothy H. Dudley and Irma Wilkinson	Rebecca A. Buck and Jean A. Gilmore	Rebecca A. Buck and Jean A. Gilmore
Contributors	16	18	34	66	68
Pages	xi + 225	viii + 294	ix + 437	xvii + 427	xi + 516
Page size	7 × 10 inches	7 × 10 inches	8 × 10 inches	8 × 11 inches	8 × 11 inches
Front matter	Foreword-1	Foreword-2	Acknowledgments-4	Introduction and Acknowledgments-2	Acknowledgments-2
			Foreword-2		Preface-1
	Introduction-3	Introduction-2	Dudley obit-1	Foreword-1	Letter from RC-AAM Chair-1
The profession					History of registration-10
				A composite job description for the registrar-2	A composite job description for the registrar-2
					The administrative placement of registration and collections care in museums-1
				The role of the registrar in the museum's web-2	The role of the registrar in the museum's web-5
				Collection roles-1	Collection roles-2
	The registration department-6	The registration department-6	The registration department-8		
		Planning ahead—the registrar's role in a building program-16	Planning ahead—the registrar's role in a building program-14	Architectural planning-9	
			A registrar's role in a natural history museum-20		
	Registration methods in a museum of science and industry-3	Registration methods in a museum of science and industry-2	Registration methods in a museum of science and industry-4		

			Registration records in a historic house museum-14		
Collection management policies					
Registration practice	Incoming and outgoing material-10	Incoming and outgoing material-10	Incoming and outgoing material-10		
		A procedure for acquiring objects—including remainder and fractional interest gifts-5	A procedure for acquiring objects, including partial gifts, at the Museum of Modern Art-5		
				Budget-2	
				Personnel and training-2	
				Quality management-2	
					Initial custody and documentation-6
					Acquisitions and accessioning-9
	The registration of objects-21	The registration of objects-25	The registration of objects-20		
	Accessioning, marking, and storing scientific collections-10	Accessioning, marking, and storing scientific collections-9	Accessioning, marking, and storing scientific collections-6		
	Accession records in a historical museum-6	Accession records in a historical museum-6	Registration records in a history museum-8	Collection management policies-3	Collection management policies-10
Provenance research in museum collections				Provenance research in museum collections-16	
Card records—their organization and duplication	Card records—their organization and duplication-8	Card records—their organization and duplication-9		Documentation: manual systems-16	Manual systems-6
Computers and registration	Computers and registration-8	Computers and registration-8	Computers and registration: a definition of terms-8		

(continued)

Table 1A.1 *Continued*

Edition	First	Second	Third	Fourth	Fifth
			Computers and registration: principles of information management-16		Computerized systems-23
			Computers and registration—a case history-5		Digital asset management-9
			Computers and registration—practical applications-15	Documentation: computerized systems-24	Types of files-5
					Documenting contemporary art-5
Documentation			Forms and records-32		
Condition reporting	The inspection of art objects and trial glossary for describing condition-9	The inspection of art objects and trial glossary for describing condition-7	Inspecting and describing the condition of art objects-8	Condition reporting-10	Condition reporting-10
Cataloging	Cataloging in the Metropolitan Museum of Art-10	Cataloging in the Metropolitan Museum of Art-13	Cataloging in the Metropolitan Museum of Art with a note on adaptations for small museums-9		
	Cataloging prints in the Museum of Modern Art-10	Cataloging prints in the Museum of Modern Art-9	Cataloging prints in the Museum of Modern Art-9		
Nomenclature and classification	A standard terminology for describing objects in a museum of anthropology-16	A standard terminology for describing objects in a museum of anthropology-16	A standard terminology for describing objects in a museum of anthropology-14		

	Classifying paintings, drawings, and prints by media-9	Classifying paintings, drawings, and prints by media-10	Classifying paintings, drawings, and prints by media, with a note on classifying constructions-11		
	A classification system for art objects-4	A classification system for art objects-5	A classification system for art objects-3		
Archives				Archives-8	Basic components of an institutional archive-10
Measuring and marking	Measuring and marking objects-18	Measuring and marking objects-21	Measuring and marking objects-24	Measuring-4 Marking-30 Numbering-30	Measuring-4 Marking-44 Numbering-3
Handling				Handling-4	Object handling-10
Preparation				Preparation-6	Preparation-7
Preventive care				Preventive care-5	Preventive care-6
Storage and care of objects	Storage and care of objects-19	Storage and care of objects-20	Storage and care of objects-24	Storage-9	Storage-7
Inventory				Inventory-3	Inventory-7
Deaccessioning				Deaccessioning-10	Deaccessioning-9
Repositories					Repositories-4
Found-in-collection					Found-in-collection-10
Old loans				Old loans-7	Old loans-15
Photography				Photography-7	Photographic services and rights and reproductions-2
Rigging				Rigging-3	Moving and rigging safely-7
Loans	Loans from museum collections-6	Loans from museum collections-6	Loans from museum collections-6	Loans-12	Loans-13
	Preparing art exhibitions for travel-18	Preparing art exhibitions for travel-14	Preparing art exhibitions for travel-22		
		The ideal container and the travel of works of art-6	The ideal container for travel of humidity-sensitive collections-6		

(continued)

Table 1A.1 Continued

Edition	First	Second	Third	Fourth	Fifth
	Packing and shipping collections-9	Packing and shipping-21	Packing and shipping-20	Packing and crating-9	Packing and crating-10
				Shipping-6	Shipping by land, air, and sea-6
	Importing and exporting museum collections-13	Importing and exporting-19	Importing and exporting-24	Import and export-4	Import and export-4
	Canadian import and export regulations affecting museums-5				
				International movement of cultural property-2	
				Couriering-5	Couriering-4
				Statement of courier practice-4	RC-AAM Courier Policy Statement-4
					In-house exhibitions-3
					Organizing loan and traveling exhibitions-5
				Hosting traveling exhibitions-7	Hosting traveling exhibitions-6
Exhibitions	Competitive exhibitions-7	Competitive exhibitions-4			
	Receiving centers for competitive exhibitions-2	Receiving centers for competitive exhibitions-2			
Rules for handling works of art			Rules for handling works of art-12		
Contracts				Contracts-6	
Risk management		Insurance-15	Insurance-17	Insurance-8	Insurance-7
				Risk management-2	Risk management-1
				Disaster mitigation planning-4	Emergency preparedness planning-3
					Emergency response and recovery-2

FIGURE IA.2 PREVIOUS EDITIONS OF *MUSEUM REGISTRATION METHODS*. TOP ROW: FIRST EDITION (1958), SECOND EDITION (1968), AND THIRD EDITION (1979); BOTTOM ROW: FOURTH EDITION (1998) AND FIFTH EDITION (2010). PHOTO BY THE AUTHOR.

conservators,"[29] but by the fourth edition (published in 1998) this statement had disappeared, and a composite job description for registrars was added. The book grew in size as well—the first two editions consisted of 225 and 294 pages, respectively (with a page size of 7 × 10 inches). The third edition, published in 1979, ran to 437 pages (with a page size of 8 × 10 inches). The fourth (1998) and fifth (2010) editions were 427 and 516 pages, respectively, but with a larger page size (8 × 11 inches).

In the first, second, and third editions of *Museum Registration Methods*, a little more than half of the text was written by Dudley and Wilkinson, the remainder consisting of specialized topics addressed by other professionals (TABLE IA.I). Although Buck and Gilmore wrote some of the text for the fourth and fifth editions themselves, their main task was to serve as editors, recruit a wide range of experts, and to integrate the contributions into a broad, comprehensive guide to professional practice. The comparison of editions is striking. The first three editions included a chapter on the registration department, but this was replaced by a chapter on the role of the registrar along with related information in other chapters in the fourth and fifth editions. A chapter on collection management policies was added in the fourth edition, the chapter on inspecting object condition was replaced by a chapter on preparing condition reports, and new topics including archives, inventory, deaccessioning, photography, rigging, courier practice, and risk management were included. The chapters on nomenclature for art and anthropological objects in the first three editions disappeared as the taxonomy in those fields was becoming more standardized. The use of computers in museums, which merited just eight pages in the second edition of the book (when computers were still large, expensive, and difficult to use) had expanded to more than thirty pages by the fifth edition (see BOX IA.I). In the second edition, the author of the computer chapter mentioned that "the punched card is now the most commonly used input medium," and then concluded:

> In the present state of the art the computer is certainly not going to eliminate the registrar's catalog cards. It won't even replace the auxiliary files though it may take over their production and upkeep. What it will do is provide special and general purpose check lists of existing collections and sources. . . . Users will be spared the drudgery of assembling a basic listing, arranging it in the desired order and, last but not least, typing.[30]

THE *BELMONT REPORT* AND ITS AFTERMATH

More changes were looming for the profession, particularly in how registrars were trained and how museums were evaluated. Ironically, the year, 1968, that the second edition of *Museum Registration Methods* was published was when the *Belmont Report* was released, which created quite a stir and prompted many changes in museums and the museum profession. *America's Museums: The* Belmont Report was the product of the Federal Council on the Arts and Humanities, commissioned by US President Lyndon B. Johnson. The report reviewed the functions, condition, staffing, and strained financial situation of museums across the country. Among the results of the *Belmont Report* were that more federal money was made available to museums

Box 1A.1 Computers and Registration

The first serious attempt at developing a computer program for museum collections took place in 1965 at the University of Oklahoma, using a records management software program called GIPSY, which stood for generalized information processing system. Although the program itself was not successful, the idea attracted the attention of a small group of museum workers who decided to form the Museum Computer Network (MCN) in 1967 to promote the use of computers in museums. Several MCN members experimented with a program called GRIPHOS (general retrieval and information processor for humanities oriented studies), but it was not until 1970 that the Metropolitan Museum of Art and the Museum of Modern Art had successful computer-based catalogs up and running. In the early 1970s, SELGEM (self-generating master) was launched by the Smithsonian Institution as a one-size-fits-all registration program, and REGIS (from Arizona State Museum's Interactive REGIStration System) made its debut in 1975 but due to the limitations of memory and the complexity of the task to be done, neither of these programs were widely adopted; information that was input into both programs had to be coded and loaded in batches, which was time-consuming. As a result of the failures of these attempts at universal museum cataloging programs, and the availability of affordable desktop computers beginning in the late 1970s, the profession turned to custom cataloging programs written for specific museums. By 1980 there were hundreds of different programs in use in museums, none compatible with any of the others. This changed with the appearance of commercial database programs based on the relational model developed at IBM, which fundamentally changed the way databases were structured and how data was stored and retrieved by organizing data into sets, and storing it in tables.

Few museums today use custom databasing programs, and it is hard to imagine doing registration in a museum without an electronic database.

Based on J. E. Simmons, *Museums: A History* (Lanham, MD: Rowman & Littlefield, 2016), 213–220.

and AAM instituted an accreditation program, providing a set of professional standards for museums to strive to meet. As stated by Buck, "The process of accreditation accelerated everything professional in museums, including creation of more positions for collection managers, collection technicians, exhibition managers, registrars, and curators" and the growth in museum studies programs.[31]

The number of postgraduate museum studies programs expanded greatly beginning in the 1970s, producing a new generation of museum workers who entered the job market with a different background than their predecessors.[32] Among other things, these new professionals were learning about the importance of preventive conservation in the care of collections. In the 1980s, a survey conducted by the Institute of Museum Services (now the Institute of Museum and Library Services [IMLS]) revealed that at least 38 percent of the collections in museums in the United States needed some sort of conservation work and that the condition of another 40 percent of collection objects was not known. In response to this information, AAM issued a report in 1984 titled *Caring for Collections: Strategies for Conservation, Maintenance and Documentation* to emphasize the need for better training of museum staff in preventive care.

The Bay Foundation funded a series of four Collections Care Pilot Training Programs (for archaeology and ethnography, fine arts, history, and natural history) that were administered by the National Institute of Conservation. The purpose the pilot training programs was to bring together collections care personnel, conservators, material scientists, and other professionals for interdisciplinary interactions and synergistic effect to explore ways to improve the training of professional collections care workers. A series of publications was produced based on these training programs under the general title *Training for Collections Care and Maintenance: A Suggested Curriculum* (TABLE 1A.2). The curricula were intended to serve as guidelines for the development of postgraduate training programs in university-based museum studies. Although the pilot training programs were of great benefit to the participants, only a few portions of the proposed curricula were incorporated into academic programs, and none were used in full by an educational institution to establish a postgraduate course in collections care as was initially anticipated. Nevertheless, the program had a significant impact in making preventive conservation a standard part of collections management and promoting improvements in collection storage environments.[33] A significant new

Table 1A.2 Publications in the Series *Training for Collections Care and Maintenance: A Suggested Curriculum*, Published by the National Institute for the Conservation of Cultural Property, Washington, D.C.

Volume	Title	Date	Training Program
I	*Archaeology and Ethnography*	1990	Arizona State Museum, University of Arizona, Tucson
II	*History*	1991	Panhandle-Plains Historical Museum, Canyon, Texas
III	*Natural Sciences*	1991	Los Angeles County Museum of Natural History, California
IV	*Fine Arts*	1991	The Art Institute of Chicago, Illinois

chapter on preventive conservation appeared in the fourth edition of *Museum Registration Methods*, making the case that preventive conservation was "the most cost-effective strategy" for museums to use to "preserve their collections in ways that are environmentally safe and sustainable and economically prudent."[34] The chapter elucidated the role of conservation in museums and advised that "registrars and collections managers should be fully informed about preventive care practices."[35]

ALPHABET SOUP—RC-AAM, SPNHC, AND ARCS

The profession continued to grow with the formation of the Registrar's Committee of the American Association of Museums (RC-AAM, now the Collections Stewardship Professional Network) in 1977, which became a driving force in the profession, producing a variety of workshops, publications, and best practice standards.[36] More than seventy members of the RC-AAM contributed to *The New Museum Registration Methods*, published in 1998.

As registrars and collections managers became more numerous in museums, several professional associations were founded. The increase in collections manager positions in natural history and archaeology brought about the establishment of the Society for the Preservation of Natural History Collections (SPNHC), founded simultaneously in Canada and the United States in 1985. The Australian Registrars Committee (now the Australasian Registrars Committee) was started in 1990, the UK Registrars Group was organized in 1991. The International Registrars Symposium held its first meeting just before the AAM annual meeting in New Orleans in 2004. The world's largest professional organization for museum registrars and collections managers, the Association of Registrars and Collections Specialists (ARCS), was founded and held its first meeting in Chicago in 2012.

THE CONSTANCY OF CHANGE AND OCCURRENCE OF CHALLENGES

Museums have survived and thrived for hundreds of years because they are adaptive and resilient institutions, but this also means that the work to be done in museums evolves and changes constantly. What registrars and collections managers are expected to do today is different in many ways from what was expected of them in the past and what will be expected of them in the future.

The introduction of preventive conservation into the management of collections, along with improvements in our understanding of how objects respond to temperature, relative humidity, light, and how materials age, have resulted in changes in environmental standards that had been recognized since the publication of the two editions of the groundbreaking book, *The Museum Environment*, in 1978 and 1986.[37] Formerly strict set points for the storage environment have been replaced by more flexible ranges that still prolong the useful life of the objects while taking into account geographic differences in climate and the capacity of building's heating and cooling systems to maintain steady, seasonally adjusted temperature and relative humidity regimens with minimal fluctuations (see CHAPTER 5I, "Preventive Care," CHAPTER 5J, "Storage," and CHAPTER 6F, "Registrars and Sustainability").[38] Registrars and collections managers are now expected to have a comprehensive understanding of the museum storage environment, its heating and cooling systems, and are tasked with environmental monitoring and reporting. Registrars and collections managers are expected to implement integrated pest management programs, know the intricacies of permits and licenses required to acquire and possess collection objects, and understand the preservation needs of modern plastics and other materials. Some registrars and collections managers specialize in indigenous and tribal museum collections, born-digital collections, or the objects that accumulate at memorial sites. Registrars and collections managers are expected to work with exhibit designers and educators to ensure that the use of collection objects is in line with preservation standards. Although far more information on collection registration and care is available both in print and online than ever before, so too is more misinformation, which means that registrars and collections managers must have good critical thinking skills to separate the wheat from the chaff. Electronic databases have improved steadily but are still far from adequate to manage collections properly. We need a new generation of collection management software systems that integrate traditional registration information with data on object use and movement, pest management, preventive conservation, environmental monitoring, and material deterioration to provide a truly useful collections management tool.[39]

Looking into a future that is likely to have ever-expanding but older collections, stagnant collection care staffing levels, and limited funding, the success of the profession will depend on finding ways to make collections management more cost-effective and for fewer personnel to better care for ever-larger collections that contain a wider variety of objects.[40]

What makes museums unique is that they use objects to help people understand the world. As Christopher Norris has pointed out, museums are the closest thing we have to time machines because with the objects in our collections we can travel back in time to see why things are the way they are now and go forward in time to glimpse what they might become.[41] This is a critically important mission, but it can only happen if museum collections are properly registered, documented, and cared for. •

NOTES

1. J. E. Simmons, *Museums: A History* (Lanham, MD: Rowman & Littlefield, 2016).

2. Simmons, *Museums*, 118–119.

3. Simmons, *Museums*, 119–120.

4. M. A. Meadow, "Introduction," in *The First Treatise on Museums: Samuel Quiccheberg's Inscriptiones 1565*, edited by M. A. Meadow and B. Robertson, pp. 1–41 (Los Angeles: The Getty Research Institute, 2013).

5. Available at: https://en.wikipedia.org/wiki/Elias_Ashmole (accessed July 26, 2019).

6. Simmons, *Museums*, 102–111.

7. Meadow and Robertson, eds., *The First Treatise on Museums*.

8. Caspar Neickel was a pseudonym for Kaspar Freidrich Jenequel. The title was *Museographia Oder Anleitung zum rechten Begriff und nützlicher Anlegung der Museorum oder Raritäten-Kammern* [*Museographica or Guide to the Correct Concept and Useful Application of the Museum or Chamber of Rarities*].

9. For a discussion of museological texts published in the 1800s, see J. P. Lorente, *Manual de la Historia de la Museología* (Gijón: Ediciones Trea, 2012).

10. R. A. Buck, "History of registration," in *Museum Registration Methods*, 5th ed., edited by R. A. Buck and J. A. Gilmore, pp. 2–11 (Washington, DC: American Association of Museums, 2010).

11. Registrar is derived from the Latin *registrum*, meaning a person who keeps a register.

12. J. E. Simmons, "Collection care and management: History, theory, and practice," in *The International Handbooks of Museum Studies. Volume 4. Museum Practice*, edited by C. McCarthy, pp. 221–247 (London: John Wiley and Sons, 2015).

13. J. E. Simmons, "Museum studies programs in North America," in *Museum Studies: Perspectives and Innovations*, edited by S. L. Williams and C. A. Hawks, pp. 113–128 (Washington, DC: Society for the Preservation of Natural History Collections, 2007).

14. Simmons, "Collection care and management," 224.

15. Buck, "History of registration."

16. *Bulletin of the Metropolitan Museum of Art* 2, no. 4 (April 1907).

17. Based on documents from the Museum of Fine Arts and cited in Buck, "History of registration."

18. Lorente, *Manual*.

19. John E. Simmons, "Natural history collections management in North America," *Journal of Biological Curation* 1, nos. 3/4 (1993): 1–17.

20. As noted by Buck (2010), the first person to hold the title of museum registrar, Stephen C. Brown, had previously been the Assistant Keeper of Reptiles at the US National Museum; the person who appointed him as registrar, George Brown Goode, was a well-known ichthyologist prior to becoming Assistant Secretary of the Smithsonian in 1881.

21. L. S. Ford and J. E. Simmons. 1997. "The diffusion of knowledge: Agassiz (1807–1873), Ruthven (1882–1971), and the growth of herpetological collections," in *Collection Building in Ichthyology and Herpetology*, edited by T. W. Pietsch and W. D. Anderson, pp. 577–593, American Society of Ichthyologists and Herpetologists Special Publication Number 3. (Lawrence, KS: American Society of Ichthyologists and Herpetologists, 1997).

22. P. S. Cato, "Summary of a study to evaluate collection manager-type positions," *Collection Forum* 7, no. 2 (1991): 72–94; B. W. Walker, "The Curator as a Custodian of Collections," *Curator* 6, no. 4 (1963): 292–295.

23. Buck, "History of registration."

24. D. H. Dudley and I. Bezold, *Museum Registration Methods* (Washington, DC: American Association of Museums, 1958), ix–x.

25. Dudley and Bezold, *Registration*, ix.

26. Buck, "History of registration."

27. Irma Wilkinson died in 1997, a year before the publication of the fourth edition, *The New Museum Registration Methods*.

28. R. A. Buck and J. A. Gilmore, "Introduction and acknowledgments," in *The New Museum Registration Methods*, 4th ed., edited by R. A. Buck and J. A. Gilmore, viii. (Washington, DC: American Association of Museums, 1998).

29. Dudley and Bezold, 57.

30. Dudley and Wilkinson, *Museum Registration Methods*, 2nd ed., 290.

31. Buck, "History of registration."

32. Simmons, "Museum studies programs in North America"; Simmons, "Collection care and management." In 2007 there were around 30 graduate programs in the United States that identified as museum studies; by 2019, there were at least 136.

33. C. L. Rose and C. A. Hawks, "A preventive conservation approach to the storage of collections," in *Storage of Natural History Collections: A Preventive Conservation Approach*, edited by C. L. Rose, C. A. Hawks, and H. H. Genoways, pp. 1–20 (Society for the Preservation of Natural History Collections, 1995); J. E. Simmons, "Application of preventive conservation to solve the coming crisis in collections management," *Collection Forum* 27, no. 1–2 (2013): 89–101; Simmons, "Collection care and management."

34. G. Fisher, "Preventive Conservation," in *Museum Registration Methods*, 5th ed., edited by Buck and Gilmore, 287.

35. Fisher, "Preventive Conservation," 287.

36. See Buck, "History of registration," for a detailed accounting of the trials and tribulations leading to the formation of the RC-AAM.

37. G. Thompson, *The Museum Environment*, 2nd ed. (London: Butterworths, 1986).

38. Image Permanence Institute, *Sustainable Preservation Practices for Managing Storage Environments* (Rochester, NY: Image Permanence Institute, 2012).

39. Simmons, "Application of preventive conservation."

40. Simmons, Application of preventive conservation."

41. C. A. Norris, "The future of natural history museums," in *The Future of Natural History Museums*, edited by E. Dorfman, pp. 13–28 (London: Routledge, 2017).

1B | THE STRAW THAT STIRS THE DRINK

The Role of the Registrar in the Museum World

ERIN MCKEEN

IT IS A GREAT TIME to work in the museum profession. Museums enjoy high levels of public trust and robust support[1] that strengthen their value in society. In addition to fulfilling the more traditional functions of exhibition, programming, and stewardship of collections, museums are playing an important role in fostering civic and cultural awareness and engagement. As this trend continues and museums continue to serve the public and increasingly global groups of stakeholders, the staff who work in these organizations are as critical as ever.

Museums serve the public by fulfilling their respective missions, which typically include collecting, preserving, interpreting, and documenting the collections they hold in the public trust in pursuit of educational endeavors and making the objects in the collections available through exhibitions, loans, and research access. Prudent collections management and registration practices are some of the most effective tools museums use to provide continuity of collections care and ensure that their obligation to the public trust is upheld.

Collections management and registration are corresponding aspects of collections care that work in concert. Whereas collections management predominately includes the hands-on aspects of collections stewardship (e.g., moving objects, integrated pest management, object rehousing, packing and storage configuration), registration is mainly focused on the documentation and risk management of collection objects. This documentation includes the creation and maintenance of records for acquisitions, cataloging, loans, deaccessions, disposals, inventory, risk management, and the management of legal issues or restrictions for collection objects. Using this documentation, it is typically the registrar who is tasked with knowing what is contained in the collections, where the objects are located, and how they legally and physically came into the museum's custody. Given the significance of this work, where should this vital position reside within the museum? When I sat down to write this, I thought it would be simple to explain the significance of the role of the registrar and its place in the organization structure. Given my own experiences, I considered myself well-versed in the myriad nuances shared by professionals who care for collections. But the more I wrote, the more I struggled with writing a single cohesive, yet comprehensive, statement about the nature of this profession. The truth is that we go by many professional titles. We work in organizations and institutions of varying sizes and make up, including many that do not bear the name museum. This includes all levels of governmental organizations, academic environments, commercial galleries, corporate offices, private collections, and for-profit and nonprofit institutions. The size, scope, history, and administrative structure of an organization are critical factors in determining staff titles and position descriptions for those who work under the banner of collections management and registration. The result may be that the duties of the registrar are collectively managed by multiple staff members across divisions or are under the supervision of a single individual.

The work of the registrar is complementary to other staff who work with collections. For example, our curatorial colleagues who build collections through their intellectual and aesthetic expertise, as well as exhibition staff who design the physical layout and presentation of exhibition content, rely on registration and collections management staff to provide physical access and accountability for collections.

As registrars and collections staff, we manage loans, facilitate intellectual and physical discovery of the collections, document the holdings to ensure accountability and future access, and provide a necessary and essential perspective and voice for preservation and use within museum-type organizations.

Although many who work in museum registration are academic generalists, those who are proficient typically possess specific knowledge, experience, and skills. Effective registration includes goal-orientation, organizational, project management, and communication skills to work with individuals from diverse backgrounds who are both internal and external to the museum. Likewise, a diplomatic and flexible demeanor is as valuable as knowledge and experience.

In addition to the skills and responsibilities enumerated in this essay, an area of specialized knowledge that is essential is a comprehensive understanding of the legal and ethical practices of museum registration. This includes legal title transfer (e.g., donations, bequests, field collecting, legal contracts related to artistic commissions, purchase contracts), loan agreements, intellectual property rights, licensing, international customs and shipping, deaccessions and disposal, tax implications related to collections care (e.g., IRS 8283 and IRS 8383 forms), grant management, donor privacy, cultural patrimony, risk management, insurance, and applicable domestic and international laws and regulations for cultural patrimony and protected species of plants and animals.

Registrars and collections managers typically have some combination of the following academic and practical knowledge:[2]

Academic Background

- BA, MA, or PhD in museum studies or the museum's specialty (e.g., history, art history, public history, fine art, anthropology, archeology, science, arts administration, information sciences).
- Graduate certificate in museum studies, collections management, arts administration, etc.

Areas of Responsibility and Oversight

- Information management in manual and electronic formats including paper-based registration files, correspondence files, catalog cards, ledgers, database records, and digital asset management systems (DAMS).

  ○ Creation and management of legal documents, provenance documentation, history of collection use, and physical documentation of collection materials, including:
  ○ Legal documents supporting acquisition, loans, deaccession, disposal, collection use including rights and restrictions
  ○ Collection catalog data, provenance research, and publication records
  ○ Conservation assessments, conservation treatment reports, and object condition reports
  ○ Exhibition, insurance, and location information
  ○ Management and implementation of inventory and accountability projects
  ○ Database management including input and coordination of data standards, data entry, and DAMS selection and maintenance
  ○ Diffusion of collections registration data to include sharing information with other departments within the museum, response to public inquiries, research access, and student access

- Collections Management

  ○ Monitoring of legal and ethical standards for collections care and use
  ○ Facilitation of care, access, and control of objects in museum custody
  ○ Development and implementation of collection management policies
  ○ Oversight of collection handling, object movement, and location tracking
  ○ Supervision and direction of collection packing and shipping logistics
  ○ Service as courier or designation of couriers
  ○ Implementation of security procedures and practices in concert with organizational security services

    ▪ Design and control of storage areas
    ▪ Determination of storage methods and standards
    ▪ Establishment of housekeeping and integrated pest management practices

  ○ Contracts outside services as needed including conservation, framing, packing, crating, photography, rigging, installation, shipping, insurance, customs brokerage, etc.
  ○ Exhibitions (traveling, in house, and on loan)

- Negotiation of loan contracts
- Procurement of insurance certificates
- Preparation of indemnity applications
- Coordination and oversight of logistics related to packing, shipping, condition reporting, and object movement
- Sharing of object information to prepare object labels
- Coordination of courier logistics

○ Collection Photography

- Management or coordination with other offices for image rights and reproduction requests
- Supervision of the creation of object photography, including image organization, storage, and use

• Administrative Skills and Responsibilities

○ Administration of department or division
○ Recruitment, evaluation, selection, and training of staff
○ Establishment and management of departmental, project, and exhibition budgets
○ Management of training and supervision of interns and volunteers
○ Procurement of departmental supplies and equipment
○ Preparation of rate structures for loans, traveling exhibits, and photo reproduction requests
○ Creation and establishment of procedures and systems for departmental practices and continuity of office operations
○ Advocacy and liaison with other museum departments

- Facility operations, systems maintenance, housekeeping, integrated pest management, and heating, ventilation, and air-conditioning (HVAC) systems
- Educational and public programming
- Governance and board representation

Although this broad list represents the general scope of responsibilities found in most museums, there are always other institutional specific duties as

well. As the fields of museum registration and collections management continue to evolve and adapt to the changing landscape of museums, additional skills will be required for future professionals.

Given current practices and trends, it can be assumed that the registrars and collection managers of the future will need to have a heightened level of technological awareness and adeptness as technology is increasingly incorporated into all facets of documentation, records management, and collections care. The ability to use digital technologies will also require more advanced data management and analysis skills to capture metrics and accurately report statistical informational for grants, budgetary justifications, and annual reporting requirements. It can also be assumed that future professionals will require a developed understanding of pertinent laws and regulations that impact museum acquisitions, intellectual property rights, donor tax implications, and ongoing changes to domestic and international laws for cultural property and protected species. These legal changes accompany the need for a greater awareness of cultural sensitivities (e.g., gender diversity, racial representation and identity, the voices and histories of disenfranchised communities) because they impact the museum's engagement with donors, stakeholders, and the general public.

The notion of the registrar as *thought leader* has been attracting attention in professional circles as greater numbers of our peers move into positions of influence within their respective organizations. Perhaps most importantly, the continued evolution of the profession will require increasing leadership skills as registrars and collections managers are given the appropriate level of authority and autonomy within the museum's web to directly participate and influence decisions made at the highest levels. The ability to offer the perspective and voice of collection care in crafting an institution's vision, goals, and priorities will require registration staff to have a solid foundation in the tools of effective governance and the ability to persuasively convey them to all who work in the museum.

After this reflection on the myriad tasks, responsibilities, and roles of the registrar, it is not surprising that those who perform this work are frequently described as *the central nervous system of the museum, risk manager for the museum,* gatekeeper of the collection, or *the straw that stirs the drink,*[3] the latter being from my own experience as I was introduced to the senior leadership on my first day at a new job. During introductions, I saw the spark of recognition on the deputy director's face as he grasped my contribution to the organization and uttered that idiomatic expression during my welcome.

Given our diversity as a profession, not everyone who does museum registration carries the title *registrar.* But all who do this work ensure that registration practices are executed in service to the public trust that museums strive so hard to uphold. A role of this significance should be afforded a position of standing so as to effectively be of service.

In ideal circumstances, the registrar functions as an independent voice that provides ethical, professional, and logistical checks and balances for our museum colleagues as we all strive to balance access and use of collections with long-term preservation and fiduciary obligations. To maximize this role, the registrar should be positioned within the organization with sufficient status to allow for direct communication with organizational leadership and to influence decision making. ●

NOTES

1. American Alliance of Museums, "Museum Facts and Data." Available at: https://www.aam-us.org/programs/about-museums/museum-facts-data/ (accessed March 2019).

2. R. A. Buck, "A composite job description for the registrar," in *MRM5: Museum Registration Methods,* 5th ed., edited by R. A. Buck and J. A. Gilmore (Washington, DC: American Association of Museums Press, 2010), 15–16.

3. Quotes taken from personal observations, anecdotal references, and communications on the American Alliance of Museums Collections Stewardship listserv.

1c | Resources for Registrars and Collections Managers

Compiled by John E. Simmons and Toni M. Kiser

Alexander, E. P., M. Alexander, and J. Decker. 2017. *Museums in Motion: An Introduction to the History and Functions of Museums.* 3rd ed. Lanham, MD: Rowman & Littlefield.

American Alliance of Museums Direct Care Task Force. 2016. *Direct Care of Collections: Ethics, Guidelines and Recommendations.*

American Alliance of Museums, Washington, DC. Available at: http://www.aam-us.org/resources/ethics-standards-and-best-practices/direct-care.

American Association for State and Local History (AASLH). Available at: https://aaslh.org/resources.

American Institute of Conservation (AIC). AIC Position Paper on Conservation and Preservation for Collecting Institutions. Available at: http://aic.stanford.edu/about/coredocs/position paper.html.

American Institute of Conservation (AIC). AIC Wiki. Available at: http://www.conservation-wiki.com/wiki/Main_Page.

American Institute of Conservation (AIC). Collections Care for Institutions. Available at: http://www.conservation-wiki.com/wiki/Main_Page.

American Institute of Conservation (AIC). 2006. *Field Guide to Emergency Response.* Washington, DC: Heritage Preservation.

American Institute of Conservation (AIC). *Field Guide to Emergency Response Supplementary Resources.* Available at: http://www.conservation-us.org/fieldguide#.Wk5fb3lG1hE/

American Library Association. Cataloguing Cultural Objects and Descriptive Terminology for Works of Art on Paper. Available at: http://www.ala.org/alcts/sites/ala.org.alcts/files/content/events/pastala/annual/06/08harpring.pdf.

Appraisal Foundation. 2005. Uniform Standards of Professional Appraisal Practice. Available at: http://www.uspap.org.

Association of Registrars and Collections Specialists. Available at: https://www.arcsinfo.org/programs/resources.

Bachman, K., ed. 1992. *Conservation Concerns: A Guide for Collectors and Curators.* Washington, DC: Smithsonian Institution Press.

Behrnd-Klodt, M. L. 2008. *Navigating Legal Issues in Archives.* Chicago: Society of American Archivists.

Benedetti, J. M. 2007. *Art Museum Libraries and Librarianship.* Lanham, MD: Scarecrow Press/Art Libraries Society of North America.

Bourcier, H. R., H. Dunn, and the Nomenclature Task Force, eds. 2015. *Nomenclature 4.0 for Museum Cataloging. Fourth Edition of Robert G. Chenhall's System for Classifying Cultural Objects.* Lanham, MD: Rowman & Littlefield.

Buck, R. A., and J. A. Gilmore. 2003. *On the Road Again: Developing and Managing Traveling Exhibitions.* Washington, DC: American Association of Museums Press.

Buck, R. A., and J. A. Gilmore. 2007. *Collection Conundrums: Solving Collections Management Mysteries.* Washington, DC: American Association of Museums Press.

Canadian Conservation Institute. Available at: https://www.canada.ca/en/conservation-institute.html.

Cassman, V., N. Odegaard, and J. Powell, eds. 2007. *Human Remains. Guide for Museums and Academic Institutions.* Lanham, MD: Rowman & Littlefield.

Cato, P. S., J. Golden, and S. B. McLaren, eds. 2003. *Museum Wise: Workplace Words Defined.* Washington, DC: Society for the Preservation of Natural History Collections.

Chmelik, S. 2015. *Museum and Historic Site Management: A Case Study Approach.* Lanham, MD: Rowman & Littlefield.

Connecting to Collections (C2C). Available at: https://www.connectingtocollections.org/.

Conservation Center for Art and Historic Artifacts. Available at: http://www.ccaha.org/publications.

Courtney, J., ed. 2015. *The Legal Guide for Museum Professionals.* Lanham, MD: Rowman & Littlefield.

Elkin, Lisa, and Christopher A. Norris, eds. 2019. *Preventive Conservation: Collection Storage.* New York: Society for the Preservation of Natural History; American Institute for Conservation of Historic and Artistic Works; Smithsonian Institution; The George Washington University Museum Studies Program.

Flynn, G. A., and D. Hull-Walski. 2001. Merging traditional indigenous curation methods with modern museum standards of care. *Museum Anthropology* 25, no. 1: 31–40.

Gardner, J. B., and E. Merritt. 2004. *The AAM Guide to Collections Planning.* Washington, DC: American Association of Museums Press.

Getty Vocabulary Program. Available at: https://www.getty.edu/research/tools/vocabularies/cco_cdwa_for_ms_prints.pdf.

Hawks, C. A., M. McCann, K. Makos, L. Goldberg, D. Hinkamp, D. Ertel, and P. Silence, eds. 2011. *Health and Safety for Museum Professionals.* New York: Society for the Preservation of Natural History Collections.

Hohn, T. C. 2008. *Curatorial Practices for Botanical Gardens.* Lanham, MD: Altamira Press.

Image Permanence Institute (IPI). Available at: https://www.imagepermanenceinstitute.org/.

Image Permanence Institute (IPI). 2012. *IPI's Guide to Sustainable Preservation Practices for Managing Storage Environments*. Rochester, NY: Image Permanence Institute.

Ingram, N. 2004. *Practical Conservation Guidelines for Successful Hospitality Events in Historic Houses*. London: English Heritage.

Jones, M. E. 2016. *Art Law. A Concise Guide for Artists, Curators, and Art Educators*. Lanham, MD: Rowman & Littlefield.

Kipp, A. 2016. *Managing Previously Unmanaged Collections: A Practical Guide for Museums*. Lanham, MD: Rowman & Littlefield.

Kuruvilla, H. H. 2016. *A Legal Dictionary for Museum Professionals*. Lanham, MD: Rowman & Littlefield.

Landrey, G. J. 2000. *The Winterthur Guide to Caring for Your Collection*. Hanover, DE: Henry Francis du Pont Winterthur Museum.

Latham, K. F., and J. E. Simmons. 2014. *Foundations of Museum Studies: Evolving Systems of Knowledge*. Santa Barbara, CA: Libraries Unlimited.

Lipinski, T. A. 2002. *Libraries, Museums, and Archives: Legal Issues and Ethical Challenges in the New Information Era*. Lanham, MD: Scarecrow Press.

Malaro, M. C., and I. P. DeAngelis. 2012. *A Legal Primer on Managing Museum Collections*, 3rd ed. Washington, DC: Smithsonian Books.

Matassa, F. 2011. *Museum Collections Management: A Handbook*. London: Facet Publishing.

McCarthy, C., ed. *International Handbooks of Museum Studies: Museum Practice*. London: Wiley Blackwell.

Merritt, E. M., ed. 2005. *Covering Your Assets: Facilities and Risk Management in Museums*. Washington, DC: American Association of Museums Press.

Merritt, E. M. 2008. *National Standards and Best Practices for U.S. Museums*. Washington, DC: American Association of Museums Press.

Miller, S. 2018. *The Anatomy of a Museum: An Insider's Text*. Oxford: Wiley Blackwell.

Miller, S. 2018. *Deaccessioning Today: Theory and Practice*. Lanham, MD: Rowman & Littlefield.

National Park Service. *Conserve O Grams*. Available at: https://www.nps.gov/museum/publications/conserveogram/cons_toc.html.

National Park Service. *Museum Handbook*. Available at: https://www.nps.gov/museum/publications/handbook.html.

National Trust. 2006. *The National Trust Manual for Housekeeping: The Care of Collections in Historic Houses Open to the Public*. Amsterdam: Elsevier.

National Information Standards Organization (NISO). 2007. *A Framework of Guidance for Building Good Digital Collections*, 3rd ed. Baltimore, MD: NISO. Available at: http://www.niso.org/publications/rp/framework3.pdf (accessed March 2, 2017).

Ogden, S., and Institute of Museum Library Services. 2004. *Caring for American Indian Objects: A Practical and Cultural Guide*. St. Paul: Minnesota Historical Society Press.

Perry, K. D. 1999. *The Museum Forms Book*. Austin: Texas Association of Museums.

Phelan, M. E. 2014. *Museum Law: A Guide for Officers, Directors, and Counsel*, 4th ed. Lanham, MD: Rowman & Littlefield.

Powell, B. A. 2016. *Collection Care: An Illustrated Handbook for the Care and Handling of Cultural Objects*. Lanham, MD: Rowman & Littlefield.

Prom, C., Rimkus, K., O'Meara, E., and Stratton, K. 2016. *Digital Preservation Essentials. Trends in Archives Practice*. Chicago: Society of American Archivists.

Registrars Committee of the American Association of Museums. 2011. *Standard Facility Report*, 2nd ed., rev. Washington, DC: American Association of Museums.

Registrar Trek. Available at: http://world.museumsprojekte.de/.

Ritzenthaler, M. L. 2010. *Preserving Archives and Manuscripts*, 2nd ed. Portland: Society of American Archivists.

Society for the Preservation of Natural History Collections (SPNHC). Available at: www.spnhc.org.

Simmons, J. E. 2018. *Things Great and Small: Collections Management Policies*, 2nd ed. Lanham, MD: Rowman & Littlefield.

Sullivan, L. P., and S. T. Childs. 2003. *Curating Archaeological Collections: From the Field to the Repository*. Walnut Creek, CA: Altamira Press.

Taberner, A. 2012. *Cultural Property Acquisitions: Navigating the Shifting Landscape*. Walnut Creek, CA: Left Coast Press.

Van Horn, D. R., H. Culligan, and C. Midgett, eds. 2015. *Basic Condition Reporting: A Handbook*, 4th ed. Lanham, MD: Rowman & Littlefield.

Visual Resource Association. 2006. *Cataloging Cultural Objects: A Guide to Describing Cultural Works and Their Images*. Atlanta: ALA Editions.

Waller, R. R. 2003. *Cultural Property Risk Analysis Model: Development and Application to Preventive Conservation at the Canadian Museum of Nature*. Göteborg Studies in Conservation No. 13. Göteborg: Göteborg Acta Universitatis Gothoburgensis.

Yeide, N. H., K. Akinsha, and A. L. Walsh. 2001. *The AAM Guide to Provenance Research*. Washington, DC: American Association of Museums Press.

Yerkovich, S. 2016. *A Practical Guide to Museum Ethics*. Lanham, MD: Rowman & Littlefield.

Young, A., ed. 2018. *Rights and Reproductions: The Handbook for Cultural Institutions*, 2nd ed. Lanham, MD: Rowman & Littlefield.

1D | CARING FOR THE NATION'S TREASURES

The National Park Service Museum Program

JOAN BACHARACH

ABRAHAM LINCOLN's rocking chair. Thomas Edison's handwritten notes. Frederick Douglass's library. Thomas Moran paintings. Theodore Roosevelt's Rough Rider outfit. Mamie Eisenhower's dinner service. Jurassic dinosaurs. The Liberty Bell. Civil War soldiers' uniforms. Everglades tree snails. American Red Cross founder Clara Barton's first aid kit. The Statue of Liberty torch. Archaeological ceramics from Mesa Verde and Chaco Canyon. Botanical specimens from Denali and Yosemite. George Washington's Inauguration Day suit. These are only a few of the more than 48 million objects and specimens and 80,000 linear feet of archives in National Park Service (NPS) museum collections. They are located in more than 385 national parks throughout the United States, from the Canadian border to the Mexican border, and from Hawaii to the Virgin Islands, making the NPS one of the largest museum systems in the world.

As collections manager in the anthropology department at the California Academy of Sciences in San Francisco, I was responsible for cataloging, collections care, and curating exhibitions. I had visited several national parks but was unaware that they had museum collections. When I became Museum Registrar for the NPS in Washington, D.C., I learned that accountability, care, and access were the core tenets of the NPS museum management strategy and that its comprehensive collections management policies and procedures were available to all at no cost. I was now part of the team responsible for developing and updating this well-respected museum guidance.

It took some adjustment from working directly with collections in a museum to writing policy in the headquarters of such a large organization. What I had not anticipated was the extraordinary professional growth that would come with this move. My work with the NPS Museum Management Program has deepened my understanding of museum and collections management, exhibition development, and my appreciation of collaborating with colleagues. It has provided deeply rewarding opportunities to participate in the stewardship of US natural and cultural heritage and to work with remarkable collections in some of the most magnificent places in the United States. To understand my NPS career, I would like to share some background information about the NPS and its museum program.

NPS MUSEUM COLLECTIONS

NPS museum collections "directly support the park mission; aid understanding among park visitors; advance knowledge in the humanities and sciences; provide baseline data for NPS managers, scientists, and other researchers; [and] preserve scientific and historical documentation of the park's resources and purpose."[1]

NPS collections are as diverse as the United States. They tell powerful stories of the United States and its peoples, from the earliest inhabitants to the present, including presidents and first families, civil rights leaders, Native Americans, and poets, farmers, and inventers. Fossil, plant, animal, and geology specimens record a tapestry of diverse habitats and ecosystems (FIGURE 1D.1). Objects, works of art, and

FIGURE 1D.1 SKULL OF *ALLOSAURUS FRAGILIS*, DINOSAUR NATIONAL MONUMENT. COURTESY OF THE NATIONAL PARK SERVICE; PHOTO BY KHALED BASSIM.

FIGURE ID.2 PORTRAIT OF FREDERICK DOUGLASS, 1878. FREDERICK DOUGLASS NATIONAL HISTORIC SITE. COURTESY OF THE NATIONAL PARK SERVICE; PHOTO BY CAROL M. HIGHSMITH.

archival items illuminate the long arc of history and the national narrative of notable events and innovative ideas (FIGURE ID.2).

The collections support the NPS mission to preserve and protect the nation's precious legacy. They are generally managed, exhibited, and interpreted where they were collected, created, or used. Collections span disciplines from archeology, archives, art, ethnography, and history, to biology, geology, and paleontology, from prehistory to the present. Many were in place at the establishment of a particular park. In recent years, archeological investigation and compliance work has generated substantial collections growth.

Each national park tells a unique story and its collections are integral to that story and the park's mission. Collections yield information for managing park resources and support scientific studies and history publications. They are used in exhibitions and in interpretation and education programs. Collections are primary source materials for future research and provide opportunities for exploration and learning.

History of the NPS Museum Program

The NPS Museum Program had its origins in a modest arboretum at Yosemite in 1904, artifacts displayed on a table at Casa Grande in 1905, and in a museum in a tent at Sequoia.[2] Early park museums grew informally within their original context before the National Park Service Organic Act of 1916 authorized the creation of the NPS. The act called for conservation of "scenery and the **natural and historic objects** and the wildlife therein and to provide for the enjoyment of the same in such manner and by such means as will leave them unimpaired for the enjoyment of future generations" [emphasis added] (16 U.S.C. 1,2,3 and 4). This legislation recognized the need to preserve, protect, and use park collections.

The groundswell to preserve natural wonders began with the establishment of Yellowstone National Park in 1872 that was "set apart as a public park . . . for the benefit and enjoyment of the people . . . [and] to provide for the preservation . . . of . . . natural curiosities . . . [and] retention in their natural condition."[3] There was a parallel movement to protect the prehistoric cliff dwellings and Spanish missions on Southwestern public lands. In 1906, President Theodore Roosevelt signed the Antiquities Act into law, giving the president authority to proclaim "historic landmarks, historic and prehistoric structures, and other **objects of historic or scientific** interest" [emphasis added] (16 U.S.C. 431-33). By 1909, when he left office, Roosevelt had proclaimed eighteen national monuments, including Mesa Verde and Grand Canyon.

Universities and museums conducted research at these locations that generated botanical, zoological, and archeological collections. Historical associations assisted in developing exhibits and furnishing historic structures. In 1918, Mesa Verde National Park exhibited prehistoric artifacts in a converted ranger cabin. In 1920, Stephen Mather, the first director of the NPS, recognized the power of collections preserved and exhibited in their original context and said, "Museums containing specimens of wild flowers, shrubs, and trees, and mounted animals, birds, and fish native to the parks, and other exhibits of this character will be established as authorized" in "every one of our parks."[4] This connection with place and context is characteristic of park museum collections.

Between 1925 and 1930, NPS museums were established in Yosemite, Grand Canyon, and Yellowstone. In the 1930s, many American Revolution and Civil War battlefields administered by the War Department were transferred to NPS stewardship, as were other parks, historic sites, and national monuments. Many came with museum collections. Park museums benefited from President Franklin Roosevelt's New Deal federal projects with the extension to the Mesa Verde museum and construction of other park museums. By 2019, 419 parks were part of the NPS, bringing many significant objects, specimens, and archival items into park collections.

Structure and Functions of the NPS Museum Program

The NPS, a bureau of the Department of the Interior (DOI), is headquartered in Washington, D.C., and holds 85 percent of the Department of the Interior's collections. The NPS Museum Management Program in the Washington Support Office provides national program leadership and coordination functions and develops policies and procedures for managing NPS museum and archival collections.

Program staff analyze service-wide collection information for strategic planning, collections management initiatives, funding, and reporting to upper management and Congress. They provide professional advice and technical assistance to the field on acquisition, documentation, accountability, preservation, protection, and the use and disposal of collections. Staff also manage the service-wide automated collections management system that includes more than 7.5 million records for the more than 48 million objects and 80,000 linear feet of archival items and oversee the NPS *National Catalog of Museum Objects*, a centralized repository of museum records that are submitted annually by park and center museum staff.

There are seven NPS regions, each providing oversight and support to the parks within its geographic boundary. Regional curators are located in Anchorage (Alaska Region); Tucson, Arizona (Intermountain Region); Omaha, Nebraska (Midwest Region); Boston, Massachusetts (Northeast Region); Landover, Maryland (National Capital Region); Atlanta, Georgia (Southeast Region); and Boulder City, Nevada (Pacific West Region). Curation centers are located in Tucson, Omaha, Tallahassee (Florida), and Landover (Maryland). Program staff work collaboratively with the Museum Management Program Council that includes regional curators and representative center and park curatorial staff.

The park superintendent, by delegation, represents the NPS director and is responsible for managing all park programs and supervising park employees, including museum staff. Headquarters and regional staff support but do not have online authority over park staff.

In 2018, 292 staff in parks and centers included curators, museum specialists and technicians, and archivists and registrars with museum responsibilities. Another 275 collateral duty staff in parks were assigned curatorial responsibilities. Park and center staff accession and catalog collections, conduct annual inventories, process loans within NPS and to non-NPS institutions, and implement collections care in accordance with NPS policies, procedures, and technical guidance. More than 1,400 NPS facilities (exhibit, storage, and administrative spaces) house museum collections. There are also NPS collections managed in more than 720 non-NPS partner institutions.

NPS Museum Policies and Procedures

In a large and geographically dispersed organization, clearly articulated written museum policies and procedures are essential to ensure uniform implementation of guidance and facilitate field support and training. In the 1920s, the NPS initiated the development of guidelines for managing and exhibiting collections in parks. Service-wide museum policies and procedures were first published in the *Field Manual for Museums* in 1941.[5] In the 1950s and 1960s, the NPS *Museum Handbook* that covered museum management topics was issued, followed by the *Manual for Museums* in 1976.[6] In 1975, the *Conserve-O-Grams* Technical Leaflet Series[7] was initiated to provide topical and easy-to-use technical information to complement the *Museum Handbook*. In the early 1980s, the *Museum Handbook* was expanded into *Part I: Museums Collections*, which addresses preservation and protection, and *Part II: Museum Records*, which covers documentation and accountability. In the mid-1990s, *Part III: Museum Collections Use* was introduced. The *Museum Handbook* and *Conserve-O-Grams* are continually updated and are available online.

In 1948, the first museum methods training course was held, and museum training workshops continue to be offered today. In 1968, exhibit, conservation, and museum services were centralized at the Harpers Ferry Center in West Virginia. The *National Catalog of Museum Objects* was established in 1977. In a drive that began with the appointment of a Chief Curator and the establishment of the Curatorial Services Division, now the Museum Management Program, at the NPS headquarters in Washington, D.C., in 1980, the NPS laid out a long-range program to bring about full accountability and sound management of its collections.

The development and ongoing updating of museum policies and procedures entails close analysis of existing guidance to determine what needs to be updated, research and in-depth knowledge of current best practices and literature in museum and related fields, and consultation with specialists and field staff. There is close collaboration with authors, as well as the writing of guidance. The process is intense and laborious, with seemingly infinite editing and review prior to issuance and aptly describes the general editor's responsibilities.

DOCUMENTING THE COLLECTIONS

My first assignment as general editor was managing the revision of the NPS *Museum Handbook*, PART II, *Museum Records*, as well as co-authoring and writing guidance. This document covers accessioning, cataloging, marking, appraisals, insurance, deaccessioning, loans, and physical inventory. Sound documentation and accountability facilitate physical and intellectual access essential to collections care, research, and exhibition. Service-wide procedures must be detailed, unambiguous, thoroughly considered, and comprehensive. Guidance has to accommodate different disciplines, from incorporating Linnaean taxonomy for natural history specimens to typologies for archeological artifacts to *Nomenclature 4.0* terminology for history objects. Collections management data such as measurements and object location are also included.

Policies have to work for collections of all kinds and sizes and for centers managing multiple park collections. Guidance must be best practice, internally consistent, logical, easy-to-follow, sound over time, and readily implementable by museum staff. User and specialist opinions have to be solicited and procedures widely reviewed and tested to avoid unintended consequences. And finally, the general editor is responsible for weighing the alternatives and then determining the most appropriate professional guidance that is to be issued.

Several automated cataloging systems were running when I joined the NPS, and so began my next challenge, overseeing the in-house development of the Automated National Catalog System (ANCS), the first service-wide automated collections management system. Disciplinary committees were established and there was extensive consultation, testing, and review. In 1987, parks began using ANCS to facilitate efficient documentation, technical support, data collection, and training. In 1998, the NPS migrated to a customized, commercial collections management system. Subsequently, the NPS oversaw the development of the Interior Collection Management System that is based on the ANCS for the Department of the Interior museum program. It is used by more than eight hundred NPS users to manage individual park databases and generate the annual park Collection Management Report and NPS Checklist for Preservation and Protection of Museum Collections used to compile and analyze service-wide statistics and trends.

In the early 1990s the Secretary of the Interior tasked the Park Service Museum Management Program with establishing the Interior Museum Property program. My tenure as Park Service Museum Registrar included leading the task force that established documentation and accountability policies and procedures for Department of the Interior collections. NPS policies and procedures were adapted and issued for collections held by the Bureau of Indian Affairs, Indian Arts and Crafts Board, Bureau of Land Management, Bureau of Reclamation, Minerals Management, US Fish and Wildlife, and the US Geological Survey.

PRESERVING AND PROTECTING THE COLLECTIONS

In 1999, I became Senior Curator responsible for NPS preservation and protection guidance issued in the *Museum Handbook, Part I, Museum Collections* and *Conserve-O-Grams*. These publications cover the museum environment, storage, biological infestations, handling, packing and shipping, conservation treatment, security, fire protection, emergency planning, and curatorial health and safety. There is close collaboration with field and center staff, conservators, engineers, facilities management, health and safety, historic architecture, and structural fire and security professionals in the development of best practice guidance.

NPS museum guidance has to address the needs of different materials, from paper to fluid-preserved specimens. It must accommodate varied local climates, from arid deserts to icy tundra and humid coastal areas, on lakeshores and seashores, and in cities, mountains, and canyons. Collections are on exhibit in park visitor centers, museums, and historic house museums. They are in storage in purpose-built facilities, curation centers, and in adapted modern buildings. Many buildings, particularly historic structures, present challenging conditions in which to maintain an optimal and stable museum environment because of design, building materials, and components (FIGURE 1D.3). Utilities such as automatic museum fire protection systems have to be minimally invasive and respect the character-defining features of historic structures. Consolidation of collections into multipark storage facilities is seen as an efficient, low-cost, and sustainable strategy to address collections growth and weather-related and funding challenges while meeting NPS preservation standards.

The *National Park Service Museum Handbook* recognizes that preservation and protection is an

FIGURE 1D.3 LINCOLN HOME, SPRINGFIELD, ILLINOIS. LINCOLN HOME NATIONAL HISTORIC SITE. COURTESY OF THE NATIONAL PARK SERVICE; PHOTO BY JOAN BACHARACH.

ongoing process. It is a bull's-eye that moves in concentric circles, from the object in its protective enclosure to the structural envelope, adjacent grounds, to the park boundary and beyond. The handbook provides easy-to-use collections planning and management tools that can be readily adapted for use by museum staff. In addition to being used by park staff, NPS publications are widely used by other museum professionals.

Making Collections Accessible

My responsibilities include managing the development of the NPS *Museum Handbook, Part III, Museum Collections Use*. It covers access and use topics such as legal issues, reproductions, publications, and the exhibition of collections in historic house museums, visitor centers, and museums. Another assignment to make collections accessible includes developing virtual exhibits, publications, object-based lesson plans, and other park museum products.

The internet provides a powerful platform to make collections available to researchers, educators, students, and the public. Virtual park museum exhibits showcase American Revolutionary War heroes, eminent Americans at home, landscape paintings and decorative arts up close, soldiers and internees in camp, and much more. Exhibit development involves collaboration with curators, archeologists, paleontologists, historians, and interpreters, as well as working with photographers to capture high-quality digital images of objects and furnished rooms. Close cooperation with web designers in presenting these images and stories in online exhibits and developing the first *Web Catalog* has made for engaging and creative experiences. NPS also administers the *Park Profiles* that include summary park collections information and has a presence on social media platforms to reach diverse audiences.

The *Teaching with Museum Collections* program was initiated to reach educators and students. Object-based lesson plans are developed in collaboration with parks to dovetail with virtual exhibits and introduce park collections to a new generation of Americans. Teaching and developing museum and collections management curriculum at NPS and Department of the Interior training workshops pro-

vides a regular and deeply satisfying opportunity to interact with staff from all over the NPS. The award-winning book and virtual exhibit, *Treasured Landscapes: National Park Service Art Collections Tell America's Stories*,[8] presents landscape art from more than fifty-five park collections together for the first time to illustrate the story of the NPS's first one hundred years. This rewarding collaboration with park museum staff celebrated the NPS Centennial in 2016.

SOME LESSONS LEARNED

- Develop best practice museum policies and procedures in collaboration with users and specialists.
- Implement stringent acquisition and deaccession policies and procedures to ensure consistent best museum practice and control collection growth.
- House collections efficiently and well to ensure long-term preservation and accessibility.
- Consider the pros and cons of an issue and always opt for preservation to ensure collections will be available for future generations.
- Good museum stewardship is an ongoing process and requires the commitment of staff, resources, and funding in perpetuity. •

NOTES
1. National Park Service, *National Park Service Museum Handbook. Part I: Museum Collections* (2006), Chapter I:4. Available at: https://www.nps.gov/museum/publications/handbook.html

2. A. Hitchcock, *NPS Museums 1904–2004*, 2004. Available at: www.nps.gov/museum/centennial.

3. B. Mackintosh, *The National Parks: Shaping the System*, rev. ed. (Harpers Ferry, WV: Harpers Ferry Center, National Park Service, 1992).

4. F. K. Lane, "National Park Policy," *Parks & Recreation* 5, no. 3 (1922): 247–249.

5. Ned J. Burns, *Field Manual for Museums* (Washington, DC: Government Printing Office, 1941).

6. Ralph H. Lewis, *Manual for Museums* (Washington, DC: National Park Service, 1976).

7. National Park Service, *Conserve-O-Grams* Technical Leaflet Series. Available at: https://www.nps.gov/museum/publications/conserveogram/cons_toc.html.

8. Joan Bacharach, ed., *Treasured Landscapes: National Park Service Art Collections Tell America's Stories* (Washington, DC: National Park Service, 2016).

PART 2 | COLLECTION MANAGEMENT POLICIES

2 | COLLECTION MANAGEMENT POLICIES

JOHN E. SIMMONS

COLLECTIONS MANAGEMENT includes everything that is done to document, care for, and develop museum collections and make them available for use.[1] There are fundamental commonalities among all collections that are summarized in the principles that form the basis for collections management policies:

1. Each object entering the museum must be documented.
2. Objects should be stabilized for long-term preservation and housed in a proper storage environment.
3. Collections must be inventoried and monitored regularly.
4. The collections storage environment must be monitored at all times.
5. All collection activities and monitoring must be documented.

The purpose of the collections management policy is to minimize risks to the collections.[2] The policy identifies who is responsible for collections care and provides a framework for management. In practice, the collections management policy is actually a set of related policies that address issues and problems specific to the institution. The core policies of acquisition, accession, loans, deaccession, access, and collections care are augmented by ethics policies, emergency preparedness policies, and collecting plans and are framed by the mission and scope of collections (TABLE 2.1). Enacting and enforcing good collections management policies helps the museum achieve its mission, demonstrates commitment to professional standards and best practices, and enables the governing authority to meet its legal and ethical obligations to protect and make accessible the collections held in the public trust.

Three fundamental concepts underlying collections management policies reflect the past history of the collections while anticipating future policy evolution:[3]

1. The collections management policies describe a relationship among the museum and its collections, its authorities and staff, and the outside world.
2. The trajectory of this relationship is set by the sum of the previous relationships among these three parties, all of which have to be taken into account whenever decisions are made.
3. These relationships are in a constant state of interaction. The policies regulate activities in the present and the future, but take their character from what has happened in the past.

The museum's organization and legal status affect some collections management policies and determine the nature of the responsibility of the governing board and the administration. In general, because a museum holds its collections in the public trust,[4] the governing authority is responsible for:

1. Maintaining the highest legal, ethical, and professional standards.
2. Establishing policies that guide the institution's operation.
3. Delegating specific responsibilities to the staff, volunteers, and consultants (by means of the collections management policies).

Collections management policies explain why a museum is in operation and how it goes about its business and define the professional standards for managing the objects in its care. Policies are accompanied by procedures, which are the detailed instructions that specify how the staff should apply the policies in their day-to-day activities. Although policies and procedures often are discussed together, it is important to understand the differences between the two. *Policies*

Table 2.1 Issues Addressed by Collections Management Policies

Administrative and Personnel Functions	Statement of authority	
	Scope of collections	
	Categories of collections	
	Ethics	Institutional code of ethics
		Discipline-specific codes of ethics
		Private collections
	Documentation	Standards
		Requirements
	Risk management	Disaster preparedness and response plan
		Insurance
	Intellectual property	Rights and reproduction
		Copyright
		Commercial use of intellectual property
	Health and safety	
Collections Acquisition and Deaccession	Collections plan	
	Acquisition of objects	
	Accession of objects	
	Documentation of objects	
	Repository agreements	
	Registration and cataloging	
	Deaccession and disposal	
	Appraisals and identifications	
Collections Care	Conservation	Standards for storage environments and housing
		Environmental monitoring
		Standards for object supports and containers
		Standards for collection storage furniture
	Organization of the collection storage array	
	Security	
	Inventory	
	Integrated pest management	
	Access and use of collections and collections information	Public access
		Professional use
		Non-professional use
		Commercial use
		Destructive sampling
		Culturally sensitive objects
	Loans	Incoming loans
		Outgoing loans
		Courier policy
		Loan insurance
	Objects in custody	
Policy Review	Compliance review	
	Policy revision	

establish the standards that regulate the museum's activities by identifying what needs to be done and provide a framework to help the staff make decisions. Policy statements must be approved by the museum's governing authority. *Procedures* tell the staff how to do things and provide the mechanism for implementing the policies in a series of succinct and unambiguous action steps. Procedures are developed at the staff level and are not approved by the governing authority. There should be separate documents to make clear what is policy and what is procedure. Because revisions of procedures do not have to be approved by the governing authority, maintaining separate documents makes it easier for the staff to adjust or revise the procedures as necessary to carry out the policies.

A policy should be created to accomplish a specific goal or address a particular issue. Collections management policies should address any issues that might have a significant impact on the collections, museum operations, staff, or collection users. Because the issues that affect collections vary from one museum to another, the set of policies will vary somewhat from one museum to another. The policies should reflect current professional standards, be sensible and logical, and be stated clearly. The individual policies that are part of the collections management policies are interrelated and may address other museum functions as well (e.g., security, pest management, or exhibitions).

Collections management policies should be written to meet the needs of a specific museum, its collections, and how those collections are accessed and used. Reviewing policies from similar institutions can be useful when preparing a policy, but wholesale adoption of documents from other institutions will prove inadequate. The policies must be institution specific, simple, and up to date. Complex, confounded, or outdated policies will simply be ignored.

The policies should define areas of responsibility (taking into account staff size, expertise, institutional mission, type and size of collections, and collections use) and delegate decision-making authority to the appropriate individuals or committees. It is important to identify who has the authority to make exemptions to the policies those rare times when it

is necessary. The policies should direct the staff to maintain complete written records regarding all collections-related decisions and activities.

DEVELOPING AND WRITING COLLECTIONS MANAGEMENT POLICIES

The most successful method of preparing collections management policies involves a team, with broad constituent input, and a deliberate process:

- A team leader is appointed, and a team is recruited from the museum staff that can provide input from all sectors of the institution.
- The team carefully reviews current legal, ethical, and professional standards and determines which policies the institution needs.
- A draft of the policies is circulated to all of the staff for comments and suggestions.
- The draft is reviewed and revised.
- The complete policy document is submitted to the institution's governing authority for endorsement.

A small museum with few staff members can solicit policy development help from colleagues in other institutions or from knowledgeable volunteers. The staff should understand how the policies are developed and should have the opportunity to participate during each stage of the process. It is recommended that several drafts of the policy documents be circulated to the staff for comment. Input from a variety of viewpoints will ensure that the policies align with the institutional mission and have support of the staff members who must implement them. More detailed information about writing collections management policies can be found in the references and in the bibliography and the end of this chapter.

Once the policies are approved, the museum staff should develop procedures to implement the policies and review the procedures periodically to make sure that they are effective and that they accurately implement the policies.

Introductory Sections

The collections management policy document should begin with the museum's mission statement, followed by an introduction briefly summarizing the institution's governance structure and history. The introduction should explain how the collections management policies were developed in the context of the museum's history, mission, and collections plan and delineate other considerations that guide the process of determining the museum's collections-related activities. Most institutions have a separate *collections plan* that establishes a vision for the collections that will best serve the museum's mission, compares the existing collections to this vision, and maps out how the museum will achieve these ideal collections.[5]

The *scope of collections* reviews the history of the collection; considers its strengths, weaknesses, and current uses; and states what the museum does and does not collect. The collections management policy should define *categories of collections* (e.g., research, exhibit, public education), if any. The policy should include or refer to the museum's institutional *code of ethics* and any discipline-specific codes of ethics the professional staff may follow. The ethics section should address personal collecting and any restrictions the institution wishes to place on staff and board members in this regard (see CHAPTER 7A, "Ethics for Registrars and Collections Managers").

The *documentation policy* sets standards for recording collections activities, including environmental monitoring and regular collections inventories. The policy should require that documentation be written in simple, plain prose (using appropriate technical terms as needed), in a permanent format (using archival materials), be legible and comprehensive, and provide guidance for which documents should be permanently archived and which can be disposed of in accordance with a documentation retention schedule.

Acquisitions

The *acquisition policy* is developed based on the collections plan and directs how objects are acquired or brought into the museum. The policy should state clearly which staff or members of the governing authority are authorized to make decisions regarding the acquisition of objects. *Acquisitions* should be relevant to the purposes and priorities of the museum. The criteria for decision, in addition to those laid out in the collections plan, may include intended and potential

use, basic integrity, the estimated cost and space for care and storage, and any special considerations for culturally sensitive objects.[6] The policy should require a receipt to be issued for any object left at the museum (e.g., for identification or consideration as a donation) and to all donors and sellers of collections. The receipt should include the owner's contact information and signature and a clear statement of intent (see CHAPTER 3B, "Acquisitions and Accessioning").

To protect the museum from liability issues, the policy should state that title (ownership) must be obtained free and clear for any accessioned material. The policy should require the staff to make appropriate efforts to ensure that accessioned collections have been obtained legally (e.g., documentation that includes permissions to possess, transport, export, and import the objects). The accession policy should be written to protect the museum from donor demands to accept restricted gifts or partial gifts or objects that do not conform to the collections plan.

Repository agreements are increasingly common in museums, particularly for archaeological and natural science collections, but other kinds of collections as well (see CHAPTER 3C, "Repositories"). Under the terms of a repository agreement, an institution takes on the responsibility for the care and management of a collection that is owned by another institution. In most cases, this means that the managing institution catalogs, cares for, and manages those collections as it does for its own. It is recommended that the repository agreement policy parallel the accession policy as closely as possible and that the required repository documentation parallel accession policy documentation as closely as possible. The repository agreement policy should require the agreement to be detailed in a written contract between the museum and the outside agency or institution with a definite beginning date, ending date, and description of what objects will be covered. The policy should specify standards for the collections storage environment, containers, and storage furniture; standards for collections care and management (which should be the same as those for the museum's own collection); required staffing; responsibility for paying to pack up and return the collections when the repository agreement terminates; and compensation (if any) due to the curating museum for the services it provides. The policy may address restrictions on a repository agreement, such as the objects covered by the repository agreement are to be studied on-site but not loaned to another institution; loans must be approved by the agency that owns the collections; and either party may terminate the agreement at any time.

Appraisals and Authentications

The *appraisals policy* must reflect the legal restrictions on donor tax deductions and ethical considerations for making appraisals (see CHAPTER 7E, "Appraisal"). In general, this means that the policy should require appraisals to be done by outside professionals to avoid conflicts of interest and should prohibit museum staff members from doing appraisals for collections or donations involving their current institution or one where they have recently worked. It is critically important to be scrupulous in avoiding both conflicts of interest and the appearance of conflicts of interest. The policy should reference internal appraisals of owned collections, which often are used for insurance purposes. The museum may allow staff to do authentications of objects for the public. If the museum does allow staff to make authentications, the policy may state that the museum is not responsible for the accuracy of determinations made by the staff.

Deaccessions

The *deaccessioning policy* covers objects that are to be removed from a collection to strengthen it (see CHAPTER 3I, "Deaccessioning and Disposal"). Deaccessioning is a way for a museum to refine and focus its collections to serve its mission better. Deaccessioning may be done when objects no longer fit the museum's mission, for legal reasons (e.g., Native American Graves Protection and Repatriation Act [NAGPRA], illegal export, theft), for various reasons dealing with the physical integrity of the object (poor condition, part/whole relationships), or because of redundancy or poor quality.

The policy should ensure that the responsibility for deaccessioning rests with more than one person and that the museum's governing board gives the final approval. The means of disposal of deaccessioned objects should be in the best interests of the museum, the public, and the professional community. Some deaccession policies require that his-

torical, cultural, and scientific material remain in a certain geographic area. The deaccession policy may promote the use of exchanges with other public trust institutions as the preferred means of disposal. The policy should mandate that deaccessioned objects will not be given or sold to museum staff, volunteers, board members, or their representatives and that any proceeds gained should be used only for the acquisition of other collection objects or the direct care of collections (direct care may include conservation studies and treatments, monitoring technology, and improvements to collection storage).[7]

Collections Care

The *collections care policy* should make it clear that all museum staff members share the responsibility for collections care, and it should identify the lead players in all areas (see CHAPTER 5I, "Preventive Care" and CHAPTER 5J, "Storage"). The policy includes risk management, conservation, storage, and environmental concerns. Documentation of the objects and the collection inventories also should be covered.

The *collections care policy* mandates the level of training required for staff members who handle museum objects and requires other users to confirm via signature that they have read and agreed to the instructions for handling collections (see CHAPTER 5B, "Object Handling"). The policy should set standards for each area—registration and cataloging, maintenance and regular monitoring of the storage environment, and inventory. It addresses collection security (in conjunction with the general institutional *security policy*) and mandates periodic collection inventories. The policy should establish a program of integrated pest management (see CHAPTER 6E, "Integrated Pest Management"). Some museums require specific policies to cover off-site storage of collections (see CHAPTER 5R, "Off-Site Storage").

Access

The *access and use policy* must balance the requirements for collections care and security with the museum's public trust responsibilities. This policy designates the staff members who may approve access to and use of collections and related information. Such access will likely be different for museum professionals than it is for the public, scholars, and commercial users. The policy should impose reasonable restrictions on access and use if such limitations are in the best interests of the collections' long-term care and preservation.

Loans

The *loan policy* should define appropriate reasons for loans of collection objects and specify that they be made to other peer institutions and not to individuals or commercial corporations (see CHAPTER 3K, "Loans"). The policy should require the use of borrowed objects or specimens be in keeping with standards in the field and with the museum's own goals.

The policy should be clear on the process and authority necessary to approve a loan to another institution or to borrow objects from another institution. The loan policy addresses insurance and documentation of loans, the length of the loan period (no loan should be open-ended), and the use of images of the objects. It should specify the physical requirements and security protocols for loans and the criteria for deciding whether to require a courier to accompany a loan object (see CHAPTER 5Q, "Couriering"). The policy should provide a mechanism for recalling loans before their due date.

Many museums have separate policies for outgoing and incoming loans and may have a policy that clarifies all work related to exhibitions produced for loans to other institutions.

Review and Revision

Each collections management policy must be reviewed and revised on a regular basis. Collections management policies, like any other policy, are useless if they are outdated, ignored, too complex to be followed, too simplistic to be useful, or not congruent with the museum's mission. A policy review should outline time intervals for policy review (typically once every three to five years or when there is evidence of policy failure). Staff should keep abreast of changes in museum standards and laws and regulations so that they can update policies when necessary. •

NOTES

1. J. E. Simmons, "Collections management: history, theory, and practice," in *The International Handbook of Museum Studies. Volume 4. Museum Practice*, edited by Conal McCarthy, pp. 221–247 (London: John Wiley and Sons, Ltd., 2015).

2. J. E. Simmons, *Things Great and Small: Collections Management Policies*, 2nd ed. (Lanham, MD: Rowman & Littlefield, 2018).

3. S. M. Pearce, *Museums, Objects and Collections: A Cultural Study* (Washington, DC: Smithsonian Institution Press, 1993), 24.

4. M. C. Malaro and I. P. DeAngelis, *A Legal Primer on Managing Museum Collections*, 3rd ed. (Washington, DC: Smithsonian Books, 2012).

5. J. B. Gardner, "From idiosyncratic to integrated: Strategic planning for collections," in *International Handbook of Museum Studies. Volume 4. Museum Practice*, edited by Conal McCarthy, pp. 203–220 (London: John Wiley and Sons, Ltd, 2015); James B. Gardner and Elizabeth Merritt, *The AAM Guide to Collections Planning* (Washington, DC: American Association of Museums, 2004).

6. See CHAPTER 7B, "The Care of Culturally Sensitive and Sacred Objects."

7. American Alliance of Museums Direct Care Task Force, "Direct Care of Collections: Ethics, Guidelines and Recommendations" (Washington, DC: American Alliance of Museums, 2016). Available at: http://www.aam-us.org/resources/ethics-standards-and-best-practices/direct-care.

REFERENCES

American Alliance of Museums. 2007. *Standards Regarding Facilities and Risk Management*. Available at: http://www.aam-us.org/resources/ethics-standards-and-best-practices/facilities-and-risk-management.

American Alliance of Museums. 2012. *Developing a Mission Statement*. Available at: http://www.aam-us.org/docs/default-source/continuum/developing-a-mission-statement-final.pdf?sfvrsn=4.

Berg-Fulton, T. 2016. "Taking a Fresh Look at Provenance." *Museum* 95, no. 4: 34–39.

Cato, P. S., and S. L. Williams. 1993. "Guidelines for Developing Policies for the Management and Care of Natural History Collections." *Collection Forum* 9, no. 2: 84–107.

Elkin, L. and C. A. Norris, eds. 2019. *Preventive Conservation: Collection Storage*. New York: Society for the Preservation of Natural History; American Institute for Conservation of Historic and Artistic Works; Smithsonian Institution; The George Washington University Museum Studies Program.

Malaro, M. C. and I. P. DeAngelis. 2012. *A Legal Primer on Managing Museum Collections*, 3rd ed. Washington, DC: Smithsonian Books.

Merritt, E. M. 2008. *National Standards and Best Practices for U.S. Museums*. Washington, DC: American Association of Museums.

Simmons, John E. 2018. *Things Great and Small: Collections Management Policies*, 2nd ed. Lanham, MD: Rowman & Littlefield.

Williams, S. L. 2005. "Policy Theory and Application for Museums." *Collection Forum* 19, no. 1–2: 32–44.

PART 3 | THE BASICS

3A | INITIAL CUSTODY AND DOCUMENTATION

REBECCA BUCK (UPDATED AND REVISED BY JOHN E. SIMMONS AND TONI M. KISER)

A N OBJECT ARRIVES at the museum for the first time; the object may be a potential gift or purchase sent on approval or a loan for exhibition or study. If arrangements have been made, and all goes according to procedure, the arriving object can be tracked forever if it enters the permanent collection, or it can be used in the short term without error or loss while it is on loan. Following established procedures enables the museum to immediately exercise physical and intellectual control over the object and accurately document its history, status, and condition. To accomplish this, the object's arrival must trigger a well-defined process, and curatorial and registration personnel must communicate with each other and follow the procedures every time, for every object.

Keeping object entry under control relates directly to the museum mission and collection management policies (see CHAPTER 2, "Collection Management Policies"). The process that emerges from those documents can strengthen a museum's ability to reduce the risks associated with abandoned property, old loans, partially processed objects, and objects that eventually become found-in-collection (FIC) objects. Guidelines and procedures for object entry should be clearly established and always followed. If the museum can control entry and allow in only those objects that are under consideration for incorporation into the permanent collection or are on loan to the museum for educational use, research, or exhibition, very few problems will arise. The better defined the guidelines are, the greater the chances of success will be. Guidelines should include the following:

- An incoming loan agreement must be in place, or a temporary receipt of custody issued, when the object arrives at the museum. The loan paperwork or receipt should include contact information for the object's owner and be signed by both the owner and a representative of the museum.

- All objects arriving at the museum must be approved by the museum's curatorial staff or administration.

- For objects under consideration for the permanent collection, the first curatorial review should be made using images of the object or on a site visit to see it. Following the initial review, arrangements for a temporary custody agreement can be made.

- No object should be accepted at the museum by front-desk personnel, guards, or other staff without prior arrangement with the collections staff and appropriate documentation of the object and its owner.

- If the museum staff engages in on-site object identification for the public, it is strongly recommended that this be done using photographs rather than objects brought to the museum without documentation (such objects too often are left at the museum accidentally or neglectfully).

- The museum should have a clear policy concerning the fate of objects left on its property without appropriate process and documentation and that applies to cases where the source is known as well as to property with no attendant identification. If undocumented objects are left at the museum, applicable state law regarding such abandoned property should be followed (see CHAPTER 3J, "Found in Collection" and CHAPTER 3H, "Old Loans and Museum Property Laws").

The initial custody procedures followed will depend on whether the object coming in to museum custody is a loan, an object destined for the permanent collection, or one intended other authorized use in the museum.

There should be a well-defined process for loans (see CHAPTER 3K, "Loans"). Most museums do not allow a loaned object to come onto their premises without a formal loan agreement in effect. The reasons for this are valid and clear, responsibilities and actions are well-defined. It is not as common for museums to require a signed agreement to be in place in advance of the receipt of objects for their permanent collections, but it is strongly advised that such a policy be established. The problems involving misunderstandings or lack of proof of intent that can lead to a museum's inability to complete an acquisition process are greatly diminished when the intent and actions are clearly defined in writing at the beginning of the process.

For objects that are intended for the permanent collection, the museum should issue a temporary custody agreement prior to the arrival of an object intended as a purchase or gift (see sample "Incoming Agreement for Temporary Custody with Conditions Governing Temporary Custody" form in the *Collection Forms* section). The custody agreement should be put in place as soon as the decision is made to consider the object for the collection. This way, if there is any question about who is responsible for loss or damage to the object (and whether that happens in a vendor's showroom or donor's apartment, or during shipment or arrival at the museum), the custody agreement will define responsibilities and allow claims that might arise to be resolved easily. For example, if the vendor closes shop or claims damage, the responsibilities for vendor and museum are clear; if a donor does not return a deed of gift or disappears into the ether, the museum will have the signature of the donor to confirm the intent to give the object to the museum and can then act on that information.

The temporary custody agreement requires significant information, some of which may be difficult to track down in advance. Contact information should include the source's name—both owner and agent, if appropriate—address, telephone, and e-mail address, with alternates where necessary. Object identification should include complete essential information including the object name; date of origin; name of artist, maker, manufacturer, or collector; title; geographic origin (if known); materials or media; and measurements. The purchase price is necessary for objects under purchase consideration, but it is always useful to get an approximate value for potential gifts. There will likely be some negotiations regarding shipping and packing costs and insurance coverage. There are many other factors to consider: Is the object local or some distance away? Are packers on-site or must they be hired? Is international movement involved? Are there applicable laws (e.g., Endangered Species Act, CITES, the UNESCO accord) that must be observed? Each transaction should be entered with an open mind, using common sense, and with the grace to keep all parties in harmony.

The potential difficulties with these procedures are obvious. The working relationships and respect between museum departments must allow them to communicate clearly and work well together. There must be adequate personnel to track down the necessary information and produce documentation. The museum's administration and governing board must understand the importance of these activities so that the process is supported. If a museum does not develop a preadmission custody agreement, it must rely for direction on a shipping receipt with basic information or an informational temporary receipt issued after an object has arrived. If no agreement is in place, the museum can initiate tracking and documentation but cannot confirm intent unless that intent is provided in supplemental documentation.

NEXT STEPS

With the temporary custody receipt signed, all is ready for the object to arrive at the museum. Most incoming objects arrive with a shipping receipt—usually a simple form noting shipment means and date that is issued at the moment of receipt or delivery. The shipping receipt may list the shipment in general terms (e.g., three crates or ten dresses) but rarely describes an object in enough detail to identify it. Nevertheless, it is important to keep a copy of all shipping documents; it is the use of receipts and standardized procedures that are most important.

Once the object has arrived most museums fill out an informational form, which may be called a temporary receipt (TR), temporary deposit (TD), or simply an incoming receipt. Using a standard form confirms the temporary custody agreement and, along with the shipping receipt, guides the first phase of the registration process.

The temporary form should include contact information, object descriptions (including measurements, if appropriate) and, if possible, an image of the object. This form should confirm the date, conditions, and terms under which a museum has received the object. If this form serves as an after-the-fact temporary custody or temporary deposit agreement, it is vital that it include intent as well as insurance, shipping, and packing information, and it is best if it can be countersigned. The registrar should process the object as follows:

1. Assign a temporary number to the transaction and to each object within the transaction (see BOX 3A.1).
2. Unpack the objects and prepare condition reports for them.
3. Tag each object with its temporary number.
4. Create database or hardcopy files for the objects, including:

   a. All contact information
   b. Reason (intent) for the entry of the object into the museum (e.g., proposed gift pending approval, purchase pending approval, bequest, loan)
   c. Description of each object (essential information to help identify each object)

5. Make images of each object and archive the images to the database, if possible.
6. Initiate tracking by noting the object's first location in storage.

The model initial object receipt described in the first edition of *Museum Registration Methods* (published in 1958) called for the inclusion of three categories of information that are no longer recommended—value or price, object location in the museum, and a record of object condition. These three categories of information are important, but we now recognize the need to keep value (price) as private as possible and, thus, record it elsewhere (e.g., in a letter or in the object file). The object's location in the museum should be a category of information in the collections management system used for all objects in the museum; object tracking is vital and must be part of the process, but object locations should not be disclosed to anyone without a direct need to know. Complete condition reports now replace the brief record of condition used in 1958.

If object information is entered in a database, the TD or TR receipt can be produced through a report. If a paper form is used, it should be filed with other acquisition documents, and the registrar who processes the information should sign the form.

BOX 3A.1 TEMPORARY NUMBERS

Temporary numbers should not be marked directly on an incoming object but, instead, should be attached with removable tags.

The name of the form and format of the temporary number are not standardized in the museum field, but internal consistency is important within each institution. Do not be surprised by the twists and turns that numbering patterns have taken in an individual institution, but do introduce and maintain as much consistency as possible. Examples of temporary receipt form names and number formats in use include:

- TR (temporary receipt)
- TR2019.1 or TR1.2019, followed by extensions for specific objects
- TD (temporary deposit)
- TD2019.1 or TD1.2019, followed by extensions for specific objects
- L (loan)
- L1.2019 or L2019.1, followed by extensions for specific objects
- No designation, simply a reverse numbering system
- 1.2019—followed by expansions for specific objects

See CHAPTER 5A, "Numbering," for a full explanation of numbers and extensions.

The curator may also keep a file of active gift transactions and purchases and, thus, may need a copy of the information that is on the receipt. A copy of the TD or TR should always be sent to the source to confirm the conditions of transfer and the safe arrival of the object at the museum. The registrar should keep a hard copy of the TD or TR in the acquisitions file. It is good practice to keep copies of the forms for all objects received each year in a binder or to record the information in a bound register book because this system allows multiple staff members to assign temporary numbers without redundancy and allows for one-stop, end-of-year reconciliation. It is important to note which objects have stayed and which have been returned to their owners or gone on to other institutions to be certain that all object tasks have been completed. If using a bound ledger, the entry should include the number assigned, curatorial sponsorship, status, reason for entry, and date of entry.

Once the TR or TD is in place and the initial registration has been completed, the tracking and documentation of the objects can be completed by following standard policies and procedures. Status changes can be made, updates in location and condition can be tracked, and, in the case of permanent collection additions, complete cataloging can take place. TR or TD files in a database can be switched to permanent collection files when appropriate.

The process described is, without doubt, the best way to avoid problems with objects that are left in the care of the museum (BOX 3A.2). Although it is time-consuming at point of entry, it saves untold hours in the long run and helps avoid problems with insurance claims, unclear donor intent, inaccurate claims by vendors, and problems in identifying objects and determining reasons why they are in the museum's custody. If instituted thoroughly, this process will prompt the museum to develop policies that do not allow objects to enter informally and will encourage sound and professional practices. •

Box 3A.2 Object Meets Museum Meets Object: Best Case and Worst Case

Best Case

- The registrar receives complete information about the object and source of each incoming gift, bequest, purchase, or loan.
- A custody agreement document, with signatures from both parties, is prepared and includes:

  ○ Names and contact information.
  ○ Intended outcome (e.g., gift, purchase, bequest, loan).
  ○ Who is responsible for insurance, packing, and shipping of the object.
  ○ A description of the object.

- All attendant information regarding special considerations, restrictions, etc.
- The registrar arranges shipping.
- The registrar receives object.
- The tracking number is assigned and informational receipt is issued.
- The object is processed in the museum.

Worst Case

- The director or curator tells the registrar that:

  ○ An object has been brought into the museum, perhaps as a gift or perhaps a purchase on approval, or perhaps neither.
  ○ An object has been dropped off that may be used in an exhibition but may be a gift.
  ○ An object was left by a member of the governing board for storage.

- The registrar receives a call from the front desk saying a visitor has left an object as a gift.
- A noncollections officer agrees to have someone drop off an unsolicited gift.

3B | ACQUISITIONS AND ACCESSIONING

JOHN E. SIMMONS AND TONI M. KISER

THE ACQUISITIONS SECTION of a collection management policy carefully defines the types of objects that are collected by the museum. It should describe all permanent collections in the museum, acknowledge special collections (e.g., those for educational use or special loans), and may reference legacy collections as well.[1] The policy stipulates the means by which decisions are made for accepting objects for the permanent collections, who is responsible for these decisions, and details the legal and ethical frameworks used by the museum for acquiring objects. The acquisitions policy is augmented by a set of procedures for processing objects that are destined for the collections and those intended for research, sale, or other uses.

All accessioned objects are acquired, but not all acquisitions are meant to be accessioned. An acquisition is made by a museum when title of an object is transferred and the museum becomes the owner. Accessioning is a three-part process of acquiring an object (acquisition), taking legal possession of it for the permanent collection of the museum (accession), and documenting it (registration). The process hinges on transfer of title to the museum.

Most museums do not accession every object that they acquire. The process of deciding which objects to accession must be clear. The word *accession* is derived from the Latin word *accessio*, meaning an increase (BOX 3B.1). As a noun, *accession* means something that is added and, thus, is used to denote an object acquired by a museum for its permanent collection. When used as a verb, *accession* refers to the act of recording or processing an object into the collection. What is important to remember is that to accession an object is the act of recording it as an addition to the permanent collection and assigning a unique number to it that connects an object to the information about it (its documentation).

If an object is a gift, the donor should be informed of the museum's intended use for the gift (e.g., for the permanent collection or to be used in educational programs) before the object comes to the museum because how the museum uses the object can

---

Box 3B.1 ACCESSION, ACCESSIONED, ACCESSIONING

In the museum literature, the word *accession* has often been used without thought to its proper definition. As Rebecca Buck[1] pointed out in her historic review of the use of the word, part of the reason for the confusion stems from the fact that accession can be used as a noun, a verb, or an adjective. Malaro and DeAngelis devoted several pages to the meaning of the word accession in the second edition of *A Legal Primer on Managing Museum Collections* (2012),[2] which is worth reviewing when title questions are addressed.

In short, when used as a verb, *accession* means "to acquire or accept and register or record an object for the permanent collection of a museum; acquisition and registration are generally linked by transfer of title."[3] When used as a noun, an *accession* means one or more objects acquired at the same time from the same source in a single transaction between the museum and the source. As an adjective, an *accession* describes an object that has been accessioned.

NOTES

1. Rebecca A. Buck, "Accession, Accessioned, Accessioning," in *MRM5: Museum Registration Methods*, 5th ed., edited by R. A. Buck and J. A. Gilmore, pp. 51–52 (Washington, DC: American Association of Museums Press, 2010), 59–63.

2. M. C. Malaro and I. P. DeAngelis, *A Legal Primer on Managing Museum Collections*, 3rd ed. (Washington, DC: Smithsonian Books. 2012).

3. Buck, "Accession, Accessioned, Accessioning."

affect the tax consequences of the gift for the donor (see CHAPTER 7E, "Appraisal"). Objects acquired by the museum may go to the permanent collection, to a hands-on loan collection, to the library or archives, or they may be accepted for use in research (which may mean the eventual destruction of the object) or be sold at a later date. See the sample "Donor Questionnaire with Warranty and Indemnification" in the *Collection Forms* section.

ACQUISITIONS

Acquisitions may be made by:

- Gift—title to the object is transferred to the museum during the life of the donor or from another entity that owns the object (see BOX 3B.2).
- Bequest—title to the object is transferred to the museum under the terms of a will or other legal document.
- Purchase—directly, at auction, in a bargain sale, by exchange
- Field collecting
- Conversion—the unauthorized assumption of ownership of property belonging to another (see CHAPTER 3H, "Old Loans and Museum Property Laws").

Gifts

Gifts may be outright, fractional, or promised and may be unrestricted (free and clear) or restricted (the donor places some stipulation on their future use or owner-

ship). See the sample "Confirmation of Gift Sample Letter" in the *Collection Forms* section.

Outright Gifts

Outright gifts are straightforward—a donor offers the museum a gift by showing intent; the museum accepts the gift; the object is delivered to the museum. Intent, acceptance, and delivery are the three necessary legal actions that transfer title. Intent may be oral, written informally, or expressed via a deed of gift (see the sample "Deed of Gift" in the *Collection Forms* section). Acceptance may be oral, but it is usually written in a formal letter and is often formalized by a countersignature on a deed of gift. Delivery is vital; the museum must take possession of the object for the transaction to be complete.

Fractional Gifts

Fractional gifts are generally made to allow the donor to maximize the tax benefit from the donation when the taxpayer's deduction in any one year is limited (see CHAPTER 7E, "Appraisal"). On advice from a tax advisor, the donor may offer the museum a percentage interest in an object (the amount of the percentage depending on the donor's allowable deduction for that year). If the museum accepts the offer, a deed of gift detailing the arrangement is produced by the museum in consultation with legal counsel or by the donor's lawyer. The deed may convey a percentage of the object only, or it may transfer title automatically to further percentages of the work over several years.

Box 3B.2 The WPA and Allocation

Allocation was the term often used by the US Works Progress Administration (WPA) to describe the transfer of title for works created in the course of its projects. The Operating Procedures section in the *Public Works of Art Program Bulletin* in 1934, stated that "For the purposes of this section 'allocated' shall mean transfer of title" (Section 32, Part A, 1st paragraph). However, the procedures also note a restriction regarding release from the responsibility of custody. In 2000, the General Services Administration (GSA) interpreted the manual to mean that allocated works included transfers of restricted title and that the "receiving agency or institution received legal title to the works of art limited by the purpose stated in the allocation forms and by the regulations."[1] Works of art produced by WPA programs are often allocated but may also be lent to an institution.

If a museum holds federal project works that it received from the federal government it is important to become familiar with GSA terms and uses. All WPA objects should be carefully checked for transfer of title, and communication with the GSA, which currently oversees WPA works, should be initiated if there is any question of status.

NOTE
1. Available at: https://www.gsa.gov/real-estate/design-construction/art-in-architecture-fine-arts/fine-arts/legal-fact-sheet.

Fractional gift laws have been evolving rapidly in the United States over the last decade, so it is important that registrars, collection managers, and curators stay abreast of changes in the laws affecting fractional gifts—check for updated information on the US Internal Revenue Service (IRS) website.[2]

A fractional gift should go through the same acquisition process as any other gift. It is important to note that by law, the object involved in the fractional gift arrangement must be physically in the museum's possession for a part of each year equal to the percentage owned by the museum. A fractional promised gift in the custody of the museum is treated as an accessioned object, as long as the pledge of the donor to the museum is binding.

Promised Gifts

Promised gifts may be made by a donor in the form of a letter (or another legal instrument) expressing the donor's intent to give a specific object to the museum at some future time. Although some museums have a draft format for promised gifts to act as a guide for donors, it is preferable to have the donor initiate the promised gift letter on the donor's letterhead before the museum and the donor sign a binding agreement. If the donor is unable to make the gift during his or her lifetime, the museum should encourage the donor to specifically include the gift to the museum in a will to ensure that the donor's intent and promise are carried out.

A promised gift that is in the custody of the museum should be treated as a loan because a promise does not confer transfer of title. Museums should be cautious about making public announcements of promised gifts because the announcement itself may convey some benefit to the donor and put the museum at risk if the promise of the gift is not later fulfilled.

Unrestricted Gifts and Gifts with Restrictions

An outright and unrestricted gift is always preferred, although there may be some circumstances in which the object is so important an addition to a collection that some restrictions are acceptable. Depending on the donor and the nature of the restrictions requested, it may be possible for museum personnel to discuss the potential restrictions with the donor to better understand the reasoning behind them, and then negotiate a more acceptable gift agreement.

The most common restrictions requested by donors are to permanently exhibit an object, to keep a collection together in perpetuity, to never deaccession an object, or to return an object to the donor or the donor's heirs if it is deaccessioned—none of these is practical, so these types of restrictions should be strongly discouraged. More reasonable restrictions include such things as including the donor's name on the label when the object is exhibited or keeping an important album of photographs together in its original binding rather than unbinding and matting each one separately. In the latter case, the museum must weigh the value of the album to the collection against the possibility that future generations will be hampered by the restriction. All restrictions must be thoughtfully considered and, if accepted, carefully documented in the object records. It is important for future registrars and collection managers to understand why restrictions were allowed when the object was accessioned.

Bequests

A bequest is a gift that passes to the museum after the death of a donor under the terms of the donor's will or some other legal instrument. It is important to have evidence of the intended transfer of title on record—usually in the form of a copy of the provision of the will that concerns the gift to the museum and a signed deed of gift—to ensure that the donor's intent to make the bequest will be carried out and not challenged by the donor's heirs.

A museum may or may not know about a bequest in advance. Museums are usually notified of a bequest by the executor (legal representative) of the donor's estate. It is important for the museum to deal with the official representative of an estate and request a copy of the will (or other legal document) that references the bequest. The museum must then decide whether to accept or refuse the gift. It is not mandatory that a museum accept a bequest. If a museum does accept the bequest and receives the object, it will usually be asked to sign both a receipt and a release—a receipt for the object and a release for the estate indicating that nothing more is expected from the estate. The museum should be aware of the fact that the transfer of the object to the museum is not final until probate of the estate is approved by the courts. The receipt and release agreements are not usually prepared until the executor is certain that the estate will be able to pay its bills and give the legatees their designated bequests.

Purchases

Purchases for museum collections can be made in a variety of ways—at auction, from dealers or galleries, or directly from individuals. Objects can be commissioned, or they may be exchanged through orchestrated deaccession of objects of like value.

Purchase from a Dealer or Gallery

If an object is purchased from a dealer or gallery, it is important that the museum have a bill of sale and proof of payment and such documents should be part of the permanent acquisition file. Provenance should always be researched and all provenance information added to the file (see sample "Dealer Provenance Questionnaire" in the *Collection Forms* section). The museum should make an effort to obtain copyright releases for contemporary works (see CHAPTER 7D, "Rights and Reproductions").

As issues of provenance and legal export and import become more important, most museums require at least a warranty of title and indemnification for the purchase of important objects. If the object purchased is of a sensitive nature or of very high value, it may be necessary to have a contract of sale to clarify all points of purchase. It is best to go beyond warranties and to confirm legality by reviewing customs papers and searching provenance indices and art loss registers as part of the provenance research.

Bargain Sale

A *bargain sale* refers to an arrangement in which a percentage of an object is purchased and the remainder of the object is donated to the museum (see CHAPTER 7E, "Appraisal") with the result that the object is sold to the museum at substantially less than fair market value with the intention of benefiting the museum by virtue of the reduced price. The vendor, therefore, is also a donor. Properly done,

there may be tax benefits for the vendor or donor. The method of transfer of title is a bill of sale, but the museum acknowledges in correspondence to the vendor or donor the fact that the price of the object has been reduced to favor the museum. It is up to the donor to establish any tax benefits with the IRS. The museum, for its part, should be certain that the sale price is substantially reduced. An independent appraisal is advisable to document the discount. The bill of sale and all related correspondence should be part of the acquisition file.

Exchange

Exchanges are, in fact, a form of purchase but with payment in kind, not in currency. In an exchange, a museum trades objects of equal value with another museum. This involves the deaccessioning of the objects that are traded; the deaccession requires full documentation as well (see CHAPTER 31, "Deaccessioning and Disposal"). The terms of an exchange should be set in a written agreement and the museum should establish the fairness of the exchange by means of appraisals or other expert opinions. The written agreement and all relevant documents should become part of the acquisition file.

Field Collecting

Field collecting is more common in natural history, anthropology, and archaeology museums than in history or art museums, but it may be part of the acquisition process of almost any collecting institution. Field collecting may include objects purchased or acquired during an expedition or scientific specimens or archaeological artifacts collected during a research project. Purchases may be made from persons who made or used the objects. The recording of provenience, materials, techniques, and use are vital to the object's record. Field collections should be accompanied by complete field notes and copies of all permits, licenses, and export and import documents.

Field collecting is subject to many legal restrictions, particularly regulations on export from the country of origin, laws dealing with repatriation to Native American or Native Hawaiian groups, and protected plant or animal species (see CHAPTER 7F, "Implementing NAGPRA" and CHAPTER 7G,

"Biological Materials—Fish, Wildlife, and Plants"). The museum must be aware of all pertinent laws and regulations and obtain necessary permits and file customs declarations (if applicable) before bringing material from the field to the museum. The registrar should research the legal title to the collections brought to the museum before the objects go through the acquisitions process.

Conversion

Sometimes objects loaned to a museum are never claimed by their owners. Several states have adopted abandoned property legislation that enables museums to acquire title to these objects if the owners cannot be located and if specified procedures and waiting periods are followed, a process referred to as *conversion* (see CHAPTER 3H, "Old Loans and Museum Property Laws"). Conversion may be necessary for found-in-collection (FIC) objects as well. Many states have statutes covering FIC objects (see CHAPTER 3J, "Found in Collection").

The Acquisition Process for Permanent Collection Objects

A cogent collecting policy that takes into account current collection strengths and weaknesses must be in place for each collecting area if the museum is to acquire collection objects intelligently. A typical museum policy sets forth the practical and legal considerations that precede an acquisition.

Practical Considerations:
- Is the object consistent with the collecting goals and museum mission?
- Will the object be useful for exhibition, educational purposes, or research and scholarship?
- Is the object in a reasonably good state of preservation?
- Can the museum properly exhibit and store the object?
- If the object is to be purchased, is the price fair and reasonable?
- Will the acquisition of the object result in major expenses for the museum for conservation or maintenance?

- Can the acquisition of the object be construed as a commercial endorsement?

Legal and Ethical Considerations:
- Can valid title to the object be acquired by the museum?
- Is the object authentic?
- Can all rights to the object be conveyed to the museum?
- Would the acquisition of the object violate any state, national, or international laws or conventions that protect the rights of an artist, an indigenous community, or the rights of a country of origin to its cultural heritage or history or threaten protected plant or animal species?
- Is the object subject to repatriation to a Native American tribe or Native Hawaiian group?
- Is the object free of donor restrictions or qualifications that inhibit the prudent use of the object by the museum?

Acquiring objects for the permanent collection is a complicated process for most museums. It must be thoughtful and undertaken with care. The process may begin with a curator who is developing a collection, but gift offers, donations, and purchase opportunities may come unsolicited. In science, anthropology, history, and archaeology museums, research-based field collecting may be an important source of collection objects.

Between the time an object becomes available and when it is actually acquired by the museum, a number of things take place (the order differs depending on the museum):

- The director, curator, or collections committee agree on the importance of acquiring the object.
- The object is transported to the museum.
- Provenance and cost research are conducted.
- A proposal for acquisitions is prepared.
- Consultation among staff, administrators, and the governing board takes place.
- Conservators are consulted regarding resources needed for preservation and conservation of the object.

- Registrars or collections managers are consulted regarding storage needs and costs.
- Legal concerns (permits, licenses, title, etc.) are reviewed.
- If the object is a gift, the intent to give is established, usually by the issuance of a deed of gift, which is sent to the donor for signature.
- If the object is a purchase, warranty of title and an indemnification agreement are executed.
- The object is placed on the agenda of the acquisitions or collections committee.

There are many variations in the acquisition process that follows after the decision has been made to pursue an acquisition, but in all cases, the registrar should be central to the process. The registrar is in charge of coordinating the object and its documentation, bringing it to the museum, and making recommendations (in conjunction with a conservator if possible) about the object's care and storage needs. The registrar is responsible for making certain that title to the object is transferred and that needed licenses and permits are acquired.

A proposal for acquisition is prepared that explains the reasons the object is desirable for the collection. The registrar begins an acquisition file and makes certain that a temporary number is assigned to the object and that proper receipts have been issued, condition reports completed, and the location of the object noted. It is also good practice to have digital photographs of the objects made at this point.

The deed of gift—a document that is drawn up with advice legal counsel—is prepared by the registrar. The deed of gift can serve as evidence of both an intent to donate and of acceptance by the museum. Three elements are normally needed to complete a gift:

- Intent to donate, preferably stated in writing. A deed of gift is the preferred instrument to demonstrate this intent.
- Proof of the physical receipt of the object by the museum.
- Written acceptance of the gift by the appropriate museum authority.

At least two copies of the deed of gift are sent to the donor with a letter requesting that the donor sign and return two copies to the museum. The signed copies are held until the acquisitions committee approves the gift, and then the designated officer for the museum countersigns them and returns one copy to the donor along with a letter of appreciation. The other signed copy goes to the registrar for inclusion in the acquisition file. Some museums do not include a copyright release provision in the deed of gift because often the donor does not hold the copyright for the object being given. If copyright is an important concern but is not covered in the deed of gift, a separate nonexclusive use agreement should be sent to the copyright holder. Be aware that donors of objects, unless they are the creators of the objects, are usually unaware of whether they hold copyright to the objects (for more details, see CHAPTERS 7C, "Copyright," and 7D, "Rights and Reproductions").

Depending on the museum's acquisition policy, gifts, purchases, bequests, and exchanges proposed for accession are usually reviewed and approved by a collections committee or acquisitions committee. The committee may be composed of board members, administrators, curatorial and collection staff members, collectors, specialists in the field, friends of the museum, and in a university museum, faculty representatives. This committee may have the authority to approve or reject acquisitions or to recommend objects to the governing board for final approval. In any case, acquisition decisions should be formally recorded in the minutes of the committee meeting.

The agenda for the acquisitions committee is usually prepared by the registrar and should include a listing of all objects to be considered for acquisition, with complete descriptions of the objects, donor or vendor names and addresses, credit lines for proposed gifts, and, as appropriate, the cost and funds to be used for purchases. If not a member of the committee, the registrar should be notified as soon as possible which objects were accepted for acquisition. Rejected objects should be returned promptly. Accepted gifts should be acknowledged with a letter of appreciation from the director or a curator that is sent with a countersigned deed of gift.

ACCESSIONING

Once an object has been approved for accession and the deed of gift signed or the sale completed, the title to the object passes to the museum. At this juncture, the registrar completes the accessioning process by recording the object as an addition to the collection. An accession number is assigned, and the information in the file that was created to track the object is transferred to the accession file. The accessioning process may include:

- Gathering all gift or purchase documents and noting the accession number on each of them.
- Creating a curatorial worksheet and sending it to the curator for approval and additions.
- Numbering the object (see CHAPTER 5A, "Numbering," and CHAPTER 5F, "Marking").
- Making images of the object (see CHAPTER 5H, "Photography").
- Entering the accession information into the registration system (which may be manual, electronic, or a combination of the two).

The information entered into the registration system may include:

- Accession number
- Catalog number (if appropriate)
- The source of the object (donor, vendor, collector, etc.)
- The geographic origin of the object
- The fund used to purchase the object
- A brief biography of the artist or maker (if appropriate)
- The location of the object in the collection storage array

The accession number associates the object with its file and all its documentation, so it is vital to have unique accession numbers that link directly to the documentation. The accession file becomes the repository of all information that comes to the museum regarding the object, including research, photography, condition reports, loans, conservation work, exhibition, and publications.

Policies and procedures should be developed to govern access to permanent collection records. Confidential information such as shipping and insurance histories, appraisals, tax documents, purchase orders, donor addresses, and telephone numbers may be available only to certain members of the professional staff. Access may also be limited to condition notes, conservation treatment reports, and some provenance information. The general public may have access to descriptive information about the object, the accession number, credit line, reference notations, and the exhibition and publication histories of an object. In developing policies to govern access to records, legal advice may need to be sought concerning applicable freedom of information or privacy laws. •

NOTES

1. Legacy collections are those few objects that may no longer serve the institutional mission but because of legal obligations, history, tradition, or popularity are retained and cared for in the museum; see J. E. Simmons, *Things Great and Small: Collections Management Policies* (Lanham, MD: Rowman & Littlefield, 2018), 40.

2. Available at: www.irs.gov.

This is an edited and updated version of the MRM *chapter by Clarisse Carnell and Rebecca Buck, which acknowledged contributions by Jeanne M. Benas, Jan W. M. Thompson, Ted Greenberg, and Marie Malaro.*

3C | REPOSITORIES

ELISE V. LECOMPTE

INTRODUCTION

FACILITIES SUCH AS museums often serve as repositories for collections that are owned by other institutions and organizations. Repository collections may be federally, state, or privately owned. Repositories usually hold collections in trust for agencies that cannot pass on legal title (e.g., governmental agencies, particularly federal agencies such as the US Fish and Wildlife Service [USFWS], the Bureau of Land Management [BLM], the Department of Transportation [DOT], or state agencies such as parks, fish and wildlife, or state DOT). For example, a government agency might contract with a museum to care for archaeological or paleontological collections made on federal or state lands, or an indigenous group may enter into an agreement with a repository to curate their historic collection.[1] Private cultural resource management (CRM) firms often contract with repositories to store project-generated collections. Sometimes the collections may belong to another country; it has become increasingly common for foreign governments to enter into agreements with US museums or other scientific institutions to house native indigenous materials or biological specimens for curation and research purposes.[2]

Different kinds of repositories have different goals depending on their institutional missions and contexts, and differing management structures affect repository activities, their perceived audiences, and their realms of accountability.[3] That said, all repositories focus on the physical well-being of the collections that they hold; therefore, all repositories have collections care and management programs. Although repositories may differ in how they manage the collections that they hold, they all face similar challenges and so have generally similar collections management programs.[4] Accessibility to repository collections is based on the same factors and concerns that guide all collections professionals: safety, appropriate research proposals, the nature of the programming, and use for heritage or religious purposes.

Staffing is usually a reflection of the repository's size, mission, and funding. In larger repositories, collections management may be the responsibility of several staff members with specialized training (e.g., registrars, collections managers, and conservators). In smaller repositories, there may be only one person in charge of collections management as well as other multiple functions within the repository (e.g., collections management, exhibits, and public programs).

Repository collections may originate from research projects, such as field expeditions or excavations, or they may be composed of objects that were confiscated. In the past, archaeological collections made up the majority of materials curated in repositories, but today, many types of collections are being cared for by repositories including natural history collections (anthropological, paleontological, geological, biological), historic, architectural, art, and archives. Collections may be site-specific, project-specific, or more general. They may contain legally protected objects or specimens. They can include the physical material (e.g., objects, specimens, or samples, comparative samples, type specimens, casts), as well as the associated documentation. The documentation might include paper records such as legal documents (e.g., proof of ownership, permits, repository agreements, loan forms), field records, survey forms, permits, analysis cards, maps, photographic materials (photographs, slides, negatives), grant proposals, research papers by students and professionals, theses and dissertations, articles, books, exhibit records, or digital files. Digital files may include digitized scans, digital photographs, or data sets related to field or analytical studies.

It is extremely important for all material related to a collection to be stored in the same repository, unless such action would fail to meet special storage, conservation, or research needs[5] to ensure the integrity and research value of the collection. Objects or records may require special security and storage conditions, fire protection, enhanced or reduced access, fiscal control, or exhibition to ensure their preservation.[6] Many types of natural history collections require specialized care that is not available at the owner's institution. For example, advanced analytical techniques now require tissue samples; to preserve these tissue samples, they must be cryogenically frozen. However, the high cost of cryogenic storage may require the collection's owner to work with partner repositories that have this type of specialized facility. For example, the National Park Service (NPS) has a service-wide repository agreement with the Ambrose Monell Collection for Molecular and Microbial Research at the American Museum of Natural History.[7] To ensure preservation, duplicate sets of specimens are often collected from a single plant for placement in separate repositories, and numerous plants of the same species collected from a single sampling area are placed in separate repositories.[8] As digital documentation has become more widespread, especially born-digital resources, recommendations have been made for depositors to consider planning and budgeting for two repositories—one for objects and hard copies of records and another for digital records.[9] The records in each repository should reference each other, and the digital files should be remotely accessible for easy access to both collections and to ensure the integrity of the collection.[10] Tracking the location of separately stored portions of a collection may be accomplished using databases and documents similar to loan forms.

Definitions

Simply stated, repositories are custodians, rather than legal owners. That is, the repository agrees to manage collections for a set period of time without taking ownership of those collections. Hurst describes a repository as a facility that "takes on the care and management of a collection, and catalogues, cares for and manages the collection as it does its own collections."[11] Sullivan and Childs declare that a repository is "a place to care for collections; it does not neces-

sarily have the public functions of a museum, such as exhibits and public programs."[12] Knoll and Huckell state that a repository is "a museum or other facility where collections are curated, managed, preserved, and made available for research or public use.[13] Simmons defines a repository as "a collections-oriented facility that provides long-term professional care and accountable curatorial services for a collection that it does not own"[14] and further explains that a repository is an institution, such as a museum, that curates collections by entering into a mutual agreement to provide care and management of collections that belong to other institutions, groups, or agencies.[15] Federal Regulation 36 CFR Part 79, *Curation of Federally-Owned and Administered Archeological Collections*, states that a repository:

> means a facility such as a museum, archeological center, laboratory or storage facility managed by a university, college, museum, other educational or scientific institution, a Federal, State or local Government agency or Indian tribe that can provide professional, systematic and accountable curatorial services on a long-term basis.[16]

Collections that are curated at a repository but owned by another cultural or scientific institution, federal or state agency, tribal government, or individual may be referred to as *reposited collections*.[17]

Repository agreements are arrangements, agreements, or contracts between the depositor and the repository. Simmons defines a repository agreement as "a contract in which an institution provides long-term professional care and accountable curatorial services for a collection that belongs to another institution or entity (e.g., a state, federal, or foreign government) in return for mutually acceptable benefits."[18] Repository agreements may be written in the form of a memorandum of understanding (MOU), a memorandum of agreement (MOA), or a contract, depending on whether or not they are legally binding. An MOU is typically a legally nonbinding agreement between two or more parties that outlines terms and details of a mutual understanding, noting each party's requirements and responsibilities but without establishing a formal, legally enforceable contract.[19] An MOA is a written document describing a cooperative relationship between two or more parties wishing to work together on a project or to meet an agreed on objective. An MOA serves as a legal document and describes the terms and details of the partnership agreement. It is more formal than a verbal agreement but less formal than a contract.[20] A contract is a legally binding agreement that recognizes and governs the rights and duties of the parties to the agreement. A contract is legally enforceable because it meets the requirements and approval of the law. Each party is legally bound to perform the specified duties such as rendering a payment or delivering goods or services.[21]

TYPES OF REPOSITORIES

A repository may be a federal, state, local, or tribal facility, or a museum, university, or other scientific or educational institution that curates collections for other agencies, organizations, companies, corporations, or individuals. Many museums, especially natural history museums, act as repositories. Sullivan and Childs[22] identify six different types of repositories—museums, academic institutions, tribal museums and cultural centers, government repositories, historical societies, and archives. They stress that regardless of the type, all repositories should meet common standards to provide the best care possible for the objects. Museums serve educational purposes through research and public outreach via exhibits and educational programs (e.g., the Florida Museum of Natural History). Academic institutions serve primarily research purposes, but may serve educational purposes as well (e.g., the Peabody Museum of Archaeology and Ethnology at Harvard University). In his article on the Erskine Ramsay Archaeological Center and David L. DeJarnette Research Center, Eugene Futato states, "our repository is not a storage building. It is an integrated part of the university's teaching and research program and that is how the university sees it."[23] Other academic institutions serve as repositories for long-term storage of collections generated by its own faculty and students. They are usually driven by research rather than public education. Tribal museums and cultural centers provide heritage and education from the perspective of the tribe. Historical societies are sometimes associated with museums, but many have a long history that predates the establishment of a museum. Government repositories can be museums or agency-run facilities. The agency-run facility will often focus more on research as its primary mission. Regional repositories have been established to care for collections owned by specific government agencies. Examples include the Anasazi Heritage Center for the BLM, and the Southeast Archeological Center (SEAC), the Midwest Archeological Center (MWAC) and the Western Archeological and Conservation Center (WACC) for the NPS.[24] An archive is primarily a repository of records related to collections that are curated elsewhere. With the explosion of digital documentation, especially born-digital records, repositories created specifically to house digital collections are becoming more common.

Guidelines for Selecting a Repository

First and foremost, a repository should be able to demonstrate that it is a legitimate, sustainable institution. Such proof may take the form of a charter, incorporation, or a government statute establishing the institution as a legally sanctioned governmental facility to house collections. For example, a Florida State statute declares that, "the Florida Museum of Natural History (FLMNH) derives its purpose, mission, and authority as the natural history museum for the State of Florida from Florida Statute § 1004.56, which formally established the institution in 1917 at the University of Florida."[25]

Collections management should be the primary function of a repository, but scholarly research based on the collections is usually another high priority activity at a repository. Depending on the nature of the repository, other functions may include developing educational programs and exhibits. To ensure long-term preservation, well-managed collection growth, and sustainability, a repository must apply professional, standard curation practices.[26] A repository should have a mission statement, long-range goals for collections care, and a strong scope of collections. Written policies, plans, and procedures such as a code of ethics, collections management policy, emergency preparedness or disaster response plan, access and use policy, and an integrated pest management (IPM) plan are essential for long-term preservation and management of a repository's collections. Other professional standards include physical integrity of the building (including health, fire, and security measures), an information management system to search for and retrieve objects and update records, and staffing expertise.[27] Federal Regulation 36 CFR 79 provides excellent guidelines for choosing a repository, methods to fund curatorial services, terms and conditions to include in contracts, memoranda and agreements for curatorial services, standards to determine when a repository is capable of maintaining long-term collections care, standards for conducting inspections and inventories, and use of the collections (TABLE 3C.1).

Table 3C.1 Basic Standards for Repositories[1]

Environmental Controls	Temperature and humidity
	Intensity and duration of visible light
	Ultraviolet light
	Pests
	Air pollution
Security	Mechanical or electrical system for detecting and deterring intruders
	Policy on access to and use of collections and associated documents, including system of visitor and researcher registration, opening and closing storage and exhibition areas, and control of keys, key cards or fobs to particular areas of the repository
Fire Protection	Fire detection and suppression equipment appropriate for the collections housed in storage and exhibition areas
	Storage of repository and collection records in appropriate fire-resistant containers that are locked when not in use
	Fire plan to prevent, detect, and suppress fire
Housekeeping	Regular cleaning of storage and exhibit spaces based on established procedures and policies
	Maintenance and calibration of monitoring equipment
	Control of pests using an integrated pest management plan
Physical Examination and Inventory	Regular examination to detect deterioration of collections' contents
	Inventory policy to regularly confirm locations of collections and prevent loss or theft
Conservation	Maintenance of objects in stable condition using professional conservation standards and practices
Disaster Planning	Policy and procedures to protect collections in the event of a natural or human-inflicted disaster
Exhibition	Consideration of how to best preserve, protect, and minimize risk to objects when planning an exhibit
	Design and use exhibit cases and areas to promote security, housekeeping, and preservation of objects

NOTE

1. Modified from L. P. Sullivan and S. T. Childs, *Curating Archaeological Collections: From the Field to the Repository*, Archaeologist's Toolkit, Volume 6 (Walnut Creek, CA: AltaMira Press/Rowman & Littlefield, 2003), 68.

When searching for an appropriate repository, the collection owner should ask the following questions:

- Does the collection to be deposited fit the repository's mission and scope of collections? Collections are usually deposited in a repository that is in the state of the collection's origin, stores and maintains collections from the same project location, or houses collections from a similar geographical location or cultural area.
- Does the repository have professional, written policies, plans, and procedures?
- Does the repository use professional standards to curate the collections?
- Does the repository have specialized staff with the expertise to curate the collections? This is particularly important if the collections cover multiple types of materials and objects.
- Does the repository have appropriate environmental controls (e.g., humidity and temperature)?
- Does the repository have lighting appropriate for different types of materials?
- Does the repository have storage facilities and methods suitable for different types of materials? For example, if the collection contains fluid-preserved specimens, does it have wet specimen storage that meets all of the necessary fire code, health and safety requirements?
- Does the repository use archival storage methods and materials?
- Does the repository have a safe, secure facility that meets local fire, building, electrical, health, and safety codes?
- Does the repository have an up-to-date emergency management plan?
- Does the repository have a functioning fire detection and suppression system?
- Does the repository have an integrated pest management program?
- What kind of access and use policy and practice does the repository have? Is it governed by professional standards that meet legal and ethical requirements? Does it match what the collection owner would allow? Is it too restrictive or not restrictive enough? For example, access may be necessary for research, programming, heritage, or religious purposes, or for monitoring fragile materials for possible conservation.[28]
- How does the repository use its own collection—for research, exhibit, education, or some combination? Does this match the ways in which the collection to be deposited is intended to be used? For example, a repository that curates collections only for exhibition and education is not appropriate for a collection with research value.
- How much object processing does the repository require before deposition of objects?
- Does adequate funding exist to fully document, preserve, and house the collection to be deposited?
- Does the repository charge a fee? If so, what kind of fee—is it annual or one time? How is the fee calculated? What services does the fee cover?
- Does the potential depositor have enough funds to prepare the collection for long-term curation according to the repository's standards for acceptance (e.g., level of pre-processing required, use of specific archival supplies, basic conservation, digitization of the collection)?

Professional digital repositories should have the following characteristics:

- Sufficient infrastructure, financial stability, and sustainable policies to ensure curation and accessibility of records in perpetuity.
- Programs in place for converting large numbers of files to archival formats, migrating files as needed, and maintaining digital files and their functionality despite rapid changes in software and technology.
- Robust storage systems with multiple backups.
- Qualified staff who can check for viruses, corruptions, and address problems when they occur.
- Sufficient cybersecurity measures to protect data from loss or breach of confidential information (e.g., site locations, collection owner's identity).
- The ability to ingest and maintain many different types of files, including remote sensing, geospatial data, photogrammetry and three-dimensional (3-D) scans.
- Systems for making the digital files searchable and accessible by remote users.

- Policy and standards requiring metadata to be associated with the digital files and to be stored with staff assistance for its creation when needed.[29]

An increasing number of commercial and open source digital preservation tools have the potential to serve as data repositories.[30] As with other kinds of repositories, the selection of a digital repository may vary by region and individual collection.[31]

It is a good idea to visit the proposed repository before making a decision. Any researcher or agency that is going to undertake fieldwork should identify a suitable repository and confirm whether that repository will take the collection; this is best done during the initial planning stages of the project.

It is standard practice for repositories to have policies and guidelines for collections preparation prior to deposition of materials. These guidelines may require that the collection (objects and records) be cleaned, labeled, cataloged, inventoried, and organized according to the repository's requirements; stored in specific sizes and types of containers; and accompanied by complete documentation and related records and that any initial conservation work on the objects be completed.[32] In some cases, the repository may ask that curation or collections management data be digitized according to set guidelines and in a manner that can be easily uploaded into the repository's collections management system. Each repository will have different preparation requirements, curation costs, and document requirements. The depositor must work closely with the repository to identify how the collections should be curated to meet the repository's requirements. Preparing collections before consulting the repository could lead to a lot of wasted time, money, and resources. If any of the repository's guidelines might interfere with planned analytical testing, the depositor should make the repository staff aware of this problem so that modifications may be made. Many repositories have check-in procedures to ensure that everything is in order when a collection arrives at the repository.[33]

Once the repository has been identified, it is vital for the depositor to initiate communication with the repository in the initial planning phases for projects that will generate the collections (e.g., an archaeological or paleontological excavation). The project director and staff that will be involved with the processing of the collection should become familiar with the identified repository's policies and procedures at this time. In addition, repository staff can provide advice and assistance regarding curation throughout the project.

Before choosing a repository for legacy collections, the depositor needs to do a collections assessment to know what the collection contains and what will be needed to begin discussions with a repository.[34] The publication, *Guidelines for Preparing Legacy Archaeological Collections for Curation*, has an excellent collections assessment questionnaire that can be used by anyone, regardless of professional affiliation.[35] The questions in this questionnaire are carefully designed to facilitate a fruitful working relationship with a potential repository. The completed assessment will help the depositor determine where the collections should go, what kind of object preparation can be anticipated, and cost considerations when readying the collections for curation.[36]

Curation of federal collections is governed by Federal Regulation 36 CFR Part 79. Section 79.9, "Standards to determine when a repository possesses the capability to provide adequate long-term curatorial services" outlines the standards to consider when choosing a repository. This list is extensive and includes, among other requirements, that the repository is able to:

1. Accession, label, catalog, store, maintain, inventory, and conserve the particular collection on a long-term basis using professional museum and archival practices.
2. Maintain complete and accurate records of the collection.
3. Dedicate the requisite facilities, equipment, and space in the physical plant to properly store, study, and conserve the collection.
4. Keep the collection in physically secure conditions within storage, laboratory, study, and exhibition areas.

5. Require staff and any consultants who are responsible for managing and preserving the collection to be qualified museum professionals.

6. Handle, store, clean, conserve and—if applicable—display the collection according to museum and archival practices.

7. Store site records, field notes, object inventory lists, computer disks and tapes, catalog records, and a copy of the final report in a manner that will protect them from theft and fire.

8. Inspect the collection for possible deterioration and damage, and perform only those actions that are absolutely necessary to stabilize the collection and rid it of any agents of deterioration.

9. Conduct inventories to verify the location of material remains, associated records, and any other federal property that is furnished to the repository.

10. Be able to make the collection available for scientific, educational, and religious uses, subject to such terms and conditions as are necessary to protect and preserve the condition, research potential, religious, or sacred importance, and uniqueness of the collection.[37]

NPS policy requires that only public, nonprofit, educational institutions can serve as partner repositories.[38] Nonfederal repositories that are contracted by the NPS must meet NPS standards for management of collections. These standards are outlined in the NPS *Museum Handbook*, Parts I, II, and III[39] as well as in Federal Regulation 36 CFR Part 79. Non-NPS partner repositories are required to submit information annually for the parks' collections management report,[40] complete the NPS Checklist for Preservation and Protection of Museum Collections,[41] and either allow NPS personnel to conduct regular inspections and inventories or submit inventories completed by repository staff. All federal agencies (e.g., BLM, DOT) that contract with nonfederal repositories require regular inspections and inventories of collections deposited at nonfederal repositories. In fact, it is good practice in general for repositories to allow or perform regular inspections and inventories. If repository staff carry out these activities on behalf of the depositor, the repository should submit a detailed report of the findings to the depositor.

Curation Standards and Best Practices at Repositories

As has been discussed elsewhere in this chapter, repositories are governed by the same professional collections management standards and best practices that museums follow. Repositories are expected to have guiding documents such as a mission statement, scope of collections, collections management policy, code of ethics, emergency preparedness or disaster response plan, integrated pest management plan, and a collections access and use policy, among others (see in particular the section, "Guidelines for Selecting a Repository"). Curatorial standards and best practices evolve over time, and repositories must stay current.

Although a museum does not accession objects that it does not own, a repository may accession a collection with the understanding that the repository is the steward of the collection, while the depositing agency or organization retains legal title.[42] This process aids in the long-term tracking and care of the collection and associated documentation. If a repository does accession a collection, it may choose to use an alternate numbering system when cataloging the objects to distinguish them from objects that it legally owns. In certain cases, federal or state collections may require specific cataloging systems that the repository will be bound to follow.

Federal Laws, Regulations, and International Conventions Governing the Management and Use of Repository Collections

There are many federal laws, regulations, and international conventions that designate legal ownership, protect anthropological and biological collections, and prescribe how these collections must be curated and managed (TABLE 3C.2). For example, the federal government asserts ownership of collections recovered from public lands under the Antiquities Act of 1906, the Archaeological and Historic Preservation Act, the Archaeological Resources Protection Act (ARPA), the National Historic Preservation Act (NHPA), Section 106 of NHPA, and Federal Regulations 36 CFR Part 79. These laws and regulations often apply to preexisting as well as new collections. Many state, local, and tribal governments have adopted laws and regulations similar to federal laws

Table 3C.2 Federal Laws, Regulations, and International Conventions Governing the Management and Use of Repository Collections[1]

Lacey Act of 1900	18 U.S.C. § 42 16 U.S.C. § 3371 Available at: https://www.fws.gov/le/pdffiles/Lacey.pdf
Antiquities Act of 1906	16 U.S.C. §§ 431-33 Available at: https://www.nps.gov/history/local-law/anti1906.htm
Migratory Bird Treaty Act of 1918	16 U.S.C. §§ 703-12 Available at: https://www.fws.gov/birds/policies-and-regulations/laws-legislations/migratory-bird-treaty-act.php
Historic Sites Act of 1935	16 U.S.C. §§ 461-471 Available at: https://www.nps.gov/history/local-law/hsact35.htm
Copyright Act of 1911, amended 1976	17 U.S.C. § § 101-810 Available at: https://www.gpo.gov/fdsys/pkg/USCODE-2011-title17/html/USCODE-2011-title17.htm
Bald and Golden Eagle Protection Act of 1940	16 U.S.C. §§ 668, et seq. Available at: https://www.fws.gov/midwest/eagle/protect/laws.html
Preservation of American Antiquities, 1954	43 CFR 3 Available at: https://www.govinfo.gov/app/details/CFR-2008-title43-vol1/CFR-2008-title43-vol1-part3
Federal Records Act of 1950, amended 2014 (overseen by the National Archives and Records Administration)	Available at: https://www.archives.gov/records-mgmt/laws
Archaeological and Historic Preservation Act of 1960, amended 1974	Available at: https://www.nps.gov/archeology/tools/laws/ahpa.htm
Convention on the Means of Prohibiting and Preventing the Illicit Import, Export and Transfer of Ownership of Cultural Property, 1970	Available at: http://portal.unesco.org/en/ev.php-URL_ID=13039&URL_DO=DO_TOPIC&URL_SECTION=201.html
Controlled Substances Act, 1970, amended 2019	Available at: https://www.dea.gov/controlled-substances-act
Reservoir Salvage Act of 1960	Available at: https://www.usbr.gov/cultural/ReservoirSalvageAct1960.pdf
Department of Transportation Act of 1966	Available at: https://www.transportation.gov/content/department-transportation-act
Freedom of Information Act of 1966	5 U.S.C. § 552, as Amended by Public Law No. 104-231, 110 Stat. 2422 Available at: https://www.foia.gov/
National Historic Preservation Act of 1966	16 U.S.C. §§ 470 et seq. Available at: https://www.nps.gov/history/local-law/nhpa1966.htm

National Environmental Policy Act of 1969	42 U.S.C. §§ 4321-70a Available at: https://www.epa.gov/NEPA
Marine Mammal Protection Act of 1972	16 U.S.C. §§ 1361-1407 Available at: http://www.nmfs.noaa.gov/pr/laws/mmpa/
Endangered Species Act of 1973	16 U.S.C. §§ 1531-44 Available at: http://www.biologicaldiversity.org/campaigns/esa/esatext.html
Federal Land Policy and Management Act of 1976	Available at: https://www.blm.gov/or/regulations/files/FLPMA.pdf
Surface Mining Control and Reclamation Act of 1977	Available at: https://legcounsel.house.gov/Comps/Surface Mining Control and Reclamation Act of 1977.pdf
American Indian Religious Freedom Act of 1978	42 U.S.C. § 1996 Available at: https://www.govinfo.gov/content/pkg/STATUTE-92/pdf/STATUTE-92-Pg469.pdf
Archaeological Resources Protection Act of 1979	16 U.S.C. §§ 470aa-470mm Available at: https://www.nps.gov/archeology/tools/laws/arpa.htm
Protection of Archaeological Resources, 1979	43 CFR 7 Available at: https://www.govinfo.gov/app/details/CFR-2012-title43-vol1/CFR-2012-title43-vol1-part7
Abandoned Shipwrecks Act of 1988	43 U.S.C. §§ 2101-2106 Available at: http://uscode.house.gov/view.xhtml?path=/prelim@title43/chapter39&edition=prelim
Federal Cave Resources Protection Act of 1988	Available at: https://www.blm.gov/sites/blm.gov/files/FCRPA-of-1988.pdf
Curation of Federally-Owned and Administered Archaeological Collections, 1990 (overseen by the US Department of the Interior)	36 CFR 79 Available at: https://www.nps.gov/archeology/tools/36cfr79.htm Available at: https://www.gpo.gov/fdsys/granule/CFR-2012-title36-vol1/CFR-2012-title36-vol1-part79
Native American Graves Protection and Repatriation Act, 1990 (overseen by the US Department of the Interior, National Park Service)	25 U.S.C. §§ 3001-13 Available at: https://www.nps.gov/archeology/tools/laws/nagpra.htm Available at: https://www.nps.gov/nagpra/
Native American Graves Protection and Repatriation Regulations, 1995, 2010, 1990 (overseen by the US Department of the Interior, National Park Service)	43 CFR 10 Available at: https://www.federalregister.gov/documents/2018/03/26/2018-06056/agency-information-collection-activities-native-american-graves-protection-and-repatriation

(*continued*)

Table 3C.2 *Continued*

National Parks Omnibus Management Act of 1998	Available at: https://www.nps.gov/gis/data_standards/omnibus_management_act.html
Paleontological Resources Preservation Act, 2009 (overseen by the US Departments of the Interior and Agriculture)	Available at: https://www.federalregister.gov/documents/2015/04/17/2015-08483/paleontological-resources-preservation
Convention on International Trade in Endangered Species of Wild Fauna and Flora (CITES)	Available at: https://www.cites.org/ Available at: https://www.fws.gov/international/cites/

NOTE

1. Does not include state, local, or tribal laws.

and regulations for collections from state, county, city, and tribal lands. Repository staff must be familiar with, understand, and be willing to abide by the legal and regulatory duties required by the depositor. Personnel must also stay abreast of any changes to these laws, regulations, and conventions because any modifications may affect the way that collections are curated and managed.

Early federal laws did not provide guidance for long-term collections curation or how to make collections publicly accessible and useful.[43] Early federal programs had no curation plans, and as a result, many collections from federal and state projects were not cared for adequately.[44] This began to change after the federal government passed the Antiquities Act of 1906. This law permitted archaeological projects to be undertaken by scientific or educational institutions with the caveat that all artifacts and data were to be permanently preserved in public museums and made accessible to the public.[45] By the 1970s, this act had become inadequate and was declared unconstitutionally sound.[46] With the passage of the Archaeological Resources Protection Act, the federal government reasserted ownership of archaeological resources from public lands, stating that "archaeological records and data will be preserved by a suitable university, museum, or other scientific or educational institution."[47] Additional laws and conventions related to cultural sites, materials, and buildings (e.g., the Archaeological and Historic Preservation Act, the National His-

toric Preservation Act, Section 106 of NHPA, and the Convention on the Means of Prohibiting and Preventing the Illicit Import, Export and Transfer of Ownership of Cultural Property) stipulate requirements for curating and managing cultural collections. Laws, regulations, and international conventions related to fauna and flora (e.g., the Lacey Act, the Migratory Bird Treaty Act of 1972, and the Convention on International Trade in Endangered Species of Wild Fauna and Flora [CITES]) regulate wildlife and plant specimens, as well as cultural objects containing any parts of protected fauna and flora.

In 1990, two laws were passed that greatly affected the ways in which repositories curated and managed their collections: Federal Regulation 36 CFR Part 79 and the Native American Graves Protection and Repatriation Act (NAGPRA). Federal Regulation 36 CFR Part 79 requires that collections generated by federal projects be curated according to professional standards and best practices in perpetuity. It provides guidance on establishing formal relationships between agencies and repositories for long-term care.[48] It acknowledges the costs involved including the obligations of federal agencies to pay for curation.[49] Ownership of collections from federal lands is retained by the federal agencies, and thus, these agencies are accountable for the collections, no longer leaving the financial onus on the repositories. The federal agency that oversees a project that recovers material remains is required to identify a suitable repository, periodically review and evaluate the curatorial services being provided by that repository, and enter into a new agreement with the repository to upgrade curation if standards are not being met or to remove the material from that repository.[50] Curation standards set forth in Federal Regulation 36 CFR Part 79 for repositories holding federal collections follow closely those developed by professional museum organizations (e.g., American Alliance of Museums, American Association for State and Local History, and the International Council of Museums). NAGPRA requires any agencies receiving federal funds to inventory their Native American human remains and associated objects and provide written summaries of unassociated funerary objects, sacred objects, and objects of cultural patrimony. Most importantly, NAGPRA requires consultation with federally recognized native tribes and organizations on the curation, management, and disposition of related human remains and cultural objects. In essence, Federal Regulation 36 CFR Part 79 and NAPGRA reinforce the need for repositories to have mission statements, collection policies, and records management systems to properly care for and manage the collections in their holdings.[51]

In 2009, the Omnibus Public Land Management Act (Public Laws 111-011) was signed by President Barack Obama, and the Paleontological Resources Preservation Act (PRPA) became law. Like the Archaeological Resources Protection Act, the PRPA requires paleontological resources and associated data and records to be deposited in an approved repository.

In general, repositories usually do not hold the copyright or other intellectual property rights to the materials that they curate for depositors. However, some repositories publish their own research reports, catalogs, and other collections-related materials to which they may hold copyright depending on the circumstances of publication.

Financial Considerations

Although some repositories curate collections as a public service or as a means of ensuring access to a collection for long-term study and use,[52] most repositories charge fees for the long-term curation of reposited collections. There is tremendous variation in the types of fees charged, the standard units on which the fees are based, the criteria used to assess fees, and the uses of the collected fees. Variation in fees across regions often relates to differences in salaries, cost of materials, utilities, and institutional affiliation.[53] Table 8.3 in Sullivan and Childs[54] provides a detailed list of key points related to curation fees based on the types of service fees charged, the standard units on which fees are based, the principal criteria used to assess fees, and the uses of the collected fees.

Many repositories now place a greater financial and physical burden on the collection's owner for the initial processing of the collection, even when the collection must be processed according to the repository's guidelines. Often the depositor is responsible for transportation costs to get the material to the repository. Contractual repository agreements have become more common because of heightened awareness of curation costs, especially as repositories stop accepting new collections because of lack of space.[55]

In general, there are two kinds of basic costs associated with curating collections in repositories: (i) the initial cost incurred for the inclusion of the objects and associated materials into the repository's facility and (ii) the costs associated with the ongoing maintenance and care of the objects and associated materials. One example is the cost incurred to replace or top off the preservative fluid used to house wet specimens such as fish and reptiles. Curation fees can be a one-time cost or an annual levy. The disadvantage of the former method is that it does not reflect the actual costs of curating the collection in perpetuity. Fees, one-time or annual, are often based on a unit of storage (e.g., number of archival cartons required, cubic or linear feet used). Fees might cover the initial processing, cataloging, and accessioning of the material or the long-term storage, inspection, inventory, maintenance, and conservation of the collection. Fees may be calculated differently for physical material compared with the associated records. If a repository chooses to curate and maintain the digital records as well as the physical material, it may charge digital preservation and data entry fees in addition to the usual curation fees.[56]

When a collection has been curated by a repository for a long period of time and needs support for improvement (e.g., rehousing, improving storage conditions, digitization), the depositor and the repository must work together to justify the needs and obtain the necessary funding.[57]

Different methods may be used to assess repository curation fees. For example, fees may be charged on an incremental basis[58] or by using a sustainable source of funds. The University of Iowa Office of the State Archaeologist (OSA) has maintained the State Archaeological Repository of Iowa since 1959.[59] Based on a historical lack of financial support from the university and the state archaeological community and a seven-fold increase in collections generated by federal projects and private consulting firms, a new financial model was created to sustain the repository on a long-term basis. The OSA's analysis of actual curation costs indicated that the only financially viable solution to in-perpetuity curation was to establish an endowment.[60] The most challenging question that the repository continues to address is, "What are the long-term costs relative to immediate needs?"[61] Assessing immediate costs is relatively easy; it requires calculating expenses related to containers, equipment, supplies, and labor.[62] Determining long-term costs is much more challenging because it involves estimating the costs associated with collection's use, loans, rehabilitation, data migration, and replacement of curatorial packaging materials, storage equipment, and building facilities.[63] The repository has also established a practice of assessing separate fees for associated records, including digital materials.[64]

Whatever method is used, the curation costs should be agreed on by the stakeholders and set down in the repository agreement prior to deposition of the collection at the repository.

Some repositories use their own staff and supplies to process the collections for which they charge a fee; other repositories will ask that the depositor do the processing before the collection comes to the repository. In the latter case, the depositor will have to include the costs of the labor and archival supplies required to curate the material according to the repository's guidelines. Some cultural resource management firms have developed successful formulas for estimating the preparatory costs of curation for their

budgets.[65] For example, some firms assess fees based on a standard number of objects per hour rate to prepare the curation processing budget; this rate includes the costs for all stages of processing a collection, including the number of person hours required.[66]

Federal Regulation 36 CFR Part 79 details a number of methods to fund curatorial services including:

1. Purchasing, constructing, leasing, renovating, upgrading, expanding, operating, and maintaining a repository that has the capability to provide adequate long-term curatorial services.
2. Entering into a cost-reimbursable or cost-sharing contract, memorandum, agreement, or other appropriate written instrument with a repository that has the capability to provide adequate long-term curatorial services.
3. Reimbursing a state for curatorial costs paid by the state agency to carry out the responsibilities of the federal agency.[67]

Removing Collections from Repositories

Sometimes a repository becomes unable to continue to adequately curate and care for the reposited collections in its holdings, or in dire circumstances, a repository may close. In such cases, reposited collections may have to be transferred from one repository to another. The depositor will then have to decide whether to provide the funds or services necessary to eliminate the deficiencies or remove the collection from the repository. If the latter option is chosen, it is up to the depositor to find another repository that has the capability to adequately curate and maintain the collection.

Certification

Currently, there is no mechanism for certifying repositories, particularly those that need to meet federal standards. For some professionals, initiating such a program is seen as costly and redundant. Organizations such as the American Alliance of Museums (AAM) and the American Association for State and Local History (AASLH) have museum accreditation programs that can serve to certify that museums that serve as repositories meet best practices and standards (Accreditation and Excellence programs for AAM and StEPs for AASLH). However, these programs do not cover nonmuseum repositories.

GUIDELINES FOR ACCEPTING COLLECTIONS

Before accepting a collection, a repository should consider the same kinds of questions that a museum does before accepting a collection:

- Who owns the material?
- Does the owning agency, institution, company, corporation, or individual have the authority to pass responsibility for the collection to the repository and the authority to sign the legal agreements?
- Will all of the legal documents (either the originals or copies) pertaining to the collection and collecting activity (e.g., field expeditions, seizures of materials from illegal operations) be made available to the repository to curate with the collection?
- Does the collection fall within the repository's mission and collecting scope?
- Can the repository adequately care for the collection according to professional standards and best practices? For example:

  1. Does the repository have the resources (e.g., labor, time, money) to care for the collection according to professional standards and best practices? If not, can it garner the necessary resources (e.g., charge a curation fee)?
  2. Does the repository have adequate space to house the collection (both the physical material and all of the associated documents and records) properly?
  3. Does any part of the collection need conservation? If so, how much will this cost and can the depositor or repository afford to pay for it?
  4. Are any of the objects fragile, and if so, what kind of care will they need? Can the repository provide such care?
  5. Are any of the objects rare? Can the repository provide proper security to house these materials adequately?

- Does the repository have the resources to make the collection accessible to the appropriate parties (e.g., researchers, the public if appropriate)?

- Does the repository have procedures in place for locating a particular collection and identifying its owner?
- Do any of the objects trigger issues of cultural heritage and sensitivity or have special storage needs (e.g., fluid-preserved specimens, radioactive objects, objects containing hazardous products, or treated with hazardous substances)? If so, is the repository prepared to address these issues in the proper manner, including housing the material according to specific guidelines (e.g., according to indigenous standards, health and safety regulations), and setting guidelines for who should have access to the collection and in what manner?

Depending on the size and organizational structure of the repository, an individual (e.g., the curator-in-charge), a committee (e.g., an institutional or board collections committee) or high-level administrator (e.g., a director or board chair) may be responsible for the decision to accept a collection. A repository may accept a collection because it supports its mission, matches its scope of collections, or supports its research and educational programming. On the other hand, a repository may turn down a collection for a number of reasons, including problems with ownership, inadequate space, insufficient funding to maintain the collection, or the physical condition of the overall collection or of specific objects or specimens. For example, materials that need extensive or complicated conservation treatment, such as waterlogged objects, are difficult for most repositories to maintain long-term.[68] The primary reasons that repositories refuse collections are unclear ownership and the inappropriate nature of the collection (i.e., the collection does not fit the repository's mission or scope of collections).[69]

Repository Agreements

The key aspect of a repository agreement is that ownership of the collection is not transferred, even though the objects in the collection are physically sent to another institution for long-term care.[70] For example, although the federal government asserts ownership of collections recovered from public lands under the Antiquities Act of 1906, the Archaeological and Historic Preservation Act of 1960, the National Historic Preservation Act (NHPA) of 1966, Section 106 of NHPA, and Federal Regulation 36 CFR Part 79, many of these collections are housed at nonfederal institutions. It is essential to have a written, signed legal agreement or contract between the depositor and the repository before any collections are handed over to the repository. All aspects of ownership must be resolved before any legal agreement is crafted and signed and the repository accepts the collection. In certain cases, repository personnel will work with the depositor and legal counsel to resolve issues relating to ownership and responsibility. The depositor and the repository should work together to develop the repository agreement or contract to address issues of concern to both parties and come to a mutually satisfactory arrangement.[71] If serious concerns related to any part of the arrangement are anticipated (e.g., matters of curation or conservation), these need to be addressed prior to formalizing the agreement or contract. Repository agreements must be signed by the designated authorized representative of the depositor and the repository. This is usually someone at a high level within the governing structure, such as the director of an institution, agency, or firm; or a repository director, board chair, department chair, provost, or sometimes a curator-in-charge with authority granted by the institution.

Repository agreements and contracts outline the roles and responsibilities of each party, fees or other financial arrangements, curation and conservation needs, special procedures or policies, access to and use of the collection, and provisions for cancellation of the agreement or contract, among other issues. Key elements of the repository agreement or contract include:

- A statement that identifies the collection and any property of the depositor that will be furnished to the repository.
- A written description of the collection.
- A detailed description of the services and funds to be provided by the depositor and the repository respectively.
- A schedule of payments (if fees are charged).
- A statement of the work to be performed by the depositor and by the repository.

- A statement that describes the expected condition upon delivery (e.g., to what degree will the collection be cataloged, in what manner will the material be housed).
- Special procedures and restrictions related to storing, handling, inspecting, inventorying, cleaning, conserving, and exhibiting the collection. Procedures and restrictions related to storing the collections, including methods and standards (temperature, humidity, light) of the storage environment and equipment and housing.
- Regulations and restrictions related to loans, destructive testing, copyright and other intellectual property rights, culling, and deaccession.
- Guidelines for access to the collection by researchers and the general public.
- When appropriate, instructions for restricting access to confidential or sensitive information.
- Start and end dates and any terms for renewal (if appropriate). For example, the NPS limits repository agreements to ten years with a renewal option.[72]
- Provisions for cancellation of the agreement by either party.
- Provisions for what to do with the collection should the repository close.

Federal Regulation 36 CFR Part 79 provides many more specific details regarding the contents of repository agreements, especially for those covering federal collections (TABLE 3C.3).

Some agreements specify that the repository cannot undertake certain activities (e.g., culling, destructive testing, deaccession) without the express written permission of the collection's legal owner. Other agreements allow the repository to make such decisions but require that regular activity reports be sent to the owner. The Florida Museum of Natural History curates an indigenous Amazonian collection for the USFWS, and as part of that agreement, museum collections staff in charge of the collection may make a decision to destroy an object if it is beyond repair. However, any such action taken must be carefully recorded and reported to the USFWS when a report is requested.

Before an agreement or contract is renewed, both parties should review the conditions set forth in the

Table 3C.3 Repositories at a Glance

This table focuses on field-generated collections. However, the points enumerated can apply to all types of reposited collections.

Repository agreement	Points to consider before an institution becomes a repository: • Is the depositor (e.g., a contractor or project director; hereafter referred to as "contractor") a member of a professional organization who upholds professional ethics (e.g., RPA)? • Does the repository already have an agreement (MOU, MOA, or contract) with the land agency with which the contractor will be working (e.g., Bureau of Land Management)? If not, does the contractor have an agreement with the agency to place the collection in a repository? Is the repository specifically named in the agreement? • Does the material fall under any legal restrictions (e.g., ARPA, PRPA, NHPA Sec. 106 mitigation, NAGPRA)? • Has the contractor obtained the proper permits? • Does the repository have adequate storage space, especially if it is a Phase III project? • Does the project fit within the repository's mission and scope of collections?
Accessioning	Points to consider when the repository accessions field-generated collections: • Does the contractor hold a current repository agreement with the repository? • Was the entire project undertaken on land owned by a single land agency or multiple agencies (federal, state, or tribal)? Are private landowners involved? • Can the contractor provide the repository with written copies of the permits and agreements from all land agencies and owners involved? • Was the work undertaken in a professional, legal, and ethical manner? • Did the contractor abide by all repository policies and procedures for processing the collection? • Did the contractor pay the agreed-on repository fees? • Did the repository or contractor notify the land agency or owner (if different than the contractor) that the collection had entered the repository?
Cataloging	Points to consider when the repository generates cataloging procedures for field-generated collections: • Has the repository been granted permission to cull the collection? If so, has the repository considered doing so (e.g., does the repository need two hundred historic aluminum cans when three representative samples are enough)? • Does the repository prefer to have the contractor process the collection (including cataloging it) prior to its being deposited or does the repository prefer to process the collection itself after it is deposited? • Does the repository provide written guidelines and instruction manuals to the contractor so that the cataloging process is clearly defined?
Packaging	Points to consider when the repository accepts field-generated collections: • Will the contractor provide the archival supplies required by the repository, or will the repository provide them for a fee? • Are requirements clearly stated so that only appropriate materials (e.g., acid-free paper and board, polypropylene or polyethylene materials, pigment ink pens, fluid-resistant paper and inks) are used for packaging and labeling the objects? • Do the repository's policies and procedures state whether multiple sites or field locations can be packaged in one container or whether each site or field location must have its own container?

ARPA, Archaeological Resources Protection Act; MOA, memorandum of agreement; MOU, memorandum of understanding; NAGPRA, Native American Graves Protection and Repatriation Act; NHPA, National Historic Preservation Act; PRPA, Paleontological Resources Preservation Act; RPA, Register of Professional Archaeologists

NOTES

1. Based on K. J. Hurst, "Chapter 3C, Repositories," in *MRM5: Museum Registration Methods*, 5th ed., edited by R. A. Buck and J. A. Gilmore (Washington, DC: The AAM Press, 2010), 58; M. C. Malaro and I. P. DeAngelis, *A Legal Primer on Managing Museum Collections*, 3rd edition (Washington, DC: Smithsonian Books, 2012), 61.

2. Culling collections is a controversial subject that is highly debated, especially in the archaeological community. A discussion regarding the ability to cull the collection should occur between the depositor and the repository before any agreement is reached. The final decision as to whether culling is permitted should be spelled out in the written repository agreement.

original document to make sure that each has upheld the conditions and wishes to continue the arrangement. Once both parties agree to renew, a new or amended written contract should be drawn up and signed by both parties.

Simmons[73] makes an important distinction between repository agreements and loans—with a repository agreement, the receiving institution is expected to manage the collection for an extended period of time, typically handling all aspects of collections care. It is notable that the NPS often uses an outgoing loan agreement to cover reposited collections.[74] This is not standard practice, however. The NPS does require that a contract for services be completed if a non-NPS repository is paid for collections management services. If a park has a substantial involvement in the collections management services, the NPS requires a cooperative agreement between the park and the repository.[75]

The following are examples of repository agreements:

- *General Agreement between the National Park Service and Smithsonian Institution for Custodianship of National Park Service Natural History Collections.* Parks may offer selected specimens to the Smithsonian Institution. If the Smithsonian accepts the offer, the Smithsonian will gain permanent custodial responsibility for the specimens. The NPA retains ownership responsibility.[76]

- *Agreement between the National Park Service and Arizona Board of Regents, University of Arizona, On Behalf of its Laboratory of Tree-Ring Research (LTRR).* This agreement covers natural history and cultural collections made on NPS lands for the purposes of tree-ring analysis. Collections are loaned to, stored, and managed by the LTRR at the University of Arizona. The agreement also covers associated records. All past collections and future collections that the NPS offers and LTRR accepts will be included in the agreement.[77]

- *Agreement between the National Park Service and the American Museum of Natural History on Management of NPS Tissue Collections.* This agreement is with the American Museum of Natural History's Ambrose Monell Cryo Collection (AMCC). The agreement provides for AMCC to manage animal tissue samples from federally listed threatened and endangered species collected on NPS land. Instructions are available for individuals collecting samples, NPS permit coordinators, NPS curators, and the AMCC curator. The tissue samples are maintained in cryogenic storage.[78]

- *Transfer Order Surplus Property.* This agreement is between the Florida Museum of Natural History and the USFWS for a seized collection of indigenous Amazonian objects and specimens. The collection contains faunal material from endangered animals, including birds, monkeys, and insects, that are illegal to import into the United States without the proper permits. The agreement states that the collection will be used for public and educational display and that the museum will publicize illegal trade in wildlife products as part of any exhibition or educational program using material from this collection (use of the collection for research is implied, but not specifically stated in the agreement).

- *Agreement between the Wanapum Heritage Center and the Department of the Army.* The Wanapum Band of Priest Rapids (Columbia Plateau) established the Wanapum Heritage Center (WHC). The WHC and the Grant County Public Utility District (GCPUD) work together to protect the natural and cultural resources as stipulated in the 2008 Federal Energy Regulatory Commission license to operate the Priest Rapids Hydroelectric Project. Article 417 of that license includes provisions to ensure that cultural artifacts related to the Wanapum are properly handled and curated.[79] The WHC wished to enter into curation agreements with federal agencies for the care of archaeological collections from their homeland—to achieve this goal, the WHC worked with the GCPUD to undergo a facility inspection and hire a qualified museum professional. The resulting facility upgrades and hiring led to a curation agreement with the Department of the Army.[80]

Federal Regulation 36 CFR Part 79, Appendix B—"Example of a Memorandum of Understanding for Curatorial Services for a Federally-Owned Collection," provides a template for a repository agreement that can be adapted for any collection. In the *Museum Handbook, Part II: Museum Records*, the NPS provides a sample repository agreement, "agreement between national park service and [Repository] on Management of NPS Natural History Collections."[81] Although specific to agreements between the NPS and a repository, sections of this sample agreement could be adapted for use by other depositors and repositories. Other helpful sample agreements and templates include the Memorandum of Understanding for Curation, University of Alaska-Fairbanks, Museum of the North, and the Repository Agreement, Minnesota Historical Society (both cited in Benden[82]). Other forms that can help the depositor prepare for entering into an agreement include the Provisional Curation Request Form, University of Alaska-Fairbanks, Museum of the North[83]; Depositors' Archaeology Repository Workflow, Minnesota History Society[84]; Checklist of Documentation Required for Acceptance of Archaeological Material, Minnesota History Society[85]; Request for Curation Services, Burke Museum[86]; and the Museum Facility Checklist for Spaces Housing DOI Museum Property.[87] An entire section of the Minnesota History Society website is devoted to instructions for obtaining repository agreements with the society.[88]

SUMMARY

Repositories are institutions that have the facilities and resources to ensure the long-term preservation of collections for other institutions, agencies, organizations, companies, and tribes. Repositories enter into repository agreements with the collections' owners to serve as custodians of the collections. As such, they play an important role in caring for many different types of collections to enable them to be used for research, interpretation, exhibition, and educational programs for present and future generations. •

NOTES

1. J. E. Simmons, *Things Great and Small: Collections Management Policies*, 2nd ed. (Lanham, MD: Rowman & Littlefield, 2018), 167.

2. Simmons, *Things Great and Small*, 167.

3. L. P. Sullivan and S. T. Childs, *Curating Archaeological Collections: From the Field to the Repository.* Archaeologist's Toolkit, Volume 6 (Walnut Creek, CA: AltaMira Press/ Rowman & Littlefield, 2003), 51, 57.

4. Sullivan and Childs, *Curating Archaeological Collections*, 59.

5. National Park Service, 36 CFR Part 79, *Curation of Federally-Owned and Administered Archeological Collections*, Title 36, Chapter I of the Code of Federal Regulations, 1990a. Available at: https://www.nps.gov/archeology/TOOLS/36cfr79.htm, Sect. 79.6, [b][2] (accessed April 6, 2019).

6. National Park Service, *Museum Handbook, Part I. Museum Collections* (Washington, DC: National Park Service, 1990b). Available at: https://www.nps.gov/museum/publications/MH1/mushbkI.html, A:14 (accessed April 6, 2019).

7. National Park Service, *Museum Handbook, Part II: Museum Records* (Washington, DC: National Park Service, 2000). Available at: https://www.nps.gov/museum/publications/MHII/mushbkII.html, H:54 (accessed April 6, 2019).

8. National Park Service, *Museum Handbook, Part II*, H:35.

9. S. R. Cofield and T. Majewski, "The preservation and management of archaeological records," in *Using and Curating Archaeological Collections*, edited by T. S. Childs and M. S. Warner, pp. 115–128 (Washington, DC: The SAA Press, 2019), 119.

10. Cofield and Majewski, "The preservation and management," 119.

11. K. J. Hurst, "Chapter 3C, Repositories," in *MRM5: Museum Registration Methods*, 5th ed., edited by R. A. Buck and J. A. Gilmore, pp. 58–61 (Washington, DC: The AAM Press, 2010), 58.

12. Sullivan and Childs, *Curating Archaeological Collections*, 3.

13. M. K. Knoll and B. B. Huckell, *Guidelines for Preparing Legacy Archaeological Collections for Curation* (Washington, DC: Society for American Archaeology, 2019), 10.

14. Simmons, *Things Great and Small*, 202.

15. Simmons, *Things Great and Small*, 166.

16. National Park Service, Sect. 79.4, [b][4][j].

17. Knoll and Huckell, *Guidelines*, 10.

18. Simmons, *Things Great and Small*, 202.

19. Investopedia, "Memorandum of understanding (MOU)." Available at: https://www.investopedia.com/terms/m/mou.asp (accessed June 5, 2019); Wikipedia, "Memorandum of understanding." Available at: https://en.wikipedia.org/wiki/Memorandum_of_understanding (accessed June 5, 2019).

20. AcqNotes, "Memorandum of agreement (MOA)." Available at: http://acqnotes.com/acqnote/careerfields/memorandum-of-agreement-moa (accessed June 5, 2019).

21. Wikipedia, "Contract." Available at: https://en.wikipedia.org/wiki/Contract (accessed June 5, 2019).

22. Sullivan and Childs, *Curating Archaeological Collections*, 46–50.

23. E. M. Futato, "A case for partnerships: one solution to the curation crisis," *Common Ground* 1, no. 2 (1996): 53.

24. National Park Service, *Museum Handbook, Part I*, 7:20.

25. Florida Senate, Florida Statutes, Title XLVIII, Chapter 1004, Section 56. Available at: https://www.flsenate.gov/Laws/Statutes/2018/1004.56 (accessed May 1, 2019); Florida Museum of Natural History, *Code of Ethics*. Available at: https://www.floridamuseum.ufl.edu/about/ethics/ (accessed May 2, 2019).

26. Sullivan and Childs, *Curating Archaeological Collections*, 80.

27. Sullivan and Childs, *Curating Archaeological Collections*, 32.

28. Sullivan and Childs, *Curating Archaeological Collections*, 51.

29. Cofield and Majewski, "The preservation and management," 121.

30. Cofield and Majewski, "The preservation and management," 121.

31. Cofield and Majewski, "The preservation and management," 122.

32. Sullivan and Childs, *Curating Archaeological Collections*, 117.

33. Sullivan and Childs, *Curating Archaeological Collections*, 97.

34. Knoll and Huckell, *Guidelines*, 3.

35. Knoll and Huckell, *Guidelines*, 6–7.

36. Knoll and Huckell, *Guidelines*, 3.

37. National Park Service, 36 CFR Part 79.

38. National Park Service, *Museum Handbook, Part II*, H:58.

39. Available at: https://www.nps.gov/museum/.

40. National Park Service, *Museum Handbook, Part II*, 5:4.

41. National Park Service, *Museum Handbook, Part II*, 5:6.

42. Hurst, "Chapter 3c, Repositories," 60.

43. Sullivan and Childs, *Curating Archaeological Collections*, 27.

44. Sullivan and Childs, *Curating Archaeological Collections*, 27.

45. Hurst, "Chapter 3c, Repositories," 58.

46. T. F. King, *Cultural Resource Laws & Practice: An Introductory Guide* (Walnut Creek, CA: AltaMira Press, 1998), 197.

47. Hurst, "Chapter 3c, Repositories," 58; M. C. Malaro and I. P. DeAngelis, *A Legal Primer on Managing Museum Collections*, 3rd ed. (Washington, DC: Smithsonian Books, 2012), 146.

48. Sullivan and Childs, *Curating Archaeological Collections*, 27.

49. Sullivan and Childs, *Curating Archaeological Collections*, 27.

50. National Park Service, 36 CFR Part 79.

51. Sullivan and Childs, *Curating Archaeological Collections*, 27.

52. Malaro and DeAngelis, *Legal Primer*, 521.

53. Futato, "A case for partnerships," 53.

54. Sullivan and Childs, *Curating Archaeological Collections*, 115.

55. L. P. Sullivan and S. T. Childs, "Being a curator: revising the curation of archaeological collections from the field to the repository," in *Using and Curating Archaeological Collections*, edited by Childs and Warner, pp. 79–89, 82.

56. Cofield and Mayewski, "The preservation and management," 122.

57. Sullivan and Childs, "Being a curator," 82.

58. S. T. Childs, K. Kinsey, and S. Kagan, "Repository fees for archaeological collections: trends and issues over a decade of study," *Heritage Management* 3 (2010): 189–212.

59. J. L. Cordell, J. F. Doershuk, and S. C. Lensink, "Dodging the repository money pit: The Iowa experience," in *Using and Curating Archaeological Collections*, edited by Childs and Warner, 151.

60. Cordell, Doershuk, and Lensink, "Dodging the repository money pit," 156.

61. Cordell, Doershuk, and Lensink, "Dodging the repository money pit," 157

62. Cordell, Doershuk, and Lensink, "Dodging the repository money pit," 157

63. Cordell, Doershuk, and Lensink, "Dodging the repository money pit," 157

64. Cordell, Doershuk, and Lensink, "Dodging the repository money pit," 157

65. R. C. Sonderman, "Before you start that project, do you know what to do with the collections?" in *Our Collective Responsibility: The Ethics and Practice of Archaeological Collections Stewardship*, edited by S. T. Childs, pp. 107–120 (Washington, DC: Society for American Archaeology, 2004), 109.

66. Sonderman, "Before you start that project," 111.

67. National Park Service, 36 CFR Part 79, Sect. 79.7.

68. Sullivan and Childs, *Curating Archaeological Collections*, 96.

69. Sullivan and Childs, *Curating Archaeological Collections*, 95.

70. Simmons, *Things Great and Small*, 167.

71. National Park Service, *Museum Handbook, Part II*, H:58.

72. National Park Service, *Museum Handbook, Part II*, 5:1.

73. Simmons, *Things Great and Small*, 167.

74. National Park Service, *Museum Handbook, Part II*, 5:1.

75. National Park Service, *Museum Handbook, Part II*, 5:4.

76. National Park Service, *Museum Handbook, Part II*, H:59.

77. National Park Service, *Museum Handbook, Part II*, H:59–H:60.

78. National Park Service, *Museum Handbook, Part II*, H:60.

79. A. Neller, "Tribal voice on archaeological collections," in *Using and Curating Archaeological Collections*, edited by Childs and Warner, 15–25, 18.

80. Neller, "Tribal voice," 18–19.

81. National Park Service, *Museum Handbook, Part II,* H:94–H:104.

82. D. M. Benden, "Finding what you need: Resources for archaeological collections," in *Using and Curating Archaeological Collections,* edited by Childs and Warner, 186.

83. Benden, "Finding what you need," 186.

84. Minnesota Historical Society, "Depositors' archaeology repository workflow." Available at: http://www.mnhs.org/collections/archaeology/reports/DepositorsReposWorkFlow.pdf (accessed June 6, 2019).

85. Minnesota Historical Society, "Checklist of documentation required for acceptance of archaeological material." Available at: http://www.mnhs.org/collections/archaeology/reports/MHSDocChecklistForm.pdf (accessed June 6, 2019).

86. Benden, "Finding what you need," 186.

87. Benden, "Finding what you need," 186.

88. Home/Collections/About the Collections/Archaeology/Curation of Archaeology Collections.

89. Hurst, "CHAPTER 3C, Repositories."

The author wishes to acknowledge Kara J. Hurst, author of the "Repositories" chapter in MRM5[89] and the numerous professionals who have researched and written about repositories, some of whom are named in this chapter's references.

3D | Provenance Research in Museum Collections

An Overview

Karen Daly

THE WORD *provenance* means "origin," yet also refers to the history of ownership, particularly of an artwork or artifact.[1] The objective of provenance research is to trace the ownership history and location of an object, ideally from its creation to the present. Documentation of the provenance of a work of art has long been a valuable component of art history research. In addition to providing insight into the history of collecting, it can serve as a way to authenticate an object. Moreover, provenance information has become necessary to determine the legal status of an object.

Museums have traditionally conducted provenance research as part of the overall curatorial research of a collection. In recent decades, there has been an increased focus on the provenance of museum objects.[2] As such, provenance has evolved to a new level of importance in museums. In effect, information that was once seen as beneficial is now further understood as crucial.

Provenance research supports a museum's mandate to ensure that all collections in its custody are lawfully held and rightfully owned; in turn, this kind of responsible stewardship helps to maintain a high level of public trust. Whether an object has been in a museum's permanent collection for many years or is being considered for acquisition, incoming loan, or outgoing loan, its documented history of ownership can be a fundamental factor in making ethical decisions in accordance with museum standards. From a collections management perspective, this chapter offers practical suggestions for the important and often complex work of provenance research and its documentation, with an emphasis on Nazi-era provenance research.[3] More than seventy years after the end of World War II and twenty years after the adoption of the Washington Principles on Nazi-Confiscated Art,[4] museums have an ongoing responsibility to research, document, and provide access to the Nazi-era provenance of their collections.

Within the diverse scope of museum professions, the field of provenance research has emerged in recent years as a specialized discipline. With expanding access to digitized archives and records, as well as increased efforts at international collaborations,[5] the tools and resources for provenance research are quickly evolving.

In the United States, the standards and practices for the museum field are ultimately determined by the museum community itself and are developed through its professional associations, primarily the American Alliance of Museums (AAM) and the Association of Art Museum Directors (AAMD).[6] With respect to Nazi-era provenance issues, the standards and guidelines developed by the AAM (*Guidelines Concerning the Unlawful Appropriation of Objects During the Nazi Era*) and AAMD (*Report of the AAMD Task Force on the Spoliation of Art during the Nazi/World War II Era*) give museums a strong basis for identifying and applying consistent methods that are most appropriate for their respective staff and collections.[7] In addressing provenance issues, each museum is entrusted to incorporate these standards and guidelines into their own policies and procedures, determine the appropriate staffing and funding, organize existing provenance information, establish their own priorities for further research, and make provenance information publicly available.

Although the focus of this chapter is provenance issues related to the World War II era, the information in this chapter will help address other provenance issues and cultural property concerns throughout a museum's collection.[8]

HISTORICAL BACKGROUND

From 1933 to the end of World War II in 1945, the Nazi regime conducted one of the largest confiscations of art and cultural property known in history.

The Third Reich enacted an elaborate and premeditated system of theft, confiscation, coercion, and destruction, with millions of objects being unlawfully and forcibly taken from their rightful owners.

After World War II, great efforts were made by the Allied forces and other governments to return objects to their countries of origin and to original owners. Many members of the US museum community played leading roles in the success of the postwar restitution effort.[9] Although large numbers of objects were restituted, some entered the art market and eventually found their way into various collections in Europe, the United States, and elsewhere, often with lost, obscured, or false provenance information.

Within the last few decades, museums have become increasingly aware of issues of looted art and restitution, particularly objects possibly misappropriated during the Nazi era. In 1998, the Presidential Advisory Commission on Holocaust Assets in the United States (PCHA) was created to study and report to the president on issues relating to Holocaust victims' assets in the United States. The Department of State and the US Holocaust Memorial Museum then cohosted the Washington Conference on Holocaust-Era Assets. This conference resulted in the release of a document with eleven principles created to help resolve issues related to art and assets looted by the Nazis.[10]

In the following years, guidelines issued by AAM and AAMD began to reshape museum policies across the United States. In a joint agreement reached with the PCHA in 2000, AAM and AAMD further recommended that museums should strive to (i) identify all objects in their collections that were created before 1946 and acquired by the museum after 1932, that underwent a change of ownership between 1932 and 1946, and that were or might reasonably be thought to have been in Europe between those dates, identified as *covered objects*; (ii) make currently available object and provenance information on those objects accessible; and (iii) give priority to continuing provenance research as resources allow. AAM, AAMD, and PCHA further agreed that the initial focus of museum research should be European paintings and Judaica.[11]

In 2003, AAM launched the Nazi-Era Provenance Internet Portal (NEPIP), which provided a searchable registry of objects in US museum collections that possibly changed hands in Europe during the Nazi era, from 1933 to 1945.[12] Through the portal, museums could submit and manage their own data on covered objects from their collections in a central location. The participating museums provided descriptive and provenance information for each object, sometimes accompanied with links to additional information on respective websites. Although the portal was a tremendous help for many museums, especially for those which had limited resources to make collections information available through their own websites, it is no longer managed and exists only as an archive. The AAMD later created the registry, "Resolutions of Claims for Nazi-Era Cultural Assets,"[13] which is a helpful resource for documenting Nazi-era museum claims. In recent years, the AAMD has taken a leading role in providing provenance research seminars and offering scholarships and information on grant opportunities.

PROVENANCE RESEARCH

Provenance research is challenging and complex work, particularly for objects possibly misappropriated during the Nazi era. Ownership records of art objects are often incomplete because many factors over time have made it difficult to locate information. Among numerous factors, the upheavals of World War II, the inaccessibility of many archives during the Cold War, destruction from natural disasters, and changing standards of recordkeeping over time have all added to the difficulty of determining a complete provenance for an object. Sometimes provenance records simply reflect a past owner's wish for anonymity. Other times, the attribution of an artwork may change over time, creating confusion in tracking the documentation.

Provenance research is interdisciplinary by its nature, requiring the ability to consult many types of sources from different fields of study. It requires an extensive knowledge of art history, the expertise to physically examine works of art, and the patience to thoroughly examine numerous sources for possible information. Particularly, provenance research for the World War II era requires a methodical investigation of the object itself, museum object records, museum archives, auction and exhibition catalogs, catalogs of collections, catalogues raisonné, dealer records, photographic archives, and publications of the wartime activities of dealers and collectors. Provenance research also requires proficiency in foreign languages, with at least a reading knowledge of German and French.

At times, provenance research requires examination of archives in other countries and access to documents that may not be publicly accessible. In many cases, museums find it necessary to employ a provenance researcher with a more specific expertise and background. Increasingly, there are online databases and digitized records available through various resources.[14]

An important provenance research resource for museums is *The AAM Guide to Provenance Research* by Nancy H. Yeide, Konstantin Akinsha, and Amy L. Walsh, published by the AAM.[15] With its extensive historical information, methodologies, indices, valuable resources, and case studies, this guide remains an essential reference for any museum addressing Nazi-era provenance and related issues. *Museum Policy and Procedures for Nazi-Era Issues*, also published by the AAM and compiled by Helen J. Wechsler, Teri Coate-Saal, and John Lukavic, is another essential resource for collection managers, registrars, and curators.[16]

At any stage of provenance research, the work can take considerable time, diligence, and expense. However, for most museums, the most substantial amount of time is required to establish and document what is already known about its collection. Subsequently, this provenance data needs to be organized and formatted in a systematic and consistent manner. For example, in *The AAM Guide to Provenance Research*, there is a suggested standard format for recording provenance.[17]

Suggested Standard Format

The provenance for an object is listed in chronological order, beginning with the earliest known owner. Life dates, if known, are enclosed in brackets. The names of dealers, auction houses, or agents are enclosed in parentheses to distinguish them from private owners. Relationships between owners and methods of

Table 3D.1 Punctuation for Standard Provenance Format

Punctuation	Meaning
[ ]	Life dates of owner, if known
( )	Dealers, auction houses, or agents (e.g., not private owners)
;	Semicolon = Direct transfer between owners
.	Period = No direct transfer is known
[#]	Footnote numbers in brackets and placed after the semicolon or period, then notes are listed in order below

transactions are indicated by punctuation. A semicolon is used to indicate that the work passed directly between two owners, and a period is used to separate two owners if a direct transfer did not occur or is not known to have occurred. Footnotes are used to document or clarify information (TABLE 3D.1).

Certainly, an institution can develop its own format provided it is explained in publications and on its website.[18] Any provenance record, whether published or included in a museum's internal database or external website, should clearly establish a sequence of ownership and document the sources of information.

Staff Roles

The work of provenance research and its documentation requires the support of an entire institution. Often, various museum departments intersect and overlap in the goal of making provenance information accurate, consistent, and available to researchers and the general public. Each museum should decide on key staff members who will undertake the necessary duties to achieve this goal.

As part of their general responsibilities, curators most often conduct and review provenance research of their respective collections. Many museums, however, need to appoint at least one additional staff member as a primary contact for provenance information and as a coordinator of the museum's provenance research. It is ideal if one person, or a small group, can oversee and organize the museum's provenance information in a centralized manner, as well as prioritize museum objects for further research. Likewise, it can be particularly helpful to have one person as a point of contact for outside inquiries on provenance and for possible claims of ownership. Whether or not an inquiry evolves into a claim of ownership, having it proceed through an initial contact can help maintain a consistency of records.[19]

As provenance research staff and their specific roles are designated, their contact information should be included in a museum directory and on the museum's website, if applicable. Many museums include a section on their museum website dedicated to the topic of provenance research, outlining the museum's efforts in this area, as well as a statement of the museum's position on provenance and other related cultural property concerns. Museums are increasingly including provenance data as part of basic object information on their websites.

At this time, the museum professionals who primarily work in the area of provenance research and related issues are curators, collection managers, registrars, and archivists. It is ideal that the staff member(s) who primarily work in this area have an extensive knowledge of the museum's collection, a familiarity with the various types of museum records, and experience working with the objects. Additionally, museum directors, senior-level administrators, and their staff are often closely involved in the supervision and management of these important issues. Furthermore, a museum's legal counsel plays a crucial role, particularly with cultural property concerns and possible claims of ownership.

Regardless of which staff members are primarily responsible for provenance research, it is clear that registrars and collection managers play a significant role in the success of any provenance research effort. As museum professionals trained to maintain the integrity of records and documentation, registrars and collections managers are often well suited to work in this area. Collections management staff typically have a comprehensive knowledge and understanding of the institution's records, related legal issues, its collection management policy, and of the collection itself.

There is an increasing call for museum professionals with expertise in provenance research and who are knowledgeable about current cultural property laws and concerns. As such, it is certain that those who work in the field of museum collections management will continue to encounter these issues and make significant contributions to this field.

Existing Collection

One of the primary objectives of provenance research of a museum's permanent collection is to ascertain what is currently known about the ownership history of the collection. In this process, it is important to establish goals and working methodologies to achieve those goals. Any methodology used should be clearly documented so the process and results can be understood and expanded upon by future researchers.

Covered Objects

The initial goal, per the AAM recommended procedures, is to determine how many covered objects are in a collection, these being

> objects created before 1946 and acquired by the museum after 1932, that underwent a change of ownership between 1932 and 1946, and that were or might reasonably be thought to have been in Europe between those dates. In the event that a museum is unable to determine whether an object created before 1946 and acquired after 1932 (a) might have been in Europe between 1932 and 1946 and/or (b) underwent a change of ownership during that period, it should still be treated as a covered object.[20]

The speed of calculating a museum's total number of potentially covered objects depends greatly on the type of museum collection. For example, if it is a small, focused collection, established mostly before the 1930s, this can be a quick and straightforward process. However, many US museum collections grew significantly after 1932 and include numerous works created before 1946. Also, numerous collections in the United States are encyclopedic and diverse in nature, with a number of different categories for consideration. From the outset, researchers are greatly aided if they can systematically search museum records, especially through an effective collections management database system.

Although it is not complex to determine how many objects were created before 1946 and acquired after 1932, it can be time-consuming to discover whether an object may have been in Europe between 1933 and 1945.

After establishing the overall number of objects that were created before 1946 and acquired by the museum after 1932, one might further refine the figure by eliminating certain categories of objects or individual objects known to have not been in Europe during the Nazi era. For example, it might be known that a group of artworks given by a certain patron were in the United States throughout the Nazi era and so can be subtracted from the overall count. Also, as AAM, AAMD, and the PCHA have recommended, the focus should first be on any Judaica and European paintings.[21] Museums should try to determine an overall timeline for those areas that need to be researched beyond holdings of European paintings and Judaica, such as sculpture, decorative arts, drawings, and prints. After those categories are completed, and if applicable, museums should estimate the time to examine any remaining potential covered objects in their collections.[22]

To make the research of covered objects a more manageable project, it helps to organize the collection into smaller groups for research, such as objects associated with a particular dealer, or a patron, or from a particular time period.

With each covered object, all related museum records should be thoroughly examined, including accession records, database entries, object files, wills, bequests, correspondence, and any exhibition and publication histories. Furthermore, it is necessary to physically examine the work in its entirety, documenting the backs of paintings and all sides of objects, looking for any kind of collector's stamps, labels, numbers, marks, auction house codes, or lot numbers. If there is no existing photography, the object should be fully photographed and documented.

When conducting this internal research, it is most efficient to concurrently document all basic information in a format through which the data can eventually be made public on the museum's website. It is recommended that museums follow AAM's "Twenty Categories of Object and Provenance Information" as a format for initially recording this information (TABLE 3D.2; see also the sample "Twenty Categories of Object Provenance Research" in the *Collection Forms* section).

Prioritizing Research
During an internal research process, some covered objects may appear more problematic than others. Therefore, the prioritization of provenance research is a necessary phase of the overall research process. It is important to critically evaluate the provenance gaps of covered objects through consideration of a few general factors.

First, there is the potential location of an object during the Nazi era. Although any gap in provenance could be problematic, it helps to look at any known locations and associations of the object. For example, a gap in the provenance history for a painting known to have been in the United States before and following the war would likely not be a candidate for misappropriation. Yet, an object associated with a German collection and with a provenance gap between 1933 and 1938 would warrant further research and higher prioritization.[23]

Another factor to consider during the research process is the identification of *red-flag* names. One of the most often cited lists of red-flag names is found in records of the Office of Strategic Services (OSS) Art Looting Investigation Unit's (ALIU) Biographical Index of Individuals Involved in Art Looting.[24] Additionally, researchers should become familiar with red-flag names of collections that are known to have been looted within this time period. Although there is no single list of names of all the victims of looting, there are various resources and archives to aid in such research.[25] It is important to keep in mind that the discovery of any type of red-flag names only indicates a need of further research. Many objects associated with these names were sold by dealers or were in collections before or after the war. Moreover, thousands of these objects were returned to their rightful

Table 3D.2 Twenty Categories of Object and Provenance Information (Template Recommended by American Alliance of Museums)

Category	Comments
Artist/Maker	To include artists' names, alternate names, and previous attributions.
Nationality of Artist/Maker	—
Life Dates of Artist/Maker	—
Place or Culture of Object	Only if artist is unknown.
Object Title or Name	To include alternate titles.
Date of Work	To include approximate date, if specific date is unknown.
Medium/Materials	—
Measurements	—
Date of Acquisition	—
Accession Number	—
Object Type	Painting, sculpture, decorative arts, etc.
Subject Type	Landscape, portrait, mythological subject, historical, religious, genre, Judaica, etc.
Signature and Marks (obverse)	To include signatures, inscriptions, and marks; for paintings, what appears on the front.
Labels and Marks (reverse, frame, mount, etc.)	To describe marks and labels (prior to 1960) on the reverse of an object (including frame, mount, etc.). Indicate if images are available.
Description	To contain description of object (its content, subject, etc.). Museums should make this a priority.
Provenance	To contain, at minimum, known owners, dates of ownership, places of ownership, methods of transfer (sale, gift, descent, etc.). To include, if known, lot numbers, sale prices, buyers, etc. To include information on unlawful appropriation during the Nazi era and subsequent restitution. Museums should ensure that provenance information is understandable and organized chronologically.
Exhibition History	—
Bibliographic History	—
Other Relevant Information	To contain anything about the object that would be useful in identifying it for this purpose. If the object fits the definition of Judaica contained in this document, so state.
Image	An image is key to identifying an object. Museums should make every effort to include an image with their records.

owners following the war, thanks to the restitution efforts of the Allied forces.

Another aspect to keep in mind is a general recognition of the types of objects highly desired and sought by the Nazis throughout this time period. Although their confiscations were wide ranging, there are certain art historical categories that were highly valued and pursued by the Third Reich officers more intensely than others, such as German art of the Renaissance period.[26]

The provenance researcher should assemble all internal information first, seeking to close any provenance gaps before going offsite to other sources. Once the internal records are thoroughly examined and the information is critically evaluated, staff should contact relevant archives, existent databases, and any art dealers, auction houses, or donors, as may be necessary. Additionally, there are scholars and other researchers who may be able to provide further information or guidance.

Making It Public: Museum Websites
Following recommendations by the AAM, AAMD, and PCHA, museums should make currently available information on their covered objects as accessible as possible. By making this information available to the public, museums help to fulfill their mandate of responsible stewardship of their collections. The internet provides the most direct way for museums to share information on objects with the public, researchers, and potential claimants, and an opportunity for others outside the museum to possibly contribute further information that may clarify the provenance of objects.

In addition to posting information on a museum website, there is the NEPIP, designed and managed by AAM on behalf of the US museum community.[27] If a museum did not have provenance information on its covered objects formatted for inclusion to the NEPIP, the museum could register on the portal as a participating museum. Initially, a museum provided a contact name, contact information, any links to their museum website, and information on whether the museum had any Judaica holdings in its collection.

As research develops and information is organized, museums can continue to submit and manage their own data on their covered objects.

Discovering Evidence of Misappropriated Objects
Per AAM, if in the process of researching a museum's existing collection, researchers find credible evidence of unlawful appropriation without subsequent restitution, there should be a procedure in place to inform key museum staff. In consultation with qualified legal counsel, the museum should make every effort to resolve the status of the object. This may include making information public and possibly notifying potential claimants. In such a situation, museums should strive to be as open and transparent as possible, seeking ways to responsibly and appropriately address the situation.[28]

Acquisitions
Among the many criteria used for determining whether an object should be added to a collection, the provenance of the object is a factor of crucial

consequence. Although museums have historically sought to obtain provenance information on objects intended for acquisition, in recent decades it has become more imperative to obtain and document such information. Currently, museums are proceeding with great caution in acquisitions, not only with respect to Nazi-era provenance but also with acquisitions of various archaeological materials and ancient art objects originating outside the United States.[29]

AAM has clearly stated that museums should take all "reasonable steps to resolve the Nazi-era provenance status of objects before acquiring them for their collections whether by purchase, gift, bequest, or exchange."[30] In recent years, museums have incorporated more rigorous guidelines and procedures into their collection management policies with respect to acquisitions and provenance.[31] For example, many museums send a provenance questionnaire to all potential donors and dealers of art considered for acquisition, including specific requests for provenance information from 1932 to 1945. For ancient art and archaeological objects being considered for acquisition, a questionnaire should also specifically inquire about ownership history of the object, as well as request any export or import documentation.[32] Often, the registrar or collections manager is directly involved in this documentation and should work in tandem with the curator in obtaining, analyzing, and documenting all provenance information.

In certain cases, it is prudent for museums to further require a warranty as part of a purchase agreement to ensure the museum obtains good title to an object, which may offer protection from potential future claims.[33] Notably, in the 1998 "Report of the Association of Art Museum Directors (AAMD) Task Force on the Spoliation of Art during the Nazi/World War II Era," the AAMD advises that museums, when purchasing works of art, "seek representations and warranties from the seller that the seller has valid title and that the work of art is free from any claims."[34]

Another due-diligence step in the acquisition process is to check the object's descriptive information and known ownership history against various databases of stolen art. Currently, there are two major organizations that most museums employ, the Art

Loss Register (ALR) and Art Recovery International (ARI), both of which are able to access databases of lost and stolen art, antiques, and collectibles.[35] These organizations have a great deal of experience with museums in providing search services, research capabilities, and expertise in a number of areas. Although their services are not free, it is a worthwhile investment and necessary expense for many museums to include in their budgets, whether related to the care and research of the collection, exhibitions, or for other related museum projects. With respect to these established databases, there is an important caveat to keep in mind. Submitting a search through these databases is just one step of due diligence for checking objects that have been registered with the databases as lost or stolen. It does not replace further research that might be warranted, nor does it guarantee any protection against possible provenance issues in the future.

Per AAM, when the provenance is incomplete or uncertain for a proposed acquisition, the museum should consider what "additional research would be necessary to resolve the Nazi-era provenance status of the object before acquiring it."[36] It falls to individual museums to determine how these decisions will be made within their institution. It is best to incorporate clear responsibilities and procedures into an acquisitions section of the museum's collection management policy and update periodically as necessary.

During the research phase of an acquisition, if credible evidence of unlawful appropriation without subsequent restitution is found, it is recommended that the museum notify the donor, seller, or estate executor of the evidence and not proceed with acquiring the object until there is an acceptable resolution and planned course of action. As circumstances and complexities can vary greatly, depending on the situation, any decisions should be made in consultation with qualified legal counsel.[37]

Once an object has been accessioned into a collection, the object and provenance information about the acquisition should be made public. Press releases on new acquisitions, published in local newspapers or on a museum's website, help to convey overall transparency. Furthermore, it is recommended that new and recent acquisitions be put on display, as is possible.

With respect to ancient art and archeological objects, the AAMD maintains an object registry for museums to document recent acquisitions of such objects, and especially reasons for acquisition if there is no provenance history dated to at least 1970, per the 1970 United Nations Educational, Scientific and Cultural Organization (UNESCO) Convention on the Means of Prohibiting and Preventing the Illicit Import, Export and Transfer of Ownership of Cultural Property.[38]

Overall, throughout the acquisition process, the museum should strive to be as open and transparent as possible, making new objects available for further research, public review, and accountability.

Loans

In recent years, issues of provenance have filtered into almost every collections-related practice within a museum. An institution's approach to loans, both to and from its collection, should include a thorough consideration of provenance information.

Incoming Loans

Per the AAM, museums should be aware of their ethical responsibility to consider the status of material they borrow as well as the possibility of claims being brought against a loaned object in their custody.[39] AAMD urges museums to review provenance information regarding incoming loans.[40]

With incoming loans, museums should request that lenders provide as much provenance information as possible. Museums may also want to consult published sources on their own for potential provenance concerns. As with provenance research for existing collections or proposed acquisitions, the borrowing museum must have and maintain clear documentation of this provenance information.

When the provenance is incomplete or uncertain for a proposed loan, the museum should consider what "additional research would be prudent or necessary to resolve the provenance status of the object before borrowing it."[41] It is recommended that museums incorporate clear responsibilities and procedures into a loans section of their collection management policies, and update as necessary.

During the research and planning phase of an incoming loan, if credible evidence of unlawful appropriation without subsequent restitution is found, the borrower should notify the lender of the nature of the evidence and should not proceed with the loan until taking action to clarify these issues.

In recent years, museums have increasingly included conditions in loan agreements and exhibition contracts that stipulate terms regarding the lender's legal status as sole owner of the loaned object(s). Some agreements stipulate that the borrower will only release or take instructions concerning the loan from the lender or the lender's authorized agent.[42] Furthermore, to limit liability during an exhibition, a borrowing museum may apply, as appropriate and necessary, for Immunity from Judicial Seizure of Cultural Objects, administered through the US Department of State.[43]

Outgoing Loans

As indicated by professional standards, potential lenders should submit to borrowers, as requested, all known provenance information on any proposed objects for loan. For loans from the collection, designated staff should conduct and document, as appropriate, a provenance review of the proposed loan. In addition to an institution's established criteria for considering loans, there are a few factors to consider with respect to provenance.

If the proposed loan has not yet been researched, efforts should be made to check internal records and publications, determining if there are potential concerns or if further research is necessary. As standard practice, the museum should clearly document all the related provenance research of any potential outgoing loans.

If any provenance concerns develop in the review process, designated staff should critically evaluate all the known ownership, exhibition, and publication history of the object(s), weighing any potential risks against the potential benefits of increased public knowledge and possible scholarship that might result from the exhibition of the object(s). In such a situation, an appropriate step of due diligence would be to submit the known information about the proposed loan to ALR or ARI for a search against their databases. Depending on where the loan is traveling to for exhibition, it is prudent to be aware of any applicable immunity from seizure laws that may be in place. Depending on the circumstances, an exhibition's organizer(s) may have secured immunity from seizure for all lenders, but it is best to confirm these details from the borrower and obtain documented evidence.

The provenance review, research information, and summary of the museum's decision regarding any provenance issues with an outgoing loan should be completely documented as part of the process.

In all incoming and outgoing loans, museums should incorporate practices that carefully consider issues of provenance, not only to protect the interests of the museum but also to responsibly participate in the shared goals of education and scholarship within the field.

Claims of Ownership

AAM states that museums should address claims of ownership of objects in their custody "openly, seriously, responsively, and with respect for the dignity of all parties involved" and, that each claim "should be considered on its own merits."[44] Furthermore, both AAM and AAMD affirm that museums should review Nazi-era related claims "promptly and thoroughly."[45]

Although these represent the important and ethical commitments of the field, the professional guidelines regarding ownership claims of objects possibly misappropriated during the Nazi era are somewhat general in nature. Realistically, when faced with such a claim, museums can find themselves in the challenging situation of attempting to respond promptly while simultaneously ensuring their responsibility of due diligence in the matter. More often than not, such claims are complicated, each one with its own unique set of challenges. The process of thoroughly reviewing a claim, while meeting a museum's fiduciary responsibility to its public, can require a significant amount of time, dedicated staff, and resources. Therefore, it is essential for museums to be as prepared as possible to respond to all inquiries and restitution claims.

Overall, the museum's goal should be to build a framework that will help support and facilitate a potential claim process. Although claims can vary greatly through unique circumstances and requirements, there are basic factors for consideration.

Whether incorporating relevant language into an existing collection management policy or creating a separate policy, museums should first consider what their response procedures would be throughout a claim process, including the designation of an internal chain of communication.[46] Included in this chain of communication should be a core group of staff members including, but not limited to, the director; senior deputy or associate level directors, as appropriate; the chief curator; the curator associated with the claimed object; the head of the museum's public relations department; collections manager or registrar; legal counsel; and provenance research staff, if applicable.[47]

The museum should determine a primary museum contact who can best correspond with the claimant or the claimant's representative. It is recommended that staff create and maintain a documented chronology of the claim, recording the claim's history, including such information as the date and content of an initial contact or correspondence; any requests for information; submission or receipt of evidence; summaries of phone calls, other contacts and communications; and summaries of evolving internal questions and opinions.[48] This documentation is an efficient way to keep key staff and trustee members clearly and consistently informed on the evolving status of a claim.

Per AAM, museums ought to conduct their own research during a claim process and should also "request evidence of ownership from the claimant in order to assist in determining the provenance of the object."[49] Depending on what is currently known and documented about the claimed object, all efforts should be made by the museum to pursue further information on the history and provenance of the object.

Although museums must individually determine what level of documentary evidence is necessary to consider restitution of an object, it is recommended that museums ask for receipt of all related information from the claimant, with specific requests for evidence that satisfactorily addresses (i) that the object

was confiscated by the Nazis or was subject to a forced sale, with no subsequent restitution or compensation; (ii) that the claimant or claimants are the sole legal heir(s) to the object, representing the entirety of those who could possibly make a claim on the object; and (iii) documentary evidence, photographic or of an adequate visual description and documentation, that clearly matches and identifies the claimed object with an actual object held in the museum's custody.

If these questions are not fully answered or adequately addressed, it can lead to a difficult situation. Although museums are committed to responding to all claims, they also hold their collections in trust for the public and have a fiduciary duty to not deaccession and restitute objects from their collection without sufficient evidence. For example, museums are not free to restitute an object to a claimant on the basis of ambiguous evidence of ownership, when a subsequent claimant might appear with evidence of ownership, thus making the museum liable to an additional claimant.

It must be noted that the due diligence that a museum must undertake before considering restitution of an object should not be dependent on a question of monetary market value. Because museums hold all of their works in trust for the public, that standard should never be based on monetary value of an object.

If, however, a museum does discover or receive evidence that supports the claim and addresses the major areas of concern, then they must determine what kind of official internal documentation is needed to proceed with a recommendation and resolution. As part of the necessary documentation of the claim process, the museum should ensure that it receives a formal request for restitution or compensation from the claimant or claimant's representative.

Both AAM and AAMD state that if a museum determines that an object in a museum collection was unlawfully appropriated during the Nazi era without subsequent restitution, the museum should seek to resolve the matter with the claimant "in an equitable, appropriate, and mutually agreeable manner."[50] Furthermore, both organizations strongly suggest that museums seek "methods other than litigation" to resolve such claims.[51] In such cases, it is ideal to negotiate any and all terms of restitution outside of litigation. A claim and restitution process are difficult and complex enough for all involved without the added expense and potential stress of litigation. When both museums and claimants are able to cooperate and coordinate all the necessary documentation and terms of an agreement, the entire process can provide an educational opportunity for a museum and its community.

Once a museum has come to a decision to resolve the claim, there are still the remaining considerations of museum procedure and documentation.

When a museum negotiates to keep the object in the collection via an agreed-on compensation to the claimant, there may be mutually agreeable conditions that guarantee the museum will educate the public about the object's provenance through gallery texts and publications. Any legal agreements should be coordinated and executed through a museum's legal counsel.

If a museum and claimant agree that the object should be removed from the collection and restituted, there are actions that must be considered and taken by a museum's governing body (e.g., its board of trustees).

Deaccession and Restitution

As part of its collection management policy, a museum should have clear deaccessioning procedures in place. These policies typically include a museum's specified criteria for consideration of the removal of an object. In preparation for possible restitution, museums may choose to update their policies by adding a criterion that conveys the need to remove works of art that "are subject to restitution or repatriation on the basis of clear evidence proving past illegal appropriations."[52]

In the case of proposed restitution, a deaccessioning recommendation should be submitted to the museum's governing board to take such an action. Ideally, the recommendation would include a summary of the claim and clearly convey the intent of restitution.

If a museum does not have a clear deaccessioning policy, museum staff may want to consider creating a special recommendation or resolution in consulta-

tion with the museum's legal counsel. This special recommendation, to be submitted to the museums' governing board for action, should summarize the claim and clearly outline the reasons for deaccession and restitution.

If a museum's governing body votes to deaccession and restitute an object, plans must be made for the transfer of ownership of the object. The museum should work with its legal counsel and the claimant or claimant's representative to prepare a satisfactory legal transfer agreement. If there are potential issues or expenses involved regarding the physical return of the object, such as packing, shipping, and insurance, those terms should be negotiated and clearly documented either prior to the transfer, or be included in the transfer of ownership agreement.

Although ownership claims for objects possibly misappropriated during the Nazi era can vary greatly in their historical context, evidence, and outcome, it is certain that throughout any claim process, the museum must follow a clear, consistent, and thorough documentation process to ensure due diligence and to meet its fiduciary responsibilities.

CONCLUSION

Within the last few decades, the museum field has experienced a paradigm shift with the increased focus on the provenance of objects acquired by museums, as well as an ever-expanding scrutiny of objects held in museum collections. As a result, there is an increased need for staff with expertise in provenance research and with extensive knowledge of current cultural property issues and laws. Museums continue to hold these collections in the public trust and remain committed to their responsible stewardship. Museums stand committed to following the highest ethical standards and professional guidelines set by the greater museum community. Therefore, they must remain vigilant in the provenance research of their collections and ensure that there are proper staff and resources for this important work.

The history of the ownership and location of an object remains a fascinating and vital aspect of art history, regardless of any potential legal claim. With the recently established field of provenance research, it is hoped that provenance information will become more visible not only through museum websites but also in the stories told in museum galleries, enriching the understanding and interpretation of museum collections. •

SUGGESTED RESOURCES FOR PROVENANCE RESEARCH IN MUSEUM COLLECTIONS

Bradsher, G. (compiler). 1999. *Holocaust-Era Assets: A Finding Aid to Records at the National Archives at College Park, Maryland.* Washington, DC: National Archives and Records Administration.

Edsel, R. M. 2006. *Rescuing Da Vinci: Hitler and the Nazis Stole Europe's Great Art: America and Her Allies Recovered It.* Dallas: Laurel Publishing.

Edsel, R. M. 2009. "Foreword." In *Beyond the Dreams of Avarice: The Hermann Goering Collection* by N. H. Yeide. Dallas: Laurel Publishing, LLC.

Edsel, R., and B. Witter. 2009. *The Monuments Men: Allied Heroes, Nazi Thieves, and the Greatest Treasure Hunt in History.* New York: Center Street.

Feliciano, H. 1997. *The Lost Museum: The Nazi Conspiracy to Steal the World's Greatest Works of Art.* New York: Harper Collins Publishers, Inc.

Howe, T. C. 1946. *Salt Mines and Castles: The Discovery and Restitution of Looted European Art.* New York: The Bobbs-Merrill Company.

Kurtz, M. H. 1985. *Nazi Contraband: American Policy on the Return of European Cultural Treasures, 1945–1955.* New York: Garland.

Lillie, S. 2003. *Was Einmal War: Handbuch der einteigneten Kunstsammlungen Wiens.* Vienna: Czernin, Vienna.

Nicholas, L.H. 1995. *The Rape of Europa: The Fate of Europe's Treasures in the Third Reich and the Second World War.* New York: Vintage Books.

Petropoulos, J. 1996. *Art as Politics in the Third Reich.* Chapel Hill: University of North Carolina Press.

Petropoulos, J. 2000. *The Faustian Bargain: The Art World in Nazi Germany.* Oxford: Oxford University Press.

Simpson, E. (ed.). 1997. *The Spoils of War: World War II and Its Aftermath. The Loss, Reappearance, and Recovery of Cultural Property.* New York: Harry N. Abrams, Inc.

Wechsler, H. J., T. Coate-Saal, and J. Lukavic (compilers). 2001. *Museum Policy and Procedures for Nazi-Era Issues.* Washington, DC: American Association of Museums.

Yeide, N. H., K. Akinsha, and A. L. Walsh. 2001. *The AAM Guide to Provenance Research.* Washington, DC: American Association of Museums.

Yeide, N. H. 2005. "Introduction." In *Vitalizing Memory: International Perspectives on Provenance Research*, pp. 9–10. Washington, DC: American Association of Museums.

Websites

Art Loss Register. Available at: www.artloss.com.

Art Recovery International. Available at: https://www.art recovery.com/.

American Alliance of Museums. Available at: https://www.aam -us.org/.

Association of Art Museum Directors. Available at: https:// aamd.org/.

Central Registry of Information on Looted Cultural Property. Available at: http://www.lootedart.com/.

Federal Bureau of Investigation National Stolen Art File. Available at: www.fbi.gov/hq/cid/arttheft/arttheft.htm

Fold3.com (World War II/Holocaust Collection). Available at: https://www.fold3.com/browse/115/

The Frick Art Reference Library. Available at: http://www.frick .org/library/index.htm

Getty Research Institute Provenance Index Databases. Available at: www.getty.edu/research/tools/provenance/

Holocaust-Era Assets: Records & Research at the National Archives & Records Administration. Available at: http://www .archives.gov/research/holocaust/

ICOM: International Council of Museums. Available at: https://icom.museum/en/

International Foundation for Art Research. Available at: http:// www.ifar.org/

The Lawyers' Committee for Cultural Heritage Preservation. Available at: http://www.culturalheritagelaw.org/

Memorial de la Shoah, Musee Centre de Documentation Juive Contemporaine. Available at: http://www.memorial-cdjc.org

Monuments Men Foundation. Available at: https://www.mon umentsmenfoundation.org/

Musées Nationaux Recupération. Available at: http://www .culture.gouv.fr/documentation/mnr/pres.htm

PREP: The German/American Provenance Research Exchange Program (PREP) for Museum Professionals, *Deutsch-Amerikanisches Austauschprogramm zur Provenienzforschung für Museen* 2017–2019. Available at: https://www.si.edu/events/prep.

Presidential Advisory Commission on Holocaust Assets in the US. Available at: http://govinfo.library.unt.edu/pcha/.

Smithsonian Provenance in the World War II Era. Available at: http://provenance.si.edu/jsp/index.aspx.

UNESCO Convention on the Means of Prohibiting and Preventing the Illicit Import, Export and Transfer of Ownership of Cultural Property 1970. Available at: http:// portal.unesco.org/en/ev.php-URL_ID=13039&URL_ DO=DO_TOPIC&URL_SECTION=201.html.

US Holocaust Memorial Museum. Available at: https://www .ushmm.org/.

US National Gallery of Art: Resources Relating to World War II. Available at: https://www.nga.gov/research/gallery-archives/ world-war-ii-resources.html.

US Department of State. Available at: https://eca.state.gov/cultural-heritage-center/cultural-property-advisory-committee.

World Jewish Congress. Available at: http://www.worldjewish congress.org/en.

NOTES

1. The term *provenience* also denotes *origin* and is most often used in an archaeological context. According to the 2019 Archaeological Institute of America glossary, *provenience* refers to "the three-dimensional context (including geographical location) of an archaeological find, giving information about its function and date." See https://www.archaeological.org/programs/educators/introduction-to-archaeology/glossary/#p.

2. After the fall of the Berlin Wall in 1989 and the dissolution of the Soviet Union in 1991, historians began to obtain access to formerly closed archives in Eastern Europe and in the former Soviet Union. This access allowed for a new awareness of the extent of looting during the World War II era, thereby raising the issue of art and assets misappropriated by the Nazis. The declassification of archival documents in the United States further contributed to the increased scholarship on this topic. In addition to concerns regarding possible Nazi loot, there are ongoing concerns about art and archaeological objects that might have been looted and illegally removed from countries of origin since the 1970 United Nations Educational, Scientific and Cultural Organization (UNESCO) Convention on the Means of Prohibiting and Preventing the Illicit Import, Export and Transfer of Ownership of Cultural Property. See http://portal.unesco.org/en/ev.php-URL_ID=13039&URL_DO=DO_TOPIC&URL_SECTION=201.html.

3. The National Socialist German Worker's (Nazi) Party was founded in 1919 and was headed by Adolf Hitler beginning in 1921. The *Nazi era* refers to the time period of 1933–1945 when the Nazi Party was in power in Germany. This time period is sometimes referred to as the *World War II era* or the *Holocaust era*.

4. In 1998, the Washington Conference on Holocaust-Era Assets set forth international standards to address the issue of museum objects with unknown Nazi-era provenance. These standards, known as the Washington Principles on Nazi-Confiscated Art, were adopted by conference representatives from forty-four governments; see https://www.state.gov/washington-conference-principles-on-nazi-confiscated-art/. These ideas were reaffirmed and strengthened through the 2009 Terezin Declaration on Holocaust Era Assets and Related Issues; see https://2009-2017.state.gov/p/eur/rls/or/126162.htm.

5. Such recent efforts include the international German/American Provenance Research Exchange Program (PREP) organized by the Smithsonian Institution and the Stiftung Preußicher Kulturbesitz (Berlin). The goal of the 2017–2019 program is to create a network of specialists from German and US art museums to improve research methods and practices pertaining to World War II–era provenance research and to publish an online guide to World War II–era provenance research resources in Germany and the United States. See https://www.si.edu/events/prep.

6. Although US museums are not overseen by a governmental regulatory agency, they must comply with all applicable laws.

7. For official guidelines and procedures regarding museums and Nazi-era provenance issues, see the American Alliance of Museum's website (https://www.aam-us.org/programs/ethics-standards-and-professional-practices/unlawful-appropriation-of-objects-during-the-nazi-era/) and the Association of Art Museum Director's website (https://aamd.org/standards-and-practices).

8. For guidelines and standards regarding museums and the provenance of archaeological materials and ancient art, see the American Alliance of Museum's website (https://www.aam-us.org/programs/ethics-standards-and-professional-practices/archaeological-material-and-ancient-art/) and the Association of Art Museum Director's website (https://aamd.org/standards-and-practices).

9. See the list of "Suggested Resources for Provenance Research in Museum Collections" at the end of this chapter for publications and websites related to this topic and time period.

10. See H. J. Wechsler, T. Coate-Saal, and J. Lukavic, comp., *Museum Policy and Procedures for Nazi-Era Issues* (Washington, DC: American Association of Museums, 2001), 93, Appendix C. The principles can also be found online at https://www.state.gov/washington-conference-principles-on-nazi-confiscated-art/.

11. See "AAM Recommended Procedures for Providing Information to the Public about Objects Transferred in Europe during the Nazi Era." Available at: https://www.aam-us.org/wp-content/uploads/2018/01/nepip-recommended-procedures.pdf.

12. Available at: nepip.org.

13. See https://aamd.org/object-registry/resolution-of-claims-for-nazi-era-cultural-assets/browse.

14. There are multiple digitized resources listed on websites such as the National Archives (http://www.archives.gov/research/holocaust/), Getty Research Institute Provenance Index Databases (www.getty.edu/research/tools/provenance/), and Fold3.com's World War II: Holocaust Collection (https://www.fold3.com/browse/115/).

15. N. H. Yeide, K. Akinsha, and A. L. Walsh, *The AAM Guide to Provenance Research* (Washington, DC: American Association of Museums, 2001).

16. Wechsler et al., *Museum Policy and Procedures*.

17. Yeide et al., *The AAM Guide to Provenance Research*, 33–34.

18. Yeide et al., *The AAM Guide to Provenance Research*, 33. Within the field, there is a lot of discussion on how to best standardize and access provenance data. There is ongoing research on ways to link provenance data among institutions. For example, see "Art Tracks Digital Provenance Project." Available at: https://cmoa.org/art/art-tracks-digital-provenance-project/.

19. These observations are based on the author's experiences and research at a museum with an encyclopedic art collection.

20. See "AAM Recommended Procedures for Providing Information to the Public about Objects Transferred in Europe during the Nazi Era."

21. Per AAM, *Judaica* is broadly defined as the material culture of the Jewish people, including ceremonial objects for communal or domestic use. Judaica comprises historical artifacts relating to important Jewish personalities, momentous events, and significant communal activities, as well as literature relating to Jews and Judaism. See "AAM Recommended Procedures for Providing Information to the Public about Objects Transferred in Europe during the Nazi Era."

22. Per AAM, museums should incorporate Nazi-era provenance research into their standard research on collections and into funding proposals for museum projects, if applicable. Depending on their particular circumstances, museums are also encouraged to pursue special funding to undertake Nazi-era provenance research.

23. See Yeide et al., *The AAM Guide to Provenance Research*, 49–51.

24. Yeide et al., *The AAM Guide to Provenance Research*, 55–56, 259–296 (ALIU lists included in indices).

25. Yeide et al., *The AAM Guide to Provenance Research*, 51, 55–68.

26. Yeide et al., *The AAM Guide to Provenance Research*, 41–44.

27. Available at: nepip.org/

28. See "AAM Guidelines Concerning the Unlawful Appropriation of Objects during the Nazi Era." Available at: https://www.aam-us.org/programs/ethics-standards-and-professional-practices/unlawful-appropriation-of-objects-during-the-nazi-era/.

29. See "AAM Standards Regarding Archaeological Material and Ancient Art." Available at: https://www.aam-us.org/programs/ethics-standards-and-professional-practices/archaeological-material-and-ancient-art/. See also "Suggested Resources for Provenance Research in Museum Collections" at the end of this chapter, which lists resources related to these issues.

30. See "AAM Guidelines Concerning the Unlawful Appropriation of Objects during the Nazi Era."

31. See Wechsler et al., *Museum Policy and Procedures*, 1–27.

32. See "2013 Guidelines on the Acquisition of Archaeological Material and Ancient Art." Available at: https://aamd.org/standards-and-practices.

33. "2013 Guidelines on the Acquisition of Archaeological Material and Ancient Art," 1–11 (examples of warranties).

34. See "Report of the Association of Art Museum Directors (AAMD) Task Force on the Spoliation of Art during the Nazi/World War II Era (1933–1945), Washington, DC, June 1998." Available at: https://aamd.org/standards-and-practices.

35. See http://www.artloss.com/ and https://www.artrecovery.com/ for more information.

36. See "AAM Guidelines Concerning the Unlawful Appropriation of Objects during the Nazi Era."

37. "AAM Guidelines Concerning the Unlawful Appropriation of Objects during the Nazi Era."

38. See https://aamd.org/object-registry/new-acquisitions-of-archaeological-material-and-works-of-ancient-art/browse.

39. See "AAM Guidelines Concerning the Unlawful Appropriation of Objects during the Nazi Era."

40. See "AAMD Standards and Practices." Available at: https://aamd.org/standards-and-practices.

41. See "AAM Guidelines Concerning the Unlawful Appropriation of Objects during the Nazi Era."

42. See Wechsler et al., *Museum Policy and Procedures*, 29–40.

43. See US Department of State, "Immunity from Judicial Seizure-Cultural Objects." Available at: https://www.state.gov/immunity-from-judicial-seizure-statute-22-u-s-c-2459/.

44. See "AAM Guidelines Concerning the Unlawful Appropriation of Objects during the Nazi Era." Note that in 2016, the Holocaust Expropriated Art Recovery Act became US law to assist claimants by removing some of the legal technicalities and obstacles often found within a claim process. See https://www.congress.gov/bill/114th-congress/house-bill/6130.

45. "AAM Guidelines Concerning the Unlawful Appropriation of Objects during the Nazi Era." See also "Report of the Association of Art Museum Directors (AAMD) Task Force on the Spoliation of Art during the Nazi/World War II Era (1933–1945), Washington, DC, June 1998." Available at: https://aamd.org/standards-and-practices.

46. See Wechsler et al., *Museum Policy and Procedures*, 65–85. See examples from museums of related procedures.

47. Museums may also include a member of their governing board in this group or designate someone to keep the board informed through the claim process.

48. This suggestion is based on shared accounts from some US museums that have experienced Nazi-era restitution claims within the last twenty years. It is informally suggested as a tool that could be adapted, updated, and changed as to the needs of a particular institution.

49. See "AAM Guidelines Concerning the Unlawful Appropriation of Objects during the Nazi Era."

50. See "AAM Guidelines Concerning the Unlawful Appropriation of Objects during the Nazi Era" and "Report of the Association of Art Museum Directors (AAMD) Task Force on the Spoliation of Art during the Nazi/World War II Era (1933–1945), Washington, DC, June 1998."

51. "AAM Guidelines Concerning the Unlawful Appropriation of Objects during the Nazi Era" and "Report of the Association of Art Museum Directors (AAMD) Task Force on the Spoliation of Art during the Nazi/World War II Era (1933–1945), Washington, DC, June 1998."

52. This language is taken from the Virginia Museum of Fine Arts (VMFA) Deaccessioning Policy, which is part of the VMFA Collections Management Policy, 2017.

3E | DOCUMENTING CONTEMPORARY ART

MARK B. SCHLEMMER

CONSERVING, DOCUMENTING, and defining the parameters of contemporary art are major issues for registrars and collection managers. It is a reality that has emerged from necessity. The issues are not new, but the volume of material that requires a nontraditional approach has increased greatly in recent years. The materials that artists choose when creating work obviously have no limits. In addition to traditional media such as wood, paint, stone, paper, and canvas, artists increasingly use ephemeral materials, detritus, and digital content to meet their creative needs. A painting or drawing may be partially defined by its two-dimensionality, but with much of contemporary art—installation art in particular—nailing down such defining parameters has become all but impossible. That is not to say that attempts to identify or give meaning to such issues were ignored or not important in the past, but rather that situations were dealt with ad hoc as they emerged. Frequently, museum professionals are forced to install, and perhaps more significantly, reinstall, contemporary work without sufficient guidelines. *The key to dealing with newly created art is in its documentation.*

Traditionally, the documentation of artwork has focused on materiality and issues of authenticity. Materials are undeniably important to the way we understand art. A working knowledge of, and familiarity with, various media will allow a registrar or collection manager to forecast storage needs, foster collections care, and recommend exhibition guidelines. In other words, the materials indeed may be important, but the conceptual core remains the essence of the work. The new challenge is how to effectively document a conceptual idea.

To document contemporary art, strategies that incorporate broader definitions of how to document, in addition to a new perspective on recording the perception of the work itself, will aid in creating the object files at the core of all museum collections.

ARTIST QUESTIONNAIRES AND INTERVIEWS

Often, the best source of information regarding how artwork is defined comes directly from the artists. It is vital for any museum that is acquiring, or thinking of acquiring, art by a living artist to devise a documentation strategy to record the artist's intent. Not only is this an ethical mandate in relation to the museum's mission to safeguard acquired artwork for perpetuity, but it is increasingly a response to protect the museum from potential litigious situations involving copyright and other artists' rights. Questionnaires and interviews are a good starting point to reach this end.

The main purpose behind documenting artists' intent via interviews and questionnaires is to record their views regarding potential changes to the parameters of subsequent installations. The interview will provide more complete results, but the questionnaire seems to be more widely used. Written questionnaires, which tend to focus mostly on factual information, such as the brand of play-back equipment (for work that incorporates video), dates of production, materials used, and so on are indeed useful to the museum. However, even art museums that advocate for the persistent use of questionnaires admit that they are not enough. Not every hypothetical situation requiring a resolution can be imagined at the time of acquisition.

Fortunately, questionnaires need not be created from scratch. *Matters in Media Art*, a research project focused on the care of time-based media art, has created resources and templates that anyone can freely adapt and use. The sample questions are straightforward and of vital importance, for example, "What are the essential vs. desirable exhibition conditions, including space requirements?" and "What can and cannot be changed in the display?"[1] These and other questions are directed at the artist to help the museum in assessing the impact the work will have if it becomes a part of the permanent collection. A deeper investigation into artists' thoughts regarding their work is often best elaborated via direct interviews.

As a response to museum professionals who were seeking guidance on formulating questionnaires, the International Network for the Conservation of Contemporary Art (INCCA) established an effective general resource guide for conducting artists' interviews for the purpose of garnering insight into their oeuvre. With a view to collecting and effectively exhibiting art in keeping with the artists' intent, the guide proposes seven approaches or methodologies to conducting artist interviews: communication via letter, questionnaire, telephone call, face-to-face conversation, brief or limited interview, extended interview, and working together with the artist.[2]

The most basic communication with the artist begins with a letter or e-mail, composed with explicit and concise questions in mind. The goal is not only to acquire insight but also to create a document for the object file. Unfortunately, the museum cannot always rely on receiving a timely or appropriate response to a letter or e-mail, and the same holds true for a more elaborate questionnaire. Letters and questionnaires demand a lot of the artist's time, and motivation to complete them may not be a top priority. As with a letter, a questionnaire cannot be depended on to elicit the breadth and complexity needed to document an artwork. Certain queries are too unwieldly to answer succinctly in a written format.

To address the relationship among the various components that comprise a total work usually requires being physically in the space with the installed work. This is especially true for work that has a highly interactive quality, is composed of complicated arrangements, or employs the accumulation of many parts of seemingly random detritus. To address such issues, oral communication is usually a better alternative.

Telephone calls are often effective in clarifying precise details or in obtaining answers to specific concerns and permit a more fluid conversation which may lead to direct questions not previously anticipated. As with any type of communication, the person initiating the call will be at the mercy of artists, and certain questions may be construed as an interruption to their work or an invasion of privacy. Additionally, not everyone communicates effectively via telephone. Face-to-face conversations may be the better all-around strategy.

The best face-to-face conversations take place in the physical presence of the artwork itself. As in all cases, extensive preparation on the part of the interviewer will provide the best results. Careful consideration should be made regarding the duration of the conversation and to judiciously controlling the direction of the dialog. These interviews can be either brief undertakings or extended investigations.

Whether a face-to-face conversation or a telephone call, it is often beneficial to prepare the artist with the content of the interview ahead of time. For brief or limited interviews, documentation techniques should be determined in advance and confirmed with the artist. Audio, video, and notes are all viable recording options, but video provides more content on which to base future conclusions.

An extended interview allows one not only to probe more deeply into particular works, techniques, or intents, but also permits far-reaching exploration of larger themes and connections in the artist's oeuvre. The questions for an extended interview are usually more open-ended and can provide deeper layers of content. The extended interview shows a commitment on the part of artists to documenting effectively as much about their thoughts and expectations as possible, providing a useful level of information.

Finally, observing artists' working sessions, or better yet, an installation of their work in which they are participating, may provide information that goes far beyond responses to questions. A certain level of trust and comfort must exist for an artist to agree to such a session. The interviewer must be able to read the situation well and know how far to take the conversation. As with all interviews, the key is in the preparation.

It is recommended that notes and annotations of the interviews always be presented to the artist for approval afterward. The end result of the interviews and questionnaires is a record that provides that museum with vital information to turn to in the future.

The timing of these interviews and of the documentation in general is important. The more time that has passed from the creation of the work to the documentation of it, the more removed the artist will be from it. Additionally, after the works are created, they take their place in art history while the artists continue to develop and advance their personal progression. Delayed documentation of a work may leave an artist too far removed from what was important and influential at the time of creation.

INCCA encourages multiple interview sessions and multiple voices in conducting the interview (curator, conservator, technician, art historian, art handler, registrar, etc.). Of course, there will be limits on the extent of these interviews depending on budget, time, and available personnel, all factors that have in the past been used as arguments or justification for not conducting interviews in the first place. It is worth emphasizing that the artist's opinion is only one to be taken into consideration. The museum has a voice, and a strong one, in making decisions as to the future of its collections. Conservators have another voice, sometimes in concert with the artist, sometimes with the museum. In the end, a collaborative agreement among all parties is the ultimate goal.

DOCUMENTING INSTALLATION ART

In recent years, more installation art has found its place among the permanent collections of art museums. The complex environments of installation art have proven to be popular with artists who seek to branch out into a fourth dimension (interactivity) with their artistic creations. However, the inherently complex nature of installation art, in particular those works that comprise elements of new or time-based media, require a new approach to museum procedures, especially the need to draw on a wide body of experts from both within and outside the museum community. Conservators, curators, registrars, collection managers, technicians, artists'

assistants, architects, and the artists themselves may be called on to help create a precisely documented account of the installation for the museum's object file. Once again budget, time, and personnel will have an impact on the extent of the documentation, but almost any institution can undertake video documentation of the installation.

The benefits of video documentation of installation art include capturing the "overall impression, visual aspects of components, relation of components, relation to space/architecture, sound, movement, choreography, time-specific aspects, interactivity and presence (and experience) of the audience."[3] All of these aspects would be extremely unruly, or even impossible, to document in written form. Just as proponents of artist questionnaires conceded the benefit of video recording, the same is seen in reverse. Video does not render written documentation obsolete, but rather augments it in ways that make a more nearly complete package. Video documentation fills in the gaps of information essential to understanding what cannot be written down.

The key to video documentation for the purpose of facilitating the reinstallation of the work is exactitude. Describing the relationship and position of individual components to each other and to the complete installation is the core of why video documentation should be used. For this information to be useful for reinstallation, this visual record must be paired with an explanation from the artist as to the importance of these relationships and the extent of their variability. Without this key idea, reinstallations could exaggerate details and relationships that are not as tightly defined in the mind of the artist.

In addition to documenting relationships, it is essential to record processes. One video documentation strategy that can capture the installation process is the use of static surveillance cameras. Long-exposure recordings, not helpful in their original form, are viewed in a sped-up or fast-forward manner to provide a record of the specific installation process that will benefit those undertaking the same in the future. However, this type of documentation lacks an essential level of detail and should only be used in a general way to steer future installations.

A complete video documentation package for the purpose of guiding reinstallation (as opposed to a publicity video, etc.) should include a general installation (static) overview, zoom views of details, recordings of sounds, and voice-overs indicating elements that may not be clear from a merely visual standpoint.[4]

Even though video documentation is the best way to guarantee a successful and accurate iteration of future installations, the issues of cost and time loom above every project. The budget will dictate to what degree video documentation takes place, and the cost to do so should be included in pre-acquisition considerations by museum acquisition committees. Videos can be prepared by staff members, contracted out to semiprofessionals, or, in the best-of-all-worlds, completed by video specialists. The latter will be able to provide the best postproduction options.

Augmented with research, the results of artist questionnaires, and other written documentation, the complexities of documenting installation art are more effectively tackled by using video for registration purposes.

FURTHER STRATEGIES FOR DOCUMENTING NEW MEDIA ART

One of the key concepts to adopt in documenting new art is the need to approach it in ways that embrace what is at the core of the work independently from how we document the media. Minimal, conceptual, and much of new media art are often not reliant on any physical object. Still, the work must be documented in a way that renders such complex realities in a usable format. *Preserving the Immaterial*, a conference at the Solomon R. Guggenheim Museum in New York in March 2001, addressed these issues head on. One of the results was the creation of *The Variable Media Approach*,[5] a strategy that remains relevant for capturing essential and core concepts in our documentation of art. At the center of this approach is a way of identifying the essence of the conceptual basis of the work.

As proposed by almost everyone involved in any aspect of documenting contemporary art, the approach to variable media is based on formulating a questionnaire and dialog with the artist to serve as a springboard for identifying non-media-specific concepts. The *Variable Media Questionnaire* is broken down into seven subtopics, each addressing a particular behavior. These ideal states are:

- *Installed*—implying that the work has more complex exhibition requirements than mounting on a wall or placing on a pedestal, issues of site-specific placement, scale, access and lighting are addressed.
- *Performed*—emphasizing that the process is integral to the end product or object created; the artist therefore provides instructions for the performers, installers, etc., in addition to specifications of sets, props, etc.
- *Interactive*—referencing not only computer-based work, but any installation in which the visitor is essential to the work through their active participation with it; this method documents how and to what extent external participation is carried out, and whether this interaction is recorded.
- *Reproduced*—documenting any medium, such as film, audio, or video in which the result of producing a copy from an original master results in a loss of quality.
- *Duplicated*—explaining that a work does not lose quality when copied from the original; most works of digital media and ready-made, mass-produced objects typically are considered as duplicated.
- *Encoded*—implying that the essence of the work is created with a computer code or special language; depending on the nature of the code, it may be possible to archive the transcript or notation separately and independently from the work.
- *Networked*—designating that the work is experienced via the internet or some other electronic system; websites, e-mail, surveillance, and so on are all networked behaviors.[6]

Identifying work in terms of behaviors references it in its ideal state. However, any changes or alterations over time, whether happening naturally or as a result of conservation interventions, produce a shift away from this ideal. The documentation of the artist's philosophy over these questions will aid the museum in making decisions about dealing with these eventual changes.

CONCLUSION

Proper documentation does, indeed, take many hours of staff time to produce correctly. Museum environments are undeniably hectic and there is always high demand on making the best use of limited staff. However, when it comes to documenting much of contemporary art, making the effort will save both time and money for the museum in the long term. Reinstallations have the potential to create an overwhelming array of problems. If registrars and collection managers can anticipate, even to a slight extent, future installation requirements, they will alleviate the burden of tedious and time-consuming tasks required to answer questions of appropriate, ethical, and realistic reinstallations. This positive outcome will become widespread only when museum administrators make proper documentation a routine undertaking.

As you search for concrete examples and further guidance on what has been successfully undertaken by others in the realm of documenting contemporary art, an additional recommended resource is the nonprofit organization Voices in Contemporary Art (VoCA). On their website[7] you can find their active blog, links to various resources, past issues of their journal, and information about upcoming workshops and talks. It is reassuring to connect with others who are dedicated to advancing the work challenges of the contemporary registrar.

In conclusion, the multivalent and complicated challenge of properly documenting the conceptual and technical variance for the reinstallation of contemporary art can be summed up by five key ideas:

1. There is no need to reinvent the wheel! Various resources already exist online that any museum can exploit to assist in preparing condition reports, installation guides, questionnaires, and so on with an emphasis on the specific needs and idiosyncrasies of contemporary art.

2. It is important to document the artist's intent. Again, by turning to existing guides for advice, registrars and collection managers can effectively formulate questions that elicit the most beneficial information for the future installations of the work.

3. Proper documentation necessitates calling on the expertise of others. Curators, registrars, collection managers, and conservators are logical allies within the museum community, but architects, technicians, preparators, and artists' assistants may all help provide essential details.

4. New media are at the same time new and familiar. To document time-based media, one must think in terms beyond aesthetics or materiality. By learning to reference the behaviors of a work, one can reach the essence of digital content.

5. Documentation involves more than creating a written record. Photography—and more importantly, video—will serve the documentation process well and permit a visual and aural record of the complicated relationships of installation components and of abstract concepts such as interactivity. Online sources can teach museum professionals the ins and outs of effectively documenting an installation with video.

Every new work of art is its own unique world; thus, it may be impossible to approach any kind of preferred practice for its documentation. Nevertheless, guidelines and suggestions from those who have studied and researched new media, conceptual, minimal, and installation art can provide insights and encouragement to aid in formulating effective strategies to assess the documentary requirements for each individual work (TABLE 3E.1). In the end, not only will the museum professionals charged with the stewardship of collections be permitted to address the specific requirements of contemporary art ethically and responsibly, they will also be providing their future colleagues with the tools they will need, and will appreciate, when called on to oversee subsequent installations. •

Table 3E.1 Documentation Tools, Guides, and Resources

"Matters in Media Art," the consortium of The New Art Trust, Museum of Modern Art (MoMA), San Francisco Museum of Modern Art (SFMoMA), and the Tate, which focuses on the stewardship of time-based works of art, has developed a range of documentation tools applicable to new media installation art. Free downloadable templates for condition reports, installation documentation guides, and other useful reference documents and practical tools are all available on their website. Available at: http://mattersinmediaart.org/

"Electronic Arts Intermix" has an excellent resource guide providing information on the exhibition, collection, and preservation of new media art. In addition, to help with dealing with installation art, the guide is also a source for single-channel video and computer-based arts. Available at: http://resourceguide.eai.org/

"Inside Installations" is an exceptional resource created as a result of a three-year study of installation art in the European Union. Though the entire project provides myriad guidelines, resources and practical tools, of particular interest is this online tutorial that teaches the museum professional the skills necessary to video document installation art. Available at: https://www.incca.org/articles/inside-installations-online-course-video-documentation-installations-2007

"The Variable Media Network," a preservation strategy developed by the Guggenheim and the Daniel Langlois Foundation, looks at ephemeral art in terms of "medium-dependent behaviors." This concept is explicitly detailed online and in the free downloadable guide, "Permanence Through Change: The Variable Media Approach." Available at: http://variablemedia.net/

The "International Network for the Conservation of Contemporary Art (INCCA)" has a detailed "Guide to Good Practice: Artists' Interviews" available on their website (articles>incca guide to good practices artists interviews). Phone interviews, letters, questionnaires, and face-to-face interview techniques are explained. Available at: http://www.incca.org/

"Voices in Contemporary Art (VoCA)" is a network of artists, conservators, curators, collectors, educators, and students who recognize the need for public forums on new forms of collaboration and documentation. Through workshops, talks, and a journal, VoCA stimulates critical discussion on the roles and working practices of all professionals involved in the production, presentation, and preservation of contemporary art. Available at: http://www.voca.network/

NOTES
1. Matters in Media Art. Available at: http://www.tate.org.uk/research/tateresearch/majorprojects/mediamatters/ (accessed March 25, 2019).

2. International Network for the Conservation of Contemporary Art, "Guide to Good Practice: Artists' Interviews, Updated Version January 2016." Available at: http://www.incca.org (accessed March 25, 2019).

3. Gaby Wijers, "Video Documentation of Installations," *Inside Installations*. Available at: http://insideinstallations.org (accessed March 10, 2008).

4. Wijers, "Video Documentation of Installations."

5. The Variable Media Approach. Available at: http://www.variablemedia.net/pdf/Permanence.pdf.

6. A. Depocas, J. Ippolito, and C. Jones, eds., *The Variable Media Approach* (New York: Guggenheim Museum Publications, 2003), 46.

7. Voices in Contemporary Art. Available at: www.voca.network.

3F | LIVING AND NATURAL HISTORY COLLECTIONS REGISTRATION

LAURA A. MORSE

THE DEVELOPMENT OF living and natural history collections begins with the institutional mission, which defines the breadth and focus of the collection, and a collection plan to guide staff activities. The collection plan sets short- and long-term collecting goals that follow ethical guidelines, takes into account the natural and social environment of the specimens, considers sustainability factors, and compliance with legal requirements (local, regional, national, and international).

Most collecting staff in living and natural history collections wear many hats, with their duties broadly defined, and with sometimes surprising undefined tasks. For living collections and natural history collections the surprising tasks add spice but also mean that we go to work most days knowing only what our basic daily routine will be.

Collection basics covered herein are deliberately discussed at a high altitude, with some unique and special collection considerations pointed out. The basics discussed in this chapter are:

1. Acquisition and accession
2. Deaccession and disposition (disposal)
3. Loans
4. Records and documentation
5. Accountability, control, and access
6. Care
7. Occupational safety
8. Wildlife laws

ACQUISITION AND ACCESSION

Acquisition

Proposed acquisitions are reviewed in the context of the collection plan for appropriateness, suitability, rationale for acquiring, and current resource availability (staff, housing or enclosure, specimen welfare, preservation, growth requirements, reproduction and propagation needs, and funding).

There are several different methods of acquiring specimens, but all methods follow the institutional collection policies and comply with applicable laws and regulations (e.g., source country, international, and domestic), and professional standards for the type of collection. Researching provenance, vetting the provider, requesting proof of legal custody of the specimen, and copies of any required permits are basic best practices. Typical acquisition methods include donation, trade or exchange, propagation (birth, hatching, or propagules), field collecting, wild caught, purchase, and loans (for propagation).

Commonly used registration terms may have different meanings, depending on the discipline and institutions. In this chapter there is a distinction between *field collected* and *wild caught* acquisitions. *Field collected* is used for preserved specimens; *wild caught* refers to a live animal specimen that is removed from the wild and held in captivity.

The most difficult part of acquisition can be the physical transportation of the specimens because they often require specialized crating, packaging, environmental conditions, and means of transport. Not surprisingly, the majority of field collecting and wild capture occurs in remote locations, often far from roads, and specimens must be hand-carried or brought out by other means.

Living Specimen Considerations

Quite often animals and plants are acquired not only for display or study purposes but also for species propagation. Propagation obligations include responsible breeding to maintain genetic diversity and mitigation of disease development and transmission. Many zoos participate in species population management programs that help ensure genetic diversity and prevent deleterious in-breeding issues. Botanical gardens may participate in clean plant programs to ensure development of healthy planting stocks.

For living collections the priority goal is specimen welfare. The living specimen must arrive at its final destination alive and in good health, suffering as little stress as possible. A variety of factors must be considered when collecting and transporting specimens, and each species may have its own unique needs. The following are typical welfare factors (but there may be others as well). In addition, there are animal welfare laws and regulations that must be followed. In the United States, the Department of Agriculture (USDA), the Fish and Wildlife Service (USFWS), and the Centers for Disease Control and Prevention (CDC) set the regulations for animal and plant transportation. Airlines worldwide follow live animal transport regulations set by the International Air Transportation Association (IATA). Transport factors include:

- Types of transport and how many are needed (e.g., by hand, sea, truck, air, or a combination)
- Number of stops during transport
- Total length of time the specimen is in a crate or enclosure (not just during transport)
- Ambient temperatures along the entire transport route, including stopovers and within the transport vehicle(s)
- Access for feeding and watering of the specimen
- Measures needed to prevent escape and prevent people from gaining access to the specimen
- Special environmental needs within the crate such as temperature, humidity, airflow, light exposure, substrate, bedding, furniture, and avoidance of sharp projections
- Social structure of the species, age of specimen, and concerns for mothers with infants
- Behavioral patterns or temperament of the specimen
- Physiological and disease issues
- Permitted, required, and best practice crating and packing materials (some materials are regulated)

Natural History Specimen Considerations

Natural history specimens present their own transport challenges and considerations. For example, fro-

zen specimens must remain frozen, and fluid-preserved specimens must remain wet (or at least moist), and all specimens need to reach their destination in good condition. Many of the coolants and preservatives used to ship specimens are classified as dangerous or hazardous substances so their use is regulated both domestically and internationally. Some specimens are considered dangerous or hazardous goods.[1] Within the United States, the Department of Transportation (DOT) regulates the transport of these materials, and airlines worldwide follow the dangerous goods regulations set by IATA. Shipping regulations pertain not only to the materials being moved but also set limits on the amounts that can be used in transport. Additionally, the use of plant-based crating or packing materials may be regulated by federal or local governments. In the United States, the use of plant-based packing materials such as wood wool, straw, and crate wood is regulated by the USDA. Typical transport considerations are listed here, but others may be relevant depending on the specimen. Transport factors include:

- Types of transport and how many are needed (e.g., by hand, sea, truck, air, or a combination)
- Number of stops during transport
- Physical hardiness or fragility of the specimen (ability to withstand vibrations, jostling, bouncing, and tipping)
- Susceptibility of the specimen to environmental changes (temperature, humidity)
- Inherent vice (radioactivity, particulates, preservation chemicals, pigments, etc.)
- Type of preservative or coolant needed
- Permitted, required, and best practice crating and packing materials (some materials are regulated)

Accession

An accession is defined as one or more specimens received from a single source at the same time. For live specimens an accession may be further delimited as a specimen or specimens of a single species from one source received at the same time. Plant accessions have the further distinction of being of identical parentage and received from one source at the same time.[2]

Acquired specimens are generally accessioned when they arrive at the receiving institution but not always. For example, an institution may gain ownership of a specimen while the specimen is in the custody of another facility for a specified period of time, such as in government quarantine or for exhibition. The accession process follows the institution's collection management policy and the professional standards for the type of collection. No matter the institution, all accessions use a numbering system. The numbering system may be numeric or alphanumeric as long as it provides an accession number that is a unique identifier specific to, and permanently associated with, that acquisition.

For zoos, aquariums, and botanical gardens, all live specimens on site, including those not owned by the institution, are accessioned due to legal and ethical requirements.

Animals are frequently transferred to other institutions for breeding purposes. In these cases, the offspring produced will be accessioned twice at birth—once by the custodial or holding institution and again by the owning institution. The two accession numbers are linked in each institution's records. An oddity of live animal collections is that an animal that has been donated to another institution may come back to its former owing institution, either on loan or as a donation. In these cases, the animal is not given a new accession number but is reassigned its old accession number with a new acquisition note made in the animal's records.

A best practice followed by living and natural history collections is the concept of reference voucher specimens. A voucher specimen can be defined as all or part of a particular specimen that is collected, preserved, and maintained for taxonomic nomenclature, taxonomic verification, or morphological representation but can also be used to verify a number of biological, ecological, and evolutionary characteristics about how and where the specimen lived.[3] Live specimens that have their provenance well documented and are not hybrids can also serve as voucher specimens for their species. Typically, a genomic sample is taken from the live specimen and deposited in a long-term biorepository. A voucher note referencing the biorepository information is made in the specimen's record. The biorepository records link back to the original specimen records.

Key to accessioning is the physical association of the accession number with the specimen. Appropriate identification of a specimen through labeling, sturdy tagging, or microchipping is important. Plants require durable tags that can withstand a variety of environmental conditions, some of which can be extreme. Tags, along with on-site location maps, help ensure the appropriate identification of specimens. A new technology increasingly used by botanical gardens is radio frequency identification (RFID) transponder tags on specimens large enough to handle the transponder capsule.[4] Two forms of identification are typically used in zoological park settings. With the advent of microchipping, most animals have a transponder inserted under the skin in positions standardized for their taxon. Leg bands, ear tags, notching, photographs featuring color patterns or scars, enclosure maps or cage cards, and other methods are used to provide a secondary form.

Associating all parts and materials of a specimen with the specimen's accession number is important in all collections. In a natural history collection, a specimen might be broken down into several parts such as a skin or pelt, skeletal material, DNA sample, and other preserved tissues. Similarly, live specimens may have preserved tissues, preserved gametes or pollen, discarded or shed materials, or samples of urine or feces associated with the accession number. Plant specimens may have an associated dried herbarium sheet or preserved DNA sample.

Special Considerations for Live Collections

Live animal numbering systems typically are sequential by arrival date and may encode a means to identify the animals' taxonomic group (e.g., mammalian, avian, herpetological, fish, invertebrate). Although the general goal of live animal collections is to have an accession number for each specimen, there are four types or classes of accessions in common use:

- Individual—specimens that can be individually identified and counted as individuals.
- Group I—specimens of the same species that are not individually identifiable (e.g., they cannot be

differentiated from one another) and are cared for as a whole but can be counted as individuals (e.g., five chinchillas in the same enclosure that all look alike but can be individually counted).[5]

- Group II—specimens of the same species that are not individually identifiable, are cared for as a group, and cannot be counted as individuals (e.g., a school of fairy wrasse fish which all look alike and may be too many to count).[6]
- Colony—specimens that must live and function as an intact unit or entity whose members cannot be counted (e.g., corals, beehives, and ant colonies).[7]

DEACCESSION AND DISPOSITION (DISPOSAL)

Deaccession

Deaccession is considered when a specimen or species no longer helps fulfill the mission of the institution. Criteria for deaccessioning can be a change in mission or scope, questionable provenance of a specimen, a specimen that is damaged beyond repair or usefulness, lack of resources for specimen care, or a specimen that should not have been collected to begin with (some institutions take the whole bag with lumps of coal to gain the one nugget of gold hidden within).

Live Specimen Collections

Live animal collections are the odd-ones-out for accessions and deaccessions. All live animals are accessioned into the collection as an individual, a group, or colony but are not typically deaccessioned as museum specimens are. This approach has to do with several factors important to maintaining accurate, linked animal records within and between institutions for breeding and animal welfare. As mentioned previously, it is not uncommon for a donated or loaned animal to come back to the institution that previously owned it. To ensure continuous records for a specific animal, the returnee is reassigned its old accession number. Another factor is that members of an accessioned group or colony can be removed and transferred to another institution while the bulk of the group or colony remains at the original institution. A final factor is that even when an animal has died, its accession number remains assigned to any retained gametes and tissues. This is particularly im-

portant for gametes because the gametes are equal to the live animal as genetic material and can be used for maintaining genetic diversity in breeding programs. Reproductive science technology now exists for the production of viable offspring from gametes stored for twenty years. Because of these factors, a single accession number can have multiple disposition transactions but not a deaccession transaction. In addition, the animal's record is not flagged as inactive or deaccessioned in the collection information system.

Disposition

As with acquisitions, proposed dispositions (disposals) should be reviewed in the context of the institution's collection plan for appropriateness, rationale, and current resource availability. All methods of disposition should follow institutional collection polices, applicable laws, and ethical considerations. Disposition may be accomplished by several methods, including donation, trade or exchange, sale, loan, or destruction. In addition, for living specimens, there is release or reintroduction into the wild, escape, and death. Some institutions use a within-institution transfer to an educational collection, educational program, or a study collection once a specimen is no longer suitable to remain in the accessioned collection.

Live Specimen Collections

Escape into the wild is unique to live collections. Animals can escape from their enclosures and facility sites, while plants escape outside of their designated growing areas by seed dispersal, runners, and fragment attachment to animals or humans.

As more species become threatened or endangered, zoos, aquariums, and botanical gardens are partnering with other organizations to create species recovery programs and assurance populations. These are species breeding programs set up to maintain genetic diversity and increase population numbers specifically for release or reintroduction into the species' former habitat range. Because of legal and ethical requirements, nonaccredited institutions that might be the receiver of live animals must undergo a facility review to ensure the receiver has the resources to continue the good care and welfare of the animal.

Loans

Natural history, zoological, and botanical specimen loans are covered by loan agreements that contain standard clauses familiar to collections professionals. The three most common reasons for loans are exhibition, research, and breeding. For each collection type, loan agreements contain clauses that are tailored for the loan purpose.

For natural history specimens, loans of indeterminate length are strongly discouraged, but most loan agreements include the possibility of loan renewal on review. The main concern is that a specimen on loan should not be used for secondary purposes, accidently incorporated into the accessioned collections, or transferred to another institution without permission. Typically, the lending institution is acknowledged in some manner, either through an exhibit label credit line or in a journal article.

Most museum loans include clauses for rights of reproduction that cover making and using images. For live specimens, the phrase *reproductive rights* refers to breeding or propagation, so this formal term is normally not used in loan agreements. Zoos and aquariums understand that animals on loan will be photographed by the visitors and by the holding institution for educational and advertisement purposes.

For live plant collections, loans are atypical and long-term loans are strongly discouraged.[8] Loans of plant specimens are usually for short-term programmatic use such as exhibitions. For live animal collections, permanent loans or loans of indeterminate length are common. Living specimens can be on loan for their entire life span, which may be as short as a few months or one hundred years or more. The loan agreement typically contains a clause to allow either party to cancel the loan prior to the death of the animal. Live specimen loan agreements contain clauses that cover ownership of specimen remains, including derived materials, ownership of offspring (animal), or propagules (plant), permits, treatment for disease, transport methods, research permission, transfer to other institutions, and notifications. In addition, all live specimens on loan are accessioned due to welfare, tracking, ethical, and legal requirements.

Exhibit Loans

Natural history exhibit loans follow typical loan agreements used by all institutions. Maintaining a specimen's exhibition history is important for the specimen's provenance and for its long-term preservation. A heavy exhibition schedule can damage a highly sought specimen. As in other museums, a natural history specimen incoming loan may be assigned an exhibit or temporary identification number so that the loan can be tracked in a systematic way.

Living specimen exhibit agreements stipulate that the loan purpose is for display only and that appropriate measures are to be taken to prevent propagation. However, despite best efforts, nature can take its course and offspring or propagules may be produced. Most exhibit loans include an accidental breeding or propagation clause that covers the disposition of offspring or propagules.

Research Loans

Nonliving research loans usually cover the activities conducted only during the research project specified in the loan agreement. The agreement contains clauses to address invasive or destructive sampling, retention of samples derived from specimens, access to retained samples, intellectual property, data ownership, and data sharing. Living specimens are rarely loaned for research purposes. However, living specimens may be participants in horticultural studies, husbandry studies, behavioral studies, and health studies. If a live specimen is already on site as a loan from another institution, permission is obtained from the owning institution prior to the specimen's inclusion in a study.

All research studies involving live animals must go through an institution animal care and use review process that focuses on the animal's welfare during the proposed study.[9] In the United States, this review is a legal requirement under the Animal Welfare Act[10] for all institutions and facilities.

Breeding Loans

Quite often live specimens are transferred between institutions for breeding purposes. For some species getting the right conditions for breeding can take years and, for genetically valuable specimens, having multiple breeding opportunities is advantageous. Loaned living specimens are covered by breeding loan agreements that specify offspring or propagule ownership. To complicate matters, advances in reproductive science are allowing the transfer of gametes between institutions rather than the live animals for use in assisted breeding such as artificial insemination (semen) and implantation (oocytes). As mentioned previously, the gametes are considered the equivalent of the live animal. These transfers are covered by specialized loan agreements that define gamete harvesting, gamete ownership, how the gametes can be used, if the gametes can be stored for future use, and offspring ownership. As additional advances are made in reproductive methods and technologies these types of agreements for the use of gametes will become more complex.

RECORDS AND DOCUMENTATION

Accurate recordkeeping, whether paper-based, digital, or a combination, is vital for any collection. Good records allow for accounting, control, and access to the physical collection and its associated information for exhibition, education, and research. Without accurate records, a collected specimen will have minimal value and use institution resources that can be better spent elsewhere. The storage of records in a digital systematic program is typically called the collections information system (CIS) or collections management system (CMS).

A specimen record is comprised of several groupings of information and documents. These groupings can be generalized as follows, but keep in mind that there is quite a bit of crossover between groupings:

Accession Records—core metadata, identification

Transaction Records—acquisition, loans, exhibits, disposition

Catalog Records—provenance, new information, research

Legal Record—permits, deeds of gift, bequests, other legal documents

Location Records or Cartographic Records—current specimen location, past locations, moves

In some institutions all of these records are held together in one master record, usually in the registrar's office, whereas in others the catalog records, field notes, and location records are held in the curatorial department.

For all collection types, there are core pieces of information that need to be captured and recorded. The terminology used for each core data field follows professional standards for the type of collection. The list of core metadata fields includes:

- Accession number
- Genus
- Species
- Date of specimen collection
- Name of specimen collector
- Location of collection (GPS or latitude and longitude coordinates preferred, area description, ecological data)
- Type of acquisition
- Date of accession
- Date of transaction
- Name of donor, seller, purchaser, owner, or legal custodian
- Number of subsets or components of specimen
- Voucher specimen or voucher components
- Storage or enclosure on site

Additional information may be included depending on collection type:

- Common name
- Field notes
- Additional identification method (e.g., leg band, ear tag)
- Catalog number
- Heritage, parentage, siblings, offspring
- Permit types and numbers
- Preservation or conservation treatments
- Habitat, behavior, nutrition, and medical notes
- Loan number
- Propagules
- Propagule sharing
- Provenance
- Images

Live Collection Considerations

For live animal collections there are two record sets, a specimen record in the collection information system and a medical record in the veterinary information system. These two record sets, along with associated pathology and gamete collections, comprise the entirety of an animal's record. Veterinary practices have specialized information and recordkeeping systems to capture medical data essential to animal health care that are not covered in this chapter.

An animal's specimen record is updated on a daily, weekly, or monthly basis depending on the animal's needs or life events. Animal keepers complete a daily report on the animals in their care that is turned in to the curator, registrar, or recordkeeper office for review. Information is pulled from these reports for inclusion in the specimen record. In North America, standards for what data to record are set by the Association of Zoos and Aquariums (AZA).[11] When an animal is moved to a new zoo or aquarium the animal's specimen record, along with its medical record, is shared with the new facility. Each facility adds to the animal's record, which helps ensure that the animal receives the best care and maintains its overall welfare through its life phases. Digitized zoological collection information systems are designed to allow ease of sharing information. Although there are a few automated systems available, there is one global system that the majority of zoos and aquariums worldwide use to store and share animal specimen records with each other, which has the benefit of real-time data access and eliminates the need for each institution to reenter core data.

An integral part of live plant specimen location or cartographic records are the detailed locator topographical maps that are based on fixed, permanent orientation markers. A standard practice for botanical gardens is to superimpose a grid pattern over the grounds and number each grid in a consistent manner from one starting point.[12] The locator maps are identified within this grid.

Natural History Collections Considerations

In natural history collections, it is common that in addition to the accession number issued by the registrars' office, each collecting department uses catalog numbers to aid in collection organization, housing, and tracking; thus, the subparts of a single accession can have different departmental catalog numbers. It is crucial for these catalog numbers to be linked to the accession number both on specimen labels and in the collection information system.

ACCOUNTABILITY, CONTROL, AND ACCESS

Accountability, control, and access to a collection begins with knowing what you have and where it is. It all starts with inventories of the collection. Inventories allow institutions to confirm (or discover) what they have, where it is located, if something is missing or simply misplaced, or if specimens have become damaged. Inventory intervals depend on the type and size of the collection. Institutions with large collections typically do spot inventories on a rotating basis in which a subsection of the collection is inventoried and then reconciled with the collection records. Any discrepancies that are found are investigated; if a significant number of discrepancies or damage is found then a larger scale inventory of the collection is conducted.

Once the institution knows what specimens it has, where they are located, and their condition, it can then make decisions about who will be allowed to use the specimens, for what purposes, and under what conditions, as well as who will care for the specimens and how. These decisions allow the institution to set up appropriate security measures to protect the collection from inappropriate access, theft, and vandalism. The institution should have a system to track the movement of specimens in and out of storage, home location, or enclosure, either to another destination within the institution or to another institution.

Accurate accounting and control of the collections aids the development of a viable disaster plan. Knowing the size and composition of the collection allows for the identification of the most vulnerable specimens to particular threats. This, in turn, enables the staff to determine the best manner to protect the collection and allocate needed resources.

Live Collection Considerations

A concern for both live animal and plant collections is found-in-collection specimens—unwanted specimens that may be dropped off without notice. Visitors have been known to slip unwanted pets or plants into enclosures or displays when the staff is not present.

Zoos and aquariums conduct annual head counts (inventories) of their live animal collections, and staff conduct daily eyes-on assessments of the animals under their direct care. If any animal is missing an alert is issued, a search team is assembled, and a search for the animal is conducted. When animals are accessioned as a group so that it is not possible to complete an accurate head count, an estimate is made. For these groups an actual count is made when their home enclosure is disassembled for refurbishing and each animal can be counted as it is caught.

Access can be a tricky issue in zoos and aquariums. Institutions must consider not only staff and researcher access but also the possibility of visitors climbing into enclosures (risking injury to themselves) or throwing objects into an enclosure, creating a risk of injury to the animals. The flip side of accessibility is control—knowing where the specimens are or should be at any given point in time allows for the timely recapture or relocation if necessary. Part of maintaining control is assessing the feasibility of an animal being able to gain access to another animal's enclosure or to the general public space. On a periodic basis, staff inspect enclosures to determine each animal's chance of escape from its home enclosure. For example, staff may find that a tree limb has grown over the enclosure fence, providing an avenue for the resident animal to climb out.

Access may be problematic for botanical institutions. Typically, plant collections are displayed in ways that allow visitors to walk up and touch specimens. Although this enhances the visitor experience it also opens an avenue for unintended damage, intentional vandalism, and theft by unauthorized removal of all or part of the specimen.

CARE

The care of an institution's collection focuses on the four primary D's—the prevention of degradation, decay, damage, and destruction. Live collections

include a fifth D, disease, and natural history collections have the fifth D of desiccation. Collection professionals continually strive to maintain the specimens in good condition for the long term. The collection type determines what kind of care is needed and how that care will be delivered. Not surprisingly each collection type has special areas of concern.

One care program that is common to all collecting institutions is the need to have an integrated pest management (IPM) plan in place to prevent, minimize, or eliminate pests (see CHAPTER 6E, "Integrated Pest Management"). The IPM program is designed to identify potential and existing pests, their sources, harborages or hiding areas, access points, removal methods, and the best way of managing these aspects with minimal impact on the collections. Most local or municipal governments regulate what types of chemical mitigation can be used in the local jurisdiction.

A best practice for all collecting institutions is to have a disaster plan that identifies the most likely events to occur for that institution, both natural and man-made and how to respond to them should they occur (see CHAPTER 6B, "Emergencies: Prepare, Respond, Recover"). All staff should have copies of the plan and know what their roles and responsibilities are during a disaster. Institutions should recognize that, depending on the size and type of disaster, staff and outside help may not be able to get to the institution site and they should plan accordingly.

An interesting note about terminology—the word *conservation* has different meanings in a museum setting and a live specimen collection. Museums use conservation to describe the activities conducted to safeguard, restore, or preserve a specimen. Zoos, aquariums, and botanical gardens use the conservation to mean saving a species or habitat. The equivalent of *preventive conservation* for live animals is *medical care* and for plants is *preservative care*.[13]

Natural History Concerns

Many natural history collections have specimens stored in fluid preservatives (usually alcohol- or formaldehyde-based). Monitoring the level of preservative is necessary to prevent the desiccation through the evaporation of the preservative.[14] Dry preserved natural history specimens must be closely monitored for pests.

Quite often research and conservation techniques require the destructive sampling of all or part of a specimen—the concern is how much of a specimen can be used in this manner before the specimen loses its value for other purposes.

Specimens degrade through exposure to environmental factors and mechanical wear. Common environmental factors that impact specimen condition include light exposure, temperature fluctuations, humidity fluctuations, and exposure to contaminants such as heavy metal salts and pesticides. Fluctuations in relative humidity may result in outbreaks of mold that can damage specimens and pose a health risk to staff. All organic and some inorganic materials undergo a decay process in which components break down that may create chemical hazards that affect other specimens or pose a risk to staff members.

Many institutions have frozen or cryopreserved specimen collections (cryopreservation uses very low temperatures). Thawing of frozen or cryopreserved specimens as a result of equipment failure is a major concern. The staff also has to consider the effects of repeated freeze-thaw cycles on the physical integrity of the specimen.

Live Collection Concerns

Caring for a live specimen collection is a continuous, multidisciplinary endeavor involving curators, keepers, nutritionists, animal behaviorists, husbandry experts, veterinarians, biomechanical experts, horticulturists, environmental control experts, water and filtration experts, soil and substrate experts, facility experts, and specialty shops. The care provided is dependent on seasonal changes and on weather conditions at given points in time.

The primary concern is the overall welfare of the animal, including its physical, social, and psychological health. Keeper staff conduct daily eyes-on checks of each animal in their care, looking for signs of illness, injury, or unusual behavior. Any changes from the norm are noted, reported, and if necessary, a veterinary examination or review of animal managing

protocols is conducted. Medical treatment is provided to resolve any issues. Quite often the care of exotic animals requires ingenious solutions and custom-made apparatuses.

Zoos and aquariums must face end-of-life care for their animals. Staff discuss the type of end-of-life care according to individual needs to maintain quality of life and to eliminate pain or suffering. It is not uncommon for the institution to provide access to grief counselors for the staff.

Many zoos and aquariums hold biological material collections derived from the animals in their custody. During medical examinations and necropsies blood samples, tissue biopsies, gametes, and other tissues may be taken and stored long term. Other things that might be saved include shed tissues (such as antlers, skin, hair, feathers, teeth, and shell fragments) that can be used for educational programs or research. Feces and urine are collected, analyzed, and stored to provide baseline health profiles. These materials are preserved and stored in the same variety of ways as natural history specimens.

The interplay of multiple variables drives the preservation program of botanical gardens and arboretums. The preservation program outlines good plant hygiene practices, maintenance cycles and activities, disease and pest control, and propagation cycles and methods to maintain plant stocks.[15] Preventive plant care is of foremost concern. Regular inspections for overall health, pruning, removing dead flowers and foliage, weeding, and appropriate cleaning or sanitizing of equipment minimize the ability of pests and disease to gain a foothold in the collection. Measures are taken to facilitate plant health in both outdoor and indoor collections. Greenhouse plants require a carefully monitored artificial environment that is independent of outdoor conditions. Some botanical gardens and arboretums collect and save dried herbarium specimens that document the collections and add valuable ancillary information on the live specimens they hold. In addition, many maintain seed banks not only for routine propagation purposes but for genetic history and genetic diversity purposes. These materials have similar collection care concerns as natural history collections.

OCCUPATIONAL SAFETY (PHYSICAL AND BIOLOGICAL HAZARDS)

Museums, zoos, aquariums, and botanical gardens present a host of challenges to keeping staff and visitors safe beyond the common slips, trips, and falls. A robust occupational safety and health (OSH) program is crucial. In general, OSH is a multidisciplinary approach to address the safety, health, and welfare of people at work (it may also be known as workplace health and safety, or WHS). An institutional OSH program includes both physical hazard and biohazard identification, biosecurity, biosafety, and physical measures to protect staff and visitors. As with any program, its success depends on the mindfulness of the staff of the hazards present and commitment to following institutional safety protocols.

All work places contain hazards but zoological, botanical, and natural history collection hazards encountered by staff are not typical.[16] The specimens themselves present issues that have to be identified and mitigated, not only from their biological components but from inherent vice. For example, some geological specimens are radioactive, some specimens may cause environmental contamination, others may be preserved or treated with chemicals that pose health hazards. In dealing with these types of specimens several terms are used to describe the hazards and the methods to mitigate the hazards, such as biohazard, biosecurity, and biosafety.

All living and dead organisms may carry germs or parasites both internally and externally, some of which cause or spread diseases. Some bacteria, viruses, and parasites can survive the death of the host organism. Some zoological and botanical specimens produce, secrete, or inject toxins (we are all familiar with poison ivy, poison dart frogs, and bee stings). A hazard that originates from a biological source is called a *biohazard*. The term *biosecurity* refers to the spread of disease between members of a species, between different species, and to humans from living and deceased specimens—the term originated in the agricultural community to describe the prevention of the spread of disease between farms and the prevention of diseases that might be imported into an unexposed population. *Biosafety* describes the methods

and measures followed to mitigate or prevent biohazards. Most biosafety measures focus on the prevention of disease and disease-causing organisms. The type of biohazard identified determines the methods and measures deployed.

Many countries have laws and regulations that determine what type of live or dead specimens can be transported, how they can be moved, and where (e.g., within a country or by import or export). In the United States, the USDA enforces these regulations by issuing permits and conducting inspections to mitigate the introduction or spread of disease to the agriculture and food chain.

Many zoological and botanical specimens present a potential for physical or mechanical injury because animals may bite, kick, scratch, hit, sting, and spit, and plants produce spines, bristles, and barbs that can scratch or pierce the skin. Large, heavy specimens, both alive and nonliving, present lifting, falling, or other movement injuries. Nonliving specimens can shed preservation salts or other chemicals that can be absorbed through skin, inhaled, or contaminate their surroundings. A good OSH program will identify these hazards and control them with appropriate mitigation methods.

Live Specimen Considerations

Live specimens arriving at a new institution undergo a quarantine period that typically lasts fourteen to thirty days, depending on the type of specimen and previous exposures. Quarantine is the act of separating the specimen from other collection specimens until the institution is assured that it is disease free. Most known diseases have an incubation period that will manifest itself within the quarantine time frame. Specimens are observed and tested during the quarantine period to see if they are diseased or carrying a disease agent. Specimens that appear to be sick, present an illness, are discovered to be carrying a disease agent, or are behaving poorly will be treated and remain in quarantine until the issue is resolved.

Additional biosecurity measures include restricting who has access to the specimen, the use of appropriate personal protection equipment (PPE), sanitizing areas and equipment, footbaths, special clothing, and other methods as deemed necessary.

During the course of cage or greenhouse cleaning care must be taken with cleaning agents to prevent plant, animal, or human exposure. Water hoses can produce a mist of mixed cleaning agents and water that may cause slippery conditions, unintended spillover, drift, or inhalation risks.

Natural History Considerations

Natural history specimens prepared as taxidermy mounts prior to about 1980 most likely were preserved with arsenic compounds, which, over time, may migrate to the surface of the specimen. The resulting dust can contaminate the surrounding surfaces and any objects it touches, including human hands. Arsenic soap was used in taxidermy until around 1990 (in some shops, its use continued much longer); thus, it is a good practice to assume that taxidermy specimens contain arsenic no matter their age, either from preparation or cross contamination.[17] In addition, gaskets on older storage cabinetry may be impregnated with mercury compounds.

Formaldehyde (formalin) has long been used to preserve specimens, and although it is now recognized as a potential carcinogen, it is still widely used.[18] Some institutions have changed formaldehyde-preserved specimens to alcohol-based preservation fluids, but alcohol, although safer for long-term human health, presents its own hazards. Inhalation of concentrated alcohol fumes can render a person unconscious, and alcohol is highly combustible.

As mentioned previously, geological specimens may also present health risks from heavy metals, radioactivity, asbestos, and other toxins.

For a review of health and safety in the workplace, see *Health and Safety for Museum Professionals*.[19]

WILDLIFE LAW OVERVIEW

There are a variety of laws that govern the protection of flora and fauna (see CHAPTER 7G, "Biological Materials—Fish, Wildlife, and Plants"). Most of these laws apply to both living and nonliving specimens and to materials and tissues derived from them. Laws can be enacted at any level—international, federal, state or provincial, and city or local municipality. In addition to legal regulations, regional customs and traditions must be respected and followed. Most countries recognize their sovereign rights to their native flora and fauna and to their traditional knowledge of plants and animals.

Primary International Treaties and Conventions

The Convention on the International Trade of Endangered Species (CITES) covers activities involving animals and plants that are listed on one of three appendices depending on their threatened or endangered status.[20] The purpose of CITES is to prevent the further decline of listed species through commercial trade, such as from overharvesting or poaching of whole organisms or their parts. International shipments of protected species require permits and for some species permits are required to move specimens between institutions within the same country.

The Nagoya Protocol on Access to Genetic Resources and the Fair and Equitable Sharing of Benefits Arising from their Utilization to the Convention on Biological Diversity (Nagoya Protocol)[21] of the Convention on Biological Diversity (CBD) has two related components that affect plant and animal specimens. One component covers access to a country's genetic resources (wild patrimony) and traditional knowledge; the other covers the fair and equitable sharing of benefits deriving from the utilization of genetic resources and traditional knowledge. Access and benefit agreements are signed by the host country and all parties prior to commencing the covered activities.

Primary US Laws of Concern

In the United States, wildlife laws are enforced by three primary regulatory agencies, USFWS, USDA, and the National Marine Fisheries Service (NMFS). These agencies regulate the possession, movement, and other activities involving wildlife. For certain animal species, the CDC regulates movement within the United States and importation into the United States. The USFWS enforces CITES, the Lacey Act, the Endangered Species Act, the Migratory Bird Treaty Act, the African Elephant Conservation Act, the Injurious Animal Act, and parts of the Marine Mammal Act.[22] The USDA enforces the Animal Welfare Act, the Plant Protection Act, and the National Animal and

Plant Health Surveillance System. The NMFS (also known as National Oceanic and Atmospheric Administration Fisheries, or NOAA) enforces parts of the Marine Mammal Act jointly with the USFWS. •

NOTES

1. J. E. Simmons, "Collections management," in *Health and Safety for Museum Professionals*, edited by C. A. Hawks, M. McCann, K. Makos, L. Goldberg, D. Hinkamp, D. Ertel, and P. Silence, pp. 515–549 (New York: Society for the Preservation of Natural History Collections and the American Institute for Conservation, 2011).

2. American Public Gardens Association, "Key Terms." Available at: https://www.publicgardens.org/programs/plant-collections-network/compass-progress-standards-excellence-plant-collections (accessed November 20, 2018).

3. V. A. Funk, M. Gostel, A. Devine, C. L. Kelloff, K. Wurdack, C. Tuccinardi, A. S. Radosavljevic, M. Peters, and J. Coddington., "Guidelines for collecting vouchers and tissues intended for genomic work (Smithsonian Institution): Botany Best Practices," *Biodiversity Data Journal* 5 (2017): e11625. Available at: https://doi.org/10.3897/BDJ.5.e11625.

4. T. C. Hohn, *Curatorial Practices for Botanical Gardens*, pp. 92–93 (Lanham, MD: AltaMira Press, 2008).

5. Institutional Data Management Scientific Advisory Group (IDMAG), *Recordkeeping Guidelines for Group Accessions*. Association of Zoos and Aquariums, 2002, revised 23 May 2014. Available at: https://www.speakcdn.com/assets/2332/recordkeeping_guidelines_for_group_accessions_final_52314.pdf.

6. IDMAG, *Recordkeeping Guidelines for Group Accessions*.

7. IDMAG, *Recordkeeping Guidelines for Group Accessions*.

8. Hohn, *Curatorial Practices*, 44.

9. J. Silverman, M. A. Suckow, and S. Murthy, eds., *The IACUC Handbook*, 3rd ed. (Boca Raton: CRC Press, 2014).

10. 7 U.S.C. § 2131 et seq.

11. Available at: https://www.aza.org/.

12. Hohn, *Curatorial Practices*, 98–100.

13. Hohn, *Curatorial Practices*, 123.

14. J. E. Simmons, *Fluid Preservation. A Comprehensive Reference* (Lanham, MD: Rowman & Littlefield, 2014).

15. Hohn, *Curatorial Practices*, 124–126.

16. C. Hawks, M. McCann, K. A. Makos, L. Goldberg, D. Hinkamp, D. C. Ertel, Jr., and P. Silence, eds., *Health and Safety for Museum Professionals* (New York: Society for the Preservation of Natural History Collections and the American Institute for Conservation, 2011).

17. F. Marte, A. Péquignot, and D. W. von Endt, "Arsenic in taxidermy collections: History, detection, management." *Collection Forum* 21, no. 1–2 (2006): 143–150. Available at: http://www.spnhc.org/media/assets/cofo_2006_V21N12.pdf.

18. Simmons, *Fluid Preservation*.

19. Hawks et al., *Health and Safety*.

20. M. C. Malaro, and I. P. DeAngelis, *A Legal Primer on Managing Museum Collections*, 3rd ed. (Washington, DC: Smithsonian Books, 2012).

21. Available at: https://www.cbd.int/abs/about/.

22. Malaro and DeAngelis, *Legal Primer*; M. E. Phelan, *Museum Law. A Guide for Officers, Directors, and Counsel*, 4th ed. (Lanham, MD: Rowman & Littlefield, 2014).

I thank Pamela Allenstein of the American Public Gardens Association for her knowledge concerning botanical garden collection care, and Judith Block, registrar emeritus, for generously reviewing drafts of the manuscript.

3G | MANAGING DIGITAL ART

GRACE T. WEISS

INTRODUCTION

MANAGING DIGITAL ARTWORKS in museum collections requires the collaboration of a spectrum of museum professionals to acquire, exhibit, and preserve these works of art that are activated when exhibited. As one of the ever-evolving genres of media art, *digital art* is "made or presented using digital technology."[1] Unlike older forms of time-based media, digital art is often *born digital*, meaning the work is created in digital form and not as a digitized copy of an analog master.[2] In a museum collection, a digital artwork exists as multiple copies of different status (e.g., master, exhibition copy, viewing copy). Common examples of digital artworks include single-channel video, installation art, computer-based art, and artwork made using custom electronics.

As with traditional media, the registrar or collections manager contributes precise knowledge of the elements acquired or loaned as part of a digital work such as digital files, media carriers, sculptural components, and dedicated equipment for play-back and display. The reproducible nature of digital works expands on the registration and collection management methods described in the other chapters of this volume. Using existing resources in the field, this chapter provides complementary guidelines for acquisitions, accessioning, numbering, exhibition, insurance, and loan processes specific to digital art collections.

ACQUISITIONS AND ACCESSIONING

Digital artwork necessitates a multistep accession process—pre-acquisition, acquisition, and post-acquisition. The registrar tracks the artwork components received at every step of the accession process and advises on the museum's long-term preservation and storage considerations. Each phase is described in detail by the interinstitutional research project, *Matters in Media Art*, a dynamic, open source website that provides resources for the complex stewardship issues posed by media arts.[3] These steps may be integrated into a museum's existing acquisition and accession procedures to address the specific considerations of collecting digital art (see CHAPTER 3B, "Acquisitions and Accessioning").

If an institution presents proposed acquisitions at an accessions meeting, viewing copy or exhibition copy files are typically received during the pre-acquisition phase for this purpose (see "Numbering" for component definitions). As the two most common types of digital derivative copies, it is essential to note this distinction when registering each file in a museum's collection management system. Web transfer via file transfer protocol (FTP) site is an accepted method to obtain pre-acquisition media; however, file-sharing platforms are not recommended to receive archival master files. Shipping the master file of an editioned digital artwork via web transfer not only creates potential for file corruption or data loss without appropriate checksum verification, but it also raises security questions around using a third-party platform's terms and conditions. Receiving master files on an external drive eliminates these risks and adds a layer of redundancy required for proper digital preservation, which is described later in this section.

Additional physical components needed to exhibit the artwork are also received during the pre-accession period. If a work has dedicated playback and display equipment, these components are generally obtained for an institution's accessions meeting. This equipment may be sourced by the institution or provided by the vendor, gallery, or artist as part of the acquisition.

Installation instructions, including a detailed equipment list, should also be acquired during the pre-acquisition phase. One of the most important pieces of ancillary materials, this document provides an institution with instructions to realize the artist's intent for a digital piece of art. Installation guides vary by artist and artwork, ranging from precise instructions to flexible guidelines.

An artist interview or questionnaire may also be administered as part of an institution's accession process (see CHAPTER 3E, "Documenting Contemporary Art"). These tools support the museum's documentation of a digital work's provenance, production notes, history, technical and physical specifications for display, acceptable parameters of change, and preservation concerns. *Voices in Contemporary Art* (VoCA) provides helpful interview resources, as well as ongoing programming, that highlight the importance of the artist's voice in contemporary art conservation.[4]

Once an accession has been approved by an institution's acquisition committee and the appropriate paperwork is in place, the registrar moves forward with the receipt of the digital work's final deliverables. Depending on the artwork, final deliverables typically include archival master files, exhibition copy files (to be used as reference for future derivative copies), and a certificate of authenticity. Digital master files are commonly received on a digital media carrier—external hard drive, flash drive, or portable computer. Because media carriers and their contents are often not unique in the traditional sense, it is acceptable to ship and receive archival digital files via overnight mailing services (e.g., FedEx). It is important to check the requested deliverables against what is received during the post-accession phase because additional materials may be included in the final transfer of objects; thus, it is essential to understand their status in relation to the entire work. To date, it is becoming more common for final payment to be sent to the vendor, artist, or gallery following receipt and review of these items.

During the post-acquisition phase, a work's digital and physical components are cataloged according to component hierarchy, which is established in conjunction with the curator and conservator. In addition to a certificate of authenticity, there are three standard groups of digital artwork constituents: (i) media components; (ii) dedicated playback and display equipment; and (iii) sculptural components.

All constituents are labeled using the record-keeping conventions described in the "Numbering" section.

Media components include archival masters, exhibition copies, and viewing copies (see "Numbering" for component definitions). All digital materials received throughout the accession process are copied to the museum's digital repository system, which takes a variety of forms depending on an institution's collection and budget. This transfer should be performed using a write-blocker, a forensic tool that prevents a computer from embedding hidden files on an external drive's contents. This device is especially useful during the initial migration of a digital work's master files.

The *Matters in Media Art* digital preservation guide offers detailed resources for designing digital storage to suit an individual collection's needs. This may take the form of a dedicated server for digital artwork or redundant array of independent disks (RAID) 5, 6, or 7 systems. An institution could consider both systems, so that the latter may act as digital temporary storage until a work is fully accessioned. Regardless of an institution's chosen system, *Matters in Media Art* confirms the key concept of digital art storage, "One copy is no copy. Save three copies of your data on at least two mediums [sic] (e.g., hard drive, server, LTO tape, flash drive, cloud) and in at least two geographic locations."[5]

Once safely backed up, archival master files undergo quality control (QC), a focused viewing of the video file in real time that acts as the work's incoming condition check. A corresponding data sheet serves as the work's condition report, which captures the file's metadata, checksum (a digital file's "unique alphanumeric sequence" that helps track corruption), provenance, technical specifications, and condition notes.[6] Any condition issues are recorded with their playback time stamp on the data sheet. Generally, a conservation-led activity, it is recommended that QC be completed in collaboration with registration. Helpful condition report templates and QC resources can be found in the documentation section of *Matters in Media Art*.[7]

Dedicated playback and display equipment is designated to activate a single collection work. Equipment becomes dedicated if it is essential to display the work or has historical or conceptual significance for the work. Dedicated equipment is handled and stored as an art object, often in its original manufacturers' packaging (if available). Ideally, the overall inventory of a work's dedicated equipment should include at least one spare of each component type required for display.[8]

Sculptural components may also be part of a born-digital artwork and are accessioned in the same manner as the physical parts of a traditional work. In some cases, dedicated equipment is sculptural in nature, embodying both an aesthetic and functional significance for the work. Sculptural components are handled, crated, and stored as art objects.

NUMBERING

At this time, there is no universal numbering standard for digital art that is shared by museums. However, by developing accession number prefix and suffix conventions to expand on an institution's existing numbering system, the following record types may be used to delineate the status of each digital artwork component in a traditional collection management system.

1. The cover record links the work's accession number to its concept, display information, and documentation. This parent record includes parts for each digital and physical component needed to activate the artwork in an exhibition space. Each of the following record types are tied to this *umbrella record* as child records.
2. Master status is assigned to the archival material that is the source of derivative exhibition formats (i.e., exhibition copies). Master records correspond to this archival content, capturing the number of accessioned components, and noting their file format (e.g., Apple ProRes 422), production information (who created the file and for what purpose), and date of receipt. Master record status may be applied to uncompressed digital video files, source code or binary files for computer-based arts, and their corresponding media carriers.
3. Exhibition copy records correspond to a derivative copy of the artwork's master made for gallery dis-

play. This record type tracks how many exhibition copies exist, their file format (e.g., H.264), and production information. Unlike traditional exhibition copies that are destroyed after display, exhibition copy files of permanent collection works are often retained internally; however, it is an institutional decision whether these compressed versions of the archival master will become accessioned digital objects.

4. A viewing copy (also known as an access copy) status is used to denote derivative material that is not meant for exhibition. Viewing copies (e.g., a multi-channel composite video) are typically provided for accessions committee meetings or curatorial viewings because their main purpose is to portray the overall sense of an artwork without it being fully installed. This record similarly notes the number of retained viewing copies, their file formats, and production information.
5. A part record convention should be established to track an artwork's dedicated equipment and non-art components (i.e., artist boxes or custom exhibition furniture). As defined in this chapter's "Acquisitions and Accessioning" section, records for dedicated equipment capture the constituent type, the number retained, each component's manufacturer and unique serial number, as well as its significance to an individual digital artwork. As consumable components, it is important to note at the time of acquisition if and how these units may be replaced.[9]

Once the component status is defined, these record types may be applied to the digital and physical parts that comprise any media work; however, each artwork is its own unique case study that requires an individualized registration and preservation approach.

Computer-based works are particularly challenging to catalog and preserve because their specialized software, operating systems, and storage devices are often combined parts that face the ongoing risk of impending technological obsolescence. The *Electronic Arts Intermix (EAI) Online Resource Guide for Exhibiting, Collecting & Preserving Media Art* is a valuable resource to help museums display, acquire, and conserve single-channel video, computer-based art and installations. The references for computer-based art are of particular note for a registrar or collections manager tasked with managing artist-made websites and specialized software.[10]

INSURANCE

Insuring born-digital artwork expands on conventional fine art insurance principles. Under an *all risks of physical loss or damage* museum fine art and collections insurance policy, an institution's archival master materials are insured at current market value. As reproducible, editioned media, market value corresponds to the cost of restoration or refabrication. However, in the event of total loss, current market value may be defined as the purchase price or commission costs plus an increase in value if the artist's work has gained renown over time. Insuring the physical components of a digital artwork depends on the object's status and replaceability. Sculptural components and artist modified equipment are insured at current market value, while exchangeable dedicated media equipment is insured at full replacement cost.

In the event of a loan, born-digital artwork is insured at the value listed on the loan agreement form. Unlike traditional media, this value often corresponds to production costs or the replacement value of its digital media carrier. For example, the valuation of a digital file sent via FTP site may be $0, while the insurance value for lending custom software on a portable computer corresponds to the replacement cost of the equipment and the software's reproduction. It is important to note this valuation distinction on the loan form agreement, especially in the event of lending media with dedicated equipment.

EXHIBITION

Exhibiting digital artwork in an in-house or traveling exhibition generally entails the creation of exhibition copy content. An exhibition copy's specifications for display vary by artwork; however, they are often a more compressed version of the master file produced according to the work's installation guidelines. The exhibition of digital media works necessitates playback and display equipment, which may or may not be dedicated to the work. In either case, it is recommended to have at least one backup unit of each type of equipment required for display[11] (see CHAPTER 3M, "Displays from Within—Considerations for Collections-Based Exhibitions," CHAPTER 3L, "Organizing Traveling Exhibitions," and CHAPTER 8A, "Hosting Traveling Exhibitions").

The registrar or collections manager facilitates the safe installation and accurate tracking of all digital and physical parts required for display. The registrar also contributes to the institution's exhibition documentation, which is a crucial part of preserving a digital artwork. Working with the artist's studio, curatorial, conservation, installation, and technical specialists, the registrar carefully documents the components used in a work's gallery presentation, as well as their order of installation for future display. This collaborative documentation process is outlined at length in CHAPTER 3E ("Documenting Contemporary Art").[12]

LOANS

Lending digital media works builds on the conventional loans processes described in CHAPTER 3K ("Loans"). The loan process for a digital artwork involves a collaborative review of the institution's holdings, as well as an in-depth dialog with the prospective borrower to ensure that the institution can fulfill the work's installation requirements and has the budget to prepare the artwork and the borrowing venue for display. In addition to these considerations, the central question of each media loan remains, what is being loaned (digitally or physically)? The answer to this query varies according to the requested artwork. In the case of single-channel videos, a digital file may be the only component shipped to the borrower, with the corresponding playback and display equipment provided by the venue. However, digital artworks with sculptural components, such as artist-modified equipment or immersive installation environments, necessitate fine art shipping and standard object lending processes.

The loan section of *Matters in Media Art* offers guidelines to develop an institution's own procedures for lending time-based media works—loan process, budget, loan agreement, facilities report, and installation documentation.[13] These resources help registrars to answer questions regarding media and equipment preparation, as well as installation and maintenance matters such as spatial requirements (i.e., a completely dark or sound proof space), voltage or amp (amperes) specifications, crew and technician stipulations, and special conditioning needs.

The summary of the final decisions reached during the review process is documented by the borrower's agreement (for outgoing loans) or loan agreement (for incoming loans). These agreements must specify the value for the digital media, sculptural components (if applicable), and dedicated equipment (if supplied by the lender). Agreements should include language about the destruction of the loan's exhibition copy material. For example, "If a loan consists of digital file(s), the Borrower must destroy said files at the end of the loan period and confirm this destruction." Loan agreements might also specify whether the lender may copy the loaned content. As with all loans, it is important for the agreed upon terms to be countersigned by both parties, and, where applicable, for the borrower to issue to the lender a certificate of insurance, before shipment takes place.

Shipping media varies according to the specific needs of the digital artwork. Single-channel digital videos are commonly shared via FTP site or shipped to the borrower on a dedicated external drive. More complex digital media works, such as synchronized multi-channel video installations, are produced by the lender and shipped on a media carrier (e.g., SD card) that corresponds to the digital artwork's specific play-back equipment. Backup copies of the digital media should be supplied by the lender. For works with specialized software, playback equipment may be purchased by the borrower and shipped to the lender to be programed with the loan's digital exhibition copy; the preloaded device is then shipped back to the borrower for its installation. At the close of the loan, the exhibition copy is deleted and the equipment is retained by the borrower. These plug-and-play approaches ensure the artwork's digital content is produced according to the artist's intent.

CONCLUSION

Like digital media itself, the museum methods used to preserve and display digital works are constantly evolving to respond to the wide range of technological innovations used by contemporary artists today. At the forefront of these developing practices, museums are now exploring how to collect and preserve virtual reality (VR). An emerging artistic medium, VR employs variable software and hardware components to create dynamic, and often interactive, immersive virtual environments.

VR software consists of a 360-degree video file or interactive software using a web-based or proprietary platform to engage with specialized VR headsets that allow viewers to experience an artist's virtual concept. Understanding the video files, source code, binary files, and operating systems needed to activate a VR artwork are at the center of developing a long-term preservation plan, as well as accurately registering the work's digital and physical components in a collection management system.[14] Once this knowledge base is collaboratively established by all museum stakeholders, the registrar may apply the collection management guidelines outlined in this chapter. For example, a VR piece's 360-degree video files, source code, and corresponding binary files (depending on its software platform) would constitute the artwork's master archival material, while its respective headset technology may be categorized as dedicated equipment. Similarly, any content generated for gallery display would be classified as an exhibition copy.

Managing digital art does not require a registrar to rewrite the book for collection management but rather to creatively build on existing institutional practice. Collaboration with colleagues is essential for the successful presentation and perpetuation of digital media works, the voices of the curator, conservator, registrar, technician, and artist are all required to thoughtfully implement a flexible preservation plan. Ultimately, each digital artwork is its own unique case study, and the methods described here may assist museums in adapting their collection management practices for these evolving art forms. ●

NOTES

1. Tate, "Art Term: Digital Art." Available at: https://www.tate.org.uk/art/art-terms/d/digital-art (accessed January 5, 2019).

2. *Electronic Arts Intermix (EAI) Online Resource Guide for Exhibiting, Collecting & Preserving Media Art*, "Glossary: Born digital." Available at: http://www.eai.org/resourceguide/glossary.html?backcoat (accessed December 31, 2018).

3. Matters in Media Art, "Acquiring media art." Available at: http://mattersinmediaart.org/acquiring-time-based-media-art.html (accessed January 25, 2019).

4. Voices in Contemporary Art (VoCA), "Interview resources." Available at: http://www.voca.network/voca-resources/ (accessed February 23, 2019).

5. All information from Matters in Media Art, "Sustaining media art." Available at: http://mattersinmediaart.org/sustaining-your-collection.html (accessed February 2, 2019).

6. See the "Implement fixity" section of Matters in Media Art for checksum resources and tips: Matters in Media Art, "Implement Fixity." Available at: http://mattersinmediaart.org/sustaining-your-collection.html#Implement-Fixity (accessed March 6, 2019).

7. Matters in Media Art, "Documenting media art." Available at: http://mattersinmediaart.org/assessing-time-based-media-art.html (accessed February 2, 2019).

8. For in-depth guidelines for managing equipment in media collections, see Pip Laurenson, "The management of display equipment in time-based media installations," *Tate Papers: Tate's Online Research Journal*, Spring 2005. Available at: https://www.tate.org.uk/download/file/fid/7344 (accessed August 3, 2018).

9. Excellent resources to help manage and identify significance for media equipment include Laurenson, "The management of display equipment," and Joanna Phillips, "Shifting equipment significance in time-based media art," *The Electronic Media Review, Vol. 1* (2012). Available at: http://resources.conservation-us.org/emg-review/wp-content/uploads/sites/15/2016/07/Vol-1_2010_Ch-6_Phillips.pdf.

10. *Electronic Arts Intermix (EAI) Online Resource Guide for Exhibiting, Collecting & Preserving Media Art*. Available at: http://www.eai.org/resourceguide/ (accessed March 2, 2019). Another valuable tool for managing computer-based arts is a version control software such as Git, that archives any necessary changes, such as migration, made to an artwork's source code over time. For more information on this platform, see Altassian: Bitbucket. Available at: https://bitbucket.org/ (accessed March 6, 2019).

11. Laurenson, "The management of display equipment."

12. Mark B. Schlemmer, CHAPTER 3E, "Documenting Contemporary Art" this volume.

13. Matters in Media Art, "Lending media art." Available at: http://mattersinmediaart.org/lending-time-based-media.html (accessed February 24, 2019).

14. Mark Hellar, interview by author, San Francisco, CA, February 28, 2019.

Special thanks to Linda Leckart.

3H | OLD LOANS AND MUSEUM PROPERTY LAWS

ILDIKO POGANY DEANGELIS (UPDATED AND EDITED BY JOHN E. SIMMONS AND TONI M. KISER)

FEW MUSEUM REGISTRARS and collections managers are spared the vexing problem of old loans and unclaimed loans (expired loans or loans of unlimited duration that are left unclaimed by lenders who cannot be readily located).[1] These objects may have come to the museum as part of a formal loan for exhibition or study by museum staff.[2] The lenders may have long since died, moved, or for some other reason failed to maintain contact with the museum. Because registrars and collections managers have the responsibility to monitor loans and to account for the objects and their documentation in the custody of the museum, it is to them that the task of resolving the old loan conundrum usually falls.

Registrars and collections managers are advised to take the time to resolve old loans because the mere passage of time will not cure the problem, only confound it further. The older the loan becomes, the harder it will be to resolve. When lacking legal title to the unclaimed objects, the museum can make only limited use of them, all the while bearing the costs and burdens of storage space, record maintenance, climate control, security, periodic inspection, insurance, and general overhead.[3]

To understand what must be done, it is important to appreciate the legal constraints involved. The basic legal relationship between the lender and the museum is a bailment, under which the museum as bailee (borrower) generally has the obligation to care for the object until the bailor (lender) comes to claim it.[4] This obligation can go on indefinitely because the passage of time will not alter this legal relationship. For example, if a lender dies, ownership interest in the object will pass to the lender's heirs. Often, determining the identity and location of heirs entitled to the object may be a difficult and time-consuming, if not impossible, task. To make things worse, returning the object to the wrong party may open the museum to liability for a claim brought by the rightful owner.

The key to resolving the old loan dilemma is for the museum to break the bailment relationship as soon as possible. Unfortunately, this is not easily done under general legal principles.

In recognition of these difficulties, many states have passed old loan statutes that specifically make this task easier for museums.[5] These old loan laws spell out the mechanisms by which the lender's ownership of the object can be cut off, making it possible for the museum to move with some assurance toward gaining title to the object. With the title secure, the museum then may use or dispose of an object as it sees fit. More will be said about these state statutes and the general approaches they take, but first a discussion of common law principles (principles that govern in absence of a statute) is in order. These principles usually prevail in states without specific old loan statutes, and a knowledge of these principles also assists in appreciating and interpreting specific old loan statutes.

THE COMMON LAW SOLUTION

In states without old loan statutes, museums are left with general principles of common law to guide them. Common law refers to principles that do not rest for their authority on any express statute but on statements of principles found in court decisions. The application of these principles to old loans has not been fully tested in court. As a result, museums are left with some legal uncertainties.[6] Nevertheless, under these principles, to break the bailment relationship, the museum must take actions inconsistent with the terms of the bailment and call the lender's attention to the fact that title to the object is being challenged and could be lost if the lender remains silent. For example, the museum should send a letter to the lender stating that the museum is terminating the loan, and unless the lender comes forward to claim the objects or make arrangements for their successful return by a certain date, the museum will take title to the objects as of that date. If the lender is aware of the museum's *conversion* (a legal term meaning unauthorized assumption of ownership of property belonging to another), the lender, under general principles of law, must come forward to protect ownership interests. If the lender fails to claim the object or to bring a claim or suit to court within a specific time after the museum's conversion of the object, the lender's ownership rights may be lost.

The specific time periods to bring claims to court are provided in state laws and are called *statutes of limitations*. Lawsuits are barred that are not brought within prescribed limitation periods. The purpose of statutes of limitations is to encourage claimants to take timely action before evidence fades and witnesses die. Statutes of limitations vary from state to state and with the nature of the claim. For example, a claim for breach of contract will have a different limitation period from a claim based on negligence causing personal injury. Although it is relatively simple to determine the length of the limitation period in any state for a claim of conversion, the more difficult issue is to determine when the limitation period begins to run against an owner to extinguish the owner's claim. The general rule is that the owner of property converted by another must bring a claim to court within the limitation period that begins after the owner's *cause of action* arises. A cause of action is a set of facts that give a person the right to file a suit in court.

Under the law of bailment, the cause of action usually arises when the lender demands return of the object and the borrower refuses. The lender's cause of action may also arise when the lender is put on notice that the borrower is claiming title to the object—in effect, refusing to return the object. Thus, to use the statute of limitations to extinguish a lender's right to an unclaimed object, the goal for the museum is to make sure the lender has notice that the museum intends to terminate the loan and to claim the loaned object as its own if the lender fails to come and get it or arrange for its return.[7]

To ensure that the limitations period is triggered, the museum should notify the lender by certified mail (return receipt requested) to prove that the lender received the actual notice of the museum's actions. Upon the lender's receipt of the notice, the limitations period should begin to run and after its expiration, the lender who has failed to take action should be barred from any further claim to the object. Title to the object, in effect, then belongs to the museum. At this time, the museum is free to do whatever it wishes with the object—to keep it, lend it, or dispose of it.

Anyone who has ever worked with old loans inevitably would ask the next question—what if the lender is unknown or the lender or heirs cannot be located? Are there any alternatives to actual notice? One court decision from the District of Columbia, in the *McCagg* case,[8] involved an old loan, and the court suggested that constructive notice to the lender might be legally sufficient where actual notice is not possible. The term *constructive notice* refers to notice to unknown or missing individuals by publication in a newspaper. If done properly, the law will presume that the notice reached the individual whether the person actually saw the notice in the newspaper. All the old loan statutes discussed herein have implemented the constructive notice approach to notify missing lenders. The question remains whether constructive notice will be legally sufficient without an applicable state statute in place that provides how and when this may be done. Until this has been tested in court, museums must face an element of uncertainty in this area. This uncertainty should not prevent museums from proceeding because doing nothing affords no chance of yielding any positive results. Each museum is urged, however, to consult with its legal counsel before initiating notice to lenders by publication.

In any event, the court in the *McCagg* case cautioned that constructive notice may be available only if actual notice is not possible. Thus, a museum must be in a position to show that the lender or heirs could not be located after reasonable efforts by the museum to do so. As to what constitutes reasonable efforts, once again there is little guidance in existing legal precedents. One commentator suggests that the following sources, in addition to the museum's own records, should be consulted in the course of a reasonable search for the lender—probate records, telephone directories, real estate records, and vital (death) records.[9] Depending on the circumstances, other avenues such as social registers or cemetery records may be available. It is absolutely essential that the museum document every effort taken to locate lenders because the museum's records may become evidence should a lender or heir suddenly surface years later and demand return of the object. The value of the object in question may have an impact on the extent of the efforts to locate the lenders. If, after reasonable efforts, the whereabouts of the lender or heirs are still unknown, the museum may try constructive notice by publication in a newspaper.

The notice in the newspapers should include as much of the following information as possible:

- Date of the notice,
- Name of the lender,
- Description of the object loaned,
- Date of the original loan,
- Name and address of the museum staff to contact, and
- Statement that the museum is terminating the loan and will take title to the object if it is not claimed by a specified date.

It is suggested that this notice should be published once a week for three consecutive weeks in a newspaper of general circulation in the county of the lender's last known address and the county or municipality where the museum is located.[10] The statute of limitations should begin to run after the date set in the notice as a deadline for contacting the museum—whether the lender or heirs have actually seen the published notice.

If the lender fails to come forward before the date given by actual or constructive notice, the museum should amend its records immediately to reflect the ownership change for the object as of that date. In addition, the museum should note in the records the date of expiration of claims under that state's statute of limitations. Although the museum asserts ownership from the date the object is accessioned, its title to the object would be subject to challenge in a claim brought to court by the lender or heirs up to the time

the applicable limitations period for filing suit had expired. Therefore, the file should note that prior to the expiration of the statute of limitations, the object should not be disposed of by the museum. For example, in the museum's published notice, the date in which title is claimed is June 1, 1995. Having failed to hear from the lender or heirs, on June 1, 1995, the museum accessions the object. Having been advised by counsel that the limitations period for conversion is three years, the museum will note in the records that the object should not be disposed of prior to June 2, 1998.

In planning a systematic approach to resolve old loans in states where no statute exists, museums are well advised to seek the advice of counsel in establishing procedures and forms for this purpose. One publication highly recommended to aid museums and their counsel in this effort is entitled *Practical Guidelines in Resolving Old Loans: Guidelines for Museums* by Agnes Tabah, which has step-by-step instructions and sample forms that may be helpful. It can be found in Malaro and DeAngelis *Legal Primer on Managing Museum Collections* (2012, 344–350).

However, because of a lack of clear precedents, even if all recommended steps are taken, there are no guarantees that claims will not be brought against the museum for conversion of the loaned object. In the worst case, a lender or heirs may surface years later and institute a lawsuit. At this point, if a court should determine that the steps taken by the museum to gain title were legally insufficient, the museum may need to return the object. If the object was disposed of in the interim, the museum may be ordered to compensate the lender for the value of the object, possibly as of the date of the lender's return. Although the risk of a legal suit with the attendant adverse publicity should not be underestimated, this risk needs to be balanced against the substantial benefits gained by freeing the museum's collections from unwanted objects that are costly to maintain, and by having reliable, up-to-date records of objects in its collections. If the objects are of little value, it is unlikely that anyone is ever going to sue. If someone does threaten a lawsuit, it is a relatively simple matter to offer to pay the claimant the value of the object to make the claim go away. If the museum has disposed of the object after acquiring title, it should have an excellent record of the object's value at the time of disposal. In any event, the museum's counsel may be able to negotiate a settlement without the need to resort to a formal legal proceeding.

LEGISLATIVE SOLUTION— STATE OLD LOAN STATUTES

A list of states that have passed old loan statutes can be found in TABLE 3H.I. For a museum located in a state with old loan legislation, resolving old loans will require following the dictates of the applicable statute. Although state old loan statutes vary in approach, they all establish specific mechanisms by which the museum may terminate the loan and take title to an object left unclaimed by a lender. In operation, the legislative solution mimics the common law approach but adds clarity and some degree of certainty about the adequacy of the procedures. In some cases, old loan statutes eliminate some cumbersome steps required under the common law approach. The usual scheme is for the law to prescribe a notice procedure by which lenders are notified by the museum that the loan is terminated. The notice procedures may apply to expired loans as well as to indefinite loans that have been at the museum for an extended period.

The notice may take two general forms. The first is by mail to the lender of record at the last known address and the second is notice by publication in newspapers. Some statutes only require notice by mail to the name and address of the lender as it appears in the museum's records. If that information is not accurate or if it is incomplete, no further search for the lender is required. Other statutes require a *reasonable search* for the lender, often not giving much guidance as to what the term means. If the lender cannot be reached by mail, the museum may proceed with notification by publication in a newspaper. If, after notice, no one comes forward to make a claim within the prescribed time period (ranging from thirty days to seven years), title to the object passes to the museum. Several states allow museums to take title to an object without giving notice if there was no contact between the museum and the lender for a long time. For example, California allows the museum to take title if there has been no contact with the lender for at least twenty-five years as evidenced in the museum's records.[11]

In addition, old loan statutes may impose obligations on lenders to notify museums of change of address and changes in ownership of the property.[12] Some statutes address the issue of undertaking conservation work on unclaimed loans.[13]

An important question not yet answered is whether these statutes will pass constitutional challenges that may be brought to court by disgruntled lenders. Such challenges to state laws may be brought under the Fourteenth Amendment of the US Constitution, alleging that the old loan statute deprives the lender of property without the due process of law. The question presented in such cases is whether the law affords owners adequate notice and opportunity to protect their ownership rights before such rights are cut off. As of 2016, there had been no published court decisions testing the constitutionality of any state old loan statute, so we have yet to see how a court may view these statutes with regard to due process questions.[14]

One unpublished study indicates that many museums may not have begun to implement applicable old loan statutes. This conclusion is based on the sparse replies to a questionnaire on implementation of old loan legislation.[15] The study posits the following reasons for this sluggishness. To use the statutes systematically, museums need to inventory their collections to determine which objects are, in fact, old loans. Inventories require time and effort and are too easily relegated to the back burner. Also, some museums may be reluctant to implement the statutes, fearing that important objects will be lost if lenders actually come forward and reclaim loaned objects. Finally, some may fear the administrative burdens that may be presented by spurious claims. The experience reported by the few museums that have implemented their legislation shows the opposite. Contrary to fears, large numbers of people did not come forward to claim objects. Moreover, implementation of the old loan statutes gave registrars a useful instrument to provide vacillating lenders incentive to make decisions on disposition of their loaned property.[16]

Table 3H.1 State Old Loans Legislation

State	Citation	Comments	FIC provision
Alabama	§ 41-6-70 to 41-6-75	Applies only to collections held by the Department of Archives and History	"Undocumented property" must be held for 5 years or longer and remain unclaimed. The museum must publish a notice at least once each week for 2 consecutive weeks with specified information. If after 90 days from the second notice, no one claims title, it become property of the department
Alaska	§ 14.57.200 to 14.57.290	Article 1 (starting with 14.57.010) applies to the State Museum only. Article 3 (starting with 14.57.200) applies to property held by museums; notifications of all Native American FIC property must be sent to all Native Corporations	"Undocumented Property" must be held for 7 years or longer, verified by museum records, with no contact or claim by any person. The museum must publish a notice once a week for 4 weeks including specified information. If the property is not Native American, the museum can claim title on the 46th day after the last notice.
Arizona	§ 44-351 to 44-356	—	"Undocumented Property" must be held for 7 years or longer, verified by museum records, with no contact or claim by any person. The museum must: publish a notice for two consecutive weeks including specified information, wait 65 days, then publish a second notice including specified information. If no claims are made, title passes to the museum.
Arkansas	13-5-1001 to 13-5-1013	—	"Undocumented Property" that is documented by the museum for 7 years, to which no person has made a claim, becomes the property of the museum. However, ownership is not vested if the undocumented property is determined later to be stolen property or property whose ownership is subject to federal law
California	§1899 to 1899.11	—	None
Colorado	§ 38-14-101 to 38-14-112	—	None
Connecticut	Connecticut General Statute § 11-81 (2012)	Allows museums to claim ownership of abandoned loans if no action is taken to recover it and proper notification is made	None
Delaware	—	No museum-specific legislation	—

State	Citation	Comments	FIC provision
District of Columbia	—	No museum-specific legislation	—
Florida	§ 265.565.1-12	—	No
Georgia	§ 10-1-529.1-7	Georgia Museum Property Act excludes American Indian human remains and burial objects	Undocumented property that is held by the museum for 7 years and remains unclaimed can become property of the museum after publishing a notice once a week for 2 consecutive weeks with specific information.
Hawaii	—	No museum-specific information	—
Idaho	—	No museum-specific information	—
Illinois	chap. 765 § 1033/1 to 1033/50	For FIC, no notice is necessary. The only requirement is for the 7-year waiting period to end.	"Undocumented Property" that is held by the museum for 7 years, to which no person has made a claim, becomes the property of the museum. However, ownership is nor vested if the undocumented property is determined later to be stolen property or property whose ownership is subject to federal law.
Indiana	§ 32-34-5-1 to 16	—	"Undocumented Property" must be held for 7 years or longer. The museum must publish a notice including specified information. If no claims are made within three (3) years of the publication of the notice, title passes to the museum
Iowa	§ 305B.l to 305B.13	—	"Undocumented Property" must be held for 7 years or longer, with no contact or claim by any person. The museum must publish a notice including specified information. If no claims are made within three (3) years of the publication of the notice, title passes to the museum.
Kansas	§ 58-4001 to 58-4013	—	"Undocumented Property" must be held for 7 years or longer, with no contact or claim by any person. The museum must publish a notice including specified information. If no claims are made within 1 year of the publication of the notice, title passes to the museum.
Kentucky	§ 171.830 to 171.849	—	A museum may initiate action to gain title to property (pursuant to KRS 171.840) after it has held property for seven (7) years, other than by the terms of a loan agreement

(continued)

Table 3H.1 *Continued*

State	Citation	Comments	FIC provision
Louisiana	§ 25.345	Applies only to Louisiana State museums	Any property that is held at a museum for 10 years or more, to which no person has made a claim, becomes the property of the museum if the museum publishes a notice once a week for two weeks containing specified information. If no claims are made within 65 days, title passes to the museum.
Maine	Title 27 § 601	—	Any property that is held at a museum for 25 years or more, to which no person has made a claim, becomes the property of the museum if the museum publishes a notice once a week for 2 weeks containing specified information. If no claims are made within 65 days, ride passes to the museum.
Maryland	—	No museum-specific information	—
Massachusetts	Chapter 200B Sections 1–8	Allows museums to assume title to abandoned loans after 7 years in the absence of claims	—
Michigan	§ 399.601 to 399.613	—	Beginning January 1, 1993, a museum may give notice on "Undocumented Property." The museum must publish a notice for 2 consecutive weeks including specified information, wait at least 60 days, then publish a second notice including specified information.
Minnesota	345.70 to 345.74	—	Effective August 1, 2004, property that: (1) is found in or on property controlled by the museum; (2) is from an unknown source; and (3) might reasonably be assumed to have been intended as a gift to the museum, is conclusively presumed to be a gift to the museum if ownership of the property is not claimed by a person within 90 days of its discovery.
Mississippi	§ 39-19-1 to 39-19-21	—	No

State	Citation	Comments	FIC provision
Missouri	§ 184.101 to 184.122	—	"Undocumented Property" must be held for 7 years or longer, with no contact or claim by any person. The museum must publish a notice including specified information. If no claims are made within 90 days of the publication of the notice, title passes to the museum.
Montana	§ 22-3-501 to 22-3-523	22-3-523. Applicability. This part applies only to property loaned to a museum on or after October 1, 1985, or to existing loaned property with a market value of $1,000 or less at the time of disposal.	No
Nebraska	§ 51-701 to 51-712	—	"Undocumented Property" must be held for 7 years or longer, with no contact or claim by any person. The museum must publish a notice including specified information. If no claims are made within 3 years of the publication of the notice, title passes to the museum.
New Hampshire	§ 201-E:1 to 201-E:7	—	Any property held by a museum within the state, other than by terms of a loan agreement, must be held for 5 years or longer, with no contact or claim by any person. The museum must publish a notice including specified information. If no claims are made within 90 days of the publication of the notice, title passes to the museum.
New Jersey	—	No museum-specific legislation	—
New Mexico	§ 18-10-1 to 18-10-5	—	No
New York	§ 233-a; § 233-aa	§ 233-a applies only to the New York State Museum. § 233-aa, signed in 2008, amends that law to include other museums in the state.	"Unclaimed or Undocumented Property" requires 3 newspaper publications, 180-day waiting period, then publication on the Unclaimed Funds Registry of the Comptroller's website. 30 days after that posting, the museum acquires the property. For "Unsolicited" property, the museum acquires rights 90 days after delivery if no one comes forward to establish ownership.

(continued)

Table 3H.1 *Continued*

State	Citation	Comments	FIC provision
North Carolina	§ 121-7(c) and 121-7(d)	Applies only to North Carolina State museums (Department of Cultural Resources)	"Undocumented Property" must be held for five years or longer, with no contact or claim by any person. The museum must publish a notice including specified information. If no claims are made within 30 days of the publication of the notice, title passes to the museum.
North Dakota	§ 47-07-14	—	No
Ohio	Title 33 § 3385.01 to 33805.10	—	No
Oklahoma	60.683.2	Pursuant to section 60.683.2(c) of the Oklahoma statutes, a museum is exempted from the provisions of the state's Uniform Unclaimed Property Act, but may avail itself of the act by complying with its provisions	
Oregon	§ 358.415 to 358.440	—	No
Pennsylvania	Title 37 § 304	Applies only to state museums	—
Rhode Island	Chapter 34-44.1-8	Provision for museums to claim abandoned loan property	Provision for museums to claim abandoned property in its possession
South Carolina	§ 27-45-10 to 27-45-100	—	No
South Dakota	§ 43-41C-1l to 43-41C-4	—	Abandoned Property: Any property that has been held by the museum for ten years or more, other than by terms of a loan agreement, shall be deemed abandoned. The museum must publish a notice with specific information. If no claims are made within 65 days, title passes to the museum.
Tennessee	§ 66-29-201 to 66-29-204	—	Abandoned Property: Any property that has been held by the museum for 20 years or more, other than by terms of a loan agreement, shall be deemed abandoned. The museum must publish a notice with specific information. If no claims are made within 65 days, title passes to the museum.
Texas	§ 80.001 to 80.008	—	No

State	Citation	Comments	FIC provision
Utah	§ 9-8-801 to 9-8-806	—	Any materials that are not accompanied by a transfer of title are considered a gift when more than 25 years have passed from the date of the last written contact between depositor or his successors and the collecting institution.
Vermont	§ 27-12-1151 to 1158	—	Any property held by a museum that is not subject to a loan agreement and has been held for 10 or more years and has remained unclaimed shall be deemed to be abandoned. The museum must publish a notice once each month for three consecutive months. After 180 days from the date of the third published notice, if no claim has been made, title passes to the museum.
Virginia	§ 55-210.31- § 55-210.38	—	No
Washington	§ 63.26.010 to 63.26.050	—	Abandoned Property: Any property that has been held by the museum for 5 years or more, other than by terms of a loan agreement, shall be deemed abandoned. The museum must publish a notice with specific information at least once a week for 2 weeks. If no claims are made within 90 days, title passes to the museum.
West Virginia	—	No museum-specific legislation	
Wisconsin	§ 171.30 to 171.33	—	No
Wyoming	§ 34-23-101 to 34-23-108	—	No

HOW TO AVOID THE PROBLEM OF OLD LOANS IN THE FUTURE

Given the time, effort, and costs involved in resolving old loans, museums should institute safeguards to avoid this problem in the future. Museums should borrow or loan objects for a limited duration only (usually one year) with the expiration date specifically stated in the loan agreement. If the object is needed longer, it is better to renew the loan than to agree to a longer initial term. More frequent contacts with lenders will also help avoid the missing lender situation. Loan agreements should specify that it is the lender's obligation to notify the museum of a change in the lender's address or a change in the ownership of the loaned object. Moreover, loan agreements should state that if, at the expiration of the loan, the museum is unable to contact the lender to make arrangements for the return of the object, the museum will store the object for a set period of years at the lender's expense. If, after this period, the lender still fails to come forward after notice by mail is sent by the museum to the lender's address of record, the museum will deem that an unrestricted gift of the object is made by the lender to the museum. In effect, the loan agreement will put the lender on notice of the museum's claim to the object after a set period of time if the lender fails to maintain contact or refuses to pick up the object.

Objects left at the museum for identification, authentication, or examination are more likely to be left unclaimed than objects borrowed by the museum for exhibition purposes. The negligible value of some of these objects may remove an incentive for their owners to return to claim them. To avoid this risk, these objects should be processed immediately by the museum. Each should be documented with a temporary custody receipt, signed by the owner. If an object was mailed unsolicited to the museum, the package should be returned within days to the sender. If more time is needed, the temporary custody receipt should be mailed to the sender for signature. The length of the museum's custody specified in the receipt should be limited to a period significantly shorter than the duration of a standard incoming loan. For example, a museum may decide that the maximum time for temporary custody is three months, subject to extension by special permission only. The temporary custody receipt should specify the exact method to be used for return of the object and include a provision, similar to one used in a formal loan agreement, that infers a gift to the museum if the object is not claimed after a limited storage period subsequent to the expiration date on the receipt.

CONCLUSION

As a public trust, a museum has a legal responsibility to make the best use of its assets. Prudent collections management dictates that museums should pursue systematic efforts to clean up old loans that eat up valuable storage space and consume scarce staff and financial resources, but procedures should also be in place to avoid these situations. It is the registrar or collections manager that usually plays a critical role in developing and implementing ways to banish the old loan problem in a museum. •

NOTES

1. Although the term *permanent loan* was used in museums many years ago, a loan is temporary by definition. It is unclear what people were thinking when the arrangements for so-called permanent loans were made. A review of a museum's records of permanent loans will often indicate that a gift was actually intended or completed. If title to the object still rests with the lender, then permanently loaned objects should be treated as loans of unlimited duration.

2. It is important to note that *old loans* do not include undocumented objects found in the museum's collections. *Found-in-collection* (FIC) objects are those that lack any documentation as to how they were acquired by the museum. This chapter deals with objects that are accompanied by documentation affirming that a loan to the museum was intended by the owner. The problem with FIC objects is that they lack evidence that someone else owns them. As discussed in CHAPTER 3J, "Found in Collection," the museum's undisturbed possession for an extended period supports a presumption that ownership was transferred to the museum at the time the objects were acquired. Therefore, unless and until someone shows up at the museum and can overcome this presumption with evidence of clearer title to a FIC object, the museum generally may treat a FIC object as its own. However, disposal of objects of unconfirmed ownership should involve further considerations and assistance from the museum's legal counsel (see the deaccession risk chart, TABLE 31.1).

3. L. K. Wise, "Old loans: A collections management problem," in *Legal Problems of Museum Administration*, ALI-ABA (1990), 44; M. C. Malaro and I. P. DeAngelis, "Figure VII.3—Practical guidelines for resolving unclaimed loans," in *A Legal Primer on Managing Museum Collections*, 3rd ed., edited by M. C. Malaro and I. P. DeAngelis, pp. 344–350 (Washington, DC: Smithsonian Institution Press, 2012).

4. For a full discussion of the legal problems of unclaimed loans and possible solutions, see Malaro and DeAngelis, "Unclaimed loans," in *A Legal Primer in Managing Museum Collections*, 319–354.

5. The Mid-Atlantic Association of Museums Registrars Committee established an Old Loan Task Force in the late 1990s to draft model legislation for that region that includes Pennsylvania, Maryland, Virginia, Washington, DC, Delaware, New York, and New Jersey.

6. In one reported court decision from the District of Columbia involving an old loan, the court held that the paintings on loan to a museum for decades had to be returned to the lender's heirs. In re: Therese McCagg, 450 A.2d 414 (D.C. 1982), the court noted that the museum had failed in that case to make a reasonable effort to notify the lender's heirs and refused to find that the loan had expired at the lender's death. However, the court noted in a footnote that if the lenders cannot be located by the museum after reasonable efforts, notice to the lenders or heirs by publication in a newspaper may be legally sufficient. Notice by publication was not directly at issue in the case.

7. In addition to the statute of limitations approach, the legal doctrines of *adverse possession* and *laches* may help a museum successfully defend a case brought by a long overdue lender

for return of an old loan. The usefulness of these doctrines is discussed in Malaro and DeAngelis, *A Legal Primer*, 81–83, and in L. A. DeAngelis, "Old loans-Laches to the rescue?" in *Legal Problems of Museum Administration* (ALI-ABA, 1992), 202. Actions taken by the museum under the statute of limitations approach discussed in this chapter will also support these alternate defenses and are not separately addressed here.

8. Malaro and DeAngelis, *A Legal Primer*, 324.

9. A. Tabah, "The practicalities of resolving old loans: Guidelines for museums," in *Legal Problems of Museum Administration*, 330–331.

10. Tabah, "The practicalities of resolving old loans."

11. California Civil Code Sec. 1899.10(b).

12. For example, see the old loan statutes of California, Wyoming, Missouri, and Kansas.

13. For example, see the old loan statutes of Indiana, Missouri, and South Carolina.

14. H. Kuruvilla, *A Legal Dictionary for Museum Professionals* (Lanham, MD: Rowman & Littlefield, 2016).

15. A. Tabah, "Old Loans: State Legislative Solutions," unpublished research paper dated December 4, 1991, prepared for the George Washington University Museum Studies Program course on Collections Management: Legal and Ethical Issues.

16. Tabah, "Old Loans."

31 | Deaccessioning and Disposal

ANTONIA MOSER

Museums acquire and accession objects to build permanent collections. Strong collections management policies and clear collections plans help museums develop collections that advance their missions, serve educational and scholarly purposes, and benefit the public. Historically, however, collecting practices have not always been as formal or well-disciplined as they are today; museums may hold objects, accessioned decades ago, that no longer meet the strict requirements or defined guidelines that are now in place for accessioning.[1] In addition, collecting priorities may change over time because museums occasionally reassess how to focus the scope of their collections to serve their missions more effectively. Museum collections, although usually intended to be permanent, are not immutable—they are "dynamic, not static."[2] Some flexibility must be granted to provide museums with a method to correct collecting mistakes of the past and to respond to the collecting needs of the present. A mechanism must be in place to allow for the thoughtful and careful removal of objects from the permanent collection.

Deaccessioning has long been considered an acceptable practice in US museums of all disciplines. It stems from the acknowledgment that museum collections must be finite.[3] Just as a museum must be selective in determining what to accession, bearing in mind its collecting criteria as well as the resources it must commit to the proper care, documentation, and use of the object, so too must the museum acknowledge that not everything in its collection truly belongs there. Removing these objects allows the museum to dedicate more resources to developing and caring for a collection that will better benefit the public trust. Because museum collecting should be "a combination of intelligent selection and thoughtful pruning,"[4] deaccessioning is considered by most museums to be an important component of proper collections management. Deaccessioning, or the process through which an object is recorded as officially removed from the museum's accessioned holdings, is usually followed by disposal, the relocation of the physical object from the museum's permanent, accessioned collection. Just as a museum must carefully document its decision to accession an object and the transfer of title to the museum, so all considerations and steps in the processes of deaccessioning and disposal must likewise be properly recorded.

Although many museum professionals recognize that deaccessioning can be important and beneficial, it can also be regarded as controversial because of what some perceive as the potential for the practice to be abused. Debates arise specifically around disposal, when a former collection object is to be sold. Critics question whether an object, once held in trust for the public in a museum collection, should be offered for public sale at all, and then face the possibility of reverting to private ownership. Even more problematic is the notion that museums might betray their public trust by monetizing collections when they are sold. Questions surround the use of proceeds realized from deaccessioned collections and how to ensure that the public trust is maintained. Despite many museums having found themselves at the center of deaccessioning controversies, stories continue to arise of museums that feel compelled to sell collections to fix budget shortfalls or to risk closing all together. Debate about this issue, and over the ethics of deaccessioning and disposal, continues (for more in-depth discussion of the ethics of deaccessioning and disposal, see CHAPTER 7A, "Ethics for Registrars and Collection Managers"). Transparent policies and procedures for thoughtful and careful deaccessioning and disposal can help museums mitigate the risk of ethical controversy.

DEACCESSIONING POLICIES

Every museum's collections management policy, in accordance with its mission, should contain a section on deaccessioning and disposal (see CHAPTER 2, "Collection Management Policies"). This policy should guide the museum through deaccessioning decisions that ensure proper collections management and accountability to the public. Important components of the deaccessioning and disposal policy include:

- Who has the authority to deaccession collections? Often, with permanent accessioned collections, this responsibility rests with the governing board of the institution, which acts with the advice of the director, curator, and collections staff. As others have noted, the "level of authority needed to remove an object from the collection should be equal to or higher than the level of authority needed to accession such an object."[5]
- For what reasons will a museum permit an object to be deaccessioned? What criteria will the museum use in making this decision?
- What methods of disposal will a museum allow?
- Are different categories of collections subject to different processes or levels of authority? For example, an object from a study or hands-on collection may require a less rigid review and may not need governing board approval for deaccessioning.
- Under what circumstances, if any, does the museum allow disposal of found-in-collection objects (see CHAPTER 3J, "Found in Collection")?
- Does the museum require a scholarly review and approval of the deaccessioning proposal from an outside party?
- Does the museum require an appraisal from a disinterested outside party, and if so, under what circumstances?
- Does the museum attempt to notify the original donors that an object they donated may be deaccessioned?
- What process does the museum follow to deaccession objects? Because deaccessioning can be complicated and must be undertaken with vigilance, deaccessioning policies may outline procedural steps required.[6]

- If a museum allows disposal via public auction, are proceeds to be used solely for acquisitions or for direct care of collections as well? How does the museum define direct care?
- What guidelines are in place to ensure that the policy complies with the museum's code of ethics?

To assist museums with developing their deaccessioning and disposal policies, professional museum organizations, such as the American Alliance of Museums (AAM),[7] the Association of Art Museum Directors (AAMD),[8] the American Association for State and Local History (AASLH),[9] the Society of American Archivists (SAA),[10] and the Association of Academic Museums and Galleries (AAMG),[11] have issued a number of directives and have included in their codes of ethics guidelines for museums to follow. Although these organizations generally acknowledge that deaccessioning is an important tool in managing a healthy collection, special attention is devoted to the ethical concerns surrounding the disposal of objects through sale and the use of those proceeds. Any profits accrued through the sale of collection objects must be used to support the collection. Codes of ethics may differ according to discipline in determining what particular activities qualify as supporting the collection. For example, while the AAMD stipulates that deaccessioning proceeds may only be used for acquisitions, the AAM and AASLH allow for direct care of collections. The term *direct care of collections* generated confusion among museums for many years—what exactly can be considered direct care, and how does one distinguish between direct care and operating expenses? As a result, AAM formed a task team that produced a white paper on the topic, released in April 2016.[12] The white paper provides guidance to help museums determine how direct care applies to their collections and makes additional recommendations to clarify deaccessioning and disposal policies (see CHAPTER 7A, "Ethics for Registrars and Collection Managers"). Museums are advised to consult the codes of ethics relevant to their disciplines to create deaccessioning policies that are in compliance with them.

State-chartered museums in New York must be aware of legal requirements established by the state's

Board of Regents in 2011. The rules delineate why museums are allowed to deaccession collections and require that proceeds from deaccessioning be used only for acquisitions or direct care; using proceeds for operating expenses is not allowed. Museums in New York State are required to submit an annual report to the State Education Committee that lists all objects deaccessioned in the previous year.

COLLECTIONS PLANS

In addition to deaccessioning and disposal policies, a museum's collections plan can provide guidance and direction for its deaccessioning activities. To justify deaccessioning decisions, the museum must have a clear understanding of the scope of its collections, what types of objects are useful for advancing its mission, and where collecting goals and activities should be focused. A collections plan is usually developed by curatorial staff based on the museum's scope of collections.[13] The plan contains a formal assessment of the strengths and weaknesses of existing collections and provides a framework for future collection growth. The assessment itself can be time-consuming—all collections staff, including curators, collections managers, registrars, and conservators, should participate in providing information about the physical condition, legal status, and intellectual or scholarly significance of collection objects. This analysis will help the museum target new acquisitions and plan for how best to use its resources for ongoing collections care. Likewise, the assessment may reveal objects that are not within the parameters of the plan and are therefore candidates for deaccessioning and disposal.[14]

Deaccessioning Criteria

A museum may consider deaccessioning a collection object under the following circumstances:

- The object is not within the scope of collections or does not serve the mission of the museum.
- The object is not likely to be useful for the museum's programs, research, exhibition, or educational purposes.

- The object is of poor quality, does not meet museum standards, or is a less important or incomplete example.
- The object is discovered to be fake or a forgery.
- The object is a duplicate of others in the collection or creates redundancy within the collection.
- The object's physical condition has deteriorated beyond conservation treatment possibilities.
- The object is composed of or contains hazardous material such that retaining the object would introduce intolerable risks to staff, visitors, or other collection objects.
- In the case of living collections, death of the specimen.
- Retaining the object is beyond the museum's resources or capabilities.
- The object is subject to restrictions that the museum is no longer able to meet.
- The object is found to be part of a set that belongs to another institution, or the object would be of greater use in the collection of another institution.
- The object is revealed to have been stolen or acquired illegally or unethically at some time in the past.
- The object is subject to a legislative mandate (e.g., NAGPRA).

Deaccessioning should never take place to satisfy the whims or tastes of individual curators, directors, or board members. It must always be an informed and thoughtful process in which multiple museum parties participate and concur. Moreover, deaccessioning is not recommended in the case of objects that were lost or stolen from the museum. These objects may someday be found or recovered, and the museum will want to reassert its ownership of them. Finally, a museum should never deaccession collections to raise operating funds, unless it is willing to face professional sanctions and public outcry.[15]

METHODS OF DISPOSAL

Although disposal is a separate (although related) process, and the proceeds gained from a disposal should never be a motivating factor in deaccessioning an object, including the planned method of disposal in the deaccessioning proposal can be prudent. Disposal can be time-consuming, may require research into appropriate repositories, and may involve difficult logistics. Without a practical disposal plan in place that has been considered and approved by the collections staff and museum management, a deaccessioned object runs the risk of languishing in storage. The most suitable method of disposal must be determined on a case-by-case basis and may vary depending on the object and the needs of the museum. No deaccessioned object should be acquired by museum staff, board members, volunteers, or their relations.[16] The following methods of disposal are generally considered acceptable.

Donation

Donation to another museum, library, archive, or nonprofit institution keeps the object in the public trust and is, therefore, the method of disposal preferred by many. Not every deaccessioned object is suitable for a collection, and it can be difficult to find an institution willing to accept a donation offer; however, for those objects that are of sufficient quality the museum may want to undertake efforts to relocate the object to another public collection.

Consider the recent well-publicized example of the transfer of the Brooklyn Museum of Art's costume collection to the Metropolitan Museum of Art in 2009.[17] On a smaller scale but equally as successful was the transfer in 2014 of a mid-nineteenth-century painting of West Point from Boscobel House and Gardens to the US Military Academy.[18]

Museums can seek out appropriate recipients through professional contacts, notices in scholarly publications, or through online resources and websites.[19] The National Air and Space Museum uses its website to promote its collections transfer program.[20] A list of deaccessioned objects designated as appropriate for transfer is posted annually; other nonprofit institutions can apply to receive these objects for their collections.

Exchange or Sale

Exchange or sale to another museum or nonprofit also keeps the object within the public trust and gives the museum the benefit of offering something back to its own public—either a new acquisition more appropriate to its mission or funds with which these new acquisitions can be purchased. Independent appraisals should be obtained to make sure the transaction is equitable.

Transfer to an Education Collection or Research Program

An object that is not appropriate for a museum collection may still be useful for scientific research, school studies, or hands-on educational programs. Even if the educational or research collection is within the same museum, the object must still be deaccessioned before it can be transferred to another collection in which it will receive a different standard of care and in which it is understood that the handling and sampling of the object may contribute to its deterioration.

Witnessed Destruction

In cases where the object's physical condition is beyond possibility of conservation treatment, or if the object is considered hazardous, then it may be destroyed. Hazardous materials should be disposed of in a safe manner, following applicable laws and in compliance with local health and safety regulations. In addition, fake or fraudulent objects may be destroyed to remove them permanently from circulation. For all objects that are destroyed, the destruction process should be thorough and full documentation including photographs should be kept, so that the museum has a complete record of the object's fate.

Repatriation or Restitution to Rightful Owner

A law such as Native American Graves Protection and Repatriation Act (NAGPRA) requires repatriation of certain objects that meet specific criteria. Objects for which the museum lacks title or which were acquired illegally (even though in good faith) or unethically should be restituted to the proper owner.

Public Auction

Some people argue that a public auction should be considered only if donation, exchange, or sale to another museum is not possible.[21] However, board members may feel an obligation to increase the acquisition funds for a museum, and thus, auction remains a frequent method of disposal. This disposition method is subject to public scrutiny, and therefore, it must be handled carefully.[22]

Interview several potential auction houses and check their references; consider their costs, their reputation for reliability, and marketing strategy. Inspect the auction's facilities, security, and handling procedures. Send requests for proposals to at least three auction houses to allow for fair competition among vendors and to provide the museum with the best option for its consignment. Be sure to discuss any questions regarding the object's provenance or attribution fully with the auction house.

The consignment agreement may need to be reviewed by the museum's legal counsel. The agreement should clarify how publicity will be arranged, who will provide photographs of the object, whether the museum will be identified in the sales catalog (and if so, how it will be identified), what commissions and fees will be charged (many auction houses offer reduced commission to museums), what reserve will be placed, how unsold materials will be handled, and what is required regarding the object's physical care and insurance coverage.

Transparency "is important to maintaining the museum's integrity"[23] so be sure to state in the sale catalog that the museum is selling the work and how it will use the proceeds.

Private sales are not encouraged as a method of disposal because they can be seen as a conflict of interest and may lack the transparency of a public auction. The same concerns make the sale of the object in the museum's gift shop an unprofessional practice. Returning an object to a private donor is not considered a good option because it may set a bad precedent and lead the public to think that donations can be recalled. It would remove an object from the public trust and return it to private hands without any compensation for the public. Returning an object to a private donor can create complications for the donor, if the donor took a tax deduction when the gift was made (currently, museums are required to file IRS form 8282 for charitable donations that are disposed of within three years of their acquisition). A

museum may, on rare occasion, consider returning an object to a donor only if it was never accessioned or was accepted with restrictions that the museum cannot keep.

DEACCESSIONING PROCESS

Each deaccessioning decision must be carefully considered, and museums should be prepared to prove how thoroughly they have undertaken this process with good documentation. Procedures should be standardized and the museum should "have the ability to demonstrate that, in fact, the procedures are followed."[24] A museum must develop a deaccessioning form or use the deaccessioning record in the collection management database to document each step. Deaccessioning documentation should include information about the object and its source, recommendations from staff members or third parties, authorizations by the museum's director and board, and all details regarding the method of disposal. The registrar plays an important role in managing this documentation, coordinating steps in this process, and providing information from museum records.[25]

Initiation and Review of Records

- The curator or the staff member most familiar with the collection and its needs usually initiates the deaccessioning process. The process should begin with a written justification explaining why the object is an appropriate candidate for deaccessioning, how it meets the deaccessioning criteria within the museum's collections management policy, and how removing the object from the collection is in line with the museum's collections plan.
- The registrar should gather any available information about the object to present with the deaccessioning proposal, including provenance, exhibition and publication history, descriptions, and photographs of the object and its physical condition. Having this information on hand will be helpful in understanding how the object fits (or does not fit) in the collection as a whole, which in turn will assist in deliberations and decisions regarding its disposition.
- The registrar should undertake a thorough review of the object's files to make sure the museum

holds clear and complete title to the object. Restrictions must be noted because they are legally binding and may cause complications that a lawyer must address. Joint ownership or shared objects will, of course, require conversations with the other owner(s) as well as with legal counsel. A review of the object files may reveal additional concerns that will need to be considered at this point, such as is the record of ownership lacking, or was the object never accessioned or fully processed? These objects may still be considered candidates for deaccessioning, but additional risks must be analyzed and extra steps may be required.

Objects without a record of ownership introduce risk into the deaccessioning process, and some museums have a policy against deaccessioning such material at all. However, in some cases, a museum may wish to weigh this risk against the benefit gained from removing an object that clearly does not belong in the museum's collection. The Deaccession Risk Chart (FIGURE 31.1) was created by Rebecca Buck to help museums counterbalance the levels of risk involved across four categories: value, disposition method, clarity of title, and object type. After checking all museum records, including loan files, for evidence of title, the registrar should assign a tracking number and create a file for the object (if this has not already been done), and, if required, enact the process

for found-in-collection objects as instructed by state law (see CHAPTER 3J, "Found in Collection"). If there is no evidence that the object is a loan, if it has been in the museum's possession for an extended period of time, and if it is not relevant to the museum's mission, then deaccessioning may be considered, despite the incomplete ownership documentation, particularly if other categories on the Deaccession Risk Chart are low (e.g., low value or the object type is "abundant" or "mass produced"). Disposition methods, however, may be limited—if the museum wished to sell the object, it would not be able to provide a warranty of title, which would impact the sales price.[26]

If the museum has proof of ownership of the object, but the object has never been accessioned, then it does not need to be taken through the full deaccessioning procedure. However, as the object is still property of the museum, a thoughtful approach to its disposal is recommended. Moreover, there is a distinction between objects not accessioned and objects not fully registered. Documentation may prove that an object was acquired with the intention to accession it into the permanent collection, but for some reason the process was not completed. Accessioning includes acquisition and registration, so it is always possible that the second of these activities was simply lost to a backlog of workflow. In these cases, an accession number should be assigned so that deaccessioning documentation can be tracked and properly filed.

	Value	Disposition method	Clarity of Title	Object type
MOST RISK	$1 million +		Clouded title	Unique
		Destroy	Undocumented/FIC	
		Return to source	Accession number only	Small series
		Sell privately	Unsigned deed of gift (no value)	
		Sell at auction	Unclear documentation	Limited edition, artist
		Exchange	Object and/or source card file	
		Repatriate	Annual reports	Limited edition, manufactured
		Give to non-profit	Report to trustees	
LEAST RISK	$0	Internal Transfer	Countersigned deed of gift/intent and acknowledgment/clear bill of sale	Mass produced (man-made) Abundant (natural)

FIGURE 31.1 DEACCESSION RISK CHART. PERMISSION FROM REBECCA BUCK.

External Opinions

- According to the requirements of the museum's deaccessioning policy, museum staff may now seek external opinions. Consultation with specialists outside of museum staff—curators, conservators, or other scholars within the discipline—and solicitation of their support of the decision to deaccession the object may strengthen the deaccessioning proposal. All details of this correspondence should be recorded.
- A disinterested third-party appraisal of value may be required. Some museums have a policy that requires external appraisals only if the object is thought to be worth over a certain amount. External appraisals of high-value objects or objects that are to be sold to or exchanged with another museum are always recommended.
- Finally, if there are any questions about the object's title or restrictions, the museum may want to seek advice from legal counsel.

Notifications

- The museum will need to consider its public and its responsibility to deaccession with transparency. Public notification of a deaccession is generally recommended;[27] consequently, the museum should now decide how and when this notification will occur. A press statement could be issued at the time of deaccessioning, worded to reassure the public that the museum's deaccessioning activities are intended to strengthen its collection and that they will be carried out with the highest accountability. Alternately, disclosure could take place at the time of disposal. Copies of any press releases should be kept as part of the deaccessioning documentation.
- Special notification may be made to the object's donor or the donor's heirs, depending on the circumstances. The museum is under no obligation to notify donors. If title to the object has been fully and freely transferred from the donor to the museum, then the donor has no legal authority to approve or object to the deaccessioning proposal.[28] Some museums want to provide this notification out of courtesy. Indeed, if a donor who is still actively involved with the museum learns through a third party or sale catalog that a gift has been deaccessioned, the museum may have an awkward situation on its hands. However, if the donor or donor's heirs have no ongoing relationship with the museum, then this notification is not necessary.
- If a work by a living artist is deaccessioned, the artist should be notified.

Authorization to Proceed

- Having gathered all the appropriate information about the object and its source, the museum staff can now determine whether to recommend deaccessioning and a disposition method to the director and board.
- Record the dates that approval is granted and have the deaccessioning proposal form signed by the proper authority.
- Mark the object's file and flag its database record as "deaccessioned."
- Follow through with efforts to remain transparent by announcing the deaccessioning decision. Museums that are AAMD members should post deaccessioned objects on their websites.

Disposal

- The registrar may now enact the disposal plan. Remove any accession numbers or other museum markings from objects that are to be sold at auction. This is considered a good practice to prevent confusion over ownership status or possible inflation of market value because of the object's past association with the museum. These objects should be tagged with removable numbers, however, to maintain inventory control throughout the disposal process. Accession numbers are usually left on objects that are donated or sold to other institutions so that the objects can be linked to the original museum's files and publications.
- Keep notes and copies of all internal discussions and correspondence as vendors or recipients are vetted and chosen.
- Make packing and shipping arrangements and record the date of the object's final transfer from the museum.
- In the case of donated objects, document the transfer of title and specify the credit line that the new institution should use.
- If an object is sold, record the date and location of the auction, keep a copy of the sale catalog, and

make note of the hammer price and net proceeds to the museum. Request a copy of the check or wire transfer receipt for the deaccessioning file, ensure the funds are deposited into a separate account restricted to the acquisition (or direct care) of collection objects, and determine what the replacement credit line will read for collection objects purchased with these funds. Many small objects sold for modest amounts can be combined into one general acquisitions fund with records kept of multiple donors' names.

- Finally, ensure that all documentation related to the deaccessioning is gathered and filed as part of the permanent history of the museum's collection, report the final outcome to the board, and include a summary in the museum's annual report on deaccession activity.

The deaccessioning process, if undertaken properly, will be time-consuming. However, a careful and thorough process is necessary to help a museum make responsible decisions about deaccessioning, to maintain accountability and transparency, and ultimately to develop a collection that effectively and efficiently serves its mission. •

NOTES

1. S. Miller, *Deaccessioning Today: Theory and Practice* (Lanham, MD: Rowman & Littlefield, 2018).

2. J. E. Simmons, *Things Great and Small: Collections Management Policies*, 2nd ed. (Lanham, MD: Rowman & Littlefield, 2018), 62.

3. M. C. Malaro and I. P. DeAngelis, *A Legal Primer on Managing Museum Collections*, 3rd ed. (Washington, DC: Smithsonian Institute Press, 2012).

4. Malaro and DeAngelis, *Legal Primer*, 248.

5. Malaro and DeAngelis, *Legal Primer*, 256.

6. Simmons, *Things Great and Small*, 74.

7. American Alliance of Museums, "AAM Code of Ethics for Museums," Ethics, Standards, and Professional Practices, amended 2000. Available at: https://www.aam-us.org/programs/ethics-standards-and-professional-practices/code-of-ethics-for-museums/.

8. Association of Art Museum Directors, "AAMD Policy on Deaccessioning," Standards and Practices, amended 10/2015. Available at: https://aamd.org/sites/default/files/document/AAMD%20Policy%20on%20Deaccessioning%20website_0.pdf.

9. American Association for State and Local History, "Statement of Professional Standards and Ethics," revised 2017. Available at: http://download.aaslh.org/Council/2017+Statement+of+Professional+Standards+and+Ethics.pdf.

10. Society of American Archivists, "Guidelines for Reappraisal and Deaccessioning," revised 2017. Available at: https://www2.archivists.org/sites/all/files/GuidelinesForReappraisalDeaccessioning_2017.pdf.

11. Association of Academic Museums and Galleries, "Professional Practices for Academic Museums and Galleries," June 2017. Available at: https://www.aamg-us.org/wp/wp-content/uploads/2018/04/AAMG-Professinal-Practices-2018-web-FINAL-rev043018.pdf.

12. American Alliance of Museums Direct Care Task Force, "Direct Care of Collections: Ethics, Guidelines and Recommendations," April 2016. Available at: https://www.aam-us.org/wp-content/uploads/2018/01/direct-care-of-collections-ethics-guidelines-and-recommendations-pdf.jpg.

13. J. B. Gardner and E. Merritt, *The AAM Guide to Collections Planning* (Washington, DC: American Association of Museums, 2004).

14. M. Morris, "Deaccessioning," in *Museum Registration Methods*, 5th ed., edited by R. A. Buck and J. A. Gilmore (Washington, DC: American Alliance of Museums Press, 2010), 101.

15. American Alliance of Museums Direct Care Task Force, "Direct Care of Collections: Ethics, Guidelines and Recommendations."

16. Morris, "Deaccessioning."

17. S. Yerkovich, *A Practical Guide to Museum Ethics* (Lanham, MD: Rowman & Littlefield, 2016), 75.

18. Miller, *Deaccessioning Today*, 37.

19. Miller, *Deaccessioning Today*, 62.

20. Smithsonian National Air and Space Museum, "Collection Items for Transfer," About the Collection. Available at: https://airandspace.si.edu/collections/about-collection/collection-items-transfer (accessed November 24, 2018).

21. Yerkovich, *Practical Guide*, 79.

22. Morris, "Deaccessioning."

23. Yerkovich, *Practical Guide*, 75.

24. Malaro and DeAngelis, *Legal Primer*, 256.

25. Morris, "Deaccessioning."

26. Malaro and DeAngelis, *Legal Primer*, 192.

27. Miller, *Deaccessioning Today*, 51.

28. Simmons, *Things Great and Small*, 67.

This chapter is based on the deaccessioning chapter by Martha Morris in the fifth edition of Museum Registration Methods. *Thanks to Rebecca Buck for the "Deaccessioning Risk Chart," to Sally Yerkovich for reviewing content, and to Johann Moser and Joanne Moser for editing and proofreading.*

3J | FOUND IN COLLECTION

REBECCA A. BUCK (EDITED AND UPDATED BY JOHN E. SIMMONS AND TONI M. KISER)

ALMOST ALL MUSEUM collections contain a few objects that are not connected with their documentation—no tag, no label, no number marked on the object, no indication of source of the object in the packaging, no characteristic that connects the object to records of gifts, purchases, or loans. Such objects are usually found during inventories, discovered during work on an exhibition, turn up in the middle of a rehousing project, or seem to magically appear when someone leaves the institution and desk drawers are emptied. These objects may have entered the collection at any time in the museum's history as gifts, purchases, bequests, or things left in spaces taken over by the museum. They may have been loans or have been left over from special events or educational programs. They may belong to a former museum staff member, have been brought in for use as decorations, or perhaps they are former utilitarian objects that, because of their age and manufacture, have attained some historical or aesthetic value. Though their status may be uncertain, it is more likely than not that if an object is found in the museum, it belongs to the museum (TABLE 3J.1).

Undocumented objects are mysteries that can sometimes be solved so that the undocumented object is restored to its correct status, but if the mystery cannot be solved, the object should properly be considered a found-in-collection (FIC) object. To protect the museum's interests should claims arise regarding these objects it is necessary to differentiate between these two categories—undocumented objects and FIC objects. Objects are considered to be undocumented if they are similar to other objects in the collections, lack numbers or any characteristics that might connect them to documentation, but their status can be resolved through careful research (thus allowing the museum to assume ownership of them). FIC objects are those undocumented objects that remain without status after all attempts to rec-

Table 3J.1 Possible Sources of Undocumented Objects

- Gifts
- Objects in temporary custody pending approval or acceptance
- Bequests, pending acceptance
- Purchases, pending approval
- Objects obtained by the institution on commission
- Unclaimed or old loan objects (see CHAPTER 3H, "Old Loans and Museum Property Laws")
- Abandoned property
- Exhibition props
- Special events props
- Objects made on site (e.g., in educational programs, arts workshops, exhibition workshops)
- Objects acquired with real property
- Decorations
- Former office or storage equipment
- Personal property of former or present staff members or board members
- Awards or trophies given to museum or staff members

oncile them with existing records of collection and loan objects have been exhausted. It is vital to track all undocumented objects from the moment they are found and attempt to connect them to existing documentation so that they may be considered museum property (e.g., perhaps through a complete inventory; see CHAPTER 5K, "Inventory"). Most FIC objects are the product of the vagaries of past collecting practices or lapses by past collection workers.

Several causes may lead to objects becoming undocumented:

- Historic documentation systems that were not regularized (usually because of inadequate staffing).

- More than one system for accessioning and documenting objects in use within the museum.
- Objects that were never processed or were misplaced by accident (particularly in natural history, history, and archaeology museums that work with large volumes of material but lack adequate staffing).
- Use of volunteers that were not adequately trained or clearly committed to finishing tasks. Supervision and confirmation of the work done by volunteers may be inadequate due to lack of professional staff.
- In the first part of the twentieth century, property transfer to museums was informal, which often resulted in inadequate recording and documentation of object transactions.
- Since the middle of the twentieth century, changes in tax laws have encouraged the recording of gifts of collection activities in a timely fashion, but before there were Internal Revenue Service incentives or mandatory reporting, timelines and record-keeping for gifts were much more casual.
- Human nature is probably the largest cause of objects becoming undocumented, particularly objects from important donors or board members who felt that the museum was an extension of their own collections and deposited, donated, and purchased objects accordingly.

POLICY

The first and arguably most difficult task is to find all undocumented objects and to reconcile as many of them as possible with existing documentation. For example, at the end of an inventory process a museum may be left with a number of objects that were lost in inventory or are undocumented. In the past, the reconciliation process was long, protracted, and difficult (searching through a card catalog or inventory books can be like searching for a needle in a haystack). The advent of electronic collection management databases has improved this process tremendously because these systems can be searched for multiple terms in multiple categories, making it infinitely easier to match undocumented objects to their records. For example, consider the case of the Northwest Museum of Arts and Culture

(MAC), in Spokane, Washington. In 1978 the institution—then the Cheney Cowles Memorial Museum—completed its first comprehensive inventory, checking each object in the collection against a set of notebooks containing accession data for the entire collection. At the end of the process there were more than two thousand undocumented objects and more than two thousand lost-in-inventory pieces. The reconciliation process included laying out all objects of one type (e.g., guns, Plateau material, textiles, domestic objects) and going through all the lost-in-inventory descriptions, matching materials with records. The result was that approximately a quarter of the objects were reunited with their documentation after a process that lasted more than six months. However, in 1994, when the last of the Native American Graves Protection and Repatriation Act (NAGPRA) inventories were being processed, staff at the MAC came across a box containing five Native American artifacts with a note dated 1978 stating that the objects had not been reconciled. The database was checked for objects without location data that had characteristics that matched the found objects and within an hour, all were reunited with their original documentation.

Most museums assign a tracking number to objects that are discovered without documentation. Tracking numbers allow the museum to begin documentation without the long process of accessioning decisions and approval. However, if the museum uses a tracking number rather than an accession number for an undocumented object, it may not make as strong a case for ownership. On the other hand, if a museum applies an accession number to an undocumented object (thus making a stronger ownership case), it implies that some thoughtful and careful process has been completed. The practical problems that arise from this conundrum are numerous: It is extremely difficult for museums with large, complex collections to complete and reconcile inventories. In fact, it can be difficult for most medium-size collections (e.g., thirty thousand to fifty thousand objects) to finish and reconcile an inventory. If records are complicated and were not clearly kept in the past, it can take years to complete a reconciliation process.

To deal effectively with the problem of undocumented and FIC objects museums should first discuss and develop a policy to provide guidance on how to proceed. If policy is not written and approved, museum staff will have to deal ad hoc with the problem, and the results will be uneven and confusing as changes in staff occur over time (see CHAPTER 2, "Collection Management Policies").

The time interval between inventory and complete reconciliation must be taken into account when the policy is established. For example, if a museum is not able to initiate or complete an inventory, then undocumented objects will probably be found from time to time during other projects. There are differences of opinion on this complex and problematic subject and laws that leave little room for opinion; some options for dealing with these problems follow, along with a recommended policy strategy.

Museum staff should first work with legal counsel to research the laws that deal with property that might be similar to undocumented or FIC objects in their state (see TABLE 3H.1). These laws may be titled lost, unclaimed, or abandoned property laws, or may be part of museum-specific laws that deal primarily with old loans. If state law makes specific demands or denies the museum title without a claim process, the first decision is made; if it does not, the museum must devise its own procedures for resolving FIC objects.

Definitions

- Undocumented objects are similar to those in the collections but found without numbers, labels, tags, information in their housing, or any characteristics that might connect them to documentation.
- FIC objects are undocumented objects that remain undocumented after all attempts to reconcile them to existing records of collection and loan objects have been exhausted.

The list of undocumented objects should not include objects with partial documentation, objects that have numbers consistent with the museum's accession numbers (even without backup documents), or objects that have not been completely processed.

A systematic process will consider how to deal with the partials, temporaries, and incompletes, but documentation should exist for most of those objects. True FIC objects are those that remain after a reconciliation process without extant clues to their origin or status.

Perceptions of Undocumented Objects in the Museum

a. The object is property of the museum.
b. The object is of uncertain status.
c. The object is an accessioned object owned by the museum that has lost the number that connects it to its documentation.
d. Undocumented objects must be processed in accordance with state museum property legislation.

Preference goes in order from option a through option d. Unless the museum has a specific state law to follow, option b may seem like a logical assumption, but in fact option a is the preferred stance and is most often used by museums. Except in unusual situations, the majority of undocumented objects are, in fact, owned by the museum in which they are found. The objects may be of uncertain status, but there is nothing to indicate that an undocumented object may belong to someone else—only a claim will bring that possibility forward.

There are times when the museum does know where FIC objects came from. Consider the use of FIC by the National Postal Museum:

In an attempt to fill gaps in the older issues, we have resurrected material set aside as "duplicate" in the 1980s. We have finished the review of a selection of good mint examples from this source and have inventoried them. Their reintroduction to the collection will be complete when they are given FIC numbers and cataloged.[1]

Records for the duplicate collection were obviously not as complete as those for the permanent collection, but there was reason to consider the objects to be owned by the museum.

A museum may accession an entire estate as a gift, including a house and its contents. An example is the Brandywine River Museum's acquisition of the N. C. Wyeth house and studio in the 1990s. If the first sweep in the process of accessioning was not complete, and if all objects were not identified and numbered, then unprocessed parts of the original accession may well become undocumented objects or FIC objects.

A second and common scenario concerns objects that have lost their accession numbers. For example, in the 1920s some collections of Native American baskets in a museum were marked by stapling small, thick, numbered paper tags to their rims. The paper was acidic and over the years it cracked and crumbled, and some of the staples rusted apart as well. This resulted in baskets with partial tags or no tags at all. However, even partial tags can be a valuable clue because an experienced museum worker may recognize the type of tag and ink used in the collection during a specific time period, or the material or format of the tag itself may point toward a single gift. In other cases, there may be no way to reconcile the basket to a record because records noting baskets in the collection may just say "coiled basket," or "woven basket," or even just "basket." The baskets with no tags must be handled as undocumented or FIC objects. It is possible that they might have come to the museum on loan (and an experienced museum worker may have a sense of whether FIC baskets might have been a gift, a purchase, or a loan).

Other characteristics of the objects can be valuable clues as well. In 1892, some valuable, long-lost scientific specimens that had been preserved in alcohol in the early 1700s were identified by the distinctive red wax seals on their jars when the British Museum acquired them from a private collector.[2]

Experienced staff members might be aware of collecting policies that were in place in the early days of their institutions. Some museums took everything that came their way and put aside material that was thought to be secondary. These secondary objects, left for future generations to deal with, might now be FIC objects. Sometimes such objects can be reconciled with some vague list, but usually they cannot.

Museums in small towns often find themselves the recipients of objects they really do not want from would-be donors who refuse to make a clear declaration of a gift but want the museum to keep the property or donors who insist on giving the museum all of the bric-a-brac they own. In some cases, even the combination of best practices, written policies, and professional association guidelines fails to convince a director or curator to take the risk offending the town's richest or most powerful citizen by declining part of a donation, with the result that the collection acquires unwanted objects that all too soon become undocumented or FIC objects.

Preliminary Actions That Should Be Taken When Dealing with Undocumented Objects

1. The undocumented objects receive tracking numbers.
2. The museum staff make every attempt to reconcile undocumented objects with existing documentation, considering objects that are not reconciled to be FIC objects.

Some museums stop at this point—tracking numbers are assigned, but no affirmative decision is made that the object is owned by the museum. However, collection management policies may state that any object found in collection is to be considered an accession or an old loan, even though it is not always possible to determine for certain which of the objects were included in a given transaction. For example, after a complete inventory, five dolls without numbers were found, and four dolls were determined to be lost in inventory. Of the four dolls that were lost in inventory, three were known to have been accessioned (in the accession documentation, one was described as a small cloth doll in bad condition, one described as a ceramic doll with blue eyes, and one was just described as a doll). The fourth doll missing in inventory was a loan to the museum, and the loan documentation described it as a cloth doll, six inches long. After reviewing all the records and carefully inspecting the dolls, it may be impossible to determine whether any of them are actually the dolls noted in the accession documentation or on the loan receipt;

in this case, it is prudent to go through an old loan process for all the dolls, listing them as from an unknown source when publishing constructive notice (see CHAPTER 3H, "Old Loans and Museum Property Laws"), and accessioning them (or deaccessioning them) when that process is complete.

FIC objects are often inferior to objects that were accessioned into the collection. Constraints on staff time generally mean that more care is taken to document and track objects that are considered valuable, whereas objects considered to be of lesser value receive less attention and less documentation. Although some FIC objects may be considered relevant to the mission of the museum, the fact that the objects were not accessioned when they first arrived at the museum is a major indicator that the objects not considered appropriate for the collection and should not be retained by the museum. The process of dealing with FIC objects is the ideal time to review each object, affirm or reject it, and if affirmed, process it into the collection.

Accessioning an object implies that it may be used in the same way other museum objects are used; it may be exhibited, loaned, photographed, published, conserved, or deaccessioned. If FIC objects receive a tracking number rather than accession number, the museum's policy should state that tracked FIC objects may also be used in accordance with policies and procedures covering accessioned objects.

Accessioning FIC Objects

The process of accessioning FIC objects begins with a decision to officially take possession of the object, following the criteria and process in the institutional collection management policy.

If a museum takes the approach that the FIC object is already theirs and that there is institutional evidence to believe that it was simply missed or has lost its documents, the process of accessioning becomes one of internal affirmation. Reporting and recording accessions with a FIC source is important so that collection size and sources are updated and transparent and can be another piece of evidence that strengthens the museum's case if a contradictory claim is later made. For this reason, the policy should require that an affidavit be signed and dated by a staff member with knowledge of possible ownership (e.g., recollection that the object was part of a group of objects coming to the museum together or knowledge of the type of material that appeared in an early collection).

Deaccession

A FIC object that is slated for disposition should go through the same deaccession process as provided in the collections management policy for owned objects. Ad hoc decisions regarding claims for title under applicable state law relating to deaccession of FIC objects may be made by a deaccession committee. FIC objects slated for deaccession may be claimed under applicable state law or court action. Keep in mind that by definition there is no evidence that the museum does not own a FIC object. Unlike old loans, the undisturbed possession by the museum of a FIC object (often for decades) is in itself evidence that supports a presumption that the title is owned by the museum. In other words, because the museum owns an object and possesses it, and there is a lack evidence for other claims of ownership, the law is generally on the side of the museum in these matters. Furthermore, clearing up the status of FIC objects is in harmony with the responsibilities of a museum that holds objects in the public trust.

If a museum adds a FIC object to its permanent collection, the worst that can happen is that a future claim may be made for ownership of the object (the chance of a successful claim will diminish as time passes). If a successful claim is made, the worst that can happen is that the object will be returned to its rightful owner, or the museum might be able to negotiate a gift of the object from the presumptive owner.

If a museum disposes of an object by sale, it may be subject to penalty should a successful claim ever be made for the object. The particular state's version of the Uniform Commercial Code will apply to the situation. In the event of a successful claim the museum may have to pay the current value of the object, rather than the value for which the object was sold. If, instead, the museum donates the object to another institution, or sells it with notice of a flawed title (in all likelihood reducing the price), there is less recourse for the owner whose claim was successful.[3]

Possible Actions If Original Documentation Is Found or a Claim Is Made

If original documentation is found for an object that has been tracked or accessioned into the collection using a FIC number, the object should be returned to its original number and the FIC number retired.

If a claim is made on a FIC object that is accessioned into the collection or has been disposed of, the museum will decide whether to accept or challenge the claim. The museum should request proof that the object claimed is, in fact, the object described in the claimant's documents, and that the claimant is either the sole owner or has complete authority from the owner or owners to make the claim. The first part may require precise documentation (e.g., "flowered vase" is insufficient to describe one of five vases from different periods made of different materials that exist in the collection with FIC documentation only). It may be difficult for a person to claim to be the only heir if more than one person inherits from the estate. If this is compounded, the greater the length of time that a museum has held an object, the less the chance for a claim to be successful.

The museum must respond to a claim promptly (as soon as it is possible to do so). If the proof is strong, the museum should return the object in a reasonable length of time. If the proof is weak, the museum should reject the claim in writing, which will start the statute of limitations time clock (usually three to six years) to bring a suit against the museum. If a suit is filed, the museum may decide whether to fight the claim or return the object; this decision often depends on the value and uniqueness of the object.

POLICY ON UNDOCUMENTED AND FIC OBJECTS

The preferred options for dealing with undocumented and FIC objects suggest the following model policy and procedures:

Policy

Undocumented objects are those objects similar to collections that are found in the collection areas with no numbers, no information in their housing, nor any characteristics that might connect them to documentation. FIC objects are undocumented objects that remain undocumented after all fair and reasonable attempts to reconcile them to existing records of permanent collection and loan objects fail. The museum will make every attempt to reconcile undocumented objects to existing documentation. Objects that are not reconciled will be considered to be FIC.

The museum considers undocumented and FIC objects to be the property of the museum. Undocumented objects will be tracked and documented from the time they are found and may be used as any permanent collection object is used. FIC objects may be accessioned into the collection or disposed of according to the approved deaccession policy. The decision to accession will be made in accordance with the accessioning policy. FIC objects accessioned into the permanent collection will be given numbers in the year of their accession.

If original documentation is found for an object that has been tracked or accessioned into the collection using a FIC number, the object will be returned to its original status and number and the FIC number will be retired. If a claim is made on an undocumented or FIC object, either accessioned into the collection or disposed of, the museum will make ad hoc decisions on accepting or fighting the claim. Unclaimed objects and FIC objects slated for disposition will follow the approved deaccession process as if they are owned objects.

Procedures

1. *Assign a tracking number.*

   Objects without documentation should be assigned a tracking number immediately.[4] The number assigned should be applied to the object immediately, using the same methods employed to mark permanent collection objects. In practice, an object may be tagged during inventory reconciliation and a permanent physical number applied only after it is reconciled and accessioned as a FIC object.

2. *Gather basic registration information.*

   Describe all undocumented objects in the system used for recording permanent collections, including measurements, images, and a condition report. Collect as much information as possible from the object itself, particularly descriptions of any marks, collector's numbers, or other characteristics that can differentiate it from other objects.

3. *Do an institutional search for information.*

Record comments from staff members who might remember details about the object for the FIC object file. For example, if someone has seen the object at a particular time or remembers using it in an exhibition a decade before it was found, or if someone remembers bringing in a group of similar materials and thinks that the object in question could be part of that group. A nondescript mark or number on the object may ring a bell with someone aware of the habits of a certain collector who marked objects in a particular way. Write down any information that is found, making sure to sign and date the document because information in an affidavit format can help formalize the museum's claim of ownership.

4. *Reconcile undocumented objects with lost-in-inventory objects.*

Inventory reconciliation is most easily accomplished with the aid of a complete inventory (trying to find a single object can be one of the most frustrating collection tasks imaginable). Records of objects that have not been found in that inventory are prime candidates for matches with objects with no numbers. If a collections management database is available, make certain that there is at least a placeholder for each object noted in either the catalog or accession ledger, and keep track of all moves in the database. Over time, even without a complete inventory, as locations are noted a history of where objects have been and are currently located emerges. Be aware that this process is long and arduous. It can sometimes be done in pieces (e.g., locate and inventory every doll in the collection; find all of the doll records; compare them). It is better if this step can be done before a tracking number is assigned in order to avoid the necessity of retiring a tracking or accession number.

When Is an Object Thought to Be Lost in Inventory Truly Lost in Inventory?

Never. Although one can never be certain that an object is truly lost, a museum may decide to claim the loss on their insurance after a careful check of all areas where the object might reasonably be (e.g., storage, conservation, exhibition, loan), and after checking with all staff who might have had reason to interact with the object. A new inventory of suspect areas and records should either find the missing object or leave the staff relatively certain that it has been inadvertently disposed of or stolen.

Records for lost property should never be removed from files or databases.

Keep a record of the tracking number that was assigned to the undocumented object. It is not always possible to eliminate or change all of the records where a number was used; the tracking number will likely pop up somewhere and will need to be linked to the current object number.

Decide Whether to Accession or Dispose

The museum's policy will outline the process for making the decision to accession or dispose of the object. Review the FIC object to determine if any federal or state laws regarding materials or origin affect the status of the object, such as whether the object is covered under the NAGPRA, the Endangered Species Act, or other laws that control the use and movement of species or specific types of material.

Dispose of an Undocumented or FIC Object

Regardless of whether an undocumented object was accessioned or just tracked, it is imperative that the complete deaccessioning process in the museum's collection management policy be followed to dispose of it. The museum board must understand that there might be a risk of future claims against the museum. As noted on the deaccession risk chart (see TABLE 31.1), it is likely that objects that are multiples, of small or no monetary value, or given to other nonprofit institutions, pose little or no risk. The museum may not have the time, staff, or resources to use legal processes to convert small or minor objects (consider, for example, how many Sears and Roebuck cast-iron irons might be claimed and whether they are worth a lawsuit. Even differentiating among five irons cataloged briefly as "clothes irons" may not be possible). Use common sense, and document everything very carefully. The risk for unique objects, especially those of high value, is a different matter. Legal counsel should be sought, and using available laws to take title to the property may prove a positive factor in fighting future claims. •

NOTES

1. Cited in *Museum Registration Methods*, 5th ed., edited by R. A. Buck and J. A. Gilmore as "Lawson, Mary H. How One Collection Is getting Its Groove Back: Revitalizing the National Postal Museum's Exhibit and Master and Reference Collection of U. S. Stamps, EnRoute, 1998."

2. J. E. Simmons, *Fluid Preservation. A Comprehensive Reference* (Lanham, MD: Rowman & Littlefield, 2014), 22.

3. For further discussion of claims, see M. C. Malaro and I. P. DeAngelis, *A Legal Primer on Managing Museum Collections* (Washington, DC: Smithsonian Institute Press, 2012), 392–395.

4. Museums have used a variety of systems for tracking numbers to indicate undocumented objects (e.g., numbers prefixed by X or N, 00 numbers followed only by sequential numbers and prefixes used on a yearly basis). It is not advisable to change what exists in records already created, but it is advisable to alter the system slightly for the present and future if a year is not indicated in the existing number system. Because of state laws, it is usually important to be able to prove how long an object has been in the museum if a claim is made so changes to the number prefix or suffix should be made accordingly.

3K | Loans

ROSE WOOD AND ANDREA GARDNER

IN AN IDEALLY MANAGED collection, any object not owned by the museum is treated as a loan. If an object is on loan to a museum, there should be a signed loan agreement between the lender (owner) and the borrower. In some cases, your museum may be the borrower and in other instances, the lender. Because most museum professionals are familiar with the terms *lender* and *borrower* and *incoming* and *outgoing loan*, we will use these to denote the parties involved and the types of loans discussed in this chapter.

The *loan agreement* is a document that gives temporary custody of something owned by one party to another party. When you think about loans it is prudent to think in the most simplistic terms first. Is the lender requesting that your museum accept a loan or is your institution asking to borrow an object? Who is the lender? Is the lender the owner or creator of the object, or agent of either? Does the lender have the right to enter into a legal agreement? Why are you taking or sending the loan? Is there more than one borrower? Knowing all of this information early in the review process can assist with making good decisions with the loan request, agreement, and management. To assist with these decisions, a written loan policy should include sections on both incoming and outgoing loans.

Your loan policy should clearly define when your institution lends objects and when it accepts them. It establishes who has the authority to approve both incoming and outgoing loans. Without a defined process, everyone will believe that they can speak for the museum and both staff and collection resources will be overcommitted.

Outgoing loan policies should address the following: (i) who receives the loan request, (ii) who reviews the request, and (iii) criteria for review such as the condition of the object, in-house use, worthiness of the project, and the ability of the borrower to properly exhibit, house, and care for the object are primary considerations. Because museums typically lend to other museums and similar cultural institutions, it is acceptable to have a prohibition for lending to private individuals and commercial entities.

The approval process should be detailed in clarifying who fulfills which role during the loan process so that efforts are not duplicated. If you follow the subsections, advice, and questions we ask, you will craft strong outgoing and incoming loan policies and be on your way to codifying your procedures. You can think of your policy as guardrails, so you do not go off course and the procedures as a step-by-step map to your destination or in this case a closed incoming or outgoing loan.

LOAN PURPOSE

Loans are made between museums or between museums and private individuals or commercial entities for a number of reasons. The reason a loan is sought should be listed on the loan agreement, kept in your permanent records, and recorded on your museum's receipts. This evidence may be vital for tracking and eventual resolution of a loan. It gives a justifiable motive for returning a loan to a lender, such as the closing of an exhibition. Lenders can become accustomed to the borrower having their loans because of several advantages, such as not having to provide physical care for the object and not having the expense of providing insurance.

Because most institutions have an exhibition program, loans for display in exhibitions are the most common type. In these cases, objects are borrowed for a specific period of time and for a specific purpose. If you have an object on long-term loan (e.g., a loan that has had multiple extensions), it is good practice to notify the lender when you include it in an exhibition, especially if that was not the original purpose. Besides reaffirming the loan's desirability, lenders also like to know when their objects are on display.

If the institution is borrowing for a traveling exhibition, the process is similar (see CHAPTER 3L, "Organizing Loan and Traveling Exhibitions"). Most of the time there will be a single organizer or two museums will join forces to organize a large exhibition. If this occurs, it is better to have one institution issue the loan agreement instead of attempting to coordinate multiple institutions' agreements, especially in regard to the sign-off of liability when the loan changes venues. Besides the internal hassle of verifying that all sets of loan agreements have similar terms and conditions, you also have the issue of making sure that lenders have signed every institution's forms. Almost as cumbersome is when each institution wants to use its own insurance instead of placing the loans under one museum's policy or purchasing a separate insurance policy for the exhibition. In cases like this, it might be best to tell the organizers that you will only lend if one museum accepts insurance liability throughout the exhibition. If this is not possible because the premium would be too costly and you want to participate in the exhibition, then it is important that the insurance responsibility for each venue is outlined in the loan agreement.

Exchange loans are often an offshoot of an exhibition loan request. An institution may request a reciprocal loan to fill a gap in its permanent exhibition galleries when another museum borrows an important work. Alternatively, exchange loans can be made for the mutual benefit of both museums such as for comparative research, examination, or conservation. If your institution requests a reciprocal loan, it is routinely added as an expense to the exhibition budget of the original borrower. The lender should be aware that a reciprocal loan places a burden on the other institution; this request should be in line with the original request of the borrower in terms of scope.

Unlike exchange loans, which are between institutions, study loans are made between museums or between museums and individuals. The purpose of the study loan is to further research on the object and is more common with science and archaeology museums than with art or history museums (see the discussion on loans in CHAPTER 3F, "Living and Nat-

ural History Collections Registration"). A loan that comes to a museum for conservation may be considered to be a study loan; in this case, the conservator should only perform services if a treatment proposal is signed and the terms of the proposal are in line with the terms of the loan agreement and vice versa.

Promised gifts in the museum's custody are loans that are in effect until title has fully been transferred to the museum. This can cause confusion because of the word *gift*. A gift is a free and clear transfer of title for an object from one party to another party; a loan is temporary possession of an object belonging to another party. If you have not received title to the gift, then the transaction is still a loan and should be treated as such. This is also the case with fractional-interest gifts. If the donor has given the museum less than 100 percent of the object, the remaining portion is considered a loan and the object should be treated as such whenever it is in the museum's custody.

Long-term loans from individuals to a museum or from one museum to another are common. Long-term loans should be entered into with caution because the museum is accepting the responsibility to care for an object for an extended period of time. If the arrangement benefits the borrowing museum more than the individual or institution making the loan, then a long-term loan may be worth the risk to the institution and the administrative headache to a registrar or collections manager. Because circumstances change over time (e.g., the lender changes address, gets divorced, dies, or institutional staff changes occur), long-term loans should have a relatively short renewal period. Best practice says to review long-term loans annually, but in practice they are often the lowest priority of loan programs. A word to the wise is to treat your long-term loans as a priority; if you do not, they may become old loans and will then require additional resources to remedy them (see CHAPTER 3H, "Old Loans and Museum Property Laws").

Another area which is often overlooked in a comprehensive loan program is gift and purchase considerations. Often the museum will use the incoming receipt, which may have minimal terms and conditions on the verso, as the temporary loan agreement with the assumption that the accession process will correct any deficiencies. However, as registrars who have had to return a gift or purchase consideration years (or even decades) later, it is best to have a formal loan agreement or purchase agreement (or what a dealer may refer to as a consignment agreement or an approval agreement) in place.

Even with a robust vetting process sometimes unsolicited objects can be received for acquisition. When objects are received, the senders should be notified immediately that the unsolicited objects will be returned at their expense and in the same manner that they were packed and shipped. Senders should be notified that they will be required to carry and pay for any insurance. Unfortunately, some unsolicited objects are dropped off in the dead of night or without a return address. In these cases, you should research your state's abandoned property laws, and for those who live in states without laws specifically for cultural institutions, you can instead research your state's unclaimed property laws (see CHAPTER 3H, "Old Loan and Museum Property Laws"). Unfortunately, there is no easy answer in these cases.

Perhaps even more vexing than unsolicited objects are objects of unknown origin in the museum's custody; the main reason for this vexation being that someone at some period knew why the object was placed in the gallery or storage area and from whom it came. Unfortunately, that staff person is now gone, and it becomes the responsibility of the current registrar or collections manager to sort these out. These objects are often called *found-in-collection* objects and should be treated as loans until the source has been identified which means spending resources on documenting them and caring for them indefinitely or going through the abandoned property process to resolve them (see CHAPTER 3J, "Found in Collection").

CONSIDERATIONS DURING THE LOAN APPROVAL PROCESS FOR INCOMING LOANS

As mentioned, every institution should have a written loan policy. Although the internal approval needed to request a loan varies from institution to institution, there are still important basics to include in any process that will help to mitigate some of the risks. In addition to a written policy, it is also advised to

have written procedures or workflows (FIGURE 3K.1) that will assist with consistency as well as departmental cooperation. Unless you are in a small institution where the registrar must be accountable for everything, some other departments or staff will need to be involved with the loan process.

If the loan is being considered for exhibition, then the request is often initiated with the director, curator, or project manager. Depending on the institution's collection management policy, these loans might need to be reported to a committee of the board often called an *Acquisition Committee* or they might just be approved internally by the curator or director. Making sure long-term loans or loans of promised gifts go through a vetting process or follow a museum's established acquisitions process is good resource management because it requires that staff think about the commitment they are about to undertake for the care of this object.

As registrars at institutions who have sometimes struggled with loan management, a way of curbing uncontrolled borrowing is to put in place a process where a written justification for taking the loan is required. It makes the transaction transparent, and administrators who are not always involved with loans are aware that resources are being used in this way. Additionally, it means the department that controls the budget for the loan arrangements must be consulted.

Protocol for requesting loans calls for the director, curator, or project manager of the borrowing institution to send the prospective lender a detailed letter describing the purpose of the exhibition or loan activity and the objects desired. The letter is often addressed to the director of the lending institution; occasionally in large institutions, this may be the curator or department head instead of the director. The loan request should contain the following key information:

- Title of the exhibition,
- Purpose of the loan,
- Length of the loan period,
- Location(s) of the exhibition with dates,
- The object's basic information including an accession or catalog number,

Example of Outgoing Loan Workflow

Loan Number: Accession Number:
Shipment Number:

Date:

_____ Arrival of Loan Request:

_____ Requested Facilities Report   Facilities Report Received: _____

_____ Preliminary Condition Report and Review for Exhibition (Matting/Framing/Conservation)

_____ Presentation at Acquisition Meeting

_____ Sent Letter of Acceptance

_____ Requested Any Work to Be Done (Matting/Framing)

_____ Schedule Conservation

_____ Requested Updated Insurance Value from Curator

_____ Complete Loan Form and Sent (Email/USPS) Loan Form Returned: _____

_____ Received Certificate of Insurance

_____ Request Crate Dimensions and Estimate for Packing

_____ Received Crate Dimensions   Crate: _____ (H) X _____(L) X _____ (D) Inches

_____ Out-Going Shipping Arrangements Confirmed   Outgoing Date/Time: _____

_____ Email to Security/Preparations/Maintenance Regarding Out-Going Shipment

_____ Courier Sheet/Arrangements

_____ Preformat

_____ Out-Going Condition Report (Emailed / Packed in Crate / USPS)

_____ Out-Going Receipt (Emailed / Packed in Crate / USPS)

_____ Invoice Expenses and Fees (See Amount Below)

_____ Incoming Shipping Arrangements Confirmed   Incoming Date/Time: _____

_____ Incoming Condition Report Updated in Collections Management System ("CMS")
                                      (No Change in Original / New Attached Report)

_____ Re-Entry Form (Emailed /USPS)

_____ Updated Location in CMS

_____ Closed Loan in CMS

_____ Complete Borrowing Institution's Documentation and Returned

Fee	Dollar Amount	Invoice No.	Emailed/Mailed Invoice	Received Date	Dollar Amount
Crate	$	R -			
Conservation	$	R -			
Framing/ Misc.	$	R -			
Loan Fee	$	R -			

FIGURE 3K.1 EXAMPLE OF OUTGOING LOAN WORKFLOW. CREATED BY AUTHOR.

- Justification for why this specific object(s) is important for the project,
- Institution(s) requesting the loan and if there is a guest curator involved,
- Loan form (with details of the arrangement),
- General facilities report for each institution that will have the loan on its premises,
- Contact name, telephone number, and email address for the person who will be able to answer the lender's questions,
- A statement that the borrower will pay for all expenses incurred,
- Anything that is unusual about your request or might need greater explanation, and
- Insurance (see CHAPTER 6D, "Insurance").

Though each institution is different, it is advisable that international loans be requested at least one year in advance and domestic loans at least six months in advance. It is best practice to ask the lender what the minimum time needed to submit a request is; institutions with active loan programs might have a longer minimum time. When a member of your institution requests information regarding the object, it is a good time to request several things from the potential lender including whether the object is currently exhibition ready, if it is stored unframed, or if it needs conservation; this could increase the amount of time needed to prepare the loan and also the cost associated with the loan.

Before a loan is requested, a borrower should have a general understanding of the costs associated with the loan. Is there a loan fee and if so, how much? Can the loan fee be waived? Will the object need to be matted or framed, and, if so, does the lender have a standard frame in stock that can be used for minimal or no charge, or will it need to be custom framed? Is it a requirement that all paintings are to be glazed? Will the lender provide an estimate of the cost before the loan is requested or only after it is approved? Is there an existing crate and what level of shipping will be required? Will the lender allow use of a fine art shuttle transport or require exclusive use? Is there a preferred shipper? Does the shipment require a courier? No lending institution wants to go to the time and expense of vetting a loan request just to be told

the loan is canceled or the budget will not allow for these expenses.

The borrower should receive a formal letter acknowledging the approval or denial of the loan. It is helpful if this letter discusses any conditions the borrower is placing on the loan and, if known, the cost of the loan's preparation. If the loan is denied, the letter should explain the reason for the denial. Depending on the importance of the loan to the project, sometimes a personal plea from a curator or director to their counterpart might reverse that decision; however, a "sorry we cannot lend" reply should be respected.

LOAN AGREEMENT CONSIDERATIONS FOR INCOMING LOANS

Once the loan is approved, each institution has its own internal process for documentation (for an example, see the sample forms for "Outgoing Loan Agreement with Outgoing Loan Conditions" and "Incoming Loan Agreement with Conditions Governing Incoming Loans" in the *Collections Forms* section). At a minimum, it should go onto a schedule, so that appropriate staff will be aware of the upcoming loan. In some cases, loans are requested years in advance. Likewise, the approval of the request should be noted by the borrower's curator and registrar so they can begin arrangements. The borrower's loan agreement should be included in the original request so that the lender's registrar may review the terms and conditions. Most museums will accept a loan form from the lender, as will most private collectors except for a select few that require their own form. Some institutions have a policy to only use a *borrower's agreement* or a loan form issued by the borrower. If the borrower wants to use their own form, then the best thing to do is to review the terms and conditions to make sure that they are acceptable to your institution before accepting their form.

Whether your loan form is used or that of the borrower, you should verify the pick-up and delivery location. If this is not in the agreement, the museum could find themselves paying significantly more in shipping than expected. This is not to say that some loans will not have different pick-up and delivery locations, but this should be negotiated up front and agreed to by all parties. This is particularly important if you are shipping internationally because additional duties and fees could be owed if the museum returns a loan to a different country than that from which it was exported.

When reviewing a borrower's agreement it is important to ascertain whether the lender is asking for absolute or strict liability (see CHAPTER 6D, "Insurance"). Though the wording might vary slightly, absolute liability will be covered if the conditions of the loan say that in the event of loss or damage, the amount paid by insurance secured in accordance with the agreement shall not limit recovery to the lender from the museum. You will want to be sure that liability is limited by the amount your insurer will pay.

If the lender requests absolute liability, you have some options: (i) do not take the loan; (ii) ask the lender to limit liability to the amount payable by insurance and agree to release the borrower from liability for any claims arising out of such a loss or damage beyond that amount; or (iii) agree to additional liability that will not exceed a certain amount.[1]

Another way for the lender to require absolute liability is to have wording in their loan agreement stating that liability shall exist when the damage to an object is found after the return of the object. As in the case of total loss, the insurance value specified in this contract would then be paid. However, for other damage, the extent of the loss would be determined by the lender. If this wording is included in the borrower's agreement, claims should be limited to a specified period after the return of the loan and by scrutinizing the insurance value before signing the agreement. We have witnessed a gallery that claimed that they did not have the time or staff to inspect the returned loan before the fifteen-day time frame stated on the outgoing receipt. In cases such as this, the borrower could offer to hire a contract registrar and a professional art handler to unpack the objects and perform the inspection. Instances in which the lender determines the loss could be made objective by having an expert appraisal commissioned in which each party selects an appraiser independently and both parties select a third appraiser together to act as an arbitrator. This would increase costs but reduce exposure to an insurance claim.

Regarding insurance for incoming loans, it is the borrower's responsibility (usually the registrar's) to know the policy limitations of the coverage. If the wording on a loan form regarding liability is not understood contact your insurance broker and ask for a reading of the loan form and an opinion on its meaning.

If you are requesting a loan from a foreign country, be aware that the loan form might say that in the case of a seizure of the loan, the borrower must cover all expenses, including legal expenses and costs of extended storage and insurance until the return of the objects to the lender. In this case, the borrower should apply for federal immunity from seizure. However, even if immunity is granted, the borrowing museum may incur costs to enforce it. It is advisable to include in your correspondence and in the terms agreed to with the lender that in the event of a seizure insurance is the sole recovery, and that in the event of a delayed return of the loan as a result of seizure, the borrower is not liable for breach of the loan agreement.

Some institutions sign both the lender's and borrower's loan form for a single loan. This is never a good idea because it produces dueling agreements if there is an issue. Additionally, some institutions' forms may state that jurisdiction over any disputes arising from the loan agreement (such as civil action or legal proceedings) must be in the courts of record of the state or country of the museum that issues the loan agreement. The terms might say that the lender and borrower must consent to the jurisdiction of such court in any such civil action or legal proceeding and waive their objection to the laying of venue. Ideally, if you are the borrower and you receive another museum's agreement with this wording, you should insist that they remain silent on jurisdiction. If the institution is foreign, ask them to agree to US courts. You should consult your insurance broker about this type of wording so that the desired arbitration or mediation venue is approved.

For incoming loans, it is the lender's job to decide if there are special requirements to lend, and it is the borrower's responsibility to decide if these requirements are within reason and if their institution is able to meet them. A borrower should never agree to anything that they cannot provide because this will put them in breach of the agreement. Conversely, it is never good practice for the lender to start preparing a loan without a written commitment from the borrower because this risks the borrower canceling the loan after resources have been expended for which the lender may not be reimbursed. If the loan agreement is complicated, a separate agreement may be necessary in which the costs are itemized and that requires the borrower to agree to pay for these costs even if the loan does not occur. This is particularly important if there is conservation work needed on the object prior to the loan.

Remember that a loan agreement is a legally binding contract between the borrower and the lender and should protect both parties by specifying all agreed-on conditions. The signed loan agreement overrides all other documents and understandings, whether written or verbal, so if a prior agreement or pre-agreement was made via e-mail the same terms should be included in the final loan agreement.

Institutions differ on who has the responsibility to sign the loan form—it may be the director, curator, loan officer, exhibitions officer, project manager, or registrar. If someone other than the registrar signs the agreement the registrar should review it first because at most institutions it is the registrar who ensures that the terms are upheld. Most institutions use a general loan contract containing standard conditions including, but not limited to, the care and handling of the objects, insurance coverage, and environmental conditions under which the objects are to be maintained. The form should include a section for special conditions or an addendum can be written and signed to address any special clauses needed for individual objects.

There may be confusion about the difference between an addendum and an amendment to a loan agreement. When there are additional special conditions to the loan, which you have already communicated to the borrower, they should be included in an addendum so that they become part of the binding agreement. However, if you have an existing signed agreement and something changes, such as the extension of an exhibition date, then the borrower and lender will sign an amendment that can be thought of as correcting the document, improving the document, or making an alteration. The signatories of the original agreement should also sign the amendment. The addendum should be added to the agreement and should include the lender's name and address and borrower's name and address. It is advisable to include the dates of the loan and exhibition dates, if known. You can include a section with wording, such as "whereas, the parties listed above wish to modify the terms of the originally stated agreement as set forth herein, and in consideration of the mutual promises herein, the parties, intending to be legally bound, hereby agree that the following constitutes additional terms and conditions of the stated contract." This is followed by a list of the special conditions of the loan. You may want to include, on the first page of the loan agreement, an asterisk and the phrase, "See addendum for special conditions." Some museums will require you to sign the addendum page as well as the original loan agreement. Because contract law is governed by each state, the rules will depend on the jurisdiction of the contract. It is advisable to always contact a lawyer who is familiar with contract law in your state when substantially amending a loan agreement.

The lender signs and returns the loan agreement along with any addenda, to the borrower. It is appropriate to include an accompanying letter to call attention to any changes. The borrower should countersign the loan agreement and return one copy to the lender. If for any reason only one signed contract is received from the lender, it is prudent for the borrower to keep the original contract and sign it and then send a copy of the endorsed contract back to the lender.

INSURANCE CONSIDERATIONS FOR INCOMING LOANS

Standard loan protocol is for the borrower to accept responsibility for insurance on the loan. At one time, the trend was for lenders to carry their own insurance and charge the borrower a premium; however, that is less common now. If you are going to accept a lender's insurance, there are a few key areas to review—limits of coverage, deductibilities, exclusions, property insured, policy terms, and terms of cancellation.

Borrowers should provide coverage that is *all risk*, and not based on *named perils*, which are less inclusive. Additionally, the coverage should be *wall-to-wall* or *nail-to-nail*. When an agreement is signed, it should allow enough time for the lender to ship and the borrower to receive the loan before it is needed, and enough time to return the loan at the end of the exhibition period. Exhibitions may be extended, so rather than having to amend the loan contract, we suggest allowing six weeks as an adequate time frame after the exhibition for any shipment that is traveling by fine art shuttle. If your own staff is delivering the returned loan, or if you are using an exclusive-use shipper, then the time can be reduced.

Understanding your insurance policy and comparing it to the terms listed on your incoming loan agreement is vital. You do not want to promise coverage to a lender that is not covered under your policy. You might want to have your insurance broker review your standard loan agreement to make sure the terms are covered under your current policy.

Reviewing the insurance value a lender places on loan object(s) is an important part of the borrower's loan review process. Unlike your own collection objects, which should be covered under the valuation clause for the purchase price or current market value, the clause that covers property not owned by the policyholder is for agreed value. This means that if you sign a loan agreement where the value is higher than current market value the underwriter will be obligated to pay this higher value. It is best practice to have someone in your institution discuss the value with the lender and prepare documentation to confirm the value if it is questioned. Because the person who requests the loan is often the most knowledgeable about the valuation, ideally this person should contact the lender. If an agreement is reached regarding the stated value, then proceed with signing the loan agreement and begin planning for the loan.

If a lender insists on a specific condition that the borrowing institution believes may be hazardous to the loan object (e.g., installing the object without a barrier, using push pins to mount an object, displaying artwork in harsh light, or allowing the general public to touch the object), the lender should be asked to sign a *hold harmless* agreement.

CONSIDERATIONS DURING THE LOAN APPROVAL PROCESS FOR OUTGOING LOANS

When a new loan request is received, the museum should initiate a systematic process to review the request. Because many museums require the loan to be approved by their governing board in addition to staff vetting, the lender's review can stretch into some months. It is not uncommon to wait for two to four months before a loan approval or denial letter is received. Occasionally requests are sent to a curator, another staff member, or chairman of the board, but in all cases, no matter who receives the loan request, it should be sent immediately to the person who is ultimately responsible for decisions related to lending the collection (e.g., the director or chairman of the board).

The director should immediately forward the original request letter to the registrar, including any initial comments on the request. It is courteous for either the office of the director or the registrar's office to then send an acknowledgment letter to the requestor verifying that the request has been received. This letter can also give the borrower an idea of the review process and timeline. If this task resides in the registrar's office it will provide an opportunity to request additional information such as a Facilities Report to properly vet the request.

After a loan request is received, the lending institution's approval procedure for outgoing loans should involve the following key players (other staff members may be involved in the process as well):

- The curator evaluates the project in general and indicates the availability of the objects requested based on any upcoming projects. It may also be helpful to consult with other curators as they may have plans to include objects outside of their curatorial purview in upcoming projects or may plan to collaborate with requesting institutions for future projects. Some institutions with robust education departments will also consult with a member of that team to make sure the object is not planned for an upcoming program.
- Provenance research should be conducted in case there are gaps in the ownership history of the requested objects. The person responsible for prov-

enance research will depend on the institution. Some museums charge their curatorial staff to complete this research but other institutions place this responsibility with the registrar. Regardless of the provenance, it is advisable that the lender request immunity from seizure for all international loans, if it is available.

- The conservator or registrar examines the condition of the objects to be loaned. Size, weight, and shipping logistics, including the routing to the borrower's location, are major factors in assessing whether the object can withstand the rigors of travel.

- The registrar also checks for other commitments during the period in question, such as other loans, and for any legal restrictions such as donor constraints, US Customs, or US Fish and Wildlife regulations.

- Final approval by the director or the board is required in many institutions after the various departments have submitted their input and recommendation.

Other key information that may be of assistance in making a decision regarding a loan request includes exhibition history of the object and a history of the institution's previous relationship with the requestor, including both lending and borrowing, which should be in the registrar's files. In many institutions it is up to the registrar to coordinate the loan review process and to make certain that the object and the borrowing institution are evaluated.

In evaluating the object's condition, the following questions should be considered:

- Is the object able to withstand the rigors of travel and additional handling?
- Does the object need conservation treatment to safely travel?
- Has the object recently traveled extensively or been subjected to long periods of light exposure (if it is a light-sensitive material)?
- Should special restrictions be placed on light levels or environmental conditions?
- Should special requirements be added to protect the object such as barriers or glazing?

- Is there a requirement for the object to be displayed in a case and if so, are there special requirements for the construction or materials used for the interior of the case?
- Does the object need a custom mount for display?
- Does the object have any special crating requirements?

If any questions arise during the loan review, such as how works on paper, textiles, lacquer, or plastics that are especially sensitive to light exposure and adverse climate conditions withstand being on loan, and you do not have the resources to answer the question (e.g., an in-house conservator), professional advice should be sought from a freelance conservator before deciding whether the object can travel safely and how best to pack it. This cost may be passed on to the borrower if the borrower is notified in advance that without this information the loan cannot be approved.

The borrower's current *General Facility Report* must be considered when evaluating a loan request. The *General Facility Report*, developed by the American Alliance of Museums (AAM), is frequently used by museums in the United States, but some institutions, particularly foreign museums, may use other facility reports. The AAM form is extremely thorough and is highly recommended. Accuracy and honesty are essential when filling out the facility report, and information on the form should be updated on a regular basis or as changes occur. Because information can be checked by the lender, false answers may jeopardize the loan or future exchanges. When reviewing the borrower's facility report, the lender should pay special attention to the sections that focus on climate, security, and fire suppression. The lender should question any unclear answers and work with the borrower to ameliorate unacceptable conditions, if possible.

The facility report should inform you if there is a safe, clear path from the point of unloading to the point of installation at the borrower's premises and whether it will fit through the borrower's doors and elevator, crated or uncrated. If it does not answer these questions and you have concerns about the facility, contact the borrower's registrar for more information. Although it is not applicable to foreign institutions, AAM accreditation usually indicates that a borrowing institution meets minimum standards.

If your museum has established standard loan terms and fees in its lending program, then shortly after the loan request has been received you should send the borrower's registrar this information. Sometimes the borrower's staff sends loan requests without doing their homework, and thus, they are unaware of these fees. A standard protocol between museums and private collectors calls for the borrower to pay all expenses related to temporary and long-term loans, incoming gifts, study or research loans, or any other loans of primary benefit to the museum. The lender may be asked to pay costs associated with loans that are of primary benefit to the lender, such as objects deposited for private conservation, photography, consideration for purchase, or exchange. Responsibility for costs should be discussed prior to the loan or prior to any charges being incurred.

Loan costs include the expenses (materials, labor, delivery, etc.) of all crating, preparation, base or mount making, matting and framing, glazing, conservation, photography, deinstallation and reinstallation, shipping, courier costs, insurance, and loan fees. Before the actual loan agreement, you may want to ask the borrower to sign a preliminary form acknowledging any unusual loan conditions such as special environmental conditions or shipping requirements. After reviewing the costs and special conditions, the borrower can decide if it is in a position to proceed with the loan request. Some museums have preprinted forms that list their general loan conditions regarding care of objects, insurance, courier costs, publication, publicity, conservation, and rights and reproduction for the objects requested for loan. The borrower is usually responsible for all the costs incurred in the loan arrangement unless this is discussed and agreed to by the lender. Some institutions have reciprocal agreements with other museums to waive certain costs, such as loan fees. In cases where the fee makes the loan impossible for the borrower, the lender may be willing to negotiate a fee reduction.

The delicate condition or high value of some objects may dictate special loan conditions. It is important that these conditions be justified and that they are essential for protecting the object. All costs or re-

quirements must be clearly stated with as much notice given as possible so that the borrower can budget adequately. These costs can include a special frame, base, mount or microclimate frame or case, alarms or barriers, requirement for a courier or supervisor, or additional security.

A museum may stipulate that a courier from the lending institution must accompany the object on loan when it is in transit, or may allow another museum professional to act on its behalf as a courier in consolidated shipments (see CHAPTER 5Q, "Couriering"). It is standard practice for a museum to have its own courier take the object to the first venue and bring it back from the final venue in the case of traveling exhibits. Transfer between exhibition venues is typically handled by the organizing institution except in special circumstances. It is typically the borrower's responsibility to arrange and pay for costs related to the courier, including transportation, lodging, and per diem. The loan agreement may stipulate the per diem amount to be allotted and any travel requirements (e.g., business class when traveling with a work of art). If not, these terms should be negotiated in advance. Preferably the courier should receive the per diem in cash on arrival; however, in some instances, this is not possible, and the lender may bill the borrower later for reimbursement of expenses. Courier arrangements should be clear and in writing.

Final approval or denial of a loan should be communicated in writing in a timely fashion once all in-house and board approvals have been received. Should a loan be denied, the reason(s) should be clearly stated so that borrowers can improve any aspects of their facilities or methods that led to the denial. If the loan is approved, the approval letters and completed loan agreement forms are signed and returned to the borrower. Any special conditions should be stated on the loan form or provided as an addendum. In-house records should be flagged or coded to indicate that the object is reserved for a loan.

Loan Agreement Considerations for Outgoing Loans

Though loan arrangements should always be fair, the lender has an inherent advantage over the borrower because it is the lender who decides whether to use the borrower's agreement or their own. Keep in mind that although you may be the lender this time, you might want to borrow from the other institution in the future.

Most institutions will sign another museum's loan agreement as long as it covers the basics. When evaluating a borrower's loan form, make sure there are loan initiation and termination dates as well as exhibition dates. Loan dates should always begin before and end after the exhibition dates because the loan starts before the object departs the lender's building and remains in effect until it is unpacked and inspected on return. Double-check that information is listed correctly, and remember that it is your responsibility as the lender to make sure the catalog information is up to date on the loan form, including the credit line.

The terms of the loan must include a statement that the borrower will exercise the same care of the loaned objects as it does in safekeeping of comparable property of its own. This ensures that the borrower understands their responsibilities and will care for the loaned objects to the best of their ability. The loan form should state that the objects will remain in possession of the borrower (or the other venues participating in a traveling exhibition) for the time specified, meaning that no other entity will be permitted to have possession of the loan. It is a standard condition that the borrower or lender reserves the right to withdraw a loaned object from an exhibition at any time thereby giving both parties the same right.

The conditions governing the loan should include that all costs for insurance, packing, crating, transportation, and courier expenses will be paid for by the borrower, that objects should be unpacked and examined immediately on return, and that the borrower is not responsible for claims made after a specific period of time following the return date. This period of time must be sufficient for the lender to complete the return loan processing. Negotiate if a longer period is needed. It is never a good policy to let returned loans sit uninspected.

If the loan includes industrially fabricated components that have been altered by an artist this should be disclosed on the loan form, and it should be stated that the insurance is for the full current value. However, if some component of the loan is off-the-shelf,

then the lender should expect compensation to be limited to the cost of the replacement.

Another clause to examine closely is the rights and reproductions portion of the agreement. Most institutions now include a broad license on their loan forms that limits the number of times that they have to go back to the lender and ask for specific rights and reproductions permission. It is acceptable to state in the loan terms that the work may be photographed, filmed, or reproduced and published in all media, in perpetuity, throughout the world, for the borrower's educational, publicity, and promotional purposes. However, the clause should state that the borrower must contact the lender if they want to use images of a borrowed object for any commercial purposes such as posters, postcards, etc.

Insurance Considerations for Outgoing Loans

The lender has the right to ask for a copy of the insurance policy from the borrowing institution. If the borrower uses an insurance broker with whom the lender is unfamiliar, it is good practice to ask to review the policy carefully. The policy should have the same terms and conditions as the lending institution's insurance. It is customary that if the borrower is insured by the same broker, the lender will accept the borrower's insurance. If you are unsure, your broker can confirm that the borrower's policy is acceptable.

A certificate of insurance or indemnity from another institution only provides evidence of coverage. Even with this certificate in hand, the borrower has no real assurance that the policy has not been amended or canceled; therefore, it is recommended to have language in the loan agreement stating that the lender is not responsible for any deficiency or lapse in insurance coverage by the borrower. The certificate should name the lender as *loss payee* and must be issued to the lender before the object is released for shipment. If the lender prefers to maintain its own coverage, the borrower should request an insurance certificate or waiver of subrogation from the lender. (see CHAPTER 6D, "Insurance"). Loans that go to multiple exhibition venues may be covered under different insurance policies, so it is important to receive a certificate of insurance for each venue if this is the case. Note when the certificate of insurance expires and request an updated one if the expiration date is less than thirty days away.

Insurance values for each object are determined by the lender. The assigned values should reflect the current market value (CMV), which is higher than fair market value (FMV) because CMV includes any buyer or seller premiums and also takes into consideration a shorter time period than FMV (e.g., a reasonable length of time to find a willing buyer at market compared with no time restraint). It is the lender's responsibility to make sure that the value is based on firm research and to keep the value updated for each object.

LOAN DOCUMENTATION

The foundation of loan documentation is a well-executed loan form; however, this is not the only documentation necessary for good loan management. The review process should be systematic; if this is not already part of departmental procedures, it is advisable to incorporate it. The museum should document its internal process for making the decision. All of this information should live in the loan file for easy reference. High-quality images of the object before it goes on the loan are necessary; if your institution cannot pay for these, the need and expense should be negotiated with the borrower. These images will assist in any dispute over condition that may arise and will be part of any claims process. The lender should issue an outgoing condition report with enough detail that a change in condition will be noted by the registrar or conservator at the borrowing institution. If there is a change in condition of an object the lender should be notified immediately. If the change in condition merits an insurance claim, the borrower's registrar should contact their insurance company and follow the claims process.

Packing instructions for the borrower should be included in the loan documentation (see CHAPTER 5N, "Packing and Crating"). This serves two purposes: it reminds the lender of the packing method that was used for the outgoing loan, and it gives the borrower guidance on how the object must be packed for shipment to the next venue or for return. Finally, receipts should be included with the loan documentation. The outgoing receipt should have a signature from the borrower's registrar to acknowledge receipt of the object in good order. As institutions become more enmeshed with the digital environment, these documents may be e-mailed instead of included with the packing. However, it is always good practice to include a copy with the packing or carried by a courier.

Packing and Shipping Arrangements

Packing and shipping arrangements must be mutually agreed on by the lending and borrowing registrars. The borrowing registrar normally contacts the lender to discuss considerations for packing, shipping methods, elevator or loading dock limitations, door heights and egress issues, scheduling, and courier needs. The borrowing registrar may wish to consolidate multiple loans to save on shipping expenses; in these instances, the borrower will sometimes provide a courier for the truck and the lender will decide if a courier from the lending institution is needed for the unpacking and installation. Specific requirements should be stated clearly in the loan agreement, such as special scheduling needs, preferred modes of transportation, or preferred vendors. Often the borrowing registrar will contact the lending registrar many months in advance to obtain estimates for packing, preparation, and courier costs to prepare a budget for the loan.

Per the Recommendations of the 9/11 Commission Act of 2007,[2] all cargo traveling on passenger aircraft must be screened by an approved method (electronic, manual, or canine). Many museums with active, outgoing loan programs choose to become Certified Cargo Screening Facilities[3] so that they may screen their shipments in advance and avoid additional handling and screening at the airport. Others choose to use a third party (e.g., commercial packers and shippers) to screen their cargo before arrival at the airport. At this point in time these regulations apply only to passenger, not cargo, aircraft, but recently airlines have begun to request that crates traveling on cargo aircraft be banded during the packing process as a deterrent to the threat of stowaways.

The packing method is determined by many factors including travel distance, route, type of conveyance, object size, media, fragility, and value. Whether soft packing for short trips or double crating for longer trips, the same packing principles apply; that is, the need to protect the object from shock, vibration, and rapid changes in temperature or humidity is of primary importance. Appropriate archival packing materials should be used. All wood must be in compliance with the International Standard for Phytosanitary Measures[4] (ISPM15), which was implemented in October 2001.

Hand-carried objects on commercial aircraft present their own challenges. With increased screening at airports, hand-carried objects are subject to the same process as any other hand-carried luggage. If hand-carrying is the best option contact the airport and ask about special screening procedures and whether a security officer from the museum will be able to accompany you to the gate. If you are traveling out of an airport that is serviced by freight forwarders, you can ask your customs agent to provide this service as their contacts at the airport may speed your departure.

If the lender has the facilities, staff, and time to do the packing, then the lender may bill the borrower for expenses. Packing charges can be based either on an exact record of the hours worked and the actual cost of materials used or on a flat rate that covers different sizes of crates. If a crate already exists for the loan object or there is an existing crate that may be retrofitted for the loan, the common practice is to prorate the cost of this existing crate or not charge the borrower. If there is no suitable crate or the capability to produce one, a commercial packer must be engaged, either by the lender or the borrower; the crate maker should be approved by both registrars. The lender must communicate particular packing, handling, or shipping instructions to the commercial packer. The commercial packer may bill the borrower directly or bill the lender who will then be reimbursed by the borrower.

The borrowing museum generally makes arrangements for transporting the loan subject to the approval of the lender because the borrower is responsible for all shipping costs. The borrowing and lending registrars should discuss the preferred routing, mode of transportation, agents, special rigging needs, consolidations, and security requirements. The shipping schedule will determine the deadline for packing and must be negotiated to make sure the dates can be

met as planned. In general, depending on the nature of the object and the cost to the borrower, the most direct route and the shortest travel time possible should be selected. Consolidated shipments may be the most cost-efficient option for the borrower as long as the safety of the object is not jeopardized in the process. Couriers may be required for a variety of reasons, such as to oversee the transit and installation of the object. Per diem payments should cover travel costs for the period the courier must attend to the loan.

International loans generally are handled through shipping or forwarding agents in the country in which the borrower is located. The borrower's registrar or the forwarding agent will contact foreign shipping agents to obtain bids for packing, shipping, and export/import documentation. The selected agent is presented to the lender for approval. Many museums select an agent through a public tender or bidding process. If the lender has a relationship with a specific domestic agent, who understands the facility and standard operating procedures, it is prudent to list this agent's company on the loan agreement as the contact for shipment. However, if there is some delay before the loan agreement is to be signed, the lending institution may want to include a condition in the acceptance letter stating that the borrower or its agent will need to contact the agent for any foreign shipments.

The agent prepares all of the necessary documentation for the export or import and may arrange packing, delivery to the airport, and airport supervision. Qualified agents can be recommended to the borrower by forwarding a list of agents to US museums that have negotiated loans with agents before and seeking their input. Some export documentation and licenses take several weeks to prepare so international loans should be arranged far in advance.

Confirm all packing and shipping arrangements as well as cost estimates in writing so that both lender and borrower are informed. Specific deadlines, special requirements, and the names and phone numbers of museum contact persons should be communicated to all vendors and agents.

Processing the Outgoing Loan

The outgoing object must be prepared adequately for travel. A conservator may need to make minor repairs, reattach loose fragments, or touch up small losses. Major conservation treatments required prior to the loan should be negotiated with the borrower in advance if the borrower will be expected to take responsibility for any of these costs. Generally, the borrower is expected to pay for all preparation expenses, but conservation treatment needed despite the loan is open for negotiation.

The registrar or preparator should check the framing, glazing, mounts, hardware, and accompanying vitrines or bases to ensure they are fit for travel. Glass should be substituted with ultraviolet-filtered Plexiglas for works on paper (excluding pastels), textiles, or other light-sensitive media that is framed. If the glass is not removed, it must be taped with low-tack tape to prevent damage should it break in transit. Any loose elements must be removed and wrapped separately. Two-dimensional framed objects should be protected with backing boards. All mounting hardware should be checked to ensure that it is adequate for display and has not become fatigued from use. Any special mounting brackets should be discussed in advance with the borrower.

If documenting images are not already in the object file, they should be taken for identification, condition, and insurance purposes. The condition report should include the frame, base, or other accompanying elements. Annotating a photograph, in addition to written notes, is an effective way of describing the object's condition. Space should be provided on the condition report form for the borrower to add comments or note any changes. All condition reports should be dated and signed by the person who prepared them. Some institutions are transitioning to electronic condition reports; these allow easy updating, electronic signatures, and sharing. The condition report can either travel within the crate itself or with the accompanying courier. The original condition report should stay with the borrower until the loan is returned; a copy can be provided while the object is on loan.

A receipt should be sent to the borrower. It is standard for two copies of an outgoing loan receipt to be sent when the loan is shipped. One copy is returned with the borrower's signature and the date on which the loan arrived; the other copy is retained by the borrower. The receipt, signed by the registrar of the borrowing institution, serves as formal notification of the loan's arrival and provides you with the borrower's official acknowledgment of the loan. The borrowing museum often sends its own receipt to document the transaction as well. The outgoing loan receipt should reiterate the conditions under which the loan has been granted and these conditions should be identical to those detailed in the loan agreement form.

Once the loan has been shipped to the borrower, the lending registrar updates internal files and databases to indicate the new location of the object. Pertinent departments (e.g., curatorial, education, information office) should be notified of the absence of the object and the estimated date for its return.

Tracking Objects on Loan

The registrar must establish a system for tracking the object while it is out of the museum. The tracking record should include the object's estimated return date or the date it is anticipated to move to the next venue. Loans occasionally are made for extended periods of more than a year. It is important that the registrar has an effective system for accounting for all objects that are out of the museum. Some museum auditors require annual confirmation of objects that are temporarily out of the museum and will send letters to borrowing museums to verify the location of objects.

Processing Returned Loans

Upon return, the object should be unpacked promptly after acclimatization (about twenty-four hours) and compared to the outgoing condition report to detect any significant changes. If changes or damage are apparent or suspected, the borrowing registrar should be contacted immediately and the two registrars should decide whether to file an insurance claim. Photographs should be taken of any changes or damage that has occurred. If the damage could have occurred during transit, all packing material must be saved and photographed as well. Be sure to check that all loan objects, as well as all parts or accessories and installation hardware, have returned. Once this is done, send an incoming receipt of loan, evidencing that you have received the objects in satisfactory condition, or sign the receipt issued by the borrower for the same purpose. Files should be updated with the new location of the object. A loan history for the object should be maintained to document its exhibition history and light exposure (see CHAPTER 4A, "Types of Records and Files"). A history file of borrowers should be kept to document problems or concerns for future reference and may include notes on agents or shippers used by the borrower that proved problematic, fees charged, extreme courier costs, or facility problems. Loan histories can be useful in negotiating later loans should you wish to borrow objects from the borrower in the future.

Shortly after the conclusion of the loan, either the registrar or the museum's business office must prepare a final invoice billing the borrower for all agreed costs related to the loan (e.g., crating, conservation, courier costs not paid directly by the borrower, insurance premiums, loan fees, etc.). Timely accounting of these costs is appreciated by both the borrowing and lending institutions. To this end, some borrowers might require the lender to bill them after each venue or after the loan is shipped. It is always advisable to request payment as soon as possible after the expense is incurred so that your institution is refunded in a timely manner. Loan expenses can also be managed by having agents' invoices sent to borrowers directly instead of paying for the expense and being reimbursed.

FINAL THOUGHTS

Whether you are a lender or a borrower, good loan management greatly reduces the risk to objects and to the museum. Having an active loan programs means that sometimes the museum will be the lender and other times the borrower. If the collection management policy or museum bylaws support a director or board approval process, it is best practice to use a justification documented during this review. If the review process is on the staff level, it is still prudent to document why decisions were made.

Understanding the terms and conditions of the loan agreement is fundamental to the loan process. Registrars should never sign a loan form they have not reviewed. Besides understanding the terms and conditions of the loan, registrars should pay special attention to loan terms that increase the risk to the object or institution. In circumstances in which it was not possible to negotiate the terms to meet the museum's risk tolerance, the museum has the option to turn down the loan request or to add a hold harmless clause to mitigate the risky part of the loan. Though the loan agreement is fundamental to lending, clear communication and documentation are also vital to having a smooth-running loan program. •

NOTES
1. L. H. Guttenplan, M. Horton Mermin, and S. B. Robinson, "Navigating red flags in loan agreements," in *Legal Issues in Museum Administration Conference*, pp. 437–445 (Los Angeles: American Law Institute: Continuing Legal Education, 2016).

2. Available at: https://www.hsdl.org/c/tl/911-commission-act-2007/.

3. Available at: https://www.securecargo.org/content/what-certified-cargo-screening-program-ccsp-0.

4. Available at: https://www.ippc.int/en/publications/640/.

We thank Sally Freitag, Cherie Summers, and Judy Cline for their assistance.

3L | ORGANIZING LOAN AND TRAVELING EXHIBITIONS

JULIE BAKKE

EXHIBITIONS ACT AS catalysts to bring museum collections and ideas to the public; they represent a way of displaying and contextualizing objects that makes it relevant and accessible to contemporary audiences. Education is at the heart of all museums mission statements. It is often necessary to successfully carry out an exhibition concept that museums augment their own collections with objects from other collections; thus, loan exhibitions are comprised primarily of objects borrowed from other institutions or private collectors.

EXHIBITION PLANNING, BUDGET AND APPROVAL PROCESSES

Planning an exhibition usually begins several years prior to the exhibition opening date. An exhibition typically starts as an idea conceived by a curator. Once the exhibition concept is approved, the curator develops a preliminary checklist, which should include basic object information such as the name of the object, the artist or maker, title, medium, and dimensions. It is at this stage that the registrar should be brought into the process to help develop an exhibition budget (see the sample "Traveling Exhibit Contract" and "Exhibition Fee Work Sheet" in the *Collection Forms* section). Besides the checklist, the curator provides the registrar with information regarding the potential lenders of the objects, such as their geographical location, as well as the proposed number and location of any venues. The registrar is usually asked to provide estimates for crating, shipping, insurance, and any other projected expenses related to the loans necessary for the exhibition, such as loan fees, courier expenses, and costs of preparing objects for loan (e.g., framing or special mounts). For international loans, the registrar contacts the museum's shipping agent who solicits bids from shipping agents in the countries where the objects are located. The agents provide estimates for packing, shipping, and export or import documentation.

As part of the budgeting process, if there are to be multiple venues, it should be decided whether a courier from the organizing institution will accompany the exhibition to each venue and if so, supervise the unpacking and installation of the objects. Factors to take into consideration include the fragility of the objects, their value, and the level of complexity of the installation. The registrar, in consultation with a conservator when possible, determines whether a courier will be needed between venues.

The internal approval process for exhibitions varies among museums. Some museums may only require approval by the director. Others may require approval by a committee of the governing board. Regardless of the number of levels in the approval process, once the budget has been established and the checklist is more or less finalized, the curator presents the exhibition and the budget to the appropriate groups for approval.

After the exhibition has been approved and the venues have been confirmed, the organizing registrar obtains facilities reports from each participating institution so that, on request, lenders can be sent copies of those reports for their own review.

EXHIBITION AND LOAN DOCUMENTATION

The exhibition, object data, and lender information should be entered into a database. If the museum has a collection database that can manage loans and exhibitions and can support multiple users, it should be used by all parties involved with the exhibition checklist to keep all changes to the checklist consistent. The museum's protocol determines who enters the data in the database, be it a curator or registrar, but it is important to have a clear understanding of who has the authority to make changes. It is also important to expect changes to the checklist and subsequently to the budget as the exhibition develops.

All documentation and correspondence related to the exhibition can be stored digitally, but it is still a good idea to also create and maintain paper files (see CHAPTER 4A, "Types of Records and Files"). A file should be created for each lender and should include the following:

- Copy of the loan request,
- Original signed loan form (contract),
- Receipts,
- Insurance documents,
- Correspondence with lenders and shippers (including email correspondence),
- Copies of shipping documents, including air waybills, proforma invoices, and bills of lading,
- Original permits or licenses (if applicable) such as CITES (Convention on International Trade in Endangered Species) or OFAC (Office of Foreign Assets Control), and
- Condition reports.

INSURANCE

It is the organizing institution's responsibility to make all of the insurance arrangements for the exhibition, and it is usually in the exhibition planning phase that the method of insurance and the insurance provider are determined (see CHAPTER 6D, "Insurance"). Four types of insurance applications may pertain to an exhibition because objects may be insured:

- By the organizing institution;
- By each venue, if there are multiple venues;
- By the lender; or
- By government indemnity.

An exhibition may incorporate any or all of these insurance arrangements. It is up to the organizing registrar to ensure that adequate and accurate coverage is provided for all objects from the time they leave the lenders' premises to the time they are returned and for providing lenders with proper documentation showing proof of coverage.

Insurance Provided by the Organizing Institution

The organizing institution may elect to cover the objects in the exhibition under its own insurance policy for the entire tour. To do so, one of the following conditions must apply:

- The total value of the exhibition must be within the policy's limits of liability.
- Extra layers of insurance may be purchased to raise the limits of liability to cover the total value of the exhibition.

Although the first method is a less costly way of insuring an exhibition, it is also the riskiest for the organizing institution because it essentially puts the institution's own collection at greater risk by borrowing a portion (or all) of its coverage. Thus, it is sometimes preferable for the organizing institution to negotiate a special insurance policy for a particular exhibition. These decisions should be made in consultation with the institution's administration and insurance provider or broker. In either case the organizing institution bears the ultimate responsibility and accountability for any damages that might occur over the course of the exhibition tour. For this reason, it is essential that the organizing registrar be familiar and comfortable with each venue's facilities and staff. When the organizing institution is carrying the insurance for the entire exhibition tour it is good practice for the organizing registrar to travel to each venue to supervise the unpacking and prepare condition reports and travel to each venue again when the exhibition closes to supervise condition reporting and packing.

Insurance Provided by Each Venue

For multiple venue exhibitions, it has become more common practice for each venue to be responsible for insuring the objects while on their premises. In these cases, the organizing registrar should review each venue's insurance policy to make sure that coverage is consistent and adequate. It is also necessary to determine who will cover the insurance during transits between venues. Usually the organizing institution proposes the insurance arrangements to each venue (see discussion in this chapter). It is also necessary to determine how the distribution of certificates of insurance to the lenders will be handled.

Government Indemnity

Application for US indemnity must be made well in advance of the exhibition opening but not more than one year and three months in advance of the start of the indemnity period. For multiple venue exhibitions, the organizing institution applies for indemnity on behalf of all of the participants. The organizing registrar must be prepared to provide detailed checklists and support documentation. The registrar should be aware of the various requirements of US indemnity and budget for the probable expenses that will be incurred as a result of these requirements (e.g., arranging for condition reports for all objects before they leave the lenders' premises and after they are returned at the close of the exhibition). The organizing registrar is responsible for providing each venue with copies of the indemnity provisions and for informing the indemnity office of any changes to the conditions outlined in the original indemnity application that may occur during the course of the exhibition, such as a change in exhibition site, exhibition dates, security, or shipping arrangements. US indemnity is available for both international and domestic exhibitions. There will be a deductible, the amount of which is based on the total value of the exhibition. The deductible applies to the exhibition as a whole (not to individual objects) and must be covered by other insurance. Objects made of certain fragile materials may be excluded from coverage and will also need to be covered by other insurance.

Insurance by Lenders

Some lenders prefer to maintain their own insurance coverage. In these cases, the organizing institution is responsible for the cost of the insurance premiums for these loans. This extra cost must be anticipated when establishing the initial exhibition budget. For multivenue exhibitions, this becomes part of the shared costs between the participating institutions (see discussion in this chapter). The organizing registrar should review all outside insurance policies, passing on any unusual stipulations to the other hosting institutions. Some things to watch out for include:

- An open-ended liability period;
- Exclusion of gross negligence or intentional misconduct; and
- A lender's policy with standard exclusions but requiring absolute liability.

The registrar should ask the lender to obtain a waiver of subrogation from the lender's insurance company and for each venue to be named additionally insured (see CHAPTER 6D, "Insurance"). The organizing registrar is responsible for obtaining certificates of insurance for these loans.

REQUESTING THE LOANS

Once the exhibition is formally approved, the loan request letters are prepared, accompanied by loan agreement forms (contracts). Although the letters are usually generated by the director, exhibitions office or curator, the loan forms most often are generated by the registrar (see CHAPTER 3K, "Loans"). Exhibition loan agreements should include the following sections:

- Exhibition title,
- Loan period,
- Exhibition venues and dates,
- Packing and transport,
- Insurance,
- Care and handling,
- Photography and reproduction,
- Environmental conditions, and
- Security.

For multivenue exhibitions, the organizing institution usually generates a single loan agreement that covers all venues rather than having each venue prepare separate loan agreements. Each venue should be given the opportunity to review the loan agreement prior to it being finalized to ensure that the conditions stated in the agreement can be met by each institution. The agreement should clearly state the proposed insurance arrangements.

As loans are approved and loan agreements signed and returned, the registrar reviews the forms and notes any special lender requirements and restrictions (e.g., light levels, security hangars, alarms, floor barriers, platforms, shipping specifications, photography, rights and reproduction limitations). The registrar distributes this information internally to the appropriate departments. It is becoming more common for lenders to send their own loan contracts in lieu of signing the borrower's agreement. In these cases, it is important to review the agreements carefully to make sure that there are no requirements that the borrower cannot fulfill or that could result in unreasonable expenses. Particular attention should be paid to the insurance requirements. The registrar needs to make sure that the requirements that are detailed in the lender's loan agreement can be met by the museum's policy and understand that liabilities beyond their coverage need formal agreement (endorsement) from the museum's insurance underwriters. Some examples of requirements that might appear in lenders' loan agreements include:

- Absolute liability;
- Designation of a specific insurance adjuster or appraiser;
- Coverage required for confiscation, seizure, or war risk;
- Jurisdiction other than institution's state or country in the event of a claim or dispute;
- A sovereignty clause (also known as a *museum clause*); and
- The basis of object valuation (e.g., agreed on value or market value or whichever is greater).

The registrar may be responsible for drafting an exhibition contract that must be signed by a representative from each participating institution. This contract should clearly delineate responsibilities—both financial and logistical—between the organizing institution and each hosting institution. However, if an institution has a separate exhibitions department, the loan contract is usually handled by that department and reviewed by the institution's legal counsel and registrar.

IMMUNITY FROM JUDICIAL SEIZURE

For exhibitions that include foreign loans, it is good practice to apply for Immunity from Judicial Seizure, a program that is administered by the US Department of State. The Immunity from Judicial Seizure statute (22 U.S.C. 2459)[1] protects certain objects of cultural significance that are imported into the United States for temporary exhibition from seizure or other judicial process. It is important to note that in order for the immunity from seizure to be valid, the determination by the US Department of State must be published in the *Federal Register* prior to the importation of the objects into the United States. The organizing registrar should apply for immunity from seizure a minimum of eight weeks prior to the earliest projected importation date. The application and instructions for submission can be found on the State Department's website.[2] If the exhibition has multiple US venues, the organizing registrar submits one application covering all venues.

ORGANIZING THE CRATING AND SHIPPING

Once the majority of the loans have been confirmed, the registrar establishes an overall shipping schedule, based on the projected installation schedule, and considers the methods of transportation available (e.g., air, overland, or a combination of both; see CHAPTER 50, "Shipping by Land, Air, and Sea"). The lenders' loan agreements should be reviewed, noting any special shipping requirements, such as courier requirements or preference for a particular carrier or shipping agent. It is helpful to create a spreadsheet to organize and keep track of the information pertaining to each loan. The spreadsheet can be organized geographically, grouping the loans by location, to produce a working list of possible ways to consolidate some of the shipments.

International loans are usually handled by shipping agents in the countries where the loans are located. The organizing registrar or US shipping agent contacts the various foreign agents for bids for packing and shipping, including export and import fees. In the United States, most domestic loans are transported by truck, so the registrar contacts one or more fine arts trucking firms and provides them with a list of loans to be collected and any other pertinent requirements, such as exclusive use, climate control, dual drivers, and courier on the truck.

Most institutional lenders arrange for their own crating. It is usually assumed that private lenders do not have crates for their objects and that the organizing registrar will need to make packing arrangements. It is helpful to group the lenders by geographic region. The registrar then obtains bids from one or more commercial fine arts packing firms in each region, providing them with a list of objects to be crated and any specific crate design requirements (e.g., thermal insulation, waterproofing, reusable closure system, travel frames; see CHAPTER 5N, "Packing and Crating"). For loans coming from smaller or remote towns where no commercial packing firms are known to the organizing registrar, it is useful to contact a colleague in a museum or gallery in close proximity to the lender to obtain names of one or more packing companies in the area. For foreign loans, most international shipping companies provide crating services as well, and it is standard practice to use the same company for both shipping and packing.

Once the various carriers, packers, and agents have been selected, the registrar contacts the lenders. Although most shipping agents will handle this entire process if necessary, it is good professional practice for the registrar to make initial contact with each lender to discuss proposed packing arrangements, shipping methods, and approximate dates and then have each commercial firm follow up directly with the lenders to confirm precise dates and times. At the same time, the registrar can gather additional information about the objects to be borrowed such as whether a work is framed, if there are any known condition problems, and if there are any logistical problems in getting the object out of the lender's residence. Most commercial crating companies are able to provide secure, climate-controlled storage and, therefore, can consolidate objects at their warehouse and do the actual crating there. Not only can this be more cost-effective for the borrower, in many cases private lenders prefer this method to on-site crating. If the registrar believes this arrangement to be appropriate it should be discussed with the lender to ensure that there are no objections or concerns about the object being transported with more minimal, but adequate, packing. However, this plan may not be an option if the object is to be covered by US indemnity because indemnity requires direct, nonstop transport or twenty-four-hour human security at all overnight facilities, which most packing and storage facilities do not have, and hiring a twenty-four-hour guard is often cost-prohibitive.

After all of the lenders have been contacted, the registrar refines the list of works that must be crated and gives it to the various packing firms, discussing in more detail the exact packing methods and crate designs desired. For exhibitions where there are several objects in one location, it is often desirable, for budget purposes, for several objects to be packed in one crate, particularly if there are many small objects. The registrar needs to take into consideration whether there are objects in the exhibition that will not travel to all of the venues; if so, those items should not be included in a crate with multiple objects.

SCHEDULING AND RECEIVING SHIPMENTS

Most, but not all, couriers will need to be on site to oversee both the unpacking and installation of objects under their care. The registrar needs to work closely with all of the departments (curatorial, conservation, production, preparations, graphics) that will be involved in the installation of the exhibition to set a workable installation schedule for objects that will be accompanied by couriers. This schedule, which is also dependent on availability and flight schedules, will drive the rest of the shipping schedule. Once the works are received at the museum, the registrar carries out the usual procedures for receiving and documenting incoming loans, including:

- Confirmation of crate dimensions, noting how each object is packed and any packing revisions that should be considered;
- Taking detailed photographs of the unpacking of the objects so they can be repacked exactly as they were received;
- Labeling or tagging each object and crate;
- Preparing incoming condition reports—in some institutions, the conservator does the incoming and outgoing condition reports; and

- Sending out receipts to the lenders, confirming safe arrival of their loans.

Condition Reports

The format for the traveling object condition report should be clear, concise, and easy to use. A good, clear photograph (printed digital image) of the object forms the basis for the condition report, thereby minimizing the need for a detailed written description. Annotations indicating preexisting conditions can be made directly on the photograph (see CHAPTER 5E, "Condition Reporting"). Some institutions have begun to do condition reports digitally, but as of this writing, most are still using paper reports. The condition report should include the following information:

- Title of the exhibition;
- Venues and dates;
- Checklist with catalog numbers for each object;
- Minimally descriptive object information (e.g., tombstone object data);
- A space for incoming condition notes, as well as notes on frame, glazing, and mounts; and
- A space for the registrar at each venue to make incoming and outgoing notes and comments. Each space should include a line for signatures and the dates of the condition checks.

If lenders send their own condition reports these should be used in lieu of the organizing institution's condition report form. Additional detailed images are taken as necessary to document any condition issues not mentioned on the lender's report.

THE EXHIBITION TOUR

Documentation

Once the exhibition has opened at the first venue, the registrar can organize the pertinent information that will be passed on to the various exhibition venues prior to the arrival of the exhibition at each site. The information packet should include the following:

- A checklist for the exhibition, including complete object data, insurance values, and credit line for each object;

- A crate and packing list including crate sizes, weights, and crate contents;
- Explicit packing instructions and packing photographs for each crate;
- A list of special equipment necessary to receive the exhibition and install the objects (e.g., forklift, gantry, crane);
- A list of display furniture, mounts, and graphics that will travel with the exhibition;
- A list of lenders' special requirements such as light levels, security hardware, barriers, photography and filming restrictions, and the use of couriers at each venue;
- A certificate of insurance naming each institution as additionally insured (if the organizing institution is insuring entire tour); and
- Indemnity documents (if applicable).

The Condition Report Notebook

All of the condition reports should be included in a master condition report notebook and sent with the exhibition to each venue. Subsequent condition notes should be made directly on each report and should be signed and dated by the person who examines the objects. If damage to an object occurs while the exhibition is on tour, it is the organizing institution's responsibility to report the damage to the lender and to determine, with the lender, the appropriate course of action (e.g., conservation treatment, insurance claim, withdrawal of the object from the exhibition). Whether the damage is significant or insignificant, the organizing institution's registrar must be contacted immediately. If it is determined that an insurance claim will be made, the prior insurance arrangements determine which institution will handle the claim. For example, if the museum in which the damage occurs is covering the insurance on their policy, that institution's registrar handles all aspects of the insurance claim, making sure to keep the organizing registrar informed during the claim process. If the organizing institution is insuring the entire tour, the organizing institution handles the claim no matter where the damage occurs. Similarly, if the exhibition is covered by US government indemnity, the organizing registrar handles the claim.

Shipping Arrangements between Venues

Several months before the exhibition is due to open at the next venue, the organizing registrar should contact the registrar at the next hosting institution to discuss the shipping schedule. The organizing registrar determines the shipping method and carrier and informs the next institution of the proposed delivery dates. The organizing registrar is responsible for making arrangements, if required, for a courier to accompany the object in transit (see CHAPTER 5Q, "Couriering"). Unless stated otherwise in the exhibition contract, the host institution's registrar usually makes per diem and hotel arrangements for any couriers.

If the exhibition is to be shipped between venues within the United States via passenger aircraft, a plan needs to be in place for screening the crates in compliance with the TSA Certified Screening Program.[3]

Dispersal of the Exhibition

Dispersal of the exhibition is usually done directly from the last exhibition venue and is customarily organized by the exhibition's organizing registrar unless other arrangements have been agreed to in the exhibition contract. The organizing registrar must be in close contact with the last venue's registrar well before the exhibition closing date to set a concise and workable packing and shipping schedule. The organizing registrar makes all of the shipping arrangements. Before the exhibition closes the registrar should review the loan list and notations regarding frames, mounts, or hanging device changes that were made during the course of the exhibition, so that the objects can be returned to the lenders in their original state (unless the lender has specifically requested otherwise). The registrar also reviews special instructions, if any, for the return of each object, such as sending it to a location other than the lender's prem-

ises. If a lender's condition report accompanied the loan, after the final condition check has been made, the registrar sends one copy of the completed condition report to the lender and retains the original in the condition report notebook. After all of the objects have been dispersed from the last venue, the organizing registrar generates receipts and sends them to all lenders for their signatures to confirm the safe return of the objects.

DEFINITIONS

Absolute liability—the borrower will be liable to lender for any loss or damage to any part of an object due to causes not covered and compensated by the insurance.

Museum clause (also known as a *sovereignty clause*)—allows that in the event of a total loss, the damaged objects (salvage) can be returned to the lender in addition to the total claim payout. This ensures that the lender always retains title to the object, even if it is totally destroyed and a total claim payout is made. This is particularly important to national and state museums because the objects may be considered national treasures that are cultural patrimony, even if they are totally destroyed or damaged beyond repair.

Open-ended liability—the borrower is liable if the loss or damage is due to circumstances for which the borrower is responsible even if the loss or damage does not become apparent until a later time. •

NOTES

1. Available at: https://www.govinfo.gov/app/details/USCODE-2011-title22/USCODE-2011-title22-chap33-sec2459.

2. Available at: https://www.state.gov.

3. Available at: https://www.tsa.gov/for-industry/cargo-programs.

3M | Displays from Within—Considerations for Collections-Based Exhibitions

MARK RYAN

Introduction

On initial inspection, collection-based exhibitions may appear to be less involved and require less effort than loan-based or traveling exhibitions—this could not be further from the truth. Collections-based exhibitions share many of the same logistical challenges as loan-based exhibitions, but may also include an additional workload associated with enhanced research and content development along with detailed, object-level assessment and the need to coordinate conservation treatment.

Exhibitions showcasing institutional holdings provide opportunities to display the depth and breadth of our collections within a broad range of conceptual frameworks. In-house exhibitions vary in both content and schedule and do not necessarily exclude noncollection objects, but do share common traits. Intended as a starting point for developing internally focused exhibitions, the following considerations provide a framework for collections-based exhibition development.

Similar to loan-based exhibitions, collection-based efforts have important benchmarks to clear and schedules to meet. These include planning sufficient time for content and design development, critical conservation treatment to be undertaken, mount and casework design and fabrication, and perhaps most importantly, allocation of adequate resources and time to ensure the smooth and orderly handling of potentially fragile, large or complicated objects.

When budgeting the appropriate amount of time to prepare for and install an exhibition, it is never too early to start. The entire process could take months or even years depending on the complexity, content, size, and anticipated duration of the exhibition at hand. The specific procedures for exhibition development and installation are unique to each museum, but all share common, core benchmarks. Each undertaking begins with conceptual design, continues through schematic and final depiction, and ends with construction and installation-ready plans that take even more time to successfully execute—again varying greatly depending on size, complexity, content, and duration.

Successful exhibition development and installation necessitates input from a variety of critical stakeholders, and it takes time to adequately vet and incorporate this input into the final product. Critical voices contributing to the end product include all museum departments (curatorial, education, security, registration, conservation, etc.), community groups, external consultants and related contractors, software/application developers, and fabricators. All exhibitions are unique; as such, a successful outcome is dependent on adequate time and the noted associated benchmarks of development to ensure they are successfully implemented.

Although internally focused exhibitions are frequently comprised exclusively of collection objects, noncollection objects are often incorporated, such as objects on loan or reproductions. Regardless of object type, all require significant time, both in terms of front-end planning and execution and may involve external parties including lenders, shippers, couriers, and intellectual property or rights holders.

Although detailed workflow checklists are useful tools to guide a registrar through the processes of developing and executing collections-based exhibitions, they are frequently framed within an institution-specific context and not therefore universally applicable. Rather than attempt to provide a one-size-fits-all approach, the following presents a responsible and preservation-centric approach for practical exhibition development and execution.

PLANNING AND DEVELOPMENT

Communication

Perhaps the most import part of any exhibition planning endeavor is consistent communication. Beginning with the initial concept and checklist development and extending through deinstallation—and involving all members of the team—the need to be in constant dialog is imperative to ensure the coordination of all related activities.

Time

Successful exhibition planning and development is an exercise in careful and concise logistical planning that incorporates the time necessary (always an overlooked and underrepresented resource) in proportion to the size and complexity of the exhibition to inform a realistic timeline.

Object Selection

Although the exhibition planning processes and staffing structures will vary by institution, the primary responsibility of selecting objects for exhibition lies with a core team—ordinarily initiated and led by curatorial staff input. From the early iterative stages of development through final selection, the essential input and perspective of the registrar is an indispensable necessity. Among other duties, the registrar ensures that object(s) selected are in suitable condition for exhibition purposes or can be brought into stable and presentable condition.

Other duties that often fall squarely on the shoulders of the registrar include drafting, reviewing, and closely coordinating the documentation associated with all of the objects in the exhibition. This includes packing and shipping, condition reporting, and photography, as well as loan and insurance agreements should the exhibit include borrowed objects.

Sensitive Objects

An auxiliary list of sensitive objects (e.g., works on paper or objects that include fugitive pigments) should be developed as an addition to the initial checklist. Sensitive objects usually need special preparation for display to ensure their safe and efficient future rotation. Beyond physically sensitive objects, we are also stewards of culturally sensitive collections that represent a wide range of worldviews. Caring for and properly displaying this category of objects requires far more than simply preserving their physical stability. When considering collections of this nature, conventional preventive conservation practice needs to also incorporate any associated aspects of spiritual care that the objects require (see CHAPTER 7B, "The Care of Culturally Sensitive and Sacred Objects" for further information).

In addition to the condition of an object, the duration of time an object should be placed on exhibition is an equally important factor. The planned rotation of sensitive objects of all types needs to be incorporated early in the process because it will impact every associated component of the exhibition from context to case design.

The Checklist

The checklist is the seminal document that guides everyone through the entire exhibition timeline. While in development, each iterative draft of the checklist should incorporate basic information about each object, including its unique identifying number (loan, accession, catalog, etc.), as well as basic descriptive content and associated photography. As planning progresses, so too will the checklist—from first draft through the final checklist. All involved parties, including staff, vendors, and contractors, will need timely access to the checklist and be made aware of any changes to it.

ASSESSING AND PREPARING THE OBJECT

Assessing an Object

There is much in the way of initial research work involved with assessing the suitability of an object for display. From thorough physical examination to a review of previous display and past conservation treatment histories, a close scrutiny of all objects is the next critical step in the process.

A major factor to consider when determining the suitability of an object to be placed on display is its susceptibility to further damage from exposure to the exhibition environment and, if deemed necessary, its potential to respond positively to environmental mitigation efforts. For example, can an acceptable microclimate be designed for the object's specific environmental requirements or can light levels be set low enough to facilitate periodic viewing while also limiting cumulative damage?

Often, remedial cleaning is all that is required (or possible) to improve the appearance of an object. This task frequently falls under the responsibility of the registrar. Given the complexities associated with cleaning any object, it is advisable to seek the guidance and recommendations of a conservator prior to undertaking any cleaning operation. Once an acceptable cleaning strategy has been established, proceed with caution and beware of well-intentioned but potentially damaging cleaning actions. Go into the process with a conservative approach in mind and know your limits. And remember—*do no harm*!

As part of an institution's overall risk mitigation approach the physical security of the objects should be incorporated into both the design and execution of the installation. The design of any security measures should conform to an object's individual needs and associated acceptable levels of risk exposure. For example, valuable or particularly vulnerable objects may have specific requirements for tamper-resistant hardware or locked casework.

If necessary, and as time and budget permit, the oftentimes necessary and complex treatment of objects requiring conservation work needs to be planned and accommodated. Allow sufficient time for the entire conservation process, including packing, transit, examination, and dialog with a conservator to inform the proposal, and of course, time for the treatment itself.

Preparing an Object for Display

After the condition of an object is well understood, the work associated with its preparation begins. This will encompass a wide range of activities including everything from proper matting and framing to designing and fabricating custom mounts and casework. The time, cost, and expertise required for these steps necessitates the early identification of an object's unique requirements in the continued development of the checklist.

For objects that include electronic components or that have specific spatial requirements (e.g., additions to the built environment), the registrar must ensure that all needs can be accommodated in the associated exhibition design and budget and that all constituent components are in good working order or are otherwise readily available.

Lastly, based on the availability or condition of the original object, the need to incorporate reproductions into the exhibition is occasionally required. Aside from the time required to arrange for the physical reproduction to be made, plan sufficient time to secure intellectual rights or reproduction permissions from the various associated rights holder(s).

PRODUCTION—EXHIBITION DESIGN AND FABRICATION

As the checklist comes into sharper focus and object-specific frames, display mounts, and casework are being conceived of, the overall exhibition design and production process gets underway. As there remains a constant potential for objects to continue to be added or removed from the checklist, timing for checklist revisions becomes critical at this stage.

Whether using in-house expertise, outside vendors, or some combination thereof, exhibition design and production is an iterative process resulting in the final design used for pricing and scheduling purposes. Beginning with an initial conceptual design and continuing through the execution of construction-ready documents, the need to incorporate preservation-specific materials and methodologies in the exhibition design is necessary.

The development of realistic preservation criteria within the established budget, space, and time constraints often necessitates compromise between potential objects and the manner in which they can be safely displayed. The use of inert materials combined with an object-focused and preservation-centric approach should drive the design and fabrication methods of all related object mounts, supports, and casework.

There are a number of resources available to help guide you through the planning processes, appropriate material selection, and casework construction. Among them are the National Park Service's *Conserve-O-Gram*[1] series and the Canadian Conservation Institute's (CCI) *CCI Notes*[2] and related technical bulletins, all of which are readily available online.

Equally important to bear in mind is incorporating desired traffic flows and adhering to code requirements and other audience-specific considerations within the overall exhibition design. Balancing these pragmatic and legal considerations while staying true to the overall curatorial position and exhibition premise is an exercise in compromise.

Lastly, plan for sufficient time to select, test, and prototype proposed materials and designs. It is essential to build in time to allow surfaces to thoroughly cure and off-gas, along with time needed for the dry-fitting of objects within all mounts and casework. These final, and often lengthy, processes need to be kept at the forefront and undertaken well in advance of actual installation.

INSTALLATION

Whether an inaugural exhibition within a new or renovated space or one following on the heels of a previously installed exhibition, gallery transitions need to be carefully planned to ensure that all selected objects are properly handled and accounted for. Prior to installation, a series of benchmarking sessions are advisable to ensure that the exhibition perimeter (shell) and associated interior temporary walls are constructed, cured, and stand ready to accept objects; that all objects are, or will be, on site; all mounts and casework are fabricated to specification; and objects fit as designed. Confirm that all available qualified staff (in house and contracted) are scheduled, briefed, and adequately prepared prior to the installation commencing.

The final exhibition design, together with the final checklist, serve as the instruction manual for how the exhibition is to be assembled and with which constituent parts. The floor plan specifies the exact location of objects and along with any models and renderings serve as essential tools to assist in strategizing the overall installation process, including sequence considerations. The sequence of installation is determined by either the schedule of couriers and technicians or is simply required to occur at a given point in time due to the need for a large or complicated installation before smaller, more straightforward installations are undertaken.

Follow best practices of limiting access to the installation space to only those needing access or to those who are otherwise authorized to be in the space. Once installed, a regular object and condition check needs to be undertaken to ensure the consistent accounting for all objects.

The need to establish clear lines of communication during the installation is imperative. It is advisable to have a single point person from whom all primary direction and communications originate on the exhibition floor—whether that individual is the exhibition manager, lead preparator, or registrar. There are often conflicting priorities with information coming from multiple sources within the dynamic setting of an exhibition installation. Establishing a defined line of communication and a clearly delineated assignment of roles and responsibilities from the start will ensure a well-orchestrated and executed installation.

Immediately prior to the exhibition opening, a dedicated walk-through with security, education, and programming staff is advised to ensure that everyone is adequately informed to undertake their particular responsibilities. For example, ensure that security staff know where to stand to have the optimal viewing perspective and are keenly aware of particularly susceptible objects. Confirm that programming staff are familiar with the layout of the exhibition. A preliminary introduction to the exhibition for all staff prior to the opening will contribute to the successful undertaking of their duties as monitors and interpreters of the exhibition.

MONITORING, MAINTENANCE, AND ROTATION

Once the exhibition is installed, the work still is not yet finished! The consistent monitoring of objects on view as well as the complete gallery environment are important practices to have in place. This vigilance serves as an extension of the preservation-centric approach necessary to provide the requisite stewardship of the objects on view throughout the life span of an exhibition.

Consistent protocols need to be in place to accurately measure, record, and—perhaps most importantly—take action on out-of-range light, temperature, and humidity readings within the specific casework and the overall exhibition space. Additionally, any need to monitor, maintain, or replenish performance-based exhibition media should be properly planned (e.g., replenish or replace humidity or pollutant absorbing media).

Lastly, it is important to maintain the aesthetic integrity and plan for the regular upkeep of the exhibition components to ensure the exhibition both looks its best and is performing as designed. Regularly scheduled downtime to address pragmatic issues such as the rotation of sensitive objects, replacement of lamps, dusting casework, adjusting label copy, and so on, needs to be predetermined to ensure the consistency and integrity of the visitor experience as well as for the safety of the objects.

DEINSTALLATION AND EVALUATION

Although straightforward in concept, the deinstallation of an exhibition involves a similar need to approach the task at hand with a preservation-centric approach and rigor. The safe transition of objects out of mounts and casework and finally back into storage—or properly packed and shipped should they be loaned objects—needs to be carefully and methodically undertaken to ensure for the well-being of all objects included in the exhibition.

Deinstallations need to be as carefully planned and coordinated as installations. They demand the same attention to details as installations do and should remain the focus of all involved until such time as objects are safely removed. All other associated activities should be held at bay until all objects are safely transitioned out of the exhibition space. Most importantly, ensure that all objects are safely removed from the space before any other transition work is undertaken (e.g., casework moved, walls demolished, walls painted, floors refinished).

Among the last, but no less important, responsibilities of the registrar is the organization of the comprehensive exhibition documentation, beginning with the initial discussions surrounding the concept development of the checklist and continuing throughout the design and installation process. The registrar tracks and documents the life span of all objects (whether selected or not) within an exhi-

bition. The story of an exhibition, its development, budget, shipping, packing, installation, and eventual deinstallation should be methodically documented within the institutional archives—from when an object is first removed from storage to when it is returned to storage, regardless of its origin. All documentation connected to the checklist, including all related correspondence, packing and shipping information, photography, object-specific display instructions, and mounts and casework design documents should be included as a historical record of the exhibition.

Understanding what worked and what did not is important to document and learn from. It is imperative, therefore, to methodically evaluate how well the exhibition delivered on content and message. Equally important is to document how the exhibition design and installation process went. How well did the cases and mounts accommodate for the scheduled rotation of sensitive objects? Did visitors struggle with labels and didactic content? Did the intended traffic pattern guide visitors through the exhibition as conceived? How did the new paint selected for the exhibition hold up? All these, and more, should be carefully documented to ensure that lessons learned are incorporated into future exhibitions.

CONCLUSION

As there will be the inevitable last-minute changes—be they deviations in floor plans, additions to the checklist, or changes of wall colors—it is important to approach any installation with as much time and contingency planning as possible to ensure success. Add equal dashes of humor, patience, and flexibility for all involved, and you have got the perfect recipe for a well-planned and executed exhibition of permanent collection objects! •

NOTES

1. Available at: http://www.nps.gov/Museum/publications/conserveogram/cons_toc.html#collectionpreservation.html (accessed December 4, 2018).

2. Available at: http://www.canada.ca/en/conservation-institute/services/conservation-preservation-publications/canadian-conservation-institute-notes.html (accessed December 3, 2018).

PART 4 | RECORDS MANAGEMENT

4A | TYPES OF RECORDS AND FILES

JOHN E. SIMMONS AND TONI M. KISER

CREATION AND MAINTENANCE of transaction and object documentation are essential tasks for a museum registrar or collections manager. Information about an object and transactions involving it were traditionally stored as paper-based documents in physical files (see CHAPTER 4B, "Manual Systems"). The files kept in a particular museum are a reflection of the kind of information stored and how it has been used in the institution. It is important to understand how the files, filing systems, and the methods used in the past govern the information about the collection that is available today (TABLE 4A.1). Although

many of the file types discussed are no longer maintained separately because of the ease with which information can be sorted and retrieved from electronic collection records, it is important to understand the organization of collection information and what information is worth saving.

Records about objects in the collection are maintained on an ongoing basis for permanent reference. Activity files are compiled, maintained, and searched while the activity itself is current. Once an exhibition is concluded or a loan has been returned, additional information may be added to a history of object use

Table 4A.1 Typical Files Maintained in Museums Prior to the Advent of Electronic Data Management Systems

Catalogs and card files	Catalogs were traditionally handwritten entries in bound leger books, but as collections grew and diversified, the use of cards that could be sorted and rearranged became much more common.[1] Object information was traditionally sorted by accession number, catalog number, object name, category, or subject, or based on a classification, taxonomy, or nomenclature such as the Linnaean system in natural history collections or the Chenhall system (now called Nomenclature for Museum Cataloging) in history museums. The old card file of the Metropolitan Museum of Art in New York occupied a line of cabinets that was a city block in length, with the cards organized by accession number.[2]
Accession number	The accession number is the traditional object identification number used in art and history museums, but the catalog number is more commonly used in natural history and archaeological collections (see CHAPTER 3B, "Acquisitions and Accessioning").
Source	Donor, collector, maker, artist, manufacturer, indigenous or cultural group, etc.
Origin	Geographic origin or place of acquisition (e.g., an Egyptian antiquity may have been purchased in Rome).
Location	Object's place in storage in the collection storage array.
Image	Photograph, sketch.
Insurance	Object-based or collection-based insurance.
Loan objects	Objects on loan to the museum or loaned to other institutions.
Exhibition	The particular exhibition the object was included in.

NOTES

1. J. E. Simmons, *Museums: A History* (Lanham, MD: Rowman & Littlefield, 2016), 86.

2. Simmons, *Museums*, 215.

BOX 4A.1 HIGHLY ECCENTRIC AND HIGHLY PERSONALIZED

The classification of objects in museums and the arrangement of information in collection catalogs has never been standardized. Which files were kept and how they are arranged has depended mostly on the ideas, philosophy, or whims of the curator or registrar as well as the types of objects in the collections and how the objects were used. Over time, this resulted in highly eccentric and personalized systems that usually worked well for one museum but were rarely transportable to another (it is still rare to find two systems that are exactly alike in different museums). When museums adopted electronic data management systems, beginning in earnest in the 1980s, these eccentric and personalized systems were converted to eccentric and personalized electronic databases, most often designed based on the assumptions, prejudices, and sometimes nonrational ideas of curators, registrars, and collections managers focused on their own institution's collections. In the early days of electronic data management, if a database system worked at least as well as the paper-based system it replaced, it was considered to be adequate. It took quite a while for museums professionals to understand the importance of having standardized information structures that enable universal database design and the ability to exchange information easily among different institutions.[1]

NOTE
1. J. E. Simmons, *Museums: A History* (Lanham, MD: Rowman & Littlefield, 2016), 213–220.

file, while the actual documents may be moved to less accessible archival storage. Some activity files—such as temporary custody, loan, acquisition—may be restarted each year with old records archived.

Because the value of storing information about objects and activities lies in its retrieval, the data should be organized in the way in that most users will logically look for it (BOX 4A.1). The arrangement of physical files may be alphabetical, numerical, or chronological, depending on the type of information and how it will be used. Retrieval from any system is easier if the information has been entered in a uniform format, with consistent spellings and modes of display. In general, filing systems should be simple, clear, and consistent. Strive for systems that can be understood even if the registrar is not there to explain them. Simple systems that are kept up to date are vastly superior to sophisticated models that are too cumbersome to be easily maintained.

Traditionally, the registrar compiled and maintained a central file that listed all of the objects in the permanent collection, usually in a ledger or card file (many museums continue to maintain card files or ledgers as backups for the information in electronic databases). However the file is maintained, it should contain a record for each object, retrievable by accession number, that incorporates essential object information. Object files sometimes include an image of the object for identification purposes, and may cross-reference other files that provide a way to identify specific objects or groups of objects by means other than the accession number (e.g., by maker, artist, donor, collector, subject matter, classification system, or geographic origin).

Maintaining a central record of all the objects in the entire collection in numerical order is essential for the accountability of the institution. The form of this central record and the complexity of data in it will depend on the resources allotted to registration functions over the history of the museum. Enough information should be in the file to distinguish each object from all others and to identify what it is, where it came from, and where it is currently located (e.g., in storage, on exhibit, on loan). The central file may be a stepping stone to the greater information that is collected about an object, may display all of that information, or may provide something between the two. Even if a bound ledger or card file has been discontinued in favor of electronically stored data, the old paper-based records should be archived as a backup to protect the information.

CATEGORY, SUBJECT, AND CLASSIFICATION FILES

A category file is based on the classification system in use, materials, or subject matter. Each discipline has its own intellectual or hierarchical categories; some are more complete or systematic than others. A museum should clearly define the standard classification systems it uses.

Category files may be difficult and time-consuming to maintain in a manual system, and are created as separate files far less often as museums adopt electronic data management systems (see CHAPTER 4C, "Computer Systems and Data Management" and CHAPTER 4D, "Digital Asset Management Systems"). Sometimes categories are not really in parallel although they reflect the way a particular museum has divided up responsibility for its varied collections. For example, a museum may have object categories such as portraits, Chinese objects, farm tools, and wood carvings. These divisions were meaningful and useful to those who started them and to those who can get used to them, but they do not always aid researchers or new staff. Form, content, and intellectual analysis can become intertwined and confused. Accurate assignment of a particular object to one of these categories may become a matter of chance.

ACCESSION, OBJECT, AND OTHER DOCUMENT FILES

Documents created by others may be appropriate for the registrar's object files, and copies of some documents may be filed in a curatorial department as well. It is important that the museum have a central location or source in which records for the entire collection may be reliably found (increasingly museums retain only electronic copies of documents for routine use, with most paper-based files stored in an archive). Accession, object, and other document files usually are kept in accession number order, sometimes further divided by curatorial department. Whether electronic or paper-based, these files usually include:

- Legal documents associated with the accession of an object, such as a bill of sale or deed of gift;
- Correspondence about the acquisition and delivery of the object (see CHAPTER 3B, "Acquisitions and Accessioning");
- Permits, permissions, and import and export documents;

- Shipping information, documents, or invoices;
- Copy of the will for a bequest;
- Images of the object;
- Acquisition or accession worksheets;
- Condition and treatment reports from the conservator;
- Valuation or appraisal information;
- Copies of research reports or correspondence, especially those documenting changes in attribution;
- Bibliographic references;
- Exhibition and loan history; and
- Deaccession information.

These files are archival in themselves because the documents are primary sources of information about the object and continue to grow throughout the history of the object, incorporating bibliographic references, appraisals and valuation, exhibition history, treatment reports, condition reports, research notes, and so forth. Information should be date-stamped when it is added to the folder. Paper-based object files are most useful when the contents are well-organized and duplicate pages removed.

MAKER, ARTIST, MANUFACTURER, OR COLLECTOR FILES

A frequently used reference is the maker, artist, manufacturer, or collector file. Like most other types of files, it is increasingly common to keep electronic originals or digitized versions of paper-based documents in an electronic database. The format of names, regardless of how the files are organized, should be consistent and clear. There are many standard references for names and titles available, but in most institutions the curator is the institution's arbiter. Collection objects or objects on long-term loan may be listed for ready capsule view. The maker—whether individual, manufacturer, or cultural group—may be described by life dates, active dates, places worked, manufacturing sites, biographical notes, nationality, or a designation for group, tribe, or culture.

SOURCE OR DONOR FILES

The source or donor file identifies the donors of objects, vendors, purchase funds, archaeological sites, expeditions, lenders, or trading institutions. It should have a consistent and clear format for names. Some source information (particularly details about donors) may be restricted and accessible only on a need-to-know basis.

LOCATION FILES

Each museum must devise a workable way to report and record object movement (e.g., in and out of storage, on and off exhibition, on loan). Location files are key to the accountability of registration. Inventory and tracking of the object is as important as descriptive information. Location files are searched or modified as often as staff need to look at or take inventory of objects or move them. This frequency of use means that location files must be easy to read and easy to update.

In large museums, a written work request often is used to initiate object movement and record new locations, with a copy to the registrar or collection manager for making changes in the object record. Some museums maintain a location log (e.g., in the storage room) in which new locations or object movements are written in as they occur and the central location file updated periodically.

Frequent object moves may be difficult to record in a timely manner. Backlogs of object movement work orders or logs in storage will soon lead to poor inventory control so periodic physical inventories must be done to confirm the accuracy of location information (see CHAPTER 5K, "Inventory"). Constant vigilance is required to enforce reports of object movement from curators and object handlers; self-discipline is required to stay up to date with location records. A location file that is simple and straightforward will be maintained better than an elegant and elaborate tracking system that requires many steps to update.

OBJECT IMAGE FILES

Images document the objects and aid identification, condition recording, insurance claims, study, research, education, exhibition planning, publication,

and publicity. Older photographic files may consist simply of a negative number with the photograph date or may encompass storage of the photographic materials themselves. Newer image files will probably be born-digital images (see CHAPTER 4D, "Digital Asset Management Systems").

Photographs may be in several formats including negatives (individual or rolls), contact sheets, black-and-white or color prints, color transparencies, color slides, snapshots, and digitized or born-digital images. The types of access needed and the materials used for image storage affect the organization of image files. If the files are used mostly by the registration staff, they can be arranged by accession number. If others need regular access, it may be more useful to organize them alphabetically by object name, artist, classification, place of origin, or medium or materials. In a good digital management system, any of these categories should be available as search terms. Choose a method that works best for the collection and for the institution's users and avoid complicated or idiosyncratic systems of organization.

It is helpful to have the negative number for film-based images in the object records. Photographs should be kept in acid-free folders. Negatives, slides, and transparencies should be kept separated from prints, in acid-free or metal boxes or in acid-free envelopes, or in Mylar D, polypropylene, or polyethylene sleeves. Prints and negatives should not be stored with rubber bands or paper clips.

INSURANCE FILES

Insurance values for individual objects are part of the continuing object documentation. Some insurance policies require a periodic schedule of new or revised values, or, as part of its own risk-management program, the museum may track object values by gallery or storage area. The organization of the information and the files depends on how the information is used by the registrar, the insurer, and the museum—for example, chronological by date of the report, location of the objects, collection group, accession number, or catalog number. Insurance values of museum objects should be restricted information. As with all files, simplicity of the system and clearly marked labels make the information easier to find and use.

INCOMING LOAN FILES

Incoming loans may be received for exhibition, research, study, long-term custody, or consideration for acquisition. Loan files document the ownership, object condition, object use, and agreed-on conditions of the loan, such as location, length of loan, or any special needs. Paperwork related to loans for temporary exhibitions should be kept with the rest of the exhibition file (see discussion in this chapter).

Loans to the museum must be recorded, stored, exhibited, or studied with the same care and level of documentation as the museum's own collection objects, but objects on loan should be tracked in a way that immediately distinguishes loaned objects from accessioned objects. Although some museums assign their own numbers to objects on loan, this practice is generally discouraged—instead, objects on loan should be tracked using the numbers that are marked on them by the loaning museum and by the loan number (usually the loan number supplied by the loaning museum). The exceptions to this are objects that arrive on loan without numbers (usually objects from a private collector). Loan records should be maintained in order in a separate file. Loan object folders will contain the loan agreement, incoming receipts, condition reports, images of objects, correspondence, and other documents. An alphabetical lender file may be useful in museums that deal with many loans to the collection, whereas a separate tickler file may alert the registrar to the return or renewal date.

The documents pertaining to the loan transaction should be annotated with the loan tracking number and filed by the activity for which the objects were borrowed. Once incoming loan transactions have been concluded and objects returned to their owners, the records should be annotated and the file marked as closed. Information about loans should be kept for future research (the history of object use is an important aspect of the history of the institution). Documents kept should include the loan agreement, official correspondence, and copies of incoming and outgoing receipts, especially those signed by the owner on return.

OUTGOING LOAN FILES

Files for outgoing loans should contain the following:

- Correspondence with the borrower about the loan;
- Loan agreement, spelling out terms of the loan (see CHAPTER 3K, "Loans");
- Shipping papers;
- Borrower's receipt;
- Condition reports; and
- Insurance certificates.

Exhibition Files

From initial planning through the opening of an exhibition, documents and notes that are used to get the work done accumulate (see CHAPTER 3L, "Organizing Loan and Traveling Exhibitions" and CHAPTER 3M, "Displays from Within—Considerations for Collections-Based Exhibitions"). The working exhibition files may include the following:

- Originals or copies of loan forms;
- Receipts;
- Correspondence with lenders, shippers, and insurers;
- An inventory of the exhibition by case, catalog, arrangement and physical location of objects in the exhibit, and object identification numbers (e.g., accession or catalog numbers);
- List of lenders;
- Contact names, telephone numbers, and e-mail addresses of lenders or others critical to the exhibition;
- Condition reports;
- Images;
- Conservator's treatment reports;
- Related in-house notes and memos;
- Shipping bids and bills of lading;
- Budget notes and estimates;
- Purchase orders;
- Related conservation or exhibit maintenance schedules;
- Insurance lists; and
- Copies of information from other departments.

This kind of working file has the order (or disorder!) that meets particular needs or time available. It is prudent to keep everything, even notes on scraps of paper during this time. At the conclusion of an exhibition, after all loaned objects have been returned and collection objects restored to storage, or once a permanent exhibit is in place, it is time to organize the contents of the file. Keep those documents with information that someone may need in later years, and organize them in a way that will aid finding them. Dispose of any redundant pages and now-irrelevant scraps and notes. A closed exhibition file should be as useful as any other research document with papers in logical order and an index or table of contents.

Exhibition files should be kept chronologically by exhibition date. All or part of the registration materials may become part of the institution's master archive file for that exhibition. Information about the logistics, lenders, shipping arrangements, insurance, and costs may be useful in future exhibition planning; the registrar may keep the information, if not the actual documents, in an exhibition planning file for reference. ●

This is an edited and updated version of the chapter originally written by Kittu Longstreth-Brown and updated by Rebecca Buck for Museum Registration Methods *(2010), who acknowledged the contributions of Anne Fuhrman Douglas, Connie Estep, Paulette Dunn Hennum, Monique Maas, and Dominique Schultes.*

JOHN E. SIMMONS AND TONI M. KISER

Creating Documentation

Managing information about the museum's collection objects and object transactions (including objects in temporary custody) is one of the primary tasks of registrars and collections managers. Several documents (with some variations) are common to most museums and form the basic paper-based records in museums using manual registration systems. These documents describe the objects, record the activities involving them, and define their legal status (e.g., ownership or custody). The format of any of these documents will be specific to the system in place in a given museum, but the functions are the same for all. In this chapter, manual registration systems are discussed, but it should be noted that the same essential information should be recorded whether the collection management system in use is fully manual, fully electronic, or a combination of the two. For discussion of the use of computer-based systems, see CHAPTER 4C, "Computer Systems and Data Management," and CHAPTER 4D, "Digital Asset Management Systems."

The essential documents in a manual documentation system include:

- Receipt of objects in the museum;
- Deeds of gift and other gift agreements;
- Internal Revenue Service (IRS) forms;
- Proofs of purchase;
- Master object or accession log;
- Worksheets;
- Condition reports;
- Copyright licenses; and
- Loan agreements.

Receipt of Objects

Information about objects coming to the museum may originate with the registrar, curator, donor, maker, vendor, or others. The original documents (those bearing signatures) should be filed and archived, and the steps between the receipt and return of an object or its accession should be carefully tracked. It is a best practice to issue receipts for all objects coming into the museum's custody for any reason. Elements of a receipt include:

- Name and address of the owner of the object, including telephone, fax, and e-mail addresses;
- Date the object was received by the museum;
- Why the object is at the museum (e.g., on loan, consideration for accessioning);
- How the object came to the museum (means of shipment);
- Description of the object;
- Temporary or catalog numbers;
- Insurance value (if appropriate) and insurer of record;
- Expiration date or duration of deposit; and
- Signatures of both the owner and a representative of the museum.

The terms and conditions under which the museum receives objects should be included. The registrar (or another authorized staff member) and the depositor sign and date the receipt. The owner of the object receives a copy, and the museum's registration office keeps one or more copies on file.

Deed of Gift

A deed of gift (also called a *gift agreement*, *deed of reconveyance*, *statement of gift*, or *certificate of gift*) substantiates the transfer of title to an object from the owner to the museum (see CHAPTER 3B, "Acquisitions and Accessioning"). The agreement is usually generated by the recipient museum and a copy is forwarded to the object owner for signature.

A deed of gift should be issued on museum letterhead or on a special form bearing the museum's legal name and address. As with all museum documents, it should be printed on acid-free paper. Three originals are generated: Two are forwarded to the owner for signature, and one is kept on file in the museum registration office. The owner signs both copies received and returns them to the museum. The museum director (or other authorized official) then countersigns both copies and returns one to the owner. This system ensures that both the owner and the museum will have signed copies of the agreement and that the museum will have a reference copy on file throughout the transaction. The museum's signed and dated gift agreement is kept in the object document file organized by donor's last name.

The gift agreement should contain the following information:[1]

- Museum's legal name, address, and telephone and fax numbers;
- Registrar's or collections managers' name, telephone number, and e-mail address;
- Donor's name, address, e-mail, and telephone number;
- A description of the object, including the type, artist or maker (if appropriate), country of origin, date of object, materials or medium, and dimensions;
- The museum's standard credit line, which the donor may have the option to change;
- Expression of intention to donate the object;
- Language waiving all right of ownership to the object;
- Language indicating that the person giving the object has the legal authority to give it;
- Language that the gift is unrestricted (any restrictions that are accepted by the museum should be written into the deed of gift; those restrictions then supplant this statement);
- Language confirming the owner's belief that the object was not exported from its country of origin in violation of the laws of that country in effect at the time of the export, or imported into the United States in violation of US laws and treaties;
- A statement that the gift was acquired legally;

- Language indicating that the owner received no goods or services in consideration of the gift;
- If dealing with the artist or copyright owner, a statement passing ownership or granting nonexclusive use to the museum;
- If not dealing with artist or copyright owner, a statement giving up all rights to the gift;
- Language acknowledging the museum's acceptance of the gift;
- A line for signature and date of signing by the owner; and
- A line for signature and date of signing by the museum representative.

Although possession of a completed gift agreement is the optimum manner of substantiating title to an object, alternate documentation—such as correspondence from a donor expressing an intent to make a gift and a gift acknowledgment letter from the museum—may serve the same purpose. However, if it is determined that the documentation on hand does not support the transfer of title, the museum may wish to have the donor sign a confirmation of gift statement, indicating that the object was donated and the date on which donation took place. If the donor is unwilling to provide such a statement, a letter should be sent to the donor by certified mail indicating that unless advised otherwise by a given date, the museum will consider the object a donation to the collection as of that date.

Fractional gifts (or gifts of fractional interest) are those in which title to a portion of a work is given to a museum; the museum often stipulates that full title must be received at a later time. It is important to note that in the case of a fractional gift, a separate gift agreement document must be issued as title for each portion of the gift is transferred to the museum, unless the initial gift contract stipulates the progressive transfer on a predetermined schedule. Legal counsel must be consulted to ensure transfer of title for fractional gifts.

A letter of acknowledgment is usually issued with the gift agreement. Sent as a cover letter to the agreement, this document serves to thank the donor for the gift and to provide instructions about completion of the gift agreement. The acknowledgment letter typically is signed by the museum director or the curator of the department and includes a description of the donated object. A copy of this letter is kept on file with the gift agreement.

IRS FORMS

The US tax code changes often as new legislation is passed and regulations are revised; therefore, it is imperative for registrars, collections managers, development officers, curators, and directors to keep abreast of new tax developments. Information in this chapter reflects laws in place at the time of writing.

The museum may be asked by a donor to complete IRS Form 8283 (Noncash Charitable Contributions) after an object has been accepted for the collection. It is the donor's responsibility to obtain and circulate Form 8283 for completion, but as a service to donors, the museum may wish to keep blank copies of IRS forms relating to donations on hand.[2] The museum is required to complete only those sections of any IRS form that apply to its action and should avoid giving any tax advice or other inappropriate assistance to a donor. The museum's signature confirms only the receipt of the gift as described on the form; it does not imply agreement with the monetary value assigned by the donor (see CHAPTER 7E, "Appraisal"). A copy of Form 8283 signed by a museum official should be placed in the object file with the gift agreement when the original is returned to the donor. If the museum sells, exchanges, or otherwise disposes of property described in Form 8283 (or any portion thereof) within three years (or the period prescribed by current law) after the date of receipt, the museum must file Form 8282 (Donee Information Return) with the IRS.

PROOF OF PURCHASE

Copies of paperwork approving purchase, an invoice or bill of sale, purchase order, or receipt for payment related to objects purchased for the collection are appropriate to include in the registrar's document files, along with any warranties the museum may require

from the vendor. Recent trends have made it imperative for the museum to have a warranty of title and indemnification for the purchase of most objects.

MASTER OBJECT OR ACCESSION LOG

Identification numbers form the link between each object and the information about that object and, thus, should be assigned as soon as an object enters the museum's custody. Sometimes the only way to distinguish objects from one another is by the number they are assigned. The number for each piece must be unique, and it must appear on the object as well as on the records (see CHAPTER 5A, "Numbering" and CHAPTER 5F, "Marking"). The numbering system selected must be adaptable, simple, and capable of expanding as the collections grow. Because descriptive information about the object will be found in the records, it does not need to be coded into an identification or accession number.

A master object file or accession log, maintained by one person, prevents numbering inconsistencies and ensures that a number is not skipped or duplicated, and provides a readily accessible running list of the institution accessions, in date order, which serves as a reference for the object catalog and other files in which object information is kept. It need not be elaborate, but should be clear, orderly, easy to read, and difficult to alter. In a manual system, the information is typically recorded a bound ledger book or in a card file. Numbers should be listed in order with enough information to identify the object and its source. More detailed information or tracking of actions is better kept in other files. On a periodic basis, the master object or accession log should be microfilmed or photocopied for offsite storage.

WORKSHEETS

Once an object has been formally accepted for the permanent collection, an information form (often called a *worksheet*, *accession sheet*, or *catalog sheet*) should be completed. This form is used to compile as much information as is available about the item and its acquisition. Although the terms *accession in-*

formation and *catalog information* are often used as synonyms, there is a distinction between them. Accession information includes a physical and material description of the object, acquisition information, current condition, and accession number. Depending on the type of museum, the monetary value and status of copyright may be included as well. Catalog information includes provenance and history, bibliographic references, an assignment into intellectual categories as followed by the museum or its discipline, and in some museums a catalog number that differs from the accession number.

CONDITION REPORTS

A condition report should be completed when an object enters the museum's custody to provide a baseline against which future examinations can be compared (see CHAPTER 5E, "Condition Reporting"). Condition reports should also be prepared when an object goes on exhibit or comes off exhibit, when an object is sent out on loan or is returned from a loan, or when monitoring a particularly vulnerable or deteriorating object. An object condition review may be part of a collection inventory (see CHAPTER 5K, "Inventory"). Condition reports on objects owned by others but in the custody of the museum are particularly important to verify the care the object received. The condition report form may incorporate a checklist or free text but should include the following elements:

- Name of the owner of the object;
- Object identification number;
- Maker or artist (if appropriate);
- Object name or title;
- Object description or type (optional);
- Classification;
- Date;
- Measurements;
- Materials;
- Condition—general and specific, using standard terminology;
- Description and condition of any accessories—base, frame, cover;
- Date, and name of person completing report; and
- Images of the object.

COPYRIGHT LICENSES

In some museums, documentation of the copyright of the object forms another part of the object record. Documentation relating to copyright should be generated at the time of object acquisition. The museum may desire to have an exclusive or nonexclusive copyright license for an object it acquires. If the item is acquired from the artist, maker, or copyright holder, language addressing copyright status can be incorporated into the gift or sale agreement. If the donor is not the copyright holder, a separate document may be sent to the owner of copyright with a request for signature (see CHAPTER 7C, "Copyright"). These documents become part of the object file.

LOAN AGREEMENTS

A loan agreement for objects coming into the museum's custody, either for exhibition or study, should be completed before the museum accepts delivery of the object (see CHAPTER 3K, "Loans"). The loan agreement describes the objects on loan, the lender and borrower, terms and conditions of the loan (including who will pay which expenses), and the beginning and ending dates of the term of the loan. Similar to a gift agreement, this form must have the museum's legal name, address, and telephone numbers clearly indicated. Other elements of the loan agreement include:

- Name, address, telephone, and fax numbers of the owner of the object(s); for institutional lenders, the name of the contact person;
- Purpose of the loan (e.g., research, exhibition);
- Beginning and ending dates of the loan arrangement;
- Credit line listing how the lender wishes to be acknowledged for catalog, label, and publicity purposes;
- Description of the object, including maker or origin, materials, dimensions, and accessories such as containers or bases;
- An insurance value and indication of which party is providing insurance (see CHAPTER 6D, "Insurance");
- Provisions for shipping;

- Permissions for photography; and
- Signatures of authorized representatives of the borrow and lender.

The loan agreement should list the conditions that pertain to the loan, with language about responsibility, notification to the lender of any damage, reference to any state laws about unclaimed property, and limits or exclusions to insurance coverage.[3]

A parallel agreement is used when a museum lends objects from the collection to another museum, using a form generated by the lending institution. The borrowing institution may negotiate changes and make modifications as its own policies dictate. The information about an outgoing loan becomes part of the object's history, so the loan agreement or reference to it is added to the object's document file or record.

MANAGING MANUAL FILES AND RECORDS

Record Maintenance

Data about objects are put in the registration files when the objects are incorporated into the collection. Over the years, information reflecting object research, exhibition, and publication history, and changes in object status should be added to the files. The addition, modification, and deletion of information must be monitored by the registrar or collections manager. In a manual system, it is often obvious that information has been changed—erasures, crossing out, different typefaces, handwriting, and different paper or card stocks tell the tale. Nevertheless, a record of who made changes and on what date will provide a means of verifying the information and its reliability. Typically, only designated staff are permitted to amend information. Subjective information (such as attributions or interpretations of subject matter) and time-sensitive information (such as condition assessments or insurance values) should be initialed and dated by the person amending the file.

Within the time constraints of the museum's activities, the registrar should assign a high priority to the timely updating of information and filing of new information or documents. In addition to maintaining and updating information, the registrar takes

physical care of the files. Acid-free paper should be used for folders, cards, and documents. Documents in folders must be protected from creasing, paper clips, and staples. If prongs are used to hold papers, care must be taken that they do not damage the documents or adjacent documents. File labels must be firmly attached, neatly printed, and replaced as required. Care should be taken that acid from an older document does not contaminate papers in physical contact with it. A long-term view of preservation is essential in organizing and maintaining these files.

Duplication and Protection

Responsibility for the safety and security of objects extends to the safety of the documentation connected with them. Disasters do happen, so steps should be taken to prevent them (see CHAPTER 6A, "Risk Management Overview"). Off-site storage of duplicate records will safeguard essential collection information in the event of loss. Various methods of duplication have been successfully employed—for example, cards and documents can be photocopied, documents can be transferred to microfilm or microfiche, or scanned for electronic storage. Duplicate records should be stored in a secure offsite area with controlled access. More than one person should know where records are stored and how to retrieve them.

Duplicate object records with basic descriptive information and an image should be made. A record of current loans with insurance values for the objects should be made and secured. Copies of acquisition records (deeds of gift or bequest, receipts of sale, etc.) should be stored off-site as well. Establish a schedule for routinely producing and storing duplicate collection records to stay up to date with new acquisitions and new versions of records. If there is an index for stored records, be sure it is updated, and keep a copy at the museum. The frequency of updating duplicate records will depend on the quantity of new records, the value of the objects, and an evaluation of the risks to registration records.

Security of Records

Registration files with information about the collection are valuable assets to the museum. The information is essential to exhibiting and interpreting as well as responsibly accounting for the collection; insurance values and object condition make a difference in situations of loss or damage. These files must be secured and the integrity of the information safeguarded. The registrar should list risks against which to secure files, periodically evaluating these risks and taking steps to protect against them (see CHAPTER 6B, "Emergencies: Prepare, Respond, Recover"). Sudden disasters that can destroy or damage records include fire, water, and theft, but slower-acting events can also cause significant deterioration or loss including dirt, exposure to light, pests, handling, acidic papers, malicious alteration of data, or well-meaning but misguided and unsupervised alteration of data.

In each museum, safeguards and solutions must be devised within the context of the building itself, the budget, support from museum administration, and the registrar's ability, resources, and creative problem solving. Safeguards for records in the registration office include:

- good housekeeping practices;
- a ban on all tobacco products;
- restrictions on food and drink;
- a regularly tested automatic fire-suppression system;
- fire extinguishers (with training for staff in how to use them);
- storing files off the floor and protecting them with water barriers;
- locking files and maintaining good key control;
- monitoring access and enforcing sign-out and sign-in procedures whenever files are removed;
- protection from ultraviolet and visible light exposure;
- clean hands and respect for materials;
- acid-free papers and folders;
- metal file containers; and
- a procedure for affecting modifications to files, including a written record of changes and clear lines of authority to make them.

Records can be considered secure if there are good, up-to-date, duplicate records off-site, personnel who understand and respect the importance of documentation, enough staff to monitor access to files, more than one reference to objects to check information against, an attentive registrar or collections manager who keeps a close eye on files and is familiar with the contents, the museum's general security practices and procedures are good and the building is protected against fire and intrusion, and access to the registration files is well controlled. ●

NOTES
1. For a detailed explanation and a model deed of gift, see M. C. Malaro and I. P. DeAngelis, *A Legal Primer on Managing Museum Collections* (Washington, DC: Smithsonian Institution Press, 2012), 235–236, 240–242.

2. Current regulations and copies of IRS forms are available from the IRS website (https://www.irs.gov/). Donors should be encouraged to obtain forms from the website to ensure that they are using the most current version.

3. For a detailed discussion of loans and a model loan invoice, see Malaro and DeAngelis, *A Legal Primer*, 273–318.

This is an edited and updated version of the article by Kittu Longstreth-Brown, updated by Rebecca Buck, from the previous edition of Museum Registration Methods *(2010), who acknowledged the contributions of Anne Fuhrman Douglas, Connie Estep, Paulette Dunn Hennum, Monique Maas, and Dominique Schultes.*

4C | COMPUTER SYSTEMS AND DATA MANAGEMENT

SUZANNE QUIGLEY (UPDATED AND EXPANDED BY CRISTINA LINCLAU)

COMPUTERS HAVE BECOME essential to the activities of preserving, interpreting, and accessing collections that are central to any museum's mission. A collections management system (CMS) is any database or other software that supports museum workflows including tracking object locations, preparing exhibitions and loans, managing images and their rights, facilitating conservation, and constructing exhibition histories and provenance. Other museum departments use this centralized record system and the CMS serves as the foundation for public access to institutional collections online. To aid registrars and collection managers—who are often CMS system administrators—in planning for and getting the most out of the museum's CMS, this section provides a comprehensive account of CMS selection, implementation, and maintenance, and briefly outlines structured data management.

COLLECTIONS MANAGEMENT SYSTEMS

System Requirements

A system consists of hardware, software, and the network on which they are used within the museum. Although these elements work in concert to automate many tasks that take hours to do manually, they are run by humans and must be carefully managed. Each museum must determine who will choose, manage, and maintain the CMS before it begins the process of implementation.

Choosing a system requires a thorough analysis of:

- The information to be stored;
- Who will enter the data;
- How, why, and by whom the data will be used;
- Present computer capabilities;
- Existing data structures; and
- Anticipated future growth of institutional needs.

Based on this analysis, the choice is among proprietary museum data management systems, professionally designed custom systems, and in-house designed or "open source" systems. Hardware should be selected only after the foregoing analysis and selection of software have been made to ensure that the hardware is appropriate for the type of data being stored, the database size, the operating system, and network capabilities. Conversely, existing hardware may limit the type of data management software that can be used.

Database Structure

A database is a collection of information in electronic format. The advantage of electronic collections data is that a computer can sort data more quickly, in many more ways, and with fewer errors than a person using a manual system can. A CMS refers to the database and the application software interface with which the user interacts.

The key to a useful electronic database is the method of data organization, that is, the database structure. Although there are a number of different types of database systems, the three most common are flat file, relational, and object-oriented. Flat file databases keep information in a single large table, whereas relational databases keep data in separate tables, each related to the others by means of a common field. The advantage of a relational database is that it creates discrete, easily parsed groupings of information that help with computation speed when searching, as well as with maintaining the integrity of data with controlled fields. The common fields that join tables to one another are referred to as identifiers or keys. Identifiers can be exposed to the general user as common reference points, such as an accession number, but more often, they are internal, ordinal numbering systems separate from common references. This allows for flexibility among the human-readable reference numbers—accession numbers can convey meaning to users (e.g., with textual prefixes such as D for deaccessioned objects; a loan number can represent the year in which the loan was initiated). An object-oriented database replaces the identifier-linked table structure of flat file and relational databases with a series of nested classes of objects that pass down attributes to subclasses. These flexible models are consistent with the languages that dominate object-oriented programming such as C++, JavaScript, and Python. Object-oriented databases use the same type of fields within the database and the application, removing the need for software to translate between the database fields and the output programming, which permits the system to run more smoothly overall. In practice, the dominance of relational database systems has given rise to hybrids—object-relational databases—which combine the extensible functionality of inheritance within a tabular system.

Flat file databases are rarely used for today's complex information management needs, though they are frequently used for simpler tasks. Relational and object-oriented relational databases have many advantages over flat files. For example, a collection might contain a number of objects given by a single donor. Although there will be a separate record for each object in the collection table, there need be only one record for the donor in the donor table, linked to every record of an object in the collection table that was given by that donor using the identifier associated with that donor. If information about the donor should change it needs to be altered in only one location in the database, thus saving work and ensuring accuracy. A cardinal rule of good database structure is that no piece of information should be entered more than once. The exceptions to this are the identifiers that link related tables together, which must be present in both tables to enable the link.

Although the terminology and precise workings vary among different software products, most computerized database systems have four components: tables, queries, forms, and reports.

Tables hold stored data. Each table comprises records, which consist of sets of data about a particular type of item, such as objects or donors. Individual pieces of information that make up a record are placed in fields, which are the equivalent of the blanks that must be filled in on a paper form, or cells in a spreadsheet. Each field has a dedicated data type—some fields only contain text data, some only numerical data, and others contain only dates. Some fields display calculations from other fields. The CMS may require that certain fields be entered (such as accession numbers), but it may leave other fields to the discretion of the data-entry operator.

Queries, also known as *searches*, extract information from a database. Queries may be simple, such as a search for a record pertaining to an object with a specific accession number, or complex, such as a request for a list of all objects given by a particular donor in a given year whose value was greater than a certain amount.

Forms generally are used for one of two purposes. Designed to represent paper records, forms visually organize and simplify the data-entry process and speed data entry. Forms can be designed to reference tables in the database to ensure that information placed in certain fields is valid and that it is correctly spelled and formatted. Forms are frequently used to specify searching or sorting criteria that are used by predefined queries selected from a menu.

Reports are the means by which the results of a query are displayed or printed. Reports may be part of the software itself, may be designed by the user, or both, depending on the capabilities of the particular software. Queries, if properly structured, can use preset reports to display or print results. If a report is not used, a query usually results in a simple list that may be displayed, printed, or exported for editing.

Functionality

It is important for a CMS to be flexible. The system should allow the museum to begin with the data it already has and to expand as needs and opportunities arise. The sum of the information about any object comes from a variety of sources, such as registrars, curators, and conservators. Each should be responsible for the timeliness and accuracy of their contributions and should be able to enter information without transmitting it to a third party. The system should incorporate methods to ensure that only authorized persons are able to enter, edit, or view various pieces of information about an object. In all but the smallest museums, this generally means a networked system of computers, with the software and data residing on a central computer called a server.

Hardware Compatibility

Many proprietary CMS and commercial database systems run locally on either Windows, Microsoft, or Linux-based operating systems. Individual workstations are commonly networked in one of two ways. One method is to have the CMS software installed on each computer and have those machines access the data by means of middleware that facilitates the delivery of content between the server and the workstations. Open database connectivity (ODBC) and Java database connectivity (JDBC) are common examples of such middleware.

Another method for enacting system connectivity is to use a virtual machine (VM), which means the CMS software is not installed on every workstation but is on a single server that users access by logging on to a remote application server (RAS). The RAS behaves like an application on the local computer, but appears as an embedded desktop, with the CMS software installed there. It can be an adjustment for users to learn how to work in a second desktop active as a simultaneous, nested environment on their workstation; care needs to be taken to export and save files on the users local machine so that they can be retrieved when the remote machine is not active on the user's workstation. However, the advantages far outweigh the disadvantages of this learning curve. Not only can the remote machine provide more flexible access because it does not rely on local CMS software installation but, for the same reason, it is also much more efficient for system administrators to upgrade, maintain, and troubleshoot a single machine rather than deal with each workstation individually.

In addition to these options, browser-based environments are being developed for commercial collection management software. Browser-based environments enable database records to be accessed from any computer, replacing the RAS connection with a common browser application such as Internet Explorer, Chrome, or Firefox. These systems have mul-tiple access points—local installations on individual workstations, VMs, or browser access—that do not dictate where the database is located. Some companies offer hosting agreements with licenses that permit access for museum staff to servers that are under the upkeep of the vendor, who then takes on many of the administrative duties that otherwise occupy dedicated staff time, such as overseeing system backups and upgrades.

Ideally, computers should be chosen only after the CMS has been selected. If this is not possible, the software must be selected so that it does not exceed the limitations of the hardware. It is important to select software that can be expanded in its capabilities as future hardware upgrades occur. Consulting a technology professional to ensure compatibility of the hardware and software is desirable, regardless of whether the selected software is a stand-alone system or a networked system. One of the advantages of browser-based commercial products is that they are relatively hardware agnostic, simplifying these systems considerations considerably. This compatibility is especially critical if the software selected runs on a network with multiple computers accessing it; in this case it is important to consult a technology professional who has experience not only with the type of server and operating system selected but also with the networking requirements of the system. The consultant will be able to advise on infrastructure upgrades needed to implement the system and will be responsible for setting up the server running the software. In many cases the vendor of a proprietary CMS will install the software on the server and networked computers. Prior to selecting the software, it is necessary that the system administrator, the technology professional, and the vendor(s) discuss the requirements of the system and the infrastructure of the institution to determine whether the software is compatible with the existing framework, such as network wiring, electrical outlets, internet speeds, and physical space requirements. If not, the institution must determine whether it is possible to upgrade its infrastructure; if an upgrade is not feasible, a different system must be selected.

The computer and server hardware must be evaluated on the basis of several criteria. The hardware should be produced by a reputable manufacturer that stands behind its warranty and should be purchased from an established vendor. A number of suppliers claim that their products are equal to those of major manufacturers; this may be true, but unless the museum is a large organization (or part of one) with an information management department that can handle alternate arrangements should the producer suddenly go out of business, a computer produced by an established manufacturer and serviced by an established vendor is worth the difference in cost.

In general, the rule is to buy the fastest, most powerful computer affordable. Speed and power are especially important if electronic documents, images, video and audio files, or other multimedia will be used as part of the CMS. The computer must have an adequate amount of random access memory (RAM), sufficient hard disk or other storage space, and hardware for internal and external backups. The computer on which the data are stored—whether a server or a stand-alone desktop computer—should have a redundancy feature called a redundant array of inexpensive disks (RAID). A RAID consists of multiple hard drives that mirror the data. In the event one hard drive fails, the computer can retrieve data from one of the other disks in the RAID. The RAID is not a substitute for external backups, however, and should be used in conjunction with backup hardware. There are a number of different RAID configurations, and a technology professional can advise on which configuration is appropriate.

If the system is a stand-alone installation the computer must have enough expansion slots to accommodate equipment additions. Connecting the computer to a network, scanner, other electronic image-capturing device, or a soundboard requires the installation of a card to handle the external connections. Some external storage hardware—such as CD-ROM, DVD-RW, tape drives, or external hard drives—could also be necessary, depending on whether the institution opts for cloud storage or not.

SOFTWARE SELECTION AND DEVELOPMENT

Software Selection
Before selecting software for a database system, the institution must decide whether it will purchase non-museum-specific commercial database software and contract with a computer programmer for configuration, employ a staff member to create or customize software, or buy a CMS from a commercial vendor. Current staffing, immediate and future budgets, long-term needs, and the stability of the museum must be considered when determining if a commercial CMS or a customized in-house database product is the right solution. Each solution has certain advantages and disadvantages, but most museums today purchase their CMS from a vendor and work with the vendor to tailor the product to the institution's specific needs.

Commercial Databases
Commercial software, such as SQL, Access, and FileMaker Pro, are economical, powerful, and flexible systems capable of being configured for collections management purposes. Although this software is designed to be customized by the user for particular applications, a reasonable knowledge of the software is required to do so. Use of commercial databases can be an economical way to begin a CMS. However, if it is not carefully thought through and managed, this option can be the most expensive and the most difficult to scale up for future needs to ensure ongoing development throughout the lifetime of the system.

One of the primary advantages of using an in-house designed system is the relatively small initial investment in equipment and software. If building a new system from scratch, the project can start out small, using the information already contained in paper records, and then expand as needs and opportunities arise. This approach is also flexible, allowing the system to be designed to fit a particular museum's needs. However, there are major disadvantages to this approach. If done by someone whose primary task is not collections management that person's time will be diverted from other duties. During the early stages of development, the amount of time required can be significant. A poorly designed system can waste time and money and in the end be worse than no CMS at all. If the person who designed it leaves the museum the database may be impossible to maintain, especially if the software in question is dated or modified to such a degree that advice and information become difficult to obtain from outside sources.

An institution with a truly customized database system may be at a major disadvantage if it decides to share its information on the internet or directly with other museums or consortiums. Creating a system using commercial database software requires recognition of and adherence to established standards and practices, as well as a broad understanding of information management practices at other institutions.

A museum no longer needs a computer guru on its staff to produce an in-house system, but if there are no dedicated staff on hand, it is recommended that the museum contract and work with a software developer to design the software. If not contracting with a developer, it is necessary to provide the person who will establish the system with training in database design, testing, and documentation. Initially, the system should be kept simple. Only when one aspect is working well should another be added; it is not wise to try to incorporate every desirable feature or function all at once. The new system should be integrated into office routines slowly, preferably by starting with the processing of new transactions. Only after the new system is functioning satisfactorily and the staff are comfortable in its use is it appropriate to ingest the entire collection.

Commercial Collections Management Systems

A commercial CMS, fully adapted for cataloging and collections management use, offers a museum many advantages. The system often comes to the museum as a complete package and can be used after system installation and initial training are finished. Technical support is often available by telephone, e-mail, or on a website; training is usually available from the vendor; and upgrades come without museum staff spending time on software development. Established vendors use client feedback to focus development and make certain that needs are met. The museum can form user groups with other clients and share information, problems, and solutions.

A major drawback of the commercial CMS can be the amount of money that must be spent for initial implementation. The commitment to a yearly maintenance agreement—which usually is based on the number of user licenses (i.e., the number of users or workstations that can access the networked system

simultaneously) a museum has purchased—is important. There may be concerns about the stability of the company that sold the program and questions about the continuance of software maintenance should the company cease to exist. There are free, open source options available that have the potential to significantly reduce startup and maintenance costs, but their drawback is that an open source CMS is not tailored to the institution's needs by a vendor, so the institution must use staff or hire a consultant to make modifications. Nevertheless, robust online communities have sprung up around open source tools that make this low-cost option more attractive.

A museum must plan the configuration and implementation of a commercial system carefully. Because development is not done in house, it is possible to overlook the careful review of data as they are collected and used by various departments. A single staff member should serve as liaison between the software company and other museum users. A second staff member should learn the program administration thoroughly and be ready to step in if needed. The program administrator is often the registrar or a member of the registration department—whoever takes the position should know collections management processes and collection information needs. Ideally, the system administrator should be a staff member dedicated solely to information and database management, help-desk functions, metadata standard implementation and oversight, report design, and communication with vendors and IT professionals.

Most commercial CMS products have room for growth. Additional users can be enabled and new features may be added at the request of the museum or included as part of an upgrade. As custom changes may be expensive to implement, it is important to anticipate future needs and select a system that already has most features present at time of installation. The popularity of commercial systems proves that they meet an extremely important need in the museum community. With the fast pace of developing technologies, it is logical that museums rely on specialists who can use new developments to improve functionality quickly. As such, proprietary CMS software have become the programs of choice in most museums.

Determining What Type of System to Select

Before software or hardware selections can be made, a comprehensive list of system requirements must be prepared. Aligning institutional requirements with available options requires some research and outreach. The Canadian Heritage Information Network (CHIN) has produced a set of resources to help museums assemble their requirements, including their *Collections Management Systems Software Criteria Checklist*, which outlines features commonly included in a commercial CMS (last updated in 2012), as well as a collection of current vendor profiles.[1] Mostly, it is helpful to interview similar institutions about which features they find especially useful.

Request for Proposal

Whether a museum has decided to purchase a commercial CMS or to hire a programmer to develop an in-house system, a request for proposal (RFP) is the appropriate document to send to a small group of selected vendors. Look for vendors who have experience working in the institution's discipline because educating the vendor about workflow will be much easier if the vendor has worked with similar institutions.

The RFP must provide the vendor with an exact, comprehensive, and clearly written outline of the product the museum needs. It must include a cover letter describing the museum and the project, a description of the existing computer environment, a functional requirement section, and instructions for submitting a proposal to the museum.

The bulk of the RFP will be the functional requirements section, which lists the desired characteristics of the CMS. It is advisable to divide this section into parts. For example, a section on system requirements will contain information about the network in place and whether the museum intends to continue to use it (if it does, the vendor's system must be compatible with the network). The museum may request that the system have an application programming interface (API) for website, kiosk, or app development, be compatible with different operating systems, or accommodate different user groups with various levels of security. Questions in the RFP should be phrased so that they can be answered by the vendor with yes, no, or modify.

Further subdivisions of the functional requirements section should address specific issues for each of the modules the museum expects to use (e.g., object tracking, exhibition registration, accessioning, multimedia).

The other significant section of the RFP contains directions for the vendors' responses:

- The deadline for the museum to receive the proposal (usually four weeks from the date of the issuance of the RFP).
- The format for the proposal (because consistency of format is important for museum staff to be able to compare proposals directly to each other).
- Clear instructions as to what must be included, including license fees, annual maintenance costs for a specified number of users, training costs, accessibility of support staff, extra costs for data transfer, and the anticipated project timeline.

It is crucial that all vendors be treated equally. Due dates must be met and the proposal must be complete for the vendor to be eligible for consideration.

Note that a vendor is legally liable for answering the RFP truthfully because it serves as the basis for a future contract.

Evaluation

Evaluation of proposals and selection of a vendor is a surprisingly labor-intensive task, and it is important to let the vendors know of your selection as quickly as possible.

Upon receipt of each proposal, check to see if all the items requested in the RFP are present. As soon as the deadline has passed, organize the proposals so that they may be easily compared. Establish a rating system that everyone agrees upon and give each person on the selection committee a set amount of time to scrutinize, compare, and rate the responses. Narrow the selection to no more than three proposals and observe the selected systems in use. If possible, ask the vendor to preload some of the museum's existing data for a demonstration. The vendor can send a representative to present an on-site demonstration, can coordinate demonstrations at a professional conference, or offer a demonstration online, using a remote desktop connection or live webcast.

After the demonstrations, contact colleagues at similar institutions who have already installed each of the systems under consideration. Ask them for a frank and honest evaluation of what they like and do not like about the systems. Ask about the vendors' responsiveness and any unanticipated costs they encountered during or after installation. If at all possible, the internal selection committee should visit other museum sites where the systems under consideration are installed and running.

The committee should then be able to reach consensus on the product.

Contract Negotiation

Once the vendor is selected it is time to buy. Even if the system is for a single user, it is advisable to have a contract with the vendor outlining exactly what is included. The proposal provided by the vendor in response to the RFP is the cornerstone of the agreement and should be referenced in the contract. The contract need not be elaborate. Many vendors will provide a sample contract that both parties are free to amend, as long as they both agree on the amendments. The contract should set dates for acceptance of the system, a schedule of payment to the vendor, return policies, training and support agreements, data conversion, and requested modifications to the system. It may also state that the source code will be placed in escrow in case the company should dissolve at a later date, but there is usually an extra cost associated with this.

IMPLEMENTING A COLLECTIONS MANAGEMENT SYSTEM

Implementation

The who, what, where, when, and how of a data management system come together in a concrete fashion during the implementation process. The adequacies of the chosen system, hardware, software, and site must be tested during the initial implementation process. The objective of this phase is to identify and correct defects so that the ultimate goals of efficiency and productivity can be achieved.

Site Preparation

Site preparation takes into account the safety and efficiency of all aspects of the system—hardware, software, and the people using the equipment. Sites can take many forms, each of which requires a different type of preparation. Sites can be centralized or dispersed, independent or connected, and permanent or mobile.

Centralized versus Dispersed

Centralized sites avoid the need for extensive networking and may allow for the design of a specialized computer room. Such a room should have requirements for temperature, relative humidity, and dust filtration similar to the collections storage areas and should provide maximum efficiency of computer use: technical support easily available, comfortable and safe working conditions, and strong security.

Dispersed sites enable customized or specialized workstations that fit the needs of particular museum users. For example, registrars can enter acquisition information, loan inventories, and so on, from their workspace without having to take materials into a central area with a higher level of traffic flow. Likewise, conservators can set up a workstation to use when doing condition and treatment reports, or secure workstations can be set up for visiting researchers in areas that will not be in the way of other museum functions.

Independent versus Connected

Whether sites are centralized or dispersed, connectivity may or may not be desirable. Connected sites permit easy communication, standardization, and control, but these networked sites almost always require a system administrator, increased security, higher costs, and modifications to architectural infrastructure. Wiring a museum for networking can be a problem; the construction of many of the old buildings that house museums is so solid that passing cables through walls, ceilings, or floors may not be possible. In these cases, wireless networks may be the solution. Thinking ahead and wiring during times of remodeling or new construction will save money and headaches in the future.

Permanent versus Mobile

The mobility of a computer site also is important to consider. Permanent workstations usually provide greater computing power, full-sized keyboards, and larger monitors. The ability to move computers, however, is advantageous in many situations. Computers can be taken into collection areas for direct data entry during inventory, condition checks, or environmental monitoring. Having the means to take digitized records or images to meetings, libraries, and off-site locations is convenient and can solve potential access and security problems. Mobile computing, however, has its drawbacks. Theft becomes a greater issue when using small, portable computing equipment and, if networking is required, using a wireless system becomes the only practical solution.

Whatever the configuration of computing sites, the computers and network equipment should be assembled and tested prior to installation. If possible, the data servers should be kept in a secure area where they are accessible to authorized personnel but protected from vandalism and theft. Backup tapes, hard drives, and other portable data storage units should be stored in a safe and secure place, preferably off-site.

Like other machinery, computer hardware should not be exposed to extreme changes in temperature and humidity and should be protected from particulates (dust, crumbs, etc.), liquids (leaky pipes, spilled coffee, etc.), and other debris. Adequate and stable energy sources and sufficient access to them should be provided to avoid data loss and undue stress on the computer hardware. Like other electrical equipment, computer hardware should be placed in a low-static area away from magnetic fields. Wires and cables should be installed so that people do not walk or trip on them, equipment does not roll over them, and animals do not chew them. Cables and the backs of computers should still be easily accessible. System disks (if any), warranty, and other legal documentation should be safely stored in a place where it will be safe but accessible when needed.

Many work-related injuries are caused by inadequate equipment and poorly designed work areas. Chairs and desktops should be ergonomically designed and organized to minimize injuries from typing at a keyboard, sitting, and viewing a monitor. Light sources should be as low as possible; focused away from computer monitors to help reduce eyestrain.

The goal of an efficient workspace is data integrity. Ideally, the workspace will have a large enough space to organize necessary paperwork and support documentation without jeopardizing the quality of data entry or the safety of equipment and objects. If accessioned objects are to be handled at the computer workstation for cataloging, condition and treatment reports, and so on, the work space must be arranged so that the risks of knocking objects over, placing documents or other objects on top of them, or losing pieces altogether are eliminated.

Schedule

The schedule for implementing a CMS can be divided into two stages: installation and execution. The actual time needed to achieve a functioning system will depend on the hardware and software planning and testing that was completed prior to implementation. The implementation process begins when a museum undertakes a needs assessment and concludes that change is needed and can be achieved. Whether a museum chooses an in-house solution or purchases a commercial CMS, a similar implementation process follows: analysis of the institution's needs, assessment of available resources, evaluation and selection of a system, followed by purchase, installation, and testing of the system.

A certain amount of time will be lost when switching between old and new systems. At a minimum, conversion to the new system will involve training existing employees to use it. If files or data are imported from another system they must be converted for use in the new system, which may be time-consuming. It is necessary to examine the information structure of the new system and clean up or reorganize existing data to correspond to it, especially if data entry in the past has been inconsistent or incomplete. Further interruption in use of the file-management system may involve hiring and training new employees to transfer data manually (initial entry from manual card files, cleanup and tweaking of existing data, etc.) and training existing employees on future applications.

Good system design results from reverse engineering. Starting with the needed results will naturally lead to appropriate software and, in turn, hardware. Some museums start a new system without knowing what they will or will not be able to do with it, which usually results in further downtime, general frustration, and low morale. How these factors affect individual institutions depends on the size, type of system, and type and frequency of use of that system. Ideally, scheduling should be structured enough to be completed at a time that is appropriate for the museum yet flexible enough to allow for unpreventable or unexpected setbacks.

Testing

Testing should be done in stages. Initial testing is best done by those designing or installing the system. Secondary testing is essential and should be conducted by those who are the day-to-day users of the system. Small, workable amounts of actual data should be used for tests. All operations of the system that are desired should be tested, as should the vendor's claims about capacity and performance. Although this may not prevent software errors that result from using larger amounts of data, more files, or different configurations of data, it is both an initial, short-term way of testing a system prior to becoming fully engulfed in its implementation, as well as a means of familiarizing staff with the software interface.

Data Management

Data are both resources and assets. The data preserved about an object give that object its meaning and value. A digitized system opens up new avenues of access to the information recorded about an object, but the functionality of any information management system rests on data entered into it. Poorly managed information in a manual system will continue to be poorly managed information when moved into a database. The expected benefits of digital recordkeeping—especially the sophisticated searching, instant retrieval of related information, and statistical reporting—will not be met if data are inconsistently entered and controlled.

In the process of choosing a system, a museum should review its requirements and the intended uses of the system. The collections database manager should undertake an inventory of existing documentation systems and standards to determine which departments or individuals collect and record data and how they do so. This not only will identify data sources within the museum, it also will help determine what data should be used in a new software system and who will provide or enter it. This will clarify how the museum anticipates a new database system will streamline existing workflow and increase capabilities by systematizing new relationships between people and processes. The institution must establish a shared understanding of what it expects of a new system before it is installed.

When the database consists of information entered by staff across multiple departments, each department must be responsible for the accuracy and consistency of the information that it enters and understand the origins of data that it is not directly responsible for. All users need a clear idea of precisely where in the system they enter their data and how their contributions relate to other information and other users. If there are many sources for the data it is a good idea to assign oversight responsibilities to one person—often a registrar, a collections information manager, or the database administrator—who can review new entries and edits for accuracy and consistency.

Data entry and upkeep are expensive processes, and the resulting database provides the facts and context that validate the value of the object(s) described therein. Much like caring for objects, the process of caring for data can be complex. Unlike many physical objects, electronic data often can be re-created and rebuilt, but the resulting cost in staff time can have an impact on other activities in the museum.

Although it is useful to access all the available information about an object in a CMS, there may be resource constraints that dictate how robust electronic records can be and how much data entry and maintenance is realistic for a given institution. At the time of the aforementioned inventory of existing information systems, the staff overseeing the database should work with curators, conservators, and registrars to decide what kinds of information will remain in analog systems with pointers from the CMS. Previous object wall texts, catalog entries, confidential donor information, bibliographic references, and detailed provenance information are examples of data that may be identified as nonessential for the database, but it is important that each external resource be acknowledged in the object record (e.g., "See Curatorial File for Provenance").

It is important to define the minimum level of completeness a record must have to meet institutional requirements for physical, intellectual, and administrative control of the object that the record represents. These three aspects of collections information management—physical, intellectual, and administrative control—broadly reference the museum's custodianship of its collection by tracking activities pertaining to location and preservation, interpretation and provenance, and institutional processes, respectively.

All information that goes into a CMS should be dictated by the museum's needs and not by the computer system. It is not necessary to enter data just because there is a field that will accommodate it. If possible, the system administrator may wish to hide unused fields to prevent users from entering information into them. Doing so will help ensure consistent locations of specific information. A realistic approach to the staff time and resources available checks the urge to catalog every field. It is also the collection information manager's responsibility to assure that the superficial layout of the program interface does not dictate the cataloging practices of the museum. Instead, cataloging should align with the table schema that supports the interface. If possible, the system administrator ought to customize the interface and reporting so that the underlying data structure is sound. This way, future design changes, software updates, or migrations to a new CMS will not be compromised by cataloging workarounds made solely to keep information front and center in a software vendor's default design settings. This concern is a moot point in home-grown CMS design, but it is worth emphasizing that the temptation for cataloging staff and researchers to see the information they consider important needs to be balanced with the integrity of the schema.

Review, compare, and select documentation and data standards that will ensure that users enter correct and complete object information. In certain institutions it may not be possible to find a perfect match, so modifying or combining data standards to fit the museum's needs will be necessary. It is usually possible to set required fields so that new records cannot be saved if they do not conform to the adopted documentation standard. Examples of such information include accession number and object location. If the date, medium, or maker information are not be available at the time of record entry it is important to eliminate future confusion by noting whether that information was omitted for administrative reasons (and ought to be obtained and entered at a later date) or if the label copy date should read "n.d." (no date), for example, implying that the matter is settled. Using a field value that consistently identifies pending label copy data has the advantage of simplifying searches on incomplete records.

Data Standards

Data standards focus on how information is structured and entered into a collections management or cataloging system (manual or automated) and how that system maintains the information and provides a framework through which the information may be retrieved and manipulated. Data standards are concerned with three elements—structure, content, and value.

Data structure standards provide guidelines for the structure of a documentation system—what constitutes a record, what fields or categories of information are considered essential information, what fields are optional, and how those fields relate to one another. Data structure standards determine how much and what kind of documentation will meet the organization's criteria for security, accountability, and access to the object. For example, the *CIDOC Conceptual Reference Model*[2] (CRM) from the ICOM International Committee for Documentation's Documentation Standards Working Group and the *Europeana Data Model*[3] (EDM) are formal, semantic ontologies for structuring cultural data. *Categories for the Description of Works of Art*[4] (CDWA) is a comprehensive set of categories for describing works of art and related images and a format for electronic exchange of information, maintained by the Getty Vocabularies.

Data content standards provide guidelines for defining each individual data element or field and what information should be entered into it. Data content standards clearly describe the content of a defined field or data element and provide guidelines for controlling the syntax, style, grammar, and abbreviations used within each field. These standards are usually adopted into internally developed cataloging rules within institutional data dictionaries and procedural manuals that outline applications of external sources such as *Cataloging Cultural Objects: A Guide to Describing Cultural Works and Their Images*[5] (CCO) from the Visual Resources Association (VRA).

Data value standards determine the vocabulary to be used for individual fields or data elements and the authority lists that will build consistency and enable interoperability. Terminology standards that are used consistently enable an electronic system to provide indexes that find like objects quickly and connect them to other objects in interesting and sometimes unexpected ways. Consistent use of data value standards protects the museum's investment in its data and provides many more points of access to an object than can be provided in a manual system. These standards may be externally or internally developed authority files, lexica, thesauri, and controlled vocabularies. For example, the Getty's *Art and Architecture Thesaurus*[6] (AAT), the *Union List of Artist Names*[7] (ULAN), the *Thesaurus of Geographic Names*[8] (TGN), *Cultural Objects Name Authority*[9] (CONA), and *Nomenclature for Museum Cataloging*[10] encourage institutions to use common terminology and reference resources.

The benefits of applying data standards within a CMS include:

- Maximized investment in the data in a system;
- Enhanced accountability for a collection;
- Easy access to records and, thereby, to objects;
- Fast retrieval of cross-referenced information;
- Improved quality and accuracy of the individual record;
- Data that adapt more easily to new technological and documentation developments;
- Data that can be exported more efficiently into a new system; and
- Simplified interoperability (the exchange of information with other programs within an institution or with other institutions).

Even when data standards have been established and are in use, it is necessary to review and revise them. There invariably will be object information that cannot easily fit into any organized system. Although the aim of using standards is to be consistent, it is also necessary to be flexible enough to accommodate unique situations. At the very least, cataloging staff should support all exceptional applications of structured (controlled dropdown) data fields with explanatory unstructured (memo-style text entry) remarks.

Terminology Control

While manual systems might use catalog cards that provide a limited number of access points for information retrieval—for instance, by accession number, classification, or maker—a CMS can provide access to not only any field in the schema but also to any combination of fields. How dependable this access is depends entirely on the precision and consistency of the language used. Establishing the consistency upon which optimal retrieval functions hinge is called *terminology control*.

Terminology control is necessary because natural language has a number of different words that mean the same thing (synonyms) and identical words that mean different things (homonyms). If synonyms have been entered in a field, it will be impossible to retrieve all the similar objects without knowing and searching for each term individually. To control synonyms in a CMS it is necessary to choose a single preferred term and use it in place of all nonpreferred terms. Some advanced systems have internal synonym rings that can retrieve all items cataloged with the words within the ring, regardless of the term entered in the query, but this requires all synonyms to be manually entered into the dictionary. If homonyms have been entered in a single field, a search on that field will retrieve irrelevant records. To control homonyms it is necessary to distinguish one homonym term from another—for instance, barrel (container) and barrel (firearm component)—otherwise, the system may not be able to differentiate one from the other in a search.

To develop a consistent vocabulary, it is necessary to use some form of terminology control such as an authority list or a thesaurus for each data element or field in a CMS for which it is determined that there are terminology control requirements. An authority list is a controlled list of terms considered to be acceptable for entry in a field. The simplest authority list may provide only a set of preferred terms, developed as a simple document or spread sheet and shared between departments. A more complex authority list may provide nonpreferred terms with cross-references to the preferred terms.

Expanding search utility even further, a thesaurus provides terms that relate to the preferred term in a broader or narrower sense. A thesaurus is a highly structured authority that defines the terms that most accurately describe an object or concept for indexing and retrieval purposes. Like any authority list, a thesaurus distinguishes instances of nonpreferred terms, synonyms, and homonyms, but it will also include variant spellings and narrower, broader, and related terms, creating a hierarchy that enables users to retrieve records that contain only their search term, or a more dynamic search that collocates records that have been cataloged with any broader, narrower, or related terms as well.

It is not necessary to control the vocabulary for every data element in a CMS record. The focus should be on those fields that will be essential for indexing and retrieval purposes. Fields that may require terminology controls include:

- Classification,
- Object name,
- Subject heading,
- Location name,
- Medium,
- Technique,
- Condition,
- Geographic place names,
- Period or style terms,
- Acquisition terms,
- Deaccession terms,

- Department names,
- Artist or maker names, and
- Artist or maker roles.

When considering what terminology controls to use in a database, it is paramount to first consider the use of established resources that are available for the entire field before developing in-house resources. On a practical level developing internal authorities can be a time-consuming and labor-intensive process. An externally developed authority may help a museum avoid repeating work that already has been done and accepted by the museum community in accordance with international standards. Adopting external standards still requires adaptation and effort because it takes coordination across departments to familiarize staff with these resources and to collaboratively navigate the descriptive vocabularies of value standards to identify terms that are most relevant to the collection. However, when an institution chooses external standards, it increases the relevance of its collection by joining a larger network and contributes to the development of consistent terminology controls throughout the museum community.

Linked Data

External standards ensure structural cohesion and terminology controls for museum collection cataloging. The established field names, styles, and values not only provide a linguistic roadmap for data entry decisions, but they also lay the foundation for broader exposure and more meaningful search in and among museum collections. In this age of networked information, external standards can be used to embed machine-readable, shared identifiers for use as entry points to collections data on the World Wide Web. The incentive for choosing external standards is not only to align institutional practice with the wider museum community but also to actively build that community by creating extensible linked data across institutions. This, in turn, has the potential to join the world's cultural collections in a seamlessly searchable virtual repository, complete with inferred relationships between records that result from mechanized self-describing data, leveraged on semantic modeling (although this is beyond the scope of this chapter, there are recommendations for further reading in the *Resources* section).

The first step to practical application of linked data is to include the universal resource identifiers (URIs) associated with chosen terms within the catalog records for every standardized entry. Begin with individual standardized fields, so that one data entry project aims to identify the artist constituent records or medium object attributes within the collections database. For example, Frida Kahlo is linked in the Getty's *Union List of Artist Names* with the URI 500030701, and in Wikidata with the URI Q5588. Similarly, copper (the metal) has the URI 300011020 in Getty's *Art and Architecture Thesaurus* while copper (the color) has the URI 300311190. These individual building blocks are small and the full benefits are still brewing in the international cultural stewardship community. Given the many developments underway and how much work there is to do, it is an exciting time to be a collections information manager, advocating for the broad implications of fully implementing external standards through linked open data strategies. These efforts will ensure the future relevance of institutional collections within the digital humanities and among the museum audiences of tomorrow.

Descriptive Standards

Many projects have developed terminology and linked data standards. Some examples include:

- *The Art and Architecture Thesaurus* (AAT) is a list of art history and architectural terminology developed as a controlled indexing language for the use of libraries, archives, and museums in cataloging book and periodical collections, image collections, and museum objects, particularly art-related objects. AAT terminology has been validated by users in the scholarly community and includes index terms that may be used to control a variety of fields in cataloging and CMSs, including object names, object genres, attributes, style and period terms, people roles, materials, and techniques. The AAT is an ongoing project that continually develops terminology and is especially responsive to user

feedback. It is available in both electronic and print editions and is sponsored by the Getty Research Institute of the J. Paul Getty Trust.

- *Nomenclature for Museum Cataloging*[11] is a standardized classification and controlled vocabulary for human-made object names. It is particularly useful for collections of historical objects. *Nomenclature* is indexed alphabetically and hierarchically. Object names are based on the original function of the object, with hierarchical divisions that include structures, building furnishings, personal artifacts, tools and equipment for materials, etc. For example, the category of *building furnishings* has subdivisions that include bedding, floor coverings, furniture, and so forth. Object terms are inverted with the noun first, followed by a comma and the modifier (e.g., chair, dining; chair, easy; and chair, folding). In an alphabetical listing of object names all chairs and like objects will display in the same place on the list. Preferred terms are displayed in capital letters and nonpreferred terms direct the user to the preferred terms. *Nomenclature* is available in a print edition and is sponsored by the American Association for State and Local History (AASLH).

- The *Thesaurus of Geographic Names* (TGN) is a list of hierarchically arranged geographic terms. Place names are arranged in terms of broader and narrower localities, and the thesaurus features preferred and nonpreferred terms. TGN is maintained by the Getty Vocabularies.

- The *Union List of Artist Names* (ULAN) is neither an authority list nor a thesaurus but was developed to serve as a terminology resource for museums, libraries, and archives. ULAN features a cluster format that displays and links all the variant spellings and versions of an artist's name as well as basic biographic data that includes life dates, roles, and nationality information. It is up to the user to choose the name that is preferred for cataloging and indexing, although ULAN provides some helpful information concerning the sources of the names and the use preferences of the sources from which the names have been drawn. ULAN is maintained by the Getty Vocabularies.

- *Iconclass*[12] is an iconographic classification system that provides subject and content terminology for art and historical images. It features a series of decimal codes within a hierarchic structure. It has ten main divisions that feature the primary subject headings of abstract, nonrepresentational art; religion and magic; nature; human being, man in general; society, civilization, culture; abstract ideas and concepts; history; bible; literature; and classical mythology and ancient history. Within these divisions are additional numbers and letters that, when combined in a string, represent important elements in an image using a descending hierarchy of concepts, beginning with a major concept such as history and ending with a specific concept, such as a precise event in history.

Iconclass is not the only system based on subject content; other projects include the Garnier System (*Thesaurus Iconographique, Systeme Descriptif de Representations*)[13] used widely in France; the Yale Center for British Art Project; and the Glass System (Subject Index for the Visual Arts) developed for the Victoria and Albert Museum.

The aforementioned projects do not form a comprehensive list of available resources. As terminologies shift and consortiums are formed to develop new dictionaries, it is useful to talk to other professionals in similar institutions to determine which thesauri they are using. If there are no existing thesauri, it can be helpful to request the lexicons of similar museums to build on their existing work.

Data Dictionary

A data dictionary provides documentation on the development and application of institutional data content standards. Foremost, it contains a scope note of each field, identifies the type of entry (free memo text, numeric, date, controlled lists, etc.), delineates the wider standard it adheres to, identifies access rights and the department or staff responsible for entering and maintaining the field, and provides data entry guidelines or defines each value of controlled lists within the field, if applicable (see discussion herein for a more extensive list). At an administrative level, the data dictionary chronicles decisions made in administering the field, which allows a museum to examine the nature of the object information it preserves and creates an explanatory record of past decisions.

Although crucial as a record of institutional memory, data dictionaries are also living documents in museums with which more than one department creates and maintains database records. When provided with a data dictionary, each department has documentation that details the scope of its own and other departments' responsibilities for entering data concerning an object. The data dictionary is the basis for an instructional cataloging manual—a visual explanation of the step-by-step procedures of records creation and management. Together, these provide a reference to guide users throughout an institution in entering data consistently.

While a data dictionary usually will be developed in house, one also may be provided by the vendor of an automated CMS. Users should review a vendor-provided data dictionary carefully, determine whether they agree with the definitions for the data elements that the vendor proposes, and revise them, if necessary, to suit their own particular needs. Concentrate on those things that assist in effective use of the documentation. A selection from the following information is useful when creating a data dictionary entry, although not all of the following information is required:

- *Module name*—In a relational database there may be more than one place in which information is entered. Identify the module (objects, locations, exhibitions, etc.) where the user will find this particular data element.
- *Field name*—The name of the category, field, or data element.
- *Table/Column Name (in relational databases)*—The name of the column and table the column resides in on the back end.
- *Field code*—The code the system uses internally.
- *Standards*—The various data standards to which the field corresponds. Such standards may include terminology dictionaries, such as the *Art and Architecture Thesaurus* or *Nomenclature* and metadata protocols.

- *Attributes*—Identify the attributes of the field, note whether it is a fixed or variable length, alphabetical or numeric, repeatable, etc. Note if there is a controlled vocabulary that will verify this field or special keystroke commands or controls associated with this field.
- *Access*—Identify which departments or users may access and enter or change data within this field.
- *Description*—Define the field, stating its purpose and the character of the information that will be entered into the field.
- *Data-entry rules*—Provide a list of conventions for data entry in this field. Note any exceptions to the rules. For example, note if dates are entered month or day first. If an authority or controlled terminology is in use for this field provide directions for using the authority and definitions of controlled terms, or direct the user to the appropriate information.
- *Examples*—Provide examples of data entered in the field.
- *Indexed*—Note whether the field is indexed.
- *Public Access*—Indicate whether the field is pushed to public repositories (online collection, aggregate repositories) or apps (mobile, kiosk).
- *Cross-reference points*—Which other modules the field is related to and where this data can be drawn into other records (e.g., object valuations available for loan insurance records, institutional or individual addresses available for loan and shipping records, etc.) or into other databases (e.g., library catalogs or digital asset management systems [DAMS]).
- *Administrative remarks*—The dates and reasons for decisions that expanded or changed the field, especially in the case of high-level authority lists such as department or classification.

A sample data dictionary entry for an accession value field might include:

Field name—Accession number
Field code—ACCNUM
Table/Column Name—Objects.ObjectNumber
Standards.

    CDWA—21.2.3. (repository number)

        21.2.3.1. (number type: "accession number")

CIDOC CRM—E42 (identifier)
ISAD code—3.1.1 (identifier)
EAD tag—<unitid>(identification of the unit)

Attributes—alphanumeric (unique value)

Access—write access for registration and administration groups, input for curatorial group for new records only, read access for all.

Description—The accession number is the unique identifier assigned to objects as they are received into the museum. For detailed accessioning and numbering procedures, refer to the Acquisition Procedures manual.

Create individual records for each object (an object refers to an item that is cataloged and displayed individually). For example, a portfolio containing seven prints would have seven or more objects, including the cover, colophon, and any additional materials. A cup and saucer are considered one object in two parts, and denoted with parts letters (a-b). In this example, each piece of the portfolio is cataloged individually, and the cup and saucer have only one record entered into the CMS.

Examples:

    2017.5
    2017.1a-c
    2017.2.1
    2017.713
    2017.7.1.1a-b
    LIB.87.2.2
    ARC.2016.011.6.1a-b

Data-entry rules:

- Always use decimal points between the numeric values of the number.
- Use hyphens between parts letters (e.g., a-c).
- For objects with special collection distinctions (LIB, ARC), insert a decimal point between the letters and the numbers.
- Do not use punctuation marks between numbers and letters.

Useful data dictionaries are not created in a vacuum. Curatorial, conservation, and registration departmental input is crucial to defining the scope of fields to assure that each department's controls are accommodated by the system and to establish each staff member as a stakeholder of collections data with an awareness of their own responsibilities for the integrity of the records. Furthermore, no matter how thorough the documentation is, there are always problems or details that will be exceptional. Meetings with users provide the opportunity to discover elements of information that each field entry in a data dictionary can and cannot accommodate. It is ideal to schedule regular meetings with a dedicated group of representatives from across the museum that are comfortable liaising on behalf of their departmental colleagues to raise issues, express preferences, and approve changes to collection information strategy.

- Meet regularly with users while the data dictionary entry is being generated.
- Listen to suggestions, and implement them.
- Use meetings as an opportunity to build consensus because data dictionary conventions that are imposed on users will be ignored.
- Always provide a reason for a convention; users are more likely to use a data dictionary that makes sense.

Finally, data dictionary entries constantly evolve and are adapted to new uses and situations. It is essential that they be kept up to date; otherwise, users will not be able to depend on them as reliable and definitive sources of information.

Training

Museums may hire information specialists with museum registration or curatorial backgrounds to manage the information needs of the institution. Information specialists should have a background in database management and understand the importance of data consistency and adherence to standards. Such personnel must bridge the protocols developed internally with the standards created by the broader museum community. Because of this, it is important to include information management staff in any discussion about cataloging, data standards, registration methods, and information access. They should share their expertise while adapting standards to existing needs.

Information specialists are often responsible for training staff to enter data into the system. Train-

ing responsibilities can be divided into two categories—initial and ongoing. Initial training is generally for those who are new to a specific software program and must be shown the basics. Training must be repeated whenever a major change in hardware or software takes place, such as the installation of a network or a new CMS, or when new staff members are hired. Ongoing training includes keeping the museum staff informed of software upgrades and new software and may be as simple as reminding staff of the importance of good housekeeping for computer files or the importance of making regular backups.

Staff training can be accomplished through different methods, including taking advantage of outside training opportunities or contracting with private companies, CMS vendors, or individuals for in-house training. Outside training means that staff must travel to another location so it must be determined whether it is a good investment for the entire staff to go for outside training or if sending one member who can come back and conduct training for the rest is more efficient. If it is decided to keep training in house, the collections information manager might establish a user group that meets periodically, send internal e-mail newsletters that offer tips, and hold office hours weekly where staff can come to troubleshoot issues or receive project-specific training. Collegial sharing of information through e-mail, user forums, and conferences greatly enhances the staff's ability to remain informed about technology advances.

Training staff to perform data entry is an exacting task in a museum because of the need to establish an accurate database. Training data-entry personnel for this task has been effectively accomplished by many museums through the use of data standards and carefully designed manuals to explain the process. The fewer decisions the data-entry person has to make, the cleaner the database.

Data Entry

Data entry into a new system can be one of the most expensive and time-consuming aspects in implementing a CMS. Furthermore, data entry is never completely done unless the collection is static. Not only does retroactive data entry often have to be done, but responsibility for ongoing data entry also must be assigned. If there are data in machine-readable form (such as an electronic spreadsheet), then there is a good chance they can be mapped by the vendor or system administrator into a new data structure. It is a good idea to plan for this conversion rather than to reenter all the data from another system manually.

When there are no data in machine-readable form, manual entry into a system is necessary. The museum may have personnel enter data from cards or catalog sheets, which is a time-consuming task because source material is often inconsistent and because there is a tendency to attempt to record all information possible for each object. Depending on the size of the collection, it is generally better to identify ten or twelve key fields of data to enter for each object to create a minimal identifying record for it. Initial records can be expanded later, as time permits. Data entry by hand can be extremely slow. Even a collection of modest size would require hiring a full-time person to do nothing but data entry.

Planning Data Entry

A commitment to record all collections management activities on the computer as soon as the database structure is up and running is important, and a plan must be made for the systematic data entry of backlogged records. Priorities for data entry may be determined by what is most important for insurance tracking and reporting or by what objects are currently on exhibit. It is logical to enter backlogged records chronologically, working from the most recent to oldest. Other approaches may be based on object type, donor or source, or objects currently on loan. Whatever the priority, a goal-oriented plan should be drawn up to complete data entry systematically and make the database useful immediately.

Establish a system for keeping track of progress, count or estimate the number of paper records, and measure daily progress against this total. Objects without accompanying records should be given numbers, listed as found-in-collection, and have minimal working fields entered for each object. Ideally, a staff member will be responsible for evaluating data entry as it is completed; this person may be the information manager, a curator, or the registrar. In some cases, it is a multiperson effort, with a few select staff members entering data into a few fields for which they are responsible. One person, such as the collections information manager, should have final authority to approve a record as correct and complete. For example, the registrar may enter an object's accession number, location, and provenance information. The curator will write a detailed description, assign a date, and identify the maker. The information manager will then check these fields for proper data entry conventions.

Data Clean-up

Raw data can be entered as it exists and cleaned up later, or it can be corrected before data entry. Conducting cleanup during data entry, especially when undertaken by multiple individuals, is problematic because it necessitates employing highly skilled data entry people who have subject-specific knowledge, understand the need for consistency, and are dedicated to the task full-time. Cleaning up data before entry will almost double the time required to get a database up and running. If all of the existing data is entirely in paper form, it must first be transcribed to a central repository with standardized formatting, and then corrected for content, spelling, and punctuation. This procedure yields good results and allows the use of minimally skilled people for data entry, but it is time-consuming.

When transferring data from one system to another, exporting the data from the old system into an electronic spreadsheet can greatly assist in data clean-up. The spreadsheet's find-and-replace, sorting, and filtering capabilities allow the data clean-up staff to find inconsistencies and missing information at a glance. The spreadsheet's most straightforward columns can be mapped to the new data structure, greatly facilitating the import of information into the new system. Depending on the quality of information in the old system, this may take a few weeks to several months. It may be useful to clean up the data in batches, by object type or department, and import it as each batch is completed. Keep a duplicate master copy available to allow staff to access the information during the data clean-up process, even if they are restricted from making changes.

Most museums cannot afford the time required to correct data before data entry and, therefore, must rely on cleaning it up after it is entered. Reports can be generated for registration or curatorial editing, with subsequent corrections made individually or globally, depending on the type and amount of information being corrected.

Proofreading

Humans make mistakes, and any computer database will reflect the mistakes made by the person who entered the data. If minimally skilled people enter data, the chances are great that many mistakes in spelling, punctuation, capitalization, and so on will occur. These mistakes may also be derived from the original paper records. It is important for the person overseeing the project to identify the source of the errors and take corrective action. Representative samples of records, selected either randomly or in conjunction with another project, should be proofread on a regular basis. Proofreading and corrections should be the responsibility of only one person (e.g., the person in charge of the project) and record approval should be indicated by the name of the proofreader and the date of approval.

SYSTEM MANAGEMENT AND INTEGRATION

System Management

Management is the backbone of a computerized file system. System management, supervised by the system administrator, involves the maintenance and protection of the system hardware, software, and data, and their integration in museum operations. Although the system administrator is the designated leader, all individuals using the system should take part in system management. Researchers and other individuals with access to the system should be trained in how to report problems, and staff members should have an efficient means for communicating their needs to the system administrator.

System management in museum settings may include scheduling with an in-house system manager, online technical support from an outside vendor,

data-logging notebooks or bug sheets that are periodically reviewed, and e-mails and telephone calls to outside technical support advisors. An institution with many computer applications may designate a system manager and a program administrator; the registrar is often one or both of these.

Maintenance

Maintenance relies on thorough and efficient communication between system users and system managers. Although scheduled maintenance tasks—such as backing up and spot-checking data—should be conducted regularly, meetings with system users to determine the continued usefulness of the system as a whole are also a part of general maintenance. If the system no longer functions at its maximum level of usefulness, upgrades and improvements should be considered. Many institutions face the simple problem of staff members who accumulate data and save it on their desktop computers; maintenance involves centralizing information so that all users can report what they have completed, what they are working on, and what projects involving the system may be ready to start. The system or program administrator should maintain a master schedule of projects and progress.

Security

A computer system, and the information it contains, represents a major institutional investment. Just as employees are informed of the general museum security plan, users of the computer system must be educated regarding electronic security. There are three main aspects to computer security, which are similar to the security requirements for a museum collection:

- The system must be protected from physical loss or damage by human actions or environmental causes.
- Information must be protected from unauthorized changes or deletion, accidental or intentional.
- Information that must remain confidential for legal, ethical, or security reasons must be safeguarded. Confidential information includes records regarding donors, valuations, storage locations, museum security systems and procedures, and employee records and personnel files.

An institution with more than two employees, or one that is part of a wider electronic network, needs password protection for its computer system. For relatively simple systems, single password entry may be sufficient, but do not rely on screen-saver password programs because they are easy to defeat. If a system has multiple users, is on a network, or relies heavily on computerized collections management data, a hierarchical system of passwords should be in place. Password protection can cover an individual's files or the official museum records. Levels of access and authority can range from read-only access to higher-level permissions to edit, add, or delete information. Confidential fields in a database may be restricted to holders of specific passwords. Take care to use best practices in password security, such that passwords for the highest levels of access and security are complex (e.g., contain a mix of letters, numbers, and symbols) and are changed periodically.

Physical security includes not only restricted access but also favorable environmental conditions. Computers should be cleaned and maintained on a regular basis. Much like collection objects, computers and computer media require a relatively high level of environmental control, and they are especially sensitive to heat. Keep computers and media at an even temperature and away from windows and internal heat sources. Avoid power surges by using a good suppressor and an outlet dedicated to computer equipment. At the very least, the data servers should be connected to an uninterruptible power supply (UPS). Other electric appliances and equipment, especially heavy power users, should be plugged into other circuits. Keep backup media in a separate, protected location, preferably off-site. Computer media must be protected from static charges and magnetic fields such as those in telephones, office magnets, and other electronic equipment.

Backups

A regular backup schedule is the key to a computer disaster recovery plan. Backup can be used as a verb (to back up) or a noun (to refer to a copy of computer files). As a precaution against information loss, backing up files is so important that it must be considered when choosing computer software and hardware. When establishing a backup schedule, the key question is how much work can the museum afford to lose? The backup frequency will depend on how often computer files are updated and how fast information is added. A full backup (a copy of everything on the computer system) can be made periodically (e.g., weekly). Incremental backup (copies of all files that have been added or amended) can be scheduled more frequently.

Active or cautious computer users may wish to maintain backups of their own files, but generally a system manager is responsible for the backup program. The process of backing up computer files on a networked system is best done during slack times such as at night or on weekends because the activity degrades computer performance and open files might not be included in the backup. The backup system can be fully automated so that a system manager need not be physically present during the process. Computer backup media exist in a number of different formats. Each type of backup medium has advantages and disadvantages based on its reliability and cost per byte of data stored. For short-term file backups the longevity of the medium is not a critical factor, but the ability to reuse it reliably in the long term is important and should be researched as part of the cost analysis conducted when selecting a system.

For long-term backup, *live storage* is the most reliable method, in which the data are continuously rewritten in multiple electronic or physical locations, ensuring that information is not degraded over time or due to the failure of a single piece of hardware. Live storage methods include *cloud computing*, in which the data are distributed across a network of servers in geographically diverse locations, or in RAIDs, in which the data are duplicated across multiple hard drives within a single server.

System Administrator

Information system managers or system administrators may interact with the museum in a variety of ways and may also be the collections information managers. Whether an outside contractor or an in-house staff member, full-time or part-time, the manager must be able to train staff, handle unforeseen problems, manage the overall system, and plays a pivotal role in the success of the system. If the system administrator is a full-time museum staff member this will be the person most likely responsible for troubleshooting, adding and deleting users on the network, and coordinating with other museum personnel for disaster preparedness and emergency backups needed during evenings, weekends, and holidays.

When selecting a system manager, museum administrators need to consider both short- and long-term costs. If a staff member is adding systems administration to an already overtaxed schedule, the short-term costs will be low because no new employees will be added, but the long-term costs can be quite high as the employee attempts to find time to get the system in running order and enable other employees to work. Contract system administrators may be cost-effective because they can be used on an as-needed basis, but scheduling these individuals may be problematic.

Ideally, a system administrator will keep a database of all of the hardware and software for each workstation within the museum. This ensures protection against problems with software licensing, crashes, theft, configuration problems, and unrelated software that tends to fill up hard drives. The system administrator may be responsible for determining whether an upgrade to the computer or network systems is needed and then coordinating the upgrade within the museum.

Managing a computer system involves not only administering hardware and software but also checking and ensuring data integrity. A systems manager should coordinate with the collections information manager to determine the percentage of a museum's records that are within the CMS, the accuracy of the information, and how up-to-date the digital records are. These data are important for insurance purposes, management, planning, and research. The system administrator may have museum staff members spot-check the data relevant to their particular area of expertise. System administrators should work with museum staff to build redundancy checks into databases. Most important of all, a comprehensive data backup plan should be maintained and duplicate data sets kept off-site.

System Manual

A system manual can be a web page or an electronic document within the museum's intranet, or a binder containing information on changes to the system or improvements in documentation. The system manual may include:

- Information on the specific hardware and software in use (including identification and serial numbers needed for access by technical assistance departments or vendors);
- The name(s) and contact information for the system manager and other technical assistance personnel;
- Policies governing systems use; and
- Instructions on how to use the systems.

An effective system manual provides employees with step-by-step guidance on how to use the system, how to enter the information, and how to get information out when it is needed. A system manual should not be a static document because as technology and computer needs change, the manual should reflect those changes. Many museums do not use systems manuals because they are seen as bothersome to produce, and some museums that have manuals do not keep them updated to avoid the cost in staff time that it takes. However, system manuals can save staff time by answering questions people have and by serving as a tutorial on systems use. Writing out instructions for what one already knows how to do may seem like an exercise in redundancy, but documenting procedures so that they can be followed by users will save an institution time and money in the long run. System manuals can help ensure that additions or changes to the system (such as new software) are compatible with existing hardware and software.

Integration into Museum Operations

The ideal CMS involves all museum records relating to collections. Museum objects (whether accessions or loans) should be continuously tracked once they enter an institution's jurisdiction. Once basic information is entered, the system should be able to produce necessary receipts, loan forms, gift agreements, and so on, directly from the database. Barcoding objects may simplify object tracking while eliminating typographical errors, and the inclusion of digital images greatly enhances identification within a CMS.

In addition to tracking objects and being a repository for object data, the CMS should make data available through direct access, integrating data between multiple internal systems through an intermediary database or application programming interface, or through reports that can be exported to multiple file formats.

Online Access

Since the 1970s, museums have been sharing their collections information online. Initially, they shared information with other museums and research institutions, but with the increase in public interest in collection holdings and the relative ease with which such information could be shared on the internet, museums began to make more information available to the public.

Providing public access to collections information serves multiple purposes. It helps fulfill the museum's mission to educate the public and prove that the objects held in public trust are used for public benefit. Sharing information with diverse groups of the public and scholars can encourage the institution to be careful with its data entry and provide the opportunity to bring oversights to the attention of museum staff. As a result, many museums are more aware of the importance of consistency in their descriptive practices, which supports basic collection stewardship.

Virtually anyone can view digital information online, so the registrar may see an increase in requests for loans and curators may see an increase in requests for additional information about collection objects. Management may become convinced that additional support for collections documentation is needed and development may look for additional funding sources for inventory and documentation. Many funding agencies (e.g., the Institute of Museum and Library Services) and private donors will fund accessibility projects that require photographing and documenting objects before their information can be placed online, and grant opportunities for collections care often have an online-access requirement.

TYPES OF ONLINE ACCESS

Museums employ a variety of methods for sharing collection information online. Today *online access* is synonymous with displaying collection items on the World Wide Web, either on the museum's website, on a consortium website, or through a third-party application or web page.

Curated Online Exhibitions

Some institutions make few collection objects available for viewing on their websites but offer a curated selection of important objects with lengthy descriptions and histories. These highlights from the collection function much like gallery exhibitions do, either informed by a specific story or self-guided by the online visitor. Supporting materials, such as video, audio, or links to related texts, may be linked to the exhibition.

The curated method of sharing collections online has the advantage of providing interpretive materials to the public, serves as a way for curators to extend exhibitions to people who cannot visit the museum, and ensures that the efforts they expend to create exhibitions live on far past the usual life span of the traditional museum presentation. The downside to the curated online display is that it requires additional effort by staff.

Database-Driven Collections Online

Some museums display information from the CMS directly in a specific online collections area of their museum's website. These database-driven pages can be extensive, displaying information about every object that has been approved for public viewing. The information displayed varies among institutions. Most museums display the accession number, title, creation date, maker, maker birth and death dates, material or medium, credit line, and an image. Some museums publish links to related materials, detailed provenance information, descriptive texts, subjects and categories, artist biographies, videos, and high-resolution images for downloading or viewing on a web browser.

Because these web pages are database-driven, any changes made in the CMS will appear automatically on the website. This may be immediate if the networking structure between the system and the web display allows it, or if administrative permissions allow immediate changes. More commonly, changes made to database records will be uploaded to the server managing the website on a nightly or weekly basis or when undertaken by an administrator. Any changes to the information should be reviewed by either the collection information manager or an editorial staff member, who should have final authority to approve the information for dissemination on the website.

Database-driven online collections may require a CMS that has a module for web-based display. Museums without such systems may hire programmers to build scripts to bridge their collections database to a website. In either case, a web designer will be needed to design the graphical layout of the web pages in which the information will be displayed. If database-driven online collection access is important to the institution (as it is to an increasing number of museums) the web-output capabilities of the system should be evaluated along with other functionalities under consideration at the time of selection. It can be helpful to view the online collections of other museums using the system for that purpose, bearing in mind that the graphical interface is often separate from the functionality of the system itself. Speaking with the staff responsible for bridging the internal system with the website can help clarify issues with the software. Another concern is that materials are presented without many explicitly defined contextual relationships, unlike curated exhibitions. Many scholars and members of the public will explore the material and make their own connections, but everyone using both mediated and unmediated displays for online collections information can be mutually supporting and enhance public education, sometimes in unexpected ways.

CONCLUSION

As demonstrated through the processes described, museum information management is an intricate process that requires dedicated effort and cooperation among staff across departments. This information is meant as a basic guide to getting up and running with a dig-itized platform starting from scratch, but even this information only begins to describe what is possible. Further considerations and creative solutions in everything from report design to network security will optimize whatever system an institution chooses to implement. Remember that colleagues in other institutions are often the best resources for guidance in issues big and small and that involvement in a community of like-minded professionals is a priceless addition to the returns on these valuable systems. ●

RESOURCES

Professional Organizations

- The Museum Computer Network[14] (MCN) promotes the development and use of computer technology in the museum community and sponsors an annual conference with workshops.
- The Canadian Heritage Information Network[15] (CHIN) offers a variety of services to Canadian museums, including an automated CMS, advice on documentation standards and new technology, and data dictionary standards. CHIN maintains three national databases for Canadian collections that cover humanities and natural sciences objects and archaeological sites. CHIN is primarily concerned with promoting and supporting the development of documentation standards and computerization in the Canadian museum community and to that end has published a number of guides and articles on their website.
- The Collections Trust[16] (previously the Museum Documentation Association) promotes the development of documentation standards in the United Kingdom. The Collection Trust publishes SPEC-TRUM, which outlines the procedures required to provide documentation for museum objects and collections management activities and describes the information needed to support those procedures. ●

Further Reading

Data Standards

Harpring, P. 2013. *Introduction to Controlled Vocabularies: Terminology for Art, Architecture, and Other Cultural Works*, 2nd ed. Los Angeles, California: Getty Research Institute.

Stewart, D. L. 2011. *Building Enterprise Taxonomies*, 2nd ed. Lexington, Kentucky: Mokita Press.

Linked Open Data
The World Wide Web Consortium[17] (W3C) is an international community that develops and disseminates web standards. Their website hosts explanatory FAQs about the history of the web and its potential, outlining the Semantic Web and Linked Open Data.

Berners-Lee, T., J. Hendler, and O. Lassila.2001. "The Semantic Web." *Scientific American*, 284(5), May.

NOTES
1. Available at: https://www.canada.ca/en/heritage-information -network/services/collections-management-systems.html.

2. Available at: http://www.cidoc-crm.org/sites/default/files/ cidoc_crm_version_5.0.4.pdf.

3. Available at: https://pro.europeana.eu/files/Europeana_ Professional/Share_your_data/Technical_requirements/EDM_ Documentation/EDM_Definition_v5.2.7_042016.pdf.

4. Available at: https://www.getty.edu/research/tools/ vocabularies/vocab_cdwa_flier.pdf.

5. Available at: http://cco.vrafoundation.org/index.php/toolkit/ cco_pdf_version/.

6. Available at: http://www.getty.edu/research/tools/ vocabularies/aat/index.html.

7. Available at: http://www.getty.edu/research/tools/ vocabularies/ulan/index.html.

8. Available at: http://www.getty.edu/research/tools/ vocabularies/tgn/index.html.

9. Available at: http://www.getty.edu/research/tools/ vocabularies/cona/index.html.

10. Available at: http://www.nomenclature.info/.

11. Available at: http://www.nomenclature.info/.

12. Available at: http://www.iconclass.org/.

13. Available at: https://gallica.bnf.fr/ark:/12148/ bpt6k33231071/f9.image.

14. Available at: http://mcn.edu/.

15. Available at: https://www.canada.ca/en/heritage -information-network.html.

16. Available at: https://collectionstrust.org.uk/.

17. Available at: https://www.w3.org/.

With thanks to Perian Sully for previous chapter revisions.

4D | DIGITAL ASSET MANAGEMENT SYSTEMS

OLIVIA ARNONE (UPDATED AND EXPANDED BY SUSAN WAMSLEY)

MOST MUSEUMS HOLD many shared images and documents on their institutional networks. A search may reveal the existence of extraneous duplicates, multiple versions, and various edits or updates of any given image or document file. It may not be apparent who created them, whether they are still viable, or if they are authentic. Knowledge of the existence of some of these files might have saved time on a previous project; eliminating redundancy among them definitely would ease the demand for network capacity. Such problems are common in the museum community, and information managers are increasingly aware of the need to control electronic files through a system that can aid in their organization, identification, searching, and retrieval in an easy, efficient, automated, and reliable manner.

To manage electronic files, many museums are turning to digital asset management systems (DAMS). These systems historically have been used by advertising and marketing professionals, but most cultural institutions now implement them to provide efficient access to files and to centralize operations. Although an asset management system can be, at its most basic level, an organized folder structure on a server, more sophisticated enterprise level or proprietary systems are designed to manage, track, display, and authenticate various types of files, their versions, and related information (or metadata) that exist within an institution's spectrum of media and document resources.

Much like any physical object cared for by a museum, digital files increasingly are recognized as valuable assets that require preservation and management. The lifecycle of a digital file—the time and money invested in its creation or capture, the frequency with which its content is used or repurposed, the amount of cross-department use of the file, and the need to archive its content as institutional history— demonstrates its value. DAMS can be programmed to facilitate the oversight of file relevance, quality, and longevity, ultimately making extremely efficient use of extant human and electronic resources. The following sections will explain the functionality of a DAMS, its various components, and the investments that an institution must consider concerning scoping, implementing, and maintaining a system.

FUNCTION

What exactly does a DAMS do? What goes into a system and how does it work? How does an institution choose a system? According to the *Guide to Good Practice in the Digital Representation and Management of Cultural Heritage Materials* from the National Initiative for a Networked Cultural Heritage[1] (NINCH) implementing a DAMS involves:

> Creating an efficient archive that can hold digital resources (such as images, audio, video and text) and the metadata used to describe them; implementing an infrastructure to ensure that these electronic data are managed and preserved in such a way that they will not become obsolete; [and] implementing search facilities that enable users to identify, locate and retrieve a digital object.

Before implementing a DAMS, the museum staff must first know what it wants from a system. For a DAMS to function properly, resources must be identified and organized in a manner that will produce positive results for these specific needs. The maintenance of files needs to be addressed for ultimate usability and preservation. This preparation involves establishing and implementing policies that address the standardization of file types, formats, sizing, and in some cases, naming.

Images

Image collections are commonly a shared resource for curators, registrars, exhibition designers, marketing teams, public relations managers, education professionals, membership departments, and web and IT staff. Although many individual departments within an institution may manage their own image collections, DAMS introduce the ability to share images of objects, archival and historical images, and activity, program, and exhibition-related images. With new forms of publication and dissemination such as blogs and podcasts come increased activity for new and existing images by various departments. As a result, the types of digital files and the frequency with which they are used and repurposed is increasing, virtually flooding shared drives with images. Before implementing a DAMS, it is important to distinguish the types of images that exist, what they can be used for, and which can be eliminated.

Master and Derivative Images

The results of a search within a DAMS interface will often display its results by listing, either by file name or thumbnail view, the various versions of an image that exist in an institution's repository or server. It is important to know the intended output format, such as a printed publication or screen use for the web or presentations, and to determine whether the available images are sufficient. Included in the available resources should be a master file—an original, high resolution, archival version.

Master files should remain the preferred and preserved archival copies of the files, stored in an uncompressed, unaltered format, such as RAW or TIFF (see section on file formats that follows). This version of an image best preserves the visual information of the object, person, or event displayed. Considering that many images are used and repurposed by many departments, it is important to preserve a master version of a file.

Depending on the storage parameters designated by your institution, master images may be stored as RAW files, which take up less space, or uncompressed TIFF files, which take up significantly more space (depending on their pixel dimensions). It is important to keep in mind that each camera model has its own RAW image setting, and these are not universally readable. For this reason, many institutions may prefer to convert RAW master images to digital negative (DNG) format, which is managed by the Adobe Corporation and, thus, is a more universally used file format. The master image should remain unaltered over time. The California Digital Library recommends that the master file should have a life span of approximately fifty years.[2]

DAMS can produce derivative files when downloaded that are commonly suitable for reuse. These files are created on demand by the DAMS and do not need to be stored. This feature can be customized for your institution's needs and should at least consist of a version that is sufficient for printing (minimally a 300 ppi JPEG or JPEG 2000), as well as a version created for digital use or web output (72-96 ppi JPEG; see CHAPTER 5H, "Photography," for more information about image sizing). It is imperative that a policy be developed to standardize the quality of master images, as well as their derivatives. The master file should be reliable enough to reproduce a variety of derivatives for many intended uses without having to rescan or recapture the original. Additionally, a DAMS should provide a function that can capture versions of files. Versioning will track assets that are edits of a master file using a text history for accountability. Not to be confused with derivative files that are merely different file sizes, versions capture the often extensive work done from a master file. For example, composite images or images with extensive digital photo alterations can be stored and linked along with the master image to retain the original as context as well as the new creation.

Careful consideration should be given to the long-term preservation of born-digital images—images that were not created using a physical medium such as film—as they remain the primary source file with no analog format to rely on as a backup. A strategy should be employed to oversee the long-term preservation of these assets so that they can be retrieved for future generations. Procedures that will preserve the accessibility, quality, and integrity of the digital master should be maintained throughout the entire lifecycle of a digital object (see CHAPTER 3G, "Managing Digital Art"). This is not the case for analog media, which are now commonly digitally reformatted to serve as the primary archival records and sources for derivative files. Digital media also serve to protect the information contained on the original analog from loss if it is misplaced, borrowed and not returned, or physically degraded over time through use or inherent vice.

Image File Formats

Long-term preservation of digital files begins with understanding the purpose and use of various file formats. *Lossless* file formats are the preferred for archival storage because the data stored in the file are not compressed in such a way that discards information; these file formats include TIFF, RAW, and DNG. *Lossy* file formats (in which some image quality is lost during compression), such as JPEG, are preferred for applications such as web pages or embedding images into collections management systems (CMS) because they are smaller in size. Lossy formats cannot, however, be used for archival purposes because the method that makes their file size smaller requires that some data be discarded on saving.

Lossless Formats

RAW—The preferred capture mode that produces a superior quality image, RAW files contain unprocessed data from a digital camera and are sometimes considered a DNG. Camera make and model determine the size of the RAW file.

DNG (digital negative)—This is Adobe's archival RAW format, the preferred archival or lossless file format to convert RAW files after image capture.

TIFF (tagged image file format)—The most widely used archival format for saving processed images. Flexible and universally supported across operating system platforms, TIFF files maintain all of the original color information and support embedded color profiles needed for printing, as well as metadata in the file.

Lossy Formats

JPEG (joint photographic experts group)—The most widely used format for distribution but not for archival purposes. Each time an image is opened, saved, and closed the image is compressed further. If it is opened and closed without saving, it is not altered.

Formats That Are Both Lossless and Lossy

JPEG 2000—Launched in 2002 as a superior alternative to the original JPEG format. This format provides both lossless and lossy compression, but it is not currently widely supported in consumer photography equipment or in internet web browsers and, thus, can cause incompatibility issues.

PDF (portable document format)—Thus is the preferred long-term storage and distribution method for text and image-based content. Universally supported across platforms, PDF files may include text, images, and graphics embedded in a single file. PDF files can be opened at any time in the future without changes. Although this format is technically proprietary because it was developed by Adobe Systems, Inc., it has been adopted by public as well as private institutions because of its reliability. Some organizations use this format for long-term storage of document files.

MOV—This is the most popular video file format, and it is widely recognized by video editing software. Depending on your storage and network, you may develop different guidelines for video. At the time of writing this, a common way to store master video files is H.264 encoded, full HD at 1920x1080p (progressive), and a high Mbps.

Unique Numbering and Persistent Identifiers

As physical objects in a collection have accession numbers, so also a unique identifier (e.g., an alphanumeric naming scheme) may be assigned to each digital asset to help locate and identify the resource.

With different versions of digital assets located in different areas of an institution's CMS and DAMS, a distinctive naming scheme will help identify the differences between the various purposes of extant versions of any given file. One option is to use qualifiers to keep all versions of a file consistently named (such as adding 001, 002, etc.). However, this number should not interfere with any existing naming conventions, such as for the page number of an album or catalog. Another easy identifier is the date. For example, an object with the accession number 25-5525 may be photographed before and after a treatment. Naming the files "25-5525_2017.TIFF" and "25-5525_2018.TIFF" would differentiate the files, alert the user to the difference, and make them easy to identify when they have been downloaded from the system. More detailed dates that include the month and day, or using predefined codes such as "bt" and "at" for "before treatment" and "after treatment" are also ways of making a file name meaningful. DAMS assign a unique ID number to every file that is uploaded into the system. It is important, however, to implement a consistent file naming system that is relevant for your institution. Once files are downloaded to a user's computer, it is extremely helpful if they contain easily identifiable information. When developing file naming conventions, there are some rules to keep in mind:

- Files should be named without the use of special characters (&, @, #, <, >, ", ?, spaces, periods, etc.).
- File names should be lowercase and be no more than 120 characters. Although most computers today can read spaces and longer file names, they cannot understand special characters, and it is good practice to ensure the files are readable across a wide range of applications.
- Consideration should be given to the way in which various perspectives or images of the same subject are named, such as aspects of three-dimensional objects, different views inside the same gallery or event, and so on.

Other Persistent Identifiers

Additional master images of the same object images that are ancillary views to the approved view of a collection object and provide persistent identifiers include:

- accessionnumber.tif (primary or main image)
- accessionnumber_01.tif
- accessionnumber_02.tif

Identification Images

Images from which no professional image has been obtained and snapshots may link records management to the CMS and are used as a record image or to document condition:

- accessionnumber_date_verso01.jpg
- accessionnumber_date_verso02.jpg
- accessionnumber_date_verso03.jpg

You can note in the file name or the metadata (preferably both) if the photo was taken for a particular department which can help with sorting, search-

ing, and the return of relevant results for users. For example, identification images could be made visible only to registrars and conservators, identified by a department code in the file name such as accession-number_date_verso01_reg.tif.

Non-Object-Related Images

Gallery views, archive images, events, and other related images are often reusable assets. For these images, it is important to retain information in the file name that will enable retrieval later. There are numerous possibilities for doing this, but the best option may be to use file names that include dates, content, or identify the departments to which the images relate. For example, images of a yearly gala event might be file names such as:

- gala_2017_001.tif
- gala_2017_002.tif
- gala_2018_001.tif
- gala_2018_002.tif

For a recurring event such as a lecture series that takes place on the first of every month you might use:

- smithlecture_20180601_001.tif
- smithlecture_20180601_002.tif
- smithlecture_20180701_001.tif
- smithlecture_20180701_002.tif

Note that the date for file names and folders should be in the form of a four-digit year, two-digit month and two-digit day (YYYY-MM-DD) to ensure that files and folders sort chronologically.

Documents

Most institutions that implement DAMS do so to manage their image and media collections. The primary concern with documents is that some formats may not be supported in the future because of regular updates and changes in proprietary software. On the other hand, the problem with choosing a nonproprietary file format (or standard) for long-term access is that the formatting preferences and design elements, such as fonts, are sometimes lost when the file is reduced to its textual elements. Currently, three standard file formats are considered preservation formats because they rely on web-based technologies:

HTML (hypertext markup language)—Widely supported on the internet to display pages and can be viewed in any browser. Commonly used for output from other systems, such as databases.

XML (extensible markup language)—Widely used for structured files, such as spreadsheets. This file format does not require licensing, is well supported and is not specific to any platform or system type, such as MAC or PC. XML is considered by some experts to be the best current and future file format because it is able to store document content along with descriptive information (metadata).

PDF (portable document format)—This is the preferred long-term storage and distribution format for text and image-based content. PDF files are universally supported across platforms and store text, images, and graphics embedded in a single file that can be opened at any time in the future without changes. Although this format is technically proprietary because it was developed by Adobe Systems, Inc., it has been adopted by public as well as private institutions for its reliability. Some organizations use this format for long-term storage of document files.[3]

METADATA

Metadata (the information attached to digital objects) are used to search for files on a server. A DAMS will display a small thumbnail image, the various versions of a file that may exist within an institution's image resources, the title, size, and other related information. There are numerous types of metadata that can be related to a file, including:

- Descriptive metadata—the content of the image, such as title, artist, date of work, or subject.
- Administrative metadata—the creator or author, input device settings, and rights information.
- Preservation metadata—information relating to the condition of the object, data migration and refreshing schedule, and technical information such as authentication and security data.

The type and amount of metadata that appear in a DAMS are entirely at the discretion of the institution and should be in compliance with policies and procedures that are place. It is good practice to confer with other institutions to determine what types of metadata they regularly embed in their assets. Some metadata are necessary to ensure the longevity and vitality of the digital file, but what is needed will differ depending on vocabularies and metadata standards developed by the Getty Research Institute,[4] such as the *Union List of Artist Names* (ULAN), a popular example of linked open data.

CMS AND DAMS: HARVESTING CONTENT AND METADATA MANAGEMENT

One of the ways to link information about images of collection objects (metadata) and other images (such as exhibition and installation or gallery images) to their sources is through an institution's CMS. The DAMS will allow a user interface to mimic the information found in cataloging information, such as tombstone or label information, creator or author identification, administrative information about the file (e.g., a creation date or input device, such as a scanner), the intellectual property or copyright status of an art object, and just about any other information the institution deems pertinent.

As information in a CMS is cataloged and updated, it can be synchronized with a DAMS as required. Through the process of performing scheduled checksums (programmed operations that check for errors and redundancies in files), which will decipher changes that have been made, and a deployment agent that systematically delivers all new information to the DAMS, the system can also be set up to feed information from the DAMS back to the CMS. To maximize access potential for future content, placeholder records can be created for catalog records that do not have matching images, indicating that there are existing media available that have not been digitized and linked to the system. The DAMS-CMS connection can be configured to collect the DAMS high-quality image files to be included in a CMS object package, making analog and digital condition-checking easier with better quality photography.

SECURITY

It is possible to program the system to be selective in its choice of information and the type of images it chooses to deploy. A security matrix can be designed to block private information or information that should not be available to end users from object records, including information about loaned objects or donor information. Default ranking—a system designed to indicate, in a specific order, the preferred file to be used for an intended output format—can be set up to maintain selectivity so as not to overload the system with substandard images.

Programming permissions for any file or folder in the repository gives an end user the limited capability of viewing, reading, or seeing a list but not permission to make changes to the information in the document or its metadata. Some institutions choose to limit the information in their DAMS to tombstone data and intellectual property information for the artwork or image and any potentially restricted uses. Permissions levels can also be set to restrict the image results that a user can find.

In addition to configuring the permission levels for objects, metadata, and users, a DAMS provides security for the museum's assets by backups of the system to protect the institution's firewalls and by tracking the history of every user action. Robust metrics reports can provide a clear view of how the museum's assets are being used and by whom.

CHOOSING A SYSTEM

Many factors contribute to choosing a DAMS for an institution. Budgetary, staff commitment, and architecture and design are the main determining factors for the system. Enterprise-level systems are time consuming and costly to implement, support, and license. Some organizations may choose an open source system or a trusted repository, both models that archives and libraries have historically used. Like an enterprise-level system, these are somewhat usable off the shelf, but require technical support from on-site staff to customize.

DIGITAL PRESERVATION

It is recommended that a strategy be enforced to manage the information in electronic records along with the media on which they are stored. The strategy should ensure that the media remain reliable and authentic without losing the integrity of the original. Preservation metadata, unlike descriptive and administrative metadata, are the information infrastructure that support the processes associated with digital preservation. Preservation metadata are defined by PREMIS (Preservation Metadata: Implementation Strategies) as "the information a repository uses to support the digital preservation process."[5] For more information on the structure and contents of preservation metadata, refer to the PREMIS Data Dictionary for Preservation Records Management Metadata.[6] More specifically, preservation metadata are necessary to:

- maintain the viability of the readable bit stream (the contiguous or noncontiguous series of bytes that make up a file [e.g., 11000011001]);
- ensure renderability (the ability of humans and computers to translate the bit stream); and
- secure understandability (the capacity of users to interpret the bit stream).

MEDIA MIGRATION

Data format and software obsolescence pose a large threat to the long-term accessibility of digital objects. As file formats continue to evolve and new versions and updates appear for software, files can become indecipherable. Media may become unreadable over time because of physical damage to the storage device or technological developments in hardware that render preexisting formats obsolete. Two strategies have been formulated to deal with these problems:

1. Media migration—Moving files from an obscure or outdated medium to a prevailing, current media format. This process applies to both file formats and storage media and ensures bit-level preservation, or preservation of the data sequence of bytes that make up a file (the 1's and 0's of a file).
2. Emulation—Allows a modern system to mimic the interface of an obsolete system for a digital object to be viewed and understood. Use of emulation software can help recover old files and migrate them to a new format.

The use of file-converter software will allow easy migration from one file format to another. Outsourcing format migration is an option, as is investing in new software technologies that can automatically scan and report the compatibility of files, which then can be selected and converted to new version formats. The Council on Library and Information Resources[7] recommends that file-conversion software:

- Read the source file and analyze the difference between it and the target format;
- Identify and report the degree of risk if a mismatch occurs;
- Accurately convert the source file(s) to target specifications;
- Work on single files as well as large collections; and
- Provide a record of conversions for inclusion in the migration project documentation.

In addition to migration and emulation, the NINCH *Guide to Good Practice*[8] also recommends:

- Enduring Care—Takes into consideration the safe storage and handling of digital objects and storage media.
- Refreshing—Moving data from one medium to another, such as from a CD to a DVD (not to be confused with migration; this process moves just the content and does not change the format of the file).

- Digital Archaeology—Rescuing content from damaged or obsolete media or hardware or software.

LIFE CYCLE MANAGEMENT AND ASSOCIATED COSTS

According to the Digital Preservation Coalition, tracking the life cycle of a digital file can be used to allocate costs.[9] The Digital Preservation Coalition based its calculation models on various studies completed by researchers interested in determining the economic impact on cultural institutions of managing these files. TABLE 4D.1 outlines a structured approach to reinforce the cyclical costs associated with the various stages in the life of a digital file.

Because of many variables, it is extremely difficult to gauge the costs associated with these stages. Open archival information systems (OAIS) developed its own reference models that describe each stage of the life cycle as a cost event. Each stage is evaluated for likely cost sources and depending on the purpose of the study, a total cost may then be calculated per item, per time period for preservation of all collection material, or per process (see TABLES 4D.2 and 4D.3). Even if these models are not used for estimating associated costs, they provide a good foundation for thinking about the cyclical nature and the accumulated activity surrounding digital files.

Table 4D.1 Typical Cost Events

Activity	Cost Events
System creation and management activities	Creating organizational infrastructure Creating repository architecture Archive administration, repository operation, and maintenance upgrades
Digital material workflow and life cycle activities	Selection, acquisition, validation, creation of digital collections, conversion of deposited material, rights negotiation and management, resource description (e.g., cataloging metadata and preservation metadata creation), storage, evaluation and revision, disposal/deaccession
Specific preservation activities	Technology planning activities, such as technology watch and long-term strategies (e.g., migration and emulation)
Specific access activities	Access to objects Access to catalogs Access to user support

Table 4D.2 Typical Cost Sources

Cost Type	Cost Sources
Digital object or data acquisition	Purchase price or licensing cost
Labor	Personnel (dedicated staff as well as varying proportions of time of senior management, supervisor, information technology staff, curatorial staff, etc.)
Technology	Hardware, software, level of requirements (e.g., speed, availability, and performance)
Nonlabor operational costs	Facilities and space (e.g., rent and electricity), materials and equipment, communications, insurance, legal costs

Table 4D.3 Life Cycle Stages of Physical and Digital Objects

Stages identified in the lifecycle of physical collections	Stages identified in the lifecycle of digitized material
Selection	Selection
Acquisition processing	Checking intellectual property rights
Cataloging and press-marking or numbering objects	Conservation check and remedial conservation costs, retrieval and re-shelving costs of physical media, capture of digitized master
Preservation, conservation, storage, retrieval deaccession	Quality assurance of digital master and production of service copies
	deaccession
	Access cost over time
	Storage costs over time

CONCLUSION

Unfortunately, by the time this book is published some of the information in this section may already be outdated. It is a disadvantage of technology that many new developments in software or hardware are replaced by something newer and greater at very brief intervals. Museums are now faced with the gargantuan task of managing digital files in a way that is conducive to access and preservation. Methods of managing information before the digital age no longer apply. We are in an era of transition, as new means of providing access to collections replace the old in exciting ways. In the meantime, as we continue to learn how to use available technologies, we must maintain and strengthen the integrity of our existing resources. ●

NOTES

1. NINCH *Guide to Good Practice in the Digital Representation and Management of Cultural Heritage Materials*, 195. Available at: http://chnm.gmu.edu/digitalhistory/links/pdf/chapter1/1.17.pdf.

2. The California Digital Library. Available at: www.cdlib.org/inside/diglib/guidelines/bpgimages/introduction.html.

3. G. S. Hunter, *Preserving Digital Information* (New York: Neal Schuman Publishers, 2000), 60–62.

4. Available at: http://www.getty.edu/research/tools/vocabularies.

5. Available at: http://preservationmatters.blogspot.com/2017/04/understanding-premis.html.

6. PREMIS Data Dictionary. Available at: http://www.loc.gov/standards/premis/v3/.

7. Council on Library and Information Resources. Available at: www.clir.org/pubs/reports/pub93/risk.html

8. Available at: http://chnm.gmu.edu/digitalhistory/links/pdf/chapter1/1.17.pdf.

9. Digital Preservation Coalition, available at: www.dpconline.org/graphics/handbook/.

SARAH RICE

4E | BASIC COMPONENTS OF INSTITUTIONAL ARCHIVES

ARCHIVES ARE CREATED AND maintained to preserve records of lasting value and to make them accessible for use. In addition to providing physical control of archival materials, a museum must consider the intended use and intellectual control of these records. The maintenance and retention of important records can be relatively simple once appropriate policies are established by the board, administration, and archivist or person serving in an archival capacity. Because there are similarities between the registrar's recordkeeping activities and the archivist's responsibilities, the registrar may be charged with administering the institutional archives in small- and medium-sized museums. There are several excellent publications on starting and maintaining an archive that will aid the successful archival administrator; some of these resources are noted in the bibliography at the end of this chapter.

Among the initial difficulties faced in establishing an archive are determining what to consider archival and understanding the terms applied to various types of materials. As stated by Julie Bressor in *Caring for Historical Records*,[1] the term *archive* can have several meanings, depending on its use, including the physical area housing the records; the agency responsible for selecting, preserving, and making the materials available; or a noncurrent record of an institution preserved because of its continuing value.

In many institutions library and archival materials are housed in the same areas for convenience of storage and handling. There are, however, some important distinctions that must be made between library and archival holdings, which differ in both form and function. Library materials generally are published resources concerning a single topic or series of related topics, whereas archival materials are generally the nonpublished and noncurrent records of an institution. These materials are usually compilations of records that are important to the operation or history of the institution but no longer active or needed for their original purpose. Some, such as annual reports, may be published. Other materials include manuscripts and printed documents and might include departmental records, correspondence, financial and personnel information, minutes, publicity, membership records, and so on. These records come in a variety of formats, including ledgers, scrapbooks, photographs, and audio- and videotapes. Computer-generated and digital records are created using a variety of formats and operating systems.

ESTABLISHMENT OF POLICIES AND PROCEDURES

For the most part, the archival records that are retained will be the products of institutional activities. A vital step in beginning an archive is to establish the policies and procedures that will govern the acquisition, arrangement, and use of both analog and digital material. The policies should be approved by and have the full support of the administration and governing body; they provide the framework for procedures and decisions. The following statements should be created.

- *Mission Statement*—Essentially a statement of purpose and goals, the mission statement should indicate the authority under which the archive is established and define its place in the overall organization of the institution. This statement may define which records will constitute the archive and who has the responsibility for carrying out the necessary tasks. Statements regarding collecting focus should be included. The mission statement should clearly indicate which materials created or compiled in the course of business are the property of the organization.

- *Statement of Authority or Organizational Placement*—A clear and concise statement of authority is necessary to establish internal support and should indicate where in the organization of the institution the archive is positioned. The higher the archival program is placed in the overall organizational structure, the greater the chance of achieving the goals set forth. This statement can be, but does not necessarily have to be, a part of the mission statement, according to Elizabeth Yakel in *Starting an Archives*.[2] It should make clear the authority, schedule, and frequency by which materials will be collected or transferred to the archive; the availability of the information; and conditions or restrictions governing the retention of materials. The policy may indicate the types of materials that will not be included because of overlap with another department. In any organization, certain materials and records have a defined period of use, beyond which the frequency of use declines. It is at that point that the materials should be transferred to the archive, provided that the information is considered to have lasting value. Establishing a schedule for transfer to the archive can facilitate the separation of the vital from the valueless and prevent the archive from becoming a storage area for unwanted records. Transfer schedules also help discourage an accumulation of inactive records that can lead to the loss of vital records through improper house cleaning. These schedules, as well as access policies, should be reviewed by counsel.

- *Access and Use Policies*—Every archive should have a policy defining the intended use of the materials in it, including statements regarding general access, restrictions, and use limitations. Procedures for requesting and copying records are based on this policy. In some cases, it may be necessary for several staff members to have daily access to the archival materials. In such cases, the development and implementation of standardized procedures regarding access is critical to maintaining good control over the records. It is important to have general statements about which records are considered open and which are subject to restrictions, about the conditions of restriction, and about the procedures required for use.

- *Collections Development or Management Policy*—The needs of the institution, its staffing, and its financial ability to maintain the records it creates are important considerations in establishing an archival collection policy. Collecting priorities should be based on input from the staff and administration. The collections policy should state what materials are acceptable and set priorities and limitations for collecting.

SCOPE OF THE COLLECTION OR ACQUISITION

Once physical control over the collection has been established, it is necessary to consider intellectual control and to make a determination regarding the permanent value of the records as this will determine what will be kept.

Various types of media, including paper, audio- or videotapes, computer-generated or digital records, photographs, film, other works on paper, and objects may be included in the archival record. Arguments can be made against the archive assuming responsibility for artifacts and some types of media. However, if no one else in the organization is able to care for these materials, the archivist may choose to assume the responsibility.

Appraisal is the process by which archivists evaluate the enduring value of records. The archival value can be assessed by projecting possible uses of the records for reference and research, determined by the information they contain on personnel, places, events, and activities. In some cases, individual items have an intrinsic value; that is, they are deemed worthy because of their creator, use, physical form, or content. Items or documents with intrinsic value are always kept in their original form.

In *Selecting and Appraising Archives and Manuscripts*,[3] F. Gerald Ham notes considerations that form the basic tools that are necessary to appraise records and identify and select those of enduring value. There should be:

- The record's functional characteristics—who created the record and for what purpose;
- The vital information contained in the record and how this information relates to other documentary sources;

- The potential uses for the record; and
- The physical, legal, and intellectual limitations on access.

THE COST OF PRESERVING THE RECORD WEIGHED AGAINST THE BENEFIT OF RETAINING THE INFORMATION

Records should be evaluated on the basis of their administrative value in addition to their long-term preservation and storage costs. Typically, institutional archival records include architectural and building plans, financial records, personnel records, board minutes, annual reports, publications, photographic records, audio- and videotapes, correspondence, departmental records, ephemera, memorabilia, and computer-generated or digital records including website(s) and social media content.

ARRANGEMENT AND DESCRIPTION OF THE COLLECTION

Archival arrangement is based on two important principles—*provenance* and *original order*. Most institutional records will come to the archive with a preexisting order indicating the particular way they were handled by the person or department that created them. The most important factor in the organization of archival records is their provenance, which includes maintaining the context in which the records were created. As stated by Ann Pederson in *Keeping Archives*,[4] the term provenance refers to the place of origin of the records (i.e., the organization or person that created, received, accumulated, and used the records in the conduct of business or life). Because archival records are the by-product of an institution, activity, or person, maintaining the context in which the record was created is essential to the future historical understanding of the organization, individual, or activity. Materials from one record creator or compiler, as Yakel notes,[5] should not be intermingled with those of another, despite similarities in subject matter.

The second principle of arrangement is original order. In other words, groups of records should be kept in their original order and not rearranged by the archivist. Any order originally imposed by the creator

of the records should be observed and followed. For example, it is not necessary to organize materials in a chronological manner if the creator did not. The original order provides information about the context of the records and rearrangement can be time-consuming and subjective. As a result, archivists tend to keep almost all existing coherent filing systems, even if they are not ideal. As Frederic M. Miller, author of *Arranging and Describing Archives and Manuscripts*[6] points out, the original order is preserved unless it is clearly detrimental to the use of the records being retained. If records do need to be rearranged, a careful plan should be prepared and outlined before any materials are actually moved. It may be necessary to remove special forms of materials from a collection (e.g., formats such as photographs or architectural drawings) to provide them with proper safe storage. If this is done, a note should be inserted identifying the item removed and its new location. This will preserve the context while allowing for safe storage. *Guidelines for Arrangement and Description of Archives and Manuscripts*,[7] a manual for historical records programs in New York State, provides these and other useful recommendations on arrangement.

Archival description is the process of gathering information about the origin, context, provenance, and original order of a group of records, as well as describing their physical and intellectual arrangement and recording that information in a standardized form. To describe a collection adequately, information should be included on the filing structure, format, scope and content, relationships with other records, and the ways in which information can be located.

For the most part, institutional records are in the form of a series, defined as a body of documents, maintained as a unit, and arranged according to a filing system. As stated by Pederson,[8] "a series consists of records which have been brought together in the course of their active life to form a discrete sequence. This sequence may be a discernible filing system, or it may simply be a grouping of records on the basis of similar function, content, or format." Typical series include minutes, correspondence, reports, newsletters, ledgers, etc. (see Frederic Miller's list of "Common Types of Functional Records Series"[9]).

The primary goal of description is to provide access to the information easily. The level of description chosen for each record should correspond to the research value and anticipated need for the information contained in the record.

When materials are transferred to the archive, the archivist must determine whether the value of the individual record is sufficient to warrant description by the item, by the file, or whether an overall description will be adequate to retrieve the necessary information.

Two excellent resources on what to consider and how to begin describing institutional records can be found in the publications *Guidelines for Arrangement and Description of Archives and Manuscripts*[10] and *Starting an Archives*.[11]

FINDING AIDS

Archives exist to house noncurrent records in a useful manner. In institutional archives, use will be primarily by staff of the institution for internal research and documentation. On occasion, the records will be used by historians and other researchers. To provide ready access to the information, finding aids are necessary. The finding aid, whether in the form of an index or narrative, should include the following:

- Information on the creator or the record;
- The volume of materials (e.g., a file folder or several boxes);
- Type of record (e.g., paper-based materials, photographs, maps, magnetic media, computer-generated, or digital records); and
- Intellectual contents and arrangement (organized by topic or medium, chronologically or alphabetically).

A condition statement is important, particularly if the materials are in poor physical condition. Any use restrictions or limitations due to condition or content should be noted.

It may be necessary to take the processing of some collections to a more detailed level than others. As varying levels of arrangement and description can be used in the processing of collections, flexibility is needed in the types of finding aids or user guides that are provided. For example, use by institutional staff may require the best stated, most current, or succinct records available; a historian or external researcher may require all available sources on a particular topic for a historical approach to the subject.

When examining a set of records, and during the arrangement and description inventory, all possible uses of the collection should be noted; this can save time when writing the finding aid for the records. Depending on the overall size of the collection, it may be necessary to provide physical finding aids for locating particular items within the collection. This is best handled by creating a container list indicating which box contains which information. Sometimes a folder list for each box is helpful or necessary.

RECORDS TRANSFER AND RETENTION SCHEDULES

The administration should establish a schedule of periodic transfer from the creator of the records to the archive. Prior to the transfer, it may be helpful to establish procedures that outline the steps to be followed when preparing the material for transfer. It may be necessary to provide a receipt for the items. Due to the nature of institutional records and record-keeping, the archive may receive transfers from the same source over time. The establishment of transfer guidelines will help ensure that the records are received in the same format and can be more easily integrated into an established series. Some records, such as personnel and financial materials, may be considered sensitive, and any restrictions on their use and access should be noted at the time of transfer.

STORAGE AND HANDLING

As with all museum collections, the storage and handling of archival materials plays a critical role in their longevity and thus comprises an important factor in the determination of the formats used to retain the information. Good storage equipment and cabinetry must be accompanied by proper handling by staff. In some cases, it will be necessary to limit use of certain records groups; any digitization, photocopying, and handling of such records should be conducted by trained personnel.

Most, if not all, of the records retained by the archive, no matter what the medium—paper, disc, tape, photographs—will deteriorate over time due to inherent vice. In paper collections, inherent vice can be the amount of acid incorporated in the paper during production. For discs and magnetic media, it could be the result of binder failure or deterioration of the binder layers. Digital formats are dependent on storage and retrieval equipment, file format, and changes in technology over time. These problems often are exacerbated by poor environmental conditions, including exposure to light, humidity, high temperature, air pollution, pests, and mold (see CHAPTER 51, "Preventive Care").

Most archival records are housed within a microenvironment provided by folders and boxes. Any materials that come into contact with records should be conservationally sound. Housekeeping is often a problem in records storage areas, so particular attention should be given to keeping these areas neat and dust free. There should be no eating, drinking, or smoking in the storage area or in any areas where the collections might be used. For a comprehensive discussion on the storage and housing of archival materials, before any new housing materials are acquired (see *Preserving Archives and Manuscripts*[12] by Mary Lynn Ritzenthaler).

SHELVING AND CABINETRY

All shelving and cabinetry used in the storage of archival records should be heavy-duty, nondamaging metal, strong enough to provide good physical support for the collection. Shelving with any physical problems such as sharp or damaged edges or rust should be avoided. To prevent falling, all shelving should be secured and bolted to the floor, to the wall, or the shelving units attached to each other across the top. The location of the storage units is important. If possible, shelving should not face windows because natural light will cause fading and produce heat. If windows are not avoidable, shades or curtains can provide some protection from light damage. It is also important to avoid placing the cabinetry units against exterior walls because the danger of moisture problems and leaks in those areas is greater. Bottom shelves should be at least six inches above the floor to guard against problems from water damage and pests.

Materials and finishes to be avoided include wood and wood products containing formaldehyde and materials that produce harmful gas as they age or deteriorate. These include press-board, chip board, plastic laminates, polyurethane paints and varnishes, and pressure-sensitive materials. Wooden shelves, drawers, and filing cabinets are not suitable for storage and should be avoided because they typically off-gas, and the acids that occur in wood can migrate to the materials stored in them. As a general rule, if the storage container or cabinet has or is producing an odor, it is not suitable storage for archival records.

STORAGE OF PAPER RECORDS

In most cases, paper boxes, folders, envelopes, and sleeves provide the best storage for archival records. Any materials that come into contact with the records should be nonacidic and buffered. Although many companies advertise archival materials, it is important to make sure that the advertising is truthful and that proper supplies are purchased.

The terms *acid-free*, *lignin-free*, and *100-percent rag* are all designations for conservationally sound materials. A variety of enclosures meet these criteria but have different features, such as reinforced hinges or a wider margin at the top. If possible, examine several different styles to determine those best suited to the collection. Paper enclosures have a number of advantages for storage; they provide support for the item enclosed, the alkaline reserve can help slow or prevent acid migration, and they are easily labeled.

One recognized disadvantage of paper enclosures is the inability to view the contents without removing them from their enclosure. This can result in mechanical damage, particularly to brittle paper. When ordering supplies, it may be best to purchase those enclosures that do not have a thumb cutout so that the contents are not always grasped in the same spot. All marking and labeling should be done in pencil, and not ink, because many inks are water soluble or can flake off when dry. Pressure-sensitive adhesive labels are not suitable because they have a tendency to peel off over time, leaving behind a sticky residue.

Plastic enclosures are available for archival material but should be used with caution. Moisture problems can develop inside plastic sleeves if there are temperature and humidity fluctuations. The plastic should not exude harmful materials or off-gas and plasticizers must not migrate into the stored materials. Good choices include polyethylene and polyester, which have a number of advantages, particularly for housing photographic collections; they are clear and allow immediate identification of the materials inside without the problem of fingerprints being transferred to the object inside. There are several disadvantages to the use of plastics: In addition to possible moisture problems, plastics can be difficult to label, they do not provide adequate support due to their inherent flexibility, and they are less permeable than paper and can trap decomposition products rather than allow them to dissipate. Plastic enclosures are not suitable for some media, such as pastels, or for any items with loosely adhered media because plastic can generate static electricity.

Both paper and plastic folders are suitable for housing in archival boxes or in hanging-file systems. For most purposes, acid-free boxes on proper shelving are considered optimum storage. Storage in boxes creates microenvironments that protect against light damage, dust, and fluctuations in temperature and relative humidity. Folders and boxes come in a variety of sizes. Housing for a collection should be determined by the physical size of the documents to be stored. Due to the depth of standard shelving units, it will be advantageous to use letter- or legal-sized supplies where possible. The size of the container used for a group of records should be determined by the dimensions of the majority of items in the set. Mixing folders of different sizes within the same box is not good practice.

Boxes should be relatively full to prevent the folders from sagging or curling and to keep the records from shifting unnecessarily when transported. The use of additional supports inside a partially full box, such as acid-free mat board interspersed with the folders, can help alleviate this problem. In some cases, it may be necessary to use a filler, such as an envelope or folder rolled into a tube or a commercially available box spacer to keep the records upright. Most plastic sleeves are flexible and will require additional support. Care should be taken not to overfill a box because this can result in mechanical damage to the records as they are removed and replaced.

Before archival objects are placed in permanent housing, nonpaper materials and metal fasteners, such as rubber bands and paper clips, should be removed because they will deteriorate over time and damage the items. The use of sticky notes (e.g., Post-it Notes) on anything considered archival is not acceptable because they are known to leave a slight residue that over time will attract fingerprints and dust. To prevent damage all papers should be unfolded and should fit inside the folder with no edges exposed.

Oversize items, such as mechanical drawings, blueprints, and maps, should be housed in cabinetry or boxes designed to accommodate them. Many vendors provide custom box services and can make enclosures to the exact dimensions needed. Storage of oversize boxes can be a problem because they need to be stored flat on a secure table. It is tempting to stack numerous boxes on top of one another, but this practice should be avoided or limited to stacks of no more than three boxes depending on the weight of the records inside. The optimum storage for oversize materials is to group them roughly by size for storage in a map or architectural file. The same rules for folders and labeling apply to oversize boxes. Many large items require additional support for storage and transport. Ideally, materials should be placed in heavyweight folders within drawers or boxes and supported by pieces of mat board cut to the size of the container and interspersed between every few folders. This will aid in the retrieval of items in the bottom. It is important to have adequate work space in areas where large records will be stored because this will minimize the distance for transport and encourage the user to take greater care in their use. Although several items may be placed in the same folder, common sense should dictate the number, based on the weight and fragility of the records.

Objects such as blueprints should be stored separately because they off-gas and are considered chemically unstable. Likewise, newsprint, which is highly acidic, should not be intermingled with other records in storage. A suitable photocopy on acid-free paper should be made to replace the newsprint in the record group and the actual newsprint itself should be stored separately.

STORAGE OF PHOTOGRAPHIC MATERIAL

Special care should be taken with photographic materials because they are highly susceptible to changes in temperature and relative humidity, light levels, and air quality. Easily damaged by environmental factors and improper handling, photographic prints and negatives require good storage and use practices to ensure their longevity. Under improper storage conditions, particularly high temperature or relative humidity, both positive and negative images may stick to an enclosure.

As with works on paper, there are several types of storage enclosures available, each with distinct advantages and disadvantages. It is important to take note of several factors in determining the proper care of photographs. Because of the diversity of photographic processes, and the inherent problems of each due to the chemical processes used, photographs are best stored individually. When organizing photographic collections care should be taken to note any materials, such as nitrate negatives, that are unstable and highly combustible; these materials should be isolated and stored apart from the rest of the collection. Ideally, a copy negative of the image should be made on safety film and the unstable materials removed to a safe storage area. Some institutions make the decision to save only the safety copies. For guidelines about preservation of film, see the Audio-Visual Conservation page by the Library of Congress.[13]

Black-and-white photographs are much more stable than color. When generating photographs as a means of documentation, good quality black-and-white film is a better choice than color. The film should be processed by a professional photographic lab, which adheres to American National Standards Institute (ANSI) standards. In some institutional archives, there is a photographic file that documents the activities of the organization. In other cases, the photographs may be supplementary information in an existing records file. In cases where a photograph will remain in another file, it is important that it be housed in a stable enclosure that separates it physically from the rest of the file.

Prints should be stored separately from negatives because of differences in the chemical stability and to guard against a complete loss in the event of disaster. Photographs taken in digital formats should follow the recommendations for organization and storage of electronic records.

STORAGE OF ELECTRONIC RECORDS AND MAGNETIC MEDIA

Increasingly, electronic records are being created and stored on a variety of media that require special storage considerations. Because technology is rapidly changing and many types of media have not been in existence long enough for guidelines for their care and use to have been established, they cannot be termed archival. Many paper-based records will deteriorate over time because of inherent instabilities, overuse and handling, and possible environmental problems. Reformatting heavily used paper items as digital or magnetic media can be essential to their preservation. The disadvantage of some of these media is that they require continual upgrading as technology changes; it will be necessary to maintain the equipment on which the media was generated to use it unless the records are transferred to another medium each time the technology changes.

The newer the technology, the less is known about its stability and longevity. The following section discusses some considerations necessary for the proper storage and handling of these media, based on current practices and information available on their longevity.

STORAGE OF MAGNETIC TAPE

Magnetic tape is comprised of a magnetic recording layer on a flexible support. Manufacturers consider the physical makeup and particular characteristics of their tapes trade secrets, which makes it difficult to obtain reliable information about the physical components of various brands. The quality of audio- and videotape varies greatly between manufacturers and types of tape. The formats currently used are housed within either a cartridge, which has one spool, or a cassette, which has two spools. Magnetic tapes housed on open or reel-to-reel spools are considered obsolete and should be reformatted. When purchasing tape for archival use, buy the best grade available. Shorter reels, although more expensive, are preferred because the tape is thicker and thought to have greater durability.

Most magnetic media are susceptible to static charge and can easily attract a variety of debris. If possible, storage of magnetic media should be in uncarpeted, unwaxed areas that are damp-mopped regularly. Storage should be on fixed metal shelving away from sources of heat, light, airborne contaminants, and mechanical equipment that might create magnetic fields. Tapes should be stored vertically in enclosures that protect them from dust and debris. The housing that tapes are purchased in is rarely suitable for storage. Good quality, inert plastic enclosures provide the best support and should include an interior hub to support the weight of the tape during storage. For long-term storage, tapes should be wound through at normal speed in the environment in which they are to be stored. On occasion, rewinding the tape can result in the breaking of the leader at the beginning of the tape; stopping in the middle of the tape can result in cinching or fold over of the tape in the pack and can irreparably damage it. Tapes should be wound through at least once every three years to help prevent sticking or transfer of information; the tape itself should never be marked, because this can introduce contamination.

Storage of Optical Disks

Digital technology that allows the storage of large quantities of information may provide the basis for records storage in the future. There are two types of optical discs—compact discs (CD) and digital versatile discs (DVD). Both are available in read-only, recordable, and rewriteable formats. No standards have been developed, and there is insufficient information at this time to judge the physical stability of the discs themselves because this technology is still in flux. According to the Digital Preservation Department of the National Archives, research suggests that recordable CDs (CD-Rs), which use a gold reflective layer and phthalocyanine-based dyes, are the most suitable for archival purposes. These often are referred to as gold/gold discs. Although differing claims as to the stability of various brands and types of discs have been made, it is believed that they will last longer than other technologies and are suitable for archival preservation. Rewritable discs should not be used as a long-term storage option. The DVD is considered a recent development and its archival qualities are not yet well understood. If used, the same recommendations as for the selection of compact discs apply.

The general storage requirements governing magnetic media also apply to discs. Discs should be handled by the edges or center hole; the recording area should not be touched. While both surfaces of the discs should be handled with caution, the upper surface is the data-carrying layer. Adhesive labels should never be used because they can damage the data layer; discs can be marked on the upper surface using water-soluble ink. Archival quality plastic cases made from inert polyester are recommended. Rigid cases should be used, as they provide greater protection than paper enclosures.

It is important never to leave any type of magnetic media in the open where it is susceptible to dust, damage, or scratching. This includes the common practice of placing the discs on top of the computer (a source of heat) between use. Use lint-free cotton gloves when handling archival storage discs to safeguard against the transfer of fingerprints and debris. Discs and tapes should be stored vertically, with support; leaning or slanting can cause distortion of the media.

Solid-State Media

Solid-state storage devices include compact flash, SmartMedia, and other formats used in digital cameras, laptops, and similar devices. Referred to as *memory cards* or *memory sticks*, these are developing technologies and, as such, are not considered suitable for archival storage. They often are used for the transfer of information and require the same standards of care in handling as other media. The contacts should not be touched, and any labeling should be applied within the approved label area.

DIGITAL ARCHIVAL COLLECTIONS

Today much of the ongoing business of institutions—large and small—is recorded digitally and fewer physical copies of information resources are produced. This includes event and collection photographs, cataloging records, correspondence, loan requests, minutes, etc. Many museums have begun to maintain digital archives for the business they conduct using digital technology as well as for other records. These collections should be retained and managed in the same manner that paper-based records are kept. Digitization allows access and use of information recorded on friable, paper-based collection documents, while creating a preservation copy of the original.

DIGITAL REPOSITORIES

Many institutions use digital formats on a daily basis. Records that once were created and stored in analog (paper) formats are now created—and must be stored—digitally. Use of digital formats requires a plan for their long-term availability and access to the information. A digital repository consists of records in digital format; some will have been created digitally, others reformatted from analog or paper records. Creating a digital archive or repository that continues the organization and retrieval historically used for institutional records produced on paper and other media will ensure continued access to information.

DIGITAL COLLECTIONS MANAGEMENT

Like the analog collections they are replacing, digital collections require a collection management strategy, an ongoing commitment to staff training, and dedicated financial resources. Unlike paper records, which can be used long after their creation even if they are poorly housed, electronic records require constant attention. Integrating a digitization policy into the normal staff workflow, along with providing written guidelines and ongoing staff training is an important component of any digital collection policy.

The choice of hardware, software, and storage (e.g., cloud-based, second- or third-party hosting, or internal) systems should be based on the type of in-formation, intended users, identified search parameters, and type of display or retrieval necessary. For example, a storage-and-retrieval system suitable for photographs may not be suitable for other types of records. The hardware and software systems must be maintained, upgraded, and converted to new formats as technologies change. Current methods for backup systems—such as external memory sticks and CDs—will be obsolete in the future, requiring continual reformatting to new technology. Otherwise, valuable information will be lost due to the inability to retrieve it.

STANDARDS

Digital technology is still considered new, and countless types of formats, hardware, and software are available. Some choices will result in a long-term commitment to a specific technology, and it may not be possible to archive formats that are dependent on specific programs or equipment as the field is rapidly developing and changing. Before undertaking a digitization effort, each institution needs to examine the purpose of the project; its ability to sustain it financially; the ability, dedication, and interest of the staff; the growth of the information over time; and the intended use of the information. The Association of Research Libraries[14] has accepted digitization as a preservation formatting method and has published accepted standards and best practices for maintaining digital collections long term. The life span of any electronic storage medium is reliant both on the physical longevity of the equipment needed to retrieve it and on the current technology.

STRATEGIES

There are numerous reformatting methods and strategies, each has strengths and weaknesses. Most institutions employ a combination of methods that suit their needs and are in keeping with their staffing and financial resources. For example, many institutions use digital cameras to record events, document incoming loans, and record individual collection objects as part of their basic condition reporting, while continuing to create paper documents for correspondence, minutes, etc. Most institutions use both paper records and e-mail records to carry out business. Each institution needs to develop a strategy for reconciling information in different formats by either printing out important e-mails or by digitizing the paper copies to have a complete record.

Libraries have taken a leading role in identifying system design and business models to sustain collections of digital objects. In addition to the standards set by the Association of Research Libraries, work is being done at the national level by the Library of Congress, which has been charged to develop a National Digital Information Infrastructure for Preservation,[15] and the National Archives and Records Administration, which has established an Electronic Records Archive.[16] These organizations can provide ongoing guidance regarding research, digital preservation, models, and strategies.

As with all museum collections, archival records should be examined periodically as a preventive measure. Because many records will be housed in folders and boxes and in a variety of formats, it may be difficult to discover developing problems unless an inventory or collections survey (if only a random sampling) is done on a periodic basis. •

SOURCES OF USEFUL INFORMATION

Boles, F. 2005. *Selecting and Appraising Archives and Manuscripts*. Chicago: Society of American Archivists.

Bettington, J., K. Eberhard, R. Loo, and C. Smith (eds.). 2008. *Keeping Archives*, 3rd ed. Australian Society of Archivists. Available at: https://www.archivists.org.au/learning-publications/keeping-archives-3rd-ed (accessed August 19, 2019).

Bressor, J. P. 1988. *Caring for Historical Records: An Introduction; Workshop Outlines, and Resource Materials*. Storrs, CT: New England Archivists Education Project.

Ogden, S. 1996. *Preservation of Library and Archival Materials: A Manual*, 3rd ed. Andover, MD: Northeast Document Conservation Center.

Roe, K. 2005. *Arranging and Describing Archives and Manuscripts*. Chicago: Society of American Archivists.

Wythe, D. (ed.). 2004. *Museum Archives: An Introduction*, 2nd ed. Chicago: Society of American Archivists.

Yakel, E. 1994. *Starting an Archives*. Lanham, MD: Scarecrow Press.

NOTES

1. J. P. Bressor, *Caring for Historical Records: An Introduction, Workshop Outlines, and Resource Materials* (Storrs, CT: New England Archivists Education Project, 1988).

2. E. Yakel, *Starting an Archives* (Lanham, MD: Scarecrow Press, 1994).

3. F. G. Ham, *Selecting and Appraising Archives and Manuscripts* (Chicago: Society of American Archivists, 1993).

4. A. Pederson, *Keeping Archives* (Sydney: Australian Society of Archivists, 1987).

5. Yakel, *Starting an Archives*.

6. F. M. Miller, *Arranging and Describing Archives and Manuscripts* (Chicago: Society of American Archivists, 1990).

7. K. Roe, *Guidelines for Arrangement and Description of Archives and Manuscripts: A Tool for Historical Records Programs in New York State* (University of the State of New York, 1991).

8. Pederson, *Keeping*.

9. Available at: http://datadrivenarchives.pbworks.com/f/Processing+Manual+St.+Johnsbury+Athenaeum.pdf (accessed June 7, 2019).

10. Roe, *Guidelines*.

11. Yakel, *Starting*.

12. Mary Lynn. Ritzenthaler, *Preserving Archives and Manuscripts* (Chicago: Society of American Archivists, 1993).

13. Available at: http://www.loc.gov/avconservation/ (accessed June 7, 2019).

14. Available at: https://www.arl.org/.

15. Available at: https://www.loc.gov/loc/lcib/0601/ndiipp2.html.

16. Available at: https://www.archives.gov/era.

This chapter has been updated from a previous chapter by K. Sharon Bennet.

PART 5 | **COLLECTIONS MANAGEMENT**

5A | Numbering

JOHN E. SIMMONS AND TONI M. KISER

To track museum collection objects—to differentiate between permanent, on-loan, and subsidiary collections, and most important, to provide access to the documentation of objects in a collection—it is vital that a systematic numbering scheme be used. The numbers assigned to objects are marked on most permanent collection objects, tagged onto objects in temporary custody, and prominently noted on all documentation associated with the objects.

Museums have tried many numbering systems over the years (BOX 5A.1). The most important thing about a number, whether permanent or temporary, is that it be unique because it is the link between the object and its documentation. Without a unique number an object is at risk of losing its context and information relating to its legal status. Sequential numbering (1, 2, 3, 4), based on early library accessioning systems, is simple and has been used by many museums (it is the current standard in most natural history collections). The system is simple—the first object gets number 1, the second object is number 2, and on into infinity. Simple sequential numbers do not show what the relationship is between objects (e.g., year of accession into the collection) so many museums choose a two-part system that incorporates the year of accession and an object number (e.g., 76.21-27, 1976.28). Simple sequential series have the advantage that sequential numbers are far easier to transcribe (particularly when entering them into an electronic database) and mark on objects without error; it is far easier to write 69482 correctly than 2019.12.342. The two-part system has the advantage of communicating some information about the object (e.g., year of accession), but the numbers are more prone to transcription error and can be long to mark on small objects as well as receipts, deeds of gift, warranties of title, etc.

Box 5A.1 Commonly Used Numbering Systems in Museums*

Description	Number	Definition
Permanent collection, legally owned objects; compound numbers	2010.1	First transaction of the year 2010
	2010.1.1	First object is a single unit
	2010.1 .1.1-10	First object is a set of ten pieces
	2010.1.1a, b	First object is a pair, two parts
Suggestions for temporary records, short and long-term loans	TR1.2010	Transaction, first of year 2010
	TR1.2010.1	First object in the transaction
	L.2010.1	First loan of the year 2010
	L1.2010	
	L2010.1.1	First object of first loan of the year 2010
	L1.2010.1	

NOTE

*Museums may also develop numbers for long-term loans to differentiate them from exhibition loans, and for long-term incoming loans. Supplemental collections may have yet another number. It is always best to keep numbering systems to a minimum and to keep them as simple as possible.

An argument can be made that there is no need for an object number to carry information because that information is recorded elsewhere; instead, the number should be simple to use and easy to transcribe. In the end, what is most important is that the number system in use be consistent. If a collection has not yet been numbered, it is worth pondering the pros and cons of simple sequential series, but if the numbering system has been in use for some time—particularly if information about the objects has been published using their object numbers—it is probably best to retain the old system.

The use of electronic databases can overcome most of the difficulties caused by various early numbering systems, as long as every number used is unique (but computers can also multiply human mistakes at an astounding rate). For example, it is possible to impose a transaction number on sequential or separated objects and pull them together in a database. If 21.3-10 and 21.15 are found to both be from the same transaction, the registrar can review the year and systematically assign a transaction number to which all pertinent object records can be attached (e.g., 1921.3).

Systems with alphabetical prefixes are popular, but they can become cumbersome if the prefix refers to a collection category, a geographical location or a department. Any of those categories may become obsolete or inaccurate with the renaming or reorganization of the referenced categories. A prefix may, however, be useful for loan collections, temporary custody, or for subsidiary collections used for teaching purposes, but is not recommended for permanent collections (BOX 5A.2).

Museums with several numbering systems may find that the systems become confused. Some museums have found it helpful to retire old, complicated systems and implement a single standard system, but in general it is inadvisable to attempt to renumber a large permanent collection (and in any case, it is likely to induce many errors). A single system applied from a certain date forward will simplify recordkeeping for current and future activity. Attempts to renumber almost always end in chaos.

It is important to be consistent in numbering once a preferred system has been selected. Separate numbering systems must be available for objects in temporary custody and permanent holdings, and each system must have its own sequence. If several departments use different systems, they must communicate and make certain that their systems do not overlap and create duplicate numbers. Because collections management databases usually use the assigned number to identify a record about an object duplicate numbers will lead to confusion.

OLD NUMBERS

Old numbers arise in collections in a variety of ways—a change in the scheme used to number objects, the acquisition of a collection assigned numbers by a previous institution, or unintended duplication within a collection. It is important that old numbers be kept as part of the institutional history of an object. However, the old number should be physically removed from the object (if it is possible to do so without harming the object) and the new number applied (see CHAPTER 5F, "Marking"). Most collection management systems have a field that allows for tracking old numbers that should be used to keep track of any old number associated with an object. These numbers will likely be referenced in old documentation, publications, catalogs, and files, so keeping old numbers associated with the object aides in tracking its whole history. Additionally, both the old numbers and the new numbers now assigned should also be recorded in any acquisition files.

Numbers for Objects in Temporary Custody

A numbering system for objects in temporary custody helps track objects and associated documentation until the objects are accessioned and or returned to their owner. The temporary number may be structured in parallel with the accession number system,

---

BOX 5A.2   PREFIXES GONE WRONG

Number prefix	Possible meanings
C	Cambodia, Ceylon, coins, crosses
P	Painting, Persia, Peru, Portugal, pottery
S	Science, sculpture

as described here, or may bear a T (Temporary,) TR (Temporary Record), or other prefix (L for loan, E for exhibition, etc.) to distinguish it. Some institutions chose to use what amounts to an accession number in reverse, that is, "16.1996" instead of "1996.16."

Accession Numbers

Perhaps the accession numbering system most widely used in the United States is a compound number separated by a point or hyphen. In this system, the first number indicates the year the object is accessioned and may be the whole year (1995) or a part year (995 or 95). The whole year is recommended to avoid confusion in the future (and if it was not used in the past, it should have been started with the year 2000). The second number indicates the sequence of the accession by which the object was formally taken into the collection such that 1995.1, 1995.2, and 1995.3 indicate the first three accessions of 1995. If there is only one object in the transaction, the two-part number typically suffices (this is common in art museums). If more than one object is included in the accession, a third number is usually assigned to each object, as in 1995.4.1, 1995.4.2, 1995.4.3. If an object is a set, portfolio, or consists of several parts, the number may have four parts (e.g., 1995.4.3.1, 1995.4.3.2). To identify component parts of an object (such as a box with a lid, a chest with removable drawers, a sculpture that can be disassembled, or a tea set) some museums prefer to use alphabetic suffixes such as 1995.4.3.a, 1995.4.3.b, etc. (see BOX 5A.3).

In a compound numbering system in which each separate object has its own distinct identification through the accession number, the transactions for each year can be easily counted. The system allows for growth because each year starts with transaction 1 and ends with the last transaction of the year. Future research that changes the intellectual classification of objects will not interfere with the number. If an object was overlooked during initial accessioning, it can be added later at the end of the sequence for an individual transaction. Number systems that use an alphabetic or numeric identifier for the objects category, site of origin, or some other information (e.g., 1995.A4.3.1 for an object from the art collection, 1995.F4.3.1 for an object from the furniture collection) can be useful but make it difficult to reclassify objects and create numbers that make transcription more problematic.

In some types of museums, most notably archaeology and natural history museums, a single accession number is applied to all of the objects received at the same time from the same source, which may be a single object, dozens, hundreds, or thousands of objects (BOX 5A.4). Rather than mark individual objects

---

BOX 5A.3 EXAMPLES OF THE STANDARD NUMBERING SYSTEM

Portfolio of eight photographs	1997.1.1.1-8
Six separate photographs	1997.1.2-7
Coffee pot with tray	1997.1.8a-c (pot, cover, tray)
Painting	1997.1.9
Pair of shoes	1997.1.10a, 1997.1.10.b
Single object purchased	1997.2

BOX 5A.4 THE NUMBERING RACKET

One of the best ways to ensure that numbers are not duplicated is to use a standardized system. In the first edition of *Museum Registration Methods* (published in 1958), Dorothy Dudley and Irma Bezold described object identification numbers in the broad context of their use for accessions, extended loans, or loans for exhibition. There was a reference to a type of catalog number they called a *curatorial number*. By the third edition (1979), however, the glossary compiled by Patricia Nauert was specific in differentiating between the two, defining an accession number as "a control number, unique to an object, whose purpose is identification, not description," and a catalog number as

a term used in a variety of ways in museums: (1) in some museums, a catalogue number is assigned to an object or specimen based on its class; its purpose is description; (2) in some museums, the number described in this book as an accession number is called a catalogue number, in which case its purpose is identification; (3) the number assigned to an object in a printed publication or catalogue of a special exhibition or collection.

with an accession number (which would result in many objects with the same number), the individual objects or specimens are marked with catalog numbers. Thus, an accession number (e.g., 1995.13) may be assigned to a group of 310 specimens of frogs collected on a single expedition to Peru in 1995, but the individual specimens in the accession will be numbered sequentially as 69012, 69013, etc. The accession record would indicate that it included specimens numbered 69012-69322 in the catalog.

Numbering Unprocessed Collections

Registrars are often faced with an array of unprocessed material from the near and distant past (see CHAPTER 3J, "Found in Collection"). To track these objects, it is recommended that they be assigned temporary numbers until their status is clarified.

Title must be transferred to a museum before an object can be considered part of the permanent collection and accessioned; thus, objects on loan are not part of the permanent collection and should receive temporary numbers for tracking (or better, use the number on the object from the loaning museum). Up until the early to mid-nineteenth century it was not uncommon that all objects coming into the museum—loans, gifts, purchases, bequests—were considered accessioned because accessioning was more about tracking than it was about the permanent collection. In current museum practice, only objects that are owned by the museum are accessioned into the permanent collection (see CHAPTER 3B, "Acquisitions and Accessioning"). •

This chapter has been edited and updated from previous chapters by Rebecca Buck with thanks to Anne Furhman Douglas, Connie Estep, Monique Maas Gibbons, Paulette Dunn Hennum, Kittu Longstreth-Brown, and Dominique Schultes.

5B | OBJECT HANDLING

DIXIE NEILSON

OF ALL DANGERS TO museum collections, the harm that can be done by human interaction is by far the most common. Although we may design elaborate systems for preventing fire, theft, and other disasters, mere common sense and a thoughtful approach can prevent us from mishandling the objects we are entrusted to safeguard. Therefore, we should handle objects as little as possible and only when absolutely necessary. The "General Rules" section in this chapter contains object-handling procedures and information applicable to most types of museum collection objects and should be reviewed before moving to more specific instructions. Further information of a more specific nature is available from sources such as the American Alliance of Museums[1] (AAM), the American Association for State and Local History[2] (AASLH), the National Park Service[3] (NPS), the Society for the Preservation of Natural History Collections[4] (SPNHC), as well as many other organizations in the museum community. The bibliography provides further resources.

WHO SHOULD HANDLE COLLECTIONS OBJECTS?

Those without prior training in museum object handling should not touch any object in the collection (education collection items excepted). This philosophy is almost universally accepted as a basic standard of care in museums. The registrar or collections manager is charged with responsibility for the collections and, therefore, has the final say in determining who may handle and move the museum's objects. Beyond that basic tenet, museums differ regarding who among the staff is permitted to handle objects. Some museums do not allow volunteers or interns to touch any of the collections, and others allow handling by a variety of staff members.

Whatever the policy may be, no one should be allowed to handle objects until they have been provided with specific training which may, at the registrar's discretion, include readings, informational videos, hands-on practice with noncollection objects, or a fairly lengthy apprenticeship—supervised time working with another, more experienced handler. Generally, curators and the director are assumed to have at least a basic knowledge of handling museum objects, and therefore, they are not prohibited from touching collections. The practices in the institution should be explained in the collections management policy (see CHAPTER 2, "Collection Management Policies").

Handling museum objects is a serious responsibility and should not be taken lightly. Those who work with objects should demonstrate an understanding of the obligations they assume as cultural stewards of the museum's collection and professional members of the staff. Individuals who are conscientious, attentive to detail, and reasonably self-assured are favored over those who are overly impulsive, impatient, or arrogant. A person who is anxious or tense may find working with objects to be too stressful to be of benefit to the department. Case-by-case judgments on handling readiness must be made by supervisors, taking into consideration, experience, general demeanor, and attitude.

Keep in mind that museums that have loaned objects to your institution may have a handling policy that differs from your practices. Before allowing untrained staff, volunteers, or interns to handle objects borrowed from other institutions be sure to review the loan agreement. If the lender stipulates who may or may not handle their objects you are under a legal, contractual duty to follow their requirements. A lender's wishes take precedence over your normal practices. Any objections to lender requests should be resolved before the loan agreement is signed.

GENERAL RULES

Museum collections are made up of many types of objects and although some handling practices can be type-specific, most procedures usually fall into just a few categories. Becoming familiar with guidelines for handling two-dimensional objects (such as paintings and works on paper) and three-dimensional items (such as sculpture, furniture, and artifacts) will prepare you for most object-handling situations.

All objects have some handling rules in common—prepare yourself, do not rush, plan ahead, and think through your procedures before laying a hand on any object. Just as a careful driver anticipates problems on the road, so should one planning to move museum objects from place to place. Ask yourself what could go wrong and if it does, what your response will be to decrease the chance of bringing harm to the object or yourself. Cultural caretakers should handle museum objects thoughtfully and with the utmost regard for each object and with appropriate consideration for culturally sensitive objects.[5] Monetary value should not be a consideration—each object should be presumed to have exactly the same value as all of the others—priceless.

All objects should be protected from overexposure to light because light damage is cumulative; objects can never regain their color, nor fabrics their flexibility and strength. We may euphemistically refer to an object in storage as resting, but this gives the false impression that we can reverse damage done by light or other environmental conditions just by leaving objects alone. Unlike living creatures, objects do not improve in a resting state; their rate of deterioration is only slowed.

Numerous studies have been done on least damaging light levels and exposure times for materials—consult a current source for the best information. Although keeping light exposure at a minimum in storage is beneficial, a muted light in an exhibition is not always ideal. Videos made to study the effects of low lighting on museumgoers show that when a museum object is too dimly lit visitors often lean in closely to see the object's details, then lean out to read the label, and then they lean in again. In our attempt to create an ideal environment for objects we cannot overlook the fact that by using light that is too low we can create a danger of a different type. A balance must be struck that works for the objects and the people viewing them. As lighting technologies evolve it is important to periodically review the museum's lighting systems and evaluate whether changes are due.

Keep all harmful materials away from the objects. Do not allow eating, drinking, or smoking in any area that contains collection objects, either in storage or on exhibit. A ban on living plants is recommended for museums because plants present a serious risk of pest infestations. Not all institutions want to prohibit plants but any area where collections are stored or exhibited should be strictly off limits to living greenery. Potted plants on desks, decorative plants in the lobby, and floral deliveries all put the collections at risk. If plants are allowed in the museum you must be extra vigilant when inspecting for pests wherever your objects are located.

Never work with tools directly above an object. When photographing an object from above keep the camera strap around your neck. Remind visitors and staff not to bring pens or markers into the exhibition galleries or storage rooms. Docents can help by announcing the no pen rule at the beginning of any tour and can provide pencils for those who wish to take notes. A notice concerning restrictions on pen usage in the galleries should be posted at the front desk, along with a supply of pencils for those unaware of the policy. Standing too close to an object while innocently pointing at it with a pen in hand (something that seems to be a notorious trait among all humans) invites damage that can leave an indelible mark on the object and on the museum's reputation.

Although it is common sense to avoid contact with known contaminants such as food, drink, and infested plants, other concerns are not so obvious. Various solvents, including some paints, plastics, new carpeting and flooring, and wood materials such as plywood and particle board all have the potential to off-gas. Off-gassing refers to the release of airborne particulates or vapors called volatile organic compounds (VOCs). Some VOCs, including benzene and formaldehyde, are suspected or known carcinogens that pose a health hazard. Objects may be harmed by off-gassing as well because the chemicals may increase rates of deterioration, especially for sensitive substances such as textiles, feathers, photographs, and silver objects, among others. Other than wood used in new construction or flooring materials, the VOCs that pose the greatest risk include those off-gassed inside new or freshly painted display and storage cases, which have low rates of air exchange.

It is difficult to say precisely how long a material needs to off-gas because chemicals and situations vary.[6] Considerations include how much of the product is used and local ventilation. Studies done in 2010 indicate a minimum of sixty days for most VOCs to sufficiently disperse and anywhere from two to eight weeks for smaller projects. Recommendations to shorten the off-gassing period include opening windows for an extended length of time, something most museums cannot do. Rather than trying to determine when VOCs have dissipated, consider using products with low VOCs. A prudent course of action is to know and understand the chemicals in use in your museum and to choose materials, particularly paints, that have a low incidence of VOCs.[7]

The US Department of Health and Human Services maintains a household products database that provides a list of the ingredients of most chemical products sold in the country, listed both by product name and by chemical name.[8] In addition, manufacturers and vendors (including retail stores) of chemical substances are required by federal law to provide a Safety Data Sheets (SDS) upon request, and there are the SDS online services as well.[9] A SDS contains information on the specific chemicals in the product, hazards associated with the chemicals, and first aid measures in case of an adverse reaction to a chemical.

When handling museum objects care should be taken to protect both the object and the handler. In most cases gloves should be worn to prevent transfer of oils and other metabolic products (including various salts) to the object. Even a trace of oil on an object attracts dust, dirt, and minute but sharp pieces of grit that can degrade the surface. A fingerprint left on a painting, drawing, or textile today can cause it to begin to deteriorate in a short period of time, with visible damage in less than five years.

Gloves provide protection to both the object being handled and to the person wearing them. White cotton gloves, once the symbol of cleanliness and care, are not appropriate for handling all objects in a museum. Rough surfaces or edges may get snagged by cloth gloves and slick surfaces are difficult to grasp and may slip from cotton gloves. Cotton gloves may absorb chemicals they come into contact with and, thus, are not always a sufficient barrier for objects that are composed of or have been in contact with hazardous materials.

Cotton gloves should be changed as soon as they get dirty or if your hands become particularly sweaty. Cotton gloves usually need to be changed several times a day. Wearing dirty gloves does not protect the objects and may spread grime and other contaminants. Keep dirty gloves in a separate container so they are not accidentally reused. Wash white cotton gloves in warm water with a mild soap with few additives, such as detergents meant for baby diapers, and rinse them twice. Do not use a separate conditioner or a dryer sheets because these products may leave oils and other chemicals imbedded in the gloves. Line dry cotton gloves if possible.

Several synthetic, rubber-like materials allow for a good grip while affording protection to the object and those handling it, including powder-free nitrile gloves (preferred for handling many objects in natural history collections), butyl gloves (that provide a chemical barrier except against petroleum and other hydrocarbons), and neoprene (a material resistant to snags, punctures, abrasions, and cuts). Latex gloves should not be used because of the high incidence of latex allergies and because latex is a poor chemical barrier.

Not all objects require the use of gloves and some museums specifically prohibit cloth gloves when handling books or other delicate paper objects because they reduce the wearer's dexterity. Bulky cotton gloves may accidentally snag objects and some materials (such as glass, ceramics, fossils or nonporous stone) are less likely to be harmed by glove-free hands. Objects with slick surfaces may slip through a cotton-gloved hand.

Evaluate the object you are preparing to handle. If you are concerned that it is not suitable for the use of gloves, wash your hands with a delicate, unscented soap before handling the object. However, keep in mind that recent conservation research suggests that washing hands accelerates the secretion of oils on fingers, making freshly washed hands oilier than they were before washing. As with any museum method, use your best judgment based on the best information available, and keep up with evolving practices.

Gloves protect the wearer. Museum collections include many objects that contain harmful toxins. Ritual objects may have traces of blood, feces, or poisons on them (e.g., curare-tipped arrows and darts). Objects may have been treated with pesticides including arsenic, mercury, or other poisons. Bones and fossils may be contaminated with radiation from the ground where they were excavated. Objects may have been exposed to particulates (e.g., asbestos, rodent feces carrying hanta virus) that present health risks. Although cotton gloves may absorb these toxins, newer synthetic glove materials are superior to cotton in protection from these risks. Stay informed, know what you are handling, and how to protect yourself when working with any object. For further protection wear a lab coat or apron that can be removed and washed separately from other clothing and, if appropriate, use a respirator to keep from inhaling anything harmful.

Each time you prepare to handle museum objects consider your route and the object to be moved. Examine your hands (whether gloved or not they should be clean). Clothing should be free of anything that could catch on an object, scratch, or tear it. To provide a snag-free surface wear a clean, bibbed apron or lab coat with empty pockets. If you wear glasses use a safety strap to ensure that they do not fall off. Remove jewelry including watches, dangling earrings, and necklaces. Tie back long hair while you work. ID badges or chains should be removed or tucked inside your clothing. Clothing should permit free movement without danger of dragging across an object. Shoes should be of a design and material that allows you to stand stable and slip-free.

Examine Your Route

Prior to picking up any object know where you will set it down again and ensure that the space is still available. Arriving at your intended destination with an object in hand and finding nowhere to put it requires some quick thinking on your part and creates an unnecessary risk for the object. Know where you are going, by what route you will get there, and make sure the pathway is clear and unencumbered. Plan how you will open doors; avoid stairs if possible. Turn on lights in advance so that you have a clear view of your path. Be aware of any cords or other obstructions lying in your path and remove them if possible. Do not hesitate to ask someone to accompany you if you need help with these maneuvers. If you must travel through public areas of the museum, it is best to do so before or after open hours when there is little traffic.

Examine the Object

Before touching an object look it over to see if there are any obvious areas of concern. Gently check that attached parts are secure but do not assume attachments can bear much weight. Review existing condition reports for information about known problems. After satisfying yourself that the object seems stable, handle it as though it is not.

Examine Your Tools

Carts, flatbeds, and dollies should be clean and free of flaking or rusting paint, and their rubber wheels in good shape. Carpet squares or padding should be soft, snag free, and clean. Carry only one object at a time, no matter how small.

When lifting heavy objects maintain proper posture—keep your back straight and let your leg muscles do most of the work (FIGURE 5B.I). Good body posture prevents or reduces debilitating back problems. Use of an industrial back support belt helps reduce the risk of injury caused by repetitive motions and acts as a reminder to use proper lifting techniques. Supervisors should monitor staff lifting techniques and ensure they are not overexerting themselves. Workplace injuries from lifting are common but preventable with correct practices and equipment.

Do not hand objects from one person to another; set the object down and have the other person pick it up. If you are alone, resist the urge to lift or move objects beyond your capacity. Wait until you have assistance.

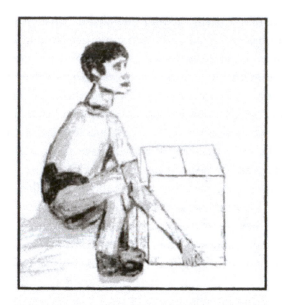

If the size or weight of an object is such that it takes two people to carry it (generally more than fifty pounds) they should communicate with each other during the entire move. Discuss in advance exactly how and where each of you will hold the object and move toward your destination. Be aware of your surroundings so that you do not bump into furniture or other objects, especially if your view is partially blocked by the object you are carrying. Neither person should walk backward while carrying the object, if possible. Have a third person to accompany you to open doors, watch as you go through doorways, and generally provide assistance. Keep the conversation focused on the move; this is not the time to discuss other matters.

Use a ladder or step-stool (never a chair) to reach objects above head height. Make sure the ladder is secure before stepping on the first rung. If the ladder has locking wheels make sure the lock is engaged before you climb on it. Have another person below, ready to receive the object from you.

Carts and flatbed trucks used to move objects should have rubber or pneumatic wheels to provide smooth transportation. If you need to push a cart over a bumpy surface, such as the floor of the freight elevator, lay down plywood to make that part of the trip as smooth as you can. Make sure the object is fully and properly placed on the cart so it cannot slip off or protrude over the edge. If necessary, carefully strap the object down to prevent movement. To protect the object place padding underneath the straps and be sure they are secure without being too tight. If needed, one person may steady the object on the cart as a second person moves the cart (FIGURE 5B.2).

Be aware of your physical limitations. Do not work while fatigued; take breaks as needed. Work at a steady pace, without hurry, and stop before either your muscles or your wits are worn out.

Do what you can to make lifting and carrying easier. Crates should have smooth hand-holds and rounded corners because a sharp angle on a handle will become uncomfortable after only a few moments of carrying. Do not overpack crates, both for the safety of the objects and to keep the overall weight at

FIGURE 5B.1 PROPER LIFTING. ILLUSTRATION BY CATHERINE PHILLIPS.

FIGURE 5B.2 MOVING AN OBJECT ON A CART.
ILLUSTRATION BY CATHERINE PHILLIPS.

an acceptable level. Attach skids to the bottom of a crate if you need to use a forklift, J-bar, or dolly (see CHAPTER 5M, "Moving and Rigging Safely").

TWO-DIMENSIONAL OBJECTS

Framed Objects

Frames offer some protection for two-dimensional and flat objects when they are being moved and often enhance your ability to carry and support them. If the frame is delicate or in poor condition, do not use it to carry the object but set it on a board and carry the board.

All objects expand and contract but the amount varies with individual object types. Although not ideal, in moderation it is not a cause for alarm. Framed objects stored in a consistent environment are less of a handling concern than those that have been subjected to fluctuations in temperature and humidity. Poor storage conditions can speed up deterioration rates and make an object less stable so all two-dimensional and flat objects should be handled as little as possible to avoid damage.

When a framed object is subjected to wide fluctuations in temperature and humidity a great deal of stress is put on it. For example, a painting consists of a number of different materials. The canvas, wood, paint, and hardware are all bound together, yet each material expands and contracts at its own rate. The result of this internal struggle may not be noticed right away but eventually stress will cause cracks to appear, the paint may begin to flake off, the frame may warp, the supports weaken, and hardware may become loose. Canvas, which serves as a support to many paintings, is vulnerable to brittleness which, over time, can lead to distortion, loss of elasticity, and tearing. These defects worsen if the work is not handled properly. The condition of objects that are subjected to poor environments should be inspected frequently.

Examine framed works visually before touching them, checking for broken or loose frame pieces. On the back check that the keys (thin wedges that stabilize and tighten corner joints) are firmly in place. If there is a wire attached as a hanging device remove and discard it because wires can scratch other paintings if they are improperly stacked together.

Always use both hands to lift and carry framed works of art. Never presume that the frame is stable or firmly attached. Never lift the painting by grasping the top of the frame because it may separate from the frame body, leaving you holding the top as the rest of the work crashes to the floor. With gloved hands, lightly but firmly hold both sides of the frame and lift, keeping your back straight with your knees and legs doing the lifting. If the object is heavy, do not attempt to move it by yourself. To carry framed works, whether by yourself or with another person, always use two hands, one at the side in a solid place and one on the bottom. Do not lift or carry a framed object by its stretcher bar, or insert your fingers between the stretcher bar and the canvas.

If possible, use a padded truck or cart to move large framed objects. Be sure the object is stable on the cart. A side cart may be used to move more than one framed object at a time (FIGURE 5B.3). Do not overload the cart, and make sure that the weight is distributed evenly on both sides. Keep the objects oriented in the direction they hang, and place similarly sized works back-to-back and front-to-front on the cart. Ensure that the frame from one object does not touch the face of another. To protect adjacent frames, insert an archival board or soft piece of foam

FIGURE 5B.3 SIDE CART. ILLUSTRATION BY CATHERINE PHILLIPS.

each time the screen is rolled out, subjecting them to unnecessary and unpredictable movement. Wires become brittle over time and can snap unexpectedly. Using wires in any circumstance increases the risk of a framed object falling to the ground. Damage from a concussion such as this may not be visible immediately, but in time a series of concentric cracks may appear in the corner closest to the impact, and in all likelihood eventually the painting will need conservation to repair flaking or loss of ground. D-rings (so named because of their shape) attached to the back of the frame and used with hanging hooks afford the most secure method of hanging framed objects on screens (FIGURES 5B.4 and 5B.5).

between them. Move only a few framed objects on a cart at one time because a heavy cart may shift its weight unexpectedly and tip over, which is dangerous to both objects and the staff moving them.

When laying out an exhibit it is a common practice to lean framed objects against the walls. In these cases, put stable frames on nonskid mats or on padded blocks, with a piece of foam between the frame top and the wall. If the frame is delicate or heavily ornamented it may not be able to support the weight without incurring damage. If the frame is gilded, the surface of the frame should not be touched. A gessoed frame should be held by the uncarved back edge and set on its back edge so the gesso is not damaged. Objects with these types of frames are best left on a cart until they can be hung. Pad blocks by wrapping them with low nap carpet, preferably older (because new carpet off-gasses) but clean. Never stack framed objects more than five deep and do not stack those that are extremely large or heavy.

The ideal storage method for framed objects is to hang them on painting screens in their correct orientation (except those with severely flaking paint, which should be stored flat while waiting for conservation treatment). Wires should never be used on screens because wired paintings will swing back and forth

FIGURE 5B.4 PAINTING SCREEN HOOK (S-HOOK). ILLUSTRATION BY CATHERINE PHILLIPS.

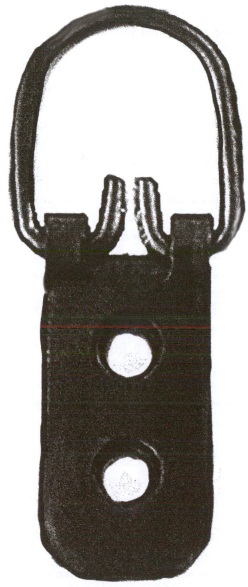

FIGURE 5B.5 D-RING. ILLUSTRATION BY
CATHERINE PHILLIPS.

In galleries, D-rings attach to hanging hardware
that is screwed into the wall. For heavier paintings,
hooks may be secured using a hollow wall bolt, such
as a toggle or molly bolt.

Hanging screens are a luxury that not all museums can afford. Screens can be made from wire fencing purchased at a hardware store and securely bolted
to the storage room walls. For ease of use, choose a
fence design that has holes large enough to accommodate sturdy hanging hooks. Monitor the condition of the fencing closely because the wire used in
fencing is not coated with the same materials as professional painting screens.

If screens are not available framed works may be
stored in bins. Remember to keep the frames oriented
the way they would be when hanging on a wall. Pad
the interior of the bins with archival board (to protect
against the acid that wood naturally contains) and secure carpet on the bin bottom, so that the frames can
easily be slid in and out. Use carpet pieces made from
an inert material or that has had sufficient time to
off-gas. Framed works in bins should be stored with
works of similar size and placed back to back and
front to front.

To prevent unnecessary handling, print the object's title and accession number on two archival
stringed tags, and attach one to each of the two D-
rings on the back of the frame. In this manner, no
matter which direction the frame is inserted into the
bin, a tag will always be at hand for identification.

Taking action to avoid unnecessary handling and
moving of objects is part of the practice of preventive
conservation—extending the longevity of the objects
and forestalling the need for conservation treatment.
When shipping framed works that are under glass,
tape the glass to provide the work some protection.
It is important to remember that taping does not
prevent the glass from breaking but protects it from
damage from glass shards. Do not use tape with a
strong adhesive because it is difficult to remove and
will cause delay and frustration when unpacking. Use
tape made specifically for glass taping, which is available in a large variety of widths. Slightly overlap the
strips of tape, covering the entire surface of the glass.
Fold each end of the tape back on itself to create a tab
to facilitate easy removal. Do not allow the adhesive
side of the tape to come in contact with the frame.
To remove the tape, pull each strip back gently at less
than a ninety-degree angle to avoid undue pressure
on the glass. Never use tape on acrylic surfaces (e.g.,
Plexiglas) because it will leave a permanent residue on
the surface (FIGURE 5B.6).

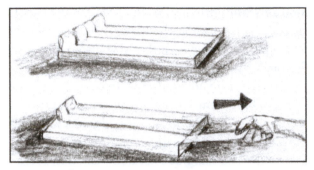

FIGURE 5B.6 REMOVING TAPE FROM GLASS.
ILLUSTRATION BY CATHERINE PHILLIPS.

UNFRAMED TWO-DIMENSIONAL OBJECTS

Without the protection provided by a frame, a two-dimensional object is at greater risk of damage from handling. Ungloved hands may leave behind fingerprints that attract dirt and dust that cause deterioration. Varnishes may be damaged from touch, resulting in a need for overall restoration.

Never touch the front surface of a painting, photograph, or work on paper. When moving an unframed work by its edges always wear thin gloves and use the lightest grip that will still ensure a good hold. To move a work a short distance, you may slip a board underneath and carry it horizontally. Be sure to orient the work properly once you reach your destination. Never stack works that do not have frames, and do not use any type of lashing or rope to secure them.

Textiles

Under no circumstances should a costume or any wearable textile object in a museum collection be worn. Textiles must be handled, stored, and exhibited with extreme caution. To prevent fading, limit light on exhibited textiles to no more than fifty lux (five-foot candles) and reduce exposure time as much as possible. Always move textiles on a support such as a hanger or mannequin, and never allow the fabric to drag on the ground. Lack of support can cause stretching or tearing of the material. Some textiles cannot be cleaned due to their material and construction. Do not exhibit textiles in the open; enclose them in acrylic or a good case.

For storage a flat textile may be rolled on an archival tube and covered with a muslin case, but do not use plastic dustsheets as they attract dust because of static charge. Attach a large tag with a color photograph of the textile and its accession number to each end of the tube to reduce handling when searching for a particular object. Tubes may be supported on racks attached to the storage room walls. Do not store rolled textiles on the floor or underneath heating, ventilation, and air-conditioning (HVAC) vents.

If textiles must be folded, pad the inside of the folds with crumpled, unbuffered, acid-free tissue and store the textiles in archival boxes. Do not store textiles with any plastic objects, such as fashion accessories, because of damaging off-gassing that may degrade the fabric or tarnish metal threads.

Do not pierce the threads of a textile to hang it. Instead, use a fabric lining on the textile to prevent dust from penetrating it from behind. Attach the lining loosely so it does not pull or stretch the fabric when moved. Mount the textile on a muslin covered board and exhibit it on a slant for easy viewing without stretch damage. If the fabric must be hung the weight should be evenly distributed along the top edge. Sew a hook-and-loop fastener (e.g., Velcro) to a band of heavy material and then hand sew this material along the top of the fabric using large stitches. Do not break the threads with the needle; insert the needle carefully between the threads. Do not sew by machine.

Accession numbers may be written on cloth tags and hand sewn to fabrics with a loose weave. Attach the tag in an inconspicuous spot that is not visible when exhibited. Include in the condition report the location of the accession number to prevent unnecessary handling.

Works on Paper

Paper objects are fragile. Not only are they subject to fading, ripping, wrinkling, and tearing, but paper is also hygroscopic so it absorbs moisture from the air. Works on paper that appear to have waves or ripples on the surface have been exposed to excessive relative humidity. In some cases, the ripples may flatten once the paper is in a drier environment, but the images on the paper are likely to be faded or blurred. When dried, the paper will be less flexible and more easily ripped or torn.

In ideal circumstances, all stored works on paper should be matted to protect the surface of the work from direct contact with those above it. All nonmatted works should be interleaved with an appropriate archival material. Most works on paper and photographs benefit from interleaving with buffered tissue, however, unbuffered tissue should be used for objects derived from animal-based proteins (e.g., blueprints, hand-tinted drawings, maps, diazo reproductions, any work with wool or silk components, and leather-bound books). Proteinaceous materials may react with the alkaline buffers by fading or discoloring. Buffering compounds are usually made from calcium carbonate (which protects the work from acidic migration). Buffered and unbuffered tissue paper look similar, but buffered papers often have a chalky feel. Rather than risk using an incorrect material as an interleaving agent, some people prefer to use unbuffered tissue exclusively.

Never lift a work on paper by its edges because this is its weakest part. Slip a thin support such as an index card or a clean spatula underneath the paper to raise it high enough to slip an acid-free board under it, then pick up and carry the paper by the board. If hand-carrying a work on paper without a support always hold the longest sides of the paper and always use two gloved hands. A work on paper that is held by one hand is subject to bending and brittle paper may rip or crack where it is held. If a work on paper must be turned over use a board underneath it as support; place a tissue on the paper's surface, then another board, and turn over the entire stack. If the work has a fragile surface, such as pastel or charcoal, this method is not advised.

Pastel and charcoal drawings should never have materials touching their surfaces; instead, they should be stored separately in shallow boxes. When framing either of these media do not use acrylic (Plexiglas), polyethylene (Mylar), or any other plastic material as glazing because these materials are subject to static charges that will pull the media off the surface of the work.

When looking for a drawing among a stack of papers (e.g., in a flat file drawer) do not bend back the works above it in your search, and do not pull one piece out from the middle of the stack. Instead, move each piece individually until you reach the one you want.

Protect unmatted works on paper in storage by making archival paper folders that are slightly larger than the sheet. Lightly write the accession number or title in pencil on the outside of the folder in the lower right-hand corner and place the work inside the folder. Never write on the folder while the object is inside to ensure that the pencil does not leave an imprint on the object. Having the number or title on the outside of the folder prevents unnecessary handling. Drawings should have their accession numbers written in pencil on the reverse, both at the top right and bottom left corners.

Do not use clips or staples on works on paper and if they are already present, remove them carefully so they do not leave impressions or rust stains. If a paper has a dog-eared corner carefully try to unfold it unless the paper is brittle. Do not attempt to unfold brittle paper because the folded corner may tear off; consult a paper conservator for advice or leave it as it is. Do not roll works on paper, no matter how large, because the fibers can become distorted and inks and pigment may flake off.

To move a group of unframed works on paper place them inside their paper folders in a Solander box or support them from below and move them on a cart. A Solander box has a hardcover surface with a hinged lid connected to its base, with a clasp to secure it shut. These boxes are designed so the side pieces nest inside the box and the top lays flat when opened. The design also protects its contents from light exposure. Solander boxes that contain works of art should always be kept horizontal because the delicate pieces inside can be damaged if the box is held or stored vertically. The reason that these boxes do not have handles is to discourage anything other than horizontal handling. Many museums prefer to store their works on paper, including photographs, inside these boxes permanently because the boxes can be stacked on top of each other and be kept on storage room shelves.

Any material that comes in contact with works on paper, such as matting or interleaving materials, must be acid free and of a high quality. Do not use wrinkled or once-folded tissue papers to interleave.

Over time the pressure created from being stacked with other materials will cause the wrinkle or fold to imprint itself on the object. Glassine, although an acid-free material when it is initially used, may eventually absorb acid. If you use glassine as an interleaving material for long-term storage change it for fresh tissue every year or so. Use a pH pen on older glassine to test for acidity.

Paper that has been exposed to high humidity or wet conditions may be subject to mold infestation. The red-brown stains often found on old paper, generally referred to as foxing, may be caused by mold, but this remains controversial as foxing may also result from the oxidation of metals in the paper (particularly iron or copper) or from chemical reactions of other substances in the paper pulp. In any case, do not attempt to remove foxing stains; consult a paper conservator concerning treatment.

Mold may appear as a light gray haze on the inside of the glass in a framed work. In this case isolate the object to prevent the mold from spreading to other objects, and check the relative humidity of the room in which the object was housed (it should be below 65 percent). Unframe the piece and move it to a drier location. Inactive mold residue may be washed off of the glass, but removal of mold from the paper surface should be left to a conservator; mold damages the surface it grows on, and may streak and permanently stain the work if removed improperly. Remove the glass from the frame before washing. Inactive dry mold should be carefully removed from frames, drawers, or other surfaces with which it has been in contact. Should conditions become humid again, dry mold may be reactivated and cause further damage.

As with most other materials works on paper should be protected from exposure to light. Keep all works on paper enclosed in drawers or boxes when they are not being used. When objects are examined, matted works should be turned face down; unmatted pieces should be covered by tissue or board to limit light exposure. Remove coverings from the objects while working on them. Never leave works exposed on a work table when you go to lunch or leave for the day. Any time you leave the room, no matter how short the duration, turn off the lights. Because light damage is cumulative, every moment you can keep the objects shielded helps to extend their life span. Remember that light damage is cumulative; objects do not recover from it, so even a series of short exposures over time can be destructive.

THREE-DIMENSIONAL OBJECTS

Books

Books should be treated gently because their appearance may mask a fragile condition. All surfaces of the shelving they sit on should be smooth. If the interior sides of the shelf have holes or grooves for adjusting the shelf height, these should be covered with glass or acid-free board to prevent imprints on book covers. Bookends should cover the entire surface of the book they touch for the same reason.

Books should be stored with other books of similar size. If stored vertically, books should remain vertical to prevent sagging pages. If a book is removed from the shelf replace it with a foam block to maintain the verticality of adjoining volumes. Particularly fragile books or those of great value should be stacked horizontally with no more than three or four to a stack. Archival book boxes can help to extend the life of books with delicate or nonexistent covers. These can be made by an archival supply company to fit the book's dimensions perfectly. Never stack open books.

Do not overstock the shelves. Each book should be easily removable without excessive pulling on the spine or the headcap (i.e., the very top of the spine). To remove a book from the shelf reach over the top of the spine to the fore-edge and gently pull it out. If this is not possible push the books on either side inward, until you can grasp the sides of the volume that you want. Lift the book, rather than dragging it off the shelf.

Do not force a book open or attempt to make it lie flat by pressing it open because this results in a cracked spine that will no longer hold the pages together. Books with loose pages or damaged bindings should be tied with a soft cotton tape (not with string or rubber bands) and sent to a conservator for repair.

When on exhibit, open books should be kept in low light conditions and, if possible, the pages should be turned every few days to prevent the open pages from fading at a different rate than the rest of

FIGURE 5B.7 BOOK SUPPORT. ILLUSTRATION BY CATHERINE PHILLIPS.

the book. If a book must be open to show a certain page, the time on view should be limited. To turn the pages, slip your fingers under the top corner of the page, and without bending it, run your fingers down the side and turn. To display an open book, place supports beneath its covers (FIGURE 5B.7).

Books with undamaged edges may be brushed infrequently with a hogs hair brush to eliminate dust. Hold the closed book firmly and brush the top from the spine to the outer edge to prevent dust from being swept into the spine. If dust has penetrated the pages, rest the open book on foam supports and brush from the inner to the outer edges. Do not attempt to clean the area of the page closest to where it is bound and do not erase marks from the pages.

Ceramics and Glass

Most ceramic or glass objects may be handled without gloves using clean and dry hands unless the ceramic is porous or unglazed. Nitrile or other synthetic gloves may also be used.

Gently grip a ceramic by its base, never by a protruding element or lip. Examine the object carefully for evidence of old repairs which may have weakened the structure or adhesives which may have broken down over time. Use caution in these areas and be aware that not all repairs are immediately evident.

Place padding between ceramic or glass objects when transporting them on a cart or in a box. Conservation pillows or snakes made from muslin or lightweight canvas and filled with BB-sized polypellets are especially helpful in keeping objects from tipping or rolling while being moved on a cart. On shelves these supports can provide security for an object whose shape may keep it from remaining upright on its own. In exhibits, these supports can be used to gently cradle open books. Note, if you make these simple supports yourself do not use metal BBs because they will oxidize over time and the rust will seep through the fabric.

When packing glassware in boxes be aware that stems and handles tend to be the most delicate parts, so give them a generous measure of padding with tissue. Pack the inside of each glass with crumpled tissue paper as well. Should the box fall or be dropped the wadded tissue inside the glass will absorb the impact, lessening the chances that the glass will break. Do not stack boxes packed with glass objects. Clearly mark the exterior of the boxes to indicate the objects inside are fragile and add a warning label not to stack other boxes on top of them. Consider using archival boxes made for glassware that include partitions. Although glass is resistant to acidic conditions, hand-painted decorations may not be. Archival boxes are usually sturdier than regular corrugated cardboard and provide better protection for glass objects.

When exhibiting glass objects in a display case, ultraviolet-filtered lighting should be external and at a sufficient distance to avoid heat buildup inside the case. Glass with incipient crizzling (tiny fissures covering the glass surface) or painted surfaces will suffer from heat-induced low humidity, causing any defects to rapidly increase. Do not spotlight any one glass object inside a case, rather use diffused light, LEDs, or fiber-optic lighting to provide a cooler environment.

Furniture

Lift and carry furniture; do not drag, push, or pull it because this strains joints and may cause damage. Use a cart or flatbed truck to move furniture, if necessary, and use pads or blankets to protect fragile edges and projections from bumps during the move. Slip pads under straps used to secure the object. Use only soft cords or cloths as straps and slip pads between the strap and surface when moving the object. Do not overtighten the straps because this may mar delicate surfaces.

Do not pick up chairs by their back or arms. Although maintaining correct lifting posture of bent knees and straight back, lift the chair from under the seat, and carry it with one hand under the seat and the other supporting the back (FIGURE 5B.8). Use the middle of your body as a brace only if you are wearing clothes without front buttons, zippers, or buckles, or if you are wearing an apron with empty pockets.

Before handling furniture, consult the condition report to learn whether there are any unstable parts that could influence how you move the piece. If furniture has component parts (e.g., dressers or bureaus with drawers) remove the components and carry them separately to reduce the piece's overall weight. Secure movable parts, such as cabinet hardware or hinged drop lids, with cotton twill tape. Collapse or remove table leaves before moving.

Large pieces of furniture should be moved by least two people working together. If your view is obstructed by the size of the furniture, enlist another person to watch for doorway overheads, stairs, electrical wires along hallway floors, or any other

FIGURE 5B.8 PROPERLY LIFTING A CHAIR. ILLUSTRATION BY CATHERINE PHILLIPS.

obstructions, and have them hold doors open as you move through.

When moving a hutch or armoire be aware that some pieces of furniture that look solid may be made of two components that are stacked together. Furniture may suffer from unnoticed wood rot or have had pest infestations that weakened its structure. Do not assume these objects are stable and do not lift any furniture component until you are certain it is securely affixed to the rest of the piece.

Grandfather Clocks

Moving a grandfather clock requires at least two people because of the unwieldy size and bulk of the piece. If the clock is especially fragile or you have concerns about your ability to move it, call a reputable clock repair specialist who can either move the clock for you or tell you how to do it. Smaller mechanical clocks, such as mantle clocks, may be carried by one person, but the preparation measures are similar; secure movable parts and move gently by hand-carrying for short distances or on a cart or flatbed for longer distances.

The two primary components of any mechanical clock are the mechanism and cabinet. When planning the move, prepare the mechanism first. Open the door to the clock cabinet to inspect the interior. Any unexpected objects such as the clock's key or unrelated articles found in the clock should be removed. Tag and box the pieces that are part of the clock so they do not get lost. Remove the pendulum by lifting it straight up and off the suspension system. Wrap the pendulum in tissue and secure it between two pieces of rigid cardboard. Label the cardboard for easy identification later.

Wind the clock until the weights are visible through the clock's doorway. Most grandfather clocks have three weights hanging from cables inside the cabinet and each has a specific function—one powers the hour-strike, one drives the time, and the third operates the chime. Clocks that do not chime will have only two weights. Before removing the weights, identify which one attaches to each of the cables and tag both the weight and the cable to ensure that the correct weight is returned to the proper cable after the move is completed. Remove the weights, wrap them in tissue, and store them in a labeled box. With the weights and pendulum removed from the clock, secure the cables so they do not become entangled during the move. Insert foam block above each pully to keep them from hitting each other during movement. Shut and secure the cabinet door with Tyvek straps so it does not open when the clock is tipped while being lifted. Similarly, secure the door in front of the clock face. Remove any elements from the clock exterior such as the winding key or the door lock key and any loose decorative objects such as spires or finials. Pack these objects in the same box as the weights to keep them from being separated or lost during the move.

To remove the bonnet, face the front of the clock and with both hands grasp the wood surrounding the clock face. With a steady but gentle forward pull, carefully slide the bonnet straight forward and away from the clock. Wrap both the bonnet and the cabinet with moving pads and secure them upright on a flatbed or cart to move. Do not transport or move clocks on their side or face down. If the clock is moved by a truck secure the upright, wrapped clock to the truck interior with straps and insert pads under the straps to prevent damage to the clock.

Once the clock has been moved, reverse the instructions to unpack it. Assemble the cabinet first, reattach accessories, and slide the bonnet back onto the clock body. Remove the foam pieces securing the cables and hang the weights from their corresponding cables. Reattach the pendulum and secure the cabinet door. If the clock is going to be running in its new location it is advisable to have the clock serviced following the move.

Musical Instruments

Cotton gloves should always be worn to protect surfaces of instruments, including polished brass and varnished wood. Instrument varnish is considered a critical aesthetic, and unlike that on a painting, should never be removed or replaced.

When moving an instrument from one area of a building to another, especially when there are differences in room temperatures, the instrument should be covered to prevent thermal shock. Instruments should not be dismantled for transportation unless under the supervision of a specialist because of the risk of damaging delicate parts.

An instrument should never be lifted by, nor rested upon, its keys, bridge, strings, or other delicate components. Avoid storage or display near exterior walls, sources of heat, air vents, or areas where condensation may accumulate.

Adhesives such as museum wax should never be used to prop up an instrument in an installation or for photographic purposes.

Natural History Specimens

Because of the prevalent use of arsenic as a preservative in the past, taxidermy mounts should not be used for hands-on demonstrations unless they have been tested and found to be free of arsenic.

Many specimens (e.g., rocks and fossils) can be extremely heavy. Special equipment such as lifts or webbing may be necessary to move them.

The surfaces of some specimens, such as shells and painted ethnographic objects, may be powdery or have fugitive dyes and paints that are easily rubbed off. Insect specimens are extremely fragile. Special care must be taken when handling these objects. In most cases, it is better to move a specimen by handling its mount or storage container than to touch it. Transport smaller specimens inside boxes padded with a neutral color material (inks and dyes in colored tissue may be transferred to the specimens). If specimens must be touched wear cotton, neoprene, or nitrile gloves.

When moving taxidermy mounts support all of the appendages and body of the object. For example, mounted animals may have arms and legs sticking out in precarious positions, and tails can be especially vulnerable to breakage. Birds may have fine, spindly feathers that stick out from the body and need special protection.

Bone, ivory, and antler materials are susceptible to chipping and fingerprint stains so they should be handled as little as possible. Bone, teeth, and ivory may crack in low humidity conditions and, thus, should be protected from the heat of examination and photographic lights.

FIGURE 5B.9 SCULPTURE WITH SUPPORT. ILLUSTRATION BY CATHERINE PHILLIPS.

THREE-DIMENSIONAL OBJECTS

As with all museum objects, inspect before touching them. Look for loose components, cracks, breaks, and areas of old repair, while being aware that not all damage may be obvious.

Objects sitting on shelves should not be lifted one over one another. When retrieving an object from the back of a shelf remove the objects in front of it before picking up the piece you want.

In general, it is best to transport objects in their most stable position, which is usually that in which they are stored or displayed. Sculpture should remain vertical in the position that best supports its weight. A horizontal placement may put stress on fragile areas. If sculpture must be laid down, insert padding underneath to support any weak areas (FIGURE 5B.9).

When moving several objects, it is easier and safer to use a cart. Objects with removable parts, such as a teapot and lid, or sculpture and base, should be separated prior to moving. Brace small or fragile objects with clean foam blocks, muslin conservation pillows, or rolled towels so they do not roll on the cart. A padded box on the cart can hold particularly fragile or small objects while in transit.

HAZARDOUS MATERIALS IN THE COLLECTION

This topic is covered in more depth in CHAPTER 6A ("Risk Management Overview"), however, the information here is relative to handling practices.

It is important to keep in mind that museum objects were once commonly treated and preserved with substances that we now know to be toxic or carcinogenic. We tend to think that the application of these substances happened long, long ago and although we know that many of those objects still exist in our collections, we may think they are no longer a safety concern. In fact, one of the most commonly used toxic compounds in museums—arsenic—was used to treat objects from the eighteenth century to the mid-1980s. Arsenic was used to preserve biological and ethnographic specimens, and mammal and bird skins, as a pesticide, and to help preserve wet specimens. Arsenic may adhere to animal fur and feathers and its toxicity does not lessen over time. Long-term exposure to arsenic may be associated with many health risks, including skin disorders, increased risk of diabetes, high blood pressure, and several types of cancer.

Recommendations for staff who handle collection objects that may have been exposed to arsenic or other toxins (primarily in natural history museums) include strict use of nitrile gloves, wearing a clean, protective lab coat and, in some cases, a fit-tested respirator. Routine practices should include regular washing of hands, discarding gloves immediately after use, and washing lab coats separately from other clothing. With these precautions rigorously observed, staff can be assured that there is little chance that they will be affected by arsenic. The National Park Service recommends that natural history collection objects collected prior to 1980 be treated with caution because they may contain arsenic or other toxic chemicals.[10] Suspected objects should be identified in museum records and always be exhibited in locked cases.

Similar concerns exist in ethnographic collections that may retain traces of ethylene oxide, Vapona (DDVP), DDT, strychnine, mercuric chloride, naphthalene, or paradichlorobenzene (PDB, or mothballs). Residues from these pesticides can be absorbed through inhalation, ingestion, or absorption through the skin. Many of these chemicals are particularly prevalent in ethnographic artifacts and have caused serious concerns in repatriation efforts. Supervisors in museums with these collections are urged to stringently enforce staff usage of personal protective equipment. Prolonged contact with these materials or working in an area with inadequate ventilation should be prohibited.

Other concerns in collections include asbestos, radioactivity (particularly radon), poisons, and pathogens. Become knowledgeable about your particular collections. Warnings about chemical hazards should be on file for each suspect object. Including this information on a condition report will inform others who may need to handle the objects. Gloves and lab coats should be worn when handling objects that are suspected of having been exposed to any chemical or process that may cause injury or risks to health.

Some objects that seem benign may have been created using chemical processes now known to be toxic. For example, mercury poisoning is a concern in museum collections containing old hats because of the common use of mercuric chloride in the felting process. Health concerns for hatters (those in the hat production industry) caused several European countries to ban the use of mercury in felt production late in the eighteenth century, however, mercury continued to be in use in the United States until the mid-1940s. The well-known term "mad as a hatter" and the Mad Hatter character in *Alice in Wonderland* are based on the historical prevalence of mercury poisoning in those who worked in the felting industry.

Exposure to mercury can harm the brain, heart, kidneys, and lungs. Although contamination risk is low, supervisors should identify problematic collection objects and limit exposure time when staff is working directly with these objects. Poisoning should be suspected if staff members become ill or exhibit unusual behavior after working with contaminated objects. Symptoms of mercury exposure include impaired vision, speech, hearing, ability to walk, and sensations such as pins and needles, muscle weakness, and extreme irritability.[11] Staff involved with handling any materials that may pose a health or safety risk should approach such objects with caution, information, and protection.

WHEN DAMAGE OCCURS

Despite careful handling procedures, mishaps may occur that result in object damage. It may be possible to prevent further harm to the object by following established procedures immediately after the incident. It is best if these procedures are included in preliminary object-handling training sessions when a calm atmosphere prevails.

Any damage should be immediately reported to the department supervisor so that incident reports and photographs may be made right away. Never try to cover up a problem, it will only prevent resolution of the situation. Blame, if any, should be dealt with after the object is properly cared for. If damage occurs on weekends or after hours, personnel should know to notify security staff who can oversee proper procedures. All museum staff should be aware that there are rules in place for this type of occurrence.

If the object is on loan to the museum, the lending institution should be notified according to instructions they provide in their loan agreement. If there are no instructions, contact the institution to report the situation the day it occurs and follow up with a written report and photographs. Depending on the severity of the damage the museum's insurance agent may need to be notified (the insurance company will request copies of the damage report and photographs).

Unless it will cause further damage, objects should not be cleaned up or removed until the report is completed and the photographs have been taken. The appropriate staff member should carefully gather up all pieces, no matter how small, and put them aside in a sealable bag. Under no circumstances should repairs be attempted or pieces fitted back together on the spot because this may cause abrasion and will greatly increase the chance that complete restoration will be impossible. Block off the area where the damage occurred and do not allow the public or staff to walk through it. If you need to go back to search for missing components it will be easier if the area has not been disturbed.

If damage occurred because of improper mounts, poorly placed pedestals, or similar reasons, the situation should be remedied before the object is returned to display.

If damage occurred during shipment do not discard any packing material or containers that the object was in. If a commercial shipper was used the company should be notified as well. Insurance claims may be negated if the shipping company is not informed as soon as the damage is discovered. Should you notice damage to any crate or box as it is being delivered, the driver should be asked to stay on the premises until the company has been contacted.

EMERGENCY PROCEDURES

As a component of a museum's emergency preparedness plan, all staff should have an introduction to the principles of object handling (see CHAPTER 6B, "Emergencies: Prepare, Respond, Recover"). This can be done in conjunction with other staff training such as fire drills, use of fire extinguishers, and other emergency procedures. Museum security guards and docents are often the only staff members present on weekends or during open evening hours. If an object is knocked off a pedestal, or should fall from the wall, staff should know what to do to prevent further damage or loss. When holding a training session for this purpose, it should be stressed that normally non-collection staff will not be expected to handle museum objects, but in the event of an emergency, without other staff present, they should know what to do. Training should focus on specific object types found in the collection and damage mitigation (see "When Damage Occurs").

When a natural disaster such as a hurricane or a flood is threatened and collections need to be moved quickly, all staff may need to be involved. One person should be designated as point person so confusion is kept to a minimum. The staff should be organized into two- or three-person teams with at least one trained object handler on each team. Keep in mind that all staff will be under stress and calm attitudes will help to smooth the process. Everyone will have personal concerns on their minds and may not be thinking clearly—encourage focused thought. Staff in areas where natural disasters may occur repeatedly over a short duration of time may suffer from *storm-fatigue*—a diminishing ability to react with the same dedication and energy as they did during previous storm preparations. Nonetheless objects must be handled carefully, just as they are in nonemergency times. Encourage all museum staff to maintain their high standards to the best of their ability.

Do not forget that staff members need to be protected as well and do not allow anyone to stay in a building longer than it is safe to do so. No matter their value, objects are objects, and nothing is more valuable than human life. •

USEFUL REFERENCES

Arthur, C. R. 1988. *North Carolina Historic Sites: Collections Care and Management Manual*. Raleigh: Historic Sites Section, Division of Archives and History, N.C. Department of Cultural Resources.

Bradley, S. 1993. *A Guide to the Storage, Exhibition and Handling of Antiquities, Ethnographia and Pictorial Art*. London: British Museum.

Canadian Conservation Institute. "Preventive conservation guidelines for collections." Available at: https://www.canada.ca/en/conservation-institute/services/preventive-conservation/guidelines-collections.html (accessed August 20, 2019)/

Fifield, B. 2013. *Museum Monday: Get Rid of Those White Cotton Gloves: Time for Nitrile*. The Still Room Blog. Available at: https://thestillroomblog.com/2013/02/25/museum-monday-get-rid-of-those-white-cotton-gloves-time-for-nitrile/

Foley, L. *Preservation 101: Preservation Basics for Paper and Media Collections*. Northeast Document Conservation Center, 2006. Available at: https://www.nedcc.org/free-resources/preservation-101.

Guldbeck, P. E. 1979. *The Care of Historical Collections: A Conservation Handbook for the Nonspecialist*. Nashville: American Association for State and Local History.

Hawks, C. A., M. McCann, K. Makos, L. Goldberg, D. Hinkamp, D. Ertel, and P. Silence (eds.). 2011. *Health and Safety for Museum Professionals*. New York: Society for the Preservation of Natural History Collections.

Huntley, M., and M. T. Simpson. 1992. *Sotheby's Caring for Antiques: A Guide to Handling, Cleaning, Display, and Restoration*. London: Conran Octopus.

Keck, C. K. 1974. *A Handbook on the Care of Paintings*. New York: Watson-Guptill Publication.

Knapp, A. M. 2000. "Arsenic Health and Safety Update." *National Park Service Conserv-O-Gram* 2/3. Available at: https://www.nps.gov/museum/publications/conserveogram/02-03.pdf.

Graham, F. "Caring for natural history collections." Canadian Conservation Institute. Available at: https://www.canada.ca/en/conservation-institute/services/preventive-conservation/guidelines-collections/natural-history.html (accessed August 20, 2019)/

Melvin, R., M. F. Mecklenburg, and R. M. Merrill (eds.) 1991. *Art in Transit: Handbook for Packing and Transporting Paintings*. Washington, DC: National Gallery of Art. Available at: https://repository.si.edu/bitstream/handle/10088/8127/mci_

Art_in_Transit_Handbook_for_Packing_and_Transporting_Paintings.pdf?sequence=1&isAllowed=y.

Odegaard, N. 1992. *A Guide to Handling Anthropological Museum Collections*. Los Angeles: Western Association for Art Conservation.

Pereira, M., and S. J. Wolf. 2001. *Physical Properties and Health Effects of Pesticides Used on National Park Service Collections*. National Park Service *Conserve-O-Gram* 2/17. Available at: https://www.nps.gov/museum/publications/conserveogram/pesticides2-17.pdf.

Powell, B. A. 2016. *Collection Care. An Illustrated Handbook for the Care and Handling of Cultural Objects*. Lanham, MD: Rowman & Littlefield.

Reeve, J. K. 1992. *The Art of Showing Art*. Tulsa: Council Oak Books.

Schultz, A. W. (ed.). 1992. *Caring for Your Collections*. National Institute for the Conservation of Cultural Property. New York: Harry N. Abrams Publishers.

Shelley, M. 1987. *The Care and Handling of Art Objects: Practices in the Metropolitan Museum of Art*. New York: Metropolitan Museum of Art.

Snyder, J. 2001. *Caring for Your Art: Guide for Artists, Collectors, Galleries, and Art Institutes*. New York: Allworth Press.

Thompson, J. M. (ed.). 1992. *A Manual of Curatorship: A Guide to Museum Practice*, 2nd ed. Oxford: Butterworth-Heinemann.

NOTES

1. Available at: https://www.aam-us.org/.

2. Available at: https://aaslh.org/.

3. Available at: https://www.nps.gov/museum/.

4. Available at: http://www.spnhc.org/.

5. See CHAPTER 7B, "The Care of Culturally Sensitive and Sacred Objects" and CHAPTER 7F, "Implementing NAGPRA."

6. J. M. Landry, M. R. Schilling, and S. C. Dusan, "Analysis of volatile organic compounds from display and storage case materials," American Institute of Conservation Objects Specialty Group Postprints, Albuquerque, New Mexico, June 1991.

7. O. Herbarth and S. Matysik, "Decreasing concentrations of volatile organic compounds (voc) emitted following home renovations," *Indoor Air* 20, no. 2 (2010): 141–146.

8. US Department of Health and Human Services, "Health and safety information on household products, household products database. National Library of Medicine." Available at: https://hpd.nlm.nih.gov/index.htm (accessed January 14, 2019).

9. SDS Online Database https://www.msds.com. Available at: https://www.msds (accessed January 14, 2019).

10. Available at: https://www.nps.gov/museum/publications/conserveogram/02-03.pdf.

11. Available at: https://www.emedicinehealth.com/mercury_poisoning/article_em.htm.

5c | DIGITIZATION

THE DIGITIZATION OF museum archives and objects draws on almost all aspects of registration and collections management. From the physical handling and preparation of materials to the catalog records, metadata storage, and the preservation files captured, the whole process encompasses a wide swath of the role of the registrar. Digitization will have a different face in different institutions. Access and outreach are often the main goals for digitization efforts, but certainly aspects of preservation, documentation, convenience, and condition play a role as well. Standards for digitization vary from one institution to another as do the methods of capture and the types of materials digitized. As with many aspects of technology, by the time one explanation is written and published standards have changed, been upgraded, or the media itself has become outmoded, so this chapter will provide general guidance on the digitization process and resources to offer guidance rather than how-to instructions.

THE DIGITIZATION PLAN

The key part of any project, digitization or otherwise, is a plan. Plans for digitization projects can be enormous in scale such as that of a collaborative effort by Duke, North Carolina State, UNC-Chapel Hill, and North Carolina Central university libraries, which digitized more than 360,000 documents related to the Long Civil Rights Movement in North Carolina,[1] or the American Museum of Natural History project that has scanned thousands of pages of scientists' and collectors' field notes.[2] Or they can be as small in scale as a single photograph, done at the urgent behest of a curator or director. Most of us are going to find ourselves somewhere in the middle.

Goals

Setting the goals of the plan is key. Goals need to take into account the many users of the museum, its collection, the services provided, and the needs to be met. Administrators' goals, curators' goals, and those of education and collections departments will differ in some, if not many, ways. Goals often fall into two categories within digitization plans: those that are more quantitative and those that are more qualitative or strategic. Defining the goals and the related outcomes sets the tone for the plan overall. Important to also keep in mind is that the goals of today may not be the goals of tomorrow. The future for how digitized images will be used is unpredictable. The key is to keep the methodology open and restrictions low so that future use is not impeded. Setting the metrics for how these goals will be evaluated should also be included in the plan. Upticks in website traffic or more research requests may be metrics, as will numbers of captured objects and rates of digitization.

In 2010 the Smithsonian Institution published "Creating a Digital Smithsonian: Digitization Strategic Plan,"[3] outlining a pan-institutional set of strategic goals with clear objectives. Using this type of format—one many administrators and boards are comfortable with—aides in clear and thoughtful decisions about digitization plans. From the overarching strategic goals, the quantitative goals can (usually) be extracted.

Common Goals of Digitization:
- Broaden access to collections through publication on the internet and intranet;
- Lessen handling of objects and archives by having digital surrogates easily available;
- Preserve obsolete media;
- Meet the legal requirements related to the Native American Graves Protection and Repatriation Act (NAGPRA), estates, or state or local laws;
- Strengthen visitor engagement; and
- Speed research initiatives.

The key to keep in mind for the goals of the digitization plan is, of course, the mission and vision of the institution. The digitization plan may have a mission and vision unto itself, but ensuring alignment with those of the institution ensures buy-in from boards, administrators, staff, and funders. In some instances, museums may have the benefit of a collections survey or assessment from which to draw digitization goals. These assessments are helpful in putting together a plan but not always necessary. Often registrars, collection managers, archivists and curators know what collections or objects are at risk, are often requested, or are a boon for researchers, etc. This institutional knowledge will help shape and define the goals of a digitization plan.

Selection

Institutional knowledge of collection use or a full survey or assessment will lead the charge in the selection of objects, archival documents, media, and so on to be scanned. The Northeast Document Conservation Center (NDCC) notes that, "at base, selection for digitization and preservation derives from the mission of the institution, and every institution should have a selection process in place to evaluate materials within that context and determine when digital conversion is most appropriate."[4] Developing selection criteria will help to further the selection process. Every institution will have criteria special to its own mission, collections, and digitization priorities. There are, however, a few general questions all digitization selection criteria should cover:

- Should the object or document be digitized? Does the collection have intrinsic value that will be worth the cost and effort of digitization? Is there enough audience demand?
- May the object or document be digitized? Are all the needed permissions and rights in place for digitization?
- Can the object or document be digitized? Is its physical state sound enough to withstand the handling involved in digitization? Is the proper metadata in place? Does the museum have the capacity to care for the digital files that will be created?

Within these criteria, each institution will have to set the standards for what makes something a good candidate for digitization. A collection of oral histories recorded on cassette tapes may not make the cut for one museum but may for another if they are at the heart of that museum's mission. Key to the selection is to be open, inclusive, and accountable.[5] By allowing curators, educators, registrars, collection managers, users, and even administrators and board members a voice in the selection process an inclusive environment will be created. However, a small selection panel or team will likely be needed to keep the process moving and to make final decisions.

Setting Standards of Digitization

An integral part of a digitization plan is the standards by which various media will be digitized. The National Archives, the Smithsonian Institution, and the Northeast Document Conservation Center along with many others have standards for capture as well as file types that are a great basis for any institution to use as a guide or model. The main components to keep in mind include the resolution of the capture (dpi for scans, bit rates for audiovisual material, ISO, etc.), the type of file to be saved (JPEG, TIFF, WAV), and how those files will be stored for both digital preservation and digital access (for more information on digital asset management see CHAPTER 4D, "Digital Asset Management Systems").

Capture standards and file types are part of the changing landscape of technology, which are often outdated as soon as printed. Resources listed are places to begin current research on standards and file types. Capture standards will also need to include the use of ruler bars, color standards, and other aids to create true to life digital surrogates. As the use of three-dimensional (3-D) scanners and printers increases in the museum field the standards for the capture of 3-D objects in addition to, or in place of photography, continue to emerge. Time-based media works, contemporary artworks, and other audiovisual material age rapidly and the upgrading and changing of file types will also need to be addressed (see CHAPTERS 3E, "Documenting Contemporary Art" and 3G, "Managing Digital Art" for more information).

Preservation master files (or archival master files), production master files, and access files also need to be addressed as part of the standards in the digitization plan. Preservation master files will be used to create the production files and the access files most users will need. Preservation masters are created at the highest capture specifications. Typically, this serves several purposes including satisfying longer-term preservation needs and can serve as a surrogate for the original if it is destroyed or the file is corrupted.[6] Preservation master files hold metadata about the images and items captured. The Online Computer Library Center (OCLC) created the "Final Report on Preservation Metadata for Digital Master Files" in 1998, and it remains a good standard for the metadata to capture.[7] Preservation masters are meant to be held for the long term and maintained in a secure storage environment.

Researchers, curators, or publishing requests for high-resolution files will be fulfilled using the production master files. These files will be used to create any derivative files needed and may be edited in various ways (e.g., stitching together a large map or a panoramic photograph). Access copies are lower resolution but still of good quality and often are used in the online publication of digitized material. The digitization plan will need to outline each of these file types, the standards needed, the long-term preservation plan, and the who, how, and when of access to each.

File naming is another key element of setting standards for the digitization plan. From 3-D objects to moving images each material type will need a standard way that each file is named. This aides in organization of digital files, the retrieval of those files, and the association of those files with the object or image captured. Accession numbers or catalog numbers, being the most common unique identifier for museum collections, will often be incorporated into the file name. However, in large rapid image capture digitization projects a nondescriptive, or numerical string, may be used as the file name. The National Archives offers advice on establishing a file naming scheme.[8]

Timeline

"How long is all this scanning going to take?" is not an easy question to answer. The digitization plan itself will account for overall goals and timelines but may be broken up into phases or discreet projects to account for the overall plan. The digitization plan provides the overview that smaller digitization projects and phases will be developed from. A good thing to remember is that any digitization plan, much like collection management policies, needs to be regularly reviewed, not only because standards change, but also so do priorities.

However, much of "How long is this going to take?!" will depend on three major factors—funding, staff time, and tools and equipment. What the digitization plan will need to account for in relation to timelines is all of these factors. Someone once told me, "There are three things you can have—good, fast, and cheap. But you can only have two of the three." These factors come together in much the same way. If you want it cheap and fast, then it will not be very good. If you want it good and cheap, then it will not be very fast. The digitization plan will need to account for each of these aspects, and note that various media types will require different levels of funding, staff time, and equipment.

Funding

Determining the cost of digitization may seem like grasping at straws at times. Pinning down equipment, obsolescence, staff time, and storage of the captured images can all quickly feel overwhelming. The Digitization Cost Calculator from the Council on Library and Information Resources (CLIR) can be helpful in guiding how much a particular project will cost.[9] Grants, directed gifts, general operating funds, or a combination of all will need to be dedicated to digitization projects. Stanford University Libraries states that "digitization costs for a particular project will vary greatly, depending on many factors such as the volume of content to be digitized as well as the nature of the content and the intended use. . . . Content format and fragility may affect handling requirements as well as the type of digitization equipment that can be applied, resulting in significant differences in terms of throughput from one project to the next."[10]

Tools and Equipment

Flatbed scanners, overhead scanners, camera, lights, tape decks, computers, software . . . the list can seem endless. Each project will have a set of equipment and tools needed for the material type being digitized. Archival materials such as documents, photographs, or maps may all be done on a flatbed scanner, but books, scrapbooks, and other bound material will require an overhead scanner. Three-dimensional objects are increasingly being scanned as well, sometimes using a flatbed scanner (e.g., for herbarium sheets[11]) but more often photographed with digital SLR cameras, studio lights, and backdrops. Microfilm, cassette tapes, VHS, and other audiovisual materials require specialized equipment to capture high resolution images. Most daily-use desktop scanners or analog-to-digital media converters are not able to provide the high resolutions needed to capture objects in a digitization project.

Each type of equipment will have its own software and hardware requirements. Other tools such as book supports, color bars, rulers, mannequins, and supports for 3-D objects must be acquired for the digitization project. Establishing a digital lab where tools and equipment specific to digitization is set up is ideal. The digital lab can be treated as an extension of the storage area to meet proper heating, ventilation, and air-conditioning (HVAC), security, fire suppression, and other established guidelines for collections care. The design of a digital lab will vary by institutional space allocated, the materials being digitized, and the equipment needed. The "Library of Congress Digital Scholars Lab Pilot Project Report" provides recommendations for digital lab design.[12]

The digitization plan must account for the inevitable obsolescence of equipment, particularly computers and software. Although discreet projects within an overall plan may not take decades, large-scale and long-term digitization plans need to account for those years when equipment and other tools will become outdated. This will closely tie into funding and overall cost projections for digitization.

Capacity of Staff

It is unfortunate that staffing for digitization is often overlooked as one of the most crucial elements of plans. Often, there is no funding or thought to provide staffing just for digitization; rather, institutions will simply add it on to the duties of registrars, collection managers, curators, and others in the collections or curatorial departments. Often on project overload, adding additional duties related to digitization can be overwhelming for smaller staffs and museums. Collection preparation, data preparation, physically retrieving and manipulating objects, tracking movements, tracking workflows, and then the return of objects, scans, and data are all time-consuming, meticulous tasks. Registrars and collection managers will need to be involved in all these steps, even if they are not directly tasked with the capturing of images. Dedicated staff for capturing images is ideal but may not be practical for all institutions. Training is key and must be based on the type of material to be imaged. Proper handling and support as well as the safety of the objects and documents is paramount. Registrars and collection managers are vital to providing the rules and guidance for this part of the process.

The rate of capture determines much of the trifecta of funding, equipment, and staff. Whether or not to capture in house or to outsource the capture process is a major consideration. Rates of capture vary from object type to object type as do the rates of speed with which equipment can capture a particular item (e.g., imaging works on paper on a flatbed scanner is faster than using a camera to image frogs preserved in alcohol). The digitization plan should factor in several aspects when deciding to capture in house or to outsource. Considerations include the size of the particular project, how complicated the objects are to capture, equipment needed, and experience within the organization. The Sustainable Heritage Network outlines the opportunities and challenges for each and also offers additional resources when considering whether to keep projects in house or outsource them.[13]

COLLECTION PREPARATION

Whether in house or outsourced, the objects and documents to be digitized will all have to be properly prepared for capture. In the case of paper materials this can involve the removal of fasteners, the flattening of curled photographs, or full conservation treatments to stabilize a book or manuscript. As part of the physical preparation process notes to scanners can be made that include handling instructions or draw attention to conditions that may alter the normal scanning process. In some cases, digitization projects will allow collections staff an opportunity to improve and upgrade the storage and housing of collections.[14] 3-D objects may also need conservation or mounts created to support them while being photographed. Similar preparations for natural history materials, audiovisual, microfilm, and other formats will need to be made.

DATA PREPARATION

Hand in hand with the physical preparation will be the evaluation and preparation of the data associated with the objects. Most museums will leverage the use of data from their collection management system to analyze the data they have about their collections. Cataloging may not have been consistent, or the use of particular terms or fields may have shifted as cataloging standards within an institution changed. The digitization plan should establish the data standards for each material type. How the data will be used, displayed, and searched should be considered as part of the standards. In some cases that data may get filled in after capture, before capture, or as part of the capture process.[15] Again, material type, time, staffing and method of capture will be factors in determining how the process of data preparation is handled.

THE DIGITIZATION WORKFLOW

The physical preparation and data preparation of the selected collections will have to be established in the overall workflow of the digitization plan. Depending on the project the workflow may vary, but there are a few key steps to keep in mind when it comes to digitization. First, the selection of collections or objects based on the criteria set in the plan. Second should be the physical assessment of the objects to ensure that they can be safely digitized and considerations for any conservation treatments made. Third, any legal and ethical issues with digitization should be considered. Fourth is preparing the data that will accompany the objects through the digitization process.

The workflow will need to account for both the digital surrogate created and the object itself, once digitized. The return of physical objects to proper storage locations is one element. The data created during or after the capture process needs to be properly entered into the database. The images created need to be properly named based on the file-naming conventions established with preservation master files saved. Then, any postprocessing that is necessary, such as adding metadata to images, cropping, or color correcting must take place.

Quality control (QC) or quality assurance (QA) should take place in all the steps of the workflow, but will be a crucial step when the capture process begins. Saving files with the proper file-naming convention, the structure and order of the folders in which those files are saved, and the quality of the images will all need to be checked regularly. This will happen more often in the beginning as new projects get started, but it can be done on a regular interval or spot checked as projects progress.[16]

The nature of a particular project will dictate the workflow once digital files are deemed of sufficient quality. Incorporating the data into the collections management system (CMS) or a digital asset management system (DAMS), publication to the web, or sharing with other institutions or internal clients are all possible next steps. The digitization plan should account for the storage of master preservation files, and access to production masters, access files, and the workflow should follow those guidelines.

EVALUATION OF GOALS

The process of digitization often feeds on itself; making collections available through digital access may increase demand for more materials to be made accessible. The influx of more standardized data, images, and physical reprocessing (or first-time processing) of collections may increase expectations from administrators, researchers, curators, and registrars and collection managers. The goals set forth in the digitization plan need to be evaluated using both the quantitative and qualitative metrics which were established. Were the goals met? Were there impediments to reaching the goals? Over time the goals should be reevaluated to ensure that they still align with the mission and vision of the museum and the plan itself. The plan may start as one that is about access but may over time evolve into supporting scholarly research or licensing opportunities. The goals within the plan will need to be reevaluated with new metrics established as digitization projects move forward.

Risks to Collections

The risks to objects must be a factor when considering digitization, and the plan should address those risks and the benefits of taking the risks. The physical stability of objects is addressed previously, but there may be instances in which because the physical state is poor, digitization is deemed the best alternative because it creates a digital surrogate. In these instances, potential loss must be taken into account. Although meticulous tracking can be in place, there is always a risk that objects could be lost or damaged during the digitization process. This can be as simple as a photograph getting placed in the wrong folder or as serious as lost shipments if outsourcing material. Objects and documents may also be damaged by inadequate supports or staff not properly trained. The workflow, standards for care and handling, and a consistent approach to providing material for digitization should mitigate these factors.

Additional risks come from the nature of the equipment used to capture the object. Light from scanners, camera lights, or other sources need to be taken into account. Although these light sources are more intense than ambient light, the duration is short so the cumulative effect on materials handled in accordance with typical digitization standards should not have severe affects. Lights often create heat, however, which is another risk factor to consider. Equipment that has been running for long hours can heat the digital lab or the glass of a scanner bed. If an object is particularly sensitive to heat it should be noted in the workflow so that care can be taken to capture an image of it before equipment or room temperatures have risen. *Preparing Collections for Digitization* by Anna E. Bulow and Jess Ahom provides more information on risks during digitization and how to mitigate them.[17]

CONCLUSION

Is digitization ever done? Probably not, unfortunately. The commitment to digitization almost always lasts beyond the scope of the initial plan. Museums need to account not only for new materials coming in, but also the migration of data from one format to another or from one media to another as standards and equipment change. The Northeast Document Conservation Center states that

> Digital copies play an important preservation role as surrogates protecting fragile and valuable originals from handling while presenting their content to a vastly increased audience. A digital version may someday be the only record of an original object that deteriorates or is destroyed. But digitization is not preservation—it is simply a means of copying original materials. In creating a digital copy, the institution creates a new resource that will itself require preservation.[18] •

GENERAL RESOURCES

Sustainable Heritage Network. Available at: http://www.sustainableheritagenetwork.org/system/files/atoms/file/2.1.06_digitizationprojectdecision-making_startingadigitizationproject_k....pdf

The Northeast Document Center. Available at: https://www.nedcc.org/free-resources/preservation-leaflets/overview.

Library of Congress. Available at: http://www.digitalpreservation.gov/.

Smithsonian Digitization Program Office. Available at: https://www.si.edu/newsdesk/digitization-program-office

Resources for Capture and File Types

The Society of American Archivists. Available at: https://www2.archivists.org/standards/external/123.

The Smithsonian Institution. Available at:https://siarchives.si.edu/what-we-do/digital-curation/digitizing-collections.

Library of Congress. Available at: http://www.digitalpreservation.gov/.

Association of Library Collections and Technical Services. Available at: http://www.ala.org/alcts/resources/preserv/minimum-digitization-capture-recommendations.

Lyrasis. Available at: https://www.lyrasis.org/Leadership/Documents/Advancing-3D-Digitization.pdf.

NOTES

1. Available at: https://blogs.library.duke.edu/bitstreams/ 2014/08/08/large-scale-digitization-lessons-ccc-project/.

2. Available at: https://www.biodiversitylibrary.org/creator/ 197368#/titles.

3. Available at: https://www.si.edu/content/pdf/about/2010_ SI_Digitization_Plan.pdf.

4. Available at: https://www.nedcc.org/free-resources/preser vation-leaflets/6.-reformatting/6.6-preservation-and-selection -for-digitization.

5. Anne E. Bulow and Jess Ahmon, *Preparing Collections for Digitization* (London: Facet Publishing, 2011), 59.

6. Available at: https://www.carli.illinois.edu/sites/files/digi tal_collections/documentation/guidelines_for_images.pdf.

7. Available at: https://www.oclc.org/research/activities/dig presmetadata/report.html.

8. Available at: https://www.archives.gov/files/preservation/ technical/guidelines.pdf.

9. Available at: https://www.diglib.org/an-update-to-the -digitization-cost-calculator/.

10. Available at: https://library.stanford.edu/research/digitiz ation-services/services/pricing.

11. Available at: https://digitalarch.org/blog/2016/2/18/plant -imaging-on-a-flatbed-scanner-creating-a-digital-herbarium.

12. Available at: http://digitalpreservation.gov/meetings/dcs16/ DChudnov-MGallinger_LCLabReport.pdf.

13. Available at: https://www.sustainableheritagenetwork.org/ system/files/atoms/file/1.20_OutsourcingvsInHouse.pdf.

14. Bulow and Ahmon, *Preparing Collections for Digitization*, 122.

15. Available at: http://www.sustainableheritagenetwork.org/ system/files/atoms/file/2.1.06_digitizationprojectdecision- making_startingadigitizationproject_k....pdf.

16. Available at: http://www.sustainableheritagenetwork.org/ system/files/atoms/file/2.1.06_digitizationprojectdecision- making_startingadigitizationproject_k....pdf.

17. Bulow and Ahmon, *Preparing Collections for Digitization*.

18. Available at: https://www.nedcc.org/free-resources/pres ervation-leaflets/6.-reformatting/6.6-preservation-and -selection-for-digitization.

5D | Measuring

HOLLY YOUNG (REVISED BY JOHN E. SIMMONS AND TONI M. KISER)

Measurements are basic to museum registration processes. They are a vital part of the initial record of an object entering a museum and serve as a baseline for publication, exhibition, and storage. Size, weight, and color should be recorded systematically. Object measurements and weights are used to determine space and material requirements for exhibit cases, storage furniture, and packing crates. Measurements can help track the condition of an object subject to breakage or dimensional changes. Standard procedures for object measurement should be defined to ensure consistency of use by individual staff members over time.

Measurement Systems

Many scientific disciplines and most countries other than the United States use the metric system, as do many US institutions. For those museums that wish to use the English system, it is best practice to record measurements in metric units as well.

An important issue to consider is the amount of precision necessary in the object measurements. In many disciplines, metric measurements are expressed in centimeters to one decimal place (or the nearest millimeter) and English measurements are expressed in inches to within 1/16 of an inch. If a measurement falls between significant increments, the reading is rounded up to the larger measurement. If increased precision is necessary, measuring implements must be selected that are more fine-tuned.

The equipment used to measure objects ranges from simple linear measuring devices to instruments that allow electronic data capture and record information directly into an electronic file. Select the kind of equipment that will be most useful for the institution, based on three major considerations: (i) the types and sizes of objects to be measured; (ii) the measurement system used; and (iii) and the amount of precision necessary.

Linear measuring devices, such as rulers, metersticks, and measuring tapes, are the most widely available and frequently used pieces of measuring equipment. They are particularly well-suited to measuring two-dimensional objects and large objects. Metal measuring tapes are the most durable but have the potential to damage the object being measured. Plastic measuring tapes have the advantage of being flexible but are easily stretched or warped, resulting in inaccurate measurements. Cloth measuring tapes and flexible fiberglass tapes are more durable than plastic and, although they can become distorted, are a good compromise.

Calipers and osteometric boards, which are useful for measuring 3-D objects, consist of a linear measuring scale with one stationary and one sliding arm, which are used to measure the distance between two points on an object. These devices yield a more accurate measurement of a 3-D object than is possible using a straight rule. Digital calipers can be used to record measurements directly into electronic data files. Calipers with both straight and pincer arms are useful; pincers are especially good for recording thickness at a particular point on the object.

Templates and gauges can be used for more precise measurements, if necessary. Color should be described using color matching systems (e.g., Munsell or Pantone). When weighing is necessary, there are a variety of electronic and spring-loaded scales and balances from which to choose. A sturdy, easy-to-calibrate triple beam balance is useful for small- to medium-sized objects. Tiny objects will require a more delicate scale or balance.

Measurement Procedures

To establish institutional measurement procedures, it is prudent to work with curatorial staff in various disciplines because they will know the standards used in their fields. Although interobserver variability can never be eliminated, it can be reduced, making measurements more reliable. Keep equipment clean, calibrated, and in good working condition and store it properly after use. Measuring equipment should be calibrated on a regular basis (as often as needed) and should be checked before use. More sophisticated and complex equipment must be calibrated more frequently.

Use particular care when handling objects for measurement. More than simply moving an object, measuring requires a certain amount of manipulation of both the object and the measuring device. For this reason, it is prudent to remove rings, watches, bracelets, pendant necklaces, or other items that may inadvertently come in contact with the object. Hands should be free of lotion or soap residues. Cotton or nitrile gloves should be worn, as appropriate (see CHAPTER 5B, "Object Handling"). Make sure that an adequate amount of space is cleared and prepared for the activity and that any necessary auxiliary materials, such as padded supports, are readily available before moving the object. When using calipers, be careful not to crush the object or damage delicate edges by applying too much pressure. To record measurements, use a pencil rather than a pen or marker (both of which can inadvertently leave a permanent mark on the object).

Two-Dimensional Objects

In general, height and width (or length) are the two basic measurements taken for flat objects. Thickness (or depth) should also be recorded for framed or mounted objects. By standard practice, height precedes width.

Paintings and other flat, rectangular objects—For square or rectangular formats, make at least two measurements from the back of the work in each direction, one at the middle, the other at an edge; record the larger measurement, if any variation occurs. Record the diameter for a circular painting or object, and the length of two axes for oval or rhombus-shaped objects. Measure the thickness of paintings on heavier supports, such as panels, and those with auxiliary supports, such as stretchers or cradles. If the frame prevents such measurements, record a sight measurement of the painting surface and the dimensions of the frame, and indicate them as sight measurements.

Textiles—This category includes two-dimensional objects such as flags, rugs, wall-hangings, and bedding. Simple woven textiles should be measured along the warp (stationary element) and the weft (moving element). Be clear as to whether or not fringe, borders, or tassels are included in the overall measurement; in any case, their length or width should be measured and noted separately. Hand-woven pieces may have the number of warps or wefts per unit of measure. More complex pieces, such as flags or quilts, should be measured in two dimensions according to their orientation in use. If a textile has a significant pile or loft, include this as a third dimension.

Works on paper—Unless otherwise indicated, works on paper are measured along the left side for height, and the lower edge for width. In addition to measuring the paper support, dimensions should be taken of the design area and plate mark, if the piece is a print. Historic documents require similar measurements, including the area covered by text. If the paper support has been hinged and matted, consider it an auxiliary support and take the measurements of the mat as well.

Three-Dimensional Objects

Generally, the overall height, length or width, and depth or thickness of these objects should be measured. Make these measurements at the point of greatest dimension. It may be practical to take a few additional measurements that are specific to the type of object and that may be important to the identification, display, or use of a particular object.

Amorphous objects—At times, objects with odd shapes and no true orientation (e.g., clumps of charred botanical materials, clods of fired adobe, crumpled pieces of metal, slag, fire-cracked rock) must be measured. Place the object on a flat surface in its most stable position, and take measurements in three dimensions from that orientation. Record the orientation or draw a simple diagram. A weight is also useful for amorphous specimens.

Boxed collections—Archival paper documents, with the exception of large format materials, are usually measured by a linear dimension (e.g., centimeter, meter, inch, foot). Large format documents, such as maps and plans, are measured by storage volume. Some repositories measure all archival collections by volume, specifically by cubic feet. This figure is determined from the compounded exterior dimensions of the storage containers. Large collections of objects and samples that are stored in boxes are similarly measured in cubic feet.

Coins—By convention, coins are measured in millimeters; if an institution uses the English system, a conversion should be made. Measure the diameter and the thickness of the coin. For coins with central perforations, give the internal dimensions of the perforation.

Furniture—The measurements for furniture may be less ambiguous if expressed as height, side-to-side, and front-to-back dimensions. Because dimensions may vary, take several measurements and record the largest. In addition to the basic measurements, measuring the height and depth of seats, and the length of aprons, table leaves, and legs may assist in developing exhibit groupings and identifying particular pieces. Because furniture is susceptible to dimensional changes, areas of loss, decay, cracks, and splits should be noted and measured.

Historic hardware and tools—Record the weight of hardware in addition to gauge. Indicate measurements of handles, including circumference, and working edges.

Natural history specimens—A wide variety of materials fall under this classification. In addition to covering the entire spectrum of animal, vegetable, and mineral, it includes auxiliary items such as nests, specimens in various stages of growth, and variously preserved specimens, including taxidermy mounts and dried or cross-sectioned specimens. It is advisable to consult the individual curatorial department for guidance. In general, overall dimensions and often weight will be useful. Specimens in containers may have the container dimensions or volume recorded, as well.

Personal items—For clothing, in addition to overall dimensions, tailoring measurements are usually taken, such as inseam length or inside waistband

FIGURE 5D.I MEASURING. CREATED BY AUTHOR.

(FIGURE 5D.I). If a standard size is marked on the object, this can be recorded, too. Accessories, such as hats or bags, should have careful measurements made of applied parts that may be subject to damage, especially feathers or trim. Component parts of jewelry should be measured—for example, the watchband or chain, as well as the watch itself. Measure diameters and restrictions for objects of personal adornment such as bracelets or labrets.

Prehistoric tools—Record basic measurements of projectile points, blades, axes, etc. For artifacts that were originally hafted, also measure hafting features, such as grooves, holes, and tangs. The hollowed-out area of artifacts such as grinding stones or mortars should be measured. Elongated artifacts such as awls, needles, or shafts should be measured for length, and diameters or thicknesses at mid-shaft and at the base.

Sculpture—Record standard dimensions; include the pedestal or other support only if it is an integral part of the sculpture. For portraits, record measurements from the proper aspect (e.g., from the depicted person's left or right, not the viewer's).

Toys—Record standard dimensions. Toys made of separate components should have a count of the pieces and a range of measurements given.

Vessels—The objects in this category can be made from many different materials, including botanical materials, ceramic, glass, and stone. For bottles and jars, measure the height and maximum diameter. Other measurements that may be taken include the orifice diameter and the neck height, where the neck is specifically delineated. Similarly, bowls should be measured for height and maximum diameter. Occasionally wall thickness is measured. At least three overall measurements should be taken for eccentric forms and other vessels such as scoops or effigies.

Weapons—In addition to basic measurements, record the length of the barrel and size of the bore for firearms. Weapons with a cutting edge should include measurements of the blade and haft.

Images and Other Machine Produced or Machine-Readable Media:

Static images—If matted and framed, these objects should be measured as flat works of art. If they are unframed, record the support and image size for positives. Record film size, length of strip (when applicable), and a count of the individual images for negatives. For slides and transparencies, give a count of the images and the size of the mount. Because these are easily duplicable, have a policy on whether or not counts should reflect unique images or include all copies of the image.

Moving images—Film and video can be measured in a number of ways, including length in feet or in playing time. Generally, the format and size of the reel or cassette are recorded.

Sound recordings—Although there are many formats, including historic cylinder and wire recordings, tapes of varying sizes and formats, and disks of different media and speeds, sound recordings are generally measured as moving images.

Digitized information—In addition to the above methods of measuring, digitized information can be measured by the byte. Other measures, such as the number of digitized images, should also be recorded. •

Thanks to Laura Andreu, Noelle McClure, and Lindsey Vogel.

5E | CONDITION REPORTING

MARIE DEMEROUKAS

A GOOD CONDITION REPORT is an accurate and informative assessment of an object's state of preservation at a particular moment in time. It provides a written and often a visual description of the nature, location, and extent of each defect in a clear, consistent manner. A condition report written by a registrar, curator, or collections manager (as discussed in this chapter) may be used for general collections management and to document incoming and outgoing loans. It is not the same as a condition report written by a conservator, which is intended for planning and performing object treatment.

A condition report can:

- Establish the exact condition of an object at a point in time.
- Benchmark the type and rate of deterioration.
- Differentiate otherwise identical objects from one another.
- Document an object's condition history, providing past evidence for the origin of future problems.
- Set priorities for conservation care and treatment.
- Make future handlers aware of seen and unseen vulnerabilities.
- Suggest an object's default monetary value in lieu of an actual value for insurance purposes.
- Provide identifying documentation for lost or stolen objects.

EXAMINATION

Prior to examination, review any previous condition reports. Examine the object in a clean, secure, well-lit work area where eating, drinking, and smoking are prohibited. For small- and medium-sized objects, pad a sturdy table or desk with polyethylene foam and cover it with clean, white, cotton sheeting or acid-free paper to help detect signs of flaking, infestation, etc. A padded flatbed dolly may be useful for larger objects. Heavy and oversized objects may need to be examined in place.

Before handling an object examine it for any inherent dangers (e.g., radioactive rocks, live ammunition, sharp-edged weapons, lead toy soldiers) and take appropriate precautions. Consult with experts and review relevant Safety Data Sheets (SDS) to determine necessary safety equipment and measures.

Wear gloves when handling objects. Nitrile gloves are smooth and less likely than cotton gloves to disrupt fragile surfaces. Nitrile gloves are especially important when working with ethnographic and natural history collections because in the past many objects were treated with pesticides and other chemicals. Follow all appropriate handling guidelines, making sure each part is properly supported. Large, awkward, or fragile objects may require several handlers. Check carefully for an object's visible faults, such as cracks, tears, and potential weaknesses, such as repaired handles or brittle veneer (see CHAPTER 5B, "Object Handling").

Make sure that lighting is adequate for the task. General lighting illuminates the object overall; raking light illuminates at an angle; transmitted light illuminates from the reverse. Good lighting can reveal a variety of surface and subsurface irregularities. Use ultraviolet (UV) light judiciously to detect adhesive residues, paints, resins, etc. An X-ray uses electronic radiation to detect subsurface cracks and losses. Avoid light damage by reducing long-term exposure, filtering UV from general lighting, minimizing intense exposure, and reducing heat buildup (see CHAPTER 5I, "Preventive Care").

To understand and identify an object's defects and weaknesses, it is important to determine its composition. Objects may be made of organic materials (e.g., bone, cotton, hair), inorganic materials (e.g., gold, clay, flint), or a combination of both. These materials may be in their original form, such as marble, or may have been modified, such as brass (an alloy of copper and zinc). Objects made from a combination of materials may suffer from a variety of problems including weak joints, dissimilar rates of expansion and contraction, or chemical incompatibility.

Damage affects an object's condition. An inherent fault (also known as *inherent vice*) is a weakness in the construction of an object or the incompatibility of materials of which it is composed, such as a thin handle on a heavy teapot or metallic salts added to nineteenth-century silks. Pests and mold, which feed on organic materials or deposits, cause biological damage as they weaken an object's structure or create problems such as riddled wood or discoloration. Physical damage is caused by mechanical stress and includes abrasion, losses, tearing, etc. Chemical damage is the result of a reaction between a material and an energy source (heat, light) or a chemical (e.g., water). It is evidenced by corrosion, tarnish, fading, etc. Other condition-related factors to keep in mind:

- Distinguish between historic and modern damage or repairs.
- Note any extraneous materials (e.g., surface dust, insect frass, and accretions such as paint splatters and adhesive residues).
- Burial may affect an object's condition (e.g., salts efflorescing on pottery) and materials that are excavated as already broken may still be considered in good condition.
- Consider that one type of damage may contribute to another (e.g., embrittlement can lead to tearing).
- Understand that some objects have important evidence of a past function (e.g., stains on a ritual blade, dried residue in a medicine bottle).

When possible, examine objects by category (e.g., hats, bird mounts, paintings) or by types of materials (e.g., stone, paper, wool). Grouping will promote consistency, thoughtful observations, and accuracy. Determine an appropriate examination pattern and follow it each time (e.g., top to bottom, proper left to proper right, front to back, exterior to interior). Some objects are made of multiple components such as a painting and its frame, a taxidermy specimen and its mount, or a tea set and its storage case. Consider reporting on each component separately.

The following equipment, tools, and supplies can be helpful when examining and documenting an object's condition.

Documentation

- Soft lead pencil (a pen can leave a permanent mark);
- White or kneaded eraser;
- Examination form and note paper (acid-free, if it will be part of the permanent record);
- Computer or tablet;
- Digital camera and SD (secure digital) cards (for still shots or video), or film camera and film; and
- Three-dimensional imaging camera or scanner (captures both visual images and measurements).

Measurement

- Cloth tape measure, without metal caps (caution: some tapes can stretch);
- Clear plastic flexible ruler; and
- Calipers.

Handling and Support

- Nitrile gloves (powder-free);
- Personal protective gear (e.g., lab coat, face mask, respirator);
- Buffered and unbuffered acid-free, lignin-free, tissue paper and board;
- Sheeting (e.g., white cotton, polyethylene closed-cell foam, nonwoven polyethylene fabric);
- Supports (e.g., padded muslin rolls and blocks, lightweight weights, book holders); and
- Flatbed dolly.

Illumination

- Flashlight;
- Pen or crevice light;
- Portable incandescent light (e.g., a mechanic's drop light);
- Headlamp; and
- UV light.

Magnification

- 10× hand lens;
- Jeweler's loupe;
- 55× microscope; and
- Head-mounted magnifier.

Miscellaneous

- Hand mirror;
- Dental mirror;
- Magnet (to identify ferrous metals);
- Natural-hair brushes in a variety of shapes and stiffness;
- Probes (dentals tools);
- Forceps (tweezers);
- Palette knife; and
- Air blower.

DOCUMENTATION

Determine what types of condition reports are required based on need, level of specificity, budget, staff availability, and collections management priorities. Condition reporting fields found within basic digital collection management systems may be adequate for a general assessment of most objects in a collection. Custom reports may be required for sizable collections of specialty items, such as glassware or archaeological materials, and for objects which are fragile, valuable, subject to loan, or are otherwise significant.

Staff-created handwritten or computer-based report forms that are customizable, budget friendly, and easy to use can be created on demand (FIGURE 5E.I; see also the "Condition Report for Paintings, Drawings, Prints, and Other Works on Paper" in the *Collection Forms* section). However uploading and annotating images, and printing and scanning completed reports, can be time-consuming. Proprietary digital reporting applications offer the convenience of quickly and seamlessly merging images and data, provide editing and annotating functions, and allow multiple users to collaborate and share. When purchasing software, consider initial costs and annual fees, the ability to customize templates, the company's reliability, the helpfulness of support staff, and the software's ability to integrate with other collection-management systems, particularly hardware compatibility.

An object's condition can be documented by text (physical description), sketch (rough representation), and photographic image (exact representation). A combination of these methods provides a complete account of an object's condition at a particular moment in time (FIGURE 5E.2). Note any issues which may impede accurate or complete condition reporting, such as an object framed behind glass or an oversize object that cannot be viewed on all sides.

Written documentation can take the form of a narrative or a checklist. Although some technical terminology will be needed for clarity, in general a report's language must be simple, straightforward, and understandable. A condition report should include:

- Identifying numbers (accession, loan, field, catalog);
- Type of object;
- Name of artist or maker (if known);
- Title of object (if any);
- Date and place of manufacture or site collection (if known);
- Dimensions (height × width × depth, diameter, circumference);
- Number of parts;
- Object composition or construction;
- Overall condition assessment;
- Types of damage and any extraneous materials;
- Extent of damage;
- Location of damage;
- Dates and cause of damage (if known);
- Previous repairs (historic, modern);
- Recommendations for exhibition or storage (based on object's condition);
- Examiner's name; and
- Date of examination.

Digital images capture the nature, extent, and location of damage, and high-resolution images can provide passive documentation of unnoticed problems for future confirmation. Notes or marks highlighting problem areas may be made within a digital file (via a word-processing or graphics-editing program) or directly on prints. If using film, consider

General Condition Report Form

Object _____ **Examiner** _____
Catalog/Loan Number _____ **Date** _____

Significance *(e.g., name of artist/maker, title of object, date & place of manufacture/site collection)*

Brief Description *(e.g., physical description, material composition, construction, number of parts)*

Dimensions *(e.g., HxWxD, diameter, circumference)*

Previous Repairs/Treatments/Alterations

Overall Condition Assessment   ___*Excellent*   ___*Good*   ___*Fair*   ___*Poor*

Specific Damage   **Location/Degree** *(negligible, slight, moderate, marked, extreme)*

Accretions
___*Soiled*
___*Residues/Deposits*
___*Tarnish*
___*Corrosion*
___*Efflorescence*
___*Other*_____

Discoloration
___*Stains*
___*Bleeding*
___*Water Damage*
___*Foxing*
___*Fading/Bleaching/*
   Darkening
___*Other*_____

Miscellaneous
___*Pest Damage*
___*Mold*
___*Shrinking*
___*Other*_____

FIGURE 5E.1A GENERAL CONDITION REPORT FORM, PAGE I. CREATED BY AUTHOR.

Structural

___*Abrasions/Scratches*
___*Wear/Fraying/Dog-Eared*
___*Dents/Gouges/Chips*
___*Tears/Splits/Cracks*
___*Losses*
___*Creases/Wrinkling/Buckling*
___*Crazing*
___*Pitting*
___*Loose Joints*
___*Delaminated*
___*Distorted/Warping*
___*Friable/Flaking/Rot/Powdering*
___*Stiff/Embrittled*
___*Detached/Missing Elements*
___*Other*_____

Images/Sketches of Damage *(note position)*

Additional Comments

Recommendations for Exhibition/Storage

FIGURE 5E.1B GENERAL CONDITION REPORT FORM, PAGE 2. CREATED BY AUTHOR.

Structural

<u>x</u> *Abrasions/Scratches*
<u>x</u> *Wear/Fraying/Dog-eared*
___*Dents/Gouges/Chips*
___*Tears/Splits/Cracks*
<u>x</u> *Losses*
<u>x</u> *Creases/Wrinkling/Buckling*
___*Crazing*
___*Pitting*
___*Loose Joints*
___*Delaminated*
___*Distorted/Warping*
___*Friable/Flaking/Rot/Powdering*
<u>x</u> *Stiff/Embrittled*
___*Detached/Missing Elements*
___*Other*_____

obv: moderate, diagonal V-shaped scratch (2.4 mm long) BC; negligible scratches in photo layer overall; entire BR portion of object missing, with slight to moderate creases in photo layer and cracks/tears in mount along missing edge; TR corner moderately dog-eared

obv/rev: marked wear/fraying at corners and along missing edge, with some loss of surface paper on secondary mount; mount markedly embrittled

Images/Sketches of Damage *(note position)*

#1 red ink(?) stain—diffuse/blurry

#2 red ink(?) stain—sharp/defined

#3 dog-ear

#4 pest damage

#5 v-shaped diagonal scratch

#6 flyspecks

obverse   *reverse*

Additional Comments

keep eye on cracks along missing edge

Recommendations for Exhibition/Storage

make reference copy for use and store original

FIGURE 5E.2 METHODS OF DOCUMENTING AN OBJECT'S CONDITION. CREATED BY AUTHOR.

black-and-white film as the contrast in tones can better highlight cracks and flaws than color film. A photographic image should include:

- Identifying numbers;
- Scale;
- Color chart; and
- Date of image.

Whether an object's condition is recorded electronically or on paper or film, make sure that the materials and methods used are archivally sound and selected for long-term preservation. Digital images should be captured at a high resolution and saved using widely available, nonproprietary lossless data compression (see CHAPTER 5H, "Photography"). View or modify a surrogate file rather than the original. If using film, keep in mind that black-and-white film is more stable than color (although modern color film is more stable than its predecessors). Process film or print digital images according to American National Standards Guidelines for longevity.

Store original and annotated images with their respective reports. Paper-based documentation should be stored in a secure and environmentally stable area. At least one set of duplicates should be housed separately, outside of the community in which the institution is located, in case of area-wide disaster. Electronic documentation should be backed-up as changes are made and maintained on external hard drives, in a networked system, or in cloud storage, depending on need and budget. Maintain more than one back-up in case problems arise with a particular hosting company. Files should be refreshed every few years to prevent degradation of media, and they should be migrated as technology changes.

When writing a condition report, consider the nature, location, and extent of damage. Completely discuss one type of damage on one portion of the object before moving on, to ensure accuracy and minimize handling. Observational skills will be honed after creating condition reports for several similar objects, so review the earlier reports and improve them as necessary. Keep all reference materials (e.g., glossaries, location nomenclature) on file for future reference. Use terms consistently. Be objective and specific.

TYPE OF DAMAGE

What is the nature of the damage? If the examiner is trained in conservation, it may be possible to determine whether damage is biological, physical, or chemical in nature or the result of an inherent fault. If the cause of damage is not apparent, leave etiological statements to the conservator. Describe damage in terms of texture, color, shape, odor, and other physical properties, as appropriate. A glossary, whether established or constructed, can be used to assign a descriptive term to a specific condition. Speculative assessments should be indicated with a question mark.

Location

Where is the damage located? When possible, use a recognized nomenclature to indicate the exact position of damage (e.g., proper left, viewer's right) or describe the damaged part of the object (e.g., for a hammer—face, neck, handle, grip, cheek). Sources for standards include museum nomenclatures, collector organizations and publications, product manufacturers, and reference texts. The object itself may provide location names (e.g., the shirt or face area on a figure in a painting, or "to the right of the handle, at the base").

A zone system (FIGURE 5E.3) provides a generalized method for locating damage on two-dimen-

FIGURE 5E.3 ZONE SYSTEM. CREATED BY AUTHOR.

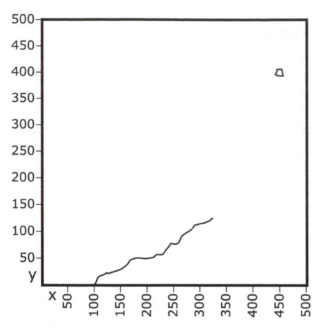

stain: center at 450, 400 mm
tear: from 100, 0 to 350, 125 mm

FIGURE 5E.4 MATRIX SYSTEM. CREATED BY AUTHOR.

sional objects. Each zone or square is labeled, such as TR (top right) or C (center), and the damage is placed within a zone. The matrix system (FIGURE 5E.4), also for two-dimensional objects, is more precise, as the damage is plotted in millimeters using the x- and y-coordinate positions. The x-coordinate represents the horizontal (bottom edge) of the object (the x-axis); the y-coordinate represents the vertical (left edge) of the object (the y-axis). A stain near the top right corner of a document might be plotted as 400 mm along the x-axis (horizontal) and 450 mm along the y-axis (vertical), and expressed as "400, 450 mm." Sketches, photographs, or digital images offer location guidance for three-dimensional objects. Measurements in the United States have been taken either metrically or in the English system, depending on the museum's discipline and traditions. However, if the English system is used, metric equivalents should be indicated as well. When possible, lay the measuring device alongside the object to avoid touching the object. Other ways to describe location include:

- Direction (horizontal, vertical, diagonal);
- Object side (obverse or reverse, interior or exterior, proper left or proper right); and
- Range (scattered, overall).

Extent

What is the extent of the damage? Proceed from the general to the specific (e.g., "object yellowed overall, especially in BR corner"). Some damage such as a tear or a loss can be readily measured. Damage, which cannot be conventionally measured, such as foxing or yellowing, can be described in standardized degrees of severity (e.g., negligible, slight, or moderate, marked, or extreme). Recognized condition standards have been established for a variety of objects (e.g., coins, stamps).

Updating Reports

When updating reports, add new condition information (including the examiner's name and date) next to the old, so past and present comments appear together. Unless there has been a change in condition, there is no need to repeat the same information for an object that is part of a long-term traveling exhibition. Rather, indicate that the comments provided in the initial report or by previous examiners are still applicable. Treat the condition report as a legal document; it may be used in title or insurance disputes.

Carefully review an incoming condition report immediately following the receipt of an object. If there is a discrepancy, a digital photo of the problem area can be made and promptly sent to the lender. When dealing with a large incoming collection, it is best to have two examiners: one person to read the report aloud (and make notes) and another to visually confirm the description against the objects.

CONDITION REPORTING GLOSSARY

The following are some common terms used to describe condition. Many are general and can be applied to a number of materials; some are material specific and are to be used in conjunction with the general terms. See FIGURES 5E.5–7 for examples of damage and the terminology used to describe it.

General Terms

abrasion—A generally superficial mechanical wearing away of the surface, often from scraping, rubbing, grinding, or friction.

accretion—External material deposited on a surface, often as a result of burial conditions or accidental

FIGURE 5E.5 LATE NINETEENTH-CENTURY MEDALLION WITH CRAZED AND STAINED ENAMEL, CONCAVITIES, AND CORROSION IN THE COPPER SUPPORT AND SURFACE LOSSES IN THE ENAMEL AS A RESULT OF EXTREME DENTS. COURTESY SHILOH MUSEUM OF OZARK HISTORY (S-66-2-892). CREATED BY AUTHOR.

FIGURE 5E.7 DETAIL OF A DOLL TRUNK WITH RUSTY NAIL HEADS, SPLITTING WOOD, AND EMBRITTLED ANIMAL-SKIN HIDE WITH MISSING FUR, TEARS, FRAYED EDGES, AND LOSSES, CIRCA 1860. COURTESY SHILOH MUSEUM OF OZARK HISTORY (S-95-100). CREATED BY AUTHOR.

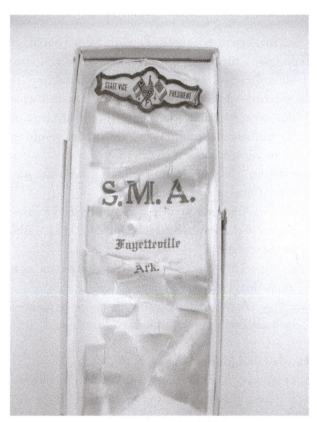

FIGURE 5E.6 DETAIL OF AN ORGANIZATION BADGE WITH SHATTERED SILK RIBBON AND A TARNISHED BAR-STYLE PINBACK WITH SOILED AND YELLOWED CELLULOID INSERT DATING FROM 1900. COURTESY SHILOH MUSEUM OF OZARK HISTORY (S-89-167-36). CREATED BY AUTHOR.

deposits such as splashes, drips, flyspecks, etc. (cf. *inclusion*).

adhesive residue—The sticky or crusty remains of glue, paste, or pressure-sensitive tape.

bleeding—The suffusion of a color into adjacent materials, often caused by water or other solvents.

break—A fracture or split resulting in the separation of parts.

chip—A defect in a surface characterized by the breaking away of material.

crack—A surface fracture or fissure across or through a material, either straight-line or branching in form; no loss is implied. A crack may be described as *blind* when it stops part way, as *hairline* when it is a tiny fissure, or as *open* when it is a large fissure.

crazing—An unintentional fine network of surface cracks in a ceramic glaze, a painting's varnish layer, or a metal's coating (cf. *crizzling*).

crease—A line of crushed or broken fibers, generally made by folding.

delamination—A separation of layers; splitting.

dent—A shallow concavity in the surface, caused by a blow (cf. *gouge*).

discoloration: A partial or overall change in color caused by aging, light, or chemical agents. Yellowing and darkening can occur, along with bleaching (the lightening of color), and fading (a loss of color or a change in hue).

disjoin—A partial or complete separation of a joint between two members of an object, as distinguished from a crack, tear, check, or split.

distortion—A misshaping of the original shape; shrinkage may occur (cf. *creep*).

draw—A local distortion at the corner of a painting or a piece of paper, marked by diagonal cockling from the corner toward the center of the mount (cf. *dishing*).

embrittlement—A loss of flexibility causing the material (e.g., paper, parchment, leather) to break or disintegrate when bent or curled (cf. *stiffness*).

friable—Able to be easily crumbled or pulverized into a powder.

gouge—A concavity in the surface where material has been scooped out (cf. *dent*).

inclusion—A particle accidentally bonded to the surface of an object during manufacture.

loss—Missing area or hole.

mildew—See *mold*.

missing element—The loss of an integral component of, or an addition or appendage to, an object (e.g., handle, tassel).

mold—Biological in nature, mold or mildew can be evidenced by a musty odor or colored, furry, or web-like surface excrescences. Some *foxing* (see below) can be caused by mold.

patina—A colored surface layer, either applied or naturally occurring.

pest damage—Surface loss, tunneling, holes, fly specks, and so on caused by insects, rodents, or other pests.

repair—The evidence of past repair such as a filled loss, a staple or rivet, or inpainting.

scratch—A linear surface loss due to abrasion with a sharp point.

sheen—A polish produced by handling. Often occurs on frequently touched locations.

soil—A general term denoting any material that dirties an object. Dust is loose soil while a smear and a fingerprint are types of localized grime.

stain—A color change as a result of soiling, adhesives, pest residue, food, oils, etc. A diffuse stain is without a distinct boundary; a discrete stain has a distinct boundary or tide line, which is darker than the general area of the stain; and a centered stain has a darker or more intensely colored center within its general area. In metallic staining, adjacent materials are discolored as a result of metal corrosion.

stiffness—The loss of flexibility and suppleness (cf. *embrittlement*).

tear—A break in fabric, paper, or other sheet material as a result of tension or torsion.

wear—Surface erosion, usually at the edges, due to repeated handling.

Ceramic, Glass, and Stone Terms

crizzling—A fine network of cracks on glass caused by the hydration of the salts in the glass as a result of the leaching of excess alkali (cf. *crazing*, *devitrification*).

devitrification—The loss of transparency in glass caused by the crystallization of the original ingredients (cf. *crazing*, *crizzling*).

efflorescence—A powdery or crystalline crust on the surface of stone, plaster, ceramics, etc. Formed when transmigrating water reacts with an object's chemical makeup or extraneous deposits from a burial.

flaking—A lifting of the surface layer (e.g., glaze, enamel); often resulting in a loss (cf. *powdering*).

iridescence—A color effect in glass or pottery that is due to the partial decomposition of the surface and the formation of innumerable thin scales, resulting in an uneven, flaky surface.

powdering—Shallow losses or flaking from the surface of stone or ceramic (cf. *flaking*).

spalling—A general weakness resulting in the exfoliation of the body or chipping off of layers parallel to the surface.

sugaring—The erosion of a marble surface creating a granulated or sugary surface appearance.

weeping—A wet, dripping surface on glass. Caused by a reaction between water and formic acid.

Leather and Skin Terms

fatty spews—A milky film found on leather as a result from previous dressing applications or the migration of natural fat in the leather.

hair loss—An area of loose or missing fur in objects and garments made of pelts. Often due to pest activity or the improper processing of the hide.

red rot—A powdery red substance found on vegetable-tanned leather objects as a result of a chemical reaction with pollutants in the air.

Metal Terms

corrosion—The chemical alteration of a metal surface caused by agents in the environment or by reagents applied purposely. Corrosion may only affect an object's color and texture without altering the form, or it may add to the form, producing hard nodules or crusts. Bimetallic (or galvanic) corrosion results from incompatible metal contact. Bronze disease (often found in unearthed archaeological objects) is a type of copper corrosion evidenced by powdery green spots. Rust is a reddish-brown corrosion that can be soft and powdery, flaking, or compact and hard. Copper stearate corrosion is a waxy green compound formed as a reaction between a copper-based metal and the oils found in leather.

pitting—Small, irregular, shallow, pinhole-sized losses scattered over the surface of metal, caused by acidic conditions or resulting from the casting process.

tarnish—A dullness or blackening of a bright metal surface.

Painting Terms

blanching—Irregular, obtrusive, pale, or milky areas in paint or varnish. Not a superficial defect like *bloom* but a scattering of light from microporosities or granulation in aged films.

blister—A separation between layers, appearing as an enclosed, bubbled area.

bloom—A whitish, cloudy appearance in the varnish layer, caused by exposure to moisture or resulting from a wax-based media.

buckling—Waves or large bulges in a canvas from a nonuniform tension around the stretcher or strainer.

chalking—A loss of a paint or emulsion layer by powdering off.

cleavage—A separation between the paint layers and the support producing tenting (gable-like ridges) or cupping (concave flakes). Caused by the contraction of the support, which forces the paint layer up and off the surface.

crackle, craquelure—A network of fine cracks that develop in the ground, paint layer, or surface coating of a painting as the materials age or dry, or as the result of a blow. Age cracks usually penetrate both paint layer and ground. Drying cracks are caused by the failure of the film to withstand its own contraction during drying. Such cracks usually do not penetrate the whole structure from support to surface. Mechanical cracks, although similar in appearance and character to age cracks, are often caused by external local pressure and frequently appear as a bullseye pattern of concentric circles.

cupping—See *cleavage*.

dishing—A defect in the stretcher caused by the torque of a drawing fabric. If the stretcher members are twisted out of a common plane, a shallow dihedral angle is formed at the corners. Dishing is a common cause of corner wrinkles in stretched canvases (cf. *draw*).

fill—The material used to replace areas of loss.

flaking—The lifting and sometimes loss of flat areas of the surface layer.

inpainting—New areas of paint added over fill to restore design or color continuity; restricted to areas of loss.

overpainting—Areas of repainting over an existing original surface.

stretcher crease—A crease or line of cracks in the ground and paint layers of a painting on fabric, following the inside edges of the stretcher members or the edges of cross-members.

tenting—See *cleavage*.

wrinkling—Small ridges and furrows of crawling paint or varnish caused by the use of improper methods or materials. Usually related to a nondrying medium and the loss of volume in the film through evaporation.

Paper Terms

cockling—A soft, concave or convex random distortion characterized by parallel, repeated ripples, usually horizontal or vertical.

dimpling—A local distortion, usually in a corner, marked by a distinctly concave area. Usually caused by local adhesion of the support to the secondary support.

dog-ear—A diagonal crease across the corner of paper-based materials (e.g., book page, pasteboard secondary mount).

foxing—Small yellow, brown, or reddish-brown spots on paper caused by mold or the oxidation of iron particles within the paper.

wrinkling—An angular, crushed distortion.

Photography Terms

ferrotyping—Glossy patches found on the surface of a photograph resulting from lengthy contact with a smooth-surfaced storage enclosure, such as polyester or glass.

frilling—The separation and lifting of the photographic emulsion from the edges of the support.

silvering—Shiny or mirror-like discoloration in the shadow areas of a photographic image, caused by the aging of excessive residual silver compounds.

Plastic Terms

bubbly area—A bubbly or blistered area in cellulose nitrate and acetate film.

creep, deformation—A change in the original shape due to chemical instability or exposure to high temperature (cf. *distortion*).

odor—The smell of sulfur, camphor, vinegar, and so on produced by the degradation of cellulose nitrate or acetate products. Strong odor indicates severe degradation.

oozing—See *sweating*.

sweating, liquid exudate—A clear or yellow oily liquid found on the surface of a deteriorated cellulose nitrate or acetate object.

Textile Terms

crocking—The rubbing off of color, resulting in the loss of dyestuff but not of fiber.

fraying—A raveled or worn spot indicated by the separation of threads, especially on the edge of a fabric.

shattering, tendering—A deterioration of threads, most common in silk. Usually caused by light, heat, use of salt mordants, exposure to perspiration, or a combination thereof. Lateral splits occur parallel to the grain of the cloth's fiber when the textile is stretched and damaged by sunlight.

weak seam—A looseness in the attachment of two adjoining pieces of fabric.

Wood Terms

alligatoring—A series of hairline cracks in old varnish, creating the appearance of alligator hide.

checking—A slight splitting along the wood grain creating a checkerboard-like pattern. Checking is usually in response to repeated dimensional change brought on by fluctuations of temperature and humidity (cf. *split*).

cupping, dishing—The warping across the width of a board, usually with the upper surface developing a concave curve.

dry rot—The decay of seasoned timber caused by fungi that consume the cellulose of wood, leaving a soft skeleton that is readily reduced to powder.

shrinkage—A loss of mass or size in response to low relative humidity conditions.

split—A crack that runs through an entire surface, such as veneer.

warping—An irregularity in wood as a result of shrinkage (e.g., furniture, a painting's wood support). Often caused by relative humidity. •

BIBLIOGRAPHY

Van Horn, D. R., H. Culligan, and C. Midgett, *Basic Condition Reporting. A Handbook*, 4th ed. (Lanham, MD: Rowman & Littlefield, 2015).

With sincere thanks to Martha Battle Jackson (North Carolina Historic Sites), Ellen E. Endslow (Chester County Historical Society, Pennsylvania), Anne Ennes (National Park Service-Harpers Ferry Center, Museum Conservation Services), Jennifer Gallatin Rigsby (Indianapolis Museum of Art at Newfields), Lena Hernandez (Museum of Science & History), Kathryn Lang (Steamtown National Historic Site), Cara Seitchek (Montgomery County Historical Society), Rachel Shabica (National Museum of the American Indian), Elizabeth Varner (US Department of the Interior, Interior Museum Program), and the authors of Basic Condition Reporting: A Handbook *(3rd edition, 1998).*

5F | MARKING

NORA S. LOCKSHIN (UPDATED AND EXPANDED FROM PREVIOUS VERSIONS BY TAMARA JOHNSTON, ROBIN MEADOR-WOODRUFF, AND TERRY SEGAL)[1]

MARKING OR LABELING museum objects with identification numbers is an important part of the registrars' and collections managers' responsibilities. The primary goal in marking an object with an identification number is to prevent dissociation (one of the established agents of deterioration) by providing a unique identifier to connect an object with its documentation.[2] Marking is a method of risk management and collections stewardship. Not all object marking is for the permanent collection; objects can also be marked temporarily for exhibition or while in the institution's custody for consideration as a purchase or gift. Marking is one of the most basic, albeit invasive, procedures undertaken in registration. Methods and materials should be selected with care and the process should be fully understood and practiced before it is implemented in the collection. This chapter includes the following topics:

- Preferred Practices;
- Choosing a Method—Temporary/Indirect, Semi-Permanent/Direct, or Permanent/Direct;
- Recommended Materials for Marking—Permanence, Lightfastness, Colorfastness;
- Location and Size of a Mark on an Object;
- Description of Methods—Step-by-Step Instructions and Alternative Strategies;
- Materials That Should Not be Used;
- Marking Specific Kinds of Objects (by Material or Object Type); and
- Materials and Supplies for Marking.

PREFERRED PRACTICES

Objects in a museum's custody, either permanently or temporarily, should be marked accordingly. Objects that are incorporated into the museum's collection by accession is an example of the former, whereas objects that are on loan, on deposit to be considered for ac-

quisition, or part of an auxiliary collection (e.g., education collections) have temporary status. It should be clear to anyone working with a museum collection, both now and in the future, which objects are part of the permanent collection and which are not, and the markings should be part of the object's history of ownership (see CHAPTERS 3B, "Acquisitions and Accessioning," and 3D, "Provenance Research in Museums—An Overview").

Each object and its constituent parts should be marked with a unique identifier. The format used depends on the type of museum and its labeling traditions. For example, in art museums the accession number is most commonly used, but in natural history museums it is the object's catalog number (see CHAPTER 5A, "Numbering"). The identifier may incorporate the year of accessioning or a code identifying the institution, and historic marks may also contain other descriptive information. Marking systems should be consistent within an institution and the assignment of identifying numbers should be centrally controlled by the registrar, based on the collection management policies and procedures (see CHAPTER 2, "Collection Management Policies"). Uncontrolled marking can lead to confusion and double numbering as well as physical damage to objects. Once an object has been assigned a number, that number should be used in perpetuity. As a general rule, accessioned objects should not be renumbered, although exceptions must be made when an accession number has been erroneously applied or an object is deaccessioned (see CHAPTER 3I, "Deaccessioning and Disposal").

When Marks Go Wrong

Occasional mistakes in object marking do occur due to lack of supervision, experience, misunderstanding, or physical errors. These mistakes must be corrected, keeping in mind that all documentation must be carefully checked before proceeding with renumbering. The need to correct mistakes brings up an important goal in object numbering—reversibility. This is a paradox because markings must be durable and persistent in the face of exposure to the agents of deterioration (physical forces, thieves and vandals, fire, water, pests, pollutants, light, incorrect temperature and humidity, and dissociation), and some markings must perform well in extreme environments, yet the markings must be eminently reversible![3] Hindsight teaches us and perspective acknowledges that, in practice, some chemical applications to surfaces may be irreversible, but with documented practices, careful analysis of material characteristics and potential interactions, and preparation of the work area and object surface, reversibility with select means and techniques can be achieved, and accidents minimized.

Marks and labels may deteriorate or be applied in a way that limits legibility, comprehension, or access. For example, letters and numbers may be confused because of the use of nonserif fonts, which do not distinguish between a lower-case l and numeral 1; symmetrical and inverted numbers read from an upside-down orientation (e.g., 6 or 9, without underlines); poorly contrasting marks; or marks applied with inappropriate supplies. Visual overviews of marks gone wrong are found in training webinars.[4]

Ethics of Removal

There are specific concerns about removing historic marks from any object held in the public trust by a cultural or scientific institution. Although historical numbering, labeling, or descriptive textual inscriptions may interfere with the appreciation of an object's meaning, aesthetics, accuracy of identification, or sacred nature, the removal of same may erase understanding of past practice, no matter how imperfect. As one interviewee put it, "in the case of ethnographic collections, that prominent writing on the object is also an example of the colonial project, the way indigenous material culture was taken and possessed by the dominant culture."[5]

If inquiring for technical advice or assistance in the removal of a mark or label, note that American Institute for Conservation offers its own *Code of Ethics and Guidelines for Practice* and commentaries by

which the professional conservator should abide that complement the protocols of whichever institution they support.[6] Statements include guidance such as "[s]ignificant non-original material that is removed prior to compensation should be documented"; "distinguish among those materials and methods that are part of currently accepted practice, those that have been superseded, and those which are still experimental. Materials and methods become part of currently accepted practice through: replicable research; objective review of past practices; professional consultation." With regard to marks or labels related to object provenance and acceptable practice, the conservator should also:

> Be cognizant of laws and regulations that may have a bearing on professional activity. Among these laws and regulations are those concerning the rights of artists and their estates, occupational health and safety, sacred and religious material, excavated objects, endangered species, human remains, and stolen property.[7]

The removal of overlarge or deteriorated marks may require an overall conservation cleaning because the underlying surface may have a different appearance that would result in a ghost image, and it may not be possible to achieve a uniform color and texture. When historic marks or labels must be removed for sake of exhibition, photography, or with intent to provide a more accurate or respectful representation, all efforts should be made to document the rationale for the decision, and to include a photographic history in the registration and conservation object records. If the mark is a historic label that can be removed, it may be considered a fragment, and documented as such by photographing it and giving it an accession part number of its own. The disposition of the rehoused label may be determined by the resources of the organization, and museums may approach this differently. In case of a deteriorated or deposed label, it may be photocopied onto permanent paper for the files, scanned and added as a child image to a collection management system (CMS), or treated or encapsulated in a permanent safe plastic enclosure and placed with the object in its housing.[8]

Keeping the label with the object is ideal to provide all end users with a sense of the object's history (see CHAPTER 3D, "Provenance Research in Museums— An Overview").

CHOOSING A METHOD

Critical Thinking, Decision Trees, and the Many Options before You

The tables found in this chapter are updated and revised versions from prior editions of *Museum Registration Methods*, but they are not exhaustive because products change, disappear from the market, and new products are released. For example, although many of the pens, pencils, and tools continue to be manufactured, others have been replaced or redesigned. No further testing was done for this edition, but a few publications offer guidance to testing and tested materials[9] or selection criteria to determine what is appropriate to the object and your resources.[10] In addition, many trusted public institutions or publications present information and options for consideration as free downloadable content.[11] All of these are excellent resources to have at the workstation in a binder to supplement written documentation of your organization's own historical practices and current protocols, for easy reference, teaching, discussion, and annotation.

Evaluating and Selecting Marking Materials

Many products that are available have stood the test of time, but others are new to the market. Excellent print resources for researching products, whether by generic name or proprietary formulation, are available[12] and updated free resources such as Conservation and Art Materials Encyclopedia Online (CAMEO),[13] which provides proprietary and generic information on products used in art and conservation, and the American Institute for Conservation (AIC) Wiki, with its lexicon and subspecialty topic pages such as adhesives.[14]

For future inquiries about products new to the market or revised in formulation, consider working with your network to engage the support of students, collections specialists, or conservators in academic or public institutions that support research and testing. See also options for do-it-yourself testing of products

you currently use, which may have changed in formulation, or ones you are considering using.

As of this writing, questions continue to be researched for emerging ink, paint, print, and adhesive technologies with which the cultural heritage community can only hope to keep pace. Permanence, durability, legibility, and potential interactions of marking and label chemistry with objects or specimens is of interest to the collaborative Materials Selection and Specification Working Group.[15] Grants may be available from research organizations to investigate potential problems or solutions to marking challenges.[16]

To keep up to date, look for updates published in journals such as *Collections: A Journal for Museum and Archives Professionals*; the Society for the Preservation of Natural History Collections' *Collection Forum*; Storage Techniques for Art, Science & History Collections and Foundation for Advancement in Conservation (STASH-c), or other resources. Use the archives and networked communities such as the CS-AAM listserv and AIC's Connecting to Collections Care Online Community to research and inquire about specific products or practices.

There are multiple variants on techniques and options from which to choose (these are summarized further in the chapter); using these and the other resources cited, investigate the possible marking supplies and methods that can be safely used to mark a particular object by its physical materials, form (parts, shape, mass), and status (ethics, loaned object). Knowledge of the object itself and the materials of which it is made are necessary. If it is not clear what the object is made of, consult a conservator or subject matter expert. In the absence of a specific material identification and its vulnerabilities, use the least invasive or indirect technique of object marking (TABLES 5F.1, 5F.2, and 5F.3).

Best practice in object marking requires an experienced registrar or collections manager to oversee all object marking. Never practice object marking on museum objects. A person may become experienced by first practicing numbering techniques on different types of non-museum objects to acquire an understanding of the effects the various methods of marking can have on different surfaces. Observe, inquire, investigate, and practice before beginning to mark any museum object.

Table 5F.1 Marking Specific Kinds of Objects by Material or Object Type

Object Types	Comments, Considerations, Locations, and Vulnerabilities
Albums (photographic and scrapbook)	For paper albums, see *Books*; for LPs, see *Audiovisual*.
Amphibians	See *Reptiles and amphibians* and *Natural history specimens*.
Armor	Mark with ink or paint over a base coat inside each element, or tie an acid-free, two- or four-ply mat board tag to the object with fabric tape or polypropylene cord. Metal tags stamped or engraved with the number are sometimes used, but more inert, nonabrasive materials are preferred.
Animal hide	See *Skins*.
Audiovisual	Many recordings have enclosures such as boxes or sleeves that can be marked. Use pencil or water-based pigment markers to mark cassettes, diskette labels, cans, film leader, or hub; or use tags with ties. Do not write directly on recording media or supports. See *Film*, *Plastics*, and *Optical discs*.
Basketry and mats (including bark cloth and other fibrous materials)	These materials can be difficult to mark. Some basket fibers are resistant to the application of varnishes and adhesives or may be too narrow for a legible written number. Mark at the center bottom of the basket or inside the rim. Choose the marking location carefully because varnishes and adhesives may stain porous fibers. The preferred method for marking is an adhered kozo paper label. If it is necessary to mark the object directly, do not apply the number directly without a varnish base coat (marking media can stain the objects and inks applied directly may bleed). If the reeds of the basket are not long or wide enough, or will not accept the application of a base coat or adhesive, tie or sew a tag or label to the fibers. It is always a good idea to use a secondary label on these types of materials, even if a label is adhered or directly marked using a barrier coat. Use caution with fine materials such as spruce root. Label or tag mats and other flat objects at one corner.
Bark cloth	Apply kozo paper labels with wheat or rice starch paste or methylcellulose at one corner.
Beads	Use a method appropriate for the material (material identification is important). Many plastics absorb ink, are etched by inks or solvents, scratched by pens, or reject inks and adhesives. Number large beads on a flat, undecorated surface, if possible. Place small beads in a padded, marked container. String loose beads with polyester thread and tag.
Birds	Number with ink on the leg or toenail. Label mounted specimens on the base near the right rear corner. Tag skeletons or number the bones directly with ink in the center or on the largest part of each bone. Attach a tag to skins around the ankle of one foot. Incompletely cleaned, salted, or dried organic specimens may continue to weep fats that can darken or transparentize tags. Use nonabsorbent tag and tie materials for oily or fatty specimens. Label fluid-preserved specimens both individually and with an inside container label. Mark dry eggs with pencil or ink, preferably above or below the opening. Use brush points to avoid scratching the shell. Tag nests or mark the tray holding the nest. See *Natural history specimens*.

Object Types	Comments, Considerations, Locations, and Vulnerabilities
Bone (including cultural artifacts and artwork. For natural history specimens see individual listings for specimen type)	Material identification is key. Many plastics can resemble bone. Bone can absorb ink, be etched by inks or solvents, scratched by pens, or reject inks and adhesives. Label less porous areas (e.g., adjacent to the epiphyses). Seal the marked area of the bone with varnish to prevent ink or paint numbers from bleeding or staining the surface.
Books (including manuscripts, printed books, autograph albums, periodicals, portfolios, scrapbooks, and sketchbooks)	Marking practices for circulating library materials, rare books, and special collections are different from those used for museum print and photograph collections. Number books with pencil on the reverse of the title page and inside the front cover at the lower right side, near the spine. If the inner cover pastedown is decorative, mark the number on the first blank page. Note that libraries' pagination practices differ from museum enumeration style of accession numbers or parts: a single accession or shelf number may be marked repeatedly through the volume, if the object is paginated; mark individually mounted photographs on leaves; inset album pages or loose prints in a portfolio may be individually numbered as a subpart of the accession number. Although this may make the catalog record unwieldy, it can help if an unbound or dismountable structure such as a screw post album is separated into individual matted display frames for exhibition and rotation. Number all loose or weakened pages, portfolios, and containers individually. Number scrapbooks in several places because they are often cheaply bound or in weakened condition and the pages are liable to separate from the binding. For books of moderate value, attach a bookplate bearing the number inside the front cover with starch paste or methylcellulose. For rare books, or books that are works of art in which every page is precious, insert an acid-free paper marker bearing the number in pencil; barcodes can be placed on a marker or polyethylene strap around board. See also *Manuscripts and documents* and *Paper and cardboard objects*.
Botanical specimens	Attach labels to herbarium sheets or write the number in pencil on the lower right corner of the sheet. Label vials or boxes containing specimens. When type photographs are made, fasten a small measurement scale with the number of the print to the herbarium sheet and photograph it along with the herbarium label of the institution to which the original specimen belongs. Use of alkaline buffered paper may negatively affect noncellulose components of plants, such as resins, and impair future study of these materials. See also *Living specimens*.
Bronzes	See *Metal objects*.
Buttons (including pin badges and costume fasteners)	Use a method appropriate for the material (identification is key). Use dating and contextual clues as well as subject matter expertise, examination under magnification, provenance description, or material analysis to distinguish ivory from pigmented celluloid. Mark on the reverse, if possible. Store small buttons in a labeled container or attach a tag. See also *Bone, Ivory, Metal, Plastics, Shell, Wood*.
Celluloid	Celluloid is the name generally used for cellulose nitrate cast objects and early motion picture or sheet film. See also *Film* and *Plastics*.

(continued)

Table 5F.1 *Continued*

Object Types	Comments, Considerations, Locations, and Vulnerabilities
Ceramic objects	Unglazed, porous ceramics may require more than one application of the base coat. Choose the location carefully because the base coat will leave a stain. Use a thickened varnish to prevent extensive penetration into porous materials. Use a solvent-based varnish on low-fired pottery because water-based materials may dissolve the surface. Apply the number with ink or paint over a base coat in an inconspicuous place not likely to be abraded by handling and not obscuring any marks. Avoid marking in cracked areas. Place the number where it will not be scraped as the object is set down or moved (the number is often placed under the base if it is recessed). If necessary, place the number near the lower edge of the back or near the base on a side not likely to be displayed. Mark vessels inside the lip. Mark pottery shards on the side without decoration, never on the break edge. Mark pottery pipes on the bottom of the bowl or on the pipe stem.
China	See *Ceramic objects*.
Clocks	Use a method appropriate for the material (identification is key). Use dating and contextual clues as well as subject matter expertise, examination under magnification, provenance description, or material analysis to distinguish ivory from pigmented celluloid. Number on the back of the case at a lower edge or corner. Number clocks with a hinged door inside the door as well.
Coins (numismatics) and medals	The preferred method of marking coins is to mark the flip they are stored in. If coin flips are used for storage, use only those made of uncoated Mylar/Melinex because they do not contain plasticizers. Do not use polyvinyl chloride (PVC) flips. In addition to the coin holder, coins should also be identified with marks on the box or envelope in which the coin is stored. Thoroughly photo document both sides of each coin. The same method may be applied to medals that fit in coin flips; if a coin must be marked directly, use a barrier coat of B-72 and a very fine point pigment-based marker. Mark on the edge or rim if possible. Do not mark coins on their obverse or reverse faces and never use permanent marks.

When using semi-permanent marks on medals, number the medal in a smooth undecorated area on the reverse. Avoid piercing attached ribbons, which are generally weaker and have solubility issues. See also *Enamel, Lacquer*. |
| Compact Discs | See *Optical discs* |
| Costumes and costume accessories | Sew a label to textiles. For details on preparing and attaching the label, see "Method 3: Sewn Labels." The label should not obscure any maker's labels. For objects composed of nontextile materials, use a method recommended for the material. Some museums choose a standard location for all garments, such as inside lower edge near the proper right side seam. Additional suggested locations follow. Standardize the location for all items of the same type. For dresses, coats, shirts, and other upper garments with sleeves, sew the label on the back neckband or, if a tag in that location would be visible on display, in one sleeve on the underarm seam or inside the cuff, usually at the left sleeve. For vests and other sleeveless garments, inside the left armhole at the side seam. For skirts, trousers, and other garments with waistbands, at the center |

Object Types	Comments, Considerations, Locations, and Vulnerabilities
	back at the waistband. For hats, inside the band at the center back; if no band, at another suitable cloth location. Mark leather, straw, or other materials at the center inside back of the crown using a method suitable for the material, or carefully attach the label to one edge, or the reverse, of the maker's label. For stockings and gloves, inside near the top edge. For neckwear and sashes on the underside at the center back or at one end. For flat objects such as handkerchiefs and scarves, mark at one corner. For carpetbags, muffs, purses, mark inside near the opening. For belts, inside near or on the buckle. For footwear with heels, mark on the bottom of the sole in the rise before the heel or on the inside face of the heel. Cloth footwear may have a textile label sewn to the inside lining at the heel end. For footwear without heels (flats, sandals, slippers), mark at the back of the shoe in the heel area. For umbrellas and canes, mark on the handle or knob or on the shaft near the handle.
Documents	See *Manuscripts*.
Dolls	Use a method appropriate for the material. Number on the back of the head at the nape of the neck; if this is not possible, on the foot. An auxiliary tag is recommended for dolls in storage so that the number may be seen without having to handle the doll. Label each item of clothing as for textiles. See also *Plastics/Polymers*, *Wood*, *Ivory*, and *Plant material*.
Drawings (including watercolors)	Mark in pencil on the reverse of the work at a lower corner. Mark two-sided drawings with separate numbers for each side of the work (e.g., 1991.1A and 1991.1B) on respective sides. If the work is mounted or hinged, mark the number on the back of the mount or on the face of the mount below the edge of the drawing. If framed, mark the frame as for paintings.
Embroideries	See *Textiles*.
Enamel	See *Glass objects*.
Ephemera (paper-based including greeting cards, postcards, trade cards, etc.)	Mark in pencil on the reverse in an undecorated or blank area, usually at one corner. Mark materials with double-sided printing on the side least likely to be displayed. Mark envelopes on the reverse at a lower corner. See TABLE 5F.4 for difficult substrates. See also *Paper and Cardboard*.
Fans (hand, folding)	Use a method appropriate for the material. See also *Plastics*, *Wood*, *Ivory*, *Paper and cardboard*, and *Feathers*. Mark folding fans on the reverse of the rear guard so that the number is visible when the fan is closed but not while on display. Mark nonfolding fans on the reverse end of the handle or stick or apply the number on the ring if wide and sound enough.
Feathers	Mark with ink or paint on a base coat applied to the shaft or on the bottom of the quill, or attach a tag. Objects that cannot be marked directly or tagged should be placed in a marked storage container or labeled on their mounts. Natural history specimens may be marked directly with ink, if permanent marks are desired.
Film, plastic (celluloid/cellulose nitrate, cellulose acetate, polyester)	For motion picture film, numbers should be written on the film leader stock attached with splices during winding and processing. *Do not splice cellulose nitrate with heat*. Motion picture or sheet film can be permanently marked in a margin, directly with India ink or film marker. See TABLE 5F.4. A preferred

(continued)

Table 5F.1 *Continued*

Object Types	Comments, Considerations, Locations, and Vulnerabilities
	means is housing film in archival photo sleeves and reel cans made specifically for film and marking the exterior before placing the film inside. Film cans and storage boxes should be marked with adhesive labels that are suitable for the storage conditions, such as cold storage.
Firearms	Use a method appropriate for the material. See also *Metal*, *Plastics*, and *Wood*. Mark on the metal butt plate, if available, on the handle or stock near the butt end, or on the underside or interior of the trigger guard. For long arms and rifles, mark on the breech end of the barrel or near the trigger on the floor plate. Mark revolvers on the cylinder, turned out-of-view while on exhibit. Mark powder horns and flasks on the back edge near the opening.
Fishes	Tag fluid-preserved specimens with solvent-resistant labels placed inside and also label the container, or tie a tag through the mouth or gill opening or around the caudal peduncle (the narrow end before the tail). See also *Fluid-preserved specimens*. For skeletal material, apply numbers with ink directly on the bone; use a base coat and top coat if permanent numbers are not desired. Place small bones in labeled containers. Label mounted specimens on the mount, that is the base to which it is fixed.
Fluid-preserved specimens	Place a label that is resistant to the preservative fluid inside the container; the container may be labeled on the exterior as well. Resistall paper may be used but is acidic. It is preferable to use 100 percent alpha cellulose, nonbuffered paper marked with waterproof, alcohol-resistant ink, Tyvek embossed with solvent-resistant ink numbers, an impact printer, or thermal transfer printer on polyester labels are recommended. Do not use Tyvek in a laser printer.
Fossils	Number on a base coat with ink or paint on a smooth, nondiagnostic flat surface, or use an adhered label but not on any part that will interfere with study (consult a conservator regarding fossil resins, which may be dissolved by solvents). For specimens consisting of several pieces, such as disarticulated vertebrates, mark the number on each fragment. Label microscopic invertebrates at one corner of the slide mount with ink or paint, or label as for *Glass*. Store microfossils in labeled vials.
Frames	Use materials appropriate to the type of frame. Frames may be accessioned as decorative arts or as part of an accession with a wall-hung work. In either case, do not mark on outer edges or corners that may be broken off. Mark in a consistent location per organization protocol. Do not mark on powdery or flaking gesso, gilding, or paint. Gummed labels may be used to record exhibition history. See also *Lacquer*, *Metals*, *Painted wood*, *Paintings*, *Paper*, *Plastics*, and *Wood*.
Furniture	Use a method appropriate for the material (see also *Metal*, *Plastics*, *Textiles*, *Wood*). Mark on a base coat with ink or paint or use a method appropriate for the material. Use a base coat that will not dissolve or damage any finished surfaces. Avoid painted areas. Attach an auxiliary tag to large pieces in storage. Number all removable parts such as shelves, keys, etc. Mark commodes and chests on the back at the bottom left or bottom right corner; mark low chests at an upper corner. Mark highboys and multiple case pieces

Object Types	Comments, Considerations, Locations, and Vulnerabilities
	at a top corner of the lower piece and the corresponding lower corner of the upper piece. For chairs and sofas, mark at the back of one leg at the height of the seat, or for less visibility on display, on the inside of the leg. If a piece is completely upholstered, sew a textile label near the left or right back leg. Mark tables on the underside of the top near one leg, on the apron, or on the inside edge of one leg just below the apron. Mark beds on the back of the rail at the head of the bed near one leg, or on the outer edge of both legs at the head of the bed. Mark lamps on the lower right-hand side at the back, or on the base, if there is one. Mark mirrors and sconces on the reverse at diagonal corners of the frame. If the object is extremely heavy, place the number on the lower edge of the frame near one corner.
Gems, precious stones	Extreme caution should be exercised when marking these objects. Gems or precious stones that are hygroscopic, fragile, or porous should not be directly marked (e.g., opals and organic objects such as pearls, ivory, and coral). Instead of marking the object directly, mark the housing or mount for the object. See also, *Stone* and *Geological specimens*.
Geological specimens (including gems, minerals, and rocks)	For nonporous minerals, mark with ink or paint on a clear base coat, placed so as not to obscure any important feature. Use a white primer or white numbers over the clear base coat on dark objects. Adhered labels may also be used; note that hygroscopic minerals may effloresce and push labels off, or grow over or through marks. Chemical by-products of some specimens, such as pyrites, may destroy labels. If the specimen is too small or too fragile to number directly, place it in a padded vial, box, or polyethylene bag on which the number is marked. See also *Stone* and *Gems*.
Glass (including enamel)	Mark on a base coat with ink or paint; use white lettering on clear glass to minimize the visibility of the number when the object is on display, or print on Mylar/Melinex or thin kozo or gampi tissues saturated with top coat after printing. Choose an adhesive with a refractive index close to that of glass when using Paraloid B-72 or B-67. Avoid directly marking etched or frosted glass or deteriorating ancient glass as well as areas of airbrushed or painted design. Make the number as small and legible as possible. Place the number on the back edge of the foot if wide enough, underneath the foot if recessed, or on a lower back edge. Mark blown glass in the recessed area near the point where the glass has been cut from the rod.
Glass, frosted or painted	See *Lacquer*.
Gold	See *Coins, Jewelry, Metal*.
Hats	See *Costumes and costume accessories*.
Herbaria	See *Botanical specimens*.
Hide, animal	See *Skins*.
Horticultural specimens	See *Living collections*. In addition to the informational labels for the public, living plants may be marked with an accession or catalog tag. Trees with a large enough trunk may have a tag attached using an aluminum nail driven into the bark; smaller plants may be tagged with a stake that is driven into the ground and wired to the plant. The tags and labels should be placed in standard locations (e.g., the south side of the specimen).

(continued)

Table 5F.1 *Continued*

Object Types	Comments, Considerations, Locations, and Vulnerabilities
Horn (antler, baleen, nails, claws, hooves)	These materials can swell and crack. Mark with ink or paint on over a Paraloid base coat. Use white ink or paint to number dark pieces. See also *Plastic/Polymer, Synthetic.*
Insects	Mark pinned specimens with pencil or ink on unbuffered, acid-free paper labels that are pinned directly below the specimen. Tag fluid-preserved specimens with solvent-resistant labels placed inside the container and label the container. Label microscopic specimens with ink on the slide mount. See also *Fluid-preserved specimens.*
Invertebrates	Use acid-free paper tags tied to the specimen for dried crustaceans. Mark mollusks with ink; use a base coat if permanent numbers are not desired. Adhered labels may also be used. See also *Fluid-preserved specimens.*
Ivory (cameos, carved, portrait miniatures, teeth)	Ivory is sensitive to water and can swell and crack. Do not mark portrait miniatures on ivory and other thin fragile ivories directly because they are highly susceptible to damage. Mark with ink or paint on a petroleum solvent-based base coat. Use white ink or paint to number dark pieces. Some ivories resist the adhesion of varnish or adhesive. Attach a tag or mark the storage container. See also *Gems.*
Japanned wood	See *Lacquer.*
Jewelry	Use a method appropriate for the material. Mark in an inconspicuous place that is not likely to be abraded by handling. If the piece is very small, attach a small acid-free tag bearing the number, loop a cloth tag marked with the number around the piece, or use a small, adhered label. Do not use paper jewelers' tags with colored strings because the paper is usually acidic and the dyes in the string may run when wet. Place numbers on the backs of pendants, watch cases, charms, and fobs.
Lace	Sew a textile label bearing the number at a corner or near the end of the piece with a small loop of thread or with one or two stitches on the reverse.
Lacquer	Painted, lacquered, Japanned, and other finished surfaces (e.g., toleware, lacquer ware, frosted or painted glass, varnished wood). A preferred method is the kozo paper method with SCMC/Jade as the adhesive. See also *Wood.* *Note on lacquer and painted surfaces*: Organic solvents used as carriers for acrylic base coats can permanently damage painted or finished objects by dissolving the surface finish; mark an unfinished area, if possible, or use a base coat composed of acrylic resins dissolved in a petroleum solvent. Mineral spirits, petroleum benzine, or related petroleum solvents are safer for more surfaces than acetone-based. Test objects carefully in an inconspicuous location to determine if the solvent affects the finish. Do not use petroleum solvents on wax or waxed surfaces.
Leather	See *Skins.*
Linen	See *Textiles.*
Living collections	Note that tags may be vectors for pathogens so hygiene protocols must be established and followed to avoid cross contamination with reuse of durable tags and equipment. See CHAPTER 3F, "Living and Natural History Collections

Object Types	Comments, Considerations, Locations, and Vulnerabilities
	Registration." For *Horticultural specimens*, in addition to informational labels for the public, living plants may also be marked with a tag. Trees with a large enough trunk may have a tag attached using an aluminum nail driven into the bark, whereas smaller plants may be tagged with a stake that is driven into the ground and wired to the plant. The tags and labels should be placed in standard locations (e.g., the south side of the specimen). For *Zoological specimens*, because live animals have specific issues for marking, each category of animal is marked in a standard way according to guidelines set out by the Association of Zoos and Aquariums.
Machinery	Mark on the right lower rear corner in close proximity to a manufacturer's plate, if present. Attach an auxiliary tag with nonabsorbent oil resistant materials on large artifacts.
Mammals	Mark bones with ink in the center of the largest part of the bone or near the proximal end of long bones. Mark skulls with ink on the cranium and mandible. Use a base coat, unless permanent numbers are desired. Limit the marking of skeletal material to bones that can be easily and legibly labeled. The numbering is done on the most completely ossified portion of the bone because marking materials will spread in porous bone, particularly bone from immature mammals. Use a thickened varnish on very porous bone. Keep small bones in numbered containers. Mark mounted specimens on the mount near the base of the right rear leg or at the back edge. Number small skins (except for study skins) in ink on the reverse, on the inner part of the neck or near the leg, or tie a tag to the ankle of the right rear leg. Number large skins on the reverse or use a label attached through a natural opening that is unlikely to tear, such as the eyes or nostrils; perforate large skins with a three-cornered awl in the middle of the lower back. For study skins, attach specimen labels or tags made of 100 percent alpha cellulose, nonbuffered paper marked with waterproof, alcohol-resistant ink. Use nonabsorbent oil-resistant tags and ties on oily specimens (e.g., marine mammals). Tag fluid-preserved specimens with a fluid-resistant label placed inside the container or attached to a rear ankle of the specimen. See also *Bone*, *Ivory*, *Horn*, and *Fluid-preserved specimens*.
Manuscript albums	See *Books*.
Manuscripts and documents	With some exceptions, it is generally inappropriate to add marks to archival manuscripts and documents because it may cause confusion as to creators' marks. Where it is necessary in archival processing to identify image copies, iterations, or paginate, pencil is preferred. Document conventions such as use of brackets around a staff's annotation, for example [exhibition copy] or [IMG 2019-10000], in a procedures manual. If marking, write in pencil on the reverse or blank side of the document near an upper or lower corner. Mark envelopes on the reverse side at a lower corner. In cases where an object cannot be marked directly (e.g., an illuminated manuscript with decorative elements extending to the edge of the paper on both sides) mark an acid-free storage sleeve or box with the number. A stamped ink identifying symbol is used for some manuscript collections but is not generally recommended for museum collections.

(*continued*)

Table 5F.1 *Continued*

Object Types	Comments, Considerations, Locations, and Vulnerabilities
Marble	See *Stone*.
Masks	Use a method appropriate for the material. Number on the inside or reverse near the bottom.
Metal	Mark with ink or paint, on a solvent-based acrylic base coat, in an inconspicuous place. Avoid areas of corrosion and painted decoration. Use a solvent-based varnish on unfinished metals. Water-based materials may initiate corrosion at the application site. Water-based acrylic emulsions may be used as a base coat on finishes that are not water soluble, but these media will not redissolve in water when dry. Organic solvents or mechanical methods needed for future removal may damage the surface.
	Avoid the use of commercial artist's acrylic media on copper, brass, or sterling silver because they may contain ammonia, which will stain the metal. Ammonia may etch resinous coatings. Do not use materials containing ammonia on copper-based metals (including sterling silver). Mark flatware on the back of the handle so as not to obscure hallmarks. If flatware is to be exhibited with hallmarks up, place the number on the other side. If the piece is too small for numbering, attach a tag bearing the number or place the object in a self-sealing polyethylene bag or other container that is marked with the number. Make one small hole in polyethylene to prevent condensation in changing environments. Use soft ties and tags to avoid scratching. See also *Coins and metal*, *Machinery*, *Tableware*, *Tools*, *Vehicles*, and *Weapons*.
Miniature paintings	See *Ivory*.
Minerals	See *Geological Specimens* and *Stone*.
Musical instruments	Determine whether the object is a composite and the associated material vulnerabilities; choose options from appropriate material types. Mark on a base coat with ink or paint. Avoid areas that will be worn if played. Mark pianos and harpsichords as for commodes and chests (see *Furniture*). Mark stringed instruments on the back of the heel at the base of the neck or on the back of the body near the base. Mark wind instruments on the underside along the shaft. Mark horns on the stem near the mouthpiece or inside the bell. Many instruments have a lacquer coating that will be dissolved by solvent-based varnishes. Use a petroleum solvent or water-based material. Do not use materials containing ammonia on copper-based metals or sterling silver. See also *Metals*.
Natural history specimens	See listings for specific types of specimens: *Birds*, *Botanical specimens*, *Fishes*, *Fossils*, *Gems*, *Insects*, *Invertebrates*, *Living collections*, *Mammals*, *Reptiles and Amphibians*, *Rocks*, *Shells*, and *Skins*. Label as appropriate to the conditions of storage environment (cold, fluid, outdoor).[1]
Optical Discs (CD, DVD, Laser Disc, Mini Disc, BluRay)	Using a water-based pigment pen (see TABLE 5F.4) to number the disc on the innermost ring or the clear inner hub or the mirror band of the disc, where no information is written onto the CD or DVD. Mark the hub as described, and key this to a list of contents printed and stored in the case or sleeve. Discs should never be marked on their recordable areas. Do not use adhesive labels on CD/DVD surfaces. More specific guidance is available.[2]

Object Types	Comments, Considerations, Locations, and Vulnerabilities
Paintings	Never write a number on, or apply a label to, the face of a painting or the reverse of a canvas. Paintings are marked on the reverse of their frames, protective backings, or supports, such as stretcher bars or panels. If the stretcher or panel is covered by a protective backing, the number is marked on the backing in the same location that it would be marked if the stretcher or panel were visible. The number can be marked on the backing with pencil or ink according to the standard practice of the institution. Ink is easier to read. For exhibition loans, a gummed paper label is sometimes pasted on the protective backing or stretcher bars. Some paintings, such as miniatures on ivory, contemporary paintings with no frame or stretcher, or reverse paintings on glass, may pose numbering problems. If in doubt as to the appropriate method for a particular piece, use a temporary method, or consult a conservator. Ivory miniatures are often thin, translucent, and extremely fragile. It is generally recommended, therefore, that the number not be applied directly to the ivory. If the miniature is framed or mounted in a case or locket, the number should be applied to the support. If the miniature is unframed, the number can be marked on its storage box. Consistently mark objects in the same location (e.g., upper right corner of the frame and panel). Mark large paintings at opposing diagonal corners so that the number can be easily located whether the work is hung high or low on a wall or storage screen. This is not necessary in the case of small works. If both sides of an object are in view (such as a two-sided painting—a painting on both the recto and the verso), mark the number on the bottom edge at one corner. See also *Drawings*, *Ivory*, and *Scroll painting*.
Painted wood and other painting surfaces	See *Frames*, *Furniture*, *Lacquer*, and *Paintings*.
Paper (includes cardboard, correspondence, papier mâché)	Use a method appropriate to the object and collection type (e.g., archive, art, library, print, photograph). Mark with soft pencil in an unobtrusive place. See TABLE 5F.4 for information regarding pencils. Place paper objects on a firm surface and write gently to avoid indentation. Mark pamphlets as for books or mark on the back cover at one corner. Mark sheet music on the reverse at one corner and also mark individual loose pages. Three-dimensional paper objects may be tagged. See also *Books*, *Drawings*, *Ephemera*, *Manuscripts and documents*, *Photographs*, and *Prints*.
Pearl, Mother of pearl	See *Gems* and *Shells*.
Photographs (including cased prints and negatives; photographs on nontraditional surfaces)	Mark prints lightly with pencil on the reverse, preferably in a nonimage area at a corner of the lower margin. Mark all items consistently in the same corner. See TABLE 5F.4 for information regarding pencils and marking pens suitable for use with photographs. If the photograph is hinged in a mount, place the number on the unhinged end. Number the mount and, if framed, mark the frame as for paintings. Interleave photographs with acid-free unbuffered tissue to prevent transfer of the marking material. For cased tintypes, ambrotypes, and daguerreotypes, apply the number on a base coat with ink or paint, on the lower back of the case by the hinge, or tag the object. Do not attempt to disassemble cased photographs without the advice of a conservator. Uncased tintypes, ambrotypes, and daguerreotypes

(continued)

Table 5F.1 *Continued*

Object Types	Comments, Considerations, Locations, and Vulnerabilities
	are not usually marked directly; place in a labeled container. Photographic film negatives cannot be labeled with pencil but can sometimes be labeled directly with inks such as India ink or film marker. The number should be placed on the nonemulsion side in a nonimage area. Because such areas are usually small, it is difficult to write the number legibly without the aid of magnification. More commonly the number is written in pencil on an archival storage sleeve before the negative is slipped in. Resin-coated and plastic-coated photographic prints (such as twentieth-century chromographic prints), and surfaces of digital print papers, if not art papers (complex layers of polymer coatings), may resist 2B or HB pencil. Digital prints may be extremely vulnerable to cracking, scratching, and crazing. Treat all photograph surfaces as sensitive when turning over to write on the verso. Protect the surface with a blotter or nontextured slip sheet. For prints on substrates other than paper, consider the substrate material and treat as framed works.
Plastics and polymers including natural bioplastics and polymers (starch-based green plastics, gutta percha, latex rubber, and tortoiseshell) and synthetic plastics and polymers (acrylic, Bakelite, cellulose esters, cellulose nitrate, cellulose acetate, celluloid, epoxies, isoprene, melamine, neoprene, nitrile, phenolic resin, polyesters, polyethylene, polyester terephthalate, propylene, polyvinyl [chloride], rubber, silicones, styrenes [poly, ABS], Teflon, urethane)	Mark on a nonplastic component if possible. Many plastic objects have painted or printed surfaces, and the marking media that is safe for the plastic may not be safe for the surface treatment and vice versa. Some plastics resist the adhesion of varnishes and adhesives; however, they may be stained by the dyes and pigments in marking media if a base coat is not used. Therefore, it is difficult to make specific recommendations. Solvents should be avoided. The most damaging solvents are acetone and toluene; alcohol and mineral spirits will damage some plastics by etching, absorbing, or changing surface gloss. The solvents used as carriers for acrylic resin varnishes (such as acetone and toluene) may dissolve the surface or cause stress cracking or crazing or may affect the gloss finish or surface texture of plastic objects. Some petroleum solvent blends may contain a small percentage of other solvents. Use reference guides, look for markings and contextual clues such as dating and casting marks to identify type.[3] Tag with acid-resistant tags and ties (Teflon, polyester, polypropylene). Some plastics off-gas acids or exude plasticizers because they deteriorate, which can damage paper and cotton tags and ties. Plastics can be numbered directly with a Berol China Marker or Schwan-Stabilo All Stabilo pencil, although the numbers may not be durable. A second (temporary means) of marking should be employed. Where possible, paint numbers on plastic directly with acrylic paints. Acrylic resins dissolved in mineral spirits pose the least possible risk for most plastics, although caution is still advised. Base coats of water-based acrylic or polyvinyl acetate (PVAC) emulsions are not a safe choice, as older plastics, such as cellulose nitrate, may be damaged by moisture, and water-based adhesives can also initiate stress cracking upon application or over time. These materials are not reversible in water when dry, and stronger solvents or mechanical methods, which may damage the plastic, will be necessary for their future removal. Numbers may not be durable as these emulsions have a tendency to peel over time. Oil paints are not recommended because both the oils and their solvents can soften or otherwise damage some plastics with long-term contact.
Porcelain	See *Ceramic objects*.
Portfolios	See *Books*.

Object Types	Comments, Considerations, Locations, and Vulnerabilities
Potsherds	See *Ceramic objects.*
Pottery	See *Ceramic objects.*
Prints	Mark lightly with pencil on the reverse, preferably in a nonimage area on the lower corner. If the print is hinged in a mat or mount, place the number on the unhinged end. Also mark the mount, and if framed, mark the frame as for paintings.
Rawhide	See *Skins.*
Reptiles and amphibians	Attach tags to the larger parts of articulated skeletal specimens or write the numbers with ink directly on each bone. Use a base coat if permanent numbers are not desired. Do not mark small bones directly if the numbers will obscure study features; store them in labeled containers. Attach tags to skins and skulls through a natural hole or opening if strong enough. Tag fluid-preserved specimens with a solvent-resistant tag tied to a leg or around the neck and also label the container. Mark dry eggs with ink above and below the opening.[4]
Reproductions	See "Permanent/Direct Marking Methods."
Resins, natural (amber, copal, dammar, kauri, balsam, mastic, rosin, and sandarac) and synthetic (acrylics, alkyds, cellulose acetate, epoxies, polyesters, polyolefins, phenolics, polystyrene, vinyls)	Distinguish between natural resin and synthetic resin. Treat natural resins the same as lacquered or painted surfaces; see also *Horn.* For synthetic (man-made) resins, see *Plastics.*
Rocks	See *Geological specimens.*
Rubber	Distinguish between natural rubber (latex, gutta percha) and synthetic rubber (butyl rubber, neoprene). Use a marking appropriate to the material, including bags or boxes, which should either be ventilated or packaged with gas scavengers.[5] Use water-based products (such as acrylic paint) on rigid rubber objects. Do not use acetone. Flexible rubbers are difficult to mark directly because marking media tend to flake or peel. Mark on a nonrubber component, attach a tag, or write the number directly with a Berol China Marker. Most rubber products are adversely affected by oils and hydrocarbon solvents and some by alcohol. Synthetic rubbers vary as widely as plastics in their properties. Take care when using inks as they often contain metallic elements that may cause degradation of the rubber. Rigid rubber objects may be marked with acrylic paint or other water-based materials. Base coats and top coats of solvent-based acrylic varnishes are not recommended because they may not adhere well and the solvents may attack the rubber, fillers, or colorants.
Rugs (including tapestries)	Sew a textile label to reverse diagonal corners so the number is easily found when the rug or tapestry is rolled. Attach a tag to the roll's tie. See also *Textiles.*
Scientific instruments	Mark on a base coat with ink or paint in an inconspicuous place near the base or use an adhered label. Number all removable parts. Number instruments that have revolving parts and revolve the part to the far side when exhibited. Metal parts may have a shellac coating, which could be damaged by solvent-based varnishes. See also *Machinery.*
Scrapbooks	See *Books.*

(*continued*)

Table 5F.1 *Continued*

Object Types	Comments, Considerations, Locations, and Vulnerabilities
Screens, folding	Use a method appropriate for the material type. Mark on a base coat with ink or paint on a lower edge when folded, near the back of the frame, near an outside corner, where it can be seen. See *Lacquer*, *Wood*, and *Textiles*.
Scroll paintings	Use a method appropriate for the material type. Mark on a base coat with ink or paint on one knob of the scroll; also mark the box. Attach an acid-free tag to the cord at the opening end of the scroll. See *Lacquer*, *Wood*, and *Textiles*.
Sculpture	Use a method appropriate for the material type. For sculpture in the round, apply the number at the lower rear base or, if there is no base, in an inconspicuous place not likely to be worn down by handling or weather exposure. Mark removable pedestals at the lower rear. Mark relief sculpture on the bottom edge (not the back) where it can be seen without lifting or moving the object. For unusual objects, such as complex abstract sculpture, note the location of the number in the object file and attach an auxiliary tag in storage.
Shell	Mark on a base coat with ink or paint in an inconspicuous place not likely to be worn by handling. Natural history specimens may be marked directly with ink. Adhered labels may also be used. See *Gems* and *Invertebrates*.
Shoes	See *Costumes and costume accessories*.
Silver	See *Metal objects*.
Sketchbooks	See *Books*.
Skins	Soft, porous leathers and skins cannot be marked directly with varnish and are permanently stained by inks and paints. Vegetable tan, brain tan, and smoke tanned leathers, salted skins, alum tawed skins, parchment, and rawhide are sensitive to water—if dyed, even more so. Chrome tanned skins may be resistant to water. Many leathers have surface finishes. Do not mark directly unless it has been determined that permanent marks are appropriate. A preferred method of marking (with exceptions—do not tag or directly mark natural history study skins) is to attach a textile label or acid-free tag with stitches passed carefully through an existing hole in the leather or around and underneath the assembly stitches, thongs, and so on, provided that the existing stitching is strong enough to withstand such manipulation, or tie to a sturdy appendage. Place the number on a metal decoration or hardware if no other suitable location can be found. Inert, chemical resistant tags and ties will be more resistant to degradation products. See TABLES 5F.6 and 5F.7. Sew cloth labels to linings or loop them around a strong appendage, such as a strap or belt loop. Adhered labels may sometimes be used, but consult a conservator and avoid painted surfaces. Hard, impervious skins (rawhide) may be sealed with a base coat of a petroleum solvent-based varnish. Use a small amount of a solvent-based varnish on a smooth, inconspicuous surface. Seal minimally, as excessive varnish may stiffen the leather and cause cracking around the varnished area. Avoid alcohol and acetone because they may cause drying or cracking. Apply the number with ink or paint.

Object Types	Comments, Considerations, Locations, and Vulnerabilities
Stamps (currency, postage, philately)	Not usually marked directly. Although the number is sometimes written lightly in pencil on the back, direct marking may lower the monetary value of stamps. Instead, place the stamp in a labeled acid-free envelope or sleeve. Number mounted stamps or stock pages with pencil on the back of the mount and if hinged, on the hinge beneath the stamp.
Stone	Some stone, such as marble, is semi-porous and easily stained. Use the kozo paper method or if marking directly on the stone, use a base coat, especially on sculpture and cultural artifacts. See *Geological specimens* and *Gems*.
Tableware	Use a method appropriate to the material. Mark the number under a recessed foot or on one side at the base and on the inside of lids. Individually mark all removable parts. See also *Ceramics*, *Glass*, *Metal objects*, *Plastics*, and *Wood*.
Tapa	See *Bark cloth*.
Tapestries	See *Rugs*.
Terracotta	Mark on a base coat with ink or paint. Extremely porous objects may need more than one application of the base coat. Use a thickened varnish to prevent extensive penetration of the varnish. Choose the location carefully because the base coat will leave a stain. Use a solvent-based varnish because water-based varnishes may dissolve or damage the surface. Place the number where it will not be scraped as the piece is set down or moved. The number may be placed under a recessed base, if the piece is small, or at the lower edge on the back. Mark roundels or medallions on the back or on the bottom edge. See also *Ceramics* and *Enamel*.
Textiles (flat textiles, including draperies, embroideries, and linens)	Sew a textile label at one corner on the reverse of small pieces, preferably along a hem or selvage. Do not sew a label directly to very deteriorated textiles. Label or tag fragile mounted textiles on the mount only. Label large textiles at opposing corners so the number is easily located when rolled. Tie a tag to the roll's tie. When textiles are wrapped on tubes or mounted on boards, also mark the support. Attach tags to fragile textiles with one loop of thread between the weave of the fabric, as for lace. Be wary of installing tags where loops may entangle with fringe or dangling material. For draperies and curtains, sew on the reverse lower left or right corner of each panel; if very sheer, sew on the reverse but on the outside corners where it will be less conspicuous. For bed coverings and quilts, sew on reverse diagonal corners. For pillow cases, sew inside the left corner of the bottom half on or near the hem. For decorative pillows, sew on the reverse lower left or lower right corner. For flags, banners, and pennants, sew on the reverse side at the top of the hoisting edge. See *Costumes and costume accessories* and *Linens*.
Toleware	See *Lacquer*.
Tools (including sports equipment)	Use a method appropriate for the material. Mark on the butt end of handles, along the shaft, or on the bottom edge of the head. Mark planes at the back of the stock; mark wedge and iron. See also *Bone*, *Firearms*, *Metals*, *Plastic*, *Rubber*, *Skins*, and *Wood*.

(continued)

Table 5F.1 *Continued*

Object Types	Comments, Considerations, Locations, and Vulnerabilities
Vehicles	Mark at the lower right rear corner of the body or stern or on the rear axle. Use a method appropriate for the material. If a manufacturer's plate is present, mark the number in close proximity to it. Attach an auxiliary tag if the direct marking is not easily located.
Vinyl	See *Audiovisual*, *Costumes and costume accessories*, *Film*, and *Plastics*.
Watercolors	See *Drawings*.
Weapons (including those with long shafts such as arrows, clubs, harpoons, knives, and spears)	Use a method appropriate for the material. Place the number on the handle of clubs and tomahawks near the butt end, on the shaft of arrows, and on the inside end of bows. Number swords and knives on the blade below the counterguard or hilt, or at the base or butt end of the handle. See *Bone*, *Firearms*, *Metals*, and *Wood*.
Wood (including lacquer)	Mark on a base coat with ink or paint in an inconspicuous place not likely to be worn by handling. Very porous wood may require more than one application of the base coat. Choose the location carefully, as the base coat will leave a stain. Use a thickened varnish to prevent extensive penetration into the wood. Avoid finished or painted surfaces or use a compatible base coat that will not dissolve or damage the finish. Base coats dissolved in a petroleum solvent will be safe for more finishes than acetone but do not use petroleum solvents on waxed surfaces. Water-based products, such as acrylic paint or PVAC emulsion, will be safer for more finishes than solvent-based varnishes but may not be as durable and will require a solvent or mechanical methods for future removal, which may damage the finish.

NOTES

1. L. Cipera, E. Range, and C. Leckie. n.d. "Labeling natural history collections," Society for the Preservation of Natural History Collections Wiki. Available at: https://spnhc.biowikifarm.net/wiki/Labeling_Natural_History_Collections#Decision_Making (accessed August 15, 2019).

2. F. R. Byers. *Care and Handling of CDs and DVDs: A Guide for Librarians and Archivists*. NIST Special Report 500–252 (Washington, DC/Gaithersburg, MD: Council on Library and Information Resources/National Institute of Standards and Technology, 2003). Available at: http://www.itl.nist.gov/iad/894.05/docs/CDandDVDCareandHandlingGuide.pdf; A. Schweikert, "An optical media preservation strategy for New York University's Fales Library & Special Collections" (2018). Available at: http://archive.nyu.edu/handle/2451/43877.

3. A. Quye and C. Williamson, "Plastics: Collecting and Conserving, National Museums of Scotland." Available at: https://www.archetype.co.uk/publication-details.php?id=60 (accessed April 19, 2017); Y. Shashoua, *Conservation of Plastics: Materials Science, Degradation and Preservation* (Abingdon, Oxon: Routledge, 2016).

4. J. E. Simmons, *Herpetological Collecting and Collections Management*, 3rd ed. Society for the Study of Amphibians and Reptiles Herpetological Circular, no. 42 (2015).

5. Canadian Conservation Institute, "Care of objects made from rubber and plastic," in *CCI Notes*, 1997. Available at: https://www.canada.ca/en/conservation-institute/services/conservation-preservation-publications/canadian-conservation-institute-notes/care-rubber-plastic.html; Quye and Williamson, "Plastics"; Shashoua, *Conservation of Plastics*.

Table 5F.2 Barrier Materials for Base and Top Coats

The use of reliable sources for technical information, including manufacturers' safety data sheets (SDS) and technical specifications, lookup resources such as Conservation and Art Materials Encyclopedia Online (CAMEO) Wiki, American Institute for Conservation (AIC) wiki, National Park Service *Conserv-O-Grams*, and *CCI Notes*, is highly encouraged for research on any material.

Material	Uses/Comments
Paraloid B-67 (formerly Acryloid in the United States) (Dow)	Used primarily as top coat. An acrylic resin (isobutyl methacrylate polymer) that contains a cross-linking inhibitor. Can be purchased in 100 percent solid pellets or as a 45 percent solution in VM&P Naphtha, or 45 percent in mineral spirits (Paraloid B-67MT) from conservation suppliers. Dissolve solids in mineral spirits or a related petroleum solvent, and not in toluene or xylene. Reversible in mineral spirits; may yellow slightly over time. The resin may need to be thinned with mineral spirits periodically as the solvent evaporates. Do not use on wax or waxed surfaces.
Paraloid B-72 (formerly Acryloid in the United States) (Dow)	Used primarily as a base coat or base and top coats. An acrylic resin—ethyl methacrylate (70 percent) and methyl acrylate (30 percent) copolymer. Can be purchased in 100 percent solid pellets, as a 50 percent solution in toluene, or as a 25 percent solution in acetone from conservation suppliers. The most stable acrylic resin used by conservators. Disadvantages are that its least toxic solvent is acetone, and it is reversible only in acetone, xylene, or toluene, which may damage some surfaces. For lower toxicity, dissolve it in acetone, and not toluene, or in an ethanol/acetone mix (at least 10 percent acetone). The resin may need to be thinned periodically because the solvent evaporates. Do not use on plastic, painted, or lacquered surfaces.
Soluvar gloss and matte varnishes (Liquitex)	Commercial preparations composed of isobutyl and n-butyl methacrylates (Paraloid B-67 and F-10). May yellow slightly over time. Easily obtained and ready to use. Reversible in mineral spirits, as well as acetone, toluene, and xylene. Mineral spirits tend to be safer for more surfaces than acetone or toluene. The gloss version is recommended because the matte version may cloud if successive layers are used and contains other additives, including a small amount of methanol. Thin with mineral spirits or a related petroleum solvent. Do not use on wax or waxed surfaces.
White base coats	Use as a base coat on dark objects, over a clear base coat to avoid leaving a white "ghost" on the object. See commercially prepared white/opaque Paraloid B-72, or white acrylic artists' paints made with titanium dioxide, or add titanium dioxide pigment to B-67, Soluvar, or B-72.
Acrylic emulsions—Rhoplex B60A (Primal B60A) (Dow); CSS Rhoplex AC-33 (Conservation Support Solutions)	Acrylic emulsions, water-based, available from conservation suppliers. May be partly soluble in ethanol or acetone, and not water, when dry. Some water-based emulsions may contain ammonia, which should not be used on copper-based metals (copper, brass, bronze, sterling silver) because it will stain the metal. Ammonia may also etch resinous coatings. Do not use water-based materials on objects that are dissolved or damaged by water. These water-based materials appear white, turn clear when dry, and are generally irreversible when dry but can be swelled in water. Sold in art supply stores as an acrylic medium; manufacturers include Golden, Liquitex, and Aqua-tec. They are not as durable as the previously listed materials.

(continued)

Table 5F.2 *Continued*

Material	Uses/Comments
Polyvinyl acetate emulsions (PVAC)—Jade 403N, Jade-R (Aabbitt Adhesives)	There are a wide variety of commercially prepared PVAC emulsions, both solvent-based and water-based. Solvent-based PVAC is soluble in ethanol or acetone when dry. The water-based emulsions are soluble in water when wet but can be difficult to remove even with stronger solvents (e.g., acetone, toluene) when fully cured. Removal of the base coat at a later date may not be possible without causing damage to the surface of the object. They are white in liquid form but turn clear as they dry. Can be hygroscopic and may turn white or swell with moisture contact, causing damage to some surfaces, including plastics. They may soften or become sticky in warm temperatures. Some release acetic acid when degrading, which can corrode metals and plastic. Most PVACs are not recommended as a base coat (acrylic resins are preferred); however, Jade 403N (a water-based PVA emulsion) performed well in pH testing conducted by the Canadian Conservation Institute (CCI). It is reversible in acetone. Jade-R is a water-reversible formulation; do not use in flood-prone areas.

Table 5F.3 Solvents

Most solvents are flammable and highly volatile (i.e., they evaporate rapidly, and vapors quickly fill an enclosed space causing both fire and health hazards). All solvents and marking materials containing solvents have the potential to be injurious to health through acute or chronic exposure, so it is important to consult safety experts before use. Use the minimal amount of the least toxic solvent you can, based on the safety data sheet (SDS) and known properties. Note that solvents are available in different concentrations and purity. Reagent grade is often mentioned in the professional literature, but it may contain up to 5 percent of unknown miscible solvents; ACS grade is of higher purity and necessarily more expensive. Use solvents in well-ventilated areas with appropriate personal protective equipment (PPE) and engineering controls for storage, ventilation, spill, and waste containment. Do not transfer solvents into any container resembling a food or drink. Use compatible containers with appropriate seals. Keep bottles tightly capped when not in direct use. Avoid skin contact by selecting appropriate gloves and wash hands frequently. Keep SDS on site for all solvents and marking materials. Do not attempt to remove coatings from the surface of an object without the advice of a conservator. If a white bloom develops on the surface of an object, discontinue use immediately. The use of reliable sources for technical information including manufacturers' SDS and technical specifications, check resources such as Conservation and Art Materials Encyclopedia Online (CAMEO) Wiki, American Institute for Conservation (AIC) Wiki.

Material	Uses/Comments
Acetone	A ketone used to thin and prepare coatings (including B-72), clean brushes, and remove coatings. It is familiar from being used in commercial nail polish remover (do not use nail polish remover; it will harm most finished surfaces and plastics). Do not use on plastics, resins, lacquered, or painted surfaces. Do not use acetone on moisture-sensitive materials such as ivory, wood, or leather because it may cause excessive drying or cracking.
Alcohols	Ethanol (ethyl alcohol) and isopropanol (isopropyl or rubbing alcohol) can be used to remove some inks and coatings, including B-72. Alcohols will damage shellac varnish finishes on wood and historic metal objects and some plastics. Do not use alcohols on moisture-sensitive materials such as ivory, wood, gems, or leather because it may cause excessive drying or cracking. Do not use drugstore ethanol or isopropanol with colored dyes in them.

Material	Uses/Comments
Mineral spirits, petroleum benzine, petroleum ether, naphtha, Stoddard Solvent, X-4, or Ligroin.	Petroleum distillate, straight chain hydrocarbon mixtures in varying degrees of purity and molecular weight. May contain aromatics such as benzene. Used to dissolve B-67 and to thin Soluvar, mineral spirits can be used to clean brushes or remove base coats and top coats of these materials. Mineral spirits are sold at hardware stores as paint thinner. Do not use on painted surfaces, wax or waxed surfaces.
Toluene, xylene, benzene	Aromatic hydrocarbons found in commercial paint thinners, polishes, and also as commercially available solvents. Xylene is found in some marking pens, which are to be avoided (see TABLES 5F.4 and 5F.5). Will harm finished surfaces and plastics.
Water	Water is a solvent! Some materials are subject to swelling, cracking, or crazing, and dyes may be water-soluble, resulting in bleeding and tidelines. Test all surfaces before using water-based adhesive or barrier coat.

Beyond the method and supplies needed, an experienced registrar or collections manager will understand where to mark an object, how large the number should be, how to provide ease of access yet manage risk by providing redundancy, and consider the aesthetics of the object (TABLES 5F.4 and 5F.5). It is advisable to develop a set of written guidelines and a list of recommended supplies that are regularly stocked by the museum. This will provide a choice of materials and methods to suit the needs of all objects in the collection and minimize the range of methods for each object type to enable staff to develop familiarity and expertise. When new staff are hired, inquire as to whether they have skills in marking to share and when appropriate, retrain staff and update procedures.

Table 5F.4 Writing Materials and Tools

Always approach new writing implements and tools with caution, and practice use on sample objects. Protect objects by draping with safe wrapping materials to avoid splatters of ink, paint, or base or top coats on areas not being numbered.

Material	Uses/Comments
Drawing or writing pencils (carbon graphite and clay)	Carbon graphite pencils are graded in terms of softness (B) or hardness (H). US standard grades are numbered 1, 2, 2.5, 3, and 4, from softer to harder. European standard grade equivalents are B, HB, F, H, and 2H. Sets of drawing pencils have softer and harder pencils around that range, all the way to 9B–9H. No. 2 or HB pencils are recommended for most paper because they will leave a dark mark with less pressure on the pencil point, and so are less likely to indent the substrate. The marks may smear slightly if rubbed. If so, numbers can be blotted gently one time, not rubbed, with a white vinyl eraser to remove excess graphite. Harder grades (F and H) are less likely to smear but may indent the substrate if applied too forcefully. Round the points of harder pencils on another surface after sharpening, before marking. No. 1 pencils may be used on some glossy papers, but check for smearing. Examine the marks on the pencil before use. In a shared workspace, beware of water-soluble art pencils such as the Stabilo or indelible copying pencils that resemble graphite. For white marks (e.g., pagination on dark album pages), use a blunt graphite pencil to achieve some reflection, or if required, a white colored pencil, avoiding water-soluble pencils.

(continued)

Table 5F.4 *Continued*

Material	Uses/Comments
Pens (for ink and paint, see TABLE 5F.5)	Pen holder with crow quill pen nibs, fine steel-nib technical pens, and disposable pigment-based markers are recommended for applying ink numbers. A variety of nib sizes (e.g., 0.1 mm very fine to 2 mm +) can be used for different size numbers. Crow quill pens can be used to write with thin, low viscosity, acrylic paints as well. Exercise caution with metal-tipped pens so as not to scratch the object, splatter, or drip ink. The ink should flow well enough to write without pressing down. Keep the ink bottle in secondary containment to avoid spills onto the work surface. If technical pens clog, try shaking the pen well away from the object, dipping the tip in water, or cleaning the pen with a recommended cleaning solution and rinsing it well. Pens should be cleaned frequently and capped when not in use. See TABLE 5F.4 for inks and paints to use with pens.
Brushes (for ink and paint, see TABLE 5F.5)	Very fine (sizes 00–00000) sable or camel's hair artist's pointed paint brushes for ink, watercolor, and oils are used to write numbers. Synthetic hair alternatives are also available. Slightly larger brushes (0–1) can be used to apply base and top coats. Larger brushes (1+) also may be used to paint numbers on large objects such as vehicles or machinery. Prepare brushes by wetting (in water for acrylics) and drain off fluid before dipping into the paint; rinse thoroughly when done to avoid drying paint in the ferrule. While working, brushes should be rinsed frequently to avoid drying and buildup that can make for poor writing. Long wooden handles can be trimmed with a wood saw and sanded at the end to make for more pen-like handling. See TABLE 5F.4 for ink and paint recommendations.
Berol China Marker (for difficult to mark materials)	These greasy crayons can be used to write directly on plastic, foil, and resin-coated photographs (such as twentieth-century black-and-white prints or negatives) but note that marks are easily abraded and may transfer to hands or adjacent objects during handling. It is hard to keep the points sharp. Do not use on photographs without interleaving between them.
Schwan-Stabilo All Stabilo pencil (for difficult to mark materials)	Can be used to write on glossy surfaces, including resin-coated photos, glass, and plastic. Available in standard pencil size and hardness, and easier to keep a fine point than with a Berol China Marker. May abrade the surface when writing. The Schwan-Stabilo All Stabilo is a water-soluble pencil that will mark clearly, densely, and legibly on any transparent, glazed surface (acetate, glass, metal, photo, film, etc.). Do not use on a porous surface. Wipes off with a damp cloth on smooth surfaces and erases on paper. #8052 Titanium White; #8008 Graphite; and #8046 Black.
Film markers	For marking photographs with a soft pencil, on margins on reverse is preferred. For semi-gloss or resin-coated papers, ownership marks for photographs can be made with a special film marking pen that passes ISO 18916. Note: Stamping or writing on the backs of photographs can readily leave an impression (embossed mark) that is visible from the front; in addition, stamp or pen ink may take a long time to dry on different kinds of photographic papers and may therefore offset onto other collection items.
Water-based pen for optical discs (CD, DVD, Blu-Ray)	Optical discs are vulnerable to scratching and interference from the dyes and solvents in most markers. Do not write on or adhere label stickers to discs. Use a felt-tip and water-based ink pen, and only label on inner clear hub (see TABLE 5F.5).

Table 5F.5 Ink and Paint Tools

The desired ink qualities include that it be quick drying, acid-free, lightfast, have good adhesion, be abrasion resistant, fluid resistant (i.e., permanent), and useful for marking on a variety of porous and nonporous surfaces. Each pen tested was claimed to have some archival qualities or was already being used by collections staff in museums around the country. Disposable pens were tested against India ink applied with a metal-nibbed pen and black acrylic paint applied with a tiny, natural bristle, size 0 paintbrush. Inks containing a mineral pigment rather than a dye are recommended for lightfastness. Inks that contain carbon are very lightfast. To date, more than one type of ink or paint will be needed for marking a variety of objects. New pens continue to come on the market and manufacturers occasionally change ink formulas of established pens. Some pens contain alcohol, xylene, or other solvents that may damage some surfaces. It is recommended that the ink be periodically tested before using it for semi-permanent or permanent marking. The table provides a starting point for choosing an ink or paint for marking. A variety of types were tested in 2006. India ink and acrylic paint are still highly recommended but are not as easy to use as the disposable pens. Note that new, thinner formulations of acrylic paint have been introduced since 2006.

Pen (tool or media)	Claim (updated from manufacturers' websites, 2019)	Quality of cover	Lightfast	Smear Test 1 (various dry time* on poly plastic)	Smear Test 2 (various dry time* on metal with B-72 base)	Acryloid Sandwich—B-72 base with B-67 top coat	Fabric test for bleeding—unbleached muslin and cotton tape
Pigma Micron (Sakura), black	Archival quality Pigma ink on paper. Waterproof. Fade and chemical resistant. Seven point sizes. Will not smear or feather when dry. Does not bleed through most papers. Meets ACMI nontoxicity standards. Not evaluated for cosmetic use on skin. Not recommended for use on fabrics intended to be washed.	Fairly consistent coverage	No noticeable fading after one month or one year	Smeared completely after five minutes and ten minutes of drying time. Smeared significantly after fifteen minutes of drying time. Not a good choice for plastic.	Completely wiped away after five minutes and after ten minutes of drying time. Smeared after fifteen minutes. Must let ink dry at least thirty minutes.	Mark was allowed to dry for fifteen minutes before applying B-67 top coat and did not smear. Longer (fifteen to thirty minutes) drying time recommended for this ink.	Marks highly legible on muslin; marks sufficiently legible on cotton tape. Best results with heat set (applying an iron).
Identi-pen Permanent Marker (Sakura) (black)	Chemically stable and water resistant. Permanent adherence on most surfaces (alcohol-based cleaners will remove ink from nonporous surfaces such as glass). A fine-line nib with protected tip that will not split. Not recommended for use on fabrics intended to be washed. Not intended for food service items or ceramics that are washed. Not evaluated for cosmetic use on skin.	Excellent coverage, opaque	No noticeable fading after one month or one year	Smeared slightly after five minutes. Smeared significantly less after ten minutes to the point that it was difficult to tell whether it had. Did not smear after fifteen minutes.	Smeared slightly after five minutes. After ten minutes, ink was set and it did not smear.	Excellent results. No smearing on any surfaces. Held up the best on Volara.	Significant bleeding on muslin and cotton tape.

Table 5F.5 *Continued*

Pen (tool or media)	Claim (updated from manufacturers' websites, 2019)	Quality of cover	Lightfast	Smear Test 1 (various dry time* on poly plastic)	Smear Test 2 (various dry time* on metal with B-72 base)	Acryloid Sandwich—B-72 base with B-67 top coat	Fabric test for bleeding**—unbleached muslin and cotton tape
				Smeared negligibly after ten minutes of drying time. Did not smear after minutes of drying time. Dry time fifteen minutes.			
Permapaque Opaque Marker-Dual Point (Sakura) (black)	Dual-Point—bullet point and chisel point on each end. Fine-Point—line width ranges from 0.5 to 1.0 mm, depending on applied pressure. Opaque. Permanent and dries quickly on noncoated paper. Suitable for acid-free environments; meets ACMI nontoxicity standards (AP seal). Not recommended for use on fabrics intended to be washed, on food service, or ceramics that are washed, and not evaluated for cosmetic use on skin. Archival quality ink—chemically stable, waterproof, and fade resistant on paper. Metallic effect shows best on coated papers. Not permanent on nonporous surfaces. Alcohol-based cleaners may remove ink from nonporous surfaces.	Contrary to its name, coverage was not opaque and was inconsistent.	Opaque black coverage dissipated after one month; very slight fading. After one year, the result remains the same, no worse.	Smeared slightly after five minutes of drying time. Did not smear after ten minutes of drying time. Drying time ten minutes.	Smeared slightly after five minutes. After ten minutes, ink was set and it did not smear.	Slight abrasion to the mark from the application of the B-67 top coat. Otherwise no smearing.	Marks are not legible. The point of the pen is too thick to make appropriate-sized marks. Additionally, marks bleed on cotton tape.

Product	Description	Coverage	Fading	Drying/Smearing	Smearing	Smearing	Bleeding
Microperm (Sakura)	Three point sizes—0.25 mm, 0.35 mm, and 0.45 mm. Protected tips will not split. Waterproof and permanent on most surfaces (alcohol-based cleaners will remove ink from nonporous surfaces). Writes on glossy and coated surfaces. Low odor, chemically stable, and waterproof on porous paper substrates. Meets ACMI nontoxicity standards. Not recommended for use on fabrics intended to be washed and not evaluated for cosmetic use on skin.	Good, consistent coverage.	No noticeable fading after one month and one year.	Smeared slightly after five minutes of drying time. Smeared negligibly after ten minutes of drying time. Did not smear after fifteen minutes of drying time. Drying time fifteen minutes.	Smeared slightly after five minutes. After ten minutes, ink was set and it did not smear.	Excellent results. No smearing on any surfaces.	Slight bleeding on muslin and on cotton tape.
ZIG, The Opaque Marker (Kuratake) (Black)	Unavailable in 2019. However, ZIG Cartoonist Mangaka appears promising. Recommend testing. ZIG Mangaka has a variable tip size and is smudge-proof, even when used with watercolors or alcohol-based markers. Lightfast, xylene free, odorless, water-based pigment						
Sharpie, black permanent marker, ultra-fine point (Sanford)	Permanent on most surfaces. Fade and water resistant. Quick-drying ink, AP certified nontoxic formula [2006]. Permanent ink marks on paper, plastic, metal, and most other surfaces. Remarkably resilient ink dries quickly and resists both fading and water; AP certified. The black ink in the Fine, Ultra-Fine, Twin Tip, Chisel, Retractable, Mini, and Super markers is permanent ink. The principle solvents are alcohols, but they also contain ethylene glycol monobutyl ether. All other Sharpie ink colors are Permchrome ink. For these the principle solvents are also alcohols, but no glycol ethers are used [2019].	Somewhat translucent cover quality. Fair coverage	Significant fading after one month. Fades to gray after one year. Not lightfast, not recommended.	Smeared slightly. Smeared slightly after ten minutes. Did not smear after fifteen minutes. Drying time fifteen minutes. Not archival.	Smeared slightly after five minutes. Did not smear after ten minutes of drying time. Not archival.	Slight smear on smooth surface objects such as glazed ceramics. Not archival.	Bleeds significantly on muslin, bleeds less on cotton tape. Not archival.

(continued)

Table 5F.5 *Continued*

Pen (tool or media)	Claim (updated from manufacturers' websites, 2019)	Quality of cover	Lightfast	Smear Test 1 (various dry time* on poly plastic)	Smear Test 2 (various dry time* on metal with B-72 base)	Acryloid Sandwich—B-72 base with B-67 top coat	Fabric test for bleeding**—unbleached muslin and cotton tape
India Ink (black) with metal-nibbed pen [Manufacturer not recorded in 2006] Only black was tested in 2006. If red is necessary, vermillion or cadmium reds have been tested in the past and hold up as well as black and white.	Semi-flat black finish on most surfaces. Water-proof, opaque, permanent, fadeless and acid-free. [2006] [see various manufacturer's technical data; and http://cameo.mfa.org/wiki/India_ink] [2019]	Good, consistent coverage.	No noticeable fading after one month or after one year.	Smeared negligibly after five minutes of drying time. Smeared negligibly after ten minutes of drying time. Did not smear after fifteen minutes. Drying time fifteen minutes.	Ink was set after five minutes of drying time. Retest at ten minutes produced no smearing.	Excellent results. No smearing on any surfaces.	Bleeds on muslin and cotton tape. Difficult to mark on textiles with metal-nibbed pen.
Acrylic paint [body/viscosity not recorded] with brush (carbon black or titanium dioxide white). Recommend testing the new Acrylic Ink and Acrylic Gouache; Fluid and High Flow, respectively. These offer finely milled particles, higher pigment and binder load, ease of use in pens or brush, and wear resistance vs. diluting thick paint. Liquitex—Acrylic Gouache (Mars Black, Ivory Black); Acrylic Ink (Carbon Black); Acrylic marker (2 and 15 mm; Carbon Black) https://www.liquitex.com/us/ Golden—Fluid Acrylics; High Flow Acrylics https://www.goldenpaints.com/technicalinfo	Both offer mineral pigments in various formulations, with detailed explanations and technical support for traditional and reformulated product lines such as the thinner acrylics listed below.	Good, consistent coverage.	No noticeable fading after one month or one year. [See manufacturer's technical info for standardized ASTM lightfastness ratings, per product]	Smeared negligibly after five minutes of drying time. Did not smear after ten minutes. Drying time ten minutes.	Paint was set after five minutes of drying time. Retest at ten minutes produced no smearing.	Excellent results. No smearing on any surfaces. Top coat prevents abrasion that might normally occur with acrylic paint marks.	Difficult to mark on textiles with paint brush. Marks rarely legible, even with skilled hand.

		Tested in a 1988 study by Rose M. Wood and Stephen L. Williams and was recommended.	Not tested in 2006	Not tested in 2006	Not tested in 2006	Not tested in 2006	Not tested in 2006
Pilot Extra Fine, item number SCAUBLK	Permanent, ultra-fine point, no xylene; writes well on most nonporous surfaces, high bleeding potential on paper and textiles; soluble in alcohol; porous plastic tip. Fair lightfastness. [2006] Xylene-free ink. Extra fine point marks permanently on most surfaces and its extra fine point provides precise delivery. [2019]	Tested in a 1988 study by Rose M. Wood and Stephen L. Williams and was recommended.	Not tested in 2006	Not tested in 2006	Not tested in 2006	Not tested in 2006	Not tested in 2006
Rotring Black; Pelikan Ink Black; ZIG, The Opaque Marker (disposable technical pens)	Unavailable by that name in 2019. Recommend testing multiple manufacturers' technical ink pen lines claiming pigment and archival, or water resistant/proof including: Alvin; Copic Multi, Kingart Inkline, (Kurutake) ZIG Cartoonist Mangaka, Marvy, Molotow, Rotring Tikky Graphic Fineliner, Uchida, Winsor & Newton Fineliner. ZIG Mangaka is smudge-proof even when used with watercolors or alcohol-based markers. Lightfast, xylene free, odorless, water-based pigment.					
KohINoor/Rotring technical pens [fillable pen] Isograph and Rapidograph	Recommend testing inks for permanence and nibs for scratching. Precision tips require cleaning after use to avoid clogs. Isograph pen and nibs (13 sizes from 0.1 to 1 mm); wear-resistant, hard chrome-plated thin tip allows working in exquisite detail. Refillable ink reservoir ideal for frequent drawers using Rotring bottled pigmented ink. Ideal for frequent drawers.					

(continued)

Table 5F.5 *Continued*

Pen (tool or media)	Claim (updated from manufacturers' websites, 2019)	Quality of cover	Lightfast	Smear Test 1 (various dry time* on poly plastic)	Smear Test 2 (various dry time* on metal with B-72 base)	Acryloid Sandwich—B-72 base with B-67 top coat	Fabric test for bleeding**—unbleached muslin and cotton tape
	Rapidograph pen and nibs (thirteen sizes from 0.1–1 mm); cartridges of Rotring pigmented ink.						
	Rotring Inks—High density of pigment particles for opacity and lightfastness, line sharpness, and adhesiveness. Fast drying on media. Waterproof. Can be used on a variety of surfaces such as lineboard, tracing paper, or vellum drawing paper. Not for any use on skin, including tattoos.						
TRIA pen, Letraset [fillable pen]	Unavailable in 2019. Tested in a 1988 study by Rose M. Wood and Stephen L. Williams and was not highly rated. Preliminary tests in 2006 showed the pen to be difficult to work with. Recommend testing: Molotow Empty Markers (1 mm +), Montana Empty Marker (0.7 mm +), Replacement Nibs.						

ACMI, Art and Creative Materials Institute; ASTM, American Society for Testing and Materials.

*Note that drying times are comparable for all the pens tested (in 2006) on a particular day in the springtime, inside a building in eastern Pennsylvania. Drying times are relative to the working environment. Drying times will vary for each pen depending on the relative humidity and temperature in which the objects are marked. Test the drying time at each marking session before assuming a medium is dry.

**Note—To test a marker on fabric, write or type a series of sample numbers on the labeling material. Rub the numbers to see if the ink smears, and eliminate any pens or ribbons that do. Second, rinse the tags in hot soapy water to see if the ink runs when wet. Third, rub each number while it is still wet. If the ink is fast in each of these tests the marking material may be used.

Health and Safety in Marking

Ergonomics should be considered in marking practices and the work environment. A suitable workspace should have adequate space to move, rest, cushion, and support the object, without clutter or obstacles that could potentially cause harm to the object or worker. Adequate light and magnification are necessary to examine surface characteristics, execute good clean work, and avoid eye, neck, and back strain that can lead to headaches or repetitive stress musculoskeletal injury (which is common in close-up work that is done for long periods of time). Assistive tools include bench-mounted lamps (with or without magnifying lenses), magnifying headgear with interchangeable lenses, magnifying readers' eyeglasses (with or without LED lights mounted in the eyepiece), traditional bench microscopes, portable microscopes that are USB compatible to a laptop or monitor (these can be bench mounted with a "third hand" vise with or without a magnifying lens) to leave your hands free or may come with an optional stand. Alternative sources for ergonomic aids for small-scale work include craft, sewing, hobby, jewelry, modelmaking, or fly-fishing suppliers (check flea markets, yard sales, and hobbyists' forums for resale items too!).

Long periods of sitting or standing for numbering can cause back, leg, and foot problems, cramps, or even circulatory problems such as faintness or blood clots. Padded standing mats are useful for work at a high table or bench but can present a trip hazard or blockage for a rolling seat. Consider your space options, ensure clearance for aisles, benches, and chairs, and for those with mobility issues. Deep concentration, steadying ones' hands, and holding one's breath to do delicate work or handle a fragile object can set up tension in the body and cause irregular breathing patterns (this author's actual experience). Use task timers to remind you to take regular breaks to refocus your eyes on middle and long distance; relax neck, hand, arms, and spine; reset your breathing pattern; change your position by getting up or walking around; change from standing to sitting, or switch from larger objects to smaller objects.

Hazardous collections—Collection objects may present hazards, either inherent (by chemical characteristics, reactivity, sharpness, friability) or ac-

quired (pesticides, deterioration effects that produce hazardous chemicals). The worker should become familiar with these through basic chemical hazard awareness safety training, selection and use of personal protective equipment (PPE), and learning what is often present and may be encountered in their own collections. Typically, in marking, exposure could come through inhalation, dermal absorption through the hands or via the hands to mucosa (eyes, nose, mouth), laceration, or proximity in handling. Mineral specimens, and some plastics may be reactive to water-based marking supplies (see CHAPTER 5B, "Object Handling").

Understanding Your Supplies: GHS and SDS, Nomenclature, Proprietary Products

In 2013, the US Office of Safety and Health Administration's (OSHA) Hazard Communication Standard (HCS) was aligned with the Globally Harmonized System of Classification and Labeling of Chemicals (GHS). In GHS practice, "material" was dropped from the new standard for Safety Data Sheets (SDS), and they were regularized to contain the same content sections so as to be more comparable. A new system of pictorial hazard warnings (pictograms) was designed for use on SDS and chemical reagent packaging and shipping labels that goes beyond the National Fire Protection Association's Hazard Identification System flammability diamond to require symbols for toxicity, marine environmental risk, and other potential hazards.[17]

GHS is designed to inform workers in the cradle-to-grave chain from manufacturers to inform shippers, handlers, resellers, end users, emergency responders, and disposal companies of hazard risks. If you are purchasing chemicals, the SDS should be provided or made available to you, directly from the manufacturer, the converter or reseller.[18] The SDS gives you an opportunity to compare products via related information, such as melting point and flash point (ignition) temperatures, reactivity with incompatible materials, potential for carcinogenic, mutagenic, and reproductive (teratogen) risks. Although most active ingredients are listed, some may be withheld for proprietary products. These data points not only serve for the safety for the worker but also give insight to potential risks for their selection and use on an object, based on its materiality. In a standard chemical hygiene and safety program that follows OSHA guidelines, up-to-date SDS should be made accessible to workers, and any inspection program that ensures compliance with these standards.[19] Along with hazard warnings posted in work areas and chemical storage, in job descriptions and procedure manuals, the areas where marking is done should have a lab safety binder of SDS for the chemical supplies that are used in marking, literature, or posted signage that explains GHS labels, selection of PPE that should be available, and job hazard analysis (JHA) forms relevant to the tasks and types of collections.

Some art supply products do not require the same type of chemical hazard labeling and bear voluntary information as certified by the Art and Creative Materials Institute, Inc., which works with partners to use standardized toxicologic testing to provide their nontoxic (AP Seal) or health warning labels (CL Seal).[20] Some manufacturers provide detailed information on product formulation, intended applications, and standardized tests (such as lightfastness, solubility, melting point) and have specialists who will speak with end users. Generally, it is sufficient to call the company and ask to speak with a technical information specialist or ask for specification sheets or technical literature, or to browse company websites for technical support.

Although there is no regulation on the use of GHS labeling on collection objects, museums are establishing better practices that align with principles of right-to-know for the worker or stakeholder. Additional training on inherent and acquired risks of collections-based hazards is found in webinars,[21] texts,[22] and networked organizations such as the American Institute for Conservation's Health and Safety working group in collaboration with the American Institute of Industrial Hygienists. Discuss with your safety professionals, collections care worker, and education staff how you might go about integrating GHS hazard warnings into collection labels or safe-handling protocols suited for diverse stakeholders (see CHAPTERS 5B, "Object Handling;" 3I, "Deaccessioning and Disposal;" 3K, "Loans;" PART 7, "Ethical and Legal Issues;" and PART 8, "Uses of Collections").

Methods and Supplies—Temporary/Indirect versus Semi-Permanent and Permanent/Direct

The words *indirect* and *direct* are joined to the rubric of temporary and semi-permanent to distinguish physical interaction, to eliminate confusion with terms of ownership or custody (e.g., object on temporary, or long-term loan), and to clarify characteristics of permanence, lightfastness, solubility (e.g., permanent marker). Conservators prefer a clearer dichotomy of indirect and direct, describing interface with surface.[23] For example, although loops and tags may interact with substrates if poorly selected or located (e.g., they may abrade feathers, block light and cause differential fading, transmit pathogens in living collections), they are not otherwise directly on or embedded in surfaces, so are truly the only temporary, indirect option.

Generally, museums have found marking the object directly with semi-permanent/direct markings to be the most suitable method for marking their permanent collections for the balanced efficacy and practicality of application. Ideally, an object is directly marked by applying the identifying number so that it cannot become physically disassociated from the object. The marking must be secure enough that it cannot be accidentally removed with normal handling, or when exposed to severe stresses such as a disaster, yet can be reversed in the future (as discussed previously).

Care should be taken that neither the initial marking of the number or the materials required for any subsequent removal of the number damage the object's surface. In view of this, irreversible, invasive, permanent/direct marking methods such as scribing, etching, or invisible dye marking are not recommended for general use; however, there may be some rare situations in which they may be preferred (see discussion herein and CHAPTER 3F, "Living and Natural History Collections Registration").

Note that not all the methods and supplies have been systematically tested or in use for a sufficient period of time to determine their long-term effects. The formulations may be changed for some products that have been relied upon for years, or they may become hard to obtain or be discontinued. Such concerns must be weighed against the value of a durable mark. When in doubt about the marking material's effect on the safety of the object, consult a conservator.

Temporary/Indirect Methods

Temporary/indirect methods of marking are easily removed and are not applied directly to the object surface. They are used for marking objects on loan, in temporary custody, and any objects that cannot be marked directly. Temporary marking methods include tying or looping a tag to the object, marking the storage box, sleeve, vial, and/or placing loose labels, tags, or entry receipts with the object, with the caveat that even when indirect marks are used, no given method can be considered completely reversible in all situations. For example, poorly placed loops and tags can cause differential fading, rubbing, or have adverse chemical interactions with the object. Supplies are discussed at length, with suggestions for various object types, below and in the tables.

Temporary marking methods should be used as the primary method for any objects, which cannot be marked directly, such as:

- Objects on loan or in temporary custody (nonaccessioned items entering the museum);
- Objects that have an unstable, highly uneven, or friable surface (e.g., weathered wood, severely corroded metals) or a powdery surface (e.g., painted ethnographic wooden objects, some leather objects);

- Very small objects, such as jewelry, coins, or stamps (although it is possible to legibly mark tiny objects, directly marking coins or stamps may decrease their value); and
- Many plastic, vinyl, and rubber objects.

Temporary marking should be used as a secondary boots and suspenders method for:

- All objects in storage;
- Large objects on which the direct marking is not easily located; and
- Objects that are stored or displayed outdoors, such as farming or military equipment, vehicles, or sculpture (when permanent marking is not appropriate or when semi-permanent marking media have proven not to remain stable in extreme heat or cold, moisture, and sunlight).

Temporary/Indirect Marking Using Tags

The most common process for marking an object with a temporary number is to loosely tie a tag, marked with the proper number, to the object. Use TABLES 5F.6 and 5F.7 to select appropriate tags (whether acid and lignin free, buffered and lignin free, plastic, metal) and ties (non-corrosive, undyed, soft, or durable). Consider all conditions to which the tags and ties will be exposed (e.g., oils and fats in incompletely processed bones, skins, or insects) and uses (e.g., frequent handling, fluid exposure, chemicals, or outdoor conditions).

Table 5F.6 Tags

Material	Uses/Comments
Acid-free card stock	100 percent cotton rag or alpha cellulose and lignin-free, pH-neutral tags are recommended for general use both to protect the object and to ensure the longevity of the tag. Tags can be purchased with cotton string ties or made from card stock. A pH testing pen can be used to check acidity. Rounded corners are preferred to prevent piercing delicate surfaces. Not waterproof or oil resistant. Alkaline-buffered materials are not recommended for use in contact with some objects, including cyanotypes, color photographs, herbarium specimens, or proteinaceous materials because the calcium carbonates have the potential to interact. 100 percent rag heavyweight permanent record paper is sometimes used for fluid preserved specimens. Can be encapsulated in Mylar or laminated for outdoor use.

(continued)

Table 5F.6 *Continued*

Material	Uses/Comments
Resistall paper	Coated or impregnated with melamine; recommended for labels placed inside containers of fluid-preserved specimens (alcohol or formaldehyde), pH 4.5 to 5.2, so it may have adverse effects in ethanol. Rounded corners are preferred to prevent piercing delicate surfaces.
Teflon tape	Nonadhesive, can be marked with a DYMO labeler (the tape must be 0.015 cm thick and 1 cm wide). Water, oil, and chemical resistant. Use for tagging plastics that give off acids as they degrade. Insect resistant.
Reemay	Tags may be cut as strips from this nonwoven polyester interfacing. Be sure it is uncoated, non-adhesive. No fusible web. It is not interchangeable with Pellon interfacing because that material may contain adhesives that may be harmful to some museum objects; there are many types of Pellon fabrics on the market with varying properties. Only nonfusible, uncoated fabrics should be used. The numbers may be written with a typewriter (if you still have one and can test the ink).
Tyvek	Spunbonded sheet from high density polyethylene resin; stiff and soft varieties available with various surface textures and weights. Soft varieties include more rigid Paper-like (Type 10 series), and Textile-like (Type 14) which are sometimes used for tagging baskets and textiles because they conform well and flex. Tyvek 1073 B is recommended but other weights may apply. Tyvek Brillion has also been recommended for higher contrast properties. Check manufacturers specifications and be sure to avoid any with coatings. Water, oil, and chemical resistant. May be used for fluid-preserved specimens (marked with solvent resistant ink). Insect resistant in general usage (dermestids may graze). Good for outdoor use. Melting point and softness of Tyvek can cause problems in conventional laser printers; see printer settings for adjustment to print on plastic films or consider alternate print methods such as screened, handwritten, or inscribed. See the manufacturers website for technical specifications, sample swatch book, and product use guide for graphics and printing. Numbers may be written with ink, impressed, or inscribed before attaching to object. Round the corners.
Mylar or Melinex, uncoated	Polyester terephthalate. Clear, inert. Round corners of sharp edges. Water and oil resistant. Insect resistant.
Metal	Limited use. Aluminum tape (nonadhesive) or aluminum sheets (such as Dibond) can be used to make tags for large industrial artifacts and machinery. Check with your exhibit shop if you have one. The numbers can be embossed with a DYMO embossing labeler or metal stamp, or an impression can be made with a pencil or stylus. Other types of metal tags are not recommended. Relatively soft but may scratch. Secure both ends of tag.
Plastic corrugated board	Water and oil resistant. Brand names include Coroplast, Primex, Cor-X. Good for outdoor use or for large machinery. Insect resistant, but tunnels may provide insect nesting area and retain water. May have sharp edges; sand them or wrap edges with stable paper and adhesive.
Formica	Carved into, routed, or etched. Water, oil, and chemical resistant. Good for outdoor use. Insect resistant.

Table 5F.7 Ties

Material	Uses/Comments
Thread and string	Undyed or natural cotton thread or string can be used to attach small tags. Polyester thread is more durable but may be too strong for use on fragile materials. Do not use jeweler's tags with colored strings; dyes may run when wet.
Fabric tape	Cotton, linen, or polyester. Use to tie string tags to large objects or mark with the number directly and loop around an object. Nonabrasive.
Cord	Unwaxed polyester or polypropylene cord can be used for large objects or strong materials such as suits of armor. Shoemaker's supply companies carry two-, three-, and four-ply polyester cords. Cotton cord is soft and nonabrasive but is not as durable. Nylon cord has a short lifetime and is not recommended.
Polyethylene straps or ties	Plastic zap straps or zip ties (of polyethylene, such as those used to tie garbage bags) and thinner ties with male and female ends can be useful for objects that have oily surfaces. Cloth or thread ties may wick oils onto paper or cloth tags. Inert and relatively nonabrasive, these materials can be used in outdoor situations although prolonged sunlight exposure may cause deterioration of the plastic ties and straps with long-term usage. They can be obtained from plastics suppliers. Use polyethylene, not nylon. Insect resistant.
Wire	Limited use. Annealed stainless steel, Monel, or aluminum wire may be used to attach aluminum tags to large-scale industrial objects or vehicles. Aluminum wire may corrode in outdoor conditions. Stainless steel will discolor but will be corrosion resistant. Caution: wire can scratch, use only in situations where other materials would not suffice. Wire can also be covered with surgical tubing or heat-shrink polyethylene tubing. Vinyl-coated stainless-steel cable, with the ends secured by a crimp connector, can also be used. Vinyl coated cable is softer and less prone to scratching until the vinyl deteriorates. Do not use polyvinyl chloride (PVC; off-gassing causes deterioration) wire or insulated copper (clue to corrosion problems associated with the copper).
Reemay	Ties may be cut as strips from this nonwoven polyester interfacing. Be sure it is uncoated, nonadhesive. No fusible web. It is not interchangeable with Pellon interfacing because that material may contain adhesives that may be harmful to some museum objects; there are many types of Pellon fabrics on the market with varying properties. Only nonfusible, uncoated fabrics should be used. The numbers may be written with a typewriter, if you still have one and can test the ink.
Tyvek	Ties may be cut as strips from this spunbonded sheet from high density polyethylene resin. Available in stiff and soft varieties with various surface textures and weights. Soft varieties include more rigid Paperlike (Type 10 series), and Textile-like (Type 14) are sometimes used for making ties because they conform well and flex. Tyvek 1422a is recommended but other weights may apply. Tyvek Brillion has also been recommended for higher contrast properties. Check manufacturers specifications and be sure to avoid any with coatings. Water, oil, and chemical resistant. May be used for fluid-preserved specimens (marked with solvent resistant ink). Insect resistant in general usage (dermestids may graze). Good for outdoor use. Melting point and softness of Tyvek can cause problems in conventional laser printer; see printer settings for adjustment to print on plastic films or consider

(continued)

Table 5F.7 *Continued*

Material	Uses/Comments
	alternate print methods such as screened, handwritten, or inscribed. See manufacturers website for technical specifications, sample swatch book, and product use guide for graphics and printing. Numbers may be written, with ink, impressed or inscribed before attaching to object. Round the corners.
Teflon dental floss	Teflon, a trade name for a polymer known as polytetrafluoroethylene or PTFE. Can be found as a dental floss (do not use traditional dental floss made from nylon, which deteriorates and may have flavors, colorings, and waxes). Teflon/PTFE resists water, oil, and chemicals. Use to tie tags on oily specimens, such as birds, oily or greasy, or acidic objects. May cut soft or fragile surfaces if stressed or pulled. Insect resistant.
Teflon thread tape (nonadhesive)	Teflon plumber's tape is chemically inert and soft and wider than floss. Can be used to tie tags onto objects with fragile surfaces. Water, oil, and chemical resistant. Good for ties for plastic, rubber, and leather objects, which may cause cotton thread or string to deteriorate. Insect resistant.

Use the same archival quality materials for tagging permanent collections and objects in temporary custody or on loan because objects temporarily in the museum sometimes remain longer than initially anticipated. Pencil is recommended for writing numbers on paper or Tyvek tags. If corrosion, resistant wire or metal tags are used, both ends of the tag should be secured to prevent the tag from moving and abrading the object. Tags should be placed in locations that will not be seen when the objects are on display so that tags can remain attached to the objects in the gallery. If tags must be removed while objects are on display, the tags should be reattached as soon as the objects are removed from their exhibition. Large sculptures might not need to be marked or tagged directly because they are unlikely to be moved. However, thefts of other outdoor works do occur for a variety of reasons. If you choose not to mark large, outdoor works, consider robust documentation of extant identifying marks. The identifying number can be included on a commemorative marker, although bronze plaques have been targeted in recent years in search of easy cash from recycling for copper content.

Temporary/Indirect Marking on Object Housing

If it is not possible to tag the object, the object should be placed in an archival sleeve, vial, box, tray, or small polyethylene or polypropylene bag, which is marked with the number; a loose tag or label should be placed inside with the object. If a poly-bagged object is to be stored in a location with wide variations in temperature, several small holes should be made in the bag, or the points of the corners should be cut off the bag, to allow air circulation and prevent condensation within the bag. Alternately, if intended for intentional cold storage, protocols for packaging and preconditioning with silica gel are to be followed. Avoid unsafe plastics such as polyvinyl chloride (PVC) or polystyrene (PS), which may exude plasticizers and other harmful substances. Tags placed inside bags should be marked with pencil, and not ink, as direct transfer of the ink or off-gassing may damage some objects (see CHAPTERS 5I, "Preventive Care," and 5J, "Storage").

Temporary/Indirect Marking on Textiles

Textile fragments may have loose tags placed in their wrappings, or the numbers can be marked in pencil on the wrappings. Matted objects may have the number marked in pencil on the reverse of the mat. Framed objects may have the number marked on the backing board in pencil, or tags may be attached to the screw eye, D-ring, or metal hanger.

Temporary/Indirect Marking for Exhibitions

For paintings, drawings, prints, and other framed works that are loaned, a label is often applied to the reverse of the protective backing paper or board support. If there is no backing, consider alternative means, such as a light pencil inscription, a looped tag, or consult the owner. The label usually includes the loan, accession, or catalog number, the title or description of the object, medium, artist or maker's name, and the title, location, and dates of the loan. This label is usually left on the backing when it is returned to the lender as a record of exhibition history. Labels in common use include both pressure-sensitive adhesive (PSA) (self-sticking) labels, as well as gummed paper labels which must be moistened with water for application. Gummed paper labels are preferred because the adhesive of many pressure-sensitive labels deteriorates and is either subject to cold-flow, leaves a sticky residue, or the adhesive and label become brittle (TABLE 5F.8). Such labels pose the risk of detachment and possible transfer to the surface of another painting or object. The adhesive can permeate wood, leaving a permanent stain and possibly a tacky residue. Often gummed labels can be removed and reapplied in a preservation quality sleeve if the backing board is replaced, thereby preserving the exhibition history of the artwork. Gummed paper or pressure-sensitive labels should never be applied directly to the object or its primary substrate (e.g., the canvas), but to a backing board or strainer. See references on paper permanence, printing permanence, and adhesive label permanence.[24]

Temporary/Indirect Marking of Natural History Specimens

Some natural history specimens require special tagging considerations. For example, fluid-preserved specimens often have two levels of labeling. Fluid-resistant tags marked with the catalog number are tied to individually cataloged specimens or placed inside the container for specimens cataloged by lot, and a label with more extensive catalog information is either inserted inside the container or attached to the outside of the container. It is important to remember that tags or labels inside the jars of fluid-preserved specimens may abrade specimens or lose their marking from abrasion or from exposure to the preservative, but labels on the outside of the jar are not as likely to be lost. Specimens may have numerous tags representing collectors, prior owners, uses, systematic identifications and nomenclatural changes, or treatments. These tags usually remain attached to the

specimen with a new tag is added when needed. If it is necessary to remove such tags for any reason, they should be documented in the collection object file and retained with the object in an indirect manner.[25] Historic tags may be made from a variety of materials (paper, metal, wood, leather) that may not meet today's standards.

Characteristics to suit particular needs may be necessary as specimens may come into contact with fluids during use, treatment, and cleaning, or may need to perform in special environments. For this reason, Resistall or other resistant coated paper has been used for tags and labels. However, the preferred pH range for labels in contact with proteinaceous tissues is 6.0 to 8.5 pH and the pH level of Resistall paper ranges from 4.5 to 5.2 pH (due to its melamine coating). A pH neutral paper (lignin-free or 100 percent rag, nonbuffered, free of optical brighteners) or an inert material (uncoated: spunbonded polyethylene such as Tyvek, spunbonded or cast polyester such as Mylar, or polypropylene) is preferred for fluid collections. However, considering the utility of historic fluid collections, which may never have been exposed to plastic contaminants in their wet environment, it may well be worth avoiding potential contamination for better comparison to specimens taken in more recent years that show evidence of biologically persistent plasticizers in marine or food chain pathways.[26]

Alkaline-buffered paper is sometimes used for labeling dry botanical specimens because it is desirable for maintaining cellulose stability. Using buffered paper in direct contact with botanical specimens should be approached with caution as the alkalinity may negatively affect noncellulose components of plants, such as resins, and impair future study of these materials (see CHAPTER 3F, "Living and Natural History Collections Registration").

Semi-Permanent/Direct Marking Methods

There are four main methods for marks that can be applied directly to museum objects, will not cause deterioration, and can be removed in the future—(i) a barrier coat with ink or paint atop; (ii) a barrier coat with an adhered label atop; (iii) sewn labels; and (iv) pencil marking. These are discussed at length, with suggestions for object types and in TABLES 5F.1, 5F.5, 5F.8, and 5F.9.

Table 5F.8 Adhered Labels

Material	Uses/Comments
Acid-free paper	Labels can be made from 100 percent alpha cellulose, chlorine-free, lignin-free paper. Paraloid lacquers, acrylic emulsions, and polyvinyl acetate (PVAC) emulsions are used to adhere labels; see discussion of PVACs in TABLE 5F.2. The number can be written with pencil, ink, or printed with a laser printer. It is possible to get kozo tissues prepared for laser feed through a bypass tray. Do not use labels printed on daisy wheel, dot matrix, or ink jet printers. Solvent-based adhesives such as Paraloid B-72 can also be used on solvent-resistant surfaces but can remove type printed with a laser printer. Use solvent-resistant ink. For the least intrusion to porous objects, apply the adhesive to the label and then apply the label to the object. Do not use on friable or painted surfaces. See print and webinar tutorials.[1]
Kozo, gampi, mitsumata papers	Whether washi, hanji, or other cultural source, long-fibered bast fiber papers are generally more flexible and translucent. Dye-free, prepared for handwriting, or laser printing. Methyl cellulose adhesive is preferable to wheat or rice starch paste, which may attract pests. Used for barkcloth, baskets, wood objects with uneven surfaces, and occasionally leather. Heat- or solvent-reactivated adhesive tissue can potentially be used for materials, such as leather, which cannot tolerate moisture and heat at the same time. Consult a conservator. Do not use on friable or painted surfaces. Saturation with an adhesive close to the refractive index of the substrate can help label disappear and allow numbers to stand out.
Mylar/Melinex	Printed with a laser printer or written on with alcohol-resistant pigment ink. Mild scuffing may help ink hold. Apply in Paraloid B72, although this may soften ink until cured.[2]

NOTES

1. Thomas J. Braun, "An alternative technique for applying accession numbers to museum artifacts," *Journal of the American Institute for Conservation* 46, no. 2 (2007): 91–104. Available at: https://doi.org/10.1179/019713607806112323; Nancy Odegaard and Gina Watkinson, "Collection labeling: Safely applying accession numbers to museum objects," presented at the Association of Tribal Archives, Libraries, and Museums (ATALM), Washington, DC, September 12, 2015. Available at: https://www.sustainable heritagenetwork.org/digital-heritage/collection-labeling-safely-applying-accession-numbers-museum-objects.

2. Braun, "An alternative technique."

Table 5F.9 Sewn Labels[1]

Material	Uses/Comments
Fabric tape (ribbon; nonadhesive)	Unbleached cotton twill tape is recommended for textile labels. Plain woven cotton, linen, or polyester tape may also be used. Sizing is sometimes used to stiffen or seal the tape but is not generally recommended. The number is written with ink. The ends are turned under 1/4 inch before sewing.
Reemay	Labels may be cut as strips from this nonwoven polyester interfacing. Be sure it is uncoated, nonadhesive. No fusible web. It is not interchangeable with Pellon interfacing because that material may contain adhesives, which may be harmful to some museum objects; there are many types of Pellon fabrics on the market with varying properties. Only nonfusible, uncoated fabrics should be used. The numbers may be written with a typewriter (if you still have one and can test the ink).
Tyvek	Spunbonded sheet from high density polyethylene resin. Available in stiff and soft varieties with various surface textures and weights. Soft varieties include more rigid Paperlike (Type 10 series), and Textile-like (Type 14) which are sometimes used for tagging baskets and textiles because they conform well and flex. Tyvek 1073 B is recommended but other weights may apply. Tyvek Brillion has also been recommended for higher contrast properties. Check manufacturers specifications and be sure to avoid any with coatings.

Material	Uses/Comments
	Water, oil, and chemical resistant. Insect resistant in general usage (dermestids may graze). Good for outdoor use. Melting point and softness of Tyvek can cause problems in a conventional laser printer; see printer settings for adjustment to print on plastic films or consider alternate print methods such as screened, handwritten, or inscribed. See manufacturer website for technical specifications, sample swatch book, and product use guide for graphics and printing. Numbers may be written, with ink, impressed or inscribed before attaching to object. Round the corners.
Thread	Cotton thread (#50 or #60), undyed and unbleached is preferred (white is acceptable) and is recommended for sewing labels on textiles. Ideally, the strength of the thread should be equal to or less than the strength of the fibers of the textile so that the thread will not tear the textile if the tag is snagged. Cotton/polyester or polyester thread may be used for very strong fabrics but may tear fragile textiles. Silk threads deteriorate quickly and are not recommended. Silk thread is also slippery, and stitches may pull out easily. Dark, colorfast thread may be used for stitching tags on dark-colored objects if the stitches will be visible on display. Test the thread to make sure that the color does not run when wet.
Needles	Fine, sharp-pointed needles (#8 quilting in-between, #9–10 crewel, #10–#12 sharps) are recommended for medium and fine textiles. Small-size tapestry or ballpoint needles are recommended for sewing labels on textiles with a heavier, open weave. Sew between warp and weft with minimal amount of stitches needed to hold down corners. A sharp-pointed needle can be blunted with fine sandpaper to avoid piercing threads.

NOTE

1. Note print and video tutorials: Museum of New Zealand Te Papa Tongarewa, *How to Apply Accession Numbers to Textiles*. Available at: https://www.youtube.com/watch?v=lInGwnjK3nA; Canadian Conservation Institute, "Applying accession numbers to textiles," in *CCI Notes 13/8* (2018). Available at: https://www.canada.ca/en/conservation-institute/services/conservation-preservation-publications/canadian-conservation-institute-notes/applying-accession-numbers-textiles.html.

Permanent/Direct Marking Methods

Permanent marks, although rarely used, may be considered for some types of objects. They should not be used without careful consideration of the ramifications of permanently disfiguring objects. Permanent marks may be useful as a deterrent to theft (e.g., in the case of firearms). It necessarily follows that although permanent marks will decrease the monetary value of objects, the gain in terms of security may be significant. The location for such marks should be chosen with extreme care. Dye-based inks have great potential to soften in appearance over time due to capillary action in hygroscopic materials. Pigment-based inks and paints applied over a semi-permanent/direct barrier layer are preferred to direct marking. Scribing and etching are never preferred.

Permanent markings may be desirable for objects used by interpreters in living history settings (such as cooking pots, utensils, and farm implements) as well as objects that are stored or displayed outdoors.

There are no means of applying and maintaining a durable, reversible mark on such collections. Additionally, reproductions and facsimiles used in demonstration collections should have permanent numbers to prevent the objects from being identified or sold as authentic should the numbers wear off. Other examples include archaeology or anthropology collections that have bone fragments or pottery shards numbering in the thousands. Such artifacts may be virtually impossible to identify, even with photography. The separation of the object from its identification number may destroy its value for future study purposes. However, the risk of permanently marking brittle or tiny objects with damaging or obscuring techniques must be weighed against better management of security protocols.

Natural history specimens are sometimes marked directly with permanent ink because the labor-intensive, semi-permanent methods may make the marking of some objects (e.g., all bones of a bird skeleton) impractical. Permanent marking methods for various types of objects are discussed herein. Note that "permanent" markers that are not pigment-based may prove problematic, as biological surfaces with remaining fats or oils may absorb or dissolve and make a blurry mess of the careful writing. For this reason, careful preparation and use of barrier methods, or direct application of a paper label with nondamaging adhesive, are preferred.

Historically, for works of art on paper, photographs, and books, the museum name or mark was often stamped on the face or back of prints; a sharpened 2H (#3) hard pencil or ink was used to indent or emboss the paper; and books were marked with permanent pigment or actinic ink in multiple locations to indicate ownership. This practice has been largely discontinued by museums because the marks are not reversible and the ink may migrate through the paper, leaving stains on the front and causing permanent damage. See the section on semi-permanent/direct marks instead.

Libraries or archive collections that wish to continue the practice of stamping materials with ink should consult the Library of Congress publication,[27] which includes advice on marking photographs and optical discs with less damaging techniques; and for their irreversibility or reversibility on photographic prints.[28] For understanding the role of bookplates and assorted marks in books that relate to provenance, see "Guidelines Regarding Security and Theft in Special Collections."[29]

For use of pigment ink or thin paint on porous materials, see TABLE 5F.5 to get a sense of the performance on ribbon labels.

Skins, leather, hides, and pelts can be marked with pigment-based ink or paint with a writing or stamping tool.

Textiles can be marked with pigment-based ink.

Wooden objects can be painted or stamped with pigment-based ink, engraved, or branded for permanent/indirect marks.

Semi-porous materials such as bone and ceramics can be marked with pigment-based ink or can be etched or imprinted with an engraving tool or stamping tool. Note that engraving can shatter brittle material.

Nonporous or impervious materials, including metals and some plastics can be etched with a scriber or engraving tool, or the number can be imprinted with a stamping tool. Some plastics will reject or absorb marks or can be scratched or crazed by marking materials, so tread carefully if you cannot confirm identification of the plastic type.[30] See also the guidelines for optical discs.

Facsimiles and Teaching Collection Objects

When marking teaching collection objects and frequently handled collection objects that are at risk of dispersal, choose the method that is least destructive to its surface. A discreet number applied with permanent ink may appear less damaging than inscribing or etching the object's surface. Do not use any method that will cause future corrosion or continued deterioration of the object. Advances have been made in microprinting for redundant and tiny security tags. Use of fluorescent dyes and optical brighteners that are imperceptible in visible light might be considered for facsimiles, although their long-term fluorescence or potential darkening or transfer will be dependent on factors of exposure. Museums often use a separate prefix or color code to distinguish reproductions or demonstration collections from the permanent collection, and the enumeration mark should reflect this.

RECOMMENDED MARKING MATERIALS— CHARACTERISTICS OF PERMANENCE, LIGHTFASTNESS, AND COLORFASTNESS

Materials used to mark objects must be as chemically stable as possible and demonstrate excellent aging characteristics to ensure the longevity, long-term legibility, and reversibility of the numbers. Previous product recommendations in *Museum Registration Methods* were based or a 1995 survey of 205 museums, pen tests performed by registrars and conservators in 2006, and a survey of registrars from 2008. Products recommended in this edition include archival quality materials that are easy to use, inexpensive, and readily available. It is recognized that many museums will not have the expertise or facilities to prepare their own solvent-based supplies. All materials discussed in this chapter are readily available online from conservation, archival, or art supply companies. See the tables for details of materials; there are advantages and disadvantages of each.

New products continue to enter the market and further testing may result in some of the materials listed in this chapter falling out of favor. Keep in mind that the performance of a commercial product may vary as formulations change over time. It is recommended that products be tested on nonmuseum objects before use. Simple tests such as exposure to sunlight, water, or solvents can be easily carried out.[31] When choosing marking materials, evaluate the risks to which objects and the markings are likely to be exposed, keeping in mind the comments on decision trees and critical thinking about methods and supplies.

- Will the objects be on exhibition for long periods of time? If so, lightfastness of marking media will be a prime concern. Check manufacturer ratings.
- Are there oils on the surface that cannot, or should not, be removed? Plastic ties and tags may be preferred in place of paper and cotton string so that the oils are not adsorbed into the tie and tag.
- Will the objects be at risk for accidental water contact, such as overhanging water pipes or outdoor display? Is the collection in a hurricane or flood prone location? Waterproof materials will be desired.
- Are pests a problem? Insect resistant materials may be preferred to paper and other natural materials that provide food for pests.

Location and Size

The number should be placed in a location that is unobtrusive while on display, yet clearly visible or easily accessible when the object is in storage. Choose an area that is unlikely to be displayed or photographed. Do not obscure maker's marks, major design elements, or old inventory numbers. Marks applied by previous owners should be retained because they contribute to the object's history. The number should not be applied to physically unstable surfaces, such as loose or flaking paint or to pitted or corroded areas, because numbers will be difficult to apply and remove and may harm the object's surface. The number should not be placed in an area that receives wear, friction, or pressure from the object's own weight or its mount. With the exception of small objects with concave bottoms or objects that have ornamentation or decoration, which would make numbering elsewhere difficult or unsightly, avoid marking the bottom of an object.

Because handling of museum objects presents the greatest single risk of damage the number should not be placed where excessive handling or ergonomic challenges will be necessary to locate it. Large, heavy objects should be marked on the reverse near the base, not on the underside, to avoid the need to lift or tip the object to read the number.

Large paintings may be marked at diagonal corners of the frame or backing so that the number can be easily located whether the painting is hung low or high on a storage screen or wall. Rugs and other large textiles or rolled formats may be marked at diagonal corners so that the labels can be easily located regardless of the direction in which the pieces are rolled for storage. If the number will not be visible in storage, an auxiliary tag should be used; the tag can be left in storage as a placeholder for the displaced object.

All detachable parts and accessory pieces (e.g., a snuffbox and cover, a knife and sheath, or fragments of a broken object) should be individually marked (e.g., 1978.120A and 1978.120B—see CHAPTER 5A, "Numbering"). The number should never be applied only to a bracket, arm, or trim piece that could become separated from the object.

Choose a consistent location on objects of the same type. When a conflict arises, the highest priority should be given to ensuring the least disruption to the object. Some objects may have no readily apparent location on which to mark the number (e.g., complex abstract sculptures, automobiles). When an object is marked in an unusual or difficult-to-find location, make note of the location in the object's file, and add an auxiliary tag if necessary.

Marks should be unobtrusive yet clearly legible. Use common sense, guided by the size of the object, the location of the number, and the marking method when determining the size of the numbers. Numbers may range from less than 1/8 inch for very small objects to 3/8 inch for larger objects. Some types of objects call for larger numbers, such as large-scale industrial artifacts or living history collections for which numbers must be located in dark historic interiors. Numbers applied to areas such as backing boards of paintings, textile storage boxes, or auxiliary tags may be as large as desired because they are not applied to the object itself or visible when on display. See TABLE 5F.1 for advice on placement for particular objects.

DESCRIPTION OF METHODS (SEMI-PERMANENT/DIRECT)— STEP-BY-STEP INSTRUCTIONS

Most of the references cited in this section can be freely accessed to see visual examples or video tutorials and alternate methods. Consider printing out your favorite resources and keeping them in a binder with your procedures.

Method l: Barrier Coat with Ink or Paint Marks and Top Coat

Recommended for most three-dimensional objects but not for paper, textiles, plastics, leathers, and fibrous materials. Examine the object to locate a suitable location for marking the number (see herein and TABLE 5F.1 for recommended locations). If an object is constructed of more than one material, place the number on the smoother, harder, less porous surface. Generally, mark on the back, on the lower right side of an object, if possible. The area to be marked should be free from dust and surface dirt. Clean the area to be marked with minimal techniques, such as dusting the surface with a soft, clean brush. Some objects may need additional cleaning before a number can be applied. Do not use a solvent (not even water) to clean an object without the advice of a conservator. If using a solvent, stop the process immediately should a change or bloom appear in the surface of the object. Never clean flaking, crazed, or unstable surfaces such as deteriorating ancient glass, or cellulose nitrate; consult a conservator.

Apply a base coat (clear or pigmented titanium white may be needed on some surfaces). Paraloid B-72 in acetone is recommended for the base coat. A base coat should be used on most surfaces, including nonporous surfaces. Ink or paint may not adhere well to smooth surfaces; some inks bead, and both ink and paint are easily abraded from nonporous surfaces. Some permanent inks are formulated to etch metal and other materials to improve their adherence, and metal oxide pigments in paints have the potential to react with the surface of metal or organic objects. A reversible base coat provides a smooth, hard writing surface and may add a measure of security for the number because it is not readily removable without the appropriate solvent. In addition, mistakes can be corrected during the process, and numbers can be removed with a solvent at a later date without affecting the surface of the object. Choose a base coat that is compatible with the surface of the object to be marked (e.g., will not dissolve or cause damage during application or removal). See the tables for recommended base and top coats and solvent compatibility. When choosing a location for the number, keep in mind that the coating may leave a permanent stain. Apply a neat rectangle of base coat just large enough to contain the identifying number with an artist's brush. Allow the base coat to dry about fifteen minutes or until it is no longer sticky to the touch before applying numbers. Drying times will vary with the temperature and humidity levels. It could take thirty to sixty minutes if it is humid. If bubbles form, it is most likely too thick, and more solvent should be added to provide a clear, smooth surface for marking. Porous materials, such as unfinished wood, may need more than one coat or an alternative method. A thickened coat may prevent extensive penetration into porous materials. Apply one coat at a time, allowing each coat to dry, until a discernible film is visible on the surface. Although drying times vary, a thicker coat will require a longer drying time. An alternative method of marking (such as adhesion) should be employed if the object is too porous.

Handwritten numbers—Write the number on the base coat with a permanent pigment-based ink, fluid acrylic paint, or acrylic ink using a fine-point technical nib pen, a flexible crow quill nib, or a fine artist's brush. Disposable pigment marking pens, such as Pigma pens, may also be used (see TABLES 5F.4, 5F.5, and 5F.6). Do not press firmly when using a flexible crow quill or metal-nib pen, as the nibs can cut through the base coat and scratch the surface. Take care not to drip inks or paints. Mask off areas with draped soft wrapping materials or paper that will not catch on textured surfaces. Practice a few numbers on a test object before attempting to mark a museum object. Choice of color is determined by the color of the object to be marked, as well as the past practice of the institution (see TABLE 5F.1). Preferred practice is to use carbon black and titanium dioxide white because these are stable pigments and should meet the needs of most collections. Dark objects are usually marked with white numbers. Alternatively, a base coat of white can be placed on the clear barrier coat before the number is written in black but this method should only be employed if the organization has used this method in the past. White numbers are commonly used on glass objects because white is less obtrusive for display purposes, but preprinted labels on Mylar or saturated with acrylic resin have also been shown to work. If another color (such as red) has been used consistently by the institution in the past, it may be acceptable to continue the practice for the sake of consistency. Check with the manufacturer regarding the lightfastness of the pigment intended for use. Red can be used successfully on many objects, except those with very dark, red, or green backgrounds; on the latter, such as patinaed bronzes, red creates an optical illusion and is difficult to read. Keep in mind that many red pigments are not lightfast and red numbers may not be as easily read by color-blind individuals. See also "Method 2: Adhered Labels" and TABLE 5F.8.

Use a compatible, nonmiscible top coat over the number—Paraloid B-67 in mineral spirits is recommended. A protective top coat is used to prevent accidental removal of the number from contact with water and other solvents. It also protects against abrasion or chipping due to handling and will help prevent number loss in the event of a disaster. Allow the number to dry approximately twenty to thirty minutes before applying a top coat. For the top coat, use a material containing a solvent that will not soften the base coat (e.g., Paraloid B-67 in mineral spirits over Paraloid B-72 in acetone, Paraloid B-72 in ethanol over Paraloid B-72 in acetone, or a water-based emul-

sion or dispersion over a base coat, according to a conservator's instructions). Load the brush and apply it in a single light stroke so that the bristles float over the base coat and do not rub the number. The top coat should be a slightly smaller rectangle than the base coat. The goal is—in the event of a mistake—to allow dissolution of the top coat but not the base coat. Allow the top coat to dry thirty minutes, or until it is no longer tacky, before moving the object.

Summary of Applying Marks using Method 1: The Paraloid Sandwich

1. Examine the object to determine what materials it is made of and the best location for the number. Determine which materials are best for marking by checking the tables.
2. Using a soft brush or lint-free cloth, clean the area to be marked.
3. Test the base coat, Paraloid B-72 in acetone, and make sure it is the right consistency for the label base (fluid, not too thick). Thin with acetone if it bubbles when set.
4. Allow the base coat to dry thoroughly (fifteen minutes, depending on temperature and humidity).
5. Write the number on the base coat with a Pigma pen, quill and nib with ink, or a tiny paintbrush and acrylic paint. Allow to dry thoroughly (ten minutes depending on the marking tool, temperature, and humidity).
6. Apply a top coat over the number. Paraloid B-67 in mineral spirits is recommended for the top coat. Allow the label to dry for at least thirty minutes before returning it to its permanent storage location.

Method 2: Adhered Labels, Written or Printed

Adhered labels may be substituted for Method 1, as discussed previously. This method is less intrusive than Method 1. Less foreign material penetrates the surface and most of the adhesive is removed with the paper, leaving only a small amount of residue that can be easily removed. This method is suitable for most objects and is ideal for flexible, porous, and irregular, uneven surfaces. As with Method 1, adhered labels should not be placed over unstable paint, flaking lacquer, or other insecure surfaces. The marking media, papers, and adhesives should be chosen carefully; several are recommended. If instituting an adhered label system for the first time, consult a conservator or practice the method on a nonmuseum object first. The label should be as small as possible and placed in an area that does not receive light exposure because the label will cause uneven fading of the object's surface.

Preprinted labels—For practical convenience, preventing errors in marking large numbers of objects, legibility at a human-readable but tiny scale, and reversibility, generating number lists from CMS in a variety of sizes and multiples and printing on a straight path laser printer has gained favor. Do not use labels printed on a daisy wheel, dot matrix, or ink jet printers because these inks are generally water soluble. Laser printers, on the other hand, use the same xerographic process as modern photocopiers. The laser toner is composed of carbon-based dry pigment with a stable thermoplastic polymer (polystyrene, acrylics, or polyesters) that is thermally fused to the paper. Printer performance and bonding to standard office papers can be checked with a standardized test.[32] Although the test may not perform perfectly on an alternative paper, if print settings are monitored to not lay down too much toner, sealing with a compatible top coat will ensure longevity. See Method 2, Option 3.[33] In addition, microscopic collections held in containers or for extreme environments, those produced on polyester by thermal transfer printers may be the only efficient means, although backup methods may be recommended. Excellent instructions with advantages and disadvantages may be found in the literature.[34] See also CHAPTER 5G, "Barcodes and RFID Tags."

Method 2, Option 1: Adhered Paper Labels for Marking for a Variety of Objects
This method can be used with laser printed labels on Perma/Dur bond paper, or kozo paper prepared for print (see other options). The advantages to using this method of numbering include:

- Fewer errors because of the ability to write the number on a secondary material, rather than directly on the object.

- It is reversible.
- It is controllable.
- Can use various types of papers.
- Can use pencil, pigment ink, acrylic paint or ink, or computer-generated numbers.
- Can make solutions in small batches as needed.
- No long drying times between bottom layers, number layer, and top coat.

Tools needed:

- Clipboard;
- Cutting mat;
- Pigma pen;
- Color shaper;
- Teflon-coated spatula;
- Dissecting forceps;
- Paintbrushes (try a short script/liner paintbrush in size 1 or 0);
- Pencil, #2 or HB;
- Scalpel;
- Ruler;
- Scissors;
- Ethafoam block;
- Silicone release paper;
- Pins;
- Blotter paper;
- Clean cloth;
- Small bottles and larger jars to nest them in as spill containment; and
- Brush rest.

Papers that can be used:

- Undyed washi, hanji, or other long fibered kozo (paper mulberry) paper.[35]
- Photo-tex, Perma/Dur Bond or other alpha-cellulose paper for opaquer label.

Adhesives that can be used:

- Paraloid B-72 granules. Synthetic resin, soluble and reversible with acetone.
- Cellofas B 3500-SCMC (sodium carboxymethylcellulose), a water-based cellulose ether that is a weak paper adhesive and is soluble in water. Alternately, generic SCMC can be mixed with water to the same concentration.

- Jade 403, internally plasticized polyvinyl acetate emulsion.
- Cellofas and Jade mixture (one part Cellofas to three parts Jade).
- Advantages to using Cellofas/Jade 1:3 include that it is water based, compatible with many materials and substrates, nontoxic, easy to use, and easy to clean up. It can be used on lacquer, most plastics, and organic materials.
- Rhoplex B-60-A.
- Krylon Clear Spray Acrylic or Lascaux Fix.

Solvents:

- Deionized or distilled water.
- Acetone, reagent grade or better is preferred.

Preparing adhesives:

- B-72 granules should be mixed with acetone 24 hours in advance of using so that the mixture is thoroughly dissolved. In a glass jar, dissolve 25 grams of granules in 75 ml of acetone, stir, and cover. B-72 must be stored in an airtight container. Make sure the lip of the jar and lid are clean of any dissolved B-72 before sealing it, or the residue will cause the lid to adhere to the jar. If the jar is sealed shut, invert the jar so that it rests on its lid (the acetone in the solution will loosen the bond) or invert the bottle in a larger container of acetone.
- Before using the B-72, add more acetone to bring the solution up to 100 ml total volume, stir, and let rest. If the stored solution has bubbles in it when it is applied or appears yellow, discard it appropriately and prepare a new solution. Ratios, order of operation, and precision matter when mixing adhesive. Develop a feel to recognize a good consistency. Experiment with adhesive mixtures on practice objects before using it on real museum objects.

Use care with interactions of paper and adhesives and matching optical reflectance and refractive index because B-72 will make thin papers translucent and the number will be difficult to see on a dark-colored object. For dark objects, use a thicker kozo tissue with the Cellofas/Jade adhesive (a more opaque adhesive) and the resulting mark will show up better on dark-colored objects. Perma/Dur Bond, being a more opaque paper, will also show up better on dark objects. Conversely, this translucency may be useful for glass or shiny objects. Experimentation with optical clearing of papers[36] may prove to yield a new method for use of preprinted labels on glass and shiny objects.[37]

Step-by-step instructions:

1. Gather the needed tools.
2. Examine the object and select an appropriate place for the number. If using ink on kozo tissue, it may be necessary to size the tissue first (by consolidating it with a thin coating of the adhesive).
3. In a well-ventilated area or outside, size the kozo with the clear acrylic or Lascaux Fix. Do not saturate the paper. Practice on scrap tissue paper first to get the feel of lightly coating the more expensive kozo. Let the tissue air-dry.
4. Stir up the B-72 solution and thin it with acetone as necessary. If using Cellofas with Jade, first prepare the Cellofas by mixing the powder with distilled water in a 1:3 ratio. Use a microspatula to mix together one part prepared Cellofas to three parts of Jade.
5. Place the tissue or paper on a clipboard.
6. Use Pigma pen or pencil to write the number on the tissue. Make sure the size of the number is appropriate for the object and where it is to be placed.
7. Draw a box around the number with a paintbrush wet with deionized water or distilled water to set up a water-tear.
8. Use a spatula straight edge to pull out the number along the wet lines of the water-tear, creating many hairs.
9. When printing numbers on Perma/Dur Bond, or when a straight edge is desired instead of the hairs, skip steps 7 and 8, and use a scissors to cut the number. It is recommended to round the corners to reduce lifting of the paper label.
10. Place the label face down on the silicone release paper.
11. Paint the back of the label with B-72 or the Cellofas/Jade mixture. Apply the adhesive from the middle outward. Pull the hairs outward with the adhesive. If using B-72, let it tack up a bit before moving onto next step.

12. Pick up label with forceps.

13. Place the label in the appropriate spot, and tamp it down gently with the color shaper. Pull the hairs out and tamp down. If using a cut number, make sure all the edges are tamped down.

14. Let the number dry before returning it to storage. Drying times will vary according to temperature and humidity conditions but generally adhered labels should dry for approximately thirty minutes.

Method 2, Option 2: Japanese Tissue Paper with Starch Paste

This method is recommended for use on bark cloth, mats, and plant materials; it may be used on some basketry items and leathers, but it requires weight on the paste until it dries:

1. Water-tear a small rectangle of kozo large enough to accommodate the number easily. Do not trim the tissue; it is important that the long fibers of the tissue are exposed to add strength to the bond.

2. Place the piece of tissue on top of blotting paper and carefully write the number on the tissue with ink. The blotting paper should draw off moisture from the ink and prevent bleeding. Be careful not to rip the paper fibers with the nib of the pen when writing; it is best to use no pressure at all. Allow the ink to dry thoroughly before proceeding.

3. Turn the piece of tissue over on the blotting paper and coat the back of it with wheat or rice starch paste or methylcellulose with a brush. Use as diluted a solution of paste as possible. The blotting paper should draw off excess moisture from the paste.

4. Lift the tissue carefully from the blotting paper with forceps and place it right side up on the object in the selected marking location. Using a stiff stencil brush, gently tamp the tissue into place to ensure good contact.

5. Place a piece of blotting paper on top of the number and gently rub it with a finger to draw off excess moisture.

6. Insert a piece of spunbonded polyethylene (Reemay) between the number and the blotting paper. If the object is flat and not brittle, a weight without sharp corners or projecting points may be

placed on top of the blotting paper. The Reemay will prevent the blotting paper from sticking to the number. Allow the paste to dry weighted for about fifteen minutes, then remove the weight, blotting paper, and Reemay and allow the paste to dry thoroughly.

7. To remove the label, roll a slightly moistened cotton swab over the paper surface until the paper is damp. After a few moments, the label may be lifted off with forceps.

Some materials, such as baskets, may require a paste with greater adhesion. A stronger adhesive can be made using equal parts starch or methylcellulose paste and an acrylic emulsion (see Method 2, Option 1).

Method 2, Option 3: Printed-Paper Labels Adhered with Acrylic or PVA Emulsion

Recommended for many three-dimensional objects with firm surfaces and useful for small objects or objects with an irregular surface because small legible numbers can be printed with a laser printer. Use either a Century Gothic or Arial type font. Century Gothic produces the most legible numbers when the character spacing is expanded by 0.3 to 0.4, but it is not always available as a font option. Depending on the font, anywhere from a 3-point to 11-point size can be used.

Step-by-Step Instructions:

1. Determine the size of lettering required for the label, which depends on the size of the object and the surface available for label placement. As a general rule, use a larger point size on large objects and a smaller point size on small objects. Remember that available light may be limited in examination situations. The numbers also will be clearer if the bold feature is selected. Semi-serifed fonts offer distinctions that prevent letter and numeral confusion.

Some guidelines:

a. Century Gothic point size 6 (97-86-543), 7 (2009-20-1), or 8 (2009-20-1) for large items.

b. Century Gothic point size 5 (97-86-543) for medium-sized items.

c. Century Gothic point size 4 for small items.

d. Century Gothic point size 3, characters expanded by 0.4, might be used in extreme cases for tiny items, but it is not generally recommended.

e. More font options and instructions are found in Braun[38] and are demonstrated in a free downloadable online webinar.[39]

2. Create numbers and sizes in the appropriate word processing package. When labeling many objects, it is most efficient to create a consecutive, columnar, single-spaced list of numbers. Consider copying and pasting that column to print in a variety of sizes on the same page to have at the ready if a number is mishandled or does not fit. Load the laser printer with the appropriate paper, probably in the bypass or envelope tray that allows a straight feed. If possible, adjust the printer settings through the print dialog to confirm black toner only will be used, and the thickness of the paper. Send the printed paper and at least one duplicate sheet for testing. Test the print permanence of the duplicate with a peel test.

3. To separate the numbers, cut the paper with scissors as close as possible along one vertical side of the numbers. Cut horizontally between each of the single-spaced numbers, then cut the paper along the second vertical side allowing the numbers to drop on the table. If possible, cut the labels with rounded, rather than square, corners. It is generally not feasible to round the corners of the smaller letter point sizes.

4. Attach the label using a base and top coat of either Jade 403 (PVA emulsion) or Rhoplex (aka Primal) B-60A (acrylic emulsion). Jade 403 results in a thicker, less shiny coat than any of the acrylics. Paraloid B-72 should be used with caution as the solvent will tend to melt printed lettering. Do not let the base coat dry before applying the paper label.

5. Cross out duplicate number columns after successfully adhering to object.

6. Allow the label to dry completely and lose its tack. In dry conditions (relative humidity below 30 percent), the drying process might be completed within an hour. In more humid situations (relative humidity higher than 45 percent), the drying process might last a day or more.

7. Before the labeling emulsion sets up or hardens, it is soluble in water. For this reason, keep a vial of water and paper towel nearby to clean the paintbrush; after drying, the emulsion is no longer soluble in water but is soluble in acetone.

8. If it is necessary to remove the number at a later date, use the tip of an acetone-dampened and blotted cotton swab to dab the surface. Once the emulsion has dissolved, the paper label can be removed and replaced. For a complete removal of the label, roll an acetone-dampened cotton swab over the surface until the remaining emulsion residue has been removed.

Method 3, Option 1: Handwritten Labels Sewn with Fabric Tape (Nonadhesive) or Spunbonded Fabrics such as Reemay

Recommended for most textiles. Do not sew a label on textiles that are disintegrating or in poor condition. May also be used for some basketry materials and leather objects, depending on structure. Several print and video tutorials are available.[40]

Tools and Materials:

- Pigma pen (SAKURA Pigma Micron recommended)
- Scissors
- Unbleached cotton tape, tight weave, 1/2"; Reemay, Tyvek, or Typar
- Natural color cotton thread
- Needle, size 7 or 8 for most things
- Deionized or distilled water
- Orvus detergent
- Clothes iron
- Drying rack

1. Choose a material for making the label. Fabric tape (cotton, polyester, or linen) is usually used for making labels for costumes, rugs, tapestries, and other textile objects. Fabric tape is available in widths from 1/4 to 1 inch and wider, but the 1/2-inch tape is the best choice for most labels. It is preferable to use fabric tape of varying size, appropriate for the size of the object, rather than

cutting a label from fabric such as unbleached muslin. The double selvages of the fabric tape will prevent the label from unraveling. Unbleached, unstarched tapes are preferred; launder material with an Orvus detergent and rinse well without bleach if unsure of preparation. Use a tape that is tightly woven, as it will make writing the number easier. Some museums use an inert material such as nonwoven polyester (Reemay) for sewn labels. An advantage of this material is that it does not ravel at the edges and can be cut to any desired size. Reemay and related materials are purchased in bolts and are available in various weights, some of which may be abrasive to delicate fabrics. Choose a lightweight material with a smooth finish dense enough to accept the number (for labeling purposes, it is not interchangeable with Pellon interfacing, another nonwoven polyester because that material may contain adhesives, which may be harmful to some museum objects; there are many types of Pellon fabrics on the market with varying properties). Only nonfusible, uncoated fabrics should be used. Soft grades of Tyvek may also be used for sewn labels. Tyvek may require sealing with B72 to prevent bleeding of the ink over textured areas.

2. Write the number on the twill tape. Leave about 1/4 inch on each side of the number for adhering to textile.

3. Iron the label to set the ink. Wash the label in a container using distilled or deionized water and Orvus detergent. Rinse several times in clear, distilled or deionized water.

4. Iron the label dry or let it air-dry on a drying rack.

5. Determine where the label should be placed. Turn under the cut ends of the label. Sew the label in place using the needle and thread. Sew between the threads of the textile (object) and not through the textile weave. For delicate or fragile textiles:

   • Reemay, 4 ml, may be used in place of cotton twill tape if the textile is delicate or fragile.
   • Do not iron the Reemay as it may melt onto the iron.

• Let the ink thoroughly dry fifteen to twenty minutes before handling and washing. Turning under the ends of Reemay will not be necessary.

Method 3, Option 2: Typed Labels on Tyvek or Reemay, Sewn

When using a typewriter with Reemay or Tyvek for textile labels, the numbers are usually typed on the nonwoven polyesters. The Reemay is cut into sheets and fed into the typewriter like a sheet of paper. Noncorrectable or one-strike carbon ribbons are recommended because they tend to be the most durable, but they are becoming obsolete and may be difficult to obtain. Most correctable carbon ribbon impressions become rough and smudge-resistant if allowed to cure two to five days after application, but some stay soft indefinitely. Fabric ribbons are not recommended as they tend to smear continually. Do not put Reemay or Tyvek in a laser printer. To test a typewriter ribbon, type a series of sample numbers on the labeling material. Rub the numbers to see if the ink smears and eliminate any typewriter ribbons that do. Second, rinse the tags in hot soapy water to see if the ink runs when wet. Third, rub each number while it is still wet. If the ink is fast in each of these tests, and endures longer, more stressful exposures,[41] the marking material may be used.

1. Choose a material for making the label.

2. Type the numbers on the fabric. Leave about 1/4 inch on each side of the number for adhering to textile.

3. Wash the fabric and let it dry before cutting the numbers apart. Laundering the tags will remove acid released by some kinds of marking inks. Some museums size the label (coating it with dilute adhesive of the same type) to provide a better writing surface or seal the label with a base coat before and after marking the number to prevent the ink from bleeding. Sizing will result in a stiffer label, which may be abrasive to some textiles. Sealing the tape should not be necessary if the earlier step for resting the ink and laundering the tag are followed. If the tape is to be sized or sealed, leave the ends untreated so that they can be turned un-

der for stitching. Reemay may be swished through an acetone bath or lightly wiped in unprinted areas with an acetone dampened to remove excess typewriter ink.

4. Stitch the label to the object.

Labels should be gently stitched, never attached with staples, pins, or adhesives. Select a sturdy area on the reverse side, preferably at the hem or near a strong selvage. Be consistent in the choice of location. See the "Marking Specific Kinds of Objects" section for suggested locations for specific objects. Place the stitches between the warp and weft threads of the fabric; do not pierce the threads. See TABLE 5F.9 for suggested needles and thread.

Although all conservators agree that the number of stitches should be limited, opinions vary as to where the stitches should be placed. Some conservators recommend stitching the label around all four sides with a loose running or basting stitch to prevent the possibility of picking up the textile by the label or accidently catching a finger in the label and thereby snagging or tearing the textile. Other conservators recommend only a few tacking stitches at each end to avoid piercing the textile in so many places. A good rule of thumb is to evaluate the specific object. How often will it be handled and by whom? Are the fabrics strong and in good condition or weak and deteriorating?

Select a stitching method that best meets marking needs with the least possible intrusion into the textile. For fragile textiles, such as lace, the label may be attached with a single loop of thread leaving the tag hanging loose. Use a loop long enough for easy positioning of the tag, yet as short as possible to avoid snagging. This method can be used for small, flat objects so the tag can be tucked out of sight when the object is on display. It may not be possible to tag directly some fragile textiles, such as silks, without causing extensive damage. Applied without magnification or finesse, the act of stitching may leave permanent holes in some textiles. Ties and tags can abrade or cut the threads due to movement. Alternatively, the number can be marked on the storage container. Permanently mounted textiles should be labeled on the mount.

Use a single strand of thread. Do not use small, tight stitches, which will cut the threads of the textile or distort the fabric. Machine-wound spool threads shrink for about a year after being unwound and may pucker the textile if the stitches are pulled tight. Begin and end the stitching with several backstitches in the label, not the textile. Do not use knots, which tend to break or disassemble or may pull through the textile, creating holes. Fabric tape should be turned under 1/4 inch at the ends to prevent raveling; tack down the corners. To remove a tag, cut each stitch, taking care not to cut the textile, and carefully pull out the individual threads.

Method 4: Pencil

Recommended for paper and photographic materials (see TABLE 5F.4).

1. Select a location for marking the number. Works of art on paper, such as prints, drawings, and photographs, should be marked on the reverse side behind a nonimage area at the lower margin. The number should be consistently placed in the same corner on each object. If the object is mounted or hinged, in addition to marking it directly, mark the number with a pencil on the back of the mount or on the face of the mount, below the object; this will eliminate unnecessary handling of the object to locate the number. Framed works on paper should be marked on the frame and backing in the same manner as framed paintings. See the "Marking Specific Kinds of Objects" section for suggested locations for other paper and photographic materials.

2. Select an appropriate pencil. Most paper objects are marked with a medium lead pencil because hard lead can crease or dent paper, whereas soft lead tends to smudge. The recommended grades are #2, HB, F, and H. For a further discussion of pencil grades, see TABLE 5F.4. If uncertain about the performance of a pencil, test it on several weights and finishes of paper prior to using it to mark objects. Modern resin-coated photographic papers and other glossy papers may resist standard pencil markings. For photographs, try a #1 pencil, a Stabilo All Graphite pencil, or a Berol China

Marker. Do not stack objects marked with these materials without interleaving with acid-free tissue to prevent the markings from transferring to the image below or place the items in individual acid-free sleeves.

3. Place the object on a lightly cushioned but firm surface and write gently to avoid indentation. This is especially important for coated photographic papers, such as Cibachrome prints, on which the emulsion is easily bruised, and thin sheets, such as tintypes, tissue, and albumen prints, particularly if the image is printed to the edge of the sheet. Do not write on metal plates or daguerreotypes, but rather their union cases and other housings. Use only #2 or HB pencils, or softer, on these objects. Dull the point of a newly sharpened pencil by scribbling on a sheet of paper. Remove excess lead by blotting once, not rubbing, with a vinyl eraser. In cases where an object cannot be marked directly see the "Temporary/Indirect Marking Methods" or the "Marking Specific Kinds of Objects" section for alternatives.

Method 5: Barcodes and Other Technology

Although a boon for many aspects of collections management, standards for sticking directly to objects apply. Do not apply barcodes directly to objects, but rather to their housings such as trays, boxes, and secondary tags. Exceptions apply for circulating library materials, however, many a barcode has been badly placed on a book that may be someday be considered rare, with significant damage to its exhibition-worthy qualities. "Tattle tale" metal security strips are backed with PSA and stuck into books, for better or worse. For aesthetically valued, rare, and special collection books, barcodes may be printed or adhered onto appropriate bookmarks, sewn or tipped in, or placed in neutral straps which are sealed around a board.[42] See also CHAPTER 5G, "Barcodes and RFID Tags."

Most CMS are now able to print out thumbnail images on labels intended for housing. Although tempting to print these in color, select the black-and-white setting only because color images will swiftly fade in stack lighting.

UNACCEPTABLE MARKING METHODS AND MATERIALS

The following materials should not be used:

- PSA tape, including cellophane, masking, mending, adhesive, cloth, and embossing tapes. Depending on the adhesive formulation (rubber, rubber-acrylic compound, or pure acrylic), it can be either aggressive and increase in hold or weaken and desiccate over time and fall off. The carrier (cloth, paper, or plastic film) can shrink and separate from the adhesive, leaving label information on the floor or missing, while the adhesive remains as a sticky residue that penetrates paper products. Some adhesives can cause corrosion to metals around the periphery of the label. After removal these labels leave irreparable dark areas on finished wood, especially wood exposed to excessive illumination. The labels also tend to fall off over time as the solvent in the adhesive evaporates. PSAs are designed for *cold flow*, which means they are mobile and retain flexibility until their plasticizers migrate by evaporation or absorption . . . into your substrate. Although rubber dries and darkens, acrylic remains transparent but tacky and mobile, with stronger hold and can transparentize the porous material it is attached to, including the paper label, causing legibility problems. Both become difficult to remove without strong solvents. Other tapes dry out and fall off, leaving behind a sticky residue or stain. Even if the tape does not fall off the object, it may discolor and stain the surface to which it is adhered.

- Pressure-sensitive labels—See tape. Depending on adhesive formulation (rubber, rubber-acrylic compound, or pure acrylic) these can be either aggressive and increase in hold or weaken and desiccate over time and fall off. The adhesive on many pressure-sensitive labels can deteriorate within several months to a sticky residue that penetrates paper products. Some adhesives can cause corrosion to metals around the periphery of the label. After removal, these labels leave irreparable dark areas on finished wood, especially wood exposed to excessive illumination. The labels also tend to fall off over time as the solvent in the adhesive evaporates.

- Gummed (water-moistened) paper labels—With the exception of use on backings to record exhibition history, these should not be used because the adhesives can stain and are difficult to remove from some materials. On other materials they have poor adhesive qualities and are not durable. They may be used on the reverse of painting frames, stretchers, or protective backings of framed art.

- Rubber cement—This adhesive goes through phases of deterioration from sticky to embrittled and desiccated and should be avoided. It can stain organic materials and tarnish metals, cause labels to fall off completely or, paradoxically, be difficult to remove.

- Silicone products—Silicones are generally nonreversible and other marking materials will not adhere well to them.

- Spray varnishes—It is difficult to control where the spray will land. In addition, the product composition may change, and some materials may yellow and become brittle or difficult to remove.

- Sticky notes—See pressure-sensitive labels. Although meant to be removable after a short duration, these leave some residue behind that can attract dirt and adhere to wrappings. Their hold can increase over time; in fact some are marketed for extra strength. The colors can run and absorb into adjacent material such as the object substrate.

- Correction fluid (also known as typewriter correction fluid)—This material is widely used as a white base coat on dark objects but should not be. Correction fluids are white paints of varying composition; most use 1-1-1 trichloroethylene as the solvent although some are water-based. Although some formulations may not harm the surfaces of objects, many correction fluids have poor durability and tend to dry out and flake as they age. Others may prove solvent resistant with age.

- Correction tape ribbon—see pressure-sensitive tape.

- Nail polish—Clear nail polish once was in wide use as a base coat and top coat. Nail polishes are usually made from cellulose nitrate, which yellows, becomes brittle, and shrinks with age. Modern formulas may be composed of more stable acrylic resins or may be a mixture of the two. The resin is dissolved in a mix of solvents, which may include acetone, xylene, alcohol, or toluene. The exact formula and aging properties of these polishes cannot be determined. Some polishes will peel with age, taking the accession number and part of the surface of the object with them.

- Nail polish remover—Commercial nail polish remover may contain additives such as perfume, oil, dyes, and gelatin, in addition to the solvent.

- Ballpoint ink—Most ballpoint inks include soluble dyes, tend to smear, and are difficult to remove. Many are not lightfast. The trackball can emboss and scratch surfaces.

- Permanent marker—Do not use permanent markers unless they are on the approved list of tested permanent marking pens. Most permanent markers are not lightfast, are dye based, will bleed easily, and are often acidic.

- Chalks—These materials are not durable. They smear indefinitely and can be difficult to remove from porous materials without using strong solvents.

- Fusible iron-on fabrics—These materials should not be used for labeling textiles. The adhesives leave a residue and may damage textiles.

- Metal-edged tags—The metal can corrode and stain objects.

- Wire—Wires can corrode or abrade objects and may tear fragile or soft surfaces. An exception is the use of aluminum or annealed stainless steel wire, or plastic or vinyl coated stainless steel for large industrial artifacts or outdoor use (see TABLE 5F.7.)

- Nails, pins, staples, screws, and other metal fasteners—Metals may corrode, thereby staining objects, cause corrosion of metal objects that they are in contact with, leave permanent holes, or cause splitting or cracking of woods and other materials. However, special types of these may be used for specimen trees and trees of note (see CHAPTER 3F, "Living and Natural History Collections Registration"). •

NOTES
1. This chapter has been updated to standardize and clarify language and provide citations that should remain sustainable and accessible to the cultural heritage community. Nevertheless, readers are encouraged to use public library and university resources such as interlibrary loan and on-site use of subscription serials to access recent professional literature. Many state or federally funded museums and cultural heritage organizations are available to advise constituents concerning new or substitute products and practices.

2. R. R. Waller and P. S. Cato, "Dissociation," *Agents of Deterioration*. September 22, 2017. Available at: https://www .canada.ca/en/conservation-institute/services/agents-deterior ation/dissociation.html.

3. N. Lockshin, "Marking collections," in *Preventive Conservation: Collection Storage*, edited by Lisa Elkin and Christopher Norris (New York: Society for the Preservation of Natural History; American Institute for Conservation of Historic and Artistic Works; Smithsonian Institution; The George Washington University Museum Studies Program, 2019). Available at: http://resources.conservation-us.org/ collection-storage/.

4. Nora Lockshin, "Marking and labeling collections," October 27, 2015. Available at: http://www.connecting tocollections.org/marking-and-labeling-collections/; Nancy Odegaard and Gina Watkinson, "Collection labeling: Safely applying accession numbers to museum objects," presented at the Association of Tribal Archives, Libraries, and Museums (ATALM), Washington, DC, September 12, 2015. Available at: https://www.sustainableheritagenetwork.org/digital-heritage/ collection-labeling-safely-applying-accession-numbers-mu seum-objects.

5. Ellen Carrlee, personal communication, 2019.

6. Available at: https://www.culturalheritage.org/about -conservation/code-of-ethics.

7. American Institute for the Conservation of Historic and Artistic Works, ed., *Code of Ethics and Guidelines for Practice (and Commentaries)* (Washington, DC: American Institute for the Conservation of Historic and Artistic Works, 1994). Available at: https://www.culturalheritage.org/about-conser vation/code-of-ethics (accessed August 29, 2019).

8. C. H. Kishinami, "Archival storage of disintegrating labels from fluid-preserved specimens," *Collection Forum* 5, no. 1 (1989): 1–4; C. A. Hawks and S. L. Williams, "Polyester film sleeves for protection of fragile or damaged specimen labels," in *Storage Techniques for Art Science & History Collections*, 1992. Available at: http://stashc.com/the-publication/labels/object- labels/polyester-film-sleeves-for-protection-of-fragile-or-dam aged-specimen-labels/.

9. H. Alten, "Testing pens helps determine applicability in museum object labeling," *Northern States Conservation Center-Collections Caretaker*, July 2010. Available at: http:// www.collectioncare.org/pubs/Jul162010.html; E. Carrlee, "Collections labeling: Alternate adhesive testing," *Ellen Carrlee Conservation* (blog), November 25, 2011. Available at: https:// ellencarrlee.wordpress.com/2011/11/25/collections-labeling -alternate-adhesive-testing/.

10. Luci Cipera, Erika Range, and Carolyn Leckie, "Labeling natural history collections," Society for the Preservation of Natural History Collections Wiki. Available at: https:// spnhc.biowikifarm.net/wiki/Labeling_Natural_History_ Collections#Decision_Making (accessed August 15, 2019); Lockshin, "Marking collections."

11. International Committee for Documentation, "CIDOC Fact Sheet No. 2, Labelling and Marking Objects." International Council of Museums, 1994. Available at: http://icom.museum/

fileadmin/user_upload/pdf/Guidelines/CIDOC_Fact_Sheet_ No2.pdf; National Park Service, Museum Management Program, *Labeling Natural History Specimens. Conserv-O- Gram*, 11/06. Available at: http://www.nps.gov/museum/ publications/conserveogram/11-06.pdf; Thomas J. Braun, "An alternative technique for applying accession numbers to museum artifacts," *Journal of the American Institute for Conservation* 46, no. 2 (2007): 91–104. Available at: https://doi .org/10.1179/019713607806112323; Collections Trust (UK), "Labelling and marking museum objects booklet," Collections Trust (UK). Available at: http://sharemuseumseast.org.uk/ download-course-handouts/.

12. J. L. Down, *Adhesive Compendium for Conservation* (Ontario: Canadian Conservation Institute, 2015).

13. Museum of Fine Arts, Boston, "CAMEO: Conservation & Art Materials Encyclopedia Online." Available at: http:// cameo.mfa.org/wiki/Main_Page (accessed August 22, 2019).

14. American Institute for Conservation, "AIC WIKI Main Page." Available at: http://www.conservation-wiki.com/wiki/ Main_Page (accessed August 27, 2019).

15. Materials Working Group, "Materials Working Group- Wiki," in American Institute for Conservation. Available at: http://www.conservation-wiki.com/wiki/Materials_Working_ Group (accessed August 27, 2019).

16. National Center for Preservation Technology and Training, "Preservation technology and training grants." Available at: https://www.ncptt.nps.gov/grants/preservation -technology-and-training-grants/ (August 27, 2019).

17. Occupational Safety and Health Administration, "Hazard communication," 2013. Available at: https://www.osha.gov/ dsg/hazcom/index.html.

18. If you have trouble getting an SDS with purchase or need to compile an SDS binder for supplies you already have on hand, it is simple enough to search on the internet for [product name] and [GHS SDS]. Alternately, an excellent resource for SDS is the Cornell University SDS List. Available at: https://sp.ehs.cornell.edu/lab-research-safety/research-safety/ hazardous-materials-shipping/Pages/MSDS-List.aspx. Look for the most recently dated version.

19. There are some discontinued products for which there are no SDS because the product ceased to be manufactured or the manufacturer ceased operations. In this case, the last issued MSDS for the product, or a similar SDS for a nonproprietary product of the exact same or very near composition may be acceptable (e.g., [brand name] Isopropyl Alcohol, 99 percent).

20. The Art and Creative Materials Institute, Inc., "Art material safety." Available at: https://acmiart.org/index.php/art- material-safety (accessed August 22, 2019).

21. American Institute for Conservation of Historic and Artistic Works, *C2CC Arsenic and Old Lace: Controlling Hazardous Collection Materials*, 2016. Available at: https:// www.connectingtocollections.org/arsenic-and-old-lace- controlling-hazardous-collection-materials/.

22. C. A. Hawks, M. McCann, K. Makos, L. Goldberg, D. Hinkamp, D. Ertel, and P. Silence. eds., *Health and Safety for*

Museum Professionals (New York: Society for the Preservation of Natural History Collections, 2012). Available at: https://www.conservation-us.org/resources/our-publications/special-projects/health-and-safety#.Wqv2x2rwZyw.

23. Rebecca A. Kaczkowski, personal communication, 2019; Odegaard and Watkinson, "Collection labeling."

24. Preservation Directorate, Library of Congress, "Preservation supply specifications—resources." Available at: http://www.loc.gov/preservation/resources/specifications/index.html (accessed March 4, 2015); N. Lockshin, "Case study: Preservation photocopying," Smithsonian Institution Archives, May 5, 2017. Available at: https://siarchives.si.edu/what-we-do/preservation/preservation-photcopying.

25. Hawks and Williams, "Polyester film"; Kishinami, "Archival storage."

26. J. E. Simmons, *Fluid Preservation: A Comprehensive Reference* (Lanham, MD: Rowman & Littlefield, 2014); J. E. Simmons, "Fluid collections," in *Preventive Conservation: Collections Storage*, edited by Lisa Elkin and Christopher Norris (Washington, DC: Society for the Preservation of Natural History; American Institute for Conservation of Historic and Artistic Works; Smithsonian Institution; The George Washington University Museum Studies Program); Cipera, Range, and Leckie, "Labeling natural history collections."

27. Library of Congress, "Ownership Marking of Paper-Based Materials." Available at: http://www.loc.gov/preservation/care/marking.html (accessed April 18, 2015); F. R. Byers, *Care and Handling of CDs and DVDs: A Guide for Librarians and Archivists.* NIST Special Report 500–252 (Washington, DC/Gaithersburg, MD: Council on Library and Information Resources; National Institute of Standards and Technology, 2003). Available at: http://www.itl.nist.gov/iad/894.05/docs/CDandDVDCareandHandlingGuide.pdf; A. Schweikert, "An optical media preservation strategy for New York University's Fales Library & Special Collections." Available at: http://archive.nyu.edu/handle/2451/43877.

28. Nancy Reinhold, Hanako Murata, Richard Stenman, Taina Meller, and Nora W. Kennedy, "Marking photographs: The impact of ink stamping practices," *Photographic Materials Group of the American Institute for Conservation of Historic & Artistic Works.* (Washington, DC: Topics in Photographic Preservation, 2007), 12: 3–14.

29. American College and Research Libraries, Rare Books and Manuscripts Section, American Library Association, "Appendix I: Guidelines for marking books, manuscripts, and other special collections materials," in *ACRL/RBMS Guidelines Regarding Security and Theft in Special Collections* (Chicago: American College and Research Libraries, 2009). Available at: http://www.ala.org/acrl/standards/security_theft.

30. Y. Shashoua, *Conservation of Plastics: Materials Science, Degradation and Preservation* (Abingdon, UK: Routledge, 2016).

31. Alten, "Testing pens"; Carrlee, "Collections labeling."

32. National Archives and Records Administration, and N. M. M. Jones, "Testing electrostatic copy quality: The Peel Test" (1999). Available at: http://www.archives.gov/preservation/technical/peel-test.html.

33. Braun, "An alternative technique."

34. William Kell and William E. Moser, "Alcoholic archival polyester specimen labels." In *14th Annual Meeting* (Washington, DC: 1999). Available at: http://www.spnhc.org/media/assets/SPNHC1999Meeting_OCR.pdf; Cipera et al., "Labeling natural history collections"; Preservation Directorate.

35. Formerly listed in many guides as Japanese tissue, options for bast fiber papers are available from diverse cultural origins. Most important considerations are weight/thickness, suitability, and ease for laser or pigment inkjet printing, free of lignin, bleaches, fillers, brighteners, coatings, or unknown inclusions. A statement of having passed the PAT or Oddy test is ideal.

36. R. S. Williams, "Optically cleared repair tissues for the treatment of translucent papers," *Book and Paper Group Annual* 37 (2018): 96–112.

37. Roger Williams, personal communication, 2019.

38. Braun, "An alternative technique."

39. Gina Watkinson, "Labeling objects with laser-printed paper labels [Tutorial]," presented at the Association of Tribal Archives, Libraries, and Museums (ATALM), Washington, DC, September 13, 2015. Available at: https://www.sustainableheritagenetwork.org/digital-heritage/labeling-objects-laser-printed-paper-labels-tutorial

40. *Labelling and Marking Textiles in Museum Collections.* Available at: https://www.youtube.com/watch?v=-zCXNphTv0U&feature=youtube_gdata_player; Museum of New Zealand Te Papa Tongarewa, *How to Apply Accession Numbers to Textiles.* Available at: https://www.youtube.com/watch?v=lInGwnjK3nA; Canadian Conservation Institute, "Applying accession numbers to textiles," in *CCI Notes 13/8* (2018). Available at: https://www.canada.ca/en/conservation-institute/services/conservation-preservation-publications/canadian-conservation-institute-notes/applying-accession-numbers-textiles.html.

41. Alten, "Testing pens"; Carrlee, "Collections labeling."

42. L. A. Blaser, "Barcoding at the Folger Shakespeare Library," Book and Paper Group Annual, 2000, no. 19. Available at: https://cool.conservation-us.org/coolaic/sg/bpg/annual/v19/bp19-28.html; J. Lloyd, "A sticky issue—Labelling library collections," in *AICCM Book, Paper and Photographic Materials Symposium*, 2010: 40–42.

This comprehensive chapter stands on the work of many authors preceding me, to whom I am indebted. We all benefit from the work of those labeled "the Mothers of Marking," gender notwithstanding, whether we have met in person, or have been indirectly taught by their contributions, colleagues, and students via their publications and teaching. Original authors, contributors and editors include Elaine Hughes, Terry Segal, and Tamara Johnston. Special thanks to Devon Pyle-Vowles, Ellen Carrlee, and my Smithsonian interviewees for leaving their mark!

5G | Barcodes and RFID Tags

MARIE-PAGE PHELPS

Barcodes

As museums become more reliant on technology and integrated collection management systems (CMS), the idea of barcoding the objects in a collection has become increasingly attractive and practical. Barcodes are essentially a form of data that can be scanned and read by a machine. Most often, the data is represented by a set of parallel lines and spaces of different widths. Each line correlates with a letter, number, or symbol that when scanned by a device is translated into recognizable data.

There are multiple barcode fonts available, and several suitable for barcoding collection objects are included in this chapter. Each font has a unique (and proprietary) association between characters and lines. When choosing a barcode font, a museum must consider the type of data being encoded to ensure that each character has a correlating line in the barcode (FIGURE 5G.1). The most common font is Universal Product Code (UPC), which consists only of numbers and can be found in most retail establishments. Code 39 includes numbers 0 to 9, letters A to Z, and a set of six common symbols. Code 128, which has three subsets (A, B, C), includes numbers 0 to 9, letters A to Z in both upper- and lowercases, and most common symbols. Each of the three subsets include a slightly different combination of these features, with Code 128B being the most inclusive.

Considerations for Use

Integrating barcodes with a CMS is useful for a variety of reasons. It can save time previously spent on entering data manually and increase efficiency by accomplishing more data entry in a shorter period of time. A barcode system can increase accuracy because using a scanner minimizes the human error inevitable in manual entry. Barcodes may improve tracking of collection objects and can create a recordable chain of custody. Another benefit is that many collection database systems allow for the integration of barcodes, creating an additional layer of information and object history.

Barcodes are particularly useful for institutions considering a collection move or for those with multiple campuses. They are an excellent resource for large collections or museums with extensive storage facilities. They can be used for temporary projects or as a permanent labeling system for cataloging collections, labeling storage spaces, and tracking collection records. The flexibility, relative simplicity, and reasonable cost of implementing a barcode system makes it a viable option for institutions of all types and sizes.

The practicality of introducing a barcode system is unique to each institution. The most important consideration is whether the implementation of barcodes will save time and create a more efficient

Barcode Type Examples	
UPC	
Code 39	
Code 128B	

FIGURE 5G.1 BARCODE TYPE EXAMPLES. CREATED BY AUTHOR.

system. If the effort and cost to integrate for a short-term project are extensive, but there is no long-term benefit, then barcodes might not be the best option. However, if creating a barcode system will add a needed layer of information or benefit future collections projects, the expense and effort might be worth it, even for a smaller undertaking or collection. The cost of barcoding, both monetarily and in terms of labor and training, should be considered carefully. Many barcode systems have yearly subscription or maintenance fees, and fonts must be purchased. These factors may outweigh the long-term benefits to an institution and should be carefully considered within the scope of collection management strategy and departmental sustainability.

Institutions should investigate whether their current CMS has the capacity to integrate a barcode system. This could be as simple as designating an unused field in a collections management database for barcodes or as complex as pulling data from a CMS into software to generate custom barcodes. In most cases, creating a separate system specifically for barcodes is not cost-effective in the long term, though some museums have found this approach satisfactory for short-term or one-time projects, such as a collection move.

Considering the implementation of a barcode system inevitably leads to the assessment of a collection's data. The prospect of a data build-out can be daunting because it often underscores existing collection problems or areas in need of work. However, perfect data and a complete inventory are not prerequisites for barcoding. Depending on the system chosen and the database fields used, relevant data groups might need to be standardized or streamlined. If there is a plan to assign barcodes to locations, facilities, or other things not strictly within the collection, then the build-out might be more extensive. It is possible to prioritize and to focus only on data useful to the new barcode system.

Implementation

The first step in implementing a barcode system is choosing which set of characters or data will make up the barcode number itself. A barcode number must be a unique identifier associated with a specific ob-

ject and its record. This can be either a completely new set of characters, assigned specifically for barcoding purposes, or an existing field of data, such as an accession number or catalog number. Institutions can purchase premade barcodes or software that generates random barcode numbers. Premade barcodes can be assigned to individual objects in the collection, usually by adding the barcode number to a previously unused field in the database, or as a second identification number.

Alternatively, there are several types of software that pull data fields from databases, which can be formatted to create custom barcodes. Most collection databases automatically assign a unique identifier key to each record as it is created. This helps the computer distinguish between records, even if the data within them change. The key can often be displayed as a field in the database, and it makes a good candidate for a barcode because it is a unique identifier already associated with an object. Some institutions opt instead to use an accession number or catalog number as the barcode number because that is also a unique identifier already associated with an object and record. This can be especially helpful if a tag is separated from an object, as most barcode interfaces allow for manual entry of numbers. It is important to keep in mind that not all barcode fonts can support all characters. For example, if an institution creates a barcode based on its accession number system that include numbers or symbols, then Code 39 or Code 128A/B must be used.

Once produced, barcodes can be printed on most materials including archival paper, polyethylene tags, and acid-free labels. Archival laser print labels are easy to find but are more suitable for outer packaging because the printer ink can smear or transfer to other surfaces. A popular choice for many museums is a thermal transfer printer, which uses heat to melt carbon particle toner onto a label substrate. Thermal transfer printed barcodes last longer, do not smear, and can be printed on materials other than paper. Several archival companies sell acid- and lignin-free adhesive labels for use in thermal transfer printers. Something to consider when printing barcodes is that certain materials allow for a slight bleeding of ink. If the barcode font is too small, this bleed may render the barcode unreadable by the scanner. Testing new brands or types of paper and labels before printing large batches will help avoid costly mistakes. Another common issue is having too large a font, which can result in a barcode being cut off midway or wrapped to another line. Barcodes will not scan unless the complete code is on one continuous line, though most will still scan if the label is upside down or sideways.

Printed barcodes are read by scanners, which come in a variety of types. The most practical type for collections management are handheld scanners, which are small, portable, allow for greater flexibility, and minimize the need to handle objects. Handheld scanners can be individual components, part of premade barcode sets, or attachments to devices such as tablets or smartphones. Scanner attachments can be particularly useful if an institution's CMS has an application or mobile component, or if the use of mobile devices has already been integrated into collections management practice.

Barcodes should never replace physically marking an object with its accession number or catalog number. Although it is possible to affix barcodes directly to objects using conservation grade materials, it is complicated, time-consuming, and not always successful. A far better option is to have barcodes closely associated with an object. Barcodes can be affixed to an artifact tag attached to the object, printed on a card next to the object, attached to an object container, on an adjacent scan sheet, or storage mat, etc. There is always the risk of a barcode being lost or disassociated from its object. This is the main reason that all objects should retain a physical number. However, having additional information on a barcode label also lessens this risk. Many institutions choose to have an object's name, maker, accession number, and even its home location on the same label as the barcode. It is important to remember that if a barcode number is changed in the database or system, the physical label must be reprinted or it will not scan.

RFID TAGGING

Radio frequency identification (RFID) is another technological tool used to augment CMS. RFID uses radio waves to transmit and read data, sending it back to a central system that records any changes. There are two main types of RFID tags—battery-powered (also known as active) and passive. Active RFID systems use tags that contain a battery and are mainly found in the form of either a beacon or a transponder. Passive RFID tags do not contain their own power source but instead use electromagnetic energy emitted by a scanner to send data. An RFID tag is essentially made up of a microchip and antenna; an active tag also contains a circuit board and battery. The tags usually contain a conductive material such as copper, as well as silicone and a plastic housing. Most are quite small, though active tags tend to be larger to compensate for the extra components. The signals that RFID tags emit are processed through readers, which decipher the information and send it back to a computer. The readers may be handheld or stationary, and in museums, they are often located near points of entry.

Considerations for Use and Implementation

For most collection management, an active RFID system is preferable because active tags continuously emit data, creating an up-to-date, live stream of information, and have a longer range than passive RFID tags. Those in the form of beacons constantly emit signals to the reader, while the transponder type emits a signal when in proximity to a reader. It is important to note that most batteries for active RFID tags have a three- to five-year life span, and as of 2018, replacement batteries were not available on the market. Once an active RFID tag has run out of battery, the whole piece must be replaced.

Passive RFID tags can be useful for institutions interested in tracking objects within smaller ranges, such as a gallery or storage area. They have the advantage of a longer life span and are available in a variety of tag materials and sizes, some of which are quite inexpensive. Unlike active tags, passive RFID tags can be inserted into live animals and plants, making them ideal for tracking living collections.

An RFID tag can store much more information than a barcode, and RFID tags have the ability to track changes in movement, temperature, humidity, and light levels. They can be programmed to send alarms and interact with complex security systems.

Like barcodes, RFID tags have unique identifiers that connect directly to an individual record and object. Although this allows for a specific tracking of one object, most RFID systems are separate from existing collections databases. This means any identifying information must be duplicated, and newly generated information integrated into an existing system. However, RFID tags have many benefits, including the ability to be read without a direct line of sight. Most scanners can read an RFID tag through a wooden crate or packing material, and several tags can be scanned at once. This can be beneficial because objects do not have to be handled frequently or unpacked to be scanned.

At this time, the cost to implement a complete RFID tagging system is prohibitive for most museums. Unlike barcodes, it is nearly impossible to implement a RFID system without the help of an outside company, though all offer customized products. As a result, some institutions have chosen to set up systems on a small scale or in stages. Tagging select objects only and setting readers up in only a few galleries can be a cost-effective way to determine whether or not RFID tagging is a viable option. It can be useful if lenders have specific requirements or if an institution has a concentration of valuable objects.

There is some debate regarding whether RFID can compete with signals from other systems, and whether the beacons and transponders are secure from outside readers. If many tags are present in a small area, it is possible to have tag *collision*, in which the reader picks up multiple RFID tag signals at the same time. This can be resolved through programming, in which the tags submit signals at different intervals. The problem of reader interference, in which multiple readers either interfere with each other's signals or try to read the same RFID tag at once, can be solved in a similar way. These concerns are specific to an institution's setup and the various companies providing RFID tagging and can often be rectified with trial and error. Institutions with metal walls or liquid specimens may also have difficulties with RFID tags reading properly and should verify that their chosen RFID company has tags specifically designed to combat this. It should be noted that RFID tags do not differentiate between their intended scanner and any other scanner. As a precaution, sensitive data, such as valuations, should not be included in a tag's data. It would also be wise to physically remove RFID tags containing identifying data from any collection objects traveling beyond the institution's boundaries and scanners. •

REFERENCES

Peak-Ryzex. "Barcode comparison chart." Available at: https://www.peak-ryzex.com/articles/different-types-of-barcodes (accessed July 22, 2019).

IDAutomation. "Barcoding for beginners and barcode FAQ." Barcodefaq.com. Available at: https://www.barcodefaq.com/barcoding-for-beginners/ (accessed July 22, 2019).

RFID Journal. "Get started." Available at: https://www.rfidjournal.com/get-started (accessed July 22, 2019).

JUSTYNA BADACH AND AMANDA SHIELDS

DIGITAL IMAGES PLAY an important role in collections management and reduce the need for an object to be moved or handled unnecessarily. Although objects constitute the primary collection holdings of any institution, a collection of related digital images is a valuable resource for many constituents in and outside the institution. For registrars, object photographs can serve as visual documentation of the collection, provide detailed views of an object's condition, record the scene of an incident and the resulting damage, or supply an appraiser with the information needed to assess an object's value. In addition, other departments in the museum use object photographs in a variety of ways. Conservation uses images for study and treatment projects. Marketing and the public relations departments use images for social-media campaigns, exhibition banners, brochures, posters, and newsletters. Exhibition designers incorporate images into their designs. Museum educators include object photographs in lesson plans and public programming. Researchers employ images in publications and online research portals.

The quality of digital cameras and monitors available on the market is rapidly evolving and currently there are few agreed-on industry standards for imaging technology. In an effort to standardize imaging practices in museums and research institutions, a consortium of federal agencies developed Federal Agencies Digital Guidelines Initiative (FADGI) in 2007.[1] FADGI is a collaborative effort to articulate common sustainable practices and guidelines for digitized and born-digital historical, archival, and cultural content. These agencies maintain a website[2] that contains a vast range of useful imaging information. Professional photographers working in the museum context should employ FADGI standards in their work.

This chapter is intended as an introduction to digital imaging terms and best practices. Because registrars are often asked to photograph objects or work directly with photographers, it is helpful to know the basics in museum photographic practices. It would be easy to dedicate an entire book to the intricacies of working with and archiving digital images in the museum context. For those readers who would like to gain more familiarity with imaging equipment or software than what we can offer here there is a world of excellent tutorials and video resources available on the internet. The best place to start is the FADGI site and camera vendor-based sites that are geared toward the professional market. Detailed information about a wide range of topics can be accessed through Adobe software tutorials, Phase One, Capture One, and Linda.com.

ASSESSING INSTITUTIONAL PHOTOGRAPHY NEEDS

Before turning off the lights to start shooting, it is important to understand how photography is used in the institution and how it relates to the mission and long-range goals.

- What types of photography does the museum currently have?
- How is photography currently used, and how will it be used in the future?
- What space is available for photo shoots for object photography?
- What financial resources can be allocated to photography?
- Is the institution just starting to photograph its collection, or has object photography been ongoing?

It is important to continually assess institutional needs for imaging.

A sound strategic plan should start with an examination of the types and scope of photography the museum already has. Most museums use a mix of several different types of images because they incorporate new photographic technologies while maintaining the previous methods as long as is practical to do so. Many institutions are digitizing some, if not all, of their analog image holdings. Analog images include old transparences (i.e., color slides), prints, black-and-white films, etc. Although there are needs that are well-served by such images, it is important to weigh the costs of digitizing and digital storage of these files against their actual use. Making all these visual resources available via collection management software can enrich the quality of visual information related to an object. Scanned analog images can provide invaluable information about the past condition of an object, installation needs, and exhibition records. But the scanning, file cleanup, and related digital data storage and maintenance of those assets comes at a cost. Many collections of old transparencies or film have not been stored properly and suffer from fading, dirt, or discoloration. An institution should involve all the related stakeholders when assessing the practicality and need for scanning analog images. There are times when an institution may need to forgo a costly scanning project to allocate resources to generating new, higher quality digital images of objects.

Most institutions understand that they need to be more open and facilitate greater access to their collections, and this is true of image archives as well. The current trend is for museums to open their archives to the public, but not every institution has the financial, technical, or staff resources to support full public access. Museums need to assess and formulate a clear policy governing who may use their images and how. Object photography is frequently used by the museum's registrar to document the collection visually and enhance object records. Although a registrar will need access to all of the object images in a database, each institution should carefully assess which of those images can be made available for public use. Object photographs represent the public face or brand of the institution, and once a digital image is made public, the institution will not be able to control how it is circulated. The institution should codify who will have access to images documenting condition issues, conservation work, or other potentially sensitive visual data related to an object. All staff should be familiar with museum policy about how and when those images can be used.

Any decisions about in-house, public use, or sharing of an image database must start with examining the institution's long-range goals and strategic plan. Does the institution have a long-term plan for the safe storage, maintenance, and ongoing upgrades of a digital archive? Are there basic metadata and image quality or file standards in place to make searching possible? Does the institution have a digital asset management system (DAMS) or collections management system (CMS) to organize and access image assets (see CHAPTER 4D, "Digital Asset Management Systems")? These questions are important if a museum intends to make any part an image database available online.

Like all programs and operations, photography requires space. A good photography space requires three things for success: enough room to house the photographic equipment, space to accommodate the object(s) to be photographed, and the capability of being completely dark. Ideally, photography should be done in a rectangular, windowless room that can be made completely dark. This type of room allows for multiple setups. However, if such a room is not available, compromises are necessary. Photography can be done nearly anywhere, although each space will have its own advantages and disadvantages. The best way to think about the size and amount of space needed for photography is to consider the sizes and types of objects in the collection to be photographed. A collection consisting of mostly works on paper will have different photographic space needs than a collection of large-scale paintings and sculpture. If options are limited and a dedicated space is not available, be creative and consider all the spaces in the museum. Galleries are often suitable for photography if they can accommodate a large number and variety of objects and photographic equipment. An auditorium stage is typically roomy enough to accommodate most types of photography as well. Another possible space for photography is the storage area, although the types and arrangement of furniture may limit its usefulness.

The final and probably most important thing to consider is the budget. The amount of money available for object photography will dictate what can be accomplished. Whatever amount the institution is able to invest in photography, it should be used to fulfill the goals of the institution.

UNDERSTANDING DIGITAL CAMERAS

Digital photography, as we know it today, was introduced by Nikon in 1986 but was not commonly available till the mid-1990s. It took another ten years for consumer digital cameras to supplant film. Although all digital cameras consist of three primary parts, they do vary in quality. This section is designed to help anyone who may need to purchase equipment or is working with a freelance photographer. When hiring a photographer it is good practice to inquire about past photography experience and the type of equipment they intend to use.

The Camera Sensor

The camera sensor plays a critical role in image size, resolution, color accuracy, and dynamic range (the accurate representation of light values from white to black). The sensor determines the overall quality of image and how much it can be enlarged. The quality of the sensor is determined by the size of its pixel array.

There are two types of sensors—charged couple device (CCD) and complementary metal-oxide semi-conductor (CMOS). CCD has been around longer and for many years was considered to be superior to CMOS. CCD sensors tended to produce less noise (unwanted color artifacts that show up as specks of light or color in the dark area of an image) and have better light sensitivity, but they have traditionally been more expensive to produce and require more power to operate. This resulted in CCD sensors being used in the more expensive professional cameras, whereas CMOS sensors are used in smaller point-and-shoot cameras that do not need to provide as much power. This trend is starting to change in the very high end of the professional camera market. When choosing a camera, you should opt for a full-frame sensor when the budget permits. There

are several advantages to using a full-frame sensor including a wider angle of view and more control over depth of field.

The Image Processor

An image processor is the camera's built-in computer and can impact image quality in several ways. First, it determines how quickly sensor data is converted into an image. A camera with a high-quality sensor and slow processor will take a long time to produce a visible image. Camera sensors are programmed to make calculated adjustments for a wide range of lighting and color scenarios. All light is made up of color and colors change, based on the time of day, shade or sun, light source, and light intensity. Shooting in light that has a color cast or in a room with colored walls will negatively impact the color accuracy of the image. A good image processor can help generate an accurate white balance and provide other image adjustments that improve image appearance and shooting speed.

The Lens

A high-quality lens is a critical component in maximizing sensor and image processor function. Cameras with high-quality digital components require a higher grade of optics to function at their optimum level. When purchasing equipment, one should buy the best possible lenses that the budget allows. There are several internet sites that post the results of lens comparison testing that can help with research before buying. A good lens will be sharp all the way through an image, have minimal chromatic aberration or color fringes along the edges in areas of high contrast, and have little to no distortion of the image.

A good initial investment is at least two fixed focal length lenses. If you have a full-frame camera, one lens should be a general 50-mm lens and the other a macro lens, used for close-up, detail images. If your camera does not have a full-frame sensor, you should consult with a reputable camera dealer for suggestions on which lenses would be the equivalent in focal length. There are other factors that may impact the price of a lens. For example, a lens that offers image stabilization will cost more. Another factor in price is the lens speed. A fast lens has a large maximum aperture opening, which is a great advantage if the goal is to properly focus and take photos in low-light situations.

File Formats

A digital image can be saved in a variety of file formats. Each format has advantages and disadvantages. When working with different file formats, keep in mind the capability of the camera, how the images will be used (viewed), and how much storage space is available for the file. Regardless of file type the amount of loss in a digital file is determined by the algorithm used to compress the image, both in the camera and once the image has gone through postprocessing software. Some camera algorithms discard no information, others discard some information, still others look for recurring patterns and replace each occurrence with a short abbreviation to reduce the image size.[3] The amount of loss determines the level of degradation within the digital image. This, in turn, will impact how the image can be used and how much storage space it will require. The most common file formats currently employed in digital imaging follow.

RAW—A RAW file is a collection of unprocessed data. This means the file has not been altered, compressed, or manipulated in any way by the computer. RAW files are often used as data files by software programs that load and process the data. A popular type of RAW file is *c*, which is generated by a digital camera. Instead of processing the image captured by the camera, the data is left unprocessed and uncompressed until it is opened with a computer program.[4]

TIFF—The tagged image file format (TIFF) file is a graphics format created in the 1980s to be the standard image format across multiple computer platforms. The TIFF format can handle color depths ranging from 1- to 24-bit. Since the original TIFF standard was introduced many small improvements have been made so there are now around fifty variations of TIFF.[5]

JPEG—The joint photographic experts group (JPEG) is a compression algorithm capable of greatly reducing the file size of a bitmap (BMP) image. The compression algorithm is *lossy*, mean-

ing that image quality is lost during the compression process. For this reason, professional digital photographers often choose to capture images in a RAW format so they can edit their photos in the highest quality possible. They typically export the pictures as JPEG (.JPG) images when they are shared or published on the web.[6]

PNG—The portable network graphics (PNG) file format for image compression is expected to eventually replace the graphics interchange format (GIF) that is widely used on the internet. The PNG format was developed by an internet committee expressly to be patent-free. Like a GIF, a PNG file is compressed in lossless fashion (meaning all image information is restored when the file is decompressed during viewing).[7]

Professional photographs start with a well-exposed camera RAW file. RAW files contain all the data that the sensor is able to register, but they do require an advanced knowledge of image-processing software, such as Adobe Bridge or Capture One. RAW offers the ability to access and display a wide range of data. When done correctly, any changes made to a RAW file during postprocessing are completely reversible. This unique ability to access image information and control over final appearance makes camera RAW a superior choice over any automated changes that can be made by an in-camera processor. However, RAW format is not appropriate for every situation or user. As of 2019, the RAW file format was not standardized across camera manufacturers. RAW files are still camera proprietary files that cannot be opened or viewed by other programs. If left in their original, unprocessed state, RAW files can become obsolete over time. The files are large in size and cannot be viewed without the appropriate software. For those who do not know how to work with RAW files or do not have the needed software, it is recommended to convert RAW files to 16-bit, Adobe RBG 1998, TIFF files. The color correct TIFF file should serve as the master file; a needed JPEG may be derived directly from the master TIFF file.

If a camera does not have an option to shoot in RAW mode or if you are not familiar with nondestructive color editing in Photoshop, the next best option is to select the high-resolution TIFF mode in the camera menu. TIFF files use a lossless compression that does not throw away file data, as is the case with JPEG files. You will not have access to the range of image information that a RAW file has, but a TIFF file will retain full image resolution and can be viewed by other programs. This makes TIFF the ideal choice for any master files that go into an image archive.

The most common file format is JPEG. This format uses different levels of image compression, allowing for reduced file size and easy sharing via the internet. Because JPEG is a "lossy" compression, each time an image is saved as a JPEG, image detail, color accuracy, dynamic range, and resolution are reduced. Repeated resaving of a JPEG file results in a degraded image that cannot be repaired. As a result, shooting in the JPEG format in the camera should be avoided when possible.

For a detailed reference of the current technical standards for digitizing different cultural objects, refer to the FADGI's *Technical Guidelines for Digitizing Cultural Heritage Materials.*[8]

Lighting and Color

Color, intensity, and light direction are the three most critical components to any photograph. Natural and artificial light sources emit a variety of color temperatures, which can affect the color accuracy of the image. One measure of light is color temperature, which is expressed using the Kelvin scale (K). Visible light temperatures cover a wide range, from 1000 K (the warm glow of a candle or late evening sunset) to the blue 6500 K cast of monitors (and some fluorescent tubes). Tungsten lighting, used in many gallery settings, emits a yellow light. A shady room with ambient window light will usually have a blue cast, as do most on-camera flash units. Daylight of around 5500 K is neutral in color and is the standard for most photographic lighting. Mixed temperature lighting or colored walls will cause changes in how object color is perceived. In the days of film photography, mixed lighting situations were difficult to properly correct for, but the advent of white balance settings and advanced postprocessing software have greatly improved our ability to accurately correct color.

There are two ways to fix unwanted color casts in an image while shooting and in postproduction. To maintain color accuracy, it is critical that the photographer maintain control over the color and quality of lighting used when photographing objects. For a registrar, who may not have a lot of photography experience, it is best to start with a set of daylight-balanced continuous LED lights. These can be mounted to light stands and are also useful when examining objects. Unlike professional flash or strobe lights, which produce a harsh light for a short duration, LED lights make it easy for anyone to see the direction and intensity of the light. If the light is too harsh, or the angle of the light is creating too many shadows, adjustments can easily be made (e.g., by moving the camera further from the object). The quality and cost of LED lights varies so it is important to work with a reputable photographic equipment dealer to determine which make and model will provide the most accurate light output for object photography.

Even when an image is made using daylight balanced lights, some white balance adjustment will still be necessary. Setting a custom white balance in your camera or adjusting the color via software while shooting tethered to a laptop is highly advised. Each camera model has specific instructions, but the fundamental steps are similar. Use a clean, smooth, white seamless piece of board or paper that is big enough to fill the frame of the camera. Make sure the paper or board you are using is not yellowed with age. Set up the light source and place the white background where your objects will be positioned, keeping it completely parallel to the camera. Focus the lens and follow the camera's custom white balance instructions to create a custom white balance profile. If the lighting or camera position are not changed this setting should render a neutral lighting color. Because the color temperature of lights can change as bulbs age, it is a good habit to do a new white balance profile each time the camera is set up.

Current best practices for museum photography dictate that a color checker or scale should be included in the image. A color checker or color scale is a precisely printed, scientific color or grayscale grid used to calibrate color balance. Each color patch has a value that matches an exact red, blue, and green

(RBG) equivalent. Color rendition charts were originally employed in the printing industry to confirm that specific colors were reproduced accurately. Color charts for photography vary in size and number of patches they display, but they should always include a black, an 18 percent gray, and a white swatch.

Placing a color checker in the frame provides important reference data for anyone doing postprocessing on the file or using the file for printed reproductions. By measuring the color on the white, black, and gray swatches, an experienced photographer can deduce information about image color and contrast range. Although this chapter is too brief to provide specific instructions, there is extensive online information on color balancing images and using color checkers and scales in combination with Adobe Bridge or Capture One software.

Color Management

In digital photography, color management begins with the color model in use—RGB, the color model used for digital capture and display, or CMYK (cyan, magenta, yellow, and black), the color model used for printing. Digital images taken in the RGB mode are device dependent "in that each different device detects and reproduces the amount of Red, Green, and Blue differently."[9] These differences are noticeable when transferring images from one device to another. To correct this problem, the International Color Consortium (ICC) was formed in 1993 to establish a universal color management system that would work across various platforms.[10] To accomplish this, the ICC created color profiles. A color profile describes the color spaces of a particular device.[11] For example, when images are transferred from camera to computer, the computer reads and converts the information into defined colors based on its color space. If the camera's color space is different from the computer's, the colors in the resulting images will be different; color profiles are used to correct this problem. The color profile describes the color space used by the camera to the computer, which then converts the information it receives into the correct colors. The result is a new image that looks as similar to the original image as possible.[12]

Color Profiles: RGB, sRGB, and CMYK

RGB, sRGB (standard red, green, and blue) and CMYK are currently the most common color models used in digital imaging. RGB is an additive color model used by any device that has a screen, including televisions, computer monitors, LCD screens, and digital camera sensors.[13] A screen or series of pixels using three primary colors—red, green, and blue—are added together in various ways to reproduce a broad array of colors. RGB can be represented as an 8-bit color (representing 256 colors most frequently used for screen-based images), 16-bit, or 24-bit color (representing 65536 or 16777216 colors, respectively). Sixteen-bit color has become the minimum standard for Photoshop or prepress images, and sRGB is the standard color profile for images that will be viewed on a screen or sent via the web. sRGB provides the best color accuracy for images viewed only on a screen, but it does not have the wide color gamut of a 16- or 24-bit Adobe RGB file and, therefore, should never be used when creating or saving a master file.

An important note on color and monitors: One of the most problematic aspects of working with digital files is the lack of industry standards for quality and accuracy of color representation across equipment. Although FADGI aims to address many of these issues, users still face numerous technical hurdles in managing the color accuracy of files. Computer monitors in particular are extremely unreliable in their display of both color and brightness levels. An image file can appear differently when viewed side by side on different monitors. To further complicate the issue, Apple and PC platforms use different display gamma settings as their standards (*gamma* is the numerical term used to describe the brightness of an image). Apple suggests using a gamma value setting of 2.2, whereas most PC monitors should be set to a gamma value of 1.8. This difference in gamma value can cause images to display either darker or lighter, depending on the type of monitor being used, and lightness and darkness inevitably impact how colors appear. This shift in appearance is often incorrectly blamed on poor file quality rather than the accuracy of the display. To better understand the problem, it is important to understand the basics about gamma.

There are three types of gamma involved in digital images:

- Image Gamma—Used by the camera or RAW image conversion software to convert the image into a compressed file (JPG or TIFF).
- Display Gamma—Used by computer monitors and video cards to adjust the output of an image. A high display gamma will create images that appear darker and with more contrast
- System Gamma—Also called "viewing gamma," this is representative of all gamma values used to display the image: essentially, the image and display gammas combined. For example, the same image viewed on a monitor with a different display gamma will not look the same because the resulting "viewing gamma" is different.[14]

How we perceive an image on a monitor is determined by the gamma setting of the monitor, quality of light in the room, the make, model, and age of the screen. It is extremely important for anyone who works with digital images to know how to calibrate their monitor on a regular basis. Monitors that are capable of extremely accurate calibration are available for specialty industries, such as medicine, where there is a demand for a high degree of precision and the funds to support the high cost of such equipment. Some specialized companies also make very good quality self-calibrating monitors for photographic imaging needs, but they do come at a much higher cost than the standard PC monitor. This brings us back to the importance of having a color checker in each image. The color data contained within digital files and their numerical values do not change just because they are viewed on different displays. A photographer can use the individual swatches on a color checker to confirm the accuracy of the numerical data by testing it with the eye dropper tool found in Photoshop. The resulting numerical readout will confirm if a perceived color issue is originating in the file data or it is caused by a monitor.

STORAGE OF DIGITAL IMAGES

When determining what storage method is right for a given situation, consider system security, asset longevity, user accessibility, and the budget. For photographs that are to be used for in-house documentation, a combination of on-site or cloud-based servers may be an appropriate storage method. If servers are not an option, a redundant array of inexpensive disks (RAID) system with secondary back up RAID can be used instead. A RAID is a system developed whereby two or more disks are physically linked together to form a single logical, large capacity storage device that offers a number of advantages over conventional hard disk storage devices—superior performance and improved resiliency. One of the techniques employed in a RAID system is mirroring. This was the first real implementation of RAID, typically requiring two individual drives of similar capacity. One drive is the active drive and the secondary drive is the mirror. The technique provides a simple form of redundancy by automatically writing data to the mirror drive when it is written to the active drive.[15] This duplication of data makes a critical loss or corruption of all of data less likely.

Because digital data is prone to becoming corrupt, regular backups of images are always recommended. Master files of images and any important derivatives should be stored on a secure system with the back-up copies stored in another location. As technology changes, the methods of storage will need to be upgraded or changed completely. For example, DVDs used to be the main method of digital storage, but as technology improved, disk technology has changed, and disks no longer can be read by many computers. Regardless of the storage method chosen, be mindful of changes and upgrade as needed. Otherwise, there is a risk that the storage method will become obsolete and unusable.

FREELANCE PHOTOGRAPHER

A crucial decision before photographing objects is determining who will do the work—a freelance photographer or a staff photographer. There are many types of photographers—commercial, fine art, and fashion to name a few. In addition, photographers come with a wide range of experience and expertise. Most object photographers are freelance or independent photographers and their clients consist of museums, galleries, and private collectors. When deciding to hire a freelance photographer, several issues must be considered.

Finding a photographer who has the studio experience necessary to photograph cultural objects and artwork and can address the institution's needs is important. If working alone, it is critical that the photographer know how to safely handle the objects. Photographers who regularly work for museums or galleries will probably be familiar with implementing FADGI standards in their workflow. The photographer should be responsible for editing, color management, metadata entry, and proper file formatting. With freelance photographers who do their own postproduction work, it is important to define the extent of this work up front. Will the institution be able to view and select images before they are processed? Who is responsible for the naming and metadata and how will the final images be delivered?

Any photographs done by a freelance photographer should be considered "work for hire," meaning that the museum is the sole copyright owner. Under US copyright law, this arrangement must be stated in writing and agreed to by both parties. If it is not, the photographer may claim to own the copyright and distribute the copies of the photographs. Any agreement should include the following language:

Work for Hire: You agree that all original works prepared by or for you in the performance of the services for the Sample Art Museum shall be "works made for hire," and the Sample Art Museum will own such works and all copyright and all other intellectual property rights therein. For any original works of authorship prepared by or for you in the performance of this agreement that, under the copyright laws of the United States, may not considered works made for hire, you agree at the request of the Sample Art Museum to convey and assign all copyright interests that may subsist in any documentation developed by you to the Sample Art Museum. This provision shall survive the termination of this agreement.

Contracts for freelance photographers should also specify if and how the photographers can use images as part of their portfolios. Will the photographers link their own website to the museum websites or provide a private link to clients? Is it ok for them to post these images on social media? Such details are particularly important if an artwork is held in copyright or is by a living artist. It should not be assumed that a photographer understands the intricacies of copyright as applied to the museum or individual works, and therefore, it is best to clarify any details concerning image use in the contract.

Details concerning the expectations for freelance photographers to use their own equipment or the use of museum equipment should also be clearly outlined. Most freelance photographers will bring their own cameras, laptops, and lights to a photo session. However, there are some large-sized accessories (e.g., paper backdrops, tables, special mounts) that may not be practical to transport and therefore may be provided by the museum.

The final issue is whether the museum will require the photographer to carry liability insurance. For example, if a photographer is hired by the museum to take pictures of an exhibition, and trips over the power cord of one of the lights and is injured, who is responsible, the museum or the photographer? Accidents will happen, and part of the museum's risk-management strategy should be to determine whether responsibility lies with the institution or with the freelance photographer.

STAFF PHOTOGRAPHER

Although most of the issues related to hiring freelance photographers also apply to staff photographers, there are differences. A freelance photographer will require an office or studio workspace, all the necessary photography equipment and a computer. A staff photographer has the distinct advantage of providing a consistent level of service and being available to respond to institutional needs as they evolve. Because the staff photographer is an employee, all the photographs are the property of the museum, and the institution would supply the necessary liability insurance.

Equipment Required for a Staff Photographer

- A good quality digital camera with lenses;
- Copy stand;
- Lighting kit (either a good quality, daylight balanced strobe light set or daylight balanced LED lights made specifically for art photography);
- Light modifiers;
- Seamless backdrop (cloth, paper, or board, white or neutral gray);
- Computer and related software;
- Tripod;
- A color checker or scale (such as the X-rite Passport);
- Light stands;
- A set of linear polarizing filters; and
- Black-and-white cards.

CONCLUSION

Object photography can play an important role in an institution, from documenting the collection in marketing and public relations. It is important to determine the role that object photography will play in the institution. Whether a museum chooses to use the services of a freelance photographer or employ a staff photographer, the goals and uses of the museum's photography program must be part of a well-defined institutional strategic plan to ensure that the money invested in object photography goes toward the fulfillment of the institution's mission. ●

NOTES

1. Available at: http://www.digitizationguidelines.gov/.

2. Available at: http://www.digitizationguidelines.gov/.

3. Rick Matthews, "Digital Image File Types Explained," Wake Forest University. Available at: http://www.wfu.edu/-matthews/misc/graphics/formats/formats.html (accessed November 24, 2008).

4. Per Christensson, "Raw file definition," TechTerms. Available at: https://techterms.com/definition/rawfile (accessed January 7, 2019).

5. Per Christensson, "TIFF definition," TechTerms. Available at: https://techterms.com/definition/tiff (accessed January 7, 2019).

6. Per Christensson, "JPEG definition," TechTerms. Available at: https://techterms.com/definition/jpeg (accessed January 7, 2019).

7. Judy Louff and David Stephenson, "PNG (portable network graphics)," Techtarget. Available at: https://searchmicroservices.techtarget.com/definition/PNG-Portable-Network-Graphics (accessed January 7, 2019).

8. Thomas Rieger, ed., *Technical Guidelines for Digitizing Cultural Heritage Materials: Creation of Production Raster Image Files*, Federal Agencies Digitization Guidelines Initiative (FADGI), September 2016. Available at: http://www.digitizationguidelines.gov/guidelines/FADGI%20Federal%20%20Agencies%20Digital%20Guidelines%20Initiative-2016%20Final_rev1.pdf.

9. Wikimedia Foundation, Inc., "ICC Profile." Available at: http://en.wikipedia.org/wiki/ICC_profile (accessed November 24, 2008).

10. International Color Consortium, "About ICC." Available at: http://www.color.org/abouticc.xalter (accessed January 10, 2019).

11. Adobe, "About color profiles." Available at: https://helpx.adobe.com/acrobat/using/color-profiles.html (accessed January 10, 2019).

12. Wikimedia Foundation, Inc., "Image: Colorspace.png." Available at: http://en.wikipedia.org/wiki/Image:Colorspace.png (accessed November 24, 2008).

13. Wikimedia Foundation, Inc., "RGB color model." Available at: http://en.wikipedia.org/wiki/RGB_color_model (accessed November 24, 2008).

14. Jo Plumridge, "Gamma: Why monitor calibration is essential," *Lifewire*. Available at: https://www.lifewire.com/what-is-gamma-493590 (accessed January 7, 2019).

15. PCTechguide.com, "RAID tutorial—the benefits of using RAID." Available at: https://www.pctechguide.com/how-to-set-up-a-raid-array/raid-tutorial-the-benefits-of-using-raid (accessed January 8, 2019).

Thanks to Scott Hankins.

51 | PREVENTIVE CARE

ROBIN BAUER KILGO

INTRODUCTION

ALL OBJECTS, sooner or later, begin to break down and deteriorate. Ten agents of deterioration, or primary threats to collection objects, have been identified as the causes of object loss in collections, and these should be the focus of long-term preventive care efforts.[1] The ten agents of collection deterioration include:

- Physical forces;
- Thieves and vandals;
- Fire;
- Water;
- Pests;
- Pollutants;
- Light, ultraviolet and infrared radiation;
- Incorrect temperature;
- Incorrect relative humidity; and
- Disassociation.

Preventive care (also called *preventive conservation*) is one of the most useful tools registrars and collection managers have for ameliorating the effects of the agents of deterioration and working toward the goal of collection preservation. Although many professional organizations have definitions for preventive care, I will use the definition developed by our colleagues at the American Institute of Conservation (AIC):

> The mitigation of deterioration and damage to cultural property through the formulation and implementation of policies and procedures for the following: appropriate environmental conditions; handling and maintenance procedures for storage, exhibition, packing, transport, and use; integrated pest management; emergency preparedness and response; and reformatting/duplication.[2]

Conservation is devoted to the preservation of cultural property through examination, documentation, treatment, and preventive care. Conservators are specially trained professionals within their specialization, but registrars and collection managers are often the ones who find themselves in charge of carrying out preventive conservation as part of their institution's preservation program, and facilities and administrative staff can frequently be good allies in establishing and maintaining the proper physical, structural, and mechanical standards within the facility.

ENVIRONMENT

The quality of the storage environment has a significant long-term effect on the preservation of objects. The storage environment refers to both collection storage areas and objects on exhibit because exhibition is a form of storage. Generally, the most critical storage environment concerns are:

- Temperature,
- Relative humidity,
- Light,
- Pollution, and
- Pests.

Taken together, these five factors establish the overall quality of the storage environment.

To create a good storage environment a holistic approach must be used that takes into account the needs of the objects (predominantly based on the materials that compose them), the building mechanical systems (heating and cooling), and institutional resources and priorities.[3]

Variations in environmental standards can cause irreversible damage to collection objects; therefore, changes to the storage environment standards must be made with the utmost care and caution, taking into consideration not only the care of the collections but also concerns for borrowed objects, the physical structure of the institution, and current information about and standards for storage environments. If these elements are not considered, then the following kinds of damage can occur:

1. Chemical deterioration—the result of chemical reactions. Reaction rates increase as temperature increases, with greater concentrations of reactants, or if there is an increase in relative humidity. An increase in chemical reaction rates in turn causes an increase in the rate of object deterioration.
2. Biological deterioration—higher temperature and relative humidity are likely to result in an increase in mold and the activity of arthropods, bacteria, and other pests, which will result in damage to collection objects.
3. Mechanical deterioration—the movement of object components due to their absorption of moisture or thermal expansion can cause splitting and warping. An increase in relative humidity is most often to blame when this occurs.[4]

Temperature and Relative Humidity

Temperature and relative humidity standards have undergone changes in recent years as research by the Image Permanence Institution[5] (IPI), the Canadian Conservation Institute[6] (CCI), and others has broadened our understanding of how materials react to changes in the storage environment. Traditionally, a universal standard of 70°F ± 5° and 50 percent relative humidity ±5 percent was encouraged for all collection storage. Although this standard was once a good rule of thumb, the emphasis now is on establishing set points for temperature and relative humidity that are based on the materials the collection objects are composed of and what the building heating and cooling systems can reasonably maintain with minimal fluctuations in a particular geographic area. Bear in mind that many external factors affect indoor temperature and relative humidity, including location and climate.

In general, conditions of lower temperatures and moderate relative humidity will extend the preservation of the collection by slowing chemical reactions

and, thus, slowing the rate of chemical decay. However, temperature and relative humidity that are too low may cause some materials to contract and become brittle.[7]

Relative humidity is the amount of water vapor in a given quantity of air compared to the amount of water vapor that same quantity of air could hold if it was saturated, expressed as a percentage.[8] Temperature and relative humidity are directly related; warm air can hold more moisture than cold air, which means that if a given quantity of air is heated, its relative humidity goes down, but if that same quantity of air is cooled, its relative humidity goes up.[9] This is why fluctuations in temperature cause fluctuations in relative humidity, which is always a concern in collection storage. For example, if warm, moist air in collection storage is cooled sufficiently the moisture in the air will begin to condense on the surface of the objects in storage because the cool air cannot hold as much moisture as the warm air. Large fluctuations in relative humidity are often the chief culprit in collection damage:

- At relative humidity higher than 65 percent, mold can begin to grow on the surface of objects composed of organic materials, and cellulose chains such as those in paper, wood, and leather will begin to absorb moisture and become limp.
- If the relative humidity drops below 20 percent, objects may become brittle and may crack and tear easily when handled.[10]

Large fluctuations in relative humidity can be avoided by creating microenvironments inside object containers, storage cabinets, or exhibit cases, using good quality materials and adding a moisture absorber such as silica gel. For oversized museum objects, polyethylene sheeting can be draped over shelving or cabinets to create a buffer for fluctuations.[11] Inside these microenvironments the relative humidity and temperature will remain more stable, which is safer for the objects they contain. Microenvironments are particularly useful when objects are moved long distances. Keeping objects in closed cabinets or exhibit cases with good seals will slow the air exchange rate so that the objects inside can adjust more slowly to fluctuations in temperature and relative humidity. The materials used to create microenvironments must be specially prepared before use.[12]

The staff at each facility need to establish a target set point or target value for temperature and relative humidity that the building's mechanical system can maintain over time (in geographic locations with widely varying climate over the year, different summer and winter set points may be chosen).[13] To determine an appropriate set point the following factors should be considered:

- The objects in the collection and the materials they are composed of.
- Annual and daily variations in temperature and relative humidity in the region.
- The annual performance of the heating, ventilation, and air-conditioning (HVAC) system.
- The design of the building and the materials it is made of.

Storage environment experts agree that avoiding large fluctuations over a short period of time is the goal that staff must aim for, but this has to be accomplished with the resources that are available and by establishing set points that can be maintained. Most heating and cooling standards are meant for human comfort rather than long-term preservation so your set points may conflict with the concept of a sustainable green building; hence, the storage environment standards will likely not be the same as environmental standards throughout the museum (see CHAPTER 6F, "Registrars and Sustainability").

Several organizations have published models and worksheets to help museums establish appropriate set points, including CCI and the IPI (which sells an *Environmental Monitoring Starter Kit*). When establishing set points, it is important to think long term and consider daily, monthly, and annual environmental cycles.

LIGHT

Although light is required to view objects, too much light can cause irreversible harm to many materials.[14] Like other forms of radiation, both the intensity and the time of exposure are critical factors for light (e.g., a short exposure to an intense radiation source can cause as much damage as a prolonged exposure to a less-intense source). Light is radiant energy that can be considered in three categories that affect objects:

- Visible radiation (visible light) is the wavelengths of light that the human eye can see. Visible light can be measured with a light meter in lux (an international unit) or as foot candles (fc), an older measurement rarely used outside of the United States.[15]
- Ultraviolet (UV) is short-wave radiation that is not visible to the human eye but is the most damaging to collection objects. UV must be measured with a UV meter. Although the typical museum measurement of UV is microwatts per lumen (μW/lumen), which is the ratio of UV in a quantity of visible light, UV can be measured directly as well (typically as microwatts per area, e.g., μW/cm^2).
- Infrared (IR) is long-wave radiation (heat) that, although damaging to objects, does not pose as much danger as UV.[16]

Damage from exposure to the different types of radiation varies, but all radiation damage is cumulative and irreversible. Examples of light damage include:

- Fading or bleaching of colors exposed to visible light. This can happen in a short period of time if the objects are sensitive, or over a prolonged exposure time.
- Yellowing, chalking, weakening, or disintegration of materials when sensitive materials are exposed to ultraviolet radiation.
- The heat from infrared radiation may damage both the surface and the interior of sensitive objects.

Direct sunlight is the most damaging form of light because it includes visible, UV and IR radiation. Equipping windows with blinds, shutters, or curtains and avoiding skylights are the easiest ways to control daylight. UV blocking film, acrylic, or glass can reduce UV damage but not that from visible light.[17]

Artificial light sources must be selected with care. There are three basic types of artificial light sources commonly used in museums—incandescent, fluorescent, and LED. An incandescent lamp has a wire filament inside a glass bulb that is heated until it glows, producing light, but also heat. Many types of incandescent bulbs produce significant amounts of UV radiation (e.g., halogen lights). Fluorescent lamps contain mercury vapor inside a glass tube that has a phosphor coating. When a fluorescent light is turned on, the electric current excites the mercury vapor, which, in turn, causes the phosphor coating to glow, producing visible light and large amounts of UV radiation, but little IR radiation. LED lamps contain semiconductors called *light emitting diodes* (LEDs) that produce light when electricity is applied to them but do not produce significant amounts of UV or IR radiation. Which light source is best depends on the situation in which it is used. Advice on selecting light sources can be obtained from lighting experts or sources such as CCI.[18] Permissible and appropriate light levels for objects in storage or on exhibit depend on a number of factors including the light sensitivity of the materials, ambient lighting in the room or gallery, how the object is stored or exhibited, etc. The traditional exposure standards for several decades was 50 lux for textiles, works on paper, watercolors, photographs, feathers, etc.; 150 lux for oil and acrylic paint surfaces, polychrome panels, and furniture, etc.; and 300 lux for stone and metal, primarily to avoid contrasting lighting. Light levels should be based on a risk management strategy that considers the fading and ease of visibility of the objects.

Visibility is an important factor to keep in mind when considering light levels because older visitors and many vision impaired visitors need more illumination than an average visitor. CCI recommends adjustments to light levels that will provide equal visibility of objects while still meeting long-term preservation goals.[19]

Once light levels are set, various tools can be used to test and calculate the rates of light deterioration. The International Standards Organization (ISO) Blue Wool Standard,[20] developed in the 1920s, is based on the light sensitivity of a special blue dye over time and can be used to estimate the amount of light-fading. The CCI has an online light damage calculator that provides assistance in determining light levels.[21]

PESTS

Damage caused by pests is a frequent issue in collection storage areas. Pests are often drawn to organic collection materials as well as storage and display materials. To prevent pest damage, institutions are encouraged to establish an integrated pest management (IPM) plan, which is an inclusive and holistic approach to prevent and deal with pests and pest infestations.[22] The practice of IPM involves monitoring for pests by examining the building and using traps, sealing entrances to the building to prevent pests from entering, and keeping areas where collection objects are stored cool and dry, and maintaining good air circulation. When pests are found, nonchemical methods of eradication are pursued first to avoid the use of pesticides that can harm objects and humans (see CHAPTER 6E, "Integrated Pest Management").

OTHER PREVENTIVE CARE CONSIDERATIONS

Contaminants

The introduction of contaminants in collection storage areas can cause many forms of damage including disintegration, discoloration, and corrosion of objects. Natural oils and salts from your hands may not appear to cause immediate damage, but over time fingerprints will permanently mar various materials, especially metal surfaces, gilded surfaces, and photographs.[23] For this reason, the use of gloves is generally encouraged. Some registrars and collection managers are promoting the idea of using clean, bare hands when handling certain types of objects because gloves reduce the sensitivity of touch, but these decisions must be carefully considered, weighing the potential of contamination by natural salts and oils against the potential damage from an insecure grip. If gloves are used, clean cotton or nonpowdered nitrile gloves are generally recommended (however, do not use nitrile gloves when handling silver).[24]

Airborne pollutants can come from outside or inside the museum. Outdoor generated pollutants include pollen, dust, fibers, and soot, which are introduced into the museum environment through open windows and doors, unfiltered ventilation systems, or on people's clothes or bodies.[25] Other significant outdoor pollutants include sulfur dioxide, nitrogen dioxide, nitrogen oxide, ozone, and reduced sulfur gases such as hydrogen sulfide. Common indoor generated gases include acetic acid, formic acid, acetaldehyde, formaldehyde, hydrogen sulfide, carbonyl sulfide, and ozone. Many of these gases are produced by the off-gassing of paints, carpets, and cleaners.[26] Of particular interest is ozone, an air pollutant that can be generated both outdoors and indoors and that can damage both organic and inorganic materials. Outdoor generated ozone is a component of smog; indoors, ozone is produced in large amounts by photocopiers and air purifiers.[27]

Pollutants should be minimized or eliminated by avoiding the source (when possible) and by the use of air filtration systems. Further protection can be provided by using neutral materials such as untreated cotton, polyethylene sheeting, and acid-free board, and by storing objects in sealed cabinets that have synthetic gaskets. Avoid placing collection objects where they are likely to come into direct contact with pollutants such as near copy machines.[28] Store chemicals—including cleaning products, paints, and any other substance that might off-gas—in a secure area well away from collection objects.

HANDLING PROCEDURES

Following appropriate handling procedures is important for ensuring the long-term preservation of collections because objects are at their most vulnerable when being handled (see CHAPTER 5B, "Object Handling"). Dents, scratches, cracks, and breaks may all result from physical forces during handling.[29] Packing and shipping may also cause damage to collections, even under the watchful eye of collections staff (see CHAPTER 5N, "Packing and Crating").

Establishing procedures to ensure object safety and guidelines for handling and moving objects and identifying materials and techniques for packing and shipping objects are all part of preventive care. Additional information can be found in chapter 6 of the *National Park Service Museum Handbook* for creating procedures for your institution.[30]

FACILITIES AND HOUSEKEEPING

Work with facilities and administrative managers to ensure that the physical plant and mechanical systems will not cause harm to the collections.[31] The CCI has a list of basic requirements that should be met by buildings and facilities that is an excellent guide for staff to use,[32] including:

- A reliable roof;
- Reliable floors, walls, windows, and doors;
- Fire detection and extinguishing systems;
- Suitable latches on doors and windows; and
- System for detection of unauthorized entry.

Mechanical systems should be energy efficient, and collection objects should not be stored near them. Attics, basements, and rooms with water pipes (other than sprinklers) or other features that could leak should not be used for collection storage. Rooms that have direct access to the outside environment should only be used for collection storage if windows and doors are properly sealed.

Housekeeping plans should cover all spaces containing collections and include the following:

- Location of museum collections;
- Routine housekeeping tasks;
- Equipment, materials, and techniques for housekeeping tasks;
- Staff responsible for housekeeping;
- Housekeeping schedule; and
- Recordkeeping.

A good housekeeping plan will prevent damage by controlling the amount of dust and grit in the collection and establishing a routine methodology for collections care and maintenance. CHAPTER 13 of the *National Park Service Museum Handbook* contains more information regarding how housekeeping plans can be created and implemented.[33]

EMERGENCY PREPAREDNESS AND RESPONSE

Emergency preparedness and response is also an element of preventive care.[34] Preventive care is defined as taking steps to prevent damage, and an emergency plan reduces the chance of damage when disaster strikes (see CHAPTER 6B, "Emergencies: Prepare, Respond, and Recover"). Practicing the emergency plan gives staff the opportunity to get to know the building better and is an excellent opportunity for facilities and frontline staff to learn about collections storage areas they might not usually access.

CONCLUSION

Recordkeeping is essential for a successful institutional preventive care program. Recordkeeping includes tracking temperature, relative humidity, and light levels; recording evidence of pests; identifying contaminants; maintaining housekeeping schedules; and organizing resources for emergencies; as well as information recorded in collection records and condition reports. All of this information is extremely useful for collections staff in combating deterioration of collection objects. Environmental records are important to identify trends and develop a long-term collection care plan based on preventive conservation, object-specific assessments, environmental and storage upgrades, and conservation management.[35]

Although preventive care may seem like a daunting task, by paying attention to the storage environment and how collections are stored and handled, deterioration of objects can be minimized in the future. •

NOTES
1. Available at: https://www.canada.ca/en/conservation -institute/services/agents-deterioration.html.

2. Available at: https://www.culturalheritage.org/about -conservation/what-is-conservation/definitions.

3. G. Fisher, "Preventive care," in R. A. Buck and J. A. Gilmore, eds., *Museum Registrations Methods*, 5th ed. (Washington, DC: American Association of Museums Press, 2010).

4. Fisher, "Preventive care."

5. Available at: https://www.imagepermanenceinstitute.org/.

6. Available at: https://www.canada.ca/en/conservation -institute.html.

7. Image Permanence Institute, *Sustainable Preservation Practices for Managing Storage Environments* (Rochester, NY: Rochester Institute of Technology, 2011). Available at: http:// ipisustainability.org/pdfs/sustainability_workbook_georgia.pdf.

8. Fisher, "Preventive care."

9. David Grattan and Stefan Michalski, "General care and preventive conservation," *Canadian Conservations Institute.* Available at: https://www.canada.ca/en/conservation-institute/ services/preventive-conservation/environmental-guidelines -museums/general-care-preventive-conservation.html (accessed December 2, 2018).

10. James M. Reilly, "Fundamentals of the preservation environment," presented April 26–27, 2010. Available at: http://www.ipisustainability.org/pdfs/western/Reilly_ FundamentalsPreservationEnvironment.pdf.

11. National Park Service, "Creating a microclimate for oversized museum objects," *Conserve O Gram*, no. 4/4 (July 1993). Available at: https://www.nps.gov/museum/publications/ conserveogram/04-04.pdf.

12. T. J. Raphael, "Airtight, humidity stabilized display cases: The practical design and fabrication of sealed exhibit cases," *Objects Specialty Group Postprints* 1 (1991): 78–87.

13. Stefan Michalski, "Agent of deterioration: Light, ultraviolet and infrared," *Canadian Conservations Institute*. Available at: https://www.canada.ca/en/conservation-institute/services/agents -deterioration/light.html (accessed December 4, 2018).

14. Fisher, "Preventive care."

15. Michalski, "Agent of deterioration."

16. Fisher, "Preventive care."

17. Fisher, "Preventive care."

18. Available at: https://www.canada.ca/en/conservation -institute/services/agents-deterioration/light.html.

19. Available at: https://www.canada.ca/en/conservation -institute/services/agents-deterioration/light.html#13.

20. Available at: http://cameo.mfa.org/wiki/Blue_Wool_ Standard.

21. Available at: https://app.pch.gc.ca/application/cdl-ldc/ description-about.app?lang=en.

22. Integrated Pest Management Working Group, *MuseumPests.net*. Available at: https://museumpests.net/ (accessed December 6, 2018).

23. Janet Mason, "Handling heritage objects," *Canadian Conservations Institute*. Available at: https://www.canada.ca/ en/conservation-institute/services/preventive-conservation/ guidelines-collections/handling-heritage-objects.html (accessed December 5, 2018).

24. Robert L. Barclay, Carole Dignard, and Lyndsie Selwyn, "Caring for metal objects," *Canadian Conservations Institute*. Available at: https://www.canada.ca/en/conservation-institute/ services/preventive-conservation/guidelines-collections/metal -objects.html (accessed December 10, 2018).

25. Fisher, "Preventive care."

26. Cecily M. Grzywacx, *Tools for Conservation: Monitoring for Gaseous Pollutants in Museum Environments* (Los Angeles: The Getty Conservation Institute, 2006).

27. Fisher, "Preventive care."

28. E. D. Duyck, "Chapter 7, Museum Collection Storage," in *The Museum Handbook Part 1: Museum Collections*, 14 (Washington, DC: National Park Service Museum Management Program, 2012). Available at: https://www.nps.gov/museum/publications/MHI/CHAP7.pdf

29. Mason, "Handling heritage objects."

30. J. S. Johnson, "Chapter 6, Handling, Packing, and Shipping," in *The Museum Handbook Part 1: Museum Collections* (Washington, DC: National Park Service Museum Management Program, 1999). Available at: https://www.nps.gov/museum/publications/MHI/CHAP6.pdf.

31. Fisher, "Preventive care."

32. Stefan Michalski, "Basic requirements for preventive conservation," *Canadian Conservations Institute*. Available at: https://www.canada.ca/fr/institut-conservation/services/conservation-preventive/lignes-directrices-collections/exigences-base-conservation-preventive.html (accessed December 11, 2018).

33. J. S. Johnson, "Chapter 13, Housekeeping," in *The Museum Handbook Part 1: Museum Collections* (Washington, DC: National Park Service Museum Management Program, 1998). Available at: https://www.nps.gov/museum/publications/MHI/CHAP13.pdf.

34. J. Levin, "Preventive conservation," *Conservation Perspectives: The GCI Newsletter* 7, no. 1 (1992). Available at: http://www.getty.edu/conservation/publications_resources/newsletters/7_1/preventive.html.

35. Fisher, "Preventive care."

5J | STORAGE

BETH J. PARKER MILLER

ACCORDING TO THE Heritage Health Information Survey (HHIS), conducted by the Institute of Museum and Library Services in 2014 and published in 2019 as *Protecting America's Collections: Results from the Heritage Health Information Survey*,[1] nearly 13.2 billion objects, plus 30.7 million cubic feet and 32.6 million linear feet of collections, are held by more than 31,290 US collecting institutions. With few exceptions, most of these heritage collections are in storage much of the time. The state of collections in storage varies depending on collection discipline, size, storage methods, location, staffing, financial resources, and institutional priorities. Of the 32 percent of institutions that reported damage or loss to collections between 2012 and 2014 in the 2019 HHIS report, 45 percent attributed the damage to improper storage or enclosures. The analysis of the survey data notes that with only 42 percent of institutions reporting completion of a general assessment of their collections, the condition of collections at more than half of US institutions remains unknown. Although many institutions have prioritized and addressed the preservation needs of their collections since the first HHIS in 2004 raised the alarm about the state of heritage collections, many other institutions still have work to do, including the development and implementation of sustainable storage solutions for the collections they hold in trust.

A carefully crafted and regularly updated collection management policy is necessary for achieving effective storage (see CHAPTER 2, "Collection Management Policies"). The collection management policy guides an institution in managing what and how much it collects and keeps by defining the scope of the collection and processes for accessioning and deaccessioning. It establishes standards for conservation, care, inventory control, and access. The policy should clearly state which staff positions have primary responsibility for development and or-ganization of storage areas and systems, for care and maintenance, and for inventory and access control. Collections storage planning and management are usually the purview of collection managers, registrars, conservators, and curators. Staff with storage responsibilities should work as a team to assess the condition of collections and storage areas, clarify priorities, develop solutions, and accomplish tasks.

For museums with limited resources, purpose-built storage solutions and archival quality materials may seem unattainable. However, large and well-funded museums also struggle with storage issues. In 2004, nearly two-thirds of US collecting institutions reported that they urgently needed improved storage.[2] Without appropriate storage, collections are neither safe nor accessible: the objects suffer damage, their lifetimes are shortened, and their usefulness is limited or lost. If a comprehensive storage improvement project is out of reach, large or small institutions can still make a dramatic impact on the lifespans of their stored collections by implementing a course of consistent, gradual improvements.

The goals of good storage should be to protect, preserve, and maintain access to collections through sustainable methods and means. These objectives can be achieved with adequate information, planning, and resources. This chapter provides guidance for storage spaces, furniture, and materials, and an overview of key risks to consider when planning and managing storage.

STORAGE AREAS

The ultimate goals for collection storage are to maintain a space that is clean, has appropriate environmental controls, is free of pests and pollutants, and protects objects from environmental and light damage, disasters, and dissociation. Storage areas vary greatly, and these differences may limit how these goals can be achieved; the limits should be taken into consideration when collections are assigned to a particular space in the collection storage array.[3]

Ideally, collection storage should be a space designed and dedicated for that purpose and separated from all other activities. Realistically, collection storage often is fitted into existing structures and is separated only marginally from noncollection spaces. Museum storage areas vary from large, centralized warehouse-type spaces, located many miles from the main campus, to hidden nooks and closets, tucked away in historic house museums. While off-site storage facilities are the solution for many museums with extensive collections and large objects, it requires additional resources to staff, monitor, and provide access to collections at the facility and to shuttle objects to and from the main campus. Some museums develop open (or visible) storage areas where the public can view collections, but this practice may mean an increase in light exposure, dust levels, and other environmental problems. Many museums in historic buildings adapt rooms or areas within their structures for their collection storage. Careful consideration should go into such adaptive uses, however, to avoid the risks associated with water and sewage pipes, windows and skylights, heat, humidity, pest infestation, potential disasters, and problematic accessibility of attics and basements.

The optimal solution for many large and small museums is to establish centralized storage where like objects are housed in separate areas or rooms within one building. Centralized storage facilitates more efficient collection management and care, and separate rooms allow for targeted environmental conditions as well as selective access control. However, decentralized storage may serve some museums better by spreading out the risks associated with fire or other loss to one structure. Special collections within a larger institution might be best located closer to the department that manages and uses them. The staff charged with collections care should determine collaboratively how best to organize and house collections to ensure that the institution's goals for preservation and access are met.

Accessibility of objects in storage is critical for retrieval and care. Each storage unit, from a room to a bank of cabinets to an individual drawer, should be clearly labeled with its contents. Positioning objects in storage with their accession or catalog numbers, labels, or tags visible; creating appropriate enclosures, especially for vulnerable objects; and maintaining up-to-date inventories greatly facilitates access and minimizes object handling. Well-organized storage creates and reserves a place for every collection object when it is not on exhibit, on loan, or removed for study, conservation, or photography.

Although access to storage areas has traditionally been limited to a subset of a museum's staff, many institutions seek creative ways to engage researchers, students, and the public with their stored collections. In addition to open storage, study storage and resource centers are among innovative storage solutions. These solutions place observation and study areas within or adjacent to storage. The goals of these spaces are to make close study of stored collections easier and to make behind-the-scenes collections activities more visible. These solutions present both exciting opportunities and challenges, as institutions must balance access with preservation and security.

Work Areas

Under ideal circumstances, separate areas that are physically distinct from the rest of storage should be established for several purposes including a temporary storage area for processing objects; a place to isolate objects that are suspected to be infested with pests, mold, or other contaminants; and a place for researchers to study the collections. Office supplies and cleaning materials should be isolated from collections storage. Temporary storage areas for processing objects moving in to or out of the museum should have environmental conditions similar to the exhibition or storage areas to which the objects will proceed next. When collections arrive from outside the museum or other areas with different environmental conditions, allow sufficient time for the objects to equilibrate to the climatic conditions of the space. The general rule-of-thumb is twenty-four hours, but the object's condition and materials may dictate other timelines. As they adjust to the new environmental conditions, the objects should be monitored for signs of pest infestation. If pests are discovered, objects should be isolated, sealed in a barrier material (e.g., polyethylene bags), and treated before they are integrated into the rest of the collection (see CHAPTER 6E, "Integrated Pest Management").

Whether erecting a new purpose-built facility or retrofitting an existing space, clear goals should be established for storage projects, such as identifying the collections to be stored, the storage furniture and methods to be used, the space required (including room for growth), and the access needs. Storage should not only provide adequate housing for collections but also make it easier (not harder) for staff to accomplish their work. Many institutions strive to ensure that their storage projects are environmentally responsible and sustainable. With clear goals and priorities, an institution can develop a manageable budget for the project and ensure the financial sustainability for long-term maintenance and staffing.

Storage Furniture

Each collection room should be outfitted with storage furniture and materials that will safely house the objects. Most objects can be properly stored in closed cabinets or on open shelving with protection from dust and light. Racks are an option for framed works, mirrors, and flat objects that can hang safely. Flat textiles can be rolled on tubes or stored folded and padded in drawers or boxes; costumes may be padded and stored in boxes or drawers or, if sturdy enough, hang on padded hangers in cabinets or on covered racks. Paper objects may be placed in folders in modular boxes, or may be matted, boxed, and placed in cabinets or on shelves. Large or unstable three-dimensional objects that cannot safely rest on a flat surface present unique challenges that may require a custom storage mount or other creative solution and must be addressed on a case-by-case basis.

Outfitting a Storage Area

- Review the objects to be stored, including material types, sizes, and numbers of objects.
- Establish how collections should be organized and accessed within the storage space.
- Check collections care literature and consult with collections colleagues for preferred storage methods, furniture, and individual object housing.

- Visit museums with similar collections, particularly those that have recently renovated storage areas, to learn the strengths and weaknesses of storage systems. Visit museums that have a similar staff size, access needs, and funding to look for innovative solutions to shared challenges.
- Consult with conservators who can clarify pros and cons of various storage options and advise on solutions.
- Develop a storage floor plan for the furniture. If using companies with museum storage expertise, seek more than one plan and cost quote.
- Plan for access and security systems.
- Plan staff responsibilities and the time needed for implementation.
- Establish a budget and funding sources.
- Order storage furniture, equipment, and materials needed to store specific objects.

Storage areas are often developed incrementally using these same steps. Upgrading or developing new storage is time-consuming and expensive and must be carefully planned and sometimes phased. Most institutions fundraise for storage projects, soliciting support from private and corporate donors and applying for grants from local, state, and national agencies.

Storage equipment designed for museums has advantages over commercial storage units designed for other purposes. Several manufacturers specialize in museum storage equipment, which varies in price depending on material, finish, capacity, and function. Museum storage equipment should be fabricated from stable materials that do not off-gas, corrode, deteriorate, or otherwise interact in a harmful way with collection objects. Preferred cabinets, shelves, and racks are constructed of powder-coated metal. Wood and wood-composite shelving and cabinets should be avoided because of the wood's natural acidity, chemical content, and flammability. If wood storage furniture must be used, the wood should be sealed with polyurethane and allowed to off-gas and cure for several weeks before use. Placing additional barriers of Mylar, Marvelseal, Ethafoam, or other stable materials between the wood and objects can slow the wood's impact on the stored collections. Ideally, wooden storage units should be used to house objects made solely of wood, stone, ceramic, or glass. Metal objects and organic materials, other than wood, are at higher risk when housed on wooden furniture.

Museum storage furniture can be specifically designed to handle particular types of collections (e.g., large racks on wheels or tracks that hold paintings and other framed works and cabinets or racks that accommodate textiles rolled on tubes). Metal cabinets are available with heavy-duty gaskets to keep out dust, and with filtered vents, if air circulation within the cabinet is necessary. Cabinet interiors may be designed with modular shelving, drawers, or hanging options to meet the needs of many types of small- to midsized objects. Biological specimens stored in fluid preservatives should be kept in airtight jars on sturdy shelving and protected from light. Safes or vaults are available for high-value and fire-sensitive objects, although their weight may require high floor-load capacity. Oversize objects such as farm wagons, sculptures, or large taxidermy specimens, can be stored on sturdy open shelving or on pallets or raised supports. If space is at a premium, and objects are stable enough to handle shelf movement, cabinets and storage units can be mounted on compactor carriages that move on rails, which eliminates the need for aisles between every bank of storage units, thereby increasing the amount of usable space in a given area.

The US National Park Service and others promote the concept of a multilayer storage system to help protect museum collections from agents of deterioration. The building envelope, the room, the storage furniture units, and the housing and materials directly surrounding the object provide successive layers of protective envelopes for collections.[4] When a storage area does not have a central climate-controlled system, good storage furniture can provide a microenvironment to help maintain a more stable storage environment. Closed cabinets with good gaskets provide a considerable buffer from exterior environmental fluctuations. Individual acid-free boxes can add another layer of insulation. Silica gel, conditioned to a specific relative humidity, can be used in individual drawers or cabinets to minimize and slow down changes in the relative humidity. These microenvironment techniques can be used to meet the humidity needs of special materials, even within a climate-controlled situation, but they do require staff time to maintain them.

Pollutants can be mitigated without a centralized air-filtration system. For example, closed cabinets minimize dust problems, and dust covers on open shelves or over individual objects are a low-cost method for minimizing exposure to particulates. Covers can be made of cotton muslin or Tyvek (if air circulation and reduced light are important), or they can be made of a stable film such as polyethylene sheeting, if reduced air movement and visibility of objects on the shelves is a priority. Objects covered with plastics should be monitored because the plastic can trap humidity, resulting in condensation and mold growth. Dust covers should not touch or rest on most objects (upholstered furniture is one exception). Closed cabinets should not house objects composed of materials that could interact negatively.

STORAGE MATERIALS

Padding and support materials protect objects from collisions and vibrations caused by normal or unanticipated activity in a storage area. Within each storage unit, each three-dimensional object should be placed on a shelf or in a drawer so that it is not in contact with other objects. Objects should not be stacked or crowded together. Objects that are hung or suspended should be supported in more than one place to prevent their weight from tearing the edges away from the hanger. Individual boxes or trays can protect objects and make removing and returning them easier.

The types of materials and supplies used in storage can directly affect collections. Many commonly used office supplies are not made of archival materials and can accelerate deterioration by chemical interactions. Preferred storage materials are those that have been Oddy-tested, analyzed by solid phase micro extraction (SPME), or otherwise characterized as appropriate for long-term storage use. Best practice is to use storage materials recommended by a conservator for specific collection situations. Test results for specific materials are available on the American Institute for Conservation (AIC) of Historic and Artistic Works wiki site.[5]

Storage Materials to Avoid

- Cellophane and masking tapes;
- Rubber bands;
- Unsealed wood, wood-pulp materials, and newsprint;
- Natural and chlorinated rubber;
- Rubber-based fabrics and carpeting;
- Rubber-based adhesives and sealants;
- Foam rubber and urethane foam;
- Sulfur-containing fabrics and fabrics containing fire retardants, sizing, or bleach;
- Plastics containing polyvinyl chloride (PVC) or plasticizers;
- Irreversible or acidic glues;
- Metal paperclips and staples;
- Materials that might snag or abrade;
- Acidic paper products, or any paper product in areas prone to silverfish;
- Wool products, which can be acidic and attractive to pests; and
- Nail polish, nail polish remover, and similar solvents.

Tested and Recommended Storage Materials

- Acid-free paper products (e.g., tissue paper, writing paper, photocopy paper, file folders, archival boxes) may be either buffered or unbuffered. Unbuffered paper has a neutral pH and is used for housing photographs, textiles, and most other types of objects. Buffered paper is impregnated with calcium carbonate, giving it an alkaline pH, and if used for storing paper objects, helps mitigate acidity of paper. However, proteinaceous materials (e.g., animal skins) should not be in contact with alkaline-buffered paper. Even acid-free storage materials may need to be replaced after a period of years if they acidify or absorb acid from other materials. Acid-free boxes and trays in modular sizes designed to fit standard cabinet drawers can be used to house a wide variety of objects.
- Unbleached and undyed cotton or linen fabrics and threads should be washed in hot water with no detergent prior to use.
- Needle-felted polyester batting (adhesive free) can be used for all sorts of padding needs, particularly textiles. Typically, a smooth fabric that is unlikely to snag on an object is placed between the batting and the collection object.
- Polyester film (e.g., Mylar) is used as a barrier between an object and a problematic surface.
- Polyethylene microfoam (e.g., Ethafoam) is a stable foam that is available in a variety of thicknesses. It has a multitude of uses in the storage environment, from lining drawers or shelves to padding and slip protection (usually 1/8-inch or 1/4-inch thicknesses) to forming special mounts or cradles (2 inches or thicker).
- Polyethylene bags are useful for containing small objects, but the bags may need a ventilation hole to prevent trapping humidity. If housing silver, bags need to be sealed and may include silica gel or a vapor phase inhibitor to maintain relative humidity and reduce tarnishing.

Be aware that manufacturers of materials may change formulas or introduce problematic additives to a product previously determined appropriate for storage. It is best to research before ordering and to monitor the performance of all storage materials over time. Archival-quality storage materials are available from a variety of museum, library, and archive suppliers. In some regions, museums have formed purchasing cooperatives to buy supplies at discounted rates. Storage materials should be kept in a clean and environmentally controlled area.

RISK MANAGEMENT IN STORAGE

An important goal of storage planning and management is to prevent or mitigate risks of damage and loss to the collections housed in those spaces. The Canadian Conservation Institute identifies ten agents of deterioration, which include the risks of physical forces, light, pollutants, incorrect temperature, incorrect humidity, thieves and vandals, dissociation, pests, fire, and water.[6]

Physical Forces

Damage resulting from physical forces includes dropping, collision, and vibration and can occur when objects are moved into, out of, or around in storage, but can also occur while an object is sitting or hanging in place. Handling objects places them at a much higher risk of damage than when they are sitting still on a shelf or in a drawer. Staff should be trained in appropriate techniques for handling the range of objects in the collections and in the use of moving equipment (see CHAPTER 5B, "Object Handling"). Precautions include using padded lifts and dollies; moving small, fragile objects on carts instead of carrying them by hand; lifting objects from underneath by their sturdiest part; and taking extra time and care when using ladders or stairs. If an object is stored in its own box, the box can be lifted, avoiding direct contact with the object. Easily visible labels and tags further minimize the need to handle objects. Measures to anchor or buffer objects may be necessary in spaces prone to vibration from earthquakes, construction, traffic, or other activities that might cause macro- or micromovements.

Light

Storage areas should be kept dark when people are not present. Light levels should be kept low when lights are needed to protect objects from both visible and ultraviolet (UV) light, which can cause fading or trigger other chemical reactions. Light damage is cumulative and irreversible, and although not all objects are equally sensitive to light, it is best practice to limit light exposure as much as possible. Windows should be eliminated or blacked out in storage areas. Use banked lighting rather than whole-room systems and turn off lights when the area is not in use. Closed cabinets minimize exposure of objects when lights are turned on in storage. Light levels can be monitored with a light meter. Light meters can be expensive, but because they are used infrequently, sharing between institutions may be possible. Fluorescent lights have a high UV output and should be fitted with filters. Incandescent bulbs, particularly halogen bulbs, emit UV and generate heat which accumulates in confined areas, initiating or exacerbating chemical decay. Light emitting diodes (LED) emit no UV and very little heat and so are preferred, but visible light from LEDs should be monitored and controlled. A little ingenuity

in arranging light placement, using different types of bulbs, and adding filters can minimize light damage.

Pollutants

Pollutants may cause deterioration of objects in storage. Pollutants come in many forms, from dust to tobacco smoke to engine fumes to chemicals in cleaning products. Certain storage materials or the objects themselves may emit corrosive gasses. Common culprits are unsealed wood (particularly plywood and composite wood products), paints and solvents, and acidic paper products. Sealing the building and designing air ducts to minimize the intrusion of dust and fumes will reduce pollutants, as will installing an air-filtration system as part of heating, ventilation, and air-conditioning (HVAC) units. Housing objects in closed containers can provide further protection. Monitoring and regular housekeeping using conservation-approved methods and materials is important for managing pollutants and other risks in storage areas.

Temperature and Relative Humidity

Conservators recommend a stable environment with minimal, gradual shifts in temperature and relative humidity (within collection-specific acceptable parameters) to prevent damage to collections. For planning and monitoring environmental conditions, dataloggers are preferred because they provide a view of temperature and humidity changes over time and insight into the timing and duration of fluctuations.

In the 1970s and 1980s the museum community worldwide adopted the ideal of strict temperature and humidity limits for museum collection environments, usually 70°F ± 2° and 50 percent ± 5 percent relative humidity. However, since the mid-2000s this rigid and problematic standard has been relaxed based on research that has shown that trying to maintain such tight parameters is unnecessary for most objects, specimens, and works of art, and may even be harmful to some.[7]

Interim guidelines offered by the American Association of Museum Directors conservation working group in 2010 suggest set points in the range of 45 percent to 55 percent relative humidity with an allowable shift of ±5 percent and a temperature range of 59°–77°F as generally acceptable for most collections. Many museums have begun adopting variations of these guidelines, as they review their collections needs and what their facilities and systems can reasonably achieve. With the implementation of less stringent temperature and humidity conditions, it is important for collections storage managers to consult with a conservator to understand specific requirements of more vulnerable collections and to design custom storage solutions for them.[8]

Although many museums rely on centralized HVAC systems to manage their collection storage environments some are exploring ways to reduce or eliminate reliance on conventional systems and the energy demands and environmental impacts of such systems. As museums seek to design and implement optimal, achievable, and sustainable environments for their collections, it is important that they understand their collections, regional climate, and building. For example:

- What are the materials and vulnerabilities of the specimens, works of art, or objects?
- What are the regional highs and lows of the transitional seasons?
- In what kind of environment has the collection been living since its creation and to what fluctuations is it already accustomed?
- Of what materials is the building constructed and how are the storage areas configured?
- Can the building's materials help buffer changes in external conditions without an HVAC system?
- Could the use of progressively nested storage enclosures (building, room, cabinet, box) help buffer an object from fluctuations in the environment?

Answers to questions like these can aid museums in designing collection-specific solutions that work for their institutions.[9]

Security
Security measures to protect collections from theft, displacement, or other loss are critical components of a good storage area. Art objects and jewelry are often thought of as theft targets, although other objects—such as prints in nineteenth-century magazines, military paraphernalia, autographed documents, certain minerals, and natural history specimens of value to collectors—are also vulnerable. High-profile, professional theft is rare. Casual theft happens more frequently, but internal theft poses the highest risk. According to the Federal Bureau of Investigation (FBI), between 70 percent and 80 percent of all solved theft cases involve insider participation of some kind.[10]

Security should start with good hiring practices and a vetting process that includes a criminal background check for anyone who will have access to collections storage. This should include interns, volunteers, visiting researchers, maintenance staff, and contract staff. Unescorted access to collections storage should be limited to the fewest number of staff whose official duties require frequent and regular access.[11]

Procedures for controlling and monitoring access to storage are critical. Curators, conservators, collections managers, and registrars who need to work regularly with collections should be able to obtain access easily, but unauthorized personnel and members of the public should not. Biometric access or key-card systems are ideal because they can be programmed and can track access on an individual level. Storage spaces that are not controlled by electronic access systems should be secured through manual keys and locks. Access can be restricted by keying separate storage areas with different but related locks. Staff needing access to one storage area can have a key that works only in that lock, and staff members who need access to many areas can have a master key. Key lists should be kept by the security officer or the staff member charged with that responsibility, and collection space keys that are signed out by authorized staff should never leave the facility or be transferred to another person. If keys are lost or stolen, locks should be changed immediately. Manual key systems and storage sign-in sheets are low-tech solutions, and their effectiveness relies on employee diligence and honesty. It is important, regardless of the method employed, to have written policies and a clear line of command protecting access to storage.

Physical changes to storage areas can improve security. Storage should be designed with a minimum of entrances and exits so access can be easily monitored. If a building is retrofitted for storage, eliminate unnecessary doors and block all windows. Alarm systems can generate an alert if unauthorized entry or departure takes place. A limited-access vault is useful for protecting high-value objects from theft and valuable documents from fire.

Monitoring the use of storage is critical to security. Closed-circuit video systems can be installed either inside or at the entrance to storage areas. It is best to develop a separate workspace outside the storage area for researchers to study collections. If researchers are permitted in storage areas, staff should always escort them and supervise their activity. All visitors to storage, whether scholars or workers installing or repairing systems, should be required to provide photo identification, sign in, and should be escorted by authorized personnel. Visitor logs should track who uses which collection objects. Good records of who had access to storage may help resolve theft or vandalism cases should such an event occur.

Regular inventories and procedures for documenting collection movements add to security by identifying missing or damaged objects and locating misplaced collections in a timely fashion. In addition to a location audit, inventories require a check of objects and identification tags against accession or catalog numbers and descriptions in collections management systems and, thus, aid in preventing the dissociation of objects from identifying information.

Collections Storage Maintenance

Established housekeeping and integrated pest management (IPM) protocols in storage areas are essential to minimize the harmful effects of particulates and pests. Collection storage should be cleaned regularly to minimize dust and potential pest attractants. Under the guidance of a person with preventive conservation expertise, staff should create a storage housekeeping and pest management plan (see CHAPTER 6E, "Integrated Pest Management"). For security and handling reasons, it is best practice for collections management or conservation staff to perform these duties rather than delegate them to janitorial staff. All staff charged with cleaning storage areas should be trained in the condition and handling concerns of the collection. Safety Data Sheets (SDS) for

cleaning solutions should be reviewed and products chosen carefully to avoid introduction of corrosive or harmful chemicals. When maintenance workers are required to be in storage areas, staff with collections responsibilities should oversee them.

Pests come in many forms, from insects to rodents, and they may infest collections of all types. Some pests are dangerous to humans as well. Routine fumigation adds toxic chemicals to the objects in the collections; therefore, it is best practice to use an IPM approach, based on intensive monitoring with sticky traps for arthropods and other traps for rodents, locating and eliminating pest entrances and harborages, and banning food and beverages in collections areas. Infested objects can be treated through freezing, carbon dioxide, or anoxic treatments, and other methods. Treatments always should be carried out with the advice of a professional conservator or museum pest management professional.

Emergency Preparedness in Storage

Emergency preparedness for large- or small-scale disasters or emergencies, whether natural or man-made, is covered in section 6, "Risk Assessment and Management." Storage-specific emergency preparedness issues include many building maintenance concerns. Some monitoring and alarm systems are mandated by law, such as fire and smoke detection and sprinkler systems, and others are highly recommended, such as water and vibration sensors. Be aware of water pipes running through storage and avoid housing objects beneath them. Keep objects elevated at least six inches off the floor in case of water leaks in the area. Store objects in closed cabinets to keep out leaking water and to provide shelter and insulation in case of fire. Mount storage furniture on vibration-dampening pads in earthquake-prone areas. Install emergency lighting and keep flashlights handy. Train staff in the locations and uses of emergency systems, such as shut-off valves, and collection emergency materials, such as tarps and water absorbent pads.

All storage areas should have a fire-detection system that complies with national and local fire protection codes, and fire-suppression systems should be installed in all storage areas. Water-sprinkler systems with air-charged pipes are intended to prevent water leaks and give time to stop the system if a false alarm is triggered, but can also mean a longer time interval between fire detection and sprinkler activation, which may cause greater damage to a collection. In most instances, the potential fire damage, possibility of the fire spreading, and smoke damage are considered higher risks than water damage from the sprinkler system, but this should be evaluated carefully for each collection with input from local fire officials and conservators. Portable fire extinguishers should be positioned strategically throughout the storage areas, whether there is a sprinkler system or not, and staff should be instructed in their use. Fire extinguishers must be checked regularly in accordance with local fire code.[12]

CONCLUSION

Ideal storage—with each object in an individually labeled, acid-free container, in a drawer or on a shelf within a metal cabinet, inside a climate-controlled room, in a well-maintained building—may seem like a daunting goal. However, incremental improvements to each layer of protection can make a significant difference. Federal, state, local, and private grants can help fund an assessment of storage situations and can support implementation of improvements. As conservators and allied professionals learn more about the nature of collections and causes of deterioration, environmental control systems and building materials, and the impact of changes in global and local environmental patterns, the definition of good storage will keep evolving. The primary storage goal is always to do no harm and to protect and preserve collections for current and future generations in as sustainable a way as possible. •

NOTES

1. The Institute of Museum and Library Services, *Protecting America's Collections: Results from the Heritage Health Information Survey* (Washington, DC: The Institute, 2019). Available at: https://www.imls.gov/sites/default/files/publications/documents/imls-hhis-report.pdf

2. Heritage Preservation and the Institute of Museum and Library Services, "A public trust at risk: The Heritage Health Index Report of the State of America's Collections," 2005. Available at: http://www.conservation-us.org/docs/default-source/hhi/hhisummary.pdf?sfvrsn=2. The full report is available at: https://www.imls.gov/publications/heritage-health-index-full-report.

3. "Guidelines and Procedures for Preventive Conservation at Winterthur Museum" (unpublished manual, Conservation Department, Winterthur Museum, Garden & Library, 2017), sec. "4.0 Storage," p. 17.

4. National Park Service, "Museum Collection Storage," in *The Museum Handbook: Part I: Museum Collections*, chapter 7, updated 2012, p. 1. Available at: https://www.nps.gov/museum/publications/MHI/CHAP7.pdf.

5. AIC Wiki, "Oddy Test," last modified February 15, 2018. Available at: http://www.conservation-wiki.com/wiki/Oddy_Test.

6. Canadian Conservation Institute, "Ten agents of deterioration," last modified September 26, 2017. Available at: https://www.canada.ca/en/conservation-institute/services/agents-deterioration.html.

7. P. Hatchfield, "Crack warp shrink flake: A new look at conservation standards," *Museum* January/February 90, no. 1 (2011).

8. Hatchfield, "Crack warp shrink flake."

9. Michael C. Henry, "What will the cultural record say about us? Stewardship of culture and the mandate of environmental sustainability," paper presented at the symposium *Gray Areas to Green Areas: Developing Sustainable Practices in Preservation Environments*, Kilgarlin Center for Preservation of the Cultural Record, School of Information, University of Texas at Austin, 2007. Available at: https://www.ischool.utexas.edu/kilgarlin/gaga/proceedings2008/GAGA07-henry.pdf.

10. Jonas Rehnberg, "Museum security: Integrated security systems to protect the priceless." Available at: https://www.securityinformed.com/insights/co-3108-ga.3200.html (accessed December 15, 2018).

11. The Cultural Properties Council of ASIS International and the American Alliance of Museums, "Suggested practices for museum collections space security," 2013. Available at: https://www.aam-us.org/wp-content/uploads/2018/01/suggested-practices-for-museum-collections-space-security.pdf.

12. The Museum, Library, and Cultural Properties Council of ASIS International and the Museum Association Security Committee of the American Association of Museums, "Suggested practices for museum security," May 2006. Available at: http://www.securitycommittee.org/securitycommittee/Guidelines_and_Standards_files/SuggestedPracticesRev06.pdf.

Many thanks are due to Lynn Swain and Rebecca Buck, authors on this topic in previous editions of this book. This chapter is grounded in their excellent work, and it has been revised with support from the current author's preventive conservation colleagues at Winterthur Museum, Garden & Library, Delaware.

5K | INVENTORY

ANGELA KIPP

O F ALL TASKS in the vast museum field, inventory is perhaps the easiest to explain to outsiders and the hardest to enforce among colleagues. It is easy to understand that to do exhibitions, guide tours, or conduct research that you first need to know where everything is. Maintaining a good inventory is a key task in every museum. In the narrow sense of the word, inventory just means to know what you have and where you have it, but in a broader sense inventory means to know why you have it (e.g., how did it end up in your collection and how does it fit into your mission) and what condition it is in.

As registrars, we are sworn into keeping our inventory always up to date:

> Registrars, through the records maintained, are accountable for the objects in custody of their museums and must be able to provide current information on each object, its location, status and condition.[1]

In museums with a long tradition of professional care you will find each object meticulously listed in the collections management system (CMS) or at least on a list in a filing cabinet or spreadsheet. In other museums the inventory might only exist in one staff member's head. The latter are the cases in which to run the museum professionally you need to conduct a complete inventory. An inventory might also be necessary to be accredited by a professional organization or as a requirement for a grant. But no matter how well-organized a museum is, it is necessary to conduct complete or partial inventories on a regular basis. Inventories discourage insider theft, help locate objects that are lost because they were put in the wrong place, help to detect hidden pests and unnoticed deterioration processes of objects, and also help detect problems with storage materials and facilities.

MAINTAINING AN INVENTORY

An inventory should reflect the current status of the collection. Keeping the inventory up to date should be a standing rule in every museum. To make sure that this really happens, the whole procedure should be mandated, preferably in a collections management policy (CMP; see CHAPTER 2, "Collection Management Policies"). You need to define which changes should be recorded, how, when, and—if you are not a staff of one—by whom. For the sake of simplicity this chapter will focus on location changes, but the basic principles hold true for other changes in an object's record such as ownership, condition, or insurance value (see BOX 5K.1).

The museum should have a stringent system of object locations[2] so that you know exactly where each object belongs. Usually the location will be in a hierarchical arrangement, from largest to smallest unit. For example: Main Building, Room 3, shelf 4, shelf board 2, box 17.

The location system must be understood by and accessible to all staff members who deal with location changes. Forms for location changes must be readily available (preferably there will be stacks of them[3] in the vicinity of every storage unit), and there should be a printable electronic version available on each computer (i.e., on the museum's intranet pages). The location change form should be easy to understand and fill out, and should not need too much required information because each additional required field reduces the likelihood that the forms will be filled out.

In larger institutions, the question of who should be allowed to update object locations in the CMS must be considered carefully and will depend on the frequency of location changes, available staff members, and level of training. Allowing just the registrar to change locations in the CMS will put pressure on

Box 5K.1 Change of Object Location

Procedure for changing a location if the staff member handling the object does not have access to the collections management system (CMS) or does not have the permission to update locations in the CMS:

1. Fill out a *location change* form with the date, accession number, object name, reason for removal, location the object will be brought to, and name of staff member filling out the location change form in legible writing.
2. Place one copy of the form at the location where the object was.
3. Give the second copy of the form to the registrar, who will update the location in the CMS.

Procedure for changing a location if the staff member has permission to update locations in the CMS:

1. Fill out the *location change* form (see above).
2. Place one copy of the form at the location the object was.
3. Change the location in the CMS.
4. Place the second copy of the form in the file folder with location changes for the current year in the registrar's office.

All location changes should be documented on the day the location change takes place. Exceptions from this rule can be granted by the registrar or collections manager and must be put in written form and signed off by the head of the department of collections.

this individual if the collection is active, and it can cause a lot of problems if the registrar is overworked or out of the office. On the other hand, if more people are allowed to update locations, it is more likely that objects will be misplaced or listed with incorrect locations or there will be failures to update the records. As a rule of thumb, the more active[4] a collection is, the more staff members should be allowed to do location changes themselves. In this case it is recommended that partial inventories be done more frequently because of the greater likelihood of misplacing objects either by handling, entering the wrong location information, or changing the location for the wrong object in the CMS.

Types of Inventories

Even in very well-organized museums, inventories are necessary and a good CMP will require them, so the museum benefits as mentioned. A complete inventory—also called a 100 percent inventory, wall-to-wall inventory, or full inventory—encompasses the whole collection and, therefore, is the most complete, but also requires the most time, staff, and money to complete. A partial inventory can take on several forms:

1. *Partial inventory by group or category*—the inventory encompasses a fraction of the collection, de-

fined by material, collection, or location (e.g., all textiles, the Middle East Collection, Room 3, or the shelf rows A–F). Because a complete inventory is a major task, a CMP might be written in a way to reach 100 percent inventory every ten years by conducting a partial inventory every year, encompassing 10 percent of the collection. However, it needs to be said that a partial inventory can never be completely reconciled against the museum records and, therefore, is never the equivalent of a 100 percent inventory.

2. *Randomized partial inventory*—in this case, a randomized fraction[5] of the collection is chosen for inventory. This is the most effective way to discover and deter insider theft.

3. *Stealth or piggy-backed inventory*—if a CMP is nonexistent or does not address inventory (which should be changed as soon as possible), and there are no resources for an inventory project, a partial inventory can still be conducted by making it part of another collections-based project. For example, when doing an exhibition on impressionism, check all impressionist paintings in the collection in addition to the ones going on exhibit. Other good occasions are collection moves, digitization, or rehousing projects. The additional resources should be planned as part of the project's schedule and budget beforehand. The downside of this

type of inventory is that it might be put on hold if it endangers the original goal of the project.

4. *Everyday spot inventory*—This is the least effective inventory strategy, but one that helps at least to maintain the quality of the existing inventory. Whenever an object is handled not only its own record but also the records of objects in its vicinity are checked. For example, when taking one object out of a box of twenty objects for a loan, the other nineteen objects in the box are checked, too.

PLANNING AN INVENTORY

It is no surprise that the better the planning of the inventory, the better the outcome and the more likely the project will stay on schedule and within the budget. If the inventory is not a requirement in the CMP (and sometimes even if it is) you will need buy-in from the director, board, or governing authority. Because they will want to know what resources are required and how long it will take, you should be prepared to provide them with a plan and a schedule.

How Detailed Should the Inventory Be?

The first consideration should be the depth of the inventory. The minimum things to be checked are:

- Accession number or catalog number (or whatever unique inventory number is used for the object); and
- Location.

These will tell you if everything is where it is supposed to be, help discover missing or misplaced objects, and will most likely resolve quite a few "found in collection" objects (FIC) (see CHAPTER 3J, "Found in Collection"). However, it will not provide any additional benefits for preservation or documentation. If your goal is to improve the documentation so that it meets a bare minimum of quality, you should also check the so-called tombstone information:

- Object title or description;
- Object medium or category; and
- Artist or maker.

The inventory will become more valuable the more information you check. A high-quality inventory might also check the catalog entry for:

- Material;
- Measurements (check existing measurements, add missing measurements);
- Dates (check for presence, add if missing);
- Nomenclature (check if correct, add if missing); and
- Other information that seems important or appropriate.

Another aspect of the inventory is the condition and the quality of object housing. You might also want to include:

- Condition (brief or long description); and
- Housing (condition; indicate if object needs a new housing, frame, mount, or support).

There are a few additional things you might want to do while taking inventory, such as adding an object photo to the documentation, marking objects directly with their accession or catalog number (see CHAPTER 5F, "Marking"), and rehousing objects that are not stored properly.

After you have an idea what you want to check in the inventory, determine whether you have the resources you need to do it. This is usually a balancing act in which you might find that you either have to cut down your wish list of things to check or increase the resources allocated for the project.

THE INVENTORY TEAM

In an ideal world, an inventory team consists of at least three:[6] a curator, a conservator, and a registrar or documentation officer. This way, you have one person who has the necessary topic-based knowledge about the objects, one who knows materials and conditions, and one who can add the information to the CMS correctly and keep the inventory process moving in a structured way. If you do an inventory with only minimum requirements it is possible to work with less specialized staff members, although it is always necessary that they have at least basic object handling and documentation training (see CHAPTER 5B, "Object Handling"). For a large inventory project, you might need several teams to get the inventory done in a reasonable time span. For an enhanced inventory project, you might want to have a photographer, an art handler, or mount-maker on board.

Sometimes you will not be able to conduct the inventory with the staff you have, and must get help from other departments or recruit interns or volunteers. Sometimes it is necessary to hire outside professionals. In any case, make sure that you communicate your needs early and clearly to everybody involved so they can schedule time for the inventory. Keep in mind that hiring professionals takes time, especially in larger institutions.

Keep in mind that a staff member who is dedicated full-time to the inventory project will be more productive than one who has other tasks to do; other projects that require attention tend to come into conflict with each other and far too often push the inventory task to a lower priority. But also keep in mind that inventory is a job that requires a high level of concentration and involves many repetitive tasks, which make it hard to stay focused. Depending on the personalities of those involved it might be wiser to assign a person to the inventory for only a few hours of the day and allow the worker to do something different for the remainder of the day. Consider the repetitive nature of the tasks when you think about the time frame and be sure to schedule enough breaks; otherwise there will be more errors caused by fatigue and routine.

Workflow and Logistics

Workflow and logistics play a huge, but often overlooked, role in planning an inventory. Often inventories are slowed down by issues that could be avoided by detecting and resolving them before starting the project. This is why it is important to think carefully about the necessary steps, how they will be done, and where they take place. Take time to identify the issues that might block an efficient working process and look for ways to make everything go smoother. Do not think only about the actual process of checking records against objects, but consider also the

things you might discover while conducting the inventory and how to handle them:

- What will you do with objects that need immediate treatment (e.g., because they are infested with pests or mold)? Will you collect them in another room? Wrap and seal them? Flag the location and move on with a second team[7] coming behind you who will take care of them? How will you flag those objects (e.g., with colored markers at the shelf or also with a database entry)?

- How will you handle objects that are not in the right location in the collection storage array? Will you leave the objects at the locations where you find them and update their database entry, collect them in a separate area, or flag them so a second team can return them to their correct location?

- What will you do with objects that don't seem to have an accession number? Will a second team try to match them with the records, or will you try to do this on the spot? Who will mark them with their accession number, and when will that be done?

- What will you do with objects that cannot be matched with any records? Will you collect them in a separate area, or will you just mark them and decide on how to handle them later?

The more complex and complete your inventory is, the more you have to think about workflow and logistics. There are quite a few decisions to make so it is best to write down the procedures that you and your team will follow. When you start the test run for scheduling is a great opportunity to give the workflow procedures a try and tweak them as necessary. You will likely run into quite a number of obstacles and have to think about possible remedies—some examples of obstacles and possible solutions are in TABLE 5K.1.

The Schedule

The next consideration is time. As a rule of thumb, the more people you have, the faster your inventory will go, but staff is not the only factor. If you cannot organize the work so that teams do not block each other, more people are useless. For example, this is often the case when working in tight spaces or when

Table 5K.1 Inventory Obstacles and Solutions

Obstacle	Solution
Objects record is long and difficult to scroll through on screen.	Create a special object record format in your CMS that holds only the fields you need to check for the inventory.
Internet connection is weak or unavailable, so the team cannot work directly with the CMS.	Prepare forms that make the physical inventory go smoothly and make the later input process easy. Print out lists with objects to check their location before the actual inventory phase starts.
The CMS runs on a desktop computer in another room.	Find out if it is possible to use the CMS on a tablet with a Wi-Fi connection in storage, or transfer the desktop computer to the storage area for the time of the inventory.
The object records are on a card catalog in the registrar's office.	Consider developing a CMS as part of the inventory project. There might be grants available to fund this. If not, take the cards to storage for the inventory.
Aisles are so narrow that objects cannot be checked directly on location.	Prepare a specialized area with enough space to examine the objects and check their records. Consider whether a cart or trolley can speed up the process of moving objects to and from the examination area.
Storage area is crammed so it is hard to get to the objects.	Consider a storage reorganization project linked to the inventory project. Consider adding an additional step of removing unnecessary clutter to speed up the inventory project. Consider whether a deaccessioning project should be part of the inventory project. Prepare a specialized area with enough space to examine the objects and check their records.
The toilet facilities are inadequate (e.g., there's only one toilet for staff of all genders, so volunteers usually leave after having worked two hours to never show up again).	Arrange for portable toilets to be installed that meet the requirements of the Occupational Health and Safety Administration.[1]

NOTE

1. Occupational Health and Safety Administration, Standard 1910.141(c)(1)(i). Available at: https://www.osha.gov/pls/oshaweb/owadisp.show_document?p_table=interpretations&p_id=22932.

the internet connection is so weak that only one team can work with the CMS.

Another factor that affects time is the level of storage organization. If the collection storage space is tidy and well-organized, with locations clearly labeled and every object marked with its accession number, the inventory will go significantly faster than in a tight, crammed storage space where it takes quite some time to find the accession number of an object or the correct name of a storage unit.

Note that checking objects against their records occupies only a fraction of the time it takes for an inventory. You will find that the physical movement of objects (e.g., taking an object off the shelf, transporting it to a table or a photographic area, unwrapping and rewrapping it, or searching for the accession number) uses up a considerable amount of time. So does the correction of database entries, which takes at least twice as much time if the necessary information must be recorded on paper before it is entered into the database.

To create a schedule that reflects reality, it is best to do a test run. After you have decided what you want to check, select a small unit such as a few shelves or several different cabinets that are a good representation of the whole collection slated for inventory. Then, assign a team (which you can be part of) to do all the inventory tasks you planned for. Monitor the workflow and the time it takes. In this way, you will encounter the first logistic hiccups and procedures that do not work well.

After the test run, you can multiply the time that the testing phase took by all the units that you will have to check in the project. Do not forget to include time for breaks, and add at least 10 percent of buffer time for the unexpected such as server failures, emergencies, and the update cycles of the CMS. Increase the amount of buffer time if you have previously known issues such as regular staff meetings, holidays, or downtime because of a major exhibit opening. You might want to adjust some of the required checks for the sake of time or plan for more staff to participate in the process.

Budgeting

After you have an idea of the things you want to check, the staff you need, and the time it will take, make a list of materials that are needed for the inventory. Depending on your plan these might include (but are not limited to) markers, notebooks, tablets, barcode scanners, printers, labels, archival packing materials, carts or trolleys, tables, and photographic equipment.

During the test run you may have discovered other things that need to be fixed before the inventory can take place such as the installation of additional power outlets, network connections, or more Wi-Fi routers in remote storage areas. Make sure you have thought of everything before calculating your budget needs.

If you need external staff such as a photographer or additional art handlers, calculate their salaries or compensation. If you plan to work with volunteers, think about perks such as snacks and coffee or a regular Pizza Friday (or other, perhaps less calorie-ridden incentives) that need to be included in the budget.

Wrap-Up and Report

As you wrap up your calculations for the schedule, needed staff, and required budget for a report to upper management, consider the organizational things you might need for management to decide. For example, the loan program and new acquisitions might interfere with inventory requirements. You might need the higher-ups to put a hold on outgoing loans during the time you will need staff members to focus on the inventory, or you might need a moratorium on new acquisitions during the inventory (or at least for acquisitions in specific collections). Depending on which staff members are available you might want to reduce or suspend other programs (e.g., guided tours or workshops) because you are in dire need of the curator who is usually assigned to do them. Make sure to spell out everything you need so upper management can decide on the whole inventory package and will not be unpleasantly surprised by more needs coming up after the inventory started.

Conducting an Inventory

As soon as resources are granted, you have the go-ahead from upper management, have purchased the necessary tools and materials, and any necessary work to improve the facilities has been done, the process of conducting the inventory can start.

Although there are generally two possible[8] ways to proceed, it is usually recommended to check which objects should be in the location according to your files and then see what you actually find in the location—that way, you will not overlook things that have gone missing. Ideally, you should empty the room you are checking and then return the objects one by one as they are inventoried. Although this adds an additional object handling step, it will ensure that nothing is overlooked, reduce the risk of knocking over an object in front as you reach for an object behind it, and it is generally the tidiest option. There are, of course, a few exceptions to this rule such as painting racks or storage units holding extremely heavy and bulky items. Either way, you will end up with three types of objects:

1. Objects that match the recorded location.
2. Objects that are at the location but have a different location entry information or no location entry information (in the worst case, they will not even have a catalog entry).

3. Objects that should be at the location, but are missing.

In an ideal world, you would be able to mitigate all of these situations as the missing objects show up in other locations. In the real world, you will always end up with a few mysterious cases.

If you have done a complete inventory, once it is finished you can be sure that you checked everything meticulously, which means that the missing objects really are missing and the things you have FIC really never came in through a formal process, or the former accessioning procedures were so shady or the documentation so badly done that you cannot really tell if the records match the objects. If you have only done a partial inventory, you will not have this satisfying state of completeness.

As for how to deal with the objects that mysteriously show up, refer to CHAPTER 3J, "Found in Collection." For the objects that are missing according to your inventory, ideally your CMP will spell out how to proceed (e.g., by filing an insurance claim, informing the authorities). If the CMP does not help, make sure it is revised so that it does in the future and work out with upper management how to proceed. The weakest form of acknowledgment is to have a location entry "missing in inventory." The most robust form is to handle it as a potential theft. Keep in mind that most thefts in museums are inside jobs, so the wishful thinking that missing objects will turn up somewhere else sometime in the future might actively help a criminal in your own ranks. Choose a procedure that aligns with the law, your professional code of conduct, and your institution's mission.

After the Inventory Is Before the Inventory

Most inventory projects have a clear start and end date, but the everyday work of the registrar or collections manager is an ongoing preparation for the next inventory—which is to say, it means making sure the next inventory goes smoother than the previous inventory by ensuring that all the policies for acquisition, accession, cataloging, marking, housing, making location changes, and condition checks are followed meticulously. In most cases, the person following the procedures is not the problem, rather it is raising awareness for the importance of following procedures among your colleagues. It requires persistence and a patient and polite way of teaching the right procedures again and again, no matter how far down on the hierarchical ladder the registrar is. Keep in mind how William James Durant put it, "We are what we repeatedly do. Excellence, then, is not an act, but a habit." •

NOTES

1. Code of Ethics for Registrars. The Registrars Committee of the American Association of Museums, accepted and endorsed on June 11, 1984.

2. A. Kipp, *Managing Previously Unmanaged Collections: A Practical Guide for Museums* (Lanham, MD: Rowman & Littlefield, 2016), 41–45, 119–124.

3. Preferably accompanied by a pencil, which is attached with a string to the storage unit, so it cannot be taken away from the forms. Probably billions of pencils get lost in storage areas every year.

4. I use the term *active* because the sheer number of collections objects is not the determining factor. A collection can have more than a million objects, but if there is only one object taken out per week documenting the location changes is far less stressful than if you have a collection with a mere handful of objects that are taken out frequently for pop-up exhibits and education programs all around the county.

5. There are numerous possibilities to decide how the randomization is done. You might write down the different collections listed in your collections policy on slips of paper and do a blind draw. You might run a numbers generator and check the equivalent object record. You might blindly draw numbers from one to twenty and then check every record that is a multiplication with this number. The possibilities are endless. The only important thing is that the result of items to be checked is not foreseeable for anyone.

6. This very wise recommendation is based on the German book on collections audits: Lina Lassak: Revision—ein Handbuch zur Durchführung, 2016, page 34. Available at: https://zenodo.org/record/157342#.XERju81CfIV (translation: Audits—a handbook for conducting them)

7. *Second team* here refers not necessarily to a real second team, it can also be the same team conducting the tasks in a later step.

8. Look what is in the location and check it against the record in the CMS (or whatever you have that holds your inventory in written form) or look what should be in the location according to your CMS and tick off what you find.

I'm eternally grateful to Maureen McCormick who wrote the original chapter on inventory in MRM5. Although I restructured the chapter by giving the maintenance of the inventory the top spot and added a few additional thoughts, the core work was done by her.

5L | PREPARATION

THE PREPARATION OF an object for a museum collection begins at the time of its acquisition, whether it is donated, purchased, or field collected. The goal is to ensure the best possible long-term preservation of the object's physical and chemical condition, considering current and anticipated use. Preparation has a continuing impact on objects, and they require ongoing maintenance once they are in the collection. Achieving this goal is dependent on an understanding of the nature of the object's material, its condition, and the types of deterioration to which it is susceptible, field collection techniques, knowledge of past preservation practices and the objects history. As always, proper handling is the first line of defense to prevent damage (see CHAPTER 5B, "Object Handling"). Ongoing documentation maintains intellectual control of the object by associating the object with the information about it.

Preparing objects for integration into a collection begins with an analysis of the object to determine its condition (usually in the form of a condition report; see CHAPTER 5E, "Condition Reporting"), needs, and labeling with a unique identifying number to associate it with its documentation (see CHAPTER 5A, "Numbering;" and CHAPTER 5F, "Marking"). At this point, it may only be necessary to place the object in a stable, environmentally appropriate location, whether in storage or on exhibit. On the other hand, further work may be required to create a proper storage or exhibition environment. This may require specialized knowledge and training or the help of conservators, preparators, mount makers, or other specially trained personnel. Some institutions may have such specialized staff, but in others much of this work may rest with one individual. Staff or volunteers without such expertise may acquire additional training, but it is important to keep actions within one's level of skill and knowledge, to document such activities, and to call in professionals when needed.

Preservation requires ongoing maintenance. Remedial work may be needed when an object's condition changes or when its function changes (e.g., by going on exhibit, on loan, or when it is used for research). Each discipline and type of material has its own requirements, methods, policies, and procedures. What may be considered appropriate for a bird specimen in a zoology collection might not be for the same specimen in a history collection. In a zoology collection preparation for use of the bird as a study skin will be quite different than preparation as a taxidermy specimen. If the bird is decoration on a hat, very little might be needed besides proper storage.

New acquisitions which are susceptible to pests should be isolated, quarantined, and closely examined for signs of infestation, and treated if necessary. All objects, especially organics, should be carefully and continually monitored for pests and not integrated into the collections until safe to do so (see CHAPTER 6E, "Integrated Pest Management"). Testing may be necessary if there is a suspicion that arsenic or other toxic contaminants were used in previous preservation or manufacturing techniques because these may pose a problem for the staff or other users, limit an object's use, require specialized storage, or have long-term preservation effects.

Preparation should be based on common principles of collection care. These principles apply to incoming loans as well, and treatment should only be undertaken with the permission of the owner:

- Consider each object's unique nature.
- Take into consideration the museum conditions and potential situations the object will be in.
- Respect the integrity of the object, its research potential, and its significance to its originating culture.
- Maintain the association of the object and its documentation.

- Use stable, nonreactive materials with collection objects.
- Use reversible, nondamaging preparation methods and materials.
- Ideally, any treatment done should be reversible; however, this may not be possible for some procedures or in the preparation of natural history specimens.
- Provide proper support, housing, and a stable storage environment.
- Document all activities affecting collections.

Conditions which pose a hazard to an object's long-term preservation should be corrected if it can be done without damaging the object or interfering with future use of the object (e.g., for research). Objects that are matted, framed, or mounted should be examined to ensure that the materials are archival and that the technique is appropriate. If not, it is generally advisable to remove the work from its existing housing and replace it with an archival housing. In doing so, markings or a record of markings should be retained for object documentation. If an object has an acidic, inappropriate, worn, fragile, or inaccurate catalog tag or label, it may be necessary to re-mark it. In this case, proper guidelines should be followed (see CHAPTER 5F, "Marking"), the procedure should be documented, and any tags or labels that are removed should be archived with other object documentation. If an old label is adhered to or written directly on an object, the services of a conservator may be necessary to remove and preserve it.

CLEANING

Objects that come into the museum may be dusty, dirty, tarnished, corroded, etc. These conditions can be damaging to the objects and attractive to pests, but cleaning objects is a difficult issue and generally best left to conservation experts. However, removal of surface dust, dirt, and fingerprints from stable surfaces may be done if proper training is received from an expert. Removing tarnish or corrosion and repairing damage are highly specialized tasks and should be done by or under the direction of a conservation professional. It is important to note that there is a difference between dust and dirt acquired due to in-

activity and lack of surface protection and dust and dirt which is evidence of historical use and thus an important part of an object's history. Any cleaning needs to be recorded in the object documentation.

Housings and Supports

Enclosed storage cabinetry is ideal for most objects (see CHAPTER 5J, "Storage," for more detailed information). However, objects may need additional housing beyond that provided by storage furniture or may need special support. These needs may change if the object is moved from storage to exhibit or is loaned to another institution. Boxes and other enclosures can provide a better environment, additional support, surface protection, can limit handling, facilitate movement, and enable safe access to the object. It is preferable that the support system be usable whether an object is on exhibit, in storage, or in transit.

Factors to consider when determining the need for an additional enclosure include:

- What kind of environment must be provided for the object?
- Is light or relative humidity control important?
- What is the potential for off-gassing of the object, the enclosure, or nearby materials?
- Does the object need a microenvironment?
- Does the object need protection from dust or touch?
- What risks from pests will be encountered?

For object supports, consider:

- Can the object stand alone without deforming or weakening?
- Are there stress points that need to be alleviated or prevented?
- Does the object need a support for proper exhibition? Will new stress points be created when the object's function is changed?
- Would a support (or container) facilitate safer handling of the object?

Materials

All materials used with museum objects, whether in direct contact with the object or in its environment, must be benign to the collection and personnel. In general, this means using acid-free (neutral pH) materials that will remain stable over time and that do not have components that can do damage should they deteriorate, such as the release of damaging gases (off-gassing), changing shape, or changing texture. Materials should not have colorants that can bleed if wet. Simple tests can be performed to identify some unsuitable materials. Materials for construction should be sturdy enough to provide proper support and suit the needs of the object. The design should be simple and easy to use. Mechanical closures are preferred. If needed, adhesives should be acid-free, stable, and kept away from objects or used with a barrier. Conservators may be consulted about materials and tests can be done for materials that you are considering for preparation (see CHAPTER 5J, "Storage," and CHAPTER 5N, "Packing and Crating," for more detail on types of materials and uses).

Coverings

If enclosed cabinetry is not available, coverings can provide protection from dust, buffer changes in relative humidity, and may protect objects from water leaks. Open cabinetry can be covered and objects individually bagged. Large objects such as furniture, dinosaur bones, and farm equipment may be best protected with a covering. Fabric (e.g., unbleached muslin) is washable, allows air circulation, is opaque, and inert; the fabric should be washed before use with a mild, unscented soap without fabric softener, and rinsed twice. Polyethylene and polypropylene sheeting or bags are relatively stable, translucent, waterproof, and low cost. However, plastics generate static electricity and must not be used in close proximity to flaking or loosely attached surfaces. If the surface is fragile or prone to crushing, coverings should not touch objects, but should be supported by a framework of other safe materials. Care should be taken to avoid the creation of an unfavorable microenvironment of high relative humidity or trap air pollutants inside enclosures. Naturally acidic objects can off-gas vapors, which may cause or hasten the deterioration of the original object as well as adjacent materials.

Containerization

Boxing and bagging objects may be a good alternative or addition to other types of housing, provide protection from environmental factors, and assist in handling. Time, material costs, availability of staff, necessary skills, and project size influence whether to buy or make enclosures. Premade boxes are more expensive than buying sheet goods, but making them allows customization, especially if only a few are needed. Consider purchasing or making boxes in a limited number of standard sizes suitable for the collection and storage furniture. Boxes must be sturdy enough to bear the weight of the contents without deforming and, if stacked, must bear the weight of the objects on top. Handling devices (e.g., handles, straps) must be effective and able to bear the weight of the box and its contents. Additional padding or support may be needed to prevent movement and vibration within the box. Even a simple tray may aid in this way.[1]

Containers made of paper products provide some relative humidity buffering but will deteriorate if they become wet. Stable plastic (e.g., polyethylene, polypropylene, acrylic) containers provide protection from water, relative humidity, and some pests. Properly sealed, they can provide a microenvironment along with the use of silica gel or other relative humidity or pollutant scavenging materials. An anoxic environment (which replaces or scavenges oxygen) is useful for certain materials whose deterioration is increased in the presence of oxygen. These can be created by using special air-tight and vapor-proof materials such as Escal (which is clear and flexible) or a laminate of aluminum and plastic (e.g., Marvelseal) to enclose an oxygen scavenging material or silica gel.[2] Glass jars, particularly the kinds used for storage of fluid-preserved specimens, can provide protection from pests for ethnobotanical collections such as seeds.

Large or heavy objects may require the structural stability of a wood or metal container. However, wood emits harmful gases (although the amount varies). Well-seasoned and appropriately coated woods off-gas less, but it is not possible to eliminate all acidic off-gassing. Therefore, wooden storage containers, especially those used for long-term storage, must be used in well-ventilated areas with a vapor barrier between the wood and the object. Wooden shelving and drawers should be lined with a vapor barrier such as an aluminum-plastic laminate (e.g., Marvelseal). Metal shelves and drawers should have a powder-coated finish or be made of stainless steel.

Enclosures

Enclosures such as mats, folders, encapsulation, and frames are used for flat or shallow objects (e.g., works on paper, paintings, and flat textiles) that need surface protection or support. The type of enclosure depends on the stability of the object's surface, the flatness of the object, the volume of material, and the available storage space, as well as time and money. Using standard-sized mats and frames throughout the collection makes storage and mounting exhibitions easier and more cost-effective but do not overstack objects that are prepared this way.

Folders are simple and quick to make and a good choice for flat objects such as paper documents, prints, and maps and have the additional benefit of making handling easier. Folders can be purchased, or you can make your own by folding in half a piece of acid-free stock or Mylar, which is large enough to enclose the object (leaving a margin) and has a weight (thickness) sufficient to support the object. If using Mylar, objects can be completely encapsulated by taping the two pieces together along all edges with archival tape, provided the adhesive is kept away from the edges of the object, though this limits access and can trap dust, other contaminants, or moisture inside.

Matting provides excellent protection for a range of materials. A mat is composed of two pieces of archival board with a window cut in the top piece to allow examination, yet limit touching. For art work, photographs, or archival materials, the object is held in place by using archival hinges, corner mounts, or rails. An interleaving sheet or tissue can be used to further protect the surface of the matted object. The surface of the window mat must project above the surface of the object that is matted and can be augmented by spacers or multiple mats. Unless they are part of a framing package, the two mats should be attached to each other with archival tape along one edge. A double-window mat (in which both windows have Mylar or fine netting covering the windows) reveals both sides of the object. Mats made from archival materials can be purchased, custom made by a specialist, or can be made in-house, but a fair degree of training and practice is required to do this, especially if exhibition is planned.[3]

For textiles, use a backing board covered with an inert padding (e.g., polyester fiberfill) and then covered with washed muslin to which the textile can be attached by lightly sewing along one edge (as when labeling a textile); this allows the reverse to be inspected. Care must be taken to avoid putting any stress on the fibers. Special training or the advice of a conservator may be necessary.

Framing

Frames provide surface protection, support, and a method of display. Many pieces of art come into museums already framed. Careful consideration must be paid to modifying, replacing, or discarding a preexisting frame and this should be a collections care, curatorial, and aesthetic decision. Frames are often an integral part of the work, especially if they are original to the work, and existing frames can have artifact status of their own.

New frames are usually purchased in either standardized or custom sizes. Whether new or old, the frame must fit the work. The painting should not touch the frame directly and the frame should be deep enough to contain the glazing (if used); a mat, separator, or barrier between the work and the frame or glazing; the artwork; and a backing. There should be room for expansion between the work and the sides of the frame (rabbets). A narrow nylon velvet ribbon, archival felt, or tape applied to the frame sides (rabbets) will protect painting edges from abrasion. If the frame is not deep enough, it may be built up on the reverse. A backing of stable, nonreactive material (such as acid-free foam core board or Coroplast) provides buffering and keeps fingers and dust away from the back of the work. Taping around the perimeter of the backing and frame prevents dust infiltration. A label with basic information is placed on the backing, not on the work itself. Mending plates are attached to the frame and hold the package together under slight pressure.[4]

Whether to glaze and what material to use depends on both aesthetic and safety concerns. Glazing can be glass or another transparent material. Glass is often preferred as it is more resistant to scratching, but it is also more susceptible to breakage than other glazing materials. If the work is a pastel or has another friable surface, then glass is preferred due to the static generated in plastics. Glazing materials are available that have ultraviolet filtering, nonbreaking, anti-glare qualities without static or distortion. If the artwork is to travel, glazing should be acrylic (except for pastels, etc.), but if glass is used, it must be taped in transit to hold glass fragments in case of breakage to prevent damage to the artwork and other contents of the container.

Any hanging hardware (e.g., D-rings, screw eyes, security hangers) should be attached to the frame and must be strong enough to hold the weight of the framed work. Old hardware may be weak or inappropriate and usually should be replaced. Do not use picture wire across the back of the frame, especially not a single strand wire. Works stored in a bin rather than hung should have any protruding mounting hardware or picture wire removed to prevent snagging and scratching and should be stored front-to-front or back-to-back with a separator between them.

Supports and Mounts

Supports and mounts provide form and stability and alleviate stress and vibrations, thereby preventing distortion, creasing, and structural damage. Supports also facilitate the transportation of objects. The design of supports is determined by the object and how it will be stored or exhibited. A successful support is not overly complex, is easily removable, provides as much visual access as possible, and does not apply stress to the object during insertion or removal. With space at a premium, supports also should be space conservative. Supports need not be elaborate and may be as simple as a flat piece of archival board, crumpled acid-free tissue, or a pillow or snake made of muslin and filled with polyester batting or polystyrene beads. Objects that are prone to collapse (such as hats, shoes, clothing, soft baskets, or bags) should have internal supports shaped to the size and shape of the object. Hats, for example, should be supported so that they are lifted off the surface, not resting on their rims, with the whole rim supported from beneath. If

the object is not stable at rest (such as a round-bottom ceramic) a ring can be constructed if inert materials to give it support and keep it from moving. There are many good sources for the construction of supports and mounts.[5]

Preparing objects for exhibition requires careful analysis of the needs both of the object and the exhibit design. Although an object may be best stored lying flat in a drawer; for exhibit, it may be desirable to have it shown in a different orientation, such as vertically, or as if in use. The condition of the piece may allow this, but only if a proper exhibit mount is made for it. Ideally, objects on exhibit should have mounts to keep them from moving if the case is bumped or subject to vibration (e.g., from an earth tremor). In earthquake-prone areas, mounts are critical for most objects both on exhibit and in storage to prevent damage.

Exhibit supports or mounts need not be invisible, but should not be visually intrusive or obscure important details of the object. They should eliminate or reduce stress on the object and prevent the object from resting on a vulnerable surface. Areas of contact must be at stable points and properly distributed for the object's weight. Supports should be made of inert materials. Metal supports should be coated with an inert material. Although mounts may be purchased or made with mat board, polyethylene foam, covered L-hooks, or other easy-to-use materials, it may be necessary to use the services of a mount maker skilled in metalworking or acrylic (Plexiglas) construction. There should always be a barrier between the object and exhibit casework or props.[6]

Clothing and Textiles

The fragile and flexible nature of textiles requires padding or special supports. Garments that are stable enough to be safely hung may be placed on padded hangers. Cotton straps sewn into the inside of a waistband can help to distribute the weight of heavy skirts to the hanger. Textiles stored flat (e.g., beaded dresses, fragile textiles) should have folds padded to prevent creasing. If flat textiles are hung for exhibition, hook-and-loop fasteners (e.g., Velcro) or a pocket for a rod may be sewn to the reverse and used for hanging. The textiles may need the additional support or protection of a muslin backing.

It is often desirable to exhibit clothing on mannequins, but commonly used store mannequins are rigid and their size and contemporary fashion proportions are not suitable for historic period clothing. Such mannequins are difficult to dress, put stress on garments, and are often aesthetically unsatisfactory. The ideal mannequin is soft-bodied, flexible, designed to fit and dress the garment being displayed without stress, and provides support throughout.

If hard-bodied mannequins must be used, one smaller than needed should be selected and covered with muslin or stockinet to provide a barrier. The covering can be padded with polyester batting as needed for form and support. Attention must be paid to the method by which the mannequin itself is supported; if the mannequin is to wear shoes, the support cannot come up through the bottom of the foot, nor should the weight of the mannequin rest on the shoes.[7]

SPECIAL PREPARATION TECHNIQUES

Some collections, particularly those with natural history specimens, have specialized methods of preparation. Often, the great bulk of these collections are for research and seldom used for exhibition. Preparation begins at the time of collection and has a great deal to do with long-term preservation. Processes focus on preservation of scientific data and maintaining research potential. However, as with any museum collection, the most stable and long-term materials and preservation techniques should be selected. Many other collections also have special considerations which affect their preparation for storage, research, or exhibition.[8]

CULTURAL COLLECTIONS
Ethnographic Collections
Increasingly, collections staff are interacting with the cultures that created the objects in their care. Cultural representatives may make arrangements with museum staff to prepare objects for storage, research,

or exhibition in their own ways. These may include the use of cornmeal, tobacco, or herbs; special ceremonies; the orientation of objects within the museum; or other preparations in order to follow traditional cultural practices.[9]

Archaeological Collections
Although some artifacts can be quite stable, others may require treatment because removal from their original buried environment can cause their deterioration. For example, salts absorbed while buried may effloresce in the museum environment and treatment or a controlled environment may be needed to prevent further damage. Previous preparation techniques can also cause problems; unstable adhesives used to reconstruct ceramics can discolor, become brittle, and fail over time, and either require removal, replacement, or additional support.[10]

ART COLLECTIONS

In addition to knowing the techniques and materials, artist rights also may determine preparation for storage or exhibit. Some pieces only exist in a digital form, others rely on documentation for knowing how to properly exhibit. Photographs have a range of materials and methods that are covered elsewhere in this publication (see CHAPTER 5H, "Photography").

NATURAL HISTORY COLLECTIONS
Botanical Collections
These contain specimens that are prepared for storage by pressing and drying plant parts, usually beginning in the field, and then mounting them for storage by adhering or attaching them to large archival sheets of herbarium paper, along with a label. The mounted plants are stored in folders that are stacked in metal cabinets. Material too bulky for attachment to herbarium sheets, such as wood samples, is placed in separate packets, which may be attached to the herbarium sheets or stored in boxes. Past chemicals used in preservation to prevent pests (such as mercuric chloride) are likely to be toxic and may require remediation.[11]

Paleontological Material

These objects can be any size from small invertebrates removed from matrix in an acid bath to dinosaurs, which are likely to have been field jacketed (encased in plaster and burlap for structural support) when excavated and are large and heavy. Supports must bear the specimen's weight, prevent it from collapsing, and assist in lifting, moving, and transporting the object, often using mechanized equipment such as a forklift.[12]

Minerology

Although rocks and minerals are commonly seen as stable, they may be quite fragile or susceptible to corrosion, oxidation, and other chemical and mechanical damage.[13]

Zoological Specimens

Techniques and materials used to prepare zoological specimens include drying, fluid preservation, skeletal preparation, tanning, taxidermy, and consolidation of bone or fossils. These methods are diverse and newer preparation methods such as freezing, thin sectioning, scanning electron microscope (SEM) preparations, and frozen tissue for sampling DNA create new challenges for storage. It is not uncommon for parts of the same specimen to be preserved in several different ways; maintaining the documentation link between the parts is critical. Because of their organic nature, zoological specimens are susceptible to pest infestation.[14]

Dry Zoological Specimens

These include study skins, skeletons, and mounted and pinned collections. Study skins are prepared by defleshing, drying, and internally padding skins to a stable form. Skeletons may be cleaned by a number of steps to remove the flesh and fats, often using dermestid beetles for the final cleaning. Some museums receive zoo animals that have died and in these cases staff must be informed of potentially hazardous infections, pest problems, and so on, that can affect workers, other specimens, or preparation techniques. For example, antibiotics may affect cleaning with dermestid beetles.

Wet Zoological Specimens

A wide range of specimens are preserved in fluids. Preparing and maintaining these collections may re-quire permits for the preserving chemicals, staff who are specially trained to deal with the hazardous materials, and specialized storage facilities. Museums that have wet collections but lack these resources should contact professionals in the field for assistance in managing these collections.

Preparing a specimen in fluid usually begins in the field by fixing specimens in formaldehyde as soon as possible after death to halt enzymatic processes. Formaldehyde is not a good long-term storage medium for most specimens, so they are usually transferred to 70 percent ethyl alcohol for storage. In the past many other chemicals, including wintergreen oil, were used to preserve wet specimens. Storage is usually in chemical resistant glass jars with tight fitting lids. The fluid levels in the containers must be regularly checked and maintained.[15]

Mounted Taxidermy Specimens

Many museum collections contain mounted animals prepared by taxidermists. Although some specimens may be considered exhibit materials only, others may be important parts of the permanent collection. Taxidermy mounts may be the only specimens of extinct species. Special problems may arise because there is great variability in taxidermy materials and techniques, with a great deal of experimentation over time. The internal supports can be a composite of materials such as plaster, metal, wood, fiber, polyurethane, or fiberglass. There is usually little or no documentation of what materials and chemicals were used, especially with older mounts. In addition, some materials are toxic; arsenic was commonly used in taxidermy to prevent pests. Hence, special handling is necessary. Because of their exhibition history and past work, the condition of taxidermy mounts may be affected and require cleaning or conservation. Careful consideration is needed to decide whether to prepare a specimen as a taxidermy mount because the process destroys much of the research use of the specimen because of the removal of tissues and the treatments and chemicals involved.[16]

Invertebrate Specimens

Insects and other invertebrates are usually prepared for storage by the technique of pinning. Typically, a specimen is captured in the field and dried. At the museum, it is relaxed (rehydrated until flexible) and positioned with an entomological pin inserted through the body; labels are stuck on the pin beneath the specimen, and it is inserted into a base in the bottom of a storage box and placed in a drawer with a tight fitting, glass-topped, lid. Because of their susceptibility to pests, these specimens are usually treated by freezing (see CHAPTER 6E, "Integrated Pest Management") before being added to the collection, as well as when returned from being on loan. Some invertebrates are stored in alcohol or other chemicals and treated as other fluid preserved specimens. Shells, corals, etc., are treated as dried specimens.[17]

Freeze-Drying

Useful for preparing specimens for exhibition and educational collections. The whole specimen is positioned and placed in a freeze-dryer, which removes the water from the tissues through freezing and sublimation. Unfortunately, a freeze-dried mount is attractive to pests and because most of the activity takes place inside the body cavity, an infestation can be well advanced before it is detected; therefore, monitoring is critical.

Living Collections

Living plants and animals have their own challenges, but many of the same preservation principles apply (see CHAPTER 3F, "Living and Natural History Collections Registration"). Collections management must not only maintain the specimens, but in some cases foster reproduction. Zoos, aquariums, arboretums, and botanical gardens have their own literature on collections management. Many museums maintain living collections for exhibition, research, and education should have staff specially trained in those disciplines or seek assistance from those trained for those activities.

CONCLUSION

Many specialized books and articles have been written on the preparation of museum collections, especially in natural history. This is a rapidly changing field as research produces new information about the best long-term care of collections. Keeping up to date with new techniques, materials, and the status of research in preparing collections is critical.[18] Equally important is documentation of what past and current practices are so the changes can be tracked and proper decisions can be made now and in the future to provide the best possible collections management. •

NOTES

1. For an example, see *How to Make a Custom Box*. Available at: https://www.thehenryford.org/docs/default-source/default-document-library/how-to-make-a-custom-box.pdf.

2. Available at: https://www.nps.gov/museum/publications/conserveogram/03-09.pdf; J. Burke, "Anoxic microenvironments: A simple guide," *SPNHC Leaflet* 1, no. 1 (1996). Available at: www.spnhc.org/media/assets/leaflet1.pdf.

3. See Canadian Conservation Institute Notes, Series 11 (Paper and Books), Canadian Conservation Institute. Available at: https://www.canada.ca/en/conservation-institute/services/conservation-preservation-publications/canadian-conservation-institute-notes.html; *Conserve-O-Gram* Series 13, Paper Objects, National Park Service. Available at: https://www.nps.gov/museum/publications/conserveogram/.

4. Canadian Conservation Institute, Note 10/8, *Framing a Painting*. Available at: https://www.canada.ca/en/conservation-institute/services/conservation-preservation-publications/canadian-conservation-institute-notes/framing-painting.html; Canadian Conservation Institute Note 10/10, *Backing Boards for Paintings on Canvas*. Available at: https://www.canada.ca/en/conservation-institute/services/conservation-preservation-publications/canadian-conservation-institute-notes/backing-boards-paintings.html.

5. *Conserve-O-Grams*, Series 5 (Ethnographic Objects), National Park Service; Storage Techniques for Art, Science & History Collections. Available at: http://stashc.com/; C. L. Rose and A. R. de Torres, eds., *Storage of Natural History Collections: Ideas and Practical Solutions* (Washington, DC: Society for the Preservation of Natural History Collections, 1992).

6. See R. L. Barclay, R. A. Bergeron, and C. Dignard, *Mount-Making for Museum Objects*, 2nd ed. (Ottawa: Canadian Conservation Institute, 2002); the 2012 special mount-making issue of the *Journal of the American Institute for Conservation* 51, no. 1; International Mountmakers Forum, available at: https://www.mountmakersforum.net; Toby Raphael, 1999. *Exhibit Conservation Guidelines* Harpers Ferry Center, CD-ROM (Harpers Ferry, WV: National Park Service, 1999).

7. L. Flecker, *Costume Mounting* (London: Routledge, 2013).

8. See C. L. Rose and A. R. de Torres, eds., *Storage of Natural History Collections: Ideas and Practical Solutions* (Washington, DC: Society for the Preservation of Natural History Collections, 1992)—information from this publication with additions is available at STASHc, Storage Techniques for Art, Science & History Collections, available at: http://stashc.com/; C. L. Rose, C. A. Hawks, and H. H. Genoways, eds., *Storage of*

Natural History Collections: A Preventive Conservation Approach (Washington, DC: Society for the Preservation of Natural History Collections, 1995); National Park Service, *Museum Handbook, Part I, Museum Collections*, Appendix Q: Curatorial Care of Natural History Collections. Available at: https://www.nps.gov/museum/publications/MHI/AppendQ.pdf/.

9. See S. Ogden, ed., *Caring for American Indian Objects: A Practical and Cultural Guide* (St. Paul: Minnesota Historical Society Press, 2004).

10. See Rose et al., *Storage of Natural History Collections*; *Conserve-O-Gram*, Series 11 (Natural History Specimens).

11. D. A. Metsger and S. C. Byers, eds., *Managing the Modern Herbarium: An Interdisciplinary Approach* (Washington, DC: Society of the Preservation of Natural History Collections, 1999).

12. See American Museum of Natural History and the Paleontology Portal, "Collections management." Available at: http://collections.paleo.amnh.org/; National Park Service, *Museum Handbook, Part I*, "Museum Collections, Appendix U; Section I: Paleontological Specimens" (National Park Service, 1999). *Vertebrate Paleontological Techniques*, Vol. 1 (Cambridge: Cambridge University Press, 1995).

13. See National Park Service, *Museum Handbook, Part I, Museum Collections*, Appendix U; Section II: Geological Collections (National Park Service, 1999). Available at: http://www.nps.gov/history/museum/publications/handbook.html;

R. E. Child, *Conservation of Geological Collections* (London: Archetype Publications, 1994); F. M. P. Howie, *Care and Conservation of Geological Material: Minerals, Rocks, Meteorites and Lunar Finds* (Oxford: Butterworth-Heinemann, 1992).

14. See National Park Service, *Museum Handbook, Part I, Museum Collections*, Appendix Q (National Park Service, 1999); H. Genoways, C. Jones, and O. Rossolimo, eds., *Mammal Collection Management* (Lubbock: Texas Tech University Press, 1988).

15. J. E. Simmons, *Fluid Preservation. A Comprehensive Reference* (Lanham, MD: Rowman & Littlefield, 2014).

16. See National Park Service, *Museum Handbook, Part I, Museum Collections*, Appendix Q (National Park Service, 1999).

17. See National Park Service, "Curation of insect specimens," *Conserve-O-Grams*, 11/8, 2006. Available at: https://www.nps.gov/museum/publications/conserveogram/11-08.pdf.

18. Several organizations provide additional information on collections preparation including the American Institute for Conservation and Foundation for Advancement in Conservation, available at: https://www.culturalheritage.org/; Canadian Conservation Institute, available at: https://www.canada.ca/en/conservation-institute/; National Park Service, available at: https://www.nps.gov/museum/; and the Society for the Preservation of Natural History Collections, available at: http://www.spnhc.org/. Professional organization within specific disciplines can provide more detailed assistance.

5M | Moving and Rigging Safety

DAVID RYAN (UPDATED AND EDITED BY JOHN E. SIMMONS AND TONI M. KISER)

Museums sometimes need to move large, heavy, and awkward objects, which might mean anything from taxidermy mounts to stagecoaches, unbalanced sculptures to huge paintings to aircraft, and many crates. In any moving or rigging task, safety is the most important consideration. Although the object being moved may be very valuable, there is nothing more valuable than human health and safety. The tragic death of artist Luis Jimenez in a rigging accident in 2006 reinforces the potentially deadly nature of some of these operations.[1]

Humans are all equipped with intuition; the gut feeling about things that defies explanation but should never be ignored. If something does not seem right, it probably is not. The careful move planner will trust that intuitive feeling and call an immediate halt to any moving project that does not feel comfortable or inspire confidence.

The number-one rule in moving is to leave an escape route open. It is one thing to steady a crate as it is being lifted or moved, but something else entirely to try to keep one from tipping over once it has started to fall. Always allow room to get out of the way immediately if things go wrong, and never allow any body part to be trapped between an object that is being lifted or is unexpectedly falling and an immovable surface.

Personal protective equipment (PPE) should be used when lifting and moving objects. PPE includes good quality gloves to protect hands from splinters and sharp edges, steel toe boots, a back brace when lifting heavy objects, and safety glasses when appropriate. All personnel in the vicinity of overhead lifting should wear hard hats.

RIGGING

Rigging enables the lifting of a heavy object (such as a sculpture, a piece of equipment, or a large artifact).

Outdoors, rigging usually involves a truck-mounted crane; indoors, a forklift, *chain hoist*, or *block and tackle* may be used. The hoist may be attached to an *A-frame gantry* or to a structural element of the building.

Although rigging is a special skill that requires training and experience beyond the experience of most registrars and collections managers, it is important to understand the concepts and terminology involved so that you will know when to call in the experts and be able to tell that contractors know what they are doing; when working in a remote location where only one local crane company is available, you must be able to evaluate whether the personnel can handle the job satisfactorily.

The first step is to determine the weight of the object to be moved. This information may be readily available from a shipping document, a label on the object, catalog information, or design drawings. More often than not, the weight will be unknown and must be estimated by calculating cubic footage and consulting a chart (see TABLE 5M.1) that gives the weights of various materials per cubic foot.

Based on the weight of the object, select equipment that is sized to lift the object within the appropriate safety margin. A crane or other lifting engine should be located as close as possible to the load because lifting capacities decrease dramatically with distance. A professional rigger will use a chart that calculates the capacity of the crane based on distance and boom angle to properly size the crane.

Safety margins are typically three-to-one, which means that the capacity of the lifting engine and the capacity of the slings, chains, cables, and hardware are rated at three times the actual weight of the object. Such a large safety margin is necessary because the capacity of a crane is calculated when a load is close to the body of the crane and the boom is retracted, but this capacity decreases with the distance a boom is extended and the angle that it is lowered. It

Table 5M.1 Weights of Common Materials in Pounds per Cubic Foot

Category	Substance	Weight in Pounds
Liquids	Alcohol	49
	Gasoline	42
	Oil	58
	Water	62
Masonry	Brick	128
	Concrete	144
	Concrete (reinforced)	150
	Marble	169
	Stone	158
Metals	Aluminum	165
	Brass	535
	Copper	560
	Iron	480
	Lead	710
	Steel	490
Miscellaneous	Clay	120
	Loose Earth	94
	Glass	160
	Ice	58
	Mud	102
	Wet Sand	128
	Tar	75
Wood	Oak	54
	Pine	34
	Walnut	41

is easy to make an error when calculating the actual weight of the object or the capacity of the crane with the boom extended and lowered. Although the hardware should be regularly inspected, it is possible the hardware may be overstressed or substandard and, thus, below its rated capacity. The operator might be less than smooth with the lift, putting an additional strain on the equipment and hardware; it is better to be safe than sorry.

The key to a safe lift is rigging to lift directly above the center of gravity. If the center of gravity is off to one side, the load will swing dangerously to the center when it is lifted. Any load swing of more than five degrees requires that the load be lowered and re-rigged. The center of gravity of the object should be below the *pick points* or *lifting points*; otherwise, the load will flip when lifted.

Loads are often lifted with slings. Sling selection will be based on the size and type of load. There are three basic types of slings: chains, wire rope, and synthetic webbing. In most museum settings, synthetic web slings are used because chain and wire rope slings may damage the surfaces of objects.

Alloy steel chain slings are strong but must be carefully inspected prior to each use because the individual links can become stretched, as evidenced by an inward bend in the oval of each link. Attached hooks should be inspected for cracks, twists, or excessive wear on the bearing surfaces. Chains and hooks should be free of gouges or nicks; any of these defects are cause to remove a chain sling from further service.

Wire rope slings are composed of individual wires twisted together to form strands. Wire rope slings must be visually inspected prior to use. Slings should be rejected if they have an excessive number of broken strands, show severe corrosion, show localized wear, kinks, *bird caging* (a strand that has become unwrapped and bulged outward), or damage to the end fittings.

Synthetic web slings are commonly made of nylon, polypropylene, or polyester. The advantages of this type of sling are its strength, load protection (webbing grips the load without marring the surface), and shock absorbency. Slings should be rejected if they have burned or melted surfaces, snags, tears, cuts, or broken stitches. Some manufacturers build in a red indicator layer below the surface of the webbing. This way, as the upper layer is stressed and torn, this red layer will show through (reject any sling showing red indicator fibers).

Sling angle is important. If two or more slings are attached to a central point, a sling angle less than forty-five degrees will place a great stress on the slings and hardware, reduce the rated capacity, and can be dangerous.

Occasionally a *spreader beam* is used as part of the sling setup. A spreader beam effectively distributes the load across the beam so it must be sized properly and its weight included in the weight of the load calculations.

Hitches are used with slings to attach the hoisting engine hook to the sling and to attach the sling to the load. An experienced rigger will know which hitch is appropriate to use for the job, based on the load. Sling hitches include single vertical hitches, bridle hitches, single- and double-basket hitches, double-wrap basket hitches, and single- and double-choker hitches.

MOVING CRATES AND EXHIBIT FURNITURE

Most moving projects involving crates or exhibition furniture depend on human power as the lifting engine. These moves occur frequently in a museum and require appropriate procedures and equipment to be done safely and efficiently (see CHAPTER 5B, "Object Handling").

Most traveling exhibits are housed in crates that arrive by truck, which means that the crates must be unloaded and moved to an unpacking area, then repacked and reloaded when the exhibit closes. Many museums store part of their collections off-site and regularly move objects from storage to the museum and back again. The tools most commonly used for these moves include four-wheel dollies (commonly known as *furniture dollies* or *piano moving dollies*) and two pieces of leverage equipment, two-wheeled hand trucks and J-bars.

Furniture dollies consist of two hardwood crossbars equipped with swivel, ball-bearing casters mounted on each end. Above these wheels and perpendicular to the crossbars are two padded bumpers attached on each end. The crossbars may be covered with rubber or carpet pads.

A good quality dolly is well worth the expense. Most dollies have a capacity of 800 to 1,200 pounds. A local moving company will know the source of such equipment and may be able to order them at a wholesale price. Large casters with soft rubber wheels are the best. The more uneven the surface to be traversed, the more important are larger diameter casters and softer wheels to reduce vibration and make the dolly easy to move. Small casters with hard plastic or rubber wheels will give satisfactory results only on a very smooth surface.

Padded rubber surface bumpers minimize the shifting of the load when rolling over an uneven surface or transitioning across a threshold (the load tends to shift much more under these circumstances). Carpeted dollies are designed to protect fragile surfaces such as the finish on a piece of furniture. Unless the dolly is used only for furniture, it is a good idea to provide further protection by placing additional padding between the carpeted bumper and the furniture. In a busy museum, furniture dollies are often used for crates and other objects, which may leave dirt and grit embedded in the carpet.

As a general rule of thumb, a healthy, strong human can lift no more than about one hundred pounds, but this must be done properly. Lifting should be done with the legs while keeping the back straight. Back injuries can occur when lifting as little as twenty-five pounds, if not done properly. A demonstration of correct techniques for lifting should be part of training in object handling.

The proper way to move a crate is to tip it up on one end, center a dolly underneath it, and then lower the crate onto the dolly. For light to medium crates, this is normally done with one or two people lifting one end of the crate. If the crate is heavy, leverage can be used. For example, using a two-wheel hand truck underneath the edge of the crate adds mechanical advantage to lifting. Pull back on the handle to lift the edge of the crate off the ground, but never apply more force on the handle than one person can muster to avoid overloading the capacity of the equipment. The handle of the hand truck can be pulled as far down as the floor if necessary to allow a dolly to be slipped underneath the crate. The bumper of the dolly should be placed as far back as necessary to center the dolly, with bumpers perpendicular to the crate. The dolly should be held up under the load (at an angle, with hands underneath the cross-bars) as the load is lowered down onto the dolly.

If the crate is too heavy to be lifted by one person using a hand truck, a J-bar (also called a *Johnson bar* or a *lever dolly*) may be used instead. A J-bar has a long (ca. five-foot) hardwood handle that is attached to a steel plate with a slight upward bend to it. Steel wheels are attached to each side of the steel plate. The leverage principle is the same as with a hand truck, but the J-bar has a much greater lifting capacity. If the lift does not raise the crate high enough for a dolly to be inserted beneath it, then 2 × 4 chocks (blocks of wood) can be placed under the crate, the crate lowered onto the chocks, and the J-bar inserted farther up under the crate to lift it higher.

Communication is key to the safety of moving operations. The person handling the hand truck should call out to the helpers, "Going up!" (or something similar) when lifting the crate. The person placing the dolly should wait until all upward movement has stopped before inserting it beneath the crate, then respond with "Come on down!" (or something similar) to signal the lifter to begin lowering the load. The lifter should reply "Coming down" before lowering the load.

Maneuvering crates through doorways and other openings requires particular care. Always plan an escape route in case the crate is inclined to tip (the taller the crate or piece of furniture, the more inclined to tip it will be). Steady the crate, but do not try to stop it from falling if it is on its way down. An escape route is needed for hands and fingers as well because they can be crushed by a heavy crate bumping into a doorjamb if hands are wrapped around the edge of the crate. Move carefully and deliberately to avoid these mishaps.

When the place to unload the crate from the dolly is reached, exercise the same care and attention as in lifting and placing the dolly. Be particularly vigilant about the location of feet to avoid crushing a foot or toes under a heavy crate as it is lowered to the floor. Communicate at all times to remain safe. Exhibition furniture should be moved in much the same way as crates. Common sense requires that objects be removed from exhibit cases or pedestals before they are moved.

Ideally, exhibit pedestals and portable walls should be constructed so that the cross braces that span the bottom just above the toe kick are spaced so that the bumpers of the furniture dolly fit just to the outside of the braces, allowing the dolly to be solidly locked in under the pedestal or wall when rolling it into position.

USING A FORKLIFT

Anyone who is a reasonably good driver can learn how to operate a forklift safely. Someone who is familiar with forklift operation should train other users in its safe operation. A good final exam is for the new operator to unstack and restack a pile of six *pallets* one at a time without spilling a cup of coffee sitting on the top pallet.

Unlike a car, a forklift steers from the back wheel, requiring considerable operating familiarization—a slight move of the steering wheel will produce a rather abrupt turn. This feature enables the forklift to turn in very tight and confined spaces, but also creates a tendency to wobble back and forth when traveling long distances. For this reason, and because the load may obscure the view forward, some operators choose to travel in reverse (looking over their shoulders) if moving an extended distance.

The first step in lifting something with a forklift is to adjust the width of the forks. Most forklifts have adjustable forks that slide back and forth to accommodate lift points of various widths. The forks are heavy, however, and it often takes two people, one slightly lifting the fork at the far end and the other pushing on the back end, to slide them into position.

Forklifts have two adjustments to the forks that are controlled by the operator—raising and lowering the forks, and tilting the forks forward and back. After manually adjusting the width, the next step is to lower the forks to just above ground level and tilt them forward until they are level. Drive forward slowly until the forks are under the load and the load is as close to the back of the forks as possible. The next step is to raise the forks to lift the load, making sure that the load is stable. The forks should then be tilted back slightly to ensure that the load will not slide off the end of the forks.

Never allow anyone to ride on the forks or to have their hands anywhere near the frame that the forks attach to when raising or lowering the forks. Drive to the destination slowly and carefully, with the load riding as low as possible. On reaching the destination, slowly straighten the forks to a level position, lower them to set down the load, and back out slowly. It helps to have a spotter who can tell the operator when the forks have reached a level position because the operator's view may be obstructed by the load or the front of the fork frame.

A forklift can be used in conjunction with nylon slings to lift an object from the top. In this case, the forks are pushed together and one loop of the sling is placed over both forks and pushed as far back on the forks as possible to prevent the loop from sliding off the front of the forks and to provide lift directly over the center of the object. This is most often done in an outdoor setting because the frame of the forks is usually too tall to clear the ceiling inside of a building. Beware of this height problem if attempting this type of lift inside a building.

When the driver leaves the seat of the forklift, the forks should be leveled and lowered to the ground. This precaution insures that no one will trip over the elevated forks and acts as an added emergency brake.

PALLET JACKS

A pallet jack is essentially a small, human-powered forklift. It differs in that the forks are fixed (not adjustable for width), lift only about six to eight inches off the ground, are raised by pumping the handle, and are lowered with a lever that releases hydraulic pressure. Pallet jacks are used mostly for moving pallets around indoors but are occasionally useful for moving heavy objects that are not on a pallet. A pallet jack is often carried in the back of a truck to enable the driver to roll a pallet to the back edge of the truck where it can then be lifted out of the truck with a forklift.

Pallet jacks have small diameter steel rollers that pivot down from the fork that contains them, thus raising the forks. Occasionally a pallet will be constructed with a cross-piece of wood attached under the pallet in a direct line with the wheels of the pallet jack. In this situation, raising the forks forces the pallet apart rather than raising it off the ground. The solution is to back out the pallet jack slightly until an open space is found for the wheels.

PULLING A LOAD

On rare occasions there may be a need to pull a load a short distance to gain access for a piece of equipment to do the lifting. For example, a heavy crate that is to-ward the front of a truck may have to be pulled toward the back before a dolly can be placed under it. This is commonly done with a chain or cable wrapped around the crate and pulled with a forklift. This can be a dangerous operation and requires extraordinary caution. If a cable breaks, it can recoil with such force as to cause grave bodily injury or death. The most likely path of recoil is directly back toward the source of the pulling power, but a cable can whip out to the side as well.

A cable is much more likely to recoil than a chain, so the best choice for pulling is a chain. The chain should be attached as low to the ground as possible. All personnel should be away from the path of the chain (at least 1.5 times the length of the chain). As an added precaution, a packing blanket should be draped over the chain while pulling. This will absorb some of the energy in any recoil, should it occur.

DESIGN IT TO MOVE

Inevitably, everything in the museum will move at least once (and probably more than once), so why not design things in a convenient way to move them? In the past, this was part of the design process. Large industrial artifacts, even old ones, were usually designed with moving *pick points* in mind. Large engines and motors almost always have *lifting eyes* and loops attached at convenient places. A thoughtful sculptor might design an element of the piece that can be removed and temporarily replaced with a lifting eye for lifting and moving, or a piece might be designed so that it can be moved with a forklift using slots at the base that accommodate the forks.

If given a choice, ask for all large incoming objects and equipment to be delivered on pallets. This will make the job of unloading and moving much easier.

Exhibition furniture should be designed so that it can be easily and efficiently moved. If the museum's mission calls for collecting or exhibiting large objects and sculpture, buildings should be designed to accommodate the moving of these pieces. Doorway dimensions, elevator dimensions, and lift capacities should all be large enough to make moving tasks simple and routine.

Rigging and moving are necessary tasks that all museums undertake. Because these activities hold inherent danger to people and objects, using common sense and working safely are goals that all should strive for.

GLOSSARY

a-frame gantry—A framework similar in appearance to a child's swing set that consists of an A-shaped framework on each end and a crossbar between them at the top. Used for lifting by attaching a chain hoist or a block and tackle to the crossbar.

bird caging—A defect in a wire rope sling whereby the wire strands become unwrapped and bulge outward so that they look similar to a bird cage.

block and tackle—An arrangement of pulleys and lines that increases lifting power for hoisting heavy loads.

chain hoist—A system of gears that allow a slight pull on a continuous chain to lift a heavy load with little effort.

lifting eye—A hardened steel loop that is bolted onto a piece of equipment and used for attaching a lifting mechanism to in order to lift the equipment.

pallet—A platform, usually constructed of wood, on which packages or pieces are loaded to facilitate handling. Usually the pallet is constructed so that it has space underneath it to permit lifting by mechanical equipment.

pick point—Also known as a *lifting point*. The actual point where the lifting power is applied. It can be a lifting eye or the point at which a sling is attached to the load.

spreader beam—A rigid beam hanging from a crane hook and fitted with a number of anchor points at different spots along its length; used to spread out the load when lifting. •

NOTE
1. Available at: https://www.dailyartmagazine.com/death-art-untimely-death-luis-jimenez/ (accessed June 13, 2009).

5N | PACKING AND CRATING

BRENT POWELL WITH JOHN MOLINI AND T. ASHLEY MCGREW
(EDITED AND UPDATED BY JOHN E. SIMMONS AND TONI M. KISER)

PACKING AND CRATING of art and artifacts involves numerous players. Thoughtful pre-planning, design and construction of crates, and proven packing techniques are employed to protect the objects from the rigors of handling and transit. Whether the object is traveling within the museum, across town, across country, or overseas, all parties involved must work cooperatively to ensure its safety.

This chapter offers a strong basic understanding of packing and crating art and artifacts for transport. Consultation with packing experts from the institutional, commercial, and conservation fields always should be considered to ensure all potential methods and materials are considered (see CHAPTER 50, "Shipping by Land, Air, and Sea").

RISK ASSESSMENT AND PACKING DESIGN

Ongoing technical developments in conservation studies combined with the cumulative practical knowledge of experienced museum packers have helped determine the best packing methods and safest materials to use. Registrars and commercial shipping agents have added to the knowledge about which combinations of transport and technical design will maximize safety. (See CHAPTER 50, "Shipping by Land, Air, and Sea.")

Pre-Planning Risk Assessments:
Who, What, Where, When

The registrar, in consultation with curators and conservators, conducts a risk assessment before arrangements are made for packing and shipping. This assessment entails careful and complete examination of the object, knowledge of the environmental conditions during transit, review of the facility report to evaluate when and where it will be displayed, and consideration of how the object will be mounted or installed at the final destination. These assessments determine the needs of the object and dictate the in-house or contractor personnel necessary to ensure the successful execution of these requirements.

Information gathered from the pre-planning risk assessment determines the design of the crate and internal packing. Consideration of transport options and the facility report ensures that the design, size, and weight of the crate can be easily managed by all parties involved and helps decide the type of equipment required for ease of movement and special handling or installation needs, including rigging and mounting. Storage requirements and the best method of safely unpacking and then repacking the object for its continued journey or return shipment also can be addressed. All these factors help create a budgetary picture that must be approved and supported.

Only experienced personnel with knowledge of museum standards should do the handling and packing. New materials under consideration should be researched and tested before being used with museum objects. It is imperative to understand the properties of materials, what type of protection they offer, and what type of interaction they may have with the object they are meant to protect. Improper use of materials can cause damage to the object.

Several designs and materials may be appropriate for packing a certain object. When in doubt, always seek advice from experienced colleagues or ask a conservator to review the design and methods.

When contracting with a commercial firm, take the time to establish a working supervisory dialog. Provide accurate instructions and measurements, and include drawings if a specific packing solution is required.

General Guidelines for Packing Museum Objects

Carefully examine the inherent properties of each object to ensure that it is structurally stable. If there are questions about the object's stability, consult a conservator, or seek the opinion of someone more familiar with the object.

When deciding on the design and construction of the packing and crating, keep the risk assessment in mind: who will transport, receive, and handle the object; the object and its inherent properties; the destination; and when the transit will occur.

Design crating and packing to protect the contents within the container against movement, shock, vibration, and abrasion. Scaled, waterproofed, and insulated containers must be constructed to retard and stabilize humidity and temperature fluctuations.

Build the appropriate container—case, box, or crate—to support the internal packing components for the rigor of transport. Always design the packing so that the person unpacking it can easily understand the design. Mark all removable packing components with written descriptions or related markings for the repacking of the objects. A superior design uses as few loose components as possible to minimize potential component loss and mistakes in repacking.

Document the packing methods with photographs or simple diagrams, and place these instructions inside the lid of the case or packing manual. Language-specific instructions should be considered for international shipments. Packing systems that provide superior visibility ensure more informed and safer handling.

CRATE DESIGN AND CONSTRUCTION

The standard packing crate is a six-sided box constructed to withstand the rigors of transit and protect the contents from impact, puncture, and weather. Plywood and wood are the most commonly used materials. Aluminum and particle- or fiberboards also have been used, although these materials may require special tools for cutting and may add cost and weight.

Materials

Generally, construction- or exterior-grade plywood (4' × 8', 1/2" or 3/4" thick) is used. It is relatively inexpensive, fairly easy to cut, and has acceptable levels of strength. Because formaldehyde is used in the manufacturing process, off-gassing is a concern, as is moisture. Lining the interior is recommended.

Tyvek, Marvelseal, Nomex, and plastic sheeting all work. Avoid waterproof papers; some contain tar, and all off-gas.

Medium density overlay (MDO; 4' × 8', 1/2" or 3/4" thick, also referred to as exterior or *marine grade*) has become the material of choice for many. Each sheet is coated with a waterproof paper, available on one side or two. Unlike construction-grade plywood, MDO has far less formaldehyde. That feature, combined with the paper coating, eliminates the need for a liner. Its composition resists warping, cuts cleanly, and has high and consistent levels of strength.

Wood Product Treatments

All woods, soft or hard, used in packaging and shipping must be compliant with the International Standards of Phytosanitary Measure (ISPM) 15, developed by the International Plant Protection Convention. This measure originated with the European Union in response to the spread of the North American Pinewood Nematode, an insect that causes pine-wilt disease. It states that all soft- and hardwoods must be heat treated (HT) to a core temperature of 132°F for thirty minutes. To be in compliance, all packages, crates, and cases assembled using these woods must display the American Lumber Standard Committee bug-free quality mark. This mark, more commonly known as the "bug stamp," is leased monthly to individuals, companies, and institutions based on their compliance. Compliance requires purchasing HT-marked lumber from approved lumber mills or vendors, keeping records of HT stock bought and used, and submitting to monthly on-site inspections. The stamp is required on opposing faces of assembled packages, crates, and cases. It is the only stamp recognized and accepted around the world. As an alternative to heat treatment, ISPM-15 allows fumigating cases with methyl bromide.

Manufactured woods (those manufactured with heat, glue, and pressure, such as plywood) currently do not need certification. Cases and crates made completely of manufactured wood must be marked with the letters NC (for nonconiferous) and the initials of the country of origin. For example, NC/US means nonconiferous/United States. More information may be obtained via phone or e-mail from

USDA/APHIS/Export Services, 301-734-4382 and the American Lumber Standard Committee, 301-972-1700, alsc@alsc.org.

Case Construction

Starting with the walls, the two most common construction types are simple pine planks and plywood with 1" × 4" pine battens along the edges. Pine planks are joined using a simple butt joint. Walls composed of plywood and pine can be joined using either a butt joint or a lap joint.

The butt joint is the simplest in both method and description: one edge butted against the backside end of the other edge forms the corner. A lap joint, on the other hand, requires setting the edges of the plywood and pine so that the materials "lap" over each other; plywood covers plywood and pine covers pine. Although a butt joint provides an acceptable level of strength, it can be compromised. High impact can knock it out of square or split the pine. Lap joints, on the whole, are more durable with greater levels of strength and tolerance for abuse.

Like walls, two types of lid and back are commonly constructed: a simple plain sheet or one fitted with pine battens along the edges. Battens that run horizontally, vertically, or both, depending on size and need, can be added for greater structural integrity. The lid and back can sit flush on the edge of the wall or be recessed so that, like a lap joint, plywood covers plywood and pine covers pine.

Handles and feet or skids are always recommended. While the former are obviously for lifting, the latter serve a dual purpose. Besides allowing safe and easy access for the blades of a forklift or pallet jack, skids reduce the points of contact between the bottom of the crate and the floor of a truck, thus reducing the amount of vibration transmitted during transit.

Assembly: Screws, Bolts, Latches, and Carpenter's Glue

Glue not only strengthens the bonds between the materials, but it also helps seal the joints against moisture and vapors. Running a bead of latex acrylic caulk or a silicone-based product along the interior seams provides additional protection. A word of caution: if choosing a product that contains silicone, make sure to read the label or specific material data sheets.

There are three ways to seal a crate: screws, a bolt-closure system, or one of several types of latches. Screws are relatively inexpensive and fairly durable. They are great for one- or two-way transit. They are not recommended for multivenue exhibitions. Bolt-closure systems, or variations of them, are extremely durable, especially if the bolt and bottom plate are tempered (a process that uses extreme heat and cooling during manufacturing that makes the metal strong, but not brittle) or made from cold-rolled steel. Tempered and cold-rolled steel components reduce the chances of the bottom-plate threads stripping out and the bolts snapping. Bolt-closure systems can be purchased from vendors such as Masterpak or manufactured at a local tool-and-die or machine shop. Obviously, bolt-closure systems cost more than screws, but their reusability far outweighs the initial cost.

Latch systems have the advantage of requiring no special tools to open. When properly installed, they provide a consistent and even pressure on the gasket. However, the disadvantage is compromised security. Because fewer latches are used on a crate—compared to screws or bolt closures—the gasket can be easily damaged during transit. Latches are also costly and difficult to install correctly and can break if improperly installed or handled.

Exteriors should be marked with dimensions, weight, cautionary symbols, and directional markings. Of course, a shipping label is necessary, but never list the contents of the container. Although painting the case or crate is not necessary, it does improve the appearance and provides a vapor and moisture barrier. If reusing crates, an application of a fresh coat of paint or a touch-up provides a clean surface for remarking.

Types of Crates

One-time/one-way crate. This is a simple crate for sending an object one-way only. It is usually destroyed after one use.

Two-way crate. This case is built to send the object there and back but not to withstand extensive travel.

Touring crate. This container is built to stand up to a multivenue tour, usually with reusable fastening hardware on the lid. It is built to withstand abuse from handling and is weather and, usually, water resistant.

Breakaway crate. This is a case that is built with removable sides and top, leaving a pallet with the object on it.

Slat crate. This crate uses a minimal amount of wood and does not have solid sides, which consist of slats instead of sheets. Although the sides are not solid, if needed they can be lined with poly sheeting, cardboard, or Coroplast. A slat crate can be constructed with a solid bottom of plywood with 1" × 4" pine battens along the edges supported by feet or skids (for three-dimensional [3-D]objects). Or it can be a simple pine collar with slats running vertically (for two-dimensional [2-D]works; also known as a *travel frame*). These crates can be used within a solid wooden crate, such as an end loader or breakaway, or as a stand-alone container.

Types of Internal Packing

Brace pack. This basic packing style for 3-D objects holds objects in place by simple wooden braces (typically 2 × 4s or T-braces), which are secured to the walls of the crate or inner crate. The most basic method secures the braces in place with screws driven through the outside of the crate. Better versions secure the braces to blocks permanently attached to the inside of the crate walls. It is critical to label and "key" each brace accurately to allow for proper repacking.

Cavity-pack/foam cut-out. The object fits into a space cut or made to conform to the shape of the object. Cavities can be lined with tissue or soft inert fabric.

Contour bracing/yokes/guillotines. This method generally is used for medium- to large-sized 3-D objects. Braces are made the same size as the crate's interior. Braces for smaller objects are made of Ethafoam. Larger or heavier objects require padded plywood braces. The yokes or guillotines are formed by cutting the shape of the object out of the brace and then cutting them in half. Braces generally are oriented on horizontal planes on different levels, designed to be in contact with the most stable portions of the object. The front half of the braces are held in slots created by two strips of wood or foam so that when the front of the crate is removed, they can slide out. The back part of the brace should be glued or screwed into place to help stabilize the container. To be effective, the braces must be cut accurately to avoid uneven distribution of shock to the object.

Foam-lined box. The object, often wrapped in poly or Bubble Wrap, is placed into a box lined with foam that does not fit the contour of the object; the voids are filled with material such as tissue paper, newsprint, or scraps of foam.

Double-crating. An inner container stabilizes the object by limiting or eliminating movement and providing a sub-environment. The cushioning takes place between the inner and outer containers. The outer container provides a rigid shell, and its design helps define how it will be handled.

Slot style. A traditional style of packing for multiple, usually 2-D, objects, and this method allows each object to be unpacked as needed without handling the others in the crate. Individual (usually framed) objects fit into their own slots, and the ability to move directly from crate to wall and the same in reverse makes for efficient and safe installation, minimizing handling of the object. Lining the slots with nonabrasive material that eliminates the need to wrap each individual object and minimizes handling enhances this packing technique. Larger objects generally are placed in side-loading crates, while smaller objects, especially works on paper, are usually packed in top-loading crates.

T-frame slots. This method incorporates multiple travel frames in a single crate, lowering crating costs and creating a more stable crate footprint than a single-painting crate. Travel frames make it easier to wrap large pieces in a vertical position, thus avoiding stress to the canvas when laying it flat.

Drawer or rack style. This sideways slot-style crate, in which individual boxes slide into the crate like drawers, provides a particularly effective method of packing traveling exhibitions containing many small 3-D objects. Each box can be removed individually, and its contents can represent the objects contained in an individual gallery or a case within a gallery.

Sliding tray. This style of packing uses rigid trays that slide out of a side-opening crate. Multiple slide-out trays may be placed at different heights within the same crate, or a single tray may be located at the bottom for larger objects. Especially with multiple trays, objects may be braced or strapped directly onto the tray. Single trays often are used in combination with yolk-style braces to facilitate loading and unloading.

Tray-pack. Objects, usually 2-D, are placed onto a flat tray typically made of cardboard, Fome-Cor, or Gatorboard and surrounded by foam on all sides cut to a depth slightly higher than the object. Trays then can be stacked on top of each other in a crate with the foam supporting the weight of the layers above it. Trays always should be stacked with the smallest sized or multiple small objects toward the bottom of the crate, and not the other way around. Placing the largest on the bottom puts the bulk of the accumulated trays (and weight) above the tray with the broadest span, increasing the potential for sagging.

Soft Packing

The term *soft packing* can be defined as a method of packing an object with materials that give the object structural protection without the conventional means of a hard-shell (wooden) crate. Soft-packing designs and materials usually are meant for a one-time handling or transport need, differing from the more elaborate multiple-use packing designs and materials used in museum loan or touring exhibitions.

Several types of handling needs can be met by soft-packing designs and techniques:

- internal movement of objects within a facility;
- regional shipments between different museum sites, local lending institutions, or to and from a collector's home; and
- hand-carrying airline shipments for domestic or international transit.

The decision to use soft-pack designs should not be made solely on the criteria of cost and time; a conservator, packer, and registrar or collections manager should be consulted before a final decision is made. The risk-assessment issues need to be thoroughly researched, discussed, and weighed so that all basics of safely moving the object are properly covered.

Internal Movement within the Museum

Soft packing is a convenient and effective method of transporting objects within the museum facility. Basic cardboard or plastic corrugated boxes or baskets can act as containers to handle the objects, which are wrapped or nestled within materials placed in the container. Materials need to support, cushion, and protect the objects from abrasion as the container is moved and handled. Materials commonly used include tissue, Bubble Wrap, polyester batting, polystyrene beads in plastic bags, and sand bags, to name a few.

Containers can be moved on carts, platform flatbeds, dollies, hand trucks, and pallets with ties, bracing, or strapping to secure these containers to the equipment. Equipment such as "sided carts" can be padded to make the cart a handling container. Custom-made pallets can be built that will properly support large or bulky objects.

Regional Movement among Museum Sites, Local Institutions, and a Collector's Home

Regional movements include transfers that involve a roundtrip journey that will take less than a normal working day. Because the transit will occur outside the museum-controlled environment, packing considerations will include temperature and humidity changes, shock and vibration, and the method of transportation.

If an object is subject to temperature or humidity fluctuations, buffering materials can be added to the support materials to help stabilize humidity and temperature fluctuations. Entire containers can be wrapped with polyethylene sheeting to create a vapor barrier and a sealed environment, if needed.

Object containers, such as cardboard boxes or plastic tubs, should be strong enough to be securely tied, strapped, or braced to the interior of a truck or van. Containers can be secured in a similar fashion inside the trunk of a car or securely strapped to the car seat using the seat belt or additional ties.

Hand-Carry Airline Shipments for Domestic or International Transit

Hand-carrying objects is a practice that has fallen out of favor over the last decade because of stringent security practices implemented by the US Transportation Security Administration (TSA) and other airline security operations around the world. Standard practices in the past, such as purchasing individual seats or placing hand-carry containers in overhead compartments, are no longer deemed reliable or guaranteed. Airport security or airline staff can take arbitrary measures that might remove the object from the courier's control and supervision during the flight.

However, if the object requires a hand-carry transit, the container must be structurally sound and comfortably portable for the person carrying it. The shell must be made of durable material, double-walled corrugate, or wood, or be a piece of hard-sided luggage. The protective shell will safeguard it from being crushed or broken in handling, especially if the container is moved from the courier's supervision to the cargo bay of the aircraft. The container must be designed to be easily opened, if required by airline security, and resecured for the remainder of the journey.

Creative Alternatives

Not every museum object can be nearly contained in a box or case. Due to the unique nature and size of many objects, it is often necessary to devise creative packing alternatives. Oversized objects can be addressed in several ways. The truck itself can become a container for large objects, with the loaded truck driven onto a cargo plane for shipment. Airplane pallets can be modified or specially constructed to accommodate large objects. Special cradles or supports can be constructed to transport large cases at angles that will permit them to ride steadily within airplanes or trucks. Airplane containers can be used as a protective external structure for objects safely po-

sitioned within. Containers can be delivered to the museum where museum staff can load them and design internal bracing for the contents.

Flatbed trucks often are used with simple frameworks and tarps to transport odd-shaped objects. When wrapping them is not possible, objects can be suspended within trucks or containers.

Using a sea container is similar to using the truck as the box. Objects placed inside sea containers must be braced for movement in all directions. Research standard practices in proper dunnage (that is, packing material used to cushion cargo on a ship) packing or bracing, or consult a shipping agent who is familiar with loading artworks into sea containers to determine the best methods.

Moving large numbers of objects down the hall or across town to an off-site storage facility can be addressed in a number of creative ways. Trays can be used to carry numerous objects that are either wrapped or divided from one another by padding. Trays can be stacked on moving carts that can be rolled onto trucks and secured for short trips. A variety of carts can be padded with tissue, cotton batting, sandbags, and so on, and used to transport objects. There is no single correct way to pack museum objects. Common sense and experience must apply to packing, along with keeping up on new materials and methods. Continued dialogue among packers, registrars, conservators, and vendors will help to protect collections more effectively.

Packing Materials

Materials used for packing art and objects possess a wide variety of characteristics. Understanding these characteristics and matching them with the needs of the object and the conditions under which it will be exposed are fundamental aspects of packing and object care.

When objects are particularly sensitive (e.g., metals and some kinds of photography) or will be kept inside their packaging (multivenue traveling exhibitions or packing that doubles as storage) care must be taken to use only archival materials. Most of these materials are the same ones that are listed as storage materials. For shorter-term packing (most situations), normal packing materials such as cardboard and Bubble Wrap are adequate for most objects. Under these circumstances, the next level of protection is provided simply by the correct choice of the material that comes into contact with the surface of the object as well as the quality of the barrier material used between the object and the rest of the packing materials.

Backer rod. This form of polyethylene foam is extruded into rods with a smooth outer skin. Usually round and gray in color, this material is used in the place of rolls of tissue in the folds of textiles. A white, triangular backer rod is also available for use as wedges or blocks on trays and storage mounts.

Blankets. These are packing blankets or pads commonly used by moving companies to cushion and protect the surface of furniture and other large objects. They must be clean and should be used with an intermediate material (e.g., tissue, Tyvek, or plastic sheeting) between the pad and the object itself. They are also helpful in mitigating vibration when placed under soft-packed objects. They can be reused if kept free of dirt, oils, and tape residue.

Blue board. This material is either single- or double-walled archival and acid-free cardboard. It can be used for boxes, trays, or mounts that may be built for storage as well as transit. Most common is a blue-gray color, but it is available in white and a white-blue combination.

Bubble Wrap. This common material consists of two layers of polyethylene, polyvinylidene chloride, or polyvinyl chloride films, which are quilted to create air-filled compartments. Air is injected into circles (1/4" to 2" in diameter), making bubble sizes typically 3/16", 5/16", and 1/2". It comes on rolls of different widths and lengths, perforated and unperforated. The material is inexpensive and tear resistant, but the bubbles will deflate over time. Some versions (e.g., Aircap) have an additional layer of nylon designed to prolong the life of the bubbles. Some varieties are treated to be static resistant (pink) or fire resistant (green). The bubble side of this material can leave circular marks if put next to a delicate surface and, therefore, should not be placed in direct contact with artwork.

Cardboard. Corrugated sheets come in various sizes and weights. Cardboard boxes, envelopes, and other packages can be constructed as a shell for the object. Inexpensive and easy to use, this material is subject to moisture breakdown, may be very acidic, and should be restricted to short-term use only.

Cellulose wadding. Often called Kimpak (now Versapak), this material consists of layers of soft, tissue-like paper, sometimes with a Kraft-paper backing. It is available in rolls and a variety of widths (12" to 48") and thicknesses (1/8" to 1/4"). It is not archival, but it has good cushioning and vibration-dampening qualities, especially when used in layers. Highly hygroscopic in a sealed environment, it can help mitigate changes in relative humidity. It is inexpensive and can be recycled with paper.

Corrugated polystyrene sheeting (Coroplast Polyflute). This translucent or white material may be used alone in soft packing or in combination with wood to make durable lightweight containers. Commonly used for making sides of transit frames, it is widely used for storage trays and boxes that may also function well in transit as inner containers.

Dartek. This thin, transparent, cast nylon film breathes and is hygroscopic. It can be used to wrap objects and makes an excellent see-through dust cover for objects in storage.

Expanded polystyrene (EPS) board. This form of Styrofoam is smoother and more rigid than the more readily recognized "headboard." This material comes in a variety of thicknesses in 4' × 8' sheets and is usually blue in color. It is used to provide thermal insulation in crates and boxes. It also provides some cushioning but can crush on initial impact.

Expanded polystyrene (EPS) peanuts (Pelspan). This common packing material should be used with caution, if at all. Heavy objects, especially, can shift and settle inside their containers. This disadvantage can be best mitigated by placing small quantities very loosely into bags. The thinner the material the bag is made of, the better the pellets can conform to the shape of the object—its best characteristic. The bag prevents scattering while handling, which creates static-attracting dirt and debris. This kind of material also is called loose fill. Its ability to provide cushioning is limited and unpredictable compared to foam.

Fome-Cor. This product consists of sheets of a styrene foam sandwiched between paper sheets; it comes in thicknesses between 3/16" and 2" and usually is sold in 4' × 8' sheets. This material can be used like cardboard, providing a cleaner appearance and surface, but it is more expensive. It, too, should be reserved for short-term use only, unless an acid-free Fome-Cor7 is used.

Gatorfoam. These sheets are similar to Fome-Cor but are denser and more rigid, and the facing is less prone to tearing.

Glassine. A glazed, semi-transparent paper, glassine typically is used to wrap paintings and other artwork or for interleaving works on paper. It is available in an acid-free version. It should not be reused for wrapping because creases caused by unwrapping create an abrasive surface.

Hot (melt) glue. This product is used for adhering cardboard, Ethafoam, Volara, and other packing materials in crates and boxes. Some approved types can be used for storage mounts.

Marvelseal. This material is plastic with a layer of metal suspended inside so that it acts as an extremely effective vapor barrier to protect objects from pollutants and changes in humidity. For the most effective barrier, it can be easily bonded to itself with heat. In packing, it often is used as a crate liner. It can be used in soft packing to provide a stable sub-environment for objects like works on paper. It also is used extensively in storage and display applications to protect objects from off-gassing of wood products in storage or materials used in display-case construction.

Microfoam. This material is a trademarked name for thin polypropylene foam. It can be identified by its obvious layers fused together with widely spaced "dimples."

Microfoam. This term is broadly used to refer to a wide range of polyethylene foams, such as Ethafoam 221. It has a smoother skin than polypropylene. Thinner versions may be used to wrap complex forms. Thicker versions can be used to cover padding where it comes into contact with object surfaces or as a material for tray or shelf lining.

Minicell (chemically cross-linked polyethylene). This material has the same characteristics as Volara, only it is available in greater thicknesses. Most commonly used in two-pound form, it can be used for cushioning pads or storage mounts.

Muslin. This plain weave, cotton fabric should be unbleached and unfinished or de-sized, and washed in hot water prior to use. In packing, this material is primarily used with textiles. In storage, it is used as an opaque dust cover.

Mylar, Melinex. This 100 percent polyester film is a chemically stable polymer with a neutral pH. It provides a barrier in packing to keep objects from contact with nonarchival materials and often is used in the form of envelopes or sleeves for paper objects.

Newsprint. Inexpensive and widely available, this old-fashioned material is still effective for use as dunnage (fill material) in soft packing. Crumpled up and stuffed around objects wrapped in plastic or Bubble Wrap, this material is for one-time, short-term use only.

Pellon. This is a 100-percent nonwoven polyester that is usually 1/8" to 1/4" thick. A thicker polyester batting, known as *bat garret*, is also available for padding.

Plastic sheeting (low-density polyethylene [LDPF]). This is the most commonly used plastic for wrapping artwork. Used both for soft packing and for creating a sub-environment inside boxes and crates, it provides a barrier against abrasion, dirt, and moisture. Although the common thickness for wrapping paintings is 4 ml, it is also made in 2-, 3-, and 6-ml thicknesses. "Virgin poly" is a term used for pure polyethylene containing no recycled materials. This allows for production methods that do not require the excessive use of plasticizers and slip agents (talc-like material).

Plastic sheeting (high-density polyethylene [HDPF]). This less commonly used plastic film has less stretch but greater strength per mil. Because it comes in much thinner weights, it conforms better to 3-D objects, and it places less pressure on delicate ones.

Polyethylene foam (Ethafoam, Polyplank). This is polyethylene plastic, which is expanded into foam, made up of many tiny, closed cells or bubbles filled with air. It is widely used in cavity packing objects, mounting forms, and padding in crates. It is inert as long as it is free of additives. Ethafoam is the best-known variety of this material and comes in different densities; 2.2 pounds is the most common.

Polyurethane-ester foam. This open-celled foam—usually a charcoal gray—is used for cushioning and thermal insulation. Positive attributes of this foam include superior vibration mitigation and a more forgiving cushioning curve (easier to calculate) than many other foams. Urethane foams are characteristically less chemically stable than some other foams (polyethylene, polypropylene). Breaking down when exposed to moisture, heat, and ultraviolet light, they can produce harmful byproducts. The ester-based urethane foam is more stable, however, than the similar, more common (and cheaper) ether-based foam. As a rule, avoid polyurethane-ether foams.

Silica gel. Used in packing, display, and storage to stabilize relative humidity, this form of silica (the same material that is the main ingredient of common sand) comes in granules and beads. It is composed of many open cells that create a large amount of surface area on a microscopic level. This makes it possible for it to wick away or absorb excess moisture in the air. Some gels can be conditioned to specific humidity levels to help maintain relative humidity in a sealed environment.

Stretch wrap (linear low-density polyethylene [LLDPE]). This variation of polyethylene often passes Oddy or off-gassing testing for archival stability, but because some types have a coating, it should not come into direct contact with the object. It is commonly used to hold in place packing blankets that have been wrapped around large objects. It also provides an extra layer of protection when applied to objects in some packing systems. Note: Stretch wrap should not be confused with shrink wrap, which actually shrinks with the application of heat and often is made of polyvinyl chloride (PVC), usually inappropriate for use in proximity to art objects.

Tapes

Blue painters' tape. This preferred variation of masking tape offers a higher quality, less aggressive adhesive that is less likely to tear Tyvek used in wrapping. It is more expensive but more stable than standard masking tape.

Double-sided tape. As the name indicates, this product has adhesive on both sides of the tape. Use only archivally safe varieties (3M #415) in proximity to artwork.

Duct tape. This tape is strong and easy to use; it is durable. Because it off-gasses, it should be for temporary use only.

Filament tape. This translucent, reinforced strapping tape is strong. It is good for short-term use to strengthen cardboard boxes.

Linen tape. This woven, gummed tape is pliable; the adhesive is acid free and is activated with water. Use this tape with archival board for making boxes, especially where they also may act as long-term housing for storage.

Packing tape. This economical tape has strong adhesion and a high-strength plastic back, primarily used for sealing cartons and plastic sheeting. Some versions of this common tape are backed with a PVC plastic film (an unstable material that can be prone to breakdown and off-gassing) and rubber-based adhesives, which vary considerably and will fail over time; short-term use only! Other packing tapes are backed with polypropylene and use acrylic-based adhesives. Both materials can make this a better choice for use where tape must perform over a longer period of time.

Reinforced paper tape. This gummed, water-activated product is a strong, waterproof tape that provides superior closure over the long run for cardboard boxes.

Tyvek tape. Tape with an archival, acrylic, pressure-sensitive adhesive applied to one side that can be used with archival board to make boxes.

Tissue. Tissues come in a range of types, textures, and forms—packing tissue, acid-free tissue, and buffered tissue. These vary from crisp, more structural tissue for stuffing out voids in boxes to soft "lens-type" tissues used with textiles to storage tissues used for interleaving. For packing purposes, start by looking at the physical characteristics called for (soft or stiff, roll or sheet). Consideration of chemical or off-gassing issues largely is related to the duration of exposure. It is important to consider that most packing is for the short term. Although the use of acid-free tissue in many packing applications appears prudent, such thinking must be tempered by the realization that it can also be wasteful of the limited resources allocated to object care in most museums. Of course, when dealing with artwork made of highly sensitive materials (e.g., some photographic prints or uncoated metals), refer to the product information available and check its appropriateness for use in long-term storage. Even then, realize that the best tissues must be replaced in time.

Twill tape. A 100 percent cotton, woven, nonadhesive tape that comes in different thicknesses and widths, twill tape is used for a number of purposes, most of which are related to attaching or securing parts of objects (e.g., lids or mounts) or pieces together. When used for storage, specify unbleached instead of white.

Tyvek. This spun, fiber-bonded olefin is composed of high-density polyethylene fibers that are bonded together under pressure and intense heat. It is strong and resists tearing, chemicals, and mildew. It is good for providing moisture protection and a clean surface. Although advertised as waterproof, this material breathes, preventing it from being a true vapor barrier. "Hard" Tyvek has a slick surface and can be used in storage applications and as a crate liner. Soft-structured Tyvek (or "softwrap") can be identified by a pattern of dimples that make the material more pliable. This version is used as a contact-wrapping material, to cover pads and cushion braces, and to line cavities cut into foam.

Velcro (hook-and-loop fastener). This material is a good solution for securing lids of inner boxes where they will be opened and closed repeatedly. It also may be used to secure lightweight objects in some crating systems. It is commonly sewn to textile gussets for display purposes.

Volara. This is fine-celled, cross-linked polyethylene foam with a smooth surface. It can be bonded to other polyethylene foams with heat or hot (melt) glue and often is used to pad objects where they come into contact with rough or hard surfaces. •

IRENE TAURINS

CHOOSING A METHOD OF transportation requires consideration of the museum object. This includes, but is not limited to, value, size, historical or cultural importance, condition, fragility, rarity, state of packing, crate and shipment size and weight, timetable, and expense. The best method offers the highest level over control to the object. Clear documentation and instructions must then be given to the carrier.

SHIPPING BY LAND

Types of Vehicles and Carriers

When using commercially available carriers, find a company experienced in transporting museum collections; recommendations on reputable carriers are best sought from other registrars and collections managers. If museum specialists are unavailable, moving companies which specialize in handling delicate electronic equipment, using vans with air suspension systems and climate control, are a next best alternative.

Common carriers (also called *regular route motor carriers*) are not generally used for shipments of fragile or high-value material. However, for heavy or bulky shipments of moderate value they provide an economical method, but this service usually involves considerable handling or *cross-docking*, which is the transfer of cargo from truck to dock to truck one or more times.

Types of Trucking Service Available

- Exclusive Use—This service deals exclusively with one institution's cargo, with all stops and deliveries determined by that institution. This is door-to-door delivery service. Exclusive use affords maximum control of timing and security. The registrar chooses the day, time, and route, and can make arrangements for special guards or museum couriers to accompany the shipment. This is naturally the most expensive service.

- Last On, First Off (LOFO)—Other freight may be on the truck, but the LOFO shipment is guaranteed to be the last freight loaded and the first unloaded. There is slightly less control of the timing and slightly less cost than with Exclusive Use.

- Expedited Use—With this service, the shipper specifies a certain finite range of dates during which your shipment as well as other freight is loaded on the vehicle; each shipment has a reserved space. This service is less expensive than Exclusive Use.

- Shuttle Service—This service is defined as *less than truckload lots* (LTL) or smaller space reservation with no special time or route restrictions. Shuttle service is the least expensive method and can be safe, but in some cases it may be more time-consuming. Ask for the details of the route and whether your cargo will be off-loaded or cross-docked.

Features to Consider

The major features to consider when booking a trucking service include air-ride suspension, double driver teams, and climate control. Air-ride is available on larger vans and trucks and provides a cushion of air to absorb road shocks. Double driver teams protect the freight if one of the drivers becomes ill or tired and allows the truck to be supervised at all times, including during rest stops. Climate control can include full-range temperature and humidity control where exact settings are determined by the kind of objects shipped; however, most climate control is temperature control only, which may be adequate for certain objects. Ideally the driver monitors and controls the climate from the cab. Some trucks are equipped to generate a graphic record of conditions during the trip. Ask vendors to specify what services they provide.

Another feature to consider is an adequate interior strapping or tie-in system. The truck should be equipped with sufficient furniture pads, dollies, and other equipment such as a J-bar (see CHAPTER 5M, "Moving and Rigging Safely"). The truck should also have lockable doors and a security system. If the load is heavy, if there is no loading dock, or if the loading dock at either end is inadequate, a lift gate on the truck will be needed to ease the crates on and off the truck.

Depending on the service required, it may be wise to choose a company that provides drivers who can double as handlers and packers, although not every company provides this service. This feature is particularly useful when picking up objects from private collectors who may not have the ability to pack their own objects. Other services to consider when booking a truck are extra security or the ability to accommodate a courier on the truck or in a follow car. These requests should be discussed fully when booking the shipment.

Good communication and understanding are important, both when booking and during the transit. For long distance or sensitive trips, make certain that the driver can be reached via cellular telephone and the owner or dispatcher of the company is available during off hours in case of emergency. Some companies track their vehicles via two-way satellite communications, in-route status reports, and on-board computer tracking.

Truck size and equipment availability vary among carriers. The size of the shipment may determine the choice of carrier. If the load is small in size, it may be best and more economical to transport it in smaller (*straight*) trucks or vans, which run from twelve to twenty-four feet. The smaller trucks can also be equipped with air-ride and climate control with varying degrees of sophistication. Height is often a determining factor in the size requirement of the truck; discuss your height requirements fully before booking a truck.

Some transports require larger (thirty to fifty-one feet) vans and tractor trailers. The determining factor is the size of the shipment, particularly height and volume, but other considerations include the distance to be traveled and the need for sophisticated climate control. Tractor trailer doors vary in height,

usually between 105 and 117 inches; more specialized high cube vans have an interior height up to 125 inches. To determine equipment needs, provide all shipping dimensions to a vendor before booking.

Trucking companies offering interstate transport were governed by the Interstate Commerce Commission (ICC) until January 1, 1996. Although the ICC is no longer a regulatory body, its guidelines are often still used for classifications, rules and regulations, rates, mileage guides and the services offered by the interstate moving companies. The Department of Transportation (DOT) is now the main agency that regulates safety in interstate transit. Each state also has intrastate regulations. Companies operating motor vans or trucks within a city or state are generally subject to the approval of regulatory bodies in each city and state. The conditions under which shipments are accepted by carriers appear on the bills of lading issued to shippers. It is a good practice to read the back of the bill of lading (see "Documentation").

It is also common and safe to engage non-commercial carriers, such as a museum-owned or staff-owned car, van, or small truck, to transport museum objects. The main advantage is that the handling is completely under the control of the museum. Care should be taken to balance the needs of the object against the potential hazards of vulnerable vehicles, lack of cushioning systems, and inadequate climate control. The same common rules for commercial vehicles should also apply here. For security, two people should travel in a car. It is best to have a mobile phone in case of emergency. Always let other museum staff know the full route, schedule, and itinerary. Be sure the vehicle is large enough to permit the object to ride safely; tie downs or other devices may be necessary to secure it from shifting (see CHAPTER 5Q, "Couriering").

Freight services offered by the railroads are not generally used for museum shipment because the ride on the tracks has too much vibration. The train, however, is an acceptable mode of transport for objects that can be hand-carried.

SHIPPING BY AIR

Airlines offer the most rapid means of transportation for long distance domestic and foreign shipments.

Ideally, all arrangements for the air shipment of valuable and fragile museum objects should be handled by museum personnel or by reliable agents. These personnel or agents must be able to supervise all movements from shippers to airports, through terminals, into planes, from planes, to and through terminals, and from terminals to final destinations. Supervision at cargo terminals is especially advisable to ensure the safe handling at airport assembly areas active with loading and unloading equipment.

TSA Certified Cargo Screening Standard Security Program

On August 3, 2007, President George W. Bush signed into law the 9/11 Commission Recommendations Act of 2007, the implementing legislation requiring the Secretary of Homeland Security to establish a system to enable industry to screen 100 percent of cargo transported on passenger aircraft at a level of security commensurate with the level of security of passenger-checked baggage, within three years. The impact of the 100 percent screening requirement is that all cargo must be screened at the piece level by TSA approved methods prior to being loaded onto a passenger aircraft. To help airlines reach this goal, the Certified Cargo Screening Standard Security Program (CCSSSP)[1] allows manufacturers, warehouses, distribution centers, third-party logistics providers, indirect air carriers, airport cargo handlers, and independent cargo screening facilities, including museums and fine arts transport companies, to organize and conduct this screening of cargo before delivery to the airlines. If they do significant passenger flight shipping museums are eligible and encouraged to become participants in the program. There is an application process, and approval, inspection, and training are necessary.[2]

Museums should consult their shipping agents to determine the best procedures to use to avoid the opening of crates at the airport, which may include joining the CCSSSP or having a fine arts company perform the screening in their certified facility.

Types of Aircraft

Different types of aircraft have certain limitations for carrying freight. Although *all cargo* planes afford the most control, all cargo aircraft and destinations have been drastically reduced in number and are therefore not readily available to every destination. However, the size of the freight may necessitate the use of planes with larger door openings. Freight taller than sixty-three inches high can only fit in an aircraft with main deck (the upper part of the aircraft generally reserved for passengers) cargo capacity, such as all cargo or *combi* aircraft. All cargo flights do not generally take passengers, but arrangements can be made to allow a courier aboard. Combi flights are part passenger and part main deck cargo, with doorways high enough to take oversized freight. It is generally easier to engage an agent to arrange cargo flights.

When using passenger flights, wide-bodied aircraft such as Boeing 747s and 767s, Douglas DC10s, Lockheed L1011s, Airbus 340s, and other Airbus models are best because cargo space is large enough to permit the loading of containers and pallets. Wide-bodied passenger planes can generally accommodate freight up to sixty-three inches in height. Containers are large receptacles, usually metal, of different configurations depending on the size of the aircraft. Always inspect containers before loading for holes and dents that could allow leaks. Pallets are low, portable platforms, usually metal, on which cargo is placed and built up to conform to the aircraft size. When shipping museum objects, ask the airline crew to place polyethylene plastic sheeting on the floor as well as over the entire buildup on the pallet or around the interior of the container to protect the cargo in case of rain or other inclement weather. The pallet must also be tied down with special straps to keep it stable. Beware of including potentially hazardous materials on the pallet.

Smaller aircraft, such as Boeing 707s and 727s and Douglas DC8s and DC9s, cannot accommodate containers or pallets. Cargo must be loaded loose, so there is significantly more handling and risk of mishap. Individual pieces are loaded and unloaded on a conveyor belt. If you do not have wide-bodied service to your destination, it is probably best to truck the objects rather than use air freight. If trucking is not possible, careful supervision is recommended.

Services

Air freight rates apply from airport to airport. Delivery to and from airport terminals can be arranged by the airlines at additional cost, but this is not recommended for museum collections because airport trucks do not follow museum standards (e.g., they will likely have a single driver, nonair-ride, nonclimate-controlled truck, and no means of securing the cargo within). If possible, make your own pickup and delivery arrangements or have door-to-door transportation arranged by reliable agents.

Air freight services will also arrange to transport door-to-door. There is a loss of control in this type of shipping, as freight is often bundled together with other freight, which may not be as sensitive. It is best to use air freight services for only the sturdiest and best-packed objects. If air freight is the only option, establish a good relationship with plenty of personal contact and communication.

Freight forwarders can be used for both domestic and foreign shipments to book the shipment, complete an air waybill, communicate effectively with airport personnel, and provide supervision (see "International Shipping and the Use of Agents").

Good supervision is important to assure the safe handling of objects at the airport. Supervision is necessary to be certain that a crate is properly placed in a container or on a pallet, that it is secure, and that it is not shipped with hazardous materials. Ideally, you or your agent should follow the freight onto the tarmac and witness the loading onto the aircraft. In today's high security climate, it has become more difficult to get beyond the *yellow line* at cargo terminals, and therefore, it is important that your agent have full security clearance to supervise. Full supervision includes staying at the airport until your flight is airborne for at least twenty minutes. On rare occasions flights are returned to the ground after takeoff, and someone should be available in this case.

A freight forwarding agent or cargo manager can help with flight planning as they have access to *cargo guides* with updated schedules and equipment types. Cargo managers can provide information about the availability and schedules of planes that will meet the requirements of shippers. They must be told the sizes and weights of the boxes when asked to reserve space on the desired flight.

Always book on a nonstop flight if possible. If a nonstop is unavailable, a flight with stops but without a change of plane is the next best routing. If a flight must stop en route, emphasize and receive assurances from the cargo manager that your freight will not be off-loaded. Avoid flights that have plane changes; if you cannot, it is advisable to contact an agent in the stopover city to supervise the transfer of the freight.

International Shipping and the Use of Agents
It is best to engage a customs or freight forwarder for export and import of museum objects. The proper documents are important, and communication is essential when choosing a customs or freight forwarding agent. For international shipments, museums generally engage customs brokers, freight forwarders, and cargo agents who are specially trained and licensed in importing and exporting. Customs brokers not only arrange for international transportation, but also make certain that shipments comply with all importing and exporting regulations. They prepare the documents required by the US Customs Service and the customs offices of other countries. They can provide supervision, an important service that will see the shipments through all the processes of handling and customs (see above and CHAPTER 5P, "Import and Export: Guidelines for International Shipping").

Freight forwarding agents or other specialized museum agents may provide help in arranging transportation, including pickup and delivery and, if desired, packing of museum shipments. Care should be taken to select agents who are well-informed about the policies and requirements desired by the museum.

SHIPPING BY SEA

Ocean transportation is not recommended for most museum objects because of the lack of control in scheduling and handling. For extremely bulky and sturdy objects, it may be an economical but slow solution. It is complicated by the fact that many documents are required, both by the carriers and by the governments of the United States and foreign countries. Museums generally engage ocean freight forwarders to handle these shipments.

Shipping by US Mail and Air-Express Service
Shipment by mail is not recommended for valuable or fragile objects because of transit and handling hazards,

the postal service's limitations on the size and weight of packages, and the limited value for which underwriters are willing to insure mail shipments. For small shipments of replaceable and nonfragile objects of low value, parcel post may prove economical and convenient. It is common practice, for example, to send some natural history specimens by mail. If mail shipment is used, special care should be taken to see that containers are strong enough to ensure protection from the weight of other parcels, from pressure and friction, and from climatic changes and repeated handling.

When shipping by mail, it is often best to use express mail. This method offers the fastest delivery and, therefore, the least amount of handling. The other options in descending order of preference are registered mail, certified mail, numbered mail, priority mail, and regular mail.

Air-express companies offer a wide range of services, from small air cargo agents who use commercial carriers and contract truckers to major forwarders who own their own planes and trucks. Their small package services have size limitations, which are marked on their air waybill or readily available by telephone. With good packing, this kind of service can be an effective option for transport, with the understanding that there will be a great deal of handling. The fastest service is preferable to limit handling and time spent on loading docks and in warehouses.

Other advice when using express mail service is to ship early in the week to avoid weekends. Use only services that can provide tracking and require signatures of delivery. Pack well, address the package clearly, and mark it "Fragile." Most importantly, develop a relationship with one or two local forwarding companies and try to elicit their help and understanding of your special needs.

INSURANCE, INDEMNITY, AND LOAN AGREEMENT CONSIDERATIONS

When deciding on the best shipping method to use, always keep in mind that guidelines from your insurance carrier, indemnity application, or loan agreement must be considered and honored; shipments must be properly insured. In most cases the insurance should be through the museum policy. Carriers assume only a limited liability, unless excess value is declared. A shipper making an excess declaration is, in effect, purchasing insurance coverage through the carrier (see CHAPTER 6D, "Insurance").

Documentation

The general rule of documentation when shipping is to always obtain a signature of receipt when transferring possession of a museum object. Always read what you are signing when your signature is requested. Receipts, bills of lading, and air waybills are contracts between shippers and carriers as well as receipts for the material accepted for shipment.

The bill of lading is a legal document, and your signature, in theory, releases the shipper from any liability for damages discovered at the time the cargo is received. Always examine the crate or package for any damage and never sign for a damaged package. Always use a disclaimer phrase such as "Condition unchecked, contents unknown," or "We are signing for the receipt only. By signing this document, we are not issuing a clean bill of lading." •

NOTES
1. TSA-ContactCenter@tsa.dhs.gov.

2. Available at: https://www.tsa.gov/for-industry/cargo-programs.

Guidelines for International Shipping

RACINE BERKOW

MUSEUMS AND GALLERIES, both large and small, may exchange collection objects via loans with their colleagues internationally. Once a loan has been negotiated and the terms and conditions approved, the planning must begin for the physical process of exporting and importing the objects from one country to another (see CHAPTER 5O, "Shipping by Land, Air, and Sea"). Although international loans are becoming more common for museums, there is still much confusion, misunderstanding, and lack of information about proper procedures. If the parties involved have not had previous experience with international transport, the first step might be to call a museum that has done international shipping and to ask for a referral to an international transportation agent. It is always best to contact more than one agent because this enables the museum or gallery to get competitive bids. That way you can be assured that you are getting the best services and the best price.

Information on export and the return import covered below is relevant only for the United States, and procedures may vary slightly from port to port within the United States. The information regarding procedures is subject to change, so the museum should always check with an agent to verify proper procedures at the port of entry or departure that the museum is using.

EXPORT FROM THE UNITED STATES

Imagine that Museum X (in the United States) is lending an important artwork from its collection to Museum Y (overseas). The terms and conditions of the loan have been agreed to, the object has been prepared, and the shipping date is approaching. It has been agreed that a courier must accompany the artwork (see CHAPTER 5Q, "Couriering"). Museum X has arranged for the piece to be crated by a crating company using wood-packaging material that meets international standards and has the appropriate international stamps on it. Museum X has secured the assistance of an agent to arrange the shipping or has agreed to work with the agent selected by Museum Y. To plan properly, the following information must be supplied to the agent by the Museum X:

- Schedule—When must the work be at the final destination? What dates are best for the courier, for installation?
- Airline—Is there a preference for which airline is used? Has Museum Y secured airline sponsorship? If so, what are the special instructions for the export agent?
- Crate Dimensions and Weight—This information is essential and must be correct because it determines the type of aircraft the object must be booked on and will determine the final flight schedule. For air transport, the dimensions should be given as length (L) × width (W) × height (H), in accordance with International Air Transport Association (IATA) regulations; the height should always be last. It is important for the agent to know if the crate can be turned or if it must be transported flat, and for the agent to know if it is possible to stack the crate with other crates during shipment.
- Special Requirements of an Object and Courier— Who is responsible for payment? What are the cost considerations? Is it okay to consolidate this shipment with other shipments or to send as a partial shipment? Is there a particular agent overseas that Museum Y wants to use or can Museum X's agent consign the shipment to an agent of its choice?
- Service Requirements—Museum X should inform the agent if trucking services, armed guard services, special security, or airport supervision are required. All details of the shipment should be discussed. The agent will offer guidance because the

agent should be familiar with museum protocol and the proper way to ship museum objects.

Paperwork

Cargo moves on paper. If the papers aren't correct, the cargo does not move. In today's shipping environment, most documents are submitted electronically, and therefore, the cargo is moved through the system electronically. The key points to remember are:

- *Power of attorney*—Museum X must grant its agent power of attorney (POA) to act on its behalf. The agent will supply the POA document to the museum; it should be signed, notarized, and returned.
- *Known shipper status*—Once the agent has the power of attorney and other relevant information, the agent will check within the Transportation Security Administration (TSA) system to determine whether the shipper is a known shipper as per TSA guidelines. This will help to determine whether the object must travel on a cargo or passenger plane. The agent will work with the shipper to define the status.
- *Commercial* or *pro-forma invoice*—A commercial invoice is required if the transfer of the object is for a sale. For a loan, a pro-forma invoice is required.

It is usually up to Museum X to prepare a commercial or pro-forma invoice. This invoice must contain the following information and be on museum letterhead:

- Shipper—Name and address and other contact information;
- Consignee—Name and address and other contact information;
- Inventory—artist (maker), title (e.g., object name), date, media, dimensions;
- Value;
- Purpose—For exhibition, sale, examination? For example, "for inclusion in the exhibition 'XXXX' from April 1–Sept. 30, 2019"; and
- Declaration, signature, and date.

If the object is an antique, it must be certified as being more than one hundred years of age. If for an exhibition and return, it should be so stated.

The documentation should be given to the export agent a minimum of three days prior to export. It is customary practice for the exporting agent to send an e-mail at least forty-eight hours prior to the arrival of the shipment with the pro-forma invoice, the air waybill, and a shipper's letter of instruction to the overseas agent receiving the shipment. This way, if there are any paperwork problems, they can be sorted out prior to tendering the shipment to the airline.

There are different information requirements for different countries. Certain objects require special documents or photographs; your agent will advise you on the rules and regulations. In any case, Museum X must supply its agent with proper documentation and information. After the museum has given the agent all necessary information, it becomes the agent's responsibility to book the shipment, prepare appropriate export filings, and to make the necessary arrangements with the airline to allow access to the airline's cargo warehouse. The agent will coordinate the trucking arrangements to the museum's specifications, provide security (if required), and coordinate arrangements with the overseas agent for Museum Y. The export agent may also procure the courier's ticket or make arrangements for the courier to board a cargo flight. The export agent, as needed, will also arrange security access. At this point, it is best for Museum X to allow the agent to do its job unencumbered; it becomes problematic if both the museum and the agent are calling the airline, truckers, etc.

RESPONSIBILITIES OF THE EXPORT AGENT

The export agent will work with the information supplied by Museum X in the following manner when planning the shipment:

Crate Dimensions and Weights Determine Type of Aircraft Required—If this information is not correct, your agent may not make the proper booking arrangements. Crates higher than sixty-four inches must be booked on freighters or combi (combination passenger/freighter) aircraft.

Flight and Installation Schedule—The agent will try to work within the requested schedule, but the museum must leave enough time for unforeseen events. For example, flights may get canceled, weather conditions can be a factor, civil unrest does occur, airplanes break down, and airlines may change equipment. These factors are beyond the agent's control, so allow several days leeway. Airline schedules change from month to month. Many airlines will not accept freight bookings more than two weeks in advance. It is good to start planning early, but the booking cannot be finalized until the airline schedule is confirmed and it is assured that the correct type of aircraft for a particular shipment will be utilized on that date.

Airline Facilitation. Different airlines have different rules and regulations. The export agent will do everything possible to arrange airline access for the courier to watch all the stages of placing the cargo on pallets and ramp access. It must be stressed that even though this may be the most important piece in your collection, to the airline it is only a box representing a minimum of revenue and a maximum of hassle. It is critical that the courier follow airline rules and procedures. Allow your agent to negotiate with the airline because the agent will have a working relationship with the airline and understands the airline's restrictions. The museum must not make unreasonable demands on the airline unless it is prepared to pay for them. For example, if you require the object to be secured in a particular way inside a container, or you will not allow the airline to load other freight touching your crate, you must be prepared to pay for the entire container.

Above all, it must be stressed that it is a privilege, not a right of the museum's courier, to be a guest in the airline's cargo area—this is a live operation area with heavy equipment in motion. The courier must cooperate with the airline and the agent for the move to be successful and avoid damage to the artwork or personnel.

Cargo Screening

Museums that have robust international exhibition programs and a number of fine art shipping companies often participate in the TSA's certified cargo screening program. Such museums may have been designated as a Certified Cargo Screening Facility (CCSF). In addition, there are a number of fine art handling companies that have CCSF approval. Having this designation enables objects to be packed in a secure area, and guarantees that the premises are following specified procedures, creating compliant documents, and that containers are sealed with a special security tape. As part of the CCSF certification the museum must follow specific guidelines when tendering cargo to an airline. Pre-screening is designed to eliminate the possibility of the TSA opening the crates at the airport; although pre-screening is a strong deterrent, it does not completely eliminate the right of the TSA to open the crates if they feel it is absolutely necessary to do so.

Crates can be screened by the airline on arrival at the cargo area. This is usually done by X-ray or by using a special swabbing technique. It is rare for an airline to demand that a crate from a reputable entity be opened. However, airlines reserve the right to do so.

ORGANIZING SPECIAL ARRANGEMENTS FOR THE OBJECT AND COURIER

If the agent is advised about the object's fragility or special temperature or humidity needs, then all precautions will be taken (e.g., climate-controlled vehicles for long truck rides both in the United States and overseas). If the packing is particularly complicated or the crate is difficult to manage, the export agent must make sure, in writing, that the overseas agent knows what to expect and has the proper equipment available at the foreign port. Special arrangements for the courier are another story. Your agent's primary concern is the proper handling and safety of the object. Your cargo agent will be able to supply your courier with a plane ticket and will make sure that the courier is met on the other side and has a place to stay. However, your agent does not want to be, nor should be, involved with the courier's personal agenda and vacation planning. Your agent can assist a first-time courier in doing their job, but the museum must be wise enough to select a courier with flexibility, stamina, maturity, interpersonal skills, and the good judgment not to antagonize customs, airline, and transport officials.

PAYMENT AND COST CONSIDERATION

These factors should be clearly defined in writing before the shipment takes place. As the details and parameters of the shipment change, so do the costs. For everyone's protection, it is best to have everything in writing. However, there are times when unforeseen circumstances necessitate schedule changes that may result in costly delays. Shipping is not an exact science, and the museum should have a budget cushion to cover contingency planning.

IMPORT

Eventually it will be time for Museum Y to return the loan to Museum X. All arrangements will be reversed, and there will be additional paperwork. In general, objects valued at more than $2,500 require a formal entry to be filed with US Customs. An individual or corporation may clear their own shipment but this is a time-consuming and sometimes complicated process, depending on what commodity is being imported. To facilitate the process, one often hires a customs broker.

In the case of the return of an object, proof of exportation will be required to avoid the merchandise-processing fee, which is levied on all imports by US Customs. A bond might also have to be posted. For the import agent to do the job properly, it is important that there be either a pro-forma invoice from the museum or shipping invoices from Museum Y. These documents must be transmitted to your US agent. If your institution wants to pick up the returned object as soon as it is available after arrival, the entry documentation must be submitted to US Customs prior to the arrival of the flight, but note that the entry package cannot be submitted for release until the aircraft is wheels-up (i.e., has departed from the foreign country). If the airline participates in the automatic manifest system (AMS), and all the documents are in order, the shipment will be released electronically by US Customs by the time the aircraft touches down in the United States.

The import agent arranges warehouse access, trucking, and security for the returning shipment, according to the museum's requirements. In most cases the agent can have access to the shipment between one and six hours after landing. Depending on what time the plane lands, the shipment and courier may arrive at the museum quite late. It is, therefore, important that the museum have adequate personnel ready to help unload the truck or allow the agent to hire sufficient labor to handle the shipment properly. These arrangements can be quite costly and must be included in the budget.

Qualifications for Agents

Import-Licensed Broker—The brokerage company should be licensed by US Customs. To obtain this license, the company must be investigated and meet the fiscal, organizational, and security requirements as described in the *Customs Regulations of the United States of America.* A licensed individual who has passed an examination and whose background has been investigated must be responsible for running the day-to-day operations of the company. The company must have a valid permit to operate at a particular port of entry, or be approved to file entries in any port in the United States. The company must be bonded.

Many companies perform import services in conjunction with a licensed broker. However, by law, the importer must be allowed to have contact with the broker directly.

Working with a licensed company guarantees that you are working with a corporation that meets stringent legal standards. To maintain its permit, the company must always comply with the most recent customs regulations. Should the company not perform in an acceptable manner, the client has the right to redress under specific procedures within US law.

Export-IATA Member-TSA Approved IAC (Indirect Air Carrier)—Your agent should be an IATA forwarding agent. In the United States, this means the agent has been endorsed by the Cargo Network Services (CNS, an IATA company). Although many companies arrange export through IATA agents, working directly with an IATA agent will assure the following:

- Your agents will issue their own air waybills in-house and book directly with the airline. The documents will not be issued or processed in any way by an intermediary party.

- Your agent or someone in the company has successfully passed both a written and oral examination of worldwide regulations and procedures that govern air cargo transport.
- Your agent's handling warehouse has been investigated and complies with international standards.
- Your agent meets the worldwide financial and security standards for necessary IATA endorsement.
- As a TSA approved IAC, the company must be in compliance with all TSA mandates and policies.

Other Considerations—Security Access
In the aftermath of September 11, 2001, a government agency called the TSA was established to secure passenger and cargo safety. This agency operates under the Department of Homeland Security. The TSA has been mandated by congress to implement a screening process for cargo, and it is responsible for all aspects of airport security. All TSA protocols for cargo and access within the secure areas of the airport must be explicitly followed; this is nonnegotiable. These policies and procedures change frequently, so your agent should be up to date on these policies and procedures and will guide you. In addition, there may be a TSA certified person within your institution who might be able to assist you with cargo screening.

Although regulations and criteria differ from airport to airport, your agent should have an airport identification pouch. At John F. Kennedy Airport (JFK) in New York City, for example, this means that the company and those individuals who have a Port Authority identification have been approved by the Port Authority Police to have access to some controlled areas. This identification pouch must be worn conspicuously when working at the airport. In addition, the agent should have a US Customs identification which allows access to customs controlled areas; it must be worn conspicuously in conjunction with the Port Authority identification. Having these badges indicates that the agent is bonded by US Customs and meets airport security standards. At JFK Airport, all companies having security ID must be licensed and bonded.

In some instances, it might be possible for airline access to be arranged by your agent directly with the airline. Certain airlines will only allow access under the *escort principle*, which means that they will assign an airline staff member to escort their clients while in the cargo area.

Import and export of museum objects is a complex undertaking. The agent you choose should have all the right credentials and must also meet the museum's needs in terms of quality of service and price. To accomplish this, the museum must specify what is wanted, and museum staff must be realistic about what the agent can actually do. The agent and museum must work together as a team, with mutual trust and respect for the international exchange to be a successful experience. •

5Q | COURIERING

CHERIE SUMMERS AND ANNE MERSMANN

A COURIER PROVIDES continuous oversight of an object as it is shipped from one location to another and supervises all handling to ensure that the object travels safely. The courier is usually a staff member of the lending institution, but may be an independent contractor or a staff member of a sister institution sharing the task. Whether the shipment consists of many large crates or one tiny stamp, a courier's responsibilities are generally the same. The courier is the eyes and ears of the lending institution and the guardian of the object while it is in transit. Should an incident occur which affects the condition of the object, the courier will notify the lending institution as soon as possible, so that the lending institution, in consultation with the courier, can make an informed decision about how to proceed. Upon arrival at the borrowing institution, the courier inspects the object for changes in condition and oversees its handling and installation.

There are many good reasons for museums to require a courier when objects travel: the object's fragility; monetary, historical or cultural value; museum policy; installation requirements; insurance requirements; political considerations; or simply the complexity of the shipment. During the initial stages of approval, the borrower should be advised of the need for and the purpose of the courier. Accommodating a courier imposes considerable expense on the borrower, so the decision to require a courier should be made thoughtfully. The lending institution should be sensitive to the costs and consider sharing a courier with another lender from the same area, especially if the two lenders have the same standards and agree to the shipping plans.

When selecting a courier to accompany a shipment, it is important to choose the appropriate person. There are many factors to consider and different expertise may be needed for different shipments. A good courier:

- Understands packing, crating, art handling, condition reporting, and fine art shipping.
- Has the appropriate expertise to understand the requirements of the specific object(s) being transported.
- Can evaluate situations quickly, assess risks, and make decisions displaying good judgment.
- Is diplomatic—knows when to be flexible and when to stand firm.
- Is discreet—shipment details should be kept confidential.

Cargo that is in transit should never be left unattended. A security escort, in addition to the courier, may be necessary during some portions of the transit, particularly if the courier must be separated from the shipment for any length of time.

For international shipments, the assistance of a freight forwarder or agent in booking the freight, clearing customs, and making courier arrangements is essential (see CHAPTER 5P, "Import and Export: Guidelines for International Shipping"). The services of a forwarder or agent can be useful for complex domestic shipments as well.

Couriers should carry the following documents with them:

- A recent condition report and photographs of the object along with instructions for how the object is to be unpacked and repacked.
- Copies of the loan agreement, evidence of insurance, and pertinent correspondence.
- Health certificate, permits, licenses, and pro forma, if applicable (see CHAPTER 5P, "Import and Export: Guidelines for International Shipping").
- List of representatives at borrowing institutions and their cellular telephone numbers.
- Contact information for forwarders or agents (including after-hours numbers), if applicable.

- Names, addresses, and confirmation numbers for hotels en route and at destination.
- Names and telephone numbers of and instructions for connecting with personnel meeting the courier at the destination.
- Names and telephone numbers of truck drivers and security guards involved in the shipment.
- E-ticket or airline ticket, valid passport, cash in the currency of the destination, or a museum credit card.

AIR SHIPMENTS

September 11, 2001 (9/11) has forever changed the way museum objects are transported. Phrases such as tarmac security, boarding security, and TSA were not in everyday vocabulary before this date and security requirements and systems change frequently to counter perceived threats. It is important to stay informed about these changes and how they affect museum objects in transit. A freight forwarder or agent is the best source of current information.

The truck carrying the object(s) from the lending institution to the airport, with the courier riding in the cab, should arrive at the airline cargo area well in advance of the close-out time. The courier supervises loading and unloading of the objects, checks the number and condition of the cases each time they are moved, brings any possible damage to the agent's or driver's attention immediately and notifies the lending institution as soon as possible. Couriers must respect the rules at each cargo warehouse as restrictions vary. At times, it may not be possible for a courier to stay with the shipment; airlines no longer permit couriers to cross the designated yellow line to observe the packing of a pallet or container, but the forwarder or agent should be able to observe the palletization or containerization on behalf of the courier. The agent should ensure that the crate(s) are placed on the pallet or in the container in the correct orientation and confirm that no liquids, flammable materials, or anything which might pose a risk are packed with the museum's shipment. Crates on pallets should be securely strapped down and covered completely with plastic sheeting before cargo netting secures the entire pallet. Crates in a container must be properly strapped in and all other cargo in the container must be secured so that nothing can move in transit and

impact the crate. The courier should take photographs of the loaded pallet or container including the pallet number embossed on the edge of the pallet or container number printed on the exterior of the container. If the plane is a commercial passenger flight that also carries cargo (called a *combi*), the courier will be taken by the agent to the passenger terminal to check in for the flight while the forwarder's tarmac security accompanies the shipment until it is loaded on the plane. Tarmac security and the courier should exchange cell phone numbers and confirm that calls between them connect. The courier should not board the plane until informed by tarmac security that the cargo is loaded onto the plane. A courier's ticket should be business class when traveling with a museum object.

On arrival at the destination airport, the courier should be met at a prearranged location by a representative of the receiving forwarder or agent and taken to the cargo terminal to observe depalletization (if possible) and loading onto the truck for transit to the borrower's premises. The name, cell telephone number, and (ideally) a photograph of the person meeting the courier should be provided to the courier in advance of the shipment. The courier should ride in the cab of the truck or in a follow car to the borrower's premises.

HAND-CARRIES

Only small and portable objects should be hand-carried, and case dimensions must conform to airline carry-on size restrictions. When transporting an object as a hand-carry, the courier should travel first or business class to arrive rested and ready to work. Under-seat dimensions should be confirmed with the airline in advance. If the packed object will not fit under the seat in front of the courier, the borrower must purchase a ticket for the seat next to the courier so that the object can be secured in this seat using a seat belt extension. The courier should not carry any baggage that may interfere with safe handling of the object. Avoid complicated packing as the courier may have to unpack and repack the object during an inspection at security, particularly if the object cannot go through the X-ray machine. A forwarder or agent should book the courier's travel, especially if customs formalities are required. Return travel without the object may be economy class, unless otherwise agreed.

SURFACE SHIPMENTS
(TRUCK, VAN, AND CAR)

Truck

Advance permission must be obtained from the shipping company for the courier to ride in the cab of a commercial truck. If the truck does not have an extended cab to accommodate a passenger, the courier may have to sit between the two drivers to enable the co-driver to assist with the trip. If the courier cannot be accommodated in the cab of the truck, the courier may travel in a follow car with a shipping agent or security escort. Before departure, the courier should confirm the exact route to the destination with the drivers and relate the planned route to the lending institution's staff. Before starting, the courier should verify that the cargo is properly secured, the side and back doors are locked and sealed, and the required climate control is set and will be monitored during the trip. If the shipment requires a security escort, the police of each state should be notified that a convoy is passing through their jurisdiction, particularly if firearms are carried. Cargo should never be left unattended. During rest or fueling stops the courier and the drivers should take turns staying with the truck. In the event of a breakdown, the courier should stay with the truck while the drivers work to fix the issue or obtain a replacement vehicle. If the replacement truck meets the requirements of the loan, the courier should oversee the transfer of all the crates with the same attention as when first loaded (see BOX 5Q.1).

Van or Private Car Shipments

Shipments by private vehicle or small van are convenient for smaller objects and can access locations that cannot accommodate a large truck or tractor-trailer. The courier should never be the driver of the vehicle. In the event of a breakdown, the courier should stay with the shipment while the driver seeks help. Staff using their own vehicles should have insurance that covers the use of their vehicle for official business. On arrival, the driver should wait until the courier and shipment are safely inside a secure area before departing.

BOX 5Q.1 ADVICE FOR COURIERS ON LONG-DISTANCE TRUCK TRANSITS

When arranging a transit longer than twelve hours, confirm with the shipping company that there will be a place for you to lie down. Space in truck cabs is limited and you should only bring a small bag with items needed for the duration of the transit with you in the truck. Your luggage will be secured in the back of the truck and will not be accessible to you until unloading at the destination. Wear comfortable clothes and dress in layers. On some trucks, you will be traveling in the equivalent of the drivers' home so be a respectful guest. Trucks traveling cross-country must stop to refuel, and hot food is usually available at truck stops. However, the selection may not always be to your taste so bring some healthy snacks with you. Because the transit is continuous, a traditional meal schedule is rarely followed, and sit-down meals are usually nonexistent (you will be surprised at how little you need to eat as your body gets used to sitting for twenty-three hours a day). Use judgment when drinking liquids and prepare yourself for a long wait between stops. Whenever you have the opportunity, get out of the cab, stretch your legs, and use the facilities. Bring earplugs; truck engines can be loud when you are trying to sleep.

AT DESTINATION

The borrowing institution is responsible for the courier's hotel accommodations and must provide the courier, on arrival, the cash per diem for expenses as previously agreed. All courier arrangements should be in place and communicated to the courier before travel commences, and the borrower is responsible for adjusting the courier's travel arrangements if travel conditions change or delays occur.

On arrival at the borrower's premises, the courier should inspect the location where the packed object(s) will be temporarily stored for acclimatization and assess the proposed display location and method. After the objects have acclimatized the courier will supervise unpacking and complete a thorough condition inspection, comparing the object's condition after travel with the condition report prepared prior to travel. The courier should photograph any changes in condition, record them on the condition report, and bring the changes to the attention of the borrower. If there is damage, the courier should contact the lending institution for directions and obtain a written agreement for any agreed-on treatment that may be required. Normally, the courier should observe installation, but if it has been agreed in advance that the courier does not need to oversee installation, the courier should approve the location where the object will be stored and installed. The borrower should sign a receipt of delivery to acknowledge accepting custody of the object. After the receipt is signed, the courier should inform the lending institution that the courier's duties are concluded.

RETURN SHIPMENT

The borrowing institution must make similar preparations for the return trip—secure reservations and bookings, and work out the transit details (such as trucking company, flight plans, hotel, per diem, time of departure, personnel and staff information, etc.). Such preparation ensures that the courier's work can be completed as quickly and smoothly as possible. Details and documentation should be in place and communicated to the courier before the courier departs. Courier travel without the object should be economy class unless otherwise agreed. Returning with the object(s) has the same requirements as detailed above. After the object has arrived at its destination and has been unpacked and inspected for changes in condition, the return of the borrowers' receipt of delivery concludes the borrower's responsibility for the loan.

Some tips on how to be a successful courier are provided in BOX 5Q.2. •

BOX 5Q.2 ADVICE FOR COURIERS

- The importance of being in good health at the start of a journey cannot be underestimated!
- Wear respectable, comfortable clothes and shoes, and be prepared to climb steep ladders, sweat in the sun, and freeze in a warehouse breezeway.
- Be prepared to carry your luggage up and down stairs (pack lightly). Travel with only carry-on luggage, if possible, to avoid having to wait for your luggage and inconveniencing others.
- Carry snacks and water; courier travel can be unpredictable. Planes may be delayed, and trucks may break down.
- Visit the lavatory just before boarding a vehicle. Facilities at airport cargo areas can be inconvenient and the distance between opportunities can be long, so use the facilities when they are available.
- Cellular telephones are essential for courier travel but can run out of battery power at inconvenient times. Carry a small portable charger because you may not be near an electrical outlet to charge your cell phone when the battery runs low.
- On a sheet of paper, record the borrower's contact information, agent and supervisor names and telephone numbers, hotel confirmation numbers, appointment times and instructions, as well as any other pertinent information because cell reception and internet access may not be available when you need them. Put an extra copy of this sheet in your luggage.
- No posting on social media until your cargo has been delivered to its destination! Routing details are confidential and should not be shared with anyone who does not have a need to know.
- Pay attention to the weather forecast for your destination and bring appropriate clothing. Do not forget that the time elapsed between trips to the same place could also mean a seasonal change requiring completely different clothes.
- You are a representative of your institution so be respectful and professional with everyone you encounter during transit and at the borrowing institution. Be on time for all appointments and meetings.
- Remember that the purpose of your travel is to be the courier for the object and your personal plans (business appointments or vacation days before or after courier travel) should not interfere with your responsibilities as a courier.
- Do your best to keep the objects safe but not at the expense of your safety. No cargo is worth your life.

   You can get through any situation if you have patience, humor, and a level head. Remember to keep the safety of the cargo as your top priority. Being a courier is a serious responsibility, but there are many rewards—the satisfaction of completing a shipment successfully, meeting colleagues from other institutions, and traveling to new and exciting places.

5R | Off-Site Storage

JOHN E. SIMMONS

How and where we store collections affects the way that the objects are used—the more difficult it is to retrieve an object, the more resources[1] it will take to access it, and as a consequence, the less likely we are to use it. Off-site storage can complicate this equation unless careful advance planning is done to make the collection as accessible as possible.

All too often, decisions about how and where to store collections are based on faulty economic reasoning. What may look like the least expensive way to store collections may not be the most cost-effective way to access the objects in the long run. It takes more time to find and retrieve objects in dense storage situations (e.g., tightly packed on shelves or in drawers and boxes), in tall or deep storage furniture (because the objects in front will have to be moved to reach the objects in back), or in off-site storage, whether immediately next door or across town (because you have to leave the main building and travel some distance to get to off-site storage). The further away off-site storage is, the longer it will take to get there and return. Dense storage, tall or deep storage furniture, and off-site storage all compound collection resource needs by making it more difficult to monitor object condition because it is harder to see individual objects when they are fit closely together, are high or deep in storage furniture, or require travel time, which means that the objects are more likely to suffer deterioration before the problem is noticed. The reason we have collections is so that the objects can be used, but the objects can only be used if they are easy to access in storage, properly housed and supported, easy to monitor, and kept in an appropriate environment.

In this chapter, six conceptual aspects of storage, budget, and management factors will be discussed to help guide decisions when creating and renovating storage facilities. There are no quick and easy answers to the best way to store collections, but there are ways to find a strategy that is both cost-effective and beneficial for the object.

Who?

Perhaps the most important of these questions is who will be responsible for the management and the security of the collection storage? It does not matter what the collection consists of—it could be Pre-Raphaelite paintings from England, quipus from the Andes, or specimens of unknown frog species from the central Congo—it is important to first identify who is going to be responsible for its care and management.

What level of training will the person in charge of the collection need to have, and what level of authority over where the objects go and how they are stored? It is all too common in collections to find workers who have the responsibility for the collections but not the authority to carry out that responsibility. The person in charge of the storage space should have decision-making authority over how the space is used and managed and how objects are arranged and stored within the space, particularly if the off-site storage is fairly remote from the main institution (because on-the-spot decisions may need to be made quickly in the event of an emergency).

Whether identifying new storage space or enlarging an existing storage space, if you have a growing collection or if you are about to expand your collection you also must consider whether you have enough collections care staff to handle the extra responsibility. If you do not have enough help, how do you plan to resolve the situation in the immediate future? If the staffing question is not addressed early on, it will become increasingly difficult to resolve it as time goes by.

What is often overlooked is that as a collection grows larger, the collections care staff must also increase—the larger the collection, the more objects it contains; the more objects a collection contains, the more places there are for objects in the collection storage array. A corollary to this is that with more locations for objects in storage, there are also more locations in which objects can be misplaced. In terms of collection growth, an *arithmetic increase* in collection size results in a *geometric increase* in needed collection care resources (including personnel).[2] In addition, more objects will mean more demand for objects for exhibit, education, or research purposes, which means more staff time spent retrieving objects for use and returning them to the collection storage array. In other words, if the collection size doubles, you do not need just double the number of people to manage it, you need to more than double the number of people, but in practice this rarely happens.[3]

What?

What types of collection objects need to be stored off-site, and how many objects are there to be stored? What sizes and shapes are the objects that need to be stored? Have all the objects been accessioned (see CHAPTER 3B, "Acquisitions and Accessioning")? Have all of the objects been cataloged? Have all of the objects to be moved to off-site storage been inventoried (see CHAPTER 5K, "Inventory")? No objects should be placed in storage until there is an accurate accounting of each and every one. If unaccounted for objects are moved into storage, the chance that some of them may be lost greatly increases because until the objects are accessioned and inventoried, you have no clear means to track them. Lost or misplaced objects may eventually become found-in-collection objects and it requires more resources to resolve their status (see CHAPTER 3J, "Found in Collection"). One of the most fundamental aspects of managing a collection is knowing where each and every object in the collection is at all times.

Are all of the objects properly housed and supported? Have the objects and the containers they are in been appropriately labeled? Are the objects and storage containers of consistent shapes and sizes? It is much trickier to plan storage for variable shapes and sizes than for consistent shapes and sizes. Do any objects to be moved require special handling or support (see

CHAPTER 5B, "Object Handling")? If so, this should be addressed prior to moving the collection off-site.

Only when these questions have been answered can you make a reasonable assessment of the collection care resources it will take to prepare the collection and move into the off-site storage space.

When?

How much time do you need to get the objects ready to move into storage? The collection will likely need to be inventoried, packed, transported, unpacked, installed in the collection storage array in the off-site space, and then inventoried again to make sure all objects were moved and properly placed in the collection storage array. When do the objects need to be installed in the off-site storage space? Keep in mind that your timeline may be different from timelines used by other people in the museum. For example, is the education department counting on using the objects before you expect them to be available? Is the director planning to bring the board in to see the new off-site collections storage area before you have finished installing the collection in it? It is critically important to integrate all the timelines together so that everyone is working under the same set of assumptions and expectations.

Be realistic with projects and expectations. Most pre-move estimates for packing, moving, unpacking, installing, and inventory are far too short. Allow yourself more time than you think you will need to accomplish these steps, then add in a fudge factor for dealing with the inevitable unexpected problems that will arise.

Where?

How far away is the off-site storage from the main museum building (or from the present collection storage space and the office of the registrar or collections manager)? Is it adjacent to the main building, within a mile or five miles of the main building, or far across town? How long does it take to travel between the museum and the storage space? Does it require the use of a vehicle and if so, does the museum have one available for use? If staff are expected to use

Table 5R.1 Options for Off-Site Storage

Option	Advantages	Disadvantages
Dedicated institutional space, either within the institution itself or in a building for which the institution is the sole occupant	The space can be customized for the unique needs of the collection and the museum. The institution directs and oversees all the activities in the space.	This is usually an expensive option. There may be many other institutional demands for the use of the space. If the space is within the institution, it may lack flexibility for how it is used.
Off-site commercial space that is leased in a multitenant building	This may be cost-effective, particularly for large collections. Such space is usually somewhat customizable and flexible.	The institution cannot control the activities that take place in areas adjacent to collection storage that may negatively affect the objects or disrupt the stability of the storage environment. The space may not meet security, fire suppression, or environmental requirements. Leased spaces are staff-intensive because the staff must travel from the main institution to the off-site space to access the collection.
Space leased from a professional museum storage company	The space is usually flexible in terms of use and expansion. The space may be less expensive than leasing commercial space that is not designed for collections (and thus must be retrofit). The space should meet security, fire suppression, and environmental requirements. This option is suitable for small collections. This option may save on staff resource requirements if the facility has its own staff.	Professional museum storage space is not available in all locations. Availability of space may be limited for very large collections. Long-term use of the space may be operationally expensive if the storage company requires use of their services. The space will likely be shared with other collections.

their personal vehicles to move objects back and forth to off-site storage, will the museum pay for the increase in vehicle insurance costs?

There are three basic options for collection storage space, and each has advantages and drawbacks (TABLE 5R.1). Which option is best will depend on the specific needs of the institution and the available resources.

There is a simple conceptual formula for estimating where the off-site storage space should be located:

$$\text{Access Requirements} + \text{Space Requirements} = \text{Location.}$$

For example, frequent access to the collection would argue for a location as close to the museum as possible, whereas infrequent access would mean cost savings by moving the storage location to a less expensive site. Ultimately, the space needs and where affordable space is located will drive the decision. The hidden factor in location is the long-term costs that accrue as the space is used. Short-term cost savings on location may well be offset by long-term access costs.

The conceptual formula for estimating how much space will be needed to store the collection is:

$$\text{Collection storage} + \text{Activities in the storage space} = \text{Space required.}$$

For example, will objects need to be packed or unpacked (e.g., when used for loans) in the off-site storage space, or will they be taken to the main building for packing and unpacking? Is there adequate space for inspection of the objects before they are placed in the collection storage array? Will condition report preparation or object conservation work take place in the off-site facility? Will object photography or collection registration activities be done at the collection storage site? If so, then a well-lit work table must be available with room to efficiently complete the necessary tasks, as well as electrical, internet, and telephone connections. Will there be permanent staff at the off-site storage location? Is the part of the collection being moved into off-site storage accessed frequently or infrequently?[4]

Can an adequate storage environment for the collection be provided in the space? A good way to assess this is to evaluate the space in terms of the ten agents of deterioration, a useful concept developed by the Canadian Conservation Institute.[5] Begin by investigating whether the existing storage space as well as the off-site storage space meet the standards for preventive conservation (see CHAPTER 5I, "Preventive Care"). To determine this, environmental monitoring of the spaces should begin well in advance of the planned collection move. Environmental monitoring means keeping track of the daily maximum and minimum of temperature and relative humidity, and how much the temperature and relative humidity fluctuate. Before moving the objects from one storage space to another, review and summarize the environmental monitoring data from the present space and the new space to make sure the objects are not subjected to a sudden change in the environmental regime.

Does the planned storage space need to be modified to make it suitable for collection storage? Is the floor loading sufficient to accommodate the heaviest part of the collection? Can compactor storage units be installed in the space? How big are the building entrances and interior doorways and hallways—are they sufficient to easily accommodate the movement of collection storage furniture and the objects to be stored? How large is the loading dock, and where is it located?

What activities will take place adjacent to the proposed collection storage space? Are the adjacent spaces clean areas (e.g., storage or offices) or dirty areas (e.g., laboratories, workshops, food-service areas, classrooms, apartments)? If the adjacent areas are used as dirty spaces, what sort of buffer or barrier can be used to protect collection storage from inappropriate environmental conditions and pests?

How?

How will the move be accomplished? Will you use an in-house moving crew? If so, who will do your regular work while you and the crew are packing, moving, unpacking, and installing the objects? If an outside crew will be used, who will train them and supervise them? What sizes of carts, hand-trucks, and other equipment will be needed to move the collection once it is packed (see CHAPTER 5M, "Moving and Rigging Safely")? Will the loaded moving equipment fit through all of the doorways and hallways it must go through? What sizes of vehicles are needed to transport the collection, and where will the vehicles come from? Will the loading and unloading facilities accommodate the moving vehicles?

BUDGET CONSIDERATIONS

Calculating the cost of off-site storage can be daunting, but the chief factors to consider include:

1. The initial acquisition purchase costs or a projection of rental or leasing fees over the anticipated life of the facility.
2. Fit-out costs (e.g., renovations, repairs, storage furniture, improvements to access).
3. Operating expenses (e.g., utilities, repair and maintenance, insurance, administration)

4. Staffing requirements (number of staff needed to operate the facility, whether they are based at the main institution or the off-site location, and staff supervision).

5. Move-in and move-out cost estimates.

MANAGING OFF-SITE STORAGE SPACE

Good management of an off-site storage facility begins with the contract terms for the space and staff. Although this is largely an administrative matter, the registrar or collections manager for the collection that will be stored off-site must be included in the contract considerations and negotiations to make sure that adequate provision for collection care is made.

A long-range strategic plan for managing the off-site facility should be prepared in advance of the collection move and evaluated after the move has been completed. In all likelihood, additional collection management policies will be needed to manage the facility, including policies governing facility access, use, and authorization to store and remove objects. Separate integrated pest management plans, risk management, and emergency response plans must also be prepared for the off-site facility, and these plans must be integrated with similar plans for the main building.

A comprehensive maintenance program will be required for the new space, with particular attention given to who will handle basic maintenance and who will supervise the maintenance staff. •

NOTES

1. In reference to museum collections, resources include time, money, and space.

2. J. E. Simmons, "Collection care and management: History, theory, and practice," in *The International Handbooks of Museum Studies, Volume 4. Museum Practice*, edited by C. McCarthy, pp. 221–247 (London: John Wiley and Sons, 2015); J. E. Simmons and Y. Muñoz-Saba, "The theoretical bases of collections management," *Collection Forum* 18, no. 1–2 (2003): 38–49.

3. Based on my experience over a career of fifty years, whether the off-site storage space is next door or several miles away, the objects in off-site storage tend to get neglected unless the off-site space has its own dedicated staff. Most of us have too much to do in our collections care jobs already, so when commuting between the main office and the off-site storage facility (even if it is just a short walk) is added, the result is that visits to the off-site space occur far less often than they should.

4. It is likely that your first space estimate will be wrong, so it is recommended that it be enlarged by 20 percent.

5. Available at: https://www.canada.ca/en/conservation -institute/services/agents-deterioration.html (accessed July 31, 2009).

This chapter is based in part on two sessions at meetings of the American Alliance of Museums, "Out of Site Out of Mind—Off-Site Storage of Museum Collections" (2013) and "Creating and Renovating Storage Facilities" (2016). I thank my fellow participants in those sessions for sharing their vast knowledge of off-site storage— Lisa Elkin, Heather Kajic, Christopher Norris, Robert Waller, and Christopher Wise.

PART 6 | RISK ASSESSMENT AND MANAGEMENT

6A | RISK MANAGEMENT OVERVIEW

PAISLEY S. CATO

IT'S A RISKY BUSINESS—there are so many reasons why the objects in our care are at risk that it is surprising that they survive as long as they do. However, we manage those risks to ensure the long-term survival of the objects. Risk management is an integral component of museum operations to maximize the life expectancy and usefulness of the objects and their documentation. Staff responsible for museum registration should be directly involved in formulating and implementing the strategies to minimize overall risks to the collections.

This section provides an overview of the concept of risk management as it applies to the tasks associated with registration and management of museum collections. Some of the key operations that are components of risk-management strategies not covered elsewhere in this book are described more extensively—disaster planning, security and fire systems, integrated pest management, and insurance. However, it is critical to remember that a risk-management approach applies to any task or function that involves objects, including handling, photography, applying accession or catalog numbers, and storage.

Risk management is the process of evaluating the chance of loss or damage to an object and then implementing steps to avoid, minimize, or eliminate the risk. Conservation researchers, including Robert R. Waller, Stefan W. Michalski, and others at the Canadian Conservation Institute (CCI) have applied risk analysis theories and methods to preventive conservation resulting in a number of publications that provide strategies for how professionals who care for museum collections can apply risk management methods as decision-making tools for preventive conservation operations in museums (see bibliography). The general steps in formulating a risk management approach include:

- Establishing the context;
- Identifying the risks and assessing the potential magnitude of each risk;
- Identifying strategies to eliminate or mitigate the risks as well as costs and benefits of each strategy; and
- Setting priorities and establishing a plan to implement strategies, along with periodic evaluation and revision or modification of the strategies.

Many collection registration operations are developed by assessing one or two major risks and implementing appropriate strategies. *Risk-based decision making* expands this to apply to the assessment of most or all risks and then managing the risks on an institution-wide basis. Clearly this involves not only the collection registration staff, but also many other staff positions, to be effectively implemented. As a result of this assessment process, an institution may determine the need to transfer the assumption of risk through the use of insurance. This situation occurs when the institution identifies limits on its ability to mitigate potential risks to the collections.

Risks to collections are categorized according to ten basic types, commonly called the agents of collection deterioration—physical forces, fire, water, thieves and vandals, pests, pollutants, light and radiation, incorrect temperature, incorrect relative humidity, and dissociation.[1] Each type of risk is assessed and ranked according to its potential magnitude. At one end of the spectrum is total, catastrophic loss of the collection and its value; at the other end a mild, gradual, low-level loss of value. The identification and analysis of the risks is an essential precursor to the development of mitigation strategies.

Strategies for dealing with these agents of deterioration are based on five stages of controlling risks:

- Avoid the source;
- Block the agent;
- Detect or monitor the agent;
- Respond to mitigate the problem; and
- Recover from the problem or treat the damage caused by the problem.

There are eight possible levels of control that should be considered for each stage:

1. Location.
2. Site.
3. Building.
4. Room.
5. Cabinet.
6. Object or specimen.
7. Policy.
8. Procedures.

These parameters are for a collection, resulting in a matrix of possible strategies for mitigation. The costs and benefits of different strategies are assessed relative to the priorities for mitigating a particular type of risk. This process makes it possible to set institutional priorities and create a plan to ensure the implementation of controls to minimize the overall risks to the collection.

This risk-management approach applies to day-to-day decisions as well collection-wide, institution-wide decision making. For example, is there a risk to the collection if there is a change in the brand of ink used to number an object? Identify the risk, assess the potential magnitude of that risk, identify strategies to eliminate that risk, determine the cost and benefit to implement that strategy, and establish a control to mitigate the risk.

It is important to understand the risk management framework to place other functions in perspective. Why should a museum implement an integrated pest management program? Or develop emergency preparedness plans? Or assess the extent and quality of fire and security systems? In all cases, it is to minimize the overall risk to the collections. There will be limitations on the resources a museum has available. The museum may decide to transfer some risk, through insurance, to a commercial entity outside the museum. •

Useful References

American Alliance of Museums. Developing a Disaster Preparedness/Emergency Response Plan. Available at: https://www.aam-us.org/wp-content/uploads/2018/01/developing-a-disaster-plan-final.pdf.

American Institute of Conservation. 2017. *Field Guide to Emergency Response*. Washington, DC: Heritage Preservation.

ASIS Standing Committee on Museum, Library, and Archive Security. 2006. *Suggested Practices for Museum Security*. Arlington, VA: American Society for Industrial Security (ASIS).

Cato, P. S., J. Golden, and S. B. McLaren (eds). 2003. *Museum Wise: Workplace Words Defined*. Washington, DC: Society for the Preservation of Natural History Collections.

Dorge, V., and S. L. Jones. 1999. *Building an Emergency Plan: A Guide for Museums and Other Cultural Institutions*. Los Angeles: J. Paul Getty Trust. Available at: www.getty.edu/conservation/publications_resources/pdf_publications/emergency_plan.pdf.

Elkin, L., and C. Norris. 2019. *Preventive Conservation: Collection Storage*. Washington, DC: Society for the Preservation of Natural History Collections, American Institute for Conservation, Smithsonian Institution, and George Washington University.

Faulk, W., and L. Sowd. 2001. *Collections Theft Response Procedures*. Los Angeles: The Getty Conservation Institute.

Hawks, C. A., M. McCann, K. Makos, L. Goldberg, D. Hinkamp, D. Ertel, and P. Silence (eds.). 2012. *Health and Safety for Museum Professionals*. New York: Society for the Preservation of Natural History Collections.

Layne, S. P. 2011. "An Ounce of Prevention—Worth MORE Than a Pound." *AASLH Technical Leaflet #253*. Nashville, TN: American Association for State and Local History.

Michalski, S., and J. L. Pedersoli Jr. 2016. *The ABC Method: A Risk Management Approach to the Preservation of Cultural Heritage*. ICCROM. Available at: https://www.iccrom.org/publication/abc-method-risk-management-approach-preservation-cultural-heritage.

National Park Service. 2000. Chapter 10. Emergency Planning. *Museum Handbook*, Part I.

National Park Service. 2002. Chapter 9. Museum Collections Security and Fire Protection. *Museum Handbook*. Part I.

Online Resources

American Association for State and Local History. Resource Center. Available at: https://aaslh.org/resources

American Institute for Conservation of Historic and Artistic Works Conservation Wiki. Available at: http://www.conservation-wiki.com/wiki/Main_Page.

Field Guide to Emergency Response Supplementary Resources. Available at: http://www.conservation-us.org/fieldguide#.Wk5fb3lG1hE.

American Institute for Conservation of Historic and Artistic Works and the Risk Evaluation and Planning Program. Available at: https://www.culturalheritage.org/resources/emergencies/risk-evaluation-and-planning-program.

ArtsReady. Available at: www.artsready.org.

Association of Registrars and Collections Specialists. Available at: https://www.arcsinfo.org/programs/resources.

Canadian Conservation Institute. Available at: https://www.canada.ca/en/conservation-institute.html.

Connecting to Collections Care (C2C Care). Available at: https://www.connectingtocollections.org.

Conservation Center for Art & Historic Artifacts Emergency Planning Guides and Fact Sheets. Available at: https://www.ccaha.org.

FEMA Federal Emergency Management Agency. Available at: https://www.fema.gov/.

Fact Sheets for salvage. Available at: https://www.fema.gov/media-library/assets/documents/113297.

Disaster Declaration Process. Available at: https://www.fema.gov/disaster-declaration-process.

Heritage Emergency National Task Force (HENTF). Available at: https://culturalrescue.si.edu/hentf/resources/planning-preparedness-and-mitigation-resources/.

Integrated Pest Management Working Group Museum Pests.net. Available at: http://museumpests.net/.

Library of Congress-Emergency Preparedness: Response and Recovery. Available at: www.loc.gov/preservation/emergprep/recovery.html.

Northeast Document Conservation Center (NEDCC). Available at: https://www.nedcc.org/free-resources.

dPlan (online program to build own plan). Available at: https://www.nedcc.org/free-resources/dplan-the-online-disaster-planning-tool.

Re-ORG (Resources for storage and documentation of collections). Available at: www.re-org.info.

NOTE
1. Available at: https://www.canada.ca/en/conservation-institute/services/agents-deterioration.html.

6B | Emergencies—Prepare, Respond, Recover

PAISLEY S. CATO

IF AN EMERGENCY HAPPENED today, what would you do? How would you respond? What would be your first step? What would be your next step? When emergencies happen it instantly triggers many small and many huge questions, and you need to be able to respond to them thoughtfully and effectively.

In an emergency, the safety of visitors and employees takes precedent, but the institution is also responsible for its significant assets—the objects in its care. The safety of the collections depends greatly on the degree to which staff have thought about, researched, planned for, and prepared to respond to a crisis. The impact of an emergency gets progressively worse if the event is not dealt with quickly in a productive manner. The registrar or collections manager will be directly involved with developing readiness plans and responding to the crisis and should be a primary advocate for the collections.

The primary objectives of an emergency planning process are to:

- Identify the potential risks to avoid or minimize damage in an emergency.
- Implement steps now that can minimize damage when emergencies do occur.
- Retain control when an emergency occurs.
- Mitigate damage as quickly as possible.

Surprise is often a significant factor during an emergency, and peoples' emotional reactions to the crisis can impact rational thought processes and responses. A carefully thought-out emergency preparedness plan can be the key to minimizing the impact of a disaster or crisis, with a focus on responsibilities of staff members and procedures to be implemented during and after the event.

THE PLAN

The specifics of an emergency plan must be written down and made available in multiple formats, accessible both on site and remotely. The final plan needs to be easy to read, understand, and use. Backup resources are critical, but the initial reaction to a crisis has to be fast and a good plan, with respect to both content and a readable design, makes that feasible.

A readiness plan, or emergency preparedness plan, should contain sections that incorporate the following types of content, customized for the institution:

- Potential risks

  - Identify the greatest risks and hazards to the collections
  - Identify what can be done immediately to prevent or minimize damage

- Contacts and responsibilities

  - Chain of command
  - Individual staff member responsibilities
  - Duties of the response coordinator
  - Identify the coordinator for volunteers
  - Local emergency responders (e.g., fire department, medical, police)

- Initial assessment and immediate response to the event

  - Evacuation procedures with floor plans for safe exit routes
  - Floor plans with other essential information (e.g., potential safety hazards; shut-off valves; highest salvage priorities)

- Assessment of damage

  ○ Documentation of the damage (text and images)
  ○ Salvage priorities

- Mitigation plans

  ○ How-to steps for initial responses to different material types
  ○ Resources for follow-up, next steps

- Supplies

  ○ Checklists and suppliers contact information
  ○ Locations of supply kits
  ○ Maintenance checklist

- Forms

  ○ Damage assessment
  ○ Post-disaster report forms

- Resources

  ○ Contact lists for external, specialty services
  ○ Appendices with more details for specific types of events or mitigation efforts

The mechanics of producing an emergency preparedness plan will vary from institution to institution. The process of developing a plan requires time to assess the specifics of the institution and the collection with respect to the potential risk and time to develop effective responses. Although the process may have a lead staff member, the success of the plan depends on the involvement of key staff throughout an institution during the development of the plan. There is no single one-plan-fits-all-institutions and risks, but there are numerous resources easily available to help.

The first step in creating a plan is research and analysis. Identify potential risks and hazards that are specific to your collections and institution. Use general conservation surveys, collection assessments, and external sources such as the US Geological Survey's *Natural Hazards Gateway*[1] and the Federal Emergency Management Agency[2] (FEMA) to identify these risks. Use worksheets, such as the American Institute of Conservation (AIC) risk evaluation and prioritization worksheet[3] to systematically consider the full range of possibilities. Rank risks according to their likelihood and envision the worst-case scenario in each situation. What damage would each disaster cause? If not impacted directly, would your institution be used as a community center, with a potential for collection damages resulting from that use?

Part of the research phase includes locating pertinent resources and suppliers. Resource information includes the obvious (e.g., police, fire, medical response teams) but also the less obvious (e.g., dehumidifiers, oversized fans, or refrigerator semi-trucks). Investigate the appropriate responses and mitigation strategies for the types of materials that exist in the collection because this will determine what supplies you might need after an event. Easy access to critical supplies for immediate, quick response is essential to minimizing potential damage in many emergencies. Some regions host coalitions of cultural institutions that develop caches of supplies for emergency purposes or willing staff to help in a crisis.

Identify priorities for the rescue of collection objects and documents. Although this needs to be completed collection by collection, there should be an institutional priority listing. Time is always an issue in responding to an emergency, so the tough decisions of prioritizing what objects or documents should be rescued first need to be made in advance.

Responsibilities for decision making and implementation of tasks must be clarified in advance (and communicated to the chain of command). Time will be critical; during the emergency event is not the time to try to decide who should do what. Identify which staff members will be needed to respond to a disaster and what their responsibilities and duties will be. Decide who has the right personality and skills to direct response and recovery efforts; this does not have to be, and often should not be, the museum's director. Assign specific jobs to specific people so that everyone knows exactly what is expected of them, which will help to prevent a chaotic environment as the emergency unfolds. Regardless of the size of the organization, roles that typically need to be assigned include a response leader, liaison to emergency responders, health and safety officer, security and facilities person, administration and financial support, supplies and equipment, communications, assessment, documentation, and salvage. Assigning one coordinator to manage volunteers is the most effective way to use this labor pool. Schedule training sessions to help everyone understand their role—and what they should not try to do.

The format of the final product should be a practical, useful document. A sectioned, three-ring binder allows for easy updating and easy access to content. Copies of the binder should be kept off-site as well as in the museum departments with key responding staff. In addition, there should be a small, shorter, and easy-to-reference response guide for all staff. The staff member who first responds to an emergency situation may not be a trained collections care staff person and, thus, will need to know how to handle decisions relating to the collection. Electronic copies of the plan are essential, but in the case of a power outage, hard copies are critical.

The plan should be reviewed and revised on a regular schedule, at least once each year. At the time of plan revision, the supply kits should be checked and replenished if necessary. Mock emergency drills allow staff to practice for visitor and employee safety as well as how to minimize damage to collections. The written emergency preparedness plan should always be considered a work in progress and should undergo regular evaluation and updating.

Response and Recovery

The first few hours and days after an emergency are critical to minimize damage and, just as importantly, to prevent additional damage from well-intentioned but incorrect actions. In addition to the immediate response, which might, in fact, take several days, weeks, or even months, there is a recovery phase during which salvage and mitigation activities occur. The recovery phase can take years but is marked by a consistent, controlled process with carefully thought-out actions to mitigate damage from the emergency.

A calm, orderly, and deliberate approach is key to a professional, effective staff response, regardless of the size of the emergency. Safety for staff and visitors is always an overarching concern and should be paramount throughout response and recovery. In the initial response, during evacuation, consciously and systematically look for hazards—frayed or loose electrical wires, fallen objects that might trip someone, broken glass, etc. Guide the staff and visitors away from hazards. Staff should not re-enter an emergency area until cleared to do so by professional emergency responders. Although this approach may seem to be common sense, we all know professionals whose first thought of safety will be for the objects and not the people!

Calm and deliberate should be the mantra for staff response. This helps defuse anxiety and deflect frantic, instinctive actions that often result in mishandling of objects and increased levels of damage. Rely on the chain-of-command structure and the response coordinator to plan and implement appropriate steps. Recognize that in a catastrophic emergency, access to collections may be significantly delayed. In a minor emergency, access should be delayed intentionally—long enough to assess the situation and think ahead to the next steps that are the appropriate and best response for this particular situation.

Steps in response to an emergency include:

- Implementation of emergency notifications;
- Securing of the area;
- Identification of the source of the problem;
- Notification of the insurance contact;
- Assembling the response team;
- Conducting the initial assessment for hazards and damage;
- Documentation;
- Protection of the highest priority collections;
- Stabilization of temperature and humidity;
- Planning the next steps;
- Gathering supplies and equipment;
- Contacting and initiating specialized services;
- Setting up work spaces and implementing salvage activities; and
- Documenting, communicating, and coordinating.

The chain of command should clarify which staff position is responsible for each of these steps. Everyone is responsible for regular, effective communication with other team members and for a calm, deliberate demeanor.

Implement the plans to assess and document conditions and damage and to protect at-risk collections with the highest priority. For example, this may involve covering collections to prevent further damage or bringing in specialized services for stabilizing temperature and relative humidity. This is one of several response steps for which advance research and planning will significantly increase the speed and efficiency of the response.

Based on the initial assessment of damage, knowledge of the extent and type of collections affected, and the areas of the institution affected, plan the next steps in the response to determine what resources are needed. The initial response should remove (or protect) as much of the collection as possible from imminent danger, and the recovery and salvage plan should slow or stop damage from the agents of deterioration. There is never one clear path that will solve all the salvage issues, so flexibility along with periodic reassessment is essential. Staff should receive advance training in basic methods for handling and salvaging materials to stabilize the objects, with the expectation that expert knowledge will be necessary at points during the recovery to assess the condition of individual objects and guide methods of mitigation.

Reinforce the need for continuing documentation, communication, and coordination among staff, volunteers, and administration. Salvage and recovery plans require flexibility, informed decision making, and revision as work continues. Recognizing that the recovery phase can extend for months, or even years, clear communication with administrators is critical to manage the recovery and obtain adequate resources for the work. Good photographic documentation can help with fundraising efforts as well as supporting insurance claims.

RESOURCES

Print and online references should continue to be updated to provide the most effective information for planning, responding, and recovering from emergencies. Become familiar with resources available through the Heritage Emergency Management Task Force[4] (HENTF)—cosponsored by FEMA and the Smithsonian Institution (an original member of the task force)—this is a partnership of forty-two national service organizations and federal agencies. Become familiar with the worksheets, fact sheets, and other resources created by or made available by professional organizations committed to collections conservation, and review updated information annually.

Locate practical tools that might help you develop your own plan and training—the American Alliance of Museum's *Developing a Disaster Preparedness/Emergency Response Plan*;[5] resources available from American Institute for Conservation,[6] including worksheets for risk identification and prioritization; videos for salvage response training; the *Field Guide to Emergency Response* (2017 update)[7] and *Emergency Response and Salvage Wheel*;[8] and online plans such as dPlan (Northeast Document Conservation Center),[9] and ArtsReady (ArtsReady.org).[10]

The best responses to an emergency are carried out by individuals and organizations that have completed advance research, planning, and repeated training. Resources are available to help, but it is incumbent on the institution to start long before the emergency occurs, and it is the role of the registrar or collections manager to be one of the primary advocates for advance preparations and planning for the safety of the collections. When an emergency occurs, with advance preparations, response team members can implement the plan, confident that they can respond safely and effectively. •

NOTES
1. Available at: https://www.usgs.gov/mission-areas/natural-hazards.

2. Available at: https://www.fema.gov/.

3. Available at: https://www.culturalheritage.org/docs/default-source/resources/emergency-resources/repp/repp-risk-prioritization-worksheet.pdf.

4. Available at: https://www.fema.gov/media-library/assets/documents/113297.

5. Available at: https://www.aam-us.org/wp-content/uploads/2017/12/Developing-a-Disaster-Plan-2018.pdf.

6. Available at: https://www.culturalheritage.org/.

7. Available at: https://store.culturalheritage.org/site/index.php?app=ecom&ns=prodshow&ref=FAIC-2.

8. Available at: https://store.culturalheritage.org/site/index.php?app=ecom&ns=prodshow&ref=FAIC-1.

9. Available at: https://www.dplan.org/.

10. Available at: https://www.artsready.org/.

6C | SECURITY SYSTEMS AND FIRE PROTECTION SYSTEMS

PAISLEY S. CATO

CONTROL OF SOME RISKS to collections will require a variety of security and fire detection and protection systems. In a risk-management framework, these systems are part of the museum's response to block or prevent a threat in advance; in the event that total prevention is not possible, these systems serve to help mitigate the effect of the threat.

Effective policies and procedures implemented by staff are critical to the effectiveness of security and fire-prevention systems. Physical components are essential, but if personnel do not consistently and correctly follow procedures, the physical components can be rendered useless. Although it is beyond the scope of this section to provide extensive descriptions of various systems, it is important to understand the basis for policies, procedures, and equipment for these controls. *Suggested Practices for Museum Security* (rev. 2006)[1] and *Health and Safety for Museum Professionals*[2] provide recommended practices for security and fire prevention that apply to collections and museums of all sizes

SECURITY

Identify the threats and assess the risks of loss. To safeguard collections, documentation, and associated digital assets from threats of theft and vandalism, evaluate the risks that are relevant to your institution considering its location (geographic region); the external grounds and building site, public areas, exhibit spaces, offices, work spaces, collection storage, and secure collection vault spaces. The process of identifying security risks at each level of possible control applies regardless of the size or location of an institution. With a better understanding of threats, it is possible to determine appropriate means and methods for mitigating the risks; for security threats, those methods include both human (policy, procedure) and equipment components.

Risk control begins with external facility elements—the design of landscaping and outside structures. Comparable digital firewalls need to be assessed for data security to protect electronically stored information from external hacking and vandalism. Collection care staff can identify possible threats by helping facility and security managers understand when and where objects and digital assets might be vulnerable.

At the points of ingress to the museum, whether by the front door or the loading dock, a significant element in a security system is *controlling access*—that is, controlling access and movement of people, parcels, and data. Control of who has the authority to enter and leave the building and individual spaces within the building is essential. Consider where individuals may travel within the building and whether an individual can enter an area unaccompanied or must be in the presence of others. Policies for access need to apply to all levels of staff, trustees, and volunteers as well as contractors, service personnel, and guests; they need to clarify when personnel at each level are permitted to enter and what individuals may or may not carry in and out with them. Procedures should specify how those policies are implemented.

Control of who has access to what types of data is equally essential. Data associated with objects can include information that is sensitive for financial, cultural, ecological, or geographical reasons. As with physical access, access to digital assets needs to be addressed by policy and procedure.

Security equipment can be used to implement access policies (e.g., key controls on a twenty-four-hour clock), to detect events that indicate a failure to follow policies (e.g., intrusion detection systems), and to summon police or guards should such events occur. The equipment is effective, however, only if it supports the policies and procedures and is used consistently and correctly.

In addition to security of the facility, the security of collections in transit (both to and from the museum and within the museum) must be addressed. Establish procedures to review each loan or object transport with respect to security. Consider not only the physical packing parameters but also the chain of custody that might be required; this varies greatly with the method of transport.

Internal security is secured by hiring honest people and by providing deterrence for dishonest behavior. Procedures for achieving these goals include routinely doing fingerprint and background security checks when hiring staff and volunteers. It also involves training to improve awareness among staff and volunteers of the security requirements of the collections and to learn how to handle situations involving potential security breaches. It is important to remember that most museum theft is insider theft.

An effective security system is structured to fit the individual museum, its staff, and its level of resources. Collections care staff advocate for the security of the objects and data, and implement policies and procedures; the director and trustees need to provide an adequate level of resources for equipment and training as part of their fiduciary responsibility for protecting the institution's collections.

The checklist in TABLE 6C.I enumerates a number of issues to consider when establishing security systems. The chapter in the *National Park Service Museum Handbook*, PART I, "Museum Collections Security and Fire Protection,"[3] provides an introduction to security systems based on a risk-assessment approach. In addition to further reading, staff should consult security experts and insurance representatives; both can provide assessments, information, and recommendations directly relevant to the institution.

See also the sample "Museum Incident Report" in the *Collection Forms* section.

FIRE PROTECTION SYSTEMS

Fire safety programs rely on a combination of human and mechanical components. Either one alone is not a sufficient safeguard, and each brings essential ele-

Table 6C.1 Checklist of Issues to Consider for Security System Components

Policies and Procedures

Staff authority for security program

- Staff position responsible for program
- Additional positions with collections responsibilities to assist

Access restrictions (who, where, when)

- Who has authority to determine access levels, approve exemptions
- Define levels of access for physical spaces
- Define levels of access for digital assets

Procedures to allow access

- Key control or password controls
- Opening and closing procedures of museum
- Opening and closing procedures for individual spaces

Procedures to monitor access

- Sign in and out
- Passes
- Identification badges

Procedures for inspection of packages (in and out)

- Who and where

Procedures for collections inventories and audits

- Who and when

Emergency response procedures

- Written plan, at least one copy off-site

Procedures for reporting and documenting events

- For theft, vandalism, intrusion, etc.
- For events of emergencies, disasters

Staff and Volunteers

Background security checks during hiring process

Formal security staff

- Visible, professional
- Contract agency or use in-house staff

Staff training and awareness

Drills for emergency responses

Drills to test security systems and procedures

Equipment

Purpose of equipment

- Intrusion detection
- Tampering detection
- Interruption of building systems (e.g., generators)
- Communication with people to initiate response

Types of contact systems (examples)

- Telephone
- Radio
- Remote monitoring or notification (e.g., text alerts, telephone calls)

Types of detection systems (examples)

- Magnetic contact
- Photo electric ray
- Ultrasonic
- Sound
- Motion
- Infrared
- Weight or pressure
- TV monitor or closed circuit

Maintenance and testing of equipment

ments to the program. The elements of a basic fire safety program include:

- Policies and procedures;
- Staff and volunteer training;
- Equipment selection and location;
- Regular inspections and maintenance; and
- Fire emergency plan.

Policies and procedures set the framework for a fire safety program, establishing who in the institution has primary authority for establishing and implementing the program. Policies clarify responsibilities of other staff positions as well as responsibilities for volunteers. Procedures for fire prevention and safety must identify and address all situations that may pose risks to the collections. For example, workspaces that require scrutiny include exhibit production, conservation labs, object and specimen preparation labs, research labs, staff and catering kitchen facilities, and building maintenance shops. Functional spaces including public areas, exhibition spaces, programming spaces, and collection storage facilities all need to be assessed. Simply stated, every function and space in the museum is subject to risks from fire; some are merely more vulnerable than others. Staff (and volunteers) involved with each function and space have a universal responsibility to implement procedures for fire prevention as well as have a plan for response to fires.

Staff and volunteer training must be a continuous process to minimize risk from fires and fire damage. Issues for training include:

- How to recognize and correct fire hazards;
- Good housekeeping standards to improve fire prevention efforts;
- Compliance with regulations (e.g., fire doors, use of open flames, smoking, etc.);
- How to store, use, and dispose of flammable and hazardous materials;
- How to notify fire department and museum staff in the event of a fire;
- How to evacuate the building and perform other duties in response to fires;
- Each staff member and volunteer should have hands-on practice using a portable fire extinguisher; and
- General knowledge about automatic sprinkler systems and location of sprinkler heads and control valves.

Sources for training can be found in most communities; your local fire department often has one or more individuals available to provide training for agencies in the region. Fire departments generally welcome opportunities to tour facilities that they might have to protect so as to become familiar with unique aspects of the museum.

Fire protection equipment includes detection systems, signaling (alert) systems, and extinguishing systems. Experts should be consulted to select and locate the most appropriate equipment for the facility, but collection care staff need to identify particularly vulnerable spaces or objects to be sure these are part of the assessment and design process. Selection of equipment also involves a thorough discussion of the maintenance needs over time because equipment that is not regularly maintained will not respond adequately if an emergency arises.

Detection systems respond to one or more of the following: smoke, heat, sprinkler water flow, or flames. Detection should trigger a signaling system that is monitored continuously by an individual responsible for dispatching appropriate response personnel. The *National Park Service Handbook*, part I, chapter 9, "Museum Fire Protection," includes a discussion of many types of fire detectors available.

Automatic sprinkler systems are the most common and most effective means of extinguishing a fire (TABLE 6C.2). These are designed so that only those sprinkler heads exposed to heat actually open and discharge water, a factor that limits water damage but suppresses flames. The most reliable and least expensive are wet-pipe sprinkler systems.[4] Pre-action or dry-pipe systems might be considered for spaces where freezing temperatures are possible. Other, less frequently chosen automatic systems are water mist and gas systems.

Occasionally fire-prevention efforts fail. Thus, it is imperative that the museum have a response plan to mitigate potential damage from fire, smoke, and water. Staff and volunteers need to undergo emergency drills to be comfortable with individual roles and responsibilities. Resources must be available to respond to the crisis (see CHAPTER 6B, "Emergencies: Prepare, Respond, Recover").

A fire safety program requires a staff that is aware of and trained to prevent and respond to fires. Registrars and collection managers generally do not have the primary responsibility for the safety program, but they should take a risk management approach to mitigate the risks: identify the threats, help develop policies, procedures, and training programs; and regularly implement and assess practices. •

Table 6C.2 Automatic Sprinkler System Descriptions

Wet-pipe

- Water is constantly maintained in the sprinkler pipes.
- Generally not used in spaces where the temperature drops below freezing.

Pre-action

- Air maintained in sprinkler pipes initially; water passes through pipes when detector is triggered.
- Can be used in spaces where freezing might occur.
- Requires functioning fire detection system to operate automatically.

Dry-pipe

- Pressurized air or nitrogen in the direct piping, holding back the water supply at a main dry-pipe valve
- Can be used in spaces where temperature falls below 32°F (0°C).

Water mist

- Water in pipes discharged through a valve to make a mist or fog of water.

Gas

- Uses a gaseous agent to extinguish fire either by displacing oxygen or removing heat.
- Inert gases include mixtures of nitrogen, argon, and carbon dioxide.

NOTES

1. Available at: http://www.securitycommittee.org/securitycommittee/Guidelines_and_Standards_files/SuggestedPracticesRev06.pdf.

2. C. A. Hawks, M. McCann, K. Makos, L. Goldberg, D. Hinkamp, D. Ertel, and P. Silence, eds., *Health and Safety for Museum Professionals* (New York: Society for the Preservation of Natural History Collections, 2012).

3. Available at: https://www.nps.gov/museum/publications/MHI/Chap9.pdf.

4. Canadian Conservation Institute. *Automatic Sprinkler Systems for Museums*, Notes 2/8. updated 2017-09-11. Available at: https://www.canada.ca/en/conservation-institute/services/conservation-preservation-publications/canadian-conservation-institute-notes/automatic-sprinkler-systems-museums.htm.

6D | INSURANCE

ADRIENNE REID

INTRODUCTION

Risk of loss or damage to museum objects is a perennial concern for museums. The risk could be a simple accident (such as a ceramic vase falling off a preparator's table), damage due to insufficient protections (such as transit damage), or even an unavoidable disaster (e.g., a flood or severe storm). As custodians of objects, museums must use risk management to recognize, analyze, and control these and many other types of risks. Risks can be avoided, accepted, or transferred. Some risks may be avoided by implementing protective measures (e.g., hire guards). Other risks may have levels of acceptance (e.g., known levels of transit vibration will cause damage to objects over time). Finally, there are risks that can be managed by transferring them to others through the purchase of insurance. Fine art insurance is a risk-transfer mechanism that provides a full or partial financial reimbursement for the physical loss or damage to objects.

Fine art insurance (insurance of museum collections) is purchased through an insurance broker (broker), who is licensed by each state's department of insurance.[1] The broker markets or offers the risk to various specialized underwriters, who work for insurance companies (insurer). The underwriter evaluates the risk, determines the pricing of premiums, and then takes on the risk (e.g., in exchange for the premium, the underwriter agrees to pay out the loss if there is a covered claim). The broker negotiates on the museum's behalf to ensure that the museum (insured) is receiving competitive pricing and coverage. Once the museum gives the broker its approval (bind order) to proceed with the quote, the broker binds the coverage with the underwriter, the insurance policy (policy) is issued, and the insurer is on-risk for the museum based on the policy terms. If there is a loss, the museum reports it to their broker, who notifies the insurer. The insurer appoints a qualified adjuster, who investigates and settles the loss based on the terms of the policy. Other parties, such as appraisers, conservators, and loss mitigation companies, may be involved in the claim process as well.

REQUEST FOR PROPOSAL PROCESS

When a museum is considering securing or renewing its insurance, the museum staff may decide that it is necessary to formally solicit insurance services from various brokers through a request for proposal (RFP) process. The RFP process gives brokers the opportunity to present to the museum their insurance services, company history and experience, and references. The museum may require oral presentations from the participating brokers and may call the references provided in order to evaluate and select a broker for the museum.

The RFP may include a request for quotation (RFQ) to solicit quotes from all participating brokers. If the RFQ is included in the RFP, the museum may prefer to provide a *market assignment* that requires the brokers to use only an assigned list of insurers. However, it is generally recommended that the RFQ be issued after the museum selects its broker so that the broker will have full and exclusive access to all available markets and be able to negotiate thoroughly on the museum's behalf. Once the museum has established a relationship with its broker, the broker may market the museum's policy to various insurers on an as-needed basis depending on the broker's assessment of changes in insurance market conditions.

POLICY RENEWAL

The museum should review its insurance policy annually as part of a renewal process. Typically, the review begins sixty to ninety days prior to the renewal date (policy expiration date). The broker will request updated information from the museum, such as the total insurable value (TIV) of the permanent collection and long-term loans at each location; top ten list (the individual values and details of the ten most valuable objects in the permanent collection); a general facility report[2] for each location; upcoming exhibition schedule with estimated values for each exhibition; and outgoing loans or other risk exposures for which the museum is responsible for insuring while off-site during the upcoming year. Once received, the broker will review the information with the museum and may request additional details. The broker negotiates the renewal with the underwriters for various limit options and presents the renewal quote options to the museum staff, who select the desired coverage level for the upcoming year and advise the broker of its bind order for the renewal. This process must be completed prior to the expiration date of the current policy so that there is no lapse in coverage. The broker will bind the renewal with the underwriter and send the policy to the museum.

INSURANCE COVERAGE BASICS

The insurance policy should cover any object that is in the museum's care, custody, or control, or for which the museum is responsible for insuring. This includes the permanent collection, jointly owned objects, residual or promised gifts, objects on approval for acquisition, long-term loans, and temporary loans. Objects should be defined in the policy's *property insured* clause to include collectible objects of every description, including but not limited to paintings, etchings, drawings, photographs (including their frames, glass, shadow boxes, and vitrines), rare books and manuscripts, numismatic objects, rugs, tapestries, antiques, sculpture, statuary, ceramics, pottery, porcelain, memorabilia, natural history specimens, historical objects, archeological artifacts, video artwork, packing crates, installation and reinstallation material, and technical equipment including video monitors, projectors, electronic data processing hardware and software of a nonartistic value used in association with, or as part of, an exhibit used in direct association with an installation or exhibition, and other bona fide works of art, or rarity, historic value, or artistic merit. The most important wording for the property insured clause is "not limited to" (e.g., the object type does not have to be specifically listed for it to be covered). In this way, the litmus test of *rarity, historic value, or artistic merit* is used to determine policy coverage. Electronic equipment, crates, and other installation material used in connection with the display of objects may be covered under the policy as well.

All-Risk Coverage

The fine art insurance policy is a form of inland marine insurance, derived from the earliest type of insurance available for objects that can be easily transported from one place to another. Inland marine policies can vary greatly by insurer and should be written as *all-risk* policies, such that all risks of physical loss or damage are covered, unless specifically excluded by the policy. In an all-risk policy, it is critical to understand the policy exclusions to be able to grasp the extent of the policy coverage.

Exclusions

Most museum insurance policies have only a few policy exclusions, such as wear and tear; gradual deterioration; inherent vice; loss or damage sustained due to or resulting from repairs, restoration, or retouching process; acts of war, insurrection, rebellion, revolution, civil war; seizure or destruction under quarantine or customs regulations; confiscation by order of any government or public authority; illegal transportation; and nuclear reaction or radiation. Many policies offer terrorism coverage as an option available for an additional premium charge. Depending on the location of the museum, the policy may have coverage restrictions or exclusions relating to earthquake, windstorm, flood, or other catastrophic events.

Valuation

Most museum insurance policies have two main clauses of valuation—valuation of the permanent collection and valuation of property belonging to others (loans). The permanent collection valuation clause should be the purchase price or current market value, whichever is greater. If there is a claim, the loss adjuster will ask the museum to provide documentation from inventory records regarding the most recent value of the object. At times, the value in the museum's inventory is either outdated or not available. If this is the case, a third-party appraiser will be assigned to appraise the object after the fact, based on the photographs and records that the museum can provide. Although seeking updated appraisals for the entire collection may not be feasible for the museum, it is strongly recommended that the museum obtain regularly updated values on at least the highest valued or most important objects in the collection. It is also a good practice to get an updated value whenever an object is requested for an outgoing loan.

For loans to the museum, the valuation method should be *agreed value*, based on the value provided by the lender on the loan agreement and countersigned by the museum. The museum is not expected to appraise the objects or verify the accuracy of the lender's values. However, if the lender provides a value that is extraordinary, the museum may ask the lender for documentation to validate the value prior to countersigning the agreement. Because the agreed value is the payoff value used in the event of a total loss claim, the values should be realistic and accurate. In all cases, it is important that all objects have an agreed value in the loan agreement and to not leave the value section blank or agree to pay current market value. This helps significantly in the claim process by avoiding possible disputes, which can prolong a claim and cause aggravation to all parties. Loan agreements should be updated and re-signed regularly (avoiding long-term loans) so that the lender's agreed value remains accurate based on current market conditions.

Partial versus Total Loss

When a claim is made, the loss adjuster will determine if the claim is a partial or total loss of the damaged object. In the case of a partial loss, the policy will pay for the costs of repair or restoration and any resulting loss in value after restoration, as agreed between the museum (or lender) and the insurer. In the case of a total loss, the full value of the object is paid by the insurer and the damaged object (called *salvage*) is either destroyed or is transferred to the insurer. The museum may be able to buy back the salvage from the insurer if it believes there is still some merit in keeping the object in the collection. The policy may include special clauses that allow certain sovereign interests to retain the damaged object even if a total loss is paid, due to the national patrimony and national importance of the object. Check with your broker if you see this requirement in a loan agreement.

Policy Limits

The insurance policy will be written with specific maximum payout limits for losses while the object is on premises, in transit, or at other locations. Usually these limits are written on a per-occurrence basis, meaning that the limit is the most the insurer will pay in any one event or disaster. The museum's limits may be considered *blanket*, and as such, claim payments will be allocated as needed in the event of a catastrophic loss that affects both the permanent collection and loans.

Premises Limit Determination

Insurance must be purchased to cover all loaned objects in the museum's care, custody, or control for which the museum is responsible for insuring. The total value of loans at any given time throughout the year should serve as the baseline for the museum when determining what *policy premises limit* it needs for the coverage year. Beyond this baseline, the museum can determine how much additional coverage it will purchase to protect the permanent collection. The museum limit determination can vary greatly depending on a number of factors, including the spread of total artwork value throughout the building(s), galleries, storage, or off-site locations; the museum's internal risk tolerance level (which may be determined by the board or director); the museum's geographic location and susceptibility to natural catastrophic events (e.g., hurricanes or earthquakes); and the concentration of value in its individual highest valued objects versus the rest of the collection. Although a museum may choose not to purchase a policy limit that reflects its collection's total value, all museums should have an educated and thoughtful means of determining what policy limit they are comfortable with for each policy year. Avoid using a straight percentage of permanent collection total value to determine the policy limit; this method is arbitrary and irresponsible because it does not account for concentration of value in various locations in the museum or the museum's exhibition schedule.

Museums may determine their policy premises limit by evaluating their probable maximum loss (PML) scenario as defined by the museum administration. The PML is generally defined as the largest loss that could result from a covered disaster (e.g., fire, flood), assuming the normal functioning of protective features (e.g., firewalls, security system) and proper functioning of most (perhaps not all) active suppression systems (e.g., sprinklers). For example, the destruction of a storage vault, a specific high value gallery, or a wing of the museum may be used to estimate PML. When calculating this figure, it is important to remember that all property owned by others for which there is a binding loan agreement (requiring the museum to maintain insurance coverage) will account for the first payment in the event of a catastrophic loss. Examine the PML estimates frequently, especially in times of rapid collection growth, museum construction, volatile markets, or increased exhibition activity. A policy limit sufficient for the museum's PML a decade ago may be absorbed by a single object today.

It may be necessary once or twice a year to increase the policy limits temporarily for a high value incoming exhibition or decrease the policy limits due to a higher value outgoing loan from the permanent collection. Depending on the length of the exhibition or loan, it may make more sense to change the policy limit for the entire coverage year rather than making a short-term change. Review the policy limit with the museum's broker in advance to determine when and how much limit change may be needed.

Transit and Any Other Location Limits
The museum's insurance policy should include a limit on insurance coverage for objects in transit. Examine the museum's transit history and total values by conveyance to determine what transit limit is needed for the coverage year. Typically, insurers will automatically include a transit limit that is a percentage of the premises limit. Similarly, the policy should include a limit for off-premises or any other location coverage. This limit is intended to cover temporary exposure

at other locations that are not listed in the policy. If objects will be at another location for an extended period of time, ask your broker if the location should be added to the policy. Keep your broker updated, especially if the museum is responsible for insuring objects at other locations in high-risk areas (e.g., high-risk seismic zones or coastal areas) because your insurer may have internal underwriting restrictions in those areas and must keep track of total exposure aggregations. As always, a high level of communication and disclosure to your broker is vital. Check the territorial limits of the policy to determine whether the transit and other location coverage is worldwide or restricted to the United States and Canada.

Acceptance of Risk—Objects Belonging to Others That Are in the Museum's Care
When negotiating loans pay close attention to the terms of the loan agreement, particularly regarding the museum's liability and insurance responsibility. Ideally, the insurance section should perfectly align with the museum's insurance coverage and limit the museum's liability to what is paid by insurance. When a loan agreement is signed that holds the museum responsible for any loss or damage, the museum makes itself directly financially liable for losses that may not be covered by its insurance. This is called *absolute liability* and should be avoided. Consult your museum's administrators for a proper course of action if this is required by a potential lender.

If the museum has a high value incoming exhibition, it may be advisable to apply for the US government's Arts and Artifacts Indemnity, which is administered by the National Endowment for the Arts.[3] The Indemnity Program was created by congress in 1975 to help minimize the costs of insuring museum exhibitions. The museum must adhere to specific guidelines and protective measures and apply to the program during set application periods. Once approved for the indemnity coverage, the specific objects in the exhibition are covered for physical loss or damage (subject to limited exclusions) by the faith and credit of the US government. Based on the medium of the object, the values submitted, and other factors, the indemnity coverage may be for the full loan agreement value of an object; a value less than the loan agreement value; or it may not cover specific objects at all. In cases where there is a shortage between indemnity coverage and the exhibition's total value, the museum should use its insurance policy or a separate exhibition insurance policy to cover the difference in value. The museum's policy should also cover the indemnity deductible, which is variable, based on the total indemnified value.

Transfer of Risk—Objects Located Outside of the Museum's Care

When objects are outside of the museum's care, custody, or control, the museum should transfer the risk by either requiring the other party (e.g., the borrower) to insure them or by purchasing a separate exhibition policy. It is most appropriate that the party that has care, custody, or control of the object be the party responsible for insurance. This insurance responsibility should be clearly defined in the loan agreement. Review the borrower's insurance terms carefully and require a *certificate of insurance* prior to the object departing the museum. If the borrower does not have insurance coverage acceptable to you as the lender, require the borrower to pay for a separate exhibition policy to cover the object so that the museum can be assured of sufficient and proper insurance coverage.

In the case of a multivenue traveling exhibition, it is ideal to purchase a separate *wall-to-wall* exhibition policy that covers the exhibition for the entire tour (during all transits and at all venues). This method of coverage simplifies the insurance so that the lender gets only one certificate of insurance (if requested), ensures that there is no confusion or dispute over who is responsible for insuring at any point in time, and allows the venues to divide the insurance costs according to their respective portions of the tour. However, if this option is not economically feasible, the individual venues may consider providing insurance by using their respective policies to cover their portion of the tour. It is critical that the insurance responsibility for each venue be clearly defined in the exhibition and loan agreements and that the transfer of insurance responsibility takes place at the time of condition reporting on packing or unpacking the objects.

CLAIMS PROCESS

When an unfortunate event occurs and an object is lost or damaged, clear and concise reporting procedures are critical to ensure a smooth claim process. The museum should have on hand the policy's claim reporting form, which will list the pertinent information needed to report a claim to the insurer. Gather the information and put it in writing as soon as possible. Take photographs of the damage, collect environmental data, and record statements from witnesses. Notify the museum's broker by telephone and in writing. The broker will contact the claims representative from the insurer to begin the claim process. In the case of a suspected theft or vandalism, contact the appropriate authorities (e.g., local police, Federal Bureau of Investigation, etc.). Once the claim has been reported, your broker should provide you with the claim number and the name and contact information of the assigned loss adjuster. The loss adjuster will be your main point of contact on the claim. The loss adjuster's role is to investigate the loss, verify coverage according to the policy terms, and recommend a claim settlement to the insurer.

If the nature of the loss is catastrophic (e.g., hurricane, fire), the insurer should be notified as soon as possible so that it can dispatch its loss adjuster immediately to assist with coordination and recovery on site. Because the priority is to contain the loss and prevent further damage, the adjuster may authorize, on behalf of the insurer, funds needed to hire additional security or provide temporary storage or mobile equipment needs, such as portable climate control or freezer units. If immediate action is required to minimize continued destruction, the museum's policy should cover the costs according to the policy terms and limits.

The museum should work closely with the adjuster to make sure that the claim stays on track and is settled properly. If the claim involves an object on loan, allow the adjuster to communicate directly with the lender to expedite communication and claim resolution. Keep in mind that museum object claims can take longer than regular property insurance claims because of the unique nature of the objects. The claim may require the consultation with a living artist due to the Visual Artists Rights Act (VARA), conservators, or appraisers, depending on the damage. Although these unique elements in a museum insurance claim do take additional time, keep in touch with the adjuster to make sure there is no unnecessary delay.

As with any insurance policy, claims on your museum insurance policy will impact the museum's future premium costs. In particular, underwriters pay close attention to frequency and severity of losses. If a museum has regular and frequent losses or if the museum experiences a major loss, underwriters may require a premium increase, a higher policy deductible, or coverage restrictions. Instead of filing a claim, the museum may decide to absorb the conservation or repair costs internally. Discuss this with your broker since it is always better to err on the side of disclosure rather than potentially risking claim declination due to late reporting (i.e., in the event that it is later determined that a claim does, in fact, need to be filed). If a claim is filed, the museum should be able to withdraw it at any point without jeopardizing the museum's loss history. The museum should closely guard and protect its loss history—not just for the interest of preservation of the objects, but also to help minimize insurance costs going forward.

CONCLUSION

Museums can successfully transfer their risks to their permanent collection and temporary loans through the purchase of fine art insurance. This unique insurance is flexible and requires the specialized oversight of the museum's insurance broker, who is the museum's advocate. Critical to the success of the museum's insurance program is thorough and proper documentation—from inventory records to loan agreements, condition reports, and exhibition schedule tracking—and a close relationship with the museum's insurance broker. Once coverage has been obtained and agreements have been signed, the museum staff can rest easy, knowing that if a loss or damage occurs, the museum will be protected.

Insurance Terminology

Additional insured. A person or entity not included in the *named insured* on an insurance policy, who is added to the policy at the request of the named in-

sured. The policy may state that owners of objects on loan are automatically listed as *additional insureds* as their respective interests may appear. On most insurance policies, the rights and responsibilities of the additional insured are generally not defined so the term's impact may be unclear. The term is more appropriately found and defined in a general liability policy.

Arbitration. A policy clause that can be triggered if the museum and the insurer do not agree on the amount of the claim settlement. The process is a clear and fair method of resolution that typically involves three appraisers—one representing each party and, if needed, a third umpire appraiser selected by the two chosen appraisers. The decision determined by the appraiser parties in the arbitration process is final.

Bailment agreements. A collector lending an object to a museum may have a financial loan in which the object is used as collateral. When this occurs, the financial lender may require the museum to sign a *bailment agreement* whereby the financial lender makes certain requirements of the museum with respect to access to the object, procedures for collateral collection (if needed due to loan default by the owner), and other conditions. From an insurance perspective, it is important that the museum ensure that the bailment agreement consistently refers back to the loan agreement (e.g., regarding the agreed insurance value of the object) and that it limits the museum's liability to what is covered by its insurance.

Cancellation. All insurance policies should include a cancellation provision that allows the insured or the insurer to cancel the policy subject to given conditions and notification requirements. Because most states have laws regarding specific insurance cancellation notification requirements, review your policy for specific terms and conditions.

Certificate of Insurance (COI). A certificate of insurance is a snapshot of the insurance policy currently in force that is used to verify the coverage for a specific object or loan. Certificates do not change the coverage on the policy, they only attest to the existence of coverage at the time of issuance. The issuance of certificates is not required for coverage to be in place for loans under a museum's policy. However, if you are a lending institution, you should request a COI from the borrowing institution to verify proper insurance coverage.

Currency fluctuation. An insurance clause that allows coverage to be applicable to loans in foreign currency. The conversion date should be specified as the date of claim settlement so that foreign lenders are paid appropriately in their country's currency when the claim is settled and the funds are transferred.

Deductible. The amount paid out-of-pocket by the museum before the insurer will pay any expenses under a covered claim. Often in museum fine art insurance policies, the deductible only applies to losses affecting the permanent collection while on premises. It is ideal for the deductible not to apply to losses affecting loans so that the museum itself does not have to make any payments out-of-pocket for covered damages to loaned objects.

Duties of the insured. A clause whereby the museum is required by the policy to use the best professional judgment and practices in protecting the object. Carefully review the policy to see if it includes any coverage warranties or conditions that may restrict or void coverage if the museum is not in compliance. If you are reviewing a borrower's policy, confirm that the borrower will comply with all policy warranties or ask that the warranties be removed.

Endorsements. Formal changes to an insurance policy. Endorsements may adjust the limits, modify coverage conditions or locations, or make other alterations, either temporarily or permanently, to the policy. Always retain policy endorsement documents in your insurance files.

Fraud or misrepresentation. Policy coverage is voided when there is intentional lying or concealment by the named insured (e.g., the museum), whether regarding material facts about the museum (e.g., past claims history or application details) or a claim. Note that fraud differs from employee dishonesty. In the case of employee dishonesty, the employees are acting on their own behalf and for their own interests and not the interest of the museum. Employee dishonesty is typically covered under a fine art insurance policy, but fraud is never covered under any insurance contract.

General liability. Insurance coverage that protects the museum from a variety of claims from others—including bodily injury, property damage, and personal injury—that can arise from the museum's business operations. For example, if a visitor slips and falls at the museum and sues the museum, the museum would turn to its general liability insurance policy to cover the visitor's medical expenses, etc. Lenders might require proof of general liability coverage from the museum if loaned objects or an installation could cause injury to a visitor (e.g., an interactive and immersive exhibit installation). In this case, it is appropriate to require the general liability COI to list the lender as additional insured so that the general liability coverage extends to the lender in the event of a claim. General liability coverage is a separate insurance policy from the museum's fine art insurance.

Gross negligence/Willful misconduct. The intentional failure to perform a manifest duty and a reckless failure to exercise ordinary care. Gross negligence and willful misconduct are both legal terms and determined by a court of law. Typically, fine art insurance policies do not exclude them. You may encounter these terms in a policy subrogation clause whereby the insurer may pursue responsible third parties if there is proof of gross negligence or willful misconduct. In this case, the terms do not impact policy coverage itself, they only impact whether the insurers may subrogate after a paid loss.

Immunity from seizure. The legal guarantee that cultural objects on temporary loan from another country will be protected against seizure during the loan period. Many countries have regulatory procedures for applying for immunity from seizure and lenders may require this to be completed prior to agreeing to loan an object. Note that seizure of an object is generally not covered by a museum insurance policy. However, separate government confiscation/seizure insurance policies are available to cover this risk.

Legal liability. A policy coverage for the museum should it be legally pursued to pay for a loss to a loaned object for which the museum was instructed not to insure (e.g., the lender elected to maintain its own insurance coverage rather than allow the museum to insure); the policy would cover the legal costs incurred to defend the museum in this case. The best defense against these types of claims is a fully executed loan agreement that includes a clearly defined insurance responsibility clause and that has been signed by representatives of both the borrower and the lender.

Limits of liability. The maximum amount to be paid in any one loss. Limits are defined on the declarations page of the policy for coverage on premises, at any other location, and in any one conveyance while in transit. Limits will be for the total costs of a claim, whether for a partial or total loss, salvage fees, or other covered expenses.

Loss buy-back. The policy provision by which the museum may choose to purchase a recovered object following a paid theft claim for it. If a total loss has been paid for an object, the object belongs to the insurer according to the terms of the policy. However, by this provision, the museum may purchase the recovered object from the insurer. Typically, the museum pays back the same amount that it received from the claim, plus loss adjustment and recovery expenses. Some policies include an interest charge as well, whereas others may require the current market value of the object to be the buy-back price. This clause varies from policy to policy.

Loss payee. A person or entity named in the policy that is entitled to all or part of the insurance proceeds in connection with a specific object for which it has a financial interest. It is appropriate to request that the owner of an object be listed as loss payee on the certificate of insurance. In a museum insurance policy, owners of the objects on loan are often automatically considered to be loss payees as their respective interests may appear.

Other insurance. A policy clause that states that should another policy or national indemnity coverage be in effect at the time of the loss, the policy may limit payment to the amount of excess or amount not paid by the other insurer.

Pairs and sets. A policy clause that addresses whether an object is a part of a pair or set of objects. The policy may allow for full payment of the entire set if there is damage or loss to a part of the set and the insured does not wish to keep the remaining parts.

In that case, the remaining parts are surrendered to the insurer. It is important that pairs or sets are clearly described and noted as such on the inventory records or the loan agreement with the value reflecting the total value of the set.

Subrogation/Recourse. The right for an insurer to legally pursue a third party who may have caused loss or damage to an object. Subrogation is done after a claim has been settled and paid. Successful subrogation can result in lowering the claim on the insured's loss history, so allowing your insurer to subrogate other parties is helpful to the museum. However, shippers or storage facilities might require a *waiver of subrogation* so that the museum's insurer is not able to pursue subrogation against them in the event of a loss. This waiver protection can be invalidated in cases of gross negligence or criminal activity, which would be determined by the court of law.

Wall to Wall or Nail to Nail. A common museum term that implies that coverage for the loaned object begins at the moment it is removed from the wall or the collection storage array at the lender's location, with coverage continuing through packing, transit, unpacking, installation at the borrowing museum, deinstallation, repacking, transit, and concludes on return to the wall or the collection storage array at the lender's location. Coverage is, therefore, in effect from the first instant the object is touched by the packers or handlers until the loan is officially terminated. Loan termination should be in writing, preferably by written receipt, and should note that the owner has accepted the object's condition as it was returned. A critical element for well-defined wall-to-wall insurance responsibility is thorough condition reports and photographs of the object at the very beginning and at the end of the loan period. •

NOTES

1. Insurance Information Institute. Available at: https://www.iii.org/.

2. *General Facility Report*, American Alliance of Museums, 2011. Available at: https://ww2.aam-us.org/ProductCatalog/Product?ID=891.

3. Available at: https://www.arts.gov/artistic-fields/museums/arts-and-artifacts-indemnity-program-international-indemnity.

GRETCHEN ANDERSON

FIGURE 6E.I PESTS. CREATED BY VERNE J. ANDERSON.

THE GOALS OF this chapter are to:

- Introduce the concept of integrated pest management;
- Provide a deeper understanding of what pests are;
- Help staff of museums, historic houses, and archives develop sustainable strategies to manage museum pests; and
- Provide resources to further learn about integrated pest management.

This chapter provides a starting point for developing an integrated pest management plan and putting it into practice in your institution. There is much that is not covered here but there are resources listed at the end of this chapter that will help.

Pest Scenario

A collections technician opens a cabinet and watches in horror as a beetle strolls across a no-pest strip that had been placed in the drawer to protect the bird study skins inside. One of the study skins was shuddering. It was full of larvae, munching away. The pesticide strip had no effect on pests.

Sound familiar? In the past, the standard way to address any infestation was to use poison or call in an exterminator (who used poison). This would solve the immediate problem, but the infestation would eventually reoccur, so poison would be applied again, and so on, and so forth—often leaving a concentration of poisons. Yet the infestation would return. In some cases, such as the one described, the pest population would build up a tolerance to pesticide. This was obviously the wrong approach. It was at that time that new ways to approach the challenge of pests were explored.

INTEGRATED PEST MANAGEMENT

Integrated pest management (IPM) is a holistic approach to reduce pest activity using a combination of methods, including environmental management, cultural actions, and reduction of pesticides. This systematic approach is dependent on a variety of strategies to reduce the presence of pests, including pest identification, environmental control, building maintenance, and improved housekeeping. There is a reliance on regular and ongoing monitoring just to make sure that a new infestation has not appeared. If there is a new infestation, then it is caught before it becomes a disaster. These methods are more environmentally sustainable than previous, pesticide dependent methods.

Traditional pest control depends heavily on the use of pesticides. In museum collections, heavy metal pesticides, including arsenic, lead, and mercury, were historically used to protect objects sensitive to infestation. Taxidermists seem to have had their own formulas using arsenic soaps and other chemicals;

these soaps were usually painted on the interior of the skins prior to mounting. During the first half of the twentieth century, neurotoxins and other organic compounds were developed, including DDT. These proved to be highly effective pesticides with increasingly worrisome side effects, both in terms of human health and the health of our planet.

IPM, as a term, was first used in the 1970s to describe less toxic methods being used to control agricultural pests, with an emphasis on integrating pest biology and cultural practices. In the early 1980s, an IPM approach began to be explored for nonagricultural needs. The National Park Service adopted IPM as the standard for pest management relating to both museum collections and to invasive species in the parks.[1] IPM is now the accepted way to manage pests in museums, and elsewhere.

Why Use IPM?

Pest Scenario

1980. The collections are stored in a basement room that flooded over a long weekend. The water has been drained, and the space is dry again, all of the cabinets are opened to air out. A pest management company is sent in to fumigate as a preventive measure against the possibility of infestation. Once the treatment is completed, the curator sends a researcher to storage to examine the most sensitive textile collections. A clothing moth is seen fluttering about. The source—an Inuit child's caribou parka—is discovered under a plastic bag. It is literally shimmering with adult clothes moths and larvae. The fumigation failed to solve the problem and the parka was damaged beyond saving.

Moral of the story: reliance on pesticides to deal with pest problems may not work. This is only one reason why collections care professionals use IPM methodology. To begin with, the history of pest control is the history of poisons. The chemicals used are effective in killing not only the targeted pest but are also detrimental to human health and to the health of the environment, as detailed in Rachel Carson's 1962 book, *Silent Spring*. Many of the chemicals used

in common pesticides remain as residues on the collection objects and in the spaces that were treated with them. A good example is mothballs. If you can smell that distinctive mothball odor you are inhaling toxic fumes. The active ingredient in most mothballs is either naphthalene or paradichlorobenzene (PDB). Technically, naphthalene is a repellent, meaning that it will discourage moths (or other pests) from eating anything around it, but it does not kill. PDB, on the other hand, is a pesticide—a neurotoxin—it kills. Naphthalene is flammable. Its effect on human health includes anemia through damage to red blood cells, dermatitis, sinus infections, fatigue, nausea, vomiting, and potentially several types of cancer. It has been banned in the European Union since 2008. PDB is less flammable and has mostly replaced naphthalene as the active ingredient in mothballs, air fresheners, disinfectants, and urinal cakes. It also is a suspected cancer causing chemical, with health effects similar to naphthalene. It is poorly soluble in water and does not break down in the ground, so it remains present in the environment. This smell is added to mothballs as a warning that there is a potentially dangerous chemical present, so that we detect it before it becomes hazardous. Not only are these chemicals bad for us, but they can be bad for the collection. They can add contaminants, cause fading, or other deterioration. PDB, for example, is a benzene ring combined with chlorine. In high enough concentrations it will cause fading.

By employing IPM methods we concentrate our efforts on using biological and cultural means to reduce infestations (see BOX 6E.1, "Definitions"). We

---

BOX 6E.1 DEFINITIONS

Biological methods—Understanding the biology and life cycle of the pest. This leads to an understanding of why it is present, what it is eating, and what environment it prefers.

Cultural methods—What we can do to reduce (or eliminate) the threat to collections (and us) from the pest. Methods include repairing holes in the building fabric, improving housekeeping, reducing attractants such as food, water, and light, thus eliminating the reasons why the pest is there.

look for the source of the pests and address the reason as to why they are there, rather than simply applying pesticides again and again and waiting for a reoccurrence. This multipronged approach is much more effective in reducing infestations and is better for the preservation of the collection.

Legalities

Many, if not most of the pesticides that were available to museums in the past are now listed as controlled substances and can no longer be purchased or used. Pesticides are highly regulated, and for good reasons; they are environmentally detrimental, causing serious damage to the biodiversity of the planet. Once used, many remain in the environment for a long time, causing significant collateral damage.[2]

There are state and federal laws governing the use and application of pesticides that include what chemicals can be used in public facilities such as museums or schools, who should apply them, and under what circumstances. For example, mothballs are no longer registered for use in museums. Mothballs can still be purchased over the counter at hardware and grocery stores, and they can be used in the home—just not in the museum. Other pesticides are registered but must be applied by a certified pest management professional (PMP). Pesticides can be used, and sometimes need to be used, but they should never be the first choice of a defense against an infestation. Always check to confirm that the pesticide used in the institution or on the grounds is registered and is properly applied.

How to Move Forward

The goal is to get rid of the pests. But how? Our toolbox is significantly reduced if we no longer can legally or ethically use pesticides. The Canadian Conservation Institute (CCI) has developed a tool to identify and reduce the risks of damage to collections, called the *Framework for Preserving Heritage Collections*.[3] Ten factors or agents of deterioration have been widely acknowledged by the conservation field, one of which is pests (the others are physical damage, thieves and vandals, dissociation, fire, water, contaminants, light, incorrect temperature, and incorrect relative humidity).[4] The agents are listed here because they interact with each other and can

be used to help control infestations. This tool identifies three levels at which the risks can be addressed—the building level, the local level, and the procedures level. Finally, five strategies are used to address the risks—avoid, block, detect, mitigate, and recover or treat the damaged object. This framework provides a practical and systematic method for addressing risks. It is a logic model designed to develop control strategies that are adaptable to any given situation or institution. The tool will be referred to throughout this chapter and provides an excellent problem-solving method for dealing with pests.

Another important resource is the Museum Pest Network.[5] This is a website, originally developed by the Society for the Preservation of Natural History Collections, designed to provide much-needed resources for pest problems. The site is meant to be a one-stop spot for information that a museum professional facing a pest challenge needs. Subjects covered include monitoring techniques, pest identifications, and treatment options. There are also additional resources and a link to join the Museum Pest Network List.

A successful integrated pest management program has six steps (see FIGURE 6E.2):

1. Monitoring.
2. Identification.
3. Solutions.
4. Prevention.
5. Treatment.
6. Evaluation and revision.

Monitoring will tell you what pests are present and leads to identification. Identifying the pests will inform the solutions that you choose to deal with them. Solutions will include a combination of exclusion (avoiding and blocking egress), improved housekeeping, and reduction of food and habitat. Treatment and recovery will reduce or remove the (hopefully) dead pests from the area and objects in the collection. Finally, you must evaluate the strategies to determine their effectiveness and revise procedures as necessary. If this last step is ignored, then it is likely that the problem will occur again. Documentation of processes, treatments, and findings is

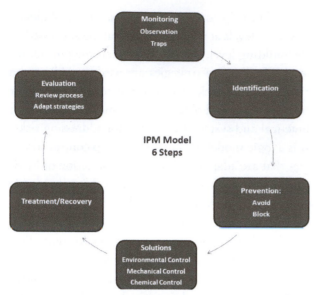

FIGURE 6E.2 THE SIX STAGES OF AN INTEGRATED PEST MANAGEMENT (IPM) PROGRAM ARE CYCLICAL. CREATED BY GRETCHEN ANDERSON.

mandatory for evaluation. You do not want to repeat the same mistakes.

Pest Identification and Risks

It is important to identify which pests specifically pose a threat to the collection. Once the pests are identified, you can make more effective decisions on how to deal with them by learning what the pests eat, how they live, what kind of environment they thrive in. With this information about their biology, we can determine why they are in the museum or historic house, and we can put our limited resources into the most cost-effective and sustainable way to meet the challenge. This is at the center of a successful IPM program.

What Is a Museum Pest?

Pests are animals and plants that come into conflict with humans. In the context of museums, archives, and historic houses, we usually mean insects, vertebrates (animals with backbones), and mold. Not all insects or vertebrates are pests. For example, there are more than a million species of insects and the clear majority are not classified as pests. The primary species we are most concerned with cause direct or indirect damage to our collections. This narrows the pool of suspicious (bad) actors even more. Some pest species are irritants; others cause serious damage, or

human health issues. The focus of the following section is specifically on museum pests—what they are, why they are present, and what we, as collection care professionals, can do about them.

Pest damage to your collection will depend on many factors, beginning with what materials your collection is composed of. For example, if the collection is primarily paper-based, then any museum pest that eats or uses cellulose (paper) or sizing will be of primary concern, including silverfish, cockroaches, and mice (there are more; this list in not complete). Silverfish and cockroaches will graze on the surface, eating the sizing as well as the paper itself. Mice and rats will happily shred paper to make their nests. This is where understanding the basic biology and the habits of the pest species helps the collection care specialist determine why the pest is present and develop sustainable strategies to reduce the impact pests have on the collection.

Understanding Pests
Pest Scenario

Collection staff report small bugs in storage and panic ensues. The staff fear an infestation. A sample is taken to an entomologist and identified as ground beetles, which live outdoors in leaf litter. Ground beetles will not survive long inside the building, nor will they cause direct damage to the collection. The danger is that they will provide a food source for actual museum pests. We call these casual invaders. The solution: check for holes in the building fabric and block them. Clean the space to make sure that most of the beetles are gone. But do not panic!

Is the creature that is in the museum a pest or a casual visitor? Has it set up residence or is it just wandering through? The answers to these and similar questions will help to determine how to address the situation in the most efficient and cost-effective manner.

The first step is to identify the potential pest (e.g., insect, rodent, etc.), to name it. This will help determine if it is a casual invader or one that will cause damage. Once you know its name, knowledge of its life habits (e.g., what it likes to eat, how it likes to live, where it nests, how it breeds) can be determined. Only

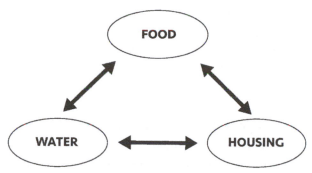

FIGURE 6E.3 ALL PESTS NEED THREE THINGS FOR SURVIVAL: FOOD, WATER, AND A HOME. CREATED BY GRETCHEN J. ANDERSON.

then can a strategy for dealing with it be built. IPM uses the biology and life habits to eliminate the risk.

IPM does not have to be too complicated. One pest control professional put it this way. There are three things that all living organisms need: food, water, and a place to live (home). If you can eliminate access to just one of these attractants, it will be easier to eliminate or reduce pest presence (FIGURE 6E.3). It is important to learn a little bit about the biology of the pests that invade your institution because the more you know, the easier it will be to find the most efficient and cost-effective way to protect the collection.

What Is in a Name?

Names can be confusing. Common or regional names are often misleading. For example, the pocket gopher (a northern US name for a specific rodent) is known as a salamander in some places in the southern United States. This is confusing because salamanders are the common name of a specific type of amphibian. Another example—have you ever heard of a palmetto bug or flying water bug? These are regional (and less pejorative) names for the American cockroach (*Periplaneta americana*), which is the large (1.5-inch-long) reddish-brown cockroach that is omnipresent throughout the United States. It originated in tropical Africa and has made its home here. It is not the same as the black native species of cockroaches, most of whom thrive outside of the urban environment. In situations like this the scientific name will clarify the animal or plant that is being discussed. Scientific names are not that hard, once you know the system (see BOX 6E.2). The scientific name is the formal name identifying a specific species, removing the ambiguity in common names. Understanding the scientific name will help communication with pest control consultants. Scientific names are written in italics, with the first word capitalized and the second lowercase. Scientific names reflect the hierarchy of biological classification. Consider the common house mouse, *Mus musculus*. The first word, *Mus* (which is the Latin word for mouse) is the genus, the second word, *musculus* (which means dim or dark, in reference to the color of the house mouse) is the species name. Only one species is referred to as *Mus musculus*, and that species has specific physical and behavioral characteristics (such as preferred

BOX 6E.2 BIOLOGICAL CLASSIFICATION

Biologists classify organisms by how similar they are to each other in a hierarchical system using Latinized names. The higher up the hierarchy of names, the broader the relationships; the lower down the hierarchy, the closer the relationships between species. When using integrated pest management (IPM) in the museum and other cultural settings, the focus is usually on the genus and species names, but often information can best be found using these in combination with the family name. For example, for purposes of identifying a museum pest, you might need to know that the American cockroach in the storage area is *Periplaneta americana*, but when looking for information about its habits, it is useful to know that it is in the family Blattidae. Here is how this looks in the hierarchy of biological classification:

Kingdom Animalia
    Phylum Arthropoda
        Class Insecta
            Order Blattodea
                Family Blattidae
                    Genus *Periplaneta*
                        Species *americana*

environment or food) not shared by other types of mice. If several species in a genus or an unknown species is referred to, the abbreviation "sp." is used; thus, you could refer to any species of mouse in the genus *Mus* by writing the name as *Mus* sp.

What Are the Pests?

There are three basic categories of pest species:

1. Arthropods (which includes insects, spiders, and centipedes);
2. Vertebrates (e.g., mice, rats, pigeons, squirrels); and
3. Mold (a fungus that grows on surfaces, often causing staining and structural damage).

Insects

Insects are the most pervasive and numerous museum pests. They are the hardest to find because they are small and often go unnoticed until the damage has been done. All insects are arthropods (which means "jointed foot"). All arthropods are invertebrates, meaning they have an external skeleton (exoskeleton), rather than an internal one like mammals or birds. There are many thousands of insect species, living under diverse environmental conditions, but all insects have six legs, and most have wings. Only a limited number of insects are classified as museum pests, and they are not the only arthropod commonly found in the museum. Spiders, centipedes, springtails, and others may be present. Pay attention to these because they may be pests or incidentals or an indicator of the presence of pest species. For example, spiders and centipedes hunt insects, so if you see them in a storage area, it is an indication that there are probably insect pests in the collection; a spider's web can indicate where insect pests are living or gaining access to the collection.

There are two types of insect life cycles to be aware of—complete and incomplete metamorphosis. Species with *complete metamorphosis* deposit eggs, which hatch into larvae. The larvae undergo multiple molts as they grow and shed their exoskeletons, and then form pupae or cocoons from which they emerge as adult beetles, moths, flies, etc. In these species, the larval stage is the most voracious (hence,

the stage we are most concerned about) and in fact some adults, such as clothes moths, do not even feed. Species with *incomplete metamorphosis* have a different life cycle. Their eggs hatch into nymphs, which generally look like small versions of the adults. The nymphs go through several molts (the intermediate stages are called *instars*) until they become adults. These insects eat throughout their life, so all of the stages may cause damage to collections. Cockroaches and silverfish are examples of insects with incomplete metamorphosis.

Cultural heritage pests are often subdivided into categories based on their food preferences:

1. Protein feeders such as dermestid beetles and clothes moths;
2. Pantry pests such as grain moths and grain beetles;
3. General feeders such as cockroaches, silverfish, and booklice; and
4. Wood feeders such as powderpost beetles and termites.

Identify the Insect Pest

Insects can be identified at any life stage. You will most commonly see either the adults, the larvae, or nymphs, but you might also find tiny dried droppings or feces, called *frass*[6] that can sometimes be used to identify pests. See BOX 6E.3 for a summary of the most common insect pests.

Protein Feeders

These are beetles and moths that exclusively feed on fur, feather, wool, leather, horn, and silk—anything that is made of protein. Collections made of these materials are at risk, including textiles, taxidermy mounts, many ethnographic objects, study skins, and horsehair furniture stuffing. The specific habits of protein feeders are species dependent. Most of the damage they do is caused by the larvae, who have voracious appetites, and the larvae may remain in the feeding mode for several years, depending on the species and environmental conditions. The adults of some protein feeders, such moths, do not feed at all. On the other hand, adult beetles (commonly called

Box 6E.3 Insect Pests

Protein feeders—Beetles and moths that go through complete metamorphosis. Among the common species to watch out for are:

Dermestids

- Carpet beetles (*Anthrenus* sp.)
- Fur beetles (*Attagenus* sp.)
- Hide beetles (*Dermestes* sp.)
- Odd beetle (*Thylodria contractus*)

Moths

- Webbing clothes moths (*Tineola bisselliela*)
- Case-making clothes moths (*Tinea pellionella*)

Pantry Pests—Insects with complete metamorphosis

- Drugstore beetles (*Stegobium paniceum*) eat starchy plant material, dried foods, plant specimens, and dried animal skins.
- Cigarette beetles (*Lasioderma sericorne*) feed on dried food, dried tobacco, plant specimens, and dried animal specimens.
- Grain beetles (*Oryzaephilu surinamensis*) feed on dried foods and grains. There are a number of related species (Family: Silvanidae) including the saw-toothed grain beetle.

General feeders—Insects with incomplete metamorphosis

- Cockroaches (*Periplaneta* sp.) feed on almost any food. There is a wide variety of roaches, from all over the world, but the most damaging species in museums are the oriental, German, and American cockroaches.
- Silverfish (*Lepisma* sp.) require high humidity and are often found in basements and under sinks. A related species, the firebrat (*Thermophila furnorum*) is more at home in hot dry climates. Both feed on starch and paper-based objects, often grazing on the surface and eating the finishes on the paper.
- Psocids (*Liposcelis bostrychophila*), commonly known as *booklice*, feed on mold. Their presence is an indication that humidity levels are too high (above 68 percent) and that microscopic mold is present. When feeding on the mold, they can damage paper.

Wood feeders—Most insects in this category go through complete metamorphosis, with the exception of termites.

- Furniture beetles (*Anobium puntatum*)
- Powderpost beetles (*Lyctus* sp.)
- Carpenter ants (*Camponotus* sp.)
- Carpenter bees (*Xylocopa* sp.)
- Deathwatch beetles (*Xestobium rufovillosum*)
- Termites (*Isoptera* sp.) often live in huge colonies that extend for miles. Complete destruction of the colony is not practical, so localized treatments are usually recommended.

dermestids) will continue to cause damage, burrowing into cardboard or wood to lay eggs. Each species has its own preferred environmental conditions. Most dermestids like warm and humid conditions, but moths tend to prefer a drier environment. Most protein feeders like dark, still areas, although some are attracted to bright colors and the light when they are adults.

Dermestids are easily identified. The larvae are generally torpedo-shaped with tufts of bristles in seg-ments of the body. They are generally 0.5–10 mm long, depending on the species and the molt. The adults are round or oval, about 2–5 mm long, depending on species. They can fly, but are most often seen crawling. Colors vary in both the larvae and the adults, depending on the species. Some will burrow into wood or cardboard to pupate. The most interesting is the odd beetle (*Thylodria contractus*), which have larvae that are orange and curl into a C-shape if threatened. The adults are sexually dimorphic, meaning the male and female are physically different in appearance. The males look like small flies and fly well. The females look like the larvae, have vestigal wings, and do not fly.

Clothes moths are small and plain looking. The adults do not fly well, avoid light, and do not eat. The larvae of both common clothes moth species are white and soft-bodied, with dark heads. The case-making clothes moth larvae create cocoons out of the material they are feeding on and their frass, thus camouflaging it as part of whatever they are eating.

Pantry Pests

Pantry pests, also known as *stored product pests*, generally eat dried and processed food products. Food sources range from flour, corn meal, and spices to crackers, nuts, and dried fruits. Beetles, moths, and ants are common pantry pests. These pests may be found in unexpected places in storage, such as in animal skins. In one case, it was discovered that a technician was using corn meal to absorb fluids while skinning animals—a perfect food for grain beetles.

General Feeders

The general feeders eat protein, mold, starch, and paper. Archives, herbaria (botanical collections), any paper-based objects or documents, and dried foods are susceptible to these pests. They may graze on the surface of paper or feathers, or burrow into an object leaving holes and tunnels. The larvae may chew their way into wood or paper products to pupate (FIGURE 6E.4).

Wood Feeders

These insects will eat or nest in wood. Carpenter ants and carpenter bees prefer moist, soft, rotting wood; most termites and deathwatch beetles prefer dried dead wood and can digest food fiber. Some wood feeders make tunnels, but the presence of tunnels in a wooden object does not necessarily mean there is an infestation because most insects that live in live wood evacuate or die as soon as the wood is dead. Although we are not particularly concerned about species that live in live wood, it is important to keep in mind that they do leave tunnels, particularly between the bark and the wood.

FIGURE 6E.4 COCKROACH. CREATED BY VERNE J. ANDERSON.

Vertebrates

Vertebrates are generally easier to spot and to deal with than insects. Rodents (mice and rats) are the most ubiquitous, but birds, squirrels, and bats can also be a concern. Most are looking for a place to live, perhaps overwinter, or maybe just something to eat. Food is the main attractant for mice. The most practical way to deal with a vertebrate problem is to learn about the habits of the animal and block its access to the building or space.

Vertebrates will cause serious damage to the building and collections. Mice and rats chew constantly because their teeth continue to grow throughout their life. They urinate as they move along walls to mark their path and territory. Mice constantly forage for food and get most of their water from what they eat. In colder climates they often come inside buildings to get out of the cold. Once a house mouse is inside it will stay if there is food and a place to nest.

The house mouse is thought to have originated in Central Asia and has spread throughout the world by hitching rides with humans. They are territorial and rarely travel more than thirty feet from their nests. House mice are prolific; females reach sexual maturity in forty-two days and live for an average of one year. They produce an average litter of six and can have up to seven litters per year, producing up to forty-four offspring during this time.

Mice are smart, curious, and sociable. They can get through openings as small as 1/4 inch; if they can fit their head through a crack or crevice, they will squeeze their body through as well. Mice are attracted to human food and love chocolate (FIGURE 6E.5).

Rats are larger than mice and can be identified by their hairless tails. There are fifty-six species of rats. The black rat or house rat (*Rattus rattus*) and the Norwegian rat or brown rat (*Rattus norvegicus*) are the ones we are most familiar with and the ones known to spread diseases to humans. Like the house mouse, most rat species are invasive and have spread through-

out the world, wherever humans live. They are attracted to human food and can cause a great deal of damage through chewing, defiling, and nesting.

Birds

By nesting in attics and roosting on roofs, birds can cause a great deal of damage. Their droppings are acidic and will cause staining and aggravate corrosion on metal and can pose human health issues. Their nests are the natural habitat for clothes moths and dermestid beetles (which keep the birds' nests clean by eating cast-off feathers and dried food).

Bats

Bats are generally looking for a place to live if they enter a building. Under the eaves or in the attic are ideal places for them to rear young and overwinter. Although bats may have a bad reputation through folklore, they are considered environmentally beneficial because of their main food sources (mosquitos and other insects) and many species are endangered through loss of habitat and contamination. However, bat guano is acidic, and like all mammals bats may carry rabies and must be dealt with carefully.[7]

Mold

We have all dealt with mold at one point or another. Mold is a fungus that spreads through spoors, which are found in the air almost everywhere. Under the right environmental conditions, mold will grow on almost any surface. Favorable conditions for mold growth usually mean relative humidity levels above 68 percent for a period of forty-eight hours or more. Mold can cause staining and structural damage to the object it is growing on, and several mold species are known to be toxic to humans. It is advisable to get the mold identified by an expert and wear personal protective equipment when dealing with it.[8]

Monitoring Strategies

To deal with a pest infestation, the first step is to identify the problem. You might see an insect flying, or a mouse scampering across the floor. You might notice that there are holes in a blanket or see tell-tale webbing on an object. A combination of observation

FIGURE 6E.5 PEST INFESTATION. CREATED BY VERNE J. ANDERSON.

and the use of traps is the best way to gather information about the pests that are present. Observation alone does not provide the complete picture—only what might be seen in a given instance. Traps provide a more complete picture of pest activity that includes around-the-clock information (what is caught or seen). The data (the pest species that are observed and trapped) should be carefully documented. These records provide information about what specific pests and occasional visitors are present, when they are likely to be seen, where they are concentrated, and where they are coming from. The documentation should include the date of the sighting (or date when the traps were checked), location of the observation or trap, the species seen, and the number of each type of pest. Systematic monitoring is the best way to gather the data needed to develop a strategy to reduce the risk to your collection.

The trap type will depend on your situation. Most of the traps discussed here are used for indoor situations, although there are traps designed for outdoor pests as well. Other types of traps may be more appropriate for your situation. Keep in mind that traps will not kill an entire population. They are used to monitor activity and show what species are present, but traps alone cannot prevent an infestation from occurring.

For most insect species, *blunder traps* are the most commonly used trap. These are also known as sticky traps or glue boards and consist of a piece of paper coated with a sticky substance. As they move about, the pests stumble on to the traps and stick to the surface. There are several inexpensive brands that are commercially available through pest management companies and hardware stores. The most common type of sticky trap is sold as a flat sheet that can be folded to form a tent or a box shape, which helps to keep dust off the adhesive. Homemade blunder traps can be made with double-sided tape placed on paper, with duct tape, or by an application of a material called Tanglefoot™. Sticky traps should be placed in out-of-the-way areas, along the junction of the floor with the wall, next to doors or windows, in cabinets, and next to (but not touching) objects. Blunder traps should be checked regularly, and the insects caught on them identified and counted. When a lot of insects are stuck to a trap, it should be replaced; a heavily loaded trap is no longer effective as a trap and may become an attractant for pests that feed on the bodies of the insects stuck on the trap. When used inside of cabinets or drawers, care must be taken not to place sticky traps where objects other than pests can become stuck to them.

Pheromone traps are available for some insect species. These consist of a sticky trap with a pheromone lure—a chemical attractant that draws the males of a specific species to the trap. Pheromone traps are available for some of the more common species such as clothes moths and pantry pests but must be placed with care because they can attract males from the outdoors into the building. Pheromone traps are significantly more expensive than blunder traps.

Light Traps are useful for many insects, such as fruit flies, that are attracted to light, particularly ultraviolet light. Light traps are usually metal boxes that contain an ultraviolet lamp and have a sticky trap in the bottom. The insects fly into the light, die, and fall onto the sticky trap. Light traps are effective and are often used in kitchens and near garbage areas. It may be necessary to clean the area around light traps frequently as not all of the insects fall on the sticky trap, and ultraviolet light traps should not be placed where the light can shine on collection objects.

The best way to monitor mice and rats is with *snap traps*, which are the most effective and least cruel of all rodent traps. With a snap trap, the rodent is almost always immediately killed when it jostles the trigger.

There are several reasons why poison should not be used for rodents. Most rodent poisons (called *rodenticides*) are anticoagulants, combined with a food bait. The mouse or rat nibbles on the bait and goes back to its nest where it slowly bleeds to death, which is inhumane. The dead body, hidden away in the nest, then becomes a food source for dermestid beetles and other pests. The poisoned bait may also be infested with grain beetles or moths.

The use of glue boards for rodents is problematic because the rodent caught on the trap dies slowly of dehydration and may drag the trap away and die in hiding. When this happens, it creates the added problem of the dead mouse or rat becoming the attractant for dermestid beetles, starting a new pest problem. Snap traps should not be set in public areas where children can get into them. When using snap traps, set them perpendicularly against a wall, with the trigger facing the wall. Mice and rats run along walls for protection and will be more likely to trigger the trap if it is positioned properly.

Live animal traps are commonly used in public areas or loading docks where snap traps are likely to be set off by vibrations. Live traps are metal boxes with entrances that the rodent can get into, but cannot get out of. Live traps must be checked frequently because trapped mice can die of dehydration within a day. I once found that a female mouse had given birth to her babies in the trap, and all had died. Remember that mice and rats are territorial and if released outside the building, they are unlikely to survive but might come right back indoors. Live traps are useful for larger pests such as squirrels and racoons. Once trapped these animals must be relocated away from the museum.

Mitigation Strategies

A gallery staff member notices a small moth fluttering toward a painting and contacts the registrar. Panic ensues (FIGURE 6E.6).

This sort of situation is what the CCI *Framework for Preserving Heritage Collections* is designed for! Once the pest has been identified, the framework can be used to help develop mitigation strategies. Examine the three levels (e.g., building, local, and procedures) at which to act and the five strategies that you can use (e.g., avoid, block, detect, mitigate, and recover).

Avoid—Can you avoid the situation? How do you avoid it? This is where you begin to apply your knowledge of the pest because if you know what attracts the pest you might be able to avoid creating a habitat that attracts it. For example, this might mean creating a sanitary perimeter around the building because mice will be hesitant to cross a three-foot space with no clutter for hiding as it leaves them exposed to predators. For mice, a sanitary perimeter might mean a three-foot-wide and two-foot-deep span of cement or rock, which they will be hesitant to cross and unlikely to tunnel underneath to reach the building.

Other landscaping choices will significantly help to reduce flying insects from entering the building:

FIGURE 6E.6 DO NOT PANIC; THERE IS A SOLUTION. IT MAY TAKE WORK AND TIME, BUT THE SOLUTION CAN BE FOUND. CREATED BY VERNE J. ANDERSON.

- Choose plants that do not attract unwanted pests (i.e., adult dermestid beetles are attracted to white flowers).
- Keep plantings away from doors and windows, trim trees so that they do not come close to the roof or exterior walls. When this simple step was taken at one museum, an ongoing carpenter ant problem was eliminated.
- Grade the ground around the building so that water flows away from the building. This will reduce mold growth from moisture moving through the foundation.
- Improve drainage by adding French drains to redirect surface water.

Avoiding pests inside the building can be done as well. If the building has interior environmental control, can it be set to discourage pests from moving in? If this can be done and the desired environment would not damage the building, then it is worth exploring. Regulating the internal environment can be done at either the building level or the local level. Use dehumidifiers and fans to better manage humidity, being careful not to create additional problems. If a dehumidifier is used, make sure that it is regularly emptied or automatically empties into a drain. An improved and controlled environment will also enhance the condition of all collections along with helping to prevent pests.

Natural history museums usually have very large collections that are susceptible to moth and dermestid infestations, which can devastate organic materials and destroy both exhibition and research specimens. If the museum has the resources, these collections can be kept cool (60°F), with stable relative humidity (45 ± 5 percent). Pests will be unlikely to want to set up shop, no matter how tasty the objects are. This is a local solution specifically for storage because it is too cold for staff, researchers, or visitors.

Block—There is a lot that can be done to block pests from entering the building or gaining access to collections. At the building level, overall good building maintenance is mandatory. Remember that the building is the first line of defense to protect the collection and, in the case of a historic house or structure, it is the collection. Make it hard for the mice to get in; look for holes into the building, especially near the ground level, and block holes in the attic and roof. This will keep squirrels, bats, raccoons and birds out. Work with a PMP to determine when the best season is to seal these holes because you do not want to close the animals inside an attic. Remove bird nests from the eaves and attics to reduce clothes moths and dermestids. Other common strategies at the building level are common sense:

- Use screens on windows and doors.
- Maintain exterior surfaces in good repair (keep wood painted, replace deteriorating mortar for brick and stone). One museum was able to eliminate a mold infestation by repairing the mortar; the infestation was discovered before it became a major issue due to the identification of minute in-

sects, which ate mold and were discovered through monitoring.
- Seal holes and cracks in the exterior walls to prevent water from coming in.
- Maintain the roof in good condition.

Eliminate sources of standing water in places such as elevator shafts, along exterior walls, and in basement mechanical rooms. Make sure that the rooms adjacent to collection storage are dry and clean. Use storage cabinets and display cases that are well sealed, especially for objects that are sensitive to pest damage.

Housekeeping, as a standard operating procedure, is a vital strategy to be used in combination with other strategies. Go back to what the pests need—food, water, and a place to live. If the museum reduces clutter and is kept clean it will be easier to find the pests and will make it more pleasant for the staff and visitors. This means establishing responsibilities for who does the cleaning, what needs to be cleaned, and how often—in other words, a housekeeping plan. Do not forget the hidden, less-trafficked areas, which are often where the most pests will be found. The plan should be reasonable according to resources (FIGURE 6E.7).

The importance of managing food cannot be overstated. Food is one of the main attractants for pests that come into the building. Establish clear rules about where human food is allowed and not allowed, and whether food may be prepared on the premises (FIGURE 6E.8). Create a food management plan that works for the institution (see BOX 6E.4) but reduces the potential of infestations (the food management plan should be closely linked to the housekeeping plan). Isolate trash bins and dumpsters or move them away from the building. One large urban museum solved a rat problem by enclosing the trash dock.

A set of written procedures should be developed for live plants in the building. In an ideal world, live plants or cut flowers should not be allowed in the museum because they increase the likelihood of attracting insect pests. However, if plants are permitted, make sure that they are healthy and well cared for. Live plants should be closely monitored for pests

FIGURE 6E.8 FOOD IN THE MUSEUM. CREATED BY VERNE J. ANDERSON.

FIGURE 6E.7 HOUSEKEEPING. CREATED BY VERNE J. ANDERSON.

BOX 6E.4 FOOD MANAGEMENT

Important elements of a food management plan include:

- Make sure that kitchens and designated eating areas are kept clean.
  - Check drains—keep them clean and keep the traps filled with water.
  - Stove and preparation areas are notoriously hard to clean, but extra effort should be made.
  - Do not allow food or garbage to stay in the building overnight.
- Use covered garbage cans and keep them clean. This will significantly reduce feeding and breeding grounds for fruit flies and other insects associated with garbage.
- Determine under what circumstances (if any) food and drink should be allowed in the galleries for special events and set strict standards for cleaning up immediately after the event. Although it is ideal that no food ever be allowed in the museum, it is understood that food at special events is often necessary.
- If your historic house or museum has a food-based educational program, develop procedures to make sure that the foodstuffs are maintained in such a way as to eliminate pantry pests. This might include defining the type of containers that dry goods (e.g., flour, sugar) are kept in or that dry goods be kept in a refrigerator or freezer.
- Determine where staff and volunteers should eat and where they can store their lunches.

(in one situation, live tropical plants were being used by a family of mice as their nesting spot!). Cut flowers may brighten a space but can also bring in pests and can cause water damage while being maintained. Take extra care to avoid damaging historic furniture if live plants are used; it is preferable to use silk flowers and plants instead because they will not attract pests. Avoid the use of wild flowers or flowers from the garden, if possible. If real flowers are mandated, use greenhouse flowers from a facility that uses systemic pesticides when growing the plants as these will be less likely to host unwanted insects.

Finally, keep monitoring, as it is an ongoing process. The only way to find out if the strategies you are engaging in are working is to be vigilant. If the methods are not as successful as you wish, then adapt. Go back to the beginning and tweak what is being done.

The best and least toxic method to deal with insects, mice, and mold is a combination of all these techniques:

1. Monitor to determine where the pests are getting into the building;
2. Block the access points in the building; and
3. Improve housekeeping and clean up any dead animals, nesting spots, or debris left behind.

Use monitoring (with snap traps) and observation to track animal movements, and remember that they move three-dimensionally, climbing wires and pipes. Eliminate all access to food and improve housekeeping, and continue to trap; this is the one instance in which a monitoring method is also key to eliminating the pest.

Pest Scenario

An intern was doing an object check in a collections storage room in the basement of a museum. He noticed white fuzz growing on some African masks. Concerned, he called the conservator and described what he was seeing. The conservator dashed down to storage to confirm his fear. Indeed, all the wooden and hide objects in two rooms were covered in mold. The rooms were located on an outside wall that had no vapor barrier or insula-

tion. Everything was removed from the rooms and mechanically cleaned. The rooms were washed with a bleach mixture and the block walls painted with a fungicidal paint used on the interior of barns. Cabinets and shelving were thoroughly cleaned. A small heating, ventilation, and air-conditioning (HVAC) unit was installed for the entire storage area. Collections were returned to the space, reorganized, inventoried and a regular monitoring program initiated. Cabinets were moved away from the outer wall to allow for greater airflow, which was about 95 percent effective. A few years later, very small spots of mold were found in one space in the corner, which was a dead area with no airflow. Fans were added to improve the airflow and that did the trick.

Treatment Strategies

The steps in treatment are straightforward, and are as follows:

1. Isolate and examine.
2. Treat objects, storage furniture, and rooms.
3. Clean objects and storage spaces.
4. Clean and examine.

When a potential infestation is discovered, it is time to take action. Both the space where the infestation is found and the objects need to be treated. As discussed, the traditional approach of indiscriminately using general poisons is not advised and is often illegal, so what are the other options? For spaces, rooms, and cabinets, housekeeping is the answer. Clean out the cracks and crevices with a high efficiency particulate air (HEPA) vacuum. A HEPA vacuum removes minute (2.5 micron) particles and contains them in a bag. Follow vacuuming with soap and water treatment using a soft scrub brush; its old fashioned, but it works. If mold is a problem, seek the advice of a mold remediation specialist. Check the spaces for holes, cracks, and other egress and address those issues. Make sure that the space is thoroughly cleaned and dried prior to returning collections.

Isolation—When an infestation is discovered, the first thing to do is to carefully isolate and examine the infested objects. Determine if the infestation is active (alive) or not (old, dead). If it is not active, remove the frass, clean the object, and continue isolation to ensure that the pests do not return. Do not return the object to storage or exhibition until you are sure that the infestation is no longer active. If the pest infestation persists, decide how to treat it. Activity should be carried out away from the main collection, so that there is less possibility of spreading the infestation to other objects.

It is best to have an isolation room as far away from collections as possible. Use it for objects that are entering the building, either new donations, or new or returning loans. Examine all objects carefully before incorporating them in collection storage or exhibitions. Many infestations have been spread through the exchange or loan of objects among museums. In fact, it has been documented that the odd beetle, which originated in Asia, has been spread worldwide by the exchange of museum objects, particularly herbarium specimens.

Be creative with isolation methods. There is never enough space. At one museum with a serious dermestid infestation and absolutely no space for a permanent isolation room for examination and isolation, the registrar and IPM technician came up with the idea of using a tent, the sort that might be used to keep mosquitos away from a picnic. It was completely self-contained, with extremely small mesh screenings. The tent could be set up anywhere as needed, even in the middle of a collection storage space. This meant that objects of concern could be brought into the space and examined without fear of exposing other objects and the tent could be completely cleaned out, even dry cleaned if necessary, when the project was done.

Treatment choice will depend on several factors. The first is what materials are the objects made of, and whether they might be damaged by the treatment. Several commonly used treatments will be briefly described, but for the most up-to-date information and more detailed procedures, check the Museum Pest Network solutions tab.[9]

Thermal treatment can be one of two types, either low temperature (freezing) or high temperature. Both are well-researched and are the safest methods

---

BOX 6E.5 PROCEDURES FOR FREEZING COLLECTIONS

- The infested object should be bagged in two layers of plastic, with as much air removed as possible. This prevents ice buildup on the object, eliminates the possibility of condensation damaging the object, and reduces fluctuation of equalibrium moisture content. Each layer of plastic should be well sealed.
- When the object is removed from the freezer it should be allowed to come up to room temperature before being unwrapped (allow at least twenty-four hours before opening the plastic bags).
- After treatment, the object should remain in isolation for at least two weeks to make sure the treatment was successful.

---

for killing insect infestations. Low temperature has been used for museum collections since the 1980s, and when done correctly, it has an excellent kill rate and will not damage most objects (see BOX 6E.5). The goal is to quickly freeze an object so that the pests in it will die. All life stages (adults, pupae, larvae, nymphs, and eggs) must be killed. The critical temperature is −22°F.[10] The length of time needed for freezing to be effective depends on the object. For small objects or specimens (e.g., pinned insects), seventy-two hours is usually sufficient. For larger objects a longer time is required.

Of course, there are several types of objects that should not be frozen, including paintings on canvas, many audiovisual materials, wax, glass, and damp plant material. However, the method is so safe that some institutions use freezing as a preventive measure when moving large quantities of collections from one place to another.

Heat treatment is also successful and easily done. Research has shown that the critical temperature for killing insects (adults and eggs) is 130°F with a short exposure time. The equipment outlay can be simple and inexpensive. There are several strategies described on the Museum Pest Network website including using an oven, a heater, and fan, or a black bag in the sun. However, there are several caveats. Any material that is subject to damage at 130°F should not be treated with heat (e.g., waxes and resins). Care must be taken to not dry out the object, which will cause damage; the best way to prevent dehydration is to double-bag the object. There are some other methods described on the Museum Pest Network site that also work.

Controlled atmosphere treatments—The key feature of controlled atmosphere treatments (CAT) is the elimination of breathable oxygen. In essence, the insect dies through suffocation or dehydration. There are three primary methods for CAT in use in museums:

1. Carbon dioxide (CO_2),
2. Inert gas (nitrogen or argon), and
3. Oxygen scavenging.

The setup for all three methods is similar. An air-tight container is needed, as any leaks in the container will reduce the effectiveness of the treatment. With CO_2 or inert gas, a vacuum is drawn to purge the container of breathable air. At the same time the CO_2 or inert gas fills the container. The relative humidity of the gas needs to be regulated so that the objects inside do not desiccate.

CO_2 treatment is considered safe for all objects. The initial expense is considerable because there are specialized systems required (called *CO_2 bubbles*), which are commercially available, and special equipment to monitor CO_2 levels. Local regulations need to be checked to determine whether a pesticide license is required. Treatment time is four weeks. Large mass treatments can be performed. Further information can be found at Museum Pest Network.[11]

Inert gas treatment is also considered safe for most objects, except for some mineral pigments, such as cinnabar and sienna, because these pigments can undergo a color transformation in the absence of oxygen. Like CO_2 treatment, these require an outlay for materials and monitoring equipment. Unlike CO_2 these gasses are not regulated as pesticides, so no license is required. More detailed description and product information is found at Museum Pest Network.[12] Treatment time varies slightly for each of these methods but is generally two to six weeks.

The easiest CAT method to use is the oxygen scavenging treatment. An oxygen scavenger (a material that absorbs oxygen from the air) is inserted into a con-

tainer with the infested object. The container is sealed and left for twenty-one days. Inside the container the scavenger absorbs oxygen and the pests die. There is no need to adjust the relative humidity. The biggest challenge is to create an air-tight container. Instructions for this are on the Museum Pest Network website.[13] This treatment can be used for almost anything with exception of the pigment Prussian Blue. Oxygen scavengers are not a registered pesticide, so no licensing is required. There are several special materials required, which are not absurdly expensive, but can add up, and large quantities of the scavenger are needed. The oxygen scavenger can only be used for one treatment and must be discarded after use.

Insect growth regulators (IGR) are synthetic pesticides that mimic certain insect hormones. They slow or halt an insect's growth and break the cycle of breeding, hence knocking down the population. IGR, like other treatments must be used in partnership with other IPM actions. For example, a natural history institution discovered a serious infestation of drugstore beetles in its storage area. The beetles were drilling into study skins to pupate. The conservator and collection manager worked with a pest management company specializing in museums to use IGR technology as part of the overall holistic strategy to eliminate the beetle. The IGRs were used to slow insect breeding while the collection was processed through low temperature treatment. At the same time the facilities maintenance department found the egress point—an unused boiler on the roof, directly above storage, that was the beetles' primary habitat. There were holes in the roof providing access to the room below. The boiler was removed, and the holes repaired. The cabinets were elevated above the floor on posts so that the floor was completely visible. The entire room and all cabinets were thoroughly cleaned, and housekeeping was improved. Ultraviolet light traps with sticky boards were placed in strategic places in storage. The monthly count of how many insects were caught on the traps went from a serious infestation to an occasional beetle being found.

Chemical Pesticide Treatments—There still is a role for pesticide treatments in museums, but they should never be used directly on collection objects but rather on the building. Localized applications of pesticides in cracks and crevices will help block insect pests from coming into the building or moving around once inside. These are residual treatments that normally are effective for about two weeks, unless the dust is washed away. If an occasional silverfish is found, an IPM professional might use a gel or powder containing diatomaceous earth to deal with the problem—as the silverfish crawls over this abrasive material the insect's exoskeleton is scratched causing it to die from dehydration.

Contracting with Pest Management Professionals
Many of the methods described in this chapter can be done in house, but there are times when it is necessary to bring in a PMP. For example, if termites threaten, then IGR or other chemical treatments will be required. Any time a registered pesticide is being used in a public institution a licensed PMP does the application. A trained PMP can be an important part of an IPM plan.

When contracting with a PMP it is important to understand what IPM is and how it relates to the institution. Define the goals and do the research. The PMP that you are seeking must have training and experience in IPM. Look at the PMP's website and interview them for the position. Ask questions and get references. Make sure that the company is registered with the National Pest Management Association (NPMA) and any state organizations, and that they are properly licensed. A good PMP, who understands the need of the institution, is a major asset. Once the decision has been made, work with the PMP on a plan to move forward, both with the immediate infestation and with ongoing monitoring.

The IPM Plan

An IPM plan is a roadmap for how to proceed to achieve the desired result. It should be relevant to the needs of the institution and the collection. It should be practical and achievable. It is a process that will evolve. It is necessary to check the efficacy of the IPM plan over time, refining it as you become more familiar with the potential and actual pests and conditions at your specific institution. Although IPM procedures can be practiced without a plan, a good

FIGURE 6E.9 IT IS IMPORTANT TO DEVELOP A PLAN AND TO SHARE IT. CREATED BY VERNE J. ANDERSON.

plan will put your actions into context, and help the staff and administration to see how everything fits together. This will help to communicate the priorities and justify expenses.

There are four key stages in developing an IPM plan:[14]

1. Recognizing and identifying priorities for action.
2. Identifying responsible staff.
3. Acting on high priorities.
4. Establishing procedures for future planning, financing, and review.

The procedures set the standards for how to go about the specific actions and treatments, describe best practices, and explain detailed actions that are to be followed to achieve the aim. They are training and reference tools, which provide consistency.

Sharing the Pain—Institutional Collaboration
Facing an infestation and building an IPM program can be overwhelming, so it is important to build collaborations to develop a team who can help. Look across the institution for roles that are natural fits for the team. Facilities and operations staff should

FIGURE 6E.10 INTEGRATED PEST MANAGEMENT
(IPM) WORKS BEST WITH A TEAM. BETTER IDEAS AND
STRATEGIES ARE DEVELOPED THROUGH EDUCATION AND
COMMUNICATION. CREATED BY VERNE J. ANDERSON.

be among your closest allies because they encounter pests, both dead and alive, on a regular basis, and so are vital to monitoring threats. Food services and special events staff deal with one of the major attractants—food—so they need to be involved. Education and frontline staff should also be included as well because they are the ones who are out in the public and see things that other staff may not. Collection staff who deal with pest risks on a regular basis are also important to include. Finally, administration and finance need to know what is going on.

Use the infestation and the IPM plan to educate your colleagues about the importance of IPM. People often find pests disgusting and gross. Use that to your advantage, empower the staff to help you with the solutions. Most often, the staff will be delighted to help get rid of the pests. Enlist the entire staff in helping to monitor by establishing a pest reporting system (paper or electronic, whichever works). Educate the staff as to what can be done without the use of pesticide and emphasize that IPM is more sustainable and environmentally friendly than the traditional methods of dealing with pest problems. Create an IPM team of key staff, making sure to include facilities staff. The more educated about pests and the building the team is, the better the chances that the solution will work.

CONCLUSION

An IPM program is a work in progress (BOX 6E.6). It is the way to gain control of the situation. It will take time, commitment, and a team effort. It will take accepting that you will never eliminate all the infestations that threaten your collection, but by working through this process, you will have a better idea of what risks your collection is facing and what to do about it.

By addressing the pest problem through holistic methods, many of the other risks to collections will also be reduced. All the actions taken to help avoid and block pests, better management of environmental conditions, and enhanced housekeeping, will improve conditions for the collections as well. Each institution is different and will require adaptations of the IPM principles. Solutions will depend on specific situations and must be determined by institutional mandate. A historic house museum, with a historic garden or natural landscape will find different challenges and solutions than an art museum in an urban

---

BOX 6E.6 PESTS, CLIMATE CHANGE, AND SUSTAINABLE PRACTICES

Climate Change

- Changes in the species, distribution, and number of pests will occur as regional climates change.

Sustainable Practices

- Make sure that traveling exhibitions are pest free to avoid the introduction of invasive species.
- Reduce the use of chemical pest control by using an integrated pest management (IPM) approach with an emphasis on prevention and targeted responses to pests.
- Consider using sanitation; thermal control with cold (–20 to –30°C) or heat (55°C); or controlled atmosphere (CO_2 or N_2) before resorting to chemical control.
- Note that although reducing the use of air-conditioning saves energy, raising interior temperatures will increase the risk and rate of growth of insect infestations.

Source: Canadian Conservation Institute (CCI). *Framework for Preserving Heritage Collections: Strategies for Avoiding or Reducing Damage*, revised. Ontario, Canada: CCI, 1994.

FIGURE 6E.II NO PESTS. CREATED BY VERNE J. ANDERSON.

setting. What is important is that IPM is a holistic system that can be creatively adapted to any cultural institution to reduce the presence of pests. •

RESOURCES

The following are books, articles, and web-based resources that are helpful when faced with an infestation. Note that a few older publications are listed which, although good for identification and basic information, include recommendations for pesticide treatments that are no longer considered appropriate. Always check the Museum Pest Network for the most up-to-date options.

Carrlee, E. 2003. "Does low temperature pest management cause damage? Literature review and observational study of ethnographic artifacts." *Journal of the American Institute for Conservation* 42: 141–166.

Florian, M. L. 1988. "Ethylene oxide fumigation: A literature review of the problems and interactions with materials and substances in artefacts." In *A Guide to Museum Pest Control*, edited by L. A. Zycherman, and J. R. Schrock. Washington, DC: Association of Systematic Collections.

Hawks, C. A., M. McCann, K. Makos, L. Goldberg, D. Hinkamp, D. Ertel, and P. Silence (eds.). 2012. *Health and Safety for Museum Professionals*. New York: Society for the Preservation of Natural History Collections.

Jacobs, J. F. 1995. "Pest monitoring case study." In *Storage of Natural History Collections: A Preventive Conservation Approach*, edited by C. L. Rose, C. A. Hawks, and H. H. Genoways, 221–231. Iowa City: Society for the Preservation of Natural History Collections.

Jessup, W. C. 1995. "Pest management." In *Storage of Natural History Collections: A Preventive Conservation Approach*, edited by C. L. Rose, C. A. Hawks, and H. H. Genoways, 211–220.

Iowa City: Society for the Preservation of Natural History Collections.

Nyberg, S. "Updated from Nov. 1987. Invasion of the Giant Spoor." *Soilinet Preservation Leaflets*. Available at: cool. conservation-us.org/byauth/nyberg/spore.html.

Olkowski, W., S. Daar, and H. Olkowski. 2013. *Common Sense Pest Control: Least Toxic Solutions for your home, garden, pets and community*. Newtown: Taunton Press.

Rose, C. L., and C. A. Hawks. 1995. "A preventative conservation approach to the storage of collections." In *Storage of Natural History Collections: A Preventive Conservation Approach*, edited by C. L. Rose, C. A. Hawks, and H. H. Genoways, 1–20. Iowa City: Society for the Preservation of Natural History Collections.

Story, K. O. 1985. *Approaches to Pest Management in Museums*. Suitland: Smithsonian Institution Conservation Analytical Laboratory.

Strang, T. 1996. "Detecting infestations: Facility inspection procedure and checklist." *CCI Note 3/2*, Canadian Conservation Institute.

Strang, T. 1995. "The effects of thermal methods of pest control on museum collections." In *Preprints of the 3rd International Conference on Biodeterioration of Cultural Property*, 199–212.

Strang, T., and R. Kigawa. "Agents of deterioration: Pests." Available at: https://www.canada.ca/en/conservation-institute/services/agents-deterioration/pests.html (accessed August 25, 2019).

Zycherman, L., and J. R. Schrock (eds.).1988. *A Guide to Museum Pest Control*. Washington, DC: Association of Systematics Collections.

Useful IPM Web Resources

Bio-Integral Resource Center. Available at: www.birc.org/IPM.htm (accessed August 25, 2019).

Canadian Conservation Institute, Agents of Deterioration. Available at: https://www.canada.ca/en/conservation-institute/services/agents-deterioration.html (accessed August 25, 2019).

Museum Pest Network, https://museumpests.net/ (accessed August 25, 2019).

Museum Study LLC, provides courses on collections care subjects, including IPM. Available at: www.museumstudy.com (accessed August 25, 2019).

National Archives. Mold and Mildew Prevention of Microorganism Growth in Museum Collections. Available at: https://www.archives.gov/preservation/conservation/mold-prevention.html (accessed August 25, 2019).

National Pesticide Information Center. Available at: http://npic.orst.edu/ (accessed August 25, 2019).

National Park Service, Integrated Pest Management. Available at: https://www.nps.gov/orgs/1103/ipm.htm (accessed August 25, 2019).

National Park Service. *Conserv-O-Grams*, Leaflets 3/4, 3/6, 3/7, 3/8, 3/9, 3/10 are about IPM. Available at: https://www.nps.gov/museum/publications/conserveogram/cons_toc.html (accessed August 25, 2019).

Society for the Preservation of Natural History Collections, Food Management. Available at: https://spnhc.biowikifarm.net.wiki/Food_Management (accessed August 29, 2019).

NOTES

1. Museum Pest Network. Available at: https://museumpests.net/history-of-ipm (accessed August 22, 2019).

2. For example, the use of DDT in Borneo. Available at: https://www.youtube.com/watch?v=17BP9n6g1F0 (accessed August 15, 2019).

3. Available at: https://pub.cci-icc.gc.ca/resources-ressources/publications/category-categorie-eng.aspx?id=20&thispubid=382 (accessed August 25, 2019).

4. Available at: https://www.canada.ca/en/conservation-institute/services/agents-deterioration.html (accessed August 25, 2019).

5. Available at: https://museumpests.net/ (accessed August 25, 2019).

6. Frass can also include debris from what is being fed on, such as sawdust or fibers.

7. Available at: http://www.batcon.org/our-work/regions/usa-canada (accessed August 25, 2019).

8. Available at: https://www.si.edu/mci/english/learn_more/taking_care/mnm.html (accessed August 25, 2019) and https://www.nps.gov/museum/publications/conserveogram/03-04.pdf (accessed August 25, 2019).

9. Available at: https://museumpests.net/solutions/ (accessed August 25, 2019).

10. Strang, "Controlling insect pest with low temperature," *Canadian Conservation Institute Note 3/3*, 1997, updated 2008.

11. Available at: https://museumpests.net/solutions-controlled-atmospherecarbon-dioxide-treatment (accessed August 25, 2019).

12. Available at: https://museumpests.net/solutions-nitrogenargon-gas-treatment/ (accessed August 25, 2019).

13. Available at: https://museumpests.net/solutions-oxygen-scavenger-treatment/ (accessed August 25, 2019).

14. Pinninger, *Integrating Pest Management in Cultural Heritage* (London: Archetype, 2015), 2.

6F | REGISTRARS AND SUSTAINABILITY

LEA FOSTER WARDEN AND SARA FRANZ (UPDATED AND EDITED BY TONI M. KISER)

At first people refuse to believe that a strange new thing can be done. Then they begin to hope it can be done. Then they see it can be done. Then it is done and all the world wonders why it was not done centuries ago.

—Frances Hodgson Burnett[1]

REGISTRARS ARE uniquely positioned to take a leadership role in fostering sustainable behavior both within their institutions and in the profession at large. First, registrars are trained to analyze and address actions that may affect the preservation of collections. Their awareness of the connections between behavior and its intentional and unintentional consequences is a vital resource for understanding and implementing sustainable practices. Second, the purview of a registrar's job is vast. Duties span many departments, requiring efficient communication and collaboration. Registrars' relationships with colleagues allow them to approach an interdepartmental project with a broad point of view, an attribute complementary to the sustainability paradigm. As detail-oriented, collaborative decision makers, registrars have the potential to increase the sustainability of their institutions.

To engage in a dialog regarding sustainability, the terms *green* and *sustainable* must be defined. In reference to the environment, the notions of *green* and *sustainable* share a similar objective—to protect and conserve natural resources. *Green* generally refers to an end result (e.g., does this product or action have a benign or positive effect on the environment), whereas *sustainability* reviews an entire system and the relationship between systems (a more holistic approach). One concise definition of *sustainable* is meeting the needs of the present without compromising the ability of future generations to meet their needs.[2] An action is rated based on whether it maintains an amicable balance among its economic, social, and environmental components—a triple-weighted scale. Therefore, a product may be *green* but ultimately not *sustainable*. Biodegradable plastic, for example, can be considered green because it degrades under certain conditions relatively safely, but it is not sustainable because more fossil fuels are consumed to manufacture biodegradable plastic than traditional polymers. *Green* products or actions are a step in the right direction, but *sustainability* is the ultimate goal.

Sustainability has become relevant within the framework of climate change. Climate change is the result of humanity's perspective that nature should be dominated or controlled. The Industrial Revolution, for example, was based on a perceived endless supply of "natural capital" and "neither the health of natural systems, nor an awareness of their delicacy, complexity, and interconnectedness, [were] part of the industrial design agenda."[3] Humans have spanned the globe, building structures and using resources at a faster rate than can be replenished. Furthermore, the loss of natural habitat coupled with species extinction continues to occur at a rapid pace. The stress that humans have placed on our fragile ecosphere is alarming. Museums play a role in this natural resource drain; standard museum operations such as the maintenance of stable microclimates and exhibitions do impact the environment.

There is growing support, both nationally and internationally, for sustainable initiatives within the museum profession. First, a number of publications are available that discuss museums and sustainability in the areas of outreach, education, exhibit design, lighting, collections care, and food service. Important resources include *The Green Museum: A Primer on Environmental Practice* by Sarah Brophy and Elizabeth Wylie and *Sustainable Preservation Practices for Managing Storage Environments* from the Image Permanence Institute.[4] Second, it is now routine for museum conferences to include some element of environmental responsibility both in program content as well as event administration. At the 2008 American Association of Museums meeting, 102 people signed up for the newly formed professional interest committee, PIC Green, now the Environmental and Climate Professional Network.[5] There are now a number of online resources such as the Sustainable Design Wiki,[6] the Green Museum Wiki,[7] the Green Building Wiki,[8] and GreenExhibits.org.[9]

LEADERSHIP IN ENERGY AND ENVIRONMENTAL DESIGN (LEED)

Building green museums is perhaps the best-known initiative within the profession. Green building methods originating from the design and engineering fields are being adopted for the construction and renovation of museums and exhibits. Many museums are also seeking LEED certification.[10] The LEED program was developed by the US Green Building Council to promote design and construction practices that reduce the industry's negative environmental impact and establish guidelines for those practices. One subset of the program is LEED for Existing Buildings and Spaces Operations and Management (LEED-EB O&M).[11] This program is designed to implement sustainable operations and maintenance practices to reduce the environmental impact of existing buildings and specifically addresses sustainable sites (including storm water management and light pollution reduction), water efficiency, energy and atmosphere (including indoor environmental quality and energy performance), materials and resources (including purchasing policy and waste performance), and indoor environmental quality (including green cleaning and integrated pest management).[12]

Green Committees

Creating a green committee that uses LEED-EB O&M guidelines is an excellent starting point to implement sustainable operations at a museum—even if certification is not an objective. However, it is important to tailor initiatives to the specific institution in question. In *Fostering Sustainable Behavior: An Introduction to Community-Based Social Marketing*, Doug McKenzie-Mohr and William Smith provide insightful strategies for instituting behavioral changes.[13] The authors note the importance of determining the barriers and benefits of a particular sustainable behavior. Because noncommunal, drastic alterations typically do not result in long-term change, establishing an open forum within a museum, in which sustainability goals are defined and potential barriers and benefits are explored, is vital to accomplish successful behavioral changes. Staff members will have varying opinions and knowledge levels about today's environmental problems, and it is important to establish an atmosphere of respect and collaboration.

The opportunity to take a leadership role in forming a green committee is ideal for the registrar given the interdepartmental nature of the position. A green committee will be most successful with the participation and collaboration of all departments. The committee's responsibility may include rethinking current needs, systems, and methodologies, and setting future goals and pathways to achieve those goals. Potential results of a Green Team include economic savings, diminished use of resources (including water and electricity), the formation of mutually beneficial partnerships with service providers, a reduction in museum consumption and waste, and improved standing among constituents and colleagues.

Registrars will find useful information in the aforementioned resources concerning energy efficient technologies and green consumer products to help launch green committee initiatives. However, much work is still needed both to consolidate and to build on data specifically geared for the registration department. Further research into new products and procedures, such as green archival products and alternative lighting strategies, is needed to develop new standards. Opportunities abound for museum studies students and established professionals alike to research and collaborate with service providers to develop, test, and apply alternative methods and materials. The following discussion, therefore, should be seen as one installment in a portfolio the authors believe will continually develop as museums bring their behaviors more in line with environmental sustainability. The topics included range from complex undertakings such as modifying lighting and climate control systems, to more mundane tasks such as the purchasing office paper.

As previously noted, several museums are now building green and seeking LEED certification. One key component of LEED certification is the installation of, or upgrade to, energy-efficient lighting and climate-control systems. The guidelines also promote the use of natural light and passive ventilation as ways to reduce energy consumption. Although these ideals do not completely conform to the standards of object preservation, there are ways to mix passive systems and energy-efficient technologies to reduce a museum's energy consumption.

Lighting

Electric lighting accounts for more than a third of all electricity consumed for commercial use in the United States.[14] Encouragingly, "due to soaring electricity prices and ever-growing environmental concerns about energy consumption and waste disposal, lighting is experiencing a technology revolution."[15] Museums' challenge with lighting has always been controlling the negative effects of light on objects, which must be exposed to light to be viewed, yet light damage is cumulative and cannot be reversed (see CHAPTER 51, "Preventive Care").

For many decades, museums have used primarily halogen or metal halide track lighting in galleries and fluorescent lighting in collection storage areas, all of which require filtering to eliminate ultraviolet (UV) radiation. Many types of filtering materials are available to protect objects from light damage, but it should be noted that the shelf life of filtering materials varies from manufacturer to manufacturer. The museum lighting paradigm is now changing, based on advances in lighting technology and the growing need to control the cost of lighting. The following presents four lighting alternatives: LED, fiber optics, hybrid solar, and diffused natural light.

Light emitting diodes (LED) are the most promising new light source with application for museum setting. LEDs consume one-fifth of energy of an incandescent bulb but last one hundred times longer. LEDs are illuminated by the movement of electrons in a semi-conductor material, which is typically aluminum-gallium arsenide. As the electrons move, photons are released—the most basic units of light. LEDs can be used in place of incandescent lights and can be dimmed without changing the color of light that is emitted—unlike incandescent lights, which become more yellow when dimmed. Although replacing incandescent lighting with LED lighting is expensive, the low-energy usage of LEDs makes them a cost-effective alternative in the long term. LEDs also produce no UV and little heat, which makes them ideal for illuminating objects.[16] LED lighting systems have steadily improved over the last twenty years and are now widely used in museums.

Fiber-optic lighting, also known as *remote source lighting*, uses plastic or glass fibers to distribute light. The fibers can be side emitting, which means the fiber itself is lighted, or end emitting, which means the light is conducted to an attachment at the end of the fiber. The benefit to using fiber optics, as noted by the Center at Rensselaer Polytechnic Institute, is that locating "the light source outside of a secured enclosure, such as a display case of costly objects, means the display area doesn't have to be opened for servicing."[17] Although fiber-optic lighting offers creative solutions, it has some drawbacks. Glass fibers dissipate UV light, but plastic fibers require UV filtering. The longer the length of fiber, the more loss of light occurs at the endpoint. Furthermore, severe bending of the fibers will result in extreme light loss, a consideration in configuring fiber placement. Finally, a museum would need to assess the environmental benefits into a cost-benefit analysis. In some cases, overall energy cost savings may not offset the expense of implementation.

Hybrid solar lighting (HSL) is one of the newest technologies in the lighting field. HSL uses solar power and fiber-optics to channel sunlight into an enclosed space while simultaneously directing infrared (IR) to a concentrating thermo-photovoltaic cell that converts it into electricity. Sunlight is tracked throughout the day using a parabolic dish. Sensors are used to maintain a constant level of illumination by supplementing sunlight with traditional electric light in special hybrid lighting fixtures.[18] Because hybrid solar lighting pipes sunlight directly to the light fixture, the process is far more efficient than photovoltaic cells, which convert 15 percent of sunlight into electricity and then change the electricity back into light, resulting in the use of only 2 percent of the original sunlight. As with all fiber-optic cables, the longer the cables are the more light they lose.[19] Because the incoming natural light is full-spectrum sunlight, light fixtures specifically designed for exhibiting objects and filters may make this technology applicable for museums in the near future.

Lastly, museums have experimented with natural light use in galleries. By diffusing direct sunlight and creating complex systems that track and control sunlight, museums can take advantage of natural light while simultaneously avoiding the harmful effects of UV rays. A report by David Behar Perahia on the use of daylight in museums cites several institutions in Europe and the United States that have successfully integrated architectural designs that use natural daylighting. The Menil Collection in Houston, Texas, uses a system of ceiling louvers, skylights, and large windows that allow for diffused full-spectrum natural lighting in the galleries. The Beyeler Foundation in Basel, Switzerland, has a glazed ceiling that also employs the use of louvers and brise-soleil.[20] Brise-soleil, an ancient architectural shading technique, appears to be experiencing a revival and is used in the new wing of the Milwaukee Museum of Art and the Louvre Abu Dhabi in the United Arab Emirates.

Ultimately, a suitable compromise between the needs of objects and museum visitors must be achieved. A report produced by the Getty Museum Lighting Research Project noted that "when applying light damage mitigation techniques simultaneously to maximize conservation, compromises are necessary—display times are limited, and light levels may be so low that they challenge perception through skewed color rendering and reduced detail."[21] David Behar Perahia attributes this challenged perception caused by inadequate lighting to museum fatigue, a well-known phenomenon identified by Benjamin Coleman in 1916.[22] David Clinard stated that "traditionally, color quality has been and still is one of the most critical concerns for displaying art objects."[23]

Creative lighting strategies throughout a museum building can benefit an institution's budget, staff, visitors, and collections. The use of motion sensor lighting and dimmers reduce both object exposure time (thus, slowing deterioration) and energy use (thus, lowering electricity bills). Other forms of nontraditional lighting such as the Solatube, a lighting strategy that redirects sunlight down a reflective tube and diffuses light within an interior space, can incorporate natural light into non-art spaces such as offices, cafes, museum stores, or meeting rooms, creating a more appealing atmosphere for staff and visitors. LEDs, fiber-optic lighting, HSL, and natural light have the potential to benefit museum objects as well as the Earth's natural environment.

Heating, Ventilation, and Air Conditioning (HVAC)

Museums use twice as much energy as typical office buildings because while office buildings usually cool, heat, and illuminate from 9 a.m. to 5 p.m., Monday through Friday, museums often have extended hours and maintain constant climate control for collections.[24] Museum HVAC systems are complex, require constant monitoring, and are one cause of museums' excessive energy use.[25]

A typical HVAC system adjusts air temperature and humidity. The air is first heated or cooled (the cooling removes humidity from the incoming air), then may be humidified by water heaters or boilers before entering the galleries or storage areas. In most systems the air passes through three filters: the first removes large particulates, the second removes fine particulates, and a carbon filter removes some vapors. These processes are controlled by electronic sensors or a central computer system. Clearly, HVAC systems use a great deal of resources and electricity.[26] Nevertheless, even in an HVAC system, there are opportunities to reduce waste and decrease costs. One alternative is the carbon filter change-outs. Usually, carbon filters are changed every twelve to eighteen months. The old filter, made of plastic, metal, cardboard, and carbon, is disposed of in its entirety. However, the carbon could be exchanged for fresh carbon and the used carbon could be sent to a reclaiming company for reactivation (discharging of the contaminants) so that it could be reused.[27] In addition to saving money and keeping filters out of landfills, this method would establish a waste-free recycling system for carbon.[28] This is just one example of how creative thinking could reduce the overall cost of operating HVAC systems.

Temperature and humidity guidelines also offer energy and cost reduction possibilities. The mechanisms of decay for objects can be attributed to three situations in humidity and temperature control—too low, too high, and too much fluctuation. The resulting damage can be chemical, mechano-physical, or biological.[29] Most museums follow the guidelines for humidity and temperature control as presented by Garry Thomson in *The Museum Environment*, first published in 1978, with a second edition in 1986.[30] Based on what was then known about how materials interact with their environment and the limitations of museum HVAC equipment, Thompson recommended a narrow range of fluctuations of humidity of ± 4 percent or 5 percent. However, Thompson stated that "the tolerance usually quoted of ± 4 or 5 percent RH is based more on what can be expected of an air-conditioning plant than on what exhibits can actually stand without deterioration, which is not known in any detail."[31] Despite this, museums long adhered to narrow ranges of fluctuations, sometimes even implementing stricter guidelines of ± 2 percent. Research published in 1994 on the specific properties of materials by Marion P. Mecklenburg, Charles S. Tumosa, David Erhardt, and Mark McCormick-Goodhart of Conservation Analytical Researchers (CAL) widened the range of humidity control to 50 ± 15 percent.[32] Although the results were considered highly controversial at the time, gradual acceptance has yielded the current Smithsonian-recommended ranges of 45 percent ± 8 percent relative humidity and 70° ± 4°F, and further research has reinforced the rationale for relaxing the old guidelines (see discussion in "The Constancy of Change and Occurrence of Challenges" in CHAPTER 1A, "A Very Brief History of the Profession," and "Section 4: Additional Information" in *Sustainable Preservation Practices*[33]).

Applying more realistic guidelines nationally could result in significant energy savings. Mecklenburg, Tumosa, Erhardt, and McCormick-Goodhart note that "ongoing implementation of the new guidelines in Smithsonian museums resulted in cost savings of $2.7 million in just the second half of 2006 (out of $32 million total energy costs for all of 2006), and $1.5 million in the first quarter of 2007."[34] Ad-ditionally, allowing for seasonal drift to occur (a slow adjustment in the humidity and temperature set points to allow for seasonal change) can result in monetary savings by maintaining an environment that correlates more closely to outside temperature and humidity. The building envelope (the separation between the interior and exterior environments) must also be considered, especially in older buildings, because introducing high humidity into the air can cause condensation to develop within the building envelope, which can then freeze and cause accelerated deterioration of the façade—thereby promoting mold growth. Acceptance of the Smithsonian-recommended temperature and humidity ranges and seasonal drift can produce substantial savings from diminished energy usage while still maintaining safe environmental controls for the objects.[35]

Materials and Products

Along with lighting and HVAC systems there are other operations under a registrar's purview that can become more environmentally friendly. One way to review daily tasks is to apply the familiar "Reduce, Reuse, Recycle" mantra, maximized by a fourth "R"—Rethink. Ask questions related to the three R's when deciding how best to accomplish a project. What is the minimal amount of material needed to properly store, display, or ship an object? Will waste be generated from the action and are there systems in place to store, recycle, or dispose of that waste properly? Is the product needed for long- or short-term use? Answers to these questions will often lead to sustainable alternatives, and such analysis is far more manageable than detangling the web of issues posed by the question, "What are the economic, social, and environmental costs to executing this task?" The following will discuss potential products and practices registrars should explore to align their departments with the goals of sustainability.

As indicated previously, there are differences between purchasing green versus sustainable products. Locating a collection care product that balances the triple weighted scale of sustainability—economy, society, and environment—is difficult in today's global economy. Comparisons between raw materials are dependent on specifying the geographic location and manner in which the resource is obtained, followed by how it is processed, where, and by whom. For example, one group claims that the agricultural plants hemp and kenaf, both rapidly renewable resources, have high yield rates, require minimal amounts of fertilizer, and have lower lignin contents than wood from trees, thus requiring fewer chemicals in the pulping process. A different group of people claims that tree plantations certified by the Forest Stewardship Council (FSC) prevent soil erosion, provide habitat for more species, and typically apply fertilizer once every crop rotation (every seven years) compared to once a year with annual agricultural crops.[36] Common among both groups is an argument against overconsumption and monoculture and agreement that even the greenest pulp mill generates some form of pollution. Ultimately, product choice is an act of compromise. However, if consumption is warranted—having first taken "Reduce, Reuse, Recycle, and Rethink" into account—it is important to support companies that have made the effort to incorporate some form of sustainability rather than none at all. The following will place the tasks of purchasing archival products, and packaging and shipping loans under the lens of sustainability.

Plant fibers are key ingredients in many archival materials. Sustainable alternatives to conventional paper products and textiles are available to other markets, but further effort is needed to bring appropriate products to the museum profession. It is possible to produce organic, nonbleached cotton cloth and to produce American National Standards Institute (ANSI)-certified archival paper from 100 percent postconsumer content without the use of chlorine.[37] Museums recognize their responsibility to educate and promote sustainability in the public sphere, so alternative products should be tested and everyday practices should be reviewed to determine their environmental impact.

Registrars can ask vendors if sustainable alternatives are available. The more the profession requests sustainable alternatives, the more industries will seek them out to maintain and build their customer base, such as the B- and E-fluted corrugated boards distributed by Gaylord Brothers are made with postindustrial waste.[38] These products meet the same archival standards as corrugated board made from single stream pulp, however, their environmentally friendly qualities are not advertised due to concerns over a potential reduction in sales. This is a good example of the importance archival vendors place on consumer trust and how the industry could be encouraged to seek sustainable alternatives with collaboration and support from registrars.

The archival industry is considered a niche market. Due to its small size and specific product requirements, the industry is not able to withstand economic forces from larger competing markets. Suppliers struggle to maintain product quantity and quality as mills close down, merge, or move overseas.[39] However, the archival industry's small scale may lend itself to the support of smaller localized farms, manufacturers, and businesses. For example, the rapidly renewable plant—kenaf—used for paper production at mills with strict environmental standards is seen as an alternative to current archival paper sources and production. The potential for creating a sustainable, archival market, integrating local suppliers, could increase with support and demand from the museum, archive, and library professions.

Switching from traditional products to green products does not necessarily solve the sustainability issue, however. Product change does not equal behavior change. For example, using bio-composite board or the FSC-certified wood products for crate exteriors instead of traditional plywood does not reduce the amount of natural resources consumed and wasted. It is the system in which crates are used that is unsustainable, not the crates in and of themselves. Although it is important to incorporate more sustainable and green products and methods into the profession, such alternatives lose their luster if used within an inefficient and wasteful system. As with product choice, registrars could fill an important leadership position by fostering the development of new norms through collaborative research with service providers.

Loans and Traveling Exhibitions
Loans and traveling exhibits are two systems managed by registrars. These systems have an admirable, educational mission but consume physical and

financial resources in a single-use manner, producing a significant amount of museum waste. Three pitfalls of the current loan system that make it unsustainable are (i) a lack of support to facilitate the reuse of packaging and crating materials; (ii) the inefficient and polluting manner in which loans are transported; and (iii) the lack of environmental responsibility when creating and disposing of museum generated products.

The *Guide to Organizers of Traveling Exhibitions* lists exhibit agencies serving museums nationwide.[40] The amount of materials consumed and discarded each year is enormous if one considers that the Smithsonian Institution Traveling Exhibition Service (SITES) currently travels more than 50 exhibitions to 250 communities each year, and ExhibitsUSA travels more than 25 exhibitions (requiring nearly 200 crates).[41] Crating and packaging is expensive and a large amount of museum resources are used to fund loans. Results from a 2007 online survey showed that out of 105 participating institutions, 29 reported ordering a total of 426 crates in 2006 for a cost of $412,108. Unfortunately, disposal fees are inexpensive, and once-valuable materials are routinely thrown away with no regard to the associated environmental costs.

There is a significant price difference between purchasing new crates and retrofitting used crates. Results from the aforementioned survey show that 30 participants reported retrofitting 510 previously used crates for a total of $38,563. This equates to an average of $75.62 per crate instead of an average $967.39 per newly built crate.[42] Retrofitting crates not only reduces waste but also saves a significant amount of money. The argument could be made that costs associated with storage, and transporting empty crates would decrease any monetary savings. However, before adequate feasibility studies have been undertaken and a true life cycle analysis between reusing and building new crates occurs, it is premature to assume that crate retrofitting would not yield savings.

To facilitate reuse, crates must be stored. The National Gallery of Art retains a large collection of crates (approximately three hundred) that are stored and managed by a local fine art shipper. The museum typically retains medium-sized crates for ver-

satility of reuse and as a rule does not use a crate if it is more than twelve inches bigger than the artwork in any one direction. Although neither the museum or the shipping company keeps track of the number of times crates are reused or which ones are used the most, the museum estimates that 95 percent of single-object loans travel in retrofitted crates, at a third less than the cost of a new crate.[43]

For those institutions that cannot afford storage, a cooperative warehouse system could be developed, managed, and collectively funded by local or regional museums. Crates could be leased, with resulting funds returning to the cooperative or to the participating museums. Alternatively, an independent third party could purchase, warehouse, and either lease or sell materials, similar to a construction salvage center. Art handling and exhibition companies could form similar partnerships and devise ways of profit-sharing when resources are needed by clients outside of the contractor's immediate service area. Although such systems would not satisfy every situation, they could reduce the production rate of new materials and provide a means for organizations to retain valuable resources. This model could also be followed for commonly used and discarded exhibition support materials beyond crates.

It is important to note that the European museum community has successfully instituted a crate leasing program. Several European crate companies have designed reusable crates, especially for two-dimensional works.[44] In general fine art crating companies in the United States do not believe a leasing system would be efficient because of the country's larger size and museum density differences in comparison to Europe. However, a modified system that approaches leasing from a regional perspective and promotes cooperation among independent crating companies should be explored in the United States if museums wish to carry out loans in a more sustainable manner.

Transport is the second aspect of loans that makes them unsustainable. Traveling exhibitions produce greenhouse gas emissions. Just one SITES exhibit, "The Burgess Shale: Evolution's Big Bang," traveled 20,044 miles, producing 38 tons of carbon dioxide. This is equivalent to 80 barrels of oil, and

6.3 passenger vehicles traveling 12,000 miles per year.[45] If traveling exhibitions are to continue, the field must develop alternative methods to rotate and transport them. Currently, where and when an exhibit travels is the outcome of variables presented by both the exhibit lender and the borrower. The content, cost, and size of an exhibit generally determine the borrower and hence the location, while the borrower's internal exhibit schedule—which may or may not be planned in advance—typically determines the dates. These variables often cause exhibits to travel great distances back and forth across the country. A new system in which lenders direct how exhibitions circulate based on geography, not time, could be developed. Exhibit companies often advertise works in progress to judge interest levels. This business strategy could be a means to establish schedules based on the location of interested borrowers. Exhibit websites could indicate when a particular exhibition would be available in a certain region. Such a system would continue to allow advanced planning for both lender and borrower but would reduce the frequency of long-distance round trips.

In conjunction with improved scheduling methods, exhibits could be transported using more energy-efficient technologies. For example, low to moderate security exhibits, especially those that do not contain collection objects, could travel by train. Comparisons between highway and rail transport have shown it is more economical to use trains for distances beyond 500 miles.[46] On average, railroads are three times more fuel efficient than trucks; railroads move a ton of freight an average of 404 miles on a single gallon of fuel. The US Environmental Protection Agency (EPA) estimates that for every ton-mile, a typical truck emits roughly three times more nitrogen oxides and particulates than a locomotive.[47] Museums and art-handling companies should consult with the railroad industry to explore current options and encourage the development of equipment and services that would facilitate a variety of museum shipments. Fine art transport companies could, therefore, expand their services to include intermodal transport. When highway transport is necessary, support should be given to companies that use energy-efficient technologies such as vehicle idling reduction initiatives

and auxiliary power units that reduce greenhouse gas emissions.[48] The EPA's website lists transport companies (e.g., rail, truck, and intermodal) that are a part of their Smartway Transport Partnership Program.[49]

Finally, museum loans and exhibitions produce vast amounts of waste. Again, reuse is rare due to a lack of storage space, and the true cost of land-filling our waste is masked by inexpensive disposal fees. Recycling packaging components, which for the purposes of this essay means implementing a secondary use for a material, is rarely practiced. There are bins for soda bottles and office paper, so why not for foam and metal? There are regionally based online recycling communities such as Freecycle, so why not "Museumcycle"? The use of various museum forums and listservs often serve as a great registrar tool to reuse or find crates, material, boxes, and even museum furniture that can be reused by other museums.

There are options to reduce the amount of waste generated from loans. Scott Carlee of the Alaska State Museum stated the following about resource-saving practices in his museum:

> We probably do more than most museums just because it is so expensive to get materials shipped up here. Therefore, material is more precious to us than to most museums. We will take apart a crate and reuse the wood for some other task or we will take apart exhibit walls and make crates out of them. For our traveling exhibits we have reusable crates that were custom-built for the shows that travel. We reuse whatever we can and when something just can't possibly be used one more time it is disposed of in a landfill. All burnable wood is usually given to someone to burn in their wood burning stove for heat. The biggest drawback is space to store the material before we can reuse it.[50]

Museums in the lower forty-eight states should perhaps adopt an Alaskan state of mind when it comes to the life cycle of museum-generated products. Redesigning crating and packaging systems to increase recycling is a necessity. For example, gluing crate joints in addition to using typical metal fasteners impedes the breakdown of crates. Wood from crates has been used by art organizations and businesses for sculptures and cabinetry or as fuel in ceramic kilns or furnaces. The use of cardboard instead of Coroplast or Gatorfoam would increase the percentage of packaging material that can enter the conventional recycling stream. Before purchasing a product, a registrar should determine whether or not the manufacturer has a recycling program. Sealed Air Corporation, the manufacturer of both Ethafoam and Bubble Wrap, for instance, has a mail-back recycling program.[51] Materials sent back to one of their seven receiving facilities is reprocessed within the company or by an outside company. DuPont has a similar mail-back recycling program for Tyvek.[52] Additionally, pack-and-ship centers frequently welcome packing supplies to support their operations, and the cleanliness and integrity are often not an issue.

CONCLUSION

Many museums and service providers are adopting green and sustainable practices. For example, Arthowe Fine Art Services uses solar panels on the company's roof, biodiesel in its fleet of vehicles, and recycles cardboard, wood, foam, and Bubble Wrap. In September 2008, the California Academy of Sciences opened the doors of its new museum, which received a LEED Platinum rating from the US Green Building Council and a second LEED Platinum award in 2011, making it the world's first double-platinum museum.[53] The building includes a 2.5-acre living roof, sixty thousand photovoltaic cells, denim insulation, and natural lighting from skylights and exterior walls of glass. The academy has an official statement on sustainability approved by its board of directors as well as a green team. Initiatives developed by the academy's green team have altered many routine operations and include the elimination of plastic bottles at all staff meetings; the reuse and recycling of packing supplies; bulk ordering; and the elimination of antibacterial soap, which is harmful to marine life. The academy recycles 60 percent to 65 percent of its garbage.[54] These institutions and individuals have taken a leadership role in the sustainable movement, and their efforts will help facilitate sustainable practices across the profession.

As stewards of the past, present, and future, registrars must continually assess how the products created for and by museums affect the world. They can update accepted standards of collection care and management to reflect environmental stewardship and take a leadership position in forming and managing a green committee within their institutions. Registrars can be active participants in the pursuit of a sustainable future by being open to new technologies, working with service providers to bring new products to the market, and collaborating with colleagues throughout the museum world. •

NOTES

1. F. H. Burnett, *The Secret Garden* (New York: Stokes Publishing Company, 1922), 353.

2. World Commission on Environment and Development, *Our Common Future* (New York: Oxford University Press, 1987).

3. W. McDonough and M. Braungart, *Cradle to Cradle: Remaking the Way We Make Things* (New York: North Point Press, 2006), 26.

4. S. Brophy and E. Wylie, *The Green Museum: A Primer on Environmental Practice* (Lanham, MD: AltaMira Press, 2008); P. Ford, P. Herzog, J. Linden, J. Reilly, and K. Smith, *Sustainable Preservation Practices for Managing Storage Environments* (Rochester, NY: Image Permanence Institute, 2012).

5. Available at: http://ww2.aam-us.org/resources/professional-networks/pic-green-network.

6. Available at: https://en.wikipedia.org/wiki/Sustainable_design.

7. Available at: https://en.wikipedia.org/wiki/Green_museum.

8. Available at: https://en.wikipedia.org/wiki/Green_building.

9. Available at: http://greenexhibits.org/.

10. Available at: https://new.usgbc.org/leed.

11. Available at: https://new.usgbc.org/leed/rating-systems/existing-buildings.

12. US Green Building Council, *LEED V4.1 Operations and Maintenance*. Available at: https://new.usgbc.org/leed-v41#om (accessed August 6, 2019).

13. D. McKenzie-Mohr and W. Smith, *Fostering Sustainable Behavior: An Introduction to Community-Based Social Marketing*, 3rd ed. (Gabriola Island, BC: New Society Publishers, 2011).

14. US Environmental Protection Agency, *Energy and the Environment*. Available at: https://www.epa.gov/energy/electricity-customers (accessed August 6, 2019).

15. J. McKenzie and M. Zoorob, Design Considerations for Intelligent Color-Changeable LED Luminaires, *LEDs*

Magazine, October 2008, 33. Available at: https://www.ledsmagazine.com/architectural-lighting/retail-hospitality/article/16695863/design-considerations-for-intelligent-colorchangeable-led-luminaires (accessed August 6, 2019).

16. Lighting Design Lab, *Advantages of LED Lighting*. Available at: http://www.lightingdesignlab.com/articles/LED_fund/led_advant.htm (accessed September 19, 2008).

17. Lighting Research Center, Lighting from Afar, *Rensselaer Polytechnic Institute*, no. 3 (1998). Available at: http://www.lrc.rpi.edu/programs/Futures/LF-RemoteSource/index.asp (accessed August 6, 2019).

18. US Department of Energy, Solar Energy Technology Program, *Solar Lighting Research and Development*. Available at: https://www1.eere.energy.gov/solar/pdfs/39081.pdf (accessed August 6, 2019).

19. US Department of Energy, Solar Energy Technology Program, *Solar Lighting*.

20. Behar, D. C. Capeluto Guedi, and L. Michael. 2007. *Light in the Art Exhibition Space*. Faculty of Architecture and Town Planning, Technion Israel Institute of Technology, Haifa, Israel.

21. The Getty, *Museum Lighting Research*. Available at: http://www.getty.edu/conservation/science/lighting/index.html (accessed September 15, 2008).

22. David Behar Perahia, PhD, Technion Israel Institute of Technology (Haifa, Israel). Telephone interview, April 15, 2007.

23. D. Clinard, Show & tell: Museum lighting, *Architectural Lighting* 17 (2002): 59.

24. S. Brophy and E. Wylie, It's easy being green: Museums and the Green Movement, *Museum News,* September/October 2006, 39.

25. Ford et al., *Sustainable Preservation.*

26. Garth Elliot, Chief Engineer, Nevada Museum of Art. Interview February 15, 2007; S. C. Sugarman, *HVAC Fundamentals* (Lilburn: The Fairmont Press, 2005).

27. The granular carbon reactivation process renders saturated carbon into reusable carbon through thermal reactivation. The spent activated carbon is treated in special kilns with steam that are devoid of oxygen at 850°C or more to release organic compounds. The volatized organics are destroyed in the furnace's afterburner. Volatile inorganics are then removed by a wet chemical scrubber. A complete description can be found at https://www.calgoncarbon.com/reactivation-services/.

28. Garth Elliot, Chief Engineer, Nevada Museum of Art, Interview October 6. 2008.

29. A. W. Brokerhof, *Applying the Outcome of Climate Research in Collection Risk Management*. Available at: http://www.padfield.org/tim/cfys/mm/brokerhof/brokerhof.pdf (accessed November 11, 2008).

30. G. Thompson, *The Museum Environment*, 2nd ed. (London: Butterworths, 1986).

31. D. Erhardt, C. S. Tumosa, and M. F. Mecklenburg, *Applying Science to the Question of Museum Climate* (November 2007). Available at: https://www.conservationphysics.org/mm/brokerhof/brokerhof.pdf (accessed August 6, 2019).

32. Originally named Conservation Research Laboratory (CRL), it was renamed Conservation Analytical Laboratory (CAL) in 1963 and Smithsonian Center for Materials Research and Education (SCMRE) in 1998. It is currently named Museum Conservation Institute (MCI); available at: https://www.si.edu/mci/.

33. Ford et al., *Sustainable Preservation.*

34. Erhardt et al., *Applying Science.*

35. See also the Getty Conservation Institute newsletter, *Conservation Perspectives*, for Fall 2018, devoted to research on managing collection environments. Available at: https://www.getty.edu/conservation/publications_resources/newsletters/33_2/index.html (accessed August 15, 2019).

36. The Forest Stewardship Council (FSC) is an international organization that has established policies and standards to protect forest ecosystems. Available at: http://www.conservatree.org/paperlisteningstudy/LSForests.pdf (accessed August 6, 2019).

37. American National Standards Institute (ANSI) oversees the creation, promulgation, and use of thousands of norms and guidelines. Cascades Fine Papers Group includes Rolland Enviro100, which is made of 100 percent postconsumer waste that is processed chlorine free in a plant that uses biogas and is a certified Permanent Paper by ANSI.

38. Postindustrial waste is leftover material created when manufacturing a product. This type of waste can be collected to be used in-house or by an outside party to make a similar or different product. In contrast postconsumer waste is material that has been used by a consumer and discarded at a recycling center such as used newspapers, plastic hordes, or aluminum cans.

39. Dolores King, Product Manager, Gaylord Brothers; interview August 25, 2008.

40. Available at: https://www.americansforthearts.org/by-program/reports-and-data/legislation-policy/naappd/guide-to-traveling-exhibition-organizers (accessed August 14, 2019).

41. ExhibitUSA, available at: https://eusa.org/exhibitions/ (accessed August 6, 2019), and SITES FAQs, available at: http://sitesarchives.si.edu/about/faqs2.htm (accessed August 6, 2019).

42. Twenty-nine museums reported ordering a total of 426 new crates in 2006 for a cost of $412,108, which averages to $967.38.

43. Johnnie Mizell, interview March 2007; Sally Freitag, Chief Registrar, National Gallery of Art, e-mail correspondence September 26, 2007.

44. Hasenkamp, two- and three-dimensional (2-D and 3-D) crates, available at: www.hasenkamp.com; Turtle Box by Hizkia Van Kralingen, Netherlands, available at: www.turtlebox.com, also www.vankralingen.com; Pegasus

Packaging Crate by Helicon: The Conservation Specialist, Netherlands, available at: www.helicon-cs.com.

45. The average tractor trailer, fully loaded, gets six miles per gallon. Carbon dioxide data was calculated using "The Greenhouse Cas Protocol Initiative's Sector Tool, CO2 Emissions" from Transport or Mobile Sources, available at: http://www.ghgprotocol.org/calculation-tools/all-tools (accessed August 7, 2019), and and US Environmental Protection Agency Greenhouse Gas Equivalencies Calculator, available at: http://https://www.epa.gov/energy/greenhouse-gas-equivalencies-calculator (accessed August 7, 2019).

46. H. Conlon, Hub Croup, Inc., interview April 5, 2007.

47. US Department of Transportation, Freight movement and air quality. Available at: https://www.fhwa.dot.gov/Environment/air_quality/research/effects_of_freight_movement/chapter02.cfm (accessed August 7, 2019).

48. Environmental Protection Agency, SmartWay Transport Partnership. Available at: http://www.epa.gov/otaq/smartway/index.htm.

49. Available at: https://www.epa.gov/smartway (accessed August 14, 2019).

50. E-mail correspondence (Warden) April 19, 2007.

51. Available at: https://sealedair.com/recycling-plastic-foam-and-paper-packaging (accessed August 14, 2019).

52. Available at: https://www.dupont.com/products-and-services/packaging-materials-solutions/industrial-packaging/articles/recycling-information.html (accessed August 14, 2019).

53. Available at: https://www.calacademy.org/press/releases/the-california-academy-of-sciences-receives-second-leed-platinum-rating-from-us-green (accessed August 14, 2019).

54. Available at: www.calacademy.org (accessed August 6, 2019).

PART 7 | ETHICAL AND LEGAL ISSUES

7A | ETHICS FOR REGISTRARS AND COLLECTIONS MANAGERS

MUSEUMS IN THE United States—whether incorporated as nonprofit organizations, created as part of larger institutions such as colleges and universities, or established as part of federal, state, or local governments—are expected to act for the benefit of the public. Laws and regulations establish minimum standards of conduct for museum operations, while professional codes of ethics promote higher standards. In the words of Marie Malaro, author of *A Legal Primer on Managing Museum Collections*, "The law is not designed to make us honorable, only bearable," while "an ethical code sets forth conduct that a profession considers essential in order to uphold the integrity of the profession."[1] Adherence to guidance provided by professional codes of ethics helps ensure that museums not only serve the public, but also do so with integrity and, in turn, obtain and maintain the public's confidence and trust.

The *Code of Ethics for Museums* of the American Alliance of Museums (AAM) states that, "museums make their unique contribution to the public by collecting, preserving and interpreting the things of this world,"[2] thereby acknowledging that collections and their care are a central concern for museums. And because museums hold their collections in trust for the public, instituting and maintaining ethical practices in managing collections is essential.

Registrars and collections managers[3] are stewards of museum collections and, as such, have an ethical responsibility to safeguard their institution's collections and collection records. This responsibility extends to all aspects of collections care from developing collections management policies to daily maintenance, from advising on the liabilities that proposed acquisitions might involve to recommending conservation treatments on permanent holdings, from overseeing incoming and outgoing collection loans to ensuring appropriate deaccessioning and disposal practices. Each of these areas should be ad-

dressed in an institution's *code of ethics*, which provides basic guidance for collections stewards.

POLICIES VERSUS PRACTICE, OR APPLYING ETHICAL PRINCIPLES TO REAL-LIFE PROBLEMS

A collections management policy should establish ethical practices regarding the museum's collections and detail procedures to be followed for acquisition; accessioning; collection care; documentation; conservation; use of objects for exhibition, education, and research; deaccessioning and disposal; and accessibility of collections and collections records (see CHAPTER 2, "Collection Management Policies"). Policies set forth best practices but do not necessarily provide guidance for all problems that arise. It is not always easy to distinguish between operational or managerial problems that have ethical ramifications and those that do not, but when a problem arises that is not easily resolved by a museum's personnel and collections-related policies, it is likely to have ethical ramifications.

The first step in resolving an ethical problem is to gather all of the facts, identifying all the people and organizations that could be affected by the resolution. Be as objective as possible; separate the relevant facts from other information that could affect your decision (e.g., emotional responses or personal opinion rather than fact). Is there an issue here that has to do with right or wrong? If so, it is likely to be an ethical issue. At this point, consult your institution's code of ethics—absent that, consult other professional codes of ethics that might apply. Then discuss the problem with colleagues, either at your own institution or others, to see if they have experience that might help guide your decision-making.

Now you are ready to formulate possible solutions to the problem (see BOX 7A.1). List your op-

Box 7A.1 Framework for Approaching Ethical Problems

1. Phase One: Formulating the Problem

   a. Collect all of the facts. Ethical problems include both hard and soft facts. Soft facts are the feelings, attitudes, beliefs, or opinions of the people and organizations directly or indirectly involved in the problem, including the public, whereas hard facts are the established or demonstrable details. Be as objective and open-minded as possible.

   b. Distinguish between pertinent and irrelevant facts. Eliminate what is irrelevant.

   c. Identify the people and institutions who are involved, both internal and external to the museum and their respective roles and perspectives. These could include, for example, museum members, community groups, the media, governmental representatives and agencies, donors and funders, and experts, depending on the circumstances. Consider any possible conflicts of interest any of them may have.

   d. Based on this information, formulate the ethical problem.

   e. Consult the provisions of relevant professional codes of ethics to see if they apply and consult with other museums or organizations that have faced similar problems to learn from their experience.

2. Phase Two: Establishing Possible Solutions and Actions

   a. Formulate possible options for resolving the problem.

   b. Consult any related laws and codes of ethics to determine whether they support these options.

   c. Consider the potential consequences of each possible solution for the museum, identifying the best- and worst-case scenarios. Consider possible responses (both internal and external to the museum) and develop a strategy to deal with negative responses.

   d. Obtain feedback from colleagues. Use the feedback to evaluate the possible solutions, make corrections as necessary, and make your decision.[1]

NOTE

1. S. Yerkovich, *A Practical Guide to Museum Ethics* (Lanham, MD: Rowman & Littlefield, 2016), xi–xii.

tions and again consult professional codes of ethics and relevant laws to be sure that your options conform. Consider the possible consequences of the solutions. Who will they impact? How will you respond? Be sure to consider both positive and negative consequences and have a strategy in place for responses that could have adverse consequences for your institution. Next, get feedback about the solutions from colleagues and use that feedback to evaluate your options, then revise them if necessary. After you make a decision, create a series of action steps for its implementation, remembering to notify stakeholders first.[4]

Finally, it is not unusual to conflate one's personal attitude or opinion about a problem (what one thinks one ought to do to resolve the situation) with what one believes a museum's position on the situation should be. Although the two are sometimes the same—for example, a registrar's personal feelings might dictate that a donors' personal informa-tion should remain private and the museum's policies mandate that all such information is confidential—there are other circumstances in which an individuals' personal attitudes do not align with the ethical obligations of the institution. In the latter case, the institution's obligations should take precedence. Thus, it is critical to understand your museum's ethics code and how it relates to the responsibilities of your position.

Acquisition

Although the decision about whether to acquire an object may rest with the museum's governing body or a collections or accessions committee, the registrar has an obligation to advise the decision-making body concerning the resources that may be necessary to acquire, store, maintain, and preserve the object in perpetuity so that the decision makers can make informed choices. The following questions should be considered:

- Is the object compatible with the museum's mission?
- Do the title documents indicate that, upon acquisition, the museum will have clear legal title?
- Do any laws prohibit or restrict acquisition and ownership, for example, the Native American Graves Protection and Repatriation Act (NAGPRA); the Lacey Act (which regulates the trade of fish, wildlife, or plants); the African Elephant Conservation Act (which regulates the movement of ivory in and out of the United States)?[5]
- Does the prior ownership history or provenance indicate that the donor or seller can convey valid legal title to the museum?
- What is the physical condition of the object?
- Will the object be endangered by movement (e.g., in shipping, routine storage, or display)?
- Is it feasible for the museum to store and maintain the object? Might storage requirements have an adverse impact on the care of other objects in the collections?
- Might the object require substantial expense for maintenance or conservation in the future?
- Will it be necessary to make provisions for an object that will deteriorate or change over time?

Answers to these questions can help the museum staff make ethical decisions about acquisitions and potentially avert problematic situations in the future. When the decision is made to acquire an object, registrars have the responsibility of formally adding the object to the museum's permanent collection by assigning a unique accession number to it and creating accession and catalog records.

It must be noted that museums are expected to use the same standards of care in accepting a loan of objects for a temporary exhibition. Consider the following:[6]

Javin Smith served in the US Army in South America and was one of the troops that were present during the capture of the dictator of a country frequently associated with terrorist activities. In a storage room adjacent to the dictator's residence, Javin and his comrades came across a cache of rocks. Javin's father is a rock collector and Javin thought he might be interested in rocks from Latin America, so he pocketed a few to take to him. When Javin's father saw the rocks, he told Javin that they were raw, semi-precious stones. Javin later learned from Army intelligence that the dictator may have been selling the rocks to fund terrorist activities. Javin considered these rocks to be souvenirs of his danger-ridden experiences in South America and had them made into bracelets for himself and for one or two of his buddies who served with him in the Army. Javin subsequently heard that the local Army museum was planning an exhibition about the US presence in Latin America that especially focused on the overthrow of the dictator. Javin approached the museum staff to ask if they would be interested in borrowing his bracelet and displaying it in the exhibition.

If you were the registrar of the museum, would you recommend that the museum accept Javin's offer of a loan for the exhibition? Would your advice remain the same if Javin were offering to donate the bracelet to your museum's collection?

Collections Care and Management
Once an object is accessioned, the museum takes on the responsibility of protecting and preserving it so that it might be used for the public's benefit in perpetuity. Collections stewards—whether curators, collections managers, or registrars—have the day-to-day responsibility for overseeing the collections and maintaining collections records, and they have an ethical obligation to notify the appropriate staff or management when one or more collection objects are at risk (e.g., when they are in irreparable condition; when the condition of one object might jeopardize other objects in the museum's permanent collection; when an object is in need of conservation treatment; or when the loan or exhibition of an object might endanger its condition).

Museums have an ethical responsibility to maintain collections records with the same care as the collections themselves, for the records provide critical documentation concerning ownership, condition, locations, exhibition, loans, and publications. Registrars oversee these records day-to-day, ensuring that the documents are secure, and determining—sometimes in consultation with curatorial staff—what information can be made public and what should remain confidential.

Collections management, although seemingly routine, brings up many challenges for collections stewards. Consider the following scenario related to collections management:

It's Monday morning. Regina Rule, the collections manager for the Museum of Regional History, walks into the collections storage area to continue an inventory of the museum's decorative arts collection. The last full inventory was completed in the 1950s, long before computer software was common in museums, so part of Regina's job now is to reconcile written records with the information entered by volunteers into the data management program purchased for the museum in the mid-1990s. Regina is especially sensitive to issues of provenance that were not so much a concern in the past; certainly provenance was not on the minds of the staff doing the last collections inventory. To date, Regina has found few discrepancies among the old record books, the data, and the decorative arts collection, so she is optimistic that she can complete the inventory in much less time than she had allocated. As she turns to the next group of objects she plans to inventory, she notices a box under a bottom shelf. Opening the box, she discovers several wooden objects, possibly tools, similar to many others in the collection. They have no accession numbers, and there is no documentation about the objects in the box.

To continue the inventory in a timely fashion, can Regina simply put the objects back in their box and make sure that the box disappears under the shelf to be dealt with at a later date, or does she have an ethical obligation to report her discovery? Would your answer be different if the box contained what appeared to be an early twentieth-century European impressionist painting?

Regina shares her discovery with one of the museum's curators who remembers that a few years before Regina was hired, her predecessor found the box under the admissions desk. The former registrar was told that the box had been dropped off at the museum over the weekend, several months previous, by someone who did not identify herself. Ms. Anonymous said she would be moving out of the country the next day and wanted the objects in the box to have a home where they would be appreciated. Before the person at the admissions desk could ask for more information or explain the museum's acquisitions policies, the woman left the museum. The former registrar, who had just been hired by another museum and was about to leave his position at the Museum of Regional History, said he would take the box and put it in collections storage. The box remained there until Regina found it.

Does this additional information change your assessment of Regina's dilemma? To whom do the objects in the box belong? Does the situation now involve abandoned property laws and add a legal dimension to Regina's problem?[7]

Sometimes a museum's ownership of an object might be called into question. For example, NAGPRA resulted in the repatriation of human remains and associated sacred objects to the Native American tribes from which they originated (discussed in CHAPTER 7F, "Implementing NAGPRA"). In the late 1990s attention was drawn to the fact that many artifacts and paintings had been unjustly confiscated during World War II and subsequently not returned to their rightful owners.[8] In 1998, as a result of the Washington Conference on Holocaust Era Assets, the *Washington Principles on Nazi-Confiscated Art* were issued, outlining the need for museums to ensure that their collections contain no material looted during World War II.[9] As a result, many museums surveyed their collections to identify objects that may have changed hands in Europe between 1933 and 1945. Although not a law like NAGPRA, the *Washington Principles* and the international declarations made thereafter place an ethical obligation on museums to ensure that their collections do not contain objects unjustly acquired during the Holocaust.[10] As a result, many museums have had to revisit the ownership history of objects that previously raised no eyebrows, and registrars might be called upon to recommend actions that should be pursued in response to inquiries about particular museum holdings. Consider the following situation:

> The Marrywell Art Museum has in its collection a small oil painting depicting a Paris urban street scene. The painting, a donation from Franklin Wellman, a well-known local collector who also happens to be one of the museum's major benefactors and a descendant of the Marrywell family, has been in the Marrywell's collection for three decades. One day the museum's director receives a letter from a woman who claims the painting belonged to her great aunt and that it went missing from the aunt's Parisian apartment in 1943. Her proof of her aunt's ownership of the painting is a photograph taken when she visited her aunt in her aunt's apartment in the early 1940s. A copy of the photo included in the letter presumably shows the women (then a child) standing near the painting which is hung over what she claims was her aunt's mantel. Although the photo is a bit blurry, the painting seems to be the painting in the Marrywell Museum's collection; the frame also appears to be the same. The woman asserts that she is the last living relative of her aunt and requests the painting be returned to her. The museum director asks the registrar about the painting and she discovers that the museum has little information about the painting's provenance. Museum records show that Wellman bought the painting at a European auction in the 1960s. The records only contain a bill of sale made out to Wellman. There appears to be no record of ownership prior to that time.

Does the registrar have enough information regarding whether the museum is the rightful owner of the painting? What facts would help the registrar make a recommendation to the director? Claims such as the one in this scenario should be taken seriously,[11] but at the same time, the museum must ensure that it has sufficient evidence to support a claim of ownership. Either unjustly retaining the painting or returning it to the wrong claimant can present problems for a museum.[12]

Accessibility

Appropriately accounting for, maintaining, and preserving museum collections, although central to a registrar's duty, is not the end-all and be-all for the objects that the museum holds. Museums maintain their collections for the benefit of the public and have an ethical duty to ensure that the collections are available for exhibitions and programs as well as for inquiry, research, and study. Museum staff who are responsible for the physical care of collections in storage need to balance requests for accessibility with concerns for the safety of the objects in the collection. Given the trend among museums to focus on visitor experience, audience development, and community engagement, collections stewardship becomes more complicated. Collections may be used in new and different ways to engage the public imagination. Nonetheless, to ensure that the collections are maintained for the public benefit, the integrity of a museum's holdings should be safeguarded while still allowing for experimentation. Museum staff most familiar with the collections and their care can contribute valuable information that would allow for using collections in novel ways without endangering them.

Sometimes, requests for access to a museum's collections can compete. Consider Ralph Registrar's problem:

> One day Ralph is approached by the Bayside Museum's curator of paintings to provide last minute access for a well-known scholar who is visiting Bayside over the weekend. He wishes to come to the museum the next Saturday to view some nineteenth-century landscapes for an article that he is writing for a prestigious national publication. The paintings have been in storage for the last five years but have recently been conserved so that they can be part of an upcoming exhibition. The scholar's article promises to

give the museum long-sought after attention to its collection. A few months ago, Ralph arranged with the Education Department for the same paintings to be part of an all-day workshop for local children who attend a school that lacks the resources to bring the students to the museum during the week. With the help of a grant, the museum is able to bring the school children to visit the museum on Saturday and participate in an intensive workshop.

What should Ralph consider in responding to the request from the curator?

Deaccessioning and Disposition

When guided by a museum's collections policy and code of ethics, deaccessioning—the removal of an object from a museum's permanent collections—is considered a routine and responsible collections practice in the United States.[13] If a museum decides to sell objects that are deaccessioned from its permanent collection, however, controversy can result, and the ensuing debate can raise ethical questions. It is important to understand the underlying ethical principles concerning disposal that are articulated in museum professional codes of ethics.

It is a basic principle of museum ethics that the decision to deaccession should be made for substantive, mission-related reasons (see CHAPTER 31, "Deaccessioning and Disposal") and should under no circumstances be motivated only by financial considerations. Nonetheless, ethical questions can arise concerning the use of funds garnered from an object's sale. A number of professional museum associations address this issue in their codes of ethics. Although specific code provisions may vary, the basic premise behind all of them is that once objects become part of museum collections they are valued for their cultural, historical, or scientific importance rather than for their resale value in the marketplace.[14]

The AAM *Code of Ethics for Museums* (1994, revised 2000) states:

Disposal of collections through sale, trade or research activities is solely for the advancement of the museum's mission. Proceeds from the sale of nonliving collections are to be used consistent with the established standards of the museum's discipline, but in no event shall they be used for anything other than acquisition or direct care of collections.[15]

Because the phrase *direct care of collections* created some confusion among museums, AAM convened a task force that produced a white paper on the subject in 2016. The white paper, "Direct Care of Collections: Ethics, Guidelines and Recommendations," acknowledges the appropriateness of deaccessioning as a means for managing collections but cautions that museums should "ensure that funds realized from the sale of deaccessioned objects are never used as a substitute for fiscal responsibility." It underscores both the critical importance of responsible collections stewardship and the cultural—not financial—value of museum collections, defining *direct care* as "an investment that enhances the life, usefulness or quality of a museum's collection."[16] The white paper provides guidance and recommendations about how to interpret the definition of *direct care* because the interpretation of this phrase could vary from museum to museum. As a result, the report encourages each museum that wishes to use funds for direct care to create specific policies concerning direct care and include them in its collections management policy.

The AAM *Code of Ethics* also prohibits the use of collections as collateral for loans, specifying that "collections . . . are lawfully held, protected, secure, unencumbered, cared for and preserved."

The *Policy on Deaccessioning* of the Association of Art Museum Directors (AAMD) states that deaccessioning should be used to "refine and improve the quality and appropriateness of the collections" to better serve the museum's mission. AAMD prohibits the use of funds realized from the sale of deaccessioned objects for "operations or capital expenses. Such funds, including any earnings and appreciation thereon, may be used only for the acquisition of works in a manner consistent with the museum's policy on the use of restricted acquisition funds."[17] In other words, AAMD's policy states that none of the proceeds from the sale of collections may be used for operating expenses not related to new acquisitions.

The American Association for State and Local History (AASLH) *Statement of Standards and Ethics* states that, "Historical resources should not be capitalized or treated as financial assets." The standards stress that deaccessioning decisions should "under no circumstances" be made because of an object's potential market value. Citing the AAM definition of *direct care of collections*, AASLH standards and ethics also stipulate that "funds from the sale of collections may be used for the acquisition of collections, or the direct care or preservation of existing collections. Funds should not be used to provide financial support for institutional operations." The standards provide similar guidance concerning the use of funds from deaccessioning for accessioned buildings and landscapes of historical properties, stating that, for these collections, institutional collections management policies should distinguish between building maintenance and building preservation.[18]

The International Council of Museums (ICOM) *ICOM Code of Ethics for Museums* stipulates that deaccessioning "must only be undertaken with a full understanding of the significance of the item, its character (whether renewable or nonrenewable), legal standing, and any loss of public trust that might result from such action." Further it states that museums should have a written policy for disposal and that "there will be a strong presumption that a deaccessioned item should first be offered to another museum." It also confirms that "museum collections are held in public trust and may not be treated as a realizable asset. Money or compensation received from the deaccessioning and disposal of objects and specimens from a museum collection should be used solely for the benefit of the collections and usually for acquisition to that same collection."[19]

The Association of Academic Museums and Galleries (AAMG) *Professional Practices for Academic Museums & Galleries* addresses the situation of museums that are part of the structure of academic institutions such as universities and colleges. It stresses that, "in addition to complying with the university's code of ethics, the academic museum must codify and formally approve its ethical responsibilities as a museum. . . . The museum's code of ethics must affirm that it puts the public trust above the interests of the university,

museum, or any individual" and that museum collections must not be considered "fungible assets used to sustain the parent institution." AAMG also affirms, along with AAM, AAMD, and AASLH that collections should be "unencumbered"; that is, they cannot be used as a collateral for a loan. Finally, "AAMG recommends that funds from deaccessioning only be used for new collections acquisitions, unless the museum is no longer acquiring objects, in which case such funds may be used for the care of the existing collection. It does, however, recognize that the American Association for State and Local History (AASLH) specifies that history museums can use such funds for acquisition or preservation of collection objects."[20]

The Society of American Archivists (SAA) *Guidelines for Reappraisal and Deaccessioning* note the ethical implications involved in the disposal of collection objects and urge transparency, adding that "reappraising and deaccessioning collections for the primary purposes of generating operating income; satisfying personal interests, aversions, or prejudices; and pleasing donors or resource allocators are not consistent actions with best practices or the SAA Code of Ethics." Although this document and the SAA Code of Ethics do not specify how funds realized from the sale of deaccessioned objects should be used, SAA refers to codes of ethics for "affiliated professions" as guidance to generate standards, noting that "many of them allow for sale proceeds to be used only for new acquisitions or direct care of collections."[21]

During deaccessioning, as with acquisitioning, the responsibility of the registrar or collections manager is largely advisory. Information provided by a museum's registrar can help a museum make ethical decisions regarding the removal of objects from its collections. A registrar's considerations might include the following:

- Does the museum have sufficient documentation evidencing ownership of the object?
- Does any such documentation restrict or prohibit the museum from disposing of the object?
- Were any conditions placed on the object that might relate to its disposition (e.g., requirements that the museum contact the donor or heirs of the donor before proceeding)?

Once the decision to deaccession an object is made, registrars should update collection records, helping to ensure that the museum fulfills its ethical obligation to maintain records of all of its collection objects, even those that have been deaccessioned.

If a museum decides to sell a deaccessioned object at public auction, care should be taken to ensure that the sale is conducted with transparency and that there are no conflicts of interest involved. Members of a museum's governing body and their families, as well as museum staff, volunteers, and their relatives, should not be allowed to purchase objects from the museum's collections. Similarly objects from the collections should not be sold in the museum's shop.

After the final disposition of a deaccessioned object, it is the registrar's responsibility to record the disposition in the object's collection records. If an object is sold and funds realized from the sale are used to purchase another object for the collection, it is appropriate to note that fact in the collection records for both the sold and the newly purchased items so that the information is available for future use by curators, researchers, and others interested in the object's history.

Conflict of Interest and Personal Collections

Museums, like other nonprofits, are required by federal law to have a conflict-of-interest policy for their governing body. All board members have a duty of loyalty that requires them to put the interests of the museum they serve above their own interests. Moreover, a conflict-of-interest policy should require that board members declare possible conflicts of interest annually. Ms. Builder, for example, owns a construction company and is a board member of a museum that is planning to renovate its galleries. Should her company compete for the renovation contract? Is it enough for Ms. Builder to recuse herself from the board's vendor selection process? This situation presents a potential conflict of interest because Ms. Builder stands to benefit if her company wins the renovation contract. While recusing oneself from the selection process might satisfy the museum's internal procedures, one must also consider how the public will perceive the situation.[22]

Many museums include in their conflict-of-interest policy provisions regarding personal collecting.

If a board member, for example, collects objects similar to those in a museum's collection, it would be appropriate for the museum to request that the board member disclose personal collecting interests so that the board member and the museum do not unknowingly compete with one another in buying objects. Similarly, if a board member purchases an object that might fall within the collecting interests of the museum, the board member should offer the object to the museum at the purchase price. The museum then has the option to buy the object.

Although some museums encourage their staff to have personal collections that relate to those of the museum, others discourage this practice. In either case, it is appropriate for the museum to have a conflict-of-interest policy concerning personal collecting by staff members. This policy might stand alone, or it might appear in an employee handbook or in the museum's code of ethics (or both). It should describe the circumstances under which it is appropriate for museum staff and volunteers to maintain personal collections that relate to the collections of the museum. Even those institutions that encourage staff members to collect in areas related to the existing museum collections need to be sure that staff understand that when personal interests and the interests of the museum conflict, the interests of the museum take precedence.

Mr. Artsy is a board member of the Big City History Museum, which has an unrivaled collection of colonial furniture. He has a fine collection of colonial chairs in which he takes great pride. He made the museum aware of his collecting interests when he became a board member and even suggested that he might bequeath a significant portion of his collection to the museum. One weekend, when Mr. Artsy is visiting an antique show in a town near his country home, he finds a chair that he believes may be a lesser known, long-missing work by one of America's best colonial chairmakers. The work is unattributed but dated to the colonial period and, as a result, is being sold for much less than Mr. Artsy feels it is worth. He snaps up the chair and is thrilled with his discovery. Observing the museum's conflict-of-interest policies, the next week he takes the chair to the Big City Museum, offering it to them at the purchase price should they wish to purchase it.

The chair falls within the museum's mission, but the museum is no longer actively collecting colonial furniture. The museum does, however, have enough money in its acquisition budget for the purchase. The curator verifies that the chair may, indeed, be the long-lost gem Mr. Artsy thinks it is, but the chair's ownership history is unclear. The museum's registrar is consulted on the purchase. What ethical considerations should be included in her decision making? Would your answer be different if the chair had been purchased by one of the museum's curators?

After conducting further research and consulting with other colonial furniture experts, the curator concludes that Mr. Artsy is correct; the chair was indeed created by the well-known artisan and would be a fine addition to the museum's collection. The curator is reluctant, however, to recommend that the museum use its acquisition funds for this chair. Mr. Artsy strongly believes that the museum should own the chair and offers to sell it to the museum at an amount that is less than what he paid for it. In his decision-making process, the curator approaches the registrar for advice.

What advice might the registrar give now? Is there a conflict of interest? Is there the potential for a perceived conflict of interest?

Other potentially problematic situations can arise when a member of the governing board, staff member, or volunteer requests the use of the museum's collections storage for their personal collections. Storing personal collections, unless they are being used for some specific museum-related educational purpose, uses museum resources inappropriately and is a conflict of interest for all involved. In addition, this situation creates a potential liability for the museum.

Authentication and Appraisals

Institutional codes of ethics often address the appropriateness of museum staff appraising and authenticating objects. The ICOM *Code of Ethics for Museums* provides the following guidance, "Valuations may be made for the purposes of insurance of museum collections. . . . However, when the museum itself may be the beneficiary, appraisal of an object or specimen must be undertaken independently."[23] Thus, when a donor offers an object to a museum and needs to have an appraisal of the object's value for income tax purposes, it is the donor's responsibility to provide the appraisal and not the museum's. To avoid a potential conflict of interest, the museum staff should not make any appraisals or even suggest the names of appraisers to the donor.

CONCLUSION

Codes of ethics issued by professional organizations and institutional codes of ethics can provide general guidance for collection stewards. Often, however, a problem is complex and involves nuances that are not addressed in a general statement of best professional practice. In these cases, there is no substitute for engaging with colleagues or museum professionals from other institutions in a dialog about a particular problem.

Even absent a real ethical dilemma, discussion about cases that raise ethical issues can be useful. The hypothetical scenarios included in this chapter can be used to spark discussion and debate within and between museums. Sharing in dialog about ethical issues related to collection stewardship can prepare registrars and collections managers to face ethical problems that arise as well as provoke reflection about conventional practice. Ethical dilemmas are not resolved by the application of hard-and-fast rules but instead through careful thought and deliberation, the separation of opinion from fact, and an understanding of an institution's mission as well as its long-term goals and objectives. Because ethical problems can arise in virtually every activity engaged in by a museum, developing ethical skills—an ethical *frame of mind*—could keep many of those situations from escalating into controversies that endanger the public's trust in museums.

The process of resolving ethical dilemmas should be shared, discussed, and enjoyed for what it teaches us about our museums and their role in responding to and complying with their obligations to the public. ●

NOTES

1. M. Malaro, *Museum Governance: Mission, Ethics, Policy* (Washington, DC: Smithsonian Institution Press, 1994), 17.

2. American Alliance of Museums, *Code of Ethics for Museums*, amended 2000. Available at: https://www.aam-us.org/pro grams/ethics-standards-and-professional-practices/code-of -ethics-for-museums/.

3. Depending on the organizational structure and resources of a museum, the institution might hire a registrar or a collections manager. In some museums, curators may have responsibility for the physical care of collection in storage. For the purposes of this essay, the term *registrar* will be used to refer to the position that is responsible for developing and enforcing policies and procedures related to the acquisition, management, and disposition of collections as well as maintaining records of the collections and overseeing loans.

4. S. Yerkovich, *A Practical Guide to Museum Ethics* (Lanham, MD: Roman & Littlefield, 2016), xi–xii.

5. The Association of Academic Museums and Galleries' *Professional Practices for Academic Museums & Galleries* provides a useful list of laws that might have an impact upon museum acquisitions. Available at: https://www.aamg-us.org/wp/best -practices/, 13–14.

6. All of the names of people and institutions in the hypothetical cases included in this chapter are fictional. The situations are composites of real and fictional circumstances and reflect actual issues faced by museums. Any resemblance to an identifiable museum is coincidental.

7. For a concise discussion of abandoned property, see H. H. Kuruvilla, *A Legal Dictionary for Museum Professionals* (Lanham, MD: Rowman & Littlefield, 2016), 3–4.

8. For accounts of some of the looting that occurred during World War II, see L. H. Nicholas, *The Rape of Europa: The Fate of Europe's Treasure in the Third Reich and the Second World War* (New York: Vintage Books, 1995); F. Feliciano, *The Lost Museum: The Nazi Conspiracy to Steal the World's Greatest Works of Art* (New York: Basic Books, 1997); and K. Akinsha and G. Kozlov, *Beautiful Loot: The Soviet Plunder of Europe's Art Treasures* (New York: Random House, 1995).

9. Available at: https://en.wikipedia.org/wiki/Washington_ Principles_on_Nazi-Confiscated_Art.

10. For a more complete discussion of the ethical issues involved in the recovery of art and other objects confiscated or looted during World War II, see "Restitution, Repatriation or Retention? The Ethics of Cultural Heritage," in Yerkovich, *Practical Guide*, 119–124.

11. See the International Council of Museums *Code of Ethics for Museums*, 6.3: "When a country or people of origin seeks the restitution of an object or specimen that can be demonstrated to have been exported or otherwise transferred in violation of the principles of international and national conventions, and shown to be part of that country's or people's cultural or natural heritage, the museum concerned should, if legally free to do so, take prompt and responsible steps to cooperate in its return." Similarly, the American Alliance of Museums *Code of Ethics for Museums* states that "competing claims of ownership that may be asserted in connection with objects in its custody should be handled openly, seriously, responsively and with respect for the dignity of all parties involved."

12. The Fred Jones Jr. Museum at the University of Oklahoma received considerable negative publicity surrounding its reluctance to return a painting (see Yerkovich, *Practical Guide*, 123), and more recently, the Leopold Museum in Austria found itself the recipient of negative publicity because the museum returned a painting to the wrong family; see David D'Arcy, "Austria returns wrong Klimt to wrong family," *The Art Newspaper*, November 13, 2018. Available at: https://www.theartnewspaper.com/news/ austria-returns-wrong-klimt-to-wrong-family.

13. For a detailed discussion of the processes of deaccessioning and disposal, see CHAPTER 31, "Deaccession and Disposal."

14. A sample of the provisions from major professional organizations are included here. Others may be found as sidebars in the American Alliance of Museums' *Direct Care of Collections: Ethics, Guidelines and Recommendations* cited in note 16.

15. American Alliance of Museums, *Code of Ethics*.

16. American Alliance of Museums, *Direct Care of Collections: Ethics, Guidelines and Recommendations*. Available at: https:// www.aam-us.org/programs/ethics-standards-and-professional- practices/direct-care-of-collections/.

17. Association of Art Museum Directors, *AAMD Policy on Deaccessioning*, issued June 9, 2010, amended October 2015. Available at: https://aamd.org/sites/default/files/document/ AAMD%20Policy%20on%20Deaccessioning%20website_0 .pdf.

18. American Association for State and Local History, AASLH Statement on Standards and Ethics. Available at: http://down load.aaslh.org/AASLH+Statement+of+Standards+and+Ethics+ -+Revised+2018.pdf.

19. International Council of Museums (ICOM), *ICOM Code of Ethics for Museums* (Paris: ICOM, 2017), 12–13.

20. Association of Academic Museums and Galleries, *Professional Practices for Academic Museums & Galleries*, 2018. Available at: https://www.aamg-us.org/wp/best-practices/.

21. Society of American Archivists, *Guidelines for Reappraisal and Deaccessioning*, issued 2012, revised 2017. Available at: https://www2.archivists.org/groups/technical-subcommittee -on-guidelines-for-reappraisal-and-deaccessioning-ts-grd/ guidelines-for-reappraisal-and-deaccession.

22. See "Conflict of Interest," in Kuruvilla, *A Legal Dictionary*, 29–30.

23. ICOM, *Code of Ethics for Museums*, 29.

KATE MACUEN

Objects are a big part of how we tell our story. They carry on the memories of the makers.

—Jordan Dresser[1]

IN 2013 A SMALL lecture series on archaeology at a museum in Miami was attended by members of the Seminole Tribe of Florida's Native American Graves Protection and Repatriation Act (NAGPRA) Committee. At the time, the NAGPRA committee was earnestly consulting on a repatriation case to return ancestors home who were then housed at a large university museum. The remains of these individuals were acquired during a dark period of US history when large numbers of human remains, sacred objects, and grave goods were taken through the heinous acts of violence, grave robbing, religious suppression, and annihilation. The remains held at this particular museum, and under review by the NAPGRA committee, were of women and children who died during their forced removal from their homelands, as well as warriors whose crania had been removed by physicians on the battlefield during the Seminole War period as a way to further study what some considered "inferior" groups of people.[2] As the repatriation case continued, the NAGPRA committee respectfully asked that although the remains of these individuals remained in the museum's collection, any analysis or research on them (including publications and presentations) be halted out of respect for the tribe's ancestors. The request was denied at the time.

The NAGPRA committee attended this lecture series for one main reason—to observe a presentation of a graduate student's research project on the Seminole ancestral remains that were in the university museum's collection. The NAGPRA committee, along with members of the public, sat through the presentation, which shared culturally sensitive photographs and scientific analysis that was done outside of consultation with the tribe, and subsequently contra-

dicted oral histories and traditional cultural views. It was in the name of science that the remains of these individuals had been taken from their resting places and almost two hundred years later, Western science was still interpreting them without consultation with the tribe.[3]

This experience is shared to illuminate some of the critical challenges that museums face—how to manage, care for, and consult on culturally sensitive and sacred objects in their collections. Although the terrain is not always easy to navigate, museums should exercise inclusivity in all of their spaces by welcoming the voices of source and descendent communities and learning how to integrate an object's cultural context with care protocols. Outside of specific laws, museums are not generally required to consult with culturally affiliated groups, which in many ways has allowed for the continuation of colonial interpretations. Therefore, adoption of strong ethical and social justice standards will help guide the care and disposition of sacred objects. While the following guidelines and best practices offer a road map for care, it is important to note that this subject matter deserves thoughtful consideration and consultation, which may be unique to each object.

DEFINING SACRED AND CULTURALLY SENSITIVE OBJECTS

We are asked to fit the sacred realm into a tidy box so that others can manage our cultural property through policy.

—Sven Haakanson, Jr.[4]

Sacred and culturally sensitive objects have come to museums through many different means. As previously noted, some of these objects were collected under painful and traumatic circumstances. Other sacred objects may be on loan to a museum, some were created with the intention of exhibition or display, whereas others were purchased or received through donation from a cultural or religious group.[5] There are several important questions that should be explored by museums as they develop policies that guide the care of culturally sensitive and sacred objects. The first and foremost question is, what is sacred or essential to a culture?[6]

How do the staff of a museum know what is sacred or religious within their collections? There is no one-size-fits-all definition for sacred and culturally sensitive objects, which understandably has caused some apprehension within the museum community. If the definition itself is unclear, then could any object be deemed sacred in a museum's collection? Although that is an unlikely scenario, it does raise a valid concern for those museums trying to better identify the objects in their collections. The key to understanding which objects are sacred is that museum staff must work closely with present-day cultural authorities in groups affiliated with the objects. Museums must be guided by the principle that "authenticity, authority, and expertise sit outside the museum as well as within it."[7] Fostering the idea that we are merely custodians of collections and not owners allows for the inclusion of spiritual and traditional cultural practices, which, in return, provides a path for reconciliation and relationship building among source communities.

Culturally sensitive and sacred objects come under the larger category of cultural property. Cultural property can include either tangible or intangible evidence or expressions of cultural heritage. Sherry Hutt writes that, "cultural property is so central to personal identity that the International Conference on Cultural Property Rights of the United Nations termed it 'ethnocide' to withhold or destroy cultural property."[8]

As a starting point for museums, several working definitions may prove useful. Both NAGPRA and the National Museum of the American Indian (NMAI) Act define sacred objects as:

Specific ceremonial objects which are needed by traditional Native American religious leaders for the practice of traditional Native American religions by their present-day adherents.[9]

NAGPRA legislation provides definitions for human remains and culturally sensitive objects, including funerary objects, and objects of cultural patrimony.[10]

The Museum of New Zealand Te Papa Tongarewa defines culturally sensitive objects as:

Objects or types of objects about which people of the culture from which the objects originate have concerns about the objects' present and future use, care, and possession.[11]

The Canadian Conservation Institute's (CCI) *Preventive Conservation Guidelines for Collections* online resource defines sacred and holy objects in this way:

"Sacred" may include objects or places that are venerated, consecrated, dedicated or protected. "Holy" is often associated with a religion or a deity. Although not all ceremonies, or the objects used in them, are religious, they may remain highly culturally significant. Sacred places and objects may be revered in a larger sense, such as those associated with the actions of cultural ancestors, or those used in the individual sense of "sacred to the memory of."[12]

Cultural significance attached to an object can change over time so it is important for museums to acknowledge the fluidity of cultural values. The CCI guidelines go on to say that it is not just "the original situation or intended use of the object that determines whether it is regarded today as sacred/sensitive heritage, but the intervening passage of time and events."[13]

Identifying Affiliated Groups

Cultural affiliation determines which individual or group will be the owner or steward of culturally sensitive and sacred objects. It is through this identifying link that tribes, religious, or cultural groups can request particular care, treatment, and disposition of sacred objects.

In 2017, the Seminole Tribe of Florida's NAGPRA Committee was confronted with several challenges during a repatriation claim of twenty-seven sets of human remains. The tribe had presented several lines of evidence to support cultural affiliation for these remains including oral histories, historical records, and ancestral land evidence. When the claim was submitted to the holding museum, the museum largely denied the request, and was only willing to repatriate four of the twenty-seven sets of human remains. All of the individuals had been removed from their original resting places in the state of Florida, yet the museum claimed that there was not a preponderance of evidence to support cultural affiliation for the remaining twenty-three. Furthermore, because not all of the remains had been originally labeled as Seminole in the archaeological record, but only identified as prehistoric, the museum asserted that they held no lineal or historic connection to the Seminole Tribe of Florida. In an effort to provide additional evidence of cultural affiliation, additional oral histories were shared about the tribe's long ancestral connection to the state of Florida. After hearing these oral histories museum staff asked if they had been written down as it would prove stronger evidence of cultural affiliation for the review committee if the oral histories had been published in a book.[14] As of 2019, cultural affiliation for the twenty-three individuals was still in dispute. Determining cultural affiliation can be a taxing and complex process, as seen in this example. Not all sacred and culturally sensitive objects were acquired by legal or ethical means. Records indicating the object's purpose or cultural context may be lost or may never have existed in the first place. Inaccurate identification of cultural groups by the original collector is not uncommon.

Cultural affiliation can be determined in a number of ways including looking at geographical and ancestral lands, kinship or biological connections, archeological evidence, linguistics, folklore, oral histories, and historical or religious records.[15] All of these lines of evidence are to be weighed equally. Museum staff must also recognize the cultural authority and collective knowledge of affiliated groups and that these groups have the right to define their own cultural practices and belief systems.

Under NAGPRA, cultural affiliation is defined as:

A relationship of shared group identity which can be reasonably traced historically or prehistorically between a present-day Indian tribe or Native Hawaiian organization and an identifiable earlier group.[16]

The first step collection management staff should take to determine cultural affiliation is to review all existing documentation and records associated with the object. If there is missing information or the affiliation is inconclusive, additional research may be necessary. Conducting new research should be done in good faith and guided by inclusive practices.[17]

Knowledge of basic human rights and legal rights is critical to the identification of culturally affiliated groups and the treatment and disposition of culturally sensitive and sacred objects. NAGPRA and the NMAI Act provide a process for cultural objects to be returned to lineal descendants and culturally affiliated Indian tribes and Native Hawaiian organizations. In addition to these two laws, museum staff must be knowledgeable about human and civil rights to ensure that no laws have or will be violated during acquisition, treatment, and disposition.

Consultation

It is through active consultation between museum staff and culturally affiliated groups that decisions on care and disposition are made. Consultation is a critical nexus to building relationships and provides a process for meaningful dialog with the affected groups. It is an opportunity for full expression of views from both the museum and the affiliated groups. Consultation is a legal requirement under NAGPRA, but experiences with consultation vary greatly, from very good to very poor.[18]

According to the National Association of Tribal Historic Preservation Officers, "mutual respect must be the basis upon which successful consultation builds, and that coming to a final agreement is not as important as building ongoing channels of communication."[19] The quality of consultation is not solely based on the outcome but on the commitment and respectful exchange of views.

Although successful consultation may take on different forms it should incorporate the following baseline practices:

- Museums are responsible for notifying official representatives of affiliated cultural groups about objects that may be deemed culturally sensitive or sacred. It is not feasible for source communities to know if a museum holds sacred objects of interest. Note that NAGPRA dictates the process for how museums notify culturally affiliated tribes.
- Meaningful consultation requires an investment of time and energy and extends beyond sending a formal letter of notification. Initial notification must be followed up with phone calls and emails. If possible, try to have a face-to-face meeting with official representatives. The effort made by museum staff will go far to build long-term, collaborative partnerships.
- Tribal governments are inundated with consultation requests each year, so be patient as it may take time to get information to the right cultural authority within an affiliated group.
- Acknowledge and actively listen to the expertise and knowledge that is shared by the source communities. Be sensitive when explaining how these objects came to be with the museum. Conclusions should not be made ahead of consultation—doing so implies that the museum is not open to hearing what representatives have to say.[20]
- Provide the delegation with all associated documentation, including accession, conservation, and research records, prior to hosting an on-site consultation. Identify any special requirements that may need to be accommodated during the visit. It is helpful to develop an agenda and to identify ahead of time which staff members will attend or assist with the consultation.
- There may be financial constraints that prevent delegations from being able to attend an on-site consultation. If possible, museums should budget for consultation expenses. National NAGPRA offers Consultation/Documentation grants to support the efforts of both museums and Indian tribes and Native Hawaiian organizations.[21]
- On-site consultation guidelines:

  ○ Provide a comfortable space for representatives to discuss, view, and handle the objects. Before the delegation arrives, it is important to discuss what will be out on view. For example, a tribe may wish to not view certain objects or human remains. Some tribes feel there is a risk to handling or improperly handling certain objects, which would cause harm to individuals or their communities.[22]

  ○ Provide a space to accommodate cultural practices, ceremonies, or rituals. If there are concerns regarding the conflict of church and state, religious rituals can be characterized as a cultural practice. If invited, museum staff may take part in ritual or ceremonial practices; however, as a protection of their rights they are not required to do so.[23]

  ○ Disclose any toxic chemicals or chemical traces on objects that may pose a health risk.[24]

- Fully document the consultation. Documentation may include written notes, updated catalog or database records, audio or video recordings, and photographs. The need for confidentiality or restrictions on information access and how a consultation is documented should be discussed prior to a consultation. Representatives are not required to disclose sacred or culturally sensitive information and may request to have private discussions during their visit.
- Museum expert Alison Edwards identifies four main questions that consultations should include: (i) What objects may be displayed or used for educational purposes? (ii) Are any of the objects essential to ongoing religious or ceremonial practices? (iii) Are there recommendations for how objects should be housed? (iv) Does the community wish to borrow objects for ceremonial purposes (this could include objects that may eventually be repatriated and objects that may stay in the museum)?[25] A few additional questions to consider include: (v) Are there any recommendations on how objects should be handled? (vi) Are there any objections to object research or testing (e.g., testing for pesticides or use in radio carbon dating)? (vii) Does the affiliated group wish to have these objects returned?
- Request for repatriation may be brought up during consultation. Laws such as NAGPRA will dictate the legal responsibility a museum has to repatriate

to Indian tribes and Native Hawaiian organizations. If the return of a sacred or culturally sensitive object is not guided by law, the museum should make clear their internal policies regarding disposition.

Successful consultation may not involve all of these practices. Each meeting, phone call, or correspondence will be unique so it is only through meaningful dialog between museums and source communities that common ground can be found. Consultation can be emotional, uncomfortable, and difficult for all parties involved; and although it is oftentimes challenging, it is a responsibility that museums must not take lightly as it can be the first step to righting past wrongs and healing communities.

Implementing and Developing Collection Care Protocols

When museums work to follow the spirit of the law and are guided by sound ethical practices, they can make their best efforts to honor specific care requests made by a culturally affiliated group. The practice of properly caring for culturally sensitive and sacred objects places an extra emphasis on the human element of collections management. Ultimately, it should bring satisfaction to the museum staff to know that they were part of a process to properly protect or return sacred objects to their source communities.

Collection care guidelines will be unique to each museum and developed through their consultation efforts. It is worth noting that not all cultural groups believe that their sacred objects need specific care protocols.[26] When developing collection care protocols, it is important that museum administration and staff are fully educated and in agreement about any special care considerations. Successful implementation of collection policy and procedures rely on all staff being well-informed.

In their NAGPRA handbook, *Finding Our Way Home*, the Little Traverse Bay Bands of Odawa Indians, in consultation with numerous tribes and museums from across the country, identified common requests that tribes have made to museums regarding how culturally sensitive or sacred objects should be cared for:[27]

- Human remains should be off limits to the general public and are to be protected by rigorous access policies.
- Human remains should be stored in appropriate containers (special boxes, certain colored cloth, special medicines included).
- Human remains should be handled only by certain individuals.
- Some tribes may conduct special ceremonies for remains and objects while they are at museums.
- Sacred items should be stored in an appropriate manner.
- Sacred objects are to be handled only by specified individuals.
- Requested objects and human remains must not be displayed.
- Videotaping and photographs are not permitted (although some tribes allow sketches of funerary and sacred items to use as future reference for reviewing inventories and summaries from different museums).

The US Holocaust Memorial Museum has integrated certain protocols for complying with Jewish religious law to appropriately care for their Judaica collections. Objects that fall under the category *tashmishey kedusha* ("accessories of holiness") are given extra care and consideration. Examples include:[28]

- Religious scrolls that are retired from use are only to be conserved and cared for by a Jewish conservator.
- A Torah that was destined for burial should not be restored.
- Special considerations are given to scrolls in regard to their coverings and treatments when out in the open.
- Consultation with a rabbi or the Jewish community should be done to develop proper care and exhibit protocols for *tashmishey kedusha*.

The integration of traditional cultural practices and treatments—while still maintaining appropriate levels of collections care—requires a balance of ethics, logistics, and available resources. Museums must work with affiliated cultural groups to know what can and cannot be done. For example, is it possible for a museum to reorientate a statue of the Buddha so that the Buddha's head is higher than surrounding objects? What about the inclusion of ceremonial feedings or offerings in an exhibit or collections storage area? Will a museum allow for smudging or smoking of culturally sensitive objects? Although many requests by cultural or religious groups may be a simple change and do not pose concerns (e.g., changing the type of materials an object is housed in), some may be more complex, needing time and resources to accommodate. Not all requests can be implemented due to constraints such as space restrictions or federal regulations. However, thoughtful curation planning and policy development will provide a means for the museum and cultural or religious groups to arrive at common ground, ensuring that sacred and culturally sensitive objects are cared for in the most appropriate ways. Within these guidelines, museums should have steps in place to address traditional practice requests. The Department of Anthropology at the National Museum of Natural History has been incorporating specific cultural procedures to care for culturally sensitive objects since the 1980s. The museum has established a three-part process that includes evaluation, implementation, and record management:[29]

1. Evaluate the submission request to change how the objects are housed. During this evaluation two questions should be addressed: (a) Does the person making the request have the authority to do so? (b) Can the request be reasonably accommodated?
2. If the request can be implemented, a plan of action should be created to identify the logistics, resources, and staff requirements needed.
3. Record all procedural changes, including the name of the individual who requested the change, the suggested treatment, and the object(s) involved. Once the request is accommodated, the requestor is notified.

Museum staff or visitors may have questions about why they need to abide by these care protocols; it is not about the person's personal belief in the cultural practices, "but asking them to respect those who do."[30] Although daunting at first, it is possible to find an effective balance between cultural care requests and traditional museum practices. Both the Alutiiq Museum and Archaeological Repository in Kodiak, Alaska, and the Ah-Tah-Thi-Ki Museum in Clewiston, Florida, are tribal museums that have received accreditation with the American Alliance of Museums. Both museums successfully navigate Western museum standards of care with the recognition and incorporation of traditional cultural methods and practices through their own internal guidelines and policies.[31]

Access

There is much discussion within the museum community about the accessibility of culturally sensitive and sacred objects. The topic of accessibility is twofold: Providing increased access for culturally affiliated and source communities and accommodating restricted access to sacred and culturally sensitive objects. It is a challenging subject that can produce ethical dilemmas as museums search for a balance between their missions as public trust institutions and their responsibilities to be inclusive of an object's cultural, sacred, and religious significance.

During consultation, representatives may request increased access to culturally sensitive, religious, or ceremonial objects. These objects may eventually be repatriated or they may stay under the care of the museum for perpetuity—as seen at the Australian Museum. Chief Jerry Taki, Ni-Vanuatu leader and traditional owner from the island of Erromango, was asked by then Director of the Australian Museum, Frank Howarth, if the people of Vanuatu would want the extensive Vanuatu collections to be repatriated back to them. Chief Jerry Taki responded no, and that it was good that the museum was caring after their objects, and that, "as long as the Ni-Vanuatu people have access to their objects then he was satisfied that they stay where they are."[32]

Some museums have implemented long-term loan agreements as a way that culturally affiliated groups can have access to a sacred object for use in ceremonies or religious practices within their own communities. The Minnesota Historical Society states in their *NAGPRA and Culturally Sensitive Objects Policy* that, "the Society will make decisions regarding loans of culturally sensitive and sacred objects in consultation with the appropriate tribes. Loans will not be made if written permission from the appropriate entity cannot be obtained. Temporary or long-term loan of the Society's culturally sensitive objects to their home communities for use in that community will also be considered."[33]

Certain restrictions to sensitive information and the handling or viewing of sensitive objects may be requested through consultation. There are many ways that museum staff can accommodate access restrictions:

- Physical access to information can be controlled through tiered security permissions within databases or electronic badge or key access to rooms that hold sensitive objects or information. Not all information is intended to be distributed to every staff member or to the public.[34]
- If space allows, certain collection objects may be placed in separate storage areas or isolated within collection rooms.
- Objects can be clearly marked with cautions concerning the handling or viewing of these objects. The restrictions should be in both the objects records and physically in the space where the object is housed. Warnings or restrictions do not need to reveal sensitive cultural information on why objects require certain care. Object labels or warning flags within a database allow staff members who wish to observe the restrictions the chance to do so.
- Respect requests to limit or cease the distribution of sensitive object information, including photographs and digital recordings. Any new or continued requests for research or analysis should be deferred to the cultural group for a decision.[35]
- Any requests pertaining to preventive conservation and conservation treatments of the objects should be respected.

The 1997 exhibit *Baule: African Art/Western Eyes*, held at the Yale University Art Gallery in corporation with the Museum for African Art in New York, successfully demonstrated how cultural viewing restrictions were accommodated during an exhibition. The exhibit, co-curated by Susan Vogel and native Baule researcher Koffi Nguessan, allowed the Baule artworks to be "seen both in the distinctive ways intended by their creators and in the traditional Western museum manner."[36] Several of the objects presented in the exhibit were placed into gender restricted spaces to honor their role in Baule sacred rituals. Although visitors were given full access to the exhibition, many of them chose to respect the restricted areas.[37]

There are debates, however, within the museum community concerning whether access restrictions should or should not be allowed. These debates stem from the foundational belief that it is a museum's responsibility to hold objects within the public trust. Some argue that to restrict access to sacred or culturally sensitive objects would take away a visitor's opportunity to be exposed and learn from the heritage of our collective humanity.[38] Museums should not be servants to any one political or religious agenda so giving the "right to religious freedom for a few over the right to intellectual freedom of the academic community as well as the education of the general public" places museums in a contradictory role.[39] These differences in belief shape how museums manage access to culturally sensitive objects and their information. Consultation is an appropriate time to inform cultural or religious groups of the institution's protocols on recordkeeping and access so that an informed decision on what information will be shared can be made.

CONCLUSION

The changes we see happening in museums surrounding culturally significant collections are encouraging. As stewards of cultural heritage, museum professionals should continue to embrace an inclusive approach to collections care that not only supports the diversity of their constituencies, but also provides strong guidance on how best to care for, conserve, handle (or not handle), and exhibit sacred and culturally sensitive objects. It may seem overwhelming to begin the transition to inclusive care practices, but even small, meaningful steps can prove rewarding.

When developing care policies and procedures, remember these key points:

- Not all objects within museum collections were acquired legally or by ethical means.
- Culturally affiliated and religious groups should be recognized and their rights to protect their sacred objects respected.
- Consultation helps build trust, relationships, and communication between the museum and culturally affiliated groups.
- Collection care protocols, including access guidelines, will be unique to each museum.
- Successful implementation of inclusive care practices relies on the education of all staff.

Although cultural property and human rights laws will guide the development of collection care policies, a museum's ethical obligations must also take precedence. The ways in which culturally sensitive and sacred objects are cared for do not always conform to what the field considers traditional museum preservation practices and may actually lead to the nonpreservation of an object or reburial of an object. Each care decision will be unique and should be based on consultation with culturally affiliated groups.

Museums are incredible places to learn and expand knowledge, and it is a museum's foundational responsibility to preserve the knowledge held within their collections. Yet information associated with culturally sensitive and sacred collections is not always represented truthfully, tainted with colonial narratives that disregard their often traumatic histories. Through thoughtful research and meaningful consultation, museums can preserve accurately both the tangible and intangible properties of these objects by engaging with source and descendent communities. The hope is that the relationships built will not just guide the care of sacred objects but influence all facets of a museum. Involving cultural authorities and communities will lead to diverse and rich experiences that will, no doubt, have a profound impact on staff and visitors alike. •

NOTES

1. Jordan Dresser, "What Was Ours," DVD, directed by Mat Hames (Austin: Alphgeus Media, Inc., 2016).

2. D. deBeaubien and K. Macuen, "Bringing the Ancestors Home," in *We Come for Good: Archaeology and Tribal Historic Preservation at the Seminole Tribe of Florida*, edited by P. N. Backhouse, B. Weisman, and M. B. Rosebrough, pp. 236–254 (Gainesville: University Press of Florida, 2017).

3. Lecture attended by author in 2013 at the National Archaeology Day event, Lowe Art Museum.

4. S. Haakanson, "Understanding sacredness: Facing the challenges of cultural change," in *Stewards of the Sacred*, edited by L. J. Sullivan and A. Edwards, pp. 123–128 (Washington, DC: American Association of Museums, 2004).

5. A. Edwards, "Care of sacred and culturally sensitive objects," in *Museum Registration Methods*, 5th ed., edited by R. A. Buck and J. A. Gilmore, pp. 408–425 (Washington, DC: American Association of Museums, 2010).

6. R. McCoy, "Is NAGPRA irretrievably broken?" 2018. Available at: https://culturalpropertynews.org/is-nagpra-irretrievably-broken/ (accessed April 20, 2019).

7. See W. R. West, "The National Museum of the American Indian: Steward of the sacred," in *Stewards of the Sacred*, edited by Sullivan and Edwards, pp. 7–18.

8. S. Hutt, C. M. Blanco, W. E. Stern, and S. N. Harris, *Cultural Property Law. A Practitioner's Guide to the Management, Protection, and Preservation of Heritage Resources* (Chicago: American Bar Association, 2004).

9. Native American Graves Protection and Repatriation Act, 25 U.S.C. 3001 et seq. Available at: https://www.nps.gov/history/local-law/FHPL_NAGPRA.pdf (accessed April 20, 2019).

10. See CHAPTER 7F, "NAGPRA Compliance."

11. Available at: https://collections.tepapa.govt.nz/category/323742 (accessed February 10, 2019).

12. Available at: https://www.canada.ca/en/conservation-institute/services/preventive-conservation/guidelines-collections/caring-sacred-culturally-sensitive-objects.html#a3 (accessed February 10, 2019).

13. Available at: https://www.canada.ca/en/conservation-institute/services/preventive-conservation/guidelines-collections/caring-sacred-culturally-sensitive-objects.html#a3 (accessed February 10, 2019).

14. Author's personal experience, 2017.

15. Native American Graves Protection and Repatriation Act, 25 U.S.C. 3001 et seq. Available at: https://www.nps.gov/history/local-law/FHPL_NAGPRA.pdf (accessed June 2, 2019).

16. 25 U.S.C. 3001 (2).

17. Edwards, "Care of sacred."

18. B. M. Mueller, "Consultation and compliance: Then and now," in *We Come for Good*, edited by Backhouse et al., pp. 255–272.

19. National Association of Tribal Historic Preservation Officers, "Tribal consultation: Best practices in historic preservation," 2005. Available at: http://www.nathpo.org/PDF/Tribal_Consultation.pdf.

20. Mueller, "Consultation and compliance."

21. National NAGPRA, 43 CFR 10.2 (e).

22. E. Hemenway, M. E. Henry, and A. L. Holt, *Finding Our Way Home: A Handbook for Tribes, Universities, Museums and Individuals Working Towards Reparation under NAGPRA* (Harbor Springs, MI: Little Traverse Bay Bands of Odawa Indians, 2012). Available at: http://www.ltbbodawa-nsn.gov/Arch/NAGPRA%20LTBB%20Manual.pdf (accessed June 10, 2019).

23. Edwards, "Care of sacred."

24. Available at: https://americanindian.si.edu/explore/collections/conservation/pesticides (accessed June 10, 2019).

25. Edwards, "Care of sacred."

26. G. Flynn, and D. Hull-Walski, "Merging traditional indigenous curation methods with modern museum standards of care," *Museum Anthropology* 25, no. 1 (2001): 31–40.

27. Hemenway et al., *Finding Our Way Home.*

28. D. Butler, "Museum approaches to Judaica: The forgotten spoils of the Nazi plunder of Europe" (master's thesis, Seton Hall University, 2017).

29. Flynn and Hull-Walski, "Merging traditional."

30. Available at: https://www.canada.ca/en/conservation-institute/services/preventive-conservation/guidelines-collections/caring-sacred-culturally-sensitive-objects.html#a3 (accessed February 10, 2019).

31. See S. Haakanson, "The Alutiiq Museum's guidelines for the spiritual care of objects," in *Stewards of the Sacred*, edited by Sullivan and Edwards, pp. 155–166.

32. F. Howarth, "Decolonizing the museum mind," 2018. Available at: https://www.aam-us.org/2018/10/08/decolonizing-the-museum-mind/ (accessed March 7, 2019).

33. Minnesota Historical Society, "NAGPRA and Culturally Sensitive Objects Policy," 2013. Available at: http://sites.mnhs.org/library/sites/sites.mnhs.org.library/files/NAGPRA%20Policy%20Final.pdf (accessed June 17, 2019).

34. See Flynn and Hull-Walski, "Merging traditional."

35. Edwards, "Care of sacred."

36. S. M. Vogel, "Baule: African Art Western Eyes," *African Arts* 30, no. 4 (1997): 64–77.

37. R. Hartfield, "Seeing and silence: Sacred encounter in museum exhibition," in *Stewards of the Sacred*, edited by Sullivan and Edwards, 51–56.

38. T. Jenkins, *Keeping Their Marbles. How the Treasures of the Past Ended Up in Museums and Why They Should Stay There* (Oxford: Oxford University Press, 2016).

39. Edwards, "Care of sacred."

7C | COPYRIGHT

MELISSA LEVINE AND CHRISTINE STEINER

THIS CHAPTER PROVIDES a broad overview of certain aspects of US copyright law focusing on three key copyright concepts—the exclusive rights of a copyright owner, the duration rules, and fair use. It briefly addresses Creative Commons licenses and open access as two important areas to be aware of in museum work. We encourage readers to consider this chapter along with CHAPTER 7D, "Rights and Reproductions." Selected resources are provided at the end of this chapter for further exploration. This chapter is intended as information to assist museum professionals in the performance of their duties; it is not intended as a substitute for legal advice. Specific intellectual property issues may require the assistance of counsel.

ABOUT INTELLECTUAL PROPERTY

Copyright is only one aspect of intellectual property, and it is helpful to have a sense of the different areas of law that are casually implied by the phrase. Intellectual property generally refers to the separate and distinct protection regimes of copyright, trademark, patent, and trade secret. The World Intellectual Property Organization[1] (WIPO) provides some helpful definitions:

Copyright—"Copyright is a legal term used to describe the rights that creators have over their literary and artistic works. Works covered by copyright range from books, music, paintings, sculpture, and films, to computer programs, databases, advertisements, maps, and technical drawings."

Trademark—"A trademark is a sign capable of distinguishing the goods or services of one enterprise from those of other enterprises. Trademarks date back to ancient times when artisans used to put their signature or 'mark' on their products."

Patent—"A patent is an exclusive right granted for an invention. Generally speaking, a patent provides the patent owner with the right to decide how—or whether—the invention can be used by others. In exchange for this right, the patent owner makes technical information about the invention publicly available in the published patent document."

Trade secret—"Trade secret is another form of intellectual property. It tends to affect museums infrequently. Broadly speaking, any confidential business information which provides an enterprise a competitive edge may be considered a trade secret. Trade secrets encompass manufacturing or industrial secrets and commercial secrets."

Why are intellectual property issues especially significant for museums today? Intellectual property rights—particularly copyright and trademark—have always been relevant for museums as they build and preserve collections, conduct research, interpret collections for the public, organize exhibitions, and provide educational programs and services. Museums reproduce works created by others for many mission-related reasons. They create original works, own collections in trust for the public (e.g., images, objects, specimens, documents, databases), sell products, and license their names for reproductions of objects and images. As educational institutions, museums in the United States and a few other countries are entitled to make fair use of the copyrighted work of others as discussed in greater detail below.

Under US copyright law, a work is protected (i.e., it is "under copyright"), or it is in the public domain—meaning that it is freely available for use by others because there is no copyright owner of the work. Some works are in the public domain because Congress excluded certain categories for public policy reasons, specifically "any idea, procedure, process, system, method of operation, concept, principle, or discovery, regardless of the form in which it is described, explained, illustrated, or embodied in such work."[2] Works of the US government are not eligible for copyright. A *work of the US government* is one prepared by an officer or employee of the government in the scope of their employment, but the government is not precluded from receiving and holding copyrights transferred to it by assignment, bequest, or otherwise. Note that the federal government may commission works that are, in turn, eligible for copyright. Typically, states retain copyright of the work of their employees unless there is a state law to the contrary. Other works enter the public domain because the copyright lapsed for failure to comply with copyright formalities or when the copyright expires through the passage of time.

Copyright in the United States

The *Copyright Law of the United States*, as codified in Title 17 of the US Code, states that copyright protection subsists in "original works of authorship fixed in any tangible medium of expression, now known or later developed, from which they can be perceived, reproduced, or otherwise communicated."[3] These three elements—originality, authorship, fixation—are threshold requirements for copyrightability. They lead to additional questions, such as is the work original or a derivative? Is there an author? Is the work fixed in a tangible medium? If the work was created in the course of employment, it is likely a work made for hire, in which case the employer is the creator and therefore the copyright owner.

Assuming the work is eligible for protection (that it is original and fixed in a tangible medium of expression), the authors (or other copyright owners to whom rights may have been assigned or transferred) are granted exclusive rights to their creative works (with the exception of limitations such as fair use, described in section 107 of Title 17). Note that the standard for originality is not high. Copyright is often referred to as a bundle of rights because one, some, or all of the rights that make up a given copyright may be owned, sold, licensed, transferred, assigned, or some combination thereof. Copyright infringe-

ment may be subject to significant civil or criminal penalties. The exclusive rights granted by copyright are the right to reproduce, adapt, distribute, publicly perform, and publicly display the works. These rights can be understood as follows.

Reproduction

This is the right to make copies of a work. It generally prevents one who is not the copyright owner from making exact or substantially similar copies without permission. Copies are defined in the act as "material objects, other than phonorecords, in which a work is fixed by any method now known or later developed, and from which the work can be perceived, reproduced, or otherwise communicated, either directly or with the aid of a machine or device. The term 'copies' includes the material object, other than a phonorecord, in which the work is first fixed."[4]

Adaptation

This is the right to prepare derivative works based on the original copyrighted work by transforming the original or altering it in some manner. This can take the form of a reproduction of, for example, a collection object in a different medium for sale in the museum shop, a translation, a musical arrangement, dramatization, or a video. Derivative works are challenging because it must be determined whether there are sufficient original elements for the work to garner its own copyright in the first place; even if there are, the copyright extends to only the added elements.

Distribution

The distribution right gives the copyright owner the right to control the initial public distribution of copies of the work by sale, rental, lease, or loan. The owner can determine the timing of the distribution, the number of copies of the work by sale, rent, lease, or loan, the place of distribution, and the like.

The distribution right is subject to an important limitation, known as the *first sale doctrine*. Under the first sale doctrine, one who owns a copy of a protected work is entitled to sell or otherwise dispose of their possession of the copy without the authority of the copyright owner. This means that although a museum may own a physical object in its collection, the museum may not hold copyrights to or associated with that object. Of course, this will depend on whether there are copyrights at all. For example, there are no copyrights intrinsically associated with natural history materials (e.g., rocks or plants), but there may be copyrights in artwork or other human-made collection objects. Although there are no copyrights intrinsic in a rock or plant specimen, a photograph or other depiction of the object may be eligible for copyright. This concept can be confusing, and the distinction between possible copyright of a physical object and possible copyright to an image of that object is an important notion for registrars. It is important when considering when and under what conditions reproductions may be made and is a vital consideration in the acquisition of collection objects. Registrars should be aware of possible copyrights and discuss those matters with donors or sellers, documenting the copyrights in the acquisition process. As a practical matter, many museums choose not to assert possible copyrights of images (particularly digital reproductions made available online for educational purposes) of collection objects that are in the public domain. These ideas are explained further in "Recommendations for Standardized International Rights Statements,"[5] a white paper for the Rightsstatements.org project noted in the Resources section.

Public Performance

This is the right to control the listening to or viewing of a copyrighted work. Under the copyright act, three types of public performances can be distinguished: (i) a performance at a place open to the public; (ii) a performance by transmission to a place open to the public; and (iii) a performance to an audience that may be separated in time, place, or both. Many activities taking place in the public spaces of museums are considered to be public performances that require the copyright holder's permission. For example, music in connection with an opening or a background in the restaurant, or an exhibition transmitted for viewing by persons in geographically dispersed locations or at different times, could constitute a public performance. There are performing rights organizations such as the American Society for Composers, Authors, and Publishers (ASCAP) and Broadcast Music,

Inc. (BMI) that administer licenses for music performances. For museums that collect motion picture, broadcast, or recorded sounds such as music, lectures, film, or other performative material there are additional considerations beyond the scope of the basic copyright framework presented in this chapter.

Public Display

The copyright holder has the exclusive right to display the copyrighted subject matter (except sound recordings). The right of public display applies to the exhibition of original works of art and to their reproduction because copyright includes any material object in which the work is fixed. When a museum acquires a work, but not the copyright (generally the case in museum practice), the copyright act places an important limitation on that exclusive right, allowing the owner of a copy of a copyrighted work to "display that copyright publicly, either directly or by the projection of no more than one image at a time, to viewers present at the place where the copy is located."[6] This public display right extends only to the immediate physical surroundings of the work. Without express authorization, the museum might not be permitted to project images of the work into other galleries, or transmit the copy of the work over computer networks for viewing at multiple locations—unless that use is a fair use, discussed later in this chapter.

How Long Does Copyright Last?

Copyright subsists from the moment of creation until expiration of the statutory duration, regardless of whether the work is hidden away or is so popular that it is used, adapted, and reproduced on a daily basis. Congress enacted the first US copyright legislation in 1790. Since then, there have been four general revisions and many amendments of the copyright law. For much of the twentieth century, the Copyright Act of 1909 provided the basic structure for protecting creative expression in the United States. Congress overhauled the copyright law when it enacted the Copyright Act of 1976, which took effect on January 1, 1978. However, the 1909 act rules continued to apply generally to works that were published or registered before January 1, 1978.

Finally, since 1976, there have been several significant amendments to the copyright law, including the Digital Millennium Copyright Act of 1998. In 1998, Congress passed the Copyright Term Extension Act, which added twenty years to the previous life plus fifty duration of copyright. The matter of orphan works (works for which the copyright owner cannot be determined or located following a diligent search), is one of great concern for museums in light of the scope and scale of museum holdings. The museum community actively engaged in shaping legislation proposed over the years to Congress. As of this writing, no new law has been enacted and the copyright act has not been further amended, although the European Union passed a directive in 2012 regarding certain aspects of orphan works in its jurisdiction (Directive 2012/28/EU).[7]

For museums, as stewards of works produced under both laws, it is important to have a working knowledge of the principles and rules of both the 1909 and 1976 acts. The publication rules were strict under the 1909 act; it is especially important regarding pre-1978 works to understand the legal distinction between published and unpublished works. The Copyright Act defines publication as "the distribution of copies or phonorecords of a work to the public by sale or other transfer of ownership or by rental, lease, or lending. . . . A public performance or display of a work does not of itself constitute publication." Publication is also a legal term of art that is not always easy to understand intuitively.

Cornell University Library maintains an invaluable chart for determining whether a work is in the public domain. It is helpful for many situations and is titled, "Copyright Term and the Public Domain in the United States" by Peter Hirtle.[8]

Works Created on or after January 1, 1978

For works created on or after January 1, 1978, copyright protection subsists from the creation of the work and lasts for the life of the author plus 70 years (previously it was for 50 years). In general, protection lasts until the end of the calendar year 70 years after the author's death. Copyrights in works of joint authorship (other than works made for hire) continue until the end of the year of the seventieth anniversary of the last surviving author's death. Anonymous or pseudonymous works (if the name of the author is not revealed) and works made for hire are protected for 95 years (previously 75 years) from the date of first publication, or 120 years (previously 100 years) from the date of creation, whichever is shorter. Nothing in the 1998 term extension law restores copyright protection for any work that entered the public domain prior to October 27, 1998, the effective date of the legislation.

Unpublished Works Created before January 1, 1978

Museums are custodians of a vast body of unpublished works such as diaries, letters, and manuscripts, many of which date to the eighteenth or nineteenth century. Many museum professionals are surprised to learn that these works may still be protected under federal copyright law. For works created before January 1, 1978, but never published or registered as unpublished works with the Copyright Office before that date, the same duration rules discussed apply, with two important differences. First, the earliest date that copyright could expire for works in this category was December 31, 2002 (if the work remained unpublished). Second, to encourage publication, the copyright term for such works was extended through December 31, 2047 (if the work was published before December 31, 2002).

Works Created and Published before January 1, 1978

The rules for determining the copyright term for works created and published before January 1, 1978, are much different and even more complex. Museums may need to be familiar with the old rules, which may remain applicable to many works in museum collections. The general rule for works created under the 1909 Copyright Act was that copyright protection began on the actual date of publication (or the date of registration for unpublished works) and lasted for twenty-eight years, subject to a renewal term of twenty-eight years, for a total potential term of fifty-six years.

To apply these rules to works created or published before January 1, 1978, a museum should be aware of three fundamental differences between the old and current copyright laws. First, under the

1909 act, the copyright term was measured from the publication or registration of the work and not from the creation of the work. Second, copyright lasted for a definite number of years rather than the indefinite period measured by the life of the author and a fixed number of years. Third, the copyright term included a mandatory renewal feature. Failure to comply with any of the formalities of publication associated with notice or renewal could cause the work to enter the public domain.

Renewal of Works Created and Published before January 1, 1978

In theory, the renewal feature of the old copyright law was a mechanism to give authors and artists a chance to regain their copyrights after twenty-eight years. In practice, renewal often caused unwary copyright owners to lose copyrights because of failure to renew. To maintain copyright protection during the second, or renewal, term, the copyright owner had to file a renewal application with the Copyright Office during the twenty-eighth year of the initial term. Failure to comply in a timely manner meant that the work entered the public domain.

In 1976, Congress abolished the two-term system. However, it retained the renewal feature for works copyrighted before 1978 and still in their initial terms before January 1, 1978. If the owner complied in a timely manner with the renewal requirements, there were substantial benefits. The copyright owner could obtain a renewal term of forty-seven years (bringing to seventy-five years the total possible period of protection for renewed copyrights). But if the copyright owner failed to comply with the renewal requirements (even if the owner was simply unaware of the requirements), copyright in the work would be lost as the work entered the public domain.

In 1992, in part to prevent forfeitures of copyright, Congress eliminated the mandatory renewal registration requirement, automatically extending the second term for works copyrighted between January 1, 1964, and December 31, 1977. The renewal term for works in this category was automatically extended to forty-seven years.

In 1998, Congress added another twenty years of protection to works in the forty-seven-year renewal term, bringing the total possible term of protection for works in their renewal term to ninety-five years from the date copyright protection was originally secured (either through publication or registration). The 1992 renewal legislation provided a number of important incentives to encourage owners to file renewal applications, the most significant of which, for museums, is that those permitted to make a derivative work based on the original work during the first term of the copyright must obtain a new license to use the work after the first term.

Today, registration is no longer required for a copyright to exist (recall that copyright arises at the moment of fixation of an original work in a tangible medium of expression). However, registration is required to bring a legal action for copyright infringement and for statutory damages. Works may be registered through the website maintained by the US Copyright Office. There is a fee for registration, but it may be well advised depending on what is invested in a given work. In addition to registration, transfers and assignments of rights may be recorded to help others to identify the copyright holder for a given work, should permission be required. The US Copyright Office's website provides information on transfers and assignments.[9]

Copyright Restoration

In 1994, Congress implemented international trade treaties that for the first time covered certain intellectual property matters. The new law affects museums because copyright was restored for certain foreign works that had previously entered the public domain in the United States for failure to comply with certain formalities required by US law. To evaluate whether a foreign work is eligible for copyright restoration in the United States:

1. Determine whether the work originated in an eligible source country.
2. Determine whether the foreign work is still under copyright in its source country.
3. Determine the period of protection for the restored work.
4. Determine the identity and rights of the owners of the restored copyright.

5. Determine whether the museum qualifies as a reliance party.

To qualify for restoration, the work must have originated in a country (other than the United States) that is a member of the Berne Convention for the Protection of Literary and Artistic Works[10] (Berne Convention) or the World Trade Organization (WTO). Given the large number of countries that participate in the Berne Convention and the WTO, works published in the last seventy years almost anywhere in the world may now qualify for copyright restoration in the United States. The restoration rules are complex, and the potential exposure makes this an issue of particular concern to museums. Further, it is often difficult to ascertain the facts needed to evaluate whether a work is subject to restoration. Copyright restoration rules typically require consultation with a specialist. That said, museums should be familiar with the basic framework governing the eligibility of foreign works for copyright restoration in the United States and the rights and remedies for infringement of restored copyrights, including the special rules for reliance parties.

What Is Fair Use?
Fair use—an equitable doctrine that balances the rights of a copyright owner with those of society—speaks to specific uses of copyrighted works that are considered fair under the US Copyright Act. Museums are both users and creators of works and may find themselves taking potentially competing positions on fair use issues.

The tension between a copyright holder's financial and security interests and society's legitimate access to intellectual property led Congress to incorporate and codify a growing body of case law when it revised the Copyright Act in 1976. Fair use strives to ensure that the author's otherwise exclusive rights do not hinder the very creativity that the law was designed to foster. The doctrine recognizes that new works draw inspiration from older works and that productive use of older works promotes the progress of science, arts, and literature. Fair use permits certain uses that, in other contexts, would be infringement. The Copyright Act identifies such uses without explicit limitation to include criticism, comment,

news reporting, teaching, scholarship, and research. There are certain other fair uses, such as parody, that are not listed in the statute.

Fair use requires case-by-case determination. An activity may qualify in one instance as a fair use, while it would be an infringing activity in another context. The fact that a work is intended for an educational purpose does not automatically make it eligible for the fair use exception. For example, educational publishing is a large segment of the publishing market. Although its audience is educational users, it is a commercial activity that relies on obtaining permission to use the copyrighted works of others. By the same token, the fact that a use is commercial in nature does not in and of itself exclude the possibility of a fair use. Museum rights departments fulfill many textbook requests at commercial rates and may or may not consider these uses to be fair uses. Similarly, a number of museum activities may not be eligible for the fair use exception although they are designed for educational purposes (see the discussion of Creative Commons licenses).

The US Copyright Office's informational circular on fair use acknowledges that the distinction between *fair use* and *infringement* is unclear and not easily defined. It provides examples of activities that the courts have regarded as fair use, including

> quotation of excerpts in a review or criticism for purposes of illustration or comment; quotation of short passages in a scholarly or technical work, for illustration or clarification of the author's observations; use in a parody of some of the content of the work parodied; summary of an address or article, with brief quotations, in a news report; reproduction by a library or archives of a portion of a work to replace a damaged copy; reproduction by a teacher or student of a small part of a work to illustrate a lesson; reproduction of a work in legislative or judicial proceedings or reports; incidental and fortuitous reproduction in a newsreel or broadcast, of a work located in the scene of an event being reported.[11]

Fair use in the context of objects and images is even more uncertain, although there are a growing number of best practice guides including those from the Association of Art Museum Directors[12] and the Center for Media and Social Impact.[13] One must determine and apply the four fair use factors (discussed herein), with all their nuances in light of new challenges presented by electronic media and without a settled body of fine art-specific case law (in the case of art museums). The growth of the internet has been accompanied by a liberal interpretation of both freedom of speech and the fair use exception. The ease and speed of downloading and manipulating images, and the mass of unrestricted images on the internet, lull many users into assuming implied licenses to copy, print, and distribute internet materials. Some liken transmitting copyrighted materials via e-mail to sharing the newspaper or showing a picture to a friend. Social media may compound infringement because distribution is quick, easy, and inexpensive.

In the 1976 Copyright Act, Congress articulated the test for determining whether a particular use is fair:

1. The purpose and character of the use, including whether such use is of a commercial nature or for nonprofit educational purposes.
2. The nature of the copyrighted work.
3. The amount and substantiality of the portion used in relation to the copyrighted work as a whole.
4. The effect of the use upon the potential market for or value of the copyrighted work.

These criteria cannot be evaluated in isolation as a mathematical formulation, but rather the test is *a totality of the circumstances* analysis. Although the flexibility inherent in the test often leaves users and providers unsure of whether the contemplated use is a fair use, these factors guide case-by-case determinations.

The Purpose and Character of the Use

Generally speaking, nonprofit uses will receive more protection than for-profit uses. However, if the use is for-profit, but serves primarily as news reporting, comment, criticism, or education, then the purpose and character of the use may be deemed worthy of fair use consideration. An overarching concept is that copyright owners should benefit from any use of their copyrighted works that generate profits. Although the commercial use of copyrighted work tends to weigh against a finding of fair use, and non-profit use tends to weigh in favor, there is nothing conclusive about these presumptions. It is important to evaluate whether the use of a protected work *adds something new* to the work, transforming *raw material* into *new information, new aesthetics, new insights and understandings*, or what has been recognized as *transformative use*.

Nature of the Copyrighted Work

Depending on the type of copyrighted work that is being used, access may be more or less important to the public interest. Access to works of scholarship may be considered more important from a social perspective than access to fictional works (and factual or scholarly works may be seen as less creative than fictional works and thus more available for fair use). Thus, more latitude tends to be granted for copying factual works.

The Amount and Substantiality Used

In determining whether a fair use defense is appropriate, a court will consider the amount and substantiality of what has been copied from the underlying work. The court may consider what proportion of the work has been copied or how important the copied portion is to the work as a whole. That is, the analysis is both quantitative and qualitative, examining how much is too much. Generally, the greater the amount taken, the less likely it is that a court will find the use fair. But how much is too much? This is not a mathematical formulation, and there are no absolute quantitative and qualitative rules. Sometimes even a small amount taken may be unfair if the borrowed material is the heart of the work. A work of visual art is generally viewed as a whole, and borrowing more than is necessary is often difficult to assess. Taking (using, reproducing) the entire work does not necessarily mean that the new use is not a fair one because the test examines all the factors.

The Effect of the Use upon the Potential Market

This final factor in determining whether the use of another's copyrighted work qualifies as fair is the commercial import of the use. Financial incentives encourage the creation of new works. When a copyright owner objects to another's use of the copyrighted work on the basis of the negative impact such use has on the owner's market, the owner need not show actual harm; potential harm is sufficient. Using this factor, a court may evaluate actual market harm caused by the particular actions of the alleged infringer and also the adverse impact on the potential market for the original. In analyzing the effect on the potential market for the original, courts are to consider traditional, reasonable, or likely markets in evaluating the marketplace effect of the use.

Kinds of Fair Use

In addition to the activities listed in the Copyright Act as fair uses (e.g., criticism, comment, news reporting, teaching, scholarship, and research), other uses of copyrighted works enjoy fair use protection. These include uses that transform the underlying work, including parody, appropriation, and other recognized categories.

Transformative Use

Transformative use means that the new work does more than simply recast the original work to create a derivative work. Instead, the creator uses the underlying work to make a different work that stands on its own as an original expression. It is often difficult to determine whether the new expression adequately transforms the underlying work, and the outcome will depend on analysis of all the facts of the use.

Parody

Parody is by nature transformative. A parody involves using someone else's work, in whole or in part, for the purpose of humor, ridicule, comment, or the like. A work parodying another will likely use some distinguishing features of the original work to make a clear association between the original and the parody. It is through this association that the parody achieves its purpose of commenting on the original work.

Although parody as fair use presents another area of highly subjective and fact-intensive analysis, the courts have attempted to craft some guidelines. From the cases decided to date, several elements emerge for determining whether parody will be found to be fair use. A parody should comment on the original work; include only as much of the original material as is needed and not enough to confuse the consumer or public, or dilute the commercial value of the original; and should not seek to replace the original in the marketplace.

Appropriation Art

Appropriation art, by its very nature, uses the work of another in a different context. The appropriated work may be protected by copyright or trademark. The purpose of the use is to alter or comment on the meaning or intention of the original work, and it may take the form of reproducing a single image, or incorporating many images into a compilation or collage. Appropriation is not always enthusiastically received by the creator of the original work. Andy Warhol, for example, was often embroiled in claims by photographers that he had misappropriated their photographic images. Appropriation art is an important means of expression for visual artists. It is equally certain that controversies will continue to arise with regard to the appropriation of works. The guidelines for free speech, fair use, and the first sale doctrine provide some guidance for the ongoing discussion and resolution of such matters.

Open Access and Creative Commons

Open access materials are available online and can be used by anyone for free without any copyright restrictions. Open access is *not* a form of copyright infringement. It is different from fair use, although they can support each other. Open access is consistent with copyright law and allows people to reuse, repurpose, and build upon materials. The Resources section has a variety of approaches including examples from the Cleveland Museum of Art, the Art Institute of Chicago, the Getty Open Content Program, and the Met Open Access Policy. The Rijksmuseum in Amsterdam was an early adopter of this approach.

Creative Commons is a tax-exempt organization that provides free legal tools to enable authors, scientists, artists, and educators easily mark their creative work with the freedoms they want it to carry. Recall that copyright today arises at the moment of fixation of an original work and that the level of originality may be very minimal. As the internet boomed in the 1990s, all kinds of creative expression—from e-mail and later social media (user-generated content)—generated copyright. Many of these copyrighted works were either meant to be shared widely or were not the kinds of works that the creators intended to control closely. The automatic formation of unintended copyrights led the founders of Creative Commons to develop a suite of easily used licenses that work with copyright law. These licenses allow creators and copyright holders to give permission to others to reproduce and otherwise use copyrighted works in any number of ways—from all rights reserved to the ability to place one's works in the public domain. The Creative Commons website[14] provides extensive, straightforward explanations of the licenses and how to use them. Each license is expressed in three ways or layers—in plain language (human readable), in formal legal language (lawyer readable), and in a machine readable version of the license, "a summary of the key freedoms and obligations written into a format that software systems, search engines, and other kinds of technology can understand."[15]

Creative Commons licenses are legally enforceable and recognized worldwide. These licenses can be used by rights holders and museums alike to both retain and manage copyrights—and still share reproductions with teachers, students, and anyone else who may be interested—thus advancing the public educational work of the museum. All Creative Commons licenses require attribution to the original creator. Some also require sharing one's new work under the same license, not making changes to the work, and not using the work commercially. Rights holders may pick and choose which license requirements they want to accomplish—whatever works for them. As long as the user complies with the terms of the license, they are free to use the work.

Should a museum make a work available online (or otherwise) with a Creative Commons license, users may contact the museum for permissions needed for uses that exceed the stated license. Individual licenses or contracts may be negotiated for particular uses as needed. Creative Commons licenses give blanket permission to make certain types of uses as needed.

Although the Creative Commons license framework is designed for the internet, it may be used with any media. Licenses may be applied to print materials (of course, without the machine-readable layer) as well as online. These licenses are now widely used in the galleries, libraries, archives, and museums (GLAM) community. They are fundamental to the success of aggregators for cultural institutions participating in Europeana and the Digital Public Library of America (DPLA).

It is critical to keep in mind that one must be the copyright holder to apply for a license. For example, an art museum may have sculptures, paintings, or other works in its collection that the museum owns but for which the museum may not hold copyright. In the process of acquisition, museum registrars can play a vital role in negotiating acceptable uses that meet the museum's need to make reproductions for educational, scholarly, and research uses. The right to make such reproductions for products—postcards, books, and so forth—may also be negotiated.

Thoughtful use of Creative Commons licenses can be helpful in agreeing on and describing acceptable uses, but they cannot be unilaterally assigned except by the copyright holder. If the museum owns the copyrights through transfer or assignment of those rights, it may, in turn, assign a license of its choice (Creative Commons licenses may be applied to work created by museum employees and contractors, provided the service contracts include provisions for the museum to be the copyright holder or licensee; this kind of museum-created or produced content is beyond the scope of this volume but is of critical importance for today's museums).

As noted, Rightsstatements.org was developed by Europeana and the DPLA as a complement to Creative Commons licenses. The rights statements are a stable uniform resource identifier (URI) designed for cultural organizations to use to describe the rights status of works in their collections as presented in an online context. Whether digital copies of analog materials or born-digital copies, museums may select the appropriate rights statements to associate with particular works. Museums today generally desire to make collections available online to the extent legally possible. The rights statements describe the status of the underlying work; they are not meant to apply to reproductions of the underlying work. One of the principles of Rightsstatements.org is that museums are expected not to assert rights to the resulting intermediate digital copy. This is explored in the formative white paper for Rightsstatements.org (in the Resource section).

Museum Policy and Practice

An understanding of the law governing copyright is not an end in itself, but it is a necessary prerequisite for museum professionals to set institutional policy and make informed judgments about specific issues. Important steps toward a comprehensive approach include a carefully crafted copyright statement for staff and volunteers that addresses such issues as work for hire, appropriate use of museum materials, a rights and reproductions policy for outside users that articulates appropriate uses and applicable fees, and a trademark policy that identifies properties eligible for trademark protection. The policy should also address departmental enforcement responsibility within the institution.

Museums make policy decisions in every department: Who has access to the collections? Who has permission to reproduce objects from the collections? May sponsors use the museum name and images, and if so, how? Should the donor be consulted if the museum plans to make a commercial use of a donated object? Should the museum require transfer of copyright when acquiring a work in its copyright term, or is a nonexclusive license more appropriate? When and how should a museum negotiate with artists' rights societies? Who clears rights that the museum does not own, the museum or the third-party user? When a museum has conducted an adequate but unsuccessful search for the copyright owner, what next? When is it appropriate to institute litigation against infringers and how aggressive should the museum be? It will reasonably be expected that different museums will approach management of intellectual property differently depending on the nature of the institution, its mission, structure, size, location, print and electronic outreach activities, product development, and a host of other factors.

The law reflects a balance of competing interests, but professional ethics may articulate a duty above the minimum threshold of the law. Museums have the right to decide how, when, and by whom the collections information is used, and they have the responsibility to exercise that right with professional judgment and in an even-handed manner. Museums also have the responsibility to respect the intellectual property of others. In the absence of a favorable fair use analysis or other applicable limitation or exception to copyright, activities implicating copyrights are ill-advised without permission. Museums have a responsibility to establish policies to vigorously monitor copyright and trademark issues in house. The principles outlined in this chapter will provide the necessary guidance. •

RESOURCES

Association of Art Museum Directors. "Guidelines for the Use of Copyrighted Materials and Works of Art by Art Museums," October 17, 2017. Available at: https://aamd.org/sites/default/files/document/Guidelines%20for%20the%20Use%20of%20Copyrighted%20Materials.pdf (accessed June 10, 2019). (The AAMD's guidelines were prepared by lawyers with deep experience in art museums. The guidelines explain fair use in an approachable and relevant way.)

Center for Media and Social Impact, School of Communication, American University. "Codes of best practices." Available at: https://cmsimpact.org/codes-of-best-practices/ (accessed June 10, 2019). (This site provides a wide range of practical, relevant resources about fair use in the context of particular disciplines with help for libraries, poets, documentary filmmakers, and more.)

Creative Commons. "About the licenses—Creative Commons." Available at: https://creativecommons.org/licenses/ (accessed June 10, 2019). (The site is well designed and provides copious material. Start with this link to material that explains the basic licenses and explore from there.)

Hirtle, Peter. "Copyright term and the public domain in the United States." Cornell University Library. Available at: https://copyright.cornell.edu/publicdomain (accessed June 10, 2019).

Hirtle, Peter B., Emily Hudson, and Andrew T. Kenyon. 2009. *Copyright and Cultural Institutions: Guidelines for Digitization for U.S. Libraries, Archives, and Museums.* Ithaca: Cornell University Library. Available at https://ecommons.cornell.edu/handle/1813/14142. (This small book is available for free under a Creative Commons license; you can print a pdf from this website, or hard copies may be purchased elsewhere for those who prefer a bound book. This book should be in the professional library of every registrar.)

Steiner, Christine, Michael Shapiro, and Brett I. Miller (eds.). 1999. *A Museum Guide to Copyright and Trademark.* Washington, DC: American Alliance of Museums. (This guide is a helpful overview of both copyright and trademark in the museum context.)

RightsStatements.org. "White paper: Recommendations for standardized international rights statements, International Rights Statements Working Group, October 2015 (last updated May 2018)." Available at: https://rightsstatements.org/files/180531recommendations_for_standardized_international_rights_statements_v1.2.2.pdf (accessed June 10, 2019). (The Rightsstatements.org website explains the need for the statements and information for applying uniform resource identifier [URI] for online collections from cultural institutions. This white paper is a valuable explanation of the purpose of the statements, the thinking behind them, and comments on policy choices for electing not to assert copyright in certain situations.)

The Cleveland Museum of Art. "Open access." Available at: http://www.clevelandart.org/open-access (accessed June 10, 2019). (An example of a museum engaged in open access work. The following three resources provide additional examples.)

The Art Institute of Chicago. "Image licensing—Open access images." Available at: https://www.artic.edu/image-licensing (accessed June 10, 2019).

The J. Paul Getty Trust. "About the Getty—Open content program." Available at: http://www.getty.edu/about/whatwedo/opencontent.html. (accessed June 10, 2019).

The Metropolitan Museum of Art. "The Met open access policy." Available at: https://www.metmuseum.org/about-the-met/policies-and-documents/image-resources (accessed June 10, 2019).

US Copyright Office. Available at: https://www.copyright.gov/ (accessed June 10, 2019). (Find information about every imaginable area of US copyright including how to register for copyright and search Copyright Office records. The search function is somewhat limited for the needs of many museums. The US Copyright Office is working on improving public access to records regarding registration as well as transfer and assignment. The New York Public Library is in the early phases of a project to improve the utility of search functions for the Catalog of Copyright Entries [CCE].)

Volmer, Timothy. "Rijksmuseum case study: Sharing free, high quality images without restrictions makes good things happen." Creative Commons, July 30, 2014. Available at: https://creativecommons.org/2014/07/30/rijksmuseum-case-study-sharing-free-high-quality-images-without-restrictions-makes-good-things-happen/.

Wikipedia. "Open access." Last modified June 2, 2019. Available at: http://en.wikipedia.org/wiki/Open_access.

World Intellectual Property Organization. "What is intellectual property?" Accessed June 10, 2019. https://www.wipo.int/about-ip/en/

World Intellectual Property Organization. "What is a Trade Secret?" Accessed June 10, 2019. https://www.wipo.int/sme/en/ip_business/trade_secrets/trade_secrets.htm

Young, Anne (ed.). 2018. *Rights and Reproductions: The Handbook for Cultural Institutions*, 2nd edition. Washington, DC: Rowman & Littlefield and American Alliance of Museums. (This is an indispensable volume that every museum professional should be aware of in addition to Copyright for Cultural Institutions noted above. Written by a professionally diverse group of experts from museums and libraries, it is well edited and deeply relevant.)

NOTES

1. Available at: https://www.wipo.int/portal/en/index.html.

2. Available at: https://www.law.cornell.edu/uscode/text/17/102.

3. Available at: https://www.law.cornell.edu/uscode/text/17/102.

4. Available at: https://www.law.cornell.edu/uscode/text/17/101.

5. RightsStatements.org, "White Paper: Recommendations for Standardized International Rights Statements, International Rights Statements Working Group, October 2015 (last updated May 2018)." Available at: https://rightsstatements.org/files/180531recommendations_for_standardized_international_rights_statements_v1.2.2.pdf (accessed June 10, 2019).

6. Available at: https://www.law.cornell.edu/uscode/text/17/109.

7. Available at: https://eur-lex.europa.eu/legal-content/EN/TXT/?uri=celex%3A32012L0028.

8. Available at: https://copyright.cornell.edu/publicdomain (accessed June 10, 2019).

9. Available at: https://www.copyright.gov/.

10. Available at: https://www.wipo.int/treaties/en/ip/berne/.

11. Available at: https://www.copyright.gov/history/1961_registers_report.pdf.

12. Available at: https://aamd.org/sites/default/files/document/Guidelines%20for%20the%20Use%20of%20Copyrighted%20Materials.pdf (accessed June 10, 2019).

13. Available at: https://cmsimpact.org/codes-of-best-practices/ (accessed June 10, 2019).

14. Available at: https://creativecommons.org/.

15. Available at: https://courses.lumenlearning.com/masteryfacultytraining1xngcxv2/chapter/understanding-creative-commons/.

We wish to acknowledge the assistance of Vicki Gambill, Director of Collections Management, The Broad; and to recognize Michael Shapiro's contribution to the copyright portion of the book, A Museum Guide to Copyright and Trademark, *noted previously, which was excerpted in the previous edition of* Museum Registration Methods.

7D | RIGHTS AND REPRODUCTIONS

ANNE M. YOUNG

RIGHTS AND REPRODUCTIONS concerns historically fall under the broad responsibilities of registrars and collections managers. For many museums, this is one of a myriad of duties that the registrar's office oversees, whereas for others there may be individual staff members who specialize in rights and reproductions. The latter may or may not be a member of the registration or collections staff; in some museums, dedicated rights and reproductions specialists[1] may comprise their own department or be staff members in a photography or media department. Yet, one constant remains no matter where on the organizational chart rights and reproductions falls—it is vital for museums to undertake the management of their intellectual property (IP) with the same care, attention, and professionalism they apply to their physical collections and historical assets. This chapter outlines, at a general level, some of the key tasks involved with rights and reproductions. Depending on whether rights and reproductions is the sole responsibility of a staff member or one part of a broader job, the amount of work and roles discussed will vary.

It is vital for rights and reproductions specialists to have a basic understanding of the IP issues, particularly copyright, that arise with collection materials. Building a strong foundation in rights management skills begins with knowing how to identify the rights issues related to each object in a museum's collection. This includes determining if a work is protected by copyright and how to find the copyright holder, as well as understanding when other issues—such as privacy and publicity rights—may come into play. Once the rights analysis has been completed, the resulting information must be properly documented and shared within the museum. In cases where a rights holder has been identified, a museum may attempt to obtain a license to guide reproductions for a wide range of purposes.

DETERMINING COPYRIGHT STATUS

Determining whether a work is still under copyright can be a complicated task even for those experienced in copyright law. Due to the many revisions to US copyright law, the rules for calculating copyright terms are based on a maze of specific factors ranging from when the work was created, the life dates and nationality of the creator, and the type of work, to whether the work has been published and where and when it was published (see CHAPTER 7C, "Copyright"). An invaluable resource developed by Peter B. Hirtle of the Copyright Information Center at the Cornell University Library helps navigate these complicated rules. First published in 1999, Hirtle's chart, "Copyright Term and the Public Domain in the United States," is available for reference online and updated annually.[2] Armed with resources such as Hirtle's chart and basic information about the work, a researcher can often identify whether the work is still under copyright in the United States or is in the public domain.[3]

As a practical matter, the simplest approach is to start broadly at the creator level to determine what the likely copyright status is for all works by a particular creator in the collection before delving deeper into the unique factors affecting the status of individual works. It is important to remember that copyright is determined on a per-object basis. Thus, it is possible for different works by the same creator to have different copyright statuses.

Some general rules of thumb can be followed in making broad copyright determinations for individual creators of literary and artistic works:[4]

- Assume all works by the creator are unpublished or unregistered until research on individual works indicates otherwise, at which point consult Hirtle's chart to calculate the term for registered or published works.

- Works by living creators or creators who died within the past 70 years are under copyright for the life of the creator plus 70 years.[5]
- Works by anonymous creators or creators whose death date is unknown, and works made for hire, are under copyright for 120 years from the date of creation.[6]

Additionally, be aware that a single work may have multiple creators and copyrights. Review all the component parts of the broader work being assessed to determine if there is more than one creator and rights owner.

It may appear conservative to begin with a blanket assumption that all works by a creator are unpublished and unregistered because this approach will likely result in assigning copyright protection to many pre-1989 works that have come into the public domain because of failure to comply with formalities. However, it can be challenging and time-consuming to determine with certainty whether an individual work has been published or registered, when and where it was *first* published, whether it was published with or without a copyright notice, and whether the registration was renewed. Many museums simply do not have the staff or budget to conduct detailed research into the publication and registration status of every potentially copyrighted work in their collections.[7] Instead, it is more likely that further research will need to be undertaken on an as-needed basis, such as prior to reproducing a work in a publication or for marketing an exhibition.

Identifying and Finding Rights Holders

Rights and reproductions specialists are greatly aided by internet search tools and the ubiquity of websites, which often make finding contact information for living creators as simple as a single online search. If this fails or when other complexities come into play—for example, common names, name changes, uncertainty about who controls an estate, works made by multiple creators, or in connection with a publisher—strong research skills and a knowledge of relevant resources are critical.

Workflow and Resources for a Rights Clearance Project

1. *Copyright Notice*—First, look at the work and determine if there are any copyright notices. The absence of a notice does not mean the work is unprotected by US copyright laws.

2. *Background Research*—Complete a basic search on the creator. Is the individual still alive? If not, when and where did the creator die? If the individual is no longer alive, heirs or other representatives of the estate likely will be the rights holder(s). Begin by searching for an obituary or other information about any remaining family. Research may point to a spouse or children who have information about or control of an estate.

3. *Check Museum Records*—If the work was acquired directly from the creator, contact information may be readily available in a collections management system or in paper records. There may even be a transfer of copyright in the original acquisition paperwork. These resources may provide contact information for a gallery representative, studio, family descendants, or the donor. Even if the contact information is out of date, it may still provide valuable clues that will aid later research.

4. *Check Aggregate Databases*—Copyright collectives and licensing agencies serve as representatives for authors, artists, and performers as well as their estates. Although numerous licensing agencies exist across industries, those most commonly referenced by museums include:[8]

- Literary works:
  - Author's Licensing and Collecting Society[9]
  - Copyright Clearance Center (CCC)[10]
  - The Copyright Licensing Agency (CLA)[11]

- Musical works and sound recordings:
  - American Society of Composers, Authors & Publishers (ASCAP)[12]
  - Broadcast Music, Inc. (BMI)[13]
  - SESAC[14]

- Visual art:
  - Artists Rights Society (ARS)[15]
  - Bridgeman Copyright[16]

○ The Design and Artists Copyright Society (DACS)[17]

These organizations negotiate uses and permissions and collect licensing fees on behalf of the represented individuals and estates. Furthermore, they act as agents for affiliated societies and copyright collectives worldwide.

In addition to licensing agencies, there are multiple organizations and resources for museums to reference:

• Writers, Artists, and Their Copyright Holders (the WATCH File)[18]
• The Library of Congress Prints & Photographs Division's Rights and Restrictions Information[19]
• National Archives and Records Administration's Source and Permission Contact List[20]

5. *Mine the Web*—If the aforementioned searches do not lead directly to contact information, deeper searches will probably bear fruit. A simple internet search on the name of the creator is often the place to start. Many creative individuals maintain their own websites and provide contact information or an online contact form. Estates often have established foundations whose management responsibilities include associated IP rights.[21] Furthermore, it is not uncommon for a gallery or publisher to act as a representative by signing on behalf of the creator or forwarding an inquiry to the appropriate individual directly.[22] Additionally, museums sometimes own both physical materials and the IP rights. These relationships will not always be obvious or readily discoverable, but may be found on a museum's rights and reproductions website page.

6. *Confer with Colleagues*—As more museums undertake rights clearance projects, a growing community of rights and reproductions specialists has amassed significant knowledge of rights holders and their contact information. An inquiry to these colleagues, via the following professional listservs, can often produce leads:

• Museum Intellectual Property[23]
• Intellectual Property SIG of the Museum Computer Network[24]
• ImageMuse[25]

• Rights and Reproductions Professional Practices Committee of the Collections Stewardship Professional Network of the American Alliance of Museums[26]
• Intellectual Property Rights Committee of the Visual Resources Association[27]

7. *Evaluate Priorities*—If, after a careful and exhaustive search, these resources do not return a definitive rights holder and associated contact information, it is important to review and prioritize the next steps on a case-by-case basis. Is the museum conducting a general copyright clearance project? If so, consider setting aside more difficult creators for more in-depth research at a later time. If, however, clearance is required for a specific, time-sensitive use, creative research skills may be necessary. In the case of some rights holders, the search will end with no clear answer. In those cases a discussion should be held with legal counsel and museum leadership about the potential risk, including whether the museum should treat the work as an orphan or apply the fair use analysis to any use of the works.

Nonexclusive Licensing Agreements

When the copyright holder for a work has been identified and contact information is available, it is advisable for a museum to request a broad nonexclusive license. Unlike one-time specific use permissions, a broad nonexclusive license can allow a museum to reproduce a work on an ongoing basis for any of the uses covered by the license, ideally for the entire duration of the term of copyright. Having a long-term licensing agreement on file saves a museum time and resources in the long run by eliminating the need to make repeated requests for permission. It can provide clarity with respect to permitted uses by clearly spelling out what the museum can or cannot do with the copyrighted work.[28]

It is important to note that a grant of a nonexclusive license is not a transfer or surrender of any rights by the copyright holder. A licensing agreement simply bestows limited rights to the museum, and the copyright holder retains the ability to grant the same permission(s) to others and to exercise all of the rights of a copyright owner under the law. Nevertheless, some rights holders may be hesitant to grant a broad nonexclusive license and will prefer to be contacted for permission for each requested use. Typically, rights holders represented by copyright collectives or licensing agencies are the least likely to agree to broad nonexclusive licensing agreements. There are several ways a museum may obtain or request a broad nonexclusive license:

1. *Negotiate with Purchase or Donation*—A museum's best opportunity for securing a broad nonexclusive license is to negotiate for one as part of the acquisition of the work. Try to make the license a condition of the purchase agreement if the work is being purchased directly from the creator or a representative of the creator or creator's estate. For gifts from creators or their representatives, it may be simplest to enclose the licensing agreement with the deed of gift.

2. *Request License upon Acquisition*—If the representative or donor is not the creator or has no connection to the copyright holder, it will not be possible to make the license a condition of purchase or part of the deed of gift. In such cases, the museum should make it a practice to request a license as soon after the work is acquired as is possible.

3. *Request License as Part of Ongoing Project or as Needed*—Because seeking nonexclusive licensing agreements as part of the acquisition process is a relatively new endeavor at many museums, large portions of the collection may not be covered by an agreement completed for new acquisitions. Depending on available staffing and resources as well as the size of the collection, a museum could tackle the backlog by undertaking a comprehensive license request project. Museums can prioritize certain works or creators, or they may choose to start at the beginning of the collection (however that is defined) and systematically work through by first identifying rights holders and then by sending out nonexclusive licensing agreements. When contacting rights holders about current works in their collections, the museum may also attempt to secure an agreement covering all the works acquired in the future by the same creator in case circumstances change and the rights holder is no longer reachable in the future.

Elements of a Nonexclusive Licensing Agreement

Although the specific wording inevitably varies from museum to museum, the following are some standard elements that should be included with any nonexclusive licensing agreement:

Introductory Cover Letter

a. Explanation of how the agreement aids the museum in fulfilling its mission
b. Outline how requests not covered by the agreement will be handled
c. Reference the museum's gift or acquisition policies, if applicable

Requested Permissions (License)

d. Identify how the museum may reproduce and use copyrighted materials, which may include some or all the following:

   i. Museum websites and other electronic media
   ii. Editorial content, press, marketing, publication, and exhibition activities
   iii. Scholarly research and educational programming
   iv. Extension of agreed-on permissions to third parties[29]
   v. Right to display and migrate the material to different formats for time-based media[30]
   vi. Extension of permissions to apply to works acquired in the future[31]

Terms and Conditions

e. Terms to govern the uses outlined in the requested permissions, which may include some or all the following:

   i. Modifications to reproductions of the work (e.g., resizing or cropping)
   ii. Credit line and notices
   iii. Ownership
   iv. Representations and warranties regarding non-infringement
   v. Indemnification
   vi. Limitation of liability
   vii. Rights reserved by rights holder
   viii. Duration and termination[32]

Object List

f. Inventory of the work(s) that the agreement covers

Contact Information

g. Request for the rights holder or authorized representative to include current and complete contact information should the museum need to contact them

Signature Line for Agreement

h. Depending on museum practice and advice of legal counsel, the nonexclusive licensing agreement may not include space for the museum to countersign the agreement[33]

Commissioning Works

Museums often commission new works either for temporary exhibition or for acquisition for the permanent collection. Vital to the creation of these new works is the execution of a well-planned commission contract that not only governs the production of the work but makes provisions for future uses of the IP inherent in the work, both by the creator and the museum.

The commission contract should clearly delineate which party retains copyright to the resultant work. Is it the creator or the museum? If the creator retains copyright to the work, it is recommended that the commission agreement include a nonexclusive license back to the commissioning museum that governs its future use(s) of the work. The contract should also specify the agreed-on credit to the work in any resulting reproductions. Furthermore, this license should detail the ownership of rights in the resultant image or video materials, and, if applicable, a license back to the creator for their own use of the museum's images or videos.

When executing a commission, contracting museums should include provisions governing the destruction, removal, or dismantling of the work in accordance with the Visual Artists Rights Act (VARA).[34] Particularly for commissions that are site-specific, intended to be temporary, or subject to unforeseen damage (by nature or human), outlining the rights of both the creator and the museum are vital.[35]

Underlying Rights

Occasionally, a work in a museum's collection (the *core work*) may depict another work of art (the *work depicted*) that is still under copyright. The term *underlying rights* is used to refer to the additional layer of copyright for the work depicted. A simple example is a photograph in the collection (core work) that shows a mural on a building (work depicted). Photographs of exhibition installations often have underlying rights because installation views typically depict multiple works.

When reproducing works with underlying rights, permission for the work depicted may also need to be obtained, depending on how visible or recognizable it is in the core work or on whether the appearance of the work depicted is really incidental in the core work. This is a judgment call to be made on a case-by-case basis depending on the specific image and the museum's risk tolerance level. Fair use for the reproduction of the work depicted may be a reasonable conclusion if the work depicted is incidental rather than the focus of the image.

Privacy Rights and the Collection

The right of privacy applies only to living people. As such, privacy rights will arise most frequently with collections of photographs, videos, or archives containing material from the last century. The right of privacy typically ends at death; some museums will agree to keep materials closed for a period after a donor's death as a condition of a gift.[36] There are four basic forms of privacy rights:[37]

1. Unreasonable intrusion on personal solitude;
2. Public disclosure of true but embarrassing private facts;
3. False light; and
4. Appropriation of name and likeness.

Privacy rights should be evaluated when a museum wishes to reproduce collection materials that depict a known or potentially living person.[38] Unfortunately, there is no simple formula to determine whether privacy rights may be violated because, as with fair use, the specific use is an important factor, as is the nature of the work.

Asking the following questions will help to identify the potential risks:

1. For what purposes does the museum wish to reproduce the work?
2. What is the context in which the person is depicted?
3. Is the person clearly identifiable?
4. Has the work been published previously?
5. Did the artist obtain a model release from the person depicted?
6. Is there another image with fewer or no privacy issues that can serve the same purpose?

Publicity Rights and the Collection

Unlike privacy rights, publicity rights may continue well after death and are governed by laws that vary from state to state.[39] The right of publicity protects against the unauthorized use of an individual's name, voice, or likeness for commercial purposes. A museum is most likely to encounter publicity rights issues in its retail operation if it produces merchandise with collection images depicting living people (or deceased individuals, in some states). However, the use of such images for other routine activities could also implicate publicity rights, regardless of the museum's nonprofit status.

Absent explicit permission or a release agreement from the person(s) depicted in the image, or from the holder of a deceased person's publicity rights, the museum should consider how *reasonable persons* would view the use—commercial, or as press or commentary? If the image is of a famous person, is the museum implying endorsement by the celebrity or gaining by association in some way, such as fundraising? Is the celebrity or their estate known to be litigious? One way to avoid running afoul of publicity rights protections is to ask for one-time permission or to obtain a release agreement for commercial uses of collection images depicting living people.

Recording and Sharing Rights Information

Once a museum has done the research to determine the rights status of a work in its collection, identified the rights holder, and successfully obtained a grant of nonexclusive license to reproduce copies of the work, the essential next step is to maintain a comprehensive and easily accessible record of the object's rights information. Maintaining accurate and updated records prevents the accidental misuse of a copyrighted work, saves time and money spent on unnecessary permissions, and minimizes potential statutory damages if a fair use reproduction that is undertaken in good faith turns out to be infringing.

In a museum, the most logical places to record rights information and store original rights documents include the collections management system (CMS), the digital asset management system (DAMS), and the central object or copyright files for the collection. Whereas a CMS and DAMS are best for recording a summary of the *current* rights status for an object in the collection, an organization's central files should serve as a repository for the complete *historical* copyright record for an object or artist. Access to each of these systems and files will likely vary for staff depending on their responsibilities; thus, duplication of elements of this information between these records may be necessary and inevitable. In such cases, it is critical to establish procedures to ensure that any updates to rights data are made concurrently.

ADDITIONAL CONSIDERATIONS

Although there are numerous forms of IP to consider when reproducing images of collection objects, rights and reproductions specialists need to be mindful of additional issues surrounding certain types and uses of works. It is not uncommon to find collection objects that raise the following considerations that the museum must address:

- Rights of indigenous peoples, including adherence to Native American Graves Protection and Repatriation Act (NAGPRA)[40] provisions;
- Contractual restrictions, as may be found in purchase, donation, or licensing agreements;
- Sensitive content and restricted materials, including obscenity, violence, and graphic depictions;
- Freelance photography with clear contractual terms governing the rights to the images; and

- Documentation of collection materials for conservation purposes that may necessitate the nondisclosure of information.

Access to Images and Reproductions of Collection Materials for External Uses

Museums spend vast amounts of time and resources developing procedures for museum uses of IP in or related to their collections, but the day-to-day focus of rights and reproductions specialist work often centers on responding to external requests to reproduce images, videos, text, or audio recordings related to works in the collections. Third parties may seek to use these materials in a wide variety of commercial and noncommercial applications. Establishing formal procedures to handle external reproduction requests results in efficiency and consistency, as well as adherence to museum policies, and aids in the documented use of collection materials. Providing image files for external reproduction purposes is one of the key ways that museums share their collections with the public.

There are several approaches to granting access to materials related to the collection:

1. Licensing when the museum holds the copyright or has a nonexclusive license from the rights holder that permits sublicensing;
2. Providing access to the materials when the requestor has permission from the copyright holder;
3. Providing access, either completely open or restricted to a specified use, to only works in the public domain; and
4. Providing access to all works; rights clearance is the responsibility of the requestor.[41]

A museum can use one or more of these approaches, depending on the rights status of its collection. The first three hold the least amount of risk for the museum but can leave large sections of the collection inaccessible if much of the collection remains under copyright. The fourth approach allows a museum to grant access to all works in its collection.[42] However, because the responsibility to clear all applicable third-party rights rests entirely on the requestor, this should be clearly spelled out in the contract or agreement that governs the use of the provided media. If a museum takes this approach, any liability associated with the third-party use should be transferred to the requestor via the terms of use in a written contract or agreement.

Information about the Request Process

No matter which approach a museum chooses to use, it is important to provide general information about the request process to the public so that a request can be handled efficiently. It should include the types of uses that will be considered by the museum as well as practical details about the information the museum needs from requestors to process their request. Here are some recommended items to include on an information page:

- Definitions for varying types of use (e.g., scholarly, commercial, personal);
- Time frame for submitting a request (e.g., at least six weeks prior to date needed);
- Information required when submitting a request (e.g., full contact and usage details);
- Link to an image request form or online submission template;
- Fees and payment process, if applicable;
- Credit line requirements;
- Number of gratis copies required; and
- Party responsible for rights clearance.

Developing a Request Form

Processing external requests can be streamlined by using a form that collects all the necessary information required to assess and fulfill the request. Key information to capture on the request form includes:

- Name of the work or object in collection;
- Name of artist or maker;
- Unique identifier (e.g., accession number or catalog number);
- Intended usage (e.g., catalog, T-shirt, movie);
- Project title;
- Author;
- Publisher;
- Expected release date;
- Print run, language(s), editions, formats (print, web, e-book, etc.);

- Geographic distribution or territory;
- Reproduction size (e.g., cover, half-page); and
- Requestor's full contact information.

Many museums offer image request forms that allow information to be submitted directly via the museum's website.[43] Online forms can streamline and automate the request procedure both for the requestor and for the museum.

Reproduction Fees

Reproduction fees vary from museum to museum for a variety of reasons. Sometimes the governing body of a museum will influence the setting of fees, with private nonprofits having more flexibility than a governmental agency. Some museums consider supplying image files as a public service and part of their mission, and thus charge reduced fees (or waive them entirely). Others may need to consider the staff resources that go into processing requests—for example, the cost of new photography or scanning—and thus structure their fees to recover those costs. Although licensing can serve as a source of revenue, previous studies conducted by the Mellon Foundation have found that most museums do not make a significant profit against expenditures in their licensing activities.[44] It is helpful for potential requestors if the museum's fee schedule is posted on its website.

When creating a fee schedule, it may be helpful to survey similar and local museums to ensure general uniformity in fee categories, while the exact fee amounts should be determined based on the museum's budget needs and philosophical approach. Just because a requestor is a nonprofit does not automatically make all its reproductions noncommercial. Consider the size of the print run and the publisher when determining what is commercial or noncommercial. Sometimes an additional fee is assessed for cover uses of an image because it can be considered more promotional or decorative than an interior use.

Electronic books (e-books) and website uses are causing many museums to re-examine their fee schedules because they do not have a traditional print run and do not fit neatly into established procedures. One way of handling e-books is to equate downloads to print runs. A museum can count downloads in ad-

dition to a traditional print run. However, duration or term length of use may be a more efficient means of measure. A museum could allow an unlimited number of downloads as long as they occur within a set time period. Time limits are the most useful and applicable when it comes to websites. Although there are few standards for determining duration and term lengths, the length used most often is a two- to five-year limit before additional permissions are required. Licensing in perpetuity may be an option for a museum, particularly given the difficulties that can arise with having to track licenses with a time limit.

Processing External Requests

Depending on the museum's approach to licensing, the following questions need to be answered internally.

1. Does the request meet the museum's policy on permitted uses?
2. What rights to license does the museum hold?
3. Is the work in the public domain?
4. If the work is under copyright, is there a nonexclusive license for the photographic representation and/or underlying work that permits sublicensing it to a third party?
5. If the work depicts sensitive content, does the request meet the museum's policy about distribution of such materials?

Once it is determined that the image can be licensed, the rights and reproductions specialist generates a contract or agreement that includes the conditions under which museum permission is granted to the requestor. This will be a legally binding agreement, and the template should be developed in consultation with legal counsel. As long as the agreement does not require alteration of the museum's template, each new request and contract should not need to be reviewed by legal counsel.[45]

The details specific to each request should be clearly outlined in the agreement, which may include some or all of the following:

- Exact use(s) being granted;
- Object attribution;

- How the museum will be credited;
- Whether cropping, text overlay, or color manipulation is allowed;
- Whether color proofs are required for approval prior to printing (if applicable);
- The approval process for the use of details, colored ink, or colored stock;
- Number of print runs, downloads, editions, or time limits (years) of use allowed before additional permissions are required;
- Number of gratis copies, or copies at cost, of the publication that must be supplied;[46]
- Licensing fees, if applicable;
- Whether advertising uses are allowed;
- Whether use on any covers without further permission is allowed;
- Any applicable terms of use;
- Any applicable geographic territory distribution limits;
- Whether the digital file must be deleted after a set time period;[47]
- If reproduced digitally, what resolution or size must be used; and
- What, if any, material will be supplied by the holding museum.

The agreement should be signed and dated by the requestor and countersigned by the authorized staff member as determined by the museum's policy.[48] It is advisable to send the materials only after the agreement has been completed and any applicable fees have been paid.

Open Access for External Uses

Open access (OA)[49] sits on the opposite end of the licensing spectrum from handling external use requests on a case-by-case basis. A growing number of museums worldwide have announced OA initiatives that offer free downloads of high-resolution public domain collection images for a range of preapproved uses.[50] Problematically, OA programs vary from museum to museum, with no consistent definition of what constitutes *open access* among them. Some museums limit uses of the downloadable OA files to noncommercial purposes, essentially only semi-open access, whereas others offer unrestricted use, includ-

ing commercial uses. Thus, it is important to read and understand the specific terms and conditions for the individual museums when using OA images from different sources.

A museum planning to offer OA should work to clearly communicate its terms and conditions and decide how best to deliver the image files given its resources. A separate microsite or website can be created to provide OA information and downloads,[51] or the museum can integrate the policy information within its existing online request pages and offer downloads from its online collection pages.[52] Whichever format is chosen, the museum should visibly label the OA content and provide cross-references on its website to help viewers find the OA images. It may also be helpful to communicate how the external requestor can request additional content that is not yet included as part of the OA distribution (either larger file sizes or perhaps a work for which an image does not currently exist).[53]

CONCLUSION

Rights and reproductions specialists need not become IP lawyers to accomplish their jobs, but they do need accurate and up-to-date resources to help them identify legal issues. Those seeking a deeper dive into rights and reproductions considerations and practices are encouraged to consult the second edition of *Rights and Reproductions: The Handbook for Cultural Institutions*,[54] which includes a variety of document and contract templates, references, and resources. ●

NOTES

1. For the purposes of this chapter, the phrase *rights and reproductions specialist* refers to anyone working at a museum who handles this type of work, including but not limited to registrars, rights and reproductions managers, archivists, librarians, and lawyers.

2. Peter B. Hirtle, "Copyright term and the public domain in the United States," Cornell University: Copyright Information Center, last modified January 3, 2020. Available at: https://copyright.cornell.edu/publicdomain.

3. There is no single, uniform, international copyright law or term for the entire world. Instead, under the rule of national treatment, US law should be applied to activities taking place in the United States regardless of a work's country of origin. Although the activities of museums may cross national boundaries, it is beyond the scope of this chapter to cover how

to determine whether a work is still under copyright outside of the United States.

4. Copyright term is calculated differently for sound recordings and architectural works. See 17 U.S.C. §§ 302, 303, 304. These are also addressed in Hirtle's chart.

5. 17 U.S.C. § 302(a). Copyright runs through the end of the day on December 31 of the seventieth year. 17 U.S.C. § 305. For example, copyright to works by an artist who died in 1955 will pass into the public domain on January 1, 2026.

6. 17 U.S.C. § 302(c).

7. Rather than specific copyright notices, the utilization of broad statements on use restrictions are advised for informing staff and outside users. A sample statement from the Indianapolis Museum of Art Archives at Newfields states: "Unpublished manuscripts are protected by copyright. Permission to publish, quote, or reproduce must be secured from the repository and the copyright holder."

8. An extensive list of global agencies can be found at "List of Copyright Collection Societies," Wikipedia. Available at: http://en.wikipedia.org/wiki/List_of_copyright_collection_societies (accessed March 13, 2018).

9. Authors' Licensing and Collecting Society. Available at: http://www.alcs.co.uk/ (accessed March 13, 2018).

10. Copyright Clearance Center. Available at: http://www.copyright.com/ (accessed March 13, 2018).

11. The Copyright Licensing Agency. Available at: http://www.cla.co.uk/ (accessed March 13, 2018).

12. The American Society of Composers, Authors and Publishers. Available at: http://www.ascap.com/ (accessed March 13, 2018).

13. BMI. Available at: http://www.bmi.com/ (accessed March 13, 2018).

14. SESAC. Available at: http://www.sesac.com/ (accessed March 13, 2018).

15. Artists Rights Society. Available at: http://www.arsny.com/ (accessed March 13, 2018).

16. Bridgeman Copyright, Bridgeman Images. Available at: http://www.bridgemanimages.com/en-US/bridgeman-copyright-service (accessed March 13, 2018).

17. The Design and Artists Copyright Society. Available at: http://www.dacs.org.uk/ (accessed March 13, 2018).

18. Harry Ransom Center, University of Texas at Austin, "Writers Artists and Their Copyright Holders," Available at: http://norman.hrc.utexas.edu/watch/ (accessed March 13, 2018).

19. The Library of Congress, Prints & Photographs Reading Room, "Rights and Restrictions Information." Available at: https://www.loc.gov/rr/print/res/index.html (accessed March 13, 2018).

20. "Source and permission contact list," National Archives. Available at: http://www.archives.gov/research/order/film-sources-contact-list.html (accessed March 13, 2018).

21. For example, see Roy Lichtenstein Foundation, "Rights & Reproductions." Available at: http://lichtensteinfoundation.org/rights-reproductions/ (accessed March 13, 2018).

22. With the caveat that it can be difficult to know whether a legal, contractual relationship actually exists—does the gallery actually have the right to sign for the artist? It is important to include language in your license so that the person signing warrants that they have this right. When galleries close down, it can also be very difficult to learn where representation, especially of estates, now resides.

23. "Museum Intellectual Property," Groups.io. Available at: https://groups.io/g/musip (accessed June 12, 2018).

24. Intellectual Property SIG, Museum Computer Network. Available at: http://mcn.edu/community/special-interest-groups-sigs/intellectual-property-sig/ (accessed March 13, 2018).

25. ImageMuse, "About." Available at: http://www.imagemuse.org/ (accessed March 31, 2018).

26. Collections Stewardship Professional Network of the American Alliance of Museums. Available at: https://www.collectionsstewardship.org/ (accessed March 13, 2018).

27. Intellectual Property Rights Committee (IPR), Visual Resources Association. Available at: http://vraweb.org/about/committees/intellectual-property-rights-committee-ipr/ (accessed March 13, 2018).

28. Retail commercial uses are often limited, or the license may specifically exclude retail and make reference to the need for a separate agreement for such uses.

29. Extension may be limited to museums borrowing the work or to fewer uses than those granted to the museum.

30. Depending on museum practice, time-based media works may also be referred to as *variable art*.

31. It is possible such a grant of rights for unspecified works may be challenged legally because at the time of the grant of rights, it was not known to which works a license might apply.

32. Duration for the full copyright term is preferable. Ideally, the license should avoid any explicit limits on the length of time of use. This way, the work may be used for the full copyright term or until the copyright holder revokes the permission. Absent any specific term for the license, the grant of rights will extend to the full term of copyright.

33. Only exclusive grants of rights must be signed by both parties. For a basic non-exclusive licensing agreement, it is sufficient for only the licensee (the rights holder) to sign. However, the licensor (the museum) should sign if the licensor also has obligations under the license. It is still good policy to have both parties sign non-exclusive licensing agreements so as to avoid any questions about the agreement in the future.

34. Visual Artists Rights Act, 17 U.S.C. § 106A.

35. Some states (e.g., California) have artist rights laws that are in addition to and not preempted by federal law. In California, some artist rights cannot be waived.

36. See generally Joseph L. Sax, *Playing Darts with a Rembrandt: Public and Private Rights in Cultural Treasures* (Ann Arbor: The University of Michigan Press, 2001).

37. It is important to note that publicity is a form of privacy rights in some jurisdictions and may apply postmortem.

38. Unless the person depicted is a public figure, it is often not possible to know for sure whether the person is still living. In such cases, simply consider the date of the work and the estimated age of the person when the picture was taken, then extrapolate the age of the person in present time. For example, teenagers depicted in a 1960 photograph are probably in their mid-seventies by the year 2020 and, therefore, likely to be still living.

39. The duration of postmortem rights varies by state. In California, for example, postmortem rights last for seventy years for famous people. Cal. Civ. Code § 3344.1(g) (West 2014).

40. Native American Graves Protection Act and Repatriation Act, 25 U.S.C. § 3001 et seq. (1990).

41. Some museums will provide works that are protected by copyright if the requestor signs an agreement regarding how the images will be used, for example stating that they will not publish the image without first obtaining permission from the copyright holder. The decision to provide access to all works should be made in consultation with the museum's legal counsel.

42. Exceptions to this might be in the case of sensitive images that may depict violence, objects covered by NAGPRA, or religious ceremonies. Native American Graves Protection Act and Repatriation Act, 25 U.S.C. § 3001 et seq. (1990).

43. For example, see the *Rights and Reproductions Request Form*, from The Sixth Floor Museum at Dealey Plaza. Available at: https://www.jfk.org/the-collections/rights-reproductions-request-form/ (accessed February 23, 2018).

44. See Simon Tanner, *Reproduction charging models & rights policy for digital images in American art museums: A Mellon Foundation study* (KDCS Digital Consultancy, 2004); and Kristin Kelly, "Images of works of art in museum collections: The experience of open access," in *A Study of Eleven Museums. Prepared for the Andrew W. Mellon Foundation* (2013).

45. However, whether an unmodified template can be used without further legal review is a determination typically made by legal counsel.

46. A museum may consider accepting digital excerpts or PDF copies in place of a printed gratis copy, which may be cost prohibitive for the external requestor to provide.

47. Increasingly, external requestors retain the digital files licensed from museums, which can make the enforceability of a term requiring its deletion impractical. Conversely, a museum may ask external requestors to use the digital file that most truly represents the work represented, which may often be the most recently created file.

48. Some museum web request forms also serve as a click-through agreement. Terms and conditions are provided to the requestor when the form is accessed, and the requestor must agree to the terms to submit the online request. This process thus eliminates the need to send contracts back and forth for signatures.

49. May also be referred to as *Open Content*.

50. For a continually updated, worldwide accounting of OA collections, see Andrea Wallace and Douglas McCarthy, *Survey of GLAM open access policy and practice*. Available at: https://docs.google.com/spreadsheets/d/1WPS-KJptUJ-o8SXtg00llcxq0IKJu8eO6Ege_GrLaNc/edit#gid=1216556120 (accessed January 29, 2019).

51. For example, see *NGA Images*, National Gallery of Art. Available at: https://images.nga.gov/en/page/show_home_page.html (accessed March 21, 2018).

52. For example, see *Open Content Program*, The Getty. Available at: http://www.getty.edu/about/whatwedo/opencontent.html (accessed March 21, 2018).

53. For example, a reference from the rights and reproductions pages of a museum's site should direct visitors to OA content, such as: "Many images of public domain works are available for free download from the Indianapolis Museum of Art at Newfields' collection pages. Simply look for the download icon to access a high resolution JPG file and begin using the image for any purpose." "Image Resources," *Newfields*. Available at: https://discovernewfields.org/research/image-resources (accessed March 21, 2018).

54. Megan P. Bryant, Cherie C. Chen, Kenneth D. Crews, John French, Walter G. Lehmann, Naomi Leibowitz, Melissa Levine, Sofía Galarza Liu, Michelle Gallagher Roberts, Nancy Sims, Deborah Wythe, and Anne M. Young, *Rights and Reproductions: The Handbook for Cultural Institutions*, 2nd ed., edited by Anne M. Young (Lanham, MD: Rowman & Littlefield, 2019).

This chapter is excerpted from the 2019 second edition of Rights and Reproductions: The Handbook for Cultural Institutions. *The author recognizes in particular the contributions of Megan P. Bryant, Cherie C. Chen, John ffrench, Melissa Levine, Sofía Galarza Liu, Michelle Gallagher Roberts, Nancy Sims, and Deborah Wythe to chapter 3, "Rights Issues for the Collection," and chapter 6, "External Uses."*

7E | APPRAISAL

LELA HERSH

THE APPRAISAL PROFESSION

AN APPRAISAL IS AN opinion of value. A good appraisal is unbiased, substantiated, and unambiguous. Appraisal reports should be prepared and delivered by a trained, reputable professional who is well versed in appraisal methodologies, and knowledgeable about the material being appraised. The appraisal profession has changed and grown considerably in the last fifty years—spurred by regulatory agencies' requirements, high prices achieved on objects in expanding markets, and technological advances that have made relevant market, ownership, and object information easier to access and share.

Even though museum staff is not allowed to appraise objects, they have a myriad of reasons to understand value. As 501(c)(3) organizations, many museums are the recipients of donations for which the donors will likely claim deductions on their tax returns. It is neither expected nor prudent for museum professionals to provide advice to their donors, yet understanding the rules and regulations will aid them in recognizing the parameters that apply to donations. This knowledge will allow museum staff to provide an appropriate level of guidance to donors and perform a valuable service by arming them with useful suggestions and information when steering them toward their accountants, appraisers, and legal advisors.

Background

In the United States, the appraisal profession is guided by the Appraisal Foundation (TAF), the principal authority of the valuation profession. The foundation was authorized in 1989 by the US Congress, which enacted the *Financial Institutions Reform, Recovery, and Enforcement Act*[1] that sanctioned the TAF as the source of appraisal standards and qualifications. TAF establishes the minimum qualifications for personal property appraisers and di-

rection for recognized valuation methods and techniques for all valuation professionals. This leadership enhances the profession by developing standards to ensure that appraisals are meaningful, independent, consistent, and objective.[2]

TAF standards are communicated through the *Uniform Standards of Professional Appraisal Practice* (USPAP)—published biannually by TAF. USPAP includes standards for various appraisal services, including real estate, personal property, business, and mass appraisal. Compliance is required for both state licensed and certified appraisers who work in real estate.[3] Personal property appraisers are neither licensed nor certified by states. Instead, they are accredited (or certified) by their own organizations. There are three nonprofit organizations that include personal property appraisers that are sponsors of TAF—the American Society of Appraisers (ASA),[4] Appraisers Association of America (AAA),[5] and the International Society of Appraisers (ISA).[6] However, there are many individuals who write appraisal reports and call themselves personal property appraisers even though they are not accredited, do not belong to a recognized society, and do not keep up with the rules, regulations and methodologies of the appraisal profession.

Uniform Standards of
Professional Appraisal Practice

Qualified appraisers in the United States follow USPAP, which helps to promote public trust and is the only nationally recognized ethical and procedural guidance for personal property appraisers. It is important to note that although some appraisers will state that they are USPAP certified, this is a misrepresentation. Simply completing a USPAP course does not entitle anyone to be a USPAP-certified appraiser because USPAP does not certify appraisers or appraisals.[7] Appraisers must be continually up to date on USPAP, and their appraisal assignments should be performed in conformity with the latest iteration of USPAP.

Museums and Value

Aside from being a repository for cultural objects, museums must care for their collections in perpetuity or at least until an object is deaccessioned. It is not unusual, and is perfectly acceptable, for a museum to assign a value to an object in certain circumstances, such as for insurance needs, bargain sales, and Internal Revenue Service (IRS) Form 990 preparation. Nevertheless, museum staff must be cautious when called upon to assign a value to an object. There are a number of disparate markets and market levels that can be referenced and applied, often resulting in different value conclusions. Mixing markets can result in confusion and inconsistencies. For example, a registrar or curator might use an auction sale, or they might call a dealer to ascertain their opinion on a value to use for insurance coverage. These numbers can be wildly different, so an understanding of values is essential.

Terminology

When discussing values, it is of paramount importance to understand the differences in appraisal terminology. Critical to understanding the vocabulary is to be aware that the term *value* is an economic concept that expresses an opinion based on the monetary relationship between properties and those who buy and sell those properties. Value is different from cost or price. For example, NASA accidentally sold an *Apollo 11*, 1969, moon bag (lunar sampler return pouch) to someone for $995 in 2015—that is the price the buyer paid. However, the pouch later sold for US$ 1.8M at Sotheby's New York in 2017.[8] Price and value can clearly be divergent.

When appraisers are asked, "What is this object worth?" they will first want to know how the value is going to be used. Appraisers call this *intended use*, and it is the first step in understanding the economics of valuation. If the object will be donated to a charity, the value is a specific number. If the questioner wants to know how much to insure the object for, the value is most likely to be a different number. If the questioner needs money immediately and plans to sell the same object at a local auction house, the value is again different. A value is not what someone pays or has paid for a similar object but depends on other factors such as timing (the *effective date*), the use of the appraisal, and the type of value sought.

Using Appraisers

There are times when a museum is required to use an appraiser. For example, the museum's collection management policy (CMP) might necessitate that any objects valued more than US$ 1M require two appraisals before deaccessioning. Or a valuation for a possible purchase might be needed so a price point can be set prior to acquisition. For both purposes, a museum's CMP should specify the type of value the museum must obtain and what staff positions are responsible for establishing the value conclusions.

As noted, there are different types of values. The museum might want *marketable cash value* (anticipated net proceeds or cash in hand that would be yielded from the sale of a property once all costs of sale were deducted—that is, the net received by the seller), *replacement value* (the price in terms of cash or other precisely revealed terms that would be required to replace one property with another),[9] or *fair market value*—which is a term from the US Department of the Treasury Regulations and is used for tax-related issues (the price at which the property would change hands between a willing buyer and a willing seller, neither being under any compulsion to buy or to sell and both having reasonable knowledge of relevant facts).

Referring Appraisers

There is no licensing for personal property appraisers. Most appraisers go through a series of classes and testing and are accredited (or certified) through their organization (AAA, ASA, or ISA). Each of the appraisal associations has different levels of credentialing for appraisers. Museums should be careful when recommending appraisers to their donors, especially in cases where the appraisal is needed for income tax purposes. There are specific qualifications required by the US Department of Treasury for appraisers who write appraisals for tax purposes.[10] If the donor has a problem with the appraisal or the appraiser, the museum could bear the brunt of their displeasure. The safest thing to do is to simply refer donors and the public to the organizations and not show a preference for an individual appraiser.

If the museum does provide a list of appraisers, make sure to alphabetize the appraisers' names so as to not show partiality. If museum staff thinks there is a need to identify some appraisers by name, it might behoove them to refer rather than recommend or to say that "other of our donors have been happy with *X* appraiser." Can the museum also direct the donor to auction houses? They can, but they should be acutely aware of potential conflicts of interest. See the *US Tax Court decision in Estate of Kollsman v. Commissioner of Internal Revenue* (2017), regarding arm's-length transactions.[11]

Hiring Appraisers

When bidding on an appraisal assignment or presenting a proposal, appraisers provide a quote based on either their rate per hour, per object, or for the total project. For obvious reasons, it is unethical to accept payment for services based on the value of the objects being appraised. The appraiser, who is hired to complete the assignment, provides a letter of agreement or contract to the museum. Appraisal agreement contents routinely include the name of the property to be appraised and its location, the intended use of the appraisal, who the appraisal is for (*intended users*), the type of value to be concluded, scope of service, what materials and information the museum and appraiser will each provide, the duration of the assignment including deadlines, payment schedules, terms, fees, and other cost, indemnifications (only if necessary and if so, both the museum and appraiser ought to indemnify each other), and privacy requirements.

After being hired, the appraiser will often request information from the donee. Object files can provide the appraiser with a wealth of information to assist in concluding value, including exhibition histories, literature citations, condition reports, and provenance. If there is any confidential information in the file, it can first be removed by staff. Providing this information to the appraiser helps save time and additional fees paid by the museum. Because it is the appraiser's

responsibility to witness, identify, and value the property to be appraised, appraising from photographs is not ideal. Caution is recommended when accepting appraisals without inspections.

Although most appraisals are written, they can be presented orally, but oral appraisals must still conform to USPAP. The appraiser does the same amount of research and analysis as for a written appraisal report, only the reporting vehicle is different (oral, not written), so this is a less costly option. When a museum or collections professional asks appraisers what they believe the value of an object to be, and the appraiser provides a number, the appraiser has just done an oral appraisal. This explains the reluctance of appraisers to answer such questions intuitively without completing the necessary research.

An appraisal report should list the people who rely on the appraisal in addition to the client (e.g., the donor's legal or financial advisor). Other readers (such as the IRS, the donee, third-party insurers, or board members) may read or receive the appraisal report, but they are not considered intended users as defined by USPAP. The appraisal report is related only to the client's use.[12] Intended users are identified by the appraiser through communication with the client.

Insurance

Museums rarely pay for appraisals to insure their entire permanent collection. The cost can be prohibitive, and some museums prefer instead to use their capital to safeguard the collection—for example, by investing in environmental controls and security provisions. Museum staff often declare their own opinions of value. The insurance industry refers to these as *agreed values* (and these are essentially the values from lenders on loan agreements). Some museums will have their entire collections insured in this manner. Other museums insure collection objects when they are traveling and at most risk. Many museums insure their collections on a loss-limit basis, in which the amount to be insured is based on a risk-management assessment and probable maximum loss. Insurers often ask museums to provide a value for their top ten objects (see CHAPTER 6D, "Insurance"). Either museum staff or a hired professional appraiser creates this type of list.

It is good practice for museums to have a system in place that addresses situations in which lenders place a value on a loan agreement that is out of sync with like properties. Accepting overinflated values on loans can place the museum in a precarious position. Some lenders want to insure based on emotional values (e.g., "this vessel was given to me by my great grandmother and is irreplaceable"). Because these values are not based on market evidence, they have no grounds. If the value is agreed on, the insurance company is obliged to pay, and the museum will be left paying higher premiums for a lower-value item. Furthermore, ethical issues could surface regarding a museum's support for an unreasonable value if the lender later relies on such a value for another use.

A museum can protect itself when receiving a loan agreement with a blank value line if the agreement states that in such a case, the museum insures the loaned property based on its own estimated value. The loan agreement should state that this value is for insurance coverage only and should not be considered an appraisal that the lender can later rely on for another purpose.[13]

Replacement values are the values that museums use to insure their collections or loans. The ASA defines *replacement value* as "the price in terms of cash or other precisely revealed terms that would be required to replace a property with another of similar age, origin, appearance, provenance, and condition, within a reasonable length of time in an appropriate and relevant market."[14] However, the museum's insurance policy will normally state that in the event of loss or damage, the basis of valuation will be *current market value*. Interestingly, the concept of current market value is almost never defined; it is specifically opened-ended. Insurance exists for the insured to be made whole again in the event of a loss or damage. Appraisers base a replacement value appraisal on the highest reasonable prices, so if there is a loss, the insured can replace the property in a timely manner. The replacement value might include shipping, crating, or assistance from a consultant, preparator, or agent, but it is not a pie-in-the-sky number.

Another type of coverage for museums was developed by the US government in its Artifacts Indemnity Act of 1975 and subsequent revisions, which seeks to "provide indemnities for exhibitions of ar-

tistic and humanistic endeavors, and for other purposes."[15] The federal Arts and Artifacts Indemnity Program[16] is a risk-management program that allows certain US nonprofit organizations to apply for additional exhibition protection for eligible objects coming in or going out of the country for temporary exhibition. In this program, the government legislates maximum sums to cover damage and losses under very strict rules. Commercial insurance covers the sliding scale deductible, and any excess of approved indemnity amounts, for validated claims for loss or damage.[17] The type of value in the indemnity program is based on fair market value.

Loss of Value

There are times when an object is damaged but can be repaired, so the result is not a total loss. Nevertheless, that repair might lessen the value of the object and the museum may request compensation. Appraisers refer to this as *diminution of value*. Diminution of value means that the object is less marketable due to repairs, and the net monetary loss is the loss of value. In situations such as these, two appraisers (one representing the insurance company and one representing the museum) usually value the damaged object and provide their value opinions based on the loss. Most insurance policies allow for a third appraiser or umpire to be hired for cases that require arbitration.

Law for Charitable Contributions

The US Internal Revenue Code (IRC) has long provided taxpayers with incentives to donate appreciated property to museums. Since the 1917 War Revenue Act, taxpayers have been able to claim deductions on charitable contributions to qualified charities.[18] The deduction was codified in Section 170 of the IRC. Numerous revisions to the statutory provisions have occurred over the years. One of the most sweeping reforms was introduced with the Tax Reform Act of 1984, which was part of the Deficit Reduction Act of 1984 (Public Law 98–369),[19] in which Congress tightened compliance provisions for contributions and required written appraisals for contributions of property for which a deduction of $5,000 or more is claimed. The act provided reporting requirements for donors and donees, including the use of Form 8283 (*Noncash Charitable Contri-*

butions)[20] and 8282 (*Donee Information Return*).[21] The guidelines also included the first explanation of who constituted a *qualified appraiser*, which was exceptionally basic. Originally, appraisers had to be someone who was not excluded[22] and who presented themselves to the public as appraisers.[23] The guidelines barred donees from providing their donors with values for their contributions. The Pension Protection Act of 2006 (PPA) and the implementing regulations provided more stringent and specific requirements.

Regulations

The Pension Protection Act was signed by President George W. Bush on August 17, 2006. Its provisions were implemented by the IRS and Treasury Department through regulations published on July 30, 2018. The new regulations provide an expanded definition of a qualified appraisal and qualified appraiser that apply to contributions made on or after January 1, 2019. Check the IRS website for a definition and more details of who is a qualified appraiser and what constitutes a qualified appraisal.[24] A qualified appraiser is someone who:

- Has an appraisal designation or
- Has verifiable experience and education valuing the specific type of property.

An individual who cannot be a qualified appraiser is someone who:

- Is the donor or donee;
- Generally, is a party to the transaction in which the donor acquired the property;
- Is employed by or related to the donor, the donee, or a party to the transaction in which the donor acquired the property;
- Is regularly used by the donor, donee, or a party to the transaction in which the donor acquired the property;
- Does not perform a majority of their appraisals for others during the taxable year (note that majority is measured by the number of items, not the number of appraisals); and
- Is prohibited from practicing before the IRS.

A qualified appraisal is one prepared by a qualified appraiser in accordance with generally accepted appraisal standards ("the substance and principles of USPAP").

The appraisal must include a sufficient property description including the object's condition and noting any restrictions on the donee's use of the property. When taxpayers make a charitable contribution, they relinquish all control, and the donee is then free to use the object as they wish for the benefit of the public. If a donor places a restriction on the disposition or use of the donated property, the fair market value must reflect that restriction.[25] Therefore, any restrictions on the donation must be disclosed in the appraisal report. Appraisers must be told about the restrictions and should be given a copy of the deed of gift. Countersigned deeds of gift should be attached to the appraisal.

Appraisers completing an assignment for a donor generally request a copy of the donee's condition report. Physical condition is a key factor for concluding a property's value for a tax-related occurrence. Appraisers may adjust value conclusions based on conditions that negatively affect the object or its potential marketability. A qualified appraisal includes information about the appraiser's credentials and knowledge about the property as well as an identification (tax ID) number. The appraisal should include a statement that the appraisal was prepared for *income tax purposes*. The *effective date* of the appraisal, the date the opinion of value applies to the property, is the date of (or expected date of) title transfer.

Neither the IRS nor USPAP requires an appraiser to inspect the appraised property, though as mentioned, it is wise that they do. If appraisers do not witness the property directly, USPAP requires them to disclose that in the certification included in the appraisal. A qualified appraisal must also include the fair market value of the property or properties, the methodology used by the appraiser, and the basis for valuation. Appraisals must be signed and dated.

Contemporaneous Written Acknowledgment

Museums must ensure that donees receive a contemporaneous written acknowledgment (CWA) for each donation. It is best practice to provide donors with a letter that is distinct from the deed of gift. The CWA should confirm that the charity provided "no goods or services" in exchange for the contribution of any donations with a value of $250 or more. Specially, the written acknowledgment required to substantiate this contribution must contain the following information:[26]

- Name of the organization;
- Amount of cash contribution;
- Description (but not value) of noncash contribution;
- Statement that no goods or services were provided by the organization, if that is the case;
- Description and good faith estimate of the value of goods or services, if any, that the organization provided in return for the contribution; and
- Statement that goods or services, if any, that the organization provided in return for the contribution consisted entirely of intangible religious benefits, if that was the case.

Any kind of barter (a taxable event) or monetary receipt from the donee (including the donee paying for the appraisal, the production of a catalog in exchange for a gift, and payment for conservation before the gift is transferred) must be acknowledged in the CWA. If donors do not have the CWA when they file their taxes, they could potentially lose the tax deduction. The burden is on donors to obtain the CWA before filing a tax return.[27] Because there is little justification for donors to be placed in that situation, the museum should send donors a separate CWA as early as possible. Sometimes, at audit time, a donor will try to argue that a variety of documents, viewed as a whole, constitute a CWA, or that a deed of gift is the CWA. See the endnotes for a recent example of a court case in which a deed was treated as a CWA.[28] Donees should keep a copy of the CWA in case donors cannot locate their copy of the document during an audit.

Publications

The appraisal prepared for a donation and written for income tax purposes concludes the fair market value of the donated property. The definition for fair market value originates from the IRC, which is the law

enacted by Congress in Title 26 of the US Code. It is often written as 26 U.S.C., or referred to as the Internal Revenue Code. Regulations, on the other hand, are the Department of the Treasury's interpretations of the IRC, which is written as the Code of Federal Regulations or 26 CFR. To best comprehend regulations, the IRS issues guidance publications that explain implementation of the regulations. The guidance publications for charitable contributions include IRS Publication 526 (*Charitable Contributions*) and IRS Publication 561 (*Determining the Value of Donated Property*). There is also guidance in the instructions for forms 8283 and 8282. Because these publications have not been updated to coincide with the newest regulations, current procedures are based on the regulations themselves.

Fair Market Value

The type of value that the appraiser uses for tax filing (as stated previously) is fair market value. The first sentence of the definition of fair market value is "the price at which the property would change hands between a willing buyer and a willing seller, neither being under any compulsion to buy or to sell and both having reasonable knowledge of relevant facts."[29] Most museum registrars have memorized this definition, but it is a shortened definition; separate definitions apply to gift tax and estate tax.

The full definition for fair market value for charitable contributions in the CFR continues,

If the contribution is made in property of a type which the taxpayer sells in the course of his business, the fair market value is the price which the taxpayer would have received if he had sold the contributed property in the usual market in which he customarily sells, at the time and place of the contribution and, in the case of a contribution of goods in quantity, in the quantity contributed. The usual market of a manufacturer or other producer consists of the wholesalers or other distributors to or through whom he customarily sells, but if he sells only at retail the usual market consists of his retail customers.[30]

Note that the word *retail* means sale to the end user, and not intended for resale. This means that the auction market can also be the retail market.

These definitions are for federal taxes. The definition of fair market value varies in some states. For example, in California, the definition states that

> the fair market value of the property taken is the highest price on the date of valuation that would be agreed to by a seller, being willing to sell but under no particular or urgent necessity for so doing, nor obliged to sell, and a buyer, being ready, willing, and able to buy but under no particular necessity for so doing, each dealing with the other with full knowledge of all the uses and purposes for which the property is reasonably adaptable and available.[31]

This state law definition specifies that the fair market value is the highest price. Other government jurisdictions have their own definitions, as do other countries. In Canada, the definition is based on judicial case precedents and states that fair market value is the "highest price, expressed in terms of money, that a property would bring in an open and unrestricted market between a willing buyer and a willing seller who are both knowledgeable, informed, and prudent, and who are acting independently of each other."[32]

As noted previously, properties that sell in different markets often sell for different prices. Prices in dissimilar markets and market levels can vary significantly. For fair market value in the United States, the appraiser bases conclusions on the market where the type of property sells most commonly to the ultimate consumer (in other words, not for resale). This could be, for example, either the auction market or gallery market. There are other markets, depending on the property type.

IRS Review

Museum donors may not always need to obtain an appraisal for their gifts. For deductions of art objects and certain other personal property, these are the general rules:[33]

- If the deduction claimed is not more than $5,000, no qualified appraisal is needed.
- If the deduction claimed is more than $5,000, the taxpayer generally needs a qualified appraisal.
- If the deduction claimed is more than $500,000, the taxpayer must attach the qualified appraisal to the return.
- For art valued at $20,000 or more, the taxpayer must attach the qualified appraisal to the return.

Note that if the value is close to $5,000, the donor can claim $5,000 or less and avoid the appraisal requirement.

Art Appraisal Services (AAS) is a department in the Office of Appeals for the IRS and is staffed by appraisers who review appraisals submitted for tax purposes. The Art Advisory Panel of the Commissioner of Internal Revenue (the Panel) is comprised of a group of volunteer curators, auction specialists, dealers, and scholars. The Panel makes recommendations to the AAS on appraisals they receive through audits that have a claimed fair market value of $50,000 or above. For art valued at $20,000 or more, the taxpayer must provide a photograph on request. For art valued at $50,000 or more, the taxpayer must attach a photograph. Rules for photographic requirements are listed on the IRS's website.[34]

Copies of Charitable Contribution Appraisals to Donees

There are good reasons for the donor to provide the donee with a copy of the appraisal report. For one thing, museums can use the thorough research provided in the appraisal, which often includes the original invoice, information on provenance, and catalogue raisonné citations. Also, reading a well-written qualified appraisal helps staff become more conversant in understanding how an argument for value is developed and defended. Museum personnel should not rely on the fair market value in the appraisal report for uses other than the value as of the date of contribution. Usually, but not always, the fair market value is less than replacement value, which would be the relevant value for insurance coverage. The museum may not be able to replace the lost or damaged property in a timely manner if they insure it based on fair market value.

Providing a copy of an appraisal to a donee can only be done if approved by the client. If the taxpayer wants to claim a deduction, the donee must be given Form 8283, which was formally known as the *appraisal summary* (an appraisal report was never an appraisal summary). However, the current regulations removed the term *appraisal summary*, and it is now simply called Form 8283. The fair market value does not have to be stated on Form 8283 when it is given to the donee.[35] Moreover, some donees prefer not to know the value because they do not want to be accused of aiding and abetting any understatement of tax liability. The client may not want the donee to know the appraiser's conclusion of value. Some museums stipulate that trustees must donate a certain amount in cash or tangible property to maintain their position on the board; this requirement is separate from the IRS rules for appraisers and donors.

Sixty-Day Rule

IRS regulations do not allow an appraisal to be completed more than sixty days prior to the date of donation. Appraisers can begin the research at any time, but the property must be valued as of the effective date (the date of donation). When the report is completed prior to the donation, the appraiser must provide the expected date of the contribution. If the title transfer date changes, the appraisal must be reissued with the new effective date, considering any changes in the market that occurred between the two dates. For this reason, it is best for museum staff not to suggest that the appraisal be completed before title transfer. Donors do not need the appraisal until their tax returns are due (including extensions) though many donors request their appraisal report earlier for planning purposes.

There are various ways for a donor to get information about an object being considered for donation. The donor can request a restricted appraisal (limited utility) or an oral appraisal (as explained previously) for tax planning. This is less expensive because even though the same amount of research and analysis must be completed for each, an extensive ap-

praisal report is not prepared for a restricted appraisal and the oral report is verbal. The donor would need another appraisal report to be completed for the donation for income tax purposes. Donors of art can also get an advanced review from the IRS before they file their income tax return. For works of art more than $50,000, they can request a *statement of value*, which is then attached to the donor's tax return. However, the appraisal report for the property must already have been completed. See the IRS website for more information on statements of value.[36]

Date of Title Transfer

The date that a museum considers to be the date of title transfer should be documented in the collection management policy. Usually title transfer is constituted by offer (letter of intent), possession, and acceptance (e.g., the letter sent after the governing board approves a gift). Sometimes, title transfer is governed by state law, so be sure to check with an attorney. The deed of gift is not always the instrument of title transfer, but there should be a document with two signatures. Sometimes a museum sends an unsigned deed to the donor clarifying that the counter signature will be returned after acceptance by the museum's governing board and firmly stating that the donor's signature does not finalize their gift. Once the gift is approved, the museum sends a fully executed agreement to the donor. Note that the effective date of the conclusion of fair market value must match the date that the donee lists on part IV of the donee acknowledgment of Form 8283, the date of title transfer or gift acceptance.

Fractional Interests

Donors can make a charitable contribution for the value of an undivided portion of their entire interest in a property. One of the changes the Pension Protection Act (PPA) enacted applies to the donation rules of fractional interests. Before the PPA, a donor could donate a percentage of a property during a calendar year and receive a tax benefit for the percentage of the full fair market value at the time of donation. This was true for the first year, and each year thereafter an additional fraction was donated; there was no limit to how long the donor could wait to donate the rest of the fractional interests. Multiple donors could donate different percentages of the same property. The rules changed after PPA enactment. Under the current rules, when donors make an additional fractional interest contribution, the deduction on their taxes is determined by using the lesser of the fair market value of the property at the time of the initial contribution, or the fair market value of the property at the time of the additional contribution, and all fractional interests must be donated to the same institution within ten years or by the time of the donor's death, whichever comes first.

The date of the PPA enactment—August 17, 2006—is significant for museums that accept long-term fractional interest donations. If the donation of a fractional interest occurred prior to this date, the old rules apply. For any fractional interest donation made after August 17, 2006, the clock starts ticking for adherence to the new PPA statutory rules. A contribution made before the date of enactment of the PPA is not to be treated as the initial fractional contribution. However, if another fractional donation was made after August 17, 2006, the fair market value at that time becomes the benchmark as the first fractional interest contribution.[37]

As an illustration, if a donor gave 20 percent of a tangible property on June 1, 2005, and then donated the final 80 percent on June 1, 2019, the donor can take the remaining percentage based on the fair market value as of June 1, 2019 (assuming all the other rules were followed). However, if a donor gave 20 percent on June 1, 2005 and then gave an additional fractional interest of 30 percent on June 1, 2019, the donor would receive a deduction of 30 percent of the fair market value as of June 1, 2019, establishing a new benchmark. That fair market value is now the highest one the donor's deduction will be based on in future gift years. Future donations will be based on the fair market value of the property on June 1, 2019 or that of the year of donation, whichever is lower. In addition, 100 percent of the gift must be donated by June 1, 2029.

Museums often refer to a percentage gift as a *partial gift*. As the term *partial interest* has a different meaning for the IRS, it would be more practical for staff to change the language and use the IRS term

fractional interest gift or *fractional gift* to comply with section 170(a) of the Internal Revenue Code.

Bargain Sales

A *bargain sale* is one in which a donor, with a charitable intent, essentially gives part of the item as a charitable contribution and sells the other part to the donee. In other words, it is a sale (or exchange) for less than the property's fair market value—part charitable contribution and part sale or exchange. In this situation, museums are expected to comment on the value of the property.[38] The museum must perform research to determine what they should pay for the object or hire a qualified appraiser to assist with *market value* (a value like fair market value but when a sale is expected within a particular time frame). The donor uses a separate qualified appraiser to prepare a qualified appraisal for their deduction, claiming the difference between the fair market value and the agreed-on sales price as their deduction.

For example, suppose a donor owns a rare manuscript that she's willing to donate to a qualified organization. She agrees to donate 50 percent of the manuscript and have the donee buy the remaining 50 percent. The donee determines that the full value is $100,000 and agrees to pay $50,000 for a 50 percent purchase. Separately, the donor obtains a qualified appraisal from a qualified appraiser who concludes a total fair market value of $80,000. The donor can take a fair market deduction of $30,000 which is the fair market value ($80,000) minus the amount paid by the donee ($50,000).

The donee's collection management policy should address the museum's guidelines for bargain sales and describe how the museum determines the price if an appraiser is not used. A museum should acknowledge in writing that it is purchasing the property for less than the fair market value. This type of donation and sale combination is reported in Part 1 of Form 8283.

Related Use and Unrelated Use

Charitable contributions can be designated for either the exempt purpose of the museum (related use) or its unrelated use. Its use is unrelated if the "use by the donee is not related to the purpose or function constituting the basis for its exemption."[39] The typical related use of a gift is for the museum's permanent collection, where normally its safekeeping is at the highest level (e.g., it is afforded preservation and conservation), and there is an opportunity to exhibit the object for the public's benefit. A typical unrelated use is accepting an object for sale in a fundraising auction, regardless of how the monies raised will be used. If the property is not for the institution's permanent collection, it would be sensible to check any gray-area uses (e.g., for a study collection or to exhibit in staff offices) with legal counsel to ensure that the charity is appropriately signing off on Section IV of Form 8283 for gifts more than $5,000.

If the donee (the museum) sells, exchanges, or otherwise disposes the property within three years after title transfer, it must submit Form 8282 within 125 days after the sale and provide a copy to the donor.[40] Museums should be cautious about including an agreement not to sell the gift on their deed because that could constitute a restriction that the appraiser would have to consider when concluding fair market value.

With some exceptions, a full gift of long-term capital gain property to a qualified 501(c)(3) organization allows donors to receive a deduction on their income taxes for the property's fair market value. If the contribution is short-term capital gain property (also known as *ordinary income property*), the donor can only deduct cost basis or fair market value, whichever is less. The donor would still need an appraisal if the property is more than $5,000 to establish which amount is smaller. In essence, ordinary income property is property that has been owned for one year or less, held as inventory by an art dealer, donated by the artist, donated by a donor who received it as a gift from the artist (who would receive the same basis as the artist), or a gift to a charity for an unrelated use. Short-term capital gain property can become long-term capital gain property if, for example, property is held longer than a year, or if a gift from an artist is inherited. In that case, the property changes character and it becomes long-term capital gain property, and there is a *step-up* in the cost basis to the fair market value on the date of the artist's death or an alternative valuation date.[41]

CONCLUSION

Finding the appropriate path to an object's value can mean having to choose from several forks in the road. Choosing the right route is easier if you know the reason for the trip, understand and respect the rules of the road, follow the trail markers, and most important, ask for help from an experienced guide. When dealing with any tax-related issue, follow best practices, and check first with the museum's accountant or legal advisors, and research online to see if there is new guidance or case law.

Working with professional appraisers can help museums navigate the ins and outs of how value is concluded and avoid the potential obstacles and consequences that can arise when best practices and laws are not followed. Understanding valuation can also help museum staff guide their patrons through the donation process, learn more about the objects in their collection, and stay current with the laws that affect their collection and overall museum policies. •

NOTES
1. Available at: https://www.govinfo.gov/content/pkg/STATUTE-103/pdf/STATUTE-103-Pg183.pdf.

2. Available at: https://www.appraisalfoundation.org.

3. Available at: https://www.appraisalfoundation.org.

4. Available at: https://www.appraisers.org/.

5. Available at: https://www.appraisersassociation.org/.

6. Available at: https://www.isa-appraisers.org/.

7. The Appraisal Standards Board, *Uniform Standards of Professional Appraisal Practice* (Washington, DC: The Appraisal Foundation, 2020–2021), FAQ 43, pg. 205.

8. Available at: https://www.chicagotribune.com/news/local/breaking/ct-moon-dust-bag-auction-met-20170720-story.html.

9. Personal Property Committee, American Society of Appraisers, Monograph #2, Type of Value, 2010, pp. 2–9.

10. 26 U.S.C. §170(f)(11)(E)(ii).

11. Available at: https://www.ustaxcourt.gov/UstcDockInq/DocumentViewer.aspx?IndexID=7051553.

12. The Appraisal Standards Board, *Uniform Standards of Professional Appraisal Practice*, FAQ 135, pp. 244–245.

13. I. P. DeAngelis and L. Hersh, *Museum News* (Washington, DC: American Association of Museums, September/October, 2001), pg. 48.

14. Personal Property Committee, American Society of Appraisers, Monograph #2, Type of Value, 2010, pp. 2–9.

15. Available at: https://www.arts.gov/sites/default/files/TheAct.pdf.

16. Available at: https://www.arts.gov/artistic-fields/museums/arts-and-artifacts-indemnity-program-international-indemnity.

17. Available at: https://www.arts.gov/artistic-fields/museums/arts-and-artifacts-indemnity-program-international-indemnity.

18. § 1201(2), 40 Stat. 300, 330 (1917).

19. Available at: https://www.irs.gov/pub/irs-tege/eotopica85.pdf.

20. November 2019 revision—used if a donee receives or any object or group of similar objects in aggragate of $5,000 or more.

21. Used if a donee who has received a donation sells, exchanges, or otherwise disposes of the donated property within three years of the effective date (title transfer). The donee must furnish a copy of Form 8282 to the donor.

22. The appraiser cannot be the taxpayer, the donee, a party to the transaction in which the taxpayer acquired the property, an employee of any of the above, or any person whose relationship with the taxpayer would cause a reasonable person to question the independence of the appraiser.

23. American Association of Museums and Association of Art Museum Directors, *Gifts of Property: A Guide for Donors and Museums* (Washington, DC: American Association of Museums, 1986), pg. 9.

24. § 1.170A–17 Qualified appraisal and qualified appraiser.

25. IRS Publication 561, April 2007, pg. 2.

26. IRS Publication 1771, March 2016, pp. 2–3.

27. 26 CFR 1.170A-13(f)(2)(ii).

28. 310 Retail, T.C. Memo 2017-164.

29. Available at: https://www.law.cornell.edu/cfr/text/26/25.2512-1.

30. 26 CFR § 1.170A-1(c)(2).

31. California Code, Code of Civil Procedure–CCP § 1263.320(a).

32. Definition stems from the decision of J. Cattanach in *Henderson v. Minister of National Revenue*, 1973 Carswell Nat 189, [1973] C.T.C. 636, 73 D.T.C. 5471.

33. IRS Publication 561, April 2007, pp. 4, 8–10.

34. Available at: https://www.irs.gov/appeals/art-appraisal-services.

35. 26 CFR § 1.170A-13(c)(4)(iv)(D) and Form 8283 instructions, pg. 7.

36. Available at: https://www.irs.gov/appeals/art-appraisal-services.

37. Available at: http://www.jct.gov/x-38-06.pdf.

38. M. C. Malaro and I. P. DeAngelis, *A Legal Primer on Managing Museum Collections*, 3rd ed. (Washington, DC: Smithsonian Books, 2012), pg. 411.

39. 26 U.S.C. § 170 (e)(1)(A)(i)(I).

40. Form 8282, April 2009.

41. Venable LLP, White paper, 2012, *Estate Planning for the Artist and the Art Collector*, pp. 6–7.

MELANIE O'BRIEN AND ANNE AMATI

THE NATIVE AMERICAN Graves Protection and Repatriation Act (NAGPRA) of 1990 gives Indian tribes, lineal descendants of Native Americans, and Native Hawaiian organizations the right to request the return of human remains, funerary objects, and other cultural objects held in museum collections. By enacting this law, the US government formally acknowledged that over the course of the nation's history, Native Americans have suffered from unjust treatment, particularly concerning their ancestral remains and funerary objects. Beginning in the colonial period, there has been a long history of excavation and collection of Native American skeletal remains and burial objects, whether in the pursuit of scientific studies, museum collections, or personal interest. In addition to ancestral remains and funerary objects from disturbed burials, other objects have been separated from their communities and are in museum collections, including objects needed for Native American religious practice and communal objects central to traditions and group histories.[1]

Although many Native American collections were acquired by museums legally, with the best intentions, or as products of their time, museums no longer have the legal right to keep certain objects in collections and away from their communities of origin. Even before the passage of NAGPRA in 1990, the museum profession acknowledged that some ancestral remains and significant cultural objects should be returned to their communities of origin for proper reburial, use in religious ceremonies, or safeguarding by traditional caretakers.[2] Beyond the legal obligations of NAGPRA, repatriation is an ethical obligation that museum professionals need to address in their collections policies.[3]

This chapter addresses NAGPRA as it relates to museum registration practices. NAGPRA also addresses discoveries of Native American cultural objects found on federal and tribal lands, the return of federal agency collections, civil penalties for noncompliance, criminal penalties for illegal trafficking, grants to Indian tribes and museums, and a review committee to monitor the compliance process.[4] NAGPRA is limited to the United States and does not extend to museums or indigenous peoples in other countries. The primary sources of information on NAGPRA are the statute itself and the implementing regulations.[5]

MUSEUMS, COLLECTIONS, AND CULTURAL OBJECTS

NAGPRA requires museums to identify certain cultural objects in their collections that may be subject to repatriation.[6] Under NAGPRA, a *museum* is any institution or state or local government agency that receives federal funds and has legal control of a Native American collection. This includes institutions not traditionally thought of as museums, such as libraries, coroners' offices, state transportation departments, university academic departments, and other organizations that have Native American collections and receive federal funds either directly or indirectly (as pass-through funds, student aid, or subgrants). The Smithsonian Institution is not included because it operates under its own repatriation law, the National Museum of the American Indian Act of 1989.

Cultural item is a general term that encompasses four specific types of Native American objects that may be repatriated under NAGPRA. (1) *Human remains* means the physical remains of a person of Native American ancestry. The term has been broadly interpreted to include bones, teeth, cremated remains, scalp locks, and biological samples. (2) *Funerary object* means an object placed with human remains, either at the time of death or later, as part of a death rite or ceremony of a culture. Funerary objects may be *associated* with human remains, meaning that the museum curates the human remains or knows the human remains are or were curated in another collection, or *unassociated*, meaning the museum does not curate the human remains, knows the human remains were not exhumed, or does not know the location of the human remains. (3) A *sacred object* is one that is needed by present-day religious leaders for traditional Native American religious practices, including objects needed to renew religious ceremonies that ceased with the loss of the object. (4) An *object of cultural patrimony* is an object with ongoing historical, traditional, or cultural importance central to the Native American group or culture. These communally owned objects could not have been separated from the group or tribe without explicit permission because they were not individually owned.

Any *museum* that has legal control of *cultural items* must identify and report all of its Native American collections through the administrative process outlined later in this chapter, consult with Indian tribes and Native Hawaiian organizations on those collections, and repatriate human remains and cultural items upon request. NAGPRA creates an affirmative duty for museums to comply with the requirements of the federal law or risk monetary penalties or civil litigation. However, if a museum proceeds in good faith through the NAGPRA process, the museum cannot be held liable for claims of breach of fiduciary duty, public trust, or violations of state law that are inconsistent with federal law.

Indian Tribes, Native Hawaiian Organizations, and Consultation

NAGPRA gives Indian tribes, lineal descendants of Native Americans, and Native Hawaiian organizations (NHO) the right to request repatriation of Native American objects. *Indian tribes* are those entities formally recognized by the US government and includes Alaska Native tribes and villages. A list of recognized Indian tribes is available from the Department of the Interior's Bureau of Indian Affairs.[7] NHOs are entities that serve and represent the interests of Native Hawaiians. A list of NHOs is available from the Department of the Interior's Office of Native Hawaiian Relations.[8]

Lineal descendants are individuals who can trace their ancestry directly and without interruption to a known Native American individual whose remains, funerary objects, or sacred objects are in a collection. Whether or not they are a member of an Indian tribe or NHO, lineal descendants have priority when requesting the repatriation of the remains or belongings of a direct ancestor. Non-federally recognized Indian groups do not have standing to make direct requests for repatriation under NAGPRA but may still be the appropriate recipients of certain objects. NAGPRA provides for the voluntary repatriation of collections to non-federally recognized Indian groups.

Museums must engage in an active exchange of information with lineal descendants, Indian tribes, and NHOs on the content of their collections. Museums are not required to consult with non-federally recognized Indian groups but may choose to do so. Consultation is integrated into every step of the NAGPRA process and should be considered an ongoing dialog between parties. Only through consultation can museums determine the identity of objects in their collections, trace relationships between people of the past and present-day Indian tribes or NHOs, and determine the proper custody, treatment, and repatriation of Native American collections. Consultation is not defined under NAGPRA, but it can take many forms, including meetings, letters, emails, text messages, and telephone calls. Given the sensitive nature of NAGPRA collections, face-to-face consultations are often necessary and are usually crucial to successfully completing the NAGPRA process. Because priorities, goals, and definitions of success can vary among the parties, the method and format for consultation should be developed collaboratively.

Museums should initiate consultation very early in the NAGPRA process. Because consultation is ongoing, museum staff need to allow time for consultation prior to making any decisions about collections. Specific and clear deadlines are often necessary to move the process forward, especially when working with multiple consulting parties. Yet, given the large amount of correspondence Indian tribes and NHOs receive, it is not feasible for them to reply to every consultation request. Most Indian tribes and some NHOs have designated NAGPRA representatives who are formally authorized to speak on behalf of the Indian tribe or organization. Museums should also designate a representative who is authorized to speak on behalf of the museum and make decisions about returning objects. Museums should determine and inform consulting parties of the timeline for the NAGPRA process and the museum's decision making. Museums should maintain an ongoing record of consultations and the decision-making process to allow progress even in the event of staffing changes or delays. Any record of consultation should not include sensitive information, as determined by the Indian tribe or NHO. In all aspects of consultation, open and transparent communication between parties is the best way to ensure a successful outcome.

Inventories of Human Remains and Funerary Objects

After consultation with lineal descendants, Indian tribes, and NHOs, museums that hold Native American human remains and associated funerary objects are required to compile an object-by-object inventory of those collections. Although inventory is a familiar collections management term, a NAGPRA inventory requires specific information on the origin of each collection of human remains, including how and when the human remains came to the museum (provenance) and, if known, who excavated or removed the human remains and from what geographic location (provenience). A NAGPRA inventory should include information on how the human remains were determined to be Native American along with a detailed description. For each set of human remains, the description may include the sex and age of the human remains, if known, and must estimate the minimum number of individuals (e.g., two left leg bones represent at least two individuals). Any associated funerary objects identified with the human remains should be described and counted in whole numbers or by lots of object type (e.g., five pieces of shell and two lots of shell beads).

Museums must consult with Indian tribes and NHOs who are likely to have a cultural or geographic connection to the human remains in a collection. Although a draft inventory may be completed by museum staff using museum records, a completed NAGPRA inventory must include evidence of and information gained through consultation with Indian tribes and NHOs. Museum records, along with general ethnographic, anthropological, and historic sources, should be used to identify those Indian tribes or NHOs the museum invites to consult on a collection. During the inventory process, consultation should focus on gathering information on the cultural and geographic connections between the human remains and present-day Indian tribes or NHOs. The primary goal of the NAGPRA inventory is to determine the *cultural affiliation* of the human remains and associated funerary objects in a collection.

Cultural affiliation is a relationship of shared group identity that can be traced between a present-day Indian tribe or NHO and an identifiable earlier group. The relationship must be reasonably traced using any of the following equally relevant types of information: geographic, kinship, biological, archaeological, anthropological, linguistic, folklore, oral tradition, historical, or other relevant information or expert opinion. Cultural affiliation establishes a reasonable connection between human remains and objects in a collection and one or more present-day Indian tribes or NHOs. Cultural affiliation should not be precluded because of gaps in the connection or because of the absence of information. Cultural affiliation is not a scientific determination, and NAGPRA neither authorizes nor requires new scientific studies or research to determine cultural affiliation.

NAGPRA established a deadline of November 16, 1995, for museums to complete their inventories of human remains and funerary objects and make determinations of cultural affiliation. Museums have two years to determine cultural affiliation and complete an inventory after receiving new or previously unreported human remains and associated funerary objects. Museums have five years to determine cultural affiliation and complete an inventory after receiving federal funds for the first time.

A NAGPRA inventory is comprised of two separate lists:

1. Culturally affiliated Native American human remains and associated funerary objects.
2. All other Native American human remains and associated funerary objects for which no cultural affiliation could be determined.[9]

NAGPRA inventories must be sent to any culturally affiliated Indian tribe or NHO and to the Secretary of the Interior, through the National Park Service's National NAGPRA Program.[10] The National NAGPRA Program maintains an online database with information from all NAGPRA inventories that have been submitted, searchable by museum or location.[11] As of 2018, nearly 190,000 individual sets of Native American human remains have been reported in NAGPRA inventories.

If a museum cannot determine the cultural affiliation of Native American human remains, NAGPRA requires that the museum consult with any geographically connected Indian tribe or NHO, meaning Indian tribes or NHOs that currently or previously occupied the location from which the human remains were removed. Although cultural affiliation is based on a relationship of shared group identity across time, geographic connection is based on the relationship between an Indian tribe or NHO and a known geographic location. A museum may use information from its NAGPRA inventory to identify whether the human remains and associated funerary objects were removed from a location that is recognized as tribal land or aboriginal land of any Indian tribes or NHOs.

Tribal land refers to land within the exterior boundaries of an Indian reservation or dependent Indian community or land in Hawaii administered for the benefit of Native Hawaiians. Regardless of whether the Indian reservation exists there today, if human remains, at the time of removal, were located within a reservation boundary, the tribal land Indian tribes have priority to request the human remains. As an example, sometime in the 1880s, Native American human remains were removed from a mound near Fort Totten, in what is today Benson County, North Dakota. The museum that curated the human remains could not determine the cultural affiliation of the human remains, but because the Spirit Lake Tribe's reservation included Fort Totten in the 1880s, the museum returned the human remains to the Spirit Lake Tribe.[12]

Aboriginal land is land that has been formally acknowledged or judicially determined to have been occupied by a specific Indian tribe or multiple Indian tribes. Treaties, acts of Congress, and executive orders are examples of documents that acknowledge the aboriginal occupants of a specific location, often as a part of a land cession or creation of a reservation. For example, the 1785 Treaty of Hopewell established a boundary between Chickasaw and Cherokee territories in present-day Tennessee. Under the Treaty of 1805, the Chickasaw and Cherokee ceded this same area of land to the US government. A museum that curated the human remains and funerary objects from Tennessee could not determine the cultural affiliation of the human remains, but used both treaties to determine a geographic connection between the human remains and funerary objects and the present-day Chickasaw and Cherokee Indian tribes.[13] Judicial determinations or adjudications of land claims such as the decisions of the Indian Claims Commission or the Court of Claims may also be used to identify aboriginal land under NAGPRA.

Online maps, websites, and reference books can assist museums in exploring geographic connections, but Indian tribes and NHOs are the best source for identifying which treaties or judicial decisions apply to a specific location in their traditional homelands. Active and engaged consultation can assist a museum in identifying geographic connection as well as cultural affiliation. When considering information on geographic connections, a museum may be able to establish cultural affiliation for the human remains and, if so, should amend its inventory.

For human remains with broad regional geographic information or without any geographic information, a museum may still repatriate the human remains to an Indian tribe or NHO. Prior to repatriating the human remains, the museum must determine that the human remains are Native American and, therefore, subject to NAGPRA, consult with the appropriate Indian tribes or NHOs, if any, and ensure no consulting party opposes the museum's plan.

Summaries of Other Cultural Objects

Museums that hold Native American collections are required to compile a general description of objects other than human remains and associated funerary objects and must invite Indian tribes and NHOs to consult. NAGPRA recognizes that without consultation museums lack the cultural knowledge needed to identify sacred objects, objects of cultural patrimony, and unassociated funerary objects in a collection. A NAGPRA summary should cover all of the objects in a collection that may be cultural items and provide information sufficient to inform consultation on specific objects that may be subject to repatriation. Using only available museum records, museum staff can complete a NAGPRA summary that estimates the number of objects, describes the general object types, and identifies the origins and provenance of objects.

NAGPRA established a deadline of November 16, 1993, for museums to complete summaries of their Native American collections. Museums have six months to complete a summary after receiving new collections that may contain cultural items. Museums have three years to complete a summary after receiving federal funds for the first time. On completion, summaries must be sent to any potentially culturally affiliated Indian tribe or NHO and to the Secretary of the Interior, through the National Park Service's National NAGPRA Program.[14] The National NAGPRA Program maintains an online database listing summaries that have been submitted and the Indian tribes and NHOs who were invited to consult on those collections.[15]

Consultation on cultural objects in a summary is usually initiated at the request of Indian tribes or NHOs. There is no obligation for an Indian tribe or NHO to consult on a NAGPRA summary, but a museum is obligated to respond and to consult when an Indian tribe or NHO asks to consult. Following consultation, an Indian tribe or NHO may choose to request the repatriation of any object in a collection. A request for repatriation of a cultural object can occur at any time and must demonstrate:

1. Cultural affiliation with the requesting federally recognized Indian tribe;
2. How the object meets the NAGPRA definition for a specific type of cultural object; and
3. That the object was acquired without voluntary consent.

In a request for repatriation, cultural affiliation should be shown by the same types of relevant information used for human remains to reasonably trace a relationship between an earlier group and one or more present-day Indian tribes or NHOs. To identify a specific type of cultural object, Indian tribes or NHOs are not required to disclose ceremonial or sacred information but must clearly state that the object meets the relevant NAGPRA definition. To demonstrate the unauthorized acquisition of a cultural object, the request for repatriation might provide specific evidence of coercion or forced removal of an object or might cite the absence of any information demonstrating voluntary consent. The repatriation request may include information on who, if anyone, had the authority to sell or otherwise transfer the cultural object, especially if the object was communally owned by the Indian tribe or a group.

After receiving a request for repatriation, a museum must evaluate the request to ensure that it satisfies these criteria. If a request for repatriation satisfies the first two criteria, but not the third, the museum may choose to assert a *right of possession* to the cultural object and refuse to repatriate it. *Right of possession* means ownership was obtained with the voluntary consent of an individual or group that had authority to sell or transfer the cultural object. A museum must only assert *right of possession* if it has sufficient information to show that the cultural object was acquired from an individual or group with the authority to transfer the cultural object and that the transfer was made voluntarily. Otherwise, the museum must repatriate the cultural object to the requesting Indian tribe or NHO.[16]

Repatriation of Human Remains and Cultural Objects

Prior to repatriating human remains or cultural objects to Indian tribes or NHOs, NAGPRA requires museums to give public notice in the daily journal of the US government, called the *Federal Register*.[17] The purpose of the notice is to formally announce the determination made by a museum under NAGPRA and to provide an opportunity for any other party to come forward and make a request. A notice provides a brief history and description of the cultural objects and the determinations made by the museum, including naming the one or more Indian tribes or NHOs who may receive the cultural objects.

The type of notice required depends on the type of cultural object. For human remains and associated funerary objects, a *Notice of Inventory Completion* is required when a museum determines human remains are culturally affiliated or agrees to repatriate geographically connected human remains to a present-day Indian tribe or NHO. For unassociated funerary objects, sacred objects, or objects of cultural patrimony, a *Notice to Repatriate* is required when a museum agrees to a request for repatriation. Museums must submit draft notices to the National Park Service's National NAGPRA Program, which publishes the notices in the *Federal Register*.[18]

A NAGPRA notice provides a thirty-day period for any lineal descendant, Indian tribe, or NHO not named in the notice to come forward and make a request for the cultural object. If a competing request is received, the museum must review all available information to identify the most appropriate requestor. Provided a museum has proceeded in good faith through the NAGPRA process, the museum cannot be held liable for claims by an aggrieved party. If no other requests for repatriation are received by the end of the thirty-day period, the museum can proceed with repatriation of the cultural objects to one or more of the parties named in the notice. Before any repatriation of human remains and associated funerary objects to an Indian tribe or NHO listed in a notice can occur, the museum must receive a formal request for repatriation of the human remains and objects.

NAGPRA requires that museums consult with the requesting Indian tribes and NHOs to determine the time, place, and manner of any physical transfer of the objects. Museums must document the repatriation (or conveyance of legal control of a cultural object) in writing prior to any physical transfer. A repatriation document can take various forms, such as a deaccession form or letter. At minimum, a repatriation document should indicate that one or more of the Indian tribes or NHOs listed in the notice are now legally in control of the cultural objects. Museum deaccessioning policies may include other requirements that need to be met and should be considered along with the NAGPRA process.

Museums should work closely with the requesting Indian tribes or NHOs to successfully and respectfully complete the repatriation of cultural objects. Although not required under NAGPRA, many museums assist Indian tribes in their repatriation efforts by contributing funding, arranging travel, or helping to identify land for reburial. Reinterment should be understood as part of NAGPRA work even though it does not fall under the scope of the law or the administrative process. Museums should acknowledge the significance of identifying a location for reinterment during consultation, and should offer assistance, if requested. Many, but not all, Indian tribes and NHOs want to reinter ancestral remains as close as possible to the original location of removal, provided the location is secure and can be protected in perpetuity. Without a reburial location, some Indian tribes will not submit a request for repatriation, and as a result, a museum may not be able to repatriate or physically transfer the human remains. Repatriation grants may be available to both Indian tribes and museums to help defray the cost of physically transferring cultural items, as well as certain costs for reburial.[19]

Case Studies

Repatriating Human Remains and Associated Funerary Objects

A new collections manager joined a small Midwestern historical society museum that held a collection of objects related to the history of the local community, including a few Native American objects. The collections manager knew about NAGPRA, but the museum's records on its compliance with the law were scarce. The collections manager searched the National NAGPRA Program's online inventory database and saw that the museum had submitted an inventory for human remains with no known cultural affiliation that included one individual and two associated funerary objects.

Even though the museum was in compliance, the collections manager wanted to do more, specifically to repatriate the human remains to Indian tribes. Accession records contained minimal information but did identify the state and county from which the human remains were removed from a burial mound, not as part of archaeological excavations, but likely by curious locals (looters), who later donated the human remains to the museum. The collections manager searched online to identify Indian tribes which might have a geographic connection with the cultural objects through treaties and land claims cases. Because there was no budget allocated to NAGPRA work, the collections manager applied for and received a NAGPRA consultation grant.

Using grant funds, the collections manager hired an intern to assist with inviting sixteen Indian tribes to consult on the collection. The intern spent considerable time searching online for contact information for the sixteen Indian tribes. The intern called each tribal office to confirm the mailing address, the current tribal leadership, and the name of the designated NAGPRA representative, if any. The collections manager mailed letters and e-mailed digital copies to tribal leadership and designated NAGPRA representatives, following up a few weeks later to confirm the letters were received and to see if the Indian tribe was interested in consulting on the human remains or other cultural objects.

Nine of the sixteen Indian tribes invited to consult participated in an in-person, multitribe consultation, using the museum's grant funds to support their travel costs. Bringing the multiple parties together allowed the tribal representatives to speak directly with each other as well as with the museum. During consultation, tribal representatives provided information to the collections manager that the human remains were part of an identifiable earlier group, based on the funerary objects, and asserted that many of the consulting Indian tribes were related to the earlier group based on linguistic, geographic, and anthropological evidence, as well as oral history. Using the information from consultation, the collections manager determined that the human remains were, in fact, culturally affiliated with several of the consulting Indian tribes. The collections manager submitted an updated NAGPRA inventory with the new determination and a draft *Notice of Inventory Completion* to the National NAGPRA Program.

After publication of the notice, one of the affiliated tribes submitted a written request for repatriation, which included support for the request from a statewide consortium of Indian tribes. The collections manager made arrangements for the return of the human remains and associated funerary objects to the requesting Indian tribe and was able to use remaining grant funds to pay for the tribal representatives to travel to the museum to pick up the human remains and associated funerary objects.

Repatriating Cultural Objects

A museum had a small collection of ten ethnographic objects identified in museum records as "Apache." A NAGPRA summary of the collection was prepared in 1993 and sent to the nine federally recognized Indian tribes who identify as Apache. In 2012, a NAGPRA representative of one of the Indian tribes contacted the museum requesting to consult on the objects. After exchanging information via telephone and e-mail, the museum hosted the tribal representatives for an in-person collection review in 2014, supported by a NAGPRA grant awarded to the Indian tribe. The museum prepared a secure temporary space in the collections storage room to examine the Native American cultural objects during consultation. After reviewing the objects, the tribal representatives identified two sacred objects, one sacred object that is also an object of cultural patrimony, and three unassociated funerary objects in the collection. The tribal representatives informed the museum that three of the objects were not NAGPRA objects, and one of the remaining objects might be a NAGPRA object but it was more likely Lakota and not Apache. During a collections review, an additional object that had not previously been cataloged as Apache was also identified by the tribal representative as a NAGPRA cultural object.

During consultation, the tribal representatives provided information about the creation of the objects and a general overview of the traditional ownership and use of the objects. Six months later, the tribal representative sent the museum a formal written request for repatriation, along with a tribal resolution and a letter from the tribal chair. The request stated that six cultural objects were culturally affiliated with the Indian tribe; met the definitions of sacred objects, objects of cultural patrimony, and unassociated funerary objects; and that there was no record of any tribal member or tribal governing body giving consent to the museum or any other person to separate those objects from the Indian tribe. Within thirty days of receiving the request, the museum reviewed the request and the record of consultation with the Indian tribe and agreed to repatriate the six cultural objects to the Indian tribe. Within sixty days of the request, the museum submitted a *Notice of Intent to Repatriate* to the National NAGPRA Program for publication in the *Federal Register*. After publishing the notice and waiting the required thirty days, the museum issued a repatriation letter to the Indian tribe, identifying the six objects and requesting input from the Indian tribe on the future care or physical transfer of those objects, now that they were under the legal control of the Indian tribe. The Indian tribe and the museum agreed on a date for the tribal representatives to come to the museum to retrieve four of the cultural objects and to sign a curation agreement for two sacred objects that had been previously treated with arsenic, which would stay at the museum with conditions for care approved by the tribe.

Repatriating Human Remains with Vague Provenience

A small university museum received a NAGPRA grant to consult on the repatriation of human remains of six individuals from known and unknown sites in the southwestern United States. The museum invited forty-six Indian tribes with a legacy of occupation in the region to consult with the goal of developing a plan to repatriate the collection to one or more of the Indian tribes. The museum decided to host a multitribe consultation in Albuquerque, New Mexico, because it was a central location convenient for many of the consulting tribes. Representatives from fifteen different tribes participated in the consultation with two museum staff and two student project assistants. The human remains came from three geographic areas: (i) four individuals removed from sites in the San Luis Valley in Colorado; (ii) one individual removed from an unknown site in the southwestern

United States; and (iii) one individual and 210 associated funerary objects removed from a cave in Colfax County, New Mexico.

The meeting opened with a traditional greeting led by one of the tribal representatives and introductions from all attendees. Museum staff went over the agenda and reviewed the NAGPRA process for repatriation of human remains to make sure everyone was on the same page because both museum and tribal participants had different levels of familiarity with the law. Tribal representatives approved the use of audio recording for documenting the meeting with the understanding they could ask for the recording to stop at any time. The meeting attendees reviewed the inventory by location and then discussed options for moving forward with repatriation. After each location group was presented, the museum staff offered to leave the room so the tribal representatives could have a private discussion. When the tribal representatives agreed on a plan, they discussed how to document their decisions—for example, by printing a document that all of the representatives present would sign. One tribal representative requested a verbal agreement, and everyone agreed. The meeting minutes served as a document of the agreement for the museum's records.

Following the meeting, a draft of the minutes along with a summary of the plan to repatriate all individuals and associated funerary objects were sent to tribal representatives for review with a deadline of thirty days to provide corrections or comments. After that time, because no one objected, the museum submitted notices to the National NAGPRA Program for publication in the *Federal Register*.

For the individual removed from an unknown site in the southwestern United States, there was not enough provenience information to determine if the human remains were removed from aboriginal lands, and therefore, the museum could not move forward with a notice.[20] With a plan in place, however, the museum requested the Secretary of the Interior to approve the plan by requesting a recommendation from the NAGPRA Review Committee. At a public meeting of the review committee, museum and tribal representatives presented the available information about the human remains and the plan to transfer the human remains to one Indian tribe, with the consent of the other Indian tribes consulted. The review committee recommended to the Secretary of the Interior that the plan be approved, and following a letter from the secretary, the museum published a notice in the *Federal Register*. After waiting thirty days, the museum deaccessioned the human remains from the collection and legally conveyed them to the Indian tribe. The museum worked closely with the Indian tribe and a state agency to identify an appropriate location for reburial. Tribal representatives instructed the museum staff on how to prepare the human remains for physical transfer and reburial. At the agreed-on time and place, the museum transferred the human remains to the Indian tribe in the manner requested.

NAGPRA Resources

NAGPRA can seem daunting to anyone new to the law or its process. Although each project is different, there are lots of resources available to support NAGPRA implementation. Here are some suggestions on how to get started.

- *Read the Law*—Keep a copy of the law and regulations for easy reference. When you have a question, look there first for the answer.
- *Call the Tribe*—If you have a question about how to consult or what information to provide, call the tribe and ask. Most tribes have a designated NAGPRA representative who can be a great resource.
- *Surf the Web*—The National NAGPRA Program website (nps.gov/nagpra) contains a wealth of information, including the text of the law, consultation resources, notice templates, and information about upcoming training opportunities. The *Federal Register* (federalregister.gov) has every NAGPRA notice that has been published and is a searchable index to all NAGPRA decision making, consultation, and collections history.
- *Take a Class*—Many online and in-person training opportunities are available. The National NAGPRA Program YouTube channel includes recorded webinars, videos, and a four-hour NAGPRA Basics Training.

- *Call the National NAGPRA Program*—If you have a question about navigating the law, possible grant projects, or training opportunities, contact the knowledgeable staff at the National NAGPRA Program whose job it is to provide you with technical assistance (nps.gov/nagpra or email NAGPRA_info@nps.gov).

Conclusion

Museum professionals have legal and ethical obligations to comply with NAGPRA and return certain museum objects to their rightful caretakers. Sometimes the work can be slow and frustrating, but it can also be extremely rewarding, both personally and professionally. Consultation with Indian tribes and NHOs can increase your knowledge about museum collections, as well as lead to other kinds of partnerships, such as community-curated exhibits and cultural programming.

As the thirtieth anniversary of NAGPRA approaches in 2020, a lot of NAGPRA work is still pending. In the coming years, it will be the dedication of museum professionals to both the letter and the spirit of the law that will ensure this important work is carried out in good faith. •

NOTES

1. For more on the history of Native American collecting, see Kathleen S. Fine-Dare, *Grave Injustice: The American Indian Repatriation Movement and NAGPRA* (Lincoln: University of Nebraska Press, 2002) and Shepard Krech and Barbara A. Hail, *Collecting Native America, 1870–1960* (Washington, DC: Smithsonian Books, 2010).

2. Before 1990, there was a broad discussion in the museum profession about the issue of repatriation. See, for example, Marie C. Malaro, "Repatriation and the Law," in *Museum Governance: Mission, Ethics, Policy* (Washington, DC: Smithsonian Press, 1994) and Harold Faber, "New York Returning Wampum Belts to Onondagas," *New York Times*, August 13, 1989. Available at: https://nyti.ms/2N8be7a.

3. For more on ethics and repatriation, see Chip Colwell, *Plundered Skulls and Stolen Spirits: Inside the Fight to Reclaim Native America's Culture* (Chicago: University of Chicago Press, 2017) and Amy Lonetree, *Decolonizing Museums: Representing Native America in National and Tribal Museums* (Chapel Hill: University of North Carolina Press, 2012).

4. For more on the development of NAGPRA and its implementation, see C. Timothy McKeown, *In the Smaller Scope of Conscience: The Struggle for National Repatriation Legislation,*

1986–1990 (Tucson: University of Arizona Press, 2013) and Sangita Chari and Jaime M. N. Lavallee, eds., *Accomplishing NAGPRA: Perspectives on the Intent, Impact, and Future of the Native American Graves Protection and Repatriation Act* (Corvallis: Oregon State University Press, 2013).

5. Native American Graves Protection and Repatriation Act, 25 U.S.C. 3001 et seq. (available at: https://www.govinfo.gov/content/pkg/USCODE-2010-title25/html/USCODE-2010-title25-chap32-sec3001.htm) and Native American Graves Protection and Repatriation Regulations, 43 CFR Part 10 (available at: https://www.ecfr.gov/cgi-bin/text-idx?rgn=div5&node=43:1.1.1.1.10).

6. Words in *italics* are terms explicitly defined by the law or the regulations. Statements using *must* and *may* are specific requirements for museums found in the law and the regulations.

7. Available at: https://www.bia.gov/bia/ois/tribal-leaders-directory/.

8. Available at: https://www.doi.gov/hawaiian/NHOL.

9. Human remains and associated funerary objects in museum collections for which no lineal descendant or culturally affiliated Indian tribe or NHO has been identified through the inventory process are labeled *culturally unidentifiable*. While this defined term is often used in NAGPRA implementation, along with the variations such as culturally unidentifiable individuals (CUI) or culturally unidentifiable human remains (CUHR), some find these terms offensive. Some argue that if human remains can be identified as Native American, they are identifiable. Some prefer the term *culturally unidentified*, indicating that cultural affiliation may be determined at a later date. Out of respect for these concerns, we have avoided the use of these terms entirely and refer instead to human remains with no known cultural affiliation.

10. NPS, "Contact Us." Available at: https://www.nps.gov/orgs/1335/contactus.htm (accessed December 20, 2018).

11. "National NAGPRA Online Databases." Available at: https://www.nps.gov/nagpra/ONLINEDB/index.htm (accessed December 20, 2018).

12. National Park Service, Interior, "Notice of Inventory Completion: Peabody Museum of Natural History, Yale University, New Haven, CT," *Federal Register* 83, no. 20

(January 30, 2018): 4263. Available at: https://www.federalregister.gov/d/2018-01710.

13. National Park Service, Interior, "Notice of Inventory Completion: New York University College of Dentistry, New York City, NY," *Federal Register* 83, no. 65 (April 4, 2018): 14492. Available at: https://www.federalregister.gov/d/2018-06829.

14. NPS, "Contact Us."

15. "National NAGPRA Online Databases."

16. To learn more, see Jaclyn Lee Schmidt, "Right of Possession: A Comparative Legal Analysis of NAGPRA," 2014, *Graduate Student Theses, Dissertations, & Professional Papers*. Available at: https://scholarworks.umt.edu/etd/4264 (accessed December 20, 2018).

17. *Federal Register: The Daily Journal of the United States Government.* Available at: https://www.federalregister.gov (accessed December 20, 2018).

18. NPS, "Notices." Available at: https://www.nps.gov/nagpra/NOTICES/INDEX.HTM (accessed December 20, 2018).

19. "NAGPRA Grants." Available at: https://www.nps.gov/nagpra/GRANTS/INDEX.HTM (accessed December 20, 2018).

20. The Department of the Interior is reviewing the required process to transfer human remains without enough provenience information to demonstrate that they were removed from aboriginal land. This paragraph describes the process required under the regulations as of July 2019.

Anne Amati would like to thank the Illinois Heritage Association for the first opportunity to write about the ideas expanded on in this work as well as the many tribal, museum, and federal mentors who have impacted her understanding and appreciation of NAGPRA. Melanie O'Brien would like to thank the National NAGPRA Program staff, especially David Tarler and Sarah Glass, who reviewed and contributed to this chapter.

WILLIAM G. THOMPKINS, ELAINE I. JOHNSON, AND JULIE L. HAIFLEY
(EDITED AND UPDATED BY JOHN E. SIMMONS)

CONSIDER THE following scenarios:

- Your museum is considering the purchase from a museum in Russia of a mahogany table with an intricate ivory inlay pattern.
- A donor offers your museum approximately 1,500 salvaged dead-bird specimens, including whole carcasses, bones, and other parts.
- Your museum is borrowing a group of Kayapo headdresses for exhibition from a museum in Brazil.
- A staff ornithologist is importing scientific study skins from a museum in Peru.
- A private trophy hunter donates an imported jaguar hide and skin acquired by hunting for sport.
- You are receiving a shipment from the People's Republic of China of unidentified herbarium specimens.
- An upcoming international traveling exhibition includes a contemporary sculpture containing trumpet corals.
- Your zoological park is shipping a live golden lion tamarin to a zoo in France on a breeding loan.
- A staff research scientist is importing frozen tissue samples collected in the field from elephants in Nepal.

If any of these situations sound familiar, museum staff should know the applicable laws and permit requirements concerning fish, wildlife, and plants. The purpose of this chapter is to outline federal laws and regulations concerning fish, wildlife, and plants and to assist registrars, collections managers, curators, and scientists in determining if, when, and how to apply for federal permits that allow an institution to engage in activities that are regulated under these laws. This is a general guide and is not intended to be definitive; the specific laws and regulations should be reviewed prior to undertaking regulated transactions.

In addition, biological material laws and regulations are periodically amended, so museum staff should refer to the most current text of relevant laws and regulations as well as consult with the appropriate regulatory agency to ensure compliance with rules.

This chapter only addresses federal laws, including the Endangered Species Act (ESA), which implements the Convention on International Trade in Endangered Species of Wild Fauna and Flora (CITES). It is important to comply with all state and local laws as well. Check with state and local authorities to determine if there are any applicable laws.

BACKGROUND

Trade in endangered, threatened, and other protected wildlife and plants has been destructive to the world's flora and fauna. In an effort to curtail activity harmful to the populations of certain species, the United States and other nations have entered into international treaties and have passed domestic legislation designed to preserve and conserve species and their habitats. These laws limit and often prohibit specific activities involving protected species. Under certain conditions, exceptions to prohibited activities are allowed by regulation or permits for purposes such as scientific research, public display, enhancement of species propagation, or survival of the affected species.

Federal regulations concerning possession, disposition, and transportation of animals and plants are complex, and compliance can be daunting. Current regulations broadly govern commercial activities involving a relatively small number of the world's species. However, such regulations significantly affect the museum community. Permits may be required when:

- Collecting, especially field collecting of plants or animals;

- Acquiring or shipping artifacts, artworks, or other objects that contain parts of protected plants or animals;
- Acquiring collections through gift or purchase;
- Lending or borrowing specimens;
- Lending or borrowing artifacts, artworks, or other objects containing parts of protected species;
- Arranging collection exchanges; and
- Transporting specimens or objects across US state boundaries, across foreign borders, or on the high seas.

It is important that museum staff be aware of the various laws when museum activities involve protected species. Museum staff who have authority to collect, acquire, dispose, loan, or transport wildlife or plant specimens[1] or objects containing wildlife or plant parts or products are responsible for determining whether the particular species is protected and for ensuring that the museum's activities are in compliance with any applicable laws and regulations. Lack of compliance, whether unintentional or deliberate, may result in delays, seizure, and confiscation of materials, personal liability for civil and criminal penalties including fines or imprisonment, and damage to personal, professional, and institutional reputations.

Collections management policies should establish an institution's standard of responsibility regarding compliance with all applicable laws and regulations (see CHAPTER 2, "Collection Management Policies"). The policy should establish authority and assign responsibility to approve, document, and ensure compliance with all legal requirements for transactions involving protected species. The institution should clearly address the delegation and responsibility of collecting authority regarding field research. Internal procedures should provide guidance for staff conducting research and collection activities regarding the acquisition, importation, exportation, and transportation of wildlife and plants and the necessary accompanying documentation.

It is not uncommon for museum staff to fail to recognize that some objects in their collections contain plant or animal parts or products that are protected by various federal laws or international treaties.

These laws and treaties prescribe that certain requirements be followed to acquire, take,[2] possess, dispose, transport, import, or export specimens or objects containing plant and animal parts or products. To comply with these laws, many routine museum practices require permits or compliance with other regulatory requirements. Laws generally apply to live or dead specimens of the protected species, as well as objects made in whole or from parts of protected species. No matter how small the object or how little of a specimen consists of an organism's parts, the laws may apply (e.g., blood, tissue, DNA samples). A valid permit is required before commencing any prohibited activity concerning a protected species. Prior to such transactions, it is advisable to review the laws and regulations relating to each activity.

Many species are protected under more than one law. Any transaction involving protected species must be in compliance with the requirements of all laws under which a particular species is protected. In some cases, it is possible to file a single permit application that fulfills the requirements of the multiple laws affecting the species. Contact the appropriate regulatory agency for guidance.

Laws governing biological materials are written broadly and authorize that specific regulations be promulgated. Federal statutes are cited as US Code volume number and section number (e.g., 18 U.S.C. § 42). Government agencies publish regulations that implement laws in the *Code of Federal Regulations* (CFR).[3] The CFR is a codification of the general and permanent rules published in the *Federal Register* by the departments of the executive branch and agencies of the federal government. The code is divided into fifty titles that represent broad areas subject to federal regulation. The regulations are cited as title number, CFR, part or section number. Title 50—Fish and Wildlife—contains most federal regulations regarding wildlife and plants. For example, migratory birds are listed in 50 CFR Part 10, subpart B; endangered and threatened wildlife in 50 CFR Part 17, subparts C and D; and marine mammals in 50 CFR Part 18. Each volume of the CFR is revised at least once each calendar year. The code is kept up to date by the *Federal Register,* which is published daily. These two publications should be used together to determine the latest version of any given regulation. The latest versions of these publications may be found at https://www.govinfo.gov/help/cfr or http://www4.law.cornell.edu/uscode/.

The Department of the Interior's US Fish and Wildlife Service (USFWS) has the primary responsibility for the enforcement of federal laws that protect most endangered species, including some marine mammals, migratory birds, fishes, and plants. The USFWS also carries out US enforcement obligations for certain international agreements affecting protected wildlife and plants. For the most current information on species under the jurisdiction of USFWS, go to http://www.fws.gov/. Other federal agencies have enforcement authority for certain laws and regulations discussed in this chapter, as described.

Helpful Hints for Obtaining Permits under Federal Wildlife Laws

1. Before Beginning the Permit Process

- Identify knowledgeable museum staff and permit procedures.
- Establish authority and assign responsibility to approve, document, and ensure compliance with legal requirements for all transactions involving protected biological material.
- Identify the species involved to the most accurate taxonomic classification reasonably practicable (be species specific and include the scientific name, common name, and country of origin); seek expert advice if necessary.
- Determine which laws cover the species and the permit requirements under each applicable law.
- Determine the provenance of the object or specimen (compile supporting documentation).
- Determine the intended uses and purposes.
- Know the type of transaction (e.g., purchase, gift, loan, exchange).
- Know the location where the permitted activity is to occur.
- Know the point of origin, destination, and all intermediary stops for any shipment of wildlife specimens.
- When field research or collecting in a foreign country is involved, staff must be aware of and comply with applicable laws and permit requirements of the foreign country.
- Foreign collecting, exportation, and importation permits should be obtained for research materials well in advance of a proposed research project.
- Live materials may require additional permits through the Animal and Plant Health Inspection Service (APHIS), of the US Department of Agriculture.[4]

2. The Permit Process

- Begin the permit process as soon as possible to allow sufficient time for the processing of permit applications and to avoid the problem of unforeseen delays.
- When filing a permit application, be as complete and detailed as possible.
- To expedite the permit process, consider sending the complete permit application by express mail or certified mail for proof of delivery.
- If an object qualifies for an exception, contact the federal or state agency for the required application and assistance.
- Under some circumstances, import and export of museum collections may be facilitated by a customs broker. Brokers are often familiar with permit requirements and can ensure compliance with the necessary procedures and documentation. However, remember that the institution remains ultimately responsible.
- Couriers and shippers must know the permit requirements of the shipment, and the institution should have a system for monitoring their compliance.
- Maintain all records documenting importation, exportation, transportation, and subsequent disposition. Retain copies of all documents relating to permit applications. It may be helpful to have multiple copies of the application and required documentation during shipment and clearance.
- Stay informed about new or modified regulations by checking the *Federal Register* and agency publications.
- If questions arise as to whether a permit is required, or concerning the permit process or

other related questions, contact the appropriate federal or state agency.

- Build a cooperative relationship with the local USFWS special agent and regional office.

3. Reporting

- There are procedures for using the permit that may include reporting, recording, declaration, and other notification requirements. These requirements and instructions are often explained on the permit or attached to it. Pay close attention to these instructions and any attachments that accompany the permit.
- It is the responsibility of the institution to make sure that timely annual reports or renewal applications are submitted.
- Any person accepting and holding a federal permit consents to and allows the entry, at any reasonable hour, by agents or employees of the permitting agency on the premises where the permit activity is conducted. Federal agents or employees may enter such premises to inspect the location of any plants or wildlife kept under the authority of the permit and to inspect, audit, or copy any books, records, or permits required to be kept.

Summary of Federal Laws Promoting Conservation of Wildlife and Plants

1. The Lacey Act
   18 U.S.C. § 42; 16 U.S.C. § 3371, et seq.; 50 CFR Part 14

The Lacey Act is the oldest and most comprehensive wildlife law in the United States. First enacted in 1900, the Lacey Act has been amended several times and its application expanded greatly. The Lacey Act Amendments of 1981 extended the protection of the act to all species of fish and wildlife, whether they are considered endangered or threatened. The Lacey Act also applies to plants but only to species indigenous to the United States and its territories that have been listed on a CITES appendix or pursuant to any state law protecting species threatened with extinction. The act establishes a single, comprehensive basis for federal enforcement of state, for-

eign, Indian tribal, and federal wildlife laws. The Lacey Act provides the legal authority for detailed regulations that implement the statute (Lacey Act provisions requiring humane treatment of live animals and protection against injurious species are discussed separately below).

The Lacey Act prohibits the importation, exportation, transportation, sale, receipt, acquisition, or purchase of any fish, wildlife, or plant that was obtained or transported in violation of any law, treaty, or regulation of the United States or Indian tribal law. Under the Lacey Act, it is illegal to import, export, or transport in interstate commerce any container or package containing any fish or wildlife, unless the container or package has previously been plainly marked, labeled, or tagged in accordance with regulations issued pursuant to the act. Making or submitting false records, labels, or identifications of fish, wildlife, or plants may violate the Lacey Act. The importer or exporter of record may be held responsible for noncompliance by its agents, such as shippers, couriers, or brokers, if the importer or exporter has not provided adequate instructions or taken appropriate steps to ensure compliance by the agent.

Regulations implementing Lacey Act requirements for importing, exporting, and transporting wildlife are found at 50 CFR Part 14. Major provisions of the regulation that relate to importing, exporting, and transporting collection material include:

a. *Designated Ports*
   Except when otherwise provided by permit or specific regulation, all regulated wildlife shipments must enter and leave the country through specific US Customs designated ports. Special ports have been designated for certain shipments to or from Alaska, Puerto Rico, US Virgin Islands, and Guam. Special port exception permits may be issued for scientific purposes, to minimize deterioration or loss, or in the case of economic hardship.

b. *Declaration of Wildlife Imports and Exports*
   At the time of importation or prior to exportation of regulated wildlife shipments, importers

or exporters must file with the USFWS a completed Declaration for Importation or Exportation of Fish and Wildlife (Form 3-177). This is not a permit, but a declaration or reporting form that must be submitted to the USFWS Law Enforcement Office at the port of entry. In addition to submitting hardcopies, the USFWS has developed an online system for filing Form 3-177.[5]

c. *Exceptions*

- Dead, preserved, dried, or embedded scientific specimens imported or exported by accredited scientists or accredited scientific institutions for taxonomic or systematic research may enter or exit through any US Customs port or may be shipped through the international mail system. This exception does not apply to wildlife that requires a permit to be imported or exported (e.g., an endangered species), or to specimens taken by sport hunting.
- Any object (other than scrimshaw)[6] that is more than one hundred years old that is composed in whole or in part of any endangered or threatened species and has not been repaired or modified with any part of an endangered or threatened species after December 28, 1973, may be imported at any US Customs port designated for such purpose.

d. *Inspection and Clearance Requirements*

- Regulated wildlife shipments imported into the United States must be cleared by a USFWS agent before they can be released from customs. Regulated wildlife shipments to be exported from the United States must be cleared by USFWS before they are packed in a container or loaded onto a vehicle for export. To obtain clearance, the importer or exporter must make available to the USFWS agent all shipping documents; all permits, licenses, or other documents required under the laws and regulations of the United States

or of any foreign country; the wildlife being imported or exported; and any documents and permits required by the country of export or reexport of the wildlife. USFWS and customs officers may detain and inspect any package containing regulated wildlife, including all accompanying documentation, upon importation or exportation.

- A USFWS or customs officer may refuse clearance of imported or exported regulated wildlife upon reasonable grounds to suspect that a federal law or regulation has been violated; the correct identity or country of origin has not been established; any permit, license, or other documentation required for clearance is not available, is not currently valid, has been suspended or revoked, or is not authentic; the importer or exporter has filed an incorrect or incomplete declaration form; or the importer or exporter has not paid fees or penalties due.

e. *Marking Requirements*

All regulated wildlife imported, exported, or transported in interstate commerce must be marked on the outside of the container with the names and addresses of the consignor and the consignee. An accurate identification of the species and the number of specimens of each species in the container must accompany the shipment.

2. The Endangered Species Act
16 U.S.C. § 1531 et seq.; 50 CFR Part 17
http://www4.law.cornell.edu/uscode/16/ch.35
.html

The ESA of 1973 is the most comprehensive US law for the preservation and protection of species that have been determined to be in danger of extinction. The ESA was designed to prevent the extinction of native and foreign species of wild flora and fauna. The law also provides for protection of the critical habitats of protected species.

The ESA defines an *endangered species* as any animal or plant that is in danger of extinction. A *threatened species* is defined as any animal or plant that is likely to become endangered within the foreseeable future. A procedure has been established under the ESA by which the USFWS determines whether a species should be listed as endangered or threatened. The determination is published in the *Federal Register* and the lists of endangered and threatened species are compiled annually in the CFR. The Endangered Species list is found in 50 CFR § 17.11. The Threatened Species list is found in 50 CFR § 17.12. For current information on a given species, contact the appropriate agency with jurisdiction over the protected wildlife or plant in question.

a. *Prohibitions Under the ESA*

The act prohibits a wide range of activities and transactions with respect to endangered species; by regulation these prohibitions have also been extended to threatened species. The prohibitions apply equally to live or dead animals or plants, their progeny, and parts or products derived from them. The act and implementing regulations prohibit:

- Importation into or exportation from the United States of any endangered or threatened species.
- Taking any endangered or threatened species within the United States or on the high seas.
- Possessing, selling, or transporting any species taken in violation of the act or regulation.
- Delivering, receiving, or transporting any endangered or threatened species in connection with interstate or foreign commercial activity (for loans and gifts, lawfully taken and held endangered and threatened species may be shipped interstate as a bona fide gift or loan if there is no barter, credit, or other form of compensation or intent to profit or gain from the transaction).
- Selling or offering for sale endangered or threatened species in interstate commerce (sales of legally acquired endangered or threatened species that take place entirely in one state are not prohibited by the ESA but may be regulated under applicable state laws).

b. *Permits under the ESA*

Under certain conditions, scientific and educational activities may qualify for permits allowing activities that are otherwise prohibited. See http://www.fws.gov/permits/. Permits may be issued for prohibited activities for the following purposes:

- Endangered species permits may be granted for scientific purposes or to enhance the propagation or survival of the affected species, and for incidental takings or economic hardship.
- Threatened species permits may be granted for scientific purposes; the enhancement of propagation or survival of the affected species; zoological, horticultural, and botanical exhibition; educational purposes; or special purposes consistent with the act.

c. *Exemptions*

Certain situations may be exempt from the prohibitions of the act. In these exempt situations, a permit is not required. The burden of proof that the specimen or activity qualifies for an exemption lies with the person engaging in the relevant activity. All supporting and authenticating documentation must be maintained with the specimens, particularly when they are in transit.

- Pre-Act Wildlife—The prohibitions applicable to ESA species do not apply in the use of wildlife, except for African elephant ivory, held in captivity or in a controlled environment on (a) December 28, 1973, or (b) the date of publication in the *Federal Register* for final listing of the species as endangered or threatened, whichever is later, provided that the wildlife has not been held in the course of a commercial activity. An affidavit and supporting documentary evidence of pre-act status is required.
- Antiques—Objects or specimens more than one hundred years old, composed in whole or in part of any endangered or threatened species, that have not been repaired or modified

since December 28, 1973, with any part of a listed species, are exempt from the ESA prohibitions. The import and export of such antiques is allowed only through a designated port and must be accompanied by authenticating documentation.

- Alaskan Natives—Alaskan Natives may take or import endangered or threatened species if such taking is primarily for subsistence purposes and is not done in a wasteful manner. Non-edible by-products of lawfully taken species may be sold in interstate commerce when made into authentic native articles of handicrafts and clothing.

- Seeds from Artificially Propagated Threatened Plants—No permits are required for interstate or foreign commerce, including import or export, of seeds from artificially propagated specimens of threatened plants. The seeds must be accompanied by a label stating that they are of cultivated origin.

- Captive-Bred Wildlife—USFWS regulations provide exceptions that allow importing, exporting, taking, and interstate commercial transactions including delivery, receipt, and sale of certain living endangered and threatened species, provided the purpose is to enhance the propagation or survival of the species. The regulation covers only living animals that are not native to the United States. The regulations prescribe detailed requirements for registration of captive breeding programs and other conditions that apply to captive breeding of protected species.

d. *Enforcement*
   Both the USFWS in the Department of the Interior and the National Marine Fisheries Service (NMFS) in the Department of Commerce enforce the ESA. By agreement between the USFWS and NMFS, the jurisdiction of NMFS has been specifically defined to include certain species, while jurisdiction is shared in regard to certain other species. USFWS is the primary agency that administers the ESA and has jurisdiction over most wildlife and plants.

For the most current information on species under the jurisdiction of USFWS, go to http://www.fws.gov/. For information on species under the jurisdiction of NMFS, go to http://www.nmfs.noaa.gov/.

3. The Convention on International Trade in Endangered Species of Wild Fauna and Flora 16 U.S.C. § 1531 et seq.; 50 CFR Part 23; http://www.cites.org/

   CITES is an international wildlife treaty that regulates the import and export of animal and plant species that are endangered and threatened by trade.[7] The USFWS oversees CITES implementation in the United States, which became a party to the treaty in June 1975. The convention, with more than 175 party nations, protects more than thirty-three thousand species of plants and animals by establishing import and export restrictions on wildlife or plants threatened by international trade. The United States implements CITES through the US ESA.

   The animals and plants protected by CITES are divided into three lists called appendices. Amendments to the lists of species in the CITES appendices are published in the *Federal Register* and listed on the CITES website. A species may be listed in any of the three appendices, depending on the degree of protection deemed necessary.

   - Appendix I includes species threatened with extinction that are or may be affected by trade.
   - Appendix II includes species that are not necessarily under present threat of extinction but may become so unless strictly regulated.
   - Appendix III includes species for which a country party to CITES has internal regulations to prevent or restrict exploitation and needs the cooperation of other parties in control of trade.

   a. *Prohibitions*
      The US laws implementing CITES prohibit the import, export, or re-export of CITES listed species without the required permits and also forbid the possession of any specimen imported, exported, or re-exported into or from

the United States in contravention of the convention. All living and dead specimens and all readily recognizable parts and derivatives are subject to the prohibitions. Note that there are some exceptions for plant parts and derivatives.

Some species protected under CITES also are protected by other US laws under which permit requirements may be more stringent, such as the US ESA, African Elephant Conservation Act, Marine Mammal Protection Act, Migratory Bird Treaty Act, Eagle Protection Act, and the Lacey Act. Permit applicants must satisfy the requirements of all laws under which a particular species is protected.

b. *Permits under CITES*
Permits are required to import or export wildlife or plants listed in Appendix I, II, or III. There are different permit requirements for importing and exporting CITES protected species, depending on which CITES appendix the species is listed in. Re-export certificates are required for the export of specimens that were previously imported, including objects subsequently converted to manufactured goods or works of art. Permits are issued by the management authority of the countries that belong to CITES. Similar documentation is required from designated authorities of countries that are not members of CITES. Permit application procedures and issuance criteria are found in 50 CFR Part 23.

c. *Exceptions*
Although CITES provides exceptions relating to some wildlife or plants listed in CITES appendices, those species may be subject to regulation under other US laws. An exception provided under CITES does not necessarily allow activities that are prohibited under other US laws. CITES permits may not be required under the following circumstances:

- Pre-Convention Specimens—Wildlife or plants held in captivity or a controlled environment prior to listing of the species in a CITES appendix do not require import or export permits. Pre-convention certificates are required to prove that a specimen qualifies for this exception.
- Captive-Bred Certificate and Certificate for Artificially Propagated Plants—No CITES permit is required if the specimen is accompanied by a Captive-Bred Certificate or Certificate of Artificial Propagation from the country of origin, staring that the wildlife or plant was bred in captivity.
- Scientific Exchange Program—Scientific institutions may register with the CITES Secretariat to facilitate importation and exportation of accessioned specimens as noncommercial loans, donations, or exchanges between CITES-registered institutions. (see CHAPTER 3B, "Acquisitions and Accessioning.")
- In-Transit Shipments—For shipments merely transiting through a country, no import or export permits issued by that country are required as long as the wildlife or plant remains in customs custody. However, this may vary from country to country; for example, specimens listed under the ESA generally may not transit the United States.

4. Marine Mammal Protection Act
16 U.S.C. § 1361 et seq.; 50 CFR Part 18, subchapter C; http://www.nmfs.noaa.gov/pr/laws/mmpa/

The Marine Mammal Protection Act (MMPA), enacted in 1972, protects all marine mammals, dead or alive, and their parts and products, including, but not limited to, any raw, dressed, or dyed fur or skin. The protected species include whales, walruses, dolphins, seals, sea lions, sea otters, dugongs, manatees, and polar bears. The taking, possession, and transportation of northern fur seals for scientific research and public display is regulated separately under the Fur Seal Act.

a. *Prohibitions*
The act prohibits the unauthorized taking, possession, sale, purchase, importation, exportation, or transportation of marine mammals and their parts and by-products. The MMPA authorizes the establishment of mora-

toria and a quota system for determining how many individuals of a marine mammal species can be taken without harm to those species or population stocks.

b. *Permits Issued under MMPA*
Permits are granted for purposes of scientific research, public display, incidental taking, commercial fishing, and enhancing the survival or recovery of the species or stock. Permit application procedures and issuance criteria are found at 50 CFR § 518.31 and 50 CFR Parts 220–222.

c. *Exceptions*

- Pre-Act Specimens—The prohibitions of MMPA do not apply in the case of marine mammal specimens or articles consisting of, or composed in whole or in part, of any marine mammal taken on or before December 21, 1972. To establish pre-act status, it is necessary to file an affidavit with the agency responsible for the management of the species in question.
- Alaskan Natives—Alaskan Natives may take marine mammals for subsistence purposes or for purposes of creating and selling authentic native handcrafts and clothing to be sold in interstate commerce.
- Marine Mammal Parts—Collection of certain dead marine mammal parts by beach collecting may be authorized, provided specific conditions are met.
- Salvaging Specimen Material—Regulations allow the utilization of specimen material salvaged from stranded marine mammals by authorized persons. Such salvaging must be only for the purposes of scientific research or the maintenance of a properly curated, professionally accredited, scientific collection and must be reported to the appropriate regional office of the NMFS.

d. *Enforcement*
By agreement, the MMPA is jointly administered by the USFWS and NMFS with jurisdiction specifically defined to include certain species. USFWS issues CITES permits for marine mammals under the jurisdiction of NMFS.

5. Migratory Bird Treaty Act
16 U.S.C. § 703–712; 50 CFR Parts 13 and 21

The Migratory Bird Treaty Act (MBTA), enacted in 1918, covers any migratory bird, any part, nest, egg, or product made from a migratory bird, part, nest, or egg. The act is administered by the USFWS. Protected bird species are listed at 50 CFR 10.13. See also http://www.fws.gov/migratorybirds/

a. *Prohibitions*
The act prohibits the taking, possession, import, export, transport, sale, purchase, barter, or offer for sale of any migratory birds, and the nests or eggs of such birds, except as authorized by valid permit.

b. *Permits under MBTA*

- Permits may be issued for banding and marking migratory birds.
- Permits may be issued to import and export migratory birds.
- A scientific collecting permit is required before any person may take, transport, or possess migratory birds, their parts, nests, or eggs for scientific research or educational purposes.
- Permits may be issued for other purposes, such as taxidermy, waterfowl sale and disposal, falconry, raptor propagation, and degradation control.

c. *Exceptions*

- Possession or transportation of specimens acquired on or before the effective date of protection of the species under the act does not require a permit. Import, export, barter, purchase, or sale of pre-act specimens is prohibited without a permit.
- The MBTA provides a general exception to permit requirements for public museums, public zoological parks, accredited institutions of the Association of Zoos and Aquariums (AZA), and public scientific or educa-

tional institutions to acquire by gift or purchase, possess, transport, and dispose of by gift or sale lawfully acquired migratory birds. The specimens must be acquired from or disposed of to a similar institution, federal or state game authorities, or the holder of a valid possession or disposal permit.

- The MBTA regulations, except for banding and marking permits, do not apply to the bald eagle or golden eagle.

6. Eagle Protection Act
   16 U.S.C. § 668; 50 CFR Part 22; http://www4.law.cornell.edu/uscode/16/668.html

   The Eagle Protection Act (EPA) protects bald eagles *(Haliaeetus leucocephalus)* and golden eagles *(Aquila chrysaetos)*, alive or dead, their parts, nests, or eggs. It was first enacted in 1940 to protect bald eagles, and amended in 1962 to include golden eagles. It is administered by the USFWS.

   a. *Prohibitions*
      The act prohibits taking, buying, selling, trading, transporting, possessing, importing, or exporting eagles or their parts, nests, eggs, or products made from them.

   b. *Permits under EPA*
      Permits may be issued for taking, possession, and transportation of bald or golden eagles, their parts, nests, or eggs, for scientific, exhibition, and Indian religious purposes. No permits are allowed for import or export, sale, purchase, or barter of bald or golden eagles.

   c. *Exceptions*
      A permit is not required for possession or transportation of bald eagles lawfully acquired before June 8, 1940, or golden eagles lawfully acquired before October 24, 1962. Pre-act specimens, however, may not be imported, exported, purchased, sold, traded, or bartered or offered for purchase, sale, trade, or barter.

7. African Elephant Conservation Act
   16 U.S.C. § 4201–245; https://www.fws.gov/international/wildlife-without-borders/multinational-species-conservation-acts-african-elephant.html

In an effort to assist in the conservation and protection of African elephant populations, the United States passed the African Elephant Conservation Act (AECA) in 1988. This act works in conjunction with the CITES Ivory Control System to protect the African elephant and eliminate any trade in illegal ivory. Currently, the African elephant is listed in Appendix I of CITES and as such most import or export must be accompanied by valid CITES documents.

a. *Prohibitions*
   The act prohibits:

   - The import of raw African elephant ivory from any country other than an ivory-producing country (any African country within which is located any part of the range of a population of African elephants).
   - The export from the United States of raw ivory from African elephants.
   - The import of raw or worked ivory from African elephants that was exported from an ivory producing country in violation of that country's laws or the CITES Ivory Control System.
   - The import of worked ivory from any country unless that country has certified that such ivory was derived from a legal source.
   - The import of raw or worked ivory from a country in which a moratorium is in effect.

b. *Exceptions*

   - Worked ivory may be imported for noncommercial purposes if the item was acquired prior to the date CITES applied to African elephants (February 4, 1977) and is accompanied by a valid pre-CITES certificate.
   - Articles more than one hundred years old may be imported or exported for noncommercial and commercial purposes under a pre-CITES certificate, provided they have not been repaired or modified with elephant ivory on or after February 4, 1977. Proof of antiquity must be provided.

8. Wild Bird Conservation Act
   16 U.S.C. § 4901; 50 CFR Part 15; http://www4.law.cornell.edu/uscode/16/4901.html

The Wild Bird Conservation Act (WBCA) was enacted in 1992 to limit or prohibit the importation of exotic birds to ensure that their populations are not harmed by trade. The act assists wild bird conservation and management in the countries of origin by ensuring that trade in species is biologically sustainable and is not detrimental to the species. The WBCA is administered by the USFWS.

a. *Prohibitions*

The act prohibits the importation of any exotic bird in violation of any prohibition, suspension, or quota on importation and the importation of any exotic bird listed in a CITES appendix that is not part of an approved list, if the bird was not bred at a qualified facility. The WBCA authorizes the establishment of moratoria or quotas for import of certain exotic birds.

b. *Permits under WBCA*

Permits to import protected species may be issued if the importation is not detrimental to the survival of the species, and is for scientific research, zoological breeding or display, or cooperative breeding programs designed to promote the conservation and maintenance of the species in the wild.

Summary of Laws Applicable to Injurious Species and Protection of Live Animals

The laws discussed above are generally intended to promote the conservation of wildlife and plant species. Activities of museums, and especially zoos and aquaria, may also be affected by laws designed to protect against potential damage caused by injurious species or to protect live animals. These laws can be quite complex and are discussed briefly here. Institutions that conduct activities with live animals or potentially injurious species should become familiar with these laws.

1. Lacey Act
   18 U.S.C. § 42; 16 U.S.C. § 1378(d); 50 CFR Parts 14 and 16

   a. *Injurious Wildlife*
      The Lacey Act, other aspects of which were discussed previously, prohibits the importation, transportation, or acquisition, without a permit, of any wildlife (or their eggs) designated as injurious to the health and welfare of humans; to the interests of forestry, agriculture, or horticulture; or to the welfare and survival of wildlife resources of the United States. The species listed as injurious wildlife are found at 50 CFR Part 16, subpart B. Permits are available for importation of such injurious wildlife for zoological, educational, medical, or scientific purposes. The permit requirements do not apply to the importation or transportation of dead scientific specimens for museum or scientific collection purposes.

   b. *Humane and Healthful Treatment of Live Animals*
      The Lacey Act prohibits the transport of wild mammals or birds to the United States under inhumane or unhealthful conditions. Detailed rules for humane and healthful transport required under the Lacey Act are set forth at 50 CFR Part 14, Subpart J.

2. Animal Welfare Act
   7 U.S.C. § 2131; 9 CFR Parts 1–4; http://www.nal.usda.gov/awic/legislat/awa.htm

   The Animal Welfare Act (AWA) was enacted in 1966 to regulate the use of warm-blooded animals for research or exhibition purposes or as pets, ensuring that they are provided with humane care and treatment. The AWA regulates aspects of transportation, purchase, sale, housing, care, handling, and treatment. Regulations provide for the licensing or registration of animal dealers, exhibitors, operators of animal auctions, research facilities, carriers, and intermediate handlers. APHIS of the Department of Agriculture is the agency responsible for administering the act.

3. Public Health Service Act
   42 U.S.C. § 216, 264–272; 42 CFR Parts 71–72; 21 CFR Parts 1240 and 1250; http://www4.law.cornell.edu/uscode/42/ch6A.html

   The Public Health Service Act (PHSA) was enacted in 1944. One of the purposes of the act is to prevent the introduction, transmission, or spread of communicable diseases from foreign countries to the United States or between states. It authorizes the surgeon general to promulgate regulations necessary to carry out this purpose. Under this authority, restrictions on importation and movement of turtles, rodents, bats, psittacine birds, and nonhuman primates have been implemented. Permits may be issued to engage in regulated activities for exhibition, educational, or scientific purposes. The Center for Disease Control and Prevention (CDC) in Atlanta is responsible for implementing the act.

4. APHIS Authorization Act and Animal Quarantine Regulations
21 U.S.C. § 101–136; 9 CFR Parts 75, 82, 92, 93–94, 98, 130; http://www4.law.cornell.edu/uscode/21/ch4.html

The APHIS Authorization Act provides authority to protect the US livestock, poultry, and agricultural industries against infectious or contagious diseases. The act regulates the importation and exportation of certain animals and animal products into the United States that are or have been affected with or exposed to any communicable disease. Permits may be issued to import or export covered species and may impose quarantine requirements and other protective measures. APHIS is responsible for implementing the act.

Endangered Species in an Art Museum?

At first glance, one might consider an art museum to be an unlikely place for US Fish and Wildlife problems to occur. With the possible exception of ivory, many materials requiring special consideration when importing or exporting works of art might be overlooked by even a conscientious museum staff member. For example, a silver dagger with a skin-covered handle, a tortoise shell hair ornament, or a hat adorned with colorful feathers could present potential problems if imported from a foreign country without proper documentation.

As in other protected species situations, the time to begin asking questions is at the beginning of any transaction involving importation, exportation, or acquisition because the export documents must originate with the foreign country of export, and sometimes it is necessary to alert the appropriate museum officials of the need to begin the application process. In the case of one exhibition coming to the Smithsonian's National Museum of African Art from Europe, it was necessary to go through the exhibition catalog and identify potential problems based on materials listed by each entry. A list of problem objects was provided to the organizing institution, which initiated the paperwork while the exhibition was still on its premises. Many questions arose about the types of materials involved, requiring correspondence with lenders, curators, and CITES officials. When the time came to ship the exhibition to the United States, the requisite documents had been obtained and the importation proceeded smoothly.

The purchaser of a 1920s Erard piano in Paris was not so fortunate. A concert pianist, the new owner arranged for air shipment of the instrument to the United States, only to have it seized by US Customs agents upon its arrival because it did not meet the requirements for exemption under the AECA. Despite the owner's protests, the ivory was eventually stripped from the keys, a sad event for all concerned.[8]

What other types of materials could be subject to CITES enforcement? For works of African art, the most common are skin and fur products, feathers, claws of mammals or raptors, primate parts (hands, feet, and tails), tortoise shell, and other types of shells. Coral, which is often used in Asian works of art such as inlaid boxes and writing instruments, is another potential problem, as is rhinoceros horn, which is used in Chinese drinking vessels as well as in ceremonial dagger handles made in Yemen. Certain types of hardwood, such as mahogany and rosewood, could also require CITES permits.

After identification of potential problem materials, the next step is to determine specific identification, including both the common name and the scientific name of the source of each material. This step can be straightforward or may require consulting with an expert or scientist. In one instance of a Kongo *nkisi* containing unidentified feathers, the assistance of a well-known British specialist was needed to determine that the feathers in question were from a domestic fowl and, therefore, not subject to CITES. In a similar situation, the crowned eagle feathers adorning a mask from Zaire were easily identified as *Stephanoaetus coronatus* by the foreign lending institution, which then applied for the required permit. If only the common name is known, one may consult the CITES appendices for the scientific name.

Perhaps the most critical information in deciding whether one needs an export or import permit or a pre-convention certificate is the date the object was made or collected. For many African works, the date of manufacture is unknown, although it may sometimes be assumed to date from the period of Western colonization. One solution to the dating issue is to request an examination of the lending institution's accession records. If the object is recorded as being in the collections of a museum before 1973, then one can be assured that it is pre-convention. However, US Fish and Wildlife may still require an *Expert's Affidavit*. To qualify as an expert, individuals must be older than twenty-one years of age, state their years of experience in the field, and swear before a witness that they have carefully examined the object in question. The witness may be another museum staff member; the affidavit does not have to be notarized. A description of each object, including an approximate date of manufacture, must accompany the affidavit (e.g., anthropomorphic face mask with wood, pigment, animal hide, and monkey hair [*Colobus abyssinicus uralensis*], Zaire, probably twentieth century, collected 1952–1956).

An exhibition date or a publication date may also be used to prove pre-convention eligibility. Authenticating documentation must accompany the shipment. A statement by the affiant, such as the following, must also be included:

> To the best of my knowledge and belief, the aforementioned objects were created before 1973 and have not been repaired or modified with any part of an endangered species on or after December 28, 1973 (50 CFR 14.22). They are, therefore, pre-convention and are exempt under the Endangered Species Act of 1973 (15 U.S.C.: 1531–43).

Another type of exemption that may be useful for shipping purposes is the *Exception to Designated Port*. Such an exception may be made for a single shipment or for a series of shipments over a specified period of time. Unless there are special circumstances precluding their use, all wildlife shipments must enter and leave the United States through a designated US Customs port.[9] Availability of direct flights, loan requirements of institutional lenders, the need for continuous supervision by museum professionals to prevent deterioration or loss, or undue economic hardship all may be grounds for an *Exception to Designated Port*. In the case of economic hardship, the applicant must provide a cost comparison for inland freight, customs clearance, bonding, trucking, associated fees, and so on between the designated port and the nondesignated port. An exception may also be granted for scientific purposes, although this factor would not be applicable for an art museum.

In addition to the federal ESA, some states have more restrictive laws. To determine whether a particular state has endangered species legislation, check with an appropriate state conservation or wildlife agency prior to the transaction.

One must anticipate CITES issues well in advance of international shipping to allow sufficient time for research and obtaining the necessary permits. The advice of experts, including CITES officials in both exporting and importing countries, can be invaluable in preparing complete documentation. Determining the date of manufacture is of primary importance. Finally, one should consider obtaining an *Exception to Designated Port*, if advantageous, and make sure all endangered species laws, both state and federal, have been reviewed for compliance. •

NOTES
1. The US Fish and Wildlife Service defines a specimen as "any animal, or part, product, including, but not limited to; tissue, egg, scale, skin, feather or fur." Available at: https://ehs.umich.edu/wp-content/uploads/2016/12/FWS-Biological-Imports.pdf (accessed August 8, 2019).

2. The term *take* means to harass, harm, pursue, hunt, shoot, wound, kill, trap, capture, or collect, or to attempt to engage in any such conduct.

3. Available at: https://www.govinfo.gov/help/cfr.

4. Available at: https://www.aphis.usda.gov/aphis/home/.

5. Available at: https://www.fws.gov/le/declaration-form-3-177.html.

6. Scrimshaw refers to worked bone, cartilage, ivory, teeth, or baleen.

7. It is important to note that the CITES appendices and the list of endangered and threatened species under the ESA do not include the same species. ESA listed species are those with threatened wild populations; CITES listed species are those threatened by trade.

8. *New Yorker*, Feb. 22, 1993.

9. Available at: https://www.fws.gov/le/designated-ports.html.

Thanks to Kim Saito, Suzanne B. McLaren, and Kristin L. Vehrs.

PART 8 | USE OF COLLECTIONS

TONI M. KISER

As an integral part of the exhibition team, the registrar plays a major role when a museum hosts a traveling exhibition. The registrar must understand the ramifications of contracts negotiated with the organizing institution, insurance providers, and shippers in the course of hosting an exhibition to ensure that the terms of these contracts are carried out. In essence, the registrar's role is to facilitate the safe shipping, handling, movement, tracking, storage, and display of the objects for the duration of the exhibition at the hosting museum. This role may extend to the care and tracking of non-collection objects, such as props, exhibition furniture, mounts, educational materials, and packing and crating materials. Through the reduction of risk, the registrar helps the museum meet its contractual obligations and ensures that the exhibition arrives at the next venue having received the best care possible.

The responsibilities assigned to the hosting registrar of a traveling exhibition vary greatly from museum to museum. In smaller museums, the registrar often assists with many of the exhibition team functions, including exhibition selection and scheduling, gallery design, collections care, preventive conservation, risk management, and gallery security. In larger museums, the role of a registrar on the exhibition team is usually more specialized. To work well with the team, it is essential that the registrar understand the team's makeup and how internal responsibility for various aspects of each exhibition is delegated. In addition, every traveling exhibition is different, each shipment presents many challenges, and every traveling exhibition project is a learning experience. Ultimately, the registrars who are able to tackle these responsibilities most effectively are the ones who are organized, flexible, and unflappable.

PLANNING

Advance planning is critical to the success of a traveling exhibition. Exhibition meetings—attended by the registrar—are the best places to plan, discuss progress, present issues, and make group decisions. The kinds of questions raised during initial exhibition meetings, which the registrar must be prepared to discuss, usually relate to the logistics of getting exhibition materials to the facility by a specified time. Early on, the registrar may be asked to provide a facility report to the organizing institution and should be prepared to discuss its contents with the organizer, if questions arise.

As soon as they are available, the registrar should review the marketing materials and legal documents provided to the exhibition team by the organizer. Marketing materials may provide basic but useful information, such as the number and types of objects, gallery environment and security requirements, and venues. Catalogs with object illustrations may be available as part of the marketing package.

As one who is knowledgeable about the museum facility from a collections-care point of view, the registrar often assists with the review and negotiation of the exhibition contract (see the sample "Traveling Exhibit Contract" in the *Collection Forms* section). The registrar reads the contract carefully and should be prepared to call attention to any requirements that cannot be fulfilled by the hosting institution. Particular attention is paid to clauses describing requirements for environment, security, insurance, and borrower responsibilities for packing, shipping, couriering, conservation, and storage of ancillary materials. Because many parts of an exhibition contract often overlap with loan agreements, the registrar checks with the organizer to determine if the contract will serve as the loan agreement, or if a separate loan agreement will be negotiated. If there will be two separate documents, both should be reviewed and discussed internally by the team and then negotiated with the organizer.

As soon as they are available, the registrar reviews inventories of objects and other exhibition materials;

the crate list and individual crate inventories; a condition report notebook with photographs, condition reports for each object, and conservation information; instructions for unpacking, handling, and installation; a full list of venues; shipping documents and copies of export and customs documents; and indemnity instructions (if applicable). These documents, which often arrive in the form of an exhibition manual, can help determine how the exhibition materials will be managed once they arrive at the museum. Crate dimensions and weights, for example, allow the registrar to determine points of entry into the museum, the number of staff required to unload and unpack the exhibition, the type of moving equipment needed, and the space required for staging and crate storage.

The registrar contributes information that helps the exhibition team formulate a project budget. Crate dimensions and weights, combined with the list of venues, may be used to obtain quotes from shippers for transporting the exhibition to or from the museum. The organizing institution may be able to provide general object inventories, packing instructions, and condition reports that may be used to create materials lists; supply catalogs then can be used to compile the estimates. Off-site storage space, couriering and customs costs, environmental monitoring devices, installation, and insurance costs may be required to fill out the budget.

EXHIBITION DOCUMENTATION

Because planning a traveling exhibition requires that information be provided in advance of the exhibition itself, records received by the registrar are usually compiled into a working exhibition file. Appropriate documents then are added to an incoming loan file when the exhibition is received. Ideally, these records are marked with a loan number and stored in acid-free folders in a locking, fire-resistant file cabinet. The loan and exhibition files might include:

- The exhibition contract;
- Loan agreement;
- Relevant checklists and instructions from the organizing institution;
- Gallery and exhibition furniture layout;
- Lists of object locations;

- Conservation records;
- Installation photographs;
- Gallery climate and pest-monitoring records;
- Purchase requisitions;
- Shipping records; and
- Correspondence relating to the exhibition.

In addition, the file may include information about where related materials, such as condition report notebooks and crates, can be found. If incoming or outgoing changes to condition reports are noted, copies of the reports should be included in the loan file as permanent documentation. If loan records are maintained electronically, backup digital copies should also be created and hard copies generated for the loan file. The loan file should be set up so that other collections staff can coordinate the tracking and return of the exhibition in the registrar's absence (see CHAPTER 4A, "Types of Records and Files").

Prior to the release of the shipment by the organizer, additional documents are usually requested from the hosting museum. For example, copies of environmental monitoring records may be requested as proof that the museum can maintain a stable climate for the exhibition. If insurance is to be provided by the borrower, the lender may request that a certificate of insurance be issued by the insurer as proof of coverage for the duration of the exhibition. If the organizer provides insurance coverage, the registrar may request a certificate of insurance naming the hosting museum as an additional insured or a waiver of subrogation from the organizer (see CHAPTER 6D, "Insurance").

RECEIVING THE EXHIBITION

It is important to become as familiar as possible with the lender's intentions for shipping and installing the exhibition. The exhibition contract may stipulate which institution is financially responsible for inbound or outbound shipping, but it might not state who will be responsible for making shipping arrangements. Although the organizer usually takes on this responsibility, the registrar of the hosting institution should be prepared, if questions or problems arise, to communicate with the packer, shipper, customs broker, freight forwarder, or courier. The registrar informs both lender and shipper about any unusual characteristics pertaining to arrival at the loading dock. Specifically, the shipper should be made aware of the museum's loading dock hours and any special equipment needs. The museum must be prepared to borrow, buy, or rent the equipment and arrange for any operators needed if they are not or cannot be provided by the shipper.

If the exhibition is to be accompanied by a courier or the organizer provides an installation team, the registrar must learn how responsibilities will be shared once the shipment arrives. Some organizers prefer to unpack, prepare condition reports, and install the exhibitions with minimal assistance; others expect the hosting institution to supply the human resources needed. Determining in advance if the courier will assist with unpacking and condition reporting, if the conservator will help with installation, and if the drivers will move crates into the facility (i.e., beyond the loading dock) allows the registrar to coordinate in-house resources more effectively.

As the hosting institution prepares to receive the exhibition, the registrar should maintain communication with the organizer's registration staff and both institutions should agree on a receiving date that takes into account the shipper's schedule, the hosting museum's loading dock hours and workload, and personnel resources. The registrar works with the shipper to determine the approximate arrival time and often must be prepared to mobilize earlier or later than expected. Security personnel should be alerted to the impending arrival of the shipment. If security personnel monitor progress at the loading dock, it can be helpful to provide them with a copy of the crate list.

In further preparation for arrival, in-house travel routes are checked and cleared in advance (see CHAPTER 5B, "Object Handling"). The loading dock is cleared of unnecessary materials and equipment, vehicles, and unauthorized persons. Any required equipment must be on hand. The route should be free of onlookers to reduce distractions and minimize the risk of damage. If entryway dimensions are restrictive, the registrar should determine alternate routes in advance and test them with prototypes, if necessary. If special environmental requirements have been requested, condition the display cases before the objects arrive.

When the exhibition arrives, the registrar meets the shipper and communicates the route to the receiving and holding areas. As crates and other exhibition materials are brought into the building, the registrar uses the crate list to account for all materials. Although the shipper may conduct an inventory, it is important that the museum keep its own institutional records and confirm that the complete shipment has arrived. The waybill should not be signed until all materials have been accounted for and a visual inspection has verified that the containers have not been damaged in shipment.

Any missing or damaged containers are noted on the waybill, and photographs are taken to document any suspected damage. At this point, the registrar determines whether it is necessary to unpack damaged containers to document the extent of damage prior to signing the waybill. After the shipment has been secured, the registrar advises the organizing institution that the shipment has been received—together they determine if materials are missing. Alternative arrangements then can be made to locate the original or obtain replacement materials.

Incoming exhibition containers should be provided a rest period prior to unpacking to allow the containers and their contents to reach an equilibrium with their new environment (the standard acclimatization period is twenty-four hours). In some cases, the temperature and relative humidity of the receiving or holding area must be adjusted to meet the requirements in the organizer's exhibition contract or loan agreement. Incoming materials should be stored in an area that meets the environmental requirements of the objects in the exhibition. If an exhibition manual, condition reports, or receipts were sent with the exhibition, the registrar determines the location of these objects and retrieves them first. The receipt then is signed, dated, and returned to the organizer to document receipt of the exhibition.

UNPACKING AND STAGING

A secure staging area is furnished with clean, padded storage equipment (e.g., tables, pedestals, shelving, and cabinetry are ideal) in preparation for unpacking. If this work is to take place in the exhibition space, which is often the case for many smaller institutions, precautions should be made to ensure that only collections staff and designated members of the exhibitions team have access to the space. Additionally, any exhibition setup work should be kept to a minimum and primarily deal with hanging, mounting, or other preparation work to complete the installation of objects.

The order of unpacking may be governed by a variety of conditions, including size or fragility of objects, space, organization of the condition reports, and installation needs. In general, it is best to work with one crate at a time, so that crate inventories can be used as a checklist to confirm receipt of each object on the object list. This way, if the registrar must step away from the unpacking, the integrity of the inventory can be maintained. In addition, packing materials (if they are to be reserved) can be replaced in the crate and the crate re-secured for storage. It is helpful to take photographs of crates and inner packing boxes as they are opened and objects are removed. Because months often pass between the opening of an exhibition and its closing, photographs can serve as an excellent reference and resource for how the objects were originally packed and shipped.

Before individual objects are unpacked, the registrar reviews their condition reports and handling instructions to get a sense of how best to handle and examine each one. As the objects are unpacked, the registrar puts notations on the crate list regarding repacking, checks that no parts of objects have been left in the packing materials, and notes whether any packing materials need to be replaced, or if existing silica gel needs to be reconditioned. With knowledge of how handling, shipping, and environmental conditions affect different types of materials, the registrar looks for evidence of changes, as well as condition information that may not have been recorded prior to shipping. By recording this information, the registrar protects the museum from claims for damage that occurred prior to receipt or during shipment.

Condition reports should be completed as soon as possible after receipt of the exhibition. If objects are placed into temporary storage for an extended period of time, the organizer may require a second review prior to installation. If the organizer does not require condition reports, it is best to produce in-house condition reports or a summary condition report and send a copy to the organizer as a safeguard against a future claim.

Other exhibition materials such as props, furniture, mounts, graphics, and educational materials are not usually treated as collection objects and may be subject to different levels of storage, handling, and security. However, these materials are part of the loan and often are included in the total value of the exhibition for insurance purposes. Therefore, the registrar tracks the condition and location of these materials as well until the exhibition moves to the next venue.

The location of each collection object should be tracked individually until the exhibition is installed. Because the objects should be handled as little as possible, it is best if staging can occur in the gallery itself provided that storage-level security is provided. If not, objects may need to be relocated to a temporary holding or staging area or to the museum's collection storage area until installation. If the storage area must be used for traveling exhibition storage, the registrar should be aware of several concerns—intellectual control must be maintained; exhibition objects must be tagged with loan numbers and segregated from the museum collection to avoid confusion with the permanent collection or misplacement of objects. In addition, there is concern regarding the potential of introducing undesirable activities and materials (such as wooden containers, organic packing materials, debris, and pests) into the storage area. To reduce these risks, the registrar checks each object thoroughly for pest activity, bags any suspect objects, isolates the objects from the permanent collection, stores the material near the storage entrance, if possible, to avoid extra activity in the storage area, and stores as much packing material as possible in an alternative location approved by the organizer.

If pest activity or active deterioration of an object is noted during unpacking and condition reporting, the registrar should contact the organizer as soon as possible. Permission may be granted to freeze infested objects or to use an in-house or contract conservator to stabilize the object. If a conservator or registrar travels with the exhibition, then the conservator will usually coordinate arrangements for treatment. However the process takes place, the registrar will receive copies of any treatment proposals, reports, and photographic documentation, and will ensure that the organizer also receives this documentation. In cases where an object cannot be stabilized for further exhibition and travel, the registrar may be asked to return it to the organizer. Keep in mind that removal or replacement of objects from a traveling exhibition affects many of the exhibition documents, including the loan agreement, certificate of insurance, object list, crate list, crate inventory, condition report notebook, and shipping waybill, which then must be modified.

INSTALLATION

During installation, the registrar provides assistance to the exhibition team with object handling, movement, tracking, monitoring, and security procedures. Objects are protected during movement by pads, weighted bags, and wedges until they are installed. If professional art handlers or installers are part of the team, the registrar provides them with handling instructions. If customized interior boxes are provided by the organizers, objects are stored and moved in them until they are installed. During installation, objects are checked off the inventory, and their new locations are noted.

Before exhibition cases and vitrines are secured, the registrar checks again to be certain gallery climate and light levels meet the specifications provided in the contract. Environmental monitoring records provide information on temperature and humidity levels in the gallery, as well as inside the cases and pedestals themselves. This information can determine how adjustments may be made to the gallery's heating, ventilation, and air-conditioning (HVAC) system or if buffering materials will be needed to meet the organizer's climate requirements. Light meters and ultraviolet meters help to measure current light levels; this information will determine how to adjust the gallery lighting or relocate light-sensitive objects. As final adjustments to casework are made, the registrar also may provide temporary security or assistance to the installers. In some instances, the registrar provides inert material for padding folds, creating protective surfaces, and otherwise cushioning objects on display to protect them from structural stress.

Prior to opening the gallery, the registrar takes a moment to review the exhibition from a security perspective. Small, valuable, and easy to sell objects are particularly vulnerable to theft or vandalism. Any concerns the registrar may have are communicated to the team member coordinating gallery security so that they may be addressed before the public opening. The registrar should work with in-house security staff or contractors to ensure that cameras, sensors, local alarms, or other monitoring equipment is in place for objects that pose a high security or theft risk.

MAINTENANCE

Once the exhibition has opened to the public, periodic inspections of the gallery are desirable and often are required by the exhibition contract. The registrar, who may be one of a number of staff keeping watch over gallery conditions, communicates with the design team and the organizer to provide solutions to any problems with educational materials or audiovisual equipment discovered during gallery inspections. If the registrar is responsible for the museum's integrated pest management program, the gallery is monitored so that potential infestation can be discovered before damage occurs (see CHAPTER 6E, "Integrated Pest Management").

If an object is damaged during the course of the exhibition, the registrar completes a condition report, photographs the damage, and works with the exhibition team to determine if the object should be removed from the gallery. A note indicating that the object has been removed from exhibition, by whom, and the removal date is left in its place, and the organizer is contacted for instructions on how to proceed. If an object is noticed to be missing from the gallery, the registrar notifies security to set internal risk-management procedures into motion. If the object is determined to have been removed without authorization and cannot be located, the organizer is notified immediately so that its procedures also may be set into motion. The registrar works with administrative staff and the organizer to provide information on the object's value and determine whether an insurance claim will be filed.

Before the exhibition closes to the public, the registrar begins planning the outbound shipment. Together with the organizer, the shipper, and the contact at the next venue, a shipping date is identified, and the waybill and any necessary permits or documents are completed and forwarded. If the next shipment is to be exported, the organizer's preferred customs broker assists the registrar with preparation of export declarations and customs documents (see CHAPTER 5P, "Import and Export: Guidelines for International Shipping"). If the organizer arranges the outbound shipping, a completed waybill is sent to the registrar, or blank waybills may be obtained in advance from the shipper.

DEINSTALLATION

Although most exhibitions are disassembled and repacked in the reverse of the order in which they were installed, some details may have changed during the course of the exhibition, especially if objects or other exhibition materials have been replaced. The registrar checks to make sure that all crating materials are sound, or have been repaired, prior to repacking. Silica gel or other buffering materials requiring conditioning are readied for packing. The organizer may request modifications to the crates, based on the information provided on the incoming condition reports. If new packing materials are required by the exhibition contract the registrar will obtain the materials and have them ready to use before the exhibition closes. After the gallery has been secured, the exhibition objects are inventoried, condition reports prepared, and objects are repacked as they were received. Props, furnishings, mounts, graphics, and educational materials must be accounted for and repacked prior to shipment. During deinstallation non-essential personnel should not be allowed in the exhibition gallery or packing space and other exhibition work should be limited to that which facilitates the packing and crating of the objects.

DISPERSAL

Occasionally, a museum that hosts the last venue of an exhibition will be asked to take on the responsibility of dispersing the exhibition objects for the organizer. Because dispersal can add complexity to the project, it is important for the exhibition team to consider the impact of the request on time, space, budget, and personnel. The exhibition contract, or a separate contract, should specify which institution will pay for shipping the objects back to original lenders, as well as crate construction or renovation costs. The contract should stipulate which organization will take possession of non-collection materials. The registrar should make sure that the organizer provides the information required to determine which objects are returned to which lenders.

SHIPPING

When the entire exhibition has been accounted for, the crate lids are secured and (if security procedures require) the crates are inspected and sealed by security staff prior to loading. The registrar uses the venue list to determine the shipping address, telephone number, and contact for the next venue. This information is added to the waybill, and address labels are affixed to the containers. Each container must be accounted for by the registrar as the exhibition is being loaded by the shipper. The registrar must be attentive to the manner in which the exhibition is loaded and discuss any unusual circumstances with the shipper and the organizer before the shipment leaves the loading dock.

After the exhibition has left for its next destination, the registrar informs the organizer and the contact at the next venue that the shipment is on its way. Copies of condition reports prepared at the hosting institution are forwarded to the organizer, along with a release that is signed, dated, and returned to the hosting institution as documentation that the museum has released custody of the materials. After the next venue contacts the registrar to confirm that the exhibition has been received, the loan files are closed, and all loan and exhibition records are maintained as part of the permanent exhibition history of the hosting museum. •

Special thanks to Deborah Slaney.

JOHN E. SIMMONS

ONE EVENING IN 1952, the famed aviator Charles A. Lindbergh (1902–1974) came to the Smithsonian's Arts and Industries building after hours, climbed up scaffolding to a platform near the ceiling, and for the last time in his life crawled into the cockpit of the *Spirit of St. Louis*, the airplane in which he had made the first nonstop flight across the Atlantic Ocean in 1927. The *Spirit of St. Louis* was hanging from the ceiling of the museum,[1] and Lindbergh needed to check the pencil markings he had made on the instrument panel during the journey for the book he was writing about the flight.[2] This is one small example of the kinds of research that are done with objects in museum collections. Lindbergh was able to obtain the information he needed because the airplane had been accessioned and preserved in the Smithsonian without alteration.

The public (and even some professionals) are usually unaware of how much and what kinds research are conducted in museums because it is largely hidden from view. As one author has noted:

> There is scarcely a major public museum of any kind anywhere whose scholarly staff is not engaged in research and publication in parts of those museums usually inaccessible to the public. The ever-increasing emphasis on exhibiting and fundraising in museums of all kinds continually constrains museum scholars from discharging their proper responsibilities as researchers seeking to add to the sum total of human knowledge, however culturally inflected.[3]

Scholarly research has long been a museum endeavor, dating back to the cabinets of curiosities of the 1600s, which were compiled to help their owners understand the world around them (collection catalogs were some of the earliest forms of published museum research).[4] By the second half of the nineteenth century, museums were widely recognized as producers of research, particularly in the United States, because universities were not yet the centers of knowledge creation that they are today.[5] Museums were where people went to see new things, to gain knowledge, not just to be entertained.[6]

One of the first scientific expeditions organized in the United States was led by the Peale Museum of Philadelphia in 1801 to excavate the bones of a mastodon (which were later exhibited in Peale's museum),[7] and some of the most ambitious long-term research programs ever undertaken in the United States have been museum research. For example, the Central Asiatic Expedition, run by the American Museum of Natural History from 1921 to 1930, conducted studies of anthropology, botany, geology, paleontology, and zoology through fieldwork and the study of extensive collections brought back to the museum in New York.[8]

There are three broad types of museum research: (i) research based on collection objects; (ii) research about the collections; and (iii) research related to museum activities and museum visitors (e.g., learning in the museum, visitor behavior).[9] Although the quantity of research done in museums now is overshadowed by that produced by universities, there is still an amazing amount of collection-based scholarly endeavor in museums, ranging from studies of the evolution of life on Earth to detailed analyses of objects and materials. Most museums engage in extensive research each time an exhibit is planned and prepared; some of the findings from this research may be published in exhibit catalogs, in separate publications about particular objects or groups of objects, or in combined publications.[10] Collection-based research includes studies on the materials the objects are made of, the historic development of material culture, and object provenance.

Persnickety object registration and long-term care provide the foundation for museum research by maintaining the integrity of the objects in the collections and the information associated with them. Most research done in museums is only possible because museums have large, systematically arranged, and well-documented objects. The collections have unique research value because of the documented history of individual objects, the diversity of objects available to researchers, the order and arrangement of the collection storage arrays (which makes it easy to access the objects and information about them), the deep temporal history of collections acquired over many decades, and because museum collections are well cared for. Going forward, museums must be ever more vigilant about how they organize and archive information associated with collections as this can have a significant impact on collections-based research.[11]

Perhaps the best-known use of museum objects in research is in natural history collections. Beginning in 1846 Charles Darwin (1809–1882) devoted eight years to an intensive study of more than ten thousand specimens of barnacles, most borrowed from museums (although some came from private collectors). Darwin's studies resulted in four books on his research and helped him clarify his ideas about natural selection and speciation before he published *On the Origin of Species* in 1859.[12] Scientists still study barnacles in museum collections, including some of the same specimens used by Darwin. Current research based on natural history collections is extremely varied, ranging from ecology to genomics, morphology, systematics, to zoonoses. Because biological collections have been collected over hundreds of years, they form chronological records of life on Earth and, thus, can be used to study such complex topics as climate change and emergent diseases.[13]

Objects in museum collections may be used for research conducted by artists, designers, forensic scientists, and historians. Collection-based research can reconstruct the history of objects or even the history of the collectors themselves, sometimes using such clues as handwriting, old labels, documents, object supports and containers, or markings on objects. Provenance research is usually thought of as simply tracing the ownership history of objects, but it can

be far more intricate and detailed, revealing much about how objects were used, the materials they are made of, and their significance in everyday use. The study of collections can reveal much about the collector, the collector's worldview, and about heritage and the history of human cultures. Museum objects have been used to elucidate history that was not recorded in written texts, such as that of women and minorities that can be found in depictions of their work, activities, and by the objects they used,[14] and to understand the role of material culture in society.[15] Studies of collections and how objects were prepared and interpreted are used in the history of science.[16] Collection-based research has informed studies of the construction of knowledge, the formation of global networks, and cultural intersections.[17] The information associated with objects in museum collections is a significant font of primary source material for researchers, who make use of everything from letters and diaries to photographs, records, field books, and operating manuals. Museum collections are also important sources for genealogical researchers.

Although not directly related to the registration and care of objects, museums often engage in studies of their visitors and how they learn through interactions with objects and with each other.[18] One of the first visitor behavior research projects in a museum was a 1924 study by two psychologists who timed visitor behavior in museums in five US cities (among other things, the researchers reported that 75 percent of the visitors turned right on entering an exhibit hall).[19] What people do in museums, particularly how visitors interact with exhibits and with each other, is now considered so important that many museums have full-time audience evaluation professionals on staff.[20]

Ultimately, museum research would not be possible without well-documented, ordered collections of objects that are carefully cared for by dedicated registrars and collections managers. In the course of our duties we are sometimes asked what the most important objects in our collections are—the best response to this question is that the most important objects are the ones that have not been studied yet because they hold the answers to questions that have yet to be asked. •

NOTES

1. The *Spirit of St. Louis* was exhibited hanging from the ceiling of the Smithsonian's Arts and Industries building from 1928 until 1976, then moved to the National Air and Space Museum.

2. Available at: https://www.usatoday.com/pages/interactives/spirit-of-st-louis-anniversary/ (accessed July 23, 2019).

3. I. Gaskell, "University and college museums: Some challenges," *Antioch Review* 74, no. 2 (2016): 229.

4. P. Findlen, *Possessing Nature: Museums, Collecting, and Scientific Culture in Early Modern Italy* (Berkeley: University of California Press, 1994); O. Impey and A. MacGregor, eds., *The Origins of Museums: The Cabinet of Curiosities in Sixteenth- and Seventeenth-Century Europe* (Oxford: Clarendon Press, 1985).

5. S. Conn, *Museums and American Intellectual Life, 1876–1926* (Chicago: University of Chicago Press, 1998).

6. A. S. Wittlin, *Museums: In Search of a Usable Future* (Cambridge: MIT Press, 1970).

7. J. E. Simmons, *Museums: A History* (Lanham, MD: Rowman & Littlefield, 2016).

8. R. C. Andrews, *Under a Lucky Star: A Lifetime of Adventure* (New York: The Viking Press, 1943).

9. K. F. Latham and J. E. Simmons, *Foundations of Museum Studies: Evolving Systems of Knowledge* (Santa Barbara: ABC-CLIO, 2014), 59–60.

10. For example, see B. Cohen, *The Colors of Clay: Special Techniques in Athenian Vases* (Los Angeles: The J. Paul Getty Museum, 2006).

11. P. F. Marty and K. B. Jones, eds., *Museum Informatics: People, Information, and Technology in Museums* (New York: Routledge, 2008).

12. D. Quammen, *The Reluctant Mr. Darwin: An Intimate Portrait of Charles Darwin and the Making of His Theory of Evolution* (New York: W. W. Norton and Company, 2006).

13. J. E. Simmons, "Adventures with a time machine: the fascinating past and challenging future of natural history museums," *The Museum Review* 3, no. 1 (2018). Available at: http://articles.themuseumreview.org/tmr_vol3no1_simmons.

14. D. Lutz, *The Brontë Cabinet: Three Lives in Nine Objects* (New York: W. W. Norton and Company, 2015).

15. For example, M. M. Andrade, ed., *Collecting from the Margins: Material Culture in a Latin American Context* (Lewisburg: Bucknell University Press, 2016).

16. I. Podgorny and M. M. Lopes, *El Desierto en una Vitrina. Museos e Historia Natural en la Argentina, 1810–1890.* (Mexico, DF: Editorial Limusa, 2008). E. G. Hancock, N. Pearce, and M. Campbell, eds., *William Hunter's World: The Art and Science of Eighteenth-Century Collecting* (London: Routledge, 2015).

17. D. Bleichmar and P. C. Mancall, eds., *Collecting Across Cultures: Material Exchanges in the Early Modern World* (Philadelphia: University of Pennsylvania Press, 2011).

18. See Simmons, *Museums*, 232–234 for a review of informal learning studies in museums; E. Wood and K. F. Latham, *The Objects of Experience: Transforming Visitor-Object Encounters in Museums* (Walnut Creek, CA: Left Coast Press, 2013).

19. E. P. Alexander, *Museums in Motion: An Introduction to the History and Functions of Museums* (Nashville: American Association for State and Local History, 1979), 167–168.

20. Latham and Simmons, *Foundations of Museum Studies*, 105.

FOR YOUR CONSIDERATION

This section contains a series of hypothetical situations, most based on the real-life experiences of various registrars and collections managers. For many of these scenarios, there are no right or wrong answers; they are designed to stimulate critical thinking in students and to challenge museum professionals to draw on their own experience and training to find creative answers to the dilemmas presented. Keep in mind that institutions and situations differ so what is the best answer at one time and place may not be at another.

It is a quiet Monday morning and as you sit down at your desk with a cup coffee prepared to tackle a pile of paperwork, one of the docents arrives at your door with a box containing an object that was left at the front desk over the weekend. The docent has no idea who was working at the desk when the object was dropped off or what is supposed to happen to it, but she thinks it is supposed to be a donation.

- How do you proceed?
- What can you do to prevent this sort of thing from happening in the future?

As the registrar, one of your duties is to carefully examine the legality of objects being considered for the collection. During one of your investigations, you find that an object's presence in the United States is questionable, and believe that this information must be made transparent to those who make decisions about acquisitions. However, the curator acquiring the piece is your direct supervisor and thinks you are just being nitpicky. The curator really wants the object for the collection and insists that no other registrar would be as obstinate as you.

- What argument(s) would you make to justify your position?
- What would you do if the curator ignored you?

While a major permanent gallery is being refurbished, two large collection objects on exhibit in the space have been carefully wrapped and sealed for protection because it would be difficult to move them. However, things are not going well—the operations department chief just called to say that there would be major delays in the refurbishing project because of staff shortages. Then you get a call from the education department that they really need an early opening of the gallery so that a class can use it; they have a long-standing and important relationship with the local university where the class is taught and had already promised them use of the space the day it was supposed to open. You have just hung up when the special events coordinator drops by to say that she forgot to tell you that they have already scheduled a wedding for this space immediately after the originally projected opening date.

- What should be the role of the registrar or collections manager in the negotiations for the use of this gallery?
- How should the conflicting demands be sorted out?

One day, as you are busily working away as a collections manager in a large natural history museum, one of the curators brings you a collection of specimens that he recently brought back from his fieldwork in the tropics. You ask the curator for copies of the collecting permits and export and import documents, but he tells you that they are not needed because the collection is on long-term loan from a tourist lodge in the country where he was working. This sounds suspicious, so you ask for a copy of the loan documents and instead the curator angrily demands that you just do your job and accession and catalog the specimens immediately.

- How should you respond in this situation?
- How should the specimens be labeled and handled until the situation is resolved?

After much consideration and staff discussion, the museum's administration has decided not to allow public photography in the galleries. This measure has been taken for reasons of safety, copyright, and security. During the first week that the new policy is in effect, you receive the following five queries. How should you respond to each?

1. A local high-school student wants to photograph an artwork on view to illustrate a paper he is writing.
2. An artist whose work is on display wants to take photos of the installation.
3. The artist-in-residence wants to make a documentary of the galleries, filmed from a drone that she will control.
4. A local television station wants to shoot opening and closing scenes for a documentary, unrelated to the museum, in the American galleries.
5. A fashion magazine wants to use the galleries as a background for an upcoming photo shoot.

In the course of a complete inventory of the collection, you discover a number of recently emptied beer cans in a back corner of the collection storage area, where food and drink are prohibited. You do not know if it is the guards, the interns, or perhaps the curator who has been drinking on the job.

• How do you proceed?

A member of the museum's governing board, a prominent local physician, asks to borrow a painting that he presented to the museum several years ago as a gift so he can display it in his office.

• What is your response?
• What if the director thinks this is a fine idea?

The educator calls you to come up to a gallery where an exhibit of paintings on loan from another institution is on display. When you arrive, the educator points to one of the paintings and says that she does not remember that one being there yesterday. You look and realize you do not recognize the painting, either.

• How do you proceed?
• What information do you need to resolve the situation?

The museum has just deaccessioned and sold more than a hundred low-value objects that have been taking up space and resources in museum storage for decades.

• How should you account for the income earned from the sale?
• How should you assign credit lines for objects acquired with the proceeds from the sale?

A young new curator, who is sensitive to the ethics of collecting, has found an object at auction that she would like for the museum to purchase. However, the object may have been purchased and imported after 1970. She comes to you, the registrar, for advice about the ethics of purchasing the work and to determine your requirements for complete provenance.

• How do you respond?

The special events coordinator has scheduled a very important (her description) Chamber of Commerce reception for the main entrance and front lawn of the museum. The date of the major event is imminent, but the weather forecast looks grim so the coordinator wants to move the event indoors and set up two bars (serving a local red wine) in a multipurpose area where only a few art objects are installed.

• What are your concerns with this proposed arrangement?
• How should you respond?

A loan request comes from a small historic house museum for an elegant wooden chest that is important for their upcoming 150th anniversary exhibit. However, being an historic house, the building is essentially without environmental controls.

• How do you respond to this request?
• What could the historic house do to make it safe to borrow this object?

A local conservator asks the museum if she could have some deaccessioned, low-value objects for her students to use as practice pieces.

- How do you respond?
- Is this a reasonable use of deaccessioned objects?

The beloved old curator of history is now himself history. Returning from the memorial service, you enter his office to remove the object files and other museum documents before his family arrives to claim his personal possessions. To your surprise, you cannot find any of the museum documents of files that you are sure he had in his office.

- How do you proceed?

The public relations director and special events manager in the historic house museum where you were lucky to get a job as collections manager have planned an exciting, crowd-pleasing activity for Halloween. In a staff meeting, they enthusiastically explain that all they want to do is exaggerate the long-standing rumors that the historic house is haunted by its previous inhabitants, open the museum late one night, and invite a local ghost hunter who uses "scientific" equipment to come in and detect paranormal activity. Meanwhile, the docents can tell people about the history of the house and the family. And it probably was not a murder anyway.

- How do you respond?
- What could go wrong?
- What could go right?

The Curator of Contemporary Art wants to acquire a sculpture made of plastic that the conservator assures you will degrade and as it does so, off-gas acidic vapors. Furthermore, the conservator says that it is not possible to preserve the artwork and that the off-gassing of the deteriorating plastic will pose a risk to other objects in the collection. The curator, however, insists that this artwork will be an important addition to the collection.

- How do you respond?
- How could this situation be resolved?

You have arrived for your first day at an anthropology museum. Settling into your new responsibilities, you find a metal cabinet in the holding area for collections containing various objects, some with handwritten notes under them, some with no notes at all. The first one you look at says, "Possibly a gift, 1982." The next one says, "M. Campbell identification request, 12/91." And the list goes on.

- What are the issues with these objects?
- How do you resolve the problems?
- What do you recommend for a system that will keep this from happening in the future?

Everything is in place for an important exhibition. The couriers for several loans have come and gone and are in agreement with placement, security, and installation. Then you receive three unanticipated requests: special events needs a bar in the entrance gallery for a major donor reception, education has come up with an innovative activity and requests that it be conducted in the exhibition space (participants will use blunt scissors and colored pencils), and adult programs calls to say that they are getting so many group requests for tours that they need to raise the number of people allowed in the gallery at one time.

- Your response?

You are called to the director's office where you are introduced to a very nice elderly woman, who explains that the family wants to donate to the museum a collection of artifacts that a cousin brought back from Turkey in the 1940s. That is, most of the family thinks this is a good idea.

- How should you proceed?
- How do you determine whether a donor has full authority to give an object to the museum?
- What do you do when you believe a gift has been finalized and another party arrives with a claim to the object?
- What are the various ways that you can prove that a gift for the museum collection has been finalized?
- What constitutes intent, acceptance, and physical receipt?

A group of rowdy, out-of-control kids running around one of the galleries knocks over a pedestal on which a sculpture, now in pieces, was mounted. Unfortunately, the sculpture was on loan from another museum.

- How should you deal with this situation?
- What are the first three things you should do?

'Twas the night before Christmas (December 24) and a major donor called, offering the museum a substantial year-end gift. However, the curator is out of the country until after the new year. The director worries about offending the donor.

- Can you accept the donation without the curator's approval?
- What procedures can you initiate to help the year-end gift-processing run more smoothly?

In a seemingly brilliant move to save paper and increase efficiency, the museum administration announces that henceforth, all museum documents must be born digital and must remain digital.

- Which documents, if any, would you insist had to be saved as paper documents?
- Would printing copies of born-digital documents be sufficient?
- What would be the advantages and disadvantages of all digital documentation?

An important long-term donor to your museum wants you to backdate a deed-of-gift for an object he is about to donate so that he can use the donation to take a tax benefit even though the deadline has passed. Your director thinks this would be okay because who would know.

- What should you do?
- If you think this is a bad idea, what arguments would you muster to support your position?

Your museum has acquired a piece by a living artist, who has supplied specific installation instructions. Unfortunately, these instructions will not provide adequate support and protection for the piece in the gallery.

- What steps can you take to find a solution?
- Would there be any difference if the piece was on loan, not acquired?

Your museum is hosting an exhibition of born-digital art. You receive on loan many DVDs with digital artwork. The insurance values differ widely: some lenders place a value on the intellectual artwork, whereas others require insurance only for the physical disc.

- How do you bring some equality to this situation?
- Do you need to?

You discover that a development staff member has accepted a donation of objects for your museum without asking. Unfortunately, it is stuff you do not want, but comes with a large donation.

- What are your options?
- How would you recommend handling this?

A trustee has for many years kept objects on deposit at your museum because he simply does not have room to store them at home. The problem is your storage space is limited as well. This trustee has been generous to the museum so the administration is concerned about offending him.

- What can you do?

During a recent inventory, you found nearly one hundred objects whose cards have been marked "deaccessioned," but the objects are clearly still present in the museum. There are no records of deaccession in the object files, and you have no idea when the deaccessioning might have been done.

- How do you proceed?

Define "found in collection" (FIC) for your museum and write a clear policy to place FIC in context. Develop as well a process to incorporate FIC intelligently into the permanent collections.

You carefully discuss all of the requirements for a large African mask that you're lending to another institution: Its crate is oversized and will need a very large door and elevator, it needs to be mounted on a pedestal with an acrylic vitrine, and the shipping estimate does not include off-site stops or offsite storage of the crate. Agreements are made. The week before you ship the mask, you receive a note from the borrower asking that you eliminate the vitrine requirement. Then, when the courier arrives with the work, it is discovered that the crate will not fit through the door, and there is no elevator.

• What can the courier do?
• Is there a positive way to resolve all issues?

You return from lunch to find a box on your desk that just arrived from another museum, probably containing some objects that were to be sent to your museum on loan. You think you see something moving—sure enough, and when you peer closer, you see that it is an evil-looking insect, crawling out of the box.

• What should you do?

How do you track in-house exhibitions?

• Discuss the importance of the checklist, the conservator's review, the creation of mounts and labels, and strategies for recording location changes.
• How do you review exhibitions after they are mounted, security checks, and condition of objects?

We rely increasingly on computers to store and manage information for us.

• Do you consider all types of paper records, such as bound accession ledgers and card catalogs, to be archaic, or do they still have their uses?
• Will the significance of paper records continue to diminish?
• How do you justify which documents should be printed and which should be stored electronically?
• How will your museum preserve electronic records so that they will be accessible for the next fifty to one hundred years, and what sort of costs would this involve?

Past inconsistencies in your museum's filing procedures have left you with some documents filed by object number and some by the donor's or vendor's name. Some documents are duplicated and filed in both source and object files. Some donor files contain documentation relating to multiple gifts and are consequently thick and disorganized. Some object files, on the other hand, are practically empty. Devise a plan to sort out your filing system and to bring some order to this chaos.

• What challenges do you anticipate?
• How might you solve the challenges?

You have accumulated a large number of digital photographs taken as records of conservation work.

• What is the best way to manage these images?
• Should the images all be linked to object records in your collections database or stored separately?
• Do you need to print hard copies for the paper files?

A donor promises that he will give a large part of his extensive collection to your museum but insists that the museum must send a registrar to his house to do an inventory of his entire collection and then he will decide which objects to donate and which to sell.

• Is this arrangement acceptable?
• Under what terms should you proceed?

Your museum receives as a gift a purse containing matching accessories: a wallet and comb. The purse is also inside of its original felt storage bag. The curator wants to accession the storage bag as well as the purse and its contents.

• How do you number this gift?
• Is the storage bag part of the purse, or a separate object?
• Do all four elements create a set?
• Are the purse and its contents one object with four parts?

An exhibit is about to close at your museum. You have limited gallery space, so you plan to pack loans for return shipment in your storage area. Your conservator, however, wants to complete outgoing condition checks in the gallery—she can see the objects better while they are still on the wall or on their pedestals.

• How do you respond?

You have been asked to oversee the numbering and marking of an acquisition of three thousand objects from an historic home that was recently acquired by your museum.

- What steps might you take to organize this project?
- How can you ensure that all pieces are numbered correctly and marked consistently?

The new curator (fresh out of curator school) informs you that the old environmental standards are now out of date, and thus, it is okay to put any object anywhere because he remembers reading somewhere that the Smithsonian said that was okay.

- How do you respond?

You are asked to keep an exhibition of hand-colored prints up for a six-month period instead of the originally scheduled three months. Then the most prestigious museum in the region asks you to loan the exhibition of prints to them for an extra three months.

- What are your concerns?
- How do you approach consensus with curators, educators, and the director about the situation?

Your museum's storage areas are below grade, overcrowded, filled with objects in cardboard boxes, and equipped with wooden shelves holding the cardboard boxes, and there is no consistent location identification scheme.

- What do you tackle first, and why?
- How do you work through each problem?

A very large sculpture is arriving at your museum. The piece is not heavy and does not require rigging, but it is so big it cannot fit through the loading dock elevator; it must be carried up the steps of the museum and through the front door. The weather is cold and icy.

- What steps must you take to ensure the sculpture is carried safely into the museum?

Decide whether to send a courier with:

1. A painting that is traveling from Cleveland to Berlin.

2. A sculpture that needs to be rigged, going from Philadelphia to Washington.
3. A delicate nineteenth-century doll going from Vermont to Boston.
4. An original historical document that is traveling from Los Angeles to Japan.
   - What criteria do you use?
   - Defend your decision.

The museum hires a well-established and respected art service company to pack and ship a fragile group of ceramics from a lender's home to the museum for exhibition. They are also contracted to help install the works in the exhibit. Everything is overseen by the museum's registrar. A vase is broken in the home of the lender and a ceramic sculpture turns up with hairline cracks at the time of deinstallation.

- Define a process of reporting, and discuss interactions with the lender, insurance company, and the art-handling company.

You are looking for new off-site storage space. You visit different sites to check their security, climate control, etc.

- What specific factors will you consider from the point of view of disaster mitigation?

A river that runs close to your museum has risen to record-breaking heights, and experts predict that it will continue to rise and flood in a matter of days. The water is seeping through walls as well as through the backup floor drains, so your precaution of keeping things off the floor has not saved the day. When you get a call from your security force, water is approximately an inch deep, and shelves containing rare books and print boxes are involved as well.

- What steps do you need to take to respond to the emergency?
- What do you need to do to mitigate the damage?
- Work out an actionable follow-up plan to keep the situation from happening again.

Your insurance broker has advised you that your insurance premiums might be lower if your disaster plan had a more thoroughly detailed section on fire prevention.

- What must you consider to revise?

You work at a historic house museum located in a downtown urban area. You have just learned that an office building next to your museum is planning a major renovation.

- What are your possible risks, and how will you mitigate them?

You have been fighting a constant battle with the administration about renting space in the museum. Now you are informed that a five-hundred-person dinner party is being given in the most value-intensive galleries at the museum. You protest but are told that the money is absolutely necessary. You walk through on the day of the event and find a microphone dangling over a statue. People are placing tables close to other sculpture. After the event you find a butter knife under one of the bases and splash marks where the cleaning table has been set up.

- How should you respond?
- What can you do to prevent something like this from happening again?

A museum commissioned a local artist to paint a panel for an upcoming exhibition. There was, however, no written contract. The curator decides to do a publication that will include not only the finished panel but also photographs of the artist working on it. She wants an accession number and a credit line.

- Is the panel the property of the museum?
- Who owns copyright?
- Can a picture of the artist be published?
- How would a contract have clarified the situation?

A photo containing a 1910 portrait by G. P. A. Healy, owned by the Sample Museum, has appeared in a *New York Times* ad for the ABC Investment firm. The ad shows the painting sitting on an easel in a sidewalk setting with a caption beside it. After some research the museum finds that a reproduction of the photograph was used on the set and that no permission had been sought.

- What is the copyright status?
- What steps might the museum take?

A request has been made to publish images of the following. What do you think is the likely copyright status of each?

- Robert Motherwell painting, 1963
- Egyptian statuette, date unknown
- Paul Cezanne painting, 1898
- Unknown artist, landscape, dated 1920
- Edward Steichen photograph, 1929
- Hopi bowl, 1950s

A donor wants to divide a gift into two parts—each part contains several objects—so that he may take a deduction in the present tax year (2019) and the next tax year (2020). He decides this after you have received the collection at the museum. He also says he wants to deal with the paperwork only once, so he asks that all of the paperwork be forwarded to him. Given that you have the intent and the delivery, which of the following do you do?

- Send him completed paperwork for both years, dating 2019 as January 1 and sending it without a museum signature on the 2020 forms?
- Ask him to sign a loan agreement or a promised gift form for the 2019 donations and send him only the 2020 gift paperwork?
- Return the 2019 material and note that the gift should be addressed in January 2020.

A museum takes in a donation for an educational collection and intends to hold and use it for at least three years. After six months of use, the objects in the collection have all been destroyed.

- What do you need to tell the donor and the IRS about the sequence?

You receive an appraisal from a donor when he sends an 8283 form to be completed by the museum, and you note that the value of the object is far too high when compared to like objects you are aware of.

- Do you have a legal or ethical obligation to intervene with the donor?
- If so, how do you approach the issue with the donor?

During an inventory of your museum's holdings the collections manager finds several slivers of bone stored with some lithics.

- Outline the steps you should take to determine what the bones are, where they have come from, and how to report them in order to maintain compliance with the Native American Graves Protection and Repatriation Act (NAGPRA).

Your curator of Native American Arts wishes to acquire a headdress that contains feathers of an endangered species (not eagle). The feathers were legally obtained by the current owner. How do the following situations affect the acquisition's process and legality?

1. The headdress is more than one hundred years old.
2. The headdress is less than one hundred years old.
3. The headdress is offered as a gift.
4. The headdress is offered by a vendor in Canada.
5. The headdress is offered by a vendor within your state.
6. The headdress is offered by a vendor who is also the artist and who is a Native Alaskan.
   - How does the situation change if the object in question is not a feather headdress, but rather a sealskin coat?

A collector in Europe wishes to donate some pieces of scrimshaw to your museum.

- How do you proceed?

GLOSSARY

abandoned property—Personal property to which the owner has intentionally relinquished all rights (e.g., property that an owner fails to claim within a reasonable length of time).

accession (n)—One or more objects acquired at the same time from a single source constituting a single addition to the permanent collection.

accession (v)—The formal process of taking possession of and recording of one or more objects for inclusion in the collection.

accession number—A unique control number used to identify the object(s) in an accession.

accession register—A paper or electronic record of accession information; a document that includes the accession number, date, and nature of acquisition (bequest, donation, fieldwork, gift, purchase, etc.), source, brief identification and description, condition, provenance, value, and name of staff member recording the information.

accreditation—Recognition of conformance to established professional standards.

acetone—Dimethyl ketone, a colorless, volatile liquid with a low boiling point, soluble in water and many other organic liquids, used as a solvent for adhesives.

acid migration—The transfer of an acid from one material to another, typically from an acidic material in direct contact with a nonacidic material.

acid free—A term generally used for materials that are neutral to alkaline (pH 6 to 11).

acidic—A substance with a pH of 7.0 or less.

acquisition—An object acquired by a museum that may later be accessioned.

adverse possession—A method of acquiring title to property by possession under certain conditions, including that the possession must be adverse to the owner, actual, continuous, and exclusive.

agent of deterioration—Something that causes damage to collection objects; the agents of deterioration are grouped into ten categories: (i) direct physical forces; (ii) thieves and vandals; (iii) dissociation; (iv) fire; (v) water; (vi) pests; (vii) contaminants; (viii) radiation; (ix) inappropriate temperature; and (x) inappropriate relative humidity.

airbill—See *air waybill*

air waybill—The basic shipping document used in airfreight that serves as both the contract of carriage between the shipper and carrier and the receipt for the shipment.

alkaline—Having a pH of 7.0 or higher.

all-cargo aircraft—An aircraft that is able to accommodate cargo but does not carry passengers except by special arrangement.

all-risk—An insurance policy that covers damage from all perils except those specifically excluded in the policy.

anoxic—Having very little or no oxygen.

appraisal—A judgment of what something is worth; an expert or official valuation, as for taxation; the process of determining the monetary value of something.

archival quality—Materials that are inert and, therefore, help extend the useful life of collection objects and records by protecting them from agents of deterioration.

archival value—The value of documentary materials preserved in an archival institution.

archive—The non-current records of an organization or institution that are preserved for the future; the institution housing archival records.

arrangement—The archival process of organizing documentary materials in accordance with archival principles.

artists rights—Rights which tie the artist, the artist's reputation, and a work of art together, as defined in the Visual Artists Rights Act of 1990 (VARA).

backup—A durable copy of electronic data saved to restore the system in case of failure.

bailee—The party who receives loaned property; the borrower.

bailment—A legal relationship created between a lender and borrower of property whereby the borrower keeps the property until the lender reclaims it.

bailor—The party who lends property; the lender.

barcode—Data presented in machine-readable strips of varying widths that can be read with an optical scanner.

bargain sale—An arrangement in which a percentage of an object is purchased and the remainder of the object is donated to the museum.

batting—Nonwoven mass of natural or synthetic fiber used for stuffing or padding.

bequest—The transfer of property to an institution under the terms of a deceased person's will.

bill of lading—The basic document used in terrestrial or ocean shipping that serves as both the contract of carriage between the shipper and carrier and the receipt for the shipment.

blanket insurance policy—An insurance contract that covers multiple classes of property at one or more locations.

boom—The arm of a crane that can be extended to the object to be moved.

born digital—An image or document that originated electronically.

brace pack—A packing style that holds three-dimensional objects in place with simple wooden braces secured to crate.

buffer—A chemical substance that resists change when a base or acid is added to it. Solutions can be buffered to an acidic or an alkaline pH (e.g., some acid-free materials contain an alkaline buffer).

caliper—A measuring device consisting of a pair of movable legs typically used to measure the distance between opposite sides of an object.

cargo close-out—The deadline for shipments to be checked in so an aircraft can be properly loaded.

cargo terminal—The building in which shipments are housed or loaded onto pallets or into containers in preparation for shipment.

case—Strong, closed, waterproof box to protect objects during shipment or storage; a crate.

catalog (n)—The list of the contents of a collection.

catalog (v)—To organize the information about accessioned collection objects into categories; the creation of a record of information specific to an object.

catalog number—A number assigned to an individual object during the cataloging process.

cause of action—Facts that give a person the right to bring a claim to court.

cavity pack—Rigid packing material that has a space cut out to conform to the shape of an object.

center of gravity—The point of balance of an object.

certificate of insurance—A document that attests that insurance is in force at the time of issuance.

Certified Cargo Screening Standard Security Program (CCSSSP)—A program implemented by the Transportation Security Administration (TSA) to screen cargo prior to loading.

chain of custody—A chronological documented trail that records the sequence of custody of an object. For shipments, refers to the control of cargo from screening until its release to the carrier.

chain fall—A reduction gear hoisting device that uses a continuous chain to raise or lower heavy objects.

claim—In insurance, a formal, written demand by the insured for payment for a loss coming under the terms of the insurance contract.

climate control—The ability to regulate the temperature and relative humidity of a space.

climate-controlled van—A shipping vehicle with climate control for the cargo area.

CMS—See *collections management system*.

coinsurance clause—The requirement that a policy holder carry insurance equal to a specified percentage of the property's value.

collection care—The activities undertaken to safeguard the integrity of collection objects and their associated information for the future.

collection management—The activities involved in the administration and stewardship of collections, including planning, development, care, conservation, and documentation; caring for a collection and making it available for use.

collection management policy—A written document, approved by the institution's governing authority, that specifies how objects will be acquired, accessioned, documented, stored, used, cared for, and disposed of.

collection storage array—The physical order in which objects are arranged in the collection storage area.

collections management system (CMS)—A database or other software that supports the internal workflows of a museum collection.

combination flight—An aircraft that carries both cargo and passengers. Also called a *combi flight*.

commercial invoice—An international shipping document that states the object name, date, country of origin, materials, value, owner, and whether or not the object will be returned.

commercial use—Use of a collection object or its associated information for sale, purchase, trade, barter, or transfer for gain or profit.

common law—Legal principles derived from practice, precedent, and court decisions rather than statutes.

compactor storage—High-density storage system consisting of movable carriages on rails.

condition—A contract provision or stipulation.

condition report—An accurate, informative descriptive report of an object's or document's state of preservation at a particular moment in time.

conditional gift—See *restricted gift*.

conservation—Maximizing the endurance or minimizing the deterioration of an object through time, with as little change to that object as possible.

conservator—A trained conservation professional.

constructive notice—The assumption that a reasonable person should have known something even if they did not have actual knowledge of it.

continuous custody—The archival principle that material should be retained by the creating organization or transferred directly to an archival institution to guarantee its integrity; the principle that noncurrent records must be retained by the creating organization or its successor in function to be considered archival.

contour bracing—Braces made the same size as the crate's interior. Also called *guillotines* or *yokes*.

copyright—Legal recognition of special intellectual property rights, distinct from the right of possession, that a creator may have for a work, including reproduction, derivative works, distribution, public performance, and public display. The rights may be given or sold to a third party by the copyright owner. Copyright protection exists for the author's lifetime plus seventy years. Copyright notice and markings are not required for copyright protection.

copyright law—The body of legislation that governs the exploitation of literary, musical, artistic, and related works. In the United States, this is contained in Title 17 of the US Code, in combination with the regulations of the Copyright Office and the cases that have interpreted Title 17 and those regulations.

country of export—The last country from which an object, animal, or plant was exported before importation into the United States.

country of origin—The country where an object was created or an animal or plant was taken from the wild, or the country of natal origin of an animal.

courier—An individual who travels with an object to ensure its proper care and safe arrival.

covered object—Any object created before 1946 and acquired by a museum after 1932, that underwent a change of ownership between 1932 and 1946, and that was or might reasonably be thought to have been in continental Europe between those dates (see AAM *Guidelines Concerning the Unlawful Appropriation of Objects During the Nazi Era*).

crane—A mobile unit equipped with a boom, cable, and draw works, capable of 360-degree rotation around a center pin.

crate markings—Symbols, numbers, and letters stenciled on the outside of a crate indicating proper handling, size, weight, or identification.

cross-docking—The transfer of a load from one truck to another before arrival at the final destination.

cultural property—Objects that for religious or secular reasons are designated by the state as important for archaeology, art, history, literature, prehistory, or science.

culturally sensitive object—An object that requires special handling or use restrictions because of its importance to a particular culture.

curation agreement—A contract between two parties detailing the curation of a collection, including a description of the state of the collection when transferred from the custody of one party to the other, responsibilities to the collection for both parties, costs, ownership, and access and use of the collection.

custody—Temporary or permanent possession of an object.

customs broker—A representative who arranges customs clearance of objects traveling between countries.

customs seal—A tag or label affixed to a shipping box by a customs official at the original port of entry to guarantee that the contents have not been tampered with.

DAMS—See *Digital Asset Management System*.

database—A structured, organized collection of information that can be accessed, managed, and edited.

datalogger—An electronic device that records temperature and relative humidity.

deaccession—The formal removal of an accessioned object from the collection.

deed of gift—A contract that transfers ownership of an object to an institution.

deferred donation—A donation in which the donor retains ownership of an object for a specific period of time (a synonym is *promised gift*).

desiccation—Removal of moisture.

digital art—Art works that are made or presented using digital technology.

Digital Asset Management System (DAMS)—A system used to control and access digital assets.

digital image—An image in electronic format composed of pixels.

digital negative (DNG)—Adobe's archival RAW format.

disposal—The act of physically removing a deaccessioned object from a museum collection.

dolly—A low, four-wheeled platform used to move objects.

domestic shipment—The shipment of objects within a country.

double-crating—The use of one box or case inside another.

DNG—See *digital negative*.

drawer case—A sideways slot-style case in which individual boxes slide into the case like drawers.

due diligence—The steps taken by an individual to meet a legal obligation, particularly in reference to a purchase or donation of an object.

endorsement—In insurance, a form attached to the basic insurance contract that alters certain provisions in the policy.

ephemera—Objects made of materials that were intended to have only short-term use.

escort—Security personnel who protect a shipment during transit.

ethics—A set of principles or values to govern the conduct of individuals.

exchange—A form of purchase in which objects of equal value are traded between two institutions.

export license—Permission to ship an object out of a country.

export shipment—The movement of an object out of a country.

extended loan—A loan that is continued beyond its original termination date by mutual agreement of both lender and borrower.

fair market value—The selling price of an object on the open market.

fair use—Use of a copyrighted work for criticism, comment, news reporting, teaching (including multiple copies for classroom use), scholarship, or research.

FIC—See *found in collection*.

fiduciary obligation—The responsibility of a museum to the collections it holds in trust, for the public.

flat-pack—Horizontal packing of objects.

foam core—A plastic foam that is laminated with a paper-based material.

follow car—A vehicle carrying an escort and sometimes a courier that follows the vehicle containing an object in transit.

foxing—A discoloration of paper caused by the action of mold on iron salts.

found in collection (FIC)—Undocumented objects that remain without status after all attempts to reconcile them to existing records of permanent collection and loan objects are completed.

fractional gift—A donation for which the museum does not receive full title but rather partial title.

freight forwarding agent—A representative who organizes shipments.

friable—Easily crumbled.

gantry—A hoist mounted on a horizontal beam that is supported by vertical sides.

General Facility Report—A publication of the American Alliance of Museums that compiles information necessary to demonstrate that a museum has suitable facilities to receive a loan of objects from another institution; formerly called the *Standard Facility Report*.

gift—The voluntary transfer of ownership of property completely free of restrictions.

glassine—A dense, slick-surfaced translucent paper that is resistant to the passage of air and dirt; used as a wrapping material or as separation sheets.

gross weight—The combined weight of a packed object, packing materials, and crate or box.

guillotines—See *contour bracing*.

hand-carry—A packed object that is carried aboard an airplane by one person, and travels under a seat or in an overhead bin.

hand signals—Standardized hand gestures to insure proper procedures in rigging an object or maneuvering a vehicle without verbal communication.

herbarium—A collection of dried plant specimens, usually mounted and systematically arranged for reference.

hitch—A method of temporarily connecting a lifting device such as a crane or gantry to an object by means of a loop, hook, or noose.

hoist—A device used to lift and or lower an object by means of ropes or chains and pulleys.

HVAC—Acronym for a heating, ventilation, and air-conditioning system.

hygroscopic material—A material capable of absorbing moisture.

hygrothermograph—An instrument that records temperature and relative humidity on a paper chart.

import shipment—The movement of an object into a country.

impounded shipment—A shipment that is seized by customs officials at a port of entry.

incoming loan—An object sent from another institution for a specified length of time without transfer of ownership.

indefinite loan—A loan that does not have a set duration or termination date.

inert material—Stable material that is not chemically reactive.

insurance claim—A formal, written demand to an insurance company for reimbursement for loss of or damage to an insured object.

integrated pest management (IPM)—The coordinated use of biological and environmental information with selected control measures to prevent, reduce, or eliminate pest damage; a holistic approach to pest management, taking advantage of all appropriate pest management options.

intellectual property—Unique products of human intelligence that have real or potential commercial value (e.g., designs, inventions, literary works, unique names, and industrial processes).

intellectual property rights—Property rights related to creative processes; nonphysical (intangible) rights to an object or record that exists independently from ownership of the physical item. Intellectual property rights include copyright, patent rights, and trademark rights.

inventory (n)—An itemized listing of objects in a collection, often including current location.

inventory (v)—The process of physically locating and recording the presence of objects in a collection.

IPM—See *integrated pest management*.

J-Bar—A lifting tool composed of a long handle with an angled or bent steel plate on one end.

JPEG—An acronym for Joint Photographic Experts Group; a file format used for distribution but not for archival storage of images.

laches—An unreasonable delay that makes it inequitable to give the relief sought by a party in court.

lacquer—A varnish coating.

load line—A line that bears the weight of a lift.

loan—A bailment; the temporary transfer of an object from a lender to a borrower; a loan does not involve change in ownership.

loan agreement—A contract between a lender and a borrower specifying the object, loan conditions, and the responsibilities of each party.

loss limit—The maximum amount an insurance policy will pay for a single loss.

lost in inventory—An object that is noted as lost following a careful check of all areas where the object might reasonably be.

lossless—A class of data compression algorithms that allows the exact original data to be reconstructed from the compressed data.

lossy—A file compression technique that does not permit the decompression of data back to 100 percent of the original.

marine mammal—A mammal that morphologically adapted to the marine environment.

metadata—Data about data.

microenvironment—A small, enclosed space around an object that in which the climate can be controlled.

MOV—A file format for digital video.

MSDS—See *Safety Data Sheet*.

Nazi era—The time period of 1933–1945 when the Nazi Party was in power in Germany, also referred to as the *Holocaust era*.

net weight—The weight of the object exclusive of the weight of the box or packing materials.

nitrile—An organic compound with a C≡N functional group used to make flexible, synthetic gloves that are resistant to many chemical compounds.

nomenclature—A system of names for things.

off-gassing—The release of volatile substances from a material (usually refers to the release of acids).

off-site storage—Collection storage at a site that is physically separated from the museum.

old loans—Expired loans or loans of unlimited duration that have been left unclaimed by lenders at the museum.

one-time crate—A simple crate intended to be used for one shipment only; also called a *one-way crate*.

original order—The archival principle that records should be maintained in the order in which they were placed by their creator.

outgoing loan—An object that is sent to another institution for a specific length of time without transfer of ownership.

ownership—The legal right of possession of title (to something); proprietorship.

pallet—A low, portable platform on which a heavy or bulky object is placed for storage or transport.

partial gift—See *fractional gift*.

patrimony laws—Legislation claiming ownership of all objects defined as part of the nation's patrimony.

PCS permit—Any document designated as a permit, license, certificate, or any other document issued by the management authority or responsible agency or office to authorize, limit, or describe activity and signed by an authorized official.

PDF—An acronym for portable document format; the preferred long-term storage and distribution format for text and image files.

permanent loan—An oxymoron used in reference to a loan with no specified ending date.

pH—A logarithmic scale used to specify acidity or alkalinity of a water-based solution.

pick—The point above the center of gravity at which an object is lifted; also called a *pick point*.

PNG—See *portable network graphics*.

policy—A guideline that regulates organizational action; policies control the conduct of people and thereby the activities of systems.

portable network graphics (PNG)—A digital file format used for image compression.

powder coating—An electrostatic coating applied as a powder and then set by the application of heat.

preventive conservation—Actions taken to detect, avoid, block, ameliorate, and mitigate the agents of deterioration that affect objects in a museum collection.

precatory restriction—A restriction on a gift that is the expressed wish of the donor.

promised gift—See *deferred donation*.

provenance—A term describing the history of ownership of museum objects; the background and history of ownership.

provenience—In archaeology, refers to the specific geographic origin of an object.

public domain—In copyright law, the right of anyone to use literature, music, or other previously copyrighted materials after the copyright period has expired.

psychrometer—An instrument for measuring relative humidity by comparing the temperature of a dry bulb and a wet bulb thermometer.

RAW image file—Unprocessed data from a digital camera, sometimes considered to be a digital negative (DNG). Camera make and model will determine the size of a RAW file.

registration—The process of assigning an accessioned object to a unique place in a serial order list of the contents of a collection.

registration number—A number assigned to an object or specimen in an accession (sometimes used as a synonym for *accession number* or *catalog number*).

relative humidity (RH)—The amount of moisture in a volume of air relative to the amount the same volume of air could hold if saturated.

repository—A collections-oriented facility that provides long-term professional care and accountable curatorial services for a collection that it does not own.

repository agreement—A contract in which an institution provides long-term professional care and accountable curatorial services for a collection that belongs to another institution or entity (e.g., a state, federal, or foreign government) in return for mutually acceptable benefits.

restitution—The return of an object or payment of compensation to an object's original owner or legal successor; the return of an object to the ownership of a source country or country that claims to be the source country.

restricted gift—The voluntary transfer of ownership of property with conditions or limitations placed upon that ownership.

RFID—Radio frequency identification tag, a device that uses radio waves to transmit and read data.

rigging—The use of slings and hitches to lift and move large or heavy objects; the equipment used in moving large or heavy objects.

risk—The chance of an undesirable change occurring.

risk management—A program of risk control that includes analyzing the probability of risks to collections, facilities, visitors, and staff as well as planning and implementing appropriate preventative measures and response methods.

Safety Data Sheet—An information sheet provided by the manufacturer of a chemical that includes data on volatility, flammability, toxicity, and safety related information (formerly Material Safety Data Sheets, or MSDS)

sale—Transfer of title in return for monetary compensation or other thing of value on terms agreed upon between buyer and seller.

SDS—See Safety Data Sheet

seal—A metal wire and numbered disc used on a lock or container to monitor tampering with the contents.

series—A body of file units or documents arranged in accordance with a unified filing system or maintained by the record creator as a unit because of some relationship arising out of their creation, receipt, or use.

shellac—A preparation of lac, usually dissolved in alcohol, and used chiefly as a wood finish.

shipping agent—See *freight-forwarding agent.*

sight line—The range of a guard's view of objects on display in which large objects do not obscure small objects.

sight measurement—An estimated measurement of an object made when the full extremities of the piece are inaccessible.

silica gel—A granular substance that has high moisture-absorbing and emitting properties and is used as a moisture stabilizer in packing, storing, and exhibiting humidity sensitive objects.

slat case—A case made with a minimal amount of wood and without solid sides.

sliding tray case—A case with rigid trays that slide out of a side opening.

slings—The rope, cables, or woven straps used in rigging.

slot style crating—A style of packing for multiple objects that allows each object to be unpacked as needed without handling the others in the crate by having individual objects fit into their own slots.

soft packed—Packing an object without enclosing it in a hard-shell box or case using soft materials

Solander box—A ready-made box of acid-free board.

specimen—Any animal or plant, or any part, product, egg, seed, or root of any animal or plant.

Standard Facility Report—See *General Facility Report.*

storage environment—The conditions under which collection objects are stored, including temperature, relative humidity, and light exposure.

stowage requirements—The structure of an object that dictates which way it can be placed in a crate, how far off center it can be tipped when handled, and which plane of travel is preferable.

straight truck—A truck with body and cab connected.

subgroup—A body of related records within a record group, usually consisting of the records of a primary subordinate administrative unit or of records series related chronologically, functionally, or by subject.

substrate—The immediate surface to which a coating or adhesive material is applied.

tagged image file format (TIFF)—An electronic image file format that preserves original color information and supports embedded color profiles and metadata.

tag line—One or more control lines that are attached to an object before a lift takes place; used to control the sway, stability, and placement of the object.

tare weight—The weight of the packing box, including packing materials, without the object.

taxidermy—The process of preparing animal skins and stuffing them in a lifelike form.

taxonomy—Classification in an ordered system; division into ordered categories; the science of naming, describing, and classifying objects or organisms.

temperature—A degree of hotness or coldness. May be expressed in Centigrade or Fahrenheit scales.

TIFF—See *tagged image file format*.

title—The possession of rights of ownership to an object or property.

touring crate—A container that is built to stand up to a multivenue tour, usually with reusable fastening hardware on the lid.

tractor and trailer—A two-part transport vehicle consisting of a tractor (which has the engine and the cab for the driver) that is attached to the trailer (which holds the freight).

travel frame—New or replacement frame used for travel instead of the original frame; a wood collar to which an object is attached for travel to allow wrapping.

traveling—Any horizontal movement.

traveling case—A case built to withstand a multistop tour.

tray pack—Objects placed into a tray or drawer using a foam cutout to cushion the object.

TSA—Transportation Safety Administration, the federal agency responsible for the security of transportation systems for public and commercial use in the United States.

two-way crate—A shipping crate built to send an object to a destination and back but not to withstand extensive travel.

unclaimed loan—See abandoned property, old loan.

undocumented objects—Objects that have no numbers, no information in their housing or any characteristics that might connect them to documentation.

ultraviolet filter—A filter that can be placed over windows, skylights, and artificial sources to remove or reduce ultraviolet radiation.

ultraviolet radiation—Wavelengths between 40 nm and 400 nm, invisible to the human eye, but damaging to most collection objects.

unlawful appropriation—Taking objects by theft, confiscation, coercive transfer, or other methods of wrongful expropriation.

useful life—The length of time during which full information can be derived from an object.

vapor barrier—A treated paper or plastic film that is moisture resistant.

varnish—A resin dissolved in a solvent or solvent mixture.

waiver of subrogation rights clause—Endorsement to a policy whereby an insurer gives up the right to take action against a third party for a loss suffered by an insured. If a museum borrows an object and someone else provides the insurance for the loan, the borrower can require a waiver of subrogation clause in the policy.

wall-to-wall coverage—Insurance that covers an object on loan from the moment it is removed from its normal resting place, incidental to shipping, through all phases of packing, transfer, consolidation, exhibition, and repacking, until it is returned to its original resting place, or a place designated by the owner.

worksheet—An informal document used to record basic catalog information pertaining to an object.

yokes—See *contour bracing*.

ABOUT THE EDITORS AND CONTRIBUTORS

Gretchen Anderson

Gretchen E. Anderson (BA, Anthropology and Art History; MA, Museum Studies and Art History) learned her craft at the American Museum of Natural History, the Smithsonian's Conservation Analytical Lab, the Canadian Conservation Institute, Getty Conservation Lab, the Los Angeles County Museum of Art, and the Minnesota Historical Society. She established the conservation department at the Science Museum of Minnesota in 1989. She is the coauthor of "A Holistic Approach to Museum Pest Management" and established a rigorous integrated pest management (IPM) program for the Science Museum of Minnesota. Since 2009, Anderson has been the Conservator at the Carnegie Museum of Natural History. She lectures and presents workshops on preventive conservation, IPM, and museum housekeeping. She has practiced IPM methods since the 1980s and been a member of the Museum Pest Network working group since 2001.

Anne Amati

As Native American Graves Protection and Repatriation Act (NAGPRA) Coordinator and Registrar at the University of Denver Museum of Anthropology, Amati is responsible for the legal aspects of the museum, including loans, acquisitions, and NAGPRA compliance activities. She is an Adjunct Instructor for the University of Denver Museum and Heritage Studies program and works closely with students on collection management and exhibit projects. Amati is the Principal Investigator for a three-year initiative to develop a network for museum professionals engaged in implementing NAGPRA, funded by an Institute of Museum and Library Services (IMLS) National Leadership Grant for Museums.

Joan Bacharach

Joan Bacharach is Senior Curator and former Museum Registrar in the National Park Service Museum Management Program and develops policies and procedures for preservation and protection and access and use for National Park Service museum collections. She is the general editor of the National Park Service *Museum Handbook, Part I: Museum Collections, Part III: Museum Collection Use,* and *Conserve-O-Gram* Technical Leaflet Series and has coauthored and authored guidance in these publications. Bacharach develops virtual museum exhibits in collaboration with parks and conducts training and curriculum development for the National Park Service and Department of the Interior museum programs. She is an adjunct professor for the Johns Hopkins Museum Studies program where she teaches a graduate collections management class and is on the board of the Mid-Atlantic Association of Museums.

Justyna Badach

Justyna Badach received her MFA in photography from the Cranbrook Academy of Art. She is the Head of Imaging at the Philadelphia Museum of Art, an exhibiting artist, and educator. Commercial clients include the Joan Mitchell Foundation, Warhol Foundation, Ed Ruscha catalogue raisonné/Gagosian Gallery, and the Art Institute of Chicago. Badach's work has been exhibited extensively throughout the United States and abroad. Notable exhibitions include the Michener Museum, Light Work Syracuse, White Columns New York, Catherine Edelman Gallery Chicago, Blue Sky Gallery (Portland) and Contemporary Art Center (Las Vegas). Badach's work is in the permanent collections of Portland Art Museum, Museet for Fotokunst Brandts (Odense, Denmark), Center for Photography Woodstock, Cranbrook Museum of Art, Rice University Library (Houston), Temple University (Philadelphia), and Haverford College. She has been awarded an artist residency from Light Work, and grants from the Pennsylvania Council on the Arts, Leeway Foundation and The Independence Foundation.

Julie Bakke

Julie Bakke is the Chief Registrar at the Museum of Fine Arts (Houston) where she has worked for nineteen years. She began her museum career in 1979 as an assistant registrar at the Philadelphia Museum of Art. In 1985 she became the Registrar at the Menil Collection in Houston, where she organized the move of the collection into the new museum facility. Bakke has extensive experience in collections management, exhibitions management, risk management, and storage planning and has participated on a number of panels related to those areas of her expertise.

Racine Berkow

Racine Berkow is president and founder of Racine Berkow Associates (RBA), Inc., a full-service international fine art transport company specializing in handling fine arts, antiques, and museum exhibitions. Prior to establishing RBA in 1987, Berkow served as Registrar at the Jewish Museum in New York and held executive positions at two international shipping companies—one based in London and one in New York. During her tenure at the museum, she was a founding member of the Registrars Committee of the American Association of Museums and a regional officer. Berkow holds a BFA from Ohio State University and professional certificates from the School of Visual Arts and the World Trade Institute. She is a member of Arttable, Inc., and Women Presidents Organization (WPO) and has served as the Chairperson of the Membership Committee of International Conference of Exhibition and Fine Art Transporters (ICEFAT). Berkow is an adjunct instructor at New York University where she teaches a course titled "International Fine Art Logistics."

Paisley Cato

Paisley S. Cato has more than thirty-five years of experience in the care, management, and documentation of collections. She has published more than forty-five articles and books (including sections for the fourth and fifth editions of *Museum Registration Methods*), and led efforts at six institutions to write policies and procedures for natural history and archaeology collections. Cato earned a BA from Smith College and an MA in Museum Studies from Texas Tech University. She holds a PhD, with emphasis in Museum Studies, from Texas A&M University. Cato worked at the Brazos Valley Museum, Texas Cooperative Wildlife Collection (Texas A&M), Denver Museum of Nature and Science, Virginia Museum of Natural History, Western Science Center, and the San Diego Natural History Museum. She has obtained more than fifteen grants from national funding agencies to improve care, management, and accessibility to collections.

Karen Daly

Karen Daly has been a museum registrar at the Virginia Museum of Fine Arts (VMFA) since 1996. In 2003, she assumed an additional role as VMFA's Coordinator of Provenance Research, serving as the museum's contact person for information related to World War II–era provenance, and as its coordinator of provenance research. Since 2012 she has been the Registrar for Exhibitions, overseeing departmental responsibilities for loan exhibitions to the museum. Daly holds a MA in Art Historical Studies from Virginia Commonwealth University and a BA in Religious Studies from Louisiana State University. She is a frequent lecturer on topics related to museums, provenance, and cultural property issues and has been published in *Vitalizing Memory: International Perspectives in Provenance Research*, and in the fifth edition of *Museum Registration Methods*. She is a participant in the 2017–2019 German and American Provenance Research Exchange Program (PREP) for Museum Professionals.

Marie Demeroukas

Marie Demeroukas is the Photo Archivist and Research Librarian at the Shiloh Museum of Ozark History in Springdale, Arkansas. She is coauthor and coeditor of *Steal This Handbook! A Template for Creating a Museum's Emergency Preparedness Plan* and *Basic Condition Reporting: A Handbook* (3rd edition) and coauthor of *Nomenclature 3.0 for Museum Cataloging*. Further professional activities include committee, board, and reviewer positions with the American Alliance of Museums, the American Association for State and Local History, the Arkansas Museums Association, the Institute of Museum and Library Services, the Registrars Committee of the American Alliance of Museums, the Southeastern Museums Conference, and the Southeastern Registrars Association.

Andrea Gardner

Andrea Gardner received an undergraduate degree in classical art and archaeology and Latin from Franklin and Marshall College in Lancaster, Pennsylvania, and a master's degree in art history from the University of Texas at Austin with a focus in ancient art. Gardner moved to Toledo in 2006 to work with Dr. Sandra Knudsen on the exhibition *In Stabiano*, featuring frescoes from villas located on the Bay of Naples. After her internship, she took a permanent position at the Toledo Museum of Art as Assistant Registrar for domestic loans and exhibitions. She was promoted to Head Registrar in July 2012 and took on the additional responsibilities of Assistant Information Officer in January 2013. In 2018 she became Director of Collections and now oversees the areas of Registrar, Exhibitions, Conservation, Library and Archives at Toledo Museum of Art.

Lela Hersh

Lela Hersh is the President of Museum and Fine Arts Consulting, LLC. She is an Accredited Senior Appraiser with the American Society of Appraisers (ASA) and an accredited member of the International Society of Appraisers, and a Senior Lecturer at the School of the Art Institute, Chicago in the graduate department of the Arts Administration & Policy program. Hersh is a twenty-year veteran of the Museum of Contemporary Art Chicago where she served as Director of Collections & Exhibitions, and a past board member of the American Association of Museums. Hersh is the former International Chair of the Personal Property Discipline and President of the Chicago Chapter of ASA. She is currently an ASA Governor for the Personal Property and on their Board of Examiners.

Claudia Jacobson

Claudia Jacobson, now retired from the Milwaukee Public Museum (MPM), has nearly forty years of experience in the field of collections management. The MPM's large and diverse cultural and natural history collections provided the opportunity to work with a range of disciplines. Starting in the Anthropology Department, she handled day-to-day collections management projects, inventory, and exhibit work. As registrar, she was responsible for museum-wide registration activities and led work in developing collections management and museum ethics policies and procedures, managed conservation activities in the absence of a conservator, and oversaw the library and photo archives. Jacobson has been active in state, regional, and national museum associations, doing programming and serving as Secretary for the American Alliance of Museums Registrars Committee and Vice President of the Wisconsin Federation of Museums. She also taught collections management and curation courses for the Museum Studies Program of the University of Wisconsin–Milwaukee Graduate School.

Robin Bauer Kilgo

Robin Bauer Kilgo holds a BA in Anthropology and an MA in History from Florida State University, as well as a graduate certificate in Collections Management and Collections Care from George Washington University. From 2005 to 2012 she worked as registrar, then as collections officer for the Seminole Tribe of Florida's Ah-Tah-Thi-Ki Museum where she developed and maintained collections management policies and emergency plans. While at the tribe's museum she was an integral member of the team that gained accreditation by the American Alliance of Museums (AAM)—the first tribally owned museum to gain this distinction. Since 2012, Kilgo has assisted institutions as a collections care consultant and acts as the Communications and Member Services Manager for the Association of Registrars and Collections Specialists. She is a member of the National Heritage Responders, an AAM Museums Assessment Program reviewer, and the Florida Representative for the Southeastern Registrars Association.

Angela Kipp

Angela Kipp is the Collections Manager of the Technomuseum in Mannheim, Germany, and as such is notorious for nagging her colleagues about demanding a correct inventory. She also works as an independent museum consultant for various museums and cultural institutions both large and small, specializing in logistics, project management, and the adaption of technology for the special needs of museums. She is especially interested in finding affordable ways to improve collections care in smaller institutions. Her blog project, *Registrar Trek*, is aimed at raising awareness of collections care in general and fostering exchanges between collections specialists around the world by publishing their articles, stories, and ideas. In her book *Managing Previously Unmanaged Collections* (2016) she gathered her own experiences and those of several colleagues to develop a framework for people confronted with a previously unmanaged, only partly managed, or just neglected collection.

Toni M. Kiser

Toni M. Kiser is the Assistant Director for Collections Management at The National WWII Museum. She overseas all aspects of registration and collection management and has worked on varied projects from large exhibit installations, digitization projects, storage moves, artifact rehousing, and cataloging and nomenclature standards. She is the author of *Loyal Forces: American Animals in WWII* and coeditor of *Museum Registration Methods*, 6th edition. Kiser serves on the Board for the Association of Registrars and Collection Specialists. She holds a BA in history from Brevard College and an MA in museum studies from George Washington University.

Elise LeCompte

Elise LeCompte is Registrar and Coordinator for Health and Safety for the Florida Museum of Natural History. She has served as collections manager, exhibit registrar, conservation technician, administrator, and consultant for museums throughout the southeast. She has several publications on collections management and artifact conservation and has organized and presented at workshops on related topics. LeCompte serves as an accreditation and museum assessment program reviewer for the American Alliance of Museums, council member and coordinator of the Southeastern Museums Conference Career Center, board member and co-chair of the Education Committee for the Association of Registrars and Collec-

tions Specialists, and Travel Grants Coordinator for the Society for the Preservation of Natural History Collections. LeCompte is an Adjunct Professor for the University of Florida Museum Studies program and holds an MA in archaeology and chemistry from the University of Florida and a BA in anthropology from Johns Hopkins University.

Melissa Levine

Melissa Levine is the Director of the University of Michigan Library's Copyright Office, providing guidance on copyright policy and practice in the university context. On any given day, questions range from open access and open data to copyright in scholarly publishing and artificial intelligence. She is a member of the library's senior management group and serves on the steering committee for the University of Michigan's Museum Studies Program. She has worked at several university museums and at the Smithsonian Institution, where she handled business affairs, including publishing and licensing matters. She served as Assistant General Counsel and Legal Advisor for the Library of Congress' National Digital Library Project. As a lecturer at the University of Michigan School of Information, she teaches a course on intellectual property and information law. She taught a fully online course on museums, law, and policy for the masters in museum studies program at Johns Hopkins Krieger School of Arts and Sciences Advanced Academic Programs.

Cristina Linclau

Cristina Linclau (MLIS, MA) is the Manager of Exhibitions and Collections Information at the Solomon R. Guggenheim Museum. She began her career in museums working to consolidate databases across nineteen curatorial departments at the Metropolitan Museum of Art. There, she learned the value of metadata standards and strategies in supporting the diverse needs of the network of specialists that make cultural preservation possible. Since then, she has served as the Senior Manager of Collections Information at the Brooklyn Museum, Image Archivist at the Felix Gonzalez-Torres Foundation, and has built an artwork database for one of the most successful contemporary painters in the United

States. Her graduate research in cultural memory and digital technologies culminated in a thesis titled "Museum Collections in the Age of Cultural Evanescence," which frames the future of museological practices within Walter J. Ong's theory of "secondary orality," and discusses the evolution of serendipity from a scientific to a cultural phenomenon.

Nora Lockshin

Nora S. Lockshin is Senior Conservator with the Smithsonian Libraries and Archives, where she provides pan-institutional services for interventive and preventive conservation, across the Smithsonian Institution and its diverse archives units. She recently authored a chapter on marking collections, for which she found this book, and dialogues with many colleagues as to their experience invaluable in recommending practices to the cultural community. Throughout her career she has had opportunities to consult on marks and substrates as varied as photographs on paper, glass, plastic, and metal; painted textiles; tapa; artists' books; geological samples; rubber sculpture; a leather flight helmet; optical discs; biological specimens; bumper stickers; composite objects such as printed bus signs; souvenir pins and medals; a box of Wheaties, a newspaper printed on asbestos, and an outrigger canoe.

Kate Macuen

Kate Macuen is the Director of the Seminole Tribe of Florida's Ah-Tah-Thi-Ki Museum. She began working for the tribe in 2009 as the Collections Manager for their Tribal Historic Preservation Office and serves on the Seminole Tribe's Native American Graves Protection and Repatriation Act (NAGPRA) committee. Macuen earned a BA in Anthropology from the University of Colorado and an MA in Museum Science from Texas Tech University.

Erin McKeen

Erin McKeen is the Collections Manager and Registrar at the Barack Obama Presidential Library, National Archives and Records Administration. Previously she worked in registration and collections management positions at the Smithsonian's National Museum of American History, US Department of the

Interior Museum, the Wolfsonian-Florida International University, and with the Fine Arts Program, US General Services Administration. She is a graduate of the Museum Studies Program at George Washington University. McKeen serves on the board of the Association of Registrars and Collection Specialists and serves as co-chair on the Education Committee.

Anne Mersmann

Anne Mersmann has been the Registrar, Collections and Technology at the Broad in downtown Los Angeles since 2014. She travels frequently as a courier for the Broad Art Foundation's active outgoing loan program. In addition, she handles exhibitions, loans, and a growing permanent collection of contemporary art. Prior to joining the Broad, she worked for seventeen years in the Collections Management Department at the Santa Barbara Museum of Art where she oversaw numerous traveling exhibitions and major collection projects including inventories and vault renovations, and a database conversion of forty-four thousand records.

Laura Morse

Laura A. Morse has been a registrar overseeing collections in both museum and zoological environments for more than twenty-five years. She has been the caretaker for live reptiles, transported live animals of every shape and size, toured with international traveling exhibits, and has been a collections management jack-of-all-trades. As the Registrar of the Smithsonian National Zoological Park and previously at the American Museum of Natural History, she has specialized in wildlife regulations and their impact on collections. At the Smithsonian Morse was on the Smithsonian Collections Advisory Committee as a grant reviewer and voting member. At present she is an independent museum consultant.

Antonia Moser

Antonia Moser is an Associate Registrar at Cooper Hewitt, Smithsonian Design Museum, where she manages off-site collections storage. She also serves as Adjunct Professor at Seton Hall University, teaching registration classes for the Masters Program in Museum Professions. Formerly she worked as a Collections Registrar at the Newark Museum. She holds degrees in English literature from Boston College and Vanderbilt University and an MA in Museum Professions from Seton Hall University.

Dixie Neilson

Dixie Neilson holds an MA in Museum Studies from Johns Hopkins University and is the Director of the Matheson History Museum in Gainesville, Florida. She has thirty years of collection care experience, including work as a collections manager and consultant, and eighteen years teaching museums studies at the graduate level. She is past chair of the Southeastern Registrars Association (SERA) and is a contributor to *Basic Condition Reporting: A Handbook* and the *Encyclopedia of Library and Information Services.* Neilson wrote and directed the DVD, *From Here to There: Museum Standards for Object Handling.*

Melanie O'Brien

Melanie O'Brien is responsible for carrying out all duties assigned to the National Native American Graves Protection and Repatriation Act (NAGPRA) Program by the Secretary of the Interior and serves as the Designated Federal Officer to the NAGPRA Review Committee. O'Brien regularly speaks about NAGPRA at national conferences for museum professionals, archaeologists and anthropologists, and tribal representatives. She has conducted extensive training sessions on the NAGPRA process to a variety of audiences. O'Brien is happy to assist museums with what is required under NAGPRA and how museums can ensure they are in compliance with both the letter and the spirit of the law.

Beth Parker Miller

After earning a BA in English and German and an MA in history with a concentration in archival and historical administration, Beth J. Parker Miller served as Associate Curator and Registrar at Hancock Shaker Village (Pittsfield, Massachusetts) and as Registrar at Hagley Museum and Library (Wilmington, Delaware). She joined Winterthur Museum, Garden & Library (Winterthur, Delaware) in 2004, where she holds the position of Registrar and Registration department head. In 2019–2020, Miller is leading a team charged with developing an accessible and sustainable institution-wide collections storage solution for Winterthur. She is a contributing author to *To Give and to Receive: A Handbook of Gifts and Donations for Museums and Donors* (2011) and *The Shakers of White Water, Ohio, 1823–1916* (2014).

Marie-Page Phelps

Marie-Page Phelps is the Registrar of Collections for the New Orleans Museum of Art, where she has directed a variety of collections relocation and inventory projects. Most recently she integrated barcodes into their collections management system while moving more than twenty thousand works of art to a new facility. She holds BA in an anthropology and has nearly a decade of collections management experience.

Sarah Rice

Sarah Rice is the Corporate Archivist at Campbell Soup Company where she is responsible for managing the historical assets of a twenty-eight-brand portfolio encompassing more than 1,600 years of combined heritage. She also serves as a board member of the Haddonfield Historical Society and Camden FireWorks, as well as a steering committee member of A New View Camden, a Bloomberg Public Art Challenge winner. She holds a BA in History from Elon University, and a MA in Museum Studies from George Washington University.

Mark Ryan

Mark Ryan has more than twenty years of experience working in the registration and collections management profession in art, historical and natural history institutions. He has been the Assistant Director for Collections & Exhibitions at the Mildred Lane Kemper Art Museum since 2016, where he is responsible for the care and management of the museum's collections and exhibitions program as well as overseeing the security and facilities departments. His formal education includes a BS in biology and a BA in history from the University of Wyoming and an MA in museum science from Texas Tech University. Ryan is an active participant, leader and advocate for collections care through a number of current and past organizations and associated activities. He currently serves on the boards of the Association of Registrars and Collections Specialists and the Midwest Art Conservation Center and has served as a peer reviewer for both the National Endowment for the Humanities and the Institute for Museum and Library Services.

Mark Schlemmer

Mark B. Schlemmer is the Registrar for Collections at the New York Historical Society in New York City. Previously, he was a member of the registrarial staff at the Solomon R. Guggenheim Museum. From 2014 to 2017, he served on the board of directors of Association of Registrars and Collections Specialists where he was the chair of the Education Committee. Schlemmer is an active trainer, author, and speaker at conferences, museums, and universities where, as part of his @ITweetMuseums initiative, he shares his insight into the benefits of cultural workers using social media platforms as a tool for professional development, networking, research, and dissemination of culture in its myriad forms. In addition to a BFA in design, and a BA in French (both from Ball State University), Schlemmer has an MA in museum professions, with a focus on museum registration and collections management, from Seton Hall University.

Amanda Shields

Amanda Shields is the Associate Registrar at the Brandywine River Museum of Art where she oversees gallery changes, extended loans, collections database management, object photography, and collection inventories. Prior to this position, she worked at the Science History Institute in Philadelphia as Curator of Fine Art and Registrar, Image Archivist, and Project Archivist. Shields earned an MA in Museum Studies from Johns Hopkins University and BA in Art History and Art Conservation from the University of Delaware.

John E. Simmons

John E. Simmons (BS, systematics and ecology; MA, museum studies) began his professional career as a keeper at the Fort Worth Zoological Park before moving on to serve as collections manager at the California Academy of Sciences and the University of Kansas. He has collected scientific specimens, taught

collections management, and presented professional training programs throughout the United States and worldwide. He is on the board of the Association of Registrars and Collections Specialists and past-chair of the Collections Stewardship Professional Network of the American Alliance of Museums. Simmons has published widely on natural history and collections management issues and serves as a reviewer for the Museum Assessment Program and the Institute for Museum and Library Services. He currently runs Museologica consulting, is Associate Curator of Collections at the Earth and Mineral Sciences Museum & Art Gallery at Penn State University, and teaches museum studies classes for the Universidad Nacional de Colombia (Bogotá) and Museum Study LLC.

Christine Steiner

Christine Steiner is an experienced art lawyer, handling transactions on behalf of diverse art-related clients such as museums, cultural organizations, collectors, artists, artist estates, foundations, auction houses, creative businesses, and universities. Prior to private practice, she served as Secretary and General Counsel of the J. Paul Getty Trust, as Assistant General Counsel of the Smithsonian Institution, as Assistant Attorney General of Maryland for state colleges and universities, and as Principal Counsel of the Maryland state public education system. She is an adjunct professor of law at Loyola Law School in visual arts law and has been a visiting professor in programs of international art law in Florence and Cambridge. Steiner speaks frequently on art law topics, currently serves on the editorial board of the *Journal of the Copyright Society of the United States*, and is active in the arts nationally. She is author of numerous publications, including a recent law review article on Art Law and the Copyright chapter of *MRM5*. She has been recognized consistently by Best Lawyers, the prestigious national peer-ranking organization, for her contributions to Art Law.

Cherie Summers

Cherie Summers' first job after graduating from New Mexico State University was at the S. R. Guggenheim Museum, later becoming Chief Registrar, then Associate Registrar at the Museum of Modern Art. On the Registrars Committee of the American Alliance of Museums she served as chair of the ethics committee, and as a Museum Assessment Program surveyor. Summers has been on the Western Museums Association board, chair of the RC-WR, and a member of ArtTable, Inc. She was on the Professional Advisory Council for the Museum of Art, Brigham Young University, and the Advisory Council for the Mesilla Valley Historical Museum. Summers has been an active workshop participant, has written articles for AAM and WMA, and sections in two editions of *Museum Registration Methods*. On the board of the Association of Registrars and Collections Specialists she chaired the Code of Ethics Committee and is currently Corresponding Secretary for the executive committee. She has been a courier on multiple shipments in the United States, Europe, Asia, and South America. She retired from the Santa Barbara Museum of Art as Chief Registrar.

Irene Taurins

Irene Taurins has been Director of Registration at the Philadelphia Museum of Art for more than forty years. As Senior Registrar, she oversees the movement of works of art into, out of, and within the museum, physically and legally. She oversees shipping, packing, and customs documentation, negotiates and administrates the fine arts insurance policies of the institution, and has been on panels and chaired several sessions at the Mid-Atlantic Association of Museums and American Association of Museums. Taurins is a founding director of the Association of Registrars and Collections Specialists (ARCS) and served as ARCS Corresponding Secretary from 2014 to 2017. She has organized and traveled many special exhibitions and has been a courier on many occasions including an "around the world" courier trip from Philadelphia to Taipei to Paris and back to Philadelphia in one week.

Susan Wamsley

Susan Wamsley has worked in the field of digital asset management for more than fifteen years. She has spearheaded major digitization projects and implemented enterprise-level DAM Systems for global institutions. Her core interest lies in creating positive user experience through intuitive interfaces, strategic metadata solutions, and efficiently integrated systems. In addition to being the Digital Asset Manager at the Solomon R. Guggenheim Museum since 2014, Wamsley is the Chair of the Digital Asset Management special interest group for the Museum Computer Network (MCN), a national organization for cultural heritage institutions.

Grace Weiss

Grace T. Weiss is the Assistant Registrar for Media Arts at the San Francisco Museum of Modern Art (SFMOMA). She has lectured and published on media registration and her work with SFMOMA's Media Arts collection, which she has managed since 2016. Weiss holds an MA in museum studies from New York University and dual BA degrees in art history and communications from Fordham University. Specializing in time-based media, her work focuses on how museums are adapting to collect and preserve the art of our time.

Rose Wood

Rose M. Wood is the Chief Registrar at the Birmingham Museum of Art. Prior to working with one of the largest art collections in the South, Wood worked for nineteen years in contemporary art at the Des Moines Art Center. After obtaining a BA from the American University, she continued her education at Texas Tech University and graduated with an MA in Museum Studies. Wood was fortunate to secure a National Endowment of the Arts' registration internship at the Indianapolis Museum of Art. For about a decade this program was dedicated to training registrars to manage all collection care aspects. In 2013 Wood completed a Master of Family and Consumer Sciences (MFCS) in Family Financial Planning with an area of concentration on how families build art collections.

Sally Yerkovich

Sally Yerkovich is Director of Educational Exchange and Special Projects at the American-Scandinavian Foundation and Adjunct Professor of Museum Anthropology at Columbia University. A cultural anthropologist with experience in museums and cultural institutions in New York and Washington, D.C., she was president and CEO of the New Jersey Historical Society, Executive Director at the Museum for African Art and first president of the Tribute NYC Museum. She currently serves on the board of trustees of the Merchant's House Museum in New York City and is currently chair of the International Council of Museums (ICOM) Ethics Committee, as well as of the Professional Standards and Ethics Committee of the American Association for State and Local History (AASLH). Yerkovich is the author of *A Practical Guide to Museum Ethics*. Her work, which draws on more than thirty years of leadership experience, is increasingly engaged with how museums will face the ethical challenges of the future.

Anne M. Young

Anne M. Young is the Director of Legal Affairs and Intellectual Property at the Indianapolis Museum of Art at Newfields, where she provides guidance and interpretation on a variety of institutional standards, policies, and procedures, including intellectual property, contracting, cultural patrimony, repatriation, and overall risk mitigation. Young was formerly the photographic archivist for the Kinsey Institute, Indiana University, and has worked for the Art Gallery of Ontario and George Eastman Museum. In 2018 she received a Master of Jurisprudence focused on intellectual property, art, and museum law from Indiana University's Robert H. McKinney School of Law. Young previously received an MA in photographic preservation and collections management from Ryerson University and a BA in art history and studio art (photography) from Indiana University.

APPENDIX COLLECTION FORMS

MRM Museum
123 Main Street, Quietville, Estado 10966
Telephone 555-555-5555

INCOMING AGREEMENT for TEMPORARY CUSTODY
For objects placed on temporary deposit

AGREEMENT
The undersigned ("Lender") hereby places the object(s) described herein in custody of the MRM Museum for the purposes, and subject to the terms and conditions, set forth.

PURPOSE: ____ Examination
    ____ Consideration for acquisition
    ____Research loan
    ____Other_____

PROJECT OR EVENT:

INCLUSIVE DATES OF CUSTODY:

MRM MUSEUM REGISTRAR:

LENDER:

Shipping Address:

Telephone: Cell phone: E-mail:

Contact Person:

OBJECT(S): Name, Title, Description, Name of artist, etc.

INSURANCE   Estimated fair market value in US $:

                MRM Museum will insure unless otherwise advised. See reverse for conditions.

SHIPPING METHOD: Incoming:
                      Return (if applicable):

Handling, installation, packing, and shipping instructions:

SIGNATURE   The lender or lender's agent acknowledges having read the conditions above and on this form and agrees to be bound by them.

Signature:
Printed Name and Date:
                Lender or authorized agent

Signature:
Printed Name and Date:
                For MRM Museum

Complete, sign, and return 2 copies to the MRM Museum Collections Office; a countersigned copy will be returned to Lender.

FIGURE 9.1 A—B INCOMING AGREEMENT FOR TEMPORARY CUSTODY WITH CONDITIONS GOVERNING TEMPORARY CUSTODY. CREATED BY AUTHOR.

CONDITIONS GOVERNING INCOMING TEMPORARY CUSTODY

Care and Handling

1. The MRM Museum ("Museum") will exercise the same care with respect to the object(s) on deposit as it does with comparable property of its own.

2. The Museum will not alter, clean, or repair objects on deposit without transfer of the object to formal incoming loan status and written approval of the Lender.

Packing and Transportation

1. The Lender certifies that the objects are in good condition and will withstand ordinary strains of packing and transportation. Evidence of damage to objects on deposit at the time of receipt or while in the Museum's custody will be reported immediately to the Lender.

2. If applicable, objects will be returned packed in the same or similar materials as received unless authorized by the Lender.

3. Costs of transportation and packing will be borne by the Lender unless agreed otherwise in advance.

4. International shipments may not be placed on Incoming Temporary Custody, but must be covered by a formal incoming loan agreement. Customs regulations will be adhered to in international shipments in this case.

Insurance

1. Unless the Lender expressly elects to maintain insurance coverage, the Museum's general insurance policy will cover the objects against risks of physical loss or damage from time of release to Museum staff authorized to receive on premises, in the case of delivery by Lender or Lender's agent. If transport is arranged by the Museum, coverage will begin at time of objects' physical release to Museum staff or to professional contract handling services designated to act as shippers/agents for Museum.

2. Insurance will be for the specified fair market value. In case of damage or loss, the insurance company may ask the Lender to substantiate the insurance value. If the Lender fails to indicate an amount, the Museum will set a value for purposes of insurance only for the period of the loan. The Lender agrees that in the event of loss or damage, recovery shall be limited to such amount, if any, as may be paid by the insurer, hereby releasing the Museum and the board members, officers, agents, and employees of the Museum from liability for any and all claims arising out of such loss or damage.

Reproduction and Credit

1. The Museum assumes the right, unless specifically denied by the Lender, to photograph the objects placed on deposit for documentation purposes only. Photography, videotaping, and reproduction for publicity, publication, and educational

purposes connected with an exhibition or research project must be covered by a formal loan agreement.

Ownership and Change in Ownership

1. The Lender hereby warrants ownership of full legal title and copyrights to objects placed on temporary custody, or is the duly authorized agent of the Owner or Owners of them.

2. The Lender will notify the Museum promptly in writing of any change of ownership of the items in custody whether by reason of death, sale, insolvency, gift or otherwise. If ownership shall change during the period of custody, the Museum reserves the right to require the new owner, prior to the return of the object, to establish right to possession by proof satisfactory to the Museum. The new owner shall succeed to Lender's rights and obligations under this agreement, including, but not limited to, the custody period and any insurance obligations.

Custody Period, Extension, Return

1. The objects in temporary custody may remain in the possession of the Museum for the time specified on the reverse, but may be returned to Lender at any time earlier by the Museum. If a time extension is requested by curatorial or administrative staff for long-term research or further examination prior to acquisition, the transaction will be transferred to a formal incoming loan agreement.

2. Unless the Lender requests otherwise in writing, the Museum will return the items only to the Lender and only at the address specified in this agreement. The Lender shall promptly notify the Museum in writing of any change of address. The Museum assumes no responsibility to search for a Lender who cannot be reached at the address specified in this agreement. The Lender will may be required to pay additional costs, if any, if the Lender requests the return of the object to another address.

3. The Museum's right to return the objects from custody shall accrue absolutely at the termination of the loan. If, after two weeks beyond termination of loan date noted above, pursuing all possible means of contact, and in accordance with any legal requirements, the Lender cannot be found or the Lender refuses to accept the return of the items on temporary custody, it shall be deemed abandoned property, and become the property of the Museum.

Interpretation

1. This agreement constitutes the entire agreement between the Lender and the Museum and may be amended or modified only in writing signed by both parties. Any changes herein of printed text or written additions must bear the initials of both parties. This agreement shall be governed and interpreted according to the laws of_____.

2. If the terms of this agreement conflict with the forms, agreements, or correspondence of the Lender, the terms of this agreement will be controlling.

DEALER PROVENANCE QUESTIONNAIRE

OBJECT: Description (name, artist, maker, title, materials, dimensions, etc.):

_____

_____

PROVENANCE:
_____

On what date did you acquire the object? _____

Name and location of the source from which the object was acquired.

_____

_____

List all known previous owners and dates of ownership: _____

_____

_____

For antiquities and archaeological materials:

When did the object leave its country of modern discovery? _____

Do you have export documents from the source country?   (Attach copies) _____

Do you have import documents?   (Attach copies) _____

EXHIBITION HISTORY: _____

_____

_____

_____

PUBLICATION HISTORY: _____

_____

_____

_____

DOCUMENTS (attach copies):

[   ] Art Loss Register Report, if any _____

[   ] Import/Export Documents _____

Signature: _____

(Vendor)

Date: _____

FIGURE 9.2 DEALER PROVENANCE QUESTIONNAIRE. CREATED BY AUTHOR.

DONOR QUESTIONNAIRE

[For objects that could have been in Nazi-era Europe (1933–1945), antiquities, and archaeological materials]

Complete the following questionnaire to the best of your ability. It is important that the MRM Museum have a complete history of objects offered as gifts. To that end, forward any additional information or documentation which you may have with respect to your ownership, the exhibition or publication history of the object, and any known prior ownership information.

Name of Donor (please print):

_____

Object description:

_____

How long have you owned the object? _____

How did you acquire it?

Purchase	Date
Inheritance	Date
Gift	Date
Found	Date
Other	Date

If this object was purchased, do you have a bill of sale, certificate, or any items relating to the transaction or authenticity?_____ If yes, please attach a copy to this questionnaire.

Were there any previous owners? _____

Please list all known previous owners and their relationship to the donor(s):

_____

Do you have any published information or press clippings about the object? _____
If yes, please attach a copy to this questionnaire.

Do you know the exhibition history of the object?   If yes, please list:

_____

_____

Have you performed any repairs, made changes to the object, or contracted a conservator to perform cleaning or repairs while this object was in your care? If yes, please list names, dates, cleanings, changes, etc., and attach copies of any pertinent paperwork and images.

_____

Do you know if this object was conserved or restored prior to your ownership? If yes, please list all known treatments, dates, and conservators used.

_____

Donor's Signature: _____   Date _____

FIGURE 9.3A–B DONOR QUESTIONNAIRE WITH WARRANTY AND INDEMNIFICATION. CREATED BY AUTHOR.

WARRANTY AND INDEMNIFICATION

This Warranty and Indemnification (the "Warranty") is made and delivered to _____ (the "Museum") as of the _____ day of _____ 20 __ from the undersigned (the "Seller/Agent"), who is (a) the seller of, or (b), the authorized agent of the owner of, the object described below and in the attached Bill of Sale dated

_____ and the Invoice previously provided to the Museum:

The Seller/Agent represents, warrants, covenants, certifies, and agrees that:

a. Seller/Agent has lawful authority to sell and transfer the object and upon the consummation of the sale, the Museum will have good and marketable title to the object, including, without limitation, any proprietary or copyright rights in the object, free and clear of all liens, mortgages, pledges, security interests, encumbrances, claims, charges or liabilities whatsoever.

If Seller/Agent is not the owner, Seller/Agent is fully authorized by the owner of the object to, and, on behalf of the owner does, enter into this Warranty and the Bill of Sale and accepts all terms and makes all representations, warranties, covenants, certifications, and agreements set forth herein.

b. The object is authentic, conforms in all respects to the description set forth above and in the said Invoice (collectively, the "Documentation") and is of the period indicated.

c. Any exportation of the object from any foreign country has been in full compliance with the laws, rules, and regulations of such country.

d. The country of origin of the object as set forth in the customs declaration for the importation of the object into the United States is true, accurate, and complete.

e. The country of modern discovery is

_____

f. Any importation of the object into any foreign country has been in full compliance with the laws, rules, and regulations of such country.

g. Any importation of the object is in full compliance with all laws, rules, and regulations.

h. No customs, tax, patrimony or other laws, rules or regulations applicable to the object, its sale, export or import have been violated.

i. Seller/Agent has provided to the Museum all information known to Seller/Agent (including after due inquiry information known to the principals and agents of Seller/Agent) regarding the object and the provenance of the object, and all information and documentation provided by Seller/Agent to the Museum with respect to the object is true, accurate, and complete in all material respects.

j. No license or other right has been granted to any person by Seller/Agent or, to Seller/Agent's knowledge after due inquiry, by any other person that would in any manner limit or restrict the Museum's rights in and to the object, including, but not limited to, any rights derived from ownership of the copyright included in the object or in any derivative of the object.

Seller/Agent agrees to indemnify, defend, and hold harmless the Museum and its trustees, directors, officers, employees, and agents from and against any and all claims, allegations (pending or threatened), costs, and fees, including without limitation attorneys' fees and costs, losses, damages, judgments or liabilities arising from, connected to, or as a result of any breach or alleged breach of this Warranty or a good faith challenge of the Museum's title to all or any part of the object or the Museum's right to the free use and enjoyment of object.

In addition to, and not in limitation of, the foregoing, in the event of any breach of this Warranty and, in connection therewith, the Museum loses or otherwise fails to have or retain the lawful right to own, possess, display, sell, enjoy, mortgage, pledge, grant a security interest in, or encumber the object, the Museum shall be entitled, at its election and without regard to any otherwise applicable statue of limitation or repose, to receive a full refund of the purchase price of the object. The foregoing shall be in addition to, and not in limitation of, any other remedies to which the Museum may be entitled and shall not be construed to limit the Museum's right to elect any of such other remedies.

This Warranty and the Documentation taken together constitute the entire agreement between the parties. In the event of any conflict between the Warranty and the Documentation, the Warranty shall control. The Warranty and the Documentation and the transactions contemplated hereby shall be construed in accordance with the laws of any State and the Warranty shall be binding upon and inure to the benefit of the Seller/Agent and the Museum and their respective successors, assigns, heirs, executors, administrators and legal representatives.

Agreed to by:

_____
Seller/Agent
_____
Name
_____
Address
_____
Telephone
_____
Date:

MRM Museum
CONFIRMATION OF GIFT

MRM Museum
123 Main Street
Quietville, Estado 10966

To Whom It May Concern:

I hereby confirm my agreement to give to the MRM Museum ("Museum"), at or before my death, the object(s) listed below or on the attachment hereto:

You have informed me that other collectors, the governing board, and friends of the Museum have indicated their intention of giving to the Museum objects which they own in order to enhance the Museum's collection. As I believe that definite commitments to make such gifts or bequests will be of great value to the Museum, I have agreed to give the above described object to the Museum on the understanding (i) that you will do your best to obtain similar commitments from others and may refer to this agreement in inducing others to make such commitments; (ii) that this agreement shall be governed by the laws of any State.

I may, according to my own convenience, give this object to you during my lifetime. Should this gift not be completed during my lifetime, it is understood that this agreement shall be binding on my heirs, executors, and administrators, and that omission from my Will of a specific bequest of this object to the Museum shall not release them from delivering the aforementioned object to the Museum in accordance herewith, or otherwise impair the force and effect of this agreement.

Neither the Museum nor I shall be under any obligation to insure this object during my lifetime. In the event I do not own this object at my death because of loss by casualty, the Museum shall have no claim against my heirs, executors or administrators with respect to this undertaking on my part.

I have entered into this agreement on the date indicated below with the full intention that I will be legally bound hereby pursuant to the applicable provisions of the law relating to written obligations and that this agreement shall be binding as well on my heirs, executors, administrators and assigns.

Very truly yours,   Notarized

(signed)   (signed)

_____   _____

(dated)   (dated)

_____   _____

                                           (seal)

We confirm that the above correctly states the agreement between

us. For the MRM Museum

(signed)   (dated)

_____   _____

FIGURE 9.4 CONFIRMATION OF GIFT SAMPLE LETTER. CREATED BY AUTHOR.

MRM MUSEUM
123 Main Street, Quietville, Estado 10966
Telephone 555-555-5555

DEED OF GIFT

Date   Page   of

Donor:
Name
Address
Telephone

Description of object(s)

Donor hereby transfers and assigns without condition or restriction all right, title and interest free of restrictions or encumbrances in the tangible personal property listed above (the "Object"), and all rights (including trade marks and copyrights) associated with it (the "Rights") to the MRM Museum Association, a corporation existing under the laws of the State of AnyState for use and disposition by the MRM Museum.

Donor warrants and represents that Donor has the full power and authority to transfer the Object to the MRM Museum Association.

Donor certifies that to the best of the Donor's knowledge, the Object has not been exported from its country of origin in violation of the Laws of that country in effect at the time of the export, nor imported into the United States in violation of United States laws and treaties.

Donor   Date

Donor   Date

Accepted for the MRM Museum

by   Date

    Director

(See reverse for additional terms)

[On back of form] This deed of gift represents an agreement between the MRM Museum and the donor(s) named on the face hereof. Any variation in the terms noted must be in writing on the face of this form and approved in writing by both parties.

Gifts to the MRM Museum are deductible from taxable income in accordance with the provisions of Federal income tax law. However, Museum employees cannot, in their official capacity, give appraisals for the purpose of establishing the tax deductible value of donated items. Evaluations must be secured by the donor at the donor's expense.

The donor received no goods or services in consideration of this gift.

Limited gallery space and the policy of changing exhibitions do not allow the Museum to promise the permanent exhibition of any object.

FIGURE 9.5 DEED OF GIFT. CREATED BY AUTHOR.

TWENTY CATEGORIES OF OBJECT AND PROVENANCE INFORMATION
Template Recommended by AAM

Category	Comments
Artist/Maker	To include artists names, alternate names, and previous attributions.
Nationality of Artist/Maker	—
Life Dates of Artist/Maker	—
Place or Culture of Object	Only if artist unknown.
Object Title or Name	To include alternate titles.
Date of Object	To include approximate date, if specific date is unknown.
Medium/Materials	—
Measurements	—
Date of Acquisition	—
Accession Number	—
Object Type	Painting, sculpture, decorative arts, etc.
Subject Type	Landscape, portrait, mythological subject, historical, religious, genre, Judaica, etc.
Signature and Marks (obverse)	To include signatures, inscriptions, and marks; for paintings, what appears on the front
Labels and Marks (reverse, frame, mount, etc.)	To describe marks and labels (prior to 1960) on the reverse of an object (including frame, mount, etc.). Indicate if images are available.
Description	To contain description of object (its content, subject, etc.). Museums should make this a priority.
Provenance	To contain, at the minimum, known owners, dates of ownership, places of ownership, method of transfer (sale, gift, descent, etc.). To include, if known, lot numbers, sale prices, buyers, etc. To include information on unlawful appropriation during the Nazi era and subsequent restitution. Museums should ensure that provenance information is understandable and organized chronologically.
Exhibition History	—
Bibliographic History	—
Other Relevant Information	To contain anything about the object that would be useful in identifying it for this purpose. If the object fits the definition of Judaica contained in this document, so state.
Image	An image is key to identifying an object. Museums should make every effort to include an image with their records.

FIGURE 9.6 TWENTY CATEGORIES OF OBJECT PROVENANCE INFORMATION. CREATED BY AUTHOR.

Loan number:

_____

MRM MUSEUM
123 Main Street, Quietville, Estado 10966
Telephone 555-555-5555
OUTGOING LOAN AGREEMENT

AGREEMENT: The MRM Museum hereby lends to the borrower identified below the object(s) described herein for the purposes and subject to the terms and conditions set forth.

BORROWER	Name:		
	Address:		
	Telephone:	Text:	
	Contact:	Title:	

OBJECT   Description (including accession or catalog number, name, artist, materials, date):

Credit Line (for use in exhibit label and catalog):

EXHIBITION   Period of Loan:

Exhibition Title:
Venue(s) and Date(s):

INSURANCE   Insurance value (in US dollars):
❏ To be carried by borrower
❏ To be carried by the MRM Museum, premium billed to borrower

SHIPPING/
PACKING   Unless otherwise specified, all objects will be released from and returned to MR5 Museum

DISPLAY   Environmental requirements (acceptable temperature, relative humidity, and light level range):

SIGNATURE   The borrower has full authority and power to enter into this agreement and has read the conditions above and on the back of this form and agrees to be bound by them.

Signature and printed name: Date:
_____   _____
     The MRM Museum
Signature: Date:
_____   _____
     Borrower
Please sign and return one copy to the MRM Museum and retain one copy.

FIGURE 9.7A–B OUTGOING LOAN AGREEMENT WITH OUTGOING LOAN CONDITIONS. CREATED BY AUTHOR.

OUTGOING LOAN CONDITIONS

Care and Preservation

Objects borrowed shall be given proper care to insure against loss, damage or deterioration. The borrower agrees to meet any special requirements for installation and handling. The MRM Museum (the "Museum") certifies that the objects lent are in condition to withstand ordinary strains of packing, transportation, and handling. The Museum is to be notified immediately, followed by a full written and photographic report, if damage or loss is discovered. If damage occurred in transit, the borrower will also notify the carrier and will save all packing materials for inspection. No object may be altered, cleaned, repaired or fumigated without the written permission of the Museum, nor may framing, matting, mounting, glazing, or other object supports be changed without written permission; nor may objects be examined by scientific methods without written permission. Objects must be maintained in a fireproof building under 24-hour physical and/or electronic security and protected from unusual temperatures and humidity, excessive light, and from insects, vermin, dirt or other environmental hazards. Objects will be handled only by experienced personnel.

Packing and Transportation

Packing and transportation arrangements for the loan must be approved by the Museum. The borrower agrees to meet any special requirements for packing and shipping. Shipping requirements include: dual drivers, air-ride and climate control truck, last on/first off, direct non-stop delivery, or exclusive use shipping. At no time should the truck be left unattended. Unpacking and repacking must be performed by experienced personnel. Repacking must be done with either original or similar materials and boxes and by the same methods as the object was received.

Insurance

Objects shall be insured at the borrower's expense for the value stated on the face of this agreement under an all-risk wall-to-wall policy subject to the following standard exclusions: wear and tear, insects, vermin, gradual deterioration or inherent vice; repairing, restoration or retouching processes; hostile or warlike action, insurrection, or rebellion; nuclear reaction, nuclear radiation or radioactive contamination. The Museum shall determine whether the borrower insures the objects or whether the Museum insures them and bills the borrower for the premium. If the borrower is insuring the objects, the Museum must be furnished with a certificate of insurance or a copy of the policy made out in favor of the Museum prior to shipment of the loan. The Museum must be notified in writing at least 30 days prior to any cancellation or meaningful change in the borrower's policy. Any lapses in coverage, any failure to secure insurance and/or inaction by the Museum will not release the borrower from liability for loss or damage.

Reproduction and Credit

The Museum will make available, through an outside service, images of objects loaned, which may be used for catalog, routine non-commercial educational uses, publicity, and registrarial purposes. No further use of such images can be made and no other reproduction of objects loaned can be made without the written permission from the Museum. Each object will be labeled and credited to the Museum in the exact format provided on the face of this contract, both for display labels and publication credits.

Costs

The borrower will assume responsibility for all expenses incurred by the Museum in work by conservators to prepare the object for loan, in packing, crating, transportation, couriers, insurance, photography, and any and all other related costs. The Museum will make every effort to provide the borrower with estimates in advance of all applicable costs.

Cancellation, Return, and Extension

The loan is made with the understanding that the object will be on view during the entire exhibition period for which it has been requested. Any intention by the borrower to withdraw the loan from the exhibition at any time must be communicated to the Museum immediately. The Museum reserves the right to recall the loan or cancel the loan for good cause at any time, and will make efforts to give reasonable notice thereof. Objects lent must be returned to the Museum by the stated return date. Any extension of the loan period must be approved in writing by the Museum Director or designate and covered by written parallel extension of the insurance coverage.

Interpretation

In the event of any conflict between this agreement and any forms of the borrower, the terms of this agreement shall be controlling. For loans to borrowers within the United States, this agreement shall be construed in accordance with the laws of the State.

Additional Conditions for International Loans

Government regulations will be adhered to in international shipments. Unless otherwise stated in writing, the borrower is responsible for adhering to its country's import/export requirements. The borrower will protect objects from possible damage during its customs inspections and will make every effort to ensure that customs examinations are made only on the borrower's premises. If the nature of the material to be exported falls within the types addressed by the UNESCO Convention, its status in the importing country should be verified before this loan agreement is signed by the borrower. The Museum requires a declaration of immunity from seizure if available. The provisions of this loan agreement are subject to the doctrine of force majeure. If US Government Indemnity is secured, the amount payable by indemnity is the sole recovery available to the Museum in event of loss or damage, and objects will be insured in US dollars at their value as of the application date. Current fluctuations affecting value of claims at a later date are not recognized under indemnity.

FIGURE 9.7A–B (CONTINUED)

MRM MUSEUM
123 Main Street, Quietville, Estado 10955
Telephone: 555-555-5555

INCOMING LOAN AGREEMENT

AGREEMENT | The undersigned ("Lender") hereby lends to MRM Museum the object(s) described herein for the purposes, and subject to the terms and conditions set forth.

EXHIBITION | Exhibition:
Dates:
Venues:
Sampler Museum Registrar:

LENDER | Lender:
Address:
Telephone: (business) (home)
Email:
Contact Person:
Credit: Lent by
(Exact wording of lender's name for catalog, labels and publicity)

OBJECT | Artist/Maker:
Object/Title:
Medium:
Date of Object:

DIMENSIONS | Painting/Print | height | in. | width | in. (unframed)
| | height | in. | width | in. (framed)
| Object | height | in. | width | in. | depth | in.
Approximate Weight | lbs
May we reframe, remat or remount if necessary for the safety of the object? _____ Yes _____ No
May we substitute acrylic for glass? _____ Yes _____ No
May we fix secure hanging devices onto frame? _____Yes _____No

INSURANCE | Total value (estimated fair market value in US $): _____
Please see reverse | MRM Museum will insure unless other wise advised.
for conditions | Do you prefer to maintain your own insurance? _____Yes _____ No
If yes, estimated cost of premium:
Do you require a certificate of insurance? _____Yes _____ No

PHOTOGRAPHY | If images suitable for reproduction are available, please state type and where they may obtained.
Please see reverse
for conditions

SHIPPING/ | Date required for receipt of loan:
HANDLING | Pick-up and/or return address if different from address above. _____Pick-up _____Return
Address:
Telephone: (business)   (home)
Name of contact if other than Lender:
Please list any special instructions for handling, packing, shipping or installation:

SIGNATURE | The Lender acknowledges full authority and power to make this loan, and has read the conditions above and on the back of this form and agrees to be bound by them.

Signature: _____ Date: _____
Lender or authorized agent

Signature: _____ Date: _____
For MRM Museum

Please complete, sign and return one copy to MRM Museum Registrar. A countersigned copy will be returned to you.

FIGURE 9.8A–B INCOMING LOAN AGREEMENT WITH CONDITIONS GOVERNING INCOMING LOANS. CREATED BY AUTHOR.

CONDITIONS GOVERNING INCOMING LOANS

Care and Handling

1. MRM Museum (the "Museum") will exercise the same care with respect to the object on loan (the "object") as it does with comparable property of its own.
2. The Museum will not alter, clean or repair the object without prior express written permission of the Lender or except when the safety of the object makes such action imperative.

Packing and Transportation

1. The Lender certifies that the object is in good condition and will withstand ordinary strains of packing and transportation. Evidence of damage to the object at the time of receipt or while in the Museum's custody will be reported immediately to the Lender. The object will be returned packed in the same or similar materials unless otherwise authorized by the Lender. Costs of transportation and packing will be borne by the Museum unless the loan is at the Lender's request. Customs regulations will be adhered to in international shipments.

Insurance

1. Unless the Lender expressly elects to maintain insurance coverage, the Museum will insure the object wall-to-wall under its fine arts policy against risks of physical loss or damage from external cause while in transit and on location during the period of the loan. The insurance coverage contains the usual exclusions of loss or damage due to such causes as wear and tear, gradual deterioration, moths, vermin, inherent vice, war, invasion, hostilities, insurrections, nuclear reaction or radiation, confiscation by order of any government or public authority, risk of contraband or illegal transportation and/or trade and any repairing, restoration or retouching authorized by the Lender.
2. Insurance will be placed in the amount specified by the Lender which must reflect fair market value. In case of damage or loss, the insurance company may ask the Lender to substantiate the insurance value. If the Lender fails to indicate an amount, the Museum will set a value for purposes of insurance only for the period of the loan. The United States Government Arts and Artifacts Indemnity Act may be applicable to this loan. If so, the Lender agrees to said coverage at US dollar valuation as specified in this loan agreement. If an object which has been industrially fabricated is damaged or lost and can be repaired or replaced to the artist's specifications, the Museum's liability shall be limited to the cost of such replacement. The Lender agrees that in the event of loss or damage, recovery shall be limited to such amount, if any, as may be paid by the insurer hereby releasing the Museum and the Trustees, officers, agents and employees of the Museum from liability for any and all claims arising out of such loss or damage.
3. If the Lender chooses to maintain insurance, the Museum must be supplied with a certificate of insurance naming the Museum as an additional insured or waiving subrogation against the Museum. If the Lender fails to supply the Museum with such a certificate, this loan agreement shall constitute a release of the Museum from any liability in connection with the object. The Museum cannot accept responsibility for any error in the information furnished to the Lender's insurer or for any lapses in coverage.

Reproduction and Credit

1. The Museum assumes the right, unless specifically denied by the Lender, to photograph, videotape, and reproduce the object for documentation, publicity, publication and educational purposes connected with this exhibition and to produce images of the object to be distributed for educational use.
2. The general public will not be allowed to photograph works on loan to MRM Museum.
3. Unless otherwise instructed in writing, the Museum will give credit to the Lender in any labels and publications as specified on the face of the agreement.

Ownership and Change in Ownership

1. The Lender hereby warrants full legal title to the object or is the duly authorized agent of the owner or owners of the object. The Lender will indemnify, defend and hold the Museum harmless from any losses, damages and expenses, including attorney's fees, arising out of claims by individuals, institutions or other persons claiming full or partial title to the object.
2. The Lender will notify the Museum promptly in writing of any change of ownership of the object whether by reason of death, sale, insolvency, gift, or otherwise. If ownership shall change during the period of this loan, the Museum reserves the right to require the new owner, prior to the return of the object, to establish right to possession by proof satisfactory to the Museum. The new owner shall succeed to Lender's rights and obligations under this agreement, including, but not limited to, the loan period and any insurance obligations.

Loan Period, Extension, Return

1. The object shall remain in the possession of the Museum for the time specified on the reverse, but may be withdrawn from exhibition at any time by the Museum. The Lender agrees not to withdraw the object during the period of this agreement without prior written consent of the Museum.
2. The terms of this agreement shall apply to any extension of the loan period.
3. Unless the Lender requests otherwise in writing, the Museum will return the object only to the Lender and only at the address specified in this agreement. The Lender shall promptly notify the Museum in writing of any change of address. The Museum assumes no responsibility to search for a Lender who cannot be reached at the address specified in this agreement. The Lender will pay additional costs, if any, if the Lender request the return of the object to another address.
4. The Museum's right to return the loan shall accrue absolutely at the termination of the loan. If, after pursuing all possible means of contact, and in accordance with any legal requirements, the Lender cannot be found or the Lender refuses to accept the return of the object, it shall be deemed abandoned and become the property of the Museum. [This clause must comply with state law.]

Interpretation

1. This agreement constitutes the entire agreement between the Lender and the Museum and may be amended or modified only in writing signed by both parties. Any changes herein of printed text or written additions must bear the initial of both parties. This agreement shall be governed and interpreted according to the laws of the State of Any State.
2. If the terms of this agreement conflict with the forms, agreements or correspondence of the Lender, the terms of this agreement will be controlling.

FIGURE 9.8A–B (*CONTINUED*)

MRM Museum
TRAVELING EXHIBITION CONTRACT

Please note: This contract is a sample only. Consult with legal counsel before adapting or using this form.

General Information

Exhibition Title:

Organizing exhibitor:
Address:
Contact:
Telephone:
E-mail:
Loan period dates:
Exhibition public opening date:
Exhibition first event:
Exhibition closing date:
Participation Fee:
Fee includes:

Shipping:
Shipping Fee:
Contents of exhibition:

Other requirements:
Insurance:
Insurance value:
Credit:

1. AGREEMENT TO BORROW

This Agreement is made on [date] between [legal name and location of organizer] ("Organizer") and [legal name and location of exhibitor] ("Exhibitor").

Organizer has prepared an exhibition for circulation entitled [title of exhibition] ("the Exhibition"). The Exhibitor desires to display the Exhibition according to the terms and conditions set forth herein. Exhibitor hereby agrees to borrow and Organizer agrees to loan the Exhibition for the purpose of the exhibition ("loan purpose") on the Exhibitor's premises (the "approved location") during the period [inclusive dates] (the "exhibition period"); [length of time] will be allowed before and after the exhibition period for transportation, unpacking/packing, and installation/deinstallation. The Exhibitor agrees to pay in consideration of the loan the amount of $ _____.

The Exhibition consists of the objects as set forth in Appendix A (which is attached and made part of this

FIGURE 9.9A–F TRAVELING EXHIBIT CONTRACT. CREATED BY AUTHOR.

agreement), object mounts and/or installation hardware, text and other panels and labels (collectively the "exhibition materials").

Exhibitor will comply with all special instructions of Organizer as outlined herein and in all written registration notes accompanying the Exhibition with respect to condition, care, handling, installation, presentation, security, and packing of the Exhibition. Care and handling instructions can be found in Appendix B, attached.

2. FEES/PAYMENT SCHEDULE

Exhibitor agrees to pay the loan fee to Organizer in two installments as follows: (1) $ _____ to be sent with the executed original of the Agreement and (2) $ _____ to be paid by the first day of the exhibition period, or not later than [date]. Organizer will provide an invoice to exhibitor for all payments. The fee for the exhibition includes use of a fully researched and assembled exhibition with labels, educational materials, publicity packet, and insurance. It also includes catalogs and/or brochures, as noted below. Packing and crating are included. All costs for the courier, who will help with installation and deinstallation, are included. If lenders require couriers for specific works, the cost of those couriers (transport and per diem), will be borne by the Exhibitor. Shipping costs are not included in the exhibition fee.

Each exhibitor is responsible for all local costs incurred in presenting the exhibition, including but not limited to its unpacking/repacking, crate storage, installation, publicity, programming, receptions, etc. The Exhibitor is also responsible for any additional costs that may be specifically outlined in correspondence between Organizer and Exhibitor.

3. INSURANCE

Organizer, as part of the exhibition loan fee, shall continuously insure the exhibition materials on a wall-to-wall basis against all risks of physical loss or damage from any external cause except wear and tear, gradual deterioration, terrorism, and other exclusions standard to fine arts policies. Exhibitor shall report to the Organizer's registrar any damage to the exhibition materials while in transit to or on the Exhibitors' premises, regardless of who may be responsible.

Exhibitor must preserve all parts, packing materials, and other evidence or result of damage and provide photographs documenting damage and action taken in response.

Exhibitor shall be held responsible for any damage to the exhibition materials that results from its negligence or failure to comply with this agreement, including but not limited to, its failure to comply with Organizer registration notes and instructions regarding security, unpacking/repacking, handling, installation/deinstallation and shipment, as well as any and all damages to the exhibition materials during the loan period which Organizer does not recover from an insurance carrier.

4. EXHIBITION DISPLAY/RESTRICTIONS

Exhibitor shall exhibit all exhibition materials as listed in Appendix A unless express written permission to the contrary has been obtained in advance from Organizer. Exhibitor will not show the Exhibition at more than one location without prior written permission from Organizer. Further, Exhibitor agrees to provide a secure and environmentally suitable storage area for any exhibition materials withdrawn from the Exhibition (as outlined in the care and handling regulations, Appendix B) for any reason and/or to pay any additional transportation or courier costs which may be incurred as a result of withdrawals of exhibition materials from the Exhibition.

Organizer shall provide Exhibitor with a detailed set of guidelines for the handling and display of the exhibition materials [length of time] before the opening of the exhibition. Exhibitor shall make such guidelines

FIGURE 9.9A–F (*CONTINUED*)

accessible to its installation and design staff, and other applicable staff, and shall be responsible for ensuring strict adherence to such guidelines.

5. CREDIT LINES/SPONSORSHIPS

The following credit shall be included on invitations and official press releases and posted at the entrance to the exhibition.

[Title] was organized by Organizer. The exhibition has received funding from the [funders names]. Additional support has been received from [foundations, corporations, and individuals]. Other promotional and related programmatic materials will carry the first sentence of the above credit.

6 . SHIPPING

The Exhibitor is responsible for the cost of shipping, which will be [pro-rated, actual, or a combination of the two] among all exhibitors. The estimated cost of shipping is $ _____ and is payable upon receipt of the exhibition materials. Adjustments to shipping payments will be made at the end of the tour of the Exhibition. For foreign venues, and for Alaska and Hawaii, the Exhibitor must pay incoming shipping costs from the port-of-exit in the contiguous 48 states of the United States in addition to the pro-rated shipping costs. The foreign exhibitor is also required to pay all charges for customs clearance the Exhibition leaving or re-entering the United States.

Organizer or the previous Exhibitor shall pack the exhibition materials for shipment to the Exhibitor and arrange for their delivery to Exhibitor not later than the first day of the loan period, by a carrier selected and scheduled in advance by Organizer. Exhibitor agrees to meet all transportation schedules required for the safety of objects and the timely shipment to other exhibitors. Exhibitor agrees that if it is unable to receive and ship the Exhibition in compliance with the necessary transportation schedule, it will absorb the cost of an acceptable interim storage facility and other expenses resulting from its inability to comply with such schedule.

7. PACKING, HANDLING, CARE, AND CONDITION REPORTING

Exhibitor shall ensure that all packing and unpacking instructions given by Organizer are followed explicitly by competent packers who are trained in museum object handling and that the exhibition materials are handled with special care at all times to protect against damage or deterioration. All unloading, unpacking, handling, repacking and reloading shall occur under the surveillance of the Exhibitor's registrar in consultation with the Exhibitor's conservators and security staff, or applicable staff. Exhibition material shall be handled with at least the same care as Exhibitor uses in handling its own property of a similar nature. In preparing exhibition materials for their outgoing shipment, Exhibitor shall ensure that the exhibition materials are packed in the same manner in which they were delivered to Exhibitor and are thus prepared for out-going shipment no later than the last day of the loan period. Exhibitor shall notify immediately, by telephone or text, the Organizer's registrar, of any loss or damage to the packing materials or packing crates which in any way might impair their ability to protect the exhibition materials. Exhibitor, at its own expense, shall, in consultation with the Organizer's registrar, replace packing materials or crates lost or damaged while in its care with comparable materials.

Exhibitor must examine the exhibition materials after a 24-hour acclimation but within seven days of their receipt and report on their condition. If any damage to the objects is discovered then or at any time, then or during the loan period, reports must be made immediately in writing, with photographic documentation and sent to the Organizer's registrar. Exhibitor agrees that it may not alter or repair any of the exhibition materials without first obtaining the express written permission of Organizer.

ADD LANGUAGE ABOUT CONDITION REPORTS, ETC.

8. FACILITIES

Exhibitor shall, at its own expense, provide adequate security and environmental conditions for the exhibition materials, and shall comply with any and all special instructions put forth by Organizer for the care of the exhibition materials. Exhibitor shall provide Organizer with a copy of its *Standard Facility Report*; Organizer will review the report as part of the contractual process.

All objects must be displayed according to guidelines provided by the Organizer.

Exhibitor shall assign security guard(s) as noted to the exhibition space during open hours. The Exhibitor must, as a security minimum during closed hours, have electronic surveillance systems that report to a central station manned 24 hours per day. Permission to use plants in the galleries must be obtained from the Organizer's registrar; food and drink will not be allowed in the exhibition galleries, storage areas, or anywhere the exhibition materials are kept.

The Exhibitor shall maintain objects in the specified environmental conditions. Light levels shall be maintained according to the guidelines provided.

The public shall be admitted to the exhibition without discrimination or segregation, and regardless of race, color, creed, sex, age or national origin. Additionally, the Exhibitor represents that there is full access to the exhibition for the physically disabled, as stipulated in Section 504 of Federal Public Law 93-112, as amended. The Exhibitor shall be in compliance with the Americans with Disabilities Act (Public Law 101-336, enacted July 26, 1990).

9. PUBLICITY

Organizer will supply Exhibitor with a press release and a selection of photographs which may be used in preparing publicity and related materials for the Exhibition. The Exhibitor agrees to clear its own press release with the Public Relations department of Organizer before use.

Exhibitor shall forward promptly to Organizer contact person, all publicity releases, reviews, and other similar matter relating to the exhibition. At the end of the loan period, Exhibitor will forward attendance figures to Organizer.

Organizer reserves to itself the right to copy, photograph, or reproduce the exhibition materials. Exhibitor shall not permit any of the exhibition materials to be copied, photographed, or reproduced, and in the event of their public exhibition, shall contain in their photography guidelines a statement advising persons attending the Exhibition that the exhibition materials may not be copied, photographed, or reproduced. Not-withstanding the foregoing sentence, Exhibitor may cause the exhibition materials to be photographed for curatorial and registrarial purposes provided that such photographs are made without removal of frames or mounts and are not released without Organizer's prior written consent and provided further that Orgainizer will be supplied with a duplicate set of prints.

Organizer will provide the Exhibitor with [number] copies of the catalog [title]. Additional copies of the catalog can be purchased at cost from Organizer.

10. DAMAGES, BREACH OF AGREEMENT

The Exhibitor must notify Organizer in writing to cancel the signed Agreement. The parties understand that it will be difficult, if not impossible, to calculate or estimate the serious and substantial damage to Organizer which would be caused by breach of this Agreement by Exhibitor, and therefore the parties agree that in the event Exhibitor cancels this Agreement prior to the beginning of the loan period, for any reason whatsoever (other than the inability of Organizer to perform hereunder), Exhibitor shall pay to Organizer, as liquidated damages and not as a penalty, the total loan fee, which balance shall be due and payable immediately upon such cancellation. However, in the event that Organizer arranges for an alternate venue for the Exhibition that is

FIGURE 9.9A–F (*CONTINUED*)

acceptable to Organizer during the loan period, the fees received from that venue, less the cost of procuring such alternate venue, shall be applied to reduce the amount payable to Organizer under this paragraph. Organizer, however, shall have no obligation to procure such alternate sponsor and the Exhibitor is entitled to no reduction of the loan fee for Organizer's failure to procure such alternate venue.

In the event Exhibitor fails to pay any amount when due under this Agreement, including but not limited to costs payable under paragraphs 1 and 3 above, such failure continuing for a period of 10 business days, the amount at the rate of 15 percent per annum from the date the unpaid amount originally was due will accrue until the late payment is received by Organizer. Nothing in this Agreement shall be construed as an express or implied agreement by Organizer to forbear in the collection of any delinquent payment. Further, this Agreement shall not be construed as in any way giving Exhibitor the right, express or implied, to fail to make timely payments hereunder, whether upon payment of such interest rate or otherwise. Should the Exhibitor not receive the first payment before the scheduled shipment date, Organizer deserves the right to cancel the contract at its own discretion.

The parties further understand that, while Organizer shall endeavor to make all reasonable effort to assure delivery of the Exhibition to Exhibitor prior to the scheduled opening as stated above:

a) In the event that Organizer is unable to perform hereunder, Organizer shall promptly refund to Exhibitor the fee already paid by Exhibitor in full and complete satisfaction of its obligation to Exhibitor. Upon prior written notice, Organizer may terminate this Agreement prior to the beginning of the loan period for events beyond its control. Exhibitor shall release, indemnify and hold Organizer harmless from and against any and all loss arising from Exhibitor's inability to display the Exhibition because of loss or damage to the exhibition materials while in transit; and

b) In the event Organizer for any reason withdraws any object from the Exhibition while it is in circulation, Exhibitor shall promptly comply with all packing and shipping instructions given by Organizer in the course of such withdrawal. Organizer shall concurrently reimburse Exhibitor for its costs and expenses of packing and shipping incurred by such withdrawal.

11. NOTICES

Except as otherwise required specifically herein, all notices and other communication provided for or permitted hereunder shall be made by hand-delivery, prepaid, first-class mail, text, or e-mail. All notices are considered delivered when delivered by hand, four days after deposit of first class mail, and when receipt is acknowledged for text and e-mail. In the case of extreme emergencies, immediate verbal consent should be sought by the exhibitor and followed as soon as possible in writing.

If to Organizer
Name and title
Address
Phone
e-mail

If to the Exhibitor
Name and title
Address
Phone
e-mail

12. SUCCESSORS AND ASSIGNS

The Agreement shall inure to the benefit of and be binding upon the successors of each of the parties. This Agreement may not be assigned by either party without the prior written consent of the other.

13. WAIVERS, REMEDIES

No delay on the part of any party hereto in exercising any right, power or privilege hereunder shall operate as a waiver thereof, nor shall any waiver on the part of any party hereto of any right, power or privilege hereunder operate as a waiver of any right, power, or privilege hereunder.

14. ENTIRE AGREEMENT

This Agreement, together with all written special instructions accompanying the Exhibition, is intended by the parties as a final expression of their agreement and is a complete and exclusive statement of the agreement and understanding of the parties. This Agreement supersedes all prior agreements and understandings between the parties with respect to the subject matter contained herein.

15. ATTORNEYS' FEES

In any action or proceeding brought to enforce any provision of this Agreement, or where any provision hereof is validly asserted as a defense, the successful party shall be entitled to recover reasonable attorneys' fees in addition to any other available remedy.

16. SEVERABILITY

In the event that any one or more of the provisions contained herein, or the application thereof in any circumstances, is held invalid, illegal or unenforceable in any respect for any reason, the validity, legality and enforceability of any such provision in every other respect and of the remaining provisions hereof shall not in any way be impaired or affected, it being intended that all of the rights and privileges contained herein shall be enforceable to the fullest extent permitted by law.

17. GOVERNING LAW

This Agreement shall be governed by and construed in accordance with the State of Any State.

18. SIGNATURES

19. APPENDICES/ATTACHMENTS/SCHEDULES

FIGURE 9.9A–F (*CONTINUED*)

MRM MUSEUM
EXHIBITION FEE WORK SHEET

Exhibition/Marketing:

Catalogs	$_____
Images	$_____
Replacement of panels or graphics	$_____
Exhibition design & installation manual	$_____
Education and marketing packets	$_____

Registrarial:

Loan Fees	$_____
Crating	$_____
Insurance	$_____
Conservation review for travel	$_____
Condition Report Book	$_____
Courier costs	$_____
Object replacement/rotation costs	$_____

Administrative:

Consultants:	$_____
Postage, Telephone, Shipping	$_____

Contingency:

Contingency: storage	$_____
Contingency: damage	$_____
Contingency: frame/crate replacement	$_____

OVERHEAD (Operating budget) $_____

     Total: $_____

A   **Divided by number of venues (_____)** $_____
B   **+ Reasonable addition to approach current fees for exhibition** $_____
C   **Profit** $_____

    Fee (A + B + C): $_____

FIGURE 9.10 EXHIBITION FEE WORKSHEET. CREATED BY AUTHOR.

MRM MUSEUM

CONDITION REPORT FOR PAINTINGS, DRAWINGS, PRINTS, AND OTHER WORKS ON PAPER

ACC.#

EXAMINER   DATE

ARTIST

TITLE

MEDIUM

STRETCHER/PANEL SIZE   H   W   IN.

SHEET SIZE   H   W   IN.

IMAGE SIZE   H   W   IN.

FRAME/MAT SIZE   H   W   IN.

SIG./DATE (HOW? WHERE?)

MARKS/LABELS (WHAT? WHERE?)

Conservation Priority   1   2   3   4   5
Curatorial Priority   1   2   3   4   5

Priority Key
Conservation Priority
1 = Object in Jeopardy
2 = Not exhibitable as is
3 = Needs minor repair or cleaning
4 = Needs further evaluation
5 = Needs no work

Curatorial Priority
1 = Needed immediately for exhibit or loan
2 = Needed in future for exhibit or loan
3 = May have some need at some time
4 = Object need never see light of day
5 = Potential deaccession

DESCRIPTION	DEFECTS	REMARKS
FRAME ❑ Framed ❑ Backed ❑ Glass ❑ Plexi ❑ Unframed Other	❑ Broken ❑ Disjoins ❑ Glazing touches ❑ Artwork ❑ Paint loss ❑ Hanging devices ❑ Insecure ❑ Accretions ❑ Abrasions Other	
AUXILIARY SUPPORT ❑ Stretcher ❑ Keys intact ❑ Strainer ❑ Secured/nails ❑ Secured/plates ❑ Cradle ❑ Matted Other	❑ Keys missing ❑ Checks ❑ Infestation ❑ Adheared to backing ❑ Acidic materials Other	
SUPPORT ❑ Fabric ❑ Lined ❑ Wax lined ❑ Wood ❑ Masonite ❑ Paper ❑ Illust. Board Other	❑ Brittle ❑ Tear ❑ Hold ❑ Dent ❑ Bulge ❑ Sagging ❑ Draws ❑ Infestation ❑ Mold Other	

Form continues on back

FIGURE 9.11A–B CONDITION REPORT FOR PAINTINGS, DRAWINGS, PRINTS, AND OTHER WORKS ON PAPER. CREATED BY AUTHOR.

DESCRIPTION	DEFECTS	REMARKS
DESIGN ❏ Oil ❏ Watercolor ❏ Tempera ❏ Pastel ❏ Gouache ❏ Pencil ❏ Ink ❏ Mixed Media Other	❏ Painter's lice ❏ Crackle ❏ Cleavage ❏ Cracking ❏ Buckling ❏ Flaking ❏ Powdering ❏ Loss ❏ Blistering ❏ Accretions ❏ Abrasions ❏ Soiled Other	
VARNISH ❏ Varnished ❏ Unvarnished	❏ Crackle ❏ Bloom ❏ Scratched ❏ Cracking ❏ Grime ❏ Accretions Other	

Action Taken upon Receipt:

Is further work needed?   ❏ yes ❏ no

Describe: ❏ new mat   ❏ new frame   ❏ repair frame
   ❏ other (itemize)

Is professional attention indicated? ❏ yes ❏ no

Conservation Record

Date	Conservator	Treatment Given

Marks and Inscriptions:

Face

Reverse

MRM Museum
MUSEUM INCIDENT REPORT

Brief description of incident:

Date and time of incident:

Location:

Accession or catalog numbers and object descriptions, if applicable:

Reported by:

Witnesses and other persons involved:

Actions taken:

Notification to:

❑ Director   ❑ Director of Facilities:

❑ Registrar   ❑ Director of Security:

❑ Curator:

❑ Other:

[on back of form]
Please describe the incident as well as possible and the condition of any objects involved.

FIGURE 9.12 MUSEUM INCIDENT REPORT. CREATED BY AUTHOR.

Index

Page references for figures are italicized.

Lightning Source UK Ltd.
Milton Keynes UK
UKHW031150080720
366179UK00003B/8

9 781538 113110